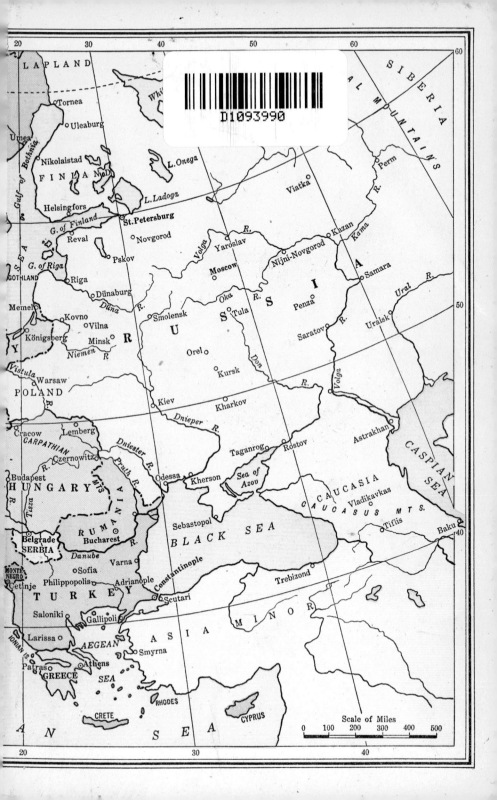

# EUROPEAN HISTORY SINCE 1870

# EUROPEAN HISTORY
# SINCE 1870

BY

## F. LEE BENNS

*Indiana University*

SECOND EDITION

F. S. CROFTS & CO. NEW YORK 1946

# PREFACE

This volume presents the history of Europe since 1870 in such a way that the reader will obtain a clear insight into the economic, social, and political forces which led to the World War and an appreciation of the profound developments which have occurred in the life of Europe since the war. Part One lays the foundation for an understanding of the period by explaining the economic and social trends in the history of Europe since 1870. Part Two traces the history of the European states down to 1914. Each country's internal problems and developments, imperialistic ambitions and achievements, and foreign policy have been woven together in order to show how they interacted upon one another. Inevitably the chapters in this part of the book reveal the driving power of nationalism, the sharp clash of imperialisms, the gradual growth of entangling alliances, the huge expansion of armaments, and the rise of international fear and suspicion which brought on the World War.

Parts Three and Four discuss the war, the peace treaties, the postwar efforts to outlaw war, the abrogation and repudiation of many provisions of the peace settlement, the failure of collective action to prevent aggressive wars by powerful states, and the eventual return to an international situation not greatly different from that existing in the years before 1914. Part Five deals primarily with the national problems of the states of postwar Europe and describes the various experiments—Communist, Fascist, Nazi, and the like—which have profoundly altered the political, economic, social, and religious life of many countries. Part Six points out how Europe in the years since 1918 has been compelled to face an ever-widening revolt of the East against domination by the West.

The author is deeply indebted to many who have made intensive studies of special topics in the history of Europe since 1870. Upon their writings he has drawn freely. Further grateful acknowledgment is due to Professor Bernadotte E. Schmitt, of the University of Chicago, who read and criticized the manuscript and helped to prevent errors from creeping in. The responsibility for the text rests, however, not upon him but upon the author.

F. Lee Benns

# PREFACE TO SECOND EDITION

The outbreak of the Second World War makes it seem advisable to expand this volume by adding Part Seven consisting of two new chapters. The first, "The Immediate Background of the War," seeks to give the reader an understanding of the fundamental causes of the conflict and of the several international crises which preceded the actual outbreak of hostilities. The second new chapter, "Warfare—New Style," outlines the course of the war itself. No one realizes better than the author that a definitive history of this period cannot be written at the present time. That fact, however, should not prevent historians from attempting to meet the present generation's desire to obtain as clear an understanding as possible of recent world-shaking events.

F. Lee Benns

# CONTENTS

## PART ONE: ECONOMIC FORCES AND SOCIAL TRENDS

CHAPTER                                                           PAGE

I   INDUSTRIALISM, IMPERIALISM, AND WORLD POLITICS . . . . 3

The Acceleration of Industrial Development after 1870 . . 3
Improvements in Transportation and Communication . . 8
The Revival of Interest in Colonial Expansion . . . . . 14
Economic Imperialism after 1870. . . . . . . . . 17
World Politics . . . . . . . . . . . . . . . 26

II   SOCIAL CHANGES, PROBLEMS, AND PROGRAMS . . . . . . 28

Growth and Urbanization of Population . . . . . . 28
Changes in Social Classes . . . . . . . . . . . 32
The Bourgeoisie versus the Proletariat . . . . . . . 33
The Rise of Socialism . . . . . . . . . . . . 35
Anarchism and Syndicalism . . . . . . . . . . 40
Bourgeois-Proletarian Compromise . . . . . . . . 42
Rise in the Standard of Living . . . . . . . . . 44
The Progress of Woman . . . . . . . . . . . 47

## PART TWO: FOUR DECADES OF PEACE

III   THE GERMAN EMPIRE. . . . . . . . . . . . . . 53

The Structure of the Imperial Government. . . . . . 53
Early Political History . . . . . . . . . . . . . 56
Economic Progress and Social Legislation . . . . . . 61
Diplomatic Ascendancy under Bismarck. . . . . . . 65
Beginnings of Colonial Expansion . . . . . . . . 71
William II and the "New Course" . . . . . . . . 75
The Scramble for Overseas Territory . . . . . . . 78
*Mittel-Europa* and the *Drang nach Osten* . . . . . . 82
The Rapid Rise of German Naval Power . . . . . . 86
Efforts to Expand the Triple Alliance . . . . . . . 91
The Eve of the World War . . . . . . . . . . 93

IV   THE THIRD FRENCH REPUBLIC . . . . . . . . . . 99

Disaster and Recovery . . . . . . . . . . . . 99
The Establishment of the Republic . . . . . . . . 103

# CONTENTS

Early Republican Measures . . . . . . . . . . . 110
Colonial Expansion and Emergence from Isolation . . . 112
The Weakening of the Royalists and Clericals . . . . . 115
The Separation of Church and State. . . . . . . . 120
Economic and Social Progress. . . . . . . . . . 124
The Creation of the Entente Cordiale . . . . . . . 127
The Moroccan Crises . . . . . . . . . . . . 130
Agitation over "Preparedness". . . . . . . . . . 136

V  THE KINGDOM OF ITALY . . . . . . . . . . . . 139

The New State . . . . . . . . . . . . . . . 139
Immediate Problems and Achievements. . . . . . . . 142
The Left in Power under Depretis and Crispi . . . . . 145
Early Attempts to Play the Role of a Great Power . . . 151
The Era of Giolitti. . . . . . . . . . . . . . 156
The Rising Tide of Nationalism and Imperialism . . . . 159

VI  THE UNITED KINGDOM AND THE BRITISH EMPIRE . . . . 164

The British Empire in 1870 . . . . . . . . . . . 164
The United Kingdom in 1870. . . . . . . . . . . 167
Gladstone and Disraeli. . . . . . . . . . . . . 175
The Conservatives in Power . . . . . . . . . . 184
Resurgent Imperialism . . . . . . . . . . . . 187
Increasing Trade Rivalry and British Policy. . . . . . 193
The Abandonment of "Splendid Isolation". . . . . . 197
The Rejection of the Conservatives . . . . . . . . 201
Reform under the Liberals. . . . . . . . . . . 202
The Irish Home-Rule Crisis, 1912–1914 . . . . . . . 209
The Triple Entente. . . . . . . . . . . . . . 211

VII  THE LESSER STATES OF WESTERN EUROPE . . . . . . . 216

The Scandinavian Monarchies. . . . . . . . . . . 216
Holland and Belgium . . . . . . . . . . . . . 220
Switzerland . . . . . . . . . . . . . . . . 225
Spain and Portugal . . . . . . . . . . . . . . 227

VIII  THE RUSSIAN EMPIRE . . . . . . . . . . . . . 232

The Vastness of Russia. . . . . . . . . . . . . 232
The Backwardness of Russia . . . . . . . . . . 235
Alexander II—Liberal or Conservative?. . . . . . . 238
Nihilism and Terrorism . . . . . . . . . . . . 243
Intervention in the Balkans . . . . . . . . . . . 245
Reaction, Repression, and "Russification" . . . . . . 254
The Introduction of Modern Industrialism . . . . . . 259
Imperialism in the Far East . . . . . . . . . . . 262

# CONTENTS

CHAPTER                                                                    PAGE

The Russo-Japanese War . . . . . . . . . . . . . . 267
The Revolution of 1905 . . . . . . . . . . . . . 269
The Eve of the World War . . . . . . . . . 279

IX  THE AUSTRO-HUNGARIAN DUAL MONARCHY . . . . . . . 284

The Habsburg Ruler . . . . . . . . . . . . . 284
The Habsburg Realm . . . . . . . . . . . . . 286
Austria's Advance into the Balkans . . . . . . . . 292
The Problem of Nationalism in Austria . . . . . . . 295
The Program of Magyarism in Hungary . . . . . 301
The Yugoslav Question . . . . . . . . . . 307

X  TURKEY AND THE BALKANS . . . . . . . . . . 313

Political Geography of the Balkans, 1878–1908 . . . . . 313
Internal History of the Balkan National States . . . . . 315
    Rumania . . . . . . . . . . . . . . . . 316
    Bulgaria . . . . . . . . . . . . . . . 319
    Greece . . . . . . . . . . . . . . . . 323
    Serbia and Montenegro . . . . . . . . . . . 327
National Aspirations of the Balkan Peoples . . . . . 330
Abdul Hamid and His Decadent Empire . . . . . 334
The Bosnian Crisis . . . . . . . . . . . . . 338
Ottoman Losses to Nationalism and Imperialism, 1908–1913 . 344


PART THREE: THE WORLD WAR

XI  THE OUTBREAK OF THE WAR . . . . . . . . . . . 357

Hopes of Peace . . . . . . . . . . . . . . 357
Causes of War . . . . . . . . . . . . . . 361
Recurring International Crises . . . . . . . . . 367
Increasing International Tension . . . . . . . . 371
The Austro-Serbian Crisis of 1914 . . . . . . . . 375
The Futile Efforts to Prevent War . . . . . . . 378
The Question of War Guilt . . . . . . . . . . 385
The Alignment of the Powers in 1914 . . . . . . . 387
Mobilization of Men and Resources . . . . . . . 390
War Propaganda . . . . . . . . . . . . 392

XII  THE PERIOD OF TEUTONIC ASCENDANCY . . . . . . . 395

The Breakdown of German Plans for 1914 . . . . . 396
German Successes of 1915 . . . . . . . . . 401
German Failure to End the War in 1916 . . . . . 410
Peace Proposals of the Central Powers . . . . . . 418

# CONTENTS

CHAPTER                                                                    PAGE

XIII   AMERICA'S INTERVENTION AND RUSSIA'S WITHDRAWAL  .  .  .  . 422

    Germany's Unrestricted Submarine Campaign . . . . . . 422
    The United States' Entrance into the War . . . . . . 425
    The Allied Offensives of 1917. . . . . . . . . . 427
    War-Weariness . . . . . . . . . . . . . . 432
    The Growing Unrest in Russia . . . . . . . . . 436
    The Collapse of Russian Autocracy . . . . . . . . 438
    The Soviets . . . . . . . . . . . . . . . 441
    Lenin and the Rise of the Bolsheviks . . . . . . 442
    The November Revolution . . . . . . . . . . 447
    The Treaty of Brest-Litovsk . . . . . . . . . 449

XIV   THE COLLAPSE OF THE CENTRAL POWERS . . . . . . . 452

    Renewed Optimism of the Central Powers . . . . . 452
    German Repudiation of the Allied War Aims . . . . 454
    Germany's Final Military Effort . . . . . . . . 456
    The Disintegration of Austria-Hungary . . . . . . 461
    Downfall of the German Empire. . . . . . . . . 464
    The End of the War . . . . . . . . . . . . 472

## PART FOUR: THE INTERNATIONAL AFTERMATH OF THE WAR

XV   THE PARIS PEACE SETTLEMENT . . . . . . . . . 477

    Preparations for the Conference . . . . . . . . 477
    The Working Organization . . . . . . . . . 478
    The Treaty of Versailles . . . . . . . . . . 481
        The Question of Including the League Covenant . . 481
        Territorial Provisions . . . . . . . . . . 483
        Limitation of Armaments . . . . . . . . . 490
        Reparations . . . . . . . . . . . . . 492
        Miscellaneous Provisions. . . . . . . . . 494
        The Signing of the Treaty . . . . . . . . 495
        The Significance of the Treaty for Germany. . . . 496
    The Treaties with Austria, Hungary, and Bulgaria . . 498
    The Minorities Treaties . . . . . . . . . . 504
    The Treaties with Turkey. . . . . . . . . . 505
    The Conflict of Ideas . . . . . . . . . . . 509
    The United States and the Peace Settlement . . . . 511

XVI   THE LEAGUE OF NATIONS AND THE PEACE SETTLEMENT . . 514

    The Structure of the League . . . . . . . . . 514
    The United States and the League . . . . . . . 520
    The League and the Preservation of Peace . . . . . 522
    The League's Role in Postwar Adjustments. . . . . 524

# CONTENTS

CHAPTER                                                                      PAGE

The Saar . . . . . . . . . . . . . . . . . 532
Mandates and Minorities . . . . . . . . . . 536
Humanitarian Activities . . . . . . . . . . 538

XVII  REPARATIONS AND WAR DEBTS . . . . . . . . . . 540

Germany's Total Obligation . . . . . . . . . 540
Germany's Default . . . . . . . . . . . . . 541
The Struggle in the Ruhr . . . . . . . . . . 545
The Dawes Plan . . . . . . . . . . . . . . 547
The Inter-Allied War Debts . . . . . . . . . 549
The Linking of Reparations and War Debts in the Young Plan 551
Economic Depression and Moratorium . . . . . . . 555
The End of Reparations . . . . . . . . . . . 558
Default on War-Debt Payments . . . . . . . . 559

XVIII  DISARMAMENT AND SECURITY . . . . . . . . . . . 562

The League's Early Efforts to Provide Security . . . . 562
French Security, 1920–1928 . . . . . . . . . . 564
Security in Central Europe and the Balkans . . . . . 567
Security in Eastern Europe . . . . . . . . . . 569
The Limitation of Naval Armaments . . . . . . . 570
The Failure of the Geneva Disarmament Conference . . 573
The Rearmament of Germany . . . . . . . . . 576
Europe's Reaction to Hitler . . . . . . . . . . 578
Diplomatic Maneuvers, 1936–1937 . . . . . . . . 581
The New Armaments Race . . . . . . . . . . 584

## PART FIVE: NATIONAL PROBLEMS AND EXPERIMENTS OF THE POSTWAR PERIOD

XIX  SOVIET RUSSIA . . . . . . . . . . . . . . . . 589

Failure to Dislodge the Bolsheviks . . . . . . . . 589
The Establishment of the Union of Soviet Socialist Republics 591
The Constitution of 1936 . . . . . . . . . . . 596
The Role of the Communist Party . . . . . . . . 598
Early Economic Experiments . . . . . . . . . . 599
The New Economic Policy . . . . . . . . . . . 601
The Rise of Joseph Stalin . . . . . . . . . . . 603
The Five-Year Plans . . . . . . . . . . . . . 608
Education and Religion . . . . . . . . . . . . 615
Soviet Foreign Policy . . . . . . . . . . . . . 617

XX  FASCIST ITALY . . . . . . . . . . . . . . . . 623

Popular Dissatisfaction with the Government . . . . . 623
Mussolini and the Rise of Fascism . . . . . . . . 626

The "Fascistization" of the Government . . . . . . 629
Fascism Constitutionalized. . . . . . . . . . . . 631
Fascist Syndicalism and the Corporative State . . . . 632
The Settlement of the Roman Question . . . . . . 635
Economic and Fiscal Problems . . . . . . . . . 636
Recovery of International Prestige . . . . . . . . 639
Italy's Conquest of Ethiopia . . . . . . . . . . 642
Italy versus the League. . . . . . . . . . . . . 647

XXI LIBERAL AND NAZI GERMANY. . . . . . . . . . . 650

The Weimar Constitution . . . . . . . . . . . 650
The Defense of the Republic . . . . . . . . . . 653
The Currency Debacle . . . . . . . . . . . . . 656
Stresemann's Policy of Conciliation . . . . . . . 658
Economic Recovery and Decline . . . . . . . . . 660
The First Decade of Politics . . . . . . . . . . 663
Hitler and the National Socialists. . . . . . . . . 666
Government by Emergency Decrees . . . . . . . . 669
The National Socialist Revolution . . . . . . . . 671
Anti-Semitism . . . . . . . . . . . . . . . 674
The Totalitarian State . . . . . . . . . . . . . 676
The "Co-ordination" of the Church . . . . . . . 678
The "Co-ordination" of Germany's Economic Life . . 682
Nazi Foreign Policy . . . . . . . . . . . . . 686
Political Developments under the Nazis. . . . . . . 688

XXII GREAT BRITAIN AND IRELAND. . . . . . . . . . . 691

Trade Decline and Unemployment . . . . . . . . 691
The Lloyd George Coalition . . . . . . . . . . 693
Free Trade or Protection?. . . . . . . . . . . . 696
Britain's First Labor Government . . . . . . . . 697
Five Years of Conservative Government . . . . . . 699
The Second Labor Government . . . . . . . . . 703
The National Government. . . . . . . . . . . . 705
Edward VIII and George VI . . . . . . . . . . 710
The British Commonwealth of Nations . . . . . . 711
The Irish Free State . . . . . . . . . . . . . 713

XXIII FRANCE AND SPAIN . . . . . . . . . . . . . . 721

Alsace-Lorraine's Return to France . . . . . . . . 721
The Problem of Reconstruction in France . . . . . 724
The Problem of National Finance in France . . . . . 725
Deflation and Unrest in France . . . . . . . . . 728
The Popular Front in France . . . . . . . . . . 731
Unrest and Discontent in Spain . . . . . . . . . 733

CHAPTER                                                                 PAGE

The Establishment of the Spanish Republic . . . . . . 736
The Struggle to Control the Spanish Republic . . . . . 739
The Spanish Civil War . . . . . . . . . . . . . 742

XXIV   POLAND AND THE BALTIC REPUBLICS . . . . . . . . 746

Poland . . . . . . . . . . . . . . . . . . 746
Danzig, Poland, and the League . . . . . . . . . 754
Lithuania, Vilna, and Memel . . . . . . . . . . 757
Estonia and Latvia . . . . . . . . . . . . . . 759
Finland . . . . . . . . . . . . . . . . . . 762

XXV   THE SUCCESSION STATES OF CENTRAL EUROPE . . . . . 765

Austria . . . . . . . . . . . . . . . . . . 765
Hungary . . . . . . . . . . . . . . . . . . 775
Czechoslovakia . . . . . . . . . . . . . . . 780

XXVI   THE TURBULENT BALKANS . . . . . . . . . . . 786

Greece . . . . . . . . . . . . . . . . . . 786
Yugoslavia . . . . . . . . . . . . . . . . . 792
Albania . . . . . . . . . . . . . . . . . . 797
Bulgaria . . . . . . . . . . . . . . . . . . 799
Rumania . . . . . . . . . . . . . . . . . . 805

## PART SIX: THE EAST IN REVOLT

XXVII   THE NEAR AND MIDDLE EAST . . . . . . . . . . . 813

The Turkish Republic . . . . . . . . . . . . . 813
Egypt . . . . . . . . . . . . . . . . . . . 817
Syria, Palestine, and Iraq . . . . . . . . . . . 821
Persia . . . . . . . . . . . . . . . . . . . 828
India . . . . . . . . . . . . . . . . . . . 830

XXVIII   THE FAR EAST . . . . . . . . . . . . . . . . 836

China, Japan, and the World War . . . . . . . . 836
The Washington Conference . . . . . . . . . . 839
Nationalist Efforts to Unite and Emancipate China . . 840
Japanese Penetration of Manchuria . . . . . . . . 842
The Establishment of Manchukuo . . . . . . . . 844
The International Crisis of 1931–1933 . . . . . . . 847
Japan and Soviet Russia . . . . . . . . . . . . 852
Japan's Advance into North China . . . . . . . . 855

## PART SEVEN: THE SECOND WORLD WAR

XXIX   THE IMMEDIATE BACKGROUND OF THE WAR . . . . . . 863

# CONTENTS

CHAPTER                                                                    PAGE

The Continuing Causes of War . . . . . . . . . 863
Hitler's *Drang nach Osten* . . . . . . . . . . . 867
  Germany's Absorption of Austria . . . . . . . 868
  Germany's Annexation of the Sudetenland . . . . 871
Franco's Triumph in Spain . . . . . . . . . 882
The Renewal of the *Drang nach Osten* . . . . . . 886
The End of "Appeasement" . . . . . . . . . 890
The Crisis of August, 1939 . . . . . . . . . 896

XXX  WARFARE—NEW STYLE . . . . . . . . . . . 902

The Nazi-Soviet Partition of Poland . . . . . . 902
Russia's Return to the Baltic . . . . . . . . . 908
The "Phony" War in the West . . . . . . . . 914
Hitler's Seizure of Norway and Denmark . . . . . 920
*Blitzkrieg* in the West . . . . . . . . . . . 926
The Battle of Britain . . . . . . . . . . . 935
Conquered France . . . . . . . . . . . . 945
The Nazi Advance into the Mediterranean . . . . 952
The Nazi Invasion of Russia . . . . . . . . 966
The War in Africa . . . . . . . . . . . 967
The War in the Far East . . . . . . . . . . 971
The War and the United States . . . . . . . . 982

SELECT BIBLIOGRAPHY . . . . . . . . . . . . . 991

INDEX . . . . . . . . . . . . . . . . . . 1035

# MAPS AND CHARTS

Europe in 1871 . . . . . . . . . . . . . . . . . *front cover*
African Possessions of European Powers about 1870. . . . . . . 18
African Possessions of European Powers in 1914 . . . . . . . . 21
Asiatic Possessions of European Powers in 1914 . . . . . . . . 25
Austro-German System of Alliances, 1887–1890 . . . . . . . . 73
Franco-Russian System of Alliances and Ententes, 1894–1909 . . . . 133
The Italian Peninsula in 1858 . . . . . . . . . . . . . . . 141
The Kingdom of Italy in 1871 . . . . . . . . . . . . . . . 141
The Balkans by the Treaty of San Stefano. . . . . . . . . . 250
The Balkans by the Treaty of Berlin . . . . . . . . . . . . 251
The Far East in 1904. . . . . . . . . . . . . . . . . . 266
The Austro-Hungarian Dual Monarchy . . . . . . . . . . . 289
The Balkans, 1885–1913 . . . . . . . . . . . . . . . . . 317
The Balkans in 1914 . . . . . . . . . . . . . . . . . . 353
Europe in 1914 . . . . . . . . . . . . . . . . . *after* 360
The Western Front in 1914 . . . . . . . . . . . . . . . . 398
The Eastern Front in 1915 . . . . . . . . . . . . . . . . 405
The Zone of Unrestricted Submarine Warfare, February, 1917. . . . 424
The War Area in the Ottoman Empire . . . . . . . . . . . 431
The Austro-Italian War Area . . . . . . . . . . . . . . . 435
The German Offensives of 1918. . . . . . . . . . . . . . . 457
The Final Allied Offensive in the West . . . . . . . . . . . 473
The Rhineland. . . . . . . . . . . . . . . . . . . . . 485
Danzig and the Polish Corridor. . . . . . . . . . . . . . 488
Political Structure of the U.S.S.R. until 1936 . . . . . . . . . 594
Political Structure of the U.S.S.R. after 1936 . . . . . . . . . 597
How Italy Conducted Her Invasion of Ethiopia . . . . . . . . 645
Germany before and after the World War. . . . . . . . . . . 661
Ireland Today . . . . . . . . . . . . . . . . . . . . . 716
The Baltic Republics and Central Europe, 1919–1937 . . . . . . . 755
Ethnographic Map of the Former Dual Monarchy, Showing the Succes-
sion States, 1919–1937 . . . . . . . . . . . . . . . . . 767
The Balkans, 1923–1937 . . . . . . . . . . . . . . . . . 789
The Near and Middle East . . . . . . . . . . . . . . . . 823
The Far East, 1920–1931 . . . . . . . . . . . . . . . . . 838
The Scene of Japan's Aggression after 1934 . . . . . . . . . 853
The Partition of Czechoslovakia, 1938 . . . . . . . . . . . . 879
The Partition of Poland, 1939 . . . . . . . . . . . . . . . 905
Scandinavia and the Baltic, 1939 . . . . . . . . . . . . . . 913
The Collapse of France, 1940 . . . . . . . . . . . . . . . 931
Merchant Marine Losses, British, Allied, and Neutral (a comparison be-
tween the two World Wars) . . . . . . . . . . . . . . . 944
The Partition of Rumania, 1940 . . . . . . . . . . . . . . 954
The Eastern Mediterranean and the Near East . . . . . . . . 963
The Far East in 1941 . . . . . . . . . . . . . . . . . . 979
Europe, January, 1939 . . . . . . . . . . . . . . . *back cover*

# ILLUSTRATIONS

FACING

INNOVATIONS IN TRANSPORTATION
An early automobile and one of the first airplanes built by the Wright
brothers . . . . . . . . . . . . . . . . . . . . . . .  8

"BISMARCK HAS RESIGNED AGAIN!"
The Iron Chancellor used to threaten to resign whenever William I
objected to his policies, whereupon the aged Kaiser would give way
to him . . . . . . . . . . . . . . . . . . . . . . . 86

"VIVE THIERS!"
French rejoicing at Belfort over the departure of the German army of
occupation in 1873 . . . . . . . . . . . . . . . . . . 102

VICTOR EMMANUEL II AND FRANCIS JOSEPH
The king of Italy playing host to the emperor of Austria at Venice in
1875 . . . . . . . . . . . . . . . . . . . . . . . . 152

THE EARL OF BEACONSFIELD
Disraeli addressing a meeting of the Conservative Party at the Carlton
Club shortly before his death in 1881 . . . . . . . . . . . 164

THE VICTIM OF A NIHILIST'S BOMB
The wounded Alexander II being conveyed to the Winter Palace . . 278

THE CONGRESS OF BERLIN
Bismarck, in the center, towers above the other delegates; Disraeli
stands with a cane in his hand . . . . . . . . . . . . . 294

THE ARCHDUKE AT SARAJEVO
The arrival of Francis Ferdinand and his wife on June 28, 1914 . . . 366

THE GERMAN HIGH COMMAND
Hindenburg, William II, Ludendorff . . . . . . . . . . 398

MOBILIZATION BEHIND THE LINES
A few of the hundreds of posters used as propaganda during the war 462

THE "BIG FOUR" AT THE PEACE CONFERENCE
Orlando, Lloyd George, Clemenceau, Wilson . . . . . . . . . 494

"THE SAAR IS GERMAN!"
Crowds in Saarbrücken giving the "Heil, Hitler!" after the announcement of the result of the Saar plebiscite. . . . . . . . . . 536

THE RESULT OF CURRENCY INFLATION
A Berlin firm's payroll in depreciated marks in August, 1923 . . . 548

ANOTHER "SCRAP OF PAPER"
The signing of the Briand-Kellogg pact, August 27, 1928. . . . . 558

A PRODUCT OF THE FIRST FIVE-YEAR PLAN
The dedication of the dam at Dnepropetrovsk in 1932 . . . . . 590

# ILLUSTRATIONS

FACING

THE "ROME-BERLIN AXIS"
The close co-operation between Fascist Italy and Nazi Germany was
emphasized by Mussolini's visit to Hitler in September, 1937 . . . . 686

DESTRUCTION IN MADRID
Loyalists made homeless by insurgents' bombs . . . . . . . 718

THE "WESTERNIZATION" OF THE EAST
Six of the seventeen Turkish women elected to the Grand National
Assembly in 1935 . . . . . . . . . . . . . . . . 814

THE PRINCIPALS AT GODESBERG
Neville Chamberlain and Adolf Hitler . . . . . . . . . . 878

WINSTON CHURCHILL IN THE BOMBED HOUSE OF COMMONS
"We would rather see London in ruins and ashes than that it should
be tamely and abjectly enslaved." . . . . . . . . . . . 910

# PART ONE

# ECONOMIC FORCES AND
# SOCIAL TRENDS

Although statesmen and political leaders usually appear as
the principal *dramatis personae* in any general history, more frequently than they realize the roles which they enact are dictated
for them by the economic and social forces of their period. The
chapters in Part One therefore explain briefly how the years
from 1870 to 1914 were marked by a rapid spread of industrialism, a lively interest in a new and intensified imperialism, a
tremendous increase and concentration of wealth, a marked
growth in population and a steady movement of people into
urban centers, a general rise in the standard of living, and a
noticeable improvement in the rights and power of labor. In general, the period may be characterized as one of bourgeois ascendancy.

CHAPTER I

# INDUSTRIALISM, IMPERIALISM, AND WORLD POLITICS

AN understanding of the history of Europe since 1870 requires at the outset an appreciation of the fact that during this period new inventions and improved methods of manufacture brought the swift expansion of industry and commerce; that cheaper and more rapid means of transportation and communication opened the way for the economic exploitation of regions far removed from Europe; that desire for increased supplies of raw materials and for wider markets for the products of an expanded and accelerated industry resulted in a new outburst of imperialism; in short, that in an era of world politics the history of Europe after 1870 was not merely the history of that continent but to a large extent the history of the world.

## THE ACCELERATION OF INDUSTRIAL DEVELOPMENT AFTER 1870

The great importance of the Industrial Revolution of the late eighteenth and early nineteenth centuries has been repeatedly emphasized. It is well known that the changes in industry and transportation inaugurated in Great Britain during that period laid the foundations for the radical economic transformation through which the world passed in the succeeding century. Mechanical power supplanted hand power; the factory system superseded domestic manufacture; and railways and steamships, by increasing the speed and decreasing the cost of transportation, bound distant regions more closely together. Nevertheless, it appears that more attention should be given to the unprecedented expansion and acceleration of industry which came in the years after 1870. These were the years in which industrialism spread most widely throughout the world, in which industrial output was most rapidly increased, in which industrial and commercial rivalry between the great powers became most keen.

Although by 1870 the new industrialism had pretty thoroughly

3

transformed the economic life not only of Great Britain but of France and Belgium as well, it had only begun to make itself felt in an effective way in Germany, Austria, and northern Italy. Prussia's large-scale iron and steel plants were not established until after 1850, and it was only in the seventies and eighties that the great industrial development of Germany really began. In the United States the era of tremendous industrial expansion came after the Civil War (1861–1865), and the establishment of modern industry in Russia and Japan did not occur until the eighties and nineties. But in both Germany and the United States, the industrial movement, once begun, worked with extraordinary rapidity; in a single generation these countries advanced into the ranks of the great industrial nations of the world. The last quarter of the nineteenth century, therefore, witnessed a vast extension of the industrialized area of the globe.

This expansion is clearly revealed by statistics for the production of iron. In 1870 Great Britain was smelting half of the world's iron, three times as much as any other country. By the close of the century, however, her share of the iron industry had diminished in a startling way. The United States had won first place, and in 1903 Germany forged ahead of Great Britain into second place. This change in position was caused not by a decline in Great Britain's production—she was smelting more iron than in 1870— but by the tremendous expansion in world production of the metal.

Prior to 1870 the chief metallic materials of construction were cast iron and wrought iron, which, because of their limitations, were not entirely satisfactory. After that date, however, new methods of manufacture greatly increased the production of steel. In the seventies the Bessemer process [1] and the Siemens open-hearth process [2] came to be generally adopted. By the former, after the iron ore had been heated until it was a molten mass, it was purified by blowing a blast of air through it while it was in a "converter." The air oxidized the carbon and some of the impurities which had been in the ore; the correct proportion of carbon was then added to the molten mass to convert it into steel. By the Siemens process, which was developed in the late sixties, the iron ore was smelted in

[1] This process, although invented by Sir Henry Bessemer in 1856, required further years of experimentation before it became a commercial success.
[2] Invented by Sir William Siemens.

a gas furnace, through which gas and hot air were forced, at a constant and controlled pressure, in order to oxidize the impurities in the ore.

Although these processes revolutionized the metal industries by greatly reducing the cost of steel as well as increasing the speed with which it could be produced, they could be used only with ores which contained no phosphorus. Fortunately, in the late seventies two British chemists, Sidney G. Thomas and Percy G. Gilchrist, perfected a method of removing the baneful phosphorus from the ore by lining the converter with a basic material—consisting chiefly of lime and magnesia—with which the phosphorus would unite. Their invention had momentous results, for it not only made phosphoric ores like those of Lorraine available for steel production,[3] but again greatly increased the speed of smelting.

Throughout the world the new processes of steel production combined to lessen the cost of steel. The price of steel rails, for example, was cut in half between 1874 and 1883, and the price of other steel commodities fell in a similar way. Superior to iron in lightness, hardness, and durability, steel came to be extensively substituted for iron. In the case of both iron and steel, however, production experienced a tremendous increase. Between 1870 and 1910 the world's production of pig iron rose from approximately 12,000,000 to more than 60,000,000 tons. In 1870 the world's steel production was only 692,000 tons; by 1910 it had increased to more than 55,000,000 tons. The Age of Steel, it appears, actually began in the years after 1870. The expansion which took place in the iron and steel industry is typical of that which occurred to a greater or less degree in the manufacture of staple products. In practically all of the older industries there came in the period after 1870 a pronounced acceleration in production.

But the great increase in the world's industrial production did not result merely from the application of new inventions and new processes to the old established industries. It was also caused in part by the rise of many new industries, which sprang into existence as the result of inventions made in the latter part of the century. The manufacture of electrical equipment is a good example of this new type of industry. In the fifties the Morse telegraph—the first

---

[3] Introduced into Germany in 1879, the Thomas-Gilchrist process helped to speed that country on its later spectacular industrial career.

practical recording telegraph—was introduced in Europe, and in the late seventies and eighties the telephone made its appearance. About 1866 the modern dynamo-electric machine was invented almost simultaneously by three men working independently of one another. Twelve years later the first efficient electric arc light was invented (1878), and in the following year Thomas Edison's incandescent lamp was produced.[4] Edison's invention of the bipolar dynamo in 1878 and his introduction of the "Edison system" of central-station power production four years later gave the first commercial importance to electric generator and power development, which thereafter progressed rapidly. Electric tramways developed in the eighties and during the last decade of the nineteenth century were introduced in the larger cities. In many cases electric power, generated near waterfalls, rapid streams, coal mines, or peat bogs and transmitted cheaply over wires, supplanted steam power in transportation and manufacturing.

The rise of the new electrical industry may be illustrated by figures from Germany. In 1882 the number employed in this industry was so insignificant that it was not listed separately in official statistics. In the last decade of the nineteenth century, however, the number of establishments manufacturing electrical machinery and equipment nearly quadrupled. The number employed in this industry increased to 15,000 by 1895, to approximately 50,000 by 1902, and to nearly 100,000 by 1910. Seventeen years later one single electrical concern in Germany employed more than 110,000 workmen. A development and expansion analogous to that of the electrical industry occurred also in the chemical and, somewhat later, in the automotive industries as well. In the postwar years, for example, the General Motors Corporation was acclaimed the greatest industrial corporation in the world.

The years after 1870, furthermore, saw the application of capital to industry on a scale formerly unknown. Huge sums were raised by the sale of stock to thousands of investors throughout the world. The phenomenal growth of industry, with its resultant increase in competition, also gave an impetus to a movement toward closer organization and concentration of industrial enterprise. While not unknown to Great Britain and France, industrial consolidation was

---

[4] By 1927 the world consumption of electric lamps had reached 950,000,000 a year.

most pronounced in the United States and Germany. In the former, competing enterprises in the same industry often amalgamated under one direction in a "trust" in order to eliminate duplication, control raw products, crush out weaker competitors, regulate prices, and increase profits. In Germany "cartels" were organized. In a cartel the various businesses remained independent in management and retained their own profits. They sought by business agreements, however, to regulate output, fix prices, and assign sales territory, and thus again to increase profits.

More and more, too, science was applied to industry, and industrial laboratories came to play an increasingly important role. In this development Germany took the lead toward the close of the nineteenth century, and eventually in that country scarcely an industry of any size and importance considered itself complete without some kind of laboratory for the carrying on of research. The movement spread to other countries, especially to the United States, which ultimately surpassed Germany in its use of laboratories and scientists in industry. Great enterprises spent large sums on expensive and complicated apparatus and employed hundreds of university-trained scientists to carry on experimental research in problems connected with industry. Countless inventions and startling advances resulted from the co-operative work of industrial scientists.

In the industrial laboratories the chemist occupied the chief position. As a result of his work substances were analyzed, altered, and imitated. By means of synthetic chemistry many products such as nitrates, indigo, leather, and rubber were made artificially. New products were manufactured from what had formerly been considered waste substances—dyes, medicines, perfumes, oils, and explosives, for example, from coal tar. Furthermore, in such processes as steel-making, glass-making, bleaching, dyeing, and tanning, chemistry wrought a sweeping revolution.

In the twentieth century a system of mass production, developed first in the United States, was gradually inaugurated in the chief industrial countries of the world. This system sought to produce large quantities of goods cheaply and well by the extensive use of automatic machinery, the extreme division of labor, and the saving of time and energy. Its essential features were the manufacture of standardized interchangeable parts and the assembling of these parts into a completed whole with the least possible use of handi-craft labor. In some enterprises automatic machinery became so highly developed that human labor was practically eliminated.

To summarize, then, the years after 1870 saw the marked expansion of most of the older industries and the establishment of new ones of equal or greater importance; the building-up of huge units of production through the large-scale application of capital and the eventual adoption of the system of mass production; the tendency toward consolidation of individual units into cartels, syndicates, or trusts; and, as an inevitable consequence of all these developments, a notable increase in the volume of industrial production.

## IMPROVEMENTS IN TRANSPORTATION AND COMMUNICATION

Simultaneous with the industrial expansion discussed above, and intimately connected with it, were the astonishing changes which occurred in the world's means of transportation and communication. Railways were enormously extended. Between 1870 and 1914 Great Britain's fifteen thousand miles grew to nearly twenty-four thousand, while France's railway system expanded from eleven thousand miles to more than thirty-one thousand. In the single generation after 1875 Germany's railway mileage more than doubled. In 1885 Russia had sixteen thousand miles of railway; two decades later she had within her empire more than forty thousand miles. By the close of the first decade of the twentieth century the trans-Siberian railway—5500 miles in length—had been built by the Russian government to link St. Petersburg on the Baltic with Vladivostok on the Pacific; Hamburg on the North Sea had been connected with Constantinople, and another line was under construction to unite the Ottoman capital with the Persian Gulf—the two systems to constitute the famous Berlin-Bagdad railway; [5] and imperialists had even dared to dream of joining South Africa with Egypt by means of a Cape-to-Cairo railway.

Mountains were tunneled and rivers were bridged in an effort to bind Europe together. In 1871 engineers completed the Mt. Cenis tunnel through the Alps to connect France and Italy by rail; ten years later the St. Gothard tunnel united the railway systems of Italy and Germany and gave the latter a railway connection with

[5] See page 84.

*New York Museum of Science and Industry*

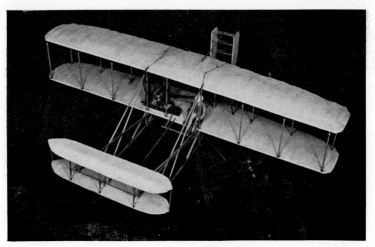

*New York Museum of Science and Industry*

INNOVATIONS IN TRANSPORTATION

An early automobile and one of the first airplanes built by the
Wright brothers.

the Mediterranean. The longest railway tunnel in Europe—more than twelve miles in length—in 1905 pierced the Alps beneath the lofty Simplon pass. By the opening of the twentieth century Europe was traversed by more than 200,000 miles of railways; and overseas, by the close of the first quarter of the present century, European capitalists and engineers had constructed nearly 150,000 more miles of railways in Africa, Asia, and Australasia.

Furthermore, in the period after 1870 railway service and facilities were vastly improved. The use of rolled steel rails made possible about 1870 the construction of a track capable of withstanding the strain of much faster and heavier trains, and thereafter the weight and capacity of freight cars were considerably increased. The introduction of the air brake reduced by 90 per cent the time and distance required to stop a train by hand brakes, and the installation of electrically controlled automatic block signals greatly increased the safety of railway operations. Both of these improvements came in the last quarter of the nineteenth century. The powerful locomotives and mile-long trains of the twentieth century were a far cry from Stephenson's light train of 1825.

The facilities for land transportation were further extended in the years after 1900 as a result of the introduction of the automobile. In the closing years of the nineteenth century Gottlieb Daimler, a German, invented a "horseless carriage" which was propelled by an internal combustion engine using gasoline. Soon thereafter inventors in other European countries and in the United States were building automobiles, but it was not until the twentieth century that they were manufactured in great numbers. The first to build a cheap, serviceable car was Henry Ford of the United States, who introduced the system of mass production in the manufacture of automobiles and thus gave a great impetus to the industry. Although no other countries nearly equaled the United States in the manufacture and use of automobiles, transportation in all of them was revolutionized as cities gradually became linked together with hard, smooth, concrete highways. By 1929, largely as a result of the influence of the automobile, the highways of the world had been extended to more than 6,500,000 miles; by 1936 the total mileage had risen to 9,900,000.

By the latter year an 8000-mile automobile road had been completed across Africa from the Cape to Cairo, and another crossed that continent from east to west. Regular automobile service was maintained on the deserts between Damascus and Bagdad, and in China automobile roads were being rapidly pushed into the interior. "Between the English Channel and the Bosporus, between mystic Saigon and teeming Shanghai, the Strait of Gibraltar and the Suez Canal," there were passable motor roads by 1937.[6]

Meanwhile great strides had been made in the improvement of ocean transportation. Down to 1870 the merchant fleet of the world consisted chiefly of sailing ships, and as late as 1880 there was as much tonnage driven by wind as by steam. The relatively slow adoption of the steamship had been caused largely by the limitations of the marine engine, which greatly restricted the amount of space available for cargo. After 1870, however, a new type of engine —the compound engine—reduced the consumption of coal by at least half, and an improved condenser not only made it possible to use the same water in the boilers for two months, but also caused a diminished consumption of coal. These two inventions reduced the cost of operating steamships and, equally important, by reducing the space required to carry coal and water, increased the space available for cargo. In the eighties steel hulls—lighter than those of iron or wood—were introduced. Since the displacement of steel ships was less in proportion to their carrying capacity than that of iron or wooden ships, they could take on more cargo than the latter before their load lines were reached. Moreover, steel ships were safer than wooden ones and cheaper than those made of iron. The compound engine, the improved condenser, and the use of steel for hulls thus greatly increased the cargo-carrying capacity of ships, and led in consequence to a phenomenal decrease in the cost of ocean transportation.

Further improvements in steamships came with the succeeding years. The introduction of the triple expansion engine brought still greater economy in fuel. More powerful engines made possible the use of screw propellers, which, although invented as early as 1836, were not extensively used until after 1870. The invention of the steam turbine to drive the screw propellers made possible, early in the twentieth century, a further development in speed, size, and economy. In this century, too, oil—cleaner, less bulky, and more

[6] Report of the highways committee of the Automobile Manufacturers Association.

economical of labor—began to displace coal as a fuel for marine engines.

To facilitate marine transportation, fueling stations, where steamships could replenish their supplies, were established along the principal routes, and mechanical appliances for rapidly loading and unloading were installed in the important harbors. Furthermore, two great obstacles to ocean transportation were removed. The Isthmus of Suez, which formerly barred the way from the Mediterranean to the Indian Ocean, was pierced in 1869 when the Suez Canal was opened in November of that year. By connecting the Mediterranean with the Red Sea, this 100-mile canal shortened by thousands of miles the sea voyage from the North Atlantic and the Mediterranean to the East. In the summer of 1914 the route to the Pacific was similarly shortened when the Panama Canal was opened through the Isthmus of Panama between North and South America. A twentieth-century commercial map of the world showed the globe crossed in every direction by definite lanes over which innumerable freight and passenger ships were regularly plying from port to port.

But man's means of transportation were not limited to land and water; the twentieth century saw him utilizing the air also. The first attempt in modern times to sail in the air had occurred in 1783 when two Frenchmen named Montgolfier launched a balloon filled with gas. One hundred and twenty years later (1903), at Kittyhawk, North Carolina, a heavier-than-air machine, propelled by its own power and carrying a man, made a sustained flight when the airplane launched by Orville and Wilbur Wright flew for less than a minute and then landed safely. After this exploit, aviation advanced rapidly. Improvements were made in the construction of airplanes, in their motors, in methods of flight, and in the study of atmosphere. The development of a light air-cooled engine prepared the way for long-sustained flights, and the magnetic compass and later the invention of an earth-inductor compass provided instruments for finding direction.

In 1909 Louis Blériot, a Frenchman, flew across the English Channel; ten years later John Alcock and Arthur W. Brown, British army officers, flew from Newfoundland to Ireland, a distance of about two thousand miles. American airplanes in 1924 flew from

California around the world by way of Alaska, Japan, China, India, Europe, Greenland, and Boston, covering the distance in 175 days. Two years later Richard E. Byrd, an American naval officer, flew over the North Pole, and in 1927 Charles A. Lindbergh, an American, astonished the world by making a sensational nonstop transatlantic flight alone from New York to Paris, a distance of 3610 miles, in slightly more than thirty-three hours. In the same year an airplane flight was made across the Pacific from California to Honolulu, and in 1928 the first westward flight across the North Atlantic was made by two German aviators, who were forced down on an island off the coast of Labrador after a flight from Dublin. Thereafter new airplane records were made almost yearly.

The twentieth century saw, too, the balloon transformed into an airship when Count Ferdinand von Zeppelin, a German, invented a dirigible with a rigid frame, immense gas bag, and hanging cabins. Although the airship never became so common as the airplane, it soon began to establish travel records. In 1919 the Atlantic was crossed for the first time in the air by a British airship; ten years later the *Graf Zeppelin,* a German dirigible commanded by Hugo Eckener, circumnavigated the globe in less than twelve days of actual flying.

By this time aviation had been put upon a commercial basis. In 1919 an air line was started between London and Paris. Eventually regular passenger, mail, and express service was established not only between the chief cities on each continent, but also between the continents. In 1937 airplanes were regularly flying between Europe and Africa, South America, Asia, and Australia and between the United States and South America and the Far East. In 1936 a German dirigible, the *Hindenburg,* carried passengers regularly between Germany and the United States during the summer months and continued the service in 1937 until an explosion wrecked it, with the loss of a considerable number of lives. Dirigible service was then suspended, pending a decision regarding the use of noninflammable helium. In this same year, however, satisfactory experimental airplane flights were made between the United States and Great Britain over the North Atlantic, and it was confidently announced that regular mail service over this route would be inaugurated in the near future. In 1937, too, the possibility of an entirely new route of travel was opened up when Russian airplanes made nonstop flights from Moscow by way of the North Pole to the United States.

Until about the middle of the nineteenth century the speed of communication was limited to the speed of transportation, for messages had, in general, to be carried from one place to another. The second half of the century, however, saw communication emancipated from its age-long dependence upon transportation. In 1866 electric communication was successfully established between Europe and North America by means of a cable laid on the floor of the Atlantic. By 1870 two more transatlantic cables were in operation, and eventually the continents came to be linked together by some thousands of cables covering hundreds of thousands of miles. In the late seventies the telephone was introduced in Europe, and by 1900 hundreds of thousands of them were in operation. The last quarter of the nineteenth century saw men transmitting messages with undreamed-of speed across oceans, seas, and continents.

But the end was not yet. In the nineteenth century Heinrich Hertz, a German physicist, confirmed the theory advanced by a British physicist that invisible electric "waves" in the ether permeate all space and matter. In 1896 Guglielmo Marconi, an Italian, availing himself of Hertz's discoveries, invented a mechanism to send and receive messages without wires by means of "Hertzian waves." In 1901 Marconi sent a wireless message across the Atlantic. Within a few years the wireless became an established and accepted means of communication. It not only enabled Europe to send messages to the most isolated places with almost lightning speed, but, applied to ships, it made possible constant contact between vessels and distant ports. Utilization of the wireless to broadcast storm warnings and to summon speedy aid to ships in distress resulted in saving the lives of thousands of voyagers.

With the development of locomotives capable of drawing heavy trains at a rate of sixty or seventy miles an hour, with the invention of engines powerful enough to drive huge ships across the Atlantic in five days, with the invention of devices to give almost instantaneous communication between the most distant places of the globe, space and time appeared to be nearly eliminated so far as the peoples of the earth were concerned. In the half century after 1870 the progress of the nations was accompanied by a notable "shrinking" of the globe.

## THE REVIVAL OF INTEREST IN COLONIAL EXPANSION

This rapid "shrinking" of the world was accompanied by a revived interest in colonial expansion. During the half century preceding 1870 there had been among European statesmen a distinct distrust of colonies. Between 1776 and 1823 Great Britain, Spain, and Portugal had all seen their great and hard-won colonial empires shattered by declarations of independence. The truth of Turgot's eighteenth-century prediction, "Colonies are like fruits which cling to the tree only till they ripen," seemed borne out by the facts, and statesmen came to view colonial dependencies with a definite aversion. Furthermore, the doctrines of free trade and *laissez faire,* which swept Europe in the first half of the nineteenth century, logically undermined the economic foundations of colonial imperialism. Colonies were, so to speak, *territoria non grata.*

But the tremendous industrial expansion and the veritable revolution in transportation and communication which came after 1870 changed all this. Each of the great industrial countries soon reached the place where it was manufacturing more than its own people could consume. Each, in other words, sought foreign markets. But none of the great industrial countries wished to be the dumping ground for another's surplus, and consequently all except Great Britain erected protective tariff barriers during the last quarter of the nineteenth century. To manufacturers looking for markets for their surplus goods, therefore, the prospect of colonies whose markets could be monopolized by the mother country began to have a great appeal in the eighties and nineties of the last century.

With the expansion of industry came, too, the need for assured and easily accessible supplies of those raw materials which went into the manufacture of finished products. Vegetable oils were required for the production of such commodities as tin plate, paint, and lubricants. Manganese was needed for steel mills, and jute for the manufacture of the millions of bags in which goods are packed for shipment. The introduction of the bicycle and later of the automobile led to a growing demand for rubber, and the development of oil-burning and internal-combustion engines tremendously increased the consumption of petroleum. Added sources of food supplies were needed, also, for the sustenance of the increased millions who were devoting themselves no longer directly to the raising of foodstuffs but to the production of manufactured goods. The rise in the general standard of living, moreover, brought an increased demand for tropical and subtropical products—fruits, coffee, cocoa, tea, and sugar. To the desire for colonies as new markets for surplus manufactures was added, therefore, the desire to have them as assured sources of foodstuffs, minerals, and raw materials.

The revolutionary changes in the means of transportation and communication which came after 1870 provided an added incentive for the acquisition of colonies. The cheapness, speed, and dispatch with which bulky and heavy goods could be transported in large and swift steamships made it increasingly profitable to bring such goods to Europe. Cheap transportation, furthermore, greatly widened the area in which Europe's manufactured products could be profitably marketed. During the eighties refrigeration was successfully installed in steamships, and a new era was opened for the tropics and for regions far distant from Europe. Without deterioration frozen or chilled meats, fresh fruits, butter, cheese, and eggs could now be brought to Europe from far-flung colonial empires.

The punctuality and regularity introduced into ocean transportation by lines of steamships which plied between important points according to stated time schedules brought a greater degree of certainty into overseas trade. This was further increased by means of the telegraph and the cable, which closely knit far-distant lands with Europe. Business communications became easier, and transactions were shortened. Consignments became less of a speculation, goods were shipped to order, and the contact between buyer and seller became more direct.

Furthermore, the lessened cost of railway construction and operation after 1870 greatly accelerated the opening up of vast new areas overseas. Railways could circumvent rapids, could cross deserts, and could surmount or tunnel through mountains. They were not, like draft animals, killed by the tsetse fly of tropical Africa. They were not vitally affected by ice or snow, tropical heat, or malaria. The fact that goods could be profitably transported to and from distant interiors encouraged the penetration of unexploited continents in the search for raw materials and markets.

In the closing years of the nineteenth century still another factor provided an incentive for the acquisition of colonies. Vast accumulations of "surplus capital," resulting from the profitable industrial and commercial expansion of the period, called for reinvestment. The same capital which would earn 3 or 4 per cent in agricultural improvements in a settled country like France, it was pointed out, would bring from 10 to 20 per cent in an agricultural enterprise in South America, Canada, Australia, or New Zealand. Sums invested in new railway construction in a country like Great Britain would earn scarcely more than 2 or 3 per cent, but they would earn up to 20 per cent in similar undertakings in new lands. The desire for opportunities to invest surplus profits in the backward places of the earth, therefore, prompted bankers to join merchants and mill-owners in the demand for colonies.

Many who were not directly concerned in the financial side of colonial expansion—who were not manufacturers, exporters, shipowners, or bankers—often came to favor the acquisition of colonies. Christian missionaries and those interested in Christian missions frequently advocated imperial expansion. David Livingstone, the famous missionary to Africa, for instance, sought to have Great Britain extend her rule over that Dark Continent in order that slavery might be destroyed and Christianity and Western civilization introduced. Sometimes missionaries in heathen lands called upon their homeland to raise its protecting flag above them; at other times they persuaded converted chieftains to swear allegiance to the government of the country from which they themselves came. At home, missionary societies and religious leaders became interested in Africa, Asia, and the Pacific isles and frequently urged statesmen to extend their own Christian government over pagan lands. Unwittingly, often, the missionary advanced the cause of the economic imperialist by teaching heathen tribes to wear Western clothes and to use Western tools. Sometimes, too, a missionary's death at the hands of pagan savages provided statesmen of the homeland with a reason or a pretext for conquest.[7]

Finally, many patriots sought to gratify their possessive instinct by increasing the "national wealth" of the homeland through the acquisition of colonies or profitable concessions abroad. They sought the confidence which came with the knowledge that their country controlled essential raw materials, that their cannon would never lack shells, their warships never be without fuel, their laboratories never seek vainly for ingredients of explosives. They sought, too, the

[7] See page 79.

comfort which came from the belief that overseas colonies provided added reservoirs of man power as well as naval bases for use in future defensive wars. They believed that colonies could serve as outlets for their country's surplus population,[8] and that their emigrants might be diverted from foreign countries to the colonies and thus retained within the empire as producers of wealth and as potential soldiers in time of war. They sought, as well, the satisfaction which came from their ability to point with pride, on the map of the world, to the various territories controlled by their particular country.

### ECONOMIC IMPERIALISM AFTER 1870

In the closing decades of the nineteenth century, accordingly, there occurred in Europe an extraordinary revival of colonial imperialism. French patriots announced that the conquest of colonies was France's *mission civilisatrice;* Italian statesmen proclaimed it a "sacred duty"; and Englishmen considered it as "the white man's burden" which no civilized people should shirk. Germany, after at first abstaining from empire-building, ultimately plunged boldly into the quest for colonies and economic concessions. Austria-Hungary strove valiantly to gain the ascendancy in the Balkans, while Russia, not content with her great realm in Europe and Siberia, "stretched acquisitive hands into Central Asia, Persia, Manchuria, and Mongolia, and looked hungrily on Turkey, Tibet, and Afghanistan." The frenzied scramble for colonies which ensued among the chief powers of the world brought conflicts far greater than those of the eighteenth century.

Down to the last quarter of the nineteenth century more than 90 per cent of Africa was as yet unappropriated by the European powers, and it constituted still an unknown and impenetrable land—the Dark Continent. The earlier period of colonization had done little more than trace the coastline of central Africa and had resulted merely in the establishment of European trading posts along the coast at the mouths of some of the rivers. In the interior most of the natives still lived in small tribal units, with here and there a little despotic kingdom. In the second quarter of the nineteenth century, however, the desire to convert these heathen Negroes prompted Christian organizations to send in missionaries, probably the most famous of whom was the Scotsman, David Livingstone.

[8] For a discussion of the rapid growth of population in Europe in the nineteenth century, see page 28.

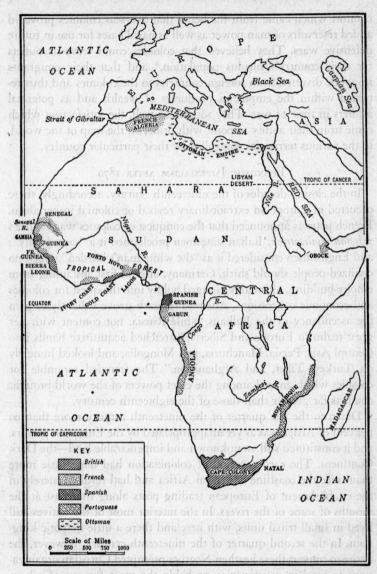

AFRICAN POSSESSIONS OF EUROPEAN POWERS ABOUT 1870

Livingstone went to Africa in 1840, but, becoming more interested in exploration than in exhortation, he ultimately decided to give up his position as a missionary and devote the rest of his life to opening up the Dark Continent. Between 1854 and 1871, at the cost of countless hardships and privations, he explored central Africa from the mouth of the Congo on the west to the mouth of the Zambesi on the east. Later Henry M. Stanley, a British-American journalist, in attempting to find Livingstone (1871) for the *New York Herald,* became himself an explorer of the Congo basin and Livingstone's most famous successor.

As, thanks to the efforts of the explorers, the map of tropical Africa began to show rivers, lakes, plateaus, and mountains, Great Britain, France, Spain, and Portugal moved their national claims inland from their trading stations on the west coast. Germany and Belgium entered the field as added competitors, and, in order to prevent the rapid partition of Africa from disturbing the general peace of Europe, international conferences were held in 1876 and again in the winter of 1884–1885. The former, at Brussels, resulted in the organization of the International Association of the Congo by the astute and grasping King Leopold II of Belgium. This association had as its purpose the exploitation of central Africa, and dispatched Stanley to that region as its agent. During the years 1879–1882 Stanley succeeded in persuading the native chieftains of the Congo basin to convert their territories into protectorates of the association—protectorates being areas where native rulers are permitted to retain the outward symbols of power but are forced to rule in accordance with the instructions of a resident foreign agent.

At the conference held in Berlin in 1884 and 1885 the rights of Leopold's association were recognized, and its African territory was organized as the Congo Free State with Leopold as "sovereign." The conference, furthermore, condemned the slave trade, advocated freedom of navigation on the Congo and Niger Rivers, and required due notification to other states of new annexations of territory. A region must be effectively occupied, it declared, before it could be recognized as a protectorate.

Africa, an unexploited continent, rich in tropical products, inhabited by backward tribes which could offer only feeble resistance to modern military conquest, now became the chief field of Europe's colonial endeavors. In the years from 1890 to 1900, particularly, a great scramble for African territory took place, some of the details of which will be given later.[9] Each power did its utmost to outwit the others in the great and thrilling game of partition. A Negro chieftain's "mark" on a treaty blank, no matter how obtained, was cited as conclusive evidence that his lands had become a protectorate of the power which held the treaty. Bribes and gifts were freely bestowed, and intimidation was far from unknown. Within a very short time, in consequence, nearly the entire continent had been appropriated by European powers, though vast areas of the hinterland were as yet ineffectively occupied.

By 1914 France, Great Britain, Germany, Italy, Belgium, and Portugal had all acquired extensive territorial possessions in Africa, and Spain had footholds on the northwest coast. Thousands of miles of railway had been constructed, steamships had been placed on rivers and lakes, valuable gold and diamond mines had been opened up, thriving cities had been erected, and the jungles were being converted into productive farmlands. In the interior, tribal wars were fast disappearing as savage tribes began to adopt the ways of Western civilization.

Although in many places native rulers still exercised nominal authority under European protection, only two regions in all Africa retained independent governments. One of these was the isolated empire of Ethiopia (Abyssinia), which was saved from incorporation in Italian Eritrea in the nineteenth century largely by the rugged nature of the country and the warlike character of its inhabitants.[10] An agreement between Great Britain, France, and Italy assured the political independence of this country, but in matters of finance and industry it was more or less dependent upon French and British capitalists. The other independent state was Liberia, founded largely by liberated Negro slaves from the United States and organized in 1847 as a free republic. But even this state was partially subject to foreign tutelage, for in matters of customs and finance it was under the joint supervision of American, British, French, and German officials. Except for these two states, however, Africa by 1914 had been brought completely under the domination of Europe.

But Africa was not the only part of the globe to feel the impress of Europe's new imperialistic impulse; the vast continent of Asia and the islands of the South Seas were also brought within its ever-ex-

[9] See pages 130–136, 154–156, 189–193.  [10] See page 155.

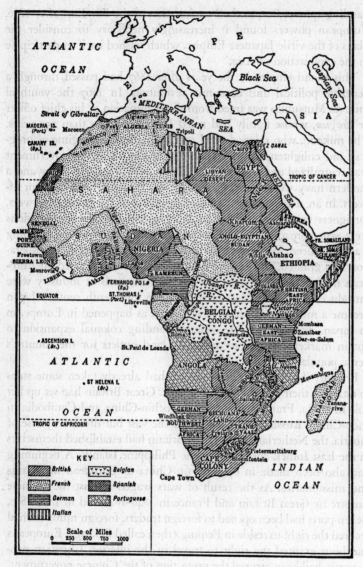

AFRICAN POSSESSIONS OF EUROPEAN POWERS IN 1914

panding sphere. But, in their exploitation of the Far East after 1870, European powers found it increasingly necessary to consider the plans of the virile Japanese Empire, which wished itself to participate in the exploitation of Asia.

This island empire in the years after 1867 had passed through a veritable political and economic revolution. In 1867 the youthful mikado Mutsuhito was freed from the domination of his chief officer or *shogun,* whose family had ruled Japan for more than 250 years. The mikado, who reigned until 1912, inaugurated a regime of progress and enlightenment. Feudalism was abolished, the government was centralized and made more efficient, and a national army and a modern navy were established under the direction of European officers. In an attempt to make Japan the equal of the Western powers, foreigners were invited into the country, and Japanese commissions were sent abroad to study European institutions. Western learning was introduced, Western codes of law were adopted, religious toleration was granted, and in 1889 a written constitution, based on European models, was promulgated. Western methods of industry were introduced, and in the last quarter of the nineteenth century Japan became a modern industrial power. And, as happened in Europe, so in Japan, imperialists were soon demanding colonial expansion to obtain markets, foods, raw materials, and outlets for the country's dense population.

Prior to 1870 the European powers had already taken some steps to establish their control in the Far East. Great Britain had set up her rule in India, France had occupied Cochin-China and Cambodia in Indo-China, Russia had appropriated the vast but dreary expanse of Siberia, the Netherlands and Great Britain had established themselves in the East Indies, and Spain in the Philippine Islands. A beginning had also been made in opening up China to European merchants and missionaries. As the result of wars waged against the Chinese Empire by Great Britain and France in 1840–1842 and in 1856–1860, eleven ports had been opened to foreign traders, foreign ministers had secured the right to reside in Peiping (then called Peking), Europeans had been granted the right to travel in the interior, Christian missionaries had been assured the protection of the Chinese government, and Great Britain had acquired the island of Hongkong and a foothold on the mainland adjoining.

During the succeeding years the vast Chinese Empire with its three hundred million inhabitants was a constant temptation to the imperialistic powers. Unlike Japan, her sister empire, China was long deterred by prejudice, a notion of self-sufficiency, and conservatism from embarking upon a program of modernization in the Western sense. Her armies and navies were therefore helpless before the powerful military and naval machines of modern imperialism and were unable to prevent the exploitation and spoliation of the empire. Gradually, however, an intense resentment developed among the Chinese, resulting, toward the close of the nineteenth century, in popular attacks on missionaries and other foreigners who were accused of undermining the ancient traditions of China.

In the year 1900 the local riots grew into an anti-European rebellion, led particularly by members of the secret society of Boxers. The latter insisted that China's misfortunes were due to the displeasure of their ancestors, whose memory was desecrated by locomotives speeding over their graves. They denounced the recently introduced machinery for throwing workmen out of employment, and called upon all patriotic Chinese to rise in defense of their country. A large part of the population of northern China was won over, and soon the European legation quarters in Peiping were crowded with frightened foreigners, besieged by the fanatical Chinese.

Great Britain, Germany, Russia, Japan, and the United States rushed troops to rescue the legations and to punish the Boxers. A relief expedition fought its way from Tientsin to Peiping and brought assistance to the beleaguered foreigners. Unfortunately, the scandalous conduct of European troops, who wantonly pillaged Peiping, sorely disgraced the Western world. The attempt of the Chinese to expel foreign influences from their country in the so-called Boxer War was severely punished. A heavy indemnity of $320,000,000 was levied,[11] and a promise to repress all antiforeign societies was exacted. The futility of attempting to shut out Western powers without borrowing from them the political, economic, and military methods which gave them their superiority was deeply impressed upon many of the Chinese.

In 1905 the dowager empress gave up her opposition to the West-

[11] Part of her share of the indemnity was renounced by the United States and was used by China to educate Chinese students in America. In 1925 the United States renounced the balance of her share in the indemnity in order that it might be used to advance scientific education in China. The balance of Russia's share of the indemnity was renounced by the Soviet government soon after it came into power in Russia in 1917.

ernization of China and began the reorganization of the Chinese army on European lines. The building of railways under Chinese control was encouraged. The ancient classical system of education was abolished, and Western science and modern languages were substituted. In 1907, yielding to pressure from the progressive group, she promised a constitution and announced that representative government would be gradually introduced. Unfortunately, the dowager empress died in 1908, leaving the throne to a two-year-old boy. The regent who was appointed was a weakling, incapable of handling the national assembly which was convened in 1910. The government's attempt to suppress certain radicals in the South, where secret societies had been organized to work for the establishment of a democratic republic, led to the outbreak of revolution in the Yangtse valley. In 1912 the struggle resulted in the deposition of the boy-emperor and the establishment of a republic.

Foreign powers immediately took advantage of the confusion in China to advance their own interests. Russia compelled the new Chinese government to recognize most of Mongolia, referred to as Outer Mongolia, as an autonomous province under conditions which made it practically a Russian protectorate. Great Britain took steps somewhat similar. When Tibet revolted against the Chinese republic, the British government forbade the Chinese to suppress the revolt, and China accordingly lost actual authority in that great province, which tended more and more to become a British sphere of influence.

By 1914 China's tributary kingdoms of Burma, Annam, Tonkin, and Korea and the great island of Formosa had been wrested from her. Four important ports had been leased to foreign powers as naval and commercial bases. The three provinces of China south of the Yangtse River had been converted into a French sphere of interest. Shantung and the Hoangho valley had become a German sphere, the Yangtse valley and the province of Shansi a British sphere, Northern Manchuria and Outer Mongolia a Russian sphere, and Southern Manchuria a Japanese sphere.

Moreover, foreigners residing in China had the privilege of extraterritoriality, that is, were exempt from Chinese laws and were subject only to the jurisdiction of their own governments. China's national tariff was regulated and administered by the Western powers rather than by the Chinese themselves. In many important Chinese cities extensive districts had been acquired by foreigners and had

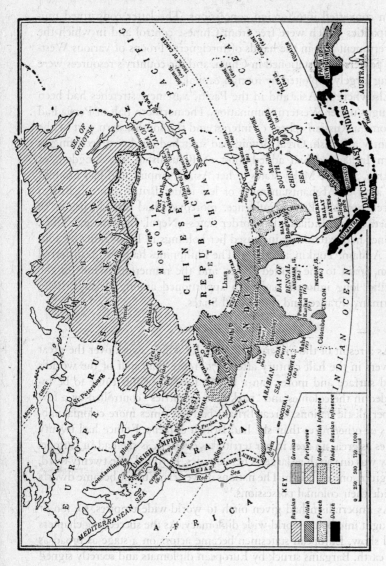

ASIATIC POSSESSIONS OF EUROPEAN POWERS IN 1914

been converted into foreign concessions. The latter constituted municipalities which were free from Chinese control and in which the government was in the hands of foreigners. Troops of various Western powers were stationed in China, and the country's resources were being largely exploited by foreign capital.

Elsewhere in Asia and in the Pacific vast new stretches had been brought under Western domination. The northern half of Persia had become a Russian sphere of interest and the southeastern part of the country a British. Great Britain had stretched out her greedy fingers from India and had added most of Baluchistan, the kingdom of Burma, and the Malay states to her Asiatic empire, and had brought the amir of Afghanistan more or less under British control. British merchants and British influence, moreover, had already begun to penetrate into India's other border states—Nepal, Bhutan, and Tibet. France had extensively increased her holdings in Indo-China by adding Annam, Tonkin, and Laos. The Philippines had been transferred from Spain to the United States, and the numerous islands of the Pacific, long ignored, had been apportioned among Great Britain, Germany, France, and the United States.

## WORLD POLITICS

As a result of the imperialistic impulse which swept over the great powers in the half century after 1870, more than half of the world's land surface and more than a billion human beings came to be included in the colonies and "backward countries" controlled by a few imperialistic nations. Great Britain had ten times more colonial subjects of other races than she had British citizens. France had twenty times as great an area in her territories overseas as she had in Europe. Italy was one sixth as large as her colonies, Portugal, one twenty-third, Belgium, one eightieth. The nations of western Europe became dwarfs beside their colonial possessions.[12]

As imperialism had given birth to world-wide empires, so, too, it brought into being world-wide diplomacy. As the succeeding chapters will show, European statesmen became actors on a stage as broad as the earth. Bargains struck by European diplomats and secretly signed in some European capital often affected the destinies of unwitting

---

[12] The above statements and much of the concluding discussion in this chapter are based upon Parker T. Moon's enlightening volume, *Imperialism and World Politics*, pages 1–4.

millions scattered over the globe. In 1904, for instance, Great Britain and France entered into an agreement which dealt with Newfoundland in America, Morocco and Egypt in Africa, Siam in Asia, and the New Hebrides Islands in the Pacific.[13] Three years later Russia and Great Britain struck a bargain which affected the future of Persians in the Middle East, Afghans on the borders of India, and the inhabitants of Tibet on the outskirts of the Chinese Empire.[14]

Alliances and ententes came to have a new meaning. Desire to protect imperial interests was the key to the Anglo-Japanese alliance of 1902.[15] Desire to increase imperial holdings was the basis of the Anglo-French entente of 1904.[16] Fears aroused by Germany's imperialistic ambitions in the Ottoman Empire were the explanation of Great Britain's willingness to drop her century-long opposition to Russia in favor of an entente with that country.[17] Common desire to advance their imperialistic schemes of aggrandizement constituted the reason for Franco-Italian agreements in 1900 and 1902.[18]

The international crises which shook Europe from time to time during the two decades just before the World War were but surface manifestations of the swift, deep current of imperialism. In 1898 Great Britain and France trembled on the verge of war in the famous Fashoda crisis,[19] and the cause was their rivalry for a million or more square miles of territory in the African Sudan. The Moroccan crises of 1905 and 1911,[20] which so nearly plunged all Europe into war, were merely two more of those explosions which were caused from time to time when the aims of imperialistic nations chanced to cross. The World War itself was in part the product of imperialism. The alignment of the European powers in that conflict was dictated not by race or democracy or kinship of culture, but by imperialism. Germany, Austria-Hungary, and Turkey were brought together by Teutonic domination of the Near East. Latin France and Teutonic Britain were united by their imperialistic bargain of 1904; liberal Britain and autocratic Russia, by their imperialistic agreement of 1907.

Europe's history after 1870 became, thus, a history not merely of that continent but of the world; her statesmen were forced to concern themselves not with continental affairs alone, but with world politics. And the root and *raison d'être* of world politics was imperialism.

[13] See page 129.    [14] See page 212.    [15] See page 200.    [16] See page 129.
[17] See page 212.    [18] See page 129.    [19] See page 128.    [20] See pages 130–136.

## CHAPTER II

# SOCIAL CHANGES, PROBLEMS, AND PROGRAMS

THE vast industrial expansion discussed in the preceding chapter not only brought a tremendous increase in manufactured goods, a reawakened interest in imperialism, and an era of world politics, but also contributed to the enormous increase and urbanization of population, the appearance of new economic and social evils, the clash of antagonistic social classes, and the formulation of new programs for the social and economic betterment of mankind. Any full comprehension of the domestic history of the chief countries of Europe after 1870 requires, therefore, a realization that, wherever modern industrialism gained a foothold, there occurred a social revolution which was in its effects both far-reaching and profound.

### Growth and Urbanization of Population

The nineteenth and twentieth centuries witnessed an amazing growth in the population of Europe, a growth which was considerably accelerated in the years after 1870. During the century ending in 1870 the increase in Europe's population had been at the rate of approximately 16 per cent for each twenty-year period. In the years from 1870 to 1890, however, the rate rose to 20 per cent, and in the succeeding twenty-year period (1890–1910) it mounted to 26 per cent. By 1901 Great Britain's population, which stood at 23,000,000 in 1871, had increased to 40,000,000. Similarly, in the forty years after 1871 Germany's population rose from 41,000,000 to 65,000,000, while that of Italy grew from less than 27,000,000 to 36,000,000.

At the opening of the nineteenth century the total population of Europe was about 175,000,000; at the outbreak of the World War it stood at approximately 450,000,000 despite the fact that some 40,000,000 Europeans had emigrated to other parts of the world. Were Europe's rate of population increase for the period from 1890 to 1910 to continue without further emigration, the end of the twentieth century would see some 1,230,000,000 persons crowded into that small continent. The relation between this rapidly increasing population and the demand for colonial expansion after 1870 has already been discussed.[1]

Two important factors made possible this phenomenal increase in population. In the first place, the conquest of disease and the throttling of pestilence brought a marked decline in the death rate and an equally notable lengthening of the span of life. Thanks to Joseph Lister's introduction of the techniques of antisepsis and to Louis Pasteur's discovery of micro-organisms and the resultant acceptance of the germ theory of disease, a relentless warfare upon bacteria was inaugurated in the eighties of the nineteenth century. The patient work of thousands of keen-eyed and painstaking men, working in clinics and laboratories, gradually exposed disease to light; vaccination and inoculation, general sanitation, and personal hygiene did much to vanquish it, especially among the infantile, juvenile, and early adult groups.

Astounding results ensued, particularly in the reduction of the rate of infant mortality. In the last fifty years of the eighteenth century half of the children born in London died before they were two years old. By 1925, however, the infantile death rate had been so reduced by modern hygiene and medicine that London was losing only about seven babies in a hundred during their first year. This was also true for England as a whole; and altogether, by 1925, thirteen countries in the world had succeeded in reducing their infantile mortality rate for the first year to not more than 10 per cent.

At the same time the campaign against infectious diseases brought down the figures for deaths from that cause in a truly marvelous way. Diphtheria, scarlet fever, and typhoid fever, it was discovered, could be largely eliminated by inoculation, yellow fever could be wiped out, and epidemics of cholera, typhus, and plague could be prevented. Cures were found, likewise, for some goiters and for syphilis; a means of relieving the symptoms of diabetes was found; and tuberculosis, though not eliminated, was lessened. In 1850 some 94 per cent of all deaths were caused by infections; in 1925 only about 50 per cent came from that cause. Gradually, therefore, the span of life was lengthened.[2]

---

[1] See page 17.

[2] "Whereas in England today at the age of fifteen the expectation of life for boys is forty-five and for girls forty-eight years, in Rome it was twenty and fifteen years respectively; whereas in England at the age of thirty the expectation of life for men is thirty-three and for women thirty-six years, in Rome it was nineteen and fourteen years respectively." E. A. Ross, *Standing Room Only?*, page 73.

During the seventeenth and eighteenth centuries, it is said, human life was being extended in Europe at the rate of about four years a century. In the first three quarters of the nineteenth century, the rate was increased to nine years a century; the last quarter of the century saw it rise to seventeen. One of the chief reasons for Europe's rapid growth in population after 1870 was, accordingly, not an increasing birth rate but a decreasing death rate.

But people, in order to live, must have something upon which to subsist, and this was the contribution of the Industrial and Agricultural Revolutions. The vast increase in the world's wealth—that is, in goods which may be used to satisfy human needs—which resulted from the Industrial Revolution has already been pointed out.[3] Although agriculture did not keep pace with industry in the application of science to production, great strides were nevertheless made after 1870 in opening up and cultivating immense wheat areas in the Americas and elsewhere. Large farms in these regions stimulated invention, and beginning in the latter part of the nineteenth century agricultural machinery was considerably improved. Rotary plows, combination harvesting and threshing machines, and tractors brought not only an increase in cultivated area but a decrease in the man power required for farming. These developments resulted in a lowered cost of production, which, combined with cheap transportation, made it possible for Europe to import large quantities of foodstuffs, paying for them in manufactured goods. The application of chemistry to agriculture in Germany and other countries, furthermore, helped to improve the productiveness of the soil and to increase the yield of foodstuffs in Europe itself. Increased food supplies, in conjunction with the extensive transportation facilities available after 1870, effectively did away with the danger of famine in most of Europe, and accordingly removed one of those checks upon population which in the Middle Ages had been so powerful.

But the Industrial and Agricultural Revolutions not only made possible the existence of a much larger population; they were responsible likewise for the great growth of cities in Europe in recent times. The building of huge factories necessitated the dwelling together in a small area of thousands of workmen, and the tendency of allied industries to locate in the same place accelerated this movement. The artisans, in turn, required others to serve them, and the consequent

[3] See page 8.

addition of "the butcher, the baker, the candlestick maker" still further increased the population of the community. Strategically located places became the centers of transportation systems, and thus still greater numbers congregated from among the transport workers. The quest for higher wages, the desire for superior industrial, social, and educational opportunities, and the lure of the city's companionships and amusements, furthermore, drew thousands from the farm to the city. A marked concentration of people in large urban centers resulted, especially in the more highly industrialized areas.

In 1871 England and Wales had thirteen cities with more than 100,000 population; twenty years later they had twenty-four. In the same period the number of their cities with 20,000 or more inhabitants increased from 103 to 185. A similar development took place also in Prussia. In 1871 the latter had only four cities of over 100,000 population; by 1895 the number had increased to eighteen. In fact, the growth of cities was pronounced throughout all Europe. At the beginning of the nineteenth century there were only fourteen European cities with more than 100,000 inhabitants; a century later there were 140 such cities.[4] Several cities came to have a population of considerably more than a million.[5] In western Europe during the nineteenth and twentieth centuries, as in the civilized centuries of antiquity, city life came to predominate over rural life.

But the growth of large cities came to constitute perhaps the greatest of all the problems of modern civilization. Out of it arose such new questions and problems as those of diminished rural labor supply, urban labor organization and unrest, dwindling district schools and overcrowded and half-time city schools, municipal transit and sanitation and taxation, poverty, the tenement house, and the "submerged tenth"—in short, a very large share of the maladjustments and physical and moral wastes of civilization.[6] On the other hand, closer association in urban communities made men's minds more open and alert, readier to question existing evils, more insistent upon changes

[4] Of only two cities—Paris and Constantinople—can it be affirmed with confidence that their population at any time during the Middle Ages exceeded one hundred thousand, although it is possible that London also attained this figure. F. A. Ogg and W. R. Sharp, *Economic Development of Modern Europe,* page 13.

[5] London grew from less than a million (1801) to over seven million (1911), Berlin from 826,000 (1871) to over two million (1910), Moscow from 751,000 (1882) to 1,617,157 (1914), and Leningrad (then St. Petersburg) from less than a million (1882) to over two million (1914).

[6] Ogg and Sharp, *op. cit.,* pages 336–337.

to remedy them, and more able through combination and co-operation to alter them. The great political, economic, and educational reform movements of recent times had their beginnings in the cities.

## CHANGES IN SOCIAL CLASSES

Wherever factories made their appearance, there too appeared inevitably the capitalist and the workingman. Machinery and factories were costly. Raw materials, furthermore, had to be purchased and wages paid before any return could be received from the sale of goods. The ordinary artisan was usually in no position to make these advances, and so, consequently, a small number of moneyed men everywhere came into possession of the new means of production and were enabled thereby to reap the financial rewards of the new era. Industrial profits were frequently large, and immense fortunes were accumulated by those who were clever and bold. Soon the industrial capitalists were in control of wealth far beyond the fondest dreams of the most avaricious aristocrats and merchants of the old regime.

Modern industrialism produced, however, not only a new capitalist class but a new wage-earning class, the proletariat. Under the factory system the machine workers, drawn largely from the farm or from the old type of handicraft, became almost wholly dependent upon the industrial capitalists for their means of livelihood. Facing the alternative of working or starving, they toiled for long hours at wages arbitrarily fixed by the factory owner. When factories came to employ hundreds of workmen, the individual was lost in the mass and became merely a numbered "hand." Between the worker and his employer there came to be no personal contact, only a "cash nexus," as it has been called. The factory-owner paid a definite sum—wages—for a definite amount of work, and, having paid it, he felt under no further obligation to his men. Furthermore, as industry expanded, the huge factories were owned no longer by a single capitalist but by great corporations which consisted of hundreds or even thousands of stockholders. Under such conditions most of the owners' knew little about the business, which they entrusted to managers; they were interested in it only as a source of dividends. That their large dividends were sometimes made possible by the evil conditions under which their workmen labored, such owners often never realized.

The new industrial capitalists became a part of the bourgeoisie and by their wealth and power tipped the scales decisively in favor of this group, which had been rising into prominence since the Commercial Revolution. The influence of the old landed aristocracy, already on the wane, in the period after 1870 definitely gave way in western Europe to the power of the wealthy bourgeoisie.[7] In fact, in many cases the landed nobleman of the later nineteenth century began to invest a portion of his wealth in the stocks of corporations managed or directed by the bourgeoisie, and thus came to be partially identified in his economic interests with this group. As the years went by, tradesmen, professional men, skilled artisans, and even some of the more thrifty peasants were occasionally able to invest small amounts in industrial stocks or bonds, and thus, almost unwittingly, linked their interests with those of the capitalist class.

The influence and power of the industrial capitalists in the years after 1870 were enormous. Millions of factory workers and their families were dependent upon them for their livelihood. Thousands of clerks and other "white-collar" office workers were hardly more free. The welfare of tradesmen and professionals in hundreds of industrial centers rested largely in turn upon the workers in factory and office to whom they catered. The closing down of a great industry was a calamity not to the factory workers of the community alone, but to thousands of others indirectly dependent upon it. Grocers and bakers, barbers and tailors, doctors and dentists, plumbers and tinsmiths, landlords and clergy all discovered that their own prosperity was linked, indirectly at least, with that of the "captains of industry." Even the peasant learned that the price of his farm products was in some way related to the prosperity of the bourgeoisie. The power which the latter wielded in directing national policies, therefore, was exceedingly great. In western Europe they became the ruling class, carrying on the nation's business, dominating its society, and in general lording it over the workingmen.

## THE BOURGEOISIE VERSUS THE PROLETARIAT

The early industrial capitalists readily adopted the economic philosophy of Adam Smith and the French physiocrats, and advocated that the government should remove all artificial restrictions which interfered with the processes of production and distribution, that the state should pursue a policy of "no interference" (*laissez faire*).

[7] In eastern Europe the decline of the landed aristocracy came more especially after the World War.

Obviously, if the government could be prevailed upon to abandon its regulative program, the bourgeoisie would be free to develop in their own way the natural resources of the world, and this was exactly what they desired. Manufacturers and capitalists believed, furthermore, in the philosophy of man's "natural rights" and held that one of these was his right to make money in whatever way he might choose. They were firmly convinced of the soundness of economic individualism, and maintained that life was, after all, essentially a struggle in which the unfit must perish and the best inevitably come to the top.

Industrial liberty, which was largely achieved for a time in the nineteenth century, was undoubtedly a great boon to the capitalists. To the new class of industrial laborers, however, it was something quite the reverse. Practically everywhere, in the early transitional stages of the modern industrial era, the factory worker was exploited and depressed. His helpless condition, without either land or tools, compelled him to accept work on such terms as were offered. Wages were accordingly low and hours of labor long. Ill-ventilated, poorly lighted, unsanitary factories menaced health and morals. The threat of unemployment, resulting from recurring industrial crises, further technological improvements, or the displacement of men by cheaper women and children, was ever present. Usually the workmen and their families were crowded together in dirty slums near the factory, where cheerless homes in cheap tenements only too often drove them to spend their "free" time in the corner saloon. Drunkenness and immorality were rife. Disease, the result of filth and the lack of hygienic necessities, periodically swept off its victims by the hundreds.

When the factory workers learned by bitter experience that they could not as individuals successfully bargain with their employers in regard to their hours, wages, and working conditions, they sought naturally to combine in self-defense with their fellow-workmen. But everywhere they encountered hostile legislation. Everywhere trade unionism in the beginning was looked upon by the governing classes as a criminal movement, and workers who joined unions or took part in strikes were liable to punishment. Not until 1824–1825 did it become lawful to organize a trade union in Great Britain, and not until the seventies were the legal restrictions removed which long interfered with the effective use of the strike. Prior to 1869 the right of labor to combine was legally denied in all German states, and in

France, although trade unions were tolerated by the government after 1864–1868, it was only in 1884 that they received full recognition. During the first half of the nineteenth century, therefore, in industrial disputes between workers and employers, the former found themselves almost helpless.

If laws stood in the way of trade unions and the workers' right to combine, then, concluded the workingmen, the laws must be changed. But here again the proletariat was handicapped. Although the middle class of France and Great Britain gained political rights in the thirties, nowhere in Europe in the first half of the nineteenth century did the workingman have power in the government which ruled him. Inevitably arose the demand for political reform. The Chartists of Great Britain, for example, during the decade from 1838 to 1848, insisted that every adult man should be given the franchise, that voting should be by secret ballot, that property qualifications for membership in the House of Commons should be abolished, and that members should receive salaries. By such reforms workingmen hoped to gain for themselves not only the right to elect members of Parliament but the right to be elected themselves. In this way, they believed, they could safeguard themselves against legislation hostile to their interests. But the Chartist movement and similar efforts failed, and not until about 1870 did workingmen gain the ballot, and then only in Great Britain, Germany, and France.[8] The struggle for democratic government, therefore, was one of the great movements carried over into the period after 1870.

## THE RISE OF SOCIALISM

Meanwhile, one of the results of the misery, inequality, and discontent caused by the new industrial conditions was the rise of socialism.[9] Although it is practically impossible to define socialism accurately because of the wide diversity of ways in which the term has been used, certain of its essential beliefs and objectives are fairly clear.

The socialist ascribes a very large measure of the world's economic ills to the fact that great masses of men have been deprived of the possession of land and capital and thus of first-hand access to the

[8] For Great Britain, see page 171; for Germany, see page 54; for France, see page 108.
[9] The term "socialism" was apparently coined in England in 1835 in connection with discussion aroused by the organization of a workers' association under the auspices of Robert Owen. In 1840 it found its way into a book published in France and became accepted in the general vocabulary of economics.

sources of wealth. Millions of men, in consequence, have been made altogether dependent for a living upon the wages they receive in the employ of men who benefit "unjustly" from their labor. The fundamental objective of socialism is the prevention of this exploitation of the workers by the capitalists and landlords. To this end they demand the abolition of private property as a basis of capitalistic production, and the transfer to the state of its ownership and control. In other words, land in general, factories, workshops, railways—all the means of production and distribution in this capitalistic era—and all forms of private wealth that might give rise to an "unearned increment" should cease to be owned by private individuals,[10] and be handed over to the state.

In the matter of government the socialists have usually regarded democracy as a necessary concomitant of their system. It follows, then, that, if all land, forests, and minerals, and all means of production, transportation, trade, and banking were nationalized, they would belong to the people as a whole. All profits which formerly went to landlords and capitalists would then accrue to the state—that is, to the people. Rent and interest would be abolished, and the only form of income would be that paid by the state to its employees. Every person in the state would contribute to the community's productiveness in accordance with his ability or capacity, and the so-called leisure class would cease to exist.

Although certain elements which enter into it may be traced back through the centuries even to Plato's *Republic*, socialism is essentially a nineteenth-century product. The founder of British socialism was the manufacturer-philanthropist, Robert Owen, a Welshman who in 1800 became manager and part owner of large cotton mills at New Lanark in Scotland, which employed more than two thousand men, women, and children. Here he improved factory sanitation, rebuilt his workmen's houses, raised wages, reduced hours of labor, and founded primary schools, with the result that what had been a degenerate and wretched population was transformed into a healthy, industrious, and contented community.

Owen maintained that the development of machine production, when organized entirely for private profit, must inevitably entail

---

[10] In general, socialists would permit the individual to have his own clothing, household possessions, money, and perhaps even his own house and a bit of ground. Communists, however, would have all property owned in common.

the poverty and degradation of the working class. Beginning in 1817, he proposed co-operation as a remedy. Men, he advocated, should be organized in groups—consisting of from five hundred to three thousand people—which should own and use in common all the means of production necessary for the welfare of the members of the group. The community should be chiefly agricultural, but should carry on a variety of occupations so as to be as nearly as possible self-sufficing. His scheme envisaged the whole country, even the world, organized on the basis of such communities, but several attempts to put his ideas into operation ended only in complete failure.

In France in the early nineteenth century several men advocated schemes which were socialistic. The founder of French socialism is usually considered to have been Count Henri de Saint-Simon. A contemporary of Owen, he was not, like Owen, a successful business man, but instead a student of political and social problems. Between 1817 and 1825 he published the socialistic program which had gradually taken form in his mind, namely, state ownership of the production and distribution of goods and payment to each man in strict proportion to his industry and skill. He did not, like many socialists, advocate the idea of equal distribution to all. During his lifetime Saint-Simon had little influence; in vain he waited for that opportunity to test his plan which never came. Charles Fourier, a younger French contemporary of Saint-Simon, was somewhat more explicit in his proposals. He proposed the reorganization of society into democratic, self-governing units of about four hundred families, which should, like Owen's, be economically as nearly self-sufficient as possible. A complicated system of distribution was outlined in which each should receive a liberal minimum, the balance of the community's profits to be given in definite proportions to capital, labor, and talent. Attempts to establish Fourier's communities, however, were, like those of Owen, usually failures.

The early socialists were essentially imaginative and utopian and apparently thought little, if at all, of making use of political machinery to facilitate the attainment of their ends. Far more practical was the French journalist, Louis Blanc, whose proposals came to have a wide appeal to the workers of France. Blanc proposed that the state, reconstructed on a democratic basis, should supply workingmen with the instruments of labor. Every man, he maintained, has a natural right to work for his own support, and, if he cannot find employment on just terms at the hands of private individuals, the state should come to his assistance. National workshops should be established by the state and placed in the control of the workers. Such factories, he believed, would gradually displace privately owned establishments, and competition would thus give way to co-operation. When that day arrived, production would no longer be carried on by capitalists who hired laborers for wages and retained the profits for themselves, but would be managed by the workers in their own interests. Blanc gained a considerable following among French workingmen, and in the revolution of 1848 he was able to force the provisional government in France to recognize in principle his program. But the attempt to inaugurate what was said to be his scheme failed.[11] In France the socialistic movement was temporarily discredited, and the socialists themselves were suppressed.

The most eminent exponent of nineteenth-century socialism, however, was none of the above-mentioned men but the gifted German Jew, Karl Marx. Born in 1818 of a middle-class family in Rhenish Prussia, Marx was given an excellent education in the universities of Bonn, Berlin, and Jena, and in 1841 received the Ph.D. degree. From his university career he emerged a bourgeois liberal, and for about a year as editor of a Rhineland newspaper he vigorously attacked the reactionary government of Frederick William IV. When his newspaper was suppressed in 1843, Marx betook himself to Paris. There he came to know Louis Blanc and, mingling with other socialists and radical exiles, formed an enduring friendship with Friedrich Engels, a fervent advocate of socialist doctrine. As the result of his environment and of his own study, Marx became a firm believer in social reform and an ardent champion of the cause of the proletariat. In 1848 he and Engels published the now famous *Communist Manifesto*,[12] which has come to be considered the first great pronouncement of modern socialism. Expelled from Brussels and again from Prussia, Marx in 1849 sought refuge in London, where he lived until his death in 1883. The latter half of his life he spent elaborating and expounding his economic views. In 1867 he published the first volume

---

[11] Blanc vigorously denied that what was done in 1848 was in accord with his proposals.

[12] Terminology in the new field of economic and social reform was not yet fixed, and "communist" was here used by Marx to indicate something which was later called socialist.

of his fundamental work, *Capital,* and left at his death two more volumes which were subsequently edited and published by Engels.

The inevitable result of modern industrialism, Marx declared, was the division of men into two great groups—the relatively small capitalist class, or bourgeoisie, and the more numerous wage-earning class, or proletariat. The former by its monopolistic control of industry waxed wealthy, while the latter, without land or capital and wholly dependent upon wages, was subjected to harsh and arbitrary exploitation. Labor, he maintained, was the source of all value, and the chief defect in the existing order was that the worker received a wage barely sufficient for the subsistence of himself and his family, the surplus product of his labor being unjustly appropriated by capitalists.

But to the workingmen Marx held out hope. Capitalism was not the final stage of economic organization, he insisted, but merely a transitional stage which would be succeeded by socialism. Final socialization of the means of production would follow the seizure of political power by the proletariat, and this step, though it might be delayed, could not be permanently prevented. In fact it was inevitable, for the proletariat was constantly increasing its numerical superiority over the bourgeoisie and sooner or later would be in a position to assert its economic will. The new socialist society could thus be brought about by peaceful steps—by evolution rather than by revolution—and to this end he emphasized the need for political democracy as its indispensable antecedent.

Marx sought to make socialism international and cosmopolitan. "Workers of the world, unite!" had been the clarion call of his early *Manifesto.* At a great public meeting of workers of many nations held in London in 1864 it was decided to establish a permanent international organization. The constitution of the International Workingman's Association, drafted by Marx, declared that the emancipation of labor was not a local or national problem but one which embraced all modern countries. This emancipation, it asserted, had hitherto failed of achievement because of (1) the lack of solidarity of the various branches of labor within individual countries, and (2) the lack of unity between the laboring classes of different countries. Elaborate machinery for the new association was created, comprehensive plans for its work were formulated, and from time to time international congresses were held.

But the International, as it came to be called, was never very successful. It was weakened from within by factional quarrels between the anarchists and the socialists, and weakened from without by the pronounced impetus given to nationalism by the Franco-German War (1870–1871),[13] and by the excesses of the Communard uprising in Paris (1871),[14] with which Marx sympathized.

After the breakup of the International, the socialist movement proceeded in the several countries independently. In order to wage an effective fight against the bourgeoisie, the socialists organized into political parties on the model of the Social Democratic party of Germany.[15] By 1914 practically every civilized country had its socialist party. With the continued growth of socialism came in 1889 the founding of the Second International, with which the various socialist parties of the world soon became affiliated. At the time of the outbreak of the World War this association had some 12,000,000 members in twenty-seven different countries. Socialism, therefore, was a force which had to be taken into account in the years after 1870.

### ANARCHISM AND SYNDICALISM

Far more revolutionary than socialism, though in the popular mind often confused with it, was anarchism, another movement which developed during the nineteenth century. Actually, socialism and anarchism are as far apart as the poles, for while, as already pointed out, the former is the acme of collectivism, the latter is the extreme of individualism. Socialists would have the state control everything for the common good of all; anarchists, on the other hand, would destroy all authority in order to establish complete individual freedom. "The only revolution that can do any good to the people," the anarchists preached, "is that which utterly annihilates every idea of the state and overthrows all traditions, orders, and classes."

Anarchism was first propounded in a way to attract attention by the Frenchman, Pierre Joseph Proudhon, who, as a matter of fact, was the one to coin the term "anarchist." Proudhon came into prominence in 1840 when he published a book entitled, *What is Property?* His answer was brief and to the point—"Property is theft." Why? Because, he asserted, "it appropriates the value produced by the labor of others without rendering an equivalent." During the next quarter century, despite occasional imprisonment or exile, he continued through his

---

[13] See pages 99–100.        [14] See page 101.        [15] See page 59.

writings to formulate and promulgate his doctrines. The capitalist system he would supplant by co-operative productive associations which would assure to the worker the product of his labor. The state he would abolish in favor of mutual protective associations. Religion, a restriction upon human freedom, he would replace with altruism. Proudhon was fundamentally a kindly and humane theorist who believed in human perfectibility. He held that man was capable of an infinite amount of self-betterment, and that he could gradually be educated to see the abuses of the capitalist system and to desire the advantages of anarchism. Proudhon therefore opposed the use of violence.

But, based upon extreme individualism, anarchism could hardly be expected to have a common platform of policies to which all anarchists adhered. Another and more aggressive group of anarchists, led in the beginning by the Russian revolutionist, Michael Bakunin, believed that violence should be used to achieve their ends. Not through peaceful political action would economic reforms be secured, they asserted, but through the "direct action" of terrorism and strikes. The dissension engendered within the International by the conflicting views of Marx and Bakunin has already been mentioned. Nevertheless, although the anarchists were expelled from that association by the Marxian socialists, they continued to gain adherents and to conspire to bomb and to assassinate. "Our task," they announced, "is destruction, terrible, total, inexorable, and universal." [16] Anarchism, however, never became popular, rarely established in any country a regular political party, and utterly failed to win the great body of workmen away from its implacable enemy, socialism.

In the latter part of the nineteenth century, however, socialism was considerably affected by a radical movement which developed among its own members. Disappointed by the failure to attain at an early date many of the things held out by earlier socialists, and alarmed at the growing moderation of some of their more practical leaders, a few socialists—more impatient and more uncompromising than the others—decided that socialism's existing methods would never achieve the sweeping changes which they sought. They determined, therefore, to adopt different methods. It was futile, they declared, to expect slow, patient work and calm, persuasive logic alone to attain

[16] In the years after 1870 rulers or statesmen in several states were assassinated by anarchists.

the great goal of socialism. Resort should be had not to parliaments, the instruments of the bourgeoisie, but to force and violence, to direct action through trade unions, the agencies which belonged peculiarly to the workers themselves. Because of its emphasis upon trade unions (*syndicats,* in French), the new movement was called syndicalism.

The syndicalists advocated that workers should be organized by whole industries, rather than by particular trades or crafts. For instance, a building-trades union should include all carpenters, plumbers, tinsmiths, iron-workers, painters, and the like. Then, when strikes were called, not one group but the members of the whole union would cease work. Through gigantic strikes the transportation and industry of any country could be paralyzed and the will of the proletariat imposed. A relentless warfare should be waged against the capitalists, but even in times of "peace" capitalist enterprises could be damaged and capitalism weakened by *sabotage* [17]—loafing on the job, injuring the machinery, spoiling the finished product.

Many of the ultimate aims of syndicalism—such as the overthrow of capitalism and the operation of the means of production for the benefit of the workers—were those of the socialists. Others, however, were quite different. It envisaged, for example, a state organized not on a democratic basis but on the basis of industries or trade unions, in which case it would be controlled by the laborers alone.[18] In its anti-government bias and its program of violent destruction of the political state it was suggestive of anarchism. Syndicalism, however, was more successful than anarchism in appealing to the workingmen, especially those in France, Italy, and Spain. Nevertheless, in Europe as a whole socialism, despite its more radical rivals, continued after the eighties steadily to increase its following.

## BOURGEOIS-PROLETARIAN COMPROMISE

To many it seemed that the lining-up of the rival forces of the bourgeoisie and the proletariat must inevitably lead to bitter civil strife between these antagonistic social classes. Although in 1917 such a struggle did occur in Russia,[19] and at the close of the World War on a smaller scale even in some other countries, in general civil and class warfare was avoided. Willingness on the part of the opposing

[17] The origin of this term is said to have been the act of certain French workmen who at the opening of a strike threw their wooden shoes (*sabots*) into the machinery to ruin it.
[18] Somewhat on the order of the Soviet government established in 1917 in Russia.
[19] See page 447.

groups to lessen somewhat their extreme demands operated in the interest of social peace. Leaders of socialism, when they found themselves at the head of large political parties with some prospect of political preferment, tended to moderate their views and to become willing to co-operate with other parties in the gradual solution of national problems. At the same time leaders of the bourgeoisie, fearful of movements more radical than socialism, became willing to surrender some of their own doctrines and to concede some of the things for which the socialists contended.

An examination of the history of Europe since 1870 reveals the fact that each group obtained some of its objectives while it abandoned or indefinitely postponed the attainment of others. The bourgeoisie gave up their earlier determined opposition to the extension of political privileges to the workingmen, and a gradual progress toward political democracy ensued. By 1914 in most of the countries of western Europe the proletariat had secured a close approximation to that full manhood suffrage which they had long sought.

Similarly, the bourgeoisie relinquished their "right" to industrial "liberty" and put aside their demand to be "let alone" in the management of their businesses. In consequence the proletariat secured, without overmuch resistance on the part of the middle classes, legislation improving their conditions of labor. Laws were enacted to regulate the employment of women and children and to control hours and conditions of labor. Factory inspectors were appointed to protect the workers in matters of light, ventilation, and sanitation. By the end of the century elaborate provisions guarded against the most patent evils of the industrial system. Furthermore, the workingmen ultimately won not only the right to combine in trade unions but the capitalists' consent to enter with them into "collective bargaining."

Free public-school education, one of the prime tenets of the socialists, was also largely secured with the "benevolent" support of the bourgeoisie, who perhaps hoped thus to wean the masses away from radicalism. In the first half of the nineteenth century Prussia alone among the great powers of Europe had a public-school system that successfully reached the children of workers. In the other countries education was largely left to churches and to private enterprises and only half-heartedly supported by the state. During the last part of the century, however, the other leading powers began to establish public and compulsory systems of primary education. Great Britain made a feeble beginning in 1870,[20] and France went much further in 1881.[21] By 1914 great strides had been made in most of the countries of western Europe toward wiping out illiteracy.

The workingmen secured, too, the enactment of laws to assure themselves at least a minimum degree of material comfort. Although at first bitterly opposed by the socialists, who feared that their strength would be undermined, social-insurance laws were enacted by Germany in the eighties and gradually adopted later in one country after another. The bourgeoisie, with the idea of increasing social efficiency and at the same time of weakening the socialists, threw their support to such legislation. National insurance against death, illness, and unemployment was introduced; old-age pensions were provided; and even minimum wages in certain industries were established.

On the other hand, the socialists were in general prevented from carrying out their program of nationalization of industry and commerce. Instead, the bourgeoisie, by availing themselves of their powerful economic position and the growing conviction among other classes that their own prosperity and welfare were indissolubly linked with that of the capitalists, were able to secure considerable legislation favorable to private industry. Despite the fulminations of the socialists, protective tariffs were erected and subsidies granted to aid capitalistic industries in practically every country but Great Britain.[22] Advantageous corporation laws were enacted, and taxation systems were, in general, drafted so as to injure business as little as possible. Finally, the policy of economic imperialism was adopted by the great powers after 1870 largely in response to the demands of the industrialists and over the protest of the socialist parties.

## RISE IN THE STANDARD OF LIVING

Every upward movement of economic progress, it is said, has been accompanied by greater social inequality, and doubtless it is true that today the difference between the economic and social status of the British multimillionaire class and that of the poverty-stricken proletariat in the East End of London is far greater than that which existed between the medieval noble and his serfs. Nevertheless, for the population of Europe as a whole the period from 1870 to the out-

---

[20] See page 176.    [21] See page 111.
[22] The postwar period saw the introduction of protective tariffs even in Great Britain.

break of the World War brought a gradually rising standard of living, a change which, though nowhere so radical as the transformation which occurred in the United States during the same period, was nevertheless very appreciable. Living conditions in Europe in the first quarter of the twentieth century were on a distinctly higher plane of convenience and comfort than they had been a century earlier. This, of course, was particularly true of the bourgeoisie, but it was also true to a lesser degree of the proletariat and even of the peasantry. Doubtless standards of living would have been raised even higher had it not been for the rapid increase in Europe's population during the period.

Modern inventions and the industrial progress of the nineteenth century introduced into housing facilities innumerable improvements. In general, hygienic and sanitary conditions became far better. Plentiful supplies of good water, often brought to urban centers from miles away, were piped into individual houses and apartments. For most urban dwellers the simple turning of a faucet supplanted the old-time trip to the well or the cistern and the burdensome carrying of water buckets. Cheap transportation facilitated the use of coal for domestic purposes and resulted in better heating; and the latter, in turn, made possible more adequate supplies of hot water. Gradually bathtubs were introduced, and bathing became more of a pleasure and less of an arduous duty. Electric lighting, gas cooking, and the introduction of many new appliances not only greatly reduced the burden of housekeeping, but also increased the comforts of life. In many modern apartment houses elevators removed the necessity for climbing long flights of stairs, and the telephone greatly reduced the need for leaving the apartment at all unless one so desired.

Cheap transportation, modern large-scale canning, and refrigeration profoundly altered the problem of food supplies. Fresh vegetables and fruits, brought from all parts of the world, became obtainable throughout the year. Fresh meats and fish could be had in abundance regardless of location. In general, man's diet was greatly enriched by the advance of modern industry and science. At the same time, large-scale production and the resultant decline in prices brought within the range of even the poor man's pocketbook many articles which in earlier centuries only the wealthy could afford. In fact, even the so-called "average man" of the twentieth century had many things far beyond the dreams of medieval nobles, while the elegantly appointed limousines, large and commodious private yachts, and luxuriously furnished mansions of the twentieth-century capitalists would have been the envy of all kings of the old regime.

The outlook of the people of Europe was greatly broadened. The application of steam and later of electricity to the printing press, the introduction of swift typesetting by means of the linotype—a mechanism, invented in 1885, by means of which type is set by manipulating a keyboard similar to that of a typewriter—and the manufacture of newsprint paper by the chemical treatment of wood pulp, all reduced the price of newspapers and brought them within means of even the poorest. At the same time, the telegraph, the cable, and the wireless made possible the quick collection of news and enabled editors to place before their readers daily—almost hourly— accounts of the happenings of the world. For many, indeed, the radio in the home eventually brought immediate contact with the world at large, enabling them at will to listen to addresses and concerts given hundreds or even thousands of miles away. Thousands of "movie" theaters brought to millions of people weekly vivid and enlightening pictures of world events. The horizon of the European became as wide as the universe.

Modern means of transportation greatly reduced the time and effort needed to cover distance. Within the cities tramcars and auto-buses enabled the masses to move from one section to another with a minimum of effort, while motorcars provided the upper classes with facilities for speeding from apartment or suburban home to office swiftly and with little effort. For hundreds of thousands of workers the humble bicycle—which came into general use in the late eighties—abolished the weary trudging to and from the factory and the shop. The modern European became far more mobile than his ancestors.

With the passing of the years the amount of leisure was increased and extended to greater and greater numbers of people. The working day was gradually shortened, holidays became more frequent, and vacations more general. Athletic sports, first popularized in Great Britain, were ultimately taken up in other industrial countries, and organized games came to play a greater part in the life of Europe than at any time since the Greeks. For many of even the "ordinary" people the coming of cheap automobiles in the twentieth century brought the opportunity to spend holidays and weekends in the countryside, and for those less fortunate reduced railway "excursion fares" and the bicycle afforded similar opportunities.

The rise of the conservative peasantry to new standards of living, however, was considerably slower than that of the urban population. Nevertheless, some of the advances which altered city life affected also the rural districts. Many a lowly peasant cottage, for example, came to be lighted by electricity. In general, the outlook of the peasant was broadened. Although he did not change his habit of staying close to home, others by motorcars, bicycles, and railways invaded his community and forced upon him some of the contacts of travel. Rural mail delivery, cheap daily newspapers, and an occasional radio, moreover, did much to end his isolation.

## THE PROGRESS OF WOMAN

The position of no class of society, perhaps, was more profoundly altered by the rise and spread of modern industrialism than that of woman. Before the Industrial Revolution woman was, as now, usually married and consequently called upon to perform the many tasks connected with the running of the old-time household. In addition to the bearing and rearing of children—often many—her time was generally devoted to cooking, cleaning, spinning, weaving, and sewing for the family. The unmarried woman found it practically impossible to engage in business or to obtain employment outside the home and was therefore driven to the necessity of living in the household of some relative. There she helped with the daily tasks, frequently devoting her time to the family's weaving and spinning—a forlorn and dejected spinster. But married or unmarried, woman in the old days, being engaged in no gainful occupation, was usually dependent for her support on some man—her husband, her father, or her brother.

Woman's inferior economic position was but one aspect, though perhaps the fundamental cause, of her general status of inferiority to man. The legal position of the unmarried woman was in no sense on a plane with that of man, while that of the married woman was even lower. In fact, the married woman had practically no rights of her own. She could not make a legal contract, could not hold property in her own name, could neither sue nor be sued in court. She had no legal existence apart from her husband, who was responsible for her as though she were a minor. She was almost completely under his authority and could legally be beaten by him for disobedience. Her property went to him upon marriage, and children born of that marriage were legally his. Possessed, supposedly, of inferior brains, the married woman led a secluded existence, rearing children, "keeping house"—in many respects little more than a domestic serf of her "lord and master."

The Industrial Revolution and the factory system, however, paved the way for a change in the status of woman by undermining or destroying the economic dependence which so long held her in a position subordinate to man. Many types of factory work could be performed as well by women as by men; some, indeed, could be better done. Women would work for less pay and were more docile, so that the new employers often preferred to hire them instead of men. Women in industrial communities, consequently, left their homes by the thousands to enter the factories. There, as earlier in the home, they engaged in spinning, weaving, canning, and the making of clothes. But there was this important difference, that, whereas formerly their toil had brought them no fixed monetary income but merely their subsistence, now they received a definitely stipulated wage. And, although in the early stages of modern industrialism this wage was pitifully low and the conditions under which it was earned were thoroughly deplorable, gradually factory legislation and economic competition led to an improvement in both wages and conditions. In the end the factory, by providing woman with an opportunity to become a wage-earner, did much to emancipate her.

For employment in the factory was only the entering wedge. Soon women began to be admitted into the semiskilled occupations and even the professions. By the close of the first quarter of the twentieth century millions of them were employed as wage-earners in factories, offices, and stores; and many types of employment, too, even began to show a tendency toward no discrimination in wages because of sex. With woman's advance into the ranks of the wage-earners came for her a measure of economic independence. No longer need the unmarried woman play the role of the humble, dependent spinster; she had advanced to the status of the "bachelor girl," independent and free.

Furthermore, hundreds of thousands of married women joined

their unmarried sisters as wage-earners and, by contributing to the family budget, not only raised their standards of living but won a degree of independence morally, if not at first legally, in the home. The lot of the middle-class married woman, moreover, likewise improved, though in another way. To her modern industry brought not an opportunity for work in a factory but a release from many of the irksome tasks in the home. With improved household appliances and conveniences, and with factories doing her spinning, weaving, clothes-making, laundry, and canning, she was enabled to enjoy a life of leisure such as her eighteenth-century predecessor had never known.

The improvement of woman's economic status strengthened her demand for an advance in her social and political status as well. Feminists, as they came to be known, inaugurated a movement to reorganize the world "upon a basis of sex-equality in all human relations; a movement which would reject every differentiation between individuals upon the ground of sex, would abolish all sex-privileges and sex-burdens, and would strive to set up the recognition of the common humanity of woman and man as the foundation of law and custom." As the result of their efforts and other influences, gradually in the course of the nineteenth century, and especially in the period after 1870, the position of woman was vastly improved.

Considered mentally inferior to man, woman was long denied access to higher education. In 1848, however, was founded Queen's College in Great Britain for the education of young women. Sweden opened the study of dentistry and surgery to women in 1861, the Swiss University of Zurich opened all its departments to them in 1863, and two years later a woman for the first time was granted a medical diploma in Great Britain. In subsequent years the institutions of higher learning throughout the world gradually opened their doors to women on equal terms with men, and ultimately were graduating thousands of them annually.

Gradually, too, woman's legal and political rights were extended. In Great Britain, for example, legislation in 1882 gave the married woman a right to hold property in her own name, and in 1886 another law finally gave the mother equal rights with the father in the control of their children. Although woman has not yet won complete legal equality with man throughout the world, the repeal of many obsolete laws and the enactment of much progressive legislation after the World War went far toward placing her on the same legal plane with man.

Politically, though slow to come, sweeping advances were eventually made in the position of woman. Despite more than a half century of education and agitation, despite the vigorous campaigns of hundreds of woman suffrage societies and a host of militant suffragettes, by 1914 Norway alone, among the sovereign states of Europe, had extended the national franchise to women. The postwar period, however, witnessed a rapid extension of political rights to them. In a score of states not only was the suffrage conferred upon them but public offices were opened to them as well. The years after 1920 saw many women elected to seats in national parliaments and some even elevated to places of importance in national cabinets. The day when woman was expected to play no part in the public life of the world was passed.

# PART TWO

# FOUR DECADES OF PEACE

In the period from 1871 to 1914 the only wars which occurred in Europe were fought in the Balkans. In each case the conflict was of relatively short duration, and only once was a great power directly involved. Generally speaking, therefore, after 1871—although some of the great powers waged imperialistic wars outside the Continent—Europe as a whole enjoyed forty years of international peace. The preceding chapters have already pointed out some of the notable economic and social trends of these years.

The chapters in Part Two, dealing with the national histories of the European states, disclose still other characteristics of the period. They reveal the advance of constitutionalism, the widening of the suffrage, and real progress toward political and social democracy. They tell of the growth of interest in popular education, of the increased reverence for science and materialism, of the diminishing loyalty to the church and the resultant rise of anticlericalism. They point out how nationalism continued to be exalted, how it entered the field of business and emerged as economic nationalism, how it operated more and more as a dynamic force in Europe's history. Finally, these chapters make crystal-clear how during four decades of peace forces were generated which in 1914 produced the most terrible war that the world has ever known.

## CHAPTER III

# THE GERMAN EMPIRE

BETWEEN 1866 and 1871, thanks to the skillful diplomacy of Prussia's great minister, Otto von Bismarck, and to the unexcelled military genius of her generals, Roon and Moltke, the situation in what had been the German Confederation was completely altered. During the first half century of its existence the confederation had been dominated by the Austrian Habsburgs. But as a result of Prussia's decisive victory in the Austro-Prussian War (1866), the Austrian Empire was expelled from the confederation and a new North German Confederation, which included all of the German states north of the Main, was organized under the hegemony of a greatly enlarged Prussia. Next, by taking advantage of a wave of chauvinism in France, Bismarck contrived to bring about the Franco-German War (1870-1871), in which the German states south of the Main fought as allies against France, and at the close of which they joined (January, 1871) with the states of the North German Confederation to establish the German Empire.

## THE STRUCTURE OF THE IMPERIAL GOVERNMENT

The constitution of this German Empire was that of the North German Confederation revised to meet the changed conditions resulting from the events of January, 1871. By virtue of this document the empire became a federation of twenty-five states—four kingdoms, six grand duchies, five duchies, seven principalities, and three free cities.[1] As in the United States, the powers of the federal government were specifically enumerated, while those of the states were broad, undefined, and residual. Nevertheless, the scope of the enumerated powers was very broad, including the control of taxation and customs duties, the army and navy, foreign and interstate commerce, postal and telegraph systems, coinage, weights and measures, patents and copyrights, banking and the issuing of paper money,

---

[1] In addition, there was the imperial domain of Alsace-Lorraine, which until 1911 occupied the position of a purely dependent territory.

and civil and criminal law. Federal laws, however, were to be executed not by federal officials but by those of the several states.

The federal legislative power was vested in two houses, the Bundesrat and the Reichstag. The former, in which the sovereignty of the empire resided, represented the constituent states and consisted of delegates appointed by the princes of the monarchical states and by the senates of the free cities. The votes in the Bundesrat were distributed more or less arbitrarily, little attempt being made to apportion them in exact relation to population, wealth, or importance.[2] Had these been considered, Prussia would have received an absolute majority. The apportionment was designed by Bismarck to convince the lesser states that they need have no fear of Prussian domination. Legally the status of the delegates was that of diplomats who spoke and voted not at their own discretion but under specific instructions of the governing authorities by whom they were appointed and by whom, also, they might be recalled and replaced at any time. Each state's vote was cast as an indivisible block, regardless of the individual opinions of the delegates.

The Reichstag, in contrast with the Bundesrat, was organized on a broadly national basis, representing not the states but the people of the empire as a whole. Its members were elected for five-year terms by the direct and secret ballot of male citizens over twenty-five years of age. The number of seats was fixed at 397, of which 235 belonged to Prussia. Although legally the legislative power of the empire rested jointly in the Bundesrat and Reichstag, actually the Reichstag came to occupy a purely subordinate position. Under normal procedure bills were prepared, discussed, and voted in the Bundesrat, submitted to the Reichstag for consideration and acceptance, and returned for further examination by the Bundesrat before their promulgation by the Kaiser. In a sense, it was the Bundesrat that made law with merely the assent of the Reichstag.

The constitution stipulated that the king of Prussia should be president of the federation and should bear the title of *Deutscher Kaiser* (German Emperor). Although technically considered merely as *primus inter pares* in a federation of territorial princes, the Kaiser was entrusted with extensive powers. He had authority to convene

---

[2] Prussia had seventeen, Bavaria six, Saxony four, Württemberg four, Baden three, Hesse three, Mecklinburg-Schwerin two, Brunswick two, and the seventeen other states one each.

and adjourn both the Bundesrat and the Reichstag, the power to appoint and remove the chancellor and all subordinate officials of the administrative hierarchy, the right to make treaties with other nations, appoint and receive ambassadors, and declare defensive war.[3] In him was vested the control of the army and navy.

The place filled in some political systems by a ministry or cabinet was, in the German Empire, occupied by a single official known as the imperial chancellor. The chancellor has been described as the Kaiser's "other self." He was appointed, and might be dismissed by the Kaiser, to whom alone he was responsible. In Germany there was no ministerial responsibility to the legislature as in Great Britain, France, and Italy. The chancellor held a position of great power. He presided over the Bundesrat; he proposed most of the legislation; he had the right to address the Reichstag; and he usually named the heads of the departments of imperial administration and supervised their work, for the various ministers were, in effect, only the heads of various bureaus of the imperial chancellory.

In order to gain the adherence of some of the larger states Bismarck had offered certain special privileges. The imperial constitution stipulated, for example, that the supreme court of the empire was to be held in Saxony; that Bavaria should have the chairmanship of the Bundesrat's committee on foreign affairs and that Saxony and Württemberg should be represented on that committee; that Bavaria should have her own postal and telegraph system and, in time of peace, should manage her own army; that Bavaria, Württemberg, and Baden should not be subject to the federal taxes on beer and brandy.

Nevertheless, it was to Prussia, the state which had created the empire and which in area and population overshadowed all the others put together, that the predominance fell. Prussia's king was *ipso facto* German Kaiser with all the extensive powers which have been enumerated. In the powerful Bundesrat Prussia was practically supreme. Her representative, as chancellor, was president of that body; the chairmanships of all permanent committees except that on foreign affairs were held by her; her votes were sufficient to block any amendment to the constitution; her delegation could prevent any change in regard to military affairs, the navy, the tariff,

[3] Treaties relating to matters controlled by imperial legislation, and the declaration of offensive war, required the consent of the Bundesrat.

and the various consumption taxes; in any tie vote her representatives had the right to cast the deciding ballot. Of the Reichstag seats she held an overwhelming majority.

### EARLY POLITICAL HISTORY

From the era before 1870 the German Empire inherited three major political parties—the Conservative, the Progressive, and the National Liberal. The Conservative Party, organized in the fifties by Bismarck and other Junkers (the Prussian aristocracy), remained distinctly Prussian. Drawn almost entirely from the agricultural classes of that state, it opposed liberalism and loyally supported the king, the army, and the Lutheran Church. On the other hand, the Progressive Party, founded in the sixties, rigorously championed true parliamentary government and with equal zeal opposed the development of militarism. Drawn largely from the professional and bourgeois classes of Prussia it stood for individual rights and limited monarchy. It had opposed Bismarck during the years when he was preparing to unify Germany "by blood and iron," and had consequently lost some of its popular appeal as a result of Bismarck's success in creating the German Empire.

The National Liberal Party, the first important German—as distinct from Prussian—party to make its appearance, was organized after the Austro-Prussian War and the formation of the North German Confederation. Delighted with the outcome of Bismarck's German policy, and gratified by his incorporation in the new constitution of provisions for the election of the Reichstag by direct and universal manhood suffrage, this party aimed to support Bismarck in his further national endeavors. Prior to 1871 it worked to promote the cause of German nationalism in South Germany. The National Liberals came chiefly from the industrial classes and were drawn in many instances from the Progressive Party. They were willing to postpone further constitutional development for a time while the central government was being consolidated and strengthened. In general, they supported the army, favored free trade, and were anticlerical.

It was upon the National Liberals that Bismarck chiefly leaned during his early years as chancellor. The Conservatives, he knew, would not be likely to oppose his policies so long as the latter did not threaten Prussia's ascendancy in Germany or their own ascendancy in Prussia. With the active support of the National Liberals, therefore, Bismarck proceeded to consolidate the empire. Believing that military strength must be the future defense of the German Empire, as it had been the chief instrument in its creation, the chancellor at once turned his attention to the army. A considerable portion of the huge French war indemnity was devoted to the construction of fortifications and to the replacement of military equipment and stores destroyed during the Franco-German War. In 1872 a uniform system of military jurisprudence, based upon Prussia's principle of compulsory military service, was adopted for the whole empire except Bavaria, and the military efficiency of the German army was assured. The peace strength of the army was placed at about 400,000 men, and the Reichstag after determined opposition was persuaded to make financial grants for the military not annually but for seven-year periods.[4]

In 1873 an imperial railway bureau was created to assist in unifying the various systems of state railways. Two years later the control of banking was transferred from the states to the federal government, and in 1876 the Reichsbank (Imperial Bank) was established under the management of the empire. Facilities were thus provided for the expeditious conduct of the nation's financial operations as well as for its economic stability. At the same time new and uniform coins, stamped with the arms of the empire and bearing the effigy of William I, silently proclaimed throughout the realm a united Germany. The North German Confederation's code of criminal law and common code for trade, commerce, and banking, promulgated in 1869, were made applicable to the whole empire, and new codes for civil and criminal procedure were drawn up and adopted.

In the early seventies a fourth political party—the Center [5] or Catholic Party—made its appearance. Having its strength principally in the South German states and in Rhenish Prussia, and being therefore essentially a states' rights party, it was from the beginning hostile to Bismarck's centralizing policies. A conflict which might eventually have arisen between the chancellor and the Catholics was made almost inevitable by other circumstances. Bismarck was suspicious of the Catholics. When many of them sought to have

[4] Bismarck had wished them to be made in perpetuity.
[5] So-called because in the Reichstag it sat between the Right and the Left.

Germany intervene in Italy in order to restore to the pope his temporal power, he accused them of trying to cause trouble between Italy and the newly established empire. Furthermore, the chancellor apparently feared that Pius IX's *Syllabus of Errors* (1864), denouncing liberty of conscience, secular education, civil marriage, and divorce as "modern errors," and the enunciation by the Vatican Council (1869–1870) of the doctrine of papal infallibility, were but foundation stones for subsequent papal interference in the domestic affairs of Germany. Firmly determined to centralize and unify the empire at all costs, Bismarck decided to attack the Catholics, who to him were the personification of separatism and localism. The conflict which he waged against them was looked upon by many liberals as a defense of contemporary civilization against a medieval church that had declared war against modern tendencies. It came to be known, therefore, as the *Kulturkampf* (Battle for Civilization).

The opening gun in the battle against the church was fired by Bismarck in 1872 when he prevailed upon the Reichstag to pass a law expelling the Jesuits from the empire. Then followed, after the breaking-off of diplomatic relations between Prussia and the Vatican, a regular barrage of laws ("May Laws" or "Falk Laws") against the church. Enacted by the Prussian Landtag, they applied not to the empire as a whole but only to Prussia; but the latter constituted two thirds of all Germany. By these laws it was stipulated that no one but a German might be appointed to an office in the Catholic Church in Prussia, that priests must have attended state schools and universities and have passed government examinations, that all ecclesiastical seminaries must be under state control, that seminaries for boys must be abolished, and that civil marriage should thereafter be compulsory. Many religious orders, furthermore, were suppressed.

An open conflict between Prussia and the church ensued when the pope declared the "May Laws" null and void and urged the clergy not to obey them. Led by Bismarck, the state fined and imprisoned disobedient priests, suspended its financial payments in several dioceses, confiscated church property, and closed over a thousand Catholic churches. The National Liberals, the Progressives, some Lutheran Conservatives, and a small minority of "Old Catholics"—schismatics who refused to accept the recently announced doctrine of papal infallibility—gave Bismarck their approval. Extreme nationalists of various types rallied to the chancellor's support against the pope, who was accused of seeking to undermine the Hohenzollern empire in the nineteeth century as his predecessors had the Hohenstaufen empire in the Middle Ages.

The great bulk of the German Catholics, however, remained staunchly loyal to the pope despite the so-called "Diocletian persecution" to which the church was subjected. To register their determined opposition to Bismarck's policies, they flocked to the support of the Center Party, which, in 1874, was consequently able to increase its representation in the Reichstag from 63 to 91, with a total poll of nearly 1,500,000 votes.

Meanwhile, another minor opposition party had made its appearance to worry Bismarck. As early as 1863 Ferdinand Lassalle, a brilliant but somewhat erratic social reformer and politician, had sought to unite the German workingmen in the cause of social regeneration. Under his leadership was founded in Leipzig in that year the Universal German Workingman's Association, designed to be developed into a great national party. A membership of less than five thousand had been obtained, however, when Lassalle's career was suddenly cut short in 1864 by a duel resulting from a love affair. In that same year, it chanced, Karl Marx commissioned one of his ablest followers, William Liebknecht, a scholar and a revolutionist in 1848, to undertake in South Germany the formation of workingmen's societies based upon Marxian principles. Liebknecht became acquainted with August Bebel, a forceful young organizer of the proletariat, and a comradeship was established which was broken only by the former's death in 1900.

In 1869 these two socialist leaders succeeded in founding the Social Democratic Workingman's Party, and six years later they persuaded Lassalle's Workingman's Association to merge with their new organization. While the Social Democrats sought ultimately to establish in Germany a Marxian socialist regime on a democratic republican basis, they announced that their first objective would be the attainment of a "free state," since political freedom was the necessary antecedent of economic freedom. They advocated reforms to bring about parliamentary government, secular education, individual liberty, and the elimination of military and clerical influences from political life. They favored the introduction of heavy income taxes, inheritance taxes, and free trade; and, being Marxians, they emphasized the desirability of internationalism rather than nationalism. In many respects their aims were the very antitheses of Bismarck's.

In the general election of 1877 the Social Democrats polled nearly half a million votes and elected twelve members to the Reichstag. Bismarck and William I viewed with alarm these triumphs of the party, and the former sought an opportunity to destroy it. In 1878 two unsuccessful attempts by socialists to assassinate the Kaiser provided the chancellor with the desired excuse. In October of that year, accordingly, the Reichstag was persuaded to pass a law of remarkable severity against them. Socialist societies were to be disbanded, socialist meetings prohibited, and socialist newspapers suppressed. The circulation of socialist literature and all efforts to spread socialist doctrine were made penal offenses, punishable by fines and imprisonment. Police were empowered to supervise labor organizations and to expel from the empire any person accused of being a socialist. Martial law might be proclaimed where considered to be expedient. Many saw in such legislation the reappearance of the reactionary spirit of the Carlsbad Decrees (1819),[6] and Bismarck was denounced as the very reincarnation of Metternich himself. Progressives and Centrists joined the Social Democrats in their invectives.

Realizing that he could not wage a destructive campaign simultaneously against both the Catholics and the socialists without running the danger of having them unite to block his cherished plans for the empire, Bismarck decided that he must make peace with one of the groups. As between the "black internationalists" and the "red internationalists," he considered the former less dangerous, and he therefore determined to come to terms with the Catholics. Pope Leo XIII, elected in 1878, was known to hold more moderate views than his predecessor, and to him the chancellor offered terms of peace which the church accepted. Diplomatic relations were again established between Prussia and the Vatican, and King William was empowered to administer the "May Laws" at his own discretion. Between 1878 and 1887 most of the anti-Catholic legislation was repealed, and the latter year saw the church once more occupying virtually its former position in Germany.

Perhaps the chief result of Bismarck's *Kulturkampf* was a per-

[6] These were enacted to suppress liberalism in the German Confederation.

manently solidified Center Party, which thereafter played an important role in German political history. In general it opposed excessive militarism and imperialism and threw its support to legislation in favor of the Catholic Church, states' rights, social and political reform, and indirect taxation. In 1912 it was the second largest political party in the empire, first place being held by the Social Democrats. For Bismarck's campaign against the socialists was no more successful than that against the church. Despite his vigorous efforts to destroy the Social Democratic Party, the latter preserved its organization and carried on an effective propaganda in Germany from the Swiss city of Zurich. Although at the first election after the enactment of the repressive legislation the socialist strength declined, thereafter it steadily rose until before the World War it was receiving practically a third of the total popular vote. Bismarck failed to defeat his opponents within the empire with the same thoroughness and dispatch with which he had defeated those abroad in the years from 1864 to 1871.

### ECONOMIC PROGRESS AND SOCIAL LEGISLATION

Although in the thirty years preceding the establishment of the empire German industry passed through those fundamental changes which are associated with the Industrial Revolution, it was only after 1870 that the growth of industry and industrial organization in that country reached such proportions as to entitle it to be called "one of the capital economic phenomena of modern times."

A number of factors contributed to Germany's startlingly rapid industrial and commercial expansion in the years immediately after the Franco-German War. In the first place, the very establishment of the empire was a great boon to German industry because of the uniform and beneficent legislation which it made possible under Bismarck. In the second place, the annexation of Alsace-Lorraine contributed a double impetus. The thriving textile industries of Alsace brought an enormous increase of resources and output and at the same time a higher standard of excellence to the manufacture of German textile goods; and the iron mines of Lorraine, thanks to the Thomas-Gilchrist process, greatly increased the empire's mineral resources and helped to lay foundations for Germany's later advance in the heavy industries. In the third place, the receipt from France of a war indemnity of five billion francs made suddenly available for German industrial expansion a vast amount of new capital.

The close of the Franco-German War, therefore, was followed by a period of tremendous industrial activity and speculation in Germany. While in the twenty-year period preceding that war only 295 stock companies with a capital of some $600,000,000 had been organized, the four-year period from 1870 to 1874 saw the establishment of 857 such companies with a capital of $800,000,000. During these "foundation years" (*Gründerjahre*), as they were known in Germany, new factories were constructed so rapidly that chimneys appeared to spring up like weeds. In 1874 this exceptional outburst of industrial activity and overspeculation culminated, however, in a severe financial and industrial crisis. The boom collapsed, and during the next decade and a half the empire was called upon to devote its energies largely to recovering its equilibrium and to building more solidly the foundation of its new economic life.

Economic depression naturally gave rise to an insistent demand for the restoration of the protective tariffs which had been gradually abandoned in the preceding two decades.[7] Free trade had never been fully accepted in Germany and had always been opposed by various powerful industrial interests. In the late seventies the demands of these industrial leaders were reinforced by those of the landowners, who, formerly favorable to free trade, were converted to protection by the competition of American and Russian grain. Both the Conservative Party, representative of the great landed interests, and the Center Party, consisting largely of peasants, pronounced in favor of protection.

Originally an ardent believer in free trade, Bismarck gradually came to the conviction that the interests of the German Empire required a return to protection. He observed, he said, that protectionist countries were prospering while free-trade countries were retrograding, that Germany, on account of her free-trade policy, was becoming the dumping ground for other countries' surplus products. Furthermore, he saw that for the rapid increase in imperial expenditures the existing fiscal system was coming to be inadequate. Increases of the customs duties, it appeared to him, not only would afford protection for Germany's economic interests but would at

[7] In 1877 ninety-five per cent of all imports entered the German Empire duty-free.

the same time increase the federal government's income and correspondingly lessen its dependence upon the states. Bismarck therefore decided to champion the cause of protection.

In 1878 the chancellor abandoned his alliance with the National Liberal Party, which was committed to free trade; and in the following year, with the support of the Center and Conservative Parties, he succeeded in enacting a tariff to protect both farm products and domestic manufactures. Although from the viewpoint of protection the new tariff was not wholly satisfactory, the customs duties, together with excise taxes and a high duty on sugar and tobacco which he secured at this time, provided the federal government with adequate income and gave it a new strength.

Bismarck's abandonment of free trade was only one aspect of his reaction against that doctrine of *laissez faire* which was so dear to the National Liberals. His repudiation of that principle was further shown by his intervention in the affairs of capital and labor through the enactment of social insurance laws, a type of legislation in which the German Empire, under Bismarck's leadership, became the pioneer. The policy of government alleviation and prevention of social distress appealed to the chancellor not only because of its broadly humanitarian aspects but because he believed it would both strengthen the empire and undermine the socialists, against whom he was then waging his repressive campaign.

Bismarck held that, according to modern Christian ideas, the state had not only the defensive duty of protecting existing rights but the positive duty of promoting the welfare of all its members, especially those who were weak and in need of help. Such activities of the state were, he believed, not only a duty of humanity and Christianity but a matter of self-interest to the state, for the unpropertied classes, constituting the most numerous and the least educated part of the population, must be led to regard the state not as an institution contrived for the protection of the better classes of society but as one serving their own needs and interests. Should not the workingman as a soldier of industry, Bismarck inquired, receive a pension as much as the soldier who had been disabled or the civil servant who had grown old in the service? If the state would show a little more Christian solicitude for the workingman, give him the right to work as long as he was healthy, assure him care when he was sick and maintenance when he was old, then, he declared, the socialists would sing their siren song in vain, and the workingmen would cease to throng to their banner.

Humanitarian desire to ameliorate the hardships of the proletariat and political desire to wean the workingmen away from socialism to the support of the empire, then, were the dominant factors which led Bismarck to adopt the policy of social legislation. This policy had already been urged by others. As early as 1878 a small group of Conservatives in the Reichstag had advocated the establishment of a system of compulsory insurance against poverty and old age, and August Bebel had even gone so far as to formulate a scheme for direct insurance by the state. The next year the Reichstag was informed that the government accepted the principle of social insurance, and in 1881 Bismarck announced his famous program. The local and voluntary workingmen's insurance systems which already existed in Germany he proposed to combine into a great national system to which should be added the compulsory feature.

Bismarck's proposal encountered vigorous opposition from two distinctly different groups. The Social Democrats, after a futile attempt to amend the first bill in order to make it more extensive in its application, finally ended by denouncing it and refusing to give it their support. The various acts they considered to be only halfway measures, and they professed to see in them nothing but bribes offered to the workers in order to win them from socialism. On the other hand the Progressives, believers in the doctrines of *laissez faire,* vigorously denounced the bills as the very essence of socialism itself. It was not until 1883 that the first of Bismarck's measures became a law; the second and third were passed in 1884 and 1889 respectively.[8]

The sickness insurance law, after amendments in subsequent years, ultimately covered all workers whose annual wages were less than two thousand marks. The insurance fund was in general sustained by the employers and the employees, and was administered by a board representing both groups. The former contributed one third and the latter two thirds, the expense to the worker rarely exceeding 3 per cent of his wage. In return the worker received free medical and surgical treatment, hospital or home care, burial

---

[8] In 1911 the Workmen's Insurance Code, containing nearly two thousand articles, replaced the earlier separate laws or series of laws in regard to sickness, accident, and invalidity insurance. This code covered practically the whole industrial population of the empire.

money in case of death, and a sick allowance ranging from one half to three fourths of his wage. If illness continued more than six months, the burden was transferred to the accident insurance fund.

The accident insurance law as later amended applied to practically every industry of importance, and nearly all workingmen, regardless of the amount of their wages, were required to be insured. In this instance the funds for the system were contributed entirely by the employers. Compensation for injury included free medical and surgical treatment plus a cash benefit depending upon the seriousness of the disability. In cases of accidental deaths compensation consisted of burial money together with pensions for widows, children, and other dependents. The system of invalidity and old-age insurance as finally revised and extended included in 1914 practically every person over sixteen years of age who worked for wages. The cost of this insurance was met chiefly by contributions from the workers and their employers in equal amounts, supplemented by payments from the federal government. The law entitled all contributing wage-earners to an invalidity annuity in case of permanent disability and to an old-age annuity after the seventieth year.

Bismarck's social legislation had far-reaching effects not only in Germany but abroad. At first looked upon by foreign governments as radical and socialistic, it came eventually to be copied and even extended by most of the other countries of Europe. Had he during his whole chancellorship succeeded in doing no more than initiate his scheme of social insurance, Bismarck would yet have been entitled to rank among the empire's greatest statesmen.

## Diplomatic Ascendancy under Bismarck

Bismarck's greatest claim to statesmanship rests, however, not upon his record in legislation but upon his achievements in diplomacy, a realm in which he stood without a peer. His spectacular success in unifying Germany and establishing the empire has already been mentioned. During the years from 1862 to 1870 his matchless skill was devoted primarily to the task of precipitating wars under circumstances which would be favorable to Prussia. Wars he sought not because he desired military glory for itself, but because he believed that they were essential to the consummation of his plan for a united Germany. During the next two decades, however, his inimitable ability as a diplomat was devoted not to the causing of wars in Europe but to their prevention. Peace, not war, he now believed to be indispensable, for the newly created empire needed most of all to consolidate the gains which had been made by the three preceding wars.

Unfortunately for the peace of Europe, Bismarck's unification of Germany had been accompanied by the annexation of Alsace-Lorraine, an act which was denounced by Frenchmen as a crime— "the brutal dismemberment of a nation." Although the German chancellor hoped to win the French eventually to accept the loss of these provinces as a *fait accompli,* he realized that in the years immediately following the Franco-German War resentment against Germany and desire for revenge were strong among the French. Of France alone he had no fear, but the possibility of France's constructing a coalition of powers hostile to the German Empire constituted for him a veritable nightmare. If he could successfully isolate France diplomatically, however, such a coalition might be prevented and the possibility of an attack upon Germany removed. In order to keep them out of the French orbit he determined, therefore, to establish close relations with the other two great powers adjoining Germany, namely, Austria and Russia.

Within a few months after the signing of the treaty of Frankfort, accordingly, Bismarck brought about friendly personal meetings on Austrian soil between William I and Francis Joseph. In the next year the latter planned to return the visit at Berlin, and Tsar Alexander II, fearful lest the two emperors might reach agreements inimical to the interests of Russia, practically invited himself also to the imperial reunion. In September, 1872, the three rulers and their foreign ministers met in Berlin for conferences. Although no definite commitments were made, the meeting served as a demonstration of reconciliation and friendship as well as an exhibition of monarchical solidarity against the rising tide of socialism. Moreover, the simultaneous visits to Berlin of Francis Joseph and Alexander indirectly strengthened Germany's position by revealing to France the latter's diplomatic isolation.

More definite steps were taken by the three rulers in 1873. Russia and Germany in a secret convention promised military assistance to each other in case either were attacked by another power. A second convention, signed at first by Russia and Austria and later by Germany also, bound all three (1) to consult one another concerning questions in which they might have divergent interests, and (2) to come to an understanding regarding a common line of action in case aggression by any other power menaced the peace of Europe. The entente of 1872 was thus transformed into the so-called League of the Three Emperors.

Unhappily for the cordial relations established by the agreements of 1873, Austria's new policy of seeking to extend her influence southeastward into the Balkans—a policy resulting from her expulsion from Germany and Italy in 1866—brought her into direct conflict with Russia's ambitions in that part of Europe. Germany was thus placed in the embarrassing position of having to choose between two friends. In 1878 at the Congress of Berlin [9] Bismarck threw his support largely to Austria, thus enabling her to secure control of Bosnia and Herzegovina and causing Russia to have to modify the treaty of San Stefano. Russia was blocked in her plan to advance in the Balkans. The tsar was not only deeply resentful but firmly convinced that Russia's misfortunes were caused by Bismarck's action. A violent outburst against Germany occurred in the Pan-Slav press, increases were ordered in Russian armaments, and Russian troops were pushed westward toward the German frontier.

In view of the danger from Russia, Bismarck at once sought a defensive alliance with Austria. He originally desired an agreement in which each would promise to aid the other in case of attack by any third power, but Austria was unwilling to undertake such a far-reaching obligation. The treaty which was signed on October 7, 1879, therefore, was directed primarily against their great Slav neighbor. If either should be attacked by Russia or any power supported by Russia, it stipulated, the other was bound to come to the assistance of the one attacked with its whole war strength. If either, furthermore, should be attacked by any power except Russia, the other was bound to observe a benevolent neutrality. The Austro-German alliance, it is seen, thus gave Bismarck a double assurance. If Russia attacked Germany, Austria would aid Germany; if France attacked Germany, Austria would at least not aid France. From the

[9] See page 252.

day of its consummation until the collapse and disappearance of the Dual Monarchy in 1918, this alliance constituted the cornerstone of German foreign policy.

But Bismarck had by no means permanently turned his back upon Russia, for he could never wholly rid himself of the fear that France might form a coalition with that power against Germany. Consequently, when in 1880 Russia sought to gain Germany's support for the closure of the Straits, Bismarck utilized the situation to restore the old harmony between the three empires which had been destroyed by the Congress of Berlin. In June, 1881, a secret treaty was finally signed between Germany, Russia, and Austria. By its provisions it was agreed that, if one of the three found itself at war with a fourth power (except Turkey), the other two would preserve a benevolent neutrality toward it and devote their efforts to localizing the conflict. In an attempt to settle the Balkan problem, it was further agreed to respect Austria's rights in Bosnia and Herzegovina under the treaty of Berlin, to make no change in the territorial status of Turkey in Europe except by common consent, to offer no opposition to the eventual reunion of Bulgaria and Eastern Rumelia, and to insist upon the closure of the Straits as laid down in the treaties on that subject. Austria, however, reserved the right to annex Bosnia and Herzegovina whenever she deemed such action opportune.

This alliance of the three emperors had definite advantages for Germany. It re-established monarchical solidarity; it tended to remove causes of conflict between Austria and Russia and thus enabled Germany to escape the dilemma of taking sides against one or the other of her neighbors; and it protected Germany against an alliance between France and Russia. All of these were, in Bismarck's eyes, desirable results. As a consequence of this alliance and the Austro-German alliance, the German chancellor now had assurance that, if France attacked Germany, both Austria and Russia would remain neutral, and that, if Russia should attack Germany, the latter would have in Austria an active ally.

In the next year (1882) Bismarck secured the promise of an active ally against France also. In this case, however, the initiative was taken not by the German chancellor but by the Italian government. The latter desired an alliance for several reasons. In the first place, there was hostility toward France. In 1881 the French had seized

Tunis in northern Africa just in time to prevent its occupation by the Italians, who had long planned to annex it.[10] In the second place, there was a lingering fear that the pope would yet attempt to regain his temporal possessions, as indeed he was trying to do through the channels of diplomacy. In the third place, there was Italian ambition. Italy not only wished to increase her national prestige by being associated in an alliance with another great power; she wished also to gain the support of such a power for her imperialistic plans in northern Africa. Enmity toward France, fear of losing Rome, imperialistic ambitions, these were the motives which led Italy to propose negotiations.

Bismarck, who had a rather low opinion of the value of Italy as a military power, was at first not especially interested in the Italian proposals. Reluctant to assume an Italian liability, he was only gradually won to the idea of an alliance. He finally concluded, however, that it would be advantageous to Germany if, in case of a European war involving the central powers, the Italian army was bound to take the field against France and not against Austria. Upon his suggestion, therefore, negotiations were initiated between Italy and Austria. The latter, perceiving the benefit which would come to herself if Italy were bound to remain neutral in case of an Austro-Russian conflict, finally acquiesced in the plan for an alliance. On May 20, 1882, therefore, Germany, Austria, and Italy united in the Triple Alliance.

Under the terms of the treaty, if Italy without direct provocation on her part were attacked by France, the other two powers were bound to come to her assistance with all their forces. On the other hand, if Germany were attacked by France without direct provocation, Italy was bound to come to the assistance of Germany. If one or two of the signatory powers were attacked and engaged in war with two or more great powers, all three were pledged to assist one another. Finally, it was stipulated that, if a great power should threaten the security of one of the signatory powers and the threatened party should find itself forced to make war, the other two powers were bound to observe a benevolent neutrality.

The Triple Alliance continued in force until 1915 and was therefore one of the most important and most stable of the European alignments. By it Bismarck still further increased the security of the

---

[10] See map on page 21; for discussion of the incident, see page 114.

German Empire. In return for the promise to come to the assistance of Italy against a French attack (a contingency very unlikely to happen), Germany obtained very real benefits. Should France attack her, French forces would have to contend also against an Italian army on the Alpine frontier. Should France and Russia jointly attack her, Germany would have the assistance of both Austria and Italy. Finally, should Russia alone attack Germany the latter would benefit from the fact that Austria, not having to fear for her Italian frontier, could send her whole strength against Russia and thus relieve the pressure on Germany's eastern front.

But the Triple Alliance did not complete the network of treaties by means of which Bismarck sought to assure the peace of Europe. With the Austrian government the German chancellor raised the question whether the "League of Peace" could be extended to include Rumania and possibly Serbia and Turkey. In a sense Serbia was already linked with the Triple Alliance by a secret treaty which she had signed with Austria in 1881, agreeing that, without previous understanding with the Dual Monarchy, she would neither negotiate nor conclude any political treaty with another government, and would not admit to her territory a foreign armed force, regular or irregular, even as volunteers.[11]

No such connections existed between Rumania and the central powers, however, and so, upon Austria's approval of the step, Bismarck opened negotiations with Bucharest. The defensive Austro-Rumanian treaty which was signed on October 30, 1883, became the basis of Rumania's adherence to the Triple Alliance. Although Russia was not named in the document, it provided in substance that if Austria or Rumania were attacked by Russia, the two would assist each other against the aggressor. Germany in another agreement signed the same day undertook the same obligations respectively toward Austria and Rumania that they had taken toward each other, and in 1888 Italy also adhered to the Austro-Rumanian treaty. The so-called Quadruple Agreement which resulted was regularly renewed and continued in force until the World War.

But the alliance of the three emperors, created in 1881 and renewed for three years in 1884, suffered a less happy fate. Once again Austro-Russian rivalry in the Balkans smashed Bismarck's diplomatic plans when, in 1887, Tsar Alexander III refused to renew the

---

[11] For a fuller discussion of this treaty see page 293.

alliance because of his distrust of Austria and her policy in south-eastern Europe. When Bismarck discovered that the tsar was un-shakable in his determination to break with Austria, he accepted with alacrity Russia's proposal for a Russo-German defensive treaty. In 1887 the two powers agreed that, if either of them were at war with a third great power, the other would maintain toward it a benevolent neutrality and would seek to localize the conflict. This provision was not to apply, however, to a war in which Russia attacked Austria or Germany attacked France. This so-called rein-surance treaty further recognized Russia's position in the Straits and in the Balkans in much the same way as it had been recognized in the alliance of the three emperors. Again Bismarck had advanced the security of the German Empire, for by the reinsurance treaty France was effectively blocked from securing Russia as an ally in an attack upon Germany.

A glance at the diagram (on page 73) of the network of defen-sive alliances which the German chancellor created in the two decades after 1871 quickly reveals the extent of France's isolation and the corresponding measure of Bismarck's diplomatic success. The peace of the German Empire was assured, for no power cared to risk a war against a country which was supported by secret alliances assuring it of the co-operation of Austria, Russia, Italy, and Rumania. The German chancellor had cured his nightmare of alliances by inoculation.

### BEGINNINGS OF COLONIAL EXPANSION

Meanwhile, the rise of German industry and trade had created "a veritable hothouse atmosphere for the culture of the colonial idea." Since Germany had made herself supreme in Europe, why, asked many German patriots, should she not extend her power upon the sea and overseas? Unfortunately, the backward and feudal con-dition of the German states at the time of the Commercial Revolu-tion and the *laissez-faire* doctrines of their various rulers during the first part of the nineteenth century had militated against the ac-quisition of colonial territory. Although German missionaries and German merchants had settlements and trading posts in Africa and the South Sea isles, not one of the component states which united to form the German Empire in 1871 brought with it a single square mile of overseas dominion.

With the establishment of the empire, however, political dis-union and economic weakness ceased to be deterrents to German maritime and colonial expansion. In the very first year of the empire the imperial admiralty was created and a naval base was established at Wilhelmshafen on the North Sea. Increasing commerce demanded naval protection, and as navalism grew it paved the way for colonies. "For a growing people," asserted Prince Albrecht, "there is no prosperity without expansion, no expansion without an overseas policy, and no overseas policy without a navy." During the early years of the empire, however, Bismarck and the ruling classes gen-erally opposed firmly the policy of imperialism. In 1874, for ex-ample, the chancellor declined to accept Zanzibar as a German protectorate even though it was voluntarily offered by the native ruler himself.

A number of factors explain Bismarck's unwillingness to en-courage colonial undertakings during the early years of his chan-cellorship. In general, he believed that colonial expansion would involve too great expense, would cause friction with other powers, and would interfere with his efforts to attain German security in Europe. He particularly desired to maintain friendship with Great Britain and was opposed to any activity which would be likely to cause friction with that power while Germany was young and her navy weak. Furthermore, during the period immediately after 1870, he was relying upon the support of the National Liberals to carry through domestic policies, and the latter were in those days still believers in the doctrines of *laissez faire*. Finally, Bismarck believed that there was no general popular demand or support for colonial-ism within Germany herself.

Nevertheless, by 1876 the chancellor had come to the conclusion that a great state like Germany could not entirely dispense with colonies, and during the next eight years he apparently played a double game. Openly and officially he continued to repudiate the policy of colonial expansion; secretly and indirectly he pursued that very policy. Governmental protection was extended to all overseas commercial enterprises, and a series of commercial treaties both inaugurated a system of overseas trade protection and endorsed the acquisition of naval stations.

Gradually circumstances came to favor Bismarck's open adoption of a policy of overseas expansion. Within the country itself there came an increase of colonial sentiment as advocates of imperialism flooded the empire with propaganda. In 1882 the Colonial Society was founded, and in January, 1884, its official organ, the *Kolonialzeitung,* was launched. By 1884 the organization had some thousands

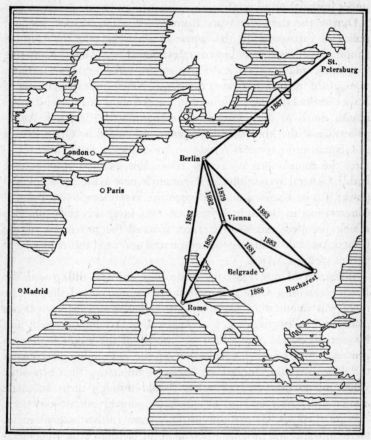

AUSTRO-GERMAN SYSTEM OF ALLIANCES, 1887–1890

of members scattered in hundreds of places throughout Germany. By that year, furthermore, with Germany's security in Europe apparently attained, the international situation seemed more favorable to German overseas expansion. Although Bismarck still believed it wise to subordinate his colonial policy to the exigencies of foreign relations, he now decided that it was no longer necessary to subordinate it to the point of negation as he had done prior to 1875. On April 24, 1884, accordingly, the chancellor publicly inaugurated the German colonial empire by telegraphing to Lüderitz, a Bremen merchant, that the latter's settlements in Southwest Africa were under imperial protection.

During the next five years Bismarck steadily pursued his new policy of expansion. In the course of the year 1884 the German Empire established four protectorates: Southwest Africa, Kamerun, Togoland, and East Africa. Early in the following year territory was gained in the Far East. A quarter of New Guinea (rechristened Kaiser Wilhelmsland), a group of the Solomon Islands and other islands north of New Guinea (later named the Bismarck Archipelago), and the Marshall Islands were recognized by Great Britain as German protectorates. Within an astonishingly short time, therefore, the foundations of a very respectable colonial empire were laid.[12] General recognition of Germany's new status as a colonial power was in a sense conceded when the first international colonial congress met in Berlin in November, 1884. Over this gathering Bismarck presided and, with France, dictated the provisions of the Congo Act [13] determining the commercial and legal future of a large part of western Africa.

When, in March, 1885, the Steamship Subsidy Bill passed the Reichstag with a large majority, Bismarck announced that at last there was manifest in Germany the "popular support" which he considered indispensable to a colonial policy. A new tone crept into his utterances. He now talked not merely of the empire's duty to protect commercial settlements but of the desirability of colonies for their own sake. Indeed, he began to emphasize their economic value and to urge that Germany should through them be made economically independent. Colonies, he pointed out, would open new markets to German industries, cause further expansion of German trade, and provide a new field for German activity, civilization, and capital.

But Bismarck did not permit his colonial ambitions to interfere with the attainment of the ends sought by his foreign policy. When relations became strained between Germany and Great

---

[12] For the location of Germany's colonies, see the maps on pages 21 and 25.
[13] See page 20.

Britain because of the latter's resentment of his new colonial policy, the German chancellor at once took steps to smooth away all causes of friction so that no *rapprochement* might result between Great Britain and France. So successful were his efforts that Gladstone, British prime minister, in the end even went so far as to welcome Germany as "our ally in the execution of the great purposes of Providence." The Anglo-German "colonial honeymoon" which began in 1885 Bismarck sought to transform into a lasting bond by negotiations for a British alliance in 1889, but in this case without result.

## WILLIAM II AND THE "NEW COURSE"

On March 9, 1888, the aged William I died and was succeeded by his son, Frederick III. The latter, however, was fatally ill at the time of his accession and died on June 15 of the same year. As a result of these circumstances there mounted the imperial throne a young man of twenty-nine years, William II, the grandson of William I. Like his grandfather a firm believer in the value of military power, William II's first imperial messages were issued not to the German people but to the army and navy. Like his grandfather, too, a loyal adherent to the divine-right theory of kingship, he did not hesitate upon occasion to assert that "the king's will is the supreme law of the land." Characterized by his own father as inclined to be vain and conceited, he was also impulsive and strongly influenced by moods. Vigorous, aggressive, and possessed of exceptional ability as a public speaker, he developed a tendency to use pompous language and to resort to spectacular public display, a tendency which seriously embarrassed the imperial government from time to time in the succeeding years. Nevertheless, he played such an important role in German and world affairs that "the Kaiser" came to be synonymous in the popular mind with "William II."

Although the new ruler resembled his grandfather in many respects, he differed profoundly from him in his attitude toward Bismarck. Despite his deep respect for the veteran chancellor's ideas and achievements, William II was himself ambitious for power and eager to rule as well as reign. He was not at all attracted by the prospect of becoming a mere imperial figurehead under the domination of Bismarck. Almost inevitably differences in viewpoint and policies developed between the young, impulsive, ambitious Kaiser and the old, conservative, powerful chancellor whom he had inherited. William II, for example, although he disliked the socialists no less than Bismarck, refused to approve or support the latter's futile antisocialist legislation, which was accordingly permitted to lapse. Bismarck, on the other hand, refused to accept a cabinet order which destroyed his position as intermediary between the other ministers and the Kaiser. Each hesitated to take the final step to sever their relations, but in 1890 William II finally demanded Bismarck's resignation. For years Bismarck had assiduously preached that the chancellor was responsible to the Kaiser and to him alone, and his words now rose to mock him. In the light of his earlier assertions, when William II withdrew his support, no course was open to him except to resign. Thereafter, until his death in 1898, Bismarck lived in retirement at Friedrichsruh.

The new chancellor was Count von Caprivi, a veteran soldier, but one who was unfamiliar with politics, largely dependent on the information and advice of others, and incapable of effective leadership. To a considerable extent William II became his own chancellor. Although many of Bismarck's policies were retained in the ensuing years, in some respects the "dropping of the pilot" appeared to be followed by the charting of a "new course." This was particularly noticeable in the realm of foreign affairs, where, despite William II's declaration that his foreign policy would remain the same as that of his grandfather, fundamental changes were soon introduced.

William I had repeatedly emphasized the need of keeping the friendship of both Russia and Great Britain, and this aim had been a cardinal point in Bismarck's successful diplomacy. When the question of renewing the reinsurance treaty with Russia was raised in 1890, however, counselors in the German foreign office, hostile to Bismarck, argued against it. The Russian treaty was, they said, contrary to the spirit of the Triple Alliance, and it might, furthermore, alienate Great Britain if its existence became known to that country. William II and Caprivi were won over by these arguments, and negotiations for a renewal of the reinsurance treaty were dropped. Thus came almost immediately the first break in the network of alliances which Bismarck had so laboriously constructed to isolate France. Russia, herself isolated, grew suspicious of the policy of the new Kaiser and soon thereafter became receptive to the solicitous proposals of France.[14]

Eventually Great Britain, too, was alienated from Germany. In this case the alienation came not as the result of the severing of treaty relations but in consequence of a fundamental change in the aims of German foreign policy. Whereas Bismarck had been content to have the German Empire a military power and the dominant state in continental Europe, William II was determined through colonial and naval expansion to make it a world power. But the aims of German world policy inevitably conflicted with the aims of Great Britain, gradually aroused the latter's suspicions and fears, and finally drove her, too, into the arms of France.[15]

To a certain extent Germany's new world policy was the natural consequence of her astounding economic development after 1890. By that year the empire had fully recovered from its economic collapse of 1874, and in the succeeding years a combination of factors carried it rapidly to the front. Little handicapped by the existence of inefficient and out-of-date industrial plants, the Germans profited by the experience of others and adopted the latest and most improved methods of manufacture. The application to industry of the excellent scientific and technical training provided by German schools and universities, furthermore, frequently brought the discovery of new methods and the introduction of greater efficiency. And the natural industriousness of the German workingman, coupled with the well-known German capacity for organization, made possible the building up of industrial enterprises that could successfully meet all competition. In the two decades after 1890 German industrial and commercial expansion was truly spectacular. The production of steel during that period, for example, increased seven times faster in Germany than in Great Britain.

Germany's industrial expansion in turn demanded world markets for her increased production, raw materials for her almost insatiable machines, and foodstuffs for her rapidly growing urban population. To obtain these William II considered it necessary for Germany, because of her late entrance into world trade, to pursue a vigorous foreign and colonial policy. New colonies were essential if Ger-

---

[14] For the Franco-Russian alliance which resulted in 1894, see pages 114–115.
[15] For these developments, see pages 129–130.

many's European hegemony were to be transformed into world power; in fact, to the Kaiser's mind colonial policy was only a branch of that world policy which the German Empire must adopt for the protection of its continental position. He accordingly placed himself at the head of the colonial movement and boldly embarked upon the "new course," departing without apparent hesitation from Bismarck's more cautious policy of subordinating colonial expansion to the exigencies of continental foreign policy.

Furthermore, to support the new world policy William II demanded the building of a powerful navy. Such a navy, he believed, would give expression to the greatness of the new Germany. It would provide the empire's growing commercial and colonial interests with adequate protection, and in case of war would remove from the German people the danger of being cut off from indispensable food supplies and raw materials. Moreover, a powerful navy might be used to back up German diplomatic arguments in the struggle for commercial and colonial advantages; it might, in fact, compel even Great Britain to make concessions in the colonial world rather than "risk" a naval struggle.

### The Scramble for Overseas Territory

The "new course" as applied to colonial policy was particularly noticeable during the decade after 1894. This period witnessed a feverish activity on the part of the Kaiser, who apparently sought by taking advantage of the embarrassments of other countries to gain for Germany a "place in the sun." During these years, according to one distinguished specialist in the diplomacy of imperialism, "the Germans made something of a nuisance of themselves by interjecting themselves into every problem and by demanding compensation everywhere and at all times." [16]

To facilitate the carrying-out of this policy, William II sought to have about him ministers who endorsed his views. For example, in 1894, when he appointed the aged Prince Hohenlohe to the chancellorship, the latter at once announced that the "support of our colonial possessions is a command of national honor and a manifestation of our national prestige." In his quest of new territories the Kaiser had also the encouragement of "big business," the Colonial Society, the Navy League, and the Pan-German League. The

[16] W. L. Langer, *The Diplomacy of Imperialism, 1890–1902*, Volume II, page 531.

latter—a patriotic organization of teachers and professors, business and professional men, and officials—was founded in the early nineties, when it announced as one of its prime aims "the promotion of an active colonial policy." It sought to further an energetic German policy of might in Europe and overseas, and above all to carry forward the German colonial movement to tangible results.

The technique of the Kaiser's "new course" was at once revealed when friction developed between Great Britain and the Boers of the Transvaal Republic during the years 1894–1895. German warships were sent to Delagoa Bay, which the British were hoping to obtain from Portugal in order to control the Boer republic's outlet to the sea; German protests were raised against Jameson's raid into the republic; and finally the famous "Kruger telegram" was sent by the Kaiser to the Boer president congratulating him on "preserving the independence" of his country.[17] Back of all these actions, apparently, was William II's real desire to land troops in order to bring about an annexation of territory for Germany, a step from which he was deterred only by the opposition of his chancellor and foreign secretary. German activities on this occasion failed to secure any territory, but they did succeed in bringing to an unhappy end the Anglo-German "honeymoon" so felicitously arranged by Bismarck.

The Kaiser's next move was in the Far East. With Germany building a bigger navy and extending her economic interests throughout the world, the possibility of securing a naval base in the Far East had been discussed for some time in German naval and colonial circles. An ice-free port which would give access to a useful hinterland was sought, and in 1897 Kiaochow on the Shantung peninsula of China was selected as a desirable site. Fortunately for the Kaiser's plans, two German missionaries were murdered by the Chinese in this very Shantung province. "We must take advantage of this excellent opportunity," William II telegraphed to the foreign office, "before another great power either dismembers China or comes to her help! Now or never!" A German squadron was immediately dispatched to Kiaochow, and in March, 1898, a treaty was wrested from China leasing to Germany for ninety-nine years some two hundred square miles of territory on the shores of Kiaochow Bay. Germany thus acquired not only a naval base in the Far East but

[17] For a fuller discussion of these incidents, see pages 190–191.

a valuable economic sphere of influence in the great Chinese Empire.[18] As significant by-products, however, she incurred the increased hostility of Great Britain, the suspicion of France, and the indignation of the rising Far Eastern power, Japan.

The acquisition of one naval base in the Pacific only whetted the Kaiser's appetite for more, and the outbreak of the Spanish-American War in 1898 appeared to offer further possibilities. At first the idea of establishing a German protectorate over the Philippine Islands was seriously considered, but the ultimate decision was to demand adequate compensations for Germany in case the islands fell into the hands of another power. Admiral von Diederichs was dispatched to Philippine waters with a large squadron in the hope of his being able to seize a naval station, but the outburst of anti-German feeling in the United States following disagreements between Admiral von Diederichs and Admiral Dewey in Manila Bay prevented such a step. Instead, Germany sought a division of the colonial spoils in co-operation with the United States, and ultimately, in return for the payment of $4,200,000 to Spain, acquired the Caroline, Pelew, and Marianne Islands.[19] Although the islands might serve as naval stations and cable landings, they were of little value economically. Nevertheless, their acquisition was described to the Reichstag by the chancellor as a milestone "along the road of *Weltpolitik.*"

Germany next took advantage of Great Britain's isolation and colonial conflicts with France and Russia [20] to try to advance her colonial program. In the view of Joseph Chamberlain, British colonial secretary at that time, she seized the occasion to "blackmail" Great Britain into making concessions in order to induce her "not to interfere where she has no right of interference." In 1898 Portugal was in need of financial assistance, and it was thought that she might be obliged to mortgage her colonies in Africa. Germany accordingly persuaded the British government to sign a treaty providing for the division of the Portuguese colonies—Angola and

[18] The lease carried with it the right (1) to fortify and administer the territory as if it were Germany's, (2) to build railways into the interior to join the projected Chinese system, (3) to exploit all mines found near the railways, and (4) to enjoy special preference for German capital and materials in the construction of public works in the whole province of Shantung.

[19] Except for Guam, which went to the United States.

[20] See pages 128 and 197.

Mozambique [21]—between herself and Great Britain as spheres of influence, should Portugal become insolvent and offer her colonies as collateral for a loan. Nothing came of the venture, but it is indicative of the Kaiser's frantic attempts to extend Germany's overseas empire.[22]

In 1899, however, Germany did manage to secure additional territory at Great Britain's expense. In that year a tripartite condominium in Samoa, participated in by Germany, Great Britain, and the United States, came to an end with the death of the native ruler. Out of the tangled negotiations which ensued, in the course of which Germany threatened to break off diplomatic relations with Great Britain, came a new arrangement for Samoa, in consequence of which Germany was enabled to add the islands of Opolu and Sawai to her empire.[23] Great Britain was obliged to be satisfied with compensations elsewhere, giving way only because of Germany's threats at a time when she was embarrassed by her own isolation.

Although in the ensuing years Germany rapidly extended her commercial activities and economic penetration in various parts of the world, she made no further territorial gains until 1911. In that year she precipitated what is known as the second Moroccan crisis [24] by seeking territorial compensation for permitting France to establish a protectorate over Morocco in northwestern Africa. At first Germany demanded that the whole French Congo be given to her; but, when France refused to make any such sweeping cession of territory and when Germany discovered that Great Britain was strongly supporting France in the crisis, Germany was obliged to moderate her demands. In the end she had to be content with a strip of the French Congo which would give German Kamerun access to the Congo River.

Taken altogether, the territory which was added to Germany's overseas empire during William II's reign was pitifully small in extent and in no wise comparable either in area or in importance to the vast stretches which Bismarck had acquired in Africa and the

---

[21] See the map on page 21.

[22] Unknown to Germany the British government practically nullified the Anglo-German treaty by a treaty of alliance negotiated with Portugal in the following year.

[23] The United States took Tutuila.

[24] See pages 134–136.

East Indies. And, unfortunately for Germany, in contrast with the great chancellor, who had secured his colonies without engendering much friction or arousing the serious hostility of other countries, William II had made his territorial acquisitions at the high cost of antagonizing three great powers: Great Britain, France, and Japan.

### MITTEL-EUROPA AND THE DRANG NACH OSTEN

Meanwhile, the Pan-German League looked with longing eyes upon the 16,000,000 people of German race in central Europe outside the empire and envisaged the day when they might be absorbed into the fatherland and make the latter a mighty state with 80,000,000 citizens of homogeneous nationality. Leaders of the league talked also of a central European customs union and even of a closer connection with Holland, Belgium, Switzerland, and Austria-Hungary, perhaps also Rumania. Such a *Mittel-Europa* would knit together under German leadership the basins of the Rhine, Elbe, Oder, and Danube. Extending from the North Sea and the Baltic to the Black Sea and the Adriatic, it would lie in a strategic position to advance German opportunities for commercial expansion.

Although the Pan-German League never had an immense membership and never gained any tremendous following in the Reichstag, it was "one of the most strident jingo societies in the world and its noise was quite incommensurate with its size." Those who have studied its activities admit that its "indirect influence was probably larger than its direct importance." [25] The theories of the Pan-Germanists found their way into much of the German political writing of the decade before the World War and inevitably caused alarm abroad, especially among the British, who feared that German economic expansion might open the way for German political domination of the Continent.

Though the Pan-German aspirations to dominion over the Low Countries and over the Adriatic were openly disavowed by the responsible statesmen of Germany, the Kaiser's project of opening up and exploiting the rich resources of the Ottoman Empire was not. Within a year of his accession William II had made an ostentatious visit to the sultan despite the opposition of Bismarck, who maintained that Germany's relations with Turkey must be kept

[25] M. Wertheimer, *The Pan-German League*, pages 210 and 217.

subordinate to her Russian policy. Throughout his chancellorship Bismarck had never forgotten that the price of Russian friendship was a free hand in the Near East, and he had deeply prized that friendship. Bismarck's cautious and skillful diplomacy was cast to the winds, however, by William II. The latter saw in the exploitation of Turkey—one of the few large and potentially rich areas of the world which had not yet been "staked out" by some great power—compensation for Germany's limited colonial opportunities outside Europe.

As early as 1888 a German syndicate had received a concession from Turkey to build a railway from the Bosporus to Angora, and the Anatolian Railway Company had been organized to carry out this project. In the following year the same German syndicate had also secured control of the Oriental Railway connecting Austria-Hungary with Constantinople. In 1893 the Anatolian Railway Company had obtained a further concession to construct a branch line to Konia in southern Anatolia, and this new project was completed three years later. Originally the German syndicate had been given to understand that it would ultimately be granted the right to extend the Anatolian Railway to Bagdad. Bismarck, however, had opposed such an extensive project, maintaining that no one should "lay on the German people the obligation to fight Russia for the future of Bagdad."

But the Kaiser was not deterred by any such ideas. In 1898 he definitely launched his plan for creating a German-Ottoman economic entente which might ultimately be transformed into a political alliance. In that year he made a second spectacular visit to the sultan, and out of that visit came the promise from Turkey of a concession to build the Bagdad Railway to connect Konia with Bagdad and the Persian Gulf. What the Kaiser and his advisers had in mind, apparently, was the construction of a unified railway system extending from the Bosporus across Anatolia to Aleppo, with one branch running from there through Syria to Arabia and Egypt and another running through Mesopotamia to the Persian Gulf.[26] When completed according to the plans, this Bagdad Railway, linked with the Anatolian Railway, the Oriental Railway, and railways of *Mittel-Europa,* would establish a gigantic road of steel, largely under Teutonic control and stretching from the North Sea

[26] See the map on page 431.

to the Persian Gulf. Such a railway system—often referred to as the Berlin-Bagdad railway—would enable German capitalists to tap the rich mineral and agricultural resources of the Ottoman Empire and go far toward giving Germany political ascendancy in that part of the world.

Although in the beginning the German bankers had been interested in the Turkish railway concessions primarily for commercial reasons, after 1899 the attitude of the German government and the German public gave the Bagdad Railway project a definitely political complexion in the eyes of foreign statesmen. Russia objected to the further construction of railways in northern Anatolia, and consequently it became necessary to alter the plan for the railway to Bagdad. In 1899 it was decided that the extension to Bagdad should start not from Angora, as originally planned, but from Konia. The British also were disturbed by the project and apprehensive for the safety of their interests in Persia and India. Great Britain accordingly took prompt steps to block the southern end of the proposed railway by making an agreement (1899) with the sheik of Koweit on the Persian Gulf. The sheik accepted British protection and promised to make no international agreements without British approval. The one possible exit to the Persian Gulf for the Bagdad Railway was thus effectively blocked.

Nothing was done by the German syndicate with the concession received in 1899 until 1903, when a new agreement was made with Turkey, and the Bagdad Railway Company was incorporated to construct and operate the proposed line from Konia to the Persian Gulf. The German promoters of the railway planned to construct it with the aid of a subsidy from Turkey and with loans floated in Germany, Great Britain, and France. According to their plans, representatives from each of these countries would be on the railway company's board of directors, but control would be in the hands of Germans.

Although the British prime minister and foreign secretary favored participation in the project and the formation of a tripartite syndicate, opposition in the cabinet and the hostile attitude of the press eventually forced the British government to abandon the plan to co-operate with the German syndicate. Possibly views expressed in a German book, *Die Bagdadbahn* (1903), may have increased

British opposition. The author, Paul von Rohrbach, declared: "England can be attacked and mortally wounded by land from Europe in only one place—Egypt. . . . We can never dream, however, of attacking Egypt until Turkey is mistress of a developed railway system in Asia Minor and Syria, and until through the extension of the Anatolian Railway to Bagdad she is in a position to withstand an attack by England upon Mesopotamia." The French government, at first benevolently neutral regarding the railway, in 1903 also turned against the project and forbade trading in the securities of the railway on the Paris Bourse. Perhaps its attitude was strongly influenced by its eagerness at that time to win Great Britain to an Anglo-French entente.

In 1908 the German syndicate surrendered to the Turkish government its concession to build the section of the Bagdad Railway from Bagdad to the Persian Gulf and thereby removed the chief ground for British hostility to the project. Directors of the syndicate, eager for British co-operation, recommended giving to the British the section of the railway from Bagdad south. The "dream of the German Bagdad Railway to the Gulf is dreamed away," wrote one of the directors. Negotiations were opened between the German and British governments, but great difficulty was experienced in reaching any agreement. The British suggested a conference of the four powers—Germany, Great Britain, France, Russia—but Germany declared that in such a conference she would be outvoted three to one.[27] The Germans, for their part, proposed that the section of the railway from Bagdad to Koweit be given over to Great Britain, provided the latter would grant Germany some concession as a *quid pro quo.* Early in 1910 the British foreign secretary declined this proposal as "one which His Majesty's Government cannot entertain."

Some progress was made in solving the Bagdad Railway problem later in 1910, however, when the tsar visited the Kaiser in November of that year. As the result of the so-called Potsdam conversations carried on at that time, Germany came to a general understanding with Russia regarding the railway. By the agreement Russia promised to put no obstacles in the way of the building of the railway

[27] France, Russia, and Great Britain had in 1907 entered into the Triple Entente. See pages 132 and 212.

and in return secured Germany's recognition of Russia's sphere of interest in Persia.[28] Early in 1914 Germany reached an agreement with France also. In this case the two powers recognized that northern Anatolia and Syria were French spheres of railway construction and that the regions served by the existing Anatolian and Bagdad Railways were German spheres. Finally, in June, 1914, the Germans and the British initialed an agreement. The latter "in recognition of the general importance which the construction of the Bagdad Railway possesses for international trade," promised not to obstruct the building and management of the railway. However, no railway connection between Basra and the Persian Gulf was to be constructed unless a complete understanding had been reached between the British, the German, and the Ottoman governments.

Although before the outbreak of the World War understandings were thus eventually reached regarding the Bagdad Railway by Germany, Russia, France, and Great Britain, the project had already done much to poison the international atmosphere. Germany had come to believe that the opposition of the three Entente powers was only part of their general policy of encirclement, which was designed to restrict and ultimately crush the German Empire. On the other hand, Russia, Great Britain, and France had become deeply suspicious of Germany's plans in the Near East and had become alarmed by her increasing influence in the Ottoman Empire. Russia, especially, had considered Germany's strong support of Austria-Hungary during the Bosnian crisis of 1908 as proof of the Kaiser's determination to persist in the *Drang nach Osten* at any cost. Russia's realization that the Austro-German advance into the Balkans and Turkey must be checked if her own plans for securing control of the Straits at Constantinople were not to be thwarted had much to do with the course of events during the fateful days of July, 1914.

### The Rapid Rise of German Naval Power

Even before William II had become the ruler of Germany he had been deeply interested in naval affairs. After ascending the throne he became increasingly convinced of the need for a larger and more powerful German navy, and in the succeeding years he constantly agitated in favor of increasing the size of the fleet. Throughout the empire it was generally felt, however, that, since Germany was main-

[28] A specific agreement was signed in August, 1911.

"BISMARCK HAS RESIGNED AGAIN!"

The Iron Chancellor used to threaten to resign whenever William I objected to his policies, whereupon the aged Kaiser would give way to him.

taining such a large military establishment, she could not hope to rank as a first-class naval power. Therefore, despite William II's desire for a more powerful fleet—which was at first looked upon as merely one of his whims—Germany in 1895 stood only fifth in naval strength among the powers. Although by that time the German Empire had risen to second place in the world in foreign trade, in sea power she ranked below even Italy.

But by the middle of the nineties the Kaiser began to be joined in his demand for a larger navy by others from many quarters. Merchants from Hamburg, professors from the universities, members of the Colonial Society, and the Pan-German League began to agitate for more warships to protect German commerce. History, it was asserted, could not offer a single example of a great commercial state that had been able to maintain its position for any length of time without the support of sea power. Gradually the members of the Reichstag became less hostile to expenditures for the navy. Hoping to take advantage of the rising sentiment in favor of naval expansion, the Kaiser in 1896 appointed as minister of marine Alfred von Tirpitz, "probably the ablest naval man produced by any country in modern times."

Tirpitz at once began to make his plans for giving Germany a modern fleet, and by October, 1897, he had put his program into form and had secured the approval of the Kaiser. His projected naval bill called for the construction by 1905 of eleven battleships, five first-class cruisers, and seventeen small cruisers. In case of a war against Russia or France or both, such a naval force, it was maintained, would enable Germany to prevent a blockade of the German coasts and thus keep open the lanes of commerce and food supply. Such a fleet, though far from being able to challenge Great Britain on the sea, might lead the latter to take a more favorable attitude toward the German Empire. When the bill was laid before the Reichstag, it received the support of the National Liberals, the Conservatives, and a majority of the Centrists, and in March, 1898, it was finally passed by the lower house.

This act, however, did not in itself provide Germany with a naval force comparable to that of Great Britain or even of France. Consequently, by the summer of 1899, even before his first program was completed, Tirpitz concluded that a new program must be prepared. It was decided to take advantage of sentiment aroused by the

Boer War,[29] when a British warship seized a German merchant ship, to introduce a second naval bill, and in December, 1899, the chancellor in an important speech in the Reichstag explained that Germany must have a navy so powerful that even the strongest naval power could not attack it without grave risk. The government's program had the support of those groups which had advocated the enactment of the first bill, but it also had the enthusiastic backing of the recently organized Navy League. The latter, heavily financed by the great steel interests of the empire, had at that time a membership of more than 100,000, a publication, *Die Flotte,* with a circulation of some 250,000, and an active corps of lecturers. The Germans were soon won to a belief in the political value of a great navy as an instrument of *Weltpolitik.*

The second naval bill was rapidly pushed through the Reichstag during the first half of 1900. Only the Social Democrats and a few of the Centrists and Progressives voted against the measure, which was passed in June of that year. The new act provided for a fleet of thirty-eight battleships to be completed in twenty years and to be built regardless of cost. Apparently what the Kaiser and his ministers desired was a fleet large enough to meet the British home fleet, which was at that time about thirty-two ships. Then, they evidently believed, Germany would appear as an attractive possible ally of Great Britain, or, failing this, of Russia or France. Unfortunately, they did not foresee that Germany's naval programs would not attract Great Britain into a German alliance but would ultimately drive her into the arms of France and Russia.

In 1905 Great Britain, taking heed of the value of powerful battleships as demonstrated in the Russo-Japanese War,[30] laid the keel of a new type of fighting craft known as dreadnoughts. The introduction of such large and powerful ships inevitably made all previous battleships largely obsolete, and at once opened the way for Germany to compete on an equal footing with Great Britain in the new category of fighting ships. Of what particular value would Britain's large fleet of obsolete ships be if Germany could have a fleet of dreadnoughts as large as the British? In 1906, accordingly, Germany passed a new navy law providing for six large cruisers of the dreadnought type to be completed in 1918.

[29] See page 192.                    [30] See pages 267–269.

As early as 1889 the British government had adopted the policy of maintaining a two-power naval standard, that is, the policy of having a navy as powerful as that of the next two naval powers combined. Naturally, therefore, Germany's determination to construct a powerful fleet disturbed the British. In 1907 the latter at the Second Hague Conference asked to have the question of armaments considered, but Germany opposed the proposal. Instead, Germany steadily progressed with her naval program—largely, it seems, to satisfy the ego of the Kaiser, who got great satisfaction from possessing and reviewing his fleet. In 1908 still another German navy law accelerated the retirement of old warships and authorized the building of four dreadnoughts yearly from 1908 to 1911 and two yearly from 1912 to 1917. When the British in 1908 attempted to reach some naval agreement with Germany, the Kaiser indignantly declared that he would fight before he would accept dictation in such matters from a foreign government. In consequence Great Britain was thrown into what has been called the naval panic of 1909,[31] and in turn proceeded to accelerate her own construction of dreadnoughts.

In 1909 Bülow, who since 1900 had played an aggressive role in international affairs as German chancellor, resigned and was succeeded by Theobald von Bethmann-Hollweg. The latter was very eager to improve relations between Germany and Great Britain. Believing that naval rivalry was largely the cause of friction between the two powers, he speedily took up with the British government the question of making some naval agreement. He proposed that each country should retard its building program in the hope of modifying public opinion in the direction of fewer ships. But he declared that the naval agreement must be accompanied by a political agreement in which Great Britain should promise not to attack Germany and to remain neutral if Germany were attacked by a third power. Unfortunately for the success of Bethmann-Hollweg's proposals, officials in the British foreign office doubted the chancellor's sincerity, professed to believe that his proposal was merely designed to get Great Britain out of the Triple Entente, and suspected that, once Great Britain's hands were tied, Germany might feel free to move against other countries. Sir Edward Grey, British foreign secretary, finally replied that the proximity of parliamentary elec-

[31] See page 213.

tions made it inadvisable to discuss naval limitation at that time.

After the second Moroccan crisis [32] German imperialists argued that their government had been weak in the face of British threats, and demanded that the German navy should be further increased until it would be powerful enough to dissuade the British from interfering with German plans. A sort of Anglophobia spread through Germany in 1911 and 1912, and many came to believe that Great Britain was the fatherland's most dangerous enemy. General von Bernhardi's book, *Germany and the Next War* (1912), voiced the feeling of German chauvinists and was designed largely to awaken Germans to the urgent need to prepare for the coming conflict. Early in 1912 the Kaiser announced to the Reichstag that a supplementary naval bill would soon be introduced.

By this time, however, certain business men in Germany and Great Britain had come to the conclusion that some effort should be made to reach an Anglo-German understanding. In January, 1912, Sir Edward Cassel, a London banker, had gone to Berlin to open the way for future discussions. Germany appeared willing to consider the British proposals and invited the British foreign secretary to confer with the Kaiser. Sir Edward Grey did not care to make the visit, however, and so Lord Haldane, the British war minister, was sent in his place. As a result of conversations between Haldane and the Kaiser, the latter agreed to retard the construction of the recently proposed ships. But again Bethmann-Hollweg desired to link the naval understanding with a political agreement of some kind. He proposed that the two countries should each promise not to join any combination of powers directed against the other, and that each should remain neutral in case the other was forced into war.

Both in Germany and in Great Britain there were those who desired the Haldane mission to fail. In Germany Tirpitz and his followers strongly opposed any change in Germany's naval program, while in the British foreign office there was great reluctance to accept the political formula suggested by the German chancellor lest it antagonize Russia and France. In April, 1912, Asquith, the British prime minister, declared that the wisdom of prolonging the discussions "about a formula" was doubtful, and in the end nothing tangible came of the Haldane mission.

In May, 1912, Germany's supplementary naval law—creating a

[32] See pages 134–136.

new squadron which would eventually include three new dreadnoughts—was passed. Although thereafter Germany slowed down
her naval construction slightly, she had risen by 1914 to second place
among the naval powers of the world. Unfortunately for the peace
of Europe, however, without actually building a navy powerful
enough to challenge Great Britain on the seas, the Kaiser by his
speeches and by his various navy bills had by 1914 succeeded in
thoroughly alarming and antagonizing the British, in whose opinion control of the seas was a matter of national existence.

### Efforts to Expand the Triple Alliance

During the nineties William II, like Bismarck in the eighties,
sought to draw Great Britain into an alliance with Germany.
Twice in 1895 he invited the British to join the Triple Alliance
under an implied threat of possible opposition by the continental
powers if Great Britain continued her policy of isolation. Apparently, too, his favorable attitude toward the Boers in 1895 and 1896
was designed in part to frighten Great Britain into closer relations
with that alliance. But all his invitations and threats were of no
avail. Although the British were willing in 1898 to conclude an
Anglo-German alliance to protect their interests in the Far East,[33]
they were not willing to enter into any alliance having to do with
Europe. Germany on her part declined at that time to ally herself
with Great Britain against Russia in the Far East, and continued
to hope that the pressure of other countries might yet drive the
British to link themselves with the Triple Alliance. During the
Boer War, when the possibility of a continental coalition against
great Britain was being discussed, Germany stood by the British in
the hope of winning their good will. Unfortunately for Germany's
hopes, her own naval law of 1900 apparently had more effect upon
Great Britain and doubtless hastened the consummation of the
*Entente Cordiale* between that country and France.

After 1904 the Kaiser turned his attention to the task of securing
an alliance with Russia. He had given diplomatic support to the
latter in her demand that Japan withdraw from the Asiatic mainland in 1895 and had urged the tsar forward in his advance into
Manchuria in 1898.[34] In 1904, after Russia with Germany's en-

[33] See pages 198–199.
[34] For these developments, see pages 264–265.

couragement had become involved in the Russo-Japanese War, the Kaiser outlined to the tsar a plan for a continental alliance of Germany, Russia, and France against Great Britain. Relations between the last and Russia were severely strained at the time, and matters actually progressed to the point where a treaty was drafted in which Germany and Russia promised mutual aid in case either should be attacked by a European power. Unfortunately for the Kaiser's scheme, however, the two rulers disagreed as to whether the treaty should be signed first and France be later informed or vice versa, and in the end the project was dropped.

In 1905, after an armistice had been signed in the Russo-Japanese War, the Kaiser again conferred with the tsar—this time near Björkö in the Gulf of Finland—and on this occasion he won the tsar over to his point of view. A treaty was signed (July 24, 1905) with terms as outlined above, and it was agreed that, after the new pact became effective, Russia should notify France of its terms and should attempt to gain her adherence also. "At last," William II joyfully informed his chancellor, "the fatherland is free from the clutch of the Franco-Russian Alliance." But much to the Kaiser's surprise, both Chancellor von Bülow and Baron von Holstein, political director of the German foreign office, severely criticized the treaty which he had so high-handedly concluded.

The somewhat simple-minded tsar was likewise astonished to discover that France would have nothing to do with the Björkö pact. Furthermore, the tsar's foreign minister did not hesitate to point out the incompatibility of the Russo-German agreement and the Franco-Russian alliance of 1894. It appeared that the friendship of France would be lost if the Björkö agreement were carried through, that Russia would have to choose between Germany and France. Financial reasons, if no others, dictated friendship with the latter, for the expenditures in connection with the Russo-Japanese War and the Russian revolution which began in 1905 made foreign borrowing absolutely necessary. Nicholas II therefore declined to let the Björkö treaty become effective, and the Kaiser's grandiose scheme for a continental alliance against Great Britain dissolved into thin air. But, obviously, if the treaty had been ratified, and if France had acceded to it, the Entente Cordiale would have been destroyed, and Great Britain would have become isolated among the European powers.

## The Eve of the World War

Meanwhile William II's determination to pursue a course of *Weltpolitik* had not gone unchallenged within Germany. In the opening years of the twentieth century the Center, Progressive, and Social Democratic Parties organized in the Reichstag a solid bloc in opposition to the Kaiser's colonial policy. The Centrists resented the expense connected with the policy, deplored the accompanying cruelties and ill treatment of the natives, and denounced the maladministration of the colonies. The Social Democrats vigorously opposed the policy on the ground that it tremendously enriched a few capitalists but brought to the mass of German workers only an increasingly heavy tax.

From 1903 to 1906 the conflict was waged in the Reichstag. Opponents of imperialism argued that Germany's trade with her colonies was so small in comparison with that with other countries that it did not warrant the expense of having them. They showed, for example, that Germany's colonial trade in 1904 constituted only half of one per cent of the country's total foreign trade, that in 1906 Togoland alone of all the German colonies was self-supporting. They pointed out, further, that most of the country's overseas territories were unsuitable for European settlement and produced figures to show that in 1903 there were in all the colonies a total of only 5125 Germans, of whom 1567 were officials and military.

Eventually, in 1906, the Reichstag drastically reduced the amounts demanded by the government for imperial purposes and thus precipitated a parliamentary crisis over Germany's colonial policy. The deadlock brought the dissolution of the Reichstag by Chancellor von Bülow, who declared that "the issue involves the question of our entire colonial policy and, what is more, of our position in the world." "Germany's position in the world is menaced," declared the *Norddeutsche Allgemeine Zeitung.* "The forthcoming election will decide whether Germany is capable of developing into a world power." The electoral campaign which ensued witnessed an unprecedented interference on the part of the imperial administration, which had the support of the various nationalist societies. The Navy League, the Pan-German League, the Colonial Society, and the Association for the Suppression of Socialism utilized their nation-wide organizations to appeal to German "patriotism" to support the government. The Progressive Party ultimately shifted over in favor of imperialism, so that only the Centrists and the Social Democrats were left in the opposition. The election returns revealed that these two parties combined had suffered a loss of more than 20 per cent of their Reichstag seats, and constituted, therefore, a decisive endorsement of the Kaiser's policy of *Weltpolitik*. Said Bülow, quoting the great and beloved Bismarck, "You have placed Germany in the saddle and now she can ride."

One explanation of the seemingly overwhelming defeat of the Centrists and Social Democrats in the election of January, 1907, was to be found in the fact that there had never been a reapportionment of the Reichstag seats since the founding of the empire. In the thirty-six years since 1871 great shifts had occurred in Germany's population as a consequence of the industrialization of the country, and the failure to recognize these changes in the empire's population resulted in a Reichstag which was no longer truly representative of the German people. Densely populated urban communities were grossly underrepresented, while sparsely settled rural regions like those in Pomerania and East Prussia were tremendously overrepresented. Such a condition, of course, constituted a very serious handicap to the parties representing the more densely populated areas. The Social Democrats vigorously demanded a redistribution of the Reichstag seats in proportion to Germany's population as it was in the industrial twentieth century.

There was in fact an increasingly widespread desire that the German Empire be democratized, a desire which was voiced not alone by the Social Democrats. The National Liberal, Progressive, and Center Parties all favored a reapportionment of representation in the Reichstag. But the Social Democrats went further by demanding that women be given the franchise, and that the chancellor be made responsible to the Reichstag, that is, that ministerial responsibility be introduced in the empire. In this last demand the Social Democrats were supported by the Progressives also. Finally, the Social Democrats, the National Liberals, and the Progressives all advocated the abolition of the three-class system of voting which had prevailed in Prussia since 1850 in the election of that state's local Landtag.[35] In the years shortly preceding the World War, accord-

[35] By this ingenious system, in which voters were divided into three classes according to the amount of taxes they paid, the wealthier citizens in the first two classes—though

ingly, Germany's semiautocratic system of government was being more and more openly attacked by her own citizens.

In 1908 an indication that the Kaiser's irresponsibility might not long go unchallenged was forthcoming when William II permitted the *London Daily Telegraph* to publish an interview dealing with Anglo-German relations. Although the Kaiser had apparently hoped by his statements to reduce the ill feeling which existed between the British and German peoples, his tactlessness resulted in infuriating them both. Bülow, the chancellor, seized the occasion to exact a promise from William II that in the future he would make no public statements without the previous approval of the chancellor. The Reichstag also, by a decisive vote, condemned the Kaiser's irresponsible action. Had all those who desired to introduce ministerial responsibility stood loyally together at this time, parliamentary government might have been obtained. But the National Liberals hung back, and no step was taken.

In 1909 the coalition of Conservatives and National Liberals which had been supporting Bülow split on the issue of his finance bill, which, to meet the rising costs of the army and navy, included an inheritance tax. The latter was distasteful to the Conservatives, who therefore deserted the chancellor and helped to defeat his budget. In July, 1909, Bülow resigned as chancellor and was succeeded by Bethmann-Hollweg. In order to dispel any rising hope that Bülow's resignation might constitute a precedent for ministerial responsibility, the new chancellor hastened to announce that, even if he should fail to secure the support of the Reichstag, he would remain at his post as long as he retained the confidence of the Kaiser. By concessions to the Conservatives in matters of taxation, however, he managed to create a bloc including them and the Centrists which lasted until 1912.

The elections of that year revealed the growing opposition to the government. Despite the chancellor's promises of future political reform and despite his vigorous attacks upon the Social Democrats, the latter won their greatest electoral victory up to that time, increasing their representation in the Reichstag from 43 to 110 seats. They now constituted the largest single group in the Reichstag and failed of electing their candidate for the presidency of that body by

constituting a relatively small minority of the total population of Prussia—were able to defeat the bulk of the voters who composed the third class.

only twenty-one votes. Eventually the government was enabled to carry on, but only by forming a Reichstag bloc which included practically all groups except the Social Democrats. Nevertheless, one fact must have caused considerable concern to the Kaiser and his chancellor—in 1912, for the first time in the history of the empire, the elections had gone decisively against the government.

Nor did developments in the Reichstag in the succeeding months bring much comfort. In 1912 Bethmann-Hollweg's government attempted to enforce a law against the Poles living in eastern Germany. This law, which had been enacted in 1908 under Bülow as part of the government's program to "Germanize" the Polish districts, provided that Polish landowners might be dispossessed of their holdings by a government commission, in case they refused to sell, so that German colonists might be settled in that region in their stead. The price to be paid to the Polish landowner would be determined by German courts. The act had originally encountered vigorous protests, but, influenced by the demands of Pan-Germans and extreme chauvinists, Bethmann-Hollweg undertook to force the sale of a few estates. The repercussion in the Reichstag was immediate and loud. In January, 1913, by a vote of more than two to one, the Reichstag resolved that the policy of the chancellor was contrary to its views, and thus passed the first vote of "no confidence" in the history of that body.

Before the year was out another vote of "no confidence" had been passed, this time as a result of events in Alsace. The German government had never succeeded in "Germanizing" or conciliating the bulk of the inhabitants of Alsace-Lorraine. At the time of their annexation in 1871 the elected representatives of the provinces had unanimously protested against being torn from France and had demanded a plebiscite on the question. Their demand had been refused, and the provinces, treated like a conquered territory, had been converted into an imperial territory (*Reichsland*) ruled by a government responsible to the Kaiser. After 1874 Alsace-Lorraine was permitted fifteen representatives in the Reichstag, and for years these deputies continued to denounce the annexation. When in the late eighties the possibility of reunion with France began to appear chimerical, the inhabitants of the provinces launched a demand for rights as Germans. They sought to obtain for Alsace-Lorraine a local government such as the other states of the empire had. For a generation their demand went unheeded, while hundreds of thousands of Germans were settled in the provinces in an attempt to "Germanize" them.

Eventually, in 1910, Alsace-Lorraine was informed that it would be given its own government, and in the next year a new constitution was voted by the German parliament. It stipulated that a bicameral legislature should be the sole source of legislation for the provinces, but the political machinery was so constructed as to retain most of the control in the hands of the imperial government. The governor of Alsace-Lorraine was appointed by the chancellor, and the ministry of the local government was responsible to this governor. Although the lower house of the legislature was popularly elected, enough members of the upper house were appointed to give the government control of that body. If the lower house attempted to impose its will by refusing to pass the budget, the government might use that of the preceding year. The fifteen Reichstag representatives of Alsace-Lorraine were popularly elected, but the three Bundesrat representatives were appointed by the governor. The constitution was a deep disappointment to the people of Alsace-Lorraine.

Relations between the appointed government of the provinces and the local legislature were far from amicable. In 1912 and in 1913 votes of censure were passed against the government. The fact that the imperial authorities kept a large army in the provinces further antagonized the inhabitants, and the overbearing attitude of the military was a constant source of complaint. In 1913 the latter were especially obnoxious in the Alsatian town of Zabern, making arbitrary arrests and imprisoning civil judges who protested against military violence. On one occasion a lieutenant slashed with a saber the forehead of an unoffending lame Alsatian cobbler. When a civil court sentenced the lieutenant to forty-five days' imprisonment, a military court promptly canceled the sentence and released the officer. This incident resulted in the Reichstag's passing another vote of "no confidence," this time by more than five to one. Although the chancellor did not resign, these votes in 1913 appeared to be symptomatic of the increasing strength and confidence of the popularly elected branch of the imperial government. It seemed that in time democratic reform must inevitably come in the German Empire.

To ward off such an eventuality as long as possible, the conservative groups began to appeal to patriotism and to cite the increasingly threatening international situation in Europe. The opportunity offered by the rise in nationalistic spirit in 1911 was immediately seized upon by the German general staff to demand an enlargement of the military forces. Those interested in further building up the army founded in 1912 the Security League, which was designed to propagandize the German people systematically with militarism. The military, although at first opposed by the civil authorities, eventually won out, and in May, 1912, a law was passed providing for a reorganization and increase in man power of the army during the succeeding five years. But the militarists were not yet satisfied. They continued to demand a still larger army because of "recent changes in the Balkans," [36] because of the "growing menace of Russian Pan-Slavism," [37] and because of "France's desire for war." [38] In April, 1913, the government introduced a new army law, which was passed on June 30. By the provisions of the new law the peacetime army of Germany would consist of about 870,000 men when the military plans were completed in April, 1914.

Within the German Empire there were, of course, great numbers who desired peace.[39] But unfortunately for the peace of Europe, the militaristic utterances of the extreme chauvinists and the above-mentioned programs of military and naval expansion almost completely overshadowed this fact. In consequence, there was steadily developing in other countries during 1913 and 1914 a profound distrust and increasing fear of Germany. The growing alarm eventually led President Wilson of the United States to send Colonel House, his personal representative, to Europe in 1914 to explore the possibilities of preventing the outbreak of a great war. When Colonel House visited Berlin in May of that year, he discovered a condition which he described as "militarism gone mad."

[36] For the Balkan wars, see pages 348–352.
[37] For Russian Pan-Slavism, see page 282.
[38] For the situation in France, see page 136.
[39] In 1912 the Union for International Understanding was organized to denounce war agitation and to work for peace. Other peace societies were founded, and it is said that pacifist literature was being more widely read between 1912 and 1914 than that of the militarists.

## CHAPTER IV

# THE THIRD FRENCH REPUBLIC

AT the opening of the year 1870 France was a monarchy presided over by Emperor Napoleon III, nephew of the famous Napoleon Bonaparte. For some time Napoleon III's prestige had been declining, as a result of his ill-fated intervention in Mexico and his failure to play an important role during and after the Austro-Prussian War of 1866. In July, 1870, therefore, the French government, in the hope of restoring the waning prestige of the Bonapartist dynasty and of weakening the position of Prussia, seized the opportunity created by an offer of the Spanish throne to a Hohenzollern prince to launch a war against Prussia. This, of course, was exactly what Bismarck ardently desired it to do. The French expected that the ensuing hostilities would occur on German soil and that the South German states would join with France in administering a decisive defeat to a common foe.

## DISASTER AND RECOVERY

But the French armies never reached German territory, the South German states fought on the side of Prussia, and in September at Sedan the French suffered a crushing defeat, the emperor himself being taken prisoner. The news of the disaster was followed in Paris by an immediate demand for the abolition of the empire and ultimately by the proclamation of the republic and the establishment of a provisional Government of National Defense. The latter placed upon the deposed emperor all blame for the war and announced that it was willing to end hostilities immediately on condition that no territory should be taken from France. But since it was the intention of German leaders to make annexations of territory as a result of the German victories, the war continued with the Germans laying siege to Paris.

Eventually the Parisians were starved into submission, and in January, 1871, an armistice was signed to permit the election of a National Assembly to decide whether or not France should make peace at the cost of losing territory. Gambetta, the outstanding leader of the republicans, favored a continuance of the war in the vain hope of preventing the loss of territory, and most of the other republican candidates took a similar stand. As a majority of the French people, especially the peasants, wanted peace and could see no possible gain to be made in waging a hopeless struggle, they voted against republican candidates, with the result that the new National Assembly consisted of a majority of royalists, who had stood for peace. The Assembly, when it met at Bordeaux, voted overwhelmingly to end the war, and elected the liberal-monarchist Thiers as "Chief of the Executive Power," with authority to negotiate with Bismarck for peace. Being predominantly royalist in its membership, the Assembly took no formal step to recognize the republic, but rather to the dismay of republicans voted to move the seat of government to Versailles, so long unfavorably connected in the popular mind with the monarchy.

But, before Thiers could conclude the negotiations for peace, he was faced with a serious insurrection at home. During the time when Paris was besieged, a new government had been organized in that city by committees of workingmen and middle-class republican national guardsmen. This was the Commune of Paris. The various elements constituting and supporting the Commune differed widely in the matter of ultimate aims, but they were agreed on at least one point, namely, that the monarchy should not be restored. Naturally, therefore, the Commune came to look with suspicion upon the newly elected, predominantly royalist National Assembly, which had hastened to make Versailles the seat of its government and had authorized the negotiation of what was bound to be a humiliating peace. Nor was this all. To the masses of Parisians, who had already suffered severely in the war, it appeared that the National Assembly was determined to heap further hardships upon them. It ordered, for instance, that the government's payment of wages to the National Guard—which included all able-bodied men in Paris—should be stopped; and at the same time it decreed that the payment of rents and debts—upon which there had been a moratorium during the war—should be resumed. To the lower classes of the city, unable to obtain employment because of the dislocation of industry and commerce resulting from the war, it appeared that the National

Assembly was the instrument of the wealthy creditor classes against the suffering masses.

The Commune of Paris therefore raised the red flag of socialism, launched a revolt against the National Assembly, and urged other communities to organize similar "communes," to join in a general movement to repudiate the Assembly's authority, and to establish a federated state in which each commune should be self-governing. In such a decentralized state, it was hoped, the industrial centers would not be outweighed by conservative peasants, and socialism might be established by the urban workingmen. Communes were set up in a number of other cities, but they were quickly suppressed. The Commune of Paris, however, was able to defend itself for weeks, thanks to the military experience of its adherents among the national guardsmen and thanks to the enthusiastic support which it received from various radical groups in the city—anarchists, socialists, and embittered republicans. The conservative elements of Paris were for a time pushed unceremoniously into the background.

In the provinces most Frenchmen were alienated by the radicalism of the Parisians and alarmed at the prospect of a bloody civil war. They therefore threw their support whole-heartedly to the National Assembly when the latter decided to use the French armies recently returned from the front to put down the Commune. In April, 1871, French troops laid siege to Paris, and after six weeks of fighting finally forced their way into the city. From then on the conflict became a bitter fratricidal struggle in which neither side showed much mercy. Outnumbered and outgeneraled, the Communards resorted to frightful acts of revenge and destruction. Prominent persons held as hostages were slain in cold blood, and famous buildings, including the Tuileries, were destroyed by fire. In retaliation, the troops of the National Assembly frequently shot down the prisoners whom they captured.

In the end the forces of the Versailles government won, and order was gradually restored in the city, which had passed through two sieges within nine months. Severe measures were taken by Thiers' government against the defeated Communards. Imprisonment, exile, and death were meted out in a sort of judicial terrorism which was inaugurated after the collapse of the revolt. By 1875, it has been estimated, over thirteen thousand Communards had been imprisoned or deported. Consequently, one result of the uprising of the Paris Commune was that the republic, with most of the radical leaders of Paris dead or in exile, was left in the hands of leaders who were for the most part moderate. Another result was that for a decade or two economic and political radicalism of any kind was held in suspicion not only in France but in other bourgeois countries as well.

In the midst of its struggle with the Paris Commune Thiers' government had concluded its negotiations with Bismarck, and on May 10, 1871, had signed the treaty of Frankfort. By the provisions of this treaty France was compelled to cede Alsace and a large part of Lorraine to the new German Empire. She was, furthermore, to pay an indemnity of five billion francs within three years and to submit to and support a German army of occupation until the indemnity was paid. In the eyes of all Frenchmen the peace terms were both severe and humiliating, and it was only with great reluctance that the National Assembly eventually ratified the treaty.

By the summer of 1871 France was again at peace both at home and abroad and in a position to turn her attention to measures of reorganization and recovery. The National Assembly, which had been elected for the purpose of making peace with Germany, declined, however, to dissolve after peace was secured. Instead, it assumed by the Rivet law of August, 1871, power both to govern France and to prepare a new constitution. For various reasons, discussed below, the latter task was difficult and somewhat long delayed. But in matters of ordinary legislation and administration the National Assembly and the government of Thiers made considerable progress.

One task which confronted the government was that of liberating the country from the occupation of German troops. The presence of foreign soldiers on French soil was a constant reminder of the nation's recent defeat. Furthermore, it constituted a financial drain on the republic's budget. But the occupying forces would not be removed until the indemnity had been paid, and might in fact be increased if payments were not forthcoming. Thiers, therefore, immediately turned his attention to the raising of funds to pay the indemnity, and through popular loans floated both in France and abroad the needed money was secured. France was happily freed of German troops six months before the end of the stipulated three-

"VIVE THIERS!"

French rejoicing at Belfort over the departure of the German army
of occupation in 1873.

year period, and Thiers was enthusiastically hailed as the "liberator of the territory."

But the French were concerned not only in getting the German troops out of France but in keeping them out in the future. The military system of the Second Empire had been seriously discredited by a defeat which, the French believed, had been caused not by lack of heroism or fighting ability on their part but by the superiority of the Prussian system. In 1872, therefore, a law was enacted introducing in France the Prussian principle of universal compulsory military service. In theory every able-bodied Frenchman was to serve five years in the active army and a longer period in the reserve. Actually, because of financial difficulties, the system was not fully enforced. Part of those subject to military training were chosen by lot for the five-year period; the rest received only six months of training in the active army. Other measures were taken, too, to strengthen France. New forts were constructed along the new German frontier, and the powerful fortifications about the capital were further strengthened. The French were still determined that, so far as military might was concerned, France should continue to be a great power. Some, in fact, even envisaged the day when France might undertake a successful war of *revanche*.

## THE ESTABLISHMENT OF THE REPUBLIC

When on September 4, 1870, France was proclaimed a republic by Gambetta and his associates, the step was taken without consulting the French people. Although the action was in accord with the desires of those staunch republicans who had long sought to restore a republic of the type that had been proclaimed in 1792 and again in 1848, it was obviously distasteful to the royalists. The latter were, in general, of three types, differentiated by their ideas regarding the dynasty which should sit on the throne of France: (1) Legitimists, conservative or reactionary royalists who desired to enthrone Henry, Count of Chambord, grandson of the last Bourbon monarch, Charles X; (2) Orleanists, liberal royalists who sought to elevate to the throne the Count of Paris, grandson of the last Orleanist ruler, Louis Philippe; and (3) Bonapartists, imperialists who sought to continue the Napoleonic dynasty which had only recently been overthrown.

It has already been pointed out that the National Assembly, elected in February, 1871, to decide upon the question of war or peace, had a strong majority of royalists. It is not surprising, therefore, that, when it first convened at Bordeaux, the Assembly took no step committing itself to a permanent continuance of the republic which had been proclaimed. Under Thiers' guidance a temporary political truce was voted in the "Pact of Bordeaux," in which the Assembly agreed that the republican government should continue temporarily without prejudice to the later claims of any party. Doubtless the thought was that, once peace had been made with the enemy, the question of France's permanent government could be settled by a test of strength of the various groups.

But when by the early summer of 1871 peace had been concluded and order restored in France, the royalist majority in the Assembly refused to permit the election of a new constituent assembly to draft a permanent constitution. Apparently the royalists were reluctant to submit the political future of France to a popular plebiscite. Instead, they forced through the Assembly the Rivet law conferring upon that body constituent powers. That is to say, the Assembly which was elected to decide upon peace or war, now, without further consulting the people of France, assumed or usurped the authority to draft a constitution. At the same time it gave Thiers, a liberal monarchist, the title of "President of the French Republic," stipulating, however, that the president should be responsible to the Assembly and presumably removable by it. Thus a crude parliamentary system of government was inaugurated, but without constitutional basis.

When the royalists next sought to restore the monarchy, they soon discovered that, though they constituted a majority in the Assembly, they were, as stated above, fatally divided among themselves. Consequently, little progress was made in the drafting of a constitution. The Legitimists were inclined to desire a France which should be reminiscent of the old regime, which should faithfully protect the interests of the aristocracy and the Catholic Church. The Orleanists, on the other hand, desired to establish a liberal constitutional monarchy somewhat on the order of the British, in which the king should reign but not rule. Obviously, it was difficult to reconcile these incompatible ideas in one constitutional document. And it was equally difficult to arrange a settlement satisfactory to the two major claimants to the throne. The Count of Chambord could not forget that his grandfather had been driven from his throne by the very revolution which had enthroned the grandsire of the Count of Paris.

The delays and uncertainties contingent upon the political maneuvering of the Legitimists and Orleanists, each group seeking to advance its own cause at the expense of the other, ultimately led Thiers to abandon his liberal monarchist ideas and to decide that a republic was after all the type of government which would least divide the French people. Thiers therefore began to advocate a conservative republic. Such views were, of course, anathema to the royalists, who, though unable to agree on many subjects, did agree that Thiers should be removed from the presidency. That aged and veteran statesman was consequently forced to resign, and to his place a dyed-in-the-wool royalist, Marshal MacMahon, was elected by the Assembly. It was believed that MacMahon would willingly resign the presidency when the royalist impasse was ultimately overcome.

Alarmed, perhaps, by Thiers' conversion to the republic and by Gambetta's active campaigning in its behalf, the royalists now redoubled their efforts to achieve their end. Eventually they persuaded the Count of Paris to seek a compromise with his cousin. Pocketing his pride, the Orleanist candidate consented to visit the Count of Chambord, who was living in Austria, and to recognize him as the head of the family. The two royalist candidates agreed that the Legitimist Count of Chambord should mount the throne as Henry V and that, since he had no children, he should be succeeded by the Orleanist Count of Paris and his heirs. The impasse, it appeared, had at length been overcome; the republic seemed doomed.

But, unfortunately for the plans of the royalists, the Count of Chambord was the type of Bourbon who had learned nothing. He had not been in France for forty years and was completely out of touch with the country; he was still thoroughly permeated by the political and religious ideas of the old regime; he was an ardent believer in the divine right of monarchs and a loyal standard-bearer of the Bourbon white flag. When all these facts were emphatically brought home to the Orleanist liberal monarchists by the Count of Chambord's announcement of his divine-right ideas and by his insistence upon the restoration of the Bourbon flag in place of the beloved tricolor, the liberal monarchists themselves drew back. The compromise plan thus came to naught.

The Orleanists now decided that it would be to their best interest to co-operate with the republicans until such time as the reactionary Count of Chambord should be removed from the scene by death. Then, they reasoned, their liberal Count of Paris might ultimately come to the throne. In November, 1873, accordingly, the Orleanists joined with the republicans to the extent of passing through the National Assembly a bill fixing President MacMahon's term of office definitely at seven years. The liberal royalists hoped that within this period events might so shape themselves that the way would be cleared for an Orleanist restoration. As it eventually proved, however, this was the first constitutional step in the definite establishment of the republic.

General distrust and more political maneuvering delayed further steps in constitution-making until 1875. Meanwhile, Gambetta and other republican leaders were busily agitating in favor of the republic. Gradually some of the royalists became alarmed lest the unsettled conditions in the country should encourage a Bonapartist revival or even lead to some radical republican regime. To them a conservative republic was much to be preferred to either of these alternatives. Consequently, by January, 1875, enough of the royalists had been won over by the republicans so that it was possible by the slim margin of one vote to enact a law making definite provision for the method of election and the re-eligibility of the president of the republic. In the succeeding months of that year the Assembly at last gave itself definitely to the drafting of further "constitutional laws." By the close of 1875 the organic laws constituting the new republican government had been completed, with provision for a president, a cabinet of ministers, a popularly elected Chamber of Deputies, and an indirectly elected Senate. With the structure of the new government completed, the National Assembly, which had governed France since 1871, was thereupon dissolved.

But the dissolution of the royalist Assembly did not bring to an end the struggle between royalists and republicans. The former had by no means given up the fight. Although, as a result of the first parliamentary elections in 1876, the republicans controlled the Chamber of Deputies, the royalists controlled the Senate. And the president, too, it must be remembered, was a royalist. President MacMahon, who sincerely believed that France should have a monarchical form of government, did his utmost to advance the royalist cause, working particularly through the army and the Catholic clergy. But the republican leaders, especially the dynamic lawyer-politician, Gambetta, were not slow in counterattacking. Throughout the length and breadth of France Gambetta, the "traveling salesman of the republic," denounced the alliance between the royalists and the church, and gradually won many anticlericals to the republican cause by his repeated assertion, "Clericalism is the enemy!"

In May, 1877, President MacMahon made another move to advance the royalist cause when, despite the republican control of the Chamber of Deputies, he forced the resignation of the republican ministry, replaced it with one consisting of royalist and clerical sympathizers, dissolved the Chamber, and called for new elections. President MacMahon asserted that he had the right to select such ministers as he chose, regardless of the wishes of the Chamber of Deputies, which asserted that the cabinet must be satisfactory to the Chamber. In the ensuing campaign the issue, therefore, was not merely royalism versus republicanism but also parliamentary versus presidential government. In other words, whether France was to be a republic or a monarchy, the question was: Should the ministry be responsible to the popularly elected Chamber, as in Great Britain, or to the titular executive of the state, as in the German Empire? In the exciting electoral campaign which ensued the various groups of republicans were fused by Gambetta into a "Federation of the Left," which, thanks largely to his enthusiasm, energy, and oratory, won a decisive victory. The new Chamber at once forced the resignation of the royalist ministry, and President MacMahon recognized the situation by appointing a cabinet which was satisfactory to the Chamber. The issue was thus settled in favor of parliamentary government.

When, in 1879, elections to the Senate gave the republicans control of that body also, President MacMahon apparently recognized the futility of his royalist campaign. Faced by a republican Senate, a republican Chamber, and a republican ministry, the royalist president resigned his office. Jules Grévy, a staunch bourgeois republican with a reputation for dignified and sound statesmanship, was at once elected president, and at last the government of the French Republic was actually in the hands of loyal republicans.

The political framework of the Third Republic, though merely pieced together by a succession of "constitutional laws" and though planned by a goodly number of those who drafted it to be only a stop-gap affair, proved to have unexpected strength and permanence, lasting with comparatively little change down to the present time. The constitution upon which it rests consists not of a single document, as in the former German Empire, but simply of a number of organic laws enacted by a National Assembly which never had been empowered to draft a constitution. It is neither systematic in its arrangement nor comprehensive in what it covers. There is nothing in it regarding the sovereignty of the people. Nevertheless, of all the great powers on the Continent, the French Republic was the only one which in the years after the World War continued its political structure unchanged.

The National Assembly did not fundamentally alter the administrative system established by Napoleon I, and the Third Republic, in contrast with the former German Empire, is a highly centralized state, divided for administrative purposes into units called departments. In each department the executive officer is a prefect, an appointee of the central government, who is assisted by an elected council with somewhat meager powers. The departments are subdivided into districts, the latter into cantons, and the cantons into communes, of which there are some 36,000 in the republic.

The legislative power of the republic rests in a bicameral parliament consisting of a Chamber of Deputies, elected directly for a four-year term by universal manhood suffrage, and a Senate, elected indirectly for nine years, one third being retired every three years. The senators are chosen by electoral colleges, one in each department, consisting of the deputies of the department, members of the local councils of the department and its districts, and representatives from each of its communes. It was originally provided that seventy-five senators should hold office for life, but this provision was later repealed. The Chamber of Deputies is the more powerful of the two houses, for, though in theory the Senate has equal authority with the Chamber, in reality it acts more as a brake on hasty action of the popularly elected house. The Chamber is the body which usually controls the rise and fall of ministries. When the Chamber and the Senate meet in joint session they constitute the National Assembly, which has power to amend the constitution by a majority vote, provided the proposal for the amendment has previously been made by the president or by a majority vote of each house.

The president of the republic is elected for a seven-year term by the National Assembly. His powers are distinctly limited. He has no veto power over legislation passed by parliament, and all his acts must be countersigned by a member of the cabinet. Under the constitution he has the authority, with the consent of the Senate, to dissolve the Chamber. So much discredit was cast upon the use of this power by President MacMahon in 1877, however, that no president since has exercised this right. As has been pointed out many times, the President of France does not reign like the hereditary King of Great Britain, nor does he rule like the elected President of the United States. He is the titular head of the republic, but neither rules nor reigns. When, in the period after the World War, a president overstepped the precedents in this respect, he was compelled to resign by the Chamber of Deputies.[1]

The actual executive power of France is in the hands of a cabinet of ministers officially appointed by the president but actually named by the leaders of parliament and directly responsible to that body. The Third Republic thus adopted the British system of parliamentary government rather than the German system with an executive not responsible to the national legislature. But the parliamentary system has operated quite differently in France than in Great Britain. Whereas some one party usually controls the British House of Commons, the French ministry, because of the many political groups in France, has to rely on coalitions or blocs. Furthermore, the French political groups are neither so well organized nor so clear-cut in their differences as the British parties, with the result that blocs once formed are forever disintegrating and permitting a ministry to fall. By resorting to his right of "interpellation" a deputy may at any time force a vote of "lack of confidence" and the resignation of the ministry. Between 1870 and 1914 the Third Republic had a kaleidoscopic succession of at least fifty different ministries. There is never any question in France of a ministry's dissolving the Chamber of Deputies to avoid resigning; the Chamber is supreme. On the other hand, the rapid change in ministries has not entailed a rapid change in policies. Frequently the new cabinet, with ministers reshuffled and with possibly a few added, supports the same policies as the one

[1] See page 726.

which fell. Instability of ministries and relative stability in policies have usually obtained.

### EARLY REPUBLICAN MEASURES

Following the triumph of republicanism, Gambetta's "Federation of the Left" dissolved, and the republican groups which emerged fell, generally speaking, into two categories: the Moderates and the Radicals. The Moderates appealed more especially to the possessing classes, definitely favored a policy of overseas expansion in order to restore French power and prestige, and were only moderately anti-clerical. Jules Ferry, serving as premier or minister of education in the years immediately after 1880, was their outstanding leader. The Radicals, on the other hand, appealed more particularly to the masses, deplored colonial expansion as likely to weaken France in Europe, and were inclined to be strongly anticlerical. Their chief spokesman and leader was Georges Clemenceau, formerly mayor of Montmartre, a radical section of Paris. During the first two decades of the republic Clemenceau was a member of the Chamber of Deputies, where he gained the title of "Tiger" because of the number of ministries he overturned. His vitriolic attacks were launched not against royalists alone but against conservative and moderate republicans as well. The republic's political situation was further complicated by the fact that the royalists and clericals constituted a Right group which seized every opportunity to embarrass the successive republican ministries. Nevertheless, the government, under Jules Ferry's guidance, was able to enact a number of important measures.

Following the triumph of the republicans, the capital of France was moved from royalist Versailles to revolutionary Paris (1880), the anniversary of the popular attack on the Bastille—July 14—was made the national holiday, and the stirring "Marseillaise" was restored as the national anthem of the republic. In 1884 the "constitutional laws" of France were modified to strengthen the republic and lessen the influence of those who might be opposed to its permanence. Proposals to modify the republican form of government were made illegal, members of former ruling families were declared ineligible for the presidency of the republic, and provision was made for the gradual abolition of the life senatorships which had originally been created.

No provision had been made in the "constitutional laws" for a bill of rights, and so the republicans enacted a number of measures to safeguard the individual liberties of the French people. In 1881 laws were passed granting freedom of speech and permitting the holding of public meetings without the necessity of securing official authorization from the government. Freedom of the press was also established. In 1884, largely through the influence of Waldeck-Rousseau, one of Gambetta's followers, full freedom to organize and to strike was granted to workingmen by a law which has been characterized as the "charter of liberties" of organized labor in the Third Republic. Under this law French trade unions expanded until their membership came to include millions of workers.

The success of the Third Republic, Ferry and his associates believed, required an intelligent, enlightened, and loyal electorate. Since the privilege of the ballot had been extended to all male adults, it was now felt that all of the youth of the country must be educated. Ferry believed, furthermore, that the best way to inculcate loyalty to the republic was through schools which were free from royalist and clerical influence. The inauguration of a system of secular schools would entail a considerable change in French education, however, for in the preceding years of the nineteenth century Catholic religious instruction had been given in most of the schools of the country, and great numbers of schools had been conducted and controlled by various Catholic teaching orders.

Nevertheless, under Ferry's inspiration and guidance, laws were enacted and administrative decrees were issued during the eighties which had, in general, two major aims: to wipe out illiteracy and to weaken the control of the Catholic Church over education. To accomplish the first of these objectives, a state-supported public-school system was established, and education in the public schools was made free. Elementary education in some school was made compulsory for all children from six to thirteen years of age, but it was left to the parents to decide whether their children should attend public or private schools. A system of secondary schools for girls was established, and higher education for women, formerly neglected, was now encouraged. Equal opportunities with men were conceded to women in most of the educational institutions of the republic. An attempt was made to guard against the influence of the clergy in the public-school system. No religious instruction might be given in the state-supported schools, and only those lay persons who held diplomas from the state's normal schools might teach in them.

To weaken the position of the Catholic Church in the field of education, religious schools were denied financial support from the state, and it was hoped that many parents might be won to send their children to the public schools because attendance at the latter was free. The Jesuit order, whose members were bitterly opposed to secular schools, was dissolved, and its members were expelled from the country. Various other teaching orders which had not been "authorized" by the state were likewise disbanded, and their members were forbidden to conduct schools. Higher institutions of learning controlled by the church were deprived of the right to grant degrees or to call themselves universities.

The anticlerical spirit of the republicans, especially of the Radicals, was further shown by legislation regarding marriage. In 1816 the influence of the clericals had resulted in the abolition of divorce in France as contrary to the doctrines of the Catholic Church. The republicans now insisted that marriage was merely a civil contract, and enacted a law stipulating that all marriages, to be legal, must be performed by civil magistrates. In 1884 they also re-established divorce by passing a law providing that marriages might be dissolved or annulled by the civil courts.

### COLONIAL EXPANSION AND EMERGENCE FROM ISOLATION

As pointed out above, Jules Ferry and his moderate republicans favored a vigorous colonial policy. Success in this field might do much to obliterate the humiliation of the Franco-German War and might even disguise the fact that the Third Republic was being forced to play a minor role on the international stage of Europe. For, during the first two decades after the establishment of the German Empire, France stood isolated among the powers of Europe, condemned to this position by Bismarck's skillful diplomacy, by her own military weakness, and by the suspicion with which the apparently unstable Third Republic was viewed by the monarchs of Europe. Although French patriots fervently hoped and ardently planned to regain for their country its lost position in Europe, although many of them were patently dominated by the idea of *revanche*, responsible French leaders clearly realized that an isolated and weak France was in no position to regain her lost provinces or to wage a successful war against the republic's powerful neighbor on the east. The day of *revanche* had therefore to be postponed.

In the meantime, within France there were strong advocates of a vigorous policy of overseas expansion. Not long after the humiliating treaty of Frankfort Professor Pierre Leroy-Beaulieu published a famous essay on modern colonization. "Colonization," he concluded, "is the expansive force of a nation, its power of reproduction, its dilation and multiplication across space. . . . The nation that colonizes is the premier nation; if it is not today, it will be tomorrow." Almost simultaneously with the publication of Leroy-Beaulieu's work, Jules Ferry and his Moderate associates, perhaps confusing colonization with imperialism, began a campaign to extend the overseas territory controlled by France. In their efforts they had the blessing of the German chancellor, Bismarck, who believed that the French people needed "satisfactions for their pride" and who hoped that such satisfactions in the form of new colonies might lead the French to forget and possibly even to forgive the loss of Alsace-Lorraine. Consequently, in the decade after 1871 he advocated for France a policy of colonial expansion and frequently assured French statesmen of his willingness to support the Third Republic diplomatically if the latter sought to extend her overseas territory. In other words, Bismarck attempted to direct France's reviving energies away from *revanche* by turning them into the field of colonial expansion.

The Third French Republic inherited a colonial empire of some 375,000 square miles, which included principally Algeria in northern Africa, Cochin-China and Cambodia in southeastern Asia, and scattered footholds on the west coast of Africa, in India, in the Pacific, and in the western hemisphere. The first imperial venture undertaken by the republic was in southeastern Asia, where Cochin-China and Cambodia were used as bases of operation. As a result of a series of military operations begun in 1874 and eventually concluded in 1887, Annam and Tonkin were secured at the expense of China and Laos from Siam. In consequence, the republic by the close of the eighties had carved out an imposing empire in southeastern Asia with an area nearly half again as large as France itself and with a population of some 20,000,000 industrious natives.[2]

[2] For the places mentioned in these paragraphs, see the maps on pages 21 and 25.

Before these conquests had been completed, the Third Republic had also launched its campaign to secure more territory in Africa. Assured of both German and British good will, in 1881 it annexed Tunis to the east of Algeria. Although this step antagonized Italy and helped to drive her into the Triple Alliance, it extended French control along the Mediterranean and improved the republic's claim to the hinterland of Africa when the time for the inevitable partition of that great continent should occur. A few years later France began to extend her control over the island of Madagascar, off the east coast of Africa. In 1885 the ruler of the island was forced to give France a port and to entrust to the republic the control of Madagascar's foreign relations. Five years later, as the result of a colonial bargain, Germany and Great Britain recognized Madagascar as a French protectorate, and in 1896 the native ruler was expelled and the island definitely annexed. Again an area greater in extent than France itself was obtained.

Meanwhile, other gains had been made at scattered points. In 1888 Jibuti, a port in Somaliland on the Gulf of Aden, had been acquired, and a foothold for expansion into Ethiopia was thus provided. On the west coast of Africa, also, the French had further extended their holdings by annexing Dahomey and establishing themselves on the Ivory Coast and in Guinea. By the close of the century the upper Niger territory had been connected with the coastal regions on the west, and the isolated French colonies there had been converted into possible commercial outlets for the extensive empire which France had carved out in the Sahara and in the western Sudan. Incidentally, France had successfully hemmed in and limited the further expansion of Kamerun, much to the chagrin of German imperialists.

But French statesmen were interested not alone in territorial expansion overseas; they were eager to remove the republic from its condition of international isolation. Consequently, they were not slow to seize the opportunity which was offered when Russia was set adrift by the German Kaiser after the dismissal of Bismarck in 1890. Immediately they determined to seek an alliance with the tsarist empire. Naturally certain obstacles had to be overcome if this was to be accomplished. Russian prejudice was strong against an alliance with the country whose Emperor Napoleon I had occupied Moscow and whose Emperor Napoleon III had helped to bring defeat to Russia in the Crimean War. Tsarist reluctance to be bound in any way with revolutionary democratic France was also a factor to be overcome.

On the other hand, Russia was as isolated as France. She likewise feared the increasingly powerful and aggressive German Empire, which had apparently decided to support its ally Austria in her imperialistic ventures in the Balkans. Furthermore, in the nineties Russia was embarking upon an industrial program which required extensive loans from abroad, and French bankers were very willing to make the necessary loans. The logical consequence of all these factors was that Russia and France came together in an entente (1891) which culminated later in a military convention creating the Franco-Russian alliance of 1894. In this convention it was provided that, if France were attacked by Germany or by Italy supported by Germany, Russia would aid France; and that, if Russia were attacked by Germany or by Austria supported by Germany, France would aid Russia. Quite evidently France was emerging from her isolation and beginning again to assume her role among the great powers.

## The Weakening of the Royalists and Clericals

Meanwhile, within France various groups had become seriously discontented with the course of events after 1879. The Radicals vigorously denounced French colonial expansion because of the great expenditures involved and because such enterprises tended to divert the government's attention from numerous domestic problems which, to their minds, urgently demanded a solution. The clericals, alarmed by the laws which had been enacted to weaken the influence of the church, were firmly convinced that the republic would have to be overturned if the Catholic Church in France were to escape from further legislation of a similar type. The royalists, continuing to lament the establishment of the republic, were quick to join with the clericals in seizing any opportunity which might present itself for discrediting or undermining the republican regime.

Conditions within France in the late eighties were such as to invite criticism. Following the death of Gambetta in 1882 and the downfall of Ferry in 1885, no outstanding personality for a time was able to dominate the political stage. Ministries succeeded one another with what appeared to be an alarming rapidity, and the efficacy of parliamentary government seemed open to question. The national budget was unbalanced, and deficits caused serious concern to those who advocated sound financial policies. On top of all this, political corruption was discovered in republican circles, involving even President Grévy's son-in-law, who had sold his influence to persons desiring to obtain membership in the coveted Legion of Honor. The resultant scandal forced the resignation of President Grévy in 1887, even though he himself was not personally involved. Jules Ferry appeared to be the logical successor to Grévy in the presidency, but the Radicals were opposed to him and were able to force the election of a compromise candidate, Sadi Carnot, who, though a Moderate, was less repugnant to the Radicals.

Many conservatives, fearful lest a republican government was too weak to meet the needs of France, began to believe that some type of "strong government" might perhaps be preferable. Moreover, many French patriots among the younger generation, dissatisfied with the peaceful policies of the Third Republic, grew more and more impatient with statesmen who would not let themselves be swayed by the idea of *revanche*. Chauvinistic Frenchmen organized societies like the "League of Patriots" to keep alive a burning desire to regain the lost provinces of Alsace-Lorraine. Naturally, they, too, desired a "strong government," though for reasons somewhat different from those which actuated the royalists, clericals, army officers, and conservatives. Among several large groups in France, therefore, the psychological state in the eighties was in many respects analogous to that preceding the establishment of fascist dictatorships in Europe in the years following the World War.

The one who for a time seemed destined to lead the forces of discontent against the republic was General Georges Boulanger, a cousin of Clemenceau. Upon the latter's recommendation, Boulanger, who was believed to be a stanch republican, was appointed minister of war. In this position he sought by various moves to win the favor of the soldiers and soon began to use his office for personal ends. He was a dashing figure on horseback and utilized the military reviews to disclose this fact. Through newspapers which he controlled he repeatedly intimated that France under his leadership might secure her *revanche* upon Germany. In order that the executive power might be strengthened, he began to advocate a revision of the constitution. Republican leaders, including Clemenceau, became alarmed at Boulanger's growing popularity and his increasingly apparent personal ambition. Fearful of the rise of another "Napoleon," they combined in 1887 to force the general not only from the ministry but also from the army as well.

Around Boulanger the various discontented groups—except the Radicals—now rallied, and ultimately the general organized the National Party, largely financed by the royalists, who hoped that he might be used to overturn the republic. Bonapartists, clericals, and even some chauvinistic republicans flocked to his support. For a time he became the storm center of France. Six times during 1888 he was elected to the Chamber of Deputies. In January, 1889, a Paris constituency elected him once again by a huge majority. At that time his friends advised him to arouse the Paris mob and with the aid of the League of Patriots to seize the government of France by force. But apparently Boulanger lacked the necessary boldness to become a dictator, for he made no overt move against the government.

The republicans, however, decided that the time for action had arrived. Temporarily laying aside their differences, they combined to defend the republic against its foe. The government ordered Boulanger's arrest on charges of conspiracy. Boulanger did not wait to be arrested, however, but fled in haste from the country. In his absence he was convicted of conspiracy against the state, and the League of Patriots which had supported him was ordered dissolved. In the general elections of September, 1889, a popular reaction against his movement gave the anti-Boulanger republicans a sweeping victory. Two years later the general committed suicide in Brussels.

Whether the republic was as much endangered by the Boulanger affair as the frightened republicans believed is uncertain. Certain it is, however, that it was definitely strengthened by the outcome and by measures taken by the government subsequently. In the first place, the belief that the republic could not be "strong" in time of need was dispelled by the government's aggressive action against Boulanger, action which went far toward destroying any lingering hope that a military dictatorship might be established. The danger of an army plot was lessened when the government retired many royalists in high military positions and filled their places with loyal republicans. In the second place, the royalists, by openly supporting

Boulanger, were in the end discredited along with the general, and their cause was therefore further weakened. Moreover, although this development was not directly a result of the Boulanger affair, many clericals deserted the royalist cause in consequence of an encyclical letter in which Pope Leo XIII urged French Catholics to accept the republic and, instead of seeking to overturn it in order to protect the interests of the Catholic Church, to attempt by constitutional means to secure the repeal of republican legislation obnoxious to the church.

The inability of the royalists to overturn the republic when presented with an opportunity like that in 1889 appeared to indicate that the royalist cause was doomed to failure. The son and heir of Napoleon III had died in 1879, thus weakening the Bonapartist cause. Four years later the Count of Chambord had died and carried with him to his grave the hopes of the Legitimists. Although the Count of Paris still lived and still asserted his right to the throne, the Orleanists were too discredited and too discouraged to make any open attempt to place him on it.

In the succeeding years the royalists and clericals were further discredited and weakened by their connection with an anti-Semitic campaign and with a notorious army scandal. In the nineties France experienced a strong wave of anti-Semitism, which was carefully fostered by a writer and journalist, Édouard Drumont. According to him the anticlerical laws of the republic were the result of Jewish influence, the oppressors of labor were Jewish capitalists and industrialists, and the reason why the army was in no position to drive the German forces out of Alsace-Lorraine was that it was constantly thwarted and betrayed by Jewish renegades. A financial scandal (1894) in connection with a French corporation engaged in constructing a canal across the Isthmus of Panama involved several Jewish bankers and members of parliament and seemed to offer ground for anti-Semitic charges. Further substantiation of the charges appeared to be forthcoming when in the same year a Jewish captain of artillery in the French army was convicted of selling military secrets to Germany.

Alfred Dreyfus, the condemned captain, was a wealthy Alsatian Jew who had been attached to the general staff. In October, 1894, he was suddenly arrested, accused of treason, convicted in a secret session by a court-martial, and sentenced to expulsion from the army and to life imprisonment on Devil's Island, a penal colony off the coast of French Guiana. The evidence against him was an unsigned document which was said to be in Dreyfus's handwriting, but later developments indicated that he was apparently being made the victim of a plot to cover the irregularities of some of his military associates and superiors. In January, 1895, he was publicly and dramatically degraded in the presence of a large detachment of the French army. So hysterical was the anti-Semitic feeling in the country at this time that mob violence was invoked against some who dared to assert that Dreyfus was innocent of the charges upon which he had been convicted.

A few Frenchmen were dissatisfied with the verdict, however, and sought to ascertain the real truth regarding the "Dreyfus affair." In 1896 a Colonel Picquart became convinced that the document in question was written not by Dreyfus but by a certain Major Esterhazy. When Picquart informed the minister of war of his belief, he was at once transferred to the army in northern Africa, and nothing was done to reopen the case. When rumors of what had happened became known, a group of radical republicans began to demand a new trial. The resultant discussions divided the French people generally into two groups: the anti-Dreyfusards, consisting of anti-Semitics, clericals, royalists, reactionaries, and chauvinists, who believed that the Dreyfus agitation was an attack on the honor of the army, and the Dreyfusards, consisting of the Radicals, certain liberal idealists among the intellectuals who opposed race hatred and believed in "fair play," and those who maintained that the army should be definitely subordinated to the civil authority.

Despite the wish of government and army leaders, the case could not be dismissed as a closed affair, and eventually Major Esterhazy was tried by a court-martial, only to be enthusiastically acquitted (1898). The distinguished novelist, Émile Zola, next sought to have the Dreyfus case reopened and ultimately forced the government to defend its action. The minister of war then produced further evidence of Dreyfus's guilt, but, unfortunately for the strength of his case, one of his documents was soon proved to be a forgery. In 1899 Major Esterhazy, who had fled from France, admitted that he had written the document which had originally been ascribed to Dreyfus. Again the latter was tried by a court-martial, with high army officers bending every effort to secure a second conviction, and again the court condemned Dreyfus. But this time President Loubet at once pardoned him and ordered his release. The Dreyfusards were still dissatisfied, however, and in 1906 succeeded in having the case submitted to the court of cassation, the highest court in France. That court ultimately ruled that the charges against Dreyfus were utterly unfounded, and that the second court-martial before which the captain had been tried had been guilty of gross injustice. Dreyfus was restored to the army with the rank of major and was invested with a decoration of the Legion of Honor.

The spectacular Dreyfus affair, which disturbed French equanimity for so many years, was significant in a number of respects. The outcome discredited and weakened still further the royalists and clericals, who were suspected of using the "honor of the army" as a screen to hide what was actually a conspiracy against the republic. Furthermore, the Dreyfus affair provided an opportunity for the civil authorities to assert their supremacy over the military. The army, still largely officered by men from the upper classes who at heart were royalists, constituted the chief instrument for the possible overthrow of the republic by a *coup d'état*. Now the army was further republicanized and made definitely subordinate to the civil authority. Both the Boulanger and the Dreyfus affair, accordingly, not only greatly weakened the royalist cause but revealed that the republican forces were sufficiently strong to maintain the republic in the time of crisis.

## THE SEPARATION OF CHURCH AND STATE

During the struggle to rehabilitate Dreyfus the Moderates and Radicals had organized in parliament a bloc of "republican defense" which included also the Socialists. Although the reaction which followed the uprising of the Paris Commune had militated against the rise of a socialist party in France, a beginning had been made in 1876 when the Labor Party had been founded by Jules Guesde upon his return from exile. In 1880 the party had become definitely socialist when it adopted a program drafted in co-operation with Karl Marx. During the eighties a number of other socialist parties had appeared, and by the nineties the various socialist groups had made considerable progress in France. The leaders of the new movement included a number of young men—among them Alexandre Millerand, Aristide Briand, René Viviani, and Jean Jaurès— who were destined to play important roles in the history of the republic. Their immediate demands were for social legislation in the interests of the workingmen, but their ultimate goal was the socialization of French industry. Through the co-operation of Briand and Jaurès a socialist newspaper, *L'Humanité,* was established in Paris to advance the cause. In the parliamentary elections of 1893 the various socialist groups gained a combined representation of about fifty in the Chamber.

In 1899 the Socialists were forced to decide to what extent they would co-operate with other parties, for in that year the bloc of "republican defense" secured control of the ministry. Pierre Waldeck-Rousseau, the new premier, wished to have a broad foundation for his government and so sought to include representatives of the Moderates, Radicals, and Socialists. On this issue the Socialists split. Although they were ready to support the bloc's program in its general outlines, the majority, led by Guesde and Jaurès, were opposed to participating in a ministry with "bourgeois" parties. Millerand, Briand, and others, however, were willing to accept office, and, when the former became the minister of commerce in Waldeck-Rousseau's cabinet, he and his supporters were expelled from the Socialist Party.

The Radicals in return for their support of Waldeck-Rousseau demanded that anticlericalism be made the foundation stone of the new ministry's policy. They openly attacked the Catholic Church, which, despite the pope's encyclical calling for support of the republic, was widely suspected of antirepublican sentiments. The church schools were accused not only of providing inadequate education for the children who attended but of deliberately inculcating royalist doctrines. Furthermore, the concordat of 1801, which regulated the relations between church and state in France, was vigorously denounced on the ground that it gave the pope excessive power within the republic and because payment of the salaries of the clergy by the government was said to constitute a heavy and unnecessary drain on the budget of the state.

In 1901 the attack against the church began with the enactment of the Associations Law, which was aimed at the religious orders, or congregations, of monks and nuns. The premier pointed out that these orders had been growing in membership and wealth at an astonishing rate, that during the last quarter of the nineteenth century the number of nuns had increased fivefold, that the property of the orders had risen in half a century from fifty million francs to more than a billion. The orders were therefore denounced on economic, educational, and political grounds, and the Associations Law was designed to alter the situation. According to the provisions of this act every congregation must be "authorized" or incorporated. Those that failed to receive authorization from the government were to be dissolved, and their property was to be confiscated. Apparently the new law was approved by large numbers of Frenchmen, for parliamentary elections in 1902 resulted in a sweeping victory for the radical republicans who came to hold a dominant position in the Chamber of Deputies.

A ministry of Radicals now took over the reins of government, and to the new premier, Émile Combes, an extreme anticlerical, was entrusted the enforcement of the Associations Law. Nearly all of the religious orders that applied for authorization were refused on the ground that they served no useful purpose socially. Both these and the orders that failed to seek authorization—some five hundred in all—were at once suppressed. The government was particularly drastic in dealing with the teaching orders. Most of their schools were closed, and their members were forbidden to teach or preach. Tens of thousands of monks and nuns thus found themselves homeless. In 1904 the Radical campaign to remove education from the hands of "royalist" clergy led to the enactment of a law directed against even the authorized orders, which were forbidden to recruit new members. Furthermore, although the act permitted authorized orders to continue their activities in the French overseas empire, it was decreed that within France all teaching by members of religious orders—whether in public or in private schools—must cease within ten years. The result sought by the Radicals was obtained; the number of children attending the public schools increased until by 1914 more than 80 per cent of them were thus included.

The next step in the anticlerical program of the Radicals was to secure the abrogation of the concordat of 1801, and in 1903 a parliamentary committee headed by Briand was appointed to draft a measure to provide for the separation of church and state. Naturally there was friction between the papacy and the French government over the suppression of religious orders, and ill feeling reached a climax in 1904 when Pope Pius X protested to the Catholic powers of Europe because the President of France paid an official visit to the King of Italy, a "usurper" in the eyes of the papacy. The Socialists in the parliament seized this occasion to denounce the pope's interference in French political affairs, and the French ambassador was recalled from the Vatican. With diplomatic relations thus broken off, a bill for abrogating the concordat was introduced, and in 1905 the Separation Law was enacted.

By the provisions of this law the concordat of 1801 was finally abrogated. No longer was the state to pay the salaries of the Catholic, Protestant, or Jewish clergy, though provision was made for payments to aged clergy and, temporarily, to those who had but recently entered the priesthood. Title to all church property remained vested in the state, where it had been since 1789, but it was stipulated that associations of laymen might make arrangements with the government for the use of church buildings for public worship. The state was to surrender all control over the appointment of Catholic bishops in France; both state and church were to be "free."

Protestants and Jews accepted the Separation Law more or less readily, and even many Catholics felt that it might be to the best interests of the church to be free from state interference and control. But Pope Pius bitterly denounced the law. In the first place, by the unilateral action of the state it abrogated an agreement originally reached through negotiation between two sovereign parties. In the second place, the act was declared contrary to canon law, which was opposed to the management of church affairs by laymen. In the third place, it was asserted that the refusal to continue state financial support to the clergy was unjust because that support was the logical consequence of the state's earlier confiscation of clerical property. Finally, the pope announced that the principle of separation of church and state was "an absolutely false thesis, a very pernicious error." The pope therefore forbade members of the church to observe the law, with the result that no associations for public worship were formed by the Catholics.

Eventually, after more than a year of friction and chaos, a new law—largely the work of Briand—was enacted by the parliament. By the provisions of the act of 1907 the use of churches was made free and was to be regulated by contracts between priests and government officials without resort to the associations of laymen which were so objectionable to the pope. In the end the religious situation for Catholics in France came to be not unlike that in the United States; that is, church and state were completely separate, the state making no contributions to the support of the clergy, and the church being free to manage its own affairs in accordance with canon law.

### ECONOMIC AND SOCIAL PROGRESS

Industrial expansion in France under the Third Republic was in no wise comparable to that which occurred in Germany under the empire. For one thing, French industry suffered a severe blow from the cession of Alsace-Lorraine. By that transfer of territory Germany had secured valuable iron deposits, important iron and steel plants, and large textile mills. Germany's gain was France's loss. It took the iron industry of France more than two decades to recover from this blow. The republic's industrial development was further handicapped in two important respects. France lacked sufficient coal, and what she had was, generally speaking, poor in quality—not good for coking. In the second place, France had no great surplus of cheap labor which might be used in industrial development. Beginning in the eighties the population of France became nearly stationary. There was a shortage of labor rather than a surplus, so that it was practically impossible to supply the workers for a large industrial system.

In two types of industry, however, there was a considerable development. When Germany required the cession of part of Lorraine, she did not—through ignorance—make her demands extensive enough to include the whole iron basin. In the northeastern part of France, therefore, the republic did possess valuable iron deposits, and here also it had some coal. In this district, accordingly, after the Thomas-Gilchrist process made these ores available for the manufacture of steel, the French made notable advances in the metallurgical industries, partly with the aid of cheap labor imported from Belgium and Italy. In steel production before the World War the republic made greater progress relatively than any other country on the Continent, though its total output was still below that of either Germany or Great Britain. During these years, too, French production of coal increased threefold and that of iron approximately fivefold. Nevertheless, because of the lack of adequate coal resources, much French iron ore was exported to the Ruhr region of Germany, there to be smelted into steel.

In another district of the country—that about Lyons—a second type of industry flourished, namely, the manufacture of silk. For a time France led the world in the production of this commodity, but ultimately she came to have a serious competitor in the Italian silk industry, and still later an even more damaging rival in rayon, a fiber made from wood pulp. Some expansion occurred also in the country's cotton textile industry. Outside the metal and textile trades, however, the typical industrial unit of France remained, down to the twentieth century, the small workshop and not the huge factory. French industrialists were slow to adopt mass methods of production, and at the opening of the century 80 per cent of the country's 600,000 industrial establishments still employed four workers or less.

With the rise of industrial labor came the demand for the right to have trade unions, a demand which was met in 1884, as pointed out above, by legislation legalizing and protecting labor combinations. Labor unions grew rapidly, and in 1895 most of them came together into the General Confederation of Labor, which aimed to unite all workers and to develop a feeling of class solidarity. At the opening of the twentieth century French trade unions became extremely radical, adopted the socialist theory of class struggle, and opposed "political" action in favor of "direct" action. In other words, the syndicalists, as French labor unionists were called, sought by strikes, sabotage, and other "direct" attacks on the captains of industry to overturn the capitalist system.

In the decade before the World War the republic was repeatedly and seriously disturbed by attempts to inaugurate "general" strikes when all labor was supposed to cease. Probably the most spectacular of these attempts was made in 1910, when a strike of railwaymen almost completely stopped traffic on the country's railway system. Much to the surprise and chagrin of the strikers, Premier Briand, who himself in his younger days had advocated resort to the general strike, turned against them. The government called the railwaymen, most of whom were reservists, to the colors, and then ordered them as soldiers under military discipline to operate the railways. The strike was thus broken, and the workers decided that, since the government could play such a decisive part in the class struggle between capital and labor, the latter had better seek to gain control of the government.

The Socialist Party was the chief gainer from this decision. In 1905 the various factions of Socialists had come together into one political group, the Unified Socialist Party, led by the able Jean Jaurès. By 1914 the representation of this party had increased in the Chamber to more than one hundred, and at that time it was believed by many that Jaurès might soon be elevated to the premiership. Although he was doomed to be only a minority leader in the years before the World War, his influence was constantly thrown on the side of those policies which aimed to bring social and industrial democracy at home and international peace abroad.

Thanks, in part, to Jaurès' efforts, in the two decades after 1890 the government enacted a number of laws for the benefit of the workingmen. Hours of labor were gradually reduced, a weekly rest day was made compulsory, minimum age limits were established for industrial workers, factory hygiene and safety were made matters of state concern, a system for the voluntary arbitration of industrial disputes was established, free medical attendance for workers and their families was introduced, a workmen's compensation law was enacted, and a system of old-age pensions was adopted. In other words, France followed somewhat tardily in the footsteps of Germany and Great Britain in the matter of social legislation and factory laws, and by 1914 she had not advanced so far in these matters as had these other countries.

Perhaps one reason for French slowness in social legislation was the fact that fundamentally, even in the twentieth century, France was an agricultural country. Before the World War more than half of the population of the republic still lived in communes which were classified as rural. The country had between five and six million landed proprietors, 99 per cent of whom owned less than one hundred acres. Contrary to the general impression abroad, although most of the *holdings* were small and were owned and tilled by the peasants, most of the arable land was held in relatively large units by landowners who rented it to tenants or let it out to workers "on shares." French agricultural products were varied and plentiful enough to make France practically self-sufficing. In addition to the staple crops, the French peasants produced for export such products as olive oil, wines, and brandies. When, because of increased and cheaper facilities for overseas transport, French agriculture began to suffer because of the import of agricultural products from abroad, protective tariffs were introduced, and government bounties were frequently extended to certain types of agricultural production. Further to assist the peasants, agricultural schools were established, cooperative societies were encouraged, and mutual loan banks and insurance agencies were given government guarantees.

At the time that the Third Republic came into being, the French, as a result of their own frugality and a period of prosperity under the Second Empire, had accumulated a large amount of capital. A considerable part of the French people had risen into the class of *rentiers,* that is, they were not compelled to engage in any productive activity but could live—sometimes rather frugally—on the income from their investments. Most of the *rentiers* had invested rather heavily in the government bonds floated by the Third Republic and therefore were vitally concerned with its perpetuation and sound financial condition. Not all of the wealth of *rentiers* could be placed in government bonds, however. In a great industrial country with rapidly expanding enterprises it might have been readily absorbed by industry, but France did not fulfill these conditions. Consequently, French investors loaned large sums of money abroad—sometimes to governments in need, sometimes to prosperous expanding industrial enterprises. As early as 1882 French foreign investments amounted to four or five billion dollars, and each year thereafter saw that figure rise markedly. This outward flow of capital in the nineties played a part in removing France from her position of international isolation. It also increased popular interest in France's role as a colonial and world power.

## THE CREATION OF THE ENTENTE CORDIALE

Meanwhile, with confidence increased by French emergence from isolation in 1894, French imperialists were becoming ever more ambitious. In the nineties they envisaged an empire which should not only include all of northwestern Africa but actually extend from the Atlantic to the Red Sea, from the Mediterranean to the Gulf of Guinea. With this in mind they planned to build a railway from Jibuti on the Gulf of Aden across Ethiopia to the Nile and to connect this vast region with French territory in central Africa. Such plans naturally conflicted with those of the imperialists of Great Britain, who, in turn, had visions of a great British empire extending unbroken from South Africa to Egypt. Great Britain therefore sought to check French expansion by encouraging Italian colonial ambitions. Italy had already secured footholds in Eritrea on the Red Sea and in Somaliland, and the British now encouraged them to conquer Ethiopia. The military disaster which overtook the Italians at Adowa in 1896 is discussed elsewhere.[3]

Even before this Italian defeat, however, the French had begun their campaign to unite their territories in western and eastern Africa. Early in 1896 two forces were organized and sent out. From French Congo Marchand with a number of French officers and some two hundred natives set out for the Sudan, while a stronger French force was ordered to march inland from Jibuti to join forces with Marchand on the upper Nile. A little later, after the battle of Adowa, Great Britain ordered Kitchener with an Egyptian army to move south to occupy the Sudan. A clash between French and British imperialism seemed inevitable, especially in view of the fact that Kitchener's progress was greatly retarded because of his decision to build a railway as he advanced.

In July, 1898, after a two-year struggle through the trackless tropical regions of central Africa, Marchand reached Fashoda on the Nile and there raised the French tricolor. Unfortunately for the strength of his position, however, the stronger French columns which were to join him from the east were delayed by swamps and fever and did not arrive. On the other hand, in the fall of 1898 Kitchener and his forces did arrive on the scene, to be welcomed to "French territory" by Marchand. Great Britain refused to recognize the region as belonging to France, an acute international crisis resulted, and the two countries came to the verge of war. But when France consulted her ally, Russia, regarding a course of action, she was advised by no means to risk an actual break with Great Britain. Furthermore, the French foreign minister, Théophile Delcassé, who had in mind the creation of a Franco-British entente as a means to other ends, believed that it would be to the best interest of France to yield at this time to the British. The French government therefore repudiated Marchand's action and ordered him to withdraw from Fashoda. A serious cause of friction between Great Britain and France was thus removed, and the crisis passed.

One reason for Delcassé's conciliatory policy at this time was that

[3] See page 155.

he had in mind the addition of Morocco to the French empire in northern Africa and for the successful accomplishment of this step needed a free hand. In 1900 Delcassé availed himself of the fact that Italy's ill will toward France had been subsiding to bring about a Franco-Italian understanding. In that year Italy agreed to give France a free hand in Morocco in return for the latter's giving her a free hand in Tripoli and Cyrenaica. The resultant good feeling between the two Latin countries led to a further agreement two years later. The two powers promised (1902) that, should either be the object of a direct or indirect aggression on the part of one or more powers, or should either, as a result of a direct provocation, find itself compelled in defense of its honor or its security to take the initiative of a declaration of war, the other would maintain a strict neutrality. In other words, should Germany attack France or should France "in defense of her honor or her security" declare war upon Germany, Italy would remain neutral. The international position of the Third Republic was considerably improved by these two agreements.

Delcassé also turned to French advantage the changing viewpoint in Great Britain, where Germany's rapid strides in industry and commerce, her adoption of a policy of vigorous colonial expansion, and her increasing demand for a place in the sun were causing uneasiness. This uneasiness was transformed into alarm after Great Britain's proffer of an alliance with Germany had been declined and the latter's apparent unfriendliness had been revealed by her encouragement of the Boers.[4] These circumstances led Great Britain to abandon her previously unfriendly attitude toward France and, skillfully used by Delcassé, resulted in the establishment of the *Entente Cordiale* (1904), which the French foreign minister had so ardently desired. Although a number of questions which had disturbed Franco-British relations were adjusted in the treaties signed at this time, perhaps the most important result was the agreement that Great Britain should have a free hand in Egypt and France a free hand in Morocco. No definite alliance or military convention was entered into, but an era of good feeling began which led Great Britain and France into closer and closer co-operation in international affairs and thus increased the Third Republic's influence as a great power.

[4] See page 190.

These treaties are good examples of what President Wilson of the United States later denounced as "secret diplomacy," for certain secret agreements in regard to Morocco and Egypt were not published. In other words, while French and British citizens rejoiced over what they thought had been signed by their responsible ministers, in reality they were being duped by those very officials. The published treaties stated that the French had no intention of altering the political status of Morocco and that the British likewise did not intend to change the political condition of Egypt. The secret clauses, on the contrary, stated that, if it became necessary to change the status of Morocco and Egypt, the former should be divided between France and Spain and Great Britain should be given a free hand in Egypt. In 1904 France also signed a secret treaty with Spain agreeing upon a future division of Moroccan territory.

## THE MOROCCAN CRISES

While Delcassé had taken secret steps to assure France of the diplomatic support of Italy, Great Britain, and Spain in case he decided to carry through his plan to convert Morocco into a French protectorate, he had neither informed Germany of his plans nor asked for her approval. Although the German chancellor, Bülow, was warned by his ambassador at London that negotiations of some sort were being carried on by Great Britain and France, the officials at Berlin firmly believed that Franco-British enmity was of too long standing to permit any pacific settlement of all their disputes. They were somewhat surprised and taken aback, therefore, when shortly before the conclusion of the negotiations Delcassé informed the German ambassador at Paris that Great Britain and France were about to conclude a general colonial agreement. Since the French foreign minister omitted the courtesy of officially informing the German government of the contents of the treaties, the latter had to obtain its information from reports in the press. It has been asserted by some that Bülow through devious channels learned of the unpublished secret agreements, and, although this fact has never been proved, his subsequent actions appear to lend color to this suspicion.

However that may be, Delcassé apparently felt so secure after the Moroccan agreements with Italy, Great Britain, and Spain that he began to prepare the way for the so-called reforms which he expected to force upon the Moroccan sultan. Bülow and Holstein, his adviser in the German foreign office, believed, on the other hand, that France's position was so weakened by Russia's war in the Far East that they might successfully utilize the occasion to advance Germany's prestige and at the same time to test the strength of the recently achieved Entente Cordiale between France and Great Britain. They therefore attempted to block Delcassé's program by encouraging the ruler of Morocco to reject the proposed reforms. Furthermore, although the Kaiser personally wished Germany to pursue a policy of hands-off so far as Morocco was concerned, the German chancellor practically forced William II to make a visit to Tangier, the chief port of Morocco on the Mediterranean. At Tangier on March 31, 1905, the Kaiser, as he was so likely to do upon occasion, in his public address said too much and said it too emphatically. His statement that he considered the Sultan of Morocco as an independent sovereign was regarded in France as an insult to the Third Republic. The international situation at once became strained.

Apparently what Bülow desired to do was to increase German prestige as a world power by indicating that nowhere on the globe was it safe to make imperialistic bargains without considering Germany's interests. The French popularly believed, however, that the German chancellor was seeking to destroy the Franco-British entente and to embarrass France in order to receive some *quid pro quo*. Shortly after the Kaiser's speech, therefore, the French premier, Rouvier, took it upon himself to ask Bülow what Germany desired in compensation for giving France a free hand in Morocco. Bülow did not ask for territorial compensation but declared that, since the status of Morocco had been fixed by the Madrid conference of 1880, France must permit her position there to be determined by an international conference of the signatory powers. The French premier, who was by no means so aggressive as his foreign minister, then suggested to the German chancellor that France and Germany might conclude a general colonial settlement similar to that which France and Great Britain had recently signed. But Bülow was at this time apparently more interested in raising German prestige than he was in settling colonial disputes, for he failed to notify the Kaiser of the French premier's proposal.[5]

Meanwhile, Delcassé had flatly refused to accept Bülow's demand for a conference, and in his stand was given full diplomatic support by the British foreign secretary, the Marquis of Lansdowne, who likewise opposed the conference. Nevertheless, the milder Rouvier, fearing the possibility of war, opposed Delcassé, with the result that the French cabinet had to choose between its premier and its foreign minister and chose to support the former. In June Delcassé was obliged to resign, and his portfolio was assumed by the more cautious Rouvier. In the face of Bülow's continued insistence upon a conference, the French premier at last gave way, and a conference was called to meet at Algeciras in Spain. It thus appeared that Germany had won a decisive diplomatic victory.

At the Algeciras conference, which convened on January 16, 1906, Germany found, however, that instead of isolating France she was herself practically isolated. Italy, Russia, Great Britain, Spain, and the United States supported France, and only Austria-Hungary voted on the side of Germany. Although the last appeared to have won her point when the fiction of Moroccan independence was preserved, France was left in a position where she could continue to increase her influence in the sultanate, and she was not compelled to give Germany compensation. The French, nevertheless, felt extremely bitter toward Germany because of the way she had forced the matter before an international conference.

In 1907 France's position as a great power was further strengthened when Russia, united with France in the alliance of 1894, and Great Britain, linked with France in the Entente Cordiale of 1904, adjusted their differences and came to an understanding.[6] Again, no binding alliance was consummated between these two powers, but the good feeling and close understanding which followed led to the designation of France, Russia, and Great Britain as the powers of the Triple Entente. Thus the great powers of Europe came to be pretty definitely divided into two groups—the Triple Alliance, created by Bismarck, and the Triple Entente, created by France. The Third Republic had successfully emerged from its long isolation and had come to occupy that central position in a system of

[5] The Kaiser later stated that such a settlement would have been acceptable to him.
[6] See page 212.

powerful alliances and ententes which Bismarck during his chancellorship had so successfully sought to prevent.[7]

Meanwhile, despite the events of 1905 and 1906, France continued

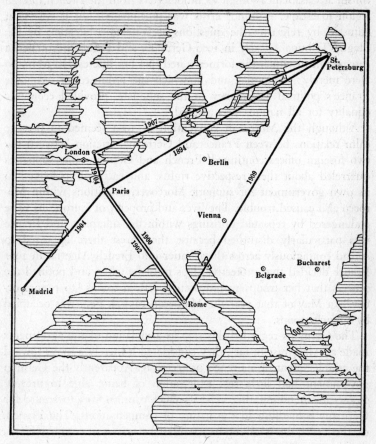

FRANCO-RUSSIAN SYSTEM OF ALLIANCES AND ENTENTES, 1894–1909

her efforts to secure control of Morocco. In the very next year after the Algeciras conference she used a civil war in the sultanate with accompanying outrages against Frenchmen as an excuse to land her

[7] A comparison of the drawings on pages 73 and 133 will reveal graphically France's emergence from isolation. In 1909 Russia and Italy also made an imperialistic bargain and entered into an entente. See page 161.

marines at Casablanca. The renewed friction which developed between Germany and France over the continued presence of French troops in Morocco was greatly increased in 1908 when the German consul at Casablanca sought to aid deserters from the French foreign legion to escape. A minor crisis was precipitated, but it was soon adjusted by referring the questions at issue to arbitration by the Hague Tribunal.[8] Early in 1909 Germany and France negotiated a convention in which the former stated that her interests in Morocco were merely "economic" and in which she promised to recognize France's political ascendancy in the sultanate, provided economic equality for all nations was assured.

Although the Moroccan convention of 1909 seemed to presage calm relations between France and Germany, friction between the two foreign offices continued. French and German concessionaires quarreled about their respective rights, and each group looked to its own government for support. Moreover, conditions within Morocco also caused trouble. The lives and property of Europeans were endangered by repeated uprisings within the sultanate, and France was particularly disturbed because the unrest there appeared to spread contagiously across the frontier into French Algeria. In 1911 France decided that protective steps must be taken and notified the powers that her troops would occupy certain towns "to restore order." In May of that year the Moroccan capital, Fez, was occupied by French troops.

The Germans regarded this step as a violation of the agreements made at Algeciras; in fact, they considered it merely a move toward the establishment of a French protectorate. Apparently the German government had little real expectation of being able to prevent France from taking this step; its chief concern was to secure for Germany something in the nature of compensations. The French, on their part, were willing to consider the matter of compensations, and in June discussions were begun. The Germans at once made rather extravagant claims as to the value of the concessions they would have to surrender in Morocco if France established her protectorate. Kiderlen, the German foreign secretary, was especially aggressive and suggested to the chancellor that the dispatch of a German warship to "protect" German interests in Morocco might

[8] For the creation of the Hague Court, see page 360.

facilitate the Franco-German negotiations. The Kaiser and Chan-cellor Bethmann-Hollweg reluctantly gave their consent to his plan, and on July 1 the German gunboat *Panther* entered the harbor of Agadir, a Moroccan Atlantic port.

Three days before the *Panther's* arrival at Agadir a new ministry had come into power in France. The new premier was Joseph Caillaux, one of the younger Radicals, a capable financier and a good administrator. He was of the opinion that France should seek a *rapprochement* with Germany as a step toward preserving the peace of Europe as well as toward lessening the heavy burden of militarism. Although Caillaux was eager to reach a pacific settlement with Germany, he was determined that the latter should receive no part of Morocco. He was willing to make concessions to her elsewhere in return for her recognition of France's protectorate, but, because of divisions within the French ministry on this subject, France delayed in making any definite offers. Eventually, on July 15, Germany demanded the French Congo. War seemed near when France refused to make any such sweeping cession of territory.

If Russia had given France any encouragement, war might actually have resulted, but Russia stated that she would not fight for Morocco and suggested that France grant suitable compensation to Germany. Officially, the British government took no steps to increase France's intransigence, though there was some concern in Britain over Germany's demand for compensation. The British, not knowing exactly what Germany wanted, jumped to the conclusion that Germany was seeking territory in Morocco, and at once feared for the safety of Britain's lines of communication with South Africa and India. On July 21, when it appeared that the Franco-German negotiations might collapse, the British foreign secretary, Sir Edward Grey, proposed that Great Britain might join Germany and France in discussing the matter of compensation. With the stage thus set, Lloyd George, a member of the British ministry, declared in a public address that Great Britain would not allow herself to be excluded from negotiations on subjects which touched her vital interests, that peace at such a price would be too great a humiliation. The natural effect of this speech was to convince both the French and the Germans that Great Britain would support France.

Although the Germans, in the face of this apparent British threat, felt that they could not retreat, the German foreign secretary did abandon his idea of driving a hard bargain with the French and therefore moderated his demands. He would, he admitted, be content with much less than the whole French Congo. Negotiations still dragged, but eventually a settlement was reached, and a treaty was signed in Berlin in November, 1911. France received recognition of her right to establish a protectorate over Morocco, provided she agreed to maintain the "open door" policy in that country. In return she ceded to Germany a portion of her Congo territory so that German Kamerun might have access to the Congo River.[9] In March, 1912, France announced her establishment of a protectorate over Morocco and began the unenviable task of pacifying the country.[10]

### AGITATION OVER "PREPAREDNESS"

In France, as a result of the crisis of 1911, the nationalists felt that Germany had interfered in matters that did not concern her and that France must be made better prepared for war so that she could take a stronger stand in defense of her rights in future crises. Caillaux's policy toward Germany, nationalists declared, had been "too conciliatory." In the Senate opposition to the Franco-German treaty which his government had signed was so strong that the Caillaux ministry was forced to resign. In January, 1912, Raymond Poincaré became premier in a ministry which was distinctly conservative and nationalistic. Poincaré, a highly successful corporation lawyer, was perhaps the outstanding spokesman of those nationalists who believed that Germany's increasing threat to French security must be met by a policy of "preparedness"—military and diplomatic—for war. He had the support of the Right and Center parties and also of those Radicals who followed the Tiger, Clemenceau. A native of Lorraine—though not of the part ceded to Germany—he was known to be unreconciled to the treaty of Frankfort, and therefore was a popular figure with French prewar chauvinists. As premier

---

[9] Germany at the same time ceded to France territory in Africa near Lake Chad. See the map on page 21.

[10] In November, 1912, a Franco-Spanish treaty handed over to Spain about 12,000 square miles of Morocco just across from Gibraltar and a small strip in the southern part of the sultanate. The important port of Tangier with some surrounding territory was internationalized. For its status, see page 641.

and minister of foreign affairs he devoted himself to strengthening France's system of alliances and ententes.

In the critical year 1913, when the international situation was tense and the fear of war was increasing, Poincaré was elected President of France. In his inaugural address he announced his belief that it was "impossible for a people to be really peaceful, except on the condition of being always prepared for war." In 1912 conscription had been extended to Algeria and West Africa, and preparations had been made to incorporate into the French army the republic's colored colonial troops. Early in 1913 the French war minister apparently learned of Germany's plans to expand her army. To meet this "threat" a new military bill was introduced in the Chamber of Deputies on March 6. To compensate for the fact that France's small and stationary population prevented a natural increase of the army under the old law, the new act proposed to raise the term of active service from two to three years.[11] The bill was strenuously opposed in the Chamber by the Radicals and Socialists, and Jaurès made a number of eloquent attacks upon it. An alternative scheme for national defense through the use of a popular militia was offered by him, but it failed to secure the approval of the military leaders. Although huge mass meetings were held by French workingmen to denounce the measure, the bill finally became a law in 1913, and for a short period France had a larger peace-time army than Germany.

But the opponents of the new law did not cease their activity with its enactment. Peace demonstrations were organized, and threats of a general strike were made. In the bitterly contested parliamentary election of 1914 the new military law was the chief issue. The outcome of the election indicated that the act was exceedingly unpopular in France, for the new Chamber was perhaps the most radical that the republic had yet had. Although Poincaré's policy appeared to be repudiated, the president resolutely refused to appoint anyone as premier unless he would first agree to retain the three-years law. After a long ministerial crisis such a government was organized. Before the rival groups in the Chamber could come to grips over the issue of militarism and presidential power, however, the crisis of

---

[11] In the preceding years, largely because of the demands of the Radicals and Socialists, the period of active service had been reduced from five years to two.

1914 broke, and the French of all types rallied to the support of the republic. When, during the crisis, Jaurès dared to raise his voice against the approaching war, he was deliberately shot down and killed by a fanatical nationalist.

## CHAPTER V

## THE KINGDOM OF ITALY

PRIOR to 1861 the Italian peninsula was politically divided and largely dominated by the Austrian Habsburgs and the Roman Catholic popes. There was no Italy in the political sense of the word; Italy was merely a "geographical expression." The transformation of this "geographical expression" into a political entity was largely the work of three famous Italians—Joseph Mazzini, Count Camillo di Cavour, and Joseph Garibaldi. The first by his inspired voice and his "Young Italy" society aroused Italian youth and awakened a nationalistic enthusiasm to liberate and unify Italy. The second by his consummate statesmanship and clever diplomacy gained French aid for Sardinia's attempt to drive the Habsburgs out of Italy in the Austro-Sardinian War (1859). The third by his dashing boldness and with his "Thousand Red Shirts" speedily conquered (1860) the Two Sicilies in the cause of a united Italy. On March 17, 1861, the Kingdom of Italy was proclaimed with Victor Emmanuel II of the house of Savoy as king. The new state did not include, however, Venetia and the Patrimony of St. Peter—the latter being a small district surrounding and including Rome. Venetia was secured from the Habsburgs as a result of the Austro-Prussian War (1866), in which Italy was Prussia's ally; Rome was taken from the pope and made the capital of the Italian kingdom during the Franco-German War (1870), when the pope was deprived of the protection of French troops.

### The New State

In 1870, therefore, for the first time since the destruction of Theodoric's kingdom in the sixth century, the Italian peninsula constituted a united and independent state. Unfortunately for this new state, however, it was from the very outset of its history seriously handicapped by its economic limitations, for it was inferior in mineral wealth, natural resources, and capital to Great Britain, Germany, and France. The coal and iron which the latter had in abundance, Italy, if she were to become an industrial country, would have to import. Even her agriculture failed to produce sufficient foodstuffs for her rapidly increasing population, for Italy, when it came to rich arable land, was less favored than Russia, Austria-Hungary, and France. Large areas of the Italian peninsula consisted of bleak, barren mountain ridges or low unhealthy swamplands. In the south, where the land reforms of the French Revolution had little penetrated, the *latifundia* were farmed in a primitive fashion by poverty-stricken agricultural laborers. In the north the peasants, though industrious, were generally too poor or too backward to use scientific methods of farming. In 1870, therefore, Italy, with a population of about 26,000,000, already had a "surplus population" in the sense that it could not be adequately supported by the existing agriculture and industry of the kingdom.

The citizens of the new state—divided by the physical features of the peninsula, separated by the previous centuries of conflict between their petty rulers, isolated by the lack of modern means of transportation and communication—were not yet fused into one people. Marked contrasts existed between different sections of the new kingdom, so marked, in fact, that Italy was once described as a country in which two stages of civilization existed simultaneously. In the north there was some modern industry and a number of large and progressive cities inhabited by a prosperous bourgeoisie and an intelligent and aggressive proletariat. In the region south of the former Grand Duchy of Tuscany, however, conditions were quite otherwise. The popes and the former Bourbon rulers had done little to improve their lands. Facilities for travel were distinctly backward; in 1860, for example, Naples had less than sixty miles of railways. There were few large cities, and the rural regions were infested with brigands who made travel a hazardous undertaking. Secret criminal societies like the *Camorra* of Naples and the *Mafia* of Sicily flourished unchecked. Everywhere the standard of living of the Italians was relatively low, and the great bulk of the population in the south was illiterate.

The government of the new kingdom was based on the constitution which King Charles Albert had granted to Sardinia in 1848. In the representative monarchical government which Italy in a sense thus inherited the king occupied a position similar to that of the British monarch, that is, he reigned but did not rule. Supreme

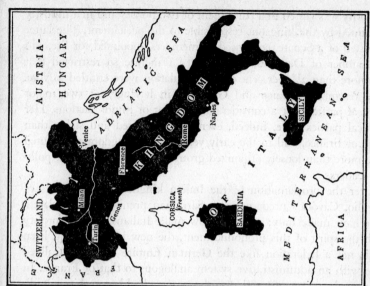

THE KINGDOM OF ITALY IN 1871

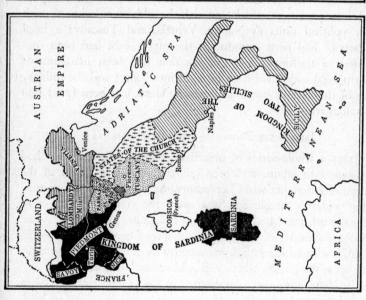

THE ITALIAN PENINSULA IN 1858

authority was vested in a parliament of two houses and in a ministry appointed by the king but responsible to the parliament. The latter consisted of a Senate, composed of members appointed for life, and a Chamber of Deputies, elected on a franchise so restricted that not more than 2½ per cent of the population were entitled to vote. Italy resembled France and Germany in having, not two major political parties, but a considerable number of minor factions. Her political parties were, indeed, even less organized and stable than those of France, and in the early years of the kingdom constituted little more than loosely organized groups attached to different political leaders.

After the proclamation of the Italian kingdom the Marquis of Azeglio, Cavour's predecessor as Sardinian premier, had declared, "We have made Italy; we must now make Italians." In conformity with the spirit of this pronouncement, the new kingdom had been made not a federation like the German Empire but a centralized state with an administrative system analogous to that of France. In the years between 1861 and 1870 the country had been arbitrarily divided into provinces which ignored the old boundaries of such earlier political units as Naples, Venetia, and Tuscany; a loyal civil service had been introduced; the public debt had been consolidated; a uniform system of taxation had been inaugurated; uniform legal codes had been brought into being; and the military forces of the various previously existing states had been fused into one Italian army.

## Immediate Problems and Achievements

By 1871 a whole series of objectives, which Italian patriots had long sought to attain, had been realized; and Italy stood at the opening of a new period in her history. As King Victor Emmanuel pointed out, the heroic age was over; the commonplace era of practical work must be begun. Poetry must now give way to prose.

To the political groups of the Right were first confided the difficult tasks with which Italian statesmen were called upon to wrestle. These were the groups which had achieved national unification and brought about administrative reforms in the years after 1859. They were chiefly representative of the upper and middle classes of Piedmont, Lombardy, and Tuscany, and in their policies were inclined to be patriotic, dignified, cautious, and somewhat antidemocratic.

Unfortunately, the one who would naturally have been their leader, Count Cavour, had died in 1861 soon after the proclamation of the Italian kingdom, so that this capable and liberal statesman was no longer available to help solve the many difficult problems which confronted the new state.

Probably the most pressing immediate problem after 1870 was that of adjusting the relations between the kingdom and the papacy. Although the seizure of the states of the church and the elevation of Rome to a position as the capital of the new state was entirely satisfactory to the great bulk of the Italian people, the pope vigorously and consistently maintained that he had been illegally deprived of his temporal possessions. In default of a general international agreement regarding the papacy's new status, an agreement in which other powers were apparently reluctant to become involved, the Italian government decided to deal with the question by domestic legislation. In 1871 parliament enacted the Law of Papal Guarantees to serve as the basis of relations between the papacy and the Italian kingdom.

By the provisions of this law the pope and his successors were guaranteed possession of St. Peter's, the Vatican and its gardens, the Lateran Palace, and the Villa of Castel Gandolfo. The head of the church was accorded sovereign rights within these possessions, including the inviolability of his own person and the authority to receive and send ambassadors. He was further granted free use of the Italian telegraph, railway, and postal systems, and guaranteed an annual subsidy from the state of approximately $645,000. Pope Pius IX refused to recognize the Law of Papal Guarantees, however, because it was a simple legislative act of the Italian government, a unilateral arrangement rather than a concordat. He and his successors refused to accept the annual subsidy, declared that they had been deprived of sovereign territory and were unable to exercise their legitimate prerogatives as sovereigns, and proclaimed themselves "prisoners of a usurping power" which they refused to recognize. From 1870 to 1929 no pope ever left the Vatican.

When successive appeals to the Roman Catholic powers failed to bring intervention, the papacy eventually adopted a policy of obstruction. In 1874 Pope Pius by a decree, *Non Expedit,* urged that Catholics should not participate in parliamentary elections nor hold office under the Italian government; and twelve years later another papal decree, *Non Licet,* expressly forbade the political activities which had earlier been declared inexpedient. These decrees were strongly resented by many Catholics who were Italian patriots, and they were never generally observed. Nevertheless, the Roman question remained, and the kingdom in its early years was deprived of the public services of many capable men who did observe the pope's injunction.[1]

Strange to say, the government continued to maintain Roman Catholicism as the state church of Italy. It paid the salaries of the clergy and passed upon the appointment of Catholic bishops. It also permitted religious instruction to be given in the public schools and even went so far as to support the church's view regarding divorce. Doubtless these policies were viewed by the government as minor concessions to satisfy the great majority of the Italian people, who were at heart sincerely loyal to Catholicism. On the other hand, the state did not hesitate to make a number of reforms which "seemed to be demanded in the interests of civil society." These included the confiscation of church property, the suppression of theological faculties in Italian universities and of spiritual directors in the public schools, the establishment of state inspection of Catholic schools, and the introduction of compulsory civil marriage.

A second problem for Italy's statesmen was economic, and, although seriously handicapped by the great expense involved, the government set resolutely to work to improve the economic conditions of the country. Highway construction was pushed as old roads were repaired and new ones built. More railways were opened until the kingdom's railway mileage increased from slightly more than 1000 in 1861 to nearly 4500 in 1876. Harbors were developed, and government subsidies were given to the country's mercantile marine. The 10,000 tons of steamships which Italy possessed in 1862 rose by 1877 to approximately a million tons. Though some progress was thus made in the years immediately after 1870, the gigantic task of bringing the various districts of the country up to an approximate level in economic well-being and Italy as a whole up to the standards of a modern state was one to engage the brains of the kingdom's most capable statesmen for decades to come.

[1] For the final settlement of the Roman question by Mussolini, see page 635.

Meanwhile, the government was moved by the desire to have Italy ranked among the great powers of Europe. Such "greatness," of course, demanded impressive military and naval forces. As the result of reforms which were made, Italy by 1873 had a peace-time army of 350,000 men, capable of being more than doubled in size in time of war. Warships were constructed, arsenals were established at Spezia and Taranto, and in 1881 an academy was opened at Leghorn for the training of naval officers.

Not unconnected with the foregoing problems, naturally, was the paramount problem of national finance. The new kingdom had assumed the debts of the various states which it had absorbed, and this indebtedness had been increased by heavy necessary expenditures coupled with the government's inadequate revenues in the decade after 1861. The national debt in 1871 amounted to the relatively huge sum of more than $1,600,000,000. An important task for the government of the Right, therefore, was that of securing a balanced budget so as to escape from the ever-embarrassing national deficits. "The great question which eclipses all others, however important," wrote one Italian statesman in 1873, "is the question of finance. All the chief problems—credit, the currency, the army, national defense, political institutions, economic development—are bound up with it." In the five years after 1870 the ordinary revenues of the Italian kingdom were increased until the Italians became the most heavily taxed people in all Europe, but in the end the fiscal battle was won—at least temporarily—and the government on March 16, 1876, was able to announce that a balanced budget had at last been achieved. Two days later the government of the Right was driven from power.

## THE LEFT IN POWER UNDER DEPRETIS AND CRISPI

The parliamentary elections of 1876 had gone in favor of the Left, for a number of factors had conspired to make the Right groups unpopular. In the first place, they had refused to extend the franchise beyond its exceedingly narrow limits and so were accused of trying to keep the mass of Italians "in bondage." The Left groups, on the other hand, stood for "democracy and progress." In the second place, a demand for educational reform had arisen which the Right group, handicapped financially, had ignored. Then, in its efforts to balance the budget, the Right had necessarily imposed heavy taxes and thus of course had aroused much hatred and opposition. Finally, the Right was denounced for its reputed favoritism toward the people of northern Italy at the expense of the rest of the country.

The Left groups now took over the reins of government with a ministry headed by Agostino Depretis, a native of Lombardy who had in his youth been a member of "Young Italy." With short interludes he was in power from 1876 to 1887, when he was succeeded by a Left colleague, Francesco Crispi, a Sicilian who headed the government during most of the time until 1896. These men derived their political support chiefly from the middle classes of Sicily and Naples, but their two decades in power were partly the result of their corrupt political "system." Depretis and Crispi developed methods of controlling parliamentary elections that were, from their own point of view, most efficient. Bribery of electors was openly practiced; registration lists were frequently altered to eliminate the names of political opponents; and gangs of ruffians— sometimes even the *Mafia* and the *Camorra*—were utilized to terrorize the opposition. Such methods usually resulted in the election of a majority of supporters. The Left leaders were also masters of parliamentary intrigue and frequently bought off an opposition leader by appointing him to a post in the cabinet. Since from that moment the new minister's main objective was to keep the government in power as long as possible so that he himself might reap material rewards, his opposition to the premier usually subsided.

The Italian people hailed the elevation of the Left to power as the coming of a new era in which a reforming government would right all the wrongs and heal all the ills from which the masses suffered. Such a program was beyond the ability of any statesman or group of statesmen to fulfill. Nevertheless, under Depretis and Crispi a number of reforms were made. In 1877 an act was passed making education compulsory between the ages of six and nine, but because of financial difficulties no adequate provision was made to carry it out. Five years later a new franchise law was enacted which lowered the age, tax, and educational requirements for voters. By this reform the Italian electorate was increased from approximately 600,000 to more than 2,000,000. The possibility of a gradual but continuous expansion of the electorate was offered by the provision that the franchise would be extended, regardless of property qualification, to all males over twenty-one years of age who had received a primary school education. Under Crispi a new communal and provincial law was also enacted, extending slightly the control of the voters over local affairs. The mayors of the larger communes, for example, were thereafter to be elected locally.

But Italy's chief problem remained economic, and all governments, whether Left or Right, were compelled to wrestle with it in the succeeding years. If adequate food supplies for Italy's growing population were to be provided by the nation, agriculture must be vastly improved. An exhaustive agrarian inquiry, authorized in 1877, brought home to the government the natural poverty of the country and led to the adoption of a far-reaching program for improvement. Though still handicapped by the lack of necessary funds, the government took a number of steps. Instruction in agrarian subjects was introduced in some of the higher schools; special agricultural schools were opened; and experimental farms and agricultural exhibitions were established. Hundreds of thousands of acres of swampland were drained and opened to agriculture. New health laws were enacted; the number of local physicians was increased; measures were taken to combat pellagra and malaria; and epidemics were considerably checked. Co-operative purchasing societies were organized among the peasants, and the importation of agricultural implements and fertilizers was increased to a marked degree. With improved methods, better seeds, and modern implements, a considerable rise in the country's agricultural production resulted, especially in northern Italy. Nevertheless, Italy still remained unable to feed her people adequately.

In industry, too, much progress was made, especially after a system of protective tariffs was erected in 1887. By the close of the century northern Italy had become considerably industrialized, the chief gains being made in the metallurgical, textile, electrical, and chemical industries. Progress in the first of these in time reached the place where the country's industries were able to take care of the nation's steel requirements so far as railway construction and naval and military supplies were concerned. In the cotton textile industry the number of operatives rose nearly 300 per cent during the two decades after 1882. The chief textile industry, however, was silk; eventually Milan surpassed Lyons as the silk-producing center of the world. But modern industry was long dependent upon steam for power, and, for the production of steam, coal—which Italy lacked —was necessary. To lessen the country's dependence upon foreign coal, Italy early embarked upon the development of hydroelectric plants. The use of electricity for industrial purposes rapidly increased, though the greatest development in this field came after the opening of the twentieth century. By 1905, however, Italy had the largest and best hydroelectric plants in Europe. Nevertheless, with a rapidly growing industry the country was still obliged to import great amounts of coal.

Although Italy's industries thus expanded, the lot of the Italian industrial workers remained hard. Because of the dependence upon foreign coal, Italian industries had to pay more for this essential commodity than those of Germany, Great Britain, and the United States. This was true also in regard to other raw materials. Italian industries could compete with those of other countries, therefore, only if Italian labor and capital received smaller returns. In general, Italian industrialists sought to hold down the costs of production by low wages. On the other hand, the protective tariff tended to increase the cost of various products within the country. As a result of these factors, Italian industrial workers were worse off than those in most of the other countries of western Europe.

In an attempt to secure sufficient foreign exchange to pay for her needed imports of raw materials and foodstuffs, Italy made special efforts to increase her exports and to improve her merchant marine. The country's foreign trade was greatly injured by a ten-year tariff war which Italy began with France in 1887, but on the other hand it was aided by the growing importance of the Mediterranean as an avenue of commerce after the opening of the Suez Canal and by a favorable commercial treaty with Germany in 1892. The latter became Italy's best customer, and the commercial and financial ties between the two countries tended to make Italy an economic satellite of the German Empire toward the close of the nineteenth century. In 1898 the Franco-Italian tariff war was brought to a close with the signing of a new commercial treaty between the two countries, and Italy's commerce benefited accordingly. During the decade after 1900 the country's foreign trade practically doubled in value.

Nevertheless, because of Italy's great need to import food and raw materials, she constantly had an unfavorable balance of trade. If, like France and Great Britain, she had had millions of dollars invested in foreign countries, this would not have constituted a particularly difficult problem, for invisible returns from these foreign investments would have enabled the country to meet its need for foreign exchange. But Italy was poor and had little income from the foreign investments of her citizens. She was, on the contrary, herself a debtor nation. Fortunately for her, however, she did possess two sources of invisible income. Hundreds of thousands of Italian emigrants by their remittances to relatives "back home" sent a steady stream of foreign exchange into the country. At the same time the thousands of tourists, who came yearly to visit the historical sites of Italy or to inspect her magnificent art galleries and museums, spent in the country a considerable sum which also thus became available for foreign payments. Further to reduce the demand for foreign exchange, the government by subsidies encouraged the building of an Italian merchant marine to carry the country's overseas commerce. By 1914 Italy's mercantile shipping was surpassed in tonnage by that of only five other nations in the world.

The Left leaders in the beginning accepted the principle of a balanced budget, and for a number of years after they came into power the national government had slight surpluses. Eventually, however, the increasing expenditures for constructing public works, for maintaining the army and navy, and for inaugurating a program of colonial expansion overtook the state's increasing revenues, and deficits again became the rule. Although expenditures for schools and for social betterment were curtailed, although taxes were increased until they became an excessive burden for the mass of the Italian people, the years between 1887 and 1898 saw accumulating deficits, which amounted by the latter year to a total of approximately $610,000,000. The Italian state appeared to be always on the verge of bankruptcy.

The economic gains enumerated above were largely offset, so far as a rise in the general standard of living was concerned, by the very high birthrate which prevailed and by the increasing pressure of population upon resources which resulted. The hard economic conditions of millions of Italians and the rather hopeless outlook which confronted so many of them, especially in southern Italy where the masses were landless and poverty-stricken, drove hundreds of thousands out of the country as emigrants. Many of them were in a sense transient laborers, who left Italy for a number of months each year to seek work in the neighboring countries of Europe or in South America. Great numbers of them, however, sought to establish homes in countries like the United States, Brazil, and Argentina, where they hoped to find more favorable conditions and greater opportunities for themselves and for their children. In the generation after 1876, according to official figures, more than eight million emigrants left Italy, though the net loss was of course not so great as this. In fact, in 1910 the figure for those who were permanently lost to Italy was officially put at about 5,500,000.

Emigration, while it helped to relieve the pressure of population in Italy, aided the country in other ways. In the regions where emigrants settled abroad they provided an expanding market for Italian commodities. Then, as stated above, Italy's international financial position was strengthened by the money sent back by many emigrants to their relatives. Naturally, also, the lot of these fortunate Italian relatives was often improved as a result of the remittances. Furthermore, many Italians, having amassed a small competence abroad, returned to Italy and introduced higher living standards in the communities where they settled.

Economic hardships in Italy had, also, an effect upon the political situation in the country and aided greatly in the rise of the Socialist Party and other radical organizations. Although both Marx and Bakunin had sought to introduce their ideas into Italy even before the country had completed its unification, it was not until the nineties that socialism made great progress. In 1882, the year in which the suffrage was widened, the Independent Workers Party was organized in Milan, but it was suppressed by Depretis four years later. About 1890, however, Antonio Labriola, in his lectures on the philosophy of history in the University of Rome, began to expound with great enthusiasm the Marxian concept of historical materialism. *Das Kapital,* translated into Italian, was also made more easily accessible to Italian readers. But more influential than Labriola in the rise of Italian socialism was Filippo Turati, who in 1891 became editor of a review in Milan which he made the medium for popularizing the *Communist Manifesto* along with other writings of Marx and Engels.

In 1891 the Italian Socialist Party was organized in Milan, and in the next year it succeeded in electing ten deputies to the Chamber. Crispi, like Bismarck, sought to destroy socialism by rigorous repressive measures. In 1894 he ordered the dissolution of all socialist organizations. Many socialists were imprisoned, and others had their names struck off the election lists. Newspapers were prosecuted, and after the end of the session of parliament in that year Socialist deputies were arrested and imprisoned. But Crispi was no more successful than Bismarck in his similar campaign. At by-elections some of the imprisoned Socialists were elected as deputies, and in the general election of 1895 the Socialist representation in the Chamber rose to twelve.

In that same year the party published its "minimum program," which, though denounced at the time, appears mild indeed today. In fact, much of what it sought had already been obtained in some of the more progressive countries of the West. For the workers it demanded the inclusion of a minister of labor in the cabinet and legislation to protect woman and child labor, to compel a day of rest each week, to provide accident and sickness insurance, to prohibit night work. For Italians generally it sought to obtain effective compulsory education, universal suffrage, payment of members of the Chamber of Deputies, and liberty of conscience, speech, press, and assembly. In the economic realm it advocated national ownership of mines and railways and the inauguration of arbitration of disputes between capital and labor. In 1896 was established the first daily newspaper of the party, *Avanti!*, edited by Leonida Bissolati, and named after the chief Socialist paper in Germany, *Vorwärts*.

## Early Attempts to Play the Role of a Great Power

Meanwhile, in international affairs Italy had been attempting to play the role of a great power. Her first venture was directed toward extending her territory to the north and the northeast. Although exalted by the achievement of national unification, Italian patriots were not slow to realize that there was still an *Italia Irredenta,* that is, territory just outside Italy's national boundaries inhabited by Italians. The Trentino in the Alps and the region around Trieste at the head of the Adriatic were the principal places now coveted by nationalistic Italians. Attempting to take advantage of the Balkan situation in 1877–1878, Depretis' government sought to acquire *Italia Irredenta* in compensation for Austria's occupation of Bosnia and Herzegovina.[2] In fact, during the summer of 1877 Francesco Crispi made a tour of the major European capitals in an effort to make such an arrangement, but without success. At the ensuing Congress of Berlin the Italian representative raised objections to Austria's occupation of Bosnia-Herzegovina and put forward a claim to the Trentino as a fair compensation for such occupation. But Italy received no support for her contention. Instead, Crispi lamented, the Italians "were humiliated at Berlin as the last people in Europe." They returned to Rome, he declared, "slapped and despised." *Italia Irredenta* and its redemption by Italy remained for more than a generation an unsolved problem.

In another sphere—that of colonial expansion—Italy was also balked in the early days of the kingdom. She was especially eager to annex Tunis, a territory in northern Africa just across from Sicily, which already contained a considerable number of Italians. In the seventies, as a result of the fiscal difficulties of the ruler of Tunis, a commission consisting principally of Frenchmen and Italians took control of the ruler's financial affairs. It seemed likely that political intervention might follow foreign financial control, and Italy sought to prepare for that intervention. But before Italy got around to intervene, France with the support of Germany and Great Britain in 1881 transformed Tunis into a French protectorate. France's action at once aroused a strong feeling of hostility in Italy and for almost two decades embittered relations between the two states.

A popular demand was now raised in Italy in favor of some alliance so that the kingdom would not be limited to the role of an unimportant neutral state. Some Italian statesmen believed that the prestige of Italy would be more likely to be enhanced if Italy would devote herself to the improvement of her economic, financial, and military strength and not seek alliances for the present. Such leaders believed that it would not be long until one of the great powers would voluntarily seek an alliance with a strengthened Italy. But Italian patriots could not wait. Consequently, Italy herself made the overtures to Germany which in the end resulted in the formation of a defensive alliance, including on Bismarck's insistence the Dual

[2] See page 293.

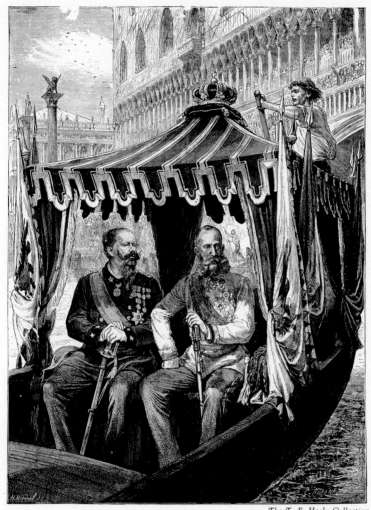

VICTOR EMMANUEL II AND FRANCIS JOSEPH

The king of Italy (left) playing host to the emperor of Austria at
Venice in 1875.

Monarchy also. The Triple Alliance [3] definitely linked Italy with two of the great powers of Europe, but otherwise Italy's gains from it were relatively unimportant. One consequence for Italy was that, now that she was allied with Austria-Hungary, it was necessary for some years to soften the demand for the acquisition of *Italia Irredenta,* and irredentist societies were therefore frequently suppressed.

In 1886 Italy sought to use the negotiations leading to a renewal of the Triple Alliance to pave the way for future Italian expansion in the Balkans and in northern Africa. In the former Italy was jealous of Austria's position and sought to check further Habsburg expansion there. Consequently, as a condition of her own renewal of the Triple Alliance she insisted upon Austria's signing a separate convention (February, 1887) in which the two powers stated their desire to maintain the *status quo* in the Balkans and promised to forestall any territorial modifications which would be injurious to either. They further agreed, however, that, if either power should be obliged to change the *status quo* "by a temporary or a permanent occupation, such occupation would take place only after previous agreement between the two powers, which would have to be based upon the principle of a reciprocal compensation for all territorial or other advantages that either of them might acquire over and above the existing *status quo,* and would have to satisfy the interests and rightful claims of both parties." This agreement became Article 7 of the treaty by which the Triple Alliance was again renewed in 1891.

In 1887, also, Italian statesmen succeeded in linking Germany with Italy's ambitions in northern Africa. In order to block France in any possible further expansion in that region and at the same time to prepare the way for her own aggression there, Italy sought to make the renewal of the Triple Alliance contingent upon German aid to Italy. Although Bismarck at first refused to consider the Italian proposal, the somewhat strained international situation in 1886–1887 eventually influenced him to accede to Italy's demand. In consequence, when the Triple Alliance was renewed in 1887, a supplementary convention was also signed by Germany and Italy. In this convention it was agreed that, if France should move to extend

[3] For the terms of the alliance, see page 69.

her hold in northern Africa and in consequence Italy should feel that she must herself take action in northern Africa "or even have recourse to extreme measures in French territory in Europe," the ensuing state of war between Italy and France would call for the aid of Germany against France. This agreement became Article 10 of the Triple Alliance when it was next renewed in 1891, and obviously by it that alliance lost its original defensive character.

In January, 1887, Italy, desiring further to block possible French expansion in northern Africa, sought a treaty with Great Britain in which the two states would agree that the *status quo* in the Mediterranean, the Adriatic, the Aegean, and the Black Sea should so far as possible be maintained, but that, if this was impossible, no modification should be permitted without a previous agreement between the two powers. Italy further desired an agreement that, in return for her support of Great Britain in Egypt, Great Britain would support Italy in Tripoli and Cyrenaica in case of encroachments on the part of a third power, and that in general the two governments would give each other support in the Mediterranean against any third power.

The British preferred a secret understanding rather than a formal treaty, however, and in February the two governments by an exchange of notes agreed on the maintenance of the *status quo* in the four seas as Italy had suggested. The British government, however, contented itself with the statement that, if it should become impossible to maintain the *status quo*, both powers desired that there should be no extension of the domination of any other great power over any portion of these coasts. The character of the two powers' co-operation, Great Britain asserted, must be decided by them, when the occasion for it arose, according to the circumstances of each case. Quite clearly, though Italy gained something by the exchange of notes, she failed at that time to secure Great Britain's definite support for her future expansion in northern Africa. The Italo-British Mediterranean agreement was further extended in 1887 by Austria-Hungary's adherence to it and by a secret exchange of notes between Italy and Spain. The last two powers agreed to attempt to maintain the *status quo* in the Mediterranean, and each promised not to co-operate with France against the other in regard to northern Africa.

Meanwhile, Italy with Great Britain's blessing had made a beginning of her colonial expansion elsewhere in Africa. Her activity had gradually centered along the Red Sea, whose importance had been increased by the opening of the Suez Canal in 1869. In 1881 Assab, which for some time had been held by an Italian navigation company, was taken over by Italy, and four years later Massaua was similarly occupied. But the kingdom's first colonial expeditions were frequently marked by incompetence and serious blunders. One instance—that of providing heavy military coats for soldiers destined to tramp the burning shores of the Red Sea—became notorious.

Italian imperialists, ardently desirous of carving out an empire in northeastern Africa, coveted Ethiopia, and Italy's subsequent attempt to extend her occupation of Massaua into the interior eventually precipitated a war with this strong empire. In 1887 Italy suffered her first colonial disaster when an Italian force was surprised and annihilated at Dogali. This tragedy was shortly succeeded by the death of Agostino Depretis and by the elevation to the premiership of his colleague Francesco Crispi.

Although Crispi had opposed the expedition to Massaua, once the occupation had occurred he was reluctant to withdraw Italian forces. In fact, in 1889 the occupation was extended, and in the next year the colony was organized and christened Eritrea. In 1889, too, the imperialistic impulse in Italy drove the government on to further steps. A new colony was founded in Somaliland on the east coast of Africa, southeast of Ethiopia. In the same year Italy aided Menelik, a local Ethiopian chieftain, to usurp the imperial throne of Ethiopia, and in return persuaded him to sign a treaty of friendship (treaty of Ucciali) which Italy at once interpreted as transforming Ethiopia into an Italian protectorate. In 1891 Great Britain signed a treaty with Italy recognizing Ethiopia as within Italy's sphere of influence.

Two years later Menelik, becoming suspicious of Italy's intentions, denounced the treaty of Ucciali. France encouraged him to take this step, and in return a French company was given the right to build a railway from Jibuti through Ethiopia to the Nile. Italy, in turn, encouraged by Great Britain, decided to force her protectorate upon Ethiopia, and in 1895 Italian armies began an advance into that country from Eritrea. Menelik long delayed giving battle, but eventually near Adowa (March 1, 1896) he disastrously defeated the Italian forces. Two Italian generals and 4600 Italian officers and men were killed, and 1500 others were taken prisoners. Overwhelmed by a wave of national grief and indignation, Crispi at once resigned. In the succeeding months Italy made peace with Ethiopia, paid Menelik an indemnity of some $2,000,000, recognized his absolute independence, and withdrew from the province which the Italian forces had occupied. Again it appeared that Italy lacked the aptitude, experience, and resources to become a great colonial power. Thereafter Adowa was to patriotic Italians a synonym for humiliating disaster.

Although the two decades prior to 1896 are usually looked upon as an unfortunate period in Italian foreign policy, nevertheless, in the view of the distinguished Italian historian, Benedetto Croce, Italy during those years "by means of Irredentism, her African ambitions, her understandings with England, the pledges given and received with regard to the Triple Alliance, and the contingent clauses contained in the treaty, laid down all the premises of her future international policy which issued at last in her participation in the World War."

### The Era of Giolitti

The downfall of Crispi in 1896 was followed by a short period of rule by the Right groups under a number of premiers. These ministries had the task of liquidating the war with Ethiopia which Crispi had begun. They also were obliged to deal with serious outbreaks of disorder within the country arising from widespread social discontent and the increasing radicalism of anarchists and syndicalists. In 1898 trouble arose among the workers of Milan, and in the ensuing conflict between the proletariat and government troops nearly one hundred persons were killed. Harsh punishments were the lot of the leaders of the insurrection, but popular unrest still continued, culminating in the assassination of King Humbert I by an anarchist on July 29, 1900. Humbert had succeeded his father, Victor Emmanuel II, upon the latter's death in 1878; he was now succeeded by his thirty-year-old son, who mounted the throne as Victor Emmanuel III. The new king early endeared himself to the Italian people by his intelligence, simplicity, and liberal tendencies, and has remained a popular figure.

In the decade before the World War the outstanding statesman-politician in Italy was Giovanni Giolitti. Back in the eighties of the nineteenth century he had been a member of the Chamber of Deputies. In 1889, because of his extensive knowledge of the country's financial problems—and perhaps also because of his attacks upon Crispi—he had been made secretary of the treasury in the latter's government. In 1892 he had even risen to be prime minister, but his government had become involved in bank scandals and had soon fallen. At the opening of the new century his influence again began to increase; in 1901 he was made minister of the interior, and in 1903 he once more became the head of the government. From then until early in 1914 Giolitti was the dominant personality in Italian political life, though not continuously the premier.

Giolitti, whether from his democratic nature or from his desire to win the political support of the masses, was sympathetic with the sufferings and needs of the poorer classes. In his efforts to aid the urban proletariat he adopted many of the planks of the Socialists for his own. To improve the lot of the workers, he recommended social legislation; to lessen the heavy burden which rested on their shoulders, he advocated tax reform. In the conflicts between capital and labor he urged the neutrality of the state and thus indirectly encouraged the workers to resort to strikes. The result was an epidemic of strikes not only among the urban proletariat but among agricultural laborers as well. In 1904 a general strike in northern Italy for a time paralyzed the economic life of that part of the country.

The trade-union movement rapidly spread during the era of Giolitti and resulted in the formation of the General Confederation of Labor with its headquarters at Turin. Railwaymen and government employees organized unions, and even university professors and public-school teachers formed associations. Radicals came to the fore with their plans for political and social revolution, and the Socialists increased their representation in the Chamber until by 1913 it totaled seventy-two. In addition, the Republicans—the political heirs of Mazzini—who advocated universal suffrage, repeal of the Law of Papal Guarantees, military preparedness, and political decentralization, in the decade before the war controlled twenty-three members in the Chamber and usually co-operated with the Socialists to form an extreme Left.

Gradually the conservative groups became alarmed. In an effort to win over the Socialists Giolitti in 1904 offered Turati a cabinet post, but the latter declined because of the Socialist Party's principle of opposition to co-operation with the bourgeoisie. A similar invitation was extended to Bissolati in 1911, but he, too, was forced to decline. The growth of radicalism eventually had its effect upon the pope, who threw his support to Giolitti's groups against the Socialists in the elections of 1904 and in the following year by an encyclical practically withdrew the earlier *Non Licet*. Catholics were now permitted to participate in politics in critical cases which affected "the highest interests of society, which must at all costs be protected." The party situation was further complicated when a Catholic political party—the Popular Party—was at once organized and soon began to play a role in the Chamber of Deputies, where in 1913 it held thirty-five seats.

Nevertheless, in the two decades before the World War many reforms were inaugurated, and considerable progress was made in improving the economic position of the masses. A great amount of social legislation was enacted. In 1898 the insurance of workers against accident was made compulsory for employers, and a voluntary system of pensions for old age and invalidity was inaugurated with government subsidies. Ten years later another of the Socialists' planks became an actuality when a weekly day of rest was ordered for industrial workmen. In 1910 a system of maternity insurance for women workers was introduced to aid in the expenses attendant upon childbirth. Further steps with a decidedly socialistic tinge were taken. In 1905 the railways of the country were nationalized, and seven years later private insurance companies experienced the same fate. The country's municipalities, moreover, were empowered to own and operate their public utilities, and the government definitely encouraged the organization of co-operative banking and commercial associations. In an effort to improve education, national legislation in 1904 required every commune to establish public schools to be maintained by local taxes, and eventually (1911) elementary education was taken over by the central government with a view to its improvement. The results were distinctly encouraging. Whereas at the opening of the twentieth century illiteracy was nearly 50 per cent, by 1914 it had been reduced to approximately 25 per cent.

In 1912 further steps toward political democracy were taken when laws were enacted providing for the payment of members of the Chamber and for the extension of the franchise. At the opening of that year, out of a population of more than thirty-four million, only 3,247,772, or less than one in ten, were entitled to vote in parliamentary elections. A new electoral law received its approval on June 30 of that year, however, and granted the suffrage to practically all adult male citizens,[4] raising the number of eligible voters to 8,635,148, of whom, it was estimated, the majority could neither read nor write. But in the ensuing elections of 1913 great numbers of the newly enfranchised citizens failed to vote, either because they feared that the electoral system was beyond their comprehension or because they felt it was not worth the trouble to cast their ballots. Many argued that the result indicated that Italy was not yet ready for manhood suffrage.

## THE RISING TIDE OF NATIONALISM AND IMPERIALISM

Meanwhile, various factors were combining to wipe out the feeling of sectionalism in the different parts of the kingdom. The thousands of miles of new railways, which increased the ease and frequency of travel within the peninsula for business men and others; the rise of modern newspapers, with their ever-widening circles of readers; the spread of business enterprises across old state boundaries, giving workers and others engaged in the same efforts an increasing feeling of solidarity; the one national capital and the one national parliament, from which emanated uniform laws for the whole country; the new administrative system, with its civil servants drawn from all parts of the peninsula; the military service, which ignored the former provincial lines and threw peasants and city-dwellers together in the same units; all of these in the course of years gradually built up in the kingdom a spirit of Italian nationalism at the expense of the older provincial loyalties.

It is not surprising, perhaps, that with a growing national consciousness there should come a recrudescence of irredentism, despite Italy's membership in the Triple Alliance. Although the statesmen of the Left had attempted to keep the question of *Italia Irredenta* in the background because of its possible effect on Italy's international relations, the opening years of the twentieth century saw the

---

[4] Besides those who had the right to vote because of their elementary school education, the new measure extended the franchise to those who had completed their military service and to those who were at least thirty years of age.

irredentist movement again gaining ground. Anti-Austrian demonstrations occurred in Italy from time to time,[5] and in 1905 friction between the Austrian and Italian governments became pronounced when the latter declined to give Austria the satisfaction demanded after the president of the Italian Chamber of Deputies had alluded to "our Trentino."

Furthermore, Italian nationalism, carefully nurtured by patriotic writers like Gabriele d'Annunzio, began to contemplate the possibility of transforming the Adriatic into an Italian lake and the Balkans into an Italian economic sphere of influence. But obviously neither these achievements nor the redemption of the Trentino and Trieste could be accomplished without bringing Italy into conflict with Austria-Hungary. To many nationalists such an eventuality was not looked upon as altogether impossible or even undesirable, for, in the words of one Italian historian, "Italy still bore in her bosom the open sores of Custozza and Lissa, always dreaming of wiping out the disgrace which she had suffered."

Therefore, although Italy's unnatural alliance with Austria-Hungary continued to exist—partly, perhaps, through inertia—in the closing years of the nineteenth century her ill will toward France subsided, and she began to gravitate toward the Triple Entente. France very definitely encouraged a *rapprochement,* and as early as 1896 signed a convention with Italy safeguarding the rights of the tens of thousands of Italians resident in Tunis. Two years later, as mentioned above, a favorable commercial treaty ended the harmful tariff war between the two Latin countries. In 1900 Italy, already casting greedy eyes upon Tripoli in northern Africa, signed a convention with France in which she gave the latter a free hand in Morocco, receiving in return the promise of a free hand for herself in Tripoli and Cyrenaica. Two years later she moved still closer to France when the two powers agreed that, should either be the object of a direct or indirect aggression on the part of one or more powers, the other would maintain a strict neutrality. Victor Emmanuel's visit to Paris and that of President Loubet to Rome in 1904 gave outward expression to the new friendship between their two countries. At the Algeciras conference in 1906 [6] France received even

---

[5] For example, when the University of Innsbruck refused to appoint Italian teachers in 1903.

[6] See page 132.

more tangible evidence of Italy's good will when the latter openly supported France rather than Germany.

For a time efforts were made by both Austria and Italy to ward off the almost inevitable conflict arising between them in the Balkans. As early as 1887 in the renewal of the Triple Alliance mutual pledges had been given. In 1900 the two states agreed to respect the *status quo* in Albania or, if it could not be maintained, to unite to establish her autonomy. Two years later, in order to conciliate Italy, Austria agreed not to oppose the former's action in Tripoli and Cyrenaica. In the succeeding years Italy continued in many ways to advance her economic penetration of the Balkans. By 1908 considerable progress had been made in Montenegro, where the tobacco monopoly of the country was in the hands of one Italian company, a concession for navigation on Lake Scutari was held by another, and the port of Antivari and a railway had been constructed by still a third. Italian business firms were also established in the Albanian towns of Scutari and Durazzo.

In 1908 the possibility of cordial relations between Italy and Austria was made more remote when the latter announced her annexation of Bosnia and Herzegovina.[7] The effect of Austria's action upon Italy's foreign policy was immediately shown when at Racconigi (1909) the latter agreed with Russia to attempt to maintain the *status quo* in the Balkans to the exclusion of all foreign domination, and in return for Russia's favorable attitude toward Italian interests in Tripoli and Cyrenaica further agreed to consider favorably Russian interests in the question of the Straits at Constantinople. Italy thus became still more closely linked with the states of the Triple Entente.

The indignation aroused in Italy by the annexation of Bosnia and Herzegovina further kindled the spirit of Italian nationalism. In 1910 the nationalists held a congress in Florence, where they demanded that the government adopt a "practical" rather than a "sentimental" policy. They established a daily newspaper, which advocated militarism and attacked liberalism. Liberty, they asserted, was a hindrance to a nation which "aspires to conquer for itself the largest share in the rule of the world." They urged a sweeping educational reform, which should include the rejection of books with timid morality and their replacement by the works of Kipling

[7] See page 341.

and Theodore Roosevelt as representative of "the morality of men who do things."

Although the more abundant fruit of this nationalist movement was not forthcoming until the Fascist period of Italian history, it had its influence on events in the years that preceded 1914. For some time Italy had been pursuing the path of economic penetration in Tripoli and had been attempting through secret agents to reach understandings with the Arab chiefs of that region. After 1908 the nationalists began to urge the conquest of this "land of promise" as a sound business proposition for Italian capitalists and as a suitable field for the colonization of "as many as two million" Italian emigrants. Others like the Socialists, however, asserted what was more nearly the truth, namely, that Tripoli had no good harbors for possible naval bases, that it had an inadequate rainfall and little possibility of irrigation, that it was merely a burning desert dotted with occasional oases, and that the long period of fighting which would be necessary to pacify the country would entail an expense far out of proportion to the value of the conquest.

But in September, 1911, Giolitti gave way before the rising tide of nationalism and imperialism. Citing the "disorder and neglect" in Tripoli and the opposition to Italian economic activities there, the Italian government on September 28 sent an ultimatum to Turkey demanding her consent to Italy's military occupation of that territory. On the next day Italy declared war. When the powers later attempted to mediate between the belligerents, Italy, in order to ward off proposals for a compromise, proclaimed Italian sovereignty over Tripoli (November, 1911). Nearly a year later Turkey in the peace of Lausanne (October, 1912) renounced her sovereignty over Tripoli and Cyrenaica, which were at once organized as an Italian colony named Libya. Turkey also left the Dodecanese Islands, which Italian forces had occupied, in Italian hands as a guarantee until all Turkish military and civil representatives were withdrawn from Tripoli. As later events proved,[8] Italy by her venture gained these islands also, and thereafter had footholds both in northern Africa and in the eastern Mediterranean.

Naturally, the Tripolitan War threw the national budget once more completely out of balance, and the increased national debt in turn required an increase in national taxes. Although the imperial-

[8] See page 639.

istic enterprise had been enthusiastically hailed by the nationalists, the parliamentary elections of 1913 appeared to leave the matter of its general popularity open to question. The Socialists, opponents of imperialism, increased their representation in the Chamber from 40 to 72, while, on the other hand, Giolitti's bloc suffered a reverse. In 1914 he was succeeded as premier by the Conservative, Antonio Salandra.

Conditions during the few months of Salandra's ministry which preceded the outbreak of the World War were hectic. Irredentism was fanned into fever heat by the dismissal of Italians from office by the governor of Trieste in 1913 and by fierce street fighting in the same city the next year between Italians, financially encouraged by the Italian government, and Slavs, encouraged by Austria. At the same time, influenced by the radical writings and speeches of the new editor of *Avanti!*, Benito Mussolini, the Socialists and Syndicalists of Italy became ever more aggressive. The government's forcible suppression of disorders in June, 1914, precipitated a general strike throughout Italy. Fighting occurred in several places, but the most radical steps were taken in Romagna and the marches, where extremists went so far as to proclaim a republic. Although this movement was quickly suppressed by Salandra's government and repudiated by Turati in the name of the Socialist deputies, it is obvious that Italy was in a weakened condition at the fateful hour when the World War broke out. How that great conflict was eventually utilized by Italian nationalists and imperialists to advance toward their goals is discussed in the later pages of this book.[9]

[9] See pages 402–403.

## CHAPTER VI

# THE UNITED KINGDOM AND THE BRITISH EMPIRE

IN 1870 what is usually referred to briefly as Great Britain included England, Scotland, Ireland, and Wales. The last of these had been absorbed by England in the sixteenth century; England and Scotland had united in the early years of the eighteenth century to form the Kingdom of Great Britain; and by the Act of Union (1800) Ireland had been joined with Great Britain to constitute the United Kingdom of Great Britain and Ireland. The United Kingdom therefore comprised the British Isles. In area it was much smaller than Russia, Austria-Hungary, Germany, or France; in fact, it was smaller, even, than Spain or Sweden. Of the so-called great powers only Italy stood below it in area and population.

But the importance of Great Britain in European and world affairs did not rest merely upon the resources and population of the British Isles. The United Kingdom was the heart and center of the most extensive and populous empire the world has ever known. Compared with its huge overseas realm, the kingdom was a tiny dwarf. The British at home and their English-speaking cousins within the empire were overwhelmingly outnumbered by the heterogeneous population which inhabited British territory in Asia, Africa, and the islands of the seas. In every section of the globe were territories and peoples which constituted parts of the British Empire.

## The British Empire in 1870

The various parts of this empire differed noticeably in their political relation to the government at Westminster. A large share of the empire, territorially speaking (but only a small part in population), was in 1870 self-governing. These self-governing areas were in general the regions which had been colonized by the British, the parts where British settlers and their descendants outnumbered the native population. Prominent in this category was the Dominion of Can-

THE EARL OF BEACONSFIELD

Disraeli addressing a meeting of the Conservative Party at the
Carlton Club shortly before his death in 1881.

ada, which had been created by the British North America Act of 1867, and which after 1878 had jurisdiction over all British territory north of the United States except Newfoundland and its dependency Labrador. Newfoundland constituted a separate self-governing colony. In Australasia there were in 1870 seven self-governing colonies: Western Australia, South Australia, Victoria, New South Wales, and Queensland in Australia proper; Tasmania, an island just south of Australia; and New Zealand, lying some 1200 miles to the southeast.[1]

In Africa there was one self-governing colony. During the Napoleonic wars the British had conquered the Dutch colony in South Africa, and at the conclusion of the wars the Congress of Vienna had ratified their possession. Most of the white inhabitants of the colony were Dutch Boers (farmers), who held a considerable number of native slaves. When Great Britain in the thirties abolished slavery in all her colonies, several hundred Boers had moved northeast and north from Cape Colony in search of new homes where they might be free from Britain's control. Natal, the colony which they established along the coast to the northeast, had been annexed by the British in 1843, but the Orange Free State and the South African Republic (the Transvaal) north of the Vaal River had been recognized as independent Boer republics in the fifties. Although Great Britain's Cape Colony had not actually been granted self-government in 1870, it obtained that privilege in 1872.

These self-governing parts of the empire had their own parliaments and ministries and managed their own domestic affairs largely as they pleased. Theoretically, Great Britain held the right to veto legislation enacted by their parliaments and to decide in the British Privy Council such judicial cases as might be appealed to it; actually, however, the British government interfered but little in their internal affairs. The various governors-general who were sent by the British government to these parts of the empire were about as powerless there as the king was in the United Kingdom itself.

By far the largest part of the population of the empire, however, lived in territories which did not have self-government. Most of this population—perhaps 80 per cent of the total of the empire—lived in

[1] The first six of these in 1900 agreed upon a plan of confederation, and each then became a state in the Commonwealth of Australia. The seventh remained outside the Commonwealth and in 1907 was raised to a rank equal to that of Canada and Australia and was thereafter called a dominion.

India, that great triangular peninsula lying south of Afghanistan
and the Himalaya Mountains in Asia. Here dwelt perhaps as many
as 300,000,000 people, who differed among themselves in race, religion,[2] language,[3] cultural standards, and economic status. Britain's
hold on India had been forged during the seventeenth, eighteenth,
and nineteenth centuries by representatives of the British East India
Company, which until 1858 had held political sway over India. In
the latter year, however, Parliament had deprived the company of
its political powers and had transferred control of Indian affairs to
the British government. In 1876 another act of Parliament designated
British India as the Empire of India, of which the British sovereign
was to be the emperor or empress. During most of the period after
1870, therefore, India was an "empire."

Supreme authority in the Empire of India resided in a British
viceroy who ruled from Calcutta with the aid of an executive
council and with practically dictatorial powers. The viceroy was
responsible to the secretary of state for India, a British cabinet member, who was assisted by a small council in London. But not all of
India was included within the Empire of India. Several hundred
"native states"—including perhaps as much as 40 per cent of the
total area—were governed by native princes who recognized British
suzerainty over them and who agreed to amicable relations with the
Empire of India and to a degree of supervision by the British
viceroy. Although most of the native princes were content with their
relation to the British Empire, many intellectuals among the natives
came to desire home rule or even complete independence for the
Empire of India. Increasingly, as the nineteenth century came to a
close, the British government was forced to reckon with the rising
spirit of nationalism within India.

In addition to the self-governing colonies and the Empire of India
the British Empire embraced a great number of other territories
scattered over the globe.[4] These, like the Empire of India, were
inhabited principally by non-English peoples, and, though differing
somewhat among themselves in the way in which they were gov-

---

[2] Hindus and Moslems, each group divided into many sects, predominated.
[3] More than two hundred languages were spoken.
[4] The more important of these scattered territories were: Bermuda, the Bahamas,
the Windward Islands, the Leeward Islands, Jamaica, Trinidad, Barbados, British Honduras, British Guiana, and the Falkland Islands in the western hemisphere; Gold Coast,
Gambia, Sierra Leone, and Natal in Africa; Gibraltar and Malta in the Mediterranean;
and Ceylon, the Straits Settlement, Hongkong, and Mauritius in Asia and the South Seas.

erned, they had as a group little home rule. Most of these possessions held in 1870 the status of "crown colonies." Their governors were appointed by and responsible to the colonial ministry in London, and were assisted by "advisory" bodies chosen from the British residents in their respective colonies. Many of the "crown colonies" provided strategically located stations for the British navy; others were of great importance to British commercial interests; still others proved their value later by serving as bases for the further extension of the British Empire.

For Great Britain's empire overseas was tremendously enlarged in the years after 1870. Although British statesmen differed noticeably in the degree of aggressiveness with which they protected or extended the empire, the forces of economic imperialism in the end drove them all to acquire ever more and more territory. Asia, Africa, and the South Seas were the chief scenes of British imperialistic activity in the ensuing years; peaceful penetration, military occupation or conquest, and diplomatic negotiation were the means used.

By 1914 Great Britain had obtained an overseas empire so vast in territorial extent and so rich in natural resources as to be a constant source of envy to the less fortunate nations of the globe. Within this empire rested the control of a large share of the world's supply of diamonds, gold, coal, iron, wool, cotton, and wheat, not to mention such other important raw materials as antimony, asbestos, copper, graphite, lead, manganese, nickel, rubber, tin, and zinc. Much of the territory was favorably located in the temperate zones. An avenue of escape for Great Britain's surplus population was thus provided within its confines, and by 1914 some 17,000,000 descendants of British stock were living in the dominions and colonies overseas. And this great empire provided a constantly expanding market for British goods. In the years immediately preceding the World War more than half of Great Britain's export trade was with her possessions. Even as early as 1870 the British Empire was absorbing 25 per cent of the goods exported from the United Kingdom.

## THE UNITED KINGDOM IN 1870

That Great Britain in 1870 was in the very heyday of her economic golden age, standing without a peer as an industrial and commerical country, was not the result of her possession of vast territories overseas, however. Her supremacy was the result primarily of two other circumstances: her possession of valuable natural resources in coal and iron and her leadership in the inauguration of the Industrial Revolution. Although other countries had adopted and were adopting the modern industrial system, the early start which Great Britain had made in this field gave her an ascendancy which in 1870 had not yet been seriously challenged. She was at that date largely the workshop of the world; from her factories and mills a steady stream of exports flowed to the uttermost parts of the globe.

In the five years beginning in 1870 the average annual value of exports from the British Isles was approximately £230,000,000—almost as much as the export trade of France and Germany combined, and more than the total for Germany and the United States. Nearly 90 per cent of the value of British exports—which consisted chiefly of cotton yarns and cloth, woolen and linen goods, pig iron, steel, rails and plate, machinery, and coal—was in goods manufactured in whole or in part in Great Britain, and to this export trade the textile, iron, and steel industries contributed most extensively. The textile mills of Lancashire and Yorkshire surpassed those to be found in any other country, and the iron and steel industries about Sheffield and Birmingham were the largest in the world. Coal production, too, was an important element in Britain's prosperity, for she not only mined enough to supply her own industrial needs but had a surplus for export to less fortunate countries.

In the early seventies the United Kingdom's foreign trade—exports and imports combined—reached the tremendous total of £669,000,000—an amount which completely dwarfed the foreign trade of any other country. And almost two thirds of the shipping which was engaged in carrying this trade was British, for in the shipping trade the United Kingdom's ascendancy was even more striking than in commerce. In 1870 the total tonnage (5,617,693) of the kingdom's merchant navy exceeded that of the mercantile fleets of the next five ranking maritime countries combined; in fact, in steam tonnage the British merchant fleet was more than twice that of the other five countries taken together. British merchantmen carried not only most of the cargoes of the homeland and the empire but a good share of those of other countries also. In the early seventies, for example, British ships carried approximately 46 per cent of the foreign trade of the United States, 37 per cent of that of France, and 33 per cent of that of Germany. Profits from the carrying trade constituted an important item in the national income.

The ascendancy of British shipping was naturally reflected in the kingdom's shipbuilding industry, for the latter constructed ships for registry both in the United Kingdom and in foreign countries as well. The Clyde district of Scotland led the world in the building of ships. But British ships contributed not only thus to British industry but also to the increase of British commerce. By their established routes and their connections with British warehouses they helped to develop a great *entrepôt* trade. Many British vessels brought their cargoes of overseas goods to British warehouses and markets, and from these centers the goods were distributed among European buyers. In a similar way European goods were brought to Britain, whence they were re-exported in British ships to many parts of the world. Of Britain's foreign trade in 1872, for example, re-exports accounted for £58,000,000.

In 1870 London was the greatest commercial port in the world; and it was also recognized as the world's financial center. British capitalists had invested great sums—as much as £1,500,000,000 in 1875—throughout the empire and in many foreign lands. Interest and dividends from these overseas investments provided a steady stream of income for the country, an income which was further supplemented by the large earnings of British bankers, brokers, and insurance companies, which served foreigners as well as the British themselves. In summary, then, it may be said that in 1870 Great Britain earned most of her national income by serving as the manufacturer, merchant, shipper, and banker for a large part of the world.

Politically, this "workshop of the world" was a constitutional monarchy in which the sovereign reigned but did not rule. In 1870 the British ruler—Queen Victoria—was a mere figurehead in the government. Although in theory she had many powers, in actual fact the powers that she appeared to exercise were controlled by her cabinet. The latter, a political device originated by the British, was a committee of members of Parliament, apparently appointed by the ruler but in reality chosen by the majority party in the House of Commons. The executive power of the kingdom was exercised by this cabinet. But the duties of the cabinet were not limited to the appointment of officials and the supervision of administration; it also assumed responsibility for and guided national legislation. All important bills were introduced in Parliament by cabinet members. The cabinet was in turn responsible to Parliament; that is, it was not appointed for a fixed term but might be forced out of office by a vote of "no confidence" in the Commons or by the failure of the latter to pass an important bill sponsored by the ministers. Two courses were open to the cabinet in case of its repudiation by Parliament. It might forthwith resign and permit the leader of the opposition to form a cabinet, or it might dissolve Parliament and call for a new election. In the latter case the voters of the kingdom decided whether or not the cabinet should resign. If a majority of the members of the new Parliament favored the cabinet, the latter continued at the head of the government; if not, it resigned.

The legislative body of the kingdom was a bicameral parliament, consisting of the House of Lords and the House of Commons. The former consisted for the most part of hereditary English peers; there were also a number of elected Scottish and Irish peers and the bishops of the established Anglican Church. Despite the fact that the Lords were not directly responsible to the voters, they exercised considerable power of a negative type in national legislation. Although by threatening to create new peers a ministry might, as in 1832, force the Lords to pass desired legislation, this device was reserved for only the most critical occasions. In general, therefore, the Lords were in a position to tone down or defeat bills that appeared to them radical or inimical to the interests of the groups they represented—socially, the landed aristocracy; politically, the Conservative Party. When the latter was not in control of the cabinet, the Lords tended to obstruct legislation. The threat "to mend or end" the House of Lords was often muttered by those who sat on the Liberal benches in the House of Commons. One power the Lords had by 1870 apparently surrendered to the Commons, namely, the power to enact the national budget. Although in principle the upper house had co-ordinate power in the drafting and adoption of the budget, precedent had established the rule that the Lords must enact money bills passed by the House of Commons. The latter during the preceding centuries had gradually risen in influence until by 1870 it was generally recognized as the predominant—although not the all-powerful—branch of the government. Its consent was necessary for all legislation; it dominated the ministry; and through its control of the "purse strings" it could, if it willed, completely paralyze the government. The House of Commons represented the British "people," and was chosen from time to time by popular election. Although elected for a maximum term of years, it might be dissolved in the name of the king by the cabinet whenever the latter wished to test the opinion of the electorate. Prior to 1832 the Commons had been largely controlled by the aristocracy, but the Reform Act of that year had so widened the electorate and changed the representation as to shift control into the hands of the middle classes. There it had remained for a generation until in 1867 a second Reform Act again altered the situation. Once more the franchise had been widened and the representation redistributed. As a consequence, in 1870 almost all townsmen, and in rural districts practically all men but the farm laborers, could vote. The act of 1867 thus for the first time had placed the Commons under the control of the mass of the people. Nevertheless, the franchise in Great Britain was not yet open to all men as in France and Germany after 1870; perhaps as many as a third of the men in the kingdom were still denied the vote.

Despite the reform measures of 1832 and 1867 the British government in 1870 was still largely dominated by the upper and wealthier classes. Obviously the House of Lords was in their control. But a large share of the seats in the Commons, most of the places in the cabinet, and the important positions in the administrative system were also held by them. Furthermore, the leadership in the two most important political parties was for the most part in their hands. In the ensuing years, however, these classes were forced more and more to cater to the desires of the masses, for without the electoral support of the latter the retention of political power was not long possible.

The two major political parties in the kingdom in 1870 were the Liberals and the Conservatives. The former, the spiritual heirs of the Whigs, had increased in strength as a consequence of the Reform Act of 1832. The Liberal Party was largely the medium for expressing the desires of the bourgeoisie, though the enfranchisement of the urban workingmen in 1867 temporarily brought into the party most of the voters from that class also. In theory the Liberals favored free trade, the further extension of the franchise, and the alleviation of the ills of Ireland; they were critical of the position and power of the established church, were not enthusiastic about imperial expansion, and usually were not particularly aggressive in foreign affairs. The Liberals have been characterized as the party of "peace, retrenchment, and reform."

The Conservatives were the successors of the Tories of the pre-1832 era. The party was dominated by the aristocracy and was to a considerable extent the champion of the interests of the landed classes. It had, for instance, long supported a protective tariff on agricultural products. It was in general hostile to "progressive" legislation and usually favored the maintenance of the *status quo*. Consequently, it supported the established church, the established peerage, the established landowning system, and the established relations with Ireland. It was more nationalistic and imperialistic than the Liberal Party and accordingly, when in power, pursued a more aggressive foreign policy and a more vigorous imperialistic program. It must be emphasized, however, that the Conservative Party was not the agent of reaction. It sought rather to apply the brakes to radical or overspeedy legislation. When, despite their opposition, progressive measures were adopted, the Conservatives acquiesced in the situation and gave up their resistance. In fact, upon occasion the Conservative Party itself championed measures which were liberal and progressive. The Reform Act of 1867 had been passed under a Conservative government.

In the seventies a third political group, the Irish Nationalists, made its appearance in the British parliament. This party drew its support from Ireland and was interested almost solely in improving the lot of the Irish. Although Ireland constituted part of the United Kingdom, it was not happy in that association. Ireland was different from Great Britain. Whereas England, Scotland, and Wales were predominantly Protestant, Ireland was largely Catholic. Whereas Great Britain had become chiefly industrial, Ireland had remained for the most part agricultural. Whereas the problems confronting the three parts of Great Britain were largely similar, those of Ireland were felt to be distinctly different. Whereas the Welsh and the Scots were generally happy in their union with the English, most of the Irish had never ceased to resent their political absorption into the United Kingdom. Their political goal was "home rule" for Ireland.

Hatred of the English had been bred into the Irish by centuries of economic exploitation and religious and political oppression. In the seventeenth century Englishmen and Scots had been "planted" in northern Ireland on lands which were taken from the native Irish; and in the seventeenth and eighteenth centuries most of the rest of Ireland had been transferred from the Irish to British landlords. The Irish had been forced to become agricultural laborers or tenants on the estates of these landlords—many of whom lived in England. As tenants—and there were 600,000 of them in 1870—they were subject to the arbitrary exploitation of their landlords, for the British government had sought to force upon Ireland a system of *laissez faire* in land. In other words, the landlords had been conceded the right to dispose of their property as they pleased, with the result that Irish peasants had been subjected to the "withdrawal of customary privileges, the ceaseless demand for higher rents, the perennial notice to quit, and the cruel eviction."

Since most of the peasants had no alternative other than to farm, the landlords could exact almost any rent they desired and could always find new tenants to succeed those evicted. Furthermore, according to the law the landlords were under no obligation to compensate evicted tenants for improvements which the latter had made during their tenancy.[5] The most pressing problem for the Irish peasants was that of securing protection against oppressive landlords. They sought legislation which would provide for fair rent, fixity of tenure, and "free sale"—the latter meaning the right to sell to their successors improvements which they had made. These demands were popularly referred to as the "three F's." The ultimate goal of the Irish peasants was, of course, the destruction of landlordism and the return of the land which had once been theirs.

Religious differences also undoubtedly played a part in the attitude of the Irish toward the British. The former had for the most part remained Catholic at the time when Great Britain broke away from the Catholic Church. But Protestant leaders in Britain had

---

[5] Although the lot of agricultural laborers and tenants of England was none too happy, nevertheless among them there was lacking the feeling that prevailed among the Irish—that their exploitation was at the hands of an alien people.

sought to win the Irish to their faith and had established in Ireland the Church of Ireland, which was in essence only the Anglican Church under another name. Irish Catholics were long forced to contribute to this established church which none of them attended and which none of them desired. Prior to 1829, also, the Catholic Irish—that is, most of the Irish—had been denied the right to represent Ireland in the parliament of the United Kingdom.

The century preceding 1870 had witnessed a notable rise of Irish nationalism, which had expressed itself in a succession of organizations under one name or another. At the close of the eighteenth century there had been formed the society of United Irishmen, including both Catholics and Protestants. Their rebellion in 1798 had precipitated the decision to absorb Ireland into the United Kingdom. Next, in the first quarter of the nineteenth century, had come the Catholic Association, led by Daniel O'Connell. This organization had made some gains for Irish Catholics by securing the removal of many civil disabilities and the granting to Catholics of the right to hold seats in the British parliament. In 1843 the Catholic Association had been dissolved and its leader imprisoned by the British government. But the suppression of O'Connell's organization had been followed almost at once by the appearance of a new and more radical society known as Young Ireland, whose members were pledged to try to establish an independent Irish republic. During the wave of nationalistic revolts on the Continent in 1848 the Young Irish had made an attempt to throw off British control, but their revolt had merely brought the suppression of their society and the punishment of their leaders.

Late in the fifties still another organization, the Fenian Brotherhood, had been formed—this time among the Irish in the United States. Although it never secured much of a following among the peasants of Ireland, the society received considerable support from Irish outside the island. In 1866 Fenians in the United States had made a foolish and abortive raid on Canada, and in 1867 other Fenians in the industrial cities of Lancashire had precipitated riots which were so serious as to lead the British government to call out troops to maintain order. Any history of the United Kingdom after 1870, it is obvious, must accordingly give attention to the situation in Ireland and to the role of the Irish Nationalist Party, which was organized in that year.

## GLADSTONE AND DISRAELI

In 1870 William Ewart Gladstone was British prime minister. He had already had a long career in Parliament, having entered the House of Commons as a Conservative in 1833. While still a student at Oxford he had attracted attention by his speeches against the Reform Bill of 1832, and as a result had been sent to Parliament for a pocket borough through the influence of the Duke of Newcastle. Almost immediately Gladstone was included in one of the Conservative ministries in a minor office, and from then on he was almost regularly a member of the ministry when the Conservatives were in power. He supported Sir Robert Peel in seeking the repeal of the Corn Laws in 1846, and thereafter became more and more liberal in his views. In 1853 Gladstone became chancellor of the exchequer in a coalition government, and at once disclosed not only his understanding of budgetary matters but his ability to explain and clarify the intricacies of state finance with an eloquence which could hold the House of Commons enthralled for hours.

In 1859 Gladstone became the chancellor of the exchequer in a purely Liberal government and thereafter was identified with the more progressive wing of the Liberal Party. For several years he supported the various efforts to secure further parliamentary reform, but to no avail, largely because Lord Palmerston, the leader of the Liberals, was opposed to such a step. Upon the death of the latter in 1865, Gladstone became the real leader of the party despite the fact that Lord Russell, an older man, held the office of prime minister. Following Palmerston's death Gladstone sponsored a parliamentary reform bill, but it was defeated in the House of Commons, and the Liberal government was forced to resign. The Reform Bill of 1867 was then passed under a Conservative government, thanks largely to the influence of Gladstone's rival, Benjamin Disraeli. The first election held under the new franchise, however, resulted in a majority not for the Conservative Party, under whose government it had been enacted, but for the Liberals.

Accordingly, Gladstone—destined in the succeeding quarter of a century repeatedly to serve Great Britain as prime minister—became head of the government for the first time (1868–1874). The Liberal leader at once turned his attention to the Irish situation and by two acts sought to alleviate the ills of Ireland. In 1869 an act of Parliament disestablished the Church of Ireland. Church and state were completely separated, and the church was dispossessed of much of its property other than church buildings. The Irish were released from their obligation to support the church—with the result that many parishes at once ceased to exist—and bishops of the Church of Ireland were deprived of their seats in the House of Lords. This measure went far toward removing all religious grounds for complaint on the part of the Irish Catholics.

A second act, the Land Act of 1870, dealt with the Irish agrarian situation. The British government abandoned its *laissez-faire* principle in regard to land and repudiated the landlords' doctrine of an absolute and infallible right in property in land. The new act forbade the arbitrary increasing of rents and stipulated that an evicted tenant should be compensated for whatever improvements he had made. It also provided that the state should lend peasants who desired to buy land a certain percentage of the purchase price. Unfortunately, the act largely failed to improve the lot of the tenants because selfish landlords were quick to discover and avail themselves of huge legal loopholes in it. While in principle it antagonized the landlords, in operation it failed to satisfy or relieve the Irish peasants.

But Gladstone was not unmindful of the need for more general reform. As in France after the establishment of the Third Republic, so in Great Britain after the wide extension of the franchise in 1867, it was felt that better provision must be made for popular education. Prior to 1870 the kingdom had no compulsory education and no state system of free education. In fact, nearly half of the children were receiving no formal instruction whatsoever. The schools that did exist were voluntary; that is, they were denominational schools, which received some slight aid from the national government, or private schools—called "public" in England—like Rugby, Eton, and Harrow. The Forster Education Act of 1870 provided for the establishment of board schools—so-called because they were put in charge of locally elected boards—to supplement the existing educational facilities. These schools, in which no religious instruction was to be given, were to be supported by national grants, by local taxes, and by student fees. The act made no requirement of compulsory school attendance, however; this decision was left to the discretion of each school board. In 1871 the doors to institutions of higher learning were also opened wider by an act abolishing the existing religious tests for admission to Oxford and Cambridge. Thereafter these institutions accepted as students dissenters and Roman Catholics as well as Anglicans.

In addition to his educational reform Gladstone favored the recently enfranchised workingmen by still other measures. The Trade Union Act of 1871 finally conferred legal status upon trade unions by authorizing them to own property and giving them the right to undertake and defend actions at law. As a consequence, trade unionism rapidly expanded in the ensuing years. In 1872 the political freedom of the masses was safeguarded when the secret or "Australian" ballot was introduced in place of voting by word of mouth. Some attention was given, also, to the condition of the workers, for in the same year a law was passed forbidding the underground employment of women and of children under twelve years of age. Gladstone also struck at the privileged position of the aristocracy by placing the British civil and military services more directly on a merit basis, thus opening them to others than the upper classes. In 1870 a system of civil-service examinations was introduced, and in the following year the purchase system, by which the wealthy had formerly been able to buy commissions and promotions in the army, was abolished.

Naturally, so many reform measures could not be introduced without antagonizing the affected classes. Many high-church Anglicans and some nonconformists were alienated by the education act with its apparently hostile attitude toward religious education. Others of the upper classes were antagonized by the reforms in the civil service and in the army. Many denounced the government's conciliatory attitude in foreign policy as pusillanimous and weak. Russia, Britain's traditional enemy, had successfully abrogated (1870) the provisions of the treaty of Paris forbidding Russian ships in the Black Sea. She had also continued practically unhindered her steady advance in central Asia toward the frontiers of India.[6] Furthermore, in 1871 Gladstone's government had agreed to express to the United States its regret at the escape of the *Alabama*

[6] See pages 234–235.

and other Confederate cruisers and to refer the assessment of damages to an international tribunal,[7] and Great Britain had been compelled to pay the United States £3,250,000 in damages. Although the method of settling this international dispute was undoubtedly enlightened and progressive, many in Great Britain felt that the outcome was a national humiliation. Disraeli, the Conservative leader, declared: "It would have been better for us all if there had been a little more energy in our foreign policy, and a little less in our domestic legislation."

It is perhaps not surprising therefore that in the general election of 1874 the Liberals were decisively defeated. A Conservative ministry, headed by Disraeli, then took over the reigns of government. In 1837 Benjamin Disraeli, like Gladstone four years earlier, had entered Parliament as a Conservative, but, unlike Gladstone, he had remained a Conservative through all the intervening years. At the beginning of his political career he had been handicapped by his Jewish descent[8] and by his striking peculiarities of manner and appearance, but he was an able man and a brilliant speaker, and in less than two decades he came to be the real head of the Conservative Party. Like Gladstone, he frequently held the office of chancellor of the exchequer, but he lacked the former's unusual ability to serve in this capacity. Disraeli enthusiastically supported the monarchical principle of government and was an ardent believer in the imperial destiny of Great Britain. In 1867 he had sought to strengthen the Conservative Party by uniting the nobility and the urban workingmen against the bourgeoisie, and had accordingly sponsored the measure which in the end became the reform act of that year. In 1868 Disraeli had been prime minister for some ten months just preceding Gladstone's first ministry.

Disraeli was a man of seventy when he entered upon his second term as prime minister in 1874. His primary interest was in foreign and colonial affairs, and he felt, furthermore, that the country was in need of a period of rest from disturbing legislation after the great number of reform measures which had been enacted in the preceding seven years. Nothing particularly startling, therefore, was

[7] During the American Civil War a number of cruisers were built in Great Britain for the Confederate government and allowed to sail out to the high seas to destroy American merchant ships. The most notorious instance was that of the *Alabama*, which was allowed to sail despite the protests of the United States government.

[8] He had received Christian baptism when a boy.

done in the field of domestic legislation. Nevertheless, under his government laws were enacted (1) forbidding children under ten to work in textile factories, (2) forbidding children under fourteen who lacked a certain amount of education from working in any industries, (3) forbidding—to protect British sailors—the use of overloaded or unseaworthy ships, (4) placing all establishments using mechanical power in the same category without respect to size, (5) permitting "peaceful picketing" by strikers, and (6) codifying the existing social legislation.

Far more striking were the achievements of Disraeli's government in the realm of colonial and foreign affairs. Queen Victoria was proclaimed Empress of India (1877); Baluchistan on the northwestern boundary of India was converted into a protectorate; and by means of the second Afghan War (1878–1881) Russia's threatening advance toward British India was checked. Steps were taken, also, to safeguard Britain's most direct route to India.

In 1869 the Suez Canal, connecting the Mediterranean with the Red Sea through Egyptian territory, had been opened and had inevitably altered the trade routes of the world. The canal had been constructed by a French engineer, Ferdinand de Lesseps, and had been largely financed by a French company. Because of the difficulty of securing sufficient funds for the project,[9] however, Lesseps had had to enlist the support of the Khedive of Egypt, who had eventually subscribed to nearly half of the shares of the company. Once the canal was constructed and in successful operation, it soon became obvious that it constituted an important link in the British Empire's "lifeline," for in the seventies two thirds of the tonnage passing through the canal was British. Great Britain, therefore, could not well be indifferent to its control. Consequently, when in 1875 the khedive found himself in financial difficulties, Disraeli, without waiting for parliamentary consent, boldly and quickly purchased his canal shares for Great Britain at the cost of £4,000,000. By this coup he at once secured for the British government an influential position on the canal's board of directors.[10]

In 1878 at the Congress of Berlin [11] Disraeli not only helped to

---

[9] Great Britain, Russia, Austria, and the United States declined to subscribe to the shares of the company.

[10] Great Britain obtained 176,602 of the total 400,000 shares.

[11] See page 252.

halt Russia's advance into the Balkans but strengthened Britain's own position relative to the Suez Canal. In return for the promise of British support against Russia, the sultan ceded to Great Britain the island of Cyprus, strategically located in the eastern Mediterranean. In the following years Great Britain's ability to control and protect the Suez Canal was further increased as the result of developments in Egypt. The khedive had been so extravagant in his expenditures as ultimately to destroy his credit and place him in an embarrassing position financially. He was accordingly forced to accept British and French financial advisers, and, when he rebelled at this, he was in 1879 removed from the throne. The new khedive was forced to accept Anglo-French financial advice, and from 1879 Egypt was subjected to the "dual control" of France and Great Britain. Elsewhere in Africa the Conservative government's imperialism was evident. In 1877 the Transvaal Republic was annexed, and two years later the British were plunged into a formidable war against the Zulus, in which they suffered a number of reverses before the natives were finally overcome.

By the close of 1879 Disraeli, now known as the Earl of Beaconsfield, was becoming unpopular. Expensive wars abroad, economic depression at home, relative inattention to domestic legislation, and increasing parliamentary obstruction by the Irish Nationalists, all reacted against his ministry. In the general election of March, 1880, the Conservatives went down in defeat, and a few weeks later Beaconsfield resigned without waiting to face the new Parliament. In 1881 the Conservative leader died and thus brought to an end the parliamentary and ministerial rivalry which had so long existed between himself and Gladstone.

The latter, himself seventy years old, in 1880 became prime minister for the second time. He was at once compelled to deal with the situation in Ireland, which was becoming more and more difficult as the result of the activities of Charles Stewart Parnell and his Irish Nationalists. Strange to say, Parnell was not a native Catholic Irishman but a Protestant of English descent. He had developed, however, an intense hatred of the British, and the attainment of home rule for Ireland had become his highest ambition. In 1877 he and his followers had inaugurated in the House of Commons a policy of obstructing all legislation until their demand for home rule should be heeded. Though Parnell himself opposed the use of force, unrest and outbursts of violence prevailed in Ireland and led Gladstone's government to push through Parliament a number of coercive measures.

At the same time, in the hope of conciliating the Irish, Gladstone had Parliament pass a new land act (1881). This act, designed to remedy the defects of the law of 1870, provided for a land court to fix the rent for a fifteen-year period during which the tenant might not be evicted except for nonpayment of rent and for certain other specified reasons. It also provided that the tenant might dispose of his interest in his holding at the best price he could get. With its adoption of the "three F's," the act thus safeguarded the tenants' rights to remain upon the land, to pay only "fair" rent, and to dispose of their interest in their holdings. It was obviously based on the principle of dual ownership and was a triumph for the Irish peasantry.

Although Gladstone's second ministry saw the enactment of laws providing for compulsory elementary education and for employers' liability, the chief legislation of this period had to do with political and parliamentary reform. In 1883 the Corrupt Practices Act limited the amount which a parliamentary candidate might spend for election expenses and made bribery for political purposes a criminal offense. In 1884 the third Reform Act was passed, extending the franchise to farm laborers and to a number of other smaller groups which had not before been included. The electorate was thus increased by some two million voters; thereafter domestic servants, bachelors living with their parents, and those having no fixed residence were the only classes of men excluded. In the following year the Redistribution Act was passed, depriving more than a hundred towns of their separate representatives and including them for purposes of representation as parts of the counties in which they lay, and reducing the representation of many others. On the other hand, more populous cities and counties were awarded increased representation. The act also provided for the division of the counties and most of the large towns and cities into electoral districts of approximately equal population, each with one representative in Parliament. After 1885, therefore, Great Britain had equal electoral districts, the secret ballot, and almost manhood suffrage for the election of Parliament. In 1882, also, the Municipal Corporations Act had given the right to vote for city officials to all men inhabiting the city, regardless of property-holding.

By this time, despite his own aversion to imperialistic ventures, Gladstone had become deeply involved overseas—thanks largely to the legacy which he had inherited from Disraeli. Popular opposition in the Transvaal against its annexation by Great Britain was strong and had eventually led to open revolt by the Boers. A brief military campaign ensued, and in February, 1881, the British were decisively defeated in a minor engagement at Majuba Hill. Gladstone had waged his election campaign in 1880 against imperialism and was prepared to recognize the independence of the Transvaal Republic. A peace treaty (1881) therefore restored self-government to the Boers under British suzerainty. A later convention (1884), however, omitted the clause regarding suzerainty and merely stipulated that the Transvaal could not conclude treaties with foreign powers without the approval of the British government. In Britain these steps were viewed with indignation by many who interpreted them as a weak surrender in the face of force.

In Egypt, too, Gladstone encountered difficulties. A strong nationalist movement soon developed in that country against the dual control of Great Britain and France. In 1881 the standard of revolt was raised, and the slogan "Egypt for the Egyptians" resounded. The British government proposed to France joint military intervention in Egypt, but France declined to participate. Great Britain then decided to proceed alone, and in 1882 a British fleet bombarded and captured Alexandria. Ultimately British troops advanced to Cairo, and the nationalist movement thereupon collapsed. Although Gladstone's government formally notified the powers that the British army would be withdrawn "as soon as the state of the country, and the organization of the proper means for the maintenance of the Khedive's authority, will admit of it," British troops continued to be stationed in Egypt. The real ruler of the country came to be the British consul-general and high commissioner, and British imperialists soon considered the Nile valley as part of the British Empire.

From Egypt the British were soon drawn into difficulties in the eastern Sudan. Egypt had attempted to establish her authority in this region along the upper Nile but had aroused strong opposition by her edicts against the slave trade and by her heavy taxes. Led by Mohammed Ahmed, who claimed to be divinely ordained to drive out both Egyptians and Europeans, the Sudanese rose in the early eighties and annihilated an Egyptian army. Gladstone's government decided that Egypt should withdraw from the Sudan and sent a small force of British troops commanded by General Charles Gordon to aid in the evacuation. Before Gordon could accomplish his task, however, he and his troops were surrounded at Khartum. Gladstone's government was dilatory in sending reinforcements, with the result that, before the latter arrived, Khartum was captured early in 1885 and Gordon was killed by native "dervishes."

Gladstone's failure to take prompt measures to relieve Gordon roused a storm of fury in Great Britain. Discontent was further increased by his government's apparently ineffective policy toward Russia's advance upon Afghanistan.[12] Even Gladstone's domestic legislation reacted against him, for his land act antagonized many of the British without fully satisfying the Irish Nationalists. In June, 1885, Parnell and his followers turned against Gladstone, who resigned and was succeeded by Lord Salisbury, the new leader of the Conservative Party. But in January, 1886, the Irish Nationalists in turn repudiated Salisbury, and Gladstone again became prime minister.

But Gladstone's third ministry was of short duration, chiefly because he espoused the cause of the Irish Nationalists. Soon after coming into power he introduced a bill to give Ireland a separate parliament for her own affairs, hoping thus to obtain peace and contentment in Ireland and the end of Irish obstruction in the British parliament. Unfortunately for his hopes, however, more than a fourth of the Liberal members of Parliament were opposed to home rule. Led by John Bright and Joseph Chamberlain, they seceded from the Liberal Party and formed the Liberal Unionist Party, which joined with the Conservatives to oppose Gladstone's Home Rule Bill. Although the eighty-six Irish Nationalist members threw their support to Gladstone, the bill was defeated in the House of Commons. Parliament was then dissolved in order that new elections might test the feeling of the country on the question.

[12] In 1885 the Russians occupied Penjdeh in Afghanistan. Instead of ousting them by military measures, Gladstone's government submitted the matter to arbitration.

The Liberals were defeated, Gladstone was forced to resign, and for the next six years the Conservatives were in power.

In the parliamentary election of 1892 Gladstone again made home rule the chief issue of his campaign. Although the Liberals failed to gain a majority of the seats in Parliament, the combined strength of the Liberals and the Irish Nationalists provided such a majority. Consequently, Gladstone for the fourth time became prime minister, and in 1893 he introduced his second Home Rule Bill. The measure, though vigorously denounced and opposed by the Conservatives and the Liberal Unionists, was this time passed by the House of Commons. But this achievement brought little satisfaction to the Irish Nationalists, for the bill was decisively rejected by the House of Lords and therefore failed to become law. Early in 1894 Gladstone at the age of eighty-four resigned the premiership and retired from public life. Four years later the "Great Commoner" died. He alone of all British statesmen had had the distinction of four times holding the office of prime minister.

### THE CONSERVATIVES IN POWER

Except for the brief interlude of Liberal government from 1892 to 1895, the Conservatives were in power for practically two decades after 1886. Until 1902 Lord Salisbury served as prime minister and as foreign secretary when the Conservatives were in office. His chief interest was in foreign affairs, and, from the viewpoint of an aristocrat and an imperialist, Britain's foreign policy was ably conducted during his period. In 1902 Salisbury was succeeded as prime minister by his nephew, Arthur James Balfour, who had been the Conservative leader in the House of Commons, and who remained at the head of the government until the Conservatives went out of power in December, 1905. Balfour was more of a philosopher than a politician or statesman. Though his parliamentary speeches were acclaimed for their scholarly open-mindedness and their philosophic and literary qualities, he did not distinguish himself particularly as a party leader.

The third outstanding figure in this period of Conservative rule—and probably the most important—was Joseph Chamberlain, who had led the Liberal Unionist secession in 1886. Chamberlain was a successful Birmingham business man. He had played an active role in the political life of his city and was well known for the political reforms he had introduced while mayor of that municipality. From 1886 to 1892 he was informally allied with the Conservatives, but, when Salisbury formed his third ministry in 1895, Chamberlain accepted the post of colonial secretary. Generally speaking, Chamberlain favored colonial expansion, closer relations between the mother country and the colonies, the erection of protective tariffs for the kingdom in conjunction with a system of imperial preference for the empire, and the enactment of further social legislation. In 1885, before he left the Liberal party, he had published a proposed program of reform which included free education, small agricultural holdings, and more democratic local government. Gladstone's indifference to these proposals had helped to pave the way for the final break which came in the following year over Irish home rule. Chamberlain's influence is apparent in the domestic legislation of the Conservative period.

In 1888 the Conservatives passed the County Councils Act transferring most of the administrative powers of the counties from the frequently old and inefficient justices of the peace to elected councils. This act had for counties much the same significance that the Corporation Act (1835) had had for towns and cities. In the realm of education two steps were taken. In 1891 the Elementary Education Act provided for the making of grants from the national treasury to denominational schools as well as to board schools in England and Wales, and made possible the practical abolition of tuition fees in the elementary schools. Eleven years later (1902) the Conservatives further strengthened the denominational schools by an act stipulating that the latter should be placed on the same footing with board schools in respect to both national grants and local taxation. Since nearly 90 per cent of the thousands of voluntary schools were controlled by the Church of England, the act was particularly distasteful to dissenters.

In the realm of labor and social legislation some slight advances were made. In 1887 the Mines Act forbade the employment of either girls or boys under twelve years of age. Five years later (1892) the Small Holdings Act authorized the county councils to buy land, to sell it in blocks of less than fifty acres each, and to loan to the purchaser as much as three quarters of the purchase price. The measure was designed to increase the number of small independent farmers in the kingdom. Steps were taken, too, to protect the workers in case of accident. In 1897 the Workmen's Compensation Act obligated employers in industry to insure their employees against accident, and three years later the act was extended to include agricultural employees also. In 1901 a comprehensive factory code was drafted to serve as the basis of Britain's industrial system.

Although the Conservatives were unalterably opposed to home rule for Ireland and did not hesitate to resort to coercion to quell the Irish Nationalists, they did enact legislation to alter the land situation in that part of the kingdom. Gladstone's land act of 1881 had applied the principle of "dual ownership," a principle which had proved to be unsound economically as well as socially. The act had been a triumph for the Irish peasantry; nevertheless, the latter remained discontented—they wanted the land. But the landlords were even more dissatisfied, for they soon discovered that "fair" rents were lower rents, and that lower rents, in the face of an organized peasantry, were just as difficult to collect as high rents. Dual ownership broke the landlords financially; for them it brought "a regime of force, fraud, and folly." From this intolerable situation they were ultimately enabled to retire with a minimum of loss as a result of a series of land purchase acts sponsored by the Conservatives.

The first of these acts was passed during Salisbury's first ministry in 1885, and other acts of a similar nature were passed in 1887, 1891, 1896, and 1903. These measures were designed to facilitate the transfer of land in Ireland from the landlords to the tenants. The act of 1903, known as the Wyndham Act, though it went further than the earlier measures, was typical. It provided that £100,000,000 should be set aside by the British government to enable Irish tenants to buy out their landlords, money being loaned to the peasants on very easy terms. By repaying annually to the government 3¼ per cent of the principal amount borrowed, a tenant could extinguish his debt—both principal and interest—in less than sixty-nine years. At the same time, in order to induce the landlords to sell at prices the tenants could or would pay, the government gave the landlords a bonus of 12 per cent of the purchase price. During the early years of the twentieth century great numbers of Irish tenants availed themselves of this act to become owners of their holdings.[13] To further placate the Irish the Local Government Act (1898) extended to Ireland the system of county and district councils which prevailed in England. Despite these measures, which were designed to "kill home rule with kindness," the Irish Nationalists nevertheless refused to withdraw their demands for a separate Irish parliament.

## RESURGENT IMPERIALISM

The fiftieth anniversary of Queen Victoria's accession to the throne, joyously celebrated throughout the kingdom, witnessed a rising tide of nationalism and imperialism. The chief ministers of the self-governing colonies, in London for the queen's jubilee, were invited to confer with British ministers on matters which concerned the empire as a whole, and their meeting blazed the way for a series of colonial conferences during the ensuing years. Also, for the "protection" of the imperial interests the Conservatives in 1889 committed Great Britain to the two-power naval standard; that is, they decided that the British navy must be as great and powerful as any other two navies combined. The building program which they inaugurated in that year called for the construction of some seventy new fighting ships.

Overseas, during this Conservative period, vast stretches of new territory were added to the empire. Although some additions were made in the Far East—notably in Borneo—the chief gains were in Africa. With Great Britain controlling territory in South Africa as well as along the lower Nile, British imperialists began to dream of a railway to connect Cape Colony with Cairo in Egypt. For a time it appeared that it might indeed be possible to construct such a "Cape to Cairo" railway through a continuous strip of British territory, for by means of protectorates or chartered commercial companies British control was established over Nigeria (1886), Somaliland (1887), British East Africa, later called Kenya Colony (1888), Rhodesia (1889), British Central Africa, later called Nyasaland (1893), and Uganda (1896).[14]

[13] By 1922 only 70,000 holdings were as yet unpurchased by their occupiers. After the establishment of the Irish Free State the latter enacted a sweeping agrarian law compelling landlords to sell their estates and tenants to purchase their holdings.

[14] International disagreements and boundary disputes were the inevitable accompaniment of such tremendous territorial expansion, but these were adjusted by various

Obviously, if the British were to control an unbroken strip of territory from Cape Colony to the Mediterranean, they could not be indifferent to the fate of the region along the upper Nile, from which they and the Egyptians had been driven by the Sudanese in 1885. Moreover, having practically converted Egypt into a British protectorate, Great Britain was inevitably forced to take an interest in the Sudan, for ownership of this territory entailed control of the waters of the Nile, which were indispensable to the agricultural life of Egypt. Consequently, although the British in the eighties were themselves unwilling to undertake the conquest of the Sudan, they were determined not to let it fall into the hands of the French. Great Britain's futile attempt to thwart French efforts to secure the Sudan by encouraging Italy's plans in Africa,[15] and the subsequent British decision to send General Kitchener with an Egyptian force to occupy the Sudan, with the resultant Anglo-French crisis over Fashoda (1898),[16] have been discussed. British imperialism triumphed, and in March, 1899, France agreed to withdraw. Great Britain then arranged with Egypt that the Sudan should be an Anglo-Egyptian condominium under the joint sovereignty of the two countries. In reality, however, the governor-general and most of the important officials were British army officers, and in the eyes of British imperialists the Sudan was British.

The way was now open for a British Cape to Cairo project, for in 1894 King Leopold, as sovereign of the Congo Free State, had made a bargain with Great Britain, by the terms of which the latter received a perpetual lease of a narrow strip of territory extending from Lake Tanganyika to Uganda. Since northern Rhodesia touched the southern shores of Lake Tanganyika, this corridor between the Congo Free State on the west and German East Africa on the east opened the way for the British to establish a

international bargains. One of the most famous of these was that with Germany in 1890. Great Britain recognized that German East Africa extended westward to the confines of the Congo Free State, and ceded to Germany (1) the island of Helgoland in the North Sea, (2) a long narrow strip of territory to connect German Southwest Africa with the Zambesi River, and (3) territory to extend German Kamerun north to the shores of Lake Chad. In return, Germany relinquished all claim to Uganda, Nyasaland, the islands of Zanzibar and Pemba off the east coast of Africa, and some disputed territory on the border of German Togoland. For the location of the territories mentioned in this paragraph, see the map on page 21.

[15] See pages 154–155.
[16] For the Fashoda affair, see page 128.

system of land and water communication under their control from Cape Colony to the Mediterranean.

By this time Great Britain had become involved in a struggle with the Boers of South Africa. Friction had been developing for some time. In the eighties British imperialists—notably Cecil Rhodes, who had come to South Africa in 1870 and had there become a dominant economic figure—had brought vast regions in Bechuanaland and Rhodesia under British control and had thus succeeded in hemming in the two Boer republics. When the Boers then sought to secure a corridor to the Indian Ocean through Tongaland, their plans had been blocked by British annexation of the latter in 1894. The only other non-British port which might be of use to the Boers was in Mozambique on Delagoa Bay. The Boers had vainly tried to secure control of this bay in 1891 and in 1893, and the British suspected that in their attempts they had had the sympathy and support of Germany. This seemed to be borne out in 1894 when a native insurrection in the vicinity of the bay led to the landing of British troops to protect British nationals. This step was immediately followed by a protest from the German government and by the arrival of two German warships. Germany's apparent interest in the Boers disturbed Great Britain, which went so far as to warn Germany about interfering in that part of Africa. Although a few months later Germany was further warned against "coquetting" with the Transvaal, German warships took a prominent part in the formal opening of the Delagoa Bay Railway in June, 1895.

The Boers, naturally antagonized by British aggressiveness in South Africa, were also irritated by the great influx of foreign miners, promoters, and adventurers—largely British—which had followed the discovery of gold in the Transvaal about 1886. The Boers became alarmed lest they should be overwhelmed in their own state by the thousands of prospectors, laborers, and others who were rushing into the Transvaal, and ultimately sought to retain political control in their own hands by restricting the privileges of citizenship. The Uitlanders (Outlanders), as they were called by the Boers, were in turn angered by this discrimination and by the fact that their enterprises were handicapped by laws of the republic imposing tariff duties, establishing dynamite and railway monopolies, and preventing importation of cheap labor. Friction between the Uitlanders and the Boers soon developed.

Eventually some of the British gold-producers and business men in the Transvaal conspired with Cecil Rhodes, then prime minister of Cape Colony, to overthrow the Boer government. A revolution was to be precipitated in Johannesburg, and then an armed force was to invade the republic. Unfortunately for Rhodes's plans, before all the arrangements had been perfected, Leander Starr Jameson, administrator of Rhodesia, with a force of about six hundred men invaded the Transvaal in December, 1895, only to be surrounded and captured within a few days. The raid proved to be a miserable fiasco, and was denounced and repudiated by the British government. Rhodes was compelled to resign the premiership (1896) and was later condemned and censured by the British Parliament. His political influence was largely ended, and in 1902 he died.[17]

The Jameson raid put a strain upon Anglo-German as well as upon Anglo-Boer relations. Before the outcome of the venture was known, the British ambassador at Berlin was informed that Germany must insist on the independence of the Transvaal, and the German ambassador at London was instructed to inquire whether the British government approved the raid. If it did, he was to demand his passports. The Kaiser desired that marines should be landed at Delagoa Bay in case of trouble in the Transvaal, but, before this could be done, the Boer government had asked that the landing of German forces be deferred pending negotiations with the British. The Kaiser apparently still harbored visions of an alliance with the Transvaal against the British with a possible protectorate over the Boer republic as the goal. The German chancellor and foreign minister, however, devoted all their efforts to dissuading the Kaiser from landing troops or seeking a protectorate and in the end were successful. As a sop to the Kaiser, he was permitted to send a telegram to President Kruger of the Transvaal expressing his "congratulations that you and your people, without appealing to the help of friendly powers, have succeeded . . . in restoring peace and in maintaining the independence of the country against attacks from without." The Kruger telegram was looked

---

[17] Rhodes left most of his huge fortune to endow scholarships at Oxford University for students from the British colonies and from the United States and Germany.

upon in Great Britain not only as "unfriendly" but as an "ingeniously worded insult," "a deliberate affront" to the British, "a piece of gratuitous insolence." It obviously helped to turn British public sentiment against the German Empire. The telegram has been characterized as "one of the greatest blunders in the history of modern diplomacy."

The Jameson raid also operated to hasten the Anglo-Boer struggle for supremacy in South Africa. The Boers thereafter were convinced that there was a plot to deprive them of their country and that the British were only awaiting a pretext for war. President Kruger accordingly became increasingly anti-British, made an alliance with the Orange Free State, and strongly encouraged the Afrikander Bond, a Boer organization in Cape Colony which sought a union of the European races of South Africa on the basis of South African nationality and independence. On the other hand, British mining interests in the Transvaal remained dissatisfied with their position and sought British intervention in their behalf. Although fundamentally their grievance was economic,[18] the British in the Transvaal emphasized their political disabilities, complaining that the Boers insisted upon a residence requirement of fourteen years for the franchise.

In the early summer of 1899 a conference was held between President Kruger and Sir Alfred Milner, the imperialistic British high commissioner of Cape Colony, in the course of which the former offered to reduce the franchise requirement from fourteen years to seven. Milner demanded that it be made five years. In August the Boers next offered a five-year franchise plan, with the proviso that Great Britain should drop her claim to suzerainty, cease interfering in the domestic affairs of the Transvaal, and agree to refer minor questions in dispute to arbitration. If Milner had been sincerely desirous of reaching an agreement, this proposal might have been used as a basis for further discussion. But Milner believed that Great Britain should remain firm. "They [the Boers] will collapse if we don't weaken, or rather if we go on steadily turning the screw," he informed Chamberlain, the British colonial

[18] British capitalists hoped, if they got control of the Transvaal government, to save £2,500,000 annually by securing an unrestricted labor supply with resulting lower wages.

secretary. The latter, therefore, in his reply to the Boer proposal accepted it *without* the proviso; in other words, from the Boer viewpoint he rejected it.

Apparently by the beginning of September, 1899, Chamberlain had decided upon war, and the subsequent negotiations were merely drawn out in order to give the British time to get troops to South Africa. He accordingly demanded the five-year franchise without conditions, but this demand Kruger rejected. The Boer government, after having asked for further British proposals and having been put off, concluded that the continuation of negotiations would be useless. Apparently hoping for victory with the possible help of Germany and other powers, Kruger in October demanded that all controversies be arbitrated and that British military preparations in South Africa be stopped. Great Britain refused to discuss this ultimatum, and on October 11, 1899, war began. In the ensuing struggle the Orange Free State made common cause with the Transvaal against the British.

In the Boer War (1899–1902) the British were forced to put into the field a greater number of troops than had ever before been used by Great Britain in a foreign war. Although the Boers never had more than 40,000 soldiers under arms at one time, the British eventually concentrated in South Africa a force of some 350,000 men—largely volunteers from Great Britain, Canada, Australia, and New Zealand. But the Boers were well acquainted with the vast territory in which they fought, they were accustomed to the use of firearms, they were led by resourceful commanders, and they fought with a courage that was indomitable. When eventually Lord Roberts with an overwhelming force succeeded in defeating the organized Boer armies and in capturing the capitals of the two Boer republics, the Boer soldiers resorted to guerrilla warfare. The British had to summon Lord Kitchener from Egypt and then had to resort to systematic "drives" and concentration camps to pacify the Boer country in small sections at a time.

Eventually the greater resources and man power of the British turned the scales, and in May, 1902, the Boers signed the treaty of Vereeniging accepting British sovereignty. In return for this acknowledgment, however, Great Britain promised to permit the use of the Dutch language in schools and courts, to grant self-government to the former republics at the earliest possible opportunity, and to pay £3,000,000 to the Boers in compensation for their destroyed farms. The Boer War brought an extensive and economically rich region into the British Empire, but the price was exceedingly high. The struggle had cost Great Britain 30,000 lives and £250,000,000.

### INCREASING TRADE RIVALRY AND BRITISH POLICY

It was hardly to be expected that Great Britain could maintain indefinitely the dominant industrial and commercial position which she held as the "workshop of the world" in the first three quarters of the nineteenth century. Attention has already been called to the great expansion and acceleration in industry which occurred in various countries in the years after 1870.[19] To this development Great Britain had directly contributed, in fact, by exporting between 1848 and 1877 capital goods—machinery and the like—valued at more than £800,000,000. Though Great Britain for a time had profited heavily by thus selling "the sinews of the Industrial Revolution" abroad, obviously her former monopoly of the new mechanical methods of production was thereby destroyed. In the end the new industries which arose in Europe and America seriously challenged Great Britain's own production.[20]

The realization of this fact first burst upon the British during the economic depression which engulfed the world in the later seventies. Exports from Great Britain fell alarmingly, while consular reports called attention to the inroads being made in foreign markets by French, Belgian, and German manufactured goods. This competition was in no sense the cause of Britain's existing economic depression, but the depression hastened her discovery of the increasing trade rivalry abroad. Though the British were somewhat disturbed by this new competition and by the rising tide of tariff protectionism in Europe and America, they were confident that their own colonies and the "half-civilized countries" of the world would provide them with markets for the continued expansion of their trade.

But the next great depression (1884–1888) shook British confidence. The reports of foreign trade rivalry of the seventies were

[19] See pages 3–8.
[20] Much of the discussion in this section of the chapter is based on R. J. S. Hoffman's study, *Great Britain and the German Trade Rivalry, 1875–1914*.

given grim substantiation in the eighties when the products of French, Belgian, German, American, and other national industries rapidly penetrated into markets formerly controlled by the British. Europe herself was fast shaking off her dependence on Great Britain for both capital and consumption goods. Outside Europe the trade rivalry of other countries was less keen, but it was growing rapidly because of the relative decline in the effectiveness of British methods and equipment for withstanding it.

The manufacturers and merchants of Great Britain tended to cling to methods which often were old-fashioned and obsolete in contrast with those used by their competitors in the newer industrial countries. Technical and commercial education was being stressed in Europe, frequently with resultant reductions in the cost of manufacturing. Knowledge of foreign languages, careful study of markets, and superior ability to exploit them successfully were powerful aids to the expansion of German, French, and Belgian commerce. In the eighties, indeed, foreign manufacturers began to compete with the British even within the United Kingdom. "Our former customers," lamented a Sheffield industrialist, "have become our competitors, and not only sell against us, but undersell us, not merely in neutral markets, but under our very noses at home."

In the eighties, too, Great Britain began to lose some of her valuable *entrepôt* trade. One reason for this decline was the increasing use of the Suez Canal. "The Commercial Revolution was reversed. The Canal did to nineteenth-century England what Vasco da Gama's voyage did to sixteenth-century Italy: it cut much of the ground from under the position of the British middleman. Trieste, Venice, Genoa, Marseilles, Odessa, and other south European ports were enabled to increase greatly their direct trade with distant lands, and instead of buying Asiatic goods in the British market they imported more and more directly from the places of origin." [21] Furthermore, as already pointed out, the world was being knit together by telegraphic communication, so that the need of laying up great supplies of Eastern goods in warehouses in Great Britain was lessened. The British were ceasing to be the great distributors and warehousemen of the world. Between 1872 and 1886, for example, Great Britain's *entrepôt* trade in raw silk declined by more than 80 per cent.

[21] Hoffman, *op. cit.*, pages 70–71.

Eventually the British awoke to the fact that their most formidable competitors in the struggle for markets were the Germans. In every quarter of the globe the latter were extending their commercial activity with steady and successful persistence. Ever keener competition, resulting in part from the rising tide of protectionism, operated to throw British and German business men against each other in various parts of the world. The press in Great Britain repeatedly cited evidences of German gains, while British commerce languished; by 1896 Germany had been singled out in the popular mind as Britain's most dangerous trade rival.

In January of that year the report of a British commission disclosed that Britain's leadership in the supply of iron and steel was passing, and it explained the advantages which the German industry had over their own. This report, coming almost simultaneously with the Kaiser's telegram to President Kruger, caused great excitement, which was increased by a book, *Made in Germany,* published in the same year. The British were severely shaken by the author's statement that "the industrial glory of England is departing and England does not know it." Germany, he warned, had entered into a deliberate and deadly rivalry with Great Britain and was battling with might and main for the extinction of the latter's supremacy. It is evident, he declared, "that on all hands England's industrial supremacy is tottering to its fall and that this result is largely German work." Perhaps it is not surprising that during the summer of 1896 the British passed through a period of hysteria over the threat of German trade rivalry. By the end of the year the alarm had largely subsided, but feeling was still so strong in 1897 that the writer of an article in a well-known weekly declared: "If Germany were extinguished tomorrow, the day after tomorrow there is not an Englishman in the world who would not be the richer."

Although in the succeeding years there was no outburst of public alarm over German trade comparable to that of 1896, nevertheless, the British steadily grew more and more acutely aware of the relentless commercial struggle with Germany. Occasionally certain definite matters served to focus attention upon the economic antagonism. Between 1899 and 1902, for instance, news of German shipping subsidies and of the German absorption of several British steamship lines caused a shipping scare and grave concern over the possible destruction of Britain's hitherto lucrative maritime carrying trade.

Chamberlain believed that one way to meet the increasing trade rivalry which Great Britain was encountering was to bind the British colonies more closely with the mother country and to link the self-governing dominions with the United Kingdom by means of a system of "imperial preference." According to his plan the dominions should reduce their tariff rates on goods coming from Great Britain, while retaining higher rates for goods from outside the empire. Such a scheme would, of course, operate to the advantage of British manufacturers and merchants. In 1897 Chamberlain utilized the occasion of Queen Victoria's second jubilee to convoke another colonial conference of the governors of the dominions in the hope that something might be done about imperial preference. Although Canada adopted a measure embodying this principle, the movement as a whole made relatively little headway. The dominions saw little to be gained for themselves by opening their doors to United Kingdom goods as long as Great Britain gave their export products—chiefly raw materials—no preference in her markets over goods from outside the empire. Imperial preference seemed logically to demand the adoption by Great Britain of some scheme of protective tariffs.

In 1903, when Germany passed Great Britain in the production of iron, thus relegating the latter to third place in world production of this commodity, Chamberlain moved on to the second point in his program and demanded a protective tariff for the United Kingdom. Under his auspices the Tariff Reform League was organized to carry on propaganda to educate the public in the need for a change in Britain's free-trade policy. Naturally the free-traders rallied their forces, and the country was subjected to a vigorous debate in the press and on the platform regarding the respective merits of the two policies. Although Balfour finally accepted the principle of protection, the Conservatives split on the issue because the prime minister declined to recommend the laws which Chamberlain demanded. The latter thereupon resigned from the cabinet but devoted his energy to the task of converting the Conservative Party to his program. Inevitably the tariff question played an important part in the next parliamentary election and contributed to the defeat which the Conservatives sustained at that time.

## THE ABANDONMENT OF "SPLENDID ISOLATION"

Although Great Britain was slow to abandon her venerated policy of free trade, world affairs did convince her that she must modify the basis of her foreign policy. During most of the latter half of the nineteenth century she had followed the policy of playing a lone hand in international affairs. Upon occasion, to be sure, she had co-operated with other powers to achieve a common end—when that end was consonant with the advancement of her own colonial and maritime interests. In the fifties, for instance, she had joined with France in the Crimean War to prevent Russian ascendancy in Turkey.[22] Again, in 1878, she had united with Austria-Hungary to force the tsar to submit the Balkan situation to the Congress of Berlin after Russia's decisive defeat of the sultan in that year.[23] And in 1887 she had entered into an agreement with Austria-Hungary and Italy to maintain the *status quo* in the Mediterranean and Black Seas.[24] On each of these occasions, which appear to mark departures from Britain's policy of isolation, the agreements had been designed to safeguard or advance the interests of the British Empire. So far as continental complications were concerned, Great Britain had steadfastly adhered to her policy of no entanglements. When in the eighties Bismarck had pressed her to enter into an alliance with Germany, she had firmly declined to become involved.[25]

By 1898, however, the international situation overseas had become so complicated that the British government began to question the wisdom of longer pursuing the policy of "splendid isolation." Germany and Russia were pushing into northern China,[26] threatening Chinese territorial integrity. France was pushing eastward in the Sudan,[27] apparently aiming to secure control of the region of the upper Nile. Friction was increasing in South Africa between the Boers and British imperialists, with the Boers receiving obvious encouragement from Germany.[28] The latter, in turn, was seeking for her own purposes to capitalize British embarrassment by pushing colonial claims in Africa and the South Seas. If Great Britain could have dealt with Russia, France, and Germany singly and at different times, the situation would not have been so alarming to

[22] See page 233.  [23] See page 252.  [24] See page 154.  [25] See page 75.
[26] See pages 79 and 264.  [27] See page 128.  [28] See page 189.

the British, but in 1898 it appeared that in a sense all three were closing in upon her and that she stood without a friend, isolated among the great powers.

For some time there had been growing in Great Britain the feeling that the kingdom must abandon its isolation and seek positive support among the other great powers. As early as 1896 one influential journal had declared: "We frankly can go no further alone, in the face of the obstacles which it is now within the power of Germany, Russia, and France to pile up in our path." Some declared that the cornerstone of British policy should be an agreement with Russia, and in 1898—when Russia was pushing into South Manchuria—Great Britain sought to reach an understanding with the tsarist government. She proposed a definition of Russian and British spheres of preponderance in both China and Turkey, but on condition that existing rights should not be altered, existing treaties violated, or the integrity of China or Turkey impaired. The British proposal was, of course, a thinly disguised move to commit Russia to a program which the latter had no intention of adopting. According to Tsar Nicholas, it merely revealed to Russia that Great Britain sought the former's friendship in order to block Russian advances in the Far East. Since the tsar's government was determined to operate with a free hand in China, nothing tangible in the way of an agreement resulted.

But Great Britain was equally determined to stop, if possible, any further Russian encroachments upon China, and next sought to secure an agreement to that end with Germany. Chamberlain, who was thoroughly convinced that Britain's isolation had become dangerous, opened negotiations in 1898 by proposing to Germany an Anglo-German alliance. The German government was at once interested, but, when it learned that the purpose of such an alliance would be to check Russia's advance beyond Manchuria, its interest perceptibly declined. Apparently what Chamberlain suggested was that China should be divided into British, German, and Russian spheres of predominance. The British sphere (in South China) would be the largest, most populous, and farthest removed from the Russian; the German sphere would serve as a buffer between the British and the Russians. But Germany had no intention of being used as a cat's-paw to protect British interests in the Far East. Furthermore, she was very willing to have Russia become involved in China; she had, indeed, deliberately encouraged Russia to take steps leading in that direction.

What the Germans on their part wanted was an alliance with Great Britain which would leave France isolated and would give a guarantee of reinsurance against Russia. But the British were not interested in any agreement having to do with Europe. Without such an alliance, however, the Germans were opposed to an Anglo-German treaty as outlined by Great Britain, for its very submission to the British Parliament—even though rejected—would increase the hostility of Russia and France toward Germany. The Germans believed, furthermore, that such an alliance with Great Britain would shift to the German frontier much of the pressure that Russia was then exerting on China. This to the Germans was altogether undesirable. Germany, therefore, concluded that she might better wait until Great Britain was still harder pressed before entering into any British alliance. Undoubtedly, future developments would make Great Britain's abandonment of isolation even more imperative, and, when the British need of an alliance became more pressing, perhaps Germany could secure better terms. Germany was little disturbed by Chamberlain's threat that, if Germany rejected Great Britain's offer, the latter might find it necessary to make separate agreements with France and Russia. .

Nevertheless, Great Britain did not wholly despair of a German alliance, and in 1899 the possibilities were again explored by Chamberlain and Bülow. When the latter appeared favorable, Chamberlain in a famous speech at Leicester went so far as to broach the subject publicly—only to have Bülow in a subsequent speech in the Reichstag apparently turn his back on the suggestion. Again in 1901 formal negotiations for an alliance were actually begun. Germany then insisted that Great Britain must join the Triple Alliance in order to afford Germany protection against Russia, but this Great Britain refused to do. According to Salisbury, the liability of having to defend the German and Austrian frontiers against Russia was too heavy in proportion to the benefit which Great Britain might derive from such an alliance. So once more the negotiations came to naught.

Meanwhile Japan, too, had become alarmed by Russia's advance into South Manchuria.[29] In 1901 Japan tried through diplomacy

[29] See page 265.

at both St. Petersburg and London to see what she could obtain to protect her interests in the Far East. At London the advances of the Japanese ambassador were cordially received, for Great Britain feared the conclusion of an agreement between Russia and Japan which might make the British position in the Far East almost hopeless. Largely to prevent such a Russo-Japanese understanding, it appears, Great Britain signed a treaty of alliance with Japan on January 30, 1902.

By the terms of the agreement the two powers recognized the independence of China and Korea and declared that they were not motivated in their agreement by aggressive tendencies. They recognized, however, that each had special interests—Great Britain in China, Japan in both China and Korea—which it would be admissible for either to safeguard if threatened by the aggressive action of any other power or by disturbances in China or Korea. If either party, in defense of its interests as defined, became involved in a war with a third power, the other party was to remain neutral; but, if the enemy were actively supported by another power, the other party was to join its ally and make war in common. In other words, should Great Britain go to war with Russia over her interests in China, Japan would stay neutral. But if Russia should be joined by France or Germany, Japan would come to the aid of Great Britain. The alliance was to last for five years, or longer unless denounced one year in advance by either party.

The Anglo-Japanese alliance constituted a landmark in British foreign policy, for it marked the abandonment of Great Britain's principle of isolation. But the Anglo-Japanese alliance was only the first step in Great Britain's new foreign policy. The next came in 1904 when she and France adjusted their various colonial difficulties in different parts of the world. Probably Britain's chief gain by these agreements was the relinquishment by France of her rights and interests in Egypt in favor of Great Britain, and the declaration by France that she would afford Great Britain her diplomatic support in case the British position in Egypt was challenged. The Entente Cordiale which resulted from these friendly agreements augured well for the future co-operation of Great Britain and France in case Germany should attempt, as in preceding years, to play one of them off against the other in order to secure something for herself.

## THE REJECTION OF THE CONSERVATIVES

During the opening years of the twentieth century the Conservatives steadily declined in popularity. Although at the outset the Boer War had the general support of the British people, before it was won a revulsion had set in against such imperialistic ventures and against those responsible for them. Conservatives were not only blamed for getting the kingdom into difficulties; they were also accused of incompetency in the waging of the conflict which resulted from their aggressiveness. At home the Education Act of 1902 by its favor to the Anglicans had alienated many dissenters, and the Taff Vale decision of the Conservative House of Lords (1901) had antagonized labor. This decision maintained that trade unions could be held responsible for financial losses suffered by employers as a result of strikes, and that trade-union funds could be attached for payment of such damages. On top of all this, Chamberlain's advocacy of a protective tariff for the kingdom was out of accord with the views of most Englishmen, the issue even causing dissension within the Conservative Party itself. After the Conservatives had lost steadily in by-elections during 1904 and 1905, Balfour in December of the latter year resigned the premiership.

Sir Henry Campbell-Bannerman then formed a ministry of Liberals and dissolved Parliament. The Liberals appealed to the country with a platform which called for the maintenance of free trade, the alteration of the Education Act of 1902 in the interest of the dissenters, the enactment of a law to modify the Taff Vale decision, more stringent national regulation of the liquor traffic, extensive legislation for social and industrial betterment, and reconciliation with the Boers of South Africa. In the ensuing election (January, 1906) the Liberal Party won a decisive victory, securing a comfortable majority over all the other parties combined. Counting the Irish Nationalist and Labor Parties as anti-Conservative, Balfour's government was repudiated by a parliamentary ratio of approximately 500 to 157.

One of the significant results of this election was the winning of twenty-nine parliamentary seats by the recently organized Labor Party. Workingmen had occasionally been returned to Parliament during the preceding generation, but they had been elected as candidates of the Liberal Party. Although in 1893 the Independent

Labor Party had been founded to put forward candidates pledged to a socialistic program, its platform had been too radical to attract many workingmen, and in 1900 it had won only one seat. After the Taff Vale decision, however, representatives of the trade unions and of a number of socialist societies determined to take more effective steps politically to safeguard the interests of the workers, and so they had organized the Labor Party. Its success in the election of January, 1906, was the first of a series which in the course of the succeeding generation made the Labor Party one of the two major political parties of the kingdom.[30]

## REFORM UNDER THE LIBERALS

The ministry which Campbell-Bannerman had organized in December, 1905, had been one of exceptional talent, reflecting the various shades of Liberal opinion and including for the first time in British history a representative of labor. The prime minister himself had entered Parliament in 1868 and thirty years later had been chosen leader of the Liberal Party. He had never shown the outstanding ability of Gladstone, but he typified the nineteenth-century liberalism of that great leader. The older group of Liberals was represented by a few other members, also. Prominent among them was John Morley, a well-known editor and author, who had only recently published his monumental life of Gladstone. Morley had entered Parliament in 1883 and had served in Gladstone's ministry three years later. Another was James Bryce, a lawyer, professor, and scholarly writer on historical and political subjects, who had entered Parliament in 1880 and had been a member of Gladstone's cabinet in 1892.

Destined to be more important in British history and in the development of the Liberal Party were several younger men in the ministry, the leader of whom was Herbert H. Asquith, a distinguished lawyer, nonconformist, and free-trader, who had entered Parliament in 1886 and had been a member of Gladstone's ministry in 1892. Since Campbell-Bannerman, the titular head of the party, was in feeble health, Asquith was the virtual leader of the Liberals. When in April, 1908, ill health forced the former to retire from public life, he was succeeded as prime minister by Asquith, who continued to serve in that capacity until the World War. Associated

[30] See pages 697–698.

with him as representatives of the younger group were Richard Haldane, Sir Edward Grey, John Burns, Winston Churchill, and David Lloyd George.

Richard Haldane, a Scottish lawyer, statesman, and philosophical writer, who had entered Parliament in 1885, became secretary for war. Sir Edward Grey, scion of a famous family of Whigs, a Liberal member of Parliament during the preceding two decades, assumed the portfolio for foreign affairs. John Burns, who had entered Parliament in 1892, was a famous labor leader in London who had frequently clashed with the government in his efforts to defend the rights of the workers. He became president of the Local Government Board. Winston Churchill was the youngest member of the group. He had had a rather adventurous career in his twenties, having served as a soldier or war correspondent in various parts of the world. At the age of twenty-nine he had entered Parliament as a Conservative (1900), but had opposed Chamberlain's tariff policy and had soon withdrawn from that party. Churchill held various positions in the new ministry, eventually becoming (1911) first lord of the admiralty.

The one who was to become the most influential figure in the Liberal Party was David Lloyd George, a Welshman, the son of a humble schoolmaster who had died when David was a young boy. Denied the advantages of a university education, Lloyd George had studied law and had become a lawyer. He was an outspoken Welsh nationalist, and in 1890 he had been elected to Parliament to represent the "common people." In general he was bitterly opposed to the landed aristocracy, to Chamberlain's imperialism and protectionism, and to the privileged position of the Anglican Church. A brilliant and courageous speaker, during the Boer War he had not hesitated to denounce the government for its aggression against the Boers. At that time he had been extremely unpopular throughout the country, but the reaction against imperialism which came as a result of the war eventually brought him back into favor. Lloyd George was at first president of the Board of Trade, but upon the reorganization of the cabinet in 1908 he assumed the important post of chancellor of the exchequer.

The Liberals at once turned their attention to the situation in South Africa. After 1902 tens of thousands of Chinese coolies had been imported into the Transvaal to provide cheap labor for the mine owners. Further importation of Chinese was stopped by the Liberals. Self-government was granted to the former Boer republics, with the result that the Boers immediately gained control of the governments in the Transvaal and in the Orange River Colony. Moreover, the Boer organization in Cape Colony—the Afrikander Bond—won the elections there also.

With the Boers in political control of three of the four British South African colonies, a movement to unite them all into one union was inaugurated. A federal constitution was drafted by a convention representing the colonies, and in 1909 it was approved as the South Africa Act by the parliament of Great Britain. In the following year the Union of South Africa—a federation consisting of Cape Colony, Natal, the Transvaal, and Orange River Colony—was established. General Louis Botha, who had fought against the British in the Boer War and had later been the prime minister of the Transvaal, at once became prime minister of the Union and served in this capacity until his death in 1919. The Boer leaders ultimately concluded that the interests of their people could best be served by co-operating with the British in South Africa under the effective protection of the British Empire.

Within the United Kingdom a number of important measures were enacted in rapid succession. The Trades Disputes Act (1906) reversed the Taff Vale decision by providing immunity for the funds of trade unions, by legalizing peaceful picketing, and by declaring that what was lawful for an individual was lawful also for a combination. In the same year the Workmen's Compensation Act made employers liable for compensation to all manual laborers and to practically all other employees receiving less than £250 a year. The Old Age Pension Act (1908) provided pensions for all resident British citizens over seventy years of age, provided they had incomes of less than £31½ yearly. The Labor Exchange Act of the same year provided for a nation-wide organization of labor exchanges to assist in bringing employers and unemployed workers together to their mutual benefit.

In 1911 the National Insurance Act, applying only to the building and engineering trades, introduced in an experimental way health and unemployment insurance. Funds for the scheme were to be subscribed partly by the employers, partly by the workers, and partly by the state. In case of sickness the benefits included weekly payments, free medical attendance, and free hospital treatments; in case of unemployment not caused by strikes or lockouts, the benefits included payments for a maximum of fifteen weeks. The unemployment feature of the act was frankly in the nature of an experiment. Attempts to pass bills regarding education, plural voting, and the liquor traffic, though successful in the House of Commons, were blocked by the Conservatives in the House of Lords. Earlier statements that the upper house would have to be "mended or ended" again began to be heard.

These somewhat abstract statements about the need for altering the House of Lords were transformed into positive demands by the Lords' rejection of the budget passed by the Commons in 1909. The budget of that year was no ordinary budget. Added naval expenditures resulting from the armaments race with Germany plus the cost of the recently enacted pension system greatly increased the need for revenues. The Conservatives asserted that the taxable resources of the kingdom were already overburdened and advocated tariffs as the only new way to expand the national revenues. Their arguments had no appeal for Lloyd George, however.

The chancellor of the exchequer was determined to use his budget not merely to provide added revenues for the state but to improve the social conditions of the kingdom. For one thing, he desired to shift the burden of taxation "from the producers to the possessors of wealth." Although Great Britain in proportion to size was probably the wealthiest country in the world, her wealth was concentrated in the hands of a relatively few. Half of the national income, it was estimated, went to 12 per cent of the people. According to Salvation Army estimates, 3 per cent of the British people were rich, 9 per cent were comfortably well off, and 88 per cent were poor. Millions were found to be living constantly on the verge of starvation. Lloyd George sought to use taxation to help change these conditions. He therefore drafted what he called a "war budget," that is, one which was designed "to wage war against poverty" in Great Britain. To strike at the wealthy his budget called for (1) increased income and inheritance taxes, (2) supertaxes on the larger incomes, and (3) higher tax rates on unearned incomes.

But Lloyd George desired particularly to use the budget as a weapon against the landed aristocracy and large landed proprietors. Great Britain was not, like France, a country of petty peasant proprietors. In England and Wales the number of persons holding more than one acre of land constituted less than ⅗ of 1 per cent of the total population. Twenty-seven lords, it was asserted, owned one tenth of England, and almost half of all the cultivated land of the country belonged to some 2250 landed aristocrats. In Scotland, according to estimates, approximately 90 per cent of the land was the property of some 1700 persons. But the concentration of land-ownership was not the only evil in the agrarian situation. The land was being used less and less for agricultural or grazing purposes and was being converted more and more to unproductive use in the form of lawns, gardens, hunting preserves, and the like.

One reason for this change was that agriculture in Great Britain was not in the twentieth century so profitable as it had been before 1870. The greatly decreased costs of transportation and the introduction of refrigeration on railways and steamships had adversely affected it. Distant parts of the world were able to sell their grains, meats, and dairy products in Britain at prices lower than were profitable to British farmers—largely tenants who were obliged to pay relatively high rents and were unable to use the more modern and large-scale methods of the newer lands. Since free-trade Britain did not give farmers the aid of protective tariffs to help meet this competition, as did Germany, France, and other countries, many of them were forced to give up the struggle. In the years just before the World War Great Britain was producing only one fifth of the food consumed by her people.

Lloyd George's budget was in part designed to help alter the land and agricultural situation in the kingdom by the imposition of certain types of taxes. Obviously, the proposed taxes discussed above might force some landowners to sell parts of their great holdings in order to pay the levies and thus lead gradually to a breaking up of the large estates. In addition, however, the budget called for (4) heavy taxes on unearned increments of land values, that is, on increases in the value of land not the result of improvements made by the owner, (5) new taxes on undeveloped idle land (formerly not taxed), particularly on game preserves, in the hope of forcing more land back under cultivation, and (6) a special tax of 5 per cent on income derived by landowners from the companies that operated mines on their properties. Although the budget included various other items of revenue, these were the chief innovations.

As might have been expected, the possessing classes at once attacked Lloyd George's finance bill on the ground that it was unfair and that it struck at the security of property. For nearly six months the measure was hotly debated in Parliament, in the press, and on the platform. Early in November it was passed by the House of Commons, but before the month was out it had been decisively rejected by the Lords. Though the latter had never formally surrendered their right to veto a budget, they had long ceased to use that right, and Prime Minister Asquith at once denounced their action as a "wanton breach of the settled practice of the Constitution."

Parliament was dissolved to ascertain the will of the voters, and the Liberals campaigned on a platform calling for the enactment of the budget, the abolition of the veto power of the Lords, and the granting of home rule for Ireland. These last two proposals were made largely to hold the support of the Irish Nationalists, who were determined to weaken the House of Lords so that a home-rule measure could be enacted. In the election of January, 1910, the Liberals lost more than a hundred seats to the Conservatives, but, since they received the support of the Irish Nationalists and the Laborites, they were enabled to continue in office. The budget was then reintroduced, and this time it was passed by the House of Lords.

With the budget safely out of the way, the Liberals next undertook to carry out their pledges to the Irish Nationalists. The Parliament Bill was introduced with three major provisions. (1) The right of the Lords to veto any money bill was abolished; any bill declared a money bill by the speaker of the Commons would become a law one month after it was submitted to the Lords, regardless of their failure to enact it. (2) Any measure not a money bill, if passed in the Commons in three successive sessions, would become a law, in spite of the veto of the Lords, provided that two years had elapsed since its first introduction. (3) The maximum life of Parliament was to be reduced from seven to five years. The House of Lords refused to accept these proposals, so again Parliament was dissolved, and for the second time in 1910 a general election was held.

Practically no change in the relative number of seats in Parliament resulted from the second election. The Liberals lost two seats, but their allies in the Commons gained four. So long as the Irish Nationalists and the Laborites supported them, therefore, the Liberal ministry was safe. Again Asquith introduced his Parliament Bill. The Lords amended the measure, but, when Asquith refused to accept the amendments and announced that the king was ready to create enough new peers to carry the measure through the Lords, the latter finally gave way and enacted the bill as passed by the Commons. The House of Lords thus ceased to be a co-ordinate part of the legislature, for it could no longer control the budget and at most could only delay for two years other legislation desired by the Commons. The Parliament Act constituted, therefore, a political revolution against the aristocracy.

The Liberal government next proceeded to reward its political allies of 1910–1911. Up to that time membership in Parliament had carried no remuneration, and therefore a workingman dependent upon his wages alone could hardly afford to accept a seat. To meet this situation the various labor unions had paid union wages to those of their members who were elected to Parliament. In 1909 the Conservative House of Lords, in what was known as the Osborne judgment, had held that it was illegal for trade unions to use money raised by the compulsory contributions of their members to pay salaries to men representing the workers in Parliament. Obviously this decision struck a severe blow at the Labor Party. To overcome the handicap under which the Labor members operated, Parliament in 1911 enacted a law providing that members of the House of Commons should receive salaries of £400 a year. Two years later another Trade Union Act empowered the unions to use their funds for political purposes if so authorized by a general ballot of their members. The labor unions were thus strengthened in their efforts to build up an adequate representation of the British workers in Parliament.

The Parliament Act of 1911 opened the way for Lloyd George to carry through his cherished plan for the disestablishment of the Anglican Church in Wales, where most of the population consisted of dissenters. In 1912 the House of Commons passed a bill separating church and state in Wales, disendowing the church of much of its property, and depriving the Anglican bishops in Wales of their seats in the House of Lords. The Lords refused to pass the measure, but, since they now had only a suspensive veto, the bill became a law in 1914. Although, because of disturbed conditions during the

World War, the act was temporarily suspended, it eventually became effective at the close of the war.

### THE IRISH HOME-RULE CRISIS, 1912–1914

The Liberals were indebted to the Irish Nationalists for support in the crisis of 1910–1911 and were committed to the introduction of a third Home Rule Bill. In April, 1912, a bill providing for an Irish parliament but not for complete autonomy was introduced in the Commons, where it was passed in January, 1913, only to be immediately rejected by the House of Lords. Again it was passed by the Commons, and again it was rejected by the Lords. Under the provisions of the Parliament Act of 1911 it appeared, however, that nothing could prevent the eventual enactment of the law in 1914 if the Commons again passed it.

But by this time the prospect of home rule for Ireland had caused a furor in that island. The Protestant Ulsterites of northeastern Ireland, largely descendants of English and Scottish settlers, opposed home rule and were determined to do everything in their power to prevent it. In their stand they were actuated to some extent by deep-seated emotions. Conflicts dating from the days of the Reformation had bred in the Protestants of Ulster a profound hatred and fear of the Catholic Irish. In view of the treatment which had earlier been meted out to the Irish Catholics when the Protestants had been in the ascendancy, the latter now dreaded possible reprisals at the hands of an Irish parliament dominated by Catholics. There was, too, an economic fear. Ulster, the industrial section of Ireland, was the wealthier and more progressive part of the island. The industrialists of that region were apprehensive lest an Irish parliament, controlled by representatives from the more backward agricultural parts of Ireland, might contrive to shift the burden of taxes to industrial Ulster or might otherwise enact legislation harmful to the economic life of that region. Racial antipathy, religious hatred, and economic fear thus led the Ulsterites to oppose home rule and to demand instead that Ireland should remain part of the United Kingdom.

Sir Edward Carson, leader of the Ulsterites,[31] believed that the Liberal government might be frightened into dropping the home-

---

[31] Carson was not an Ulsterite. In Parliament he represented the University of Dublin —an Episcopalian institution.

rule project if Ulster showed its determination not to submit. "We will stop at nothing," he declared, "if an attempt is to be made to hand the Loyalists of Ireland over to those whom we believe to be the enemies of our country." In Ulster great mass meetings and demonstrations were held; a volunteer army of 100,000 was organized; and over 237,000 Unionist men bound themselves by a "solemn covenant" never to submit to an Irish parliament. In his decision to organize demonstrations among the Protestants of Ulster, Carson was supported by the leaders of the Conservative Party, who not only favored the maintenance of the United Kingdom but hoped to embarrass the Liberals and possibly put a stop to their "socialistic" legislation by driving them from power.

Carson believed that any government would ponder long before it dared "to shoot a loyal Ulster Protestant devoted to his country and loyal to his King." Asquith did ponder long, and eventually he sought to find some compromise which might be acceptable to both the Unionists and the Irish Nationalists. But as soon as the Liberals began to waver, the Irish Nationalists, led by John Redmond, in turn started to raise a force of "Irish volunteers" to support their demand for the granting of home rule to the whole island. Civil war appeared to threaten in Ireland if the Home Rule Bill should actually be passed. The situation for the Liberal government was made still more difficult and perplexing when several high officers of the British army which was destined for service in Ireland resigned their commissions rather than fight against the Unionists of Ulster.

Nevertheless, despite the threatening situation in Ireland, the Home Rule Bill was passed for the third time by the Commons in May, 1914. In July, with conditions in Ireland growing constantly more menacing, King George [32] went so far as to call a conference at Buckingham Palace of the representatives of the Liberals, Conservatives, Irish Nationalists, and Ulster Unionists. "For months," he said, "we have watched with deep misgivings the course of events in Ireland. The trend has been surely and steadily towards an appeal to force, and today the cry of civil war is on the lips of the most responsible and sober-minded of my people." Despite the

[32] Queen Victoria was succeeded in 1901 by her son, Edward VII, and the latter in turn by his son, George V, in 1910.

king's anxiety, however, no agreement could be reached at the conference, and the crisis continued.

When the World War broke out in August, 1914, the seriousness of the international situation led the various groups involved in the home-rule struggle to reach a compromise agreement. The Irish Nationalists gained their point—the Home Rule Bill was enacted into law in September. But the Ulster Unionists and British Conservatives secured the simultaneous enactment of a law suspending the Home Rule Act for the duration of the war. Actually, therefore, the existing political status of Ireland was left undisturbed, and the settlement of the home-rule problem was merely postponed until a later time. Before that time had arrived, however, the demands of the Irish Nationalists had gradually become so extreme that they were then unwilling to accept a settlement such as that proposed in the Home Rule Act of 1914.[33]

## THE TRIPLE ENTENTE

Meanwhile, in the decade preceding the World War, Great Britain—having abandoned her isolationist policy—had been drawn ever deeper into international understandings and entanglements. During the first Moroccan crisis, precipitated by Germany in part to test or even destroy the Entente Cordiale,[34] France had sought to transform the Entente into an alliance by securing from Great Britain the latter's promise of assistance. The British government, however, desiring to keep its hands free, had declined to accede to the French request. But Sir Edward Grey, the foreign secretary, had gone so far as to authorize the carrying on of military conversations between the general staffs of the two countries, so that, if Great Britain should ever decide to go to the aid of France in time of war, the French and British armies could co-operate effectively. Thereafter, in the words of Winston Churchill, "the relations of the two staffs became increasingly intimate and confidential." The British army was reorganized to prepare it for participation in a European war, and conversations were even inaugurated with the Belgian general staff regarding military aid which Great Britain might extend to Belgium if the latter's neutrality should be violated by Germany.

[33] See pages 713–720.      [34] See pages 131–132.

In 1906 the British government took still another step in its program of adjusting Britain's colonial difficulties with other powers. It has already been pointed out that Great Britain as early as 1898 had sought to reach an understanding with Russia, only to be rebuffed. Other overtures—equally futile—had been made to Russia in 1903 and 1904. But Sir Edward Grey believed that an understanding with Russia was desirable, and in the spring of 1906 negotiations between the British and Russian governments were again inaugurated. By this time circumstances had been so altered as to make Russia more ready to consider an understanding. She had been checked in the Far East by Japan,[35] and was once more casting her eyes on the Near East in search of a possible outlet to the seas.

What Russia now desired was to secure the opening of the Straits at Constantinople to Russian warships. But in the Ottoman Empire by 1906 the ascendancy had passed from Great Britain to Germany. If Russia was to be successful in carrying through her Straits policy, therefore, it appeared that she must smooth away the causes of friction between herself and Great Britain in order to strengthen her position against Germany. She was given to understand that, if Great Britain and Russia could adjust their differences over Tibet, Afghanistan, and Persia, "the effect upon British public opinion would be such as very much to facilitate a discussion of the Straits question if it came up later on."

The negotiations between the two countries dragged on for months, and it was not until August, 1907, that an agreement was finally reached. By it disputes between the two powers were adjusted in the Middle East. Neither was to attempt to seize Tibet, which was recognized as part of the Chinese Empire. Russia further agreed that Afghanistan was outside her sphere of influence. But the most important provision of the settlement had to do with Persia, which was divided into three spheres of influence. It was agreed that northern Persia was a Russian sphere, southeastern Persia a British sphere, and central Persia a neutral zone. Both powers recognized in principle the territorial integrity and political independence of Persia. Russia, furthermore, recognized Great Britain's special position in the Persian Gulf. Great Britain, it is apparent, gained more by the settlement than did Russia.

Although the Anglo-Russian agreements in no way constituted an

[35] For the Russo-Japanese War, see pages 267–269.

alliance and Germany was not mentioned in them, the two signatory powers had established cordial relations between themselves
and were thus free to unite against Germany if their interests were
challenged by her. The Anglo-Russian understanding of 1907, together with the Anglo-French agreements of 1904, constituted what
came to be called the Triple Entente.

Developments in other fields also tended to drive the British into
closer relations with France and Russia. Although Great Britain
shared in the tremendous expansion of world trade which occurred
in the decade before the World War to such an extent that from
1910 to 1913 her export trade yearly reached a new record peak,
German commercial rivalry was nevertheless a powerful factor in
shaping British national policy. It not only provided a source of
fear which alarmists exploited; it also engendered suspicion, jealousy, and alarm. J. Ellis Barker, a distinguished British writer on
Germany's economic life, declared in 1908 that fate "has placed
Great Britain and Germany in the same reciprocal position into
which it put Rome and Carthage two thousand years ago. Germany
wishes to possess that which Great Britain wishes to keep, and it is
difficult to see how, under the circumstances, a collision between the
two countries can be avoided." There seems little doubt that German
trade rivalry bred resentment and fear in Great Britain and that
these in turn caused a dislike of Germany that rose in time to the
level of hatred.

Anti-German sentiment was further fed by Germany's naval laws
of 1906 and 1908 providing for the construction of dreadnoughts.[36]
In Great Britain the Liberal government, upon coming into power,
had abandoned the existing plan of constructing four dreadnoughts
annually and instead had ordered only three in 1907 and two in 1908.
Many Englishmen were thrown into something like a panic by the
fear that Germany might be able successfully to challenge Great
Britain's supremacy on the sea. In 1909 a wave of naval agitation
swept the kingdom, and in response to it the Liberals again presented naval estimates calling for the construction of four dreadnoughts. Although Sir Edward Grey informed Parliament that
Great Britain's relations with Germany were excellent, the Conservatives moved a vote of censure of the government on the ground
that it was neglecting the defense of the empire. Chauvinists raised

[36] See page 89.

the cry, "We want eight, and we won't wait," and in the end the Liberal government was forced to give way and order eight dreadnoughts for 1909.

Meanwhile, in the Bosnian crisis of 1908–1909 Great Britain had given Russia full diplomatic support when the latter demanded that Austria-Hungary's annexation of Bosnia-Herzegovina should be submitted to a conference and that Serbia should be given compensation.[37] Similarly, as already pointed out, she loyally supported France at the time of the second Moroccan crisis in 1911. In the latter year the Anglo-French military conversations, which had been begun in 1906, were completed, and the details of the plan for the British to fight by the side of the French were settled.

In 1912, after the failure of the Haldane mission [38] and the decision of the German government to continue to expand its navy, Great Britain moved still closer to France by entering into a naval understanding with her. Disturbed by Germany's naval program, the British decided to withdraw some of their ships from the Mediterranean so that they might successfully meet any possible challenge of the German navy in the North Sea. In order that the combined forces of Austria-Hungary and Italy might not thereby gain the ascendancy in the Mediterranean, Great Britain induced France to concentrate her whole fleet in that sea.

The French, in turn, sought some promise of protection for their northern coast and persuaded the British government to an exchange of notes on this subject. It was agreed that, if either government had grave reason to expect an unprovoked attack by a third power, it should at once discuss with the other whether both countries should act together to prevent aggression and, if so, what measures they would take in common. If the latter involved action, it was agreed, the plans of the general staffs would immediately be considered, and the governments would then decide what effect should be given to them. Plans for naval co-operation were subsequently drafted by the French and British admiralties.

In 1914 Russia sought to bring about a still closer union of the powers of the Triple Entente by having it converted into a formal and public alliance. The British government opposed this step as being not then feasible, but did inform the Russian government of

[37] For the Bosnian crisis, see pages 341–343.
[38] See page 90.

the contents of the notes exchanged by France and Great Britain in
1912. Great Britain thus revealed to Russia the plans for probable
close co-operation between the other two members of the Entente.
She went even further, however, and permitted the inauguration of
Anglo-Russian naval conversations similar to those held earlier between the French and British admiralties. But when, early in July,
1914, the Russian government again urged an alliance, the matter
was once more postponed on the ground that the British government
was then too busy with the Irish situation to give the question the
necessary consideration.

It is thus obvious that, although by 1914 Great Britain had actually
entered into no alliance so far as treaties were concerned, she had
established cordial relations with both France and Russia and by
exchanges of notes had largely transformed—in spirit, at least—the
Entente Cordiale into a defensive agreement against Germany. It
is also clear that, although in the decade before the World War the
British government considered that it had retained freedom of action in time of crisis, morally it had obligated Great Britain to take
certain steps in defense of France. The British position was mis-
leading and dangerous. The government's declaration that Britain's
hands were free led Germany to think that the former would remain
neutral in case of a European war. The Anglo-French exchange of
notes and the military and naval conversations, on the other hand,
convinced French leaders that "the principle of an eventual co-
operation of the military and naval forces of France and England"
had been established. When the great crisis came in 1914, events
proved that the French view was correct. Great Britain was no
longer isolated and free but was rather entangled in the plans
and ambitions of Russia and France.

## CHAPTER VII

## THE LESSER STATES OF WESTERN EUROPE

IN western Europe in addition to the four great powers—Germany, France, Italy, and Great Britain—there were before the World War eight so-called lesser powers. Most of them, however, were inferior only in respect to total resources, population, military and naval establishments, and ability to play a dominant role in international affairs. In personal liberty, economic well-being, achievements in science and literature, and progress in political, social, and economic institutions, some of them were not surpassed by any of the great powers. The lot of the citizens of many of these lesser states was far happier than that of their contemporaries in some of their more powerful neighbors.

### THE SCANDINAVIAN MONARCHIES

Among the more progressive states of Europe were the three Scandinavian countries—Denmark, Norway, and Sweden—which had much in common. The inhabitants of all three were "Nordics"; they spoke Teutonic languages which were closely related; and most of them were Lutheran Protestants in their religion. The economic life of all three was based primarily upon agriculture, commerce, and fisheries, though they differed slightly in the emphasis given to each. In all of them popular education was exalted and illiteracy reduced to the vanishing point. Although they all retained the monarchical form of government, they nevertheless introduced democratic principles and were among the first to grant full political and civil rights to women. In all three countries the twentieth century saw socialism become an influential force in their political and economic life. Their producers' co-operatives, consumers' co-operatives, and dairymen's associations were carefully studied and frequently imitated by even the great powers. Although ranked among the lesser states, they stood in the vanguard of Western civilization.

In 1870 the Danish kingdom, the smallest of the Scandinavian countries,[1] consisted of the Jutland peninsula, the neighboring islands in the Baltic, and the Faroe Islands lying midway between the Shetlands and Greenland. It was then governed under a constitution, adopted in 1866, which provided for a bicameral legislature. In the upper house a minority of the members were appointed for life by the king, and the rest were chosen by the large taxpayers. The lower house was elected by a wide but not manhood suffrage. Denmark thus had a constitutional form of government, but the constitution was frequently ignored by King Christian IX, who ruled until 1906.[2] Throughout most of his reign a struggle was waged by the lower house to force the king to recognize the principle of ministerial responsibility, but not until 1901 did Christian finally yield on this point. After that year, however, parliamentary government prevailed in Denmark.

In the decade before the World War strenuous efforts were made by the Liberals and the rising Socialists to bring about the democratization of the government. Ultimately, in 1914 and 1915, constitutional amendments were adopted introducing manhood and womanhood suffrage in the elections for both houses of parliament, the age requirement being twenty-five for the lower house and thirty-five for the upper. Moreover, the life memberships in the latter were abolished, and a system of proportional representation was adopted. Denmark thus took her place among the most democratic countries of the world.

Meanwhile, progress had also been made in the country's economic life. Although some attention was given to fisheries and, increasingly with the passing years, to industry, the greatest percentage of the population derived its livelihood from agriculture. Danish peasants specialized in the production of butter, eggs, and bacon for export to neighboring countries, particularly to Great Britain—which took more than two thirds of the kingdom's exports—and to Germany. To aid the peasants in marketing their products, borrowing money, and securing expensive equipment, numerous cooperative societies were organized. Also, with the increase in the number of employees in industry [3] and commerce, social legislation

[1] Denmark's population in 1930 was 3,550,656.
[2] Christian IX was succeeded by Frederick VIII (1906–1912) and he in turn by Christian X.
[3] Industrial factories in 1925 employed 392,000 persons.

was enacted to provide labor exchanges and accident, sickness, old-age, and unemployment insurance.

After 1870 some changes were made in the territorial and polit-ical status of the kingdom's overseas possessions, which at the open-ing of the period consisted of Iceland, Greenland, the Faroe Islands, and three islands in the West Indies. In 1874 Iceland was granted home rule and was thereafter governed by her own parliament; in 1918 her complete independence was recognized by Denmark, and thereafter Iceland was united with the former only because they both had the same king. In 1917 the Danish West Indies (the Virgin Islands) were sold to the United States. The Faroe Islands being an integral part of the kingdom, Denmark's only colony today is Greenland. In 1920 the kingdom's area in Europe was slightly in-creased by the addition of a strip of territory in northern Schleswig.[4]

In 1870 Norway and Sweden [5] were united in a personal union. Each kingdom had its own parliament and own ministry, but they had a common ruler and common ministers of war and foreign affairs. Generally speaking, the Norwegian government was more liberal than that of Sweden, probably because Sweden had a strong aristocracy and a dependent peasantry, while Norway was largely a land of peasant proprietors and sturdy fishermen. Supreme author-ity in Norway was vested in an indirectly elected parliament over whose acts the king had only a suspensive veto; in Sweden the parliament was controlled by the aristocracy, and the king had an absolute veto over its acts.

This union of the two kingdoms had existed ever since the Con-gress of Vienna had transferred Norway from the King of Denmark to the King of Sweden at the close of the Napoleonic wars. At that time Norwegian nationalism had been so strong that the inhabitants of Norway consented to the transfer only after the Swedish king had agreed to recognize Norway as "a free, independent, and indi-visible kingdom united with Sweden under one king." And in the succeeding years Norwegian nationalism had continued to be strong. Eventually the Norwegians demanded their own flag and their own consular service, separate from Sweden's. These demands

[4] See page 486.

[5] Norway is a little larger than Italy and in 1930 had a population of 2,814,154; Sweden is only slightly less in area than postwar Germany and in 1933 had a popula-tion of 6,211,566.

arose in part from the fact that by the opening of the twentieth century Norway had become an important commercial country.

But King Oscar II (1872–1907) refused to sanction the appointment of Norwegian consular agents, alleging that such a step might ultimately lead to a double foreign policy. Consequently, in 1905, after the consular question had been discussed for more than a decade, the Norwegian parliament voted unanimously to separate Norway from Sweden and to depose Oscar II. In many cases such a step might have precipitated war, but this was averted when the Swedish government decided to recognize the dissolution of the union if the step was approved by a popular plebiscite in Norway. The plebiscite was held and resulted in an almost unanimous vote in favor of separation. In the subsequent treaty of dissolution the two powers agreed (1) to demilitarize their common frontiers and (2) to refer to the Hague Tribunal any future disputes between them which could not be settled through the ordinary channels of diplomacy.

Norway offered her throne to a Swedish prince, but, when he declined, she turned to the royal family of Denmark. In 1906 a Danish prince was crowned as Haakon VII.[6] The kingdom was then further democratized. Direct elections for the parliament were introduced in 1906; women were granted suffrage on the same basis as men in 1913; the suspensive veto of the king was abolished in the same year; and women were made eligible for membership in the cabinet in 1915. With direct and proportional representation, universal manhood and womanhood suffrage, ministerial responsibility, and a merely honorary king, Norway became a thoroughly democratic country.

Although Norway is large, most of it is barren and mountainous. Over 72 per cent of her territory is unproductive, and less than 4 per cent is under cultivation. But forests constitute one of the kingdom's chief sources of wealth; almost one fourth of Norway is in forests, and among her chief exports are wood pulp, paper and cardboard, and timber. Of her population 30 per cent gain their livelihood (1930) from agriculture and forestry and 28 per cent

---

[6] This title was assumed to indicate the continuity of the independent kingdom of Norway, Haakon VI having been the last king of Norway before she was united with Denmark in the Middle Ages.

from industries related largely to forestry. Navigation and transportation provide the economic basis for 10 per cent of the country's population, for Norway's merchant marine has long been important. In 1934 it was exceeded in total tonnage only by those of Great Britain and the United States. Approximately 100,000 Norwegians are engaged in the fisheries industry, cod and herring constituting an important export commodity. The working people of Norway have gained considerable political influence; in the postwar years the Laborites were by far the largest political party in the kingdom.

Meanwhile, Sweden, too, had entered the ranks of the democratic nations. After the death of Oscar II and the accession of his son, Gustavus V, universal manhood suffrage was introduced for the election of the lower house of the parliament; the property qualification for electors of the upper house was decreased; proportional representation was provided for both houses; and ministerial responsibility was inaugurated. At the close of the World War the suffrage was extended to women, also, on the same basis as to men.

In the years after 1870 Sweden became increasingly industrialized. At the opening of the period only 12½ per cent of her population depended for their livelihood upon industry and commerce, but fifty years later the percentage had increased to 44. By 1933 nearly 400,000 workers were employed in factories. Iron mining also was important, especially in the arctic regions of the country. Politically, with the increase of industrial workers came the rise of the Socialist Party. In the parliamentary elections of 1914 it obtained more than a third of the seats in the lower house, and eighteen years later the kingdom had its first Socialist ministry. During the postwar economic depression Sweden attracted the attention of the world by her experiment with a "managed" currency.

## HOLLAND AND BELGIUM

Although each of these states is smaller than Denmark, Norway, or Sweden, the population of each is considerably larger than that of the most populous Scandinavian country. In fact, the Netherlands—popularly referred to as Holland [7]—and Belgium are the two most densely populated countries in Europe, each having (1930) more than 8,000,000 inhabitants. Special circumstances account for

[7] Holland is only one—but the largest and richest—of the eleven provinces in the Kingdom of the Netherlands.

the ability of these two small kingdoms to support such relatively large populations.

Holland possesses an overseas empire of approximately 788,000 square miles with more than 60,000,000 inhabitants. Most of this empire is located in the East Indies, where the Netherlands control rich and populous Java, Sumatra, Celebes, most of Borneo, and approximately half of New Guinea, besides innumerable small islands.[8] In the western hemisphere she possesses Dutch Guiana on the northern coast of South America and Curaçao and a number of smaller islands in the Caribbean. The East Indian empire provides the Netherlands with a steady stream of wealth in the form of rubber, coffee, palm oil, tea, and tobacco. Moreover, the administration of the islands offers profitable careers to many Netherlanders, while the exploitation of their resources is very profitable to Dutch merchants and bankers.

But Holland's economic life is based, in part, upon two other factors also. The country is strategically located not only from a military but from a commercial viewpoint. Rotterdam and Amsterdam serve as *entrepôts* for a considerable amount of trade between central Europe and countries overseas. This exchange of goods across Holland's territory brings income to Dutch carriers and middlemen and provides a livelihood for many Netherlanders. Furthermore, Holland is also a rich agricultural land and is advantageously located between Great Britain and Germany. Neither of these countries produces sufficient foodstuffs for its population, and therefore they provide the Dutch peasants with ready markets for their agricultural and dairy products. Holland's wealth and her economic importance in world affairs are therefore much greater than her limited area in Europe would seem to indicate.

Political democracy was somewhat slower to develop in Holland than in some of her neighbors. In 1870 the kingdom had a bicameral parliament with ministerial responsibility, but the ruler [9] still held an absolute veto over all legislation. The upper house of the parliament was elected by the legislatures of the eleven provinces, and the lower house was chosen by those who paid a heavy property tax. The government, therefore, was largely in the hands of the wealth-

---

[8] For the location of the Dutch East Indies, see the map on page 25.
[9] King William III ruled until 1890, when he was succeeded by his minor daughter, who became Queen Wilhelmina.

ier classes. The succeeding years saw some progress, however. In 1887 and again in 1896 the electorate was enlarged by modifying somewhat the property qualifications. Ultimately, in 1917, further reforms introduced proportional representation and manhood and womanhood suffrage at the age of twenty-five for the election of the lower house. In the postwar period the two most important political parties were the Catholic and the Social Democratic.[10]

The economic foundation upon which Belgium rests is quite different from that of her neighbor to the north. Although some 60 per cent of the country is under cultivation and, thanks to the use of intensive methods and co-operative enterprise, agriculture has continued to be profitable, only a small percentage of the Belgians gain their livelihood from farms. For Belgium is rich in coal and iron, and early in the nineteenth century she experienced the Industrial Revolution. She was not only the first continental country to become industrialized, but she became the most highly industrialized of them all. Eventually, those engaged in industry came to outnumber those employed in agriculture by four to one (1930). In trade and commerce, too, Belgium came to occupy an important place. Before the World War the volume of her foreign trade—chiefly with France, Great Britain, Holland, and Germany—was almost a third again as large as that of Italy. In 1930 the number of Belgians engaged in commerce and transportation exceeded the number of agriculturists by more than 15 per cent.

Belgium has an extensive colonial realm, which, although not so rich perhaps as that of the Netherlands, is still of considerable value to the kingdom. The establishment of the Congo Free State under the sovereignty of Leopold II has already been discussed.[11] At first Belgium as a state had no control over this territory. But the cruel treatment of the natives in attempts to force them to provide exploiting companies with ivory and rubber was later reported by the missionaries, and the disclosures led to insistent demands that reforms be introduced. In 1908, accordingly, the sovereignty of the

[10] From 1815 to 1890 the rulers of the Netherlands were also the rulers of the Grand Duchy of Luxemburg, a tiny state lying between France and Germany just east of Belgium. In 1890 the grand duchy did not pass to Queen Wilhelmina, however, but went to one of her father's male relatives, Adolphus of Nassau. The little state was included in the German customs union, and its industrial life was largely dominated by Germany. In 1867 Luxemburg had been neutralized and forbidden to have any armed force except local police.

[11] See page 20 and the map on page 21.

region was transferred from Leopold to the Kingdom of Belgium, which ruled it thereafter as a colony. Belgium's economic strength was thus further increased, for the Congo is particularly rich in rubber and also supplies the kingdom with gold, diamonds, copper, palm oil, cotton, coffee, and ivory.[12]

The Belgians are not, like the people of the Scandinavian countries and Holland, homogeneous linguistically and racially. Those in the southern part of the kingdom are Walloons, who are closely akin to the French and speak French. Those in the north are Flemings, who are closely related to the Dutch in race and language. Throughout the country, however, French is generally used by the so-called upper classes and was in the nineteenth century the only official language of the state. At times the linguistic and racial division of the people had a very noticeable influence upon the political life of the kingdom.[13]

In 1870 Belgium was a constitutional monarchy with a bicameral parliament and ministerial responsibility but with a suffrage limited by a relatively high property qualification. Only a small percentage of the population could vote, and most of the urban workers were disfranchised. The two most important political parties were the Liberals and the Catholics. The former were anticlerical and accordingly favored secular education; the latter desired to have religious instruction in the schools and wished it to be controlled by the Catholic clergy. Until 1884 the Liberals were generally in power, with the result that religious instruction was not given in the schools.

In the eighties, however, the Liberal Party began to lose many of its members to the Socialists, and in 1884 the Catholic Party came into power and thereafter retained control of the government until after the World War. As might be expected, religious instruction was introduced in most of the schools. But the Catholic Party also responded to the demand for political reform and social legislation. After the country had experienced a great general strike (1893) in which the workers demanded manhood suffrage, the government in 1894 made a concession and extended the franchise to practically all men twenty-five years of age. But in order to protect the prop-

---

[12] After the World War a small part of German East Africa was added to the Belgian Congo as a mandate of the League of Nations and was rechristened Ruanda-Urundi.

[13] During the World War the German government of occupation tried to weaken Belgium by arousing hostile feelings between the two groups of Belgians.

ertied class somewhat, the principle of plural voting was introduced; that is, additional votes were allotted to those men who could meet certain property qualifications. Under this law a man might have as many as three votes. In the succeeding years the Socialists raised the slogan "one man, one vote."

To appease the workingmen as well as to improve their condition, legislation was enacted to regulate factories, legalize trade unions, provide old-age pensions, and erect workers' dwellings. To satisfy the Flemish-speaking peasants and workingmen, Flemish was in 1898 made the official language of the state along with French. Thereafter both Flemish and French had to be used in governmental publications and the like. In the next year proportional representation was introduced for the election of members of the parliament. Eventually, in 1921, the constitution was further revised to provide for manhood suffrage at twenty-one years of age for both houses of the parliament and to grant the ballot to a limited number of women.[14] The reforms of 1899 and 1921 weakened the Catholic Party.[15]

Situated as she is between France and Germany and just across the Channel from Britain, Belgium occupies a highly strategic military position in Europe. Through her territory run the easiest routes over which either France or Germany may invade the other, and from her shores may an offensive against Britain be most easily launched. Fear that one of the great powers might gain the ascendancy in the little kingdom and eventually utilize it for military purposes had led Great Britain, France, Prussia, Russia, and Austria to sign a treaty in 1839 neutralizing Belgium. By the provisions of this agreement Belgium was to be an independent and perpetually neutral state, and was bound to observe such neutrality toward all other states. The great powers placed this article of the treaty under their guarantee.

Nevertheless, in the opening years of the twentieth century, Belgium became alarmed by the growing tension between the great powers and by Germany's construction of strategic railways up to

[14] The franchise was extended to widows whose husbands or sons had been killed in the war and to women who had suffered imprisonment at the hands of the German authorities.

[15] In 1919 it lost the parliamentary majority which it had held since 1884, and six years later it lost first place to the Socialists, who secured places in the ministry. For a time their able leader, Émile Vandervelde, was prime minister of the kingdom.

the Belgian frontiers. To protect her neutrality Belgium strengthened the fortresses around Liége and Namur until they were considered almost impregnable. She also carried on negotiations with Great Britain and France looking to the defense of her neutrality in case of a German invasion. Finally, in 1913, she introduced compulsory military service for all of her young men.

## SWITZERLAND

In the years before 1914 Switzerland was probably the most democratic country in the world. This small republic was a confederation of twenty-two cantons [16] which had gradually come together for mutual protection during the preceding centuries. The confederation as a whole was not homogeneous in its population, however. Of its inhabitants approximately 65 per cent (1914) were German; 23 per cent French, and 12 per cent Italian. Besides differing in language and customs the Swiss also differed in religion, 57 per cent (1930) being Protestant and 41 per cent Roman Catholic. Furthermore, in the years after 1870 the Swiss came to differ noticeably in their economic activities. To the herdsmen of the mountains and the petty farmers of the valleys were added increasingly the industrial workers of the cities.

The ability of these diverse groups to live together contentedly within one state was the result in part of three circumstances. In the first place, the cantonal governments had extensive powers, for in the confederation only certain delegated powers belonged to the national government. Although all of the cantons recognized the principle of popular sovereignty, they differed among themselves in the organization of their local governments. While some of the more populous adopted the representative type of government, some of the smaller cantons long retained a type of pure democracy —all the electors meeting at one time in one place to make political decisions by oral voting. Extensive local government, therefore, made it possible for each canton to manage its own local affairs as it chose.

In the second place, the confederation was divided into so many cantons that in each of them the population was fairly homogeneous racially and linguistically, and so there was lacking the feel-

---

[16] Three of the cantons were divided so that technically there were nineteen cantons and six half-cantons.

ing that one racial group was being dominated or exploited by another. In the third place, no one of the racial groups was distinctly favored by or in the national government. All three languages were recognized as official; any one of them might be used in discussions in the parliament; the presidency of the confederation went by rotation to the different nationalities; and the central government usually sought to exercise its authority in such a way as not to antagonize any of the cantons on racial, linguistic, or religious grounds.

Under the constitution of 1848, as amended in 1874 and again in 1891, the federal legislature consisted of an upper house with two representatives from each canton and a lower house popularly elected in proportion to population. The republic had a plural executive, called the Federal Council, which was chosen by the parliament, and the chairman of this council—though differing little from the other members in power—bore the title of President of the Swiss Confederation. But the legislative power of the national government was not entirely or finally in the hands of the parliament, for, by means of the referendum, laws passed by the parliament might be rejected by popular vote, and, by means of the initiative and referendum,[17] laws might be popularly adopted even though not enacted by the parliament.

The economic life of Switzerland had for the most part a threefold basis. Agriculture and dairying predominated in many of the cantons, and the manufacture of cheese and condensed milk constituted one of the republic's chief industries. In a number of the cities—notably Zurich, Basel, Geneva, and Bern—a considerable amount of modern industry developed and provided employment for some hundreds of thousands of Swiss workers.[18] Silk and artificial-silk goods, watches, embroidery, coal-tar dyes, and electrical goods were among the exports from this little state. In addition to agriculture and dairying and industry and commerce, the third important source of income for the Swiss was the tourist trade. Hotel-keeping provided a livelihood for thousands of people, and it might well be said that one of Switzerland's chief businesses was the sale of scenery.

---

[17] The principle of the popular referendum was adopted in 1874, that of the initiative in 1891.

[18] In 1929 factories employed 409,083 workers in Switzerland.

## SPAIN AND PORTUGAL

In the years between 1870 and the World War Spain and Portugal were undoubtedly the most backward of the lesser states of western Europe. In 1870 Spain was in the midst of a political upheaval which had resulted from the overthrow of the Bourbon ruler, Queen Isabella II, in 1868. At that time universal manhood suffrage had been proclaimed, and freedom of religion and of the press had been guaranteed, and subsequently the Cortes had drafted a constitution providing for a liberal monarchy based upon the principle of popular sovereignty. A new monarch was then sought, and eventually Prince Leopold of Hohenzollern was selected. Although in the end Leopold declined the throne, the Prussian minister, Bismarck, so manipulated events that out of Leopold's candidacy emerged the Franco-German War of 1870-1871. In November, 1870, Amadeo—the second son of King Victor Emmanuel of Italy —finally accepted the Spanish throne. But continual political strife, occasioned by the opposition of republicans, Carlists,[19] and legitimists, soon discouraged the new monarch, and in 1873 he abdicated.

In February, 1873, the Cortes proclaimed a republic, but the new government from its very inception was denounced and opposed by the royalists of all types, by the clergy, and eventually by the military leaders. It was furthermore embarrassed by wars with the Carlists and regionalists at home and with the Cubans overseas. Late in 1874 the army declared in favor of the restoration of the Bourbons, and early in the next year the son of Isabella II returned to Spain to rule as Alfonso XII. In 1876 a new constitution was adopted providing for a parliamentary government with ministerial responsibility and with a franchise based upon a property qualification.

Although parliamentary in name, the government of Spain during the ensuing years was really controlled by cliques of politicians and military leaders, who fell generally into two opposing groups: the Conservatives, organized and led by Canovas del Castillo, who had worked to overthrow the republic; and the Liberals, led by

---

[19] The Carlists were the successors of those who in 1833 had asserted, on the basis of the Salic law, that the legal successor of Ferdinand VII was not his daughter, Isabella, but his brother, Don Carlos. The chief supporters of Don Carlos during the so-called Carlist wars of the thirties had been the nobility, the clergy, and those who favored royal absolutism.

Mateo Sagasta. There was relatively little difference between the views and policies of the two groups, although perhaps the Conservatives were more sympathetic with the nobility and clergy of the old regime. The two leaders ultimately reached an agreement in accordance with which their parties rotated in office by controlling the elections. This rotation of office-holding, with its privilege of distributing patronage, continued down to the opening of the twentieth century. Political corruption and coercion were general. In protest against this type of regime Canovas was assassinated in 1897.

But corruption and inefficiency were not limited to the kingdom alone; they were found also in Spain's colonies overseas. In 1878 a revolt which had raged in Cuba for ten years was put down partly by military force and partly by the promise to introduce reforms in that island. But the reforms had not been forthcoming, and so in 1895 the Cubans again raised the standard of rebellion. In attempting to suppress this revolt Spain was handicapped by an uprising in the Philippines and ultimately defeated by the intervention of the United States. At the close of the Spanish-American War (1898) Spain gave Cuba her independence and ceded Puerto Rico and the Philippines to the United States. In the next year she sold her other islands in the Pacific to Germany. Of her once proud overseas empire Spain at the opening of the twentieth century possessed only small strips of territory in Africa and a few islands in the eastern Atlantic.

In 1902 Alfonso XIII came to the throne.[20] Although he was personally popular, the new king's reign was almost continually disturbed by social unrest and the demand for far-reaching reform. To a large extent the latter was the result of changing economic conditions within the country. Spain is predominantly agricultural, and hard-working peasants constitute the bulk of her population. In the nineteenth century, however, the landed aristocracy and the numerous and privileged clergy were the most influential classes. But Spain also has considerable deposits of iron, copper, coal, zinc, and lead, and the closing years of the nineteenth century saw the introduction of some modern industrialism, especially in the regions around Barcelona, Madrid, Seville, and Bilbao. They saw, too, the

[20] He was the posthumous son of Alfonso XII, who had died in 1885. During the years from 1885 to 1902 Maria Christina, the queen-mother, had ruled as regent.

rise of an industrial and financial bourgeoisie and an urban proletariat.

The industrial workers were soon attracted by the doctrines of the socialists, syndicalists, and anarchists and consequently became more and more radical in their views. And since manhood suffrage had been introduced in 1890, the radicals were able to make their influence felt in politics. The twentieth century, therefore, witnessed increasing conflict between the upholders of the old regime and those who sought to modernize Spain and bring her institutions abreast of those in the more progressive countries. The former consisted largely of nobility, clergy, and adherents of the *status quo* generally; the latter included most of the bourgeoisie, intellectuals, and proletariat.

In 1902 state supervision of elementary schools was authorized, and seven years later elementary-school attendance was made compulsory. Nevertheless, the facilities for popular education were inadequate and inefficient, and a large percentage of the Spanish people continued to be illiterate. Some progress was made in the realm of social legislation—trade unions were authorized, factories regulated, employers' liability for accidents introduced—but here, too, Spain lagged behind the progressive states. In 1907 the Conservatives, in an attempt to nullify the radicalism of the proletariat by the conservatism of the peasantry, made the exercise of manhood suffrage compulsory.

Despite this step, anticlerical sentiment began to make itself felt, and in 1910 a Liberal government, pledged to an anticlerical program, came into office. Diplomatic relations with the papacy were thereupon severed, taxes were placed on industrial enterprises conducted by religious orders, and the establishment of additional religious houses without the sanction of the government was forbidden. But, when it was rumored that church and state were to be separated and education secularized, the reactionary and conservative groups organized such strong opposition that the Liberal government was forced to give way, and the Conservative premier who came into power resumed relations with the pope and prevented further anticlerical legislation. The struggle between the clericals and the anticlericals was carried over into the postwar period.[21]

[21] See pages 739–745.

With the growing differentiation between industrial Catalonia and the agricultural sections of the kingdom, an autonomist movement began to develop in the northeastern section of the country. The regional consciousness of this district was deep-rooted, for it had emerged as a separate entity back in the ninth century when Charlemagne created the Spanish March. Not until the fourteenth century had it been conquered and gradually merged into what became the Spanish monarchy, and during the intervening centuries it had developed a separate language and literature and its own parliament. Even down until the nineteenth century many of its liberties had been retained, though during this century the last vestiges of its former independent existence were destroyed by the highly centralized government at Madrid. Catalan nationalism survived, however, and in the years before the World War a states' rights program was being advocated. On the eve of the war, therefore, the permanence of the centralized Bourbon monarchy in Spain was being challenged by those favoring republicanism, socialism, syndicalism, and regionalism.

But in the neighboring kingdom of Portugal the Braganza line of rulers was not permitted to remain on the throne even down to the war. Political life in Portugal in the years from 1870 to 1910 was very similar to that in Spain with its corresponding manipulation of elections and rotation in office of leaders of the two principal political parties. As in Spain, too, there was the gradual growth of radicalism, which expressed itself in the programs of the republicans, socialists, syndicalists, and anarchists.

Although under Louis I (1861–1889) conditions appeared to be fairly stable, popular discontent was being engendered by the prevalence of political corruption, the burden of heavy taxes, and the government's indifference to social reform and popular education. Under Carlos I (1889–1908), who was inclined to resort to dictatorial methods to accomplish his ends, unrest became greater and more widespread. Eventually, in 1908, both the king and the crown prince were assassinated. Carlos's second son then mounted the throne as Manuel II. But the new ruler's reign was short. The republicans redoubled their efforts to bring about the downfall of the monarchy and sought especially to win over the organized armed forces.

In 1910 a republican revolt broke out when both the army and the navy mutinied and seized the capital. Manuel fled from the country, and a provisional government proclaimed a republic. In 1911 a democratic constitution, closely resembling that of the Third French Republic, was adopted, and Manuel Arriaga, long a leader of the Portuguese republicans, was elected president. Then followed a series of anticlerical laws, which resembled those enacted earlier in France. Diplomatic relations with the pope were broken off; church and state were separated; religious orders were suppressed and their property confiscated; and a system of free, secular education was introduced.

But the establishment of the republic brought neither political stability nor general content. Socialists were dissatisfied with the bourgeois character of the new regime; monarchists intrigued to restore the old regime; and army leaders repeatedly meddled in political affairs. Great strikes, frequent riots, and occasional insurrections and coups prepared the way for the establishment of the fascist dictatorship which was eventually inaugurated in Portugal after the World War.

Although one of the smaller states of Europe, Portugal possesses one of the largest overseas empires. Before the war only the empires of Great Britain, France, and Germany exceeded it in area. Most of this overseas territory is located in Africa, but some of it is in India and the Far East.[22] Unfortunately for Portugal, her empire is not so rich as that of the Netherlands, and by many the expenses entailed in administering so large a colonial realm are considered beyond her financial ability. Germany's prewar interest in the possibility of obtaining some of this territory, in case the Portuguese government went bankrupt, has already been discussed.[23]

---

[22] The Cape Verde Islands off the west coast of Africa; Portuguese Guinea, Angola, and Mozambique in Africa; Goa, Damaun, and Diu in India; part of Timor in the Malay archipelago; and Macao in China. The Azores and the Madeira Islands are not colonies but are considered integral parts of Portugal.

[23] See page 80.

## CHAPTER VIII

# THE RUSSIAN EMPIRE

WITHIN Russia, the great Slavic power of northern and eastern Europe, the half century preceding the World War witnessed an unending struggle between liberals and radicals, on the one hand, who sought to bring the institutions of the empire more nearly into harmony with those of the progressive countries of the West, and conservatives and reactionaries, on the other, who were determined to perpetuate the old regime as long as possible. In this struggle the Romanov dynasty and government were as a general rule closely aligned with the latter group. Plots and counterplots, assassinations and executions, imprisonment and exile, revolution and repression were the accompaniments of the conflict, which was hard-fought and bitter. Although some progress was made, the empire in 1914 was still far from the goal which liberals and radicals envisaged.

In international affairs Russia's role during this period was dominated largely by the centuries-old desire to obtain a suitable warm-water outlet to the high seas. In the quest for such a port her statesmen schemed and intrigued both in Europe and in Asia, but on each occasion their plans were thwarted by one or more of the great powers. In 1914 Russia's renewed determination to gain an outlet through the Straits had much to do with precipitating the World War.

## THE VASTNESS OF RUSSIA

In 1870 the Romanov Tsar Alexander II ruled over the largest country in Europe both in area and in population. But his empire was not limited to Europe any more than the British Empire was limited to the British Isles. Across the Ural Mountains intrepid trappers, gold-seeking miners, aggressive merchants, political refugees, escaped serfs, and adventurers generally had pushed the Russian frontier ever onward into Siberia. Long before the nineteenth century they had extended Russian territory to the northern Pacific

Ocean; in fact, they had even appropriated in the name of the tsars the Alaskan region [1] of North America. By the time of Alexander II the tsar ruled an empire second in size only to the British, an empire which had been created not by overseas expansion but by constantly advancing its frontiers over land.

From the days of Peter the Great Russia's diplomacy and policy of territorial expansion, so far as they may be said to have had a conscious dominating motive, had been directed toward the acquisition of a satisfactory outlet to the high seas. Peter himself had secured an access to the Baltic, and Catherine the Great had gained a foothold on the Black Sea. Neither of these outlets was satisfactory, however; the former because it was not an ice-free port throughout the year, and the latter because the fortified Bosporus and Dardanelles, connecting the Black Sea with the Mediterranean, were in the control of the Ottoman Empire and might be closed to Russian commerce or to the passage of Russian warships almost at the whim of the sultan's government.

One of Russia's major aspirations, accordingly, was to secure the control of the Straits, and during the nineteenth century she schemed in various ways to attain this end. At times it appeared that her interests could best be advanced by partitioning or destroying Turkey and bringing under Russian control the territory along the Straits. At other times it seemed that the desired outlet could best be secured by maintaining the territorial integrity of the Ottoman Empire and at the same time gaining for Russia a privileged position as a sort of guardian of Turkey. In pursuing the former policy Russia eagerly sought to avail herself of unrest among the sultan's subject races in the Balkans in order by intervention to gain territory for herself and the good will of the Balkan peoples. In pursuing the second policy she posed either as the defender of Turkey —in return for privileges in respect to the Straits (as in 1833)—or as the protector of the Greek Christians in Turkey—in order to secure opportunities to interfere in Turkish affairs.

At the time when Alexander II mounted the throne (1855) Russia was engaged in the Crimean War, a struggle which had been precipitated by her attempt to carry out the second of these policies. Great Britain and France had come to the aid of Turkey, and in 1856 the tsar was compelled to withdraw from the struggle. By the

[1] Alaska was sold to the United States in 1867.

subsequent treaty of Paris Russia was compelled to cede to Moldavia (later called Rumania) a valuable strip of Bessarabia at the mouth of the Danube, and was forced to agree to the neutralization of the Black Sea. No warships were thereafter to be stationed in that sea, and no arsenals were to be permitted on its shores.[2] The treaty appeared to constitute a definite check, at least temporarily, to any Russian advance in the Near East.

Blocked in that direction, the empire's energies were next turned to expansion into other regions, particularly into the Middle East and the Far East. South of the Russian Empire, between Chinese Turkestan on the east and the Caspian Sea on the west, lay a vast territory which was organized into Moslem khanates and peopled largely by nomadic tribesmen. The latter occasionally conducted raids northward into Russian territory and from time to time attacked Russian caravans. They thus provided the tsar's foreign minister, Gorchakov, with an opportunity to justify Russia's subsequent conquests on the ground that the constant inroads of lawless tribes made Russian advances unavoidable until the frontiers of some well-ordered states should be reached. In an apparent effort to reach such frontiers Russia pushed steadily southward toward Persia, Afghanistan, and India.

In 1865 a number of strongholds, including Turkestan and Tashkend, were captured, and the conquered region was eventually organized (1867) into a governor-generalship named Turkestan. Almost at once a conflict began between the Russian governor-general of Turkestan, General Kauffmann, and the ruler of the neighboring khanate of Bokhara. In 1868 the Russians captured the sacred city of Samarkand and forced the ruler of Bokhara to recognize the suzerainty of the tsar. Five years later Russian troops under the command of General Kauffmann invaded Khiva from Turkestan and from the Caspian Sea and soon completed its conquest. Part of the Khivan territory was annexed to Russia outright, and part became a vassal state. Next, in the middle seventies, a civil war in the khanate of Kokand was seized upon by the Russians as an opportunity for an attack, and in 1876 Kokand was incorporated in the Russian Empire as a province with the name Fergana.

Still pushing southward, a Russian army leader entered Kabul,

[2] During the Franco-German War Russia announced her abrogation of these provisions regarding the Black Sea.

the capital of Afghanistan, and persuaded the ruler of that country to sign a treaty (1878) placing his country under Russia's protection. This, at last, had the effect of moving the British to action, for, despite Gorchakov's efforts to allay their fears, they had for some time been alarmed at Russia's steady advance toward India. The British had hoped that a neutral zone might be established in the Middle East between their possessions and Russia's and had urged the tsar to recognize the Amu River as the boundary between his territory and Afghanistan, the latter supposedly being in the British sphere of influence. As soon as the Russian treaty with Afghanistan became known, therefore, Great Britain launched a war against the Afghan amir and eventually (1881) succeeded in placing on the throne of Afghanistan a ruler who was favorable to Great Britain's interests. Russia's further southward expansion was therefore checked in this part of the Middle East by British troops and diplomats.

Meanwhile, in the Far East other important territories had been acquired. In 1858 the governor-general of Eastern Siberia annexed the region on the left bank of the Amur River together with the great stretch of territory on the right bank lying between the Amur and the Pacific and extending south as far as the present city of Vladivostok. Here was a good harbor which was ice-bound only three or four months of the year, and here Russia planned to build a new city and port to provide a better outlet to the Pacific. In 1860 all this territory was formally ceded to the tsar by China. In the same year Russia also secured the northern half of the valuable island of Sakhalin, and fifteen years later the rest of the island, which had been in Japanese possession. As a result of these acquisitions of territory Russia was thereafter in a position to play an increasingly important role in the affairs of the Far East. Incidentally, she now possessed an empire variously estimated as including from one seventh to one sixth of the land surface of the globe.

## THE BACKWARDNESS OF RUSSIA

Although by far the largest of the states of Europe, Russia, when judged by the standards of Western civilization, was decidedly the most backward of the great European powers. In fact, if the institutions of the empire are considered as they existed when Alexander

II began to rule, it is obvious that the Russians were lagging far behind the peoples of the other great powers, were, in fact, actually living amid conditions which were not greatly different in many respects from those which had existed in western Europe centuries before.

The social life of the empire was organized in a distinctly medieval fashion. As in western Europe in the Middle Ages, the great bulk of the population consisted of peasants who lived in village communities known in Russia as *mirs*. The great majority of these peasants were serfs. Most of them were bound to the soil. They worked on the great estates of the landed aristocracy and in their personal lives were in many ways subject to the demands of their overlords. Some, however, had been released from agricultural work but were still obligated in various other ways to their lords and masters. As in medieval times, the privileged group in Russia consisted of the aristocracy and the clergy. Relatively speaking, the bourgeois class was small and of little influence; at the middle of the nineteenth century less than 8 per cent of the population lived in towns or cities.

In her economic life, too, Russia was still largely medieval. Despite its wealth of mineral resources, the empire was chiefly dependent upon agriculture for its economic well-being. And in agriculture the system of cultivation was that of the inefficient and out-of-date three-field system, with the serfs holding dispersed or scattered holdings which were periodically redistributed by the mir. A large share of the peasant's time was spent on the lord's domain, the rest on his own strips. The agricultural revolution had not yet reached Russia.[3] Industry was largely of the type found under domestic and guild systems, since the Industrial Revolution had as yet made practically no headway in the empire. Domestic commerce was carried on largely over water and caravan routes, for facilities for travel and trade were still not greatly different from those which existed in medieval times. In the middle of the nineteenth century, according to one Russian authority, the total length of the railways in operation in the vast Russian Empire was not more than 660 miles.

[3] Even as recently as the decade immediately preceding the war the average yield of wheat in Russia was per acre only two thirds of that in the United States and less than half of that in France.

Politically, Russia was still back in the age of Louis XIV—in the period of the old regime. The government was an absolute monarchy, supposedly controlled entirely by the divine-right Autocrat of all the Russias, who from 1855 to 1881 was Alexander II. There was no constitution to restrict the tsar. There was no national legislature to determine the laws which were to govern the Russians and bind their ruler. Although the tsar was assisted by a sort of cabinet, the Council of the Empire, ministerial government in the Western sense of the term did not exist; the ministers were appointed by and were responsible to the tsar, whose decrees constituted the law of the land. Naturally, in an empire as far-flung as the Russian, the government, although centralized in St. Petersburg, was administered chiefly by a large number of officials, with most of whom the tsar never came in contact. Unfortunately for the permanence of the tsarist regime, many of these officials not only oppressed the people but administered the government with gross inefficiency and widespread corruption. Probably one reason why the autocratic regime lasted as long as it did was the naïve belief of the Russian peasants that their ills were not the fault of their "little father," the tsar, but were caused by those corrupt officials whom he himself would remove from office if he but knew the real situation.

As in the Middle Ages, education and culture in Russia were the privilege of the few. Illiteracy was largely the rule, and even those who received education were sometimes thwarted in their search for truth by the interference of the tsar's government, which occasionally dictated what might and might not be studied. In religion the dominant faith was the Greek Orthodox, and there was a close union between this church and the state. The tsar himself appointed the procurator of the holy synod, who in turn dominated the church. Although in Russia's great population there were also Roman Catholics, Uniates, Protestants, Jews, Moslems, and others, the government openly favored the Greek Orthodox Church and frequently persecuted those of other faiths. Among the Greek Orthodox believers there was much that was suggestive of the Middle Ages. "The pilgrims, dressed like Tannhäuser in the third act, with staves in their hands and wallets at their sides, who wander through Russia on their way to pray at the Holy Sepulchre, belong to the age of the Crusades. The ascetic who spends his life in prayer and fasting and wears chains about his body seems to have found his way into modern Russia from the Egyptian Thebaid of the fourth century."

Finally, the Russian Empire, like most states in early medieval times, was not a homogeneous nation but was inhabited by a conglomeration of races and varying linguistic groups. The Slavic Russians—the Great Russians, the Little Russians (Ukrainians), and the White Russians, who spoke languages that were akin—constituted more than 70 per cent of the empire's population. They inhabited most of the central and eastern provinces of European Russia and were the predominant element in the central part of the empire in Asia. The other 30 per cent of Russia's population consisted of Poles in Poland, Lithuania, and the Ukraine; Jews in Poland, Lithuania, and the Ukraine; Finns and Swedes in Finland; Germans, Lithuanians, Letts, and Estonians in the Baltic provinces; Rumanians in Bessarabia; Tatars in the Crimea and the southeastern provinces; Armenians, Georgians, and Circassians in the Caucasus; Mongols in Siberia; Moslem tribes in central Asia; and many other groups like the Lapps and Eskimos in northern Siberia. Although among the Poles and Finns—and to a less extent, perhaps, among the Rumanians, Lithuanians, Estonians, and Letts—there was some feeling of national rebellion against being ruled by the alien tsar, most of the other subject groups were as yet undisturbed by the dynamic spirit of nationalism which existed in the West.

### ALEXANDER II—LIBERAL OR CONSERVATIVE?

In the early years of his reign Alexander II by various measures gained the reputation of being a reformer, a ruler who was desirous of liberalizing Russian institutions so that they might be brought into harmony with those of the other great states of the West. Whether in the beginning the tsar was a sincere liberal or was merely moved to modernize the empire so that it might escape in the future a disastrous defeat like that suffered in the Crimean War, it is difficult to say. According to some Russian historians, Alexander in his political views did not differ greatly from his father, Nicholas I, and at heart held the ideal of enlightened despotism.

The young tsar opened his reign most auspiciously by attacking the institution of serfdom. For more than a century there had been an increasing realization in Russia that serfdom should be abolished, a realization which was hastened from time to time by the outbreak of peasant disorders. While many were influenced by the moral and social evils inherent in a servile system, perhaps more were swayed by the economic and military defects. It was found that forced labor was inefficient and wasteful, and that lack of the incentive which usually comes from private ownership of property dampened the serfs' zeal for labor. In the army it was emphatically brought home by the Crimean War that Russian servile soldiers were no match for the free men of western Europe in the matter of intelligence and initiative. The military strength of Russia, resting largely on servile troops, was found to be greatly exaggerated. The old regime in Russia had proved to be incapable of organizing an effective defense of the empire. It was therefore decided that the system of serfdom must be abolished.

In the reign of Alexander I the serfs of the Baltic provinces had been set free without any land and had immediately become an agricultural proletariat. By many this was considered to be an unsatisfactory solution of the problem. Alexander II was determined that land allotments should be provided for the emancipated peasants, but the adjustment of relations between freedmen and landed aristocrats and the setting of the price to be paid for the land given to the peasants called for careful study. For three years a committee worked on the general plan of emancipation and on the details of its execution. In a manifesto issued in March, 1861, the project was eventually confirmed by the tsar.

By the terms of Alexander's edict household serfs were given their personal freedom without redemption and without any form of compensation. But all the millions of serfs who had worked on the land were to receive in addition to their personal freedom their homesteads and certain allotments of land. Generally speaking, about half of the cultivated land was handed over to the peasants. The land allotments were not given to the peasants directly in full personal ownership, however, but to the mirs, which consisted of the heads of the families in the peasant villages. The mirs, in turn, were periodically to divide the land among the peasants roughly in proportion to the size of the different families. Nor were the land allotments surrendered by the estate-owners without compensation. In most cases the government paid the landowner for the land which he surrendered to the mir, and the latter was obligated to repay the government over a period of forty-nine years. The millions of serfs on the royal appanages and on the state lands were given their freedom in 1863 and 1866 respectively.

Although Alexander's edict of emancipation gained for him the title of "Tsar Liberator," the provisions and execution of the edict of emancipation were unsatisfactory to most of those involved. In the first place, the peasants maintained that all the land of the proprietor should have been given to the peasants. In general the peasants received allotments of land which before 1861 had absorbed only half of their labor.[4] In the second place, the peasants asserted that the land should have been given to them as individuals rather than to the mirs. The incentive of private ownership was still largely lacking when the peasants did not know how long they would retain their own particular strips of land. Furthermore, in a sense the peasant still found himself unfree, for the mir not only allotted him his strips of land but determined his portion of the land tax and even decided whether or not he might leave the mir. On the other hand, the landed proprietors often had difficulty in obtaining satisfactory labor to till the land which they still held after the peasants were no longer required to work for them.[5] Many proprietors gave up the attempt to exploit their own domains, sold parts or all of their holdings,[6] and moved to the cities.

After the emancipation of the serfs, other reforms were made which went far, it was thought, toward modernizing the character of the Russian state. In 1864 the tsar took a step which was believed by many to be second in importance only to his freeing of the serfs. By an imperial decree of that year he introduced a system of local self-government by the creation of zemstvos or assemblies. In each county of the thirty-four administrative provinces, or "governments," of Russia, a local zemstvo was created and empowered to levy local taxes and to look after such matters as roads, hospitals,

[4] Though the size of the peasant holdings after emancipation varied in different provinces, the average was slightly more than twenty-two acres.

[5] Apparently the small allotments of land to the peasants were designed in part to make the latter willing to work for the landed proprietors in order to supplement their own incomes.

[6] It has been estimated that by 1905 half of the land possessed by the nobility after emancipation had passed into peasant hands.

education, public health, and public welfare generally.[7] For the purpose of choosing the zemstvos the electorate of each county was divided into three classes—the private landowners, the mirs, and the townspeople—each of which elected representatives. The local zemstvos in turn chose provincial zemstvos. Although the zemstvos were authorized to deal only with matters with which the central government had not concerned itself, they provided political training in responsible administration and came in time to serve as critics of the tsar's regime. In 1870 town government was likewise reformed, and municipal *dumas* or councils, elected on a three-class system analogous to that in Prussia,[8] were established.

In the sixties, too, reforms were made in the judicial system of Russia, which had stood almost untouched since the days of Catherine the Great. By decrees of Alexander II civil and criminal cases were taken out of the hands of local administrators—usually landed proprietors—and turned over to a system of lower courts, which were freed of all class distinction and made independent of the administrative officials. The tsar's purpose appeared to be to institute in his empire a judicial system similar in its general outlines to that which existed in western Europe. Provision was therefore made for jury trial in criminal cases, for public rather than secret trials, for the appointment of prosecuting attorneys, for adequate remuneration of the judges, and for the use of private lawyers. The system, as completed, provided for justices of the peace, elected by the local zemstvos,[9] district and circuit judges, and a senate, the latter serving as the empire's highest court of appeal.

While reform was still the order of the day, the tsar also gave permission for travel abroad, restored a considerable measure of academic freedom to the universities, made easier of access the institutions of higher learning, encouraged the establishment of primary and technical schools, and considerably weakened the censorship of the press. The results of these steps, however, were not particularly pleasing to Alexander. Numerous publications at once began to use their liberty to criticize the gross incompetence of the tsar's administrative system; the views of the intelligentsia began

[7] The central government in St. Petersburg reserved to itself all police and military authority.

[8] See footnote on pages 94 and 95.

[9] Actually, however, the peasants in most cases involving small civil litigations were not allowed to use the new courts.

to be expressed through new magazines which catered to the professional and educated classes; and the wider opening of the doors of the universities tended to make more democratic and more critical the student bodies of those institutions.

If, as many aver, Alexander II was not at heart a true liberal, it is probably not surprising that he was easily and rather quickly turned against reform when incidents occurred to frighten or alarm him. Perhaps the first incident which led him to question the advisability of continuing as a liberal was the revolt which occurred in Russian Poland (1863), where groups of poorly armed patriots sought to throw off the Russian yoke. Although the insurrection was quickly suppressed by the tsar's army, Russian reactionaries and Slavophiles—those who cherished Russia's ancient institutions and opposed the introduction of Western ideas—were not slow to argue that the difficulties in Poland were the inevitable result of the tsar's liberal concessions. If he continued with his reform program, they declared, similar unrest and possibly insurrections might be expected in Russia proper. Their arguments were doubtless given added potency in the tsar's mind when an unbalanced communist attempted to shoot him in 1866.

In the ensuing years, therefore, Alexander II pursued a policy of reaction, as a result of which some of the chief reforms which he had introduced were greatly curtailed. The zemstvos, whose institution had been so gladly welcomed by public-spirited Russians, were within two years of their creation placed under the control of local governors, were restricted in the matter of publicity for their debates, and in 1868 were considerably limited in the matter of taxation. The reform of the judiciary was likewise never carried to its completion. The government failed to observe the principle that local judges were irremovable, and gradually different types of offenses were withdrawn from the jurisdiction of local courts. In 1878, for instance, it was ordered that political cases should be referred to courts-martial. The press, too, was increasingly subjected to new restrictions entailing limitation of subscribers and the necessity for advance censorship.

Attempts were also made to control advanced education in order to prevent the too widespread dissemination of dangerous ideas. History, modern languages, and geography were definitely subordinated to such supposedly nonrevolutionary subjects as Latin,

Greek, and mathematics. Science, on the other hand, was taken out of the curriculum altogether. In an effort to crush not only tendencies toward liberalism but tendencies toward nationalism as well, the government sought to suppress everything having to do with the Ukrainian (Little Russian) language and literature. It was ordered, for example, that Ukrainian should not be used in printing or on the stage, and that specialists in the study of the Ukrainian language and literature should be removed from university faculties. Similar steps were taken also against the Poles.

## NIHILISM AND TERRORISM

But at the very time when Alexander's government was becoming more and more reactionary, certain groups in the empire were seeking and demanding further liberal reforms. These demands were in part the rather natural consequence of the critical spirit which had been developed among the younger intellectuals during the sixties by the writings of two Russians, Alexander Herzen and Michael Bakunin. In 1857 the former, an exile in London, had founded a weekly journal—the *Kolokol* (*Bell*)—which was smuggled into Russia and which came to have a limited circulation among the intellectuals of that country. Through the *Kolokol* Herzen attacked various Russian institutions and advocated something in the nature of utopian socialism. But he was, after all, rather moderate in his demands, and so he has been called the father of Russian liberalism. Bakunin, on the other hand, was an extreme radical who is usually considered to have been the father of both Russian anarchism and terrorism. While a student in Germany he had come under the influence of the philosopher, Hegel, and later in Paris under that of the anarchist, Proudhon. During the fifties he had spent some years in Russian prisons, but he eventually escaped from Siberia and lived the rest of his life an exile from Russia. Through his writings Bakunin advocated the breaking of the restrictive bonds of religion, the state, and even the family in order that mankind might stand forth free and unshackled by conventions or authority. Such a change could be brought about, he declared, only by violence.

Although the Russian intellectuals did not at once take up Bakunin's program of violence, they did adopt a critical attitude toward Russian institutions and ideals. According to them, reason and science must be the yardsticks for judging institutions, and nothing of the old regime in Russia should be respected or accepted unless it measured up to these standards. The Russians who held these views became known as nihilists (*nihil* being the Latin for nothing). "A nihilist," wrote the Russian novelist, Turgenev, "is a man who does not bow down before any authority, who does not take any principle on faith, whatever reverence that principle may be enshrined in." In their role, therefore, the Russian nihilists of the nineteenth century were not unlike the French enlightened critics of the preceding century. Although they were not primarily interested in altering the political institutions of Russia, the critical attitude which they exalted inevitably reacted against the tsarist regime.

Before long many of the young intellectuals threw off the restraint of bureaucratic tradition and conservatism and began to demand civil equality, bona fide trial by jury, complete freedom of conscience and of the press, police reform, popular control of legislation and finance, and ministerial responsibility. Strange as it may seem, the intellectuals received some support from the nobility. Many of the latter believed that, since the nobles had been deprived of social and economic privileges by the abolition of serfdom, they should receive in exchange a part of the governing power of the empire. During the seventies there was a steadily increasing demand that elective representation should not be limited to the local zemstvos and dumas but should be extended to some national legislative body as well.

The younger intellectuals eventually came to the conclusion that to gain results they must first propagandize the masses, who were, of course, the peasants. In the seventies, therefore, hundreds of students went out to live among the peasants as teachers, laborers, physicians, nurses, clerks—in fact, they took any kind of job they could obtain. But the mission of these *narodniki* (men of the people) proved to be an utter failure. The government at once arrested and imprisoned or exiled several hundred participants in the movement. It was not difficult to identify them, of course, because radical intellectuals were bound to be conspicuous in a peasant village. The peasants themselves had little realization of the significance of the doctrines advocated by the *narodniki* and remained largely inert. It soon became evident to the intellectuals that the peasants were not interested in politics, or in socialism, but only in acquiring more land.

Thwarted in their efforts to enlighten the masses, many of the members of the *narodniki* became radical revolutionists and turned definitely to the use of terrorism as advocated earlier by Bakunin. "Terrorist activity," wrote one radical, "consists in the destruction of the most harmful persons in the government, the protection of the party from spies, and the punishment of official lawlessness and violence in all the more prominent and important cases in which such lawlessness and violence are manifested. The aim of such activity is to break down the prestige of governmental power, to furnish continuous proof of the possibility of carrying on a contest with the government, to raise in that way the revolutionary spirit of the people and inspire belief in the practicability of revolution, and, finally, to form a body suited and accustomed to warfare." In pursuance of this program spies and policemen were frequently assassinated, but gradually the terrorist campaign turned to high officials and ultimately came to center on Alexander himself. In 1873 a second futile attempt was made on his life. But when, shortly thereafter, the tsar embarked on another venture designed to gain for Russia the coveted outlet to the Mediterranean, it was hoped by many that a foreign war and an aroused national enthusiasm might ultimately engulf and destroy the menacing terrorists.

## INTERVENTION IN THE BALKANS

In the middle seventies conditions in the Balkans were such as again to encourage Russia to hope that she might benefit by intervention in that troubled part of Europe. Although, as the Ottoman flood had receded during the first half of the century, some of the Christian peoples had begun to emerge as national states, the sultan in 1870 still controlled the greater part of the Balkan peninsula. Despite the fact that the Greeks had established a small independent kingdom in the south, and the Rumanians, Serbs, and Montenegrins had carved out autonomous principalities in the north, the Ottoman Empire stretched across the Balkans from the Black Sea on the east to Austrian Dalmatia and the Adriatic on the west. Included within this Turkish realm was a heterogeneous population of Bulgarians, Macedonians, Greeks, Serbs, Albanians, and Bosnians, the great bulk of whom were Christians.

The Turks had never succeeded in assimilating these various peoples, largely because of the differences in religious faith and more lately because of the strong national sentiment which had begun to develop among them. On the other hand, the mutual jealousies and rival territorial ambitions which divided and weakened the subject peoples had enabled the sultan to retain his hold in the Balkans much longer than might otherwise have been expected. Because the subject Christian peoples, the *"rayahs"* (cattle), had been almost continuously exploited by their Moslem overlords, the powers, in the treaty of Paris (1856), had forced the sultan to promise to introduce reforms to safeguard the rights of these subjects. In practically every case, however, the half-hearted attempts at reform had broken down because of the inefficiency of Turkish officials and because of the opposition of the Moslem population.

In the summer of 1875 affairs in the Balkans reached a crisis when, as a result of the Moslem attempt to collect extortionate taxes, the Yugoslav populace of the little province of Herzegovina raised the standard of rebellion. Soon other uprisings occurred in Bosnia, where the rebels were strengthened by volunteers from the neighboring Yugoslav state, Serbia. The Bulgarians, probably the most downtrodden of the sultan's subject peoples, next took heart and seized the occasion to rise against their Turkish masters, only to be slaughtered without mercy by Ottoman forces. A tremendous wave of popular indignation swept through the Yugoslav peoples of the Balkans, and in response to it the rulers of the small principalities of Serbia and Montenegro declared war on Turkey, and the former immediately invited a Russian general to command the Serbian army. At once there arose the fear that from the Balkan war a general European conflict might develop.

In accordance with agreements reached in 1873 when the League of the Three Emperors had been created,[10] the emperors of Austria, Russia, and Germany, in January, 1876, sent a joint note to the sultan demanding reforms in the interests of the latter's Christian subjects, but the Balkan insurgents were not satisfied with the sultan's promises and continued to fight on. In May the three em-

[10] See page 67.

perors again intervened to demand an armistice, but without effect. Two months later Emperor Francis Joseph and Tsar Alexander met at Reichstadt to consider the Balkan situation. At that time they agreed not to intervene for the present, but further agreed that if Russian intervention with resultant territorial changes should occur, Austria should receive the provinces of Bosnia and Herzegovina. Apparently, too, it was agreed that Russia should regain the strip of Bessarabia which she had lost in 1856 and should make additions of territory along the eastern shores of the Black Sea. Provision was also made for the territorial enlargement of Serbia, Montenegro, and Greece, for the establishment of Bulgaria and Rumelia as autonomous states, and for the transformation of Constantinople into a free city.

Military operations had meanwhile continued in the Balkans, and by the autumn of 1876 it appeared that the Turkish forces would capture Belgrade, the capital of Serbia. In October, therefore, Russia intervened with an ultimatum demanding an armistice, which was this time accepted. Great Britain now concluded that, unless the plight of the Christian subjects of the sultan was at once alleviated, Russia would probably declare war upon Turkey. In a war in behalf of fellow-Christians against what the British Liberal leader, Gladstone, called the "unspeakable Turk," Russia would undoubtedly have the popular sympathy of Europe and might therefore be in a position to recover that informal protectorate over Turkey which she had sought and lost in 1853–1856. Great Britain accordingly invited the powers to a conference at Constantinople to consider means of adjusting the Balkan situation without territorial gains to any of the great powers.

Such a conference opened in December, 1876, but when Sultan Abdul Hamid II refused to weaken his independence by giving the powers any authority in his empire, the conference disbanded two months later without tangible result. In March, 1877, the powers, meeting in London, reached another agreement looking to the protection of the Turkish Christians, but the sultan obstinately refused to consider even this more moderate proposal, citing the treaty of Paris to prove that Turkey was absolutely independent of outside intervention. Feeling was by this time so high in Russia that, despite a warning of bankruptcy by his minister of finance, Alexander II declared war against Turkey on April 24, 1877. Russia was later joined in the war by the neighboring principality of Rumania.

For a time Russia's military progress was not great, for she was handicapped by the fact that her army reforms had not yet been completed.[11] She was also hampered by the perennial evils of incapable leadership, peculation in army contracts, and administrative abuses. Nevertheless, victories finally came. In November, 1877, Kars was taken; in December the main Turkish army was captured with the fall of Plevna, and the Russian troops began to cross the Balkan Mountains; in February, 1878, the tsar's forces were approaching Constantinople and were at last in sight of their long-sought goal.

But unfortunately for Russia's plans, the nearer her forces approached the coveted Turkish capital, the more other powers appeared to prepare to intervene. Austrian forces were moved into the Carpathians, where, if called upon, they could strike at the flank of the Russian army; and a British fleet, at first concentrated in the eastern Mediterranean, in February entered the Straits, where it would be in a position to bombard the tsar's forces if they attempted to take Constantinople. Furthermore, the British government let it be known that Russia's entrance into that city would constitute a cause for war. Accordingly, when Abdul Hamid offered to open peace negotiations, the tsar considered it the better part of wisdom to accept without actually entering the Ottoman capital. The treaty which resulted took its name from San Stefano, a village not far from Constantinople.

Ignoring the agreements which had been reached by Alexander and Francis Joseph at Reichstadt in 1876, Russia now dictated a treaty which left to the sultan in Europe only an area in the vicinity of the Straits, including Constantinople and Adrianople, and the detached district of Albania along the Adriatic in the west. Rumania, Serbia, and Montenegro were to be enlarged territorially and to be recognized by the sultan as entirely independent politically. A new Christian state, Bulgaria, was to be created with boundaries to include not only Bulgaria proper but most of Macedonia from the Aegean to Albania. Such a Bulgaria would be the largest of all the Balkan states. It would still in theory belong to the Otto-

---

[11] In 1874 Alexander II had begun reforms which were designed to organize the Russian army according to the Prussian system of universal military service.

man Empire and would pay an annual tribute to the sultan in recognition of this status, but it would have its own prince and make its own laws. Bosnia and Herzegovina were also to receive a measure of autonomy in the interests of their Christian subjects; nothing was said about handing these provinces over to Austria-Hungary.

But the tsar was not unmindful of the interests of his own empire. Russia was to obtain part of Armenia, where her armies had been victorious, a strip of the Dobrudja adjoining Rumania,[12] the destruction of all Turkish fortifications along the Danube, the opening of the Straits to the commerce of all nations, and a large war indemnity. In addition to advancing his empire in the region across the Caucasus, he had, he hoped, greatly increased his influence if not his territorial holdings in the Balkans, for it was rather to be expected that the new Bulgaria, brought into being by the tsar and not yet completely independent of the sultan, would become a satellite of the Russian Empire. It was hoped, too, that the other Balkan states which would benefit by the treaty of San Stefano might out of gratitude be loyal to the tsar's interests. Finally, it is possible that the tsar expected that the sultan's inability to pay the large war indemnity would provide Russia with an excuse to interfere in Turkish affairs. The net result of the treaty of San Stefano seemed particularly favorable to the tsar.

That fact was also abundantly clear to both Austria-Hungary and Great Britain. Quite apparently the tsar had flagrantly violated the agreement reached with Francis Joseph at Reichstadt. The Habsburg hope of eventually securing a suitable port on the Aegean now seemed blocked by the creation of a big Bulgaria. Austria-Hungary, therefore, was bitterly opposed to the treaty of San Stefano. But so also was Great Britain. Statesmen of the latter feared, or professed to fear, that an advance of Russia's interests either in Asiatic Turkey or in the Balkans would endanger British dominance in the eastern Mediterranean and seriously menace Britain's route to India. In fact, British desire to keep Russia back from the Mediterranean had been increased by the opening of the Suez Canal in 1869. Consequently, Great Britain and the Dual Monarchy decided to block Russia by refusing to accept the treaty

[12] Russia planned to exchange the strip of the Dobrudja for the strip of Bessarabia which had been transferred from Russia to Rumania by the treaty of Paris (1856).

THE BALKANS BY THE TREATY OF SAN STEFANO

THE BALKANS BY THE TREATY OF BERLIN

of San Stefano and in this decision were supported by Serbia and
Greece, both of which were alarmed by the creation of a big Bulgaria.

Austria-Hungary, therefore, announced that Russia had no right
to revise the treaty of Paris by her unilateral action, asserted that
the Balkan situation was one which concerned all the powers that
were signatories of that earlier treaty, and demanded that the treaty
of San Stefano be submitted to a general conference of the signatory powers. The aggressive, imperialistic Lord Beaconsfield (Disraeli) immediately aligned Great Britain with the Dual Monarchy
and even threatened war if the tsar did not accede to their demand.
Alexander was extremely reluctant to submit his treaty to an international conference, but he soon discovered that Russia stood
isolated among the great powers and, mindful of the outcome of
the Crimean War, eventually gave way to Austro-British pressure.
Upon the invitation of Bismarck, who promised to act as an "honest broker" for the interested powers, the ensuing congress met at
Berlin in the summer of 1878.

In general, the Balkan states fared worse under the new treaty
of Berlin than they had by the treaty which Russia had dictated.
The big Bulgaria created by the San Stefano agreement was split
into three parts: Bulgaria proper, the northern section, was made
an autonomous principality subject to annual tribute to the sultan;
Eastern Rumelia, the southeastern section of the proposed big Bulgaria, was granted some administrative autonomy with a Christian
governor but under the military and political control of the sultan;
the rest of the proposed big Bulgaria was restored to the sultan
without restrictions. Thus, at the expense of Bulgarian nationalism,
the great powers endeavored to thwart Russia's hopes of increased
influence in the Balkans. Rumania, Serbia, and Montenegro were
formally recognized as independent, but the last two received less
in territory than Russia had planned to give them. Of all the
Balkan states, perhaps Greece fared best, for the congress recommended that Turkey cede her Thessaly, and this was done in 1881.

Russia, the victor in the war, received from Rumania [13] the small
strip of Bessarabia, which she had lost by the treaty of Paris, and
the region around Batum, Ardahan, and Kars, which she had con-

---

[13] Rumania was forced to content herself with the annexation of part of the Dobrudja,
with a population largely non-Rumanian.

quered in the Caucasus. Austria-Hungary and Great Britain each
took part of the spoils. The former gained the right to occupy and
administer Bosnia and Herzegovina, the right to garrison Novibazar, and special commercial privileges in Serbia and Montenegro.
The latter, in a separate Turco-British convention, obtained the island of Cyprus in the eastern Mediterranean in return for her
promise to uphold the territorial integrity of the Ottoman Empire
against any future Russian attack. To Russia it appeared that,
though she had sacrificed thousands of lives and spent millions of
rubles to improve her position in the Balkans, the Austrians and
British, merely by cleverly playing the game of diplomacy, had secured in the final settlement greater gains.

Russia's humiliation at the Congress of Berlin contributed not at
all to Alexander's popularity among Russian patriots, nor did the
reactionary measures which his government had begun to take even
before the Russo-Turkish War add to his popularity among the
liberals and radicals. In fact, the liberal desire for a constitution
was still further accentuated when Bulgaria, the little Slavic state
created largely as a result of the tsar's efforts, received a constitution. In 1879 the terrorists published the tsar's "death sentence,"
and thereafter pursued more vigorously than ever their campaign
of violence. Late in that year an attempt was made to wreck the
tsar's train while it was on the way from the Crimea to the capital;
and in February, 1880, the dining room of the Winter Palace was
blown up, the tsar escaping death only because his expected guest
was a half hour late. On the other hand, during these years the
government redoubled its efforts in a countercampaign of oppression.

Ultimately Alexander decided that he must give way to liberal
sentiment. He therefore appointed a commission headed by the
minister of the interior, Loris Melikov, conferred upon it dictatorial
powers, and authorized it to find a solution for the situation. Melikov believed that revolutionary activities could not be stopped by
repressive measures alone. He argued that, if the government could
placate the liberals by granting a moderate constitution, it could at
the same time deprive the radicals of the moral support of this
group. In February, 1881, the minister of the interior submitted to
the tsar a scheme for associating popularly elected representatives
with the government in legislative work. On March 13 the tsar

signed Melikov's project, but later that same day, while driving on the Catherine Canal, he was assassinated by a nihilist's bomb. "The bomb that killed Alexander put an end to the faint beginnings of Russian constitutionalism."

## REACTION, REPRESSION, AND "RUSSIFICATION"

The new tsar, Alexander III, although undoubtedly courageous, industrious, and honest, was by intellect and education greatly limited in his outlook. He had opposed his father's return to a policy of liberalism in 1881, and for him his father's assassination was sufficient proof of the futility of such a course. Furthermore, by his intimate advisers—especially by Constantine Pobiedonostsev, his former tutor—Alexander III was strongly urged to abandon liberalism and to withhold from publication the projected scheme for political reform. It is not surprising, therefore, that the new tsar departed from his father's course and in his accession manifesto openly proclaimed his faith in the power and right of autocracy. The plan for establishing a sort of representative government, which had been devised by Melikov and accepted by Alexander II, was accordingly never executed. Instead, a policy of reaction and repression, at once inaugurated, was vigorously pursued throughout his reign.

Upon his death in 1894 Alexander III was succeeded by his twenty-six-year-old son, who ascended the throne as Nicholas II. Lacking most of the qualities of a statesman and leader, Nicholas was not particularly interested in political matters, but he was firmly determined to maintain the principle of autocracy unchanged. He was easily influenced by those surrounding him, and since in the early years of his reign many of his intimate advisers were inherited from his father, it is not surprising that he adopted and put into effect the political program of Alexander III. The granting of a constitution and the establishment of an imperial parliament were, in the words of Nicholas II, only "senseless dreams." From 1881 to 1917, therefore, Russia was subjected almost continuously to a policy of reaction, repression, and "Russification," though in the last decade of this period the accumulated popular discontent was usually at or near the explosive point.

The directing genius in this policy of repression was Pobiedonostsev, who held the office of procurator of the holy synod. He formulated for the tsarist policy of reaction a political theory based on a deep distrust of human intellect and human nature. "If all representatives of the people were saints," he wrote, "a parliamentary regime would be the very best kind of all; but as the morality of popular representatives is usually more than dubious, a parliamentary regime is the worst." To his mind democracy of the Western type was rotten, and only the Russian patriarchal system of government was still sound. Parliaments, freedom of the press, secular education, jury trials were all to him anathema. His position as lay chairman of the governing body of the Russian Orthodox Church he deliberately utilized to crush liberalism and foster reaction. Sermons of clergymen were censored, and village priests were instructed to report to the police any of their parishioners who appeared to be "politically untrustworthy."

Assisting Pobiedonostsev in the execution of the policy of repression was Viatscheslav Plehve, the director of the department of secret police in the ministry of the interior. Through the agency of the so-called "Third Section," which was authorized to make arrests without warrants and to punish without trials, Plehve sought to crush all opposition to the tsarist regime. Ubiquitous spies and secret police diligently ferreted out and mercilessly suppressed the liberals and radicals. Imprisonment, exile, or death was the lot of those who dared to oppose the government. Thousands were sent to penal colonies in the wilds of Siberia, while other thousands sought safety by flight to foreign countries.

In accordance with Alexander III's "cold storage" policy for Russia—that is, his policy of preserving Russian autocratic institutions by keeping them from being contaminated by contact with Western ideas—the program of repression was directed particularly against education and the press, the avenues through which a free public opinion might be expected to manifest itself. Children of the lower classes were excluded from the secondary schools, and Pobiedonostsev even made a futile attempt to have the primary schools transferred from the control of the local zemstvos to the church. The universities were deprived of all autonomy, and student clubs were forbidden. Courses of study were modified by government decree, and many well-known books by foreign authors were excluded from use by Russian intellectuals. When student demonstrations were staged against such measures, they were ruthlessly suppressed by troops. Many students were expelled from the universities; many were sent into exile. Intellectuals who were suspected of "revolutionary" political tendencies were placed under police supervision, while control of the press was made complete by subjecting most magazines and newspapers to a "preliminary censorship" of government agents.

To strengthen itself against the forces of liberalism and radicalism, the government sought to win the support of the nobles. Special privileges were extended to them in the realm of local government, and steps were taken to bring the peasants partly back under their control. For this purpose, apparently, the office of land captain was created. These land captains were appointed by the government from the nobility and were placed under the direct control of the tsar's minister of the interior. They were given not only administrative power in local affairs but also authority to act as judges over the peasants. Moreover, the system of representation in the zemstvos and dumas was deliberately altered so as to increase the influence of the nobility and of the wealthier classes, and at the same time other measures were inaugurated which were designed to weaken the influence of the peasants. After 1890, for instance, the latter were permitted to elect only candidates for the zemstvos, the actual peasant representatives being finally chosen by the governors from the list of candidates. Despite this alteration in the system of representation, however, the zemstvos and dumas continued to be suspected by the government, which deliberately weakened their powers while increasing those of the government-appointed provincial governors.

Accompanying the government's policy of reaction and repression was that of "Russification." It has already been pointed out that a considerable part of the population of the Russian Empire consisted of non-Russians. To Alexander III and his Slavophile ministers this situation constituted a challenge, and they inaugurated measures which were designed to meet it. They sought to achieve within the empire uniformity in such matters as language, religion, and general cultural ideals, and to this end vigorous steps were taken to crush all national feeling in the non-Russian parts of the realm—particularly in Finland, Poland, and the Baltic provinces.

Finland at the time of her conquest had been granted autonomy by Alexander I, and in the minds of the Finns their country was bound to Russia only by a personal union through the tsar. In accordance with the policy of "Russification," however, Finland's political rights were progressively ignored. In the nineties Russians began to supplant Finns in the higher administrative offices, and ability to use the Russian language became necessary for an office-holder in even the lower ranks of the administration. By an imperial decree (1899) the diet of Finland was arbitrarily reduced to the status of a mere consultative body, and a Russian was appointed secretary of state for Finland in defiance of the Finnish constitution. Eventually, Russian was made the official language of Finland (1900), the independent Finnish army was abolished and replaced by the Russian military system (1901), all administrative offices in Finland were opened to Russians (1902), and the tsarist system of espionage, arbitrary arrest, and imprisonment was extended to that grand duchy (1903).

Even under Alexander II repressive measures against the Poles had been initiated as a result of the Polish uprising of 1863, and under Alexander III further steps were taken to crush Polish nationalism. As a consequence, the use of the Polish language was made illegal, and all teachers were compelled to use Russian— even when they were giving instruction in Polish literature and language! The use of the Russian language on business and trade signs was made obligatory. Public offices in Poland were closed to Poles, and for more than a decade after 1885 Poles might not legally sell land to non-Russians. In the Baltic provinces of Estonia and Latvia, where German barons had long held an ascendancy over the peasants, the Slavophile goal was the destruction of the cultural dominance of the Germans. Russian was made the official language instead of German, and eventually in these provinces "Russification" went so far as to force the change of German place names to Russian and to forbid the use of German in both public and private educational institutions.

"Russification" also led to various measures of repression against the adherents of religious faiths other than Russian Orthodoxy. In the Baltic provinces, for example, the erection of Lutheran churches was made dependent upon the consent of the procurator of the holy synod, and Lutheran schools were placed under the control of the tsarist government. In Poland the government interfered with the

Roman Catholic Church, depriving it of its revenues and converting parish priests into salaried state officials. Following the Polish
uprising of 1863, many Roman Catholic monasteries had been suppressed and their property confiscated. In Lithuania and White
Russia the "uniate" Catholics [14] were persecuted, their marriages
and their children being officially considered as illegitimate.

The five million Jews who lived within the empire suffered particularly from the policy of "Russification." Since they differed from
the great bulk of the Russians in race, religion, language, and social customs, their loyalty was suspected by the government, and
they were openly discriminated against. During the eighties and
nineties a number of anti-Jewish measures were introduced which
definitely marked the Jews as a class apart. As a consequence, they
became legally restricted in respect to their residence, their political
rights, their educational opportunities, and their economic status.

In the matter of residence, all Jews were expected to live within
the so-called Jewish Pale, which comprised the Ukraine, Poland,
and Lithuania. Exceptions were offered for certain classes of Jews
—university graduates, wealthy merchants, professional men, and
artisans—who might, if they were fortunate, obtain special licenses
from the government permitting them to reside outside the Pale.
Within the Pale the Jews were generally compelled to live in towns
and cities under the surveillance of the government. They were
forbidden to move into the smaller villages. Their political rights
were definitely restricted, for they could not vote for members
of the dumas in the cities in which they lived but had to be content with such representatives as the governor might appoint. In
the matter of education the number of Jews who might enter secondary schools and universities was limited to a fixed percentage
of the student body which ranged from 3 per cent to 10 per cent,
depending upon the location of the institution. Many were forced
to leave Russia in order to obtain the education which they desired.

Economically, the Jews were subjected to numerous restrictions.
They could not legally buy or lease land in rural districts. Practically all public employment was closed to them. Authority had to
be secured from the government before a Jew could become a law-

[14] The Uniates—members of the United Greek Church—retained many of the practices
of the Greek Orthodox Church, but recognized the leadership of the pope at Rome.

yer, for the government sought to limit the number of Jews in the various professions. The number of Jewish stockholders in any industrial corporation was definitely limited. Although obliged to serve in the army, they might not rise to the rank of officer. As a result of these restrictions, many Jews became, almost of necessity, bankers or retail merchants. In these capacities they frequently won the hatred of the peasants because of their high rates of interest or high mercantile profits.

It must not be thought, of course, that all of these laws were always and everywhere enforced. Russian officials were frequently open to corruption, and Jews by "paying the price" might gain a certain precarious immunity. On the other hand, Russian officials sometimes went to the other extreme and did not afford the Jews the protection to which they were legally entitled. At times anti-Jewish riots—pogroms—broke out, at which time Jews were more or less systematically subjected to plundering and even massacre while the police looked on with toleration. Perhaps the most notorious of these pogroms occurred in 1903 in the Bessarabian city of Kishinev, when the Jewish quarter of the city was raided and hundreds of Jews were killed or wounded. Anti-Jewish legislation and pogroms such as this led hundreds of thousands of Jews to migrate from Russia to the United States, carrying with them their deep-seated and bitter hatred of the tsarist regime.

## THE INTRODUCTION OF MODERN INDUSTRIALISM

Despite the government's policy of reaction and repression, economic developments during the reigns of Alexander III and Nicholas II were producing certain classes which were destined eventually to challenge and destroy the government responsible for that policy. Until about the time of Alexander III, Russia had remained almost exclusively an agricultural country, a land of peasants dominated by a landed aristocracy and an Orthodox clergy. There was no strong and ambitious bourgeois class and no numerous and aggressive group of industrial workers. Beginning in the eighties, however, this condition was gradually altered by the introduction of modern industrialism of the Western type.

A number of factors made possible Russia's relatively rapid industrial development in the succeeding years. In the first place, the empire possessed considerable quantities of such basic raw materials as coal, iron, and petroleum. In the second place, an abundant supply of cheap labor was available during these years because of the rapid growth of the peasant population after emancipation, with the consequent pressure of rural population on the inadequate land-holdings.[15] In the third place, in the late eighties Russia began to borrow extensively from abroad and thus secured funds not only for stabilizing her currency and for military purposes, but also for railway construction and for loans to private industrial enterprises as well. And what the Russian government did in these respects Russian bankers and private industrialists did also. By 1914 foreign loans totaling billions of dollars had been utilized, in part, to provide the needed capital for the development of Russia's resources.

The one who did most, perhaps, to hasten the advent of modern industrialism in Russia in the period before the World War was Sergius Witte, "the Colbert of Russia." After having served as head of the government's department of railways and as minister of communications, in 1892 he became Alexander III's minister of finance, a post in which he was retained by Nicholas II until 1903. Not without considerable opposition from Slavophiles—who looked upon the development of Russian industrialism as an injury to the peasants and a menace to autocracy—Witte did his utmost to encourage the rise of industry and the expansion of railway facilities within the empire. He assiduously sought foreign loans to finance both industry and transportation and deliberately pursued a policy of high protective tariffs to aid the former.

The economic consequences of Russia's adoption of modern industrialism soon became obvious. By 1895 the railway mileage within the Russian Empire had risen to approximately 22,000; by 1914 it had increased to more than 40,000. Railways transformed the economic situation in Russia, for with railways it became possible to link together the vast resources of the empire, to transport commodities from places of abundance to areas of scarcity, to get goods more readily and assuredly to markets both at home and abroad. In consequence, mines were opened, factories were constructed, and commerce was increased. From the Donets basin by 1914 came annually millions of tons of coal; from the region about Baku came other millions of tons of petroleum. By 1914, too, Russia was pro-

[15] Between 1850 and 1900 the population of Russia doubled.

ducing more than four million tons of pig iron being exceeded in this respect only by Great Britain, the United States, and Germany. But the most important branch of Russia's industries was the manufacture of textiles. By 1914 Russia was able not only to satisfy her home demand for cotton goods but to compete successfully in foreign markets as well. In the production of cotton goods she stood fourth in the world.[16]

The introduction of modern industrialism into Russia and the consequent need for obtaining large loans from abroad had an influence also upon the government's foreign policy. Before the eighties Russia's foreign loans had been floated largely in Germany, but during that decade the increased demand for funds to advance Germany's own industrial and imperial programs began to absorb German capital. Furthermore, Bismarck sought to bring political pressure on Russia by excluding her bonds from the Berlin stock exchange. But Russia was increasingly in need of foreign financial assistance, and when a group of French bankers offered in 1888 to grant a loan to her, she turned to France as the source of her future borrowings. Naturally, the relations between the two governments became more cordial. Consequently, when in 1890 Germany declined to renew the existing reinsurance treaty with Russia [17] and the latter found herself cast adrift and isolated among the powers, it was almost inevitable that she should look with favor upon suggestions of a *rapprochement* when they were made by French statesmen. The result, as has already been pointed out,[18] was the Franco-Russian entente of 1891, which led in 1894 to the Franco-Russian defensive alliance against Germany.

Connected, also, with Russia's industrialization were the efforts made under Witte's direction to advance Russia's economic penetration of regions adjoining the empire. In the early nineties, for instance, Witte called attention to the economic opportunities which were open to Russia in Persia. In consequence, a Russo-Persian bank was organized, and, supported by the tsarist government, it undertook to finance Russian concessions and Russian trade

[16] Because of the protective tariffs, however, the great bulk of the Russians—the peasants—had to pay higher prices for many commodities than they had paid before the advent of industrialism in Russia.

[17] See page 76.

[18] See page 115.

in Persia. In the succeeding years Persia became the principal foreign market for Russia's cotton industries, which were able successfully to compete there with British goods.

But Witte's attention was not focused merely on the Middle East. Under his direction the construction of a trans-Siberian railway was begun in the nineties in order that European Russia might have a railway connection with Vladivostok, her port on the Sea of Japan. For more than a decade thereafter the work was pushed forward with funds provided largely by loans floated in France. In 1905 the 5000-mile, single-track railway was finally completed, and railway communication between St. Petersburg and Vladivostok was actually inaugurated.

## IMPERIALISM IN THE FAR EAST

The construction of the trans-Siberian railway constituted part of Russia's century-long search for a suitable outlet to the high seas. Her attempts to advance to the Mediterranean, made earlier in the nineteenth century, had been resolutely checked by the great powers. Her move southward through central Asia had likewise been stopped—at least temporarily—by Great Britain in the eighties. In the nineties Russia temporarily laid aside her ambitions in the Balkans [19] and determined to seek a warm-water port in the Far East. She saw no reason why, if the powers were bent upon dismembering China, she should not secure her share, especially since by pushing southward through Chinese territory she might obtain an all-year ice-free port. Russia apparently marked out for her immediate expansion the Chinese territories of Manchuria and Korea. These, if annexed to the Russian Empire or if converted into Russian spheres of influence, would provide excellent ports to supplement Vladivostok, which was closed for part of each year. Control of Manchuria, moreover, would enable Russia to build across that province a shorter and more direct line to Vladivostok.

Probably, if Russia had had to deal only with the "backward" Chinese, she would have succeeded in carrying through these plans in the Far East with a large degree of success. But unfortunately for Russia's ambitions, she was forced to deal not only with the Chinese but with the Japanese as well. As already pointed out, Japan in the second half of the nineteenth century had been rapidly

[19] For the Austro-Russian treaty of 1897, see page 337.

adopting many Western ideas and institutions, had rapidly industrialized herself, and by the closing decade of the century was ready to embark upon a program of imperial expansion. She was especially desirous of securing Korea, a tributary kingdom of China lying on the Asiatic mainland just across Tsushima Strait from Japanese territory. As a result of Japanese interference in Korean affairs a war was precipitated between China and Japan in 1894.

The Sino-Japanese War of 1894–1895 quickly revealed that the Chinese were no match for the Japanese, who had modernized their military and naval forces. By the treaty of Shimonoseki, which Japan dictated to China, the latter agreed (1) to cede to Japan the island of Formosa and the Liao-tung peninsula in southern Manchuria, (2) to pay an indemnity of $150,000,000, and (3) to recognize Korea as an independent kingdom. Independence for Korea was generally recognized as merely a step preliminary to absorption by Japan. Naturally, Japan's acquisition of a foothold on the Asiatic mainland in territory desired by Russia was particularly distasteful to the latter. If Korea came into the hands of Japan, the latter would control both sides of Tsushima Strait, the southern outlet of the Sea of Japan upon which Vladivostok was located. Should Japan also secure Port Arthur and the Liao-tung peninsula, Russia would be prevented from obtaining a warm-water port in that region.

Russia therefore determined to force Japan to withdraw from the Asiatic mainland and turned to France and Germany for support in this program. France, which had only recently succeeded in securing Russia as an ally, naturally responded with alacrity to the Russian request for joint intervention in the Far East. At the same time the Kaiser, desiring Russia's support for Germany's contemplated plans in the Far East,[20] willingly lent his support to the Russian plan of intervention. Possibly the Kaiser even hoped to weaken the Franco-Russian alliance by helping one member of that alliance to become so deeply involved in the Far East that it would be unable to play an aggressive role in the West.[21]

Soon after the conclusion of the treaty of Shimonoseki the three powers in a joint note "advised" Japan to refrain from annexing any part of the Chinese mainland. Japan had not yet proved her mettle

[20] See page 79.
[21] "We must try," wrote the Kaiser in 1895, "to nail Russia down in eastern Asia, so that she may occupy herself less with Europe and the Near East."

against any of the great powers of the West and could not contemplate with equanimity a clash between herself and a coalition consisting of Russia, Germany, and France. She therefore gave up her claim to territory on the Asiatic mainland and in return received from China an additional indemnity of $22,500,000.

Russia, posing as the defender of Chinese territorial integrity, next sought to advance her own position in China. In 1896 a treaty of friendship was concluded between Russia and China in which the former undertook to aid the latter in case she were attacked by a third power. China, on her part, was persuaded to permit the establishment of the Russo-Chinese Bank,[22] which was to assist the Chinese government to meet its indemnity payments to Japan and and which was also authorized to embark upon various types of financial and economic enterprises in China. Later in the same year this newly organized bank secured a concession to build the Chinese Eastern Railway from Chita in Siberia across Manchuria to Vladivostok. Such a railway would obviously connect Russia's port in the Far East with inland Siberia and European Russia by a much shorter and more direct route than that of the circuitous trans-Siberian railway. The political nature of the proposed railway was indicated by the fact that its bonds were to be guaranteed by the Russian government and that Russian military guards could be stationed along the railway to maintain order even in time of peace.

In 1898 Russia further strengthened her position in the Far East by securing (1) a twenty-five-year lease of about five hundred square miles of territory—including part of the region surrendered by Japan in 1895—at the end of the Liao-tung peninsula, and (2) the right to construct a branch line to connect this territory with the Chinese Eastern Railway at Harbin.[23] Subsequently the harbor of Dalny was improved for commercial use, and a powerful fortress and a naval base were constructed at Port Arthur. At last Russia had a warm-water outlet for her trans-Siberian railway. Moreover,

---

[22] It was organized as a Russian corporation.

[23] Great Britain attempted through diplomacy to prevent Russia's acquisition of these bases, but Russia was supported by Germany and France and secured Japan's acquiescence by concessions to the latter in Korea. In the end Great Britain had to be content with the lease of Weihaiwei on the northern coast of the Shantung peninsula, on the southern coast of which Germany had just secured a foothold at Kiaochow (see page 79). France joined in the scramble for leases and obtained a concession on the shores of Kwangchow Bay.

Manchuria, it appeared, must inevitably come under Russia's economic and military dominance, for the railways would largely control the commerce of the province,[24] and would greatly facilitate the movement of Russian troops. Furthermore, the stationing of Russian guards along the railway routes and the presence of Russian military and naval forces at Port Arthur presaged ill for Chinese sovereignty in Manchuria. During the Boxer rebellion (1900), in fact, Russia sent troops into the province apparently with a view to detaching it from China, and after the rebellion she neglected to withdraw them.

Russia's apparent decision to annex Manchuria was particularly distasteful to the Japanese. The latter therefore protested against the former's military occupation of the province, and Russia promised to withdraw her forces—but again neglected to do so. Actually Russia was determined to hold Manchuria and even had visions of adding Korea also. Russians were already trying to gain concessions and political influence in that kingdom. But Korea, though nominally independent, had since 1895 been considered by the Japanese as their special sphere. They naturally became alarmed. For a time, however, Japanese statesmen were divided as to the correct policy to pursue. Some argued that Japan might better come to a compromise agreement with Russia and permit the latter to seize Manchuria. Others held that a war against Russia was inevitable and that Japan should seek to secure an anti-Russian alliance with Great Britain.

In 1901 Japan opened negotiations with both St. Petersburg and London. As it chanced, Great Britain also was alarmed by Russia's activities in the Far East and was ready to abandon her long-cherished policy of isolation for an Anglo-Japanese alliance. The treaty concluding such an alliance was signed in January, 1902.[25] The terms of the alliance assured Japan that, if war occurred between herself and Russia, Great Britain would remain neutral, and that, if any power assisted Russia in such a war, Great Britain would come to the aid of Japan. By thus choosing to ally herself with Great Britain, Japan, it appeared, had determined to check Russian expansion in the Far East even at the cost of war.

[24] The Chinese Eastern Railway was given mining rights along its route.
[25] For the terms, see page 200.

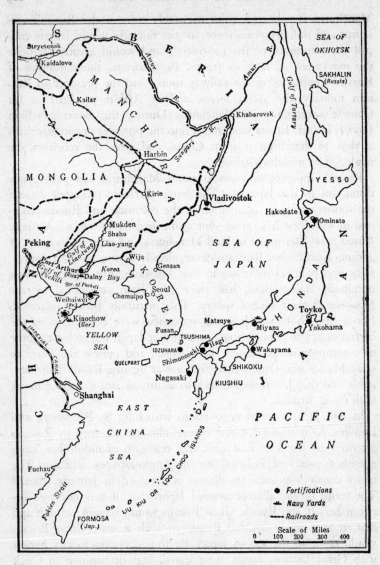

THE FAR EAST IN 1904

## THE RUSSO-JAPANESE WAR

In 1903 Japan attempted to reach an agreement with Russia. As a preliminary she demanded that the latter withdraw her troops from Manchuria. She suggested, however, that she might be willing to recognize Russia's ascendancy in the greater part of that province if Russia would recognize Japan's right of intervention in Korea and if Japan might build a railway from Korea into Manchuria to connect with the Chinese Eastern. When Russia hesitated to commit herself and delayed making a definite reply, the Japanese government became impatient and broke off diplomatic relations. Japanese statesmen apparently believed that Russia by her dilatory tactics was merely trying to postpone the inevitable conflict until her strategic railways in the Far East should be completed and until her Pacific war fleet should be freed from the handicap of winter's ice. They decided not to wait for Russia's convenience and on February 8, 1904, Japan launched a surprise attack upon the Russian warships at Port Arthur. Two days later she formally declared war. A struggle to determine which power should dominate the Far East was thus inaugurated.

To the casual observer it appeared that the war was to be a conflict between a powerful giant from the West and an inexperienced, weak pigmy from the East. But superficial appearances were altogether deceiving. Although Russia was vastly superior in man power and resources, she was seriously handicapped from the very outset by her inability to bring her full strength to bear. The scene of the conflict was far distant from the heart of Russia, and her troops and supplies had to be transported thousands of miles over the single-track trans-Siberian railway. Furthermore, although the Russian troops were probably not greatly inferior to the Japanese, they lacked enthusiasm for the war, whose purpose they either did not understand or did not approve. In fact, the war never received the whole-hearted support of the Russian people. Moreover, the twin evils of inefficiency and corruption, which had so often undermined Russian armies in the past, were again present and operative. Finally, it was Russia's misfortune to have a supreme command which lacked initiative and strategic ability.

Japan, on the other hand, had a highly disciplined, efficient, and enthusiastic military force, which was ably directed by its commanding officers and loyally supported by the populace at home. Furthermore, she was in close proximity to the seat of hostilities and in a position to place her forces in the field with a minimum of difficulty. Perhaps most important of all, as a result of her surprise stroke against the Russian warships Japan was in complete control of the sea. Without such control, in fact, she could hardly have maintained an army on the Asiatic mainland. It was the realization of this fact that had led her to cripple Russia's fleet by a surprise attack before war was formally declared.

With the Russian fleet at Port Arthur severely damaged, Japan proceeded to rush her troops into southern Manchuria. There they cut off Port Arthur, drove the tsar's forces back to the north, and in the autumn of 1904 succeeded in defeating the main Russian army under General Kuropatkin in a great battle at Liaoyang. Early in 1905 Port Arthur, besieged by land and blockaded by sea, surrendered to the Japanese. In March the Russian army was again decisively defeated, this time in a ten-day battle farther north at Mukden. Following this disaster, the possibility of a Russian victory in the war appeared to hang on the fate of a Russian fleet which was even then on its way to engage the Japanese.

In September, 1904, thirty-six Russian warships, commanded by Admiral Rozhestvensky, had left the Baltic bound for Japanese waters. Part of the fleet had gone eastward through the Mediterranean while the main detachment had proceeded around Africa, and not until the spring of 1905 had the reunited fleet eventually reached Far Eastern waters. At the time of the defeat at Mukden it was slowly feeling its way northward through the South China Sea and up the Chinese coast. If the Russians could win the impending naval engagement and gain control of the sea, they would be in a position to isolate the Japanese army in Manchuria and even to bombard Japanese coast cities and towns. Japan might be forced to withdraw from the war. But an increasing sense of despair prevailed among the men in the Russian fleet, who realized that an incompetent government had sent them on a mad naval venture. Already absent eight months from their Baltic bases, having steamed halfway around the world, they were destined to meet in its home waters an efficient modern fleet of proved mettle and with a capable commander in the person of Admiral Togo.

On May 15 the Russian warships encountered Admiral Togo's

whole fleet off the coast of the Japanese island of Tsushima. In the ensuing battle the Russians were outnumbered, outmaneuvered, and outshot. Almost before they knew what had struck them they were disastrously defeated. Most of the Russian ships were sunk or captured by the Japanese. A half dozen or so escaped to neutral ports, where they were interned. Only three of the smallest vessels succeeded in reaching their destination in the harbor of Vladivostok. Russia's dramatic effort to wrest the control of Far Eastern waters from Japan had proved a dismal failure; the naval disaster rang the death knell on Russia's hope of final victory.

Both the German Kaiser and the American President Roosevelt now urged peace upon the belligerents. Although Russia with her vast resources and man power might possibly have sent new armies to continue the struggle in the Far East, popular discontent and revolutionary outbreaks at home were alarming the tsar's ministers, who were therefore not unwilling to consider peace proposals. On the other hand, the Japanese by their military efforts had nearly bankrupted themselves and so were quite ready to halt their military operations. On President Roosevelt's invitation a peace conference was opened at Portsmouth, New Hampshire. Sergius Witte ably represented the tsar at the conference and succeeded in saving Russia from the worst consequences of her disastrous defeat. By the treaty of Portsmouth (September 5, 1905) Russia's lease of the Liaotung peninsula, Russia's railway from Port Arthur north to Changchun, and Russian coal-mining rights in southern Manchuria were all transferred to Japan, thus converting southern Manchuria into a Japanese sphere of influence. Russia recognized Japan's preponderant interest in Korea and her right to control and protect the Korean government. In addition, Russia surrendered to Japan the southern half of the island of Sakhalin, which Japan had occupied during the war. Clearly the Japanese had administered a definite check to Russian expansion in the Far East. They had furthermore demonstrated not only to the tsar but to the world at large that a new great power had appeared which must thereafter be considered in dealing with affairs in that part of the globe.

## THE REVOLUTION OF 1905

Perhaps the chief reason why the tsarist government gave up so soon its struggle against Japan in the Far East was that it was being

confronted at home by widespread unrest and revolutionary outbreaks. As between the loss—perhaps only temporary—of prestige
and power and territory in the Far East and the complete collapse
of autocratic government within Russia the tsar considered the
former as the less of the two evils. And in 1905 the downfall
of Russian autocracy seemed imminent. The repressive policies of
Alexander III and Nicholas II had signally failed to crush out
liberal and radical opposition to the tsarist regime. Discontent had
remained general and had grown with the passing years. And the
introduction of modern industrialism in Russia had further contributed to the growth of unrest, for it had increased both in number
and in strength the bourgeois capitalist class and the industrial proletariat.

In the opening decade of the twentieth century there were several
distinct groups which sought to introduce political and economic
changes in Russia. The proletariat, deprived of any real voice in
the government and oppressed by an industrial system which forbade the organization of trade unions,[26] had offered a fertile field
for socialist propaganda. Marxian socialists had soon gained the
attention of the factory workers, and in the nineties industrial
strikes had begun to occur. Eventually, in 1898, the Social Democratic Party was organized in Russia, and its members began to
plan for the time when political power might be theirs, when factories might be seized, the capitalists turned out, and a millennium
of shorter hours, increased wages, and better conditions ushered in.
They therefore sought to overthrow the empire in order to erect
in its stead a socialist republic.

In 1903 the Social Democratic Party, at a congress held outside
Russia, split into two wings: the *Bolsheviki* or majority, led by
Nicholas Lenin, and the *Mensheviki* or minority, led by George
Plekhanov. Originally they differed only in matters of party organization, but in the course of years they came to differ fundamentally
on the question of party tactics as well. The Bolsheviks were the
extremists, opposed to any co-operation with bourgeois parties, opposed to the policy of gradual reform, in favor of a cataclysmic
upheaval which should establish the regime of the proletariat. The

[26] Although the government restricted the development of trade unions, it did attempt
to improve the lot of the industrial workers. Various laws limited hours of work, regulated the employment of children, and provided for accident compensation.

Mensheviks, on the other hand, were the moderates, willing, if necessary, to bring in the socialist regime gradually through the slow education of the masses, even with the co-operation of the moderately liberal groups. In other words, the Bolsheviks were more "revolutionary," the Mensheviks more "evolutionary."

Another socialist group, founded about 1900 and known as the Socialist Revolutionary Party, undertook to advance the interests of the peasants. Its members were interested chiefly in the land problem and sought to transform the land from private property into "the property of the whole people." The lands which the peasants had been permitted to buy at the time of their emancipation had been inadequate to support them, and the steady increase in population and subsequent subdivision of estates had considerably reduced the per capita holdings. In consequence, millions of land-hungry Russians gazed enviously upon the remaining estates of the crown, the church, and the aristocracy and longed for the time when they might be seized and parceled out. The Socialist Revolutionary program, therefore, aimed at the destruction of both the political and the social regime of Russia for the benefit of the peasant masses.

What may be called a liberal group was also eventually organized and consisted largely of the professional classes of the cities and the more progressive elements of the nobility, who had been active in the district and provincial zemstvos. Utilizing the latter as a medium for discussion, these nobles had sought to secure better educational facilities, a fairer electoral system, removal of restrictions upon the zemstvos, and the crowning of the zemstvo system by the establishment of an elective national zemstvo. In 1903 secret conferences held outside Russia resulted in a union of the bourgeois liberals with the progressive zemstvo leaders in an organization called the Union of Liberation. The liberals, as well as the Socialist Revolutionaries, were interested in the land question, and they advocated a policy of compensated expropriation of the holdings of the aristocracy and the state in order to improve the lot of the peasants. Their political program called for a democratic, parliamentary monarchy like that of Great Britain. The "unifying influence of tsardom," they believed, was essential for the preservation of Russian national unity.

But discontent was not limited to the Russians proper. It was inevitable that the government's policy of "Russification" should also arouse strong opposition among the oppressed national groups within the empire. This was particularly true of the Finns, who never ceased to demand that the domestic independence of their grand duchy be respected. It was likewise true of the Poles and Jews, who had suffered severely at the hand of the tsarist government. Groups like these awaited only a favorable opportunity to implement their discontent and could be counted upon with a fair degree of certainty to align themselves with or take advantage of any Russian revolutionary movement in order to force the tsar to make concessions to them.

The outbreak of the Russo-Japanese War in 1904 had greatly increased popular discontent in Russia, partly because most of the people had no clear idea why it was being fought, and partly because evidences of corruption and inefficiency were at once revealed in the lamentable failure to supply the army with adequate munitions, equipment, and supplies. The growing unrest within the country received a startling confirmation when, in July, 1904, the tsar's reactionary minister of the interior, Plehve, was assassinated. Temporarily it seemed that Nicholas II might become less reactionary. Prince Mirsky, a liberal, was appointed to succeed Plehve, and in November, 1904, the government even permitted representatives of the zemstvos and dumas to meet informally in a national congress. From the latter came a petition requesting Nicholas II not only to guarantee individual liberties, but to extend local self-government and to establish a national parliament. In response to this petition the tsar's government did grant a few reforms but very carefully refrained from taking any step to provide for a national parliament. The liberal and radical groups remained, therefore, far from satisfied, and popular agitation continued unchecked.

In the early days of 1905 St. Petersburg was paralyzed by a strike which involved tens of thousands of workers. A priest, Father Gapon, sought to lead some of the strikers and drafted a petition to Nicholas requesting a number of moderate economic and political reforms. On Sunday, January 22, 1905, Father Gapon led a procession of several thousand people—men, women, and children —to the Winter Palace to present this petition to the tsar personally. Although the priest and his followers gave no indication of desire to provoke disorder or to start a revolt, the procession was fired upon by the military as it approached the palace. As a consequence, several hundred persons were killed and nearly three thousand were wounded. When news of the events of "Bloody Sunday" became known, it was at once answered by further strikes and political demonstrations. The government now became genuinely alarmed and decided to suppress popular unrest by resort to force. The liberal Mirsky was therefore summarily dismissed from office, and the reactionary General Trepov was instructed to restore order in the capital.

But the brutal measures of the latter failed to cow the radicals. In February Grand Duke Sergius, the tsar's uncle, was assassinated, and others less prominent in government circles from time to time suffered a similar fate. The popular movement for reform—now become, in fact, revolutionary—continued unabated. Political meetings and banquets were held despite police activities. Influenced by Social Democratic leaders, workers in nearly every type of industry struck. The transportation and communication systems were disrupted. At the height of the movement the strange spectacle was presented of restaurant waiters, university professors, chorus girls, drug clerks, newspapermen, college students, skilled workers, manual laborers all striking in an attempt to force the tsar to grant reforms. In rural regions the peasants under Socialist Revolutionary leaders showed their dissatisfaction by attacking the landed aristocracy, burning their homes, and pillaging their barns. Subject nationalities in Poland and in the Caucasus seized upon the occasion to try to secure national concessions. Revolt spread even into the imperial navy, where the crew of the battleship *Potemkin* joined the revolutionary movement.

With the greater part of his armed forces thousands of miles away in Manchuria, the tsar was in no position to suppress such a widespread movement by force and decided that he must bend before the revolutionary storm. In an attempt to weather the popular hurricane—without actually surrendering his autocratic power—Nicholas II in a succession of decrees granted religious toleration, relaxed the enforcement of anti-Jewish legislation, remitted the land payments of those peasants who were in arrears, conceded the right of Poles and Lithuanians to use their languages in private schools, placed the trial of political offenders in the hands of the regular courts, promised to call a national assembly, dismissed Trepov,

Pobiedonostsev, and many others, and called Witte—who had just negotiated peace with Japan—to serve as his chief minister. Such concessions, designed to win the support of the peasants, subject nationalities, and moderate liberals, left the political structure of Russia practically unchanged, however, and were themselves subject to arbitrary alteration in the future if the tsarist autocracy continued. The revolutionary storm, therefore, did not subside. Instead, the empire's economic life was brought almost to a standstill. Faced by this crisis, the tsar was at length forced to give way.

In October, 1905, Nicholas II issued a manifesto granting freedom of speech, of the press, and of association, promising the institution of a national legislature, the Duma, to represent all classes of the people, and proclaiming the "immutable rule" that no law would thereafter be considered binding without the consent of the Duma, that to the people would be given "the power to exercise an effective supervision over the acts of the officials." In an effort to win greater popular support a decree was issued reducing by 50 per cent the peasants' land payments for 1906 and canceling all payments after January 1, 1907.[27] Further to strengthen the government, another decree in December, 1905, made suffrage for the new Duma practically universal. To appease the Finns, who had inaugurated a general strike, their grand duchy was given back its right of local autonomy, and the Finns were conceded the authority to draft a constitution to take the place of the one suppressed by the tsar in 1899.

It is quite obvious that the popular movement which had forced the tsar thus to grant concessions rested upon the support of many and diverse elements of the Russian people, and that, once some of the groups had attained their ends, the united front would begin to disintegrate. Many of the more moderate liberals, for instance were willing to accept the tsar's October manifesto as satisfactory and final. The Octobrists, as they were soon called, consisted chiefly of liberal nobles and industrial capitalists who favored a government in which the Duma should play a role subordinate to the divine-right monarch, somewhat as did the Landtag of Prussia. They advocated the continuation of a centralized regime and were

---

[27] According to the calculations of the government these payments would not have ended legally until 1931.

somewhat sympathetic with the Slavophile policy of "Russification." Their most outstanding leader was Alexander Guchkov.

On the other hand, the more pronounced liberals, who organized the Constitutional Democratic Party under the leadership of
the distinguished Russian historian, Paul N. Miliukov, considered
the tsar's manifesto only the beginning of necessary political reform. The Constitutional Democrats or "Cadets," as they were
called, advocated a constitutional government based on the doctrine
of popular sovereignty. They urged that the first Duma should
not confine itself to legislative functions but should act as a constituent assembly to draft a constitution for Russia. This constitution, according to them, should transform the tsar into a mere
titular head of the empire and give real executive power to a ministry responsible to the Duma. In short, the Cadets envisaged the
conversion of Russia into a democratic, parliamentary monarchy
like the British. Many of them, moreover, advocated a federal structure of government which would make possible a greater degree of
cultural and political autonomy for the subject peoples of Russia.
The Cadets were drawn chiefly from the professional classes, university men, and more progressive bourgeoisie.

Naturally the October manifesto failed to satisfy the Social Democrats. But among the latter there were differences of opinion as to
what should be done, now that the tsar had made concessions. The
Mensheviks believed that Russia was not yet ready for socialism,
that the most that could be expected at that time was the establishment of a democratic republic in which the masses could through a
national parliament work for socialist institutions and the improvement of the lot of the working people. A soviet or council of
workers' delegates—largely Mensheviks—had been organized in St.
Petersburg and had played an important role in directing the general strike which had paralyzed the economic life of Russia. This
soviet, which came largely under the influence of Leon Trotsky
after his arrival in October, 1905, planned to push the political
revolution still further by renewed strikes.

But many of the Bolshevik leaders, including Nicholas Lenin,
who returned to Russia in November, held aloof from the soviet
movement. They were not so much interested in democracy under
capitalist auspices as they were in the overthrow of capitalism itself.

These Bolshevik leaders condemned the Mensheviks' willingness to co-operate with the liberals, and Lenin's attitude did much to undermine the soviet. In fact, the first experiment with a workers' soviet was short-lived. A second general strike called by it in November was a failure, and in December another attempt to launch such a movement met with little response. Following Witte's arrest of nearly two hundred leaders of the workers, the soviet movement utterly collapsed. An armed insurrection in Moscow, instigated by the Bolsheviks near the end of the year, was likewise eventually suppressed.

By this time many of the moderate elements in Russia, genuinely alarmed by the continued violence of the radicals, had begun to rally to the side of the tsar, who naturally received also the support of most of the beneficiaries of the old regime. Eventually, with the gradual return of Russian troops from the Far East after the signing of the treaty of Portsmouth, the moment of fear which had impelled the tsar to make his liberal concessions passed away, and then—in spite of Count Witte's opposition—came a systematic attempt on the part of the governmental clique to restore as much as possible of the autocratic system. The nationalistic revolts in the Caucasus and in Poland were violently suppressed. To intimidate opposition in other quarters a veritable reign of terror was inaugurated through the agency of pogroms and the activities of the "Black Hundreds"—gangs of hoodlums who were encouraged to attack the people. In the rural regions the peasants were forcibly pacified by troops loyal to the government. Thousands of Russians were arrested or executed in the ensuing months.

In March, 1906, the tsar undertook to annul the October manifesto so far as its most important features were concerned. By a new decree an upper house, the Council of the Empire, was created and given power co-ordinate with the Duma. Of its two hundred members, half were appointed by the tsar and the rest were chosen by various institutional organizations. Obviously, the purpose of this second house was to act as a check upon the popularly elected Duma in the interest of tsarist autocracy. It was also decreed that the fundamental laws of the empire were not to be within the power of the Duma, and that foreign affairs, the army, and the navy belonged exclusively to the tsar's jurisdiction. It was provided that between sessions of the Duma any matter might, in case of emergency, be dealt with by executive decree, the latter to become law in case the Duma did not enact legislation on the subject during the first two months of its next session. Finally, in case the budget or laws concerning army recruits had not been passed by May 1 of any year, the government might legally use the figures for the preceding period. Thus the Duma was effectively blocked in advance if it should attempt to use "the power of the purse strings" to coerce the tsar. The increasing influence of the reactionaries was further revealed when on May 2, 1906, shortly before the first Duma was to convene, Witte was dismissed as prime minister and was succeeded by Goremykin, an old man who was largely the tool of the supporters of autocracy. Another strong reactionary, Peter Stolypin, was given the important position of minister of the interior.

Meanwhile, elections for the first Duma had been held. The Social Democrats and the Socialist Revolutionaries as parties both boycotted the elections because they wanted not a legislative but a constituent assembly. A group of radicals, called the Labor Party, however, secured somewhat more than a hundred seats, and unorganized peasants, chiefly interested in agrarian reform, obtained about two hundred. The supporters of the government consisted chiefly of a small number of Octobrists and a few conservatives and reactionaries. Of all the organized groups the Constitutional Democrats held the most seats and largely dominated the Duma. The outcome of the elections might possibly have been more alarming to the tsar except for the fact that shortly before his resignation Count Witte had secured from French and British bankers a loan of $450,000,000. With this sum available the government was in a position to treat somewhat cavalierly the demands of the Duma.

The latter soon after convening petitioned the tsar to abolish the Council of the Empire, to recognize ministerial responsibility to the Duma, to permit the expropriation of the estates of the landlords for the benefit of the peasants, and to grant amnesty for political prisoners. Since the tsar had no intention of granting such reforms, a deadlock ensued, for the Duma on its part then refused to enact the few laws requested by the government. In the end the Duma was dissolved by the tsar. In a futile attempt to rally popular support for the Duma, the Cadet deputies and a few others thereupon assembled in Viborg in Finland and issued a manifesto appealing to the Russian people to refuse taxes and military service. When a few spasmodic antigovernment revolts occurred, however, they were quickly suppressed by tsarist forces, and many revolutionaries were executed or exiled to Siberia. The signers of the Viborg manifesto themselves were disfranchised, with the result that the Constitutional Democratic party lost many of its more aggressive leaders.

Elections were eventually held for a second Duma, and, despite the government's efforts to influence the vote, the result was practically the same as before. Opponents of the system of autocracy controlled an overwhelming majority of the seats. And the fate of the second Duma was the same as that of the first; in June, 1907, it was likewise arbitrarily dissolved. The tsar thereupon issued what amounted to a constitutional amendment drastically altering the electoral system. The representation of the subject nationalities was greatly reduced, in some cases abolished altogether; and the political influence of the landlord class was much increased by the introduction of a system of indirect representation on a class basis something like that existing in Prussia. As a result of these measures, the third Duma, elected in the autumn of 1907, was satisfactory to the tsarist government. The Cadets and the Left groups altogether controlled less than seventy-five seats, while the Octobrists and others on the Right held approximately four times as many. The new Duma was accordingly permitted to function until the expiration of its term; the fourth Duma, elected in 1912, was also acceptable to the government and was still in existence when Russia entered the World War.

Looking back upon the events of 1905 and the two succeeding years, opponents of the autocratic regime felt that all their efforts to secure for Russia a liberal parliamentary government had been largely futile. With the tsar reserving to himself the right arbitrarily to alter at any time the constitutional basis of the imperial government, as he had done in 1907, Russia could hardly be said to have a constitutional government in the true sense of the term. With the imperial ministers responsible to the tsar alone, parliamentary government as it was understood in the West was entirely lacking in Russia. Finally, with so many state matters excluded from the jurisdiction of the Duma, the latter could hardly be considered even a legislative body in the full meaning of the term. Thanks largely to the military support of a loyal army, the financial and moral support of foreign governments, and the division among the revolu-

THE VICTIM OF A NIHILIST'S BOMB

The wounded Alexander II being conveyed to the Winter Palace.

tionists, Russian autocracy came through the upheaval of 1905 with only minor political losses.

## THE EVE OF THE WORLD WAR

In the years from 1906 to 1914 the situation in Russia largely resembled that which had preceded the revolutionary movement of 1905. On the side of the government reaction and repression were again in the ascendancy. Year by year scores—sometimes hundreds— were sentenced to death for their political activities, while a more or less steady stream of Russians passed as exiles into Siberia or fled in desperation to foreign countries. Once more, too, the policy of "Russification" was vigorously pushed, particularly against the Jews, the Finns, the Poles, and the subject nationalities in the Caucasus. On the other hand, the revolutionists, slowly recovering from their despair, began again to lay plans and hatch plots to assassinate officials and ultimately to bring about the overthrow of the tsarist regime. Eventually, Social Democratic propagandists once more aroused the industrial workers to strikes and riots with political as well as economic purposes.

Stolypin, who had succeeded Goremykin as prime minister in 1906, hoped to rally the bulk of the Russians to the tsar's side. Most of the nobility—who, however, were declining in importance —could be counted upon for support. In addition, most of the industrial capitalists, who looked upon autocracy as protection against labor unions, labor unrest, and socialism, appeared willing to uphold the tsarist regime. Their political representatives, the Octobrists, largely dominated the Duma in the succeeding years and usually threw their influence in favor of government measures. The peasants, the overwhelming majority of the population, Stolypin sought to win by his agrarian reforms.

During the revolution Witte had secured a decree canceling further land payments to the government after 1906, and this measure had of course removed a heavy burden from the shoulders of the peasants. Stolypin now sought to increase the amount of land available for the peasants and to create a class of independent petty landowners who, like those in France, might come to constitute a conservative force within the country. In October, 1906, accordingly, a decree was issued giving the peasants the right to purchase crown lands. To facilitate the transfer of not only the crown lands but those of the nobles as well, the Peasants' Bank was authorized to loan peasants the necessary funds at low rates of interest. Since, after the events of 1905 and 1906, many nobles were alarmed lest their estates should be seized without compensation, much of their land subsequently passed into peasant hands.

Another decree, in November, 1906, permitted peasants to withdraw completely from the control of the mir. The head of any peasant family might demand that his share of the common land be given to him in a solid block, which thereafter would be his to do with as he pleased. In other words, collective ownership was to give way to individual ownership, with a resultant increased incentive to improved methods of agriculture. By 1914 more than a third of the heads of peasant families had become petty landed proprietors. Greater inequalities among the peasants soon developed, however, as a result of this decree. Some—less capable or more restless—sold their lands and moved to the cities, while others— more competent or more ambitious—bought up the land of those who wanted to leave and rose to the level of fairly well-to-do farmers (the *kulaks*). The average peasant, however, was still land-hungry and continued to look with covetous eyes upon the remaining lands of the crown, the nobility, and the church. Many of the dissatisfied, with the encouragement of the government, sought to better their condition by emigrating to Siberia. In the years between 1906 and the World War more than 350,000 peasants yearly moved into Asiatic Russia.

Although unrest among the peasants was somewhat lessened by these developments, that among the urban workers was not. After 1910 strikes became more frequent, and political assassinations once more began. In September, 1911, Stolypin was killed, but his removal from the premiership in no way altered the general trend of policy. The ministers who succeeded him were of the same type as he. Although in 1912 a law was enacted giving the peasants the benefit of the general judicial system of the empire by displacing land captains with justices of the peace, and although in the same year the industrial proletariat was conceded an employers' liability act with provision for accident and sickness insurance, the policies of the government continued to be basically repressive and reactionary. Popular unrest therefore continued to grow. By 1914 the industrial strikes had taken on a definite political complexion. In the early summer of that year the working people of St. Petersburg were filled with revolutionary ideas, the capital was convulsed by revolutionary strikes and even open street fighting. "Demonstrations and meetings were held, tramway cars were overturned, telephone and telegraph poles were cut down, and barricades were built." According to Alexander Kerensky, later head of the provisional government after the downfall of the tsar,[28] if the World War had not broken out, revolution "would have come not later than the spring of 1915, perhaps even at the end of 1914."

In Russian foreign policy, meanwhile, developments had occurred of deep significance. In 1906 Alexander Izvolsky had become foreign minister. The latter had as his chief objectives the strengthening of Russia's position in Constantinople, the opening of the Straits to Russian warships, and perhaps ultimately the acquisition by Russia of control of the Straits themselves. The Straits had become vitally important to Russia economically, for through them was exported a great part of the country's wheat crop. But Izvolsky realized that Russia could not successfully pursue such a policy in Europe if she were handicapped by misunderstandings and clashes in Asia. Accordingly, he sought to reach agreements in the Far East in order that Russia's hands might be free in Europe. To this end he concluded in 1907 a convention with Japan, which was followed by a second and fuller treaty in 1910. By the terms of these agreements Japan was recognized as having a preponderant influence in southern Manchuria and Russia in northern Manchuria. Japan and Russia thus came to an amicable agreement regarding their positions in the Far East.

Izvolsky felt, however, that Russia was still too involved in Asiatic complications to make it safe for her to pursue a vigorous policy in the Balkans. Friction and rivalry disturbed the relations between Russia and Great Britain in the Middle East, particularly in Persia, Afghanistan, and Tibet. But Russia, Izvolsky believed, could not afford to quarrel with Great Britain if she desired to strengthen her position in Europe. Consequently, when Great Britain suggested an Anglo-Russian agreement which should settle all difficulties between the two countries, Izvolsky readily fell in with the idea. Moreover, the members of the Duma, hoping that liberalism might be advanced in Russia if the latter co-operated

28 See page 446.

with Great Britain, willingly approved such a step. In 1907, accordingly, an Anglo-Russian treaty was signed in which the two powers came to an understanding regarding their positions in the Middle East.[29] This agreement and the others already made between Russia and France (1894) and France and Great Britain (1904) completed what came to be called the Triple Entente.

Beginning in 1908 Izvolsky's foreign policy was chiefly concerned with advancing Russia's position in the Near East. In other words, thirty years after the treaty of Berlin had decisively checked the expansion of Russian power in the Balkans, the tsarist government once more directed its attention to that part of Europe. Thwarted in the Far East by Japan and in the Middle East by Great Britain, Russia in 1908 was more than ever determined to secure her long-coveted outlet to the sea through the Near East. It was in accordance with this policy that Izvolsky attempted to make a bargain with Austria-Hungary in 1908, only in the end to suffer a diplomatic reverse.[30] It was in pursuance of this plan that, having been checked in 1908, he reached in the following year an agreement with Italy (1909),[31] by the terms of which the two powers promised to co-operate in blocking Austria-Hungary's further advance in the Balkans.

It was in accordance, too, with Russia's desire to advance in the Balkans that Pan-Slavists assiduously sought to cultivate the friendship of Slavs outside the empire. Russia was held up as the great elder brother of oppressed and thwarted Slavs everywhere, but special efforts were made to win the Slavs within the Habsburg realm to this viewpoint. With Russia's benediction Pan-Slavic congresses, attended particularly by the Slavs of Serbia, Bulgaria, and Austria-Hungary, were held during the years from 1908 to 1911. As a result of this policy, in the years before 1914 great numbers of Slavs in central and southeastern Europe came to consider Russia as their natural protector and possible benefactor.

When Izvolsky was transferred from the foreign office to the Russian embassy at Paris (1910), he used his new position to advance his Balkan policy. Under his personal direction determined efforts were made to "Balkanize" the Franco-Russian alliance in

---

[29] For the terms, see page 212.
[30] For these negotiations and the Bosnian crisis of 1908, see pages 338–343.
[31] See page 161.

order that the French should be won to support Russia's policy in the Near East. At the same time, in the foreign office at St. Petersburg, Izvolsky's successor, Sergius Sazonov, Stolypin's brother-in-law, largely continued Izvolsky's Balkan policy. Under Russia's tutelage the Balkan League [32] was created in 1912 chiefly for the purpose of thwarting Austria-Hungary's attempt to advance through Macedonia to the Aegean. During the Balkan crisis of 1912–1913 [33] Russia strongly supported Serbia's attempt to gain an outlet on the Adriatic because that little Slavic country had become an anti-Habsburg pawn of the tsarist empire. But again, chiefly because of Austria-Hungary's opposition, Russian diplomacy was obliged to recede from the stand which it had taken.

The diplomatic defeat which Russia suffered at that time, as well as the one which had occurred four years earlier in connection with Austria's annexation of Bosnia, Russian patriots and Pan-Slavists ascribed to the military unpreparedness of the empire. Stolypin's government had sought to rebuild the Russian navy as rapidly as possible after the Russo-Japanese War and had endeavored to reorganize and strengthen the Russian army, but in 1912 the Russian military and naval forces were still far from adequate for a great war. In 1912 and again in 1913, however, large loans were secured in France for the improvement of the army and the construction of strategic railways, and in 1914 a five-year program of military and naval expansion, involving billions of dollars, was inaugurated. In the latter year, also, the term of active service in the Russian army was lengthened by six months, and more than a hundred thousand recruits were added to the peace-time army. To observers of international affairs it appeared that the foreign policies of Russia and Austria-Hungary must inevitably lead to a clash in the Balkans, and Russia was doggedly determined to be prepared to defend her interests when the next crisis should occur.

[32] See page 347.          [33] See page 349.

CHAPTER IX

## THE AUSTRO-HUNGARIAN DUAL MONARCHY

IN the early centuries of modern European history the German Habsburg dynasty had expanded its territorial holdings to include many non-German peoples at a time when the latter were incapable of fulfilling their mission as states. The result was that during the last half century preceding the World War that dynasty ruled over a polyglot empire which had become an anachronism. The history of Austria-Hungary, therefore, differed from that of most of the countries of western Europe in that it was "not so much the history of a people or a country as the history of a state."

Within the state, during these years, the Habsburg dynasty was compelled to struggle almost constantly with what the distinguished Austrian historian, Alfred Pribram, has called "the irreconcilable antagonism of the different nationalities which aimed at an independence incompatible with the idea of imperial unity and of the ascendancy which the Germans had enjoyed for hundreds of years." Abroad, during the same time, the dynasty felt compelled to push its influence into the Balkans in order to check the disruptive forces of Yugoslav nationalism both within and without the empire. When the propaganda of the Serbian Yugoslavs increased in fervor and eventually appeared actually to menace the integrity of the Habsburg realm, Austro-Hungarian leaders were won to the belief that only by military measures against Serbia could the Dual Monarchy be preserved.

### THE HABSBURG RULER

The head of the Habsburg dynasty was Francis Joseph. Born in 1830, elevated to the throne as a result of the inundating wave of revolt that swept over the Austrian Empire in 1848, he held the throne for almost "three score years and ten." Death brought his reign to a close (1916) in the midst of the fateful World War, which paved the way for the complete disintegration of his realm only two years later. During all these years he was, in the last analysis, responsible for all important decisions of the government.

From the beginning of his reign Francis Joseph apparently held the divine-right idea of kingship, and to his last days he firmly believed that the ruler's will should consistently be the strongest political force in the realm. Proud of the dynasty which he represented, he was never content that as its head he should become a mere figurehead, a shadow ruler. He took his position seriously, was an industrious monarch, conscientiously rising at an early hour to take care of the routine work of his empire. The later hours of his days were almost regularly occupied with audiences to ministers and other high officials, for he sought to keep in close contact with his responsible political servants. In matters of policy Francis Joseph could upon occasion display a watchful patience that was admirable, and at other times could show a firmness, even a stubbornness, which brought dismay to his ministers. What he lacked in intellectual ability and imagination, he in part made up for as his reign progressed by his long years of experience in dealing with perplexing political problems. The fact that the complicated machinery of the Dual Monarchy actually functioned with a fair degree of smoothness would seem to testify to the emperor's political ability.

Throughout his reign Francis Joseph's major political aim was that of preserving his realm intact despite the friction which occasionally developed between the two halves of his empire, and despite the ever-rising tide of nationalistic opposition among the subject races. When driven to extremities, he sought to overcome his difficulties by compromises, but even here his innate conservatism led him to depart as little as possible from established tradition. He had little real comprehension of the political significance of the changes which were taking place in the world as a result of the transformation in industry, transportation, and communication which came in the late nineteenth and the early twentieth century, for his emphasis upon the proprieties of social distinction and his somewhat rigid isolation through his system of court ceremonials prevented him from coming into close touch with the bourgeoisie or with public opinion. Nevertheless, there is little doubt that in his later years the venerable Habsburg ruler constituted a personal bond of union for his millions of subjects, who could not be held together as in most countries by the abstract tie of nationalism.

A second aim to which Francis Joseph seemed to cling after 1867 was that of peace. Having in his early years seen his empire lessened in extent and in international prestige by the wars of 1859 and 1866, the emperor was determined at almost any price to prevent the Dual Monarchy from being drawn into war. Even as an old man in his eighties, when confronted by men like Conrad von Hötzendorf, chief of staff, and Count Berchtold, foreign minister, who sought to precipitate a war against Serbia, Francis Joseph had to be tricked by a forged telegram before a declaration of war could be wrung from him.[1]

## THE HABSBURG REALM

Despite the losses sustained in the wars of 1859 and 1866,[2] Francis Joseph after 1867 ruled a realm which in area stood second among the states of Europe, being surpassed in this respect only by the Russian Empire. From north to south it stretched from the plains of the Vistula to the shores of the Adriatic; from east to west, from the bounds of Rumania to the heart of the Alps. The greater part of this territory—the Danube valley—constituted a geographic, economic, and military unit. But the realm as a whole was not so completely unified. Galicia and Bukowina, cut off by the Carpathian Mountains, seemed more naturally to belong to Poland or Russia than to the Dual Monarchy. Similarly, the Adriatic coastlands, cut off from the Danube valley by the Dinaric Alps, were probably more easily accessible to Italy than to those living in the heart of the Habsburg empire. The Adriatic territory, however, did provide the Dual Monarchy with valuable outlets to the sea at Trieste and at Fiume.

Racially, Austria-Hungary was inhabited by a very heterogeneous population. The two most numerous races were the Germans and the Magyars,[3] who, generally speaking, occupied the center of the

---

[1] See page 379.                    [2] See page 139.
[3] The census of 1910 showed the races divided approximately as follows:

| | | | |
|---|---|---|---|
| Germans | 12,011,081 | Serbs | 2,041,889 |
| Magyars | 10,067,917 | Croats | 2,888,171 |
| Czechs | 6,643,059 | Slovenes | 1,371,256 |
| Slovaks | 1,967,520 | Italians | 771,054 |
| Poles | 4,977,642 | Mohammedan Slavs | 612,137 |
| Ukrainians | 3,999,100 | Others | 367,853 |
| Rumanians | 3,224,728 | | |

For the distribution of the races in the monarchy, see the map on page 767.

empire, although they also constituted large minorities in various other sections of the country. The next most numerous element were the Czechs, who dwelt chiefly in Bohemia, Moravia, and Silesia, where in the beginning they constituted the lower classes, largely controlled by a minority of Germans. To the east of Moravia were the Slovaks, akin to the Czechs but dominated by the Magyars. Across the Carpathian Mountains to the north were the Poles in western Galicia, and in eastern Galicia the Ukrainians, who were largely exploited by the Poles. In Bukowina, Transylvania, and the Banat of Temesvar the majority of the inhabitants were Rumanians, largely tenants and workers on the estates of the great Magyar landlords. To the south of the Magyars dwelt the Serbs, Croats, and Slovenes—Yugoslavs who were akin to the peoples living farther south in Serbia, Bosnia-Herzegovina, and Montenegro. In the Trentino, in Trieste, in part of Istria, and in some towns along the Dalmatian coast the Italians predominated. Although in a general way the population of the Habsburg empire was grouped in large national blocks, the races were so interspersed that it would be impossible to draw political boundaries for national states in such a way as not to leave fairly large minorities as ethnic islands in most of the states.

Politically, this Habsburg realm had been divided in 1867 into two almost completely separate states by the *Ausgleich* or compromise of that year. By the terms of the *Ausgleich* the former Austrian Empire had been transformed into the Dual Monarchy. Under this unique political system the whole realm was divided into two autonomous parts: the Empire of Austria, which included Lower Austria, Upper Austria, Salzburg, Tirol, Vorarlberg, Bohemia, Moravia, Silesia, Galicia, Bukowina, Styria, Carinthia, Carniola, Gorizia and Gradisca, Istria, Trieste, and Dalmatia; and the Kingdom of Hungary, which included Hungary proper, Transylvania, Croatia-Slavonia, and the district of Fiume.

The two countries constituted separate states, each with its own constitution, parliament, ministry, courts, administration, and language. They were, however, united under one flag and had one common sovereign, who in Austria was known as emperor and in Hungary as king. Certain interests common to both, such as foreign affairs, war, and finance, were controlled by joint ministers, appointed by the emperor-king but responsible to a body known as

the Delegations. The latter consisted of 120 members, half elected
by the Austrian parliament and half by the Hungarian parliament,
and they not only supervised the joint ministers but voted the
budget for the army and for foreign affairs. The delegations met
alternately at Vienna and Budapest, the capitals of the respective
states. Usually they sat separately, meeting in joint session only
in case of failure to agree, and then simply for the purpose of voting and not for debate. Matters concerning tariffs, trade, currency,
and railways were settled between the two countries by treaties
renewed every ten years by the Delegations.

Each half of the Dual Monarchy had its own constitution. In
Austria a parliament known as the Reichsrat consisted of an aristocratic upper house of nobles and officials and a lower house
elected by the seventeen provincial diets. In Hungary the upper
house was aristocratic and largely hereditary, and the lower house
was elected on a franchise so highly restricted as also to keep power
in the hands of the upper classes of the Magyars. In neither half
of the Dual Monarchy was the government democratic.

Economically, the realm over which the Habsburg ruler presided
was essentially an agricultural state, possessed of rich grain fields,
extensive pasture lands, and deep forests. As late as 1910 more than
56 per cent of the population of the empire was engaged in agricultural pursuits. In certain regions the land was held for the most
part in great estates. In Hungary proper a relatively small number
of large holdings, the *latifundia,* included 40 per cent of the total
area.[4] Some of these estates were of tremendous size, running from
186,000 up to 570,000 acres in a single holding. In fact, 324 of these
*latifundia,* averaging at least 41,000 acres each, included more than
19 per cent of the total area of Hungary. The church also possessed
great areas of farm land, one Roman Catholic bishop, for instance,
holding as much as 266,000 acres. Not more than a third of the
land in Hungary was actually owned by those who personally cultivated it; and four fifths of the agricultural population—nearly half
of the total population of Hungary proper—held less than 20 acres
per family.

Although the great estates were most numerous in Hungary, they
were found also in Croatia-Slavonia and Bohemia. In the latter, for

[4] These figures for landholding are for the year 1913, and are based on statements in
O. Jaszi's *The Dissolution of the Hapsburg Monarchy, passim.*

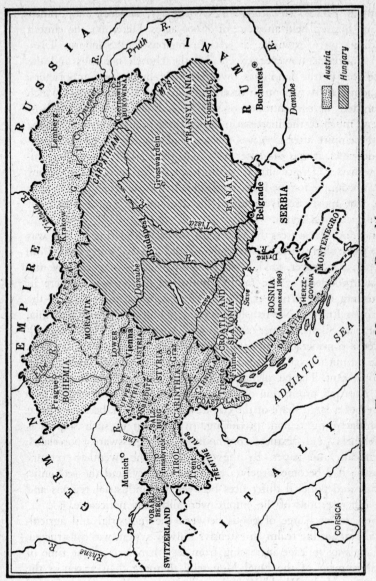

The Austro-Hungarian Dual Monarchy

example, Prince Schwartzenberg owned 437,000 acres, and Francis Joseph himself held an estate of 86,000 acres. Here, too, the church holdings were extensive. In certain regions like Salzburg, Tirol, and Carinthia, however, except for the church holdings and the state forests, the land was owned chiefly by peasant proprietors. Although there was much dissatisfaction with a land system which permitted the concentration of such large holdings in the hands of a few, much of the increase in agricultural production which came in the empire after 1870 was the result of the activities of the great landowners. It was the latter who took the lead in introducing improvements in agricultural technique, and in these respects they set an example for the lesser peasantry. It was the great landowners, too, who most effectively voiced the demand for a protective tariff on agricultural goods.

In mineral resources the Habsburg realm, considering its size, was not particularly rich. To be sure, it did possess some coal, iron, copper, lead, silver, gold, and petroleum; but in 1907 the raw materials produced by the mining industries of the empire were in value not quite a fifth of those produced in the same year in the German Empire. Nevertheless, certain regions—northern Bohemia, Moravia, Silesia, Upper and Lower Austria, and Styria—experienced a considerable industrial development in the years after 1870. The output of coal in Austria increased between 1876 and 1913 by 370 per cent. The petroleum resources of Galicia provided the basis for Austria's production of refined oil and paraffin. Bohemia, possessed of a large share of the empire's coal and iron, became a great manufacturing region, producing, in addition to such staples as machinery and textiles, commodities like glassware, porcelains, chemicals, and paper. By the opening of the twentieth century Austria had become largely a capitalist country, and the economic, social, and political differences between the industrial regions and the other sections of the empire were distinctly noticeable.

For the exchange of goods between the industrial and agricultural parts of the realm an extensive railway system was constructed, the railway mileage increasing from less than 4000 at the time of establishment of the Dual Monarchy to more than 27,000 at the outbreak of the World War. In a sense the regions of the empire which were less developed industrially—Galicia, Hungary, and the Yugoslav territories—became agricultural colonies of the more advanced industrial sections. The industrial leaders, running true to form, soon demanded and obtained protective tariffs for their infant industries and thus practically forced the agricultural regions to buy their manufactured goods. When eventually efforts were made to establish industries in Galicia, Bukowina, Hungary, Transylvania, and the Yugoslav regions, the capital was to a considerable extent furnished by the German bankers of Austria, so that the inhabitants of these districts felt that they were still largely subject to the "exploitation" of Viennese financiers. Eventually the great landowners struck back and demanded and secured a protective tariff on agricultural products. After 1887, therefore, both industrial and agricultural products were protected, and the cost of living for both urban and rural classes became in consequence greater than it might otherwise have been.

By the opening of the twentieth century the numbers of the bourgeoisie and of the proletariat had greatly increased, not only in the essentially industrial regions of the empire but also in various more or less isolated districts elsewhere. In Austria-Hungary as in other countries the workers were soon demanding the introduction of universal, equal, and direct suffrage. But industrialism not only helped to strengthen the demand for democratic reform; it also accentuated the differences between the Germans and the subject races. In the great majority of cases the leaders of the new large-scale industries established in the non-German parts of the empire were Germans. Frequently the proprietors of the already existing small industrial enterprises were of non-German stock. Naturally, the latter feared and opposed the new great industrialists and, in an effort to maintain their own positions, appealed to their fellow nationalists to support them by buying their products. In the second place, the workers in the new factories were generally of non-German stock, so that the anticapitalist feeling which was present among the proletariat in all countries was in Austria-Hungary further sharpened by a nationalistic rebellion against "exploitation by foreign capitalists." Finally, in the more advanced industrial region of Bohemia a prosperous bourgeoisie developed among the Czechs. The children of these bourgeois Czechs were privileged to secure an advanced education in high schools and in the Czech university in Prague, and as a result became more and more permeated by Czech national ideals. Industrialism, therefore, although it tended in many ways to unite the Habsburg realm, also helped to complicate the problems arising from the nationalism of the subject races. These problems were made still more difficult by the acquisition of new territory in 1878.

### Austria's Advance into the Balkans

By the treaties resulting from the Austro-Prussian War of 1866 the Habsburgs had been effectively ousted from their earlier positions of influence in both Germany and Italy. For a time Francis Joseph nursed the faint hope of revenge against the Hohenzollerns, but the weakening of France in the Franco-German War and the establishment of the powerful German Empire in 1871 definitely ended the possibility of any future Habsburg ascendancy in central Europe. Similarly, the completion of Italian unification by the acquisition of Rome in 1870 seemed to augur ill for any further meddling by the Habsburgs in that region. In fact, it even raised the question as to how long they themselves might retain their remaining Italian subjects against a rising irredentist movement on the other side of the Alps.

Shut out of Germany and Italy, the statesmen of the Dual Monarchy were not slow to realize that Austria-Hungary's hope of future expansion must be to the southeast into the Balkans. Indeed, as early as 1868 Count Beust, Francis Joseph's chancellor, had expressed this view. Such a policy was not, of course, altogether new, for ever since the days of Prince Eugene the Habsburgs had pursued more or less consistently a policy of southeastern penetration. After 1871 the idea of extending the empire in that direction again came to the fore and with it the realization that for such a policy a reconciliation between the Habsburg and Hohenzollern rulers was essential. This reconciliation, sought also by Bismarck, was brought about in 1872 and 1873.[5] Within two years thereafter uprisings among the Christian populations of the Balkan peninsula provided an opportunity for Austro-Hungarian diplomats to begin fishing in troubled waters.

After the Balkan uprisings against Turkish oppression broke out, Francis Joseph and Alexander II of Russia, each doubtless suspicious of the other's projected plans in southeastern Europe, met for a

[5] See page 66.

conference in July, 1876, at Reichstadt. The former persuaded the tsar to agree that Austria-Hungary should receive the provinces of Bosnia and Herzegovina, adjoining the Dual Monarchy on the south, if Russia should intervene in the Balkans and territorial changes should result. When, however, Russia after her victorious war against Turkey (1877–1878) completely ignored her commitments to Austria-Hungary in the subsequent treaty of San Stefano, the Dual Monarchy united with Great Britain in a determined effort to prevent Russia from carrying through her Balkan program.[6]

In the new settlement which was reached at the Congress of Berlin (1878) Austria-Hungary for all practical purposes gained two new provinces in the Balkans, a fact which Andrássy admitted in private when he declared that the occupation of Bosnia-Herzegovina was only an annexation "very badly disguised." Furthermore, in securing the right to garrison the province of Novibazar, she not only succeeded in driving a territorial wedge between Serbia and Montenegro but gained control over what was then thought to be an excellent route for a railway to Saloniki. In addition, she secured commercial privileges in Serbia and Montenegro, including the right to use Antivari in the latter as a "free" port for her mercantile and naval ships. Incidentally, of course, she succeeded in thwarting Russia's attempt to secure the ascendancy in the Balkans. It is obvious, therefore, that Austria-Hungary strengthened her position and influence in southeastern Europe as a result of events between 1875 and 1878.

In 1881 the Habsburg government further improved its Balkan position diplomatically by linking Serbia with the Dual Monarchy. Serbia, as a consequence of the outcome of events at Berlin in 1878, was temporarily alienated from Russia. Moreover, cut off from Montenegro by the Austrian-garrisoned province of Novibazar and almost enclosed on three sides by Austro-Hungarian territory, she had been made extremely dependent upon the Habsburg empire for her economic well-being. Francis Joseph's government hastened to take advantage of the situation created by these circumstances and persuaded Serbia to sign a convention which made the latter almost a protectorate of the Dual Monarchy. In return for Austria-Hungary's future support of Serbia's claims in Macedonia, Serbia

[6] For a fuller account of this crisis of 1878, see pages 249–253.

agreed to abandon her aspirations in Bosnia-Herzegovina. She promised, further, that she would conclude no political treaties with other states without a previous understanding with Austria-Hungary, and would not admit to her territory any foreign armed forces of any kind. This treaty, one Serbian statesman indignantly pointed out, placed Serbia in the same relation to Austria as Tunis to France. Serbia's need of Habsburg assistance was made abundantly clear in 1885, however, when it was necessary for Austria-Hungary to intervene to prevent the destruction of the little kingdom at the hands of Bulgaria.[7]

Meanwhile, although Russia's reaction to events at Berlin had been so threatening that Germany and Austria-Hungary had concluded a defensive alliance in 1879,[8] thanks to Bismarck's skillful diplomatic maneuvers the three eastern empires were again brought together in 1881. In the treaty signed at that time Russia agreed to respect Austria-Hungary's recently acquired rights in Bosnia-Herzegovina, and the two powers promised to make no territorial changes in European Turkey in the future except by common consent.[9] Two years later Austria-Hungary's position in the Balkans appeared to be still further strengthened when Rumania, alienated from Russia by her loss of Bessarabian territory to that country by the treaty of Berlin, was persuaded by Bismarck to make a defensive alliance with the Habsburg empire against the tsar.

By the close of 1883, therefore, Austria-Hungary appeared to have advanced far toward obtaining for herself a dominating position in the Balkans and had apparently mapped out the course which she was to attempt to follow thereafter in southeastern Europe. The Dual Monarchy contained millions of Yugoslavs and Rumanians who would naturally be more and more drawn toward Serbia and Rumania, the adjoining states of their kinsmen. It therefore became the Habsburg policy after 1878 to endeavor to keep these increasingly nationalistic little states under Austria-Hungary's influence. By so doing Francis Joseph hoped to prevent that disintegration of his polyglot realm which might otherwise result from an active propaganda launched among the subject nationalities of his monarchy by Serbs and Rumanians.

[7] See page 321.                    [8] See page 67.
[9] For other terms of the agreement, see page 68.

THE CONGRESS OF BERLIN

Bismarck, in the center, towers above the other delegates; Disraeli
stands with a cane in his hand.

### The Problem of Nationalism in Austria

Francis Joseph had made his first compromise with the spirit of nineteenth-century nationalism within his realm when he signed the *Ausgleich* of 1867 recognizing the Kingdom of Hungary as a separate political entity under the domination of the Magyars. But this concession failed to end his difficulties. Within the German-dominated Austrian half of the Dual Monarchy, the Slavs were grievously disappointed that no provision had been made to recognize their separate statehood. The Czechs and Poles, especially, protested against the new settlement and demanded an autonomy similar to that which had been granted to the Magyars. The Poles, in fact, refused outright to send representatives to the Austrian Reichsrat.

In an effort to satisfy the national yearnings of at least one of the Slavic groups the Austrian government, controlled by the German Liberals, made another concession to nationalism in 1869 by granting the province of Galicia complete autonomy. It was thereafter to have a Polish governor appointed by the emperor, an autonomous Polish school system with eventually two Polish universities, a Polish bureaucracy, and recognition of the Polish language as official within the province. Furthermore, in accordance with the well-established Habsburg policy of *divide et impera,* the Poles were given political and economic ascendancy over the Ukrainians of eastern Galicia, and were thus largely won to a loyal support of the government at Vienna.

But the Czechs continued to rebel against their status under the Austrian constitution of 1867. They asserted that the Reichsrat in Vienna had no right to legislate for Bohemia and Moravia, and declared that Bohemia was historically an independent kingdom joined with the rest of the Habsburg realm only by a common sovereign. They refused to attend the Bohemian provincial diet which had been authorized by the new Austrian constitution, and vehemently demanded that the Bohemian kingdom be restored with its own independent central government located in the ancient capital, Prague. Eventually, to placate the Czechs and to win their loyalty, Francis Joseph went so far as to promise to recognize the existence of the Kingdom of Bohemia by coming to Prague to be crowned and by giving the Prague government legislative control over all questions distinctly Bohemian. To win the numerous Germans of Bohemia to accept this new arrangement, he promised that in Bohemia the German language would be placed on an equality with the Czech, and that so far as possible the administrative districts of the kingdom would be arranged to separate the Germans from the Czechs.

But strong opposition was immediately voiced by powerful elements in the Dual Monarchy. Naturally, the Germans of Bohemia sought to prevent an arrangement which would subject them to the domination of the more numerous Czechs, and they were strongly supported in their efforts by the Germans elsewhere in the empire. The Magyars, too, perhaps for fear of the influence of such a move on their own minor nationalities, strongly opposed the carrying out of the emperor's promises. In the face of these developments Francis Joseph reversed his position and quickly withdrew his promises to the Czechs. So thoroughly did the emperor change his views that it was later made a crime to circulate the message which he himself had voluntarily sent to the Czechs! In deep disgust, the latter decided to resort to passive resistance and so refused to send representatives to either the Austrian Reichsrat or the Bohemian diet. They failed, however, to alter the emperor's latest decision.

But the boycotting of the Reichsrat by the Czechs and some of the other subject peoples appeared to cast discredit upon the imperial regime. In 1873, accordingly, a new electoral system was inaugurated which provided for the election of deputies to the Reichsrat not in a block by the diet of each province but directly by the voters themselves. Under the already existing electoral law the right to vote for members of the provincial diets was vested in four different classes: landowners, cities, chambers of commerce, and rural districts. By the reform of 1873 it was provided that each of these four classes should elect directly a certain number of deputies to the Reichsrat. The system was quite definitely weighted in favor of the landowning and upper bourgeois classes, however. For instance, deputies elected in the rural districts each represented 11,600 voters (1890) while those elected by the landowners each represented only 63 voters. The new electoral system made it practically impossible for the dominant national group to control the election of all of the deputies from any province and thus largely prevented a 100-per-cent boycott of the Reichsrat by any province.

For fourteen years, from 1879 to 1893, the Austrian government was headed by Count Taafe, a boyhood friend of the emperor and of all the Austrian ministers after 1867 perhaps the one who most nearly represented the views of Francis Joseph himself. His long ministry was doubtless the result in part of this fact, but it was also in part the result of his success in placating some of the nationalities and in cleverly playing off at times one group against another. There were those, too, who felt that bribery was a factor in his long retention of power. However that may be, he managed to persuade the Czechs to take their seats in the Reichsrat and, aided by the political divisions among the Germans, succeeded in creating a parliamentary majority of Poles, Czechs, Slovenes, and Christian Socialists.

The latter—members of a Catholic party somewhat like the Center Party in the German Empire—consisted principally of peasants and lower bourgeoisie of German stock with a sprinkling of Poles and Czechs. They favored greatly extending the franchise, enacting social legislation, and increasing the rights and privileges of the subject nationalities. Beginning in the eighties they exerted considerable influence in favor of imperial legislation to improve the status of the factory workers. Between 1884 and 1888, for instance, laws were enacted to regulate hours and conditions of labor in factories and mines, to limit the industrial employment of children and women, to legalize labor unions, and to provide at least a start in social insurance.

Meanwhile, to retain the support of the Czechs, Count Taafe was repeatedly compelled to make concessions of one sort or another. The Czech language, for example, was placed on an equality with German in the administrative system of Bohemia. In the realm of education, particularly, the Czechs made national gains. The number of Czech elementary schools was increased, Czech high schools and technical schools were established, and eventually (1882) a Czech university was founded in Prague. Politically, the Czechs obtained an electoral law which enabled them to control a majority in the Bohemian diet, and were further given so many positions in the bureaucracy that the Germans of Bohemia in protest took their turn at boycotting the diet in Prague.

But Taafe's position was ultimately undermined by the rise in Bohemia of the "Young Czechs," a group whose leaders were politically more democratic and economically more radical than the "Old Czechs" who had been supporting his government. The distinguished intellectual leader of this new group was a professor of philosophy in the Czech university in Prague, Thomas G. Masaryk,[10] who had risen to this position from the humble home of a Slovak blacksmith on one of the large estates in the empire. Under his guidance the Young Czechs devoted themselves enthusiastically and energetically to improving the cultural and economic conditions of Bohemia and Moravia as a means of increasing the political influence and power of the Czechs. Their strength was disclosed when, in 1890, Taafe attempted to satisfy the Germans of Bohemia in the matter of the bureaucracy of that province by a compromise arrangement. His plan, which provided for two sets of officials—one of Germans, and one of Czechs—in all districts with mixed populations, at once encountered the vigorous opposition of the Young Czechs, who were instrumental in having the scheme rejected. His position, thus weakened, was later made altogether untenable by the attacks which were made upon his government by certain groups when he proposed to widen the suffrage to include the lower classes. In 1893 Count Taafe resigned the premiership.

In 1897, however, a slight electoral reform was made during the ministry of the Polish Count Badeni, as the result of which a fifth electoral class, which included all men at least twenty-four years of age, was to elect seventy-two deputies to the Reichsrat. Obviously, the new system bestowed a double vote upon those who were already included in one of the other four classes. Its inconsistency with democracy is further revealed by the fact that, whereas the 1,700,000 voters in the first four classes together chose 353 deputies, the 5,500,000 voters in the fifth class were permitted to elect only 72. The measure was far from popular with those interested in advancing the cause of democracy.

In an effort to keep the Czechs satisfied, Badeni issued orders that brought his downfall. In 1897 he decreed that all Bohemian officials should know both German and Czech. The Germans, most of

[10] At the close of the World War he became the first president of the new Republic of Czechoslovakia. See page 463.

whom had not gone to the trouble of learning the Czech language, immediately denounced his order and demanded its withdrawal. To enforce their demand, the German deputies in the Reichsrat deliberately resorted to obstruction in order to prevent that body from carrying on its work. Epithets and inkstands were hurled with abandon in the legislative halls, while riots occurred in the streets outside. In despair Badeni's government resigned, and his orders were withdrawn. The Czechs, dissatisfied with the outcome of the affair, now in turn resorted to riots, until peace was restored by the proclamation of martial law in Prague. One of the paradoxes of the Austrian situation seemed to be that the more the national claims of any group were granted the more that group considered itself oppressed.

The success of the German parliamentary obstruction at this time set a precedent for years to come. Thereafter dissatisfied groups of deputies by their noise and disorder frequently prevented the Reichsrat from going on with its work until a ministry in desperation resigned or resorted to a dissolution of the ineffective legislative body. A visitor to the Reichsrat in 1914 was told that each faction in the national legislature had transformed its committee room into an arsenal in which were locked away a complete assortment of such noise-makers as whistles, sleigh bells, cow bells, harmonicas, and trombones for use in making impossible the conduct of business when it so desired. It thus appeared that the principle of parliamentary government could not succeed in a state where an increasing nationalism repeatedly drove the various parties to a mutual hostility.

Francis Joseph had long maintained that Austria could not be governed parliamentarily, and now more or less readily resorted to the use of Article 14 of the Austrian constitution, which gave the government the authority to issue emergency decrees if they became necessary when the Reichsrat was not in session. In the succeeding years, therefore, the government usually dissolved the Reichsrat when it became altogether obstructive and then resorted to legislation by way of emergency decrees. In the leading universities constitutional lawyers were soon found who constructed a right on the part of the state to defend itself against obstruction, and so the system went merrily on.

As a result, while Austria in the years preceding the World War nominally had a constitutional parliamentary government, in actual fact she had a government which was a bureaucratic absolutism functioning under a "constitutional cloak." Parliament became largely a sham affair. In it the national groups continued to voice their demands and to obstruct legislation; outside it, by means of emergency decrees and the granting of occasional concessions to some of the opposition groups, the government continued to function more or less unhindered. In theory Austria possessed a government in which the ministry was responsible to the Reichsrat; in actuality she had one in which the responsibility was to the emperor. And to help him maintain his dominant position above parliamentary obstruction, Francis Joseph had (1) a powerful German-officered imperial army, (2) a reliable and loyal bureaucracy, and (3) a Roman Catholic clergy who used their influence to strengthen the Habsburg hold on the lesser nationalities.

The Russian revolution of 1905 excited the subject races and the more radical elements in Austria and resulted in popular demonstrations, long parades, and, when the government attempted to use repressive measures, bloodshed. In 1906 a new prime minister, Baron Beck, decided to see what the effect of introducing universal suffrage would be. A number of political leaders believed that the lower classes were really far less influenced by nationalism than the upper enfranchised groups, and that the nationalistic movements within the empire might be weakened by granting universal suffrage. By the reform measure of January, 1907, the old class system was abolished, and all men twenty-four years of age were given the right to vote. The most startling result of the first exercise of the new franchise was the election (1907) of eighty-seven Social Democratic deputies to the Reichsrat.[11]

But the new electoral law in no wise lessened the government's difficulties with the various nationalities. The Slav groups took to holding Pan-Slavic congresses to keep alive their nationalistic objectives. After the government of the German Empire enacted its laws to dispossess the Poles of their land in Germany,[12] the Poles in Galicia turned their wrath against all things German, and re-

[11] The effect of introducing universal manhood suffrage is seen in other figures on parliamentary deputies. Counting the Liberals, the Christian Socialists, and the Social Democrats as "German" parties, the Germans controlled only eighteen more seats than the subject nationalist groups taken together.

[12] See page 96.

sorted to a boycott even of goods made by Austrian Germans. The government, in order to embarrass the Poles, thereupon began to encourage Ukrainian nationalism, with the result that acute friction developed between the Ukrainians and the Poles in Galicia, where riots became of frequent occurrence. In 1912 the Ukrainians took their turn at paralyzing the Reichsrat by resorting to noise-making devices, and not until after the government had promised to establish a Ukrainian university in Lemberg did the few Ukrainian deputies cease their obstruction. Eventually even the Polish government of Galicia had to make concessions to the Ukrainians in order to secure a cessation of their obstructionist activities in the provincial diet.

A veritable wave of nationalistic obstruction swept over Austria on the eve of the World War. In 1912 the Italians by resort to such measures forced the government to dissolve the diet in the province of Tirol. In 1913 street riots broke out among the Italians of Trieste when the provincial governor began dismissing Italians from office, and in an effort at conciliation the government was led to promise to establish an Italian university in that city. In Bohemia the Germans succeeded in paralyzing the provincial diet because of their dissatisfaction with concessions which had been made to the Czechs. Finally, to cap the climax, the Czechs themselves in 1914 returned to the use of obstruction [13] and by their measures forced a dissolution of the Reichsrat. Thereafter Austria functioned without a national legislature until, in the third year of the World War, the exigencies of that conflict made necessary its convocation.

## THE PROGRAM OF MAGYARISM IN HUNGARY

Although it is usually asserted that the *Ausgleich* of 1867 gave control of Austria to the Germans and that of Hungary to the Magyars, each a minority in its own realm, it is obvious from what

---

[13] The following is a description by an eye-witness of a session in the lower house of the Reichsrat in March, 1914: "About a score of men, all decently clad, were seated or standing each at his little desk. Some made an infernal noise violently opening and shutting the lids of these desks. Others emitted a blaring sound from little toy trumpets; others strummed jew's-harps; still others beat snare drums. And at their head, like a bandmaster, stood a grey-bearded man of about 65, evidently the leader of this wilful faction, directing the whole pandemonium in volume and in tempo. The sum of uproar thus produced was so infernal that it completely drowned the voice of a man who was evidently talking from his seat in another part of the house, for one could see his lips moving and the veins in his temples swelling. Bedlam let loose! That was the impression on the whole."

has been written about the Taafe ministry in Austria that at times the subject races had considerable political influence in that half of the Dual Monarchy. This was never the case in Hungary. The government of the latter was almost entirely in the hands of the Magyar aristocracy, a very small minority of the total population of the kingdom. The upper house of the national legislature was frankly aristocratic and mostly hereditary, and the lower house, too, was largely responsive to the desires of the landed aristocrats. Elected on a franchise so restricted that only about 6.5 per cent of the population had the ballot (1914), it consisted to a large extent of representatives of the aristocrats and of those who might be called the gentry. In addition to the limited franchise, the aristocracy in order to protect itself resorted to gerrymandering of electoral districts, open voting, official pressure, and bribery. As might be expected, the bureaucracy, too, consisted almost wholly of Magyars. So far as Hungary was concerned, therefore, the result of the *Ausgleich* was to confer home rule upon the Magyars and for all practical purposes upon only a small fraction of them—the aristocracy.

The Magyar aristocrats presided over a country which as late as 1914 was largely a land of the old regime. Although the revolution of 1848 had legally destroyed feudalism and had given land to some of the peasantry, a relatively small number of leading families still dominated the political, economic, and social structure of the monarchy. A great part of the peasants lacked land of their own and as an agricultural proletariat continued in economic dependence upon the large landed proprietors. And the latter were nearly all Magyars, for of the 1657 owners of estates of more than 1420 acres in Hungary (1914), only 142 were not Magyars. According to one distinguished Hungarian historian, three or four leading families dominated in most of the counties, and all of the more prominent officials of the kingdom were related to one another directly or by marriage.[14]

At first it appeared that the government of the restored Hungarian kingdom might be inclined to deal liberally with its racial minorities. In 1868 an enlightened law drafted by Francis Deák

[14] A Hungarian publicist, writing at the close of the nineteenth century, likened the Schönborn estate with its more than 340,000 acres and its two hundred villages to a small medieval state. Although the estate was inhabited by some 70,000 Ukrainian peasants, the two representatives from this district in the lower house of the Hungarian parliament were regularly chosen by the owner of the estate.

was enacted, guaranteeing the equal rights of nationalities in the matters of languages and schools, and in the same year a compromise was reached with the Croats which granted autonomy to Croatia (Croatia-Slavonia) under a Magyar governor. The official language of this province was to be Croatian, and the Hungarian government was to be limited in its control of Croatia to such matters as trade, finance, and the army. The Croats, furthermore, were conceded the right to have five of the sixty Hungarian representatives in the Austro-Hungarian Delegations, and three members in the upper house and forty members in the lower house of the Hungarian parliament. When, however, the Rumanians, the Slovaks, and the Ukrainians sought to secure similar separate institutions, they met with stern refusals. Even the proclamation of a federation of the non-Magyars by representatives of these three peoples (1869) failed to move the dominant Magyar leaders.

Following the death of the liberal Deák in 1875, all pretense of compromise with the minority races of Hungary was dropped by the Magyar leaders, prominent among whom were Count Julius Andrássy and Count Stephen Tisza. The liberal law guaranteeing the equal rights of nationalities soon became a dead letter. Instead, an intensive campaign of "Magyarization" was inaugurated. Innumerable steps were taken to wipe out the non-Magyar languages. Except in Croatia no high schools or universities were permitted unless instruction was in Magyar, and figures for 1913 reveal that 82 per cent of those who graduated from high schools and nearly 90 per cent of the students in colleges and universities were Magyars. In some parts of the kingdom even primary schools using a non-Magyar language were closed.[15] Only the use of Magyar was permitted in the postal, telegraph, and railway services, and even family names and place names were subject to "Magyarization." The press was also utilized to advance this program, for more than 80 per cent of all the newspapers and periodicals published in Hungary were (1909) limited to the Magyar language. Upon occasion even the funds raised to keep alive the language and literature of the subject nationalities were ruthlessly confiscated by the Magyar government.

Because of the highly restricted franchise in Hungary, the lesser

---

[15] The effect of such a policy is seen in the figures for illiteracy. As late as 1910 more than 31 per cent of the population over six years of age in Hungary proper was illiterate.

nationalities were largely excluded from the parliament and therefore precluded from using that body to set forth their grievances. In 1881, however, Rumanian representatives drafted demands for the restoration of political autonomy to Transylvania, the appointment of Rumanians as officials in that region, and state aid for Rumanian schools, but their demands received little consideration. When later they made an attempt to go over the head of the Hungarian government to present their grievances to Francis Joseph himself, the chief result was that they themselves were brought to trial on the charge of "incitement against the Magyar nationality." Evidence of the deep dissatisfaction which prevailed among the subject nationalities is seen in the heavy emigration of these classes from the Hungarian kingdom after the policy of "Magyarization" became effective. Between 1876 and 1910 more than 3,500,000 left the country.

Although the Magyar leaders could almost unanimously agree on the policy of Magyarizing the subject peoples in the kingdom, the last decade of the nineteenth century saw a serious split among the Magyars over the question of maintaining the *Ausgleich* unchanged. One group, the Liberals, continued to be satisfied with the benefits which the Magyars derived from that "compromise." Another, organized as the Independence Party, became increasingly dissatisfied with the *Ausgleich*. Its members were the spiritual heirs of those who had stood with Louis Kossuth in 1848–1849 and were now led by his son, Francis Kossuth. They demanded the end of the *Ausgleich*, the destruction of the dual structure of Austria-Hungary. They sought the abolition of the Delegations and the joint ministers, and desired instead a purely personal union with Austria through the Habsburg Francis Joseph.

Consequently, though the Hungarian parliament escaped the obstructionist activities of subject nationalities such as paralyzed the Austrian Reichsrat, it was seriously handicapped at times by the Independents. The latter joyfully resorted to obstructionist tactics whenever it came time to renew the decennial agreements with Austria. In the nineties they denounced the proposed commercial treaty with Austria with such force that they brought the downfall of the Liberal government, which under one premier or another had been in power since 1867. But this proved to be a futile achievement, for the commercial agreement was completed nevertheless.

The Independents next directed their attack against the use of the German language in the Austro-Hungarian army. They demanded that Magyar should be made the language of service and command in all regiments recruited in Hungary, despite the fact that more than half of the soldiers from Hungary were Slovaks, Ukrainians, Rumanians, Croats, Serbs, or Germans. If they could carry their point in this matter they stood to gain in two ways. Magyar nationalism would be exalted by having the Magyar language placed on a plane of equality with German in the army. And, in the second place, the army could thereafter be used as an efficient instrument for the "Magyarization" of the subject races of Hungary.

Although Francis Joseph had apparently cared not at all what the Magyars did to the minor national groups in Hungary so long as they adhered to the Dual Monarchy, he did object strenuously to the destruction of the unity of the Habsburg army and to the loss of his unlimited imperial and royal command over the military forces of his realm. He therefore refused to consider this proposal of the Independents and insisted that the command of the Austro-Hungarian army was his special royal prerogative. Again the Independents by their obstructive tactics brought the dissolution of the parliament; and later, in 1905, Count Tisza, the Liberal premier, was forced out of office when the Liberals were defeated in an election in January of that year. But Francis Joseph refused to surrender. On the contrary, he himself took the offensive. First he prorogued the parliament, and next he proposed a scheme for universal suffrage in Hungary. Obviously such an innovation would be a boon for the subject races and a disaster for the Magyars. Then, early in 1906, he actually dissolved the existing parliament but issued no call for the election of another.

These steps secured the desired results for the Habsburg ruler. The Independents—chiefly Magyars—decided to make a bargain with the Hungarian king in order to rid themselves of the menace of universal suffrage. In return for Francis Joseph's promise to call new elections and to postpone indefinitely his plan for universal suffrage, the opposition agreed to pass the budget, renew another commercial treaty with Austria, and postpone indefinitely further discussion of the army language question. A coalition government, largely representative of the Magyar aristocracy but containing a number of Independents also, was then organized under Wekerle.

On the important matter of his supreme control of the Austro-Hungarian army, however, Francis Joseph had triumphed. As late as 1910 some 85 per cent of the officers in the Habsburg army were Germans.

But the Independents soon found other matters about which to agitate. In 1908 the charter of the Austro-Hungarian Bank, with its head office in Vienna, was due to expire. The Independents speedily seized this occasion to demand that there should not be one Austro-Hungarian Bank for the whole Dual Monarchy but a separate bank for each of the two states. Again they met the opposition of Francis Joseph, who once more threatened to bring forward his proposal for universal suffrage. Parliamentary life in Hungary during the ensuing months became exceedingly hectic; but when, in 1909, the parliament failed to pass the budget, the government carried on as usual regardless of that fact.

Meanwhile, conditions both at home and abroad had begun to give the more moderate Magyars cause for concern. Nationalism among the subject races, especially the Slavs, was noticeably on the increase. Russia's growing interest in and encouragement of the Pan-Serb movement seemed to threaten the very existence of the Hungarian kingdom. In the international crisis of 1908–1909 [16] Austria-Hungary had seemingly won against Serbia and Russia only because of the vigorous support which she had received from the German Empire. To many thoughtful Magyars the situation seemed wholly unfavorable for a conflict within the Dual Monarchy. The Independence Party, accordingly, was weakened by defections of the more moderate Magyars, and in the election of 1910 the Liberals once more won control of the parliament. Nevertheless, again in 1912 the Independents returned to the attack by renewing their efforts to limit Francis Joseph's supreme command over the army, and again they resorted to parliamentary obstruction. Count Tisza, in June, 1913, once more became premier, and this time he defeated the obstructionists, though he had to resort to police action to do it. From 1913 until after the death of Francis Joseph this iron-handed premier, despite occasional attempts to assassinate him, remained at the head of the Hungarian government.

Grave concern over the rising nationalism of Hungary's subject

[16] See pages 338–344.

races led Tisza in his last ministry to attempt to conciliate the 3,000,000 Rumanians living in Transylvania. Ever since the establishment of the Dual Monarchy the Rumanians had sought autonomy. The government's refusal to consider their demands, together with its policy of "Magyarization," its efforts to control the Rumanian Church, and its refusal to recognize the Rumanian intelligentsia in the state government or in the local administration had led eventually to an irredentist movement which aimed at the union of Transylvania with the Kingdom of Rumania. Although Rumanian irredentism was never so aggressive as the Yugoslav— partly because it was discouraged by King Carol of Rumania— it was increasing rapidly among the intelligentsia and the middle classes in the second decade of the twentieth century. Tisza's negotiations with the Rumanians in 1914, in a half-hearted effort to conciliate them, therefore proved futile.

### THE YUGOSLAV QUESTION

The most threatening menace to the territorial integrity of the Dual Monarchy in the twentieth century came from the Serbs, Croats, and Slovenes, who were collectively referred to as Yugoslavs. As early as 1848 Croat leaders had envisaged the creation of some kind of Yugoslav state, linked with the rest of the Habsburg realm in a personal union through Francis Joseph. In the revolution of that year they had aided the emperor to put down the Magyar movement for independence in Hungary, but had themselves obtained little from Francis Joseph in return for their support. Not until late in the sixties did they receive any encouragement. In 1867 a Yugoslav Academy was created to keep alive their cultural heritage; in the next year they were given a limited political autonomy by the Magyar government at Budapest; and in 1874 they secured a Slavic university at Agram. Meanwhile, a National Party had grown up in Croatia, aimed at the creation of a large Yugoslav state to include, besides Croatia-Slavonia, the Serbs in southern Hungary, the Austrian province of Dalmatia, and the Hungarian port of Fiume.

The acquisition of Bosnia and Herzegovina, whose inhabitants consisted chiefly of Serbs and Croats, further complicated the Yugoslav problem. At the very beginning there was strong opposition to Habsburg rule, and several army corps had to be sent into the provinces before Austro-Hungarian control could be actually established. The provinces were never annexed to either of the partners of the Dual Monarchy but remained apart as a sort of colonial realm governed by the imperial minister of finance. Although in the years after 1878 some material improvements were made—such as the construction of roads and railways, and the abolition of brigandage—the provinces were denied self-government, and remained largely in a condition of feudalism and illiteracy. In 1910 more than four fifths of the population of Bosnia and Herzegovina over six years of age were unable to read and write. The Habsburg government, in order to offset the influence of the Croats, had sought in a way to create a feeling of Bosnian nationalism, but it only succeeded in building up a pro-Serb sentiment instead. Increasingly with the passing of the years the Bosnians dreamed of union with a greater Serbia.

As early as 1878 Austro-Hungarian leaders had begun to fear the rise of a greater-Serbia movement, and at the Congress of Berlin they had insisted that the narrow province of Novibazar should be turned over to the military occupation of the Habsburg army. This they had demanded partly in order to prevent direct contact between the two Yugoslav states, Serbia and Montenegro. In the eighties Austria-Hungary had taken advantage of Serbia's exigencies at that time to make her almost a dependency in order to bring her into line with Austro-Hungarian policies. The treaty of 1881 had never been popular in Serbia, and the pro-Austrian Obrenovich ruler who had signed it was denounced in Serbia for his action. A group in the little kingdom were soon plotting to overthrow the reigning dynasty in favor of a member of the rival Karageorgevich line.

Although even before 1903 the Serbs had begun to turn from Austria to Russia, the revolutionary seizure of the throne of Serbia by the pro-Russian Karageorgevich King Peter in that year gave a great impetus to Pan-Serbianism and to the rise of a strong anti-Habsburg sentiment. The latter was further increased in 1906 when Magyar landlords managed to prevent the renewal of the commercial treaty between Austria-Hungary and Serbia. As a result of the tariff war that followed, Serbia lost practically all of the market for her products in the Dual Monarchy, and since the Serbs exported chiefly pork, the quarrel was popularly referred to as the "pig war." Serbian peasants suffered greatly from this loss of markets, and as might be expected the denunciation of the Habsburgs was extremely bitter. Serbia's need of an outlet to the sea was realistically brought home to the Serbs. Added fuel was thus provided for the already burning desire of many Serbs to create a great Yugoslav kingdom which would embrace the Yugoslavs of Serbia, Montenegro, Bosnia, and the Habsburg empire as well.

While Serbian propagandists sought to inculcate these ideals among their kinsmen across the border, the repressive measures of the Magyar government of Hungary helped the movement along by alienating the Yugoslavs within the Dual Monarchy. In 1905 deputies from Croatia, Dalmatia, and Istria, meeting at Fiume, demanded, in total disregard of the dividing line between the Austrian Empire and the Kingdom of Hungary, that Dalmatia and Croatia-Slavonia be united in one state. In the same year this Yugoslav movement was further strengthened when Dalmatian Serbs and Croats, meeting at Zara, proclaimed that the Serbs and Croats constituted one nation, and demanded that steps be taken by the Habsburg government to give substance to the Fiume resolutions. Those who supported these resolutions came to be known as the Serbo-Croat coalition. Apparently the repressive measures of the Magyars had led most of the Roman Catholic Croats and the Greek Orthodox Serbs to waive their differences in order to present a united front to the Magyars.[17] In 1906 the coalition elected a majority of the diet of Croatia. Two years later it again won control, and the governor, unable to secure support in the diet, dissolved that body and ruled autocratically.

In an effort to discredit the Serbo-Croat coalition, Magyar leaders sought to prove that many Serbs in Hungary had actually become traitors to the kingdom by becoming linked with the Serbian government at Belgrade. During 1908 and 1909 scores of Serbs were brought to trial, and many were condemned to prison. In the latter year, too, an article based on documents in the government archives and written by Heinrich Friedjung, a well-known Austrian historian, appeared in a Vienna newspaper. The writer described Serbia's intrigues against the Dual Monarchy, and, at least by implication, accused the leaders of the Serbo-Croat coalition of trea-

---

[17] The Croatian Nationalists, who feared future domination by the Serbs, were bitterly opposed to the Serbo-Croat coalition.

son. The article proved to be a boomerang against the government, however, for, in the celebrated Friedjung trial which resulted when the leaders of the coalition sued for libel, it was proved that some of the documents which the historian had used were forgeries. Furthermore, Professor Masaryk, the leader of the Young Czechs, investigated the documents later and in 1911 announced his conviction that both the Austrian minister at Belgrade and Aehrenthal, the Austro-Hungarian foreign minister in Vienna, had been involved in the forgery.[18] Although the Magyars by their accusations of treason had succeeded in largely destroying the influence of Supilo, the leader of the Serbo-Croat coalition, they brought down on the Habsburg government a veritable hornet's nest of criticism, which further alienated the Yugoslavs within the empire and made Europe as a whole suspicious of the policies and purposes of the Dual Monarchy. This was especially so after the somewhat discredited Austro-Hungarian minister at Belgrade was elevated to the position of under-secretary of state in the Habsburg foreign office.

The government still wrestled valiantly, if perhaps mistakenly, with the Yugoslav problem. The railway systems and economic interests of Bosnia-Herzegovina and Dalmatia were deliberately separated to hinder co-operation between these two districts. In 1910 a constitution was granted Bosnia, and a diet, with a franchise so contrived as to prevent the appearance of any national party, was established. But, though the government managed to control the diet, Yugoslav enthusiasts caused trouble in other ways. In the very year that the constitution was granted, an unsuccessful attempt was made on the life of the governor. It was not long till the new constitution was suspended and Bosnia was temporarily put under military rule.

In Yugoslav districts outside Bosnia the situation became still worse. Eventually, in 1912, even the more passive Slovenes of Austria became aroused to the extent that they proclaimed their determination to attempt to unite their district with Croatia-Slavonia. In the latter, although the Serbo-Croat coalition declined in strength after the discrediting of Supilo, it did not give up the fight. The Croatian schools were filled with Yugoslav propaganda. In 1912

[18] It is probable that both of these men had been deceived by a Serbian adventurer regarding the authenticity of the documents involved.

the Croatian university at Agram had to be closed for a time because of nationalistic activities among its students, and many high schools suffered a similar fate. More and more the tendency to resort to violence became evident. The governor of Croatia dissolved the diet and established a dictatorship, with the result that in 1912, in 1913, and in 1914 attempts were made to assassinate him and his successor. The spirit of violence spread also to the neighboring city of Fiume, where in 1913 an attempt was made to blow up the governor's residence.

There were some within the Dual Monarchy who felt that perhaps the best way to meet the Yugoslav menace was to permit the creation of a large Yugoslav state within the empire and to concede to this state a status equal to that of Austria and Hungary. That is to say, such reformers advocated changing the Habsburg empire from a dual to a "trial" or triple monarchy. They urged that such a step would go far toward drowning out the siren song of the Yugoslavs outside the empire, who were advocating that all Yugoslavs should be gathered into a greater Serbia. The Croats had a civilization and an economic well-being which was undoubtedly on a higher plane than that which prevailed in the Serbian kingdom. Because they were the literary and cultural leaders of the Yugoslavs, they had an influence out of all proportion to their numbers. Give them political equality within the Habsburg empire, the advocates of "trialism" declared, and their desire to be part of a Serbian-dominated state would soon disappear. Archduke Francis Ferdinand, the heir-apparent to the Habsburg throne, was drawn more and more to favor some such reorganization of the Habsburg realm in the early years of the twentieth century.

But the Magyar leaders, who were chiefly responsible for the alienation of the Yugoslavs, were not willing to consider any reform which might decrease the importance of the Hungarian kingdom or lessen their own power within it. They were therefore opposed to any experiment in the matter of "trialism," and were more inclined to favor those in the Dual Monarchy who in desperation concluded that the only way to save the empire from disintegration as the result of Yugoslav propaganda was utterly to destroy Serbia or at least to bring her definitely under Habsburg domination. An advocate of such measures was Conrad von Hötzendorf, who became chief of staff of the Habsburg army late in 1912. Until the outbreak of the World War he steadily urged an attack upon the little Serb kingdom as the only way to end the menace of Yugoslav nationalism. To prepare the Habsburg army for such a war—which, of course, might involve Russia—two years of peace-time service in the army were made compulsory (1912), with the result that the standing army of the Dual Monarchy was increased to 450,000 men. Perhaps the concluding tragedy of Francis Joseph's long reign was that it was Hötzendorf's ideas rather than those of Francis Ferdinand which were in the ascendancy in Austria-Hungary just prior to 1914.

## CHAPTER X

## TURKEY AND THE BALKANS

ALTHOUGH the territory which is usually referred to as the Balkans constitutes a small part of Europe, within that area in the century before the World War there existed such a tangle of conflicting nationalistic programs and clashing imperialistic ambitions as to make peace within the peninsula almost an impossibility. The difficult problem of handling this complex Balkan situation in such a way as to satisfy the interested powers—large and small—has frequently been reduced to the two words, "Eastern Question." A German historian, writing in the nineteenth century, grasped the importance of the Balkan situation in a way that was almost uncanny. "Amongst the great problems of our age," he wrote, "none is more fitted to occupy the thoughts, not only of the professional statesmen but of every keen-sighted individual who takes an interest in politics, than the so-called Eastern Question. It is the pivot upon which the general politics of the century now drawing to an end are turning, and it will be so for the coming century also." How correct he was in his historic prophecy the events recorded in this and the next succeeding chapter offer abundant proof.

### POLITICAL GEOGRAPHY OF THE BALKANS, 1878–1908

As a result of changes made by the treaty of Berlin [1] and by events in the immediately succeeding years, the political map of the Balkan peninsula after 1878 was far different from that which had existed a few years earlier. The northernmost of the Balkan states, the one which adjoined both Russia and Austria-Hungary, was Rumania, which was bounded by the Pruth and Danube Rivers on the northeast, the Carpathian Mountains on the west, the Danube River on the south, and the Black Sea on the east. In 1878 it was the largest and strongest of the Balkan states. South of Rumania, extending from the Black Sea on the east to Serbia on the west and to the

---

[1] It would be profitable for the student to reread here the account of events leading to the treaty of Berlin. See pages 245–254.

Balkan Mountains on the south, was the newly created principality of Bulgaria, which was still a tributary state of the sultan. It was a very disgruntled state in 1878 because the Congress of Berlin had deprived it of territory running down to the Aegean which the treaty of San Stefano had originally allotted to it. South of the Balkan Mountains was the autonomous district of Eastern Rumelia, ruled by a Christian governor appointed by the sultan. Its inhabitants were largely Bulgarians and ardently desired to have their territory incorporated in Bulgaria.

To the west of Bulgaria was the little independent principality of Serbia, which was separated from Austria-Hungary on the north by the Save and Danube Rivers. On the east it bordered on Rumania and Bulgaria; on the west and southwest it was hemmed in by the Habsburg-administered province of Bosnia and by the narrow strip of Novibazar, which was occupied by Austro-Hungarian military forces. One reason for Austria's insistence upon her military occupation of this little province had been that a way might be open for the possible construction of an Austrian railway to the port of Saloniki. A second reason had been the Habsburg determination to keep Serbia and Montenegro, the neighboring little Yugoslav principality, from having direct contact with each other. Serbia was a landlocked state—the only one in the Balkans—and therefore largely dependent commercially upon Austria-Hungary. To the west of Serbia, separated from her by Novibazar, was the tiny principality of Montenegro, which for all practical purposes had been independent for more than three quarters of a century, though that fact had not been legally recognized until 1878. In the treaty of Berlin it had been given a seaport on the Adriatic, though with conditions attached which made it somewhat subordinate to Austria-Hungary.

The southernmost part of the peninsula and a number of the islands adjoining it in the Mediterranean and Aegean Seas constituted the independent kingdom of Greece, the first of the Balkan states to gain legal recognition of its freedom. In 1881, as a result of agreements made at the Congress of Berlin, Greece received additions of territory in Thessaly. All of the territory from Greece's northern boundary to the southern limits of Montenegro, Novibazar, Bulgaria, and Eastern Rumelia belonged in 1878 to the Ottoman Empire, as did Crete and most of the other Greek-inhabited islands in the Aegean. On the European mainland the sultan's realm included the important cities of Constantinople, Adrianople, and Saloniki, and extended from the Black Sea through Thrace, Macedonia, Epirus, and Albania to the Adriatic.

Although the great powers at Berlin had solemnly pledged themselves to guarantee the integrity of the remaining territorial holdings of the Ottoman Empire, some of them apparently did not take their pledges very seriously. Within three years after the treaty of Berlin, Russia, Austria-Hungary, and Germany agreed (1881) not to oppose the eventual union of Bulgaria and Eastern Rumelia. With three of the great powers in this tolerant state of mind, it is not surprising that the national leaders of Bulgaria and Eastern Rumelia should conspire to overturn the Berlin settlement. In 1885 the two states united to form one principality.[2]

For a quarter of a century after 1885 the national states in the Balkans continued to maintain the *status quo* territorially. Perhaps this was in part the result of the increasing jealousies and rivalries of a number of the great powers, each of which feared that another might advance its position and prestige if any further change did occur in the Balkan peninsula. In 1887 agreements looking to the maintenance of the *status quo* in the Balkans were made by Italy and Austria-Hungary and by Italy and Great Britain,[3] and a decade later by Russia and Austria-Hungary. Fear that any territorial change or any war in the Balkans might precipitate a general European conflict also led the great powers for a time to oppose any attempt to change the *status quo*.

### INTERNAL HISTORY OF THE BALKAN NATIONAL STATES

Although, in the minds of many, Rumania, Bulgaria, Greece, Serbia, and Montenegro in some vague way constituted before 1914 a sort of amorphous mass in southeastern Europe which was called the Balkans, in reality each of these states in the years before the World War had its own individuality, its own problems, its own hopes and aspirations. Before an account is given of further changes in the political geography of the Balkans, it would be wise to learn something of the domestic history of these states which played such an important role in reducing the territory of the sultan in Europe.

[2] For a fuller discussion of this step, see pages 320–321.
[3] See pages 153–154.

## RUMANIA

During the quarter century from 1856 to 1881 numerous changes had been made in the political status of the Rumanians who dwelt in Moldavia and Wallachia. After the Crimean War the treaty of Paris (1856) had made these two provinces of the Ottoman Empire autonomous but separate political units; three years later the provinces had each elected the same man, Alexander Cuza, as its prince; and in 1862 the sultan had accorded legal recognition to the principality of Rumania formed by their union. Finally, at the close of the Russo-Turkish War of 1877–1878, the treaty of Berlin had recognized the complete independence of Rumania, which in 1881 proclaimed herself a kingdom. Meanwhile, the native prince who had first ruled Rumania had been forced to abdicate (1866) because he had made reforms which were unpopular with the powerful landed aristocracy and clergy. The one who became the first king of Rumania was Carol (Charles), of the German family of Hohenzollern-Sigmaringen, a younger brother of the one who was offered the throne of Spain in 1870.[4] In 1881 this Hohenzollern prince was crowned King Carol I of Rumania.

Carol rather naturally was inclined to pursue a pro-German policy and to align his kingdom with the two great Germanic empires. Furthermore, Rumanian public opinion—what there was of it—was in the eighties opposed to Russia because the latter had forced Rumania to surrender a valuable strip of Bessarabia in 1878. It is not surprising, therefore, that Rumania signed a defensive alliance with Austria-Hungary against Russia and that almost to the day of Carol's death (1914) she remained a loyal satellite of the Austro-German alliance. In her domestic political institutions, too, Rumania under Carol imitated the Hohenzollern kingdom of Prussia in having a government which was largely aristocratic and which conferred great power upon the monarch. Another Prussian institution which King Carol admired was the army. He accordingly increased his own army in numbers, installed German instructors, and modernized its equipment, with the result that Rumania in the succeeding years had the largest military force of all the Balkan states.

Three causes of popular dissatisfaction and unrest existed within Rumania during the years from 1878 to 1914. One was economic.

4 See page 99.

THE BALKANS, 1885–1913

The country was predominantly agricultural, and the majority of its inhabitants were peasants. But the land was held for the most part by powerful landed proprietors who were reluctant to make any concessions which might weaken their positions. Rumania therefore had an agrarian problem. With the steady increase of the rural population the danger of peasant uprisings became imminent. In an attempt to improve the agrarian situation—without antagonizing the landed proprietors—the government provided (1889) for the sale of public lands to the peasants, but this step naturally failed to solve the problem permanently. So strong did the unrest become that a great uprising occurred in 1907, when the peasants demanded sweeping land reforms. A large part of the army was mobilized to suppress the revolt, but following its collapse a number of measures were enacted in an effort to placate the peasants. Nevertheless, in 1914 nearly half of the total agricultural area of the country was still in the hands of large landowners, who constituted scarcely more than half of one per cent of the total number of agriculturists. On the other hand, a million peasant proprietors in 1914 each had farms of less than twenty-five acres. Not until after the World War was agrarian legislation enacted to put the land of Rumania in the hands of the peasants.[5]

A second cause of popular dissatisfaction was political, for the Rumanian government was far from democratic. The kingdom had a national parliament which was very similar to the Prussian Landtag in that the lower house was elected on a three-class system of suffrage which gave a small percentage of the wealthier Rumanians a predominant voice in legislation. Out of a population of approximately 7,500,000 in 1914 fewer than 200,000 were entitled to participate in national elections. Furthermore, King Carol, like the ruler of Prussia, had an absolute veto on all laws which the parliament might enact. Despite agitation in behalf of a more liberal system of government, little progress was made, and it was not until the closing years of the World War that the franchise was actually widened.

A third cause of unrest was the presence within Rumania of a considerable number of Jews. They lived for the most part in the towns, where they were often the chief merchants and moneylenders, and as a group they constituted the bourgeoisie of the country, as they did in parts of Russia. The Congress of Berlin, in order

[5] See page 807.

to protect the Jews, had stipulated when it recognized Rumania as an independent state that all citizens must be granted equal rights regardless of their religion. But Rumania, in order to destroy any political power of the Jews, passed a law which classified Jews as aliens [6] and therefore not entitled to the rights of citizenship. Naturally, this caused great dissatisfaction among the Rumanian Jews. Furthermore, in order to turn criticism from themselves, the landed proprietors occasionally aroused the peasants against the "money-lending, anti-Christian" Jews. This was not particularly difficult to do when anti-Jewish pogroms were occurring at frequent intervals in neighboring Bessarabia. Not until 1917 were the Rumanian Jews admitted to citizenship, but even this step failed to stop the agitation of the anti-Semites within the kingdom.

Despite these disturbing factors, noticeable economic—if not cultural—progress was made in the kingdom in the period before 1914. As in Hungary, the great landowners led the way in introducing improved agricultural methods and machinery, and the soil was naturally rich. The country therefore came to be one of the important grain-producing regions of Europe. As a result of cordial relations with Germany and Austria-Hungary, capital from these states entered Rumania and helped to develop railway facilities and the country's rich oil fields. As part of the ramifications of the famous Berlin-Bagdad railway scheme, Rumania was linked by rail with Constantinople, and by 1914 she had more than two thousand miles of state-owned railways.

### BULGARIA

By the terms of the treaty of Berlin, establishing Bulgaria as an autonomous principality tributary to the sultan, this new state was to be administered by a Russian commissar until a constitution had been drafted and adopted by a popular assembly. In 1879 the Russian commissar submitted the draft of a conservative constitution to an assembly of Bulgarians, who immediately transformed it into a democratic instrument of government, providing for universal manhood suffrage, a one-house parliament, and ministerial responsibility. The assembly next turned to the matter of selecting a ruler for the new state and unanimously chose Alexander of Battenberg, twenty-two years old, an intelligent and honest but obviously in-

[6] Somewhat as Nazi Germany did after the World War. See pages 674–676.

experienced German prince. Perhaps the most important reason for his election was that he was a nephew of Tsar Alexander II and was favored by him for the throne.

Starting with a provisional directive position in Bulgaria, the tsar apparently hoped to transform the new principality into something like a Russian protectorate to serve as a Romanov outpost in the Balkans. To accomplish this end he relied on the gratitude and political inexperience of the Bulgarians and upon the subservience of the young prince, who could not help feeling that in a sense he was a representative of the tsar. The democratic constitution of Bulgaria had never been popular with Prince Alexander's Russian advisers, and after a number of conflicts between the parliament and the prince, the latter with Russian support in 1881 suppressed it. For two years Prince Alexander ruled as a quasi autocrat—on the surface. But he knew, and many of his subjects suspected, that he was only a figurehead for the tsar, for during this period two Russian generals dominated his ministry, and other Russians held high positions not only in the army but in the government as well.

Eventually the young ruler became irritated by his position of subordination to Russia, and looked about for a way of escape. He thought he found it in the presence within Bulgaria of a group of patriots who were hostile to his domineering Russian advisers. To free himself from absolute dependence upon the Russian tsar, Prince Alexander sought a reconciliation with his patriotic subjects. In 1883 he restored the democratic constitution, replaced many of his Russian advisers with Bulgarians, and regained popular favor—at the cost of incurring the tsar's enmity. Thereafter, for a time, Russia's policy was designed to keep Bulgaria weak. Events in 1885, however, further strengthened the principality.

In that year a group of conspirators expelled the governor of Eastern Rumelia, proclaimed the union of this district with the principality of Bulgaria, and sent a delegation to invite Prince Alexander to become the sovereign of Eastern Rumelia. The prince was momentarily deterred by fear of the displeasure of the tsar, but in the end, moved by the national enthusiasm of his Bulgarian subjects, he accepted the throne of Eastern Rumelia and sent Bulgarian military forces to occupy that district. Obviously all this was in flagrant violation of the treaty of Berlin, and among the great powers an exchange of diplomatic notes at once began in an effort to decide upon a course of action. The tsar, to show his displeasure, immediately ordered the withdrawal of all Russian officers from the Bulgarian army.

But the repercussion of events in Bulgaria was greater in the Balkan states than among the great powers. Both Greece and Serbia announced that the Balkan equilibrium had been upset by Bulgaria's enlargement and consequently demanded territorial increases for themselves as compensation. Serbia, in fact, went so far as to mobilize her army and invade Bulgaria, hoping perhaps that the latter's army would be demoralized by its recent loss of Russian officers. Contrary to all the expectations of the powers, Serbia, the older and supposedly the better-organized state, more than met her match in the war that ensued. The Bulgarians valiantly rallied to defend their recently enlarged national state, and, three days after the invasion of Bulgaria began, the Serbs were overwhelmed by a disastrous defeat. The victorious Bulgars then drove the Serbs back across the frontier and started for Belgrade. They had hardly launched their invasion, however, when they were met by an ultimatum from Austria-Hungary. Under pressure from the latter, Bulgaria was compelled to sign a truce, which was later followed by a peace treaty. Thanks to Habsburg intervention Serbia neither lost territory nor had to pay an indemnity, and thus escaped from what might have been the disastrous results of her attack upon her neighbor.

Bulgaria's defeat of Serbia apparently had its effect also upon any plans which the great powers may have been formulating to prevent the union with Eastern Rumelia. Although the powers at first protested and stated that they would not recognize the union, in the end they did nothing to prevent what the Bulgarian people had so enthusiastically achieved. In fact, Great Britain's desire to utilize the Balkan states to check Russia's future expansion toward the Mediterranean led British statesmen to exert pressure upon the sultan in favor of recognizing the union of the two principalities now that enmity existed between Bulgaria and the tsar. By April, 1886, the sultan, in need of Great Britain's friendly support, had formally recognized the *fait accompli,* and the other powers had acquiesced. Bulgaria thus emerged from the crisis greatly increased in area and population. On the other hand, Prince Alexander's position was weakened, for by strengthening his principality he had further antagonized the tsar.

In the end the latter's opposition cost Alexander his throne. Utilizing the discontent of certain Bulgarian army officers, the Russian government succeeded in hatching a conspiracy which resulted (1886) in the seizure of the prince, who was compelled to sign his abdication and was then carried off to Russian Bessarabia. Although he was later released and was recalled to the throne by those who had driven the pro-Russian conspirators from the capital, Prince Alexander apparently had lost his nerve. When he learned from the tsar that the latter would not approve his return to Bulgaria, he appointed a regency, in September, 1886, and then rather abjectly resigned his throne.

Within Bulgaria a political struggle now ensued. On the one side the pro-Russians wished to consult the tsar regarding a new ruler and were in general content to have the principality constitute a sort of Russian protectorate. On the other side the Bulgarian nationalists desired to pursue a policy of freedom and independence from outside control. The latter were led by Stefan Stambulov, president of the parliament, a somewhat coarse Bulgarian peasant but a man of vigor, courage, and intelligence. Stambulov's group eventually won, and the second Russian attempt to gain the ascendancy in Bulgaria was thus thwarted. Almost a year passed, however, before the parliament chose a new ruler. Again they turned to Germany, this time electing Prince Ferdinand of Saxe-Coburg, who, though young, apparently had sufficient courage and self-reliance to accept a difficult position among an alien people. That he understood the national sentiment of his adopted land seemed evident when he chose as his prime minister Stefan Stambulov.

The election of Prince Ferdinand had been made against the protest of Russia, and consequently the tsar's government would not formally recognize the new ruler. Russia's attitude in turn deterred the other powers from taking such a step. Despite Russian conspiracies against him, however, Ferdinand managed to hold his throne. During the first seven years of his reign he was apparently content to study the Bulgarian situation and to let Stambulov manage the government. The latter, a Russophobe at heart, energetically devoted himself with every means at hand to advancing the independence and security of Bulgaria. Inclined to use high-handed measures to achieve his ends, when he considered them necessary, he naturally created numerous bitter enemies within the country.

By 1894 Prince Ferdinand had arrived at the place where he desired

to be recognized by the governments of Europe, and he was clever
enough to realize that, if he could win the support of the Russian
tsar, his quest for recognition would be facilitated. Furthermore, he
had begun to grow weary of Stambulov's rather arbitrary rule. Consequently, it was not difficult for friction to develop between the ruler
and his Russophobe prime minister, and eventually (1894) Stambulov
submitted his resignation.[7] Prince Ferdinand next availed himself of
a change of rulers in Russia to seek a reconciliation with the new tsar,
Nicholas II. In this he was successful, and, following recognition by
the Russian government, Prince Ferdinand's position as ruler of
Bulgaria was speedily accepted by the other states of Europe. In 1908,
after the Young Turk revolution,[8] Ferdinand successfully proclaimed
the complete independence of Bulgaria and changed his title from
Prince to King.

Bulgaria, in contrast with Rumania, was a land of petty peasant
proprietors and so was not disturbed by agrarian agitation advocating the seizure of great estates. She was, also, politically democratic,
though the peasants were all too often inclined to permit politicians
to manage the government. Economically, the country advanced
steadily in the generation before the Balkan wars. Roads and railways were constructed to facilitate communication within the country, and Varna on the Black Sea and ports on the Danube were
improved to take care of the foreign trade. A good public-school
system was established, and education was made compulsory for
boys and girls. By 1914 the percentage of illiterates in the Bulgarian
army was much lower than that in any other Balkan state. Her
army, too, at the opening of the Balkan wars, was one of the strongest to be found in the Balkan peninsula.

### GREECE

When the Ottoman flood began to recede in the Balkans in the
nineteenth century, Greece was the first national state to emerge
and to receive legal recognition of its independence by Turkey and
the European powers. In the thirties it was established as a kingdom,
and Otto I, the second son of King Louis I of Bavaria, reigned in
Greece from 1833 to 1862. In the latter year nationalistic dissatisfaction with the king's numerous German advisers and with his lack

---

[7] In the following year Stambulov met death at the hands of an assassin.
[8] See page 344.

of strong aggressive efforts to secure additional territory for Greece led to a popular uprising which drove him from the country. In 1863 a new monarch, secured this time from Denmark, mounted the throne of Greece as George I. In order to help popularize the new ruler with his subjects at the very outset of his reign, Great Britain in 1864 ceded to Greece the Ionian Islands off the west coast of the Balkan peninsula. In 1881, as already explained, Greece also secured Thessaly from Turkey as a result of the recommendation of the Congress of Berlin.

Soon after the accession of King George a new constitution was adopted which laid the foundation for the political life of the Greek kingdom until after the World War. Greece established a one-chamber parliament (*Boulé*) elected by universal suffrage. Unfortunately, the widespread illiteracy and political inexperience of the masses and the tendency of many Greek leaders to resort to political corruption in the interests of their diverse factions militated against stability in government. The reign of George I saw on an average at least one ministry come and go each year.

Arnold J. Toynbee, an English historian well versed in the history of the Near East, succinctly summed up the history of Greece before the World War when he stated: "The Greek nation's present was overshadowed by its future, and its actions paralyzed by its hopes." Patriotic Greeks, it appeared, were more concerned with adding to the kingdom the many Greeks who lived under the Turkish flag than they were in improving the lot of those that already lived under the Greek flag. Fundamentally, Greece was a poor agricultural country, and in the seventies its rural population was illiterate and backward. In the early days of King George's reign the country was lacking in railways and inadequately provided with roads, bridges, and means of communication. This had the effect of encouraging brigandage in some of the isolated districts. Although the kingdom was advantageously situated for playing a mercantile role in the eastern Mediterranean, for years its port facilities were neglected and its commerce remained insignificant. The national treasury was almost continuously on the verge of bankruptcy.

Crete was one of the territories which frequently held the attention of the Greeks to the detriment of progress in Greece herself.

Crete was a large island lying to the southeast of Greece and was inhabited almost entirely by Greeks. The Cretans were as eager to become part of the Greek kingdom as the patriots of Greece were to bring about their annexation. Uprisings and insurrections against the Turkish government were of frequent occurrence on the island, and at the Congress of Berlin the great powers had attempted to remove the cause of Cretan unrest by compelling the sultan to grant the islanders a local assembly with a Christian majority.

But the Turkish government failed to carry out its promises, and the Cretans refused to be satisfied with their new status. Doubtless, even if the sultan had faithfully lived up to his agreements, unrest would have continued because of the strong national sentiment which had been aroused in favor of union with Greece. In February, 1897, the Cretans once more rose against their Turkish overlords, and in Greece a great outburst of national sentiment compelled King George to send warships and troops to aid the insurgents. A little later, on the mainland, other Greeks, organized as irregular troops, began raiding across the border into Turkish territory in the Balkans. The Ottoman government thereupon declared war, and its troops began an invasion of Greece.

In May, 1897, the great powers intervened and compelled the belligerents to sign an armistice, and in the course of the succeeding months a treaty was negotiated. To pay for her ill-prepared and hot-headed attack upon the Turks, Greece was compelled to cede to the sultan a small strip of Thessaly and also to pay an indemnity. For Greece the outcome of the venture, therefore, was harmful both to her national prestige and to her national treasury. The insurrection did bring some improvement in the status of the Cretans, however. The four great powers—Great Britain, Russia, France, and Italy [9]—persuaded the sultan to retain only nominal suzerainty in Crete and to withdraw from the island all Turkish troops and civil officials. The protecting great powers, apparently sympathetic with Greek nationalism, then appointed as governor of Crete Prince George, the second son of the Greek king.

The insurrection of 1897 helped to raise to prominence a Cretan who was destined to play a prominent role in Greek affairs for more

[9] Apparently in deference to the Kaiser's desire to secure the ascendancy in Turkey, both Germany and Austria-Hungary declined to be involved in the new settlement.

than a quarter of a century. This was Eleutherios Venizelos, whose ancestors had migrated from Greece, after a futile revolt in the eighteenth century, while that country was still part of the Ottoman Empire. As a youth he had come under the influence of Greek nationalism, for he had received his collegiate degree from the University of Athens. Following his graduation from the university, Venizelos had returned to Crete thoroughly imbued with a determination to advance the Pan-Hellenic program by adding his island to the Greek kingdom. As might be expected, therefore, he had played a prominent part in the uprising of 1897, and in recognition of his political importance in Crete Prince George gave Venizelos a position in his government. But since the former sought to maintain the autonomous status of Crete while the latter aimed to bring about its union with Greece, they naturally disagreed on policies. Venizelos ultimately organized a political opposition to Prince George's government and in 1906 was instrumental in forcing the latter's resignation as governor. Prince George was then succeeded in his office by a Greek who, the great powers permitting, received his appointment at the hands of King George of Greece. Further recognition was thus accorded by the powers to Greek nationalism.

In the Greek parliamentary elections of 1910 Venizelos—who because of his ancestry was considered a citizen of Greece—entered the campaign as a candidate from a district in Athens and was elected. A strong nationalist organization in the country then forced King George to accept Venizelos as his prime minister. During the years that immediately preceded the World War, therefore, Venizelos was the guiding genius in Greek history. He apparently had two principal aims: in domestic affairs to modernize and strengthen the kingdom; in foreign affairs to bring about a system of alliances which could be utilized to advance Greece toward the ultimate consummation of her Pan-Hellenic dream. To accomplish the first of these aims he made many changes in Greek institutions. These included the revision of the constitution, the creation of an efficient civil-service system, the improvement of the nation's finances, the inauguration of free and compulsory education, the enactment of progressive social legislation, and the reorganization of the army and navy. His successful efforts to secure alliances and to obtain further territory for Greece are discussed in later pages of this chapter.

## SERBIA AND MONTENEGRO

Serbia, a small, primitive, agricultural country—cut off from the high seas in every direction by the intervening territory of other states—had inaugurated her revolt against the Ottoman Empire as early as 1804, when she was led by a swineherd known as "Black" ("Kara") George. Kara George, however, had been defeated and driven from the country by the Turks, but another insurrection occurred a few years later under the leadership of Milosh Obrenovich. In 1830 the little country was granted its autonomy by the sultan and from then on had practically an independent status, an independence which, as already pointed out, was formally conceded in the treaty of Berlin. In 1882 Serbia was raised to the rank of a kingdom.

Two important questions disturbed the history of Serbia down into the opening years of the twentieth century. Within the country there was the question whether the Obrenovich or the Karageorgevich dynasty should sit on the Serbian throne. In 1817 Milosh Obrenovich had murdered his rival for power, Kara George. Milosh then ruled in Serbia until 1839, when he was forced from power by adherents of the rival dynasty. In 1842 a Karageorgevich prince gained the throne, but in 1858 he in turn was driven from power to be succeeded by the aged Milosh Obrenovich. The latter lived only two years. In 1868 his son, Michael, was murdered by the Karageorgeviches, but the latter failed to secure the throne. In 1870 the Prince of Serbia was Milan Obrenovich.

Milan's abortive war against the Turks in 1876–1877 did not enhance his popularity with his subjects. Neither did Serbia's meager gains at the subsequent Congress of Berlin. A few years later his popularity suffered a further distinct decline when his secret convention (1881) surrendering Serbian aspirations in Bosnia and converting the principality into a satellite of Austria-Hungary became known. Whatever rise in popular favor resulted from his assumption of the title of king in 1882 was wiped out three years later by his disastrous attack upon Bulgaria, especially since the war brought increased taxation for the Serbs. Had his personal life been above reproach, his situation might not have been quite so hopeless, but his life was known to be scandalous, and there was little popularity to be gained by referring to it. From time to time, too, the king had to deal with anti-Obrenovich conspiracies and attempts at insurrection. Eventually, in 1889, after having proclaimed a liberal constitution for his kingdom, he resigned in favor of his son, who mounted the throne as King Alexander I.

Unfortunately the new king was not much of an improvement on his father. Apparently he had no thought of being a liberal monarch, for he abrogated the constitution which his father had granted and sought to rule without restraint. In the early years of his reign he increased his unpopularity because, like his father, he aligned Serbia in international affairs with Austria-Hungary. Finally, he shocked and antagonized a good share of his subjects by allowing his personal life to take precedence over his official position. While on a vacation at Biarritz the king chanced to fall in love with Draga Masin, the somewhat elderly divorced wife of a Serbian army officer; and despite the objections of his people, he married her and placed her on the throne as Queen Draga. From the beginning the new queen was unacceptable to those at court, and Alexander's tendency to favor her relatives added to his own unpopularity. Some army officers finally entered into a conspiracy with partisans of the Karageorgevich line to get rid of the Obrenovich dynasty. In 1903 King Alexander, Queen Draga, and a considerable number of their ministers and attendants were foully murdered in a palace revolution.

The throne of Serbia was now offered to Peter Karageorgevich, who accepted it and was crowned as King Peter I, but many of the European powers for a time refused to recognize the new government because of the manner in which it had come to power. The new monarch restored the constitution of 1889, with modifications widening the franchise, introducing proportional representation, and providing for special representation of the educated classes. King Peter accepted the idea of parliamentary government and chose his ministers from the majority party in the national legislature. The new king and his able premier and adviser, Nicholas Pashich, at once set out to strengthen the nation's financial condition and to increase its military forces so that Serbia might be prepared to grasp any favorable opportunity to redeem the Yugoslavs living beyond the kingdom's borders. So far as the question of dynasty was concerned, however, it appeared to be settled, for the murdered Alexander had been the last legitimate representative of the Obrenovich line.

The second important question which long disturbed the prewar history of Serbia was that of deciding whether the little state should align itself with the neighboring Dual Monarchy or with the more distant Russian Empire. In favor of the former was the fact that it was close at hand and could offer a favorable market for Serbia's products. Against an alliance with Austria-Hungary, however, was the fact that the latter included within her bounds great numbers of those who were akin to the Serbs. It appeared almost inevitable that a conflict must ensue between the powerful Austro-Hungarian monarchy and the little Serbian state when the Habsburgs, on the one hand, should try to extend their influence and territory down toward Saloniki, and the Serbs, on the other, should seek with increasing nationalism to redeem their Yugoslav kinsmen. For this reason it seemed to many Serbs more logical that their country should seek the backing and support of the great Slavic Russian Empire.

It has been pointed out that the outcome of the Congress of Berlin temporarily alienated Serbia from Russia and that in the following decade Serbia by treaty and otherwise became a sort of dependency of the Dual Monarchy.[10] This course of events was not particularly favored by the Serbian people, who showed their displeasure with the policy increasingly with the passing of the years. The Austrian alliance was one of the factors contributing to the unpopularity of both Milan and Alexander. So strong had become the nationalistic sentiment against Austria that even King Alexander shortly before his assassination had begun to turn in his international outlook from Austria to Russia. It was quite clear to King Peter when he assumed the crown that the only popular foreign policy for him would be one which was firmly anti-Austrian. This policy, accordingly, he adopted as his own, and from 1903 Serbia became more and more anti-Austrian and increasingly pro-Russian in her sentiment.

Serbia's change in foreign policy had a very real effect upon the domestic conditions of the country. In 1905, when the Serbian government was reorganizing its army and was about to purchase big guns, Austria-Hungary demanded that they should be bought from Austrian manufacturers instead of from French. Apparently the Habsburg government hoped to control the little kingdom's munitions supply and thus indirectly dominate its foreign policy also.

[10] See pages 293-294.

When Pashich refused to permit Austria-Hungary to decide where Serbia should buy her munitions, the Dual Monarchy as punishment raised a customs barrier against Serbian exports and initiated the already discussed "pig war." This step only increased Serbian nationalism to a higher pitch than ever, and in the end it led to an improved economic status as well. In 1906 the Ottoman government granted Serbia a lease on part of the harbor at Saloniki and conceded her the right of free entry and export. With a way thus opened to the high seas, Serbian exporters eventually found new markets in other countries, and Serbia to a considerable extent gained her military and economic freedom from Austria-Hungary. But Serbian patriots fully realized that they were still without a seaport of their own and that their free access to overseas countries continued to depend upon the good will of some one of Serbia's neighbors. So far as the question of foreign policy was concerned, however, it had been almost unanimously decided in favor of co-operation with Russia.

This was also the foreign policy of Prince Nicholas, the ruler of the diminutive Yugoslav state of Montenegro. Inhabited by Serbs, Montenegro was inclined in foreign affairs to co-operate with Serbia as she had done in 1875 and as she was destined to do again in 1912, in 1913, and in 1914. Until 1905 Montenegro was ruled in a patriarchal manner, but in that year her ruler so far gave way to the spirit of the times as to grant his subjects a democratic constitution. Five years later Nicholas sought to exalt his small country by raising it to the rank of a kingdom. In the years before the World War the King of Montenegro, like the King of Serbia, was enamored of the idea of bringing all the kinsmen of the Serbs into some kind of Yugoslav state.

### National Aspirations of the Balkan Peoples

None of the Balkan peoples organized in independent states after 1878 were content with the national boundaries which had been forced upon them largely as the result of the decisions of the great powers. The annexation of Eastern Rumelia by Bulgaria in 1885 and the attempted annexation of Crete by Greece in 1897—discussed in the pages above—were both indicative of the strong nationalist sentiment which existed in Bulgaria and Greece. But the Bulgarians and the Greeks were not the only Balkan peoples to be moved by nationalist aspirations. The people of every Christian state in the Balkans were ambitious to liberate and unite within the bounds of their own state the great numbers of kinsmen who dwelt outside their political frontiers; and each felt that their right to do this was as justifiable as had been the unification of Italy and Germany a few decades earlier or the consolidation of France and Great Britain some centuries before. For a clear understanding of subsequent developments in the Balkans and in Europe, a knowledge of the nationalist aspirations of each of the Balkan states is therefore essential.

On the surface it appeared that the Rumanian nationalists had a very difficult problem to solve, for their kinsmen were not all located in one foreign country, like those of Greece, for example. In Russian Bessarabia, to the north of Rumania across the river Pruth, the bulk of the population—the peasants—was chiefly Rumanian in the twentieth century despite the Romanov policy of "Russification." To the west of Rumania, in the Austrian province of Bukowina and in the Hungarian district of Transylvania,[11] the greater part of the people—again the peasants—were also Rumanians. Obviously, if Rumanian nationalists were to attain their goal completely, it would have to be won at the expense of both the Dual Monarchy and the Russian Empire.

To a minor state like Rumania this appeared to be an impossible task. A partial nationalist success, it was believed, must temporarily suffice. That is to say, Rumania by allying herself with either the Habsburgs or the Romanovs must be content for the time to gain territory at the expense of the other. There was some division of opinion within the country as to which policy should be adopted, but Rumania's loss of territory to Russia in 1878 turned the scale in favor of an alliance with Austria-Hungary against Russia. Such an alliance was signed in 1883.[12] Furthermore, the Rumanian King Carol I was stanchly pro-German in his sentiment, and so down until 1913 Rumania remained a faithful ally of the Hohenzollern and Habsburg rulers, and fondly dreamed of a future opportunity to wrest Bessarabia from Russia.

The program of the Bulgarian nationalists appeared more likely to be realized at the opening of the twentieth century than that of

---

[11] See the linguistic map on page 767.
[12] See page 70.

the Rumanians, for the territory which they coveted lay within the already decadent Ottoman Empire. Their program had in a sense already been outlined for them in the treaty of San Stefano which Russia had dictated in 1878. In 1885, to be sure, the Bulgarians had achieved part of their ambition, but they still aspired to "liberate" and annex Macedonia, of which they had been deprived by the Congress of Berlin. After 1878 a "map marking the lost territory of Macedonia hung in every Bulgarian school, and every Bulgarian peasant brooded over its loss and resolved in his sullen, dogged fashion to win it back." [13] Macedonia had not constituted a separate political unit for centuries, and its boundaries in consequence were somewhat difficult to define. In general, it included the valleys of the Vardar and Struma Rivers and the peninsula of Saloniki. It extended from Thrace on the east to Albania and Epirus on the west, and in the north it merged into the Sanjak of Novibazar.

Meanwhile, south of Macedonia the nationalists of Greece had become thoroughly permeated and dominated by Pan-Hellenic dreams of a "greater Greece," which should bring within the bounds of their kingdom the millions of Greeks who lived in what had once been the Hellenic world around the Aegean. Their nationalistic program included the eventual acquisition of Epirus, parts of Macedonia, Thrace, Constantinople, parts of Asia Minor including the important city of Smyrna, the islands of the Aegean, and Crete. If and when their nationalist dreams came true, the Greeks would once more have a realm which might rival that of the former Byzantine Empire. Although the territorial ambitions of Greece all lay within the realm of the Ottoman Empire, part of what the Greeks sought fell within the bounds of the territory coveted by Bulgaria.

It has been repeatedly indicated in connection with other topics that the closing years of the nineteenth century saw the rise of a strong national sentiment among Serbian patriots, who envisaged the creation of a great Yugoslav state under the leadership of Serbia. In the twentieth century, before the World War, this desire for Yugoslav unification became a burning passion among chauvinistic Serbs. The "greater Serbia" would include not only Serbia herself but Montenegro, the Austrian provinces of Dalmatia and Carniolia, the Hungarian kingdom of Croatia-Slavonia, the Austro-Hungarian imperial territory of Bosnia-Herzegovina, and part of Turkish Mace-

[13] H. W. V. Temperley, *History of Serbia*, page 315.

donia. The Yugoslav threat to the territorial integrity of the Dual Monarchy has already been discussed.[14] It should be observed here that the "greater Serbia" program constituted a menace, also, to Bulgaria's ambitions in Macedonia.

It will be obvious, therefore, that Macedonia constituted a veritable apple of discord for at least three of the Christian states of the Balkans. Bulgaria, Greece, and Serbia all laid claim to the district on historic grounds. The successive Balkan migrations had all passed through the Vardar valley, and each had left its impress on the population. Furthermore, as any student can see by consulting a historical atlas, at one time or another Macedonia had been within the political bounds of states dominated by Greeks, Serbs, or Bulgarians. Historic grounds alone could not settle the problem. Serbia and Bulgaria laid claim to the territory also on linguistic grounds. But, since the Serbs and Bulgars were themselves kindred nationalities, speaking similar languages, it was difficult to determine to which of them the intermediary dialects belonged. Furthermore, the Greeks claimed that in Saloniki and the coastal towns a majority of the people were Greeks; while, to make the situation still more complicated, even the Rumanians entered the controversy by claiming kinship with isolated groups of Vlachs.

By the closing years of the nineteenth century a triangular struggle for possession of Macedonia—when finally the Turks should be ousted—had developed, with Bulgaria, Greece, and Serbia as the contestants. Because of the earlier and more vigorous activities of the Bulgarian Church, it appeared that Bulgaria had won a majority of the Macedonians to favor union with her, though here again the situation became more complicated in 1893 when a Macedonian revolutionary committee began to agitate for complete autonomy for a Macedonia which should be independent of any one of the three claimants.[15] But the fate of the region was to a considerable extent connected with the course of events within the Ottoman Empire, to the history of which it is now necessary to turn.

[14] See pages 307–312.

[15] "It [the Macedonian question] presents, on the one hand, such a medley of jarring races, long-standing animosities, and ever-recurring atrocities, and, on the other hand, such a jumble of ethnographic riddles, philological controversies, psychological uncertainties, unreliable statistics, assertions and counter-assertions flatly contradictory on every point, that one almost despairs of an idea as to how it ought to be settled, or of the hope of ever seeing it settled at all." C. H. Haskins and R. H. Lord, *Some Problems of the Peace Conference*, pages 267–268.

### Abdul Hamid and His Decadent Empire

The ruler who held the throne of Turkey throughout most of the period included in this chapter was Sultan Abdul Hamid II, who had mounted the throne in 1876 after his two immediate predecessors had both been deposed within a few months, and who held it for more than a generation until he himself was deposed in 1909. Abdul Hamid had been elevated to his position by a small group of liberals who hoped that by reform the national unrest within the Balkans might be quieted and the empire be freed from threatening international intervention. But, unfortunately for their liberal hopes, they chose the wrong man to be sultan. "Dry, unimaginative, and pedantically devoted to labor of a purely clerical sort, . . . an old-fashioned Turk with a mentality bounded by the Koran," Abdul Hamid developed an absolutism "of which the main elements were deceit and fear, and which to operate . . . required a tireless subterranean plotter, a creature half fox, half rat." [16]

To be sure, when, shortly after his accession, the great powers had intervened in Ottoman affairs, the wily sultan had hastily promulgated a constitution which seemed designed to Westernize and liberalize his realm. But his trick had failed to convince the powers that the millennium had arrived in Turkey, and so they had demanded that the sultan undertake a program of reform in the Balkans under foreign supervision. When Abdul Hamid refused thus to compromise his independence, war with Russia had resulted, and further territory had been lost by the Ottoman Empire in the resultant treaty of Berlin. [17]

Probably it was inevitable that a far-flung empire like that of the sultan would disintegrate in an age which was coming to be dominated by the forces of nationalism, industrialism, and imperialism. To begin with, it was a polyglot state, necessarily subject to the devastating ravages of the rising and dynamic nationalism of its subject peoples, aided and abetted as they were by their kinsmen who resided in the neighboring national states. If ever the latter could lay aside their national jealousies and enmities long enough to unite against their common foe, they were almost bound to bring disaster upon Turkey in Europe.

---

[16] F. Schevill, *History of the Balkan Peninsula,* page 423.
[17] For an account of events in Turkey from 1870 to 1878, see pages 245–253.

In the second place, the empire was so located that in 1878 it presented a tempting morsel to at least three imperialistic powers. Its territory commanded the Suez Canal, the vital link in the trade routes between the Western world—especially Great Britain—and the East. It stood athwart the important Straits connecting the Black and Mediterranean Seas, and thus blocked Russia in her "historic mission" to acquire control of the Bosporus and Dardanelles. Its territory intervened between the Dual Monarchy and Saloniki, the port on the Aegean which Austria-Hungary hoped eventually to acquire to free her from dependence upon the Adriatic. In fact, one reason for Austria-Hungary's stipulation at Berlin (1878) that her military forces should be permitted to occupy Novibazar—the narrow strip of Ottoman territory lying between Serbia and Montenegro—was that she thought it offered a good railway route to Saloniki.

In the third place, the Ottoman Empire was economically in no position to defend itself against the great powers. It was still predominantly an agricultural country, having been hardly touched by the Industrial Revolution. Moreover, its agriculture was carried on largely by methods which were primitive and inefficient. Aside from agriculture, its natural resources were, in the nineteenth century, largely undeveloped. A backward country, therefore, inhabited by a population both sparse and poor, it was totally unable to raise enough revenues to enable an inefficient and corrupt government to support military and naval forces adequate for defense against the great industrial powers.

As a result of territorial losses to the great powers and to the national states established by the subject races, the Ottoman Empire by 1878 had shrunk to a mere shadow of what it had been in the seventeenth century. The sultan's loss of sovereignty over Rumania, Serbia, Montenegro, and Thessaly and his loss of all control—though technically retaining sovereignty—over Bulgaria, Bosnia, Herzegovina, and Cyprus—all in consequence of arrangements made at the Congress of Berlin—have been pointed out. But further losses were soon forthcoming. In 1881 France converted Tunis into a French protectorate, and in the next year Great Britain, in order to strengthen her hold on the Suez Canal, established a virtual protectorate over Egypt,[18] which was at least in name a dependency of

[18] See page 182.

the sultan. Again in 1897, as mentioned above, the sultan, for all practical purposes, also lost Crete when that island was granted autonomy under a Greek governor.

That Turkey in Europe was not entirely destroyed during the nineteenth century was the result not of her ability to defend herself militarily but of her policy of playing one great power against another. From 1854 to 1856 she had relied upon British and French support to defeat an aggressive Russia in the Crimean War. Two decades later she had escaped almost complete expulsion from Europe at the hands of Tsar Alexander II only because Austria-Hungary and Great Britain came to her assistance diplomatically—for a price. After the British became less vitally interested in checking Russia's expansion into Turkey—they themselves having obtained Cyprus and Egypt to safeguard their interest in the Suez Canal—Turkey turned more and more to Germany as a possible protector against the Russian Empire. William II's increasing interest in Turkey has already been discussed.[19]

Thus Abdul Hamid, in order to meet the threat to his empire from abroad, continued the old policy of double-dealing with the great powers. His domestic policies were no more admirable. As soon as he again felt secure on his throne, the powers at Berlin having solemnly sworn to uphold the integrity of his empire, he adjourned the recently created parliament and firmly and indefinitely suspended the constitution of 1876. As someone has pointed out, the sultan's interest in liberal reform appeared to fluctuate directly with the danger of foreign intervention. For thirty years Abdul Hamid ruled as an absolute autocrat.

So far as popular unrest was concerned, his aim was not to nurse and coddle it but to suppress it with every means at hand. To ferret out individual political enemies he relied on an elaborate system of espionage; to rid himself of them, he did not hesitate to resort to assassination. When unrest appeared among groups of his Christian subjects, he resorted to a system of terrorism by encouraging the less civilized Moslems to massacre them. An instance of the latter came in the nineties when his Christian Armenian subjects in Anatolia rebelled (1894) and were punished by having the Moslem Kurds turned loose upon them. All Europe shuddered at the fearful butch-

[19] See page 82.

ery of tens of thousands of Armenians, and Abdul Hamid came to be known as "Abdul the Damned."

The situation which finally brought Turkish affairs to a crisis developed in Macedonia, to which the sultan in the treaty of Berlin had promised to grant an autonomous regime. But Abdul Hamid, perhaps fearing that the grant of local autonomy was but the first step toward an inevitable surrender of authority, failed to carry out his promise, and the great powers for various reasons never took any steps to force his observance of the treaty. Doubtless one reason for the lack of activity among the great powers was the fear that any real intervention might again lead to complications, as in 1875–1878, and to the advancement of the Balkan interests of one power at the expense of some other. A *rapprochement* between the two great powers most directly interested in the Balkan problem—Russia and Austria-Hungary—came about in 1897 when they avowed their determination to maintain the *status quo* and abjured for the time being any designs of conquest in the Balkans.

Meanwhile, conditions in Macedonia improved not at all; in fact, they grew steadily worse. Unrest in this region continued unabated, fomented to a considerable extent from Bulgaria, where the hope of eventually creating a "big Bulgaria" still survived. It was fomented, too, by Turkish misgovernment, by brigandage, and by widespread misery. The list of murders, the names of victims of kidnapers, and the story of burning villages were spread far and wide by the foreign newspapers. Eventually, in the face of another Macedonian insurrection (1903), the statesmen of Europe were forced to turn their attention once more to the Balkans. Under pressure from Great Britain, what became known as the Mürzsteg program was drafted by Russia and Austria-Hungary. Since this program was supported by all the great powers of Europe, it was perforce accepted by the sultan. The plan provided for maintaining peace in Macedonia by means of an international mounted police, each of the five great powers being responsible for its allotted sector. The scheme never succeeded in completely pacifying Macedonia, however, largely because of the activities of Bulgars, Serbs, and Greeks, who continually plotted to redeem their kinsmen.

By this time, among the Turks themselves forces were being engendered which were to topple Abdul Hamid from his throne. The sultan's efforts to suppress all liberals within the empire drove many Turks to other countries. These liberals gathered in some of the democratic centers of western Europe and there became more than ever determined to liberalize and reform the Ottoman Empire. By resort to propaganda through secret agents as well as through newspapers and pamphlets, they ultimately gained a considerable following among the younger generation of Turks. In fact, the Young Turks, as they came to be called, made such headway in winning over the officers of the sultan's army that they dared in 1906 to transfer the headquarters of their organization, the Committee of Union and Progress, from Paris to Saloniki.

The Young Turks were still discussing plans for a possible insurrection against the sultan when in 1908 they learned that the great powers were once again considering intervention in anarchic Macedonia. Fearful that this region, too, might be lost to the Ottoman Empire unless steps were taken at once to reform conditions there, they launched a revolt in the army in Macedonia and at the same time voiced demands for a constitution. So widespread was the military revolt that Abdul Hamid at once saw the futility of resistance. In July, 1908, he again proclaimed the constitution of 1876, and issued a writ summoning the national parliament. Thus with almost no bloodshed a political revolution was consummated in the empire. Everywhere and among all classes there was deep rejoicing "while Christians and Mohammedans, Bulgars and Greeks, Albanians and Serbs passionately embraced in church, mosque, and public square, comporting themselves as if they verily believed that all men had become brothers."

## THE BOSNIAN CRISIS

The leaders of the Young Turks, while residing in western Europe, had absorbed not only liberalism but nationalism as well. The Committee of Union and Progress therefore did not limit its pronouncements to such topics as liberty and democracy; it likewise discussed with what appeared to be great assurance its plans for removing the foreign-imposed restrictions upon Turkey's authority in such regions as Bosnia, Herzegovina, Crete, Macedonia, and even Bulgaria. In some quarters of Europe it actually began to be feared that the Ottoman Empire might be rejuvenated and under the guidance of the Young Turks become a power of some consequence.

Such a development did not fit in with the plans of certain European governments, notably those of Austria-Hungary and Russia.

In the years just before 1908 developments within the Dual Monarchy were such as to lead the Habsburg government to increase its activity in the Balkans. In 1906 Count Aehrenthal, who hoped to meet the Yugoslav menace within Austria-Hungary by more aggressive action in the Balkans, became the Habsburg foreign minister, and Conrad von Hötzendorf, who urgently advocated a protective war against Serbia, became the new chief of staff. As part of Austria-Hungary's more aggressive Balkan policy plans were outlined for the construction of a new railway through Novibazar to link Vienna and Budapest with Saloniki and Constantinople.[20] In January, 1908, before the Young Turk revolt, Aehrenthal announced his plan for the new railway which would give the Dual Monarchy access to the Aegean through territory which was wholly Turkish.

Later in the year, however, the Austro-Hungarian general staff apparently came to the conclusion that the province of Novibazar was in no way suitable for a military railway, that the best military route to Saloniki was that followed by so many migrations in earlier centuries, that is, through Belgrade, Nish, and the Vardar valley.[21] In other words, Belgrade constituted the real gateway from Austria-Hungary into the Balkans. Obviously, an Austrian advance toward Saloniki through Serbia could be successfully executed only if Serbia were a Habsburg dependency or were crushed by overwhelming force. Austrian military plans therefore called for the weakening of the little Serb kingdom if not for its actual absorption by the Dual Monarchy.

This military decision seemed to coincide very closely with the desires of Habsburg diplomats, for Aehrenthal's foreign policy called for similar action in order to put an end to the pro-Serb agitation which was being carried on among the Yugoslav subjects of the Dual Monarchy. Apparently Aehrenthal believed that one effective way to check the spread of revolutionary fever from Serbia into the Habsburg provinces to the west "was to sterilize Bosnia-Herzegovina by the antiseptic process of annexation." So long as these provinces

---

[20] The principal existing railway—through Serbia—was no longer considered secure for Austria-Hungary after the latter lost Serbia's favor in the opening years of the twentieth century.

[21] Since the cost of building a railway through mountainous Novibazar was too great to warrant its construction for other than military reasons, the project was dropped.

were formally recognized as being under the sultan's sovereignty, so long would the Serbs carry on their propaganda in the hope that, when Turkish rule in the Balkans finally and completely crumbled, the Yugoslavs of Bosnia-Herzegovina might be united with their kinsmen in Serbia. Aehrenthal hoped that the outright annexation of the provinces by Austria-Hungary might give the death-blow to the "greater Serbia" idea. By various agreements Austria-Hungary's right to annex the provinces at her own discretion had already been recognized. She had secured Russia's consent in 1876 and again in 1881, Germany's approval in 1881, and Italy's promise (1887 and 1905) that their annexation would not be considered a change in the Balkan *status quo* in the meaning of the terms of the Triple Alliance.[22]

Meanwhile, Russia's defeat in the Far East by Japan (1905)[23] and her subsequent agreements with Great Britain in regard to the situation in the Middle East (1907)[24] had had the effect of turning her attention once more to the Near East. Her diplomats now increased their activity in the Balkans and were eager to advance their Pan-Slavic program and to take advantage of Serbia's recently regained friendship. Shortly after Aehrenthal's announcement of plans for the new railway through Novibazar, for example, Izvolsky, the tsar's foreign minister—probably to win Serbia's good will—announced Russia's intention to build a railway across the Balkan peninsula from the Danube to the Adriatic and thus not only to provide Serbia with her long-sought access to the sea but also to link the Slavic countries more closely together.

The primary aim of Izvolsky's foreign policy in 1908, however, was to secure for Russia the right to send her warships through the Straits. In July of that year he suggested to Aehrenthal that they might discuss in the spirit of reciprocity their countries' desires in respect to Bosnia-Herzegovina and the Straits. After the Austro-Hungarian ministerial council had actually decided (August 19) to annex the provinces, Aehrenthal informed Izvolsky that, although Austria-Hungary considered the provinces her own, an Austro-Russian agreement might possibly be made. Russia might promise to show a benevolent attitude if circumstances should compel Austria-Hungary to annex the provinces, and in return Austria-Hungary

---

[22] For these various agreements, see pages 68, 153, 247.
[23] See pages 267–269.      [24] See pages 212–213.

might promise that, if the question of the Straits was raised, she would be willing to have a confidential exchange of views on the subject with Russia.

In the middle of September Izvolsky and Aehrenthal met at Buchlau and reached a number of agreements. The former gave his consent to the annexation of Bosnia-Herzegovina, provided Austria-Hungary withdrew from Novibazar; the latter agreed to the opening of the Straits to Russia's warships, provided the same right was extended to the warships of the other countries bordering on the Black Sea, and provided Turkish territory was left inviolate. Izvolsky now set out to secure international approval for altering the status of the Straits, but, before he had made any headway, Aehrenthal announced (October 6) the annexation of the provinces.

Naturally, this step caused great resentment at Constantinople, though even the Young Turks must have realized in their hearts that Bosnia and Herzegovina were already lost to the Ottoman Empire. Nevertheless, to show their opposition, the Turks began a boycott of Austro-Hungarian goods. Serbia's reaction to the annexation was much more vigorous than that of Turkey, for the little kingdom now saw rapidly disappearing all its own hopes of eventually annexing the provinces. Public opinion in both Italy and France was inclined to be indignant, but the governments of these states did not go so far as that of Great Britain. The latter at once denounced Austria-Hungary's action as a violation of the treaty of Berlin—though it must be admitted that this was not the first violation.

The Kaiser, on his part, feared that the annexation might alienate Turkey from the Teutonic powers and thus ruin their project for a *Drang nach Osten*. Ultimately, however, Bülow, his chancellor, won him to the view that Germany must stand by Austria-Hungary now as the latter had stood by Germany at Algeciras in 1906.[25] The German government made every effort to pursuade Turkey to recognize the annexation in return for the payment of an indemnity by Austria-Hungary, and in February, 1909, the Ottoman government did sign a protocol to that effect.

Meanwhile, among the diplomats of the great powers probably the loudest protests against Aehrenthal's step had come from Izvolsky. Apparently the latter, when he had thought that by co-operating

[25] For the Algeciras conference, see pages 131-132.

with Austria-Hungary he might gain for Russia the coveted freedom of passage through the Straits, had cared little about the national aspirations of the Serbs. But Premier Stolypin in St. Petersburg saw the situation in a different way. What particularly worried him was the possible reaction of the Russian Pan-Slavists if they discovered that Russia's foreign minister had consented to betray Serbia's interest in Bosnia. He therefore sent specific instructions to Izvolsky not to abandon Serbia, but instead to protest against the annexation and insist that again, as in 1878, the Balkan situation must be dealt with by a general European congress. Stolypin maintained, too, that Aehrenthal's step was a violation of the understanding between Russia and Austria-Hungary that neither would disturb the *status quo* in the Balkans.

During the winter of 1908–1909 the international situation was particularly strained. On the one hand, the Serbs and the Pan-Slavs denounced Austria-Hungary; on the other, the Habsburg government attempted to scotch the Yugoslav peril by its notorious trial of Austrian Yugoslavs for treason at Agram.[26] Feeling ran high, and the danger of war was great. But Austria-Hungary was comforted by assurance from Germany that, if the former invaded Serbia and Russia in consequence attacked her, Germany would join the war on the side of the Habsburgs.

For a time it looked as though war might actually break out between Serbia and Austria-Hungary. The Serbian parliament by a unanimous vote demanded that Turkish sovereignty be maintained over Bosnia-Herzegovina. In view of the annexation, Serbia's "irreducible minimum" demand was that a strip of Bosnian territory should be ceded to her in order to give her contact with Montenegro and at the same time afford both states an outlet to the Adriatic. When news of the Austro-Turkish protocol of February, 1909, reached Belgrade, the Serbian army was mobilized, and an appeal was made to the Entente powers for assistance. The latter were inclined to give Serbia their support, but Austria, with the backing of Germany, stood firm. Since British and French support of Serbia was limited to diplomatic measures, the question of military assistance rested wholly with Russia.

The latter's decision not to give Serbia military aid at this time was doubtless hastened by a note from Bülow. The German chan-

26 See page 309.

cellor had agreed to give the powers signatory to the treaty of Berlin
an opportunity to sanction the recently concluded Austro-Turkish
protocol, provided Izvolsky would first promise that Russia's approval would be forthcoming when requested. In this way the fiction that the treaty of Berlin could not be altered, except with the
consent of all of the signatories, would be maintained. When Izvolsky appeared to hesitate to commit himself on this proposal, Germany notified him that, if he declined to accept it, she would "let
things take their course." At St. Petersburg this statement was interpreted to mean that Germany would not restrain Austria from
attacking Serbia (as the Austrian general staff was eager to do), and
that, if Russia attacked Austria in behalf of Serbia, Germany would
enter the war against Russia. The Russian government, realizing
that it must fight alone and that its military recovery from the
Russo-Japanese War was not yet complete, decided not to intervene.

Serbia was therefore left without military support and was placed
almost at the mercy of Austria-Hungary. Had the Austrian military
leaders been given free rein, a preventive war against Serbia might
have been fought in 1909, but Francis Joseph firmly opposed such a
conflict. Furthermore, Great Britain through diplomatic channels
sought to save Serbia from military disaster by discovering some
formula for a note which Serbia might send to Austria-Hungary in
order to mollify the latter. In March the British foreign secretary,
Grey, finally secured a formula which Aehrenthal agreed to accept
if Serbia used it. Perhaps his willingness to accept the formula was
influenced by the fact that consent to Austria-Hungary's modification
of the treaty of Berlin had been secured from all the powers signatory to the treaty except Great Britain. On March 31, 1909, Serbia
in a note to Austria-Hungary recognized without reservation the
latter's annexation of Bosnia and Herzegovina, and pledged herself
"to live in the future on terms of good neighborliness" with the
Dual Monarchy. Aehrenthal declared the Serbian note acceptable,
and Great Britain then agreed to Austria's alteration of the treaty of
Berlin.

After nearly six months of severe strain on the international situation, the crisis thus passed. Russia had been obliged to postpone
her plan to aid Serbia, and Austrian chauvinists had been compelled
to abandon, at least temporarily, their plan to smash Serbia. But the
crisis was particularly unfortunate, for it intensified Serbia's hatred

of Austria-Hungary and led Russia to bend every effort to improving her position so that in the future she might thwart the plans of the Teutonic powers for a *Drang nach Osten*. In fact, Russia at once laid plans not only to create some kind of Balkan league but to "Balkanize" the already existing Franco-Russian alliance.

### OTTOMAN LOSSES TO NATIONALISM AND IMPERIALISM, 1908–1913

Austria-Hungary was not the only state to take advantage of the weakness of the Ottoman government following the Young Turk revolution. Urged on by Aehrenthal, Bulgaria, which was still tributary to the sultan, seized the occasion to forestall any future steps to reintegrate her territory with a rejuvenated Ottoman Empire. On October 5, 1908, Prince Ferdinand proclaimed Bulgaria's complete independence of the sultan, and to indicate his country's new status he himself assumed the title King. The Young Turks, who probably realized the absolute impossibility of holding Bulgaria within their empire, merely demanded the payment of an indemnity in return for the sultan's surrender of his legal prerogatives under the treaty of Berlin. As was to be expected, the governments of Bulgaria and Turkey could not agree on the amount to be paid, but thanks to Russia's mediation and apparent generosity [27] an agreement was reached, and in April, 1909, the sultan signed a treaty recognizing the complete independence of Bulgaria.

In October, 1908, anti-Turkish steps were taken in Crete also. On October 12, after a bloodless revolution had been staged five days earlier, the assembly of the island formally proclaimed the union of Crete with Greece. The office of high commissioner was abolished, and the government was entrusted temporarily to a committee of Cretans which included Eleutherios Venizelos. Although the union was not actually effected at this time, Turkey's shadowy claim to Crete faded still more, for the great powers in 1909 withdrew their troops from the island and 'left Venizelos in full control. All that remained for the Cretans and the Greeks was to secure eventually the formal acknowledgment of the sultan's loss of sovereignty.

At Constantinople, meanwhile, the situation was confused and uncertain. Although the foxlike Abdul Hamid had promptly pro-

---

[27] Russia, again seeking to build up her influence in Bulgaria, agreed to pay the difference between what Turkey demanded and what Bulgaria offered. Of course, Russia's payment was to come out of her own claims on Turkey.

claimed a constitutional government, he was not content to surrender his autocratic power without a struggle. When he saw the Young Turks embarrassed by the actions of Austria-Hungary, Bulgaria, and Crete, when he saw that many of those about him were tempted to question the wisdom of entrusting the fate of the empire to the inexperienced and, it appeared, unsuccessful Young Turks, he sought to arouse among his subjects a movement in his own behalf. In April, 1909, he was able to stage a counterrevolution—but it was only short-lived. Troops loyal to the Young Turks soon arrived from Saloniki, and on April 27 Abdul Hamid was deposed. A new sultan, Abdul Hamid's brother, was proclaimed as Mohammed V. During the succeeding years the real power in the Ottoman government, however, was in the hands of the Young Turk ministry which assumed power upon the deposition of Abdul Hamid. The ministry, in turn, was practically the tool of the Committee of Union and Progress, which, in turn, was supported by the military. Probably the most influential leader in Turkish affairs was the strongly nationalist Enver Bey.

Those at the head of the Ottoman government after the downfall of Abdul Hamid were extremely nationalistic and soon embarked upon a vigorous policy of "Turkification." Their plan called for the revival of the empire by the joint process of nationalization and centralization. Armenians in Anatolia; Arabs in Syria, Mesopotamia, and Arabia; Greeks, Bulgars, and Serbs in Macedonia; the herdsmen of Albania; all these were to be "Turkified." This, to the extreme nationalists, necessitated the use of Turkish alone as the official language of the empire and the institution of a system of Turkish national schools. To strengthen the empire for its new role in international affairs, they decided to adopt the principle of compulsory military service, and secured German officers to reorganize the army. Similarly, they sought to improve the naval forces of the empire with British assistance.

Thus it was that the subject nationalities of the Ottoman Empire, after their first thrill of joy over the proclamation of a constitution and the subsequent deposition of the hated and feared Abdul Hamid, awoke to find their lot not better but perhaps even worse than before 1908. Centralization under the Young Turks appeared to mean, so far as the subject races could see, merely a continuation of the despotism of the deposed sultan. "Turkification" was soon found to entail repression of the non-Turk nationalities, accompanied by bloody measures as of old. In the spring of 1909 several thousand Armenians were massacred in cold blood at the instigation of Turkish authorities. Naturally, such Young Turk policies and measures not only failed entirely to win the loyalty of the subject groups but quickly drove them into active opposition. A home-rule movement was begun by the Arabs in Syria, and an insurrection in behalf of complete independence broke out in Arabia. In Macedonia and Albania nationalistic plots and conspiracies, accompanied by severe repressive measures at the hands of the Ottoman government, once more became the rule.

With the Ottoman Empire thus violently shaken by the nationalistic reactions of its subject peoples, the Turkish government had next to meet an imperialistic attack on its territorial integrity—this time at the hands of Italy. The Tripolitan War, which began in 1911, has already been discussed,[28] as has Turkey's recognition of her loss of sovereignty over Tripoli and Cyrenaica by the treaty of Lausanne in 1912. The sultan's government was thus ousted from control of the last sections of that great empire in northern Africa which it had once ruled.

The Tripolitan War had its effect, also, in Russia. Shortly after the war began, the tsar's ambassador to Turkey proposed a Russo-Turkish league in which, in return for Russia's guarantee of Turkey's territorial integrity, the latter was to grant free passage of the Straits for Russian warships. The proposal failed, however, because both the British and the German government secretly opposed it, and the sultan in consequence refused to grant the right of passage. Russia's inability to solve her problem by direct negotiations with Turkey naturally increased her desire to create a Balkan league which might be used indirectly to help change the *status quo* of the Straits. This desire was further strengthened when during the war the Ottoman government closed the Straits because Italian warships bombarded the forts along the Dardanelles. The closing of the Straits, in turn, prevented the accustomed flow of Russian exports from the Black Sea area, and entailed the loss of millions of rubles to Russian merchants.

Another effect of the Tripolitan War was to increase the likelihood that a Balkan league would be established, for the small Balkan

[28] See pages 162–163.

states reasoned that, if Italy could despoil the Ottoman Empire with impunity, perhaps they could do the same. Furthermore, if the great powers could not or would not force reforms in Macedonia to lessen the burdens borne by their despairing kinsmen, why should not the Balkan states undertake to "liberate" them? Success would, of course, necessitate some sort of understanding among the Balkan states in order to bring effective co-operation. Russia readily gave her blessing and assistance when the rulers and statesmen of Bulgaria, Greece, and Serbia sought to come to an understanding.

Negotiations for an alliance between Bulgaria and Serbia, begun in October, 1911, resulted in a secret treaty in March, 1912, in which the two states mutually guaranteed their political independence and territorial integrity and agreed to oppose with all their forces any attempt by a great power to seize any part of the Ottoman Balkan territory if either of them considered such action hostile to its interests. Annexed to the treaty of alliance was an agreement on the future division of Turkish Macedonia. Here Bulgaria made some concessions, for she had formerly demanded autonomy for Macedonia in the hope that she herself might eventually secure it all. The Serbo-Bulgar delimitation agreement assigned Struga, Uskub, and Kumanova to Serbia, and Okhrida, Monastir, and Ishtip to Bulgaria. A "contested zone" was left for future delimitation and was to be settled by the arbitration of the Russian tsar in case the two powers could not agree. In May, 1912, a secret military convention was signed by the two powers. In the same month Bulgaria and Greece also agreed on united action in case of war with Turkey, but reached no definite understanding regarding a division of Macedonian territory. Apparently Montenegro, too, became linked more or less formally with the other three powers in this Balkan league.

No precise time had been set by the Balkan states for their contemplated war on Turkey. Nevertheless, events so shaped themselves during the summer of 1912 as to hasten an attack. In the first place, Turkey was engaged in a war with Italy which was rapidly turning into a decisive defeat. If the Balkan powers wished to strike while Turkey was embarrassed elsewhere, they must strike soon. In the second place, Turkish concessions to the Albanians greatly alarmed the Balkan allies. Soon after the Young Turk revolution the Albanians had begun to agitate in favor of an autonomous national state. In 1909 their separatist policy had led the Turks to at-

tempt to suppress them by military force, but the Turks soon discovered that it was an extremely difficult task to carry on a successful war against the herdsmen in the Albanian hills. When, in 1911
and 1912, Turkey found herself compelled to deal also with Italian
imperialism, the Ottoman government decided to treat with the
Albanians, and in the summer of 1912 the latter were conceded extensive home rule under the suzerainty of the sultan. But the part
of the treaty which particularly alarmed the Balkan states was that
which delimited Albania so as to include the four districts of Scutari,
Janina, Monastir, and Kossovo. If this plan for an autonomous Albania should actually be executed, each of the four Balkan states
would find itself excluded from a district which it had planned to
annex.

The Balkan allies accordingly decided upon an immediate war
against Turkey. Formal demands for Macedonian reforms were
dispatched to Constantinople. On September 30, 1912, Bulgaria,
Greece, and Serbia all ordered mobilization; eight days later little
Montenegro made the fateful plunge and declared war. Although
Russia and Austria-Hungary in a joint note thereupon announced
that they would permit no modification of the territorial status of
European Turkey at the end of the conflict, Serbia, Greece, and Bulgaria declared war on October 18. Meanwhile, Turkey had made
peace with Italy, and now planned to hurl all her German-trained
forces against the Balkan allies. It was apparently expected by the
great powers and even feared by the Balkan states themselves that
the Ottoman army would be formidable.

But the actual course of events proved the very opposite. Each of
the allies operated in a separate area, and each was soon successful.
The Bulgars, advancing in the Maritza valley, at once defeated the
main Turkish army at Kirk Kilissé. After a second defeat at Lule
Burgas the Ottoman forces fled until they reached the Chatalja line
of fortresses only twenty miles from Constantinople. Siege was laid
by the Bulgars to the fortified city of Adrianople. The Greeks successfully bottled up the Turkish navy in the Dardanelles, occupied
most of the Turkish islands in the Aegean, and captured Saloniki.
The Serbs, operating in the Morava and upper Vardar valleys, were
also victorious, capturing Uskub and advancing into Macedonia as
far as Monastir. Then, seeing her way to the sea down the Vardar

valley blocked by Greek and Bulgarian forces, Serbia turned west in search of an outlet to the Adriatic, and late in November her forces occupied Alessio and Durazzo on the Albanian coast. The Montenegrins, at the same time, laid siege to the strong fortress of Scutari. The Albanians, now thoroughly alarmed, declared their independence of Turkey in a last-minute attempt to preserve their district from being divided among the victorious allies.

By this time developments in the Balkans had ceased to be a concern of Turkey and the Balkan allies alone, for the attack on Turkey precipitated another crisis among the great powers of Europe. Austria-Hungary feared that, if Serbia got an outlet to the Adriatic, the excitement and enthusiasm for the little kingdom which would be aroused in the Yugoslav districts of the Dual Monarchy would endanger the territorial integrity of the Habsburg realm. At the very outbreak of the Balkan conflict, therefore, Austria-Hungary had decided that she would go to war if necessary to prevent Serbia from gaining an outlet to the Adriatic. On the other hand, Russia feared that the Dual Monarchy might utilize the war as an occasion to seize more territory in the Balkans or might avail itself of this new opportunity to attack Serbia. The tsar's government accordingly decided that it would go to the aid of Serbia if Austria-Hungary attacked.

The crisis among the great powers was actually precipitated when the Serbs finally fought their way to the Adriatic. To check the Serbs, Austria-Hungary and Italy at once proclaimed the establishment of a new state, Albania. Some years earlier the Habsburg government had secured the approval of both Russia and Italy for this projected step.[29] Serbia had naturally never been consulted on this matter, however, and now persisted in her determination to secure an adequate outlet to the sea. Russia, despite her earlier agreement, was inclined to sympathize with Serb aspirations, and France gave Serbia strong support throughout the ensuing crisis. Germany, France, and Great Britain were all eager, however, to keep the Balkan War from spreading to the rest of Europe and engulfing the great powers. Upon Poincaré's suggestion, therefore, Sir Edward

[29] In 1897 Austria-Hungary and Russia had agreed that such a state should be created if the territorial status in the Balkans could not be maintained, and three years later Italy had acceded to this agreement.

Grey proposed that informal discussions should be held in London by himself and the ambassadors of Russia, Austria-Hungary, Germany, France, and Italy, and his proposal was accepted.

Accordingly, when Turkey—with her holdings in Europe practically reduced to Constantinople and the three besieged cities of Adrianople, Janina, and Scutari—signed an armistice on December 3, 1912, the subsequent peace conference was held in London under the supervision of the diplomats of the great powers. The peace conference was broken up in January, 1913, however, when the aggressive Enver Bey by a *coup d'état* seized power in Constantinople and resumed the war. On March 6 the Greeks captured Janina; on March 26 the Bulgars and Serbs entered Adrianople; and on April 22 the Montenegrins occupied Scutari in defiance of the orders of the London conference of ambassadors, which had meanwhile continued to hold frequent meetings.

The action of the Montenegrins increased the international tension. At London the statesmen of the six great powers had been attempting to reach an agreement on the size of the new Albania. Russia, representing Serbia, and Italy, hoping to dominate a weak Albania, desired to create a small state, while Austria-Hungary, desiring to check Serbia and to make Albania strong enough to repel Italy's penetration, argued for a large state. France supported Russia's views. Germany and Great Britain were chiefly interested in achieving a compromise which would prevent the spread of the Balkan War. But when little Montenegro went so far as to refuse to evacuate Scutari in the face of a joint note from the six great powers, it appeared that the war might engulf at least one great power, for in May Austria-Hungary decided to attack Montenegro. Her decision, however, quickly led the King of Montenegro to announce that he would at once withdraw his forces from Scutari, and so Austria-Hungary withheld her hand. But the course of events had taught her that the threat of force might thereafter prove effective in dealing with the Yugoslav states.

Meanwhile, in April, Turkey—now holding in Europe little more than the district about Constantinople—again sued for an armistice. Negotiations were resumed, and a treaty was signed in London on May 30, 1913. By the treaty of London—which was never ratified—Turkey lost all territory in Europe except a narrow strip extending from Constantinople to a line drawn from Enos on the Aegean to

Midia on the Black Sea. If all the territory taken from the sultan had been turned over to the victorious Balkan allies, perhaps the latter could have pacifically reached a more or less satisfactory division of the spoils. But, as pointed out above, the great powers had intervened to create Albania, to which Montenegro and Serbia were to be compelled to surrender territory and ports captured by their military forces.

As a consequence of the loss of territory which she had conquered to give herself an access to the Adriatic, Serbia demanded that the territorial agreements reached with Bulgaria before the war should be revised. She now desired that her territory should be extended through Macedonia to the northern boundary of Greece so that she might be able to have at Saloniki an access to the sea through territory of a friendly power. Serbia and Greece held the territory which now came into dispute, for, while Bulgaria had been engaged in driving the Turks back through Thrace toward Constantinople, these two powers had occupied most of Macedonia. They now urged Bulgaria to be satisfied with the acquisition of Adrianople and Thrace.

But Bulgaria, whose desires in Thrace had been partly thwarted at London by Russia, was determined to acquire Macedonia and refused to consider any change in the original Serbo-Bulgar agreement. The immediate result of Bulgaria's attitude was the conclusion (June 1, 1913) of a defensive military convention against her by Serbia and Greece. Russia was alarmed at the possibility of the destruction of her Balkan league and urged restraint upon both Bulgaria and Serbia. The latter's future expansion, Russia pointed out, should be at the expense of Austria-Hungary rather than Bulgaria. "A break between Bulgaria and Serbia," Russia declared, "would be a triumph for Austria." The situation was further complicated by the attitude of Rumania, which during the First Balkan War had demanded that Bulgaria should surrender part of the Dobrudja to her in order to maintain the Balkan equilibrium.

Bulgaria's intransigence at this time was partly the result of encouragement from Austria-Hungary, whose statesmen were busily engaged in attempting to separate Bulgaria from her allies so that the Balkan league might be wrecked. Moreover, the Habsburg government was strongly opposed to a further material and moral strengthening of hostile Serbia at the expense of Bulgaria. Austria-

Hungary was willing, in return for a friendly attitude on the part of Bulgaria, to give active support to the latter's aspirations in the Balkans, provided Bulgaria by compensations could keep Rumania neutral. Shortly after Bulgaria learned of the Habsburg attitude, she ordered her troops to attack the Serbs (June 29). The Second Balkan War—this time between the Balkan states—was thus launched. Greece and Montenegro at once entered the conflict against Bulgaria. And, although Bulgaria had agreed to cede some territory to Rumania, the latter also declared war against her. Bulgaria was therefore forced to fight against invading armies from the south, the west, and the north.

The Second Balkan War was of short duration, for Bulgaria was no match for her numerous foes. With the Bulgars sure to be defeated, Turkey also entered the fray and sent her army up the Maritza valley to retake Adrianople. King Ferdinand sued for peace, and an armistice was concluded on July 31. Ten days later a new peace treaty was signed by the Balkan states at Bucharest, and on September 29 another treaty was signed between Bulgaria and Turkey. Bulgaria suffered by the terms of both treaties. She was forced to hand over part of the Dobrudja to Rumania, to cede Adrianople and Kirk Kilissé to Turkey, and to content herself with a mere bit of Macedonia in the vicinity of Strumitsa and with central Thrace and an outlet to the Aegean at the unsatisfactory port of Dedeagach. And the boundary between Turkey and Bulgaria was so drawn that the only railway to Dedeagach was partly under Turkish control.

Greece got probably the best part of the spoils, for she acquired Epirus with the city of Janina, a large share of western and southern Macedonia with the two excellent ports of Saloniki and Kavalla, Crete, and most of the Aegean islands.[30] Serbia, although she did not secure the territory which she sought on the Adriatic, did obtain all of "Old Serbia," including Monastir and the Vardar valley down to Gevgeli. It was expected that she would secure an economic outlet to the Aegean through the Greek port of Saloniki. Serbia and Montenegro divided the district of Novibazar between them and thus at last came to have their long-desired common frontier.

In the western part of the Balkan peninsula, commanding the

[30] Rhodes and the Dodecanese—which from the viewpoint of nationalism belonged to Greece—had been occupied since the Tripolitan War by Italian troops. The great powers made no move to force them out in favor of Greece.

THE BALKANS IN 1914

eastern shore of the Strait of Otranto and effectively cutting off Serbia from access to the sea, the great powers established the new sovereign state of Albania. To this new state—a principality—they gave a German ruler, Prince William of Wied. In March, 1914, the latter arrived in Albania, which as yet had nothing resembling a modern government. When the new ruler attempted to set up his authority, many of the Albanian mountaineers—long free from outside restraint of any kind—rebelled. The country was soon in a turmoil, and when, a few months after his arrival, the World War broke out, Prince William withdrew from his recently acquired principality, never to return.

A comparison of the map of the Balkans in 1914 with that in 1870 will reveal the extent to which the Ottoman Empire had been driven from Europe during the intervening years; it had almost ceased to be a European power. A study of the maps will also show how the small Balkan states had been greatly enlarged at the expense of Turkey. Nevertheless, despite the considerable degree of success which each Balkan people had had in extending its national territory, in 1914 none was yet content. Bitterness was the lot of Bulgaria, which was still determined to gain the territory in Macedonia which the ill-fated treaty of San Stefano had allotted her. Restless ambition, whetted by partial success, still disturbed Greece, Serbia, and Rumania, each eyeing with longing the foreign territory occupied by her kinsmen. Increased hatred of Austria-Hungary for her part in forcing the creation of Albania poisoned the heart of Serbia. The Balkans in 1914 still constituted a region where a terrific explosion might occur at any time.

# PART THREE

# THE WORLD WAR

During the four decades from 1871 to 1911 Europe largely escaped the horrors of war. Nevertheless, as preceding chapters have shown, within this period forces were engendered which inevitably brought clashes between national aims and ambitions. Consequently, there occurred in the early years of the twentieth century a succession of international crises which ultimately culminated in that of 1914. The failure of Europe's statesmen to surmount this crisis, as they had successfully surmounted those of the preceding decade, let loose upon Europe and the world the most dreadful war of all history. The chapters in Part Three explain the fundamental causes of the World War, discuss the tangled negotiations of July, 1914, consider the problem of "war guilt," trace the military and diplomatic history of the ensuing struggle, and show how the war released revolutionary forces which brought the downfall of three imperial dynasties.

## CHAPTER XI

# THE OUTBREAK OF THE WAR

DESPITE the many hopes and plans for international peace which encouraged the world in the two decades before 1914, it is obvious that certain fundamental causes of international conflict seemed to be irresistibly drawing the great powers of Europe toward war. Crisis followed crisis in the years after 1904. Each left its heritage of suspicion, fear, and hatred; each led the nations to strengthen their armed forces to prepare to defend themselves against attack. By 1914 the tension between the powers had become so great that, in the face of Austria-Hungary's determination to crush Serbia, all efforts to preserve peace proved unavailing, and Europe found herself plunged into the most terrible war of her long history. Until the very outbreak of the World War, however, many still clung to their hopes of peace.

## HOPES OF PEACE

To many people in the years before 1914 one of the most hopeful signs of peace among the nations was the fact that since 1871 no war had occurred between the great powers of Europe. Although some of the countries had carried on wars outside Europe, those who longed for world peace hoped that, once all the unclaimed areas on other continents had been appropriated and all the "backward" regions of the world had been Europeanized, war might finally be banished from the face of the earth.

These seekers after peace—the pacifists—pointed to many circumstances which seemed to indicate that the world might outgrow war. The nineteenth century, they argued, had witnessed the rise of businesses on such a scale that nations could no longer exist economically as isolated units but had become dependent upon one another for their economic well-being. The very magnitude of foreign investments, the rapid development of international credit and exchange, they declared, inevitably worked to promote mutual confidence among the nations. The improved means of communication and the introduction everywhere of cheap newspapers, they asserted, tended to create a world community and made possible the development of a world opinion against war. The interchange among the nations of professors and students and the spread of scientific discoveries across national borders helped to provide the peoples of the world with a common cultural background. In fact, the nineteenth and twentieth centuries, they pointed out, had gone far toward the development of a world community with increasingly uniform ideas and ideals.

They pointed out also—these advocates of peace—that the nations were becoming more and more accustomed to co-operation in spheres which were nonpolitical. In the seventies of the nineteenth century, for example, thirty states had organized the Universal Telegraph Union; twenty-three states had agreed to use the metric system of weights and measures; and sixty states had created the Universal Postal Union with its headquarters in Bern, the capital of Switzerland. Thanks to this last step, uniformity of postal laws, low rates, and speedy delivery had resulted for international mail. Soon hundreds of millions of letters and packages were being delivered throughout the world with a degree of safety that was remarkable. Other international agreements which helped to bring world solidarity were entered into by many nations. During the eighties conventions to standardize patent laws and copyright laws were ratified by a number of states.

The tendency toward world co-operation and world solidarity appeared, also, in many spheres of activity outside the control of national governments. Catholic Christians in 1881 began a series of eucharistic congresses, which were held successively in different parts of the world and were attended by clergy and laymen of many countries, and Protestant Christians likewise convened in world gatherings. In 1889 the Socialists organized the "Second International," and thereafter they held congresses of the workers of the world. In 1889, too, an international Parliamentary Union was set up to aid in spreading throughout the world the idea and practice of parliamentary government. Organizations such as the Rotary Club and the Boy Scouts extended across national lines, and they, also, held their world congresses. Especially significant were the numerous world gatherings of scholars and scientists with their resultant exchange of ideas in all realms of knowledge. By 1914 there were more

than thirty international organizations that concerned themselves
with "international science." It was hoped by pacifists that enlightened leaders everywhere might come to have a world outlook and
that they, in turn, might exert their influence to lead mankind to
think not merely in terms of one country but internationally.

To facilitate the growth of internationalism and to aid in the
movement for world peace, the pacifists had begun early to organize.
Prior to 1870 various peace societies had been established in Great
Britain, the United States, Switzerland, and France. By 1914 the
number of organizations of this type had increased until there "were
55 in Italy; 36 in France; 22 in Great Britain; 17 in the United
States; 8 each in Austria and Sweden; 7 in Latin America; 4 in
Australia; 3 each in Hungary, Norway, Russia, Spain, Japan, and
Denmark; and 1 in Canada—a total of 160 organizations with many
branches and an enormous membership." Probably one weakness in
the peace movement was its failure to crystallize into one great international society with a definite and uniform program. After 1889,
however, peace advocates held yearly international congresses, and
in 1891 they located the permanent headquarters for their international peace movement at the capital of Switzerland.

Many were drawn into the peace movement not merely because
of their hatred of the brutality and suffering which always accom-
pany war, but also for economic reasons. In an effort to be "prepared" against an attack by another country, each of the great
powers levied ever-increasing taxes. If war could be abolished, it
was argued, a heavy financial burden could be lifted from the shoulders of mankind. Furthermore, it was maintained, the cost of a great
war in the twentieth century would be so tremendous as to stagger
the imagination. Writers of keen vision pointed out that such a
conflict would be disastrous for even the victors. Ever since Bismarck
had made the Franco-German War "pay" by successfully collecting
an indemnity of five billion francs from defeated France, it had been
thought in many quarters that, if a war was won, the cost of waging it
could be placed on the shoulders of the defeated. In 1898, however,
Ivan Bloch, a Polish Jew, revealed the futility of this fond hope by
pointing out in his book, *The Future of War,* that war under modern conditions would inevitably bring general bankruptcy and starvation. His thesis received added support in 1910 when Norman
Angell, an Englishman, asserted in his volume, *The Great Illusion,*

that the economic and social conditions of the twentieth century made a military victory in war a mere illusion so far as improvement in the national well-being was concerned.[1] Other men like Alfred Nobel, a Swedish chemist and manufacturer of dynamite, Andrew Carnegie, an American steel manufacturer, Count Leo Tolstoi, a Russian novelist and social reformer, and Baron d'Estournelles de Constant, a French senator and publicist, gave abundantly of their wealth, their ability, and their time to advance the cause of peace.

Of course, it was realized that differences among nations would inevitably arise to cause ill feeling and friction. But, it was argued by peace-lovers, no differences could arise that could not be peaceably adjusted through diplomatic channels, use of arbitration, or resort to the mediation of other powers. A number of famous international controversies had been thus settled without recourse to war, perhaps the most famous being the *Alabama* case (1871–1872), the Bering Sea controversy (1892), and the Alaskan boundary dispute (1903), all between the United States and Great Britain; the colonial differences between Germany and Spain (1886); the dispute over the Samoan Islands (1899), between Great Britain, Germany, and the United States; the boundary dispute between Argentina and Chile (1902); and the differences between France and Germany over Morocco (1905–1909). By 1909 some eighty treaties making arbitration compulsory had been concluded between the various countries, and it has been estimated that during the century preceding 1914 arbitration in some form had been used to settle nearly three hundred international disputes.

In 1899 what was considered to be a notable step forward in the cause of international arbitration occurred when the first Hague Peace Conference [2] created the Permanent Court of Arbitration, popularly referred to as the Hague Court because it met at the capital of the Netherlands. This court was hardly a permanent tribunal in the full sense of the term, for it consisted merely of a list of the names of 132 distinguished jurists from which disputing states might, if they wished, select arbitrators. It had, moreover, no compulsory jurisdiction over any state and no way to enforce its decisions. The court was eventually housed in a magnificent peace

---

[1] Of course certain individuals—the war profiteers—might profit.
[2] See page 364.

# EUROPE
## IN 1914

ICELAND

*Arctic Circle*

FAROE IS.
(Den.)

SHETLAND IS.
(Br.)

ORKNEY IS.

HEBRIDES

BRITISH
ISLES

SCOTLAND
Aberdeen
Edinburgh
Glasgow
Newcastle

Londonderry
Belfast
IRELAND
Dublin
Cork
C. Clear
Irish
Sea

Manchester
Liverpool
WALES
ENGLAND
Birmingham
Bristol
London
Plymouth
Lands End

Brest

NORWAY
Trondhjem
Bergen
Stavenger
Christiansand
Christiania
Upsa
Norrk
Göteborg
SWEDE
ÖLAND
BAL

NORTH
SEA

DENMARK
Malmö
Copenhagen
Kiel
Hamburg
Bremen
Hanover
Leipzig
Berlin
Stettin
Dan
Oder R.
Dresden
Prague
EMPI

HELGOLAND
(Ger.)
Amsterdam
The Hague
Rotterdam
NETHERLANDS
Antwerp
Brussels
BELGIUM
Cologne
Frankfurt
GERMAN
Elbe
EMPI

English Channel
St. of Dover
CHANNEL IS.
(Br.)
Havre
Seine
Paris
Orleans
LUXEMBURG
Metz
Strassburg
Nuremberg
Danube
R.
Vienna
AUSTRIA

Nantes
Loire
FRANCE

Bay of
Biscay
San Sebastian
Santander
Oviedo
Vigo
Oporto
C. Finisterre

Bordeaux
St. Etienne
Bayonne
Garonne
Toulouse
PYRENEES
Ebro

Basel
Berne
SWITZERLAND
Geneva
Lyon
Rhone
Milan
Turin
Po
Genoa
Nice
ALPS
Munich
Venice
Graz
Trieste
Fiume
Di
Sa
ADRIATIC
Zara
Sar

Valladolid
SPAIN
Madrid
Duoro
Tagus
R.
Toledo
PORTUGAL
Lisbon
Seville
Cadiz
Malaga
Granada
Cartagena
Str. of Gibraltar
Gibraltar
(Br.)

Marseille
Toulon
CORSICA
Ajaccio
Florence
ITALY
Rome
Naples

Valencia
Barcelona
Saragossa

BALEARIC IS.
MINORCA
MAJORCA
Palma

SARDINIA
Cagliari

Palermo
Messina
SICILY

MALTA
(Br.)

MEDITERRA

A F R I C A

ATLANTIC OCEAN

30    20    10    0    10

50

40

0

10

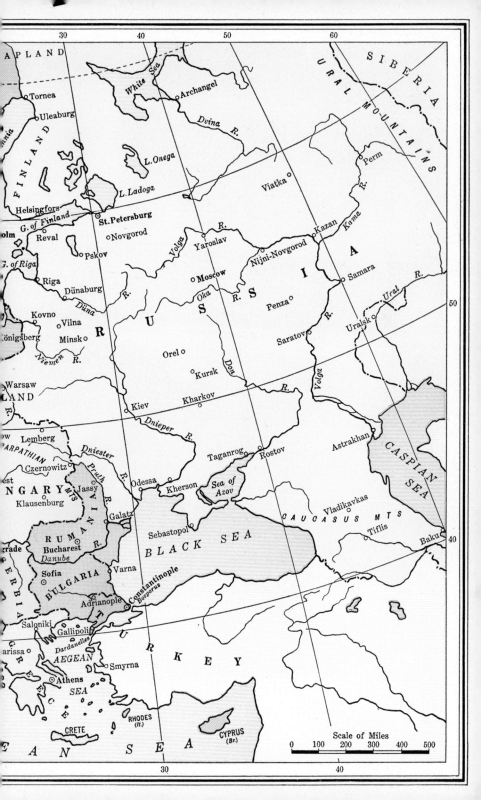

palace erected at the Hague with funds provided by Andrew Carnegie. By 1914 eighteen important cases and a number of lesser ones had been settled by this tribunal. On the other hand, even after the establishment of the Hague Court the great powers—Russia and Japan—resorted to war to settle their differences (1904–1905), Italy waged war against Turkey to gain colonial territory in northern Africa (1911–1912), and the Balkan states rose in arms against the sultan to advance their nationalist programs (1912–1913).

## CAUSES OF WAR

It is obvious from the foregoing statement that, at the very time when more and more attention was being given to the matter of preventing war, in the very years after machinery had been set up at the Hague for the pacific settlement of international disputes, wars were being fought in rapid succession by the nations of Europe. Why was this? In the first place, it was because the more deeply engrained spirit of competitive nationalism proved to be stronger than the more recently awakened ideal of international conciliation. In the second place, it was because various types of competition had developed among the nations, each of which was determined either to attain some objective or to prevent another power from attaining its objective, regardless of the justice of either's cause, and even at the cost of war if a reasonable chance of victory seemed present. And in the third place, it was because the nations of the world in their international relations lived in a "state of anarchy."

Although since 1914 much has been written on the subject of "international anarchy," it may be well to explain what is meant by the term and what its significance was—and is—in the history of the world. In 1914 Europe consisted of some twenty-five sovereign states, each in theory the equal of every other. They were called sovereign states because each refused to recognize any authority higher than its own will and its own interests. Each claimed the right to make its own decisions and steadily refused to accept or adopt any procedure which seemed to encroach upon its complete independence—independence to enter into alliances, to make war, to conclude peace, to do as it pleased. None would concede the right of any higher international authority to make decisions binding it, and none would admit its obligation to appeal to any arbiter except force where matters of "national honor" or "territorial integrity" were involved. In other words, the states of Europe lived in a condition of anarchy in the sense that each recognized no authority outside itself.

In such circumstances war was very likely to occur whenever some ambitious "sovereign" power believed that the situation was favorable for it to obtain some objective for which it was competing with other powers. And international competition was present in many fields in the years before 1914. Rival national plans clashed in numerous places. The preceding chapters have given many instances of wars resulting from imperialism and of diplomatic conflicts—arising from the same cause—which at times brought Europe to the verge of war. Unfortunately for the peace of the world, in 1914 many imperialistic programs still remained unfulfilled to constitute a disturbing element to the course of international relations.

Austria-Hungary still sought to push her way into the Balkans in order to check the anti-Habsburg propaganda emanating from Serbia. Germany was inclined to support Austria-Hungary's Balkan program, for she herself planned to exploit the rich resources of Asia Minor and for the latter purpose needed a railway route through friendly territory in the Balkans as well as predominance in Constantinople. Obviously the German and Austrian plans for a *Drang nach Osten* conflicted with Russia's desire to accomplish her "historic mission" of acquiring Constantinople and the Straits, together with domination in the Balkans. The ambitions of the two Teutonic empires militated, also, against the realization of Italy's hopes for territorial expansion, for the latter—in addition to her ambitions in Africa and Asia Minor—desired to control the eastern coast of the Adriatic in order that she might transform that sea into an Italian lake. And Great Britain and France, despite the fact that they possessed the first and second largest overseas empires respectively—or because of that fact—were disturbed lest some power might seek to obtain a "place in the sun" at their expense. Imperialism thus produced conflicting national aspirations, bred mutual fears and suspicions, and created an atmosphere which made a great war possible.

Not unrelated to the clash of imperialistic programs had been the construction of numerous entangling alliances. By 1914 Europe had come to be divided, in a general way, into two rival groups of heavily armed, ambitious powers. On the one hand, it will be recalled, there was the system of defensive alliances centering around

Germany and Austria-Hungary which Bismarck had created between 1879 and 1883.[3] These included the Austro-German alliance (1879) and the Austro-Rumanian alliance (1883), both against Russia, and the Triple Alliance (1882), which was aimed primarily against France. On the other hand, there was the Franco-Russian alliance (1894), defensive against Germany, and the Triple Entente (1904, 1907), which, though not specifically aimed against any particular power, was largely facilitated by a common fear of Germany.[4] Italy was linked with both sets of alliances, for, despite her membership in the Triple Alliance, she had made a colonial agreement (1900) and a military agreement (1902) with France and an imperialistic bargain (1909) with Russia,[5] which tended to wean her away from the Teutonic powers. Therefore, although on paper Germany's system of alliances seemed more closely and more definitely knit together than France's group of alliances and ententes, it is doubtful if that was actually so.

These ententes, alliances, and counteralliances, though defensive in their original character, eventually created an atmosphere favorable to war. Naturally, the number of "danger spots" which might embroil all Europe in a serious international conflict was increased as states became more and more entangled in the plans and aspirations of their allies. At the same time, believing that if attacked they would have the active assistance of their allies, states became less willing to make concessions in times of diplomatic clashes. Finally, as the international situation became more tense, members of each alliance became reluctant to concede anything to members of the other lest their action be interpreted as weakness and their group suffer a loss of prestige.

Accompanying the rise of entangling alliances, and undoubtedly accelerated by the fear engendered by these alliances, was the growth of huge national armaments. After the Austro-Prussian and Franco-German wars, the system of conscription which seemed to have enabled Prussia to gain an easy victory in each case was rapidly adopted by the other states on the Continent. One after another the national armies were reorganized on the Prussian model. Year by year the number of young men called to serve in the various national armies

[3] For an account of the creation of Bismarck's system of alliances, see pages 65–71.
[4] For an account of France's alliances and ententes, see pages 115, 129, and 132.
[5] For these agreements, see pages 160–161.

was increased until Europe came to be a veritable armed camp. All of this was done in the name of peace, for it was argued that the best insurance against war was national preparedness. Many taxpayers complained, however, of the ever-increasing tax burden laid upon them for armaments which some pacifists maintained would not assure peace but might rather provoke war. The latter viewpoint was well presented by H. N. Brailsford, an Englishman, who in *The War of Steel and Gold* (1914) asserted that preparedness inevitably brought war.

At the close of the nineteenth century a feeble attempt was made to limit armaments by international agreement. In 1898 Tsar Nicholas II of Russia invited the powers to assemble at the Hague to consider the possibility of some such agreement. Whether he was moved to this step by a sincere personal desire to promote the cause of peace or merely because the financial burden which armaments entailed was becoming too great for Russia to carry, is not clear. It soon became apparent, however, that most of the statesmen of the great powers were opposed to any international limitation on armaments. When the Hague Peace Conference convened in 1899 with delegates from twenty-six states present, no agreement was reached on this subject. In general, Germany stood out as the power most opposed to limitation of land armaments, and Great Britain blocked all steps which might weaken her control of the seas.

A second Hague Peace Conference, held in 1907, was attended by the representatives of forty-four states, but again the nations failed to agree upon any limitation of armaments. A number of rules were adopted to regularize and make more humane the conduct of war, but these, as the succeeding pages disclose, were largely ignored when the World War finally came. Attempts to arrive at some agreement limiting naval armaments were also carried on by direct negotiations between Great Britain and Germany, but these, too, proved futile.[6] And so the armaments race went madly on. By 1914 the five major continental powers had millions of men in their peace-time standing armies, to say nothing of other millions trained and organized in the reserves.

Such a situation did much to create an atmosphere favorable to war. In the first place, it engendered international fear and suspicion. Although each power professed to be preparing merely to defend

[6] For these negotiations, see pages 90–91.

itself against aggression, each in turn suspected the others of preparing *for* aggression. In the second place, the knowledge that great military establishments were back of them undoubtedly increased the reluctance of statesmen to make concessions which might appear in the nature of national diplomatic defeats and, conversely, increased their determination to press for some advantage which might appear to be a national diplomatic triumph. In the third place, in all countries to some extent, but more particularly in Germany, the growth of armaments contributed to the development of a state of mind usually summed up in the one word "militarism." [7] In the fourth place, with the growth of great military machines there developed in each country a general staff of leaders and experts, one of whose chief concerns was to prevent the army of another power from "getting the jump" on them in time of international crisis. These general staffs worked out carefully calculated "timetables" of what must be done if war should break out, and in every international crisis there was always the danger that some chief of staff, in an effort to maintain the schedule on his "timetable," might force an order for mobilization and thus precipitate a war. Finally, the existence of great military establishments produced a group of armament manufacturers in all of the important countries who were at times not averse to the spread of warlike ideas as a means of increasing their own profits.

A fourth factor which disturbed the course of European international affairs and constituted an ever-present potential cause of war was the increasing desire of certain groups of people of the same race, speaking the same language or kindred dialects, having in general the same customs and traditions, and inhabiting contiguous territories, to unite into one state independent of foreign domination. This was the goal of nationalism. The years before 1914 had witnessed a considerable advance toward this nationalist ideal in the creation of the German Empire and the Italian, Greek, Belgian, Serbian, Rumanian, and Bulgarian kingdoms. Nevertheless, in 1914

---

[7] "Militarism is an attitude of approval of war as an elevating, ennobling occupation, as the purifying salt in the otherwise nauseous human compound; . . . usually, the approval rises to a desire for national glory as the product of military success, welcoming quarrel in order that war's beneficent influence may have full operation; and . . . the approval and desire have, as a result, the endowment of the military profession with a rank and worthiness higher and more meritorious than attaches to avocations of civil character." J. S. Ewart, *The Roots and Causes of the Wars (1914–1918)*, Volume I, pages 479–480.

national statehood was as yet unattained or only partly attained in various parts of Europe. In general, Austria-Hungary and Russia constituted the chief obstacles to its consummation.

Although the desire for national unity was a force in Italy, which since her consolidation had cast longing eyes upon the Trieste and Trentino territories of Austria-Hungary wherein dwelt "unredeemed Italians," and in France, where the desire to regain the lost provinces of Alsace-Lorraine was still strong in the hearts of many, it constituted a more active factor in the Balkans. Here, though considerable advance toward national statehood had been made, each state was possessed of nationalist dreams as yet unfulfilled. Greece desired to obtain Thrace, some of the Aegean islands, and parts of Asia Minor in order to reconstruct the ancient Byzantine Empire. At the same time Bulgaria hoped to secure most of Macedonia and Thrace in order to round out her territory and gain an adequate outlet to the Aegean. Rumania longed to bring within her boundaries the millions of "unredeemed" Rumanians dwelling in Transylvania, Bukowina, and parts of Bessarabia. Serbia aspired to liberate her kinsmen who dwelt within the Habsburg empire and to gain a foothold on the Adriatic. Naturally, this unrest in the Balkans constituted a standing menace to the peace of Europe, the more so since states like Russia and Austria-Hungary sought to turn the Balkan aspirations to their own advantage. The possibility that some Balkan group would attempt to complete its "unification" and thus precipitate a war in which the great powers might participate was always present.

And if the statesmen of any power—great or small—led their country into war, they were almost certain to receive the enthusiastic support of the great majority of their fellow citizens. Patriotic history and literature magnified the former glory and future promise of each nation, while patriotic writers devoted themselves to extolling the superiority of their own racial group. "Patriotic state education taught unquestioning loyalty to state or dynasty as the first principle of moral conduct, carefully obscured any questionable occurrences or policies in the national past, and frowned on national criticism and proposals of radical reform." In every country some jingo or venal newspapers stood ready upon the least pretext to inflame public opinion by criticizing and misrepresenting the acts or policies of other states. In many countries international antipathies had been

THE ARCHDUKE AT SARAJEVO

The arrival of Francis Ferdinand and his wife on June 28, 1914.

assiduously cultivated, with the result that national suspicions, fears, and hatreds were deep-seated. Such was the spirit of this type of nationalism that in each state the people felt that their government was always honest and upright in its dealings with others, that if war occurred it was because some other state was the aggressor.

## RECURRING INTERNATIONAL CRISES

Many careful observers of the course of international events during the decade before 1914 were not altogether surprised by the outbreak of the World War, for a series of international crises accompanied by an increasing tension among the great powers had revealed a noticeable drift toward war. These crises have been discussed in the preceding chapters, but it will be well to recapitulate briefly in order to get the international situation in 1914 clearly in mind.

The first crisis, it will be recalled, was precipitated in 1905, when the Kaiser landed at Tangier and proclaimed his support of the Moroccan sultan in maintaining the political sovereignty and territorial integrity of his country. War between France and Germany might have resulted from this step and the latter's subsequent demands, but it was avoided because the French government gave way and permitted the Moroccan situation to be settled at the Algeciras conference.[8] Although the outcome of this conference was largely favorable to France, the latter deeply resented Germany's interference in French plans. At the same time Germany was disturbed by finding herself and Austria-Hungary almost isolated in the deliberations of the Algeciras conference, for Italy had voted in favor of France against her own ally. Apparently this fact was not lost on the Kaiser, who, at the close of the conference, sent a telegram to Francis Joseph referring to Austria-Hungary as his "faithful ally," evidently implying that Italy had proved unfaithful to the Triple Alliance.

If the German government's plan in precipitating the crisis had been to destroy or weaken the recently consummated Entente Cordiale between France and Great Britain, it had failed miserably. At the very outset of the crisis British public opinion supported France, and the German ambassador at London had notified Berlin that British newspapers were even "more French than the French."

[8] For an account of the first Moroccan crisis, see pages 130–133.

In fact, during the crisis Sir Edward Grey, British foreign secretary, went so far as to inform the German ambassador that, if Germany actually attacked France, Great Britain could hardly keep out of the war. Furthermore, after consulting the prime minister and the minister of war, Grey permitted British army leaders to work out with French and Belgian military men provisional plans for British aid against a German attack in case Great Britain should ever decide to go to the aid of these two countries. The crisis therefore served to consolidate the Franco-British entente, while increasing the tension between France and Germany.

The next event which placed a severe strain upon the peaceful course of international relations came in 1908 when Austria-Hungary announced her annexation of Bosnia and Herzegovina.[9] From one viewpoint the ensuing crisis was of nationalist genesis, for the annexation aroused the Serbs almost to a frenzy because it appeared to block their plans for a "greater Serbia." From another viewpoint the crisis was imperialistic, for the Russian government was inclined to support Serbia's demand for an outlet to the sea in order to strengthen Russia's own position in the Balkans. Again war might easily have resulted between Serbia and Russia, on the one hand, and Austria-Hungary and Germany, on the other, had not Russia yielded and permitted the annexation of the provinces without a conference of the powers.

There is little doubt that in this crisis the Teutonic powers gained a decisive diplomatic victory. But the price they paid was high. Serbia now hated Austria-Hungary more bitterly than ever. By her promises to Austria-Hungary she had gained immunity from immediate attack; but in the following years she pushed the reorganization of her army with feverish activity, obtaining from France guns, munitions, and military advice. Although she had officially undertaken not to carry on propaganda inimical to Austria-Hungary, the promise had little likelihood of being fulfilled so far as the secret agitation of the various Serbian patriotic societies was concerned. The Yugoslav threat to the territorial integrity of the Dual Monarchy was not destroyed by the annexation of Bosnia-Herzegovina.

In the second place, Russia, after her humiliation, definitely began to make preparations for a war which she regarded as inevitable. In order to block the plans of the Teutonic powers and at the same

[9] For an account of the Bosnian crisis, see pages 338–344.

time strengthen her own position in the Balkans, she at once turned her attention to the creation of a Balkan league. In 1909 she proposed to Bulgaria a military convention designed to protect each against the Teutonic powers and Turkey. Although the convention seems never to have been actually signed, Russia's attitude is disclosed in one article which stipulated "that the realization of the high ideals of the Slavic peoples in the Balkan peninsula . . . is possible only after a favorable outcome of Russia's struggle with Germany and Austria-Hungary." In France, at the same time, Russia began a campaign to "Balkanize" the Franco-Russian alliance, that is, to convert the French to the view that developments in the Balkans which were vital to Russia were important likewise to France.

In the third place, the annexation strained relations between Italy and Austria-Hungary and led the former to take one more step toward the Triple Entente. During the crisis, when anti-Austrian agitation in Italy was so feverish, Austria-Hungary had concentrated forces in the Trentino. Apparently the Habsburg chief of staff had even contemplated an attack on Italy as well as on Serbia. Russia took advantage of the increasing anti-Habsburg feeling in Italy to come to an agreement with that power (October, 1909) in which each promised to attempt to maintain the *status quo* in the Balkans.[10] Apparently both had in mind the possibility of checking further Habsburg expansion to the southeast. Italy's double-dealing at this time becomes obvious when it is pointed out that only a few weeks later (December, 1909) she signed another Balkan agreement with Austria-Hungary in which each renewed professions of loyalty to the Triple Alliance.[11]

Within less than three years after the settlement of the Bosnian crisis Europe was again pushed to the verge of war by Germany's demand for extensive territorial compensation as her price for permitting France to transform Morocco into a French protectorate.[12] In this crisis Great Britain gave her whole-hearted diplomatic support to France. Had the French government positively refused to make any territorial concessions to Germany or had the latter failed

[10] For the agreement of Racconigi, see page 161.
[11] Austria-Hungary agreed that, if she should be compelled to occupy Novibazar, either temporarily or permanently, the obligation to make territorial compensation to Italy would become effective.
[12] For an account of the second Moroccan crisis, see pages 134–136.

to moderate her demands upon France, war might have followed, but fortunately neither government wanted war, and so eventually a pacific settlement was reached. But so strong was the feeling caused in France by this crisis that the pacific Caillaux ministry was overturned and was succeeded by one headed by the strong nationalist, Poincaré.[13] The latter immediately set out to strengthen the ties between France and Russia. In Germany many felt that their government had been blocked in its demands for compensation by Britain's control of the sea and consequently demanded further increases in the German navy. Germany's new naval program, in turn, increased the tension between Germany and Britain, especially after the Haldane mission failed to check their naval rivalry.[14]

Hardly had the statesmen of Europe regained their breath after the second Moroccan crisis before an equally grave crisis was precipitated, when, despite the opposition of the great powers, the Balkan league made a concerted attack upon Turkey in 1912. The two Balkan wars that ensued and the crisis which developed among the great powers in consequence were discussed in the preceding chapter.[15] Suffice it to point out here that the wars of 1912–1913 had farreaching effects on the general European situation.

They nearly doubled the area and population of Serbia, greatly increased her self-confidence, and strongly stimulated her hope of a speedy realization of that dream of a "greater Serbia" which envisaged the ultimate acquisition of Bosnia-Herzegovina, Dalmatia, Croatia-Slavonia, and the Serb-inhabited districts of southern Hungary. They greatly increased the size and importance of Greece, where enthusiasm for a further advance toward the realization of its aims led the Greek government to purchase two warships from the United States in preparation for seizing any future opportunity which might present itself for the reconstitution of the Pan-Hellenic empire. They converted Bulgaria into a defeated and humiliated power which was eager for revenge upon her erstwhile allies and was therefore prepared to join with any great power that seemed in a position to bring to her the Macedonia which she had twice lost within a single generation.

They turned over to Greece and Serbia former Turkish territory

---

[13] See page 136.
[14] For an account of the Anglo-German naval rivalry and the Haldane mission, see pages 89–91.
[15] See pages 348–352.

through which Austria-Hungary had planned to secure railway connection with the Aegean, at the same time placing in more powerful hands her existing railway route to Constantinople. They obviously made more difficult of realization the proposed Berlin-Bagdad railway under German influence. They revealed that Rumania was no longer a trusty satellite of the Teutonic powers, and at the same time smashed Russia's recently created Balkan league. The net result seemed unfavorable to the Teutonic powers. In fact, so alarmed was the Austrian government over developments in the Balkans at this time that in the summer of 1913 it seriously contemplated a preventive war against Serbia in order to keep that country from becoming too powerful and too attractive to the Yugoslav people within the Dual Monarchy. The latter was on the point of launching an attack against the little Slav kingdom and was deterred only by the opposition of Germany and Italy.

## INCREASING INTERNATIONAL TENSION

During the years 1912–1914, when the governments and peoples of Europe displayed an "excessive nervosity," existing alliances and ententes were tightened up and new ones were projected. Definite steps were taken, for instance, to bring France and Great Britain into closer relations. After the failure of the Haldane mission,[16] Great Britain transferred most of her Mediterranean fleet to the North Sea in order quickly to balance there the increase in strength which Germany was planning to gain in the ensuing years by the execution of her naval program. In view of the weakening of the Entente naval power in the Mediterranean by the withdrawal of British ships, Great Britain urged France to station most of her navy in that sea. Naturally, the latter was reluctant to leave her Atlantic coast undefended unless she received some guarantee from Britain. Eventually, with the consent of the British cabinet, personal notes were exchanged (November, 1912) between Grey and Cambon, the French ambassador at London. Grey explicitly stated that, if either country suspected that it was about to be the victim of an unprovoked attack, "it should immediately discuss with the other whether both governments should act together to prevent aggression and preserve the peace, and, if so, what measures they would be prepared to take in common." This correspondence, obviously, went

16 See pages 90–91.

far toward transforming the Entente Cordiale into a Franco-British alliance against Germany. Apparently the French government so regarded it, for it soon transferred its Atlantic fleet to the Mediterranean. Furthermore, Marshal Joffre later stated that French military plans were developed with the assumption of active British support.

In 1912, too, steps were taken to bring France and Russia into a closer understanding regarding the Balkans. Although in August of that year Poincaré informed Sazonov that France would not go to war over a Balkan question, he qualified his statement by adding the clause, unless Russia is attacked by Germany. Later in the year Izvolsky, the Russian ambassador at Paris, reported to St. Petersburg that Poincaré realized that an attack upon Serbia by Austria might force Russia to give up her passive attitude and take diplomatic steps followed by military measures against Austria. According to Poincaré, Izvolsky reported, Russia could count on French diplomatic support and, if Germany should come to the military aid of Austria, military support as well. Whether Izvolsky exaggerated or truly reported what Poincaré had said is not clear, but the effect upon the Russian government at St. Petersburg would have been the same in either case. The statement seemed to indicate that the Russian ambassador at Paris had at last succeeded in "Balkanizing" the Franco-Russian alliance. At the same time, in order to make the French people "Balkan-conscious," the French press was extensively subsidized by Izvolsky with funds secured from Russia. Meanwhile, to implement the alliance more effectively, a Franco-Russian naval convention was concluded, and the general staffs of the two countries conferred annually to perfect their plans for a joint offensive against Germany in case of war. Finally, in 1914 Russia was informed of the exchange of letters between Grey and Cambon in November, 1912, and negotiations were opened between Russia and Great Britain looking to a naval agreement.

Nor were the powers of the Triple Alliance inactive. Although that alliance was not due to expire until July, 1914, the treaty was renewed in December, 1912, and extended until July, 1920. Italy announced, however, that in case of war she would be unable to send any of her military forces north of the Alps, as she had always promised to do during the preceding quarter of a century. France's transfer of her whole navy to the Mediterranean, however, frightened her enough so that she was willing to sign a naval convention with the other partners in the Triple Alliance. In June, 1913, agreements were reached defining the action of the Mediterranean fleets of Germany, Austria, and Italy in case of war. Provision was specifically made for attacking French troop ships operating between North Africa and France. And in the spring of 1914 Italy once more promised to send troops into Germany to fight against France in case Germany should be attacked by the latter. So far as agreements on paper were concerned, therefore, the powers of both the Triple Alliance and the Triple Entente were more closely bound together in 1914 than they had ever been before.

In the Balkans, meanwhile, both Russia and Austria-Hungary were busily engaged in trying to construct or reconstruct alliances. During the wars of 1912-1913 Berchtold had managed to destroy Russia's Balkan league, but he was not content with this achievement. He next sought to overcome the threat of a "greater Serbia" by the creation of a Balkan alliance against Serbia, with Bulgaria as the pivot but with Greece, Turkey, and possibly Rumania also included. During 1914 negotiations were carried on between the Dual Monarchy and Bulgaria which had progressed far enough by July of that year so that Bulgaria was able to secure a loan from Berlin. On the other hand, Russia, whose diplomacy had received something of a blow by the destruction of her Balkan league, was desperately attempting to reconstruct the league by substituting Rumania for Bulgaria.

In 1913 and 1914 both sets of great powers were also attempting to improve their positions at Constantinople, where the Turkish government was trying to reorganize its military and financial departments after the Balkan wars. An Englishman was invited to reorganize the empire's finances; a Frenchman was asked to train the gendarmerie; a German general, Liman von Sanders, was invited to reorganize and train the army; and a British admiral was asked to do the same for the navy. The growing international tension in Europe is clearly revealed by the fact that, as soon as Sazonov learned of the Sanders mission, he entered a determined protest against giving a German command of an army corps in the Ottoman capital, where, he declared, the sultan would be deprived of all liberty of action. The Russian foreign minister wished to use the occasion to force Germany to draw back. But Great Britain, whose admiral's powers over the Ottoman navy were probably greater than those of Sanders over the army, declined to support Russia, and France likewise refused to exert pressure at Berlin.

In January, 1914, at a Russian council meeting Sazonov urged an immediate attack upon Germany unless the latter abandoned the Sanders mission. The council, however, decided for peace. The German government, in order to appease Russia, offered a compromise arrangement by the terms of which Sanders was not to command troops in Constantinople but was to function merely as inspector of the Turkish army. But Sazonov was still dominated by the idea that Russia must not permit Germany to secure control of Constantinople and the Straits, and during the early weeks of 1914 Russian military and naval officers worked on plans for seizing the Straits in case of necessity. In a council meeting in February of that year it was decided that Russian operations against the Straits could not be inaugurated with any assurance of success without a general European war.

Meanwhile, Russia's willingness to support Serbia in order to block Austria-Hungary's advance into the Balkans continued unchecked, as was indicated by the tsar's statement to Premier Pashich of Serbia when the latter had a conference with him in St. Petersburg in January, 1914. "For Serbia," declared Nicholas II, "we shall do everything." Russia directed her immediate efforts toward securing a union of Serbia and Montenegro and in 1914 began to bring pressure to bear on the ruler of the latter state. Such a union not only would increase the size and population of Serbia, but would at the same time provide the latter with an outlet to the Adriatic. The Austrian government, however, had come to the conclusion that, if this union were ever consummated, it would demand that the coast of Montenegro should go to Albania. Such a transfer of territory would have at least two significant results. It would again prevent Serbia from securing an outlet to the sea, and it would extend Albania's territory northward to the Austrian frontier. The latter possibility was particularly alarming to the Italians, because they believed it would increase Austria's influence over Albania, which the Italians themselves wished to dominate. Consequently, in the late spring of 1914 Italy again wavered in her loyalty to the Triple Alliance.

These brief glimpses of the diplomatic situation in Europe in

1913 and 1914 somewhat resemble the pieces of a jig-saw picture, none of which alone gives a complete or true idea of the picture as a whole. Possibly enough of the pieces have been fitted together, however, to indicate that just before the crisis of 1914 international rivalry and friction in Europe were being more and more localized and centered in the Balkans and the Near East. And as the fears and suspicions increased, so did the measures for expanding the various national armies and navies. Europe as a whole was perhaps never so well prepared to wage war as in the summer of 1914.[17]

Gradually the international situation became more tense. In Austria-Hungary "the feeling that the nations are moving toward a conflict, urged by an irresistible force," grew from day to day. In Russia the military began to realize that "we are preparing for a war in the West. Not only troops but the whole nation must accustom itself to the idea that we arm ourselves for a war of annihilation against the Germans, and the German empires must be annihilated." In France the "atmosphere of hate and defiance has become heavier owing to the discussions on the Three Years' Law." "Russia is ready. France must be ready too," proclaimed the headlines of an article in the St. Petersburg *Bourse Gazette* in June, 1914, whereupon the Kaiser wrote: "Any German who still disbelieves that Russia and France are working full steam for an early war against us . . . , is fit for the madhouse." "The whole of Germany is charged with electricity," wrote Colonel House, after visiting Berlin in May, 1914. "Everybody's nerves are tense. It only needs a spark to set the whole thing off." "Peace," the German ambassador in Paris reported, "remains at the mercy of an accident."

## THE AUSTRO-SERBIAN CRISIS OF 1914

Such was the atmosphere in Europe when Francis Ferdinand, nephew of the Habsburg emperor and heir to the Austrian and Hungarian thrones, set out for his visit to the capital of Bosnia. In going to Sarajevo at this time the archduke took his life in his hands, for Bosnia was honeycombed with propaganda of two Serbian societies, "National Defense" and "Union or Death," and men were not lack-

[17] For the military and naval preparations of Germany, France, Russia, Austria-Hungary, and Great Britain, see the following pages, respectively: 98, 137–138, 283, 312, 213–214.

ing to undertake his assassination in the interest of the "greater Serbia" movement.[18] Even before the announcement of the proposed visit of the archduke, the latter of these societies had marked him for assassination. His presence in Sarajevo provided the sought-for occasion, and plans were laid under the direction of Colonel Dimitriyevich, a member of the society and chief of the intelligence division of the Serbian general staff. Three Bosnian young men who volunteered to carry out the plot were furnished with the necessary pistols, ammunition, and bombs in Belgrade, and smuggled back across the frontier into Bosnia. Apparently still others were in Sarajevo on that fateful day as "reserves" in case the attempts of these three should fail.

On the morning of June 28, 1914, the archduke's party arrived in Sarajevo shortly before ten o'clock. A few minutes later, when the party was on the way to the town hall to be welcomed by the mayor, a bomb was hurled by one of the trio of conspirators. It missed its mark, however, and exploded under the car behind the one in which Francis Ferdinand and his wife were riding. Later, when the archduke was returning from the town hall, a second conspirator suddenly jumped on the running-board of the car and assassinated both the archduke and his wife.

Once more events in the Balkans precipitated a European crisis. Count Berchtold, Austro-Hungarian foreign minister, determined to use this occasion for that final reckoning with Serbia which had been desired but postponed in 1913. The Austro-Hungarian government held that Serbian propaganda, seeking to unite all Yugoslavs under the Serbian flag, must encourage such crimes and endanger the Habsburg dynasty and empire if not stopped. Austria-Hungary's efforts must now "be directed to isolating Serbia and reducing her size." Austria-Hungary consulted her ally and learned that Germany would fully support her in *whatever* action she might decide to take. This promise, given shortly after the assassination (July 6), constituted what was later called Germany's "blank check" to Austria-Hungary. Germany, naturally, was anxious to have her one dependable ally maintain her strength undiminished, and concurred in her belief that this necessitated military action against Serbia. Austria-Hungary

[18] Many Serbs feared that the archduke's scheme for transforming the Dual Monarchy into a Trial (triple) Monarchy with autonomy for the Slavs might wean their kinsmen in the empire away from the "greater Serbia" movement.

desired only a local war between herself and Serbia, and Germany in the beginning urged rapidity of action in order to forestall intervention. Both recognized, however, the possibility that Russia would intervene in Serbia's behalf.

Berchtold now proceeded to pave the way for the desired military action. On July 7 at a ministerial council [19] meeting in Vienna the foreign minister proposed a surprise attack upon Serbia. To this Count Tisza, the Hungarian premier, objected, and so the matter was postponed. One week later, however, Tisza consented to a short-term ultimatum purposely designed to be so severe that Serbia could not accept it. Said Berchtold after the ultimatum had been drafted, "The text of the note, to be sent to Belgrade, as it was settled today, is such that we must reckon with the probability of war."

The ultimatum asserted that Serbia had broken her promise "to live on good neighborly terms" with Austria-Hungary by encouraging propaganda aimed against the Dual Monarchy, and declared that the latter was thus compelled to abandon its attitude of benevolent and patient forbearance in order to put an end "to the intrigues which form a perpetual menace to the tranquillity of the monarchy." The ultimatum then made several peremptory demands, the most important of which were: (1) that the Serbian government officially condemn the anti-Austrian propaganda of its citizens; (2) that it suppress all publications and societies which incited hatred and contempt of the Dual Monarchy; (3) that all anti-Austrian teachers and books be eliminated from the public schools; (4) that the public officials implicated in the anti-Austrian propaganda be dismissed; (5) that two Serbian officers, named in the ultimatum, be arrested at once; (6) that Serbia accept the collaboration of Austrian officials in the suppression of the anti-Austrian propaganda within her borders; and (7) that Serbia accept the help of Austrian officials in the investigation of those implicated in the Sarajevo crime. On July 23 the ultimatum, with a demand for an answer within forty-eight hours, was presented to Serbia.

The Entente powers' request that Austria-Hungary extend the time limit beyond the stipulated forty-eight hours was bluntly refused. Serbia consequently submitted her reply within the designated pe-

---

[19] Matters of foreign policy were usually settled by the ministerial council, which included the Austro-Hungarian joint ministers of foreign affairs, war, and finance, the prime ministers of both Austria and Hungary, and sometimes their finance ministers.

riod. She offered to accede to all the demands of the ultimatum except the ones referring to the participation of Austro-Hungarian officials in the suppression of anti-Austrian propaganda and in the investigation of the Sarajevo crime. These, she asserted, would be a violation of her rights as a sovereign state. Serbia offered, however, to refer the whole matter to the Hague Court or to a decision of the great powers, if Austria considered the reply unsatisfactory. The reply was conciliatory, and most of the powers considered that it laid the basis for negotiation. The Kaiser himself believed that it removed "every reason for war." Nevertheless, Austria-Hungary asserted that the reply was unsatisfactory, severed diplomatic relations with Belgrade, and ordered partial mobilization against Serbia—which had already mobilized her army. "Vienna burst into a frenzy of delight, vast crowds parading the streets and singing patriotic songs till the small hours of the morning."

## The Futile Efforts to Prevent War

Serbia's attempt to prevent war by having Austria-Hungary's ultimatum referred to the Hague Court or to a conference of the great powers had failed because of the Habsburg government's unwillingness to accept that means of settlement. Perhaps the latter still remembered how Germany had fared at the Algeciras conference. The great powers now offered various plans and made various proposals for a pacific settlement. On the day after the ultimatum was delivered to Serbia Sir Edward Grey, British foreign secretary, proposed that Great Britain, France, Germany, and Italy should exert a moderating influence simultaneously in Vienna and St. Petersburg. Nothing came of this plan, however, largely because of the attitude of France and Russia, which demanded pressure on Austria-Hungary.

In this crisis Russia was determined to support Serbia and asserted that she would agree to a settlement only in so far as it involved no humiliation of the latter as an independent state. Furthermore, she believed that her own position in the Balkans demanded a strong and independent Serbia to block the way of her rival, Austria-Hungary. Apparently the tsar's foreign minister, Sazonov, hoped to prevent war by bluffing Austria-Hungary into moderation by a show of force. On July 25 the Russian government issued orders for the "period preparatory to war," and on the next day notified

Austria-Hungary that, if the latter's forces crossed the Serbian frontier, the Russian army would be mobilized against the Dual Monarchy. At the same time Sazonov requested Berchtold to discuss the ultimatum with him. Meanwhile, in St. Petersburg there were many who felt that war was inevitable and that now was Russia's chance for a final reckoning with Germany and the acquisition of Constantinople and the Straits. Sazonov characterized the Austrian ultimatum as highly provocative and expressed the hope that Great Britain would proclaim her solidarity with Russia and France.

As in 1913, so now, however, Grey was chiefly interested in mediation in the interests of peace. He believed that France, Germany, Italy, and Great Britain—the powers which had no direct interest in Serbia—might act jointly in Vienna and St. Petersburg. On July 26, therefore, he proposed that these governments instruct their ambassadors in London to meet in conference with him for the purpose of discovering an issue which would prevent complications. He contemplated a procedure similar to that followed during the Balkan crisis of the preceding year. France and Italy promptly accepted the proposal, but Germany declared that she could take part in mediation only at Austria-Hungary's express wish. The latter had no such wish, and so the plan was rejected.

Germany, in turn, advocated direct conversations between Russia and Austria-Hungary, and on July 26 such conversations were initiated between Sazonov and the Austro-Hungarian ambassador in St. Petersburg. Sazonov requested that the latter be authorized to discuss a redrafting of certain points in the Austro-Hungarian ultimatum in such a way as to satisfy Austria-Hungary's chief demands and at the same time be acceptable to Serbia. Berchtold, who was resolved not to enter into negotiations regarding issues between Serbia and Austria-Hungary, at first evaded Sazonov's request and later rejected it on the ground that war had already been declared against Serbia. The declaration of war had been issued on July 28 for the specific purpose of evading further proposals for mediation. Opposed to war to the very last, Francis Joseph was tricked into giving his consent by a forged telegram stating that Serbian forces had already entered Austria-Hungary. The bombardment of Belgrade, an unfortified city, began on July 29.

This action on the part of Austria-Hungary furnished further basis for Russia's belief that the former was planning "to gobble up Serbia." At the same time it gave Russian military officers an opportunity to exercise pressure for war preparation. They felt that a war between Austria-Hungary and Serbia was necessarily a war between Austria-Hungary and Russia, and therefore between Germany and Russia; while Sazonov believed that Germany was supporting Austria-Hungary and would continue to do so unless Russia made it clear that she would threaten Austria-Hungary with force in order to protect Serbia. On July 29 Russia declared mobilization against the Dual Monarchy. France approved the Russian policy and, far from exerting a moderating influence, telegraphed the promise of full French aid.

On July 29, also, Russia requested Great Britain again to press for mediation with a view to the suspension of military operations. The latter then suggested to Germany as a good basis for mediation that Austria should occupy Belgrade or other towns as pledges, while mediation should seek "to procure for Austria all possible satisfaction." This same plan had already been proposed by the Kaiser, and came to be known as the "pledge plan." Information on Russia's action together with Great Britain's attitude now caused Germany at once to address sharp warnings to Austria-Hungary, pointing out that the latter's refusal "to exchange views with St. Petersburg would be a grave mistake." Berchtold thereupon permitted the renewal of conversations at St. Petersburg the next day, but limited them to an explanation of the ultimatum and to a discussion of Austro-Russian—not Austro-Serbian—relations.

On July 30 the German ambassador at Vienna presented to Berchtold Great Britain's "pledge plan," together with Bethmann-Hollweg's urgent request for its acceptance. "If Austria refuses all intervention, we are thus faced with a conflagration in which England would go against us, and, according to all indications, Italy and Rumania not with us, and we two would have to face four great powers. . . . Austria's political prestige, the honor of her arms as well as her legitimate demands on Serbia, could be amply preserved by the occupation of Belgrade or other places. . . . Under these circumstances we most urgently and earnestly submit to the considerations of the Vienna cabinet that it should accept mediation under the honorable terms specified. The responsibility for the consequences which will otherwise result would be uncommonly serious for Austria and for ourselves." Later in the day the Kaiser also sent a telegram of somewhat the same tenor to Francis Joseph. The German government thus—a little late, perhaps—finally brought a moderating influence to bear upon its Habsburg ally.

The Habsburg foreign minister, however, declined to commit himself on the thirtieth, but ordered a meeting of the ministerial council for July 31. But before the council met on that day, the Austro-Hungarian government had received other messages from German officials. When on July 30 Moltke, the chief of the German general staff, learned that the tsar had declined to stop Russia's military preparations, he at once advised Austria to mobilize against Russia and promised German aid. When Berchtold saw Moltke's telegram, he exclaimed, "Who is in charge, Bethmann or Moltke?" After news of Russia's order of general mobilization reached Berlin on the morning of July 31, Moltke again urged Austria-Hungary to proceed at once with general mobilization.

When the Austro-Hungarian council met on the morning of July 31 to formulate its own plans, therefore, it had two types of messages from Germany to consider: Bethmann-Hollweg's urgent advice to accept Great Britain's pledge plan and Moltke's equally urgent advice to order immediate general mobilization. Berchtold himself believed that warlike operations against Serbia must continue, that Austria-Hungary could not negotiate concerning the British offer so long as Russian mobilization had not been stopped, and that Austria-Hungary's demands must be accepted integrally without negotiation. The council of ministers adopted Berchtold's views, and practically repudiated the mediation proposals, as Francis Joseph clearly realized when he wrote to the Kaiser: "I am aware of the implication of my decisions, and have made them with entire confidence in the justice of God and with the certainty that your armed forces will range themselves with unalterable fidelity in favor of my Empire and the Triple Alliance." On that day Austria proclaimed mobilization against Russia, some hours after the latter had herself ordered general mobilization against Austria and Germany.

As early as July 26 Russia had begun to take far-reaching measures preparatory to general mobilization. Three days later, after news of the bombardment of Belgrade, mobilization had been ordered against Austria-Hungary. Finally, in the afternoon of July 30, the consent of the tsar to general mobilization was obtained, and on the following morning public announcement of the mobilization was made. According to Russian army orders of 1912, mobilization was not the signal for beginning hostilities. Nevertheless, it was generally understood between the French and Russian experts that mobilization was equivalent to a declaration of war, and Great Britain had warned Russia as early as July 25 "that if Russia mobilized, Germany would not be content with mere mobilization or give Russia time to carry out hers, but would probably declare war at once." On July 30, France, her ally, had urged Russia to "take no immediate steps that may give Germany any pretext for the total or partial mobilization of her forces." Germany herself had warned Russia that mobilization was a highly dangerous form of diplomatic pressure since "the purely military consideration of the questions by the general staffs would find expression, and if that button were once touched in Germany, the situation would get out of control." Yet, despite all these warnings, and at a time when Germany was at length endeavoring to restrain her ally, and when the Kaiser and the tsar were in telegraphic communication, Russia proclaimed general mobilization.

Apparently Germany had at first decided to remain quiescent unless Russia actually attacked Austria-Hungary or actually commenced war preparations against herself. But Germany's chances for success in war depended upon rapidity of action, while Russia, because of her area and her deficient transportation facilities, needed time for mobilization and concentration of her troops. In the words of Jagow, German secretary for foreign affairs, Germany "had the speed and Russia had the numbers, and the safety of the German Empire forbade that Germany should allow Russia to bring up masses of troops from all parts of her wide dominions." The German military leaders naturally failed to see the wisdom of the tsar's suggestion that both Russia and Germany carry out their mobilizations without recourse to war, while the diplomats continued "to negotiate for the welfare of our two countries and the universal peace which is so dear to our hearts." Upon receiving news of Russia's general mobilization, therefore, Germany immediately proclaimed a "threatening state of war," and later the same day, upon the demand of Moltke, presented an ultimatum demanding that Russia stop every measure of war against Germany and against

Austria-Hungary within twelve hours, or German mobilization would follow. No answer was forthcoming, and on August 1 Germany declared war upon Russia.

The system of entangling alliances now began to operate, for Germany well understood that France was bound to come to the aid of Russia in just such a contingency as now existed. The German general staff had years before planned that in case of a war against Russia and France, Germany's first thrust must be against France because the latter could mobilize much more rapidly than Russia. With France defeated by an overwhelming attack, German forces could then turn against more slowly moving Russia. It was the essence of the German military plan, therefore, that attack on France should not be delayed. Germany could not wait for France to decide to attack in accordance with the latter's treaty obligations. As early as July 31 she inquired from France what course the latter would pursue in the event of war between Germany and Russia. It is now known that she was prepared to demand the handing over for the duration of the war of Toul and Verdun in case France promised neutrality. Even if the French government had aimed to stay neutral, this demand for the two fortresses would have forced France into the war, for no French government would have consented to hand over to the Germans the fortresses of Toul and Verdun, even temporarily. Germany had no opportunity to make her second demand, however, for on August 1 France replied that she would consult her own interests, and began to mobilize. On August 3 Germany declared war on France.

Meanwhile, on July 31 Great Britain had asked France and Germany whether, in case of war, they would engage to respect the neutrality of Belgium, and France had given the desired assurance. Germany, however, had declined to state her attitude. Both France and Germany had signed treaties to respect the neutrality of Belgium and Luxemburg, but, as pointed out above, German military leaders years before had decided that in order to crush France quickly it would be better to violate the neutrality of Belgium than to make a frontal attack on the French fortified eastern frontier. On August 2 German troops occupied Luxemburg despite the protests of that little state. On the same day Germany presented an ultimatum to Belgium demanding within twelve hours permission to move her troops across that country into France. She promised, if permission were granted, to guarantee Belgian independence and integrity and to pay an indemnity. On the other hand, she threatened that, if any resistance were encountered, she would treat Belgium as an enemy, and the "decision of arms" would determine her subsequent fate. Belgium refused to grant Germany's request and appealed at once to Great Britain for diplomatic support in upholding her neutrality. On August 4 German troops crossed the Belgian frontier, and Bethmann-Hollweg admitted to the Reichstag that "this is a breach of international law . . . the wrong we thereby commit we will try to make good as soon as our military aims have been attained."

The invasion of Belgium had its immediate effect in Great Britain, where up to this time public opinion had strongly opposed entrance into the war. Although Sir Edward Grey himself believed that Great Britain's interests demanded that she should range herself beside France and Russia if war came, the British cabinet was divided on the question. For a time, therefore, Great Britain kept her hands free and refused to commit herself regarding future action. On July 29 Bethmann-Hollweg made a strong bid for Great Britain's neutrality, promising that Germany if victorious would take no territory from France in Europe, would respect the neutrality of the Netherlands, and—if Belgium did not take sides against Germany—would respect her neutrality after the war. Grey's immediate reaction was that he could not for a moment entertain the chancellor's proposals.

Germany having failed in her effort to secure a promise of British neutrality, France next sought to attach Great Britain more closely to herself. On July 30 Cambon, the French ambassador at London, reminded Grey that their two countries had agreed in 1912 that, if peace was threatened, they would immediately discuss with each other what should be done. Cambon declared that now was the time for such discussions and suggested that the British government might promise to come to the aid of France in case of aggression by Germany. On the next day Grey stated that his government could not then give any pledge, and on August 1 he informed Cambon that "France must make her decision without reckoning on an assistance that we are not now in a position to promise."

On August 2, however, in view of Germany's declaration of war on Russia and her anticipated attack on France, Great Britain assured the latter that the British fleet would undertake to protect French coasts and shipping, should the German fleet come into the Channel or through the North Sea to attack them. This she did because as a result of her request in 1912 the French fleet was in the Mediterranean, and the northern and western coasts of France were undefended. Great Britain felt in honor bound to protect the latter, though the offer brought the resignation of two members of the cabinet.

On the following day came news of the German ultimatum to Belgium. This action threatened a cardinal principle of British foreign policy, namely, that the little countries across the narrow seas should not be absorbed by any great imperial system which might be hostile to Great Britain. In part because of this determination, Great Britain had fought against Louis XIV and Napoleon I, and had insisted during the Franco-German War that both sides respect Belgian neutrality. When, therefore, on August 4 news reached London that German troops had actually crossed the frontier into Belgium, Great Britain dispatched an ultimatum to Germany demanding assurance by midnight that Germany would respect Belgian neutrality. Germany, while admitting that Belgium's protest was just and that a wrong was being committed, refused on the ground that "necessity knows no law," and accused Great Britain of making war "just for a scrap of paper." The next day Great Britain announced that a state of war existed between herself and Germany.

By August 24 Austria-Hungary had declared war on Russia and Belgium; France and Great Britain had declared war on Austria; Serbia had declared war on Germany; and Montenegro had joined Serbia against Austria and Germany in another struggle to fulfill their common political aspirations. Early in September Russia, France, and Great Britain transformed their entente into a wartime alliance by signing the pact of London, in which each agreed not to conclude peace separately nor to demand peace terms without a previous agreement with the others.

## THE QUESTION OF WAR GUILT

Much time has been spent in trying to determine which country was primarily responsible for the outbreak of the World War. Probably no decision will ever be reached which will satisfy all.

It is obvious that the crisis of 1914 was precipitated as a consequence of propaganda carried on within the Dual Monarchy by Serbs who ardently sought to attain the national unification of all Yugoslavs. It is equally clear that fear of alienating the Magyars deterred the Habsburg government from giving the Yugoslavs within Austria-Hungary a place co-ordinate in political power with Austria and Hungary and led rather to repressive measures. The latter, in turn, made the Bosnians a fertile field for pro-Serbian propaganda, and from these disaffected Bosnians came the assassins of the archduke.

There is little doubt that after the assassination Count Berchtold and Conrad von Hötzendorf determined to end the Yugoslav menace by crushing Serbia with military force, and that Germany definitely encouraged Austria-Hungary to take military measures against the small Slav kingdom. It seems reasonable to believe that, if Austria-Hungary had not early in the crisis received this encouragement from Germany, she would never have dared to be so intransigent in the succeeding days. At the same time it is very clear that Russia, in order to thwart Austria's further advance into the Balkans, to enhance her own prestige, and to bring herself nearer the accomplishment of her "historic mission," was determined from the outset of the crisis to go to war if necessary to prevent Serbia from being weakened in her political sovereignty or territorial integrity. And early in the crisis Russia, in turn, was encouraged by the French government, which stated that it approved of Russia's stand and that it would give her loyal support.

Great Britain, while declining to commit herself to either set of powers, repeatedly sought, as in 1912–1913, to find some way out of the crisis short of war, and offered a number of plans for settlement. It appears, however, that on this occasion Germany did not co-operate with Great Britain so closely and so wholeheartedly as she had in the previous crisis. Nevertheless, it must be admitted that eventually—perhaps after it was too late to influence Russia effectively—Germany did apparently exert considerable pressure upon Austria-Hungary in favor of moderation and mediation. This is more than can be stated in regard to French influence upon Russia.

On the other hand, so far as mediation is concerned, both Russia and France appeared generally more willing to accept the various plans offered than did Austria-Hungary and Germany. Whether Russia's willingness to accept mediation was dictated by her belief that thus she might gain more time for her mobilization is not clear. What is clear, however, is the fact that Austria-Hungary steadily declined to accept any and all schemes for a pacific settlement of her dispute with Serbia, even when toward the end of the crisis her own ally, Germany, strongly urged her to accept, and even though she knew her attack on Serbia would probably precipitate a general war.

It is, of course, undisputed that Russia—perhaps seeing in Austria-Hungary's actions nothing but a determination to crush Serbia and in Germany's stand nothing but a decision to support her ally—was the first great power to order general mobilization with its inevitable fatal effect on the general staffs of all the other countries. On the other hand, it is perfectly evident that Germany was the first great power to declare war on another great power, thus automatically and unavoidably transforming the Austro-Serbian war into a great European conflict. There is so much evidence which may be used against at least four of the great powers that the decision as to primary responsibility seems to be largely a matter of arranging the evidence according to the already existing bias of each investigator.

Probably the truth is that each statesman and each country did about what could be expected under the circumstances, that the sole responsibility cannot be placed on any one person or state, that they were all being driven into the abyss of war by certain fundamental or underlying forces. Anyone who will carefully study the crisis cannot help seeing that those who directed the destinies of the nations were largely the victims of the forces about them. Nationalism, imperialism, militarism, and entangling alliances all played a part in the final denouement, and the development of a great war out of the crisis was made more easy and inevitable because the countries of Europe lived in a state of international anarchy.

## THE ALIGNMENT OF THE POWERS IN 1914

Two of the countries which were linked with Germany and Austria-Hungary did not join the Teutonic powers in the World War. Berchtold had not taken Italy into his confidence in respect to his plans for sending an ultimatum to Serbia, and thus antagonized Italy at the very outset. Immediately upon learning of the ultimatum, however, the latter began to demand compensation under Article 7 of the Triple Alliance [20] and intimated that the Trentino might be considered as acceptable. Although Germany urged Austria-Hungary to offer some compensation to Italy, Berchtold was reluctant to cede any Austrian territory. In view of the Habsburg foreign minister's attitude, Italy informed her allies, just before the outbreak of hostilities between Germany and Russia, that, since the impending war was aggressive on the part of the Dual Monarchy, Italy was released from her obligations to them under the terms of the Triple Alliance. Although Berchtold stated that Austria-Hungary would be willing to consider a partition of Albania if Italy would join the Teutonic powers, the Italian government on August 3, 1914, formally declared its neutrality.

The secret Franco-Italian treaty of 1902 [21] had provided that in just such a contingency as existed in August, 1914, Italy should remain neutral. Nevertheless, it was not Italy's treaty obligations that dictated her policy so much as what her prime minister, Salandra, called "sacred egoism." In this respect, of course, she differed little from the other powers. She had always feared to lay her coasts open to attack by the British navy; her own army and navy had not yet recovered from the exhausting struggle in Tripoli; and *Italia Irredenta,* which she longed to incorporate within her own frontiers, lay within the territory of Austria-Hungary. During the opening weeks of the war Italy continued to carry on negotiations with both sets of powers to determine what she could gain from each, but her neutrality during this period contributed very materially, if indirectly, to the German defeat on the Marne by releasing French troops from the southeast for use against Germany.

Even before the outbreak of the World War the Austrians had decided that, despite the treaty of 1883,[22] Rumania could hardly be counted a loyal ally. She was, of course, in an advantageous position to receive bids for her aid from both sets of powers during the crisis. Russia started by offering Transylvania and a guarantee of the territory in the Dobrudja which Rumania had recently taken from Bulgaria. Austria-Hungary countered by offering Bessarabia. Although King Carol apparently advocated Rumania's entrance into the war on the side of Austria in accordance with her treaty obligations, Rumanian statesmen preferred a policy of watchful waiting.

[20] For this article, see page 153.
[21] See page 160.          [22] See page 70.

On August 3 the crown council decided in favor of neutrality, but Rumania, like Italy, continued to negotiate with both sides. Eventually, in fact, Rumania and Italy agreed (September 23, 1914) to follow the same course during the war.

Before the year was over, however, each set of belligerents was reinforced by one more power. Early in August Great Britain asked Japan for assistance under the terms of the alliance concluded in 1902 and renewed in 1905 and 1911. Germany was already busy with warlike preparations in Kiaochow, her naval base in the Shantung peninsula, and her warships in the Far East constituted a serious menace to British commerce. One of the objects of the Anglo-Japanese alliance was the defense of the special interests of the contracting parties in eastern Asia, and Japan decided to comply with the British request and, if necessary, declare war upon Germany. Doubtless in reaching this decision Japan was more especially actuated by the desire to lessen by one the number of powers competing with her in the exploitation of China. On August 15, therefore, Japan sent an ultimatum to Germany demanding that the latter should withdraw all warships from Chinese and Japanese waters and deliver up the entire leased territory of Kiaochow before September 15 "with a view to the eventual restoration of the same to China." When Germany refused to comply with the demands of the ultimatum, Japan declared war on August 23.

The last country to be drawn into the conflict in 1914 was Turkey. In the years just preceding the World War, German influence—political, military, commercial, and financial—had steadily increased at Constantinople, so that it was almost inevitable that Turkey should enter the struggle on the side of the Teutonic powers. This was particularly likely in view of the fact that her traditional foe, Russia, was one of the Entente powers. Upon the assassination of the archduke the Ottoman government at once sought to connect itself with the Triple Alliance. The German government, at first reluctant to consider any definite commitment to Turkey, ultimately came to look with favor upon such an alliance; and a treaty, hurriedly drafted, was accordingly signed by Germany and Turkey on August 2 at the very height of the diplomatic crisis. Drawn up before the conflict had become one between the great powers, it provided that Turkey should enter the war on the side of the Teutonic powers in case Russia intervened.

While the Entente powers, unaware of this secret alliance, sought through diplomacy to secure Ottoman neutrality, the Turks utilized the weeks spent in futile negotiations to carry out extensive military preparations. Gradually Turkey's connection with the Teutonic powers became evident. Upon the outbreak of the war two German cruisers in the Mediterranean took refuge in the harbor at Constantinople. When their officers refused either to put to sea or to be interned, the Entente powers protested, but to no avail. Later in the year Turkey closed the Dardanelles to commerce, thereby cutting Russia's communication with the Mediterranean, and again protests had no effect. On October 29 one of the German cruisers, masquerading as a Turkish ship, shelled Russian towns on the Black Sea, and three Turkish torpedo boats raided the port of Odessa. In consequence Russia, on November 3, declared war on Turkey and was followed in this action two days later by both France and Great Britain. At the close of the year, therefore, the military alignment stood: Germany, Austria-Hungary, and Turkey against Russia, France, Great Britain, Japan, Belgium, Serbia, and Montenegro. The two conflicting groups soon came to be generally called the Central Powers and the "Allies."

## MOBILIZATION OF MEN AND RESOURCES

Even before the declarations of war were issued, mobilization of the various national armies had begun. In the belligerent countries on the Continent millions of men were under arms in time of peace, but they were scattered about the countryside and at the outbreak of the war had to be rushed to protect threatened frontiers or concentrated for the purpose of opening projected offensives. Other millions in the reserve armies had to be called to the colors. From the farm, the factory, the store, from every walk of life men were summoned for military service. The problem of transportation was tremendous; nonmilitary service on the railways was temporarily set aside as thousands of trains hurried men and supplies to the fronts.[23]

In a war where more ammunition was used in two weeks on some of the sectors than in the whole Boer War, the men at the front re-

[23] Of the principal belligerents, Great Britain alone had no system of conscription. Lord Kitchener, veteran of many wars, was appointed head of the war office, and immediately laid plans for creating an army of seventy divisions. In the World War British divisions consisted of about 15,000 men each; French and German, of about 12,000.

quired scores of thousands of field guns, hundreds of thousands of machine guns, millions of rifles, billions of shells, hundreds of billions of rounds of ammunition for small arms, besides high explosives, gases, airplanes, and tanks. Existing armament firms were not equipped for the tremendous demands made upon them. Old factories had to be extended, new ones built, and others converted into war work.[24] In Great Britain, especially, new factories had to be erected, new machine tools made and set up, material assembled, and labor gathered and instructed.

But the mobilization of resources was not limited to munitions. The millions at the front had also to be fed and clothed. Gradually agriculture, manufacture, transportation, and commerce became submilitary activities. As the military needs became more pressing, national boards were established, section after section of industry and transportation was brought under the direction of the governments, and standardization of products was introduced. In order to supply war requirements, production was diverted into new channels, new processes were initiated, wages and prices were fixed, strikes and lockouts were forbidden, and millions of women were mobilized for war work in factories.

The financing of the war was a task in itself and required sums far greater than any ever before raised. Eighty per cent of the total war expenditures was met by borrowing, the belligerent powers repeatedly resorting to great bond issues. National bonds were offered in amounts in some cases as low as ten dollars, and millions of people in each of the principal belligerent countries participated in the loans. Single issues were brought out and successfully floated which a few years earlier would have been considered impossible by even the best-informed financiers. Single loans of different governments ranged from $3,500,000,000 to nearly $7,000,000,000. Extensive advertising campaigns and methods of "high pressure" salesmanship were used to arouse the patriotism of those in a position to subscribe. For those who were unable to buy bonds except with borrowed money, special credit facilities were established. It

[24] A neutral observer, describing the situation in Berlin in December, 1914, wrote: "A talking machine factory is busy trimming shrapnel shells to prepare them for explosive filling; a piano factory makes cartridges; a bicycle factory turns out iron bedsteads for military hospitals; a wood-working establishment makes barracks to set up where wanted to accommodate prisoners of war; and a sewing machine factory is producing shrapnel."

soon became obvious that the prewar statements of financiers that it would be impossible for any country to finance a modern war for many weeks were in error. When the Central Powers finally collapsed, it was not because of lack of money but because of the lack of essential commodities.

## WAR PROPAGANDA

The prospect of a war in which the casualties might mount into the millions led each belligerent government to seek to throw the responsibility for the conflict solely upon its foes. Soon after the outbreak of hostilities each government published what purported to be the diplomatic documents exchanged during the crisis. These volumes, which took their names from the distinctive colors of their covers, became known as the white book (Germany), the blue book (Great Britain), the orange book (Russia), the red book (Austria-Hungary), and the yellow book (France), and are sometimes referred to as the "rainbow books." Of them all the British blue book was probably the most truthful and nearly complete. By each of the other great powers documents unfavorable to its own cause were frequently suppressed or altered in order to mold the minds of its own citizens as well as those of neutral countries.

Before the war was many months old, agencies were organized by most of the belligerent countries to carry on systematic campaigns of propaganda. These campaigns usually had at least three major objectives: (1) to keep up the morale of the country's own citizens so that they would willingly make the sacrifices of men and money which would be necessary in order to bring victory; (2) to gain the good will, benevolent neutrality, or active participation in the war of those neutral countries whose assistance would be valuable in winning the struggle; (3) to weaken or destroy the morale of the citizens of the enemy countries so that the latter would be seriously handicapped in their conduct of the war.

On both sides stories of atrocities were widely circulated. When actual atrocities were not available, stories were frequently fabricated to serve the same purpose. The treatment of Belgium by the Germans, their reference to treaties as "scraps of paper," and their destruction of the lives of women and children by submarine warfare were eagerly seized upon by Allied propagandists to arouse enthusiasm for the war at home and to turn sentiment against the Central

Powers in neutral countries. The severe hardships which fell upon the noncombatant population in the Teutonic countries as a result of the Allied blockade, on the other hand, were not so spectacular for propaganda purposes. Nor, apparently, did the Teutonic propagandists understand the psychology of the neutral peoples so well as did those of the Allies.

As the war progressed, each government sought to explain to the world and to its own people why it was fighting. In every case the war was defensive. The Germans, for example, were told that they were fighting to keep back the Slavic hordes of "freedom-slaying tsarism," whose triumph would bring the "end of the German people," that they were struggling to break the iron ring which the Allies had forged around Germany for the purpose of crushing the fatherland. The Allied peoples, on the other hand, were informed that they were fighting to protect the world from an aggressive and brutal militarism, to defend the sanctity of treaties and the rights of small nations. Eventually the Allied governments maintained that they were engaged in a "war to end war," a struggle "to make the world safe for democracy."

The mental state of the people of each of the belligerent great powers—the result of the efficient and widespread propaganda of their governments—is clearly and truly depicted by the writer of the following lines: [25]

> I was a peasant of the Polish plain;
> I left my plough because the message ran:
> Russia, in danger, needed every man
> To save her from the Teuton; and was slain.
>> I gave my life for freedom— This I know;
>> For those who bade me fight had told me so.
>
> I was a Tyrolese, a mountaineer;
> I gladly left my mountain home to fight
> Against the brutal treacherous Muscovite;
> And died in Poland on a Cossack spear.
>> I gave my life for freedom— This I know;
>> For those who bade me fight had told me so.

[25] "Five Souls," by W. N. Ewer, in *Quotable Poems*, Volume II, pages 121–122.

I worked at Lyons, at my weaver's loom,
When suddenly the Prussian despot hurled
His felon blow at France and at the world;
Then went I forth to Belgium and my doom.
    I gave my life for freedom— This I know;
    For those who bade me fight had told me so.

I owned a vineyard by the wooded Main,
Until the Fatherland, begirt by foes
Lusting her downfall, called me, and I rose,
Swift to the call; and died in fair Lorraine.
    I gave my life for freedom— This I know;
    For those who bade me fight had told me so.

I worked in a great shipyard by the Clyde,
There came a sudden word of wars declared,
Of Belgium peaceful, helpless, unprepared,
Asking our aid; I joined the ranks, and died.
    I gave my life for freedom— This I know;
    For those who bade me fight had told me so.

## CHAPTER XII

## THE PERIOD OF TEUTONIC ASCENDANCY

THE World War differed from previous conflicts not only in the gigantic size of the armies directly engaged and the appalling numbers of casualties suffered, but in the tremendous mobilization of men and resources behind the lines for war purposes. The struggle was not confined to the battlefields alone, but was waged in factories, laboratories, and banks, on farms, railways, and merchant ships. In the World War nations fought nations, and strained every nerve, utilized every resource for victory.

For waging the war each side had certain distinct advantages. To begin with, the Central Powers possessed a much closer unity of command than did the Allies. Almost from the opening gun, and certainly after 1916, Germany overshadowed her allies, whose plans she came to direct, whose armies her officers frequently came to command. Among the Allies, on the other hand, until the very closing months of the war, lack of unity existed, and diversity of plans and lack of co-ordination resulted. The Central Powers, too, possessed a distinctly strategic advantage in their geographical position. Its compactness and the splendid network of railways made possible the prompt and efficient transfer of troops from one military front to another. Without interference from the Allies, troops could readily be shifted from the German front in France to the Austrian front in Galicia or, after 1915, even to the Turkish front in Mesopotamia. The Allies, on the other hand, were widely separated geographically. From the beginning, Russia was almost completely isolated from her allies in the west. The resources of Great Britain's far-flung empire could be utilized only after they had been gathered from the seven seas and transported through the perils of the sea to the front where they were needed. Japan was thousands of miles from the main theaters of the war and confined her activities chiefly to the Far East.

Nevertheless, the Allies possessed several very important advantages, especially in case of a long war. They greatly outnumbered the Central Powers in man power and economic resources. If the war dragged on long enough to enable the Allies to tap their unlimited human reservoirs, the Central Powers might be overwhelmed by sheer weight of numbers. Especially was this true since the wealth of the Allies greatly exceeded the total wealth of the Central Powers. Moreover, the Allies possessed a naval supremacy which enabled them not only to marshal their own resources but to trade with neutral countries overseas. Thus they were able to utilize the food-producing and munition-producing facilities existing in extensive regions outside their own frontiers. At the same time Allied naval supremacy brought with it the power to blockade the coast lines of the Central Powers and, to a large extent, force them to depend on their own resources for the sinews of war. Throughout the conflict the Allies cheered themselves with the thought that time was on their side.

## The Breakdown of German Plans for 1914

But Germany did not intend that the war should be of long duration. She aimed to strike a decisive blow at France immediately, then to wheel upon the slower-moving Russians and to defeat them in more leisurely fashion. With this end in view the "Schlieffen plan" called for the delivery of the blow not on the Franco-German frontier, which was lined with impregnable fortresses and defended by the Vosges Mountains, but through the neutral buffer states of Luxemburg and Belgium. The best railways and roads from Berlin to Paris ran through Belgium, and the French fortifications on this frontier were feeble compared with those at Belfort, Toul, and Verdun. The plan, therefore, held out the promising possibility of rolling up the French left by a wide encircling movement.[1]

On August 5 German troops attacked the Belgian fortified city of Liége, and, though temporarily halted by the stubborn defense of the Belgian army, they entered the city two days later. For a week longer some of the outlying forts held out, but on August 15 the last of them was captured, and German troops poured into the country in overwhelming numbers. On August 23 the Germans won the first resounding success of the war when they captured the reputedly impregnable fortress of Namur after a three days' bombardment by heavy howitzers. The way was at length cleared for a

[1] For the French front, see the maps on pages 398, 457, and 473.

German invasion of France, but, because of Belgian resistance, eighteen days had been required for the march to the French frontier.

Meanwhile the French and British prepared to meet the German advance. France had failed to concentrate her forces on the Belgian frontier and so was now faced with the necessity of shifting some of her armies to that front. The British Expeditionary Force crossed the Channel without mishap and on August 22 took up positions on the French left in accordance with prearranged plans. But French fighting at Charleroi and British at Mons failed to stop the German advance, and the Allied armies began a general strategic retreat. The Germans disregarded the Channel ports, which might easily have been seized at this time, and rushed on toward Paris, their goal.

Not until September 5, at the very gates of Paris, did Joffre give up his Fabian policy of retreat. On the next day came his order "to attack and repel the enemy." For seven days (September 6–12) the first battle of the Marne raged over a front extending from Paris to Belfort, engaging more than two millions of men. But now, at length, Germany's long-planned scheme broke down under the burden of overworked troops and the impossible task of co-ordination and control which was placed on general headquarters. In the end—thanks to Joffre's strategy and the heroic efforts of Gallieni, Foch, Castelnau, and others—Paris was saved, the first German plan of campaign was wrecked, and the forces which were to have crushed France in a month were hurled back.

The main German armies now retreated to a strong position on the river Aisne, where trenches had been prepared for the infantry and concrete foundations for the big guns. From this position the Allies were unable to dislodge them in the first battle of the Aisne. Meanwhile, the lines of both armies were extended westward and northward, the French in an effort to outflank the Germans, the latter in an effort to protect themselves and to seize the Channel ports. Though the Germans succeeded in occupying Ghent, Bruges, and the coast towns of Zeebrugge and Ostend, their attempt to push on to Dunkirk, Calais, and Boulogne was thwarted by the determined resistance of the Allies, especially the British in the terrible first battle of Ypres. Thereafter the conflict in the west ceased to be a war of movement and maneuver, and settled down to trench warfare over a line extending some six hundred miles from the Channel to the Alps.

Although the Germans had failed to carry through their plans in the west, they had made conquests which were later of tre-

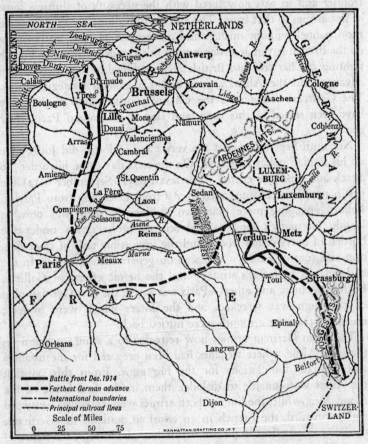

THE WESTERN FRONT IN 1914

mendous assistance to them in carrying on the war. They were in complete possession of most of Belgium and of a fairly large strip of northern France. These regions of Europe were highly developed industrially and were now added to the resources of the Central

THE GERMAN HIGH COMMAND

Hindenburg, William II, Ludendorff.

Powers. Especially valuable to Germany were the coal fields of Belgium and northern France and the iron mines of French Lorraine. In proportion as the Central Powers were strengthened by these conquests, France and the Allies were weakened. In fact, had the paths of commerce not been kept open for France by the British navy, it is difficult to see how the French could long have waged an effective war.

Meanwhile in the east, the Russian armies were mobilized more rapidly than Germany had expected. Even before German troops had reached the French frontier through Belgium, Russian soldiers were pouring into East Prussia and threatening Königsberg.[2] Russia was jubilant. In St. Petersburg the sum of $100,000 was raised to be given to the first Russian soldier to enter Berlin. In alarm, the German government summoned from retirement General Paul von Hindenburg, reputed to be a specialist in the strategy and geography of a war with Russia, and appointed General Ludendorff, chief quartermaster of the Second Army in the west, as chief of the general staff of the Eighth Army in the east, with Hindenburg in command. The battle of Tannenberg which followed (August 26–31) put an end to Russian plans in East Prussia even more completely than the Marne did to German plans in the west. The bulk of the Russian army in this area was captured or destroyed; less than a third escaped. Hindenburg at once became the popular idol of the Central Powers.

But one defeat, no matter how decisive, did not mean that Russia was out of the war. Her man power was so great that she had planned to press her attack on more than one front. Simultaneously with her advance into East Prussia came her drive against the Austrians in Galicia. By September 3 the Russians had captured not only the outposts at Tarnopol and Halicz but Lemberg, the capital of Galicia, also. They then promptly followed up their victory by driving the Austrians back into Jaroslav and Przemysl. To the latter, a strongly fortified city, the Russians laid siege; the former they captured on September 23. By the end of the year Russia was in complete occupation of nearly all of Galicia.

Russian successes in Galicia interfered disastrously with the Habsburg plan to punish Serbia in 1914. Austria opened the war by bombarding Belgrade on July 29, and thrice attempted a conquest of the kingdom. Although in their third attempt the Austrians suc-

[2] For the Russian front, see the map on page 405.

ceeded in capturing Belgrade (December 2), they had held it less than two weeks when a crushing defeat at the hands of the Serbs and Montenegrins drove them out of the country. The year ended with not a single Austrian soldier on Serbian soil. But, on the other hand, Serbia's attempts to "liberate" her kinsmen in Bosnia-Herzegovina from Habsburg control had likewise met disaster. For the next few months the Austro-Serbian front was comparatively inactive.

But fighting was not restricted to Europe. Great Britain was not in a position in 1914 to be of great assistance to her allies with her armies, but she played a vital role with her fleets. Almost immediately her naval superiority swept Germany's merchant marine from the seas, and thus largely prevented the latter from importing foodstuffs and munitions of war and from marketing her products. Furthermore, the British navy, by hunting down and destroying isolated German warships, by forcing others into neutral ports, where they were interned, and by blockading the German battle squadron in its own home waters, gradually cleared the seas of these threats to Allied shipping, and made possible the gathering of Allied troops and supplies from the uttermost parts of the earth. All this was not done without some losses, however. At least ten British warships were sunk in 1914 by German submarines and mines. A number of minor naval engagements also occurred. Off the coast of Chile near Coronel (November 1, 1914), a superior German fleet defeated a British squadron, sinking two ships; but a few weeks later (December 8) a more powerful British squadron sighted the same German fleet off the Falkland Islands and destroyed every ship but one.

Not only on the seas but overseas events went against Germany, owing largely to the fact that the British navy made it impossible for her to send assistance to her colonies. Immediately after her declaration of war on Germany, Japan had begun a blockade of Kiaochow; a few days later troops were landed and a siege was begun. By November 6, 1914, the forts had been silenced, and on the tenth the German base was surrendered to Japan. By this time, too, Germany's various island possessions in the Pacific had been captured by Japanese or British colonial forces. In Africa, where the chief German colonies were located, operations were begun by Allied forces, and Togoland was soon conquered by Anglo-French armies. The other colonies held out longer, but it was only a question of time until they too would be captured.[3]

## GERMAN SUCCESSES OF 1915

In 1914 it had been Germany that had taken the offensive against France; in 1915, upon Russia's suggestion, Great Britain and France decided to undertake an offensive at the Dardanelles.[4] A successful outcome here would be especially advantageous for the Allies. In the first place, it would open a much desired communication with Russia from the Mediterranean and would relieve her from Turkish pressure on the Caucasian front. It would diminish the danger of attack on the Suez Canal and Egypt. Obviously, it would isolate Turkey from her allies and at the same time cut Germany's proposed Berlin-Bagdad railway. Finally, a decisive Allied victory here might have considerable influence in converting Greece, Rumania, or Bulgaria to the Allied cause.

The first plan called for a naval attack on the Dardanelles in the hope of forcing the heavily fortified strait. For this purpose a powerful fleet of British and French battleships was gathered, and on February 19, 1915, they began a heavy bombardment of the forts at the entrance to the Dardanelles. These forts were more or less in the nature of outposts and were soon silenced. But when, on March 18, the Allied fleet attempted to force the narrows, powerful guns on shore and floating mines in the strait wrought havoc among the ships. The Allies were forced to retire with a loss of three battleships and two thousand men.

It was next decided that the strait must be opened by troops rather than ships. Unable to persuade any of the Balkan states to espouse their cause, the Allies were forced to provide an army of their own. At length a force made up chiefly of Australian, New Zealand, Indian, and French colonial troops was gathered together for the purpose. On April 25 the Allied troops began their Gallipoli campaign, forcing a landing on the peninsula at terrible cost. But the Turks had used the interval since the naval failure at the Dardanelles to strengthen the fortifications on the hills, so that the Allied soldiers were called upon to drive from almost impregnable

---

[3] German Southwest Africa was conquered in 1915, Kamerun in 1916, and German East Africa finally on November 14, 1918, after the signing of the armistice.

[4] See the map on page 353.

positions a much stronger Turkish army under the command of a skillful German general. The Allies had expected that Russia would help divide the Turkish forces by landing 100,000 men from the Black Sea and seizing the northern outlet of the Bosporus, but this she was prevented from doing by a terrific Austro-German attack near Gorlice.[5] Three costly attempts to capture the peninsula netted the Allies nothing but the loss of some 55,000 men. The strait remained closed until the end of the war.

While the Dardanelles and Gallipoli campaigns were being waged, it had been hoped that Italy might be persuaded to join the Allies and not only relieve Russia by engaging Austrian troops in the south but also contribute some forces for use against Turkey. At the time of the outbreak of the war in 1914 Italy, as already pointed out, proclaimed her neutrality on the ground that the Central Powers were waging an offensive war and also on the ground that Austria-Hungary had not lived up to Article 7 of the Triple Alliance.[6] Even as early as the crisis of 1914 Italy had sought to obtain part of *Italia Irredenta* by demanding compensation of Austria in accordance with this article. Austria, however, had refused to discuss the question. On February 21, 1915, Italy forbade further Austrian operations in the Balkans until an agreement had been reached, and Austria on March 9 finally announced that she was willing to discuss the cession of territory. Then followed a period of bargaining, for, late in February, the Allies also began to offer Italy inducements to join them against the Central Powers. Naturally, the advantage in the bidding lay with the Allies, for they could generously offer Italy larger slices of Austrian territory than Austria herself was disposed to concede.

On April 26, 1915, Great Britain, France, and Russia signed with Italy the secret treaty of London. In this treaty the Allies promised Italy the Trentino and southern Tirol up to the Brenner Pass, Gorizia and Gradisca, Trieste and the Istrian peninsula, North Dalmatia and the islands facing it, Avlona and a military zone about it, the Dodecanese in the Aegean, rights to the province of Adalia in case Turkey should be partitioned or divided into spheres of influence, and the extension of her possessions in Eritrea, Somaliland, and Libya in case Great Britain and France should gain colonial

---

[5] See page 404.
[6] For this article, see page 153.

territory in Africa at the expense of Germany. The Allies further promised Italy a loan, a share in the war indemnity, and their support in preventing the pope from taking any diplomatic steps for the conclusion of peace or the regulation of questions arising from the war.

On May 23 Italy declared war on Austria, but not until fifteen months later did she declare war on Austria's more powerful ally. On September 5, 1915, she signed the pact of London, further binding herself not to make peace except in concert with the Allies. But the military hopes of the latter, based on Italy's entrance into the war, were sadly disappointed in 1915. Italy sent no troops to aid in the Gallipoli campaign, asserting, like France, that they could not be spared from the home front. Furthermore, in spite of her field army of a million and her reserve force of two million, Italy's attacks along the Isonzo and in the Trentino made little headway because of the difficult terrain [7] and apparently contributed not at all to relieving the increasing Teutonic pressure on Russia.

And Russia, by this time, was in need of all the assistance she could get. At the opening of the year her prospects had, indeed, looked bright. During the preceding months she had occupied nearly all of Galicia, and on March 22, 1915, she had finally captured the powerful Austrian fortress of Przemysl, besieged since the preceding November. In Allied countries it was believed that the year would see Russian troops pouring over the Carpathians on to the Hungarian plains. By 1915, however, Russia's supply of munitions was getting low, and the possibilities of adequate replenishment were scant. Russia was primarily a peasant country; her factories for the manufacture of munitions were few; and her means of importing and transporting war material to the front were inadequate. Corruption, too, had already begun to undermine her armies and to sap their strength.

On the other hand, the Central Powers were generously supplied with heavy guns, shells, rifles, and other war material. This year, trusting the trench system to hold with fewer men in the west, they transferred thousands of seasoned German troops to the east until, by April, 1915, they had a combined Austro-German army of two million men, with heavy batteries numbering at least 1500 guns. This force, which was probably the strongest that had ever been

[7] For the Italian front, see the map on page 435.

placed under one German commander, they entrusted to General Mackensen. Suddenly, on May 1, the tables were turned on the eastern front; Russia ceased to be the attacker and became the attacked. The heavy Teutonic batteries were loosed against the Russian lines near Gorlice in Galicia, and the Russian trenches were simply blown out of existence. The Russians, inadequately equipped with heavy guns, could not check the attack. With the capture of Gorlice, their defense collapsed. In less than two months nearly all of Galicia, with its oil wells, mines, and other resources, was regained by the Central Powers. With it, too, came the temporary abandonment by Rumania of her thought of joining the Allies.

But the reconquest of Galicia was only one phase of the projected Austro-German campaign to put the Russian armies out of action. Success in this phase, however, rendered the next step more easy, for the Russian armies in Poland were now open to attack from both the north and the south. Pressure from both directions was brought to bear by the Central Powers, whose consistent successes led, on August 4, to the Russian evacuation of Warsaw and Ivangorod. Not content with the capture of these strongholds, the Teutonic troops pushed on, taking Kovno, Brest-Litovsk, Grodno, Pinsk, and Vilna, finally driving the Russians behind the Pripet marshes. With winter coming on, the Central Powers had no desire to court the fate of Napoleon, so they now halted their advance. At the close of the campaign, therefore, the Central Powers had driven the Russians out of most of Galicia, all of Poland and Courland, and part of Lithuania. Thanks largely to the masterly retreat conducted by Grand Duke Nicholas, the Teutonic forces had neither captured nor destroyed the Russian armies: but they had rolled them back a safe distance and had undoubtedly put them temporarily out of action.

By September, 1915, the Central Powers were free to look for other fields to conquer. As a result of their campaigns against Russia they had shortened and straightened their eastern front so that they could now hold that advanced position with fewer men than the old line required. The developments on the western front during the year had proved that the German entrenched positions there could not be broken by the Allies with the men and munitions which they then had at their disposal. Italy's efforts along the Isonzo and in the Trentino were being defeated largely by the terrain. In these circumstances, the Central Powers determined to administer to Serbia her long-delayed chastisement. Much was hoped from a decisive success in this part of Europe. It was expected to remove the Yugoslav danger and the threat to Austria's flank, to insure the

THE EASTERN FRONT IN 1915

safety of the Dardanelles and the final isolation of Russia, to open new possibilities of operations in Asiatic Turkey, to affect the attitude of Rumania, and finally to increase the supply of foodstuffs and copper for the Central Powers. Before the end of August the

Central Powers had begun to shift troops from the Russian to the Serbian front.

Meanwhile, under pressure from Teutonic general headquarters negotiations were being pushed with Bulgaria looking toward her joining the Central Powers in the contemplated attack upon Serbia. It proved to be not particularly difficult to win this country to the cause of the Central Powers, for in 1915 the latter seemed to be the winning combination in the war, and the territory which Bulgaria desired to annex in Macedonia lay chiefly within the Serbian frontiers. At length, on September 3, a military convention was signed, according to which the Central Powers and Bulgaria were to have their troops on the Serbian frontier ready for operations early in October, and General Mackensen, who had been largely responsible for the German success at Gorlice, was to take supreme charge of all troops. Bulgaria promised to allow absolutely unrestricted transport of Teutonic troops and material to and from Turkey as soon as the way through Serbia should be open; while Germany, on the other hand, agreed to grant Bulgaria a loan and to supply her with munitions to the extent that her own needs would permit. Bulgaria was to receive Serbian Macedonia; Saloniki and Epirus, in case Greece joined the Allies; and a large portion of the Dobrudja, if Rumania attacked her. Furthermore, in order to neutralize possible offers of the Allies, the Central Powers compelled the Ottoman government to promise Bulgaria territory in eastern Thrace. The Bulgarians had never been satisfied with the boundary between their country and Turkey as drawn in 1913.

On October 7 the forces of the Central Powers crossed the Danube into Serbia. Four days later the Bulgarians crossed the eastern frontier, striking the Serbians on the flank. The latter were overwhelmingly outnumbered in men and material, and within the next two months Belgrade, Nish, Novibazar, Prisrend, and Monastir were taken by the Central Powers. The Serbian army, reduced to scattered bands of retreating refugees, fled into Montenegro and Albania. But even there they found no safety, for the Austrians pushed on into the former and completely conquered it. By the end of February, 1916, Austrian and Bulgarian forces had expelled the Serbs and Montenegrins from northern Albania, capturing Tirana, the capital, and Durazzo, one of the chief Adriatic ports. Only on the Greek island of Corfu, where they were protected by Allied naval batteries, did the Yugoslavs eventually find a safe refuge from the Central Powers.

The Allied attempt to come to the aid of Serbia had been an inglorious failure. Trusting until too late that Bulgaria would not join the Central Powers or that, if she did, Greece would carry out her part of the Greco-Serbian alliance,[8] the Allies had made no preparations to aid Serbia before September, 1915. As soon as Bulgaria actually mobilized, Greece did likewise, and the Greek premier, Venizelos, asked the Allies to send a force of 150,000 men to co-operate with Greece in support of Serbia. But King Constantine later decided that the interests of Greece could best be served by neutrality, dismissed Venizelos, and refused to enter the war. The Allied forces which landed at Saloniki on October 5 were not only too few to render effective aid to Serbia; they were so few that their own position soon became precarious in view of the successes of the Central Powers. After repeated and loud appeals for help from General Sarrail at Saloniki, the Allies eventually permitted the forces at Gallipoli to be transferred from that disastrous venture to one which, till that moment, had been only a little less disastrous.

Not only on land but on the sea as well Germany launched an offensive in 1915. Her naval leaders, during the early part of the war, held the view that an offensive by the German battle fleet was advisable only under extraordinarily favorable circumstances because the risk of a decisive action against the infinitely superior naval forces of the Allies was too great. An offensive with a view to forcing a decision by this means was therefore not undertaken. The Allies, however, were using their naval superiority to prevent the importation of war materials by the Central Powers, whose merchant ships had been swept from the seas. Great Britain not only seized and searched neutral vessels which might be carrying contraband, but gradually extended the definition of contraband. The United States, the chief neutral country of the world, was concerned with preserving open routes to the neutral countries of Europe and

---

[8] In 1913 Greece and Serbia had signed a treaty and military convention in which it was provided that "in case of a sudden attack by . . . the Bulgarian army against the Hellenic or Serbian army, the two states . . . promise to each other mutual military support, Greece with all her land and sea forces, and Serbia with all her land forces." Constantine maintained that this applied only to a Balkan war, not to a general European war.

an open market in Europe for noncontraband goods, and accordingly proposed that the declaration of London (1909) regarding contraband should be generally accepted. This declaration had left such articles as copper and rubber on the noncontraband list and would have permitted the importation of foodstuffs by the Central Powers. But Great Britain had never ratified this declaration and refused the American suggestion.

Early in 1915, therefore, Germany decided upon the unrestricted use of submarines against all vessels of the Allied countries. Her naval staff believed that the submarines would prevent Great Britain from bringing her military forces to play on the Continent to the same extent as hitherto, and that this would have the effect of breaking the fighting spirit of the other members of the Entente. Accordingly, on February 4, 1915, Germany designated the waters about the British Isles as a "war zone" in which enemy merchantmen would be sunk, and in which even neutral merchantmen might accidentally suffer a like fate. This step she justified on the ground of self-preservation and as a justifiable countermeasure against "the war of starvation which had been initiated against the noncombatant population of Germany" by Great Britain's classifying as contraband all foodstuffs intended for consumption in that country.

In response to an American note on the subject, Germany asserted that, if Great Britain would permit the importation of food and raw materials in accordance with the declaration of London, Germany would abandon her unrestricted submarine campaign. Great Britain, while willing to permit the importation of food in case Germany lifted the submarine blockade, refused to allow the importation of raw materials, and announced on March 1 that she intended to intercept all overseas trade with Germany, to detain all goods, and to bring neutrals into British ports for search. The situation for neutrals came to resemble that at the time of the British and Napoleonic decrees in the early years of the nineteenth century. Anti-British feeling which was rising in the United States subsided, however, when a German submarine sank without warning the great British liner *Lusitania,* with a loss of some twelve hundred lives, of which over one hundred were American. The fact that the ship was carrying cases of munitions for the Allies (denied at the time) in no way lessened the horror which the deed evoked, and a wave of anti-German sentiment swept over the United States.

Within a week an American note demanded that Germany disavow the sinking, make reparation, and take immediate steps to prevent the recurrence of such acts. When the German government sought to extenuate the tragedy, a second American note convinced Bethmann-Hollweg that the United States was determined to resist the submarine campaign as then being waged. Allied countermeasures, moreover, and the scarcity of submarines had prevented the campaign from exerting any perceptible influence on Great Britain's warlike operations. Germany therefore decided that the slight results did not warrant a policy which might bring the United States into the war, and ordered her submarine commanders to cease attacking passenger vessels. No public announcement of this decision was made at the time, however. It was only in September that Count Bernstorff, German ambassador to the United States, promised that liners would not be sunk without warning by German submarines, provided the liners did not try to escape or offer resistance.[9] Although nearly a thousand Allied and neutral ships were put out of use by the submarine campaign during 1915, Germany's counter-offensive on the seas during this year was a failure and was so recognized by German headquarters.

Teutonic achievements in 1914 and 1915, however, had done much to realize the German dream of a *Mittel-Europa* and a *Drang nach Osten*. The industrial regions of Belgium and northern France, Poland, parts of Lithuania and the Baltic provinces, Serbia, Montenegro, and northern Albania had all been successively conquered and held. Bulgaria and Turkey had become subsidiary allies, and the latter's repulse and final capture (Kut-el-Amara, April 29, 1916) of the British force which, under General Townshend, had attempted to conquer Bagdad, augured well for the future. All that seemed to remain to be done was to defeat decisively the Allied forces in the west, and then dictate a peace commensurate with Teutonic achievements. German headquarters clearly realized that Germany could not be content to stand on the defensive, because the Allies, thanks to their superiority in men and material, were increasing their resources much more than the Central Powers. If this situation

---

[9] Early in 1916 the German government finally expressed regret for the death of Americans caused by the sinking of the *Lusitania*, recognized Germany's liability therefor, and promised reparation by the payment of an indemnity.

continued, the time would come when the balance of numbers itself would deprive Germany of all remaining hope. The German people, too, were growing impatient of victories which brought no decision in the war. A decisive blow must therefore be struck in 1916.

### German Failure to End the War in 1916

During the winter of 1915–1916 the Teutonic powers considered which of the principal Allies should be their victim. Austria pressed for an overwhelming Austro-German attack upon Italy, but German headquarters vetoed this proposal, pointing out that victory on this front would aid only Austria and not influence the war as a whole, that it would have no effect on the attitude of France and Great Britain. Besides, it was argued, domestic conditions in Italy would soon make her further active participation in the war impossible. The same argument held good for Russia, whose rapidly multiplying domestic difficulties were expected to force her to give in within a relatively short time. The western front was therefore chosen as the area of attack, but one more decision remained to be made. Should the German forces be hurled against British or French sectors? A drive against the British was finally discountenanced because there was no good objective within reasonable reach. The German goal would have to be nothing less than the complete expulsion of the British from the Continent, and unless that were attained the attack would have been useless. Furthermore, Germany felt quite sure that even this achievement would not put Great Britain out of the war.

The French lines in the west, therefore, were finally chosen for the decisive campaign of 1916, and Verdun was selected as the object of attack. The French lines at this point were only about ten miles from the German railway communications. An Allied drive here might conceivably render the whole German front in France and Belgium untenable. Furthermore, the German leaders felt that France had already strained herself almost to the breaking point; the breaking point might be reached if Germany could convince the French that in a military sense they had no further ground for hope. Verdun was an objective for the retention of which the French would be compelled to throw in every man they had. If they did so, Germany argued, the forces of France would bleed to death; if they did not do so, and Germany captured the city, the effect on

French morale would be disastrous. Finally, one of the prime purposes of the campaign was to lure the Allies into a counterstroke. German headquarters realized that the Allies were preparing to make simultaneous advances on all fronts in 1916, and greatly feared the consequences. They confidently expected that the terrific German drive on Verdun would frustrate this plan by provoking the Allies into a premature counteroffensive. This in turn would wreck the scheme for a great simultaneous advance and enable the Central Powers to defeat it piecemeal.

On February 21 the German attack was opened by a bombardment even more terrific than that which had preceded the campaign against Russia in the spring of 1915. "For twelve and a half hours guns of every calibre poured 100,000 shells per hour on a front of six miles. History had never seen so furious a fire. It blotted out the French first lines, it shattered the communication trenches, it tore the woods into splinters, and altered the very shape of the hills." [10] Then, after scouts had ascertained that the bombardment had accomplished its work of destruction, after the German guns had changed their range and placed a "curtain of fire" behind the French trenches, the German infantry at a quarter to five in the evening moved forward and occupied the French first line with comparative safety. The Germans expected to be in Verdun in four days.

But the Germans had miscalculated the date of their entrance into Paris in 1914; they soon discovered that they had again erred in 1916. Pétain, who had been successful in conducting French offensives at Arras and in Champagne in 1915, was immediately put in command, and reinforcements were rushed to the scene. Responding to the battle cry, "They shall not pass," the French held on while the conflict raged back and forth about the city. With only a slight slackening of effort on either side, the struggle continued through March, April, and May. With a determination little less than that of the French, the German troops fought doggedly on toward their objective. In June, when the Germans got within four miles of the city, even Joffre doubted whether Verdun could be held. But the French struck back and on June 30 recovered ground and neutralized the German advantage. On the following day the British launched a drive on the Somme, and the center of activity shifted farther to the west, where the Germans, in turn,

[10] J. Buchan, *A History of the Great War*, Volume II, pages 547–548.

were now forced to stand on the defensive. Intermittent fighting continued in the Verdun sector during the summer and fall, but for all practical purposes the battle of Verdun was ended.

The outcome was a distinct victory for the French. The Germans had failed to achieve any of the results which they had expected from their attack. They had not broken the French front, nor entered the city of Verdun, nor bled France to death. They had not even lured the British into a premature offensive, as they had hoped. They had won a few square miles of territory, but the price they had paid in the irreparable loss of troops was out of all proportion to the gain which they had made. Fighting against the French in the west, they discovered, was quite different from fighting against an ill-equipped foe in the east. Falkenhayn was dismissed, and Hindenburg was elevated to the supreme command of the German armies, with Ludendorff as his assistant.

While the struggle for Verdun was in progress, the most important naval engagement of the war was fought in the North Sea. As already pointed out, German naval policy was not to risk a decisive action until, by the process of attrition, British forces had been so weakened as to give the German fleet good prospects of victory. With a view to destroying part of the British fleet, Vice-Admiral Hipper with scouting forces was ordered to demonstrate off the southwest coast of Norway in the hope of luring a British squadron out. The German battle fleet, under Vice-Admiral Scheer, was to remain out of sight until the British squadron appeared, when it would rush in to annihilate it. Early in the morning of May 31 the German fleet sailed forth.

Unknown to the Germans, however, the British battle fleet on May 30 was ordered to concentrate in the North Sea. Early in the following afternoon the British scouting squadron under Vice-Admiral Beatty and the German squadron under Hipper made contact. The latter, hoping to draw the British on, fell back toward the German battle fleet some fifty miles distant. A running engagement occurred until Beatty discovered that he had encountered the more powerful German battle fleet, whereupon the British light squadron turned and attempted to draw the Germans toward the British high-seas fleet. Late in the afternoon the latter came in sight and succeeded in placing itself between the German fleet and its home base. The scene seemed to be set for a gigantic naval engagement, more than 250 ships being present in the two fleets.

But the German fleet maneuvered with the sole object of avoiding an engagement and returning to its base. This the British prevented so long as it was light, and planned on a decisive engagement on the following day. During the night, however, the German fleet managed to cut its way through a weaker section of the British battle line, and returned to Helgoland. The question of victory was a matter of dispute at the time, and the battle of Jutland is still being fought by experts. Nevertheless, although the British lost fourteen ships to the Germans' eleven and suffered more than twice as many casualties, they were left in control of the sea. Only once afterward did the German high-seas fleet venture forth from its base, and then, upon being warned of the approach of the British battle fleet, it at once fled.

Meanwhile, although German headquarters had vetoed the Austrian suggestion of a combined Austro-German attack upon Italy when the proposal had been made during the preceding winter, the Austrian general staff determined to carry out the plan with its own resources. It chose as its point of attack the salient of the Trentino, which ran down to the Lombard plain, threatening the Italian left flank. The Austrian objective was to be the Venetian plain, through which ran the two railway lines which were the main communications with the Isonzo front. If they could cut one, the Isonzo army would be crippled and compelled to retreat; if both, it might be pocketed and disastrously defeated. For the projected drive a force of about 400,000 men was gathered in the Trentino and placed under the command of Archduke Charles, heir apparent to the Habsburg thrones.

On May 14 the preliminary bombardment began with over two thousand guns on a thirty-mile front. The Italians fell back, suffering heavy casualties. Cadorna, commander-in-chief of the Italian armies, immediately summoned his reserves to assemble around Vicenza, a stronghold protecting the northern railway line to the east, but the transfer of a new army of nearly a half million from the reserve lines of the Isonzo required time. The Italian brigades strove heroically to hold back the Austrians in the ensuing days, in some places sacrificing more than half of their strength. Nevertheless, on June 4 the Austrian troops were only eighteen miles from Vicenza. But by this time Cadorna had received his reinforcements, and soon thereafter the Italian troops repulsed what proved to be the last of the great Austrian attacks. Within a few days Cadorna began to move forward in a counterstroke. The Austrian plan to force the retirement or capture of the Italian army on the Isonzo front had failed.

One of the chief reasons why the Austrians were forced to relax their efforts against the Italians in the Trentino was the unexpected launching of a Russian attack on the eastern front on June 4. The Austrian lines in the east had been weakened not only by the withdrawal of troops for use in the Trentino offensive but by the withdrawal of artillery as well. When, therefore, the Russians suddenly attacked along almost the entire front from the Pripet marshes southward to Rumania, they met relatively little resistance. Near Lutsk they broke through the Austrian lines and within two days opened a gap fully thirty miles wide. By June 16, in twelve days of fighting in this vicinity, they had taken Lutsk and Dubno, had advanced some fifty miles from their original lines, and had reached the Galician frontier. Thousands of men had been captured, together with numerous guns and great quantities of war material. Meanwhile, in Bukowina, Czernowitz had been taken on June 10; and a week later the Russians were in possession of most of the province.

The Russian headquarters had not anticipated such a sweeping success, however, and failed to have at hand adequate reserves to take advantage of their opportunity. Teutonic forces were rushed to the threatened area from the French, Italian, and Balkan fronts, and Austrian operations were put more completely under the control of German headquarters. Opposed by German and more trustworthy Austrian divisions, the Russian advance slackened. Some Russian gains were made during July and August, but by the middle of the latter month the drive had spent itself, and it came to an end principally for lack of war materials with which to carry it on. Nevertheless, the effect of the Russian drive had been favorably felt by Allied armies before Verdun, on the Somme, in the Trentino, and along the Isonzo.

Just before the conclusion of the Russian offensive, the Italians succeeded in pushing back the Austrians a safe distance in the

Trentino, and then transferred their heavy guns to the Isonzo front, where they launched an attack on August 4. Five days later, in spite of stubborn resistance by the Austrians on the heights beyond the river, Gorizia fell and the immediate Italian objective was attained. Because of the difficult terrain in which they operated, however, they were still a long way from capturing the coveted port of Trieste.

By now the western front was once more ablaze, this time the Allies taking the offensive. The British had chosen to wait until ample reserves of troops and munitions were at hand for a prolonged effort. In the first months of the Verdun drive, therefore, no great counterblow was delivered on the western front, much to the consternation of German headquarters. But when, at length, Italy had checked the Austrians in the Trentino, the Russians had put nearly half a million Austrians out of action by their unexpected drive in the east, and the British forces were well equipped with all the materials of war and thousands of reserve troops,[11] then, finally, the Allies determined to make a supreme effort in the west, and chose as their field of operations the valley of the Somme.

The aims of the Allies were threefold: to relieve the prssure on Verdun; to prevent the transfer of large bodies of troops from the western front to meet the Russian advance in the east; to exercise a steady and continuous pressure for a long period of time on one definite section of the German lines for the purpose of depleting the Teutonic forces. The Allies had created a military machine which they believed at last to be superior to that of the enemy. During all the last week of June they subjected the German lines in the Somme valley to a terrific bombardment in an effort to wipe out the opposing trenches. In that week more munitions were used by the big guns each day than the total amount manufactured in Great Britain during the first eleven months of the war. Then, on July 1, along a twenty-five-mile front the Allied infantry leaped to the attack. From then until November 18, when the weather finally rang down the curtain on the drama in the west, the battle raged with only one intermission in September. "Before July 1 Verdun had been the greatest continuous battle fought in the world's history; but the Somme surpassed it in numbers of men engaged, in the tactical

---

[11] Dissatisfied with the results of the system of voluntary enlistment, Great Britain in January, 1916, had adopted a system of conscription.

difficulty of the objectives, and in its importance in the strategical
scheme of the campaign."

To the general public the Allied drive on the Somme seemed a
failure, for it wrested only about 120 square miles of territory from
the enemy. Nevertheless, it did succeed in doing three things. It
relieved Verdun, and transferred the offensive in the west from Germany to the Allies; it held the bulk of the German army on the western front; and it wore down the German forces tremendously.
Although German casualties were considerably fewer than those
of the Allies, the situation was such that the latter could better
afford to suffer such losses than the Central Powers. The major
purpose of the campaign, the acute attrition of German forces, was
attained. Still more tangible evidence of the success of the drive
was to be given in the spring of 1917.

The German failure at Verdun and the Austrian failure in the
Trentino, followed by the Russian advance into Galicia and Bukowina, the Allied drive on the Somme, and the Italian capture of
Gorizia, all had their effect on Rumania, which, up to this time,
had remained a restless and uneasy neutral. In 1914 King Carol
had urged Rumania's intervention on the side of Austria in accordance with the treaty of 1883, but the Rumanian crown council had
overruled him in favor of neutrality. Germany's suggestion that
Francis Joseph should offer Rumania territorial compensations was
vetoed by the Hungarian premier, Tisza. On the other hand, Russia's offer of Transylvania and a guarantee of the territory in the
Dobrudja which Rumania had recently taken from Bulgaria likewise failed to bring about her intervention. Russia's disastrous defeat in 1915, followed by the intervention of Bulgaria and the Teutonic conquest of Serbia, soon drove from the minds of Rumanian
statesmen any thought of immediate entrance into the war on the
side of the Allies.

But with Russia's spectacular drive against the Austrians in June,
1916, came another change in Rumania. With every advance of the
Russians, Falkenhayn complained, the Rumanian attitude toward
the Central Powers became less favorable. During the summer
Allied statesmen negotiated with Rumania in the attempt to gain
her support. In the end a secret treaty was signed between Great
Britain, France, Russia, Italy, and Rumania, promising to the latter
the Banat of Temesvar, Transylvania, and Bukowina. In addition

the Allies promised the simultaneous assistance of both the Russian forces in Bukowina and the Allied forces at Saloniki. On August 27 Rumania declared war on Austria, asserting that "Rumania, governed by the necessity of safeguarding her racial interests, finds herself forced to enter into line by the side of those who are able to assure her the realization of her national unity."

Apparently the entry of Rumania gave the Allies a powerful recruit. It lengthened the battle line of the Central Powers in the east by several hundred miles; it added some 250,000 trained soldiers to the Allied armies; it cut off from the Central Powers the grain, petroleum, and other economic resources which were so much needed to resist the British blockade. But all this was more apparent than real. Rumania's entry into the war was not unexpected to Germany and perhaps not altogether unwelcome.

On August 28 Rumanian troops, in an effort to close in on the Austrians from the north and the south, crossed the frontier into Transylvania at eighteen different points.[12] But, for several reasons, they advanced not to victory but to defeat. In the first place, they were fatally short of heavy guns, airplanes, machine guns, and even rifles, and they had no great reserve of ammunition. Russia had guaranteed an ample supply of munitions, but the promise was not fulfilled. In the second place, they failed to receive the promised cooperation of the Allied armies. Russia's progress in the Carpathians was counted upon to divert the Austrian left wing in Transylvania, and Sarrail's advance from Saloniki was expected to engage the attention of Bulgaria; but neither of these developments occurred. Exhaustion of men and munitions, after a four months' campaign against Teutonic troops, prevented the Russian armies from carrying out their part of the bargain; and Sarrail, with a large but heterogeneous and poorly equipped army at Saloniki, hesitated to strike northward in a vigorous offensive lest a hostile Greek army attack him suddenly from the rear.

During the first three weeks of her campaign Rumania conquered about a quarter of Transylvania. But Mackensen was immediately dispatched to command a Bulgar-Teutonic army on the southern frontier of Rumania, while Falkenhayn took charge of the Austro-German forces facing the Rumanians in Transylvania. Heavy guns and immense supplies of munitions were rushed to the

[12] For the Rumanian front, see the map on page 353.

east. A simultaneous advance on the Transylvania and Dobrudja
fronts then followed, and the Rumanian armies were soon in flight
for safety. By the middle of October Transylvania had been cleared
of Rumanian troops, and the invasion of Rumania itself began.
Constanza fell on October 22, Bucharest on December 6. By the
middle of the following month, the Central Powers had occupied
all the Dobrudja, all Wallachia, and a portion of southern Moldavia,
and had driven the Rumanian government to Jassy.

The net result of Rumania's entry into the war thus seemed favorable to the Central Powers. The fertile grain fields and rich oil wells
of that unfortunate country were added to *Mittel-Europa's* economic
resources. The menace of Rumania's long-delayed intervention was
removed, and the Central Powers now held their lines in the east
with actually fewer men than had formerly been required. Teutonic
prestige, which had been badly shaken by earlier events of the year,
was once more restored. The Central Powers determined to capitalize this latest achievement and to seize the favorable position
created by the fall of Bucharest to make a peace offer.

## PEACE PROPOSALS OF THE CENTRAL POWERS

For some months Germany had been hoping that the President
of the United States would propose mediation. Almost from the beginning of the war President Wilson had considered mediation, and
in January, 1915, he had sent Colonel E. M. House to Europe as his
private and personal representative to discover, by conversations
with persons of high authority in the belligerent countries, the possible attitude toward mediation. In 1915 Colonel House had found,
however, that, although everybody seemed to want peace, nobody
was willing to concede enough to get it; that none of the belligerents
was willing to yield an iota of its aspirations; that France and Germany especially wanted annexations; and that both the Allies and
the Central Powers expected to win the war and to impose their
own terms. "Mothers and wives, fathers and brothers," he had discovered, desired peace, but not the governing groups.

A year later, in February, 1916, Colonel House made another move
toward possible mediation when he informed the British government in confidence that President Wilson was ready, on hearing
from France and Great Britain that the moment was opportune, to
propose that a conference should be summoned to put an end to

the war; and that, should the Allies accept this proposal and should Germany refuse it, the United States would probably enter the war against Germany. And, since the United States was not offering assistance merely for the sake of enabling the Allies to satisfy their national aspirations and to destroy Germany politically and economically, Colonel House outlined what he considered reasonable terms of peace.[13] But the Allies were determined to fight until the utter collapse of Germany, were confident of ultimate victory, and stated that the time was premature for mediation.

Although the Allies were not interested in President Wilson's proposed mediation, the Central Powers had reached the place where they were favorably disposed toward peace proposals. When, for various reasons, President Wilson delayed making any open proposal of mediation, therefore, the Central Powers at length decided to make one themselves. They believed that, in view of their decisive defeat of Rumania, they would run little risk of damaging their prestige or showing signs of weakness, and that, if the Allies rejected their offer, the odium of continuing the war would fall upon them.

Accordingly, on December 12, less than a week after the fall of Bucharest, Germany transmitted a note to France, Great Britain, Russia, Japan, Serbia, and Rumania. Animated "by the desire to stem the flood of blood and to bring the horrors of war to an end," the Central Powers proposed peace negotiations. Although the latest events had demonstrated that the war could not break their resisting power, they professed to have no desire to crush or annihilate their adversaries. They felt sure that the propositions which they would bring forward in the negotiations would be such as to serve as a basis for the restoration of lasting peace. But if, in spite of this offer of peace and conciliation, the struggle should continue, the four Central Powers were resolved to carry it on to the end, "while solemnly disclaiming any responsibility before mankind and history." As to the final outcome in the latter case, there could be little doubt, for Germany and her allies had already given proof of their indestructible strength in winning successes at war.

---

[13] These included: (1) complete restoration of Belgium and Serbia; (2) return of Alsace-Lorraine to France; (3) cession of Constantinople to Russia; (4) surrender of *Italia Irredenta* to Italy; (5) creation of an independent Poland; (6) compensation for Germany outside Europe; (7) abolition of competitive armaments; (8) guarantees against military aggression.

The weak feature of the German note was the absence of any definite terms of peace. In respect to this matter Germany was in an embarrassing position. If she proposed terms which would be moderate enough to invite serious discussion by the Allies, the German people would question the much-advertised success of the Central Powers, and their morale might be weakened or destroyed. On the other hand, if she formulated terms in accordance with popular expectations and the demands of her military leaders, the Allies could assert that peace with victorious Germany would mean a Germanized world, and Allied morale would be enormously strengthened.[14]

An official reply to Germany was presented on December 30 in the collective name of Russia, France, Great Britain, Japan, Italy, Serbia, Belgium, Montenegro, Portugal, and Rumania. The mere suggestion, without statement of terms, that negotiations should be opened, was not, they asserted, an offer of peace but a war maneuver, a calculated attempt to influence the future course of the war, and to end it by imposing a German peace. The object of Germany's overtures, they declared, was to create dissension in public opinion in Allied countries, and to stiffen public opinion in the Central Powers, "already severely tried by their losses, worn out by economic pressure and crushed by the supreme effort which has been imposed upon their inhabitants." They denied that the Central Powers had

[14] The terms upon which the Central Powers would have been prepared to take part in peace negotiations were later transmitted in confidence to President Wilson in a telegram of January 29, 1917, and are quoted by Count Bernstorff in *My Three Years in America*, page 377. They were:

"The restitution to France of that part of Upper Alsace occupied by her. The acquisition of a strategical and economic safety-frontier-zone, separating Germany and Poland from Russia.

"Colonial restitution in the form of an understanding which would secure Germany colonial possessions compatible with the size of her population and the importance of her economic interests.

"Restoration of those parts of France occupied by Germany, on condition that certain strategic and economic modifications of the frontier be allowed, as also financial compensation.

"Restitution of Belgium under definite guarantees for the safety of Germany, which would have to be determined by means of negotiations with the Belgian Government.

"Economic and financial settlement, on the basis of exchange, of the territory invaded by both sides, and to be restituted by the conclusion of peace.

"Compensation for German undertakings and private persons who have suffered damage through the war.

"Renunciation of all economic arrangements and measures, which after the peace would constitute an obstacle in the way of normal commerce and trade, with the conclusion of corresponding commercial treaties.

"The freedom of the Seas to be placed on a secure basis."

won the victory; the "war map" of Europe represented nothing more than "a superficial and passing phase of the situation, and not the real strength of the belligerents." The Allied governments, therefore, fully conscious of the gravity of the moment, but equally conscious of its requirements, refused to consider a proposal which was "empty and insincere."

The rejection of the German proposal was followed by a new German note to the neutral governments, stating that the Central Powers had made an honest attempt to terminate the war and pave the way for an understanding among the belligerents; that it had depended solely on the decision of the Allies whether the road to peace should be taken or not; that the latter had refused to take this road, and on them fell the full responsibility for the continuation of bloodshed. As for the Central Powers, they would prosecute the fight with calm trust and confidence in their good cause until a peace had been gained. "In your just anger at the boundless frivolity of our foes," the Kaiser proclaimed to his troops, "in your firm will to defend our holiest possessions, your hearts will turn to steel. Our enemies have not desired the hand of understanding I have offered them. With God's help our arms will compel them to accept it."

CHAPTER XIII

## AMERICA'S INTERVENTION AND RUSSIA'S WITHDRAWAL

ALTHOUGH the Central Powers had presented a bold front in their proposals for peace negotiations in December, 1916, they realized that time was running against them. They had hoped by a tremendous blow to capture Verdun in 1916 and force the Allies to consent to a peace. But their blow had been parried, and they in turn had been forced to take the defensive on the Somme, on the Isonzo, and on the Sereth. Their attempted submarine campaign had failed and had had to be abandoned; their high-seas fleet had met the British at Jutland and been forced to flee for safety to the protective guns of Helgoland. The Allied blockade had already created such an alarming food situation within their territories that riots had begun to break out and a practical food dictatorship had been established. In the face of all these developments the Central Powers realized that their spectacular triumph over Rumania counted for little; hence their desire for immediate peace negotiations at the close of 1916.

### GERMANY'S UNRESTRICTED SUBMARINE CAMPAIGN

The Allied reception of their peace proposal brought little comfort to the Central Powers, and still less did the subsequent announcement of the Allied war aims. On December 20, 1916, shortly after the Central Powers had made their peace proposals, President Wilson invited the various belligerents to state "their respective views as to the terms upon which the war might be concluded." While the Central Powers in their reply to the President did no more than "propose an immediate meeting of the delegates of the belligerent states at some neutral place," the Allied Powers went into greater detail. Their war aims, they said, implied: (1) the restoration of Belgium, Serbia, and Montenegro, with the compensations due them; (2) the evacuation of the invaded territories in France, Russia, and Rumania, with just reparation; (3) the restitu-

422

tion of provinces formerly torn from the Allies by force or against
the wish of their inhabitants; (4) the liberation of the Italians, the
Slavs, the Rumanians, and the Czechoslovaks from foreign domination; (5) the setting free of the populations subject to the bloody
tyranny of the Turk; (6) the expulsion from Europe of the Ottoman Empire as decidedly foreign to western civilization. The prospect of such terms drove the German government to a new decision.

For some time both Hindenburg and Ludendorff had been urging
the resumption of unrestricted submarine warfare. They had come
finally to the conclusion that only by this means could Germany
force the Allies to accept peace. But Bethmann-Hollweg had wished
to try first his peace proposal, and general headquarters had consented. Toward the close of December, however, Hindenburg again
insisted that Germany's dangerous economic and military position
made the unrestricted submarine campaign absolutely essential. The
chancellor at length gave way, and on January 9 a German crown
council decided that unrestricted submarine warfare should be resumed on February 1, 1917. That this move on the part of Germany
would force the United States to join the Allies, they had little doubt;
but they believed that the war would be ended long before the
United States could raise, train, equip, and place in Europe any great
number of troops. Furthermore, in an attempt to embarrass the
United States in case of war, Alfred Zimmermann, secretary for foreign affairs, instructed the German minister in Mexico to propose
an alliance with that country as soon as an outbreak of war appeared
certain. He was to propose that Germany should give general financial support, and Mexico should "reconquer the lost territory of
New Mexico, Texas, and Arizona."

On January 31, 1917, Germany announced that beginning the next
day all sea traffic within certain zones adjoining Great Britain,
France, and Italy and in the eastern Mediterranean would, "without
further notice, be prevented by all weapons." All vessels, neutral or
belligerent, were to be sunk by German submarines. Special permission was granted for one regular American passenger steamship to
sail in each direction between the United States and Great Britain
each week, provided a number of hard and fast rules were observed.
Germany was confident that this measure would "result in a speedy
termination of the war and in the restoration of peace which the
Government of the United States has so much at heart."

American exasperation with the Central Powers had been increasing for some months. Both groups of belligerents had been eager to influence public opinion in the United States and had carried on an active propaganda by means of subsidized newspapers and

THE ZONE OF UNRESTRICTED SUBMARINE WARFARE, FEBRUARY, 1917

public speakers. But the Central Powers had not been content with propaganda; their diplomatic representatives had further proceeded to organize and support a staff of conspirators. Passport frauds had been committed, strikes had been instigated in munition plants, and bombs had been manufactured for the destruction of factories and ships. Late in 1915 the United States had demanded the recall of the Austro-Hungarian ambassador and the military and naval attachés of the German embassy because of their improper activities. Now, on February 3, the German ambassador was handed his passports, and President Wilson announced to Congress the severance of diplomatic relations with Germany.

President Wilson did not believe that Germany would actually do with her submarines what she had announced, and preferred to await "overt acts" before taking further steps. Nevertheless, the immediate result of the German decree was a practical embargo on American shipping, since most shipowners refused to risk the loss of their vessels. During the first week following the break in diplomatic relations not a single American ship left New York for the war zone. On February 26 the President pointed out to Congress this practical embargo on American shipping and asked for authority to maintain armed neutrality "to protect our ships and our people in their legitimate and peaceful pursuits on the sea," but the measure was defeated in the Senate by the obstructionist tactics of a few members.

Meanwhile, the British steamship *Laconia* was sunk without warning on February 26 with the loss of eight American lives. Three days later the "Zimmermann note" to Mexico, which had been intercepted and deciphered by the British government, was published in the United States. The President was therefore accorded popular support when, on March 12, the government issued an order for arming American merchant ships by executive authority. Then followed within a week the sinking (March 16–17) of three homeward-bound American ships with the loss of American lives; and by the first of April thirty-five more Americans had been drowned. These attacks undoubtedly constituted "overt acts," and anti-German sentiment rose to a high pitch in the United States.

### THE UNITED STATES' ENTRANCE INTO THE WAR

On April 2 President Wilson came before a joint session of the Senate and the House of Representatives and advised that "Congress declare the recent course of the Imperial German Government to be in fact nothing less than war against the government and people of the United States." During the next two days Congress adopted a declaration of war by large majorities, and on April 6, 1917, President Wilson issued a proclamation declaring that "a state of war exists between the United States and the Imperial German Government."

The United States now began the task of preparing to aid the Allies and to defeat Germany. French and British missions to America pointed out that the United States could best assist by contributing (1) money, (2) food and ships to convey food, (3) help against the submarines, (4) men. In respect to the first, Congress on April 24 passed the War Finance Act authorizing the raising of seven billion dollars and the lending to the Allies of three billion. These funds were raised by "Liberty Loans." By the end of June over one billion dollars had been advanced to the Allies—chiefly for the purpose of purchasing food, cotton, metals, and other war materials. By October the amount appropriated to cover loans to the Allies had risen to the immense sum of seven billion dollars. America's entry into the war saved the Allies serious financial difficulties during the early part of 1917.

Every effort was made to increase the quantity of foodstuffs and war materials which could be shipped to the relief of the Allies and to expedite their transportation to Europe. In July the President made Herbert Hoover "food-controller"; in August Congress passed food-control and shipping acts. To counteract the menace of the submarine, the United States immediately seized all enemy merchant ships in American waters and inaugurated, under the direction of the United States Shipping Board Emergency Fleet Corporation, a tremendous shipbuilding program which called for the rapid construction of great numbers of standardized steel ships. In addition, a considerable flotilla of American destroyers was soon dispatched to co-operate with the British fleet against the German submarines in British waters.

At the time of the declaration of war upon Germany, the United States regular army consisted of only slightly more than 165,000 men, of whom more than 25,000 were scattered in outlying possessions and overseas posts. In consequence, less than five full divisions [1] were available for dispatch to the front in Europe, where divisions were numbered by the hundreds. To remedy this situation the Selective Service Act was passed in May, authorizing the President (1) to increase the regular army by voluntary enlistment to the maximum war strength, (2) to draft into federal service the national guard, and (3) to raise by conscription a force of 500,000 men, with 500,000 more if deemed necessary. On June 5 some nine and a half

---

[1] A division in the United States army consisted of 28,000 men.

million men between the ages of twenty-one and thirty years were registered, and on July 20 the drawing of 625,000 men to form the first selective army took place at Washington. During the summer the national guard was mobilized, but not until September was the mobilization of the new national army begun. Germany was correct in her calculation that it would be months after the resumption of the unrestricted submarine campaign before the military forces of the United States could play an effective role in Europe.

## THE ALLIED OFFENSIVES OF 1917

Meanwhile, on the western front the year opened with the voluntary relinquishment of about one thousand square miles of French territory by the German armies. As early as November of the preceding year the retreat had been decided upon, and for various reasons. The Allied drive on the Somme, although a disappointment to the Allies, had struck a deadly blow at Teutonic strength and had badly dented the German line. Further Allied gains at this point might endanger the whole Teutonic western front. Allied superiority in troops in the west had risen to thirty or forty divisions, and retirement to a shorter and more defensible line would enable the Central Powers to meet this situation more readily. Finally, a strategic retreat to a stronger line might nullify the extensive preparations which the Allies were making for a gigantic offensive in 1917. During the winter, therefore, a fresh system of trenches was constructed in front of Cambrai and St. Quentin, and the new bulwark of defense was christened the "Siegfried Line." The Allies, however, persisted in calling it the "Hindenburg Line." In March the Germans began to withdraw to their new position, devastating the surrendered territory as they went.

But the Germans were not left long undisturbed in their new positions. On April 9 the British opened a drive against the north end of the new line along a forty-five-mile front in the vicinity of Arras. During the first three days of the battle the British advanced rapidly, capturing one of the most cherished German observation posts, Vimy Ridge, and part of the new Hindenburg Line itself. Thereafter the advance slowed down, but at the end of a month the British had taken more than 20,000 prisoners and hundreds of heavy guns, trench mortars, and machine guns. In respect to the attrition of the German forces and the decline of their morale, it had been even more successful. The boasted new defenses had proved to be no more impregnable than the old. In an attempt to hold them, Germany had been obliged to throw in large numbers of her best troops. The Central Powers were thus sustaining heavy losses and using up their reserves.

While the battle of Arras was in progress, a new experiment was tried by the French in the second battle of the Aisne. Certain groups in France had become impatient with the slow, costly tactics used by Joffre, and clamored for a change in leadership. As a result, Joffre on December 16, 1916, had been succeeded as generalissimo by Nivelle, hero of the Verdun counteroffensive of that year. The latter believed that new methods might be discovered and that the enemy's strength might be broken by some other means than slow sapping. He envisaged "limitless objectives, the end of trench fighting, victory within two days." The capture of Laon he looked for as a result of the first day's fighting. Although his plan appeared doubtful to Painlevé, minister of war, and to Foch and Pétain, he was finally authorized to try it.

But certain circumstances rendered success almost impossible. In the first place, the terrain was difficult, and practically everywhere the Germans held the dominating positions. In the second place, the enemy through the capture of prisoners with documents was fully forewarned. In the third place, Nivelle's scheme demanded fresh, enthusiastic, loyal troops, but "the French armies were weary, dispirited, out of temper, doubtful of their leader, and in the mood to listen to treasonable tales. . . . Many had had no leave for two years, and the small comforts which keep troops in good humor had been neglected." Finally, Nivelle's purpose was to break through a strong enemy defense, but his methods differed little from those already used for less ambitious objectives.

The first day's battle, April 16, ended in driving sleet; the second day's began in a hurricane of wind and snow. By the close of the fifth, the French had taken all the banks of the Aisne from Soissons to Berry-au-Bac and all the spurs of the Aisne heights. They had captured 21,000 prisoners and 183 guns. All but sixteen of the fifty-two German reserve divisions had been thrown in to meet the attack. But the French themselves had suffered 75,000 casualties, of whom 15,000 were dead. And they were still very far from Laon. An abrupt reversion of feeling in favor of the cautious tactics of Pétain and

Foch resulted. Nivelle's tactics had failed, and he fell from command as suddenly as he had risen. In May Pétain was appointed to succeed Nivelle as commander-in-chief of the French forces, Foch becoming chief of the general staff.

The needless sacrifice of men provoked a near-crisis in the French army. No adequate preparation had been made for the care of the wounded, who were sent to various parts of France where they spread despondency by the tale of their needless sufferings. The depression which resulted found vent in mutiny, which, beginning about May 20, broke out in ten divisions. Pétain immediately set to work to remedy this menacing situation. For the remainder of the year, however, the French limited themselves on the western front chiefly to the policy of attrition, seeking by minor attacks to wear the Germans down in man power, war materials, and morale.

Throughout most of the summer and fall the British carried on operations in Flanders, and eventually they succeeded in capturing the important German observation point, Passchendaele Ridge. Late in November, with scarcely any artillery preparation but aided by a large number of huge tanks, they started a drive toward Cambrai. Several villages were captured, and German occupation of Cambrai was rendered most precarious. But before the British had consolidated their newly won position, they were compelled to meet a German counteroffensive which forced them to surrender about two thirds of the territory they had gained. The battle of Cambrai closed the campaign of 1917 on the western front. While all these offensives brought the Allies comparatively few miles of new territory, they did strengthen the Allied lines, and, more important than all, they inflicted serious losses upon the Teutonic armies, which, for almost the entire year, were compelled to stand on the defensive in France.

Allied disappointments in the West were to some extent balanced by successes in Mesopotamia and the Near East. To retrieve the British disaster at Kut-el-Amara early in 1916, the British forces at the head of the Persian Gulf were strengthened by reinforcements from India and Great Britain and put under the command of General Sir Stanley Maude. The latter part of the year was spent in preparing for an advance up the Tigris, and in December the march began. In February, 1917, Maude recaptured the city of Kut-el-Amara, where a British army had been forced to surrender to the

Turks only ten months before. The British pursued the retreating Turkish army and on March 11 entered the coveted city of Bagdad. By so doing they restored British prestige in the East, deprived the Central Powers of one of the famous goals of their *Drang nach Osten,* raised the morale and enthusiasm of the Allies, and correspondingly depressed the spirits of the Turks.

Events elsewhere were similarly depressing for Germany's ally in the East. In November, 1916, the Sherif of Mecca proclaimed the independence of the Arab kingdom of Hejaz and received the prompt recognition of the Allied powers. The moving spirit in the negotiations leading to the Arab revolt was T. E. Lawrence, a young Oxford University graduate who had learned colloquial Arabic while working in excavations in Syria and Mesopotamia before the war. Late in 1916 Lawrence had joined the Arabs, had won their confidence, had helped them organize their armies, and had persuaded them to co-operate with the British against the Turks. Beginning in 1917, the sultan's forces were compelled to fight not only against the invading Allies but against the revolting Arabs as well.

The latter were of considerable indirect assistance to General Murray in his efforts to protect the Suez Canal and to build a railway across the Sinai peninsula, preparatory to an advance into Palestine. The railway was at length completed, but attempts to capture the strongly entrenched Turkish position at Gaza were repulsed in April and May. During the summer Murray was succeeded by General Allenby, who renewed the offensive in October. On November 1, Beersheba was taken by a surprise attack, and five days later Gaza fell. The British continued to push northward, took Jaffa, the port of Jerusalem, on November 16, and on December 11 occupied the Holy City itself. The year closed with the British holding a line running from the Mediterranean to the Dead Sea north of Jaffa and Jerusalem, while in Mesopotamia they had advanced to within a hundred miles of Mosul. Turkey was beginning to crumble, and, in response to the urgent pleas of the distressed Turks, Teutonic headquarters rushed to their assistance a German "Asia corps" under the command of Falkenhayn.

For a year and a half the Allied forces at Saloniki had been practically impotent to advance against the Central Powers largely because of their fear of the possible action of Greece in their rear. The year 1917 saw the Greek situation finally clarified and the Saloniki

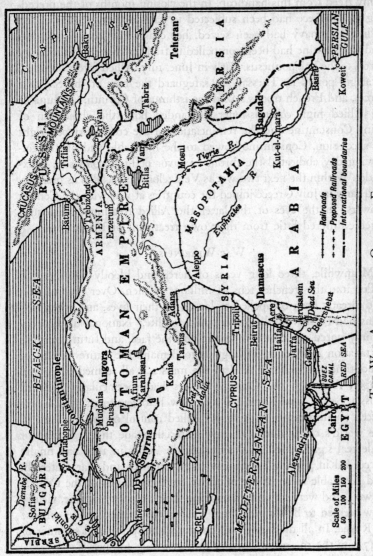

THE WAR AREA IN THE OTTOMAN EMPIRE

army freed from this handicap. In the closing months of the preceding year Greece had been subjected to various coercive acts of the Allies. Her navy had been seized, her coasts had been blockaded, and Constantine had been compelled to transfer most of his military forces to the Peloponnesus. Early in June, 1917, Allied forces occupied strategic points in Thessaly to safeguard the rear of the Saloniki forces, and French troops seized the isthmus of Corinth. On June 11 an Allied high commissioner demanded both the abdication of King Constantine and the renunciation of the crown prince's right of succession. Constantine bowed to the inevitable and on the following day abdicated the throne in favor of his second son, Alexander. Within the next two weeks Venizelos was recalled as premier, and early in July Greece joined the countries at war with the Central Powers. In the eyes of the latter the Allied treatment of neutral Greece differed little from their own treatment of Belgium.

## WAR-WEARINESS

Meanwhile, three long years of fierce and bloody fighting had called into the trenches tens of millions of men. Over four million had already been compelled to lay down their lives, and other millions had been wounded or crippled for life.[2] National bankruptcy plainly stared each country squarely in the face, and future burdens of taxation loomed up so large as to demand the entire surplus of peace-time production.[3] And to the masses it all seemed futile and empty. Although the Central Powers had spectacularly defeated Russia, Serbia, and Rumania, and now held territories which produced an impressive "war map," Allied control of the seas and of the world's chief sources of raw materials made that war map of little real significance. And although the Allies in 1916 had finally succeeded in gaining superiority in man power and war materials, had been able to wrest the offensive from the hands of the Central Powers, and were seriously damaging their military machine, victory now seemed to be slipping from their grasp because of the collapse of Russia. In all the belligerent countries the spring and summer of 1917 saw the masses war-weary and yearning for peace.

In the Austrian Empire this war-weariness was reflected in the

[2] The loss of life in the first two years of the war was greater than the total death toll of all the important wars from 1790 to 1914.

[3] The total cost of the war for the first three years was about $90,000,000,000.

report of the foreign minister, Count Czernin, to Emperor Charles [4] (April, 1917), pointing out that "the burden laid upon the population has assumed proportions that are unbearable," that the "dull despair of the population increases day by day," that "our military strength is coming to an end," that "another winter campaign would be absolutely out of the question," that "in the late summer or in the autumn an end must be put to the war at all costs," and that it "will be most important to begin peace negotiations at a moment when the enemy has not yet grasped the fact of our waning strength." It was seen in the unrest and nationalistic demands of the Poles, Czechs, and Yugoslavs, in the downfall of the ministry, in the weakening of the Dual Monarchy's loyalty to Germany, and finally in Emperor's Charles's secret overtures to France (March–May) looking toward a separate peace, even at the expense of granting Serbia access to the sea.

Within the German Empire the same feeling was revealed by the increase in the number of Socialists who opposed the war, by the Bavarian Prince Rupprecht's desire for peace, by the conversion of the Center Party's leader, Erzberger, from a peace of conquest to a peace without annexations, by unofficial statements in London and Paris that the Kaiser was disposed to peace, and finally by the Reichstag's resolution (July 19) that it strove "for a peace of understanding and the permanent reconciliation of the peoples," and that with such a peace "forced acquisitions of territory and political, economic, or financial oppressions are inconsistent." But the Pan-Germanists and the general staff disagreed with the Reichstag resolution and refused to accept it as coming from the entire country. And since Germany, in the words of Bethmann-Hollweg, had now come to be governed by a military dictatorship, no definite steps were taken to give the resolution substance.

War-weariness in the Allied countries was manifested during 1917 in what has been called the "defeatist movement," the essence of which was that peace could not be won through victory, but must be attained through negotiations—a "peace without victory." Anti-imperialist Socialists, bankers and capitalists who feared the effect of endless war on the world's financial structure, religious leaders, pacifists, and even some aristocrats were won over to the movement, which naturally had a tremendous appeal to the suffer-

[4] He had succeeded Francis Joseph in November, 1916.

ing, heartsick masses. In France and Italy the tendency was especially strong. The mutiny in the French army in 1917 has already been mentioned. But behind the lines newspaper proprietors, financiers, senators, and deputies became interested, and ex-Premier Joseph Caillaux was extremely active in spreading the doctrines. The re-action ultimately came, however, valiantly led by the aged veteran, Georges Clemenceau, who insisted upon a "peace through victory." Two ministries fell as a result of his fierce attacks, and he himself finally became premier and minister of war on November 16, 1917. Not many weeks later Clemenceau, in order to crush defeatism in France, took the drastic step of ordering Caillaux's arrest on the charge of having endangered the security of the state.

In Italy the defeatist movement was encouraged by secret agents of the Central Powers and by representatives of the Russian Bol-sheviks. Both the illiterate peasants and the radical proletariat So-cialists became imbued with the doctrines. Even the army became infected. In August rioting occurred in Turin, one of the chief mu-nition centers, and mutiny broke out among the troops sent to quell the disorder. In consequence, exemption from military service was canceled for many of the munition workers, who were organized into battalions and sent to the Italian front. By chance they were placed in the very sector where the Central Powers had decided to strike in an effort to cut off the Italian Second Army, on the Isonzo north of Gorizia, and the Third Army, which held the line from Gorizia to the Adriatic.

On October 24 the Central Powers launched an attack in the Julian Alps. A breach was made in the Italian lines at Caporetto, and Teutonic troops rushed through. Cadorna was forced to move his headquarters from Udine to Padua. By the twenty-eighth the Austro-German troops had reached the Friulian plain, had taken Cividale, and were menacing Udine. The Italian Second Army, weakened by the discontent and treason of its recently acquired Turin battalions and broken by the impact of new Teutonic tactics, became "a fugitive rabble." The Italian Third Army, in a desperate effort to escape capture by retreat, precipitately withdrew from Gorizia.

The plight of this Third Army was most serious. The Tagliamento River was the first halting-place for Cadorna's retreat, and the Third Army was as far from that river as were the advance forces of the

enemy. For a time it seemed doomed. "A million of men were retreating along the western highways, encumbered with batteries
and hospitals and transport, while by every choked route peasants
and townsmen fled for refuge from the Austrian cavalry." But the
Third Army was not captured; with heavy losses and by the nar-

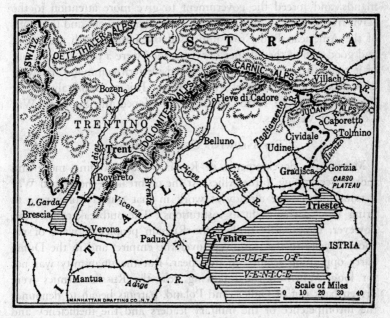

THE AUSTRO-ITALIAN WAR AREA

rowest margin it escaped. On November 1 it was in position on the
western bank of the Tagliamento with the river between it and the
enemy. Its successful retreat made an Italian stand possible and deprived the Teutonic forces of their expected triumph. But on November 3 the enemy crossed the river and began to move west along
the edge of the hills. On the seventh the Italians abandoned the
Tagliamento, halted temporarily on the Livenza, and by the tenth
were back on the Piave. Here the retreat ended.

French and British reinforcements were at once dispatched from
the western front. Diaz supplanted Cadorna as commander-in-chief.
Italian boys of seventeen and eighteen, many with little military
training, were rushed to the battle line. Italian monitors off the coast

contributed their constant shelling to the defense. During November and December desperate fighting continued, but the Teutonic advance was finally checked. The disaster had cost Italy some 800,000 effectives in addition to great quantities of war materials. Yet in the end it aroused Italy's fighting spirit, brought reforms in her commands, and forced the government to give more attention to the "civil front." The aid of the British and French troops and the work of the American Red Cross impressed the Italians with the extent and good will of the alliance of which they were a part. Finally, out of it came the movement for a unified western command. Early in November the premiers of France, Great Britain, and Italy met at Rapallo, and from their conference developed the Supreme War Council of Versailles.

## The Growing Unrest in Russia

Meanwhile, developments in Russia were becoming more and more discouraging to the Allies. At the outbreak of the World War various forces were already at work in that country preparing to bring about a change in its institutions.[5] The outbreak of the war, however, temporarily unified the Russian people. A wave of patriotic loyalty to the tsar swept over the empire, and in the Duma party opposition seemed to disappear. But the unanimity was not for long. When in the following year the Russian armies were driven back out of Galicia and Poland, patriots began to denounce the incompetence of the military leaders and the inefficiency and corruption of the government. And, as defeat succeeded defeat, as the number of killed and wounded mounted into the millions, as the vast crowds of homeless refugees poured eastward before the retreating armies, denunciations became louder and angrier. The vigorous prosecution of the war and the punishment of criminally inefficient commanders and officials were openly demanded. Serious riots in the cities and strikes in the munition factories occurred.

Nevertheless, the tsar in February, 1916, elevated to the premiership Boris Stürmer, an ultraconservative landed aristocrat, a man of German descent and of suspected pro-German sympathies, later accused of deliberately planning the Rumanian defeat as part of his scheme for a separate Russo-German peace. Furthermore, the imperial family fell beneath the spell of the long-haired, illiterate

[5] See pages 270–272.

scoundrel, charlatan, and reputed monk, Gregory Rasputin, who was thought by many to be in close contact with a pro-German organization in Petrograd.[6] Gradually the conviction gained ground among men of widely different classes that certain "dark forces" were attempting to paralyze the country, that, if the German staff itself were in control of Russia, it could not have brought to pass conditions more to its advantage than those created by the Russian government. During 1916 both conservative and liberal groups in Russia gradually came to the conclusion that victory in the war was impossible so long as the methods of autocracy prevailed. In the fall of that year preparations for a *coup d'état* were begun in various circles which included military men of both Petrograd and Moscow, and Duma members of as high standing as Rodzianko, the president. Most of the plans envisaged the abdication of Nicholas II.

At the same time the army with its millions of peasants from every part of Russia was discouraged, discontented, and weary of the futile struggle, which seemed to be waged not only against the Central Powers at the front, but against the forces of inefficiency, corruption, and even treason in the rear. The great bulk of Russian troops—perhaps as many as ten million—never reached the front lines but were for the most part concentrated in the large towns and cities. Here enforced idleness gave them plenty of time to brood over their privations and wrongs and to become fertile ground for revolutionary propaganda. By the winter of 1916–1917 the army was already in process of dissolution. "Unwillingness to fight, decline of discipline, distrust and suspicion of officers, desertion in the rear" were present. One of the essentials for successful revolution—a discontented and disloyal army—thus existed in Russia by the spring of 1917.

Among the masses, meanwhile, discontent and unrest were greatly accentuated by the economic conditions. The relative cost of living increased during the war by leaps and bounds. During the winter of 1916–1917 a coal shortage developed which made itself felt in the progressive closing down of industries in which its use was essential. The transportation system, none too efficient at best, collapsed under the strain of the war. Passenger traffic had to be stopped for weeks at a time to enable military and supply trains to go through to the

6 In September, 1914, the name of the capital was changed from St. Petersburg to Petrograd.

front. Finally, the shift of millions of peasants from the farms into the armies,[7] the tremendous demand for food to feed these armies, the peasants' unwillingness to part with food for depreciating paper currency, and the collapse of the transportation system, all conspired to produce an acute food shortage in the larger towns and cities. Short rations and bread lines became more and more frequent. In a winter which was bitterly cold, many Russians were hungry. "Bread!" became the dominant cry.

### THE COLLAPSE OF RUSSIAN AUTOCRACY

On March 8, 1917, spontaneous riots occurred in Petrograd when crowds of people from widely separated parts of the city poured into the streets, shouting "Bread!" On the same day between eighty and ninety thousand workmen went on strike and joined the demonstrating masses in the streets. The more radical elements at once sought to turn the situation to their advantage, and soon red flags and revolutionary placards began to appear. In the evening bakers' shops were looted by workmen unable to get bread. During the next day some fraternization began between the crowds and the troops of the Petrograd garrison, who gave assurance that the soldiers would not fire on the people.

On Sunday, March 11, incidents of considerable significance occurred. One of the companies of the Petrograd garrison mutinied when ordered to fire upon the people, and had to be disarmed by the Preobrashensky regiment, the flower of the household troops. During the day the military governor of Petrograd posted notices ordering the strikers to return to their work; and Premier Galitzin, using a decree which had been signed but left undated by the tsar before he left Petrograd, sent Rodzianko an order proroguing the Duma. But the strikers, instead of returning passively to work, established the Soviet (Council) of Workmen's and Soldiers' Deputies and set to work organizing the masses and converting the soldiers to their cause. Even the Preobrashensky regiment now mutinied and shot some of its officers. Other regiments followed suit until by noon 25,000 soldiers had thrown themselves on the side of the workmen. By evening of the twelfth, revolutionary workers and soldiers were in control of the capital, and former dreaded tsarist

---

[7] It has been estimated that 14,000,000 soldiers were under arms in 1917, in Russia alone.

officials were either surrendering themselves or being arrested by the revolutionary forces.

Meanwhile the Duma, while not venturing to defy the tsar's order officially, had met "informally" and had authorized the appointment of a temporary committee with limited powers. The latter, headed by Rodzianko, on the thirteenth undertook to assume executive functions and began to issue orders to the Petrograd garrison. At the same time the Petrograd soviet, representing the "revolutionary democracy" of the factory workers and soldiers of the city, elected a temporary executive committee and began doing the same thing. Thus there were, almost from the beginning of the revolution, two centers of authority; the temporary committee of the Duma and the temporary executive committee of the soviet.

An attempt was made to amalgamate the two groups in a provisional government which was projected on March 14, when the temporary committee of the Duma proposed a government consisting for the most part of bourgeois ministers, but with two places reserved for representatives of the soviet. The executive committee of the soviet, however, declared that representatives of the soviet could not take office in the provisional government because the government and the whole revolution were "bourgeois." But the executive committee was overruled by the soviet delegates, and Alexander Kerensky, a Socialist Revolutionary member of the Duma, was permitted to enter the new provisional government, which was composed, however, primarily of members of the Octobrist and Constitutional Democratic parties. Although Kerensky was the only member drawn from the Left group, the Petrograd soviet approved the government by an overwhelming vote.

On the fourteenth the tsar attempted to reach Petrograd, but his train was compelled to stop because workmen had pulled up the tracks. Meanwhile, he had dispatched an army under General Ivanov, the hero of the first Galician campaign, to take Petrograd, but most of his troops went over to the revolution. On March 15 the tsar decided to give way and grant a responsible ministry, but it was too late. The demand was now for his abdication. As to what should follow his abdication, there were differing views, but the majority of the temporary committee favored the regency of Grand Duke Michael during the minority of the tsar's son, Alexis. Confronted with the information that his troops had deserted him, advised by his generals that abdication was his only possible course, Nicholas II at length surrendered his throne, requesting only that it go directly to his brother Michael rather than to his young son, Alexis.

But by this time the Petrograd soviet was demanding a republic. A delegation of the Duma thereupon visited Grand Duke Michael and informed him that the popular demand was for his renunciation of the regency and his surrender of all powers to the provisional government until a constituent assembly could decide upon the future. The grand duke in turn bowed to the revolution and announced his intention to accept the supreme power only if it should be conferred upon him by a constituent assembly "elected on a basis of equal, universal, and secret suffrage." He closed his declaration by requesting all Russians to obey the provisional government until the meeting of a constituent assembly. The provisional government at once announced that it assumed all the financial and treaty obligations of the state incurred by the old regime.

With the appointment of the first provisional government of Russia the bourgeois stage of the revolution began. The ministry represented a coalition of the moderate parties. The new premier was Prince George Lvov, creator and president of the Union of Zemstvos. Associated with him as foreign minister was Paul N. Miliukov, eminent historian and leader of the Constitutional Democrats. The war minister was Alexander Guchkov, leader of the Octobrists and formerly chairman of the military commission of the Duma. Kerensky, a Socialist Revolutionary, became minister of justice. The ministry was chiefly representative of the landowning, capitalist, manufacturing, and professional classes—obviously a bourgeois group. And the aims of the first provisional government were distinctly bourgeois aims: the establishment of constitutional, democratic, parliamentary government, perhaps even a monarchy; the active prosecution of the war in close co-operation with the Allies; the protection of the rights of private property; the settlement of the land question by a constituent assembly, but no alienation of land without compensation; the accomplishment of all changes in Russian institutions only through a legally elected constituent assembly. To the onlooker, Russia had at length apparently become one of the liberal democratic states of the world. Formal recognition of the new regime was soon forthcoming from the United States, Great Britain, France, Italy, and Japan.

## THE SOVIETS

Meanwhile, the Russian masses had begun to organize in order to make themselves articulate. Following the example of the workmen of Petrograd, they established throughout the country extralegal soviets, chosen in the towns by the factory workers, in the rural districts by the peasant communes, in the army by military units. These soviets were controlled largely by the Socialist Revolutionaries and the Menshevik Social Democrats, groups which were practically unrepresented in the provisional government.

The aims of the groups which found representation in the soviets were radically different from those of the provisional government. Both the urban proletariat and the peasants desired a thoroughgoing social revolution in addition to political change. Both sought the overthrow of the bourgeoisie. Specifically, the peasants wanted the great estates seized and divided up without compensation to the owners, while the proletariat hoped for the expulsion of the capitalists and the introduction of a socialistic scheme of workers' control in the factories. All were war-weary and discouraged; while not at once demanding the immediate cessation of the war, they did desire a revision of its aims and a final peace "without annexations and indemnities." They were eager for the early convocation of a constituent assembly, which they expected to provide the panacea for all their wrongs.

The masses had an opportunity to express their views on something like a national scale for the first time when an "All-Russian Congress of Soviets," composed largely of Menshevik Social Democrats and moderate Socialist Revolutionaries, met early in April, 1917. It was almost inevitable that a clash in policies should occur between a congress, thus representing the Russian masses, and the provisional government, representative of the bourgeoisie. The congress demanded the abandonment of imperialism, the acceptance of the principle of self-determination, and the conclusion of peace without annexations and indemnities. It voted to continue the war and to support the provisional government only if it adopted the views of the congress.

On May 1, however, Foreign Minister Miliukov sent a note to the Allied governments stating Russia's resolve to conclude no separate peace, but to carry the war to a "decisive victory" in conformity with her past agreements with the Allies.[8] This note immediately evoked the disapproval of the Petrograd soviet. Meetings of protest were held in the capital and in Moscow. Workmen, on leaving the factories in the evening, marched in processions through the principal streets bearing red flags with inscriptions hostile to the government, and "Down with Miliukov!" was the cry. A number of regiments paraded with banners demanding the resignation of Guchkov, minister of war, together with Miliukov. The government hastened to explain to the Petrograd soviet that "decisive victory" did not preclude Russia's renunciation of territorial conquests. Nevertheless, as a result of the crisis, both Guchkov and Miliukov resigned.

Up to this time the Menshevik leaders in the Petrograd soviet had declined to assume any responsibility for policies of the provisional government, had refused to co-operate with it, and had sought merely to exercise upon it the pressure of an opposition. Now, however, the provisional government demanded that the soviets should be officially represented, and in the new government which was organized the Mensheviks and moderate Socialist Revolutionaries each had three representatives. Lvov remained as prime minister and Kerensky succeeded Guchkov as minister of war. The immediate result of the change in the government was a reversal of Miliukov's earlier announced war policy. Imperialism was definitely repudiated in a manifesto of the provisional government (May 19) which adopted as its aim "the re-establishment of a general peace which shall not tend toward domination over other nations or the seizure of their national possessions or the violent usurpation of their territories—a peace without annexations or indemnities and based on the right of nations to decide their own affairs."

### Lenin and the Rise of the Bolsheviks

One explanation of the Petrograd soviet's decision to enter the government and to give active support to its policies was the alarm with which Menshevik and moderate Socialist Revolutionary leaders viewed the increasing activity of the Bolsheviks. Although the outbreak of the revolution had found the latter's organization practically broken up, although they had taken no serious part in the overthrow of the tsar, they had finally been galvanized into action

---

[8] Professor Miliukov later admitted that this was the weakest point in the provisional government's program.

by the arrival of Nicholas Lenin on the evening of April 16 and by his dramatic speech at the railway station demanding a second revolution.

The real name of this "plump little man, with a high bulbous forehead, a snub nose, and bald head," whose tremendous will power and boundless energy so dominated the Bolsheviks that he might well have said, *"Le parti c'est moi,"* was Vladimir Ilyich Ulianov. He was born in Simbirsk (now called Leninsk) in 1870, the son of a district inspector of schools whose family descended from a stock of impoverished nobles. His elder brother, Alexander, was executed for his part in the attempted assassination of Alexander III in 1887, and doubtless Lenin was in sympathy with his views, for he himself was soon expelled from the University of Kazan because of revolutionary agitation. Later he passed the bar examinations in Petrograd, but soon gave up the practice of law, joined a secret organization of professional revolutionists, became a Social Democrat, and was even exiled for a time to Siberia because of revolutionary activities among the working classes of the capital. The split in the Social Democratic Party which occurred in 1903 was largely due to Lenin, who repudiated co-operation with the liberals and sought a violent outbreak of class war. To a certain extent, therefore, Lenin may be considered the father of Bolshevism. During the revolution of 1905 he was again in Petrograd, but his role was rather unimportant, his chief endeavor being to incite violence and hostility against the Duma and the Constitutional Democrats. At the conclusion of the revolution he left the country, and from 1906 to 1917 lived abroad as a professional revolutionary, giving himself exclusively to the work of revolutionary organization and secret propaganda.

The revolution of 1917 found Lenin in Zurich, Switzerland, but the general pardon of political offenders proclaimed by the provisional government opened the way for his return to Russia. Refused the right to pass through territory of the Allies, he at length secured permission to cross Germany from the Kaiser's government, which hoped to weaken Russia by sowing dissension behind the lines. Upon his return to Petrograd, Lenin immediately began his attack. The food difficulties, the protracted war, the delay in summoning a constituent assembly, all these he exploited for his own ends. Upon the provisional government he placed the blame for all that went wrong.

Gradually Lenin gathered about him a group of followers: doctrinaire fanatics, masters of intrigue and propaganda, ambitious opportunists, sentimental visionaries, crazy degenerates, sincere idealists —yet withal many extremely energetic and capable men whose names, Zinoviev, Bukharin, Chicherin, Kamenev, Rykov, Stalin, Dzerzhinsky, have since been prominent in Russian affairs. While Lenin unquestionably held first place in the Bolshevik Party, second place soon went to a new recruit, Leon Trotsky, who did not finally join the Bolsheviks until after the March revolution. Trotsky, whose real name was Leon Davidovich Bronstein, was a Russian middle-class Jew who had early become imbued with revolutionary ideas. Twice he had been exiled to Siberia, and twice he had escaped. The revolution found him in New York City, where he had recently gone after having lived in exile for several years in Vienna and Paris. When he attempted to return to Russia, he was arrested in Halifax, but on the application of Kerensky, upon whom the Petrograd soviet brought pressure to bear, he was released and permitted to sail for Russia.

The program which these Bolshevik leaders offered was bound to make a tremendous appeal to the masses, who, with the sole exception of the announced change in war aims, could see little difference between the policies of the old and those of the new provisional government. No order for the confiscation and subdivision of the great landed estates was forthcoming. No step toward the overthrow of the capitalistic system of industry was taken. Not even a call for the early meeting of a constituent assembly was sent out. Instead of these, what they saw were vigorous efforts to prepare for a renewed military effort at the front. On the other hand, the Bolsheviks drafted a program which called for what the mass of the people wanted: (1) immediate conclusion of a general peace; (2) immediate confiscation of landed estates without compensation and without delay for legal forms; (3) possession and operation of factories by the workmen; (4) national control of production and distribution; (5) the substitution of soviets of workmen, peasants, and soldiers for all existing agencies of government; (6) the exclusion of the propertied classes from political rights.

Meanwhile, War Minister Kerensky was bending every effort to prepare for a successful offensive against the Central Powers, believing that a Russian victory would strengthen the provisional government and raise the morale of both soldiers and civilians. Discipline was so well restored, at least in the southern divisions on the Austrian front, that an offensive was projected for July. The plan called for local attacks to hold the German troops in the north while the main blow was delivered against the weaker Austrian lines. But Russian deserters betrayed the plan to the enemy, and German reinforcements were sent to the Austrian rather than to the German front. After weeks of feverish activity on the part of Kerensky and his assistants, the Russian advance began at the very close of June. For a few days all went well. Thousands of prisoners and vast quantities of war material were captured, and an advance of some twenty miles was made. Wherever the Austrian lines were not stiffened by Germans, they gave way. But on July 19 a heavy concentration of German troops began a drive in the direction of Tarnopol. Not yet recovered from the exhaustion of their own attack, the Russians fell back under German pressure. Discipline and organization again broke down; entire regiments shot their officers and refused to fight. The whole Russian line in Galicia precipitately took to flight, and the Russian gains of 1916 were completely wiped out.

And behind the lines things were going no better. On July 16 the Bolsheviks made their first serious attempt at an armed uprising in Petrograd. Part of the Petrograd garrison, honeycombed with Bolshevik propaganda, revolted. In company with armed workmen they paraded through the city with banners inscribed, "Down with the capitalist ministers," "Down with the war," "All power to the soviets." Red flags appeared among the crowds, and speeches by Trotsky and Zinoviev were greeted with thunderous applause. From the front, Kerensky telegraphed demanding that the government take active steps to suppress the Bolsheviks, and dispatched sixty thousand loyal soldiers to assist in this task. After two days of desultory fighting in the streets, both the disloyal troops and the Bolsheviks were defeated. While their support in Petrograd was strong, the Bolsheviks were still weak in the country and in the army as a whole. After this "reconnoiter" of Bolshevik and government strength, Lenin abandoned his cry for the immediate overthrow of the provisional government, and decided that special efforts must now be made to win not only the Petrograd garrison but the whole army to the Bolshevik program.

In the midst of defeat at the front and uprising in the capital, the provisional government itself passed through a crisis, as the result of which Kerensky succeeded Lvov as prime minister. Although the former at once took steps to strengthen the government, it was soon menaced from another direction. The July rising of the Bolsheviks gave a great impetus to the activities of the extreme Right. "Pale and trembling with indignation, the respectable citizen now called for the strong man," and the forces of reaction and militant monarchism raised their heads. The Bolsheviks had sought the "dictatorship of the proletariat"; the conservatives now sought the dictatorship of the military. Early in September, under orders from General Kornilov, troops advanced from the front upon Petrograd. At the same time Kornilov dispatched an ultimatum to Kerensky demanding the proclamation of martial law in Petrograd and the resignation of the provisional government. But Kerensky refused to accept the ultimatum, was given dictatorial power by the cabinet, and in the end arrested Kornilov himself.

The Kornilov affair brought a distinct reaction toward the Bolsheviks. The mass of the people—peasants, proletariat, soldiers— were in deadly fear lest "tsarist generals" might immediately bring about the restoration of the repressive system of the old regime. It was rumored that Kerensky had been in sympathy with the plot and had turned against it only under pressure from the soviet. Whether or not this was true, the Bolsheviks seized upon the rumor and used it so effectively that within a few days the confidence of the bulk of the people in the provisional government was completely destroyed. The soviets became more revolutionary. Within a week after the crushing of the Kornilov rebellion, the Bolsheviks gained control of the executive committee of the Petrograd soviet for the first time.

The moderates were waging a losing fight. The odds against them were too great. Russia was falling into chaos. The military situation became more and more desperate. Desertions were on the increase, and the mass of soldiers threatened to leave the trenches, whole regiments at a time. The Germans continued to advance, captured Riga, and threatened Petrograd. Kerensky's government prepared to move to Moscow. In the villages a general seizure of land was going on. Food riots in the cities were frequent. Russia's finances and industries were sinking into a state of collapse. Reactionary propaganda, Bolshevik propaganda, German propaganda, separatist propaganda were everywhere present and flourished in proportion as the domestic situation became more chaotic. Then Kerensky made the fatal blunder of postponing the elections to the constituent assembly from September 30 to November 25—fatal because it still further weakened the confidence of the masses in him and played directly into the hands of the Bolshevik leaders, who claimed that the provisional government did not really wish to introduce the long-sought popular reforms. With redoubled energy the Bolsheviks sounded their slogan: "Peace to the army, land to the peasants, control of the factories to the workmen!"

The inevitable result was that the Bolsheviks rapidly increased in numbers and strength. Throughout the country land-hungry peasants, who cared not so much for victory over Germany as for the overthrow of the landlords, began to approve the Bolshevik program. In the cities the workers, so long at the mercy of their government-protected employers, became enamored of the Bolshevik promise of complete control of industry. And the active soldiers, maltreated, betrayed, defeated in the war, compelled to endure untold hardships, and at the same time yearning for the war to end in order that they might return to claim their share of the confiscated lands, gladly enlisted under the Bolshevik banner of peace. Regiment after regiment declared it would recognize only the Petrograd soviet's commissioners.

## THE NOVEMBER REVOLUTION

Lenin now made up his mind that the time to strike was at hand. Late in October he returned to Petrograd and held a "conspiratory meeting" of the central committee of the Bolshevik Party. By an almost unanimous vote an armed insurrection against the government was decided upon. The occasion was to be the assembling of the All-Russian Congress of Soviets, which was set for November 7. A large majority of those who had been elected to this congress were Bolsheviks, and there was thought to be little doubt that the congress would declare itself in favor of handing over power to the soviets. But the Bolsheviks felt that such a resolution must be backed by force. Furthermore, it was argued, an insurrection under the cry of protecting the rights of the Congress of Soviets would have a much more effective appeal than one under the mere cry of seizing power for the Bolsheviks.

With everything ready for the coup, therefore, the Bolsheviks proclaimed to the masses on the evening of November 6: "The counterrevolution has raised its criminal head. The Kornilovists are mobilizing forces in order to annihilate the All-Russian Congress of Soviets and the Constituent Assembly." During the night the public buildings of Petrograd were occupied by Bolshevik troops. Railway stations, telegraph and telephone offices, bridges, power plants, and even the Bank of Russia came into their control. On the morning of the seventh another Bolshevik proclamation announced that the provisional government had been overthrown. "Long live the revolution of the workers, soldiers, and peasants!" Late in the day the members of the provisional government, with the exception of Kerensky, who escaped, were arrested and imprisoned. That same night the All-Russian Congress of Soviets approved the *coup d'état* and passed a resolution formally taking over the government, which thereupon became the soviet government. On the next day the same congress established a new provisional government, called the "Soviet of the People's Commissars," of which Lenin was chairman and Trotsky commissar for foreign affairs.

Nevertheless, on November 25 elections for the Constituent Assembly were held according to schedule, the vote being based on equal, direct, universal, and secret adult suffrage. The assembly, therefore, was more representative of the Russian people than any other body which had ever been called together in that country. The Bolsheviks had hoped to control a majority of the delegates, but the elections revealed that they actually represented a small minority of the Russian people. A large majority of the total membership was composed of moderate Socialist Revolutionaries. From a parliamentary point of view the Bolsheviks should now have turned the administration of the government over to the Socialist Revolutionaries.

But the Bolsheviks had no such idea. They intended either to control or to destroy the assembly, and managed to postpone its first meeting from December to January. Finally, however, the Constituent Assembly, "the object of the struggles and hopes, the symbol of the people's sovereignty for so many generations of Russian revolutionaries," convened in Petrograd on January 18, 1918. Although many of the conservative members absented themselves through fear for their personal safety, although the assembly met under the menace of "Red Guards," the Socialist Revolutionaries were numerous enough and courageous enough to block the plans of the Bolsheviks. In consequence, the latter left the assembly, and early the next morning dissolved it by force, charging that it was a counter-revolutionary bourgeois body.

## The Treaty of Brest-Litovsk

Within two weeks after the November revolution Commissar for Foreign Affairs Trotsky had sent to the foreign diplomats in Petrograd a note stating that the Soviet government intended "to propose to all peoples and their respective governments an immediate armistice on all fronts, with the purpose of immediately opening *pourparlers* for the conclusion of a democratic peace." The Allies ignored Trotsky's note and refused to have anything whatever to do with the Bolshevik peace proposal. On the other hand, the Central Powers, which were naturally eager to have Russia withdraw from the war, responded with alacrity. Negotiations for an armistice were begun at Brest-Litovsk on December 3, and twelve days later a definite truce was signed between representatives of Russia on the one hand and of Germany, Austria, Bulgaria, and Turkey on the other.

On December 22 the first peace conference of the war was formally opened at the same place. The task of the Russian delegates was not an easy one. They realized well enough that military force was on the side of the Central Powers. They doubtless clearly saw that, if they resisted a peace dictated by the Central Powers, Russia would continue to be invaded and the Bolsheviks themselves might be confronted by a rebellion at home on the part of those who had been promised an immediate peace. On the other hand, if they yielded too much or too easily, they might prevent further German invasion, to be sure, but they might also bring upon themselves the wrath of Russian patriots for having betrayed the national interests. Faced by this dilemma, they played for time. They first secured a suspension of the peace conference on the pretext of enabling the Allies to participate, and then in the meantime they attempted by propaganda to incite the German people to revolt against their "imperialistic" government. But the Allies did not participate, nor did the Germans revolt, and the Bolsheviks failed to benefit by their procrastination.

The Bolsheviks next desired to transfer the negotiations to Stockholm, where they would be less under the domination of the Central Powers, but the Germans objected, and the conference was at length resumed on January 10, 1918, at Brest-Litovsk. The chief obstacle to an agreement was the treatment of the Russian territory occupied by troops of the Central Powers. The Bolsheviks demanded that the forces of the latter should evacuate Poland, Courland, and Lithuania and permit plebiscites to determine the fate of these regions. This the Central Powers refused to do, the Kaiser ordering the German delegates to demand without plebiscites not only Courland and Lithuania but Livonia and Estonia as well. As a result of the consequent impasse the conference broke up again four days later and adjourned *sine die,* the only positive achievement being the extension of the armistice to February 12.

Two days before the expiration of the armistice, Trotsky handed the Germans a note which is considered unique among war documents: "We are going out of the war; but we feel ourselves compelled to refuse to sign the peace treaty." But Germany was determined to have a signed peace. On February 18, therefore, German armies on the eastern front once more began to advance into Russia. The following day Lenin and Trotsky capitulated and agreed to sign. The German government now made a new offer of peace, more drastic than the first, and attached a forty-eight-hour time limit for its acceptance. Although some of the more fiery Bolsheviks counseled armed resistance, Lenin advised acceptance in order that Bolshevism might have time to organize and strengthen itself within Russia.

Peace negotiations were, accordingly, once more resumed and resulted in the treaty of Brest-Litovsk, signed on March 3, 1918. Russia agreed: (1) to give up Poland, Courland, and Lithuania, and to let Germany and Austria determine the future status of these territories in agreement with their populations; (2) to evacuate Livonia, Estonia, Finland, and the Åland Islands; [9] (3) to evacuate

---

[9] These regions were soon brought within the orbit of the Central Powers. In April, 1918, German troops landed in Finland, and not long afterward the throne was offered to Prince Charles of Hesse, brother-in-law of the Kaiser. On April 21 the Kaiser himself "accepted" the invitation of Estonian Balts to be the ruler of that country. In March Germany recognized the independence of Lithuania, which in July received Prince William of Urach, a younger member of the ruling house of Württemberg, as king. In April German and Austrian troops, entering the Ukraine as allies, occupied the whole country and established a military dictatorship under the pro-German General Skoropadski.

the Ukraine and to recognize the treaty signed between the Ukrainian People's Republic and the Central Powers; (4) to surrender to Turkey the districts of Ardahan, Kars, and Batum; (5) to discontinue all Bolshevik propaganda in the territory of the Central Powers and in the territories ceded by the treaty.

Thus the Bolsheviks gained peace for Russia, but for a Russia reduced to an area less than that which Peter the Great had inherited back in the seventeenth century. Profoundly altered both politically and territorially by the revolution, Russia was finally "at peace" with the world; and the Bolsheviks were now free to try their great experiment—the "dictatorship of the proletariat."

CHAPTER XIV

THE COLLAPSE OF THE CENTRAL POWERS

EARLY in 1918 the Central Powers confidently announced that that year would see the final conclusion of the war and that the end of the conflict would be achieved by the decisive victory of Teutonic arms. Their prediction of the end of the war was truly fulfilled, but their expected victory proved to be only a mirage which faded with the passing of the months. In 1918 the overwhelming resources of the Allies were at last successfully brought to bear against the Central Powers, already weakened economically by long years of blockade and undermined politically by nationalist propaganda in Austria-Hungary and liberal and radical propaganda in Germany. The outcome of the conflict was the final and decisive defeat of the Teutonic armies and the utter collapse of the Central Powers.

RENEWED OPTIMISM OF THE CENTRAL POWERS

The opening of the year 1918 saw in German circles a spirit of optimism which was entirely lacking in the previous year. During the summer and autumn of 1917 the Central Powers had passed through a critical period of discouragement and war-weariness. They had even talked of a peace "without annexations and indemnities." But that had been at a time when they were losing their superiority in man power and war materials on the western front, when they were being compelled to stand on the defensive on nearly all fronts, when it was beginning to be apparent that their unrestricted submarine campaign was not going to bring Great Britain to her knees in a few months, if ever.

For the submarine campaign had proved to be a bitter disappointment to the Central Powers. In the early months of 1917 Allied shipping losses were tremendous, and the Teutonic threat to the sustenance of the British people and to the munitioning of the Allied armies was extremely grave. But gradually in two ways the menacing blow was countered. In the first place, shipping losses were ultimately cut down. This was accomplished by weapons of offense against the submarine itself—the submarine chaser, the destroyer, the decoy ship, the submarine, the airplane, the bomb, and the depth charge; and by methods of defense—the camouflaged ship, the convoy system, and the barrage. In the second place, Allied shipping losses were made good by the rapid construction of new tonnage, particularly in the United States, where the construction of standardized steel ships reached such a degree of efficiency that a completed vessel could be turned out in seventy days. In the end, German submarines were being destroyed about as rapidly as they could be built, and Allied shipping was being constructed faster than submarines could sink it.

Nevertheless, the Italian disaster in the fall of 1917 and Russia's withdrawal from the war during the winter restored the German hope of ultimate victory in 1918. The disappearance of the eastern front nullified the Allied campaign of attrition, and the Central Powers could once more confront the Allies in the west with a numerical superiority. The defection of Russia, furthermore, had completely isolated Rumania, which was finally compelled to sign a peace treaty with the Central Powers on March 7, 1918. This left Austria-Hungary free to concentrate practically her whole army for what should be a decisive blow against the recently defeated Italians, while German troops should finally smash the Allied line in the west and compel exhausted France to sue for peace.

The Allies, it appeared, would be unable to duplicate the sudden increase of Teutonic man power in the west. France was so nearly exhausted that she could not even keep her units at full strength. The gaps in the British armies occasioned by the late offensives of 1917 had not been adequately filled; in fact, British infantry strength in March, 1918, was 180,000 less than in the same month of the previous year. American forces, since the landing of the first contingent in France on June 25, 1917, had increased slowly; but at the rate of approximately 25,000 men a month it would be many months before they could offset the sudden increase of Teutonic effectives in the west. These facts led Hindenburg and Ludendorff to lay their plans for 1918 with every expectation of final victory for the Central Powers in that year. It was this expectation of a speedy triumph, in turn, that led the political leaders of the Central Powers to treat so cavalierly the Allied announcements of war aims.

## German Repudiation of the Allied War Aims

Early in 1918 the Allied war aims had been further clarified and formulated as a result of two notable addresses—that of Premier Lloyd George before the British trade unions on January 5, 1918, and that of President Wilson before the United States Congress three days later. The two statesmen were in general agreement, and their aims may be discussed in the order of President Wilson's famous "Fourteen Points," destined to play such an important part in the final settlement. They were:

1. "Open covenants of peace, openly arrived at."
2. "Absolute freedom of navigation upon the seas, outside territorial waters, alike in peace and in war."
3. "The removal, so far as possible, of all economic barriers and the establishment of an equality of trade conditions among all the nations."
4. Reduction of national armaments "to the lowest point consistent with domestic safety."
5. "A free, open-minded, and absolutely impartial adjustment of all colonial claims, based upon a strict observance of the principle that in determining all such questions of sovereignty the interests of the population concerned must have equal weight with the equitable claims of the government whose title is to be determined."
6. "The evacuation of all Russian territory and such a settlement of all questions affecting Russia as will secure the best and freest co-operation of the other nations of the world in obtaining for her an unhampered and unembarrassed opportunity for the independent determination of her own political development and national policy."
7. The evacuation and restoration of Belgium without any limit to her sovereignty.
8. The evacuation and restoration of French territory, and the righting of "the wrong done to France by Prussia in 1871 in the matter of Alsace-Lorraine."
9. A readjustment of Italian frontiers "along clearly recognizable lines of nationality."
10. "The freest opportunity of autonomous development" for the peoples of Austria-Hungary.
11. The evacuation and restoration of Rumania, Serbia, and Montenegro, with "free and secure access to the sea" for Serbia.
12. Secure sovereignty for the "Turkish portions" of the Ottoman Empire; security and autonomous development for "the other nationalities which are now under Turkish rule": the permanent opening of

the Dardanelles "as a free passage to the ships and commerce of all nations under international guarantees."

13. The erection of an independent Polish state including "the territories inhabited by indisputably Polish populations" with "a free and secure access to the sea," and with an international guarantee of her "political and economic independence and territorial integrity."

14. The formation of "a general association of nations . . . for the purpose of affording mutual guarantees of political independence and territorial integrity to great and small states alike."

The British premier, in his address, did not include within his war aims anything covering the first three of President Wilson's points. Neither did he take a stand in behalf of Russia such as President Wilson did in his sixth point. Here Lloyd George apparently let disappointment and vindictiveness dominate his statement that "if the present rulers of Russia take action which is independent of their Allies we have no means of intervening to arrest the catastrophe which is assuredly befalling their country." On all the other points of President Wilson's program, however, he held a practical identity of views, and concluded by laying down "three conditions" for a permanent peace:

First, the sanctity of treaties must be re-established. Secondly, a territorial settlement must be secured, based on the right of self-determination or the consent of the governed. Lastly, we must seek by the creation of some international organization to limit the burden of armaments and diminish the probability of war.

These announcements of Allied war aims evoked no enthusiasm among the leaders of the Central Powers, whose views were set forth on January 24 in addresses by Count Hertling, the German chancellor, and Count Czernin, the Austrian foreign minister. On the first four points they admitted that "an understanding might be reached without difficulty." The fourteenth point Czernin accepted much more whole-heartedly than did Hertling, the former stating his belief that it would "nowhere meet with opposition in the Austro-Hungarian Monarchy," the latter only grudgingly conceding that "the Imperial German Government is gladly ready, after all other pending questions have been settled, to approach the examination of the basis of such an association of nations."

But not even a grudging acceptance was vouchsafed the remaining points. The fifth would have to be discussed "at the reconstitution of the world's colonial possessions, which we . . . absolutely demand." Great Britain must "come to terms with this proposal" of President Wilson. The question of Russia was one which concerned the Central Powers and Russia alone, and Germany declined all interference. She also refused to agree in advance in regard to the treatment of Belgium; this question belonged "to the complex of questions . . . which will have to be settled by the war and peace negotiations." Under no circumstances would Germany countenance the cession of Alsace-Lorraine, and even the evacuation of France "must take into account Germany's vital interests." The future of Poland was a question for the decision of Germany, Austria-Hungary, and Poland. In regard to the remaining points Germany was prepared to "do everything for the attainment of peace by Austria-Hungary, which takes into account her just claims," and to give her energetic support to her "loyal, brave, and powerful ally, Turkey." The Allied war aims, Count Hertling asserted, reflected the Allies' belief that they were the victors and that it was the Central Powers who were the vanquished.

The leaders of the Entente must therefore free themselves from this point of view and this self-deception. And in order to facilitate this aim I would like to recall what the position really is. They may take it from me that our military position has never been so favorable as it is at the present time. Our brilliant military leaders face the future with undiminished confidence in victory. Unbroken joy of battle inspires the entire army—officers and men. . . . God is with us, and will continue to be with us.

## GERMANY'S FINAL MILITARY EFFORT

In February Hindenburg and Ludendorff explained their military plans for 1918 to a secret session of the Reichstag, which approved the undertaking even though it called for Germany's loss of a million and a half men. Their aim was to obtain a decision in the field in four months, before the United States could bring her tremendous resources and man power fully to bear. As the first step in their campaign, they proposed to isolate the British army by rolling it up from its right and then driving it into the sea or holding it in an entrenched camp between the Somme and the Channel. The first drive, therefore, was to be directed against that point in the line where the British and French forces met, on the supposition that the lack of unified command among the Allies would lead to confusion here at the moment of attack. German divisions were withdrawn from the Italian and Balkan fronts, half of the 1920 class of recruits was prepared for service, and some half

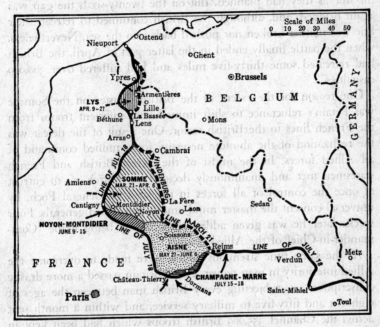

THE GERMAN OFFENSIVES OF 1918

million men were transferred from the east. By March Hindenburg was on the western front with the "whole German manhood for the first time united in a single theater of war, ready to strike with the strongest army that the world has ever known." In addition to superiority of forces, the German high command counted further upon new tactics the effectiveness of which had been proved at Riga and Caporetto in 1917. The essence of these new tactics was the absence of preliminary massing of troops near the front and of long artillery preparations, the use of highly specialized shock troops, and the assault in open order by a method called "infiltration."

After preliminary threats on the Champagne and Ypres fronts, the Germans on March 21, 1918, suddenly hurled a force of over half a million men against a fifty-mile sector between Arras and La Fère. The British, outnumbered three or four to one,[1] gave way and on the second day lost contact with the French on their right. It appeared that the Germans would succeed in breaking through the line as they had planned. But on the twenty-sixth the gap was again bridged, and, although the British continued to retreat, their line was neither broken nor pushed back into the sea. Nevertheless, when the battle finally ended in the latter part of April, the British had retreated some thirty-five miles and had suffered over 300,000 casualties.

One reason for the extent of the British disaster on the Somme was Pétain's reluctance to shift immediately sufficient troops from the French lines to the British sector. One result of the defeat was the realization of the absolute necessity for a unified command of all Allied forces. In the midst of the retreat British and French statesmen met and unanimously decided, on March 26, to entrust at once the control of all forces in the west to General Foch, by universal consent the master mind among the Allied generals. Four weeks later he was given added authority by being made "Commander-in-Chief of the Allied Armies."

At the same time strenuous efforts were made to overcome the Allied inferiority in man power. Great Britain passed a more drastic conscription act, subjecting every British man between the ages of eighteen and fifty-five to military service, and within a month sent across the Channel 355,000 British troops which had been kept in England to meet a possible invasion. By herculean efforts, during May, June, and July over 675,000 American soldiers were rushed across the Atlantic to France—more than twice the number sent in the whole preceding year. On April 28 the first American regular army division, after long training in quiet sectors, began active fighting on the Picardy front.

Meanwhile, on April 9, shortly after the first offensive died down, the Germans struck their second blow against the depleted British left wing between La Bassée and Armentières, where there seemed to be a possibility of breaking through to the Channel ports. During

---

[1] At Verdun between February 21 and March 21, 1916, the French had to face 20½ German divisions; between March 21 and April 17, 1918, the British were attacked by 102 German divisions.

April the Germans employed on this sector forty-four divisions of the cream of their army. But the British troops responded to General Haig's plea that "there must be no retirement. With our backs to the wall . . . each one of us must fight on to the end." And, although in some places they retreated from fifteen to twenty miles, the British stemmed the German flood, kept their lines intact, and held the enemy far back from the coveted Channel ports.

These two tremendous drives with their spectacular results temporarily encouraged the German people to make still further sacrifices, although the German armies had already incurred something over half a million casualties. Ludendorff's attempts to rebuild his forces with men returned from hospitals and with boys of the 1920 class were suffered in silent anguish in the hope that a "German peace" would be won before autumn. By the last week of May Ludendorff had succeeded in replacing more than 70 per cent of his losses. On the twenty-seventh he struck his third terrific blow, this time against the French between Soissons and Reims. Within two days the Germans captured Soissons, and on the thirty-first they reached the Marne valley, down which they hoped to advance toward Paris. Now at length the American forces began to play a decisive role. The second division and parts of the third and twenty-eighth divisions were thrown into the line and helped to bring the German drive to an end. Not only did they halt the Germans; they recaptured from them some of the positions which they had already taken.

But again the Germans had made a tremendous advance of over thirty miles in three days. They had seized the Marne bank for ten miles and had taken between 30,000 and 40,000 prisoners. But their position was such that it offered no safe resting place. They must continue the battle or relinquish their gains. So far they had established two salients threatening Paris; they now sought to convert them into one by a fourth attack (June 9–15) on a front of twenty-two miles between Montdidier and Noyon. But this time the French army, expectant and reinforced, resisted firmly and stopped the drive after an advance of only six miles. In this they were assisted by the American first division, which had proved its mettle earlier (May 28) by capturing and holding Cantigny.

No sooner had this offensive subsided in the west than the Austrians launched what they hoped would be a decisive drive against the Italians on the Piave. But General Diaz learned of the Austrian plans, and knew even the hour set for the attack, which was to begin at three in the morning of June 15. He therefore anticipated the assault by an Italian bombardment of the Austrian troops and succeeded in seriously upsetting their assembly. Nevertheless, promptly at the designated hour the advance began, the Austrians attempting to use the tactics which had been so successfully employed by the Germans in France. They had succeeded in crossing the river with nearly 100,000 men when suddenly, on the afternoon of the seventeenth, the flooding of the Piave turned that broad, shallow stream into a raging torrent which swept away ten of the fourteen bridges upon which the Austrians depended. On the next day Diaz with reinforcements began the counterattack. Within a week the whole of the west bank of the Piave was once more in Italian hands. Austria, instead of putting Italy out of the war, had lost 20,000 prisoners and had suffered at least 150,000 casualties. It was Austria's last great effort. She was broken in spirit, and great numbers of her people were starving. Mutinies and desertions menaced her armies, and disruptive nationalist aspirations threatened the empire. Germany must now continue the struggle practically alone.

But in the west the Germans were preparing to do this. They planned a great *Friedensturm,* or "peace offensive," which was to strike the French line to the east and west of Reims, capture that city, split the French front, cut the vital railway from Paris to Nancy, and enable German troops to sweep down the Marne valley to Paris. At midnight on Sunday, July 14, the sound of great guns to the east told Paris that the final struggle for her capture had begun. Four hours later, at dawn, the Germans began an advance, the importance of which was recognized by both sides. "If my offensive at Reims succeeds, we have won the war," said Ludendorff. "If the German attack at Reims succeeds, we have lost the war," admitted Foch. The Germans succeeded in crossing the Marne between Château-Thierry and Dormans, but they got little farther. On the southeast an Italian corps blocked their way, while on the southwest they encountered American troops who stopped them and pushed them back across the Marne. East of Reims French and American troops held back the German rush and prevented the capture of the city. In the three days' battle the Germans advanced barely six miles at the farthest point. The day of their terrific sledgehammer blows was past. Paris was again saved, and thereafter the offensive rested in Allied hands.

For Foch was now in a position to undertake a general advance. Thanks to American reinforcements, the Allies once more had superiority in rifle strength, a superiority which continued to increase during the rest of the war. The decisive turning point in the conflict had come. Henceforth the collapse of the Central Powers was speedy and sure. A series of Allied offensives rolled back the German armies without cessation until their final surrender in November. Château-Thierry fell on July 21; in August, Soissons, Fismes, Montdidier, Bapaume, and Noyon were recaptured, and the Allies crossed the Somme. In six weeks they captured 130,000 German prisoners, 2000 heavy guns, and 14,000 machine guns.

On August 8 a terrific British attack convinced Ludendorff that the war could not be won, and at a conference at general headquarters at Spa five days later he advised the initiation of "peace feelers." The German chancellor was given a free hand to act at his discretion. Early in September the German army chiefs informed Chancellor Hertling that they must have peace as soon as possible. On September 15 Austria issued an appeal "to all belligerents to send delegates to a confidential and nonbinding discussion on basic principles," an appeal which was declined by President Wilson on the ground that his terms had already been stated.

### The Disintegration of Austria-Hungary

By this time the Habsburgs were in dire straits, for they were waging a struggle not only against foes without their empire but also against foes of disintegration within. The long pent-up national aspirations of the various subject peoples were seeking concrete expression. In January, 1918, Czech, Polish, and Yugoslav deputies in the Reichsrat had drafted a program calling for the establishment of a sovereign constituent assembly for every local area in which a specific language was spoken, the settlement of boundary disputes by means of plebiscites, and the right of each nation to form whatever political ties it desired. Three months later Czechs and Yugoslavs in a great public meeting in Prague had taken a solemn oath to "persist in the struggle for independence in all circumstances and unto the end."

Meanwhile, abroad, energetic steps had been taken to present the claims of the various subject nationalities. Before the war was a year old, national leaders of the Czechoslovaks, Yugoslavs, and Poles were busily at work seeking to gain the sympathy of the Allies and the official recognition of the justice of their cause. Representing the Czechoslovaks abroad were Thomas G. Masaryk, long the leading exponent of the Czech nationalist movement, Edward Beneš, one of his young colleagues at the Czech University of Prague, and Milan Štefánik, a distinguished Slovak scientist. By them the Czechoslovak National Council was organized in Paris, and "bureaus" were established in France, England, Italy, and the United States to create a sentiment favorable to Czechoslovak national aspirations.

Similarly, under the leadership of Ante Trumbich, a deputy in the Austrian Reichsrat, the Yugoslav Committee was organized in London. The aim of the Yugoslav leaders was set forth later in the declaration of Corfu, drawn up jointly by Trumbich and the Serbian premier, Pashich, and forecasting the "Kingdom of the Serbs, Croats, and Slovenes." These three peoples, according to the declaration, constituted a single nation, and it was definitely agreed that they should become united under the Karageorgevich dynasty in a constitutional, democratic, and parliamentary monarchy, the constitution for which should be drafted, after peace had been attained, by a constituent assembly elected by universal suffrage.

In the early years of the war somewhat less vigorous steps were taken abroad in behalf of the Poles under the leadership of Paderewski, world-renowned pianist, and Sienkiewicz, the famous Polish novelist. Eventually, the Polish National Committee, seeking the resurrection of a free and united Poland, located its headquarters in Paris and appointed Paderewski to represent it in Washington. By the middle of 1918 the subject nationalities had succeeded in winning from the Allied governments official recognition of the justice of their cause.

But the military collapse of the Dual Monarchy was a necessary prerequisite of the final independence of the subject races, for the Habsburg government steadily refused to consider any such eventuality. To this collapse the subject nationalities contributed both directly and indirectly. On the one hand, they offered their regiments to swell the Allied forces; by 1918 Czechoslovak, Yugoslav, and Polish legions were fighting on the Allied side. On the other hand, they persistently sought to undermine and weaken the Teu-

Mobilization behind the Lines

A few of the hundreds of posters used as propaganda during the war.

tonic forces from within. Munition plants were blown up, mutinies became frequent both in the army and in the navy, and desertions by the thousands continued unchecked. Leaflets bearing the Allied assent to the freedom of the subject nationalities, which were scattered by airplanes over the Austrian armies in 1918, undoubtedly contributed to the destruction of the morale of the troops.

Military developments in the Near East also contributed to the undermining of that morale. On September 15 the Allied forces on the Saloniki front finally began their oft-delayed advance. In the battle of the Vardar, Serbian, French, British, and Greek troops attacked the Bulgarians, who were routed and forced to retreat. As soon as the latter's territory was actually invaded, the Bulgarian government sued for an armistice, and on September 30 the first of the Central Powers went out of the war. Her means of transportation, now placed at the disposal of the Allies, opened the way for an attack upon Turkey from the west. But Turkey did not wait for any such eventuality. Cut off from the Central Powers, driven back three hundred miles by a rapid Allied advance which captured Damascus, Beirut, Tripoli, and Aleppo in the single month of October, fearful for the safety of Mosul in Mesopotamia and Adrianople in Thrace, the Turks likewise appealed for an armistice, and withdrew from the war on October 31.

The defection of Bulgaria threw the burden of maintaining the Balkan front on weakened Austro-German forces, which were further demoralized by events within the monarchy. Early in October the German-Austrian deputies of the Reichsrat constituted themselves a provisional national assembly and proclaimed the establishment of a new Austrian state. On October 5 representatives from all Yugoslav territories of the empire met at Zagreb and elected a Yugoslav national council to defend their interests. Two days later at Warsaw Polish representatives issued a manifesto promising a national government and a freely elected diet for a reunited Poland. On October 14 Beneš informed the Allied governments that the Czechoslovak National Council in Paris had been transformed into a provisional government with Masaryk as president, Beneš as foreign minister, and Štefánik as secretary for war; and France recognized the provisional government on the next day.

In a last desperate effort to save his realm from complete disintegration Emperor Charles issued a manifesto on October 16,

1918, announcing the policy of federalization. Austrian Poland might freely unite with the independent Polish state, but the rest of Austria was to be transformed into a federal state in which every race should "create its own constitutional status" in the territory in which it dwelt. In Hungary, the issuing of the imperial manifesto was regarded as the destruction of the *Ausgleich,* and the Hungarian government at once declared that the Dual Monarchy was dissolved. This resulted, in turn, in the immediate assertion of the right of self-determination by the Rumanians and Slovaks of the Hungarian kingdom. Nor did the emperor's program win the approval of the various Slav peoples; the day when federalization would satisfy the subject nationalities had passed. Their aim was now absolute independence. During the succeeding ten days the empire went completely to pieces, and the various districts came under the political control and administration of different national councils—Polish, Ukrainian, Yugoslav, Czech, German, Magyar, and Rumanian. National popular governments supplanted the Habsburg dynasty.

On the field of battle, meanwhile, the Habsburg forces were being relentlessly driven back. On October 12 they lost Nish, and two days later Durazzo and Novibazar. By the nineteenth their line near the Rumanian frontier was back on the Danube. On the twenty-fourth the Allies launched an attack in the Trentino and on the Piave, which resulted a week later in the complete routing of the Austrian forces on these fronts. On November 1 the Serbians recaptured Belgrade; two days later the Italians made their triumphal entry into Trieste. On that same day (November 3) the Habsburgs, beset behind and before, capitulated and signed an armistice with the Allied Powers. Eight days later Emperor Charles formally surrendered his Austrian throne. Of *Mittel-Europa,* Germany alone remained a belligerent.

### Downfall of the German Empire

Meanwhile, in the west the Germans by September had been driven back to the Hindenburg Line, having suffered a million and a half casualties since they had left it less than six months earlier. But the Allies continued their attacks unceasingly. In the middle of September over half a million American soldiers wiped out the long-standing St. Mihiel salient. Farther west the Allied troops smashed through the Hindenburg Line and drove the Germans back out of Péronne, Lens, and Dixmude. By September 28 Ludendorff concluded that all was lost and so informed the Kaiser at a conference at Spa the next day. On the thirtieth Hertling resigned as chancellor, and the Kaiser announced that "the German people shall co-operate more effectively than hitherto in deciding the fate of the Fatherland." On October 1 Hindenburg insisted that a peace offer should be made at once, and two days later made his demand more peremptory.

The Kaiser now appointed Prince Max of Baden German chancellor, with a coalition ministry admitting two Socialists into the government for the first time in the history of the empire. On the following day the new government sent a note to President Wilson appealing for a cessation of hostilities, and announcing Germany's readiness to accept the President's "Fourteen Points" together with his later pronouncements as a basis for the discussion of peace terms.[2] But the obtaining of an early armistice was not the only nor perhaps the most important task which rested upon the shoulders of the new chancellor. He had also to attempt to preserve the Hohenzollern empire against the forces which were by now apparently determined to bring about its downfall.

For the situation within Germany in 1918 was very different from that which had existed four years earlier. Then, firm in the belief that the fatherland was being maliciously attacked by an overwhelming coalition of opponents, the German people of all parties had sprung forward as a nation to repel the foes. Even the Social Democrats, who had long denounced all war as in the interest of capitalists alone, recognized the duty of defending the homeland against tsarist Russia, whose triumph their leader, Haase, declared "would be the end of the German people."

But to the Germans the war had brought ever-increasing hardships, privations, and sorrow. These in turn had led to disappointment, disillusionment, and a loss of faith in the government. In consequence, the succeeding years had witnessed a gradual decline in enthusiasm for the war and for those who in the popular mind had come to be held responsible for its continuance. In 1916 this feeling had split the Social Democrats when Haase denounced the

---

[2] On July 4 and September 27 President Wilson had restated the purposes of the war and in the latter address had laid down five principles for the foundation of a league of nations.

continuance of the war and was in consequence read out of the party. In the following year he and his followers had organized the Independent Social Democratic Party. Thereafter they had devoted their efforts to denouncing the war as a crime and had even begun to work for the overthrow of the empire.

Even more destructive in their activities than the Independents were the Spartacists, led by Karl Liebknecht and Rosa Luxemburg, both of whom spent a considerable part of the war period in prison. This group had developed on the left wing of the Independents and took its name from the so-called Spartacus letters, the first of which had appeared in 1916 on the Kaiser's fifty-seventh birthday. These letters had denounced the war as one of imperialistic aggression and had summoned Germans to employ all possible obstructive tactics against it.

For the revolutionary agitators in Germany during the closing years of the war, a fertile field for propaganda was created by the dire distress of the urban masses, caused largely by the Allied blockade. Millions lived on the verge of starvation, while the death rate steadily climbed. Bread, butter, milk, sugar, meat, eggs, and potatoes were rationed out in very limited quantities, while pork, bacon, ham, fresh fish, cheese, coffee, tea, and spices gradually disappeared altogether. For weeks during the "turnip winter" of 1916–1917 potatoes were not to be had, and coarse fodder turnips had to be substituted. The discontent with such conditions was greatly magnified by frequent breakdowns in the government's rationing system, which resulted in profiteering and in an inequitable distribution of the foodstuffs that were actually available. In consequence of this, the wealthy could usually obtain most of the necessaries and some of the luxuries of life, while the poorer people were forced to suffer privation. "To be continually hungry, to rise from the table hungry, to go to bed hungry, was the universal experience of all but the very well-to-do." Cold, miserable, dispirited, many recalled the prewar Socialist doctrine that all wars are the work of the capitalist classes, that existing governments everywhere are obstacles to the coming of a true universal brotherhood of men.

After the Russian Bolshevik revolution and subsequent peace of Brest-Litovsk the "poison gas of Leninism" was wafted back upon Germany. Even before the treaty of Brest-Litovsk, emissaries of the Bolsheviks, well supplied with money, entered the empire by secret routes and worked with Germans in sympathy with their cause. After the establishment of a Bolshevik embassy in Berlin, the leaders of the Spartacists and Independent Socialists were supplied with money, arms, and literature, and from the Russian embassy a staff of men worked to overthrow the very government to which it was accredited. The Spartacists now became definitely imbued with communistic doctrine and began to advocate the immediate socialization of industry and a world revolution of the proletariat. In preparation for the latter they sought to transplant into Germany the methods of Russian Bolshevism, and set out to establish revolutionary workmen's and soldiers' councils throughout Germany and even at the front.

By the beginning of 1918 the influence of these revolutionary groups had reached such proportions in the capital and in the industrial sections of Westphalia that a great political strike was called in Berlin and Essen. For over a week a half million men refused to work. In Berlin they presented an ultimatum to the government demanding a speedy peace without annexations or indemnities, the participation of workingmen's delegates of all countries in the peace negotiations, the release of all political prisoners, freedom of assembly and the press, democratization of state institutions, and woman suffrage.

The government's ruthless suppression of this pacific strike convinced the Independent Socialists that only an armed revolt of the proletariat could free the nation from the menace of imperialism and capitalism. They therefore made the definite decision to overthrow the government. Their revolutionary committee in Berlin redoubled its efforts to establish connections with comrades at the front and with industrial workmen in the capital, and aimed to seize the moment when military defeat should discredit the Hohenzollerns to establish a socialistic republic.

A further disastrous result of this January strike came from the punitive measures adopted by the government. Many of the strikers were men subject to military duty who had been kept in indispensable industries at home, but thousands were now promptly drafted into the army in punishment for their activity during the strike. This practice of "using the army as a prison establishment, and the trenches as cells" proved most unwise, however, for the men thus punished became ardent propagandists of socialism and peace, and carried to the front lines not only rifles but germs of revolution as well.

In the army, too, during 1918, revolutionary propaganda found a fertile field among men who were beginning to be hungry and ill-clad,[3] and who were dispirited by complaints from home folks of increasing privations and suffering. The doctrines of Bolshevism, which the troops transferred from the east brought with them, found ready listeners in men who, subject to the discomforts of mud, vermin, and crowded quarters of the front-line trenches, had come to resent the arbitrary orders and arrogance of the officers—especially the newer, youthful ones during the closing period—who lived in comparative luxury and ease miles in the rear of the battle lines. This discontent was immeasurably increased when the tremendous wastage of men during the first half of 1918 brought only military defeat. Even in the highly disciplined German army desertions by the thousands occurred in the closing three months of the war.

The German defeat in the second battle of the Marne and the fearful collapse of the entire western front during the following months had an effect not only in the army itself but behind the lines as well. Everywhere was the belief that the nation had been duped and deceived, and that there was but one road to salvation —the overthrow of the regime which had brought this immense misery upon the people. The destruction of the military dictatorship of general headquarters and the democratization and parliamentarization of the empire became the program, late in September, of the National Liberals and Centrists, who signified their desire to work toward this end in co-operation with the Majority Socialists.[4]

A menacing situation thus confronted Prince Max when he assumed the chancellorship early in October. But the government went

---

[3] "With the coming of the fourth year conditions began to grow bad even at the front, and the winter of 1917–18 brought a marked decrease of rations, both in quantity and quality. Cavalrymen and soldiers belonging to munition or work columns ate the potatoes issued for their horses. They ground in their coffee-mills their horses' scant rations of barley and made pancakes. . . . Not only were the soldiers hungry by this time, but they were insufficiently clad. Their boots were without soles, and they had neither socks nor the *Fusslappen* (bandages) which most of them preferred to wear instead of socks. A shirt issued from the military stores in the summer of 1918 to a German soldier-friend of the writer was a woman's ribbed shirt, cut low in the neck and gathered with a ribbon."—S. M. Bouton, *And the Kaiser Abdicates*, pages 72–73.
[4] After the founding of the Independent Social Democratic Party, those who remained in the original Social Democratic Party became known as Majority Socialists.

desperately to work to avert revolution by transforming the former quasi-autocratic state into a parliamentary monarchy. The new chancellor hoped that by rapidly democratizing the constitution and the government he might save the Kaiser and the Hohenzollern dynasty. Reform was now the order of the day. Ministerial responsibility was established, the sanction of war and peace was placed in the hands of the Reichstag, the military was brought under the control of the civil authority, amnesty was granted to political prisoners, and freedom of press and assembly was established. Prince Max thus ended the personal regime of the Hohenzollerns and gave the German Empire its first parliamentary government. These changes constituted, in fact, a veritable political revolution. The Kaiser remained merely as the symbol of German unity.

But by this time William II was doomed. The Kaiser's position, already undermined by Socialist and enemy propaganda, became altogether untenable when President Wilson demanded, as the prerequisite of peace negotiations, "the destruction or reduction to virtual impotency of the arbitrary power which has hitherto controlled the German nation." When the German people learned "that the nations of the world do not and cannot trust the word of those who have hitherto been the masters of German policy," that, if the United States "must deal with the military masters and the monarchical autocrats of Germany now, or if it is likely to have to deal with them later in regard to the international obligations of the German Empire, it must demand, not peace negotiations, but surrender," a revulsion of popular feeling set in against generals, emperors, and kings, and even against the monarchy itself. Early in October the question of the Kaiser's abdication began to be discussed among the people, and by the end of the month the demand had apparently gained the support of the bulk of the nation as the only means to assure a cessation of hostilities and bearable terms of peace. On the evening of October 29 the Kaiser, feeling insecure in Berlin, fled from the capital to general headquarters at Spa.

The final crisis was precipitated when the admiralty, realizing that the armistice terms would undoubtedly demand the surrender of the German navy, ordered the fleet to steam out to engage the British in a final decisive battle. When the men realized that, with armistice negotiations actually under way, the lives of 80,000 subordinates were to be recklessly sacrificed, their bitter opposition was aroused. "If the English attack us," they declared, "we will defend our coasts to the last, but we will not ourselves attack. Farther than Helgoland we will not go." This of course constituted only mutiny, not revolution.

But it soon became revolution. On November 4 the sailors' revolt became general. Soldiers' councils were elected, the red flag was hoisted, and the cry "Long live the Republic!" was raised. On the next day the workers of Kiel joined the revolt and formed workmen's councils. What had originally been a naval mutiny now became a great revolutionary movement. Demands were made for the abdication of the Hohenzollerns, the abolition of the state of siege, and the introduction of universal, equal, and secret suffrage. The movement spread rapidly through the coast towns, where the proletariat united with the sailors. Hamburg, Bremen, Lübeck, Wilhelmshaven, and Hanover soon joined the revolt, and by the close of the first week in November the revolution had triumphed along the German coasts. In spite of the government's attempt to isolate the area of contagion by cutting the arteries of communication, the success of these uprisings became known in the interior, and town after town raised the revolutionary standard. The contagion swept swiftly through the empire, claiming Munich, Frankfort, Cologne, Düsseldorf, Leipzig, Stuttgart, Magdeburg, and Brunswick by the evening of November 8.

By this time Prince Max had come to the conclusion that the only way to save the monarchy and to preserve the Hohenzollern dynasty was to have both the Kaiser and the crown prince abdicate in favor of the Kaiser's young grandson, and he so informed the Kaiser. But the latter flatly refused to consider the chancellor's proposals. All day on the eighth the wires between Berlin and Spa were kept busy in an attempt to force the Kaiser to see the light, and that evening the chancellor talked with the Kaiser over the telephone and, "as a relative," informed him that his abdication was "necessary to save Germany from civil war." Furious, the Kaiser rejected all proposals, announced that his intention not to give way was unshaken, that at the head of his army he would reduce his country to order.

That night the Majority Socialist leaders instructed the workers that, if the Kaiser's abdication was not announced in the early morning papers of the ninth, they were to leave their work and hold big demonstrations. The Independent Socialists, likewise, decided to begin their revolution on the same morning, announcing, "We do not demand one person's abdication, we demand the republic." By ten o'clock on the morning of the ninth, therefore, thousands of unarmed workmen, preceded by women and children, were marching toward the center of the city, carrying placards inscribed, "Brothers, no shooting!" But the appeal was hardly necessary, for the troops in Berlin were already mutinying and forming soldiers' councils.

All these facts were passed on to Spa by telephone, together with the insistent demand for immediate abdication. Shortly after eleven o'clock came the message that the Kaiser had resolved on abdication in principle, that he was now simply engaged in the formulation of the statement which would be received in half an hour. The half-hour passed without the promised announcement. The Majority Socialists resigned from the government, and talk of deposition was in the air. In order to forestall the latter, the chancellor now took the decisive step of notifying the press that William II had decided to abdicate his thrones, that the crown prince had resolved to renounce his rights of succession, that a regency would be set up, that Prince Max intended to propose the appointment of Friedrich Ebert, leader of the Majority Socialists, as chancellor, and that a German constituent assembly would be convoked. When a deputation of Majority Socialists demanded that the government be entrusted to men who had the full confidence of the German people, Prince Max surrendered the chancellorship to Ebert. At two o'clock that afternoon the Majority Socialist leaders proclaimed the German Republic.

At general headquarters, on the same day, the Kaiser learned from the army heads that the troops would no longer fight either abroad or at home, that they would not defend the Kaiser's life against German republicans, and that there was little chance, therefore, of his being able to reconquer Germany with their help. Confronted with these facts, the Kaiser at length agreed to a conditional abdication. In the afternoon came the message that "His Majesty is ready to abdicate as German Kaiser, but not as King of Prussia." That night in a special train he fled to the Dutch frontier.

## The End of the War

In the meantime, during October, the Allied troops had completed their smashing of the Hindenburg Line by an "arpeggio" of attacks, which forced the Germans almost completely out of France and compelled them to surrender the Channel ports and a considerable portion of Belgium. At the same time, farther east a disastrous blow had been struck by the American forces in their Meuse-Argonne offensive, "beyond compare the greatest ever fought by American troops." [5] For nearly seven weeks the battle raged, with 1,200,000 American soldiers advancing through tangled woods and underbrush toward the Sedan-Mézières railway. This was the principal line of supply for most of the German forces in the west, and, if it were cut, a German retirement on the whole front must result. Slowly American troops pushed back the best of the German divisions until, on November 6, they reached the outskirts of Sedan, cut the Sedan-Mézières railway, and made the German line untenable.

The day before the Americans entered Sedan, President Wilson finally informed Germany that she might apply for an armistice to Marshal Foch. On the following day a delegation headed by Matthias Erzberger was dispatched to receive the terms which on November 8 were laid down by Foch, subject to rejection or acceptance without amendment within seventy-two hours. The position of the delegates was most difficult. Mutiny had already broken out in the navy. Even while they considered the armistice terms, the government of Prince Max was forced to give way to a Socialist ministry headed by Friedrich Ebert, and the Kaiser fled precipitately from general headquarters to Holland. Behind them was a Germany in chaos; before them, a document most severe.

According to the thirty-five clauses of the terms, Germany was to evacuate Belgium, Luxemburg, France, and Alsace-Lorraine within two weeks, and all the territory on the left bank of the Rhine within one month. Allied troops were to take over all of this territory and were to occupy the bridgeheads of the Rhine at Mainz, Coblenz, and Cologne to a depth of thirty kilometers on the right

[5] "The actual weight of the ammunition fired was greater than that used by the Union forces during the entire Civil War."

bank. A neutral zone ten kilometers wide was to extend along the right bank of the Rhine from Holland to the Swiss frontier. All German troops in Russia, Rumania, and Turkey were to be withdrawn. Within two weeks 5000 locomotives, 150,000 railway cars, and 5000 motor trucks in good working order were to be delivered to the Allies. A specified number of submarines and warships were to be surrendered, and the rest, together with the naval aircraft, were

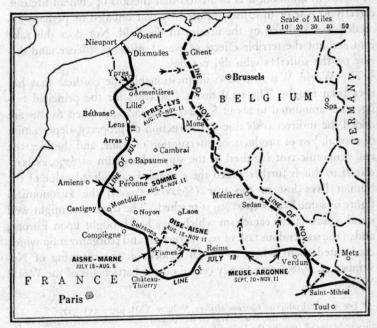

THE FINAL ALLIED OFFENSIVE IN THE WEST

to be disarmed. There was to be an immediate repatriation, without reciprocity, of all Allied prisoners. Finally, the existing blockade of the Allies was to continue unchanged, and all German merchant ships found at sea were to remain liable to capture. These terms were in no sense peace terms. They were designed merely to bring about a cessation of fighting, and to render it utterly impossible for Germany successfully to resume hostilities. At five o'clock on the morning of November 11 the news was flashed to an anxious and expectant world that in a little clearing in the former royal forest of Compiègne these armistice terms had been accepted and signed by the German delegates, to take effect at 11 A. M.

Undoubtedly the World War was the bloodiest that has ever been fought. The conflict mobilized the tremendous total of 65,000,-000 men.[6] Of these millions of the most able-bodied of the nations, nearly 9,000,000 lost their lives and about 22,000,000 were wounded in battle. In addition, it is estimated that the loss of civilian life due directly to war or to causes induced by war equaled or perhaps exceeded that suffered by the armies in the field. Nor does this take into account the terrible effects of war, famine, pestilence, and disease on the sufferers who did not die.

The World War was also unquestionably the costliest that has ever been fought. The total direct war costs for the principal belligerents amounted to about $186,000,000,000,[7] and when to this are added the indirect costs due to destruction of property, depreciation of capital, loss of production, interruption of trade, and the like, the real economic cost is raised to the stupendous sum of $270,000,000,-000. If to this is further added the estimated capitalized value of the human lives lost in the war ($67,000,000,000), the astronomical figure of some $337,000,000,000 is reached.[8] The statesmen might well stand aghast at the cataclysm which they had brought upon Europe, and at the stupendous task of reconstruction and reorganization which confronted them when, at eleven o'clock on the morning of November 11, 1918, firing finally ceased on the battlefields of the World War.

[6] See statistical tables in *Current History*, Volume XXII, pages 355–357.

[7] The direct cost of the World War to the United States was nearly enough to pay the entire cost of running the United States Government from 1791 up to the outbreak of the World War.—U. S. General Staff, *The War with Germany: A Statistical Summary*, page 135.

[8] As distinct from the money cost or actual expenditures of the belligerent governments for war purposes, the British economist and statistical authority, Mr. Edgar Crammond, estimated that the war actually decreased the national wealth of Great Britain 12.7 per cent, France 25 per cent, Italy 20 per cent, and Germany 26 per cent. —*The Economic World*, July 3, 1920, page 19.

# PART FOUR

# THE INTERNATIONAL AFTERMATH
# OF THE WAR

During the World War mankind dreamed of a new international order which should be ushered in at the close of "the war to end war," and many hoped that the ensuing peace conference would lay the foundation for this new era. The chapters in Part Four point out the problems, achievements, and mistakes of this peace conference. They discuss the postwar efforts through international organizations and international treaties to reduce armaments and to lessen or abolish war. They reveal how grievously mankind's hopes for the creation of a new world order were disappointed, for they show how clashes between national aims again turned the nations to entangling alliances, huge armaments, and in general to a state of "international anarchy" which differed little from that existing in 1914.

PART FOUR

THE INTERNATIONAL AFTERMATH
OF THE WAR

## CHAPTER XV

# THE PARIS PEACE SETTLEMENT

THE signing of the armistice was not followed immediately by the drafting of the peace treaties. For various reasons, two full months elapsed between the cessation of fighting and the first preliminary meeting of the peace conference. In the first place, even with modern means of travel it required several weeks for the duly appointed representatives to gather from all the belligerent powers, for this had been a world war. In the second place, the heads of the delegations of two of the most important states were unable to come to the conference immediately. President Wilson decided to lead personally the peace delegation from the United States, and it was impossible for him to arrive in Europe before the middle of December. Premier Lloyd George decided that his government ought to appeal to the British people for a vote of confidence before it represented them at the conference, and so called an election for December 14. This and the subsequent reorganization of the government prevented him from attending until four weeks later.

## PREPARATIONS FOR THE CONFERENCE

In the meantime, however, attempts were made to gather up and organize the great mass of information—historic, geographic, ethnographic, economic, and the like—which had been prepared by the various elaborate research agencies of the chief Allied states for use at the inevitable peace conference. Great numbers of experts had been working for months gathering facts which might have a bearing on the solution of the many intricate and complex problems which would have to be met. For the tasks which confronted the Allied statesmen at the close of the World War were incomparably greater than those of any previous peace conference, and the need for an adequate knowledge of the facts in connection with the various problems was imperative.

In recognition of the heroic part played by France in the war,

Paris was designated as the seat of the peace conference, and early
in 1919 the national delegations began to arrive. In some cases their
members numbered into the hundreds—"trained diplomats, soldiers, sailors, airmen, civil administrators, jurists, financial and economic experts, captains of industry and spokesmen of labor, members of cabinets and parliaments, journalists and publicists of all
sorts and kinds"—together with their clerks and typists. Whole
hotels—sometimes several—were needed to accommodate the various groups. At the head of each delegation were the plenipotentiaries, of whom there were seventy representing the thirty-two
Allied and Associated Powers. Although there was a noticeable absence of crowns and gold lace, the plenipotentiaries constituted a
distinguished assemblage of the responsible statesmen of the world,
including besides the President of the United States at least eleven
prime ministers and twelve foreign ministers. Among them were
such outstanding men as Clemenceau, Pichon, Tardieu, and Cambon of France; Lansing and House of the United States; Lloyd
George, Balfour, and Bonar Law of Great Britain; Orlando and
Sonnino of Italy; Hymans of Belgium; Dmowski and Paderewski
of Poland; Pashich and Trumbich of Yugoslavia; Bratianu of Rumania; Kramář and Beneš of Czechoslovakia; Venizelos of Greece;
and Smuts and Botha of South Africa. No delegations from the defeated powers were present during the drafting of the peace terms,
for theirs was a role which called merely for the signing of the
completed documents. This was to be a dictated, not a negotiated,
peace.

## THE WORKING ORGANIZATION

On January 12, 1919, the two ranking delegates of the United
States, of Great Britain, of France, and of Italy in an informal meeting decided that those states which had declared war on, or had
broken off relations with, Germany should be represented at the
conference, and that the number of plenipotentiaries of each state
should vary from one to five, the five great powers to have the
latter number.[1] A plenary session of the conference was to consist
of the plenipotentiaries of all the powers, but the main organ was

---

[1] Belgium, Brazil, and Serbia had three each; Australia, Canada, China, Czecho-
slovakia, Greece, Hejaz, India, New Zealand, Poland, Portugal, Rumania, Siam, and
South Africa, two each; Bolivia, Cuba, Ecuador, Guatemala, Haiti, Honduras, Liberia,
Nicaragua, Panama, Peru, and Uruguay, one each.

to be the Council of Ten, in a sense an outgrowth of the Supreme Inter-Allied War Council which had acted on matters of military policy during the last year of the war. This council should consist of two representatives of each of the five great powers,[2] and should have the right to decide what questions were to be referred to the general conference, and to reserve to itself all questions which it considered needed preliminary treatment. It was further decided that the great powers should be represented on all committees or commissions, the others being represented only when questions directly affecting them were being discussed. Although in theory all decisions of the conference required the approval of a plenary session, as a matter of fact only six plenary sessions were held before the treaty with Germany was signed. For all practical purposes, therefore, the Council of Ten constituted the peace conference during the first two months. Its meetings were secret, but representatives of the other powers were given an opportunity to appear before the council in order to present their claims.

The intricate facts that underlay most of the problems which it was called upon to solve, facts which were constantly being made more difficult to ascertain because of the steady stream of propagandist pamphlets, treatises, ethnographic maps, and petitions which flooded the conference, soon convinced the Council of Ten that it must be assisted in its investigations. The result was the appointment of special commissions, varying greatly in size, to which difficult questions were referred for preliminary study and report. France, Great Britain, Italy, and the United States always had representatives on each commission, and other powers had seats on some of the larger ones. Before the treaty with Germany was completed, fifty-two of these commissions had been appointed to consider various problems. Although their reports were in no sense binding upon the council, many of the articles in the final treaties were taken bodily from the reports of commissions.

By the middle of March, two months after the opening of the conference, the only parts of the treaty with Germany which had been finally agreed upon were the military, naval, and air terms.

[2] At the peace conference, the United States, Great Britain, France, Italy, and Japan were designated as the "Principal Allied and Associated Powers," the rest being designated merely as the "Allied and Associated Powers." For the sake of brevity, the former will be referred to as the "principal Allies" or the "great powers," the latter as the "small powers."

None of the important and complex territorial questions had yet been decided, and commissions were still considering the financial and economic settlement. It must not be forgotten, of course, that the necessity for dealing with a great many of what may be called executive matters, in connection with bringing order out of chaos in central and eastern Europe, prevented the Council of Ten from devoting its whole attention to treaty-making. Nevertheless, the alarming conditions in Europe urgently demanded greater speed on the part of the conference. The resultant demand for an early peace and a definite ending of the war was most insistent.

The desire for greater speed in the drafting of the treaty together with the need for secrecy during the period of compromise between the great powers led to a change in the organization of the conference. On March 25 it was announced that informal conferences of the chief plenipotentiaries would take the place of the former meetings of the Council of Ten. The "Big Four"—Wilson, Lloyd George, Clemenceau, and Orlando—ceased to attend the sessions of the Council of Ten. Since thereafter the first ranking delegate of Japan also ceased attending the sessions of that council, the latter from March on consisted of only five men. It came to be known as the Council of Five and sank to the position of a sort of superior commission. As such it considered the reports of the commissions already appointed, and transmitted them with its findings to the "Big Four." The latter, beginning with purely personal and informal conversations, finally constituted themselves the supreme Council of Four, which made almost all the important decisions of the conference in respect to the treaty with Germany.

It was an interesting personnel which composed this council: Clemenceau, the dauntless Tiger, stolidly silent save when some remark disclosed his dry humor or stinging sarcasm, inclined to be cynical and dogmatic, inflexibly and courageously fighting for one object, the security of his beloved France; Lloyd George, the nimble-minded, responsive politician, shrewd, alert, dynamic, ingenious, more and more inclined to be lenient with the defeated powers, seeking by compromise and adjustment to bring speedily a peace which would facilitate Britain's much-needed revival of trade; Wilson, idealistic spokesman of the moral and spiritual forces of the world, clear-minded and resolute, tirelessly working to construct the League of Nations which he firmly believed would be the salvation of mankind; Orlando, learned, warm-hearted, eloquent, destined to play a relatively subordinate part in the general settlement, nevertheless struggling to satisfy the ambitions of his enthusiastic compatriots.

Almost inevitably conflict arose among these four statesmen when the time came for the various personal and national programs to be presented for fulfillment, for the abstract "Fourteen Points" to be transformed into definite treaty provisions. In the latter case, the very elasticity and vagueness which had made it easy for the powers to accept some of the "Points" in principal made it likewise easy for differences in interpretation to arise when they came to be examined from the conflicting nationalistic points of view. In fact, even before the peace conference the Allies had made a number of reservations. The chief problem of the statesmen at Paris was to draft terms which would reconcile the opposing viewpoints of the Allied powers. No one man could dominate a group like the "Big Four." Agreement was possible only through compromise, though frequently affairs had to reach an actual crisis before a settlement was finally effected. On one occasion President Wilson in despair ordered his ship, the *George Washington,* to come for him; on another Orlando and his delegation went even so far as to withdraw from the conference and return to Rome. Despite the strain and stress which prevailed at such times as these, however, the peace conference managed to hold together and eventually completed its work.

## THE TREATY OF VERSAILLES

Although more than a dozen treaties and conventions were eventually drafted and signed in the attempt to settle the many and complex problems raised by the World War—treaties between the Allies and the defeated powers, between the principal Allies and some of the newly created states, and even between some of the Allies themselves, undoubtedly the treaty with Germany was the greatest single achievement of the peace conference.

### THE QUESTION OF INCLUDING THE LEAGUE COVENANT

At the very outset of the conference an acute difference of opinion arose as to whether the Covenant of the proposed League of Nations should be included in the treaty with Germany or should constitute a separate document. There was little doubt, of course, that the conference was expected to create such an organization. Even before the war much thought had been given to the possible prevention of international wars, and various societies had been organized both in Europe and in America to work toward that ultimate goal. The World War with its terrible bloodshed and suffering gave a great impetus to the movement, and during the final year of the conflict the idea of creating an international organization to prevent war made a tremendous appeal. By the time the peace conference assembled in Paris there was a general demand that this great international assembly should create some common agency for the prevention of war. The spokesman of world opinion on this subject was President Wilson, who had asserted early in 1918 that for a just and stable peace a "general association of nations must be formed under specific covenants for the purpose of affording mutual guarantees of political independence and territorial integrity to great and small nations alike."

Wilson maintained that the League Covenant should be an integral part of the treaty with Germany. Others, however, in view of the serious European situation, desired the speedy conclusion of a preliminary treaty of peace, which need not wait for the drafting of the Covenant. This treaty could settle such important questions as the boundaries and military establishment of Germany, could definitely end the war, and make possible the raising of the blockade of the Central Powers. Wilson, on the other hand, felt that the preliminary treaty would in reality be the main treaty and that to leave the Covenant out would be to weaken the League, if not to postpone its creation indefinitely. Only by making it necessary for the nations to adopt the Covenant of the League in order to gain the benefits of the peace treaty, he believed, was it possible to secure their immediate and unanimous approval of the various provisions of the Covenant.

The second plenary session of the conference, on January 25, 1919, voted that the Covenant should be an integral part of the peace treaty, and entrusted the drafting of it to a special commission of which Wilson was chairman and upon which sat ultimately the representatives of fourteen states. This commission considered a number of drafts, among which the most important were undoubtedly those of General Smuts and Lord Robert Cecil, and at another plenary session of the conference, on February 14, Wilson presented the report.

The draft Covenant of the League at once encountered considerable criticism. From the United States, especially, came an insistent demand that the Monroe Doctrine be safeguarded. In order to satisfy this demand, Wilson, after consulting various political leaders in the United States, brought forward an amendment to the Covenant, which he so worded as to avoid placing the United States in the position of asking a special favor. He proposed that:

Nothing in this Covenant shall be deemed to affect the validity of international engagements, such as treaties of arbitration or regional understandings like the Monroe Doctrine, for securing the maintenance of peace.

The French, desiring a more exact definition of the Monroe Doctrine, objected to this amendment. The British and Italians, however, gave it their support, and Wilson, after an impassioned speech, secured its adoption by the commission. The amendment became Article 21 of the Covenant of the League, and for the first time in history the European powers gave their official diplomatic recognition to the Monroe Doctrine. The Covenant in its final form was definitely approved at a plenary session of the conference on April 28, and became the first twenty-six articles in the treaty with Germany as well as in the treaties with the other defeated powers. These articles are discussed in the next chapter.

### TERRITORIAL PROVISIONS

When the statesmen came to consider the territorial provisions of the peace treaty, it was readily agreed that, in order "to redress the wrong done by Germany in 1871 both to the rights of France and to the wishes of the population of Alsace and Lorraine," these two territories should be restored to French sovereignty. Clemenceau demanded, in addition, that in the interest of French security [3] Ger-

[3] The original French program of security as presented at the peace conference has been summarized as follows:

"(1) French military control of the Rhine: (2) a permanent alliance of the Great Powers to help France hold it: (3) a group of smaller allies to menace Germany from the east: (4) territorial reduction of the German Empire: (5) crippling of the German political organization: (6) disarmament of Germany but not of the Allies: (7) a crush-

many's western frontier should be fixed at the Rhine, that the ten thousand square miles of territory lying on the left bank of the Rhine between Alsace and Holland should be detached from Germany and erected into an autonomous and neutral state. A secret treaty of 1917 with Russia had, in fact, stipulated that such a state should be created and that it should be occupied by French troops until all the terms of the final treaty of peace had been fulfilled by Germany. Although it was admitted that the inhabitants of the territory were thoroughly German in speech and life, Clemenceau argued that the Rhine constituted the one advance line which could not be turned and which guaranteed France against invasion.

From the outset Lloyd George opposed the creation of such a buffer state, and repeatedly insisted that "another Alsace-Lorraine" must not be created. The French plan was also consistently opposed by President Wilson. In the end Clemenceau surrendered his demand for the creation of a separate state on the left bank of the Rhine. In return, however, he secured the occupation of this territory by an Inter-Allied force for at least fifteen years, as a guarantee of Germany's execution of the peace treaty, and the permanent demilitarization of the left bank together with a strip of territory fifty kilometers wide on the right bank. Finally, and in addition, Lloyd George and Wilson promised France a guarantee treaty of security which provided that their two countries would come to the aid of France in case of an unprovoked attack by Germany.

Clemenceau also advanced a claim to the Saar basin, a highly industrialized and densely populated area of about seven hundred square miles, most of which had been French before the second treaty of Paris had taken the whole district from France and given it to Prussia and Bavaria in 1815. The basin was of great economic value because it included one of the richest and most concentrated coal beds on the Continent. Furthermore, the Saar mines lay on the outer edge of Germany, they were within a dozen miles of the new French frontier, they were already linked with the industries of Lorraine which were to become French, and with two exceptions they were the state property of Prussia and Bavaria. Clemenceau demanded the political annexation of the territory which had been

ing indemnity: (8) deprivation of economic resources: (9) a set of commercial agreements preferential to France, prejudicial to Germany."—R. S. Baker, *Woodrow Wilson and World Settlement,* Volume II, page 20.

French before 1815 and the full ownership of the mines but not the political sovereignty of the rest of the basin.

In view of the deliberate destruction of French coal mines by the Germans in 1918, and in view of the fact that prewar Germany had

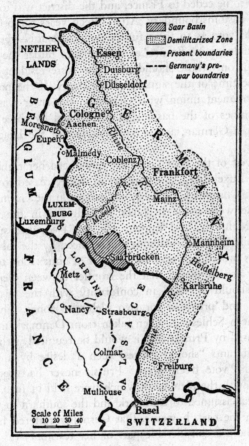

THE RHINELAND

a large surplus of coal, the Allied statesmen looked with favor upon French acquisition of the Saar coal mines. The acquisition of these mines might justly balance the destruction of the French mines, and any excess value might be credited to Germany's reparations account. But neither Lloyd George nor Wilson favored the political annexation of the district by France. Again a compromise resulted. Germany for the time was to retain the political sovereignty of the region, but was to hand over the government of the district to a commission under the League of Nations for fifteen years. The coal mines were to be ceded to France, and the district was to be within the French customs boundary. After fifteen years the people of the basin should vote as to their future political status—reunion with Germany, union with France, or continuance under the League of Nations; but only those should vote who were resident in the territory at the time of the signing of the treaty. If the popular vote favored permanent union with Germany, the latter was to repurchase the mines of the basin at a price fixed by three experts, a Frenchman, a German, and a representative of the League of Nations.

To the west of the Saar Germany renounced her rights over the railways of Luxemburg, and this grand duchy ceased to be part of the German Customs Union. Slight changes in the German-Belgian frontier line were made in favor of Belgium in the vicinity of Moresnet, Malmédy, and Eupen. The last two were subject to a sort of plebiscite, which—although denounced by the inhabitants as unfair in its procedure—resulted in favor of annexation to Belgium. The treaty also stipulated that the frontier between Germany and Denmark should be fixed in conformity with the wishes of the population, and provided for two plebiscite zones. This was because northern Schleswig, when taken from Denmark in 1864, had been promised by Prussia that it would be reunited with Denmark if the inhabitants "should express such a desire by a vote freely given." This "vote freely given" Prussia never had permitted. In accordance with the plebiscites, which were held in 1920, the northern zone was assigned to Denmark and the southern to Germany.

It was in the east, however, that Germany suffered her greatest losses, for here a considerable part of her territory was allotted to the new Polish republic. It has already been pointed out that during the World War the Allies committed themselves to the restoration of a "united and independent Poland." But how large this Poland should be or where her boundaries should be placed none of the "Big Four" knew. The only thing that was definitely known in the beginning was the Allied statement that the new Poland should include the territory inhabited by a population indisputably Polish, and "should be assured a free and secure access to the sea." To provide the latter, experts recommended that a corridor through the province of West Prussia, including both banks of the lower Vistula and the city of Danzig, should be given to Poland.

But this recommendation was vigorously attacked, especially by Lloyd George. He argued that such an arrangement would dismember Prussia, that it would separate East Prussia from the rest of Germany and turn it into "a German island floating in a Slavic sea." It would compel a German going by land from Berlin to East Prussia to cross Polish territory. Furthermore, he pointed out, the population of the city and district of Danzig, which exceeded 300,000, was overwhelmingly German, as was also the population in the narrow belt of territory around Marienwerder on the east bank of the Vistula.

On the other hand, Polish statesmen, backed by Clemenceau, maintained that either Germans must cross Polish territory to go by land to East Prussia or Poles must cross German territory in order to carry their commerce to the Baltic. They pointed out that East Prussia's most important item in trade had always been the export of timber by ship, and that Germans could easily carry on their commerce with East Prussia by sea. Furthermore, they asserted, the rights and needs of the people in Poland ought to take precedence over those of the 1,500,000 in East Prussia. It was freely admitted that the population of Danzig and the Marienwerder district was predominantly German, but Wilson was quoted to the effect that every state had the right to conditions that would assure its economic life. Danzig was the natural port of Poland and of the Vistula river basin, and had been for many centuries outside the political frontiers of Germany. The possession of the Marienwerder district was necessary in order that Poland might control the lower Vistula and the one direct railway between Danzig and the Polish capital, Warsaw.

Ultimately it was decided that in order to insure Poland's economic interests in Danzig without actually annexing it to that republic, a district of about seven hundred square miles around the port should be established as a free city under the protection of the League of Nations. The Allies undertook to negotiate a treaty between Danzig and Poland which should bring Danzig within the Polish customs lines, should insure to Poland free use of all waterways and docks necessary for Polish commerce together with the

control and administration of the means of communication between Poland and Danzig, and should give to Poland the conduct
of the foreign relations of the free city. The executive of Danzig
was to be a high commissioner appointed by the League of Nations.

DANZIG AND THE POLISH CORRIDOR

In the treaty, therefore, Germany was compelled to recognize
the independence of Poland and to renounce in the latter's favor
about five sixths of the former province of Posen and the greater
part of the former province of West Prussia. In East Prussia two
plebiscites were to be held in districts in the vicinity of Allenstein
and Marienwerder, chiefly to determine whether Poland should con-

trol territory on both banks of the Vistula. Both districts later voted for union with Prussia and were retained practically intact. In industrial Upper Silesia a plebiscite was likewise to be held; but in this case the final division of the district was favorable to Poland.[4] Germany also surrendered a small section of Upper Silesia to Czechoslovakia. The Baltic cities of Danzig and Memel, together with a certain area in the vicinity of each, were renounced in favor of the principal Allied and Associated Powers. The former, as discussed above, was established as a free city under the League of Nations; the latter was assigned in 1923 to Lithuania.

Before the peace conference, it was generally taken for granted among the Allies that Germany's conquered colonies would not be returned, and, when the question of disposing of them first came up in January, the great powers of Europe favored outright annexation. Wilson, however, opposed this procedure and pronounced in favor of a mandatory scheme which apparently had been conceived earlier by both General Smuts and Colonel House. This plan provided that to the various colonies which were "inhabited by peoples not yet able to stand by themselves under the strenuous conditions of the modern world, there should be applied the principle that the well-being and development of such peoples form a sacred trust of civilization." The various colonies should, therefore, be distributed among the powers as mandates which the powers should administer in trust for the League of Nations, to which they must make an annual report. The mandates might differ in character according to their conditions, but to all members of the League there should be equal opportunity for trade and commerce.

Wilson saw in this novel scheme an opportunity to increase the influence of the League of Nations and at the same time to prevent an out-and-out annexationist policy on the part of the European states. Others saw in it an opportunity to deprive Germany of her colonies without having to credit their value to the reparations account. Although French colonial circles were inclined to question the practicability of the proposal, the only open opposition came from Australia, New Zealand, and the Union of South Africa. In the end, however, the mandatory system was adopted, Germany renouncing overseas "all rights, titles and privileges whatever in or over territory which belonged to her or to her allies." Her former

[4] See page 528.

colonies were later distributed among Great Britain, France, Belgium, the Union of South Africa, Australia, New Zealand, and Japan as mandates of the League of Nations.

The fate of Germany's concession in Shantung caused an acute crisis at the conference. Early in the war Japan had joined the Allies and had captured the German fortress of Tsingtao; later, in 1917, Great Britain, France, and Italy had promised her Shantung and the German islands north of the equator. Definite engagements had thus been entered into which now arose to embarrass the conference. The Chinese government also had declared war on Germany, and at the conference the Chinese delegates demanded the restoration of Kiaochow to China. Wilson supported the Chinese in their demand and desired that Germany's rights in the Shantung peninsula should not be surrendered to Japan but should be returned directly to China.

But Japan was in possession of the district involved, and her delegates were inflexible in their demand for the concession. Taking advantage of the strained situation at the time of the withdrawal of the Italian delegation, they insisted that the Japanese claim to Shantung be granted at once, else they would leave Paris and refuse to sign the treaty or join the League. For a week the Shantung question monopolized the conference. Lloyd George and Clemenceau finally stated that they considered themselves bound by the pledges of 1917. Fearing that, in the face of these developments, the Covenant of the League of Nations might finally fail of adoption, Wilson yielded. It was agreed that the peace treaty should stipulate that Japan obtained the former German rights in Shantung. On the same day that the agreement was finally reached, however, Japan promised that she would return the Shantung district to China in full sovereignty, keeping only the economic rights which had formerly been granted to Germany, and the right to establish a settlement at Tsingtao. This promise was carried out by Japan in 1923.

### LIMITATION OF ARMAMENTS

In the interest of French security as well as in the interest of general disarmament, the peace conference deliberately sought to weaken Germany's military and naval forces and to limit her in the use of those which were actually left in her control. The treaty specifically stated that, after March 31, 1920, the army of the states constituting Germany "must not exceed one hundred thousand men, including officers and establishments of depots." There were to be neither military nor naval air forces. The great German general staff was to be abolished and might not be re-established in any form. The manufacture of arms, munitions, and other war material was strictly limited, and the importation or exportation of war material was forbidden. Neither the manufacture nor the importation of poisonous gases was permitted. Universal compulsory military service was abolished. In order to prevent the extension of military training to a greater number of men, by having a rapid turnover in the personnel of the army, the treaty stipulated that the enlistments of officers must be for at least twenty-five consecutive years and those of privates for at least twelve, and that the number of officers or privates discharged in any one year must not exceed 5 per cent of the total effectives.

Germany was definitely restricted in the use of her military forces even within her own frontiers. She was forbidden to maintain or construct any fortifications in her territory on the left bank of the Rhine, or on the right bank to a distance of fifty kilometers eastward. Those already existing were to be disarmed and dismantled. In this demilitarized area she was forbidden to maintain either temporarily or permanently any armed forces or to conduct any military maneuvers. Germany's violation of these articles would be regarded as a hostile act against the signatory powers. On the southern and eastern frontiers Germany must limit her system of fortified works to its existing state.

The German navy was restricted to six of the larger battleships, six light cruisers, twelve destroyers, and twelve torpedo boats, and she was forbidden to construct or acquire any warships except to replace units already in commission. Germany might not have any submarines, even for commercial purposes; and all existing submarines must be handed over to the Allied powers or destroyed. As in the army, so in the navy the personnel was limited. The fortifications and harbor of Helgoland were ordered destroyed, never to be reconstructed.

Inter-Allied commissions of control were provided for in the treaty to supervise the execution of the disarmament clauses. They were given the right to establish their organizations in Berlin, to send agents into any part of Germany, and to demand information and aid from the German government. The upkeep and cost of these commissions of control and the expenses involved in their work were to be borne by Germany.

## REPARATIONS

In a prearmistice note of November 5, 1918, the Allies had demanded that compensation should "be made by Germany for all damage done to the civilian population of the Allies and to their property by the aggression of Germans, by land, by sea, and from the air." Nevertheless, in the opening weeks of discussion at the peace conference, the British and French delegates contended for the inclusion of all war costs in the amount which Germany should pay, arguing that only thus would the settlement really be based on justice. The American delegates, on the other hand, maintained that the demands which might be made upon Germany were limited by prearmistice agreements and that, consequently, only reparation of damage should be collected, and not the costs of the war. After Wilson had vigorously asserted that the inclusion of war costs was "clearly inconsistent with what we deliberately led the enemy to expect," the other three members of the "Big Four" gave way and agreed that Germany's reparations obligations should be limited to what might be called actual damage, the costs of the war being excluded.[5] The justification for the reparations demands was set forth in the now famous or infamous Article 231:

The Allied and Associated Governments affirm and Germany accepts the responsibility of Germany and her allies for causing all the loss and damage to which the Allied and Associated Governments and their nationals have been subjected as a consequence of the war imposed upon them by the aggression of Germany and her allies.

The next difficulty arose over the meaning of the term "damage" as distinct from "war costs." At first thirty-one different categories of damages were considered, but the number was gradually reduced to ten upon which there was general agreement except as to pensions and separation allowances. The Allied statesmen vigorously urged the inclusion of these items, and argued that there should be compensation for damage to the homes and families behind the

[5] A single exception was made in the case of Belgium; Germany was to pay all of her war costs down to the signing of the armistice.

front as well as for damage to the houses at the front. "Payment for a destroyed chimney was not to be placed above compensation for a lost life or a pension for a blinded or wounded soldier." The unanimous approval of the "Big Four" for the inclusion of war pensions and separation allowances was finally gained by a memorandum submitted by General Smuts.

Next came the question of the amounts, periods, and method of payment to be required. The American delegates contended for a fixed and reasonable sum. They argued that it would be well for the Allies to know exactly what they could depend upon to aid them in the rehabilitation of their own economic and financial situation and equally advantageous for the defeated powers to know exactly what they had to pay so that they could set about paying it. But the Allies could not agree on the amount which Germany could pay, and they felt that she should pay all that she could.

In the end it was decided that it would be unwise politically to fix any definite total in the peace treaty. Clemenceau asserted that whatever amount might be agreed upon would fall far short of the expectations of the French people and would bring the downfall of the government which accepted it. Lloyd George, recalling the campaign arguments of the election of 1918, readily fell in with this view. A provisional solution was therefore eventually agreed upon. Germany, by May, 1921, should pay in gold or its equivalent a total of $5,000,000,000, an amount which the experts in general asserted she could pay from her quick, realizable surplus assets. Out of this amount the expenses of the Inter-Allied army of occupation were first to be met, and the balance then applied to the reparations account. The question of further payments was left unsettled but was to be determined by that date, and the power to fix the final sum was to be vested in a Reparations Commission. In case of default by Germany in the performance of any of her reparations obligations, the commission should give notice of such default to each of the interested powers, and might make recommendations as to the action to be taken in consequence of such default.

The measures which the Allied and Associated Powers shall have the right to take, in case of voluntary default by Germany, and which Germany agrees not to regard as acts of war, may include economic and financial prohibitions and reprisals and in general such other measures as the respective Governments may determine to be necessary in the circumstances.

### MISCELLANEOUS PROVISIONS

In addition to the provisions already discussed, the treaty when finally completed made a number of miscellaneous requirements of Germany. She consented to the abrogation of the treaties of 1839 which had established Belgium's neutrality, and also adhered to the termination of the regime of neutrality of the Grand Duchy of Luxemburg. She acknowledged and promised to respect strictly the independence of Austria, and agreed "that this independence shall be inalienable, except with the consent of the Council of the League of Nations."

In articles on waterways, the conference sought to provide access to the sea for landlocked countries of Europe by establishing international control over rivers which flowed through more than one country. International commissions were set up to control the Rhine, Oder, Elbe, Niemen, and Danube. In the control of three rivers considered as German—the Rhine, Oder, and Elbe—Germany was therefore placed in a minority. The treaty provided for free zones for Czechoslovakia in the harbors of Hamburg and Stettin. Finally, the Kiel Canal was to be free and open on terms of equality to the mercantile and war ships of all nations at peace with Germany.

In response to the aroused public sentiment in Allied countries during the war and just following it, the treaty publicly arraigned "William II of Hohenzollern, formerly German Emperor, for a supreme offense against international morality and the sanctity of treaties." A special tribunal was to be constituted to try the ex-emperor; but the Allied request for his extradition by the Netherlands was refused by the latter, and the trial never took place. In respect to German "atrocities," Germany recognized the right of the Allied powers to bring before military tribunals persons accused of having committed acts in violation of the laws and customs of war, and agreed to hand over such persons as the Allied powers should specify.[6]

---

[6] In the face of German protests, however, the Allies later gave way and permitted trials in Leipzig to be substituted for the trials established by the treaty. Only about a dozen of the hundred or more accused were ever brought to court, and most of them

THE "BIG FOUR" AT THE PEACE CONFERENCE

Orlando, Lloyd George, Clemenceau, Wilson.

Certain guarantees for the execution of the treaty of Versailles were stipulated in the treaty itself. German territory to the west of the Rhine, together with the bridgeheads, was to be occupied by the Allied troops for a period of fifteen years from the coming into force of the treaty. If the conditions of the treaty were faithfully carried out by Germany, the occupation would be gradually restricted. At the expiration of five years the Cologne area would be evacuated; at the end of ten years, the Coblenz area; at the end of fifteen years, the Mainz area and all other German territory under occupation. If before the expiration of the fifteen years Germany should comply with all the undertakings resulting from the treaty, the occupying forces would be withdrawn immediately. If, on the other hand, the guarantees against unprovoked aggression by Germany were not considered sufficient by the Allied governments, the evacuation of the occupying troops might be delayed to the extent regarded as necessary for the purpose of obtaining the required guarantees. Finally, it was provided:

In case either during the occupation or after the expiration of the fifteen years referred to above the Reparation Commission finds that Germany refuses to observe the whole or part of her obligations under the present Treaty with regard to reparation, the whole or part of the areas . . . will be reoccupied immediately by the Allied and Associated forces.

### THE SIGNING OF THE TREATY

On May 7, 1919, the draft treaty was presented to the German delegates who had at last been summoned to the conference, and they were informed that they would have three weeks in which to make written observations on the terms but that no oral discussions with the Allied delegates would be permitted. The counterproposals of the Germans reached the Council of Four on May 29, and were immediately submitted to ten Inter-Allied committees of experts for consideration. The Allied reply granted a few concessions, but in general left the treaty substantially unchanged. Germany was required to declare her willingness to sign the treaty, as modified, within five days, or the armistice would terminate and the Allies would take the necessary steps to enforce their terms. In Germany

received merely light sentences as a result of the perfunctory trials conducted by the Germans themselves.

the feeling was most bitter, and the Scheidemann government resigned rather than sign the treaty. In the end, however, a new government, in which Gustav Bauer was chancellor and Hermann Müller foreign minister, agreed to accept it. Müller and Johannes Bell, minister for the colonies in the new German government, were appointed German plenipotentiaries for the formal signing.

Although none of the meetings of the conference had been held in the great palace of Versailles, arrangements were made to have the final ceremony in connection with the German treaty in the famous Hall of Mirrors in which, years before, the King of Prussia had been proclaimed German Emperor. There on June 28, 1919, the fifth anniversary of the assassination of the Austrian archduke, the final scene was enacted. When the delegates of all the Allied and Associated Powers—except China [7]—were seated, at three o'clock the German delegates were admitted. "Müller was pale and nervous, Bell held himself erect and calm. They were led to their seats just opposite the table of rose and sandalwood on which the book of the Treaty was placed." Upon Clemenceau's invitation the German delegates signed. After them the other delegates signed in the alphabetical order of their countries according to the French names, President Wilson signing first for *Amérique du Nord*. While the signatures were still being affixed the guns began to boom outside. At 3:40 P.M. the ceremony was over. In the gardens, whose gorgeous fountains were playing for the first time since the outbreak of the war, cheering throngs greeted the delegates as they came from the historic palace of Versailles.

### THE SIGNIFICANCE OF THE TREATY FOR GERMANY

The effects of the treaty upon Germany were far-reaching. Of her territory in Europe she was deprived of more than 25,000 square miles; of her population she lost about 6,000,000. But her loss of raw materials was far greater and much more serious. Her prewar resources of iron, coal, oil, potash, lead, zinc, and foodstuffs were all greatly diminished. With Alsace-Lorraine went iron, petroleum, and potash; with the Saar basin went coal. With the removal of Luxemburg from the German industrial system went still more iron.

---

[7] As a protest against the Shantung settlement, the Chinese delegates refused to sign the treaty of Versailles.

With the lost regions in Upper Silesia, next to the Ruhr the most important industrial district in prewar Germany, went coal, zinc, lead, together with many foundries and mills. Altogether, Germany was compelled to surrender approximately 65 per cent of her iron-ore reserves, 45 per cent of her former coal wealth, 72 per cent of her zinc ore, 57 per cent of her lead ore, from 12 to 15 per cent of her principal agricultural products, and about 10 per cent of her manufacturing establishments.

Overseas, Germany lost an area of about one million square miles with a population of more than 12,000,000 natives. With this region went about 25 per cent of her prewar rubber supply, besides valuable oils and fibers. Her merchant marine, before the war totaling nearly 5,500,000 tons, was reduced to 400,000 tons. Many of the bases of her prewar foreign commerce, such as her special privileges, capitulations, and concessions in China, Siam, Morocco, Liberia, and Egypt, were destroyed. She forfeited many of her prewar commercial treaties with the Allied powers, was for a short period forbidden to discriminate against the commerce of any of the Allies, and in several respects had to grant without reciprocity most-favored-nation treatment to the Allies for a period of five years.

Possessing before the war the mightiest military machine in the world, she was reduced by the treaty to a peace army less than one eighth as large as her prewar establishment, and with no reserves. Her navy, from being second only to that of Great Britain, was reduced to comparative insignificance. Foreign armies were stationed in her territory, there to be maintained at her expense. Foreign commissions, likewise maintained at her expense, were given power to interfere in her economic and military life. On top of it all, she was committed to a reparations bill of unknown size which gave every indication of mounting into the tens of billions of dollars. It was a severe treaty, but it was in response to popular demand in the Allied countries, and should always be read in connection with the treaty which the Central Powers dictated to Russia at Brest-Litovsk.[8] Furthermore, it was President Wilson's idea that most of the treaty provisions would be more or less temporary, while the League of Nations would endure and eventually operate to correct the evils which might later appear.

[8] See pages 449–451.

### The Treaties with Austria, Hungary, and Bulgaria

After the signing of the treaty of Versailles,[9] other treaties were signed in 1919 with Austria and Bulgaria, and in the following year with Hungary and Turkey. In the drafting of the subsequent peace treaties, the treaty of Versailles served as the general model. Many of its clauses were transferred bodily into the later treaties, and many of its principles were simply modified to fit the other states.

The treaty with Austria takes its name from St. Germain, near Paris, where it was signed. While the Germans were still considering their fate, the second of the peace treaties was presented to the Austrians on June 2, 1919. Like the Germans, they were given permission to make written observations. The Austrian delegates asserted that their state, "German Austria," was a new state, created after the armistice, and had never been at war with the Allies. It was just as much a successor state of the Habsburg empire, they declared, as Czechoslovakia, Poland, and the others. But they failed to convince the Allies, who insisted that Austria was an old state simply shorn of certain of its outlying provinces and endowed with a new government. Accordingly Austria was forced to drop the modifying "German" from her title and was further compelled to accept responsibility for the loss and damage inflicted upon the Allied powers "as a consequence of the war imposed upon them by the aggression of Austria-Hungary and her allies."

One reason why the Austrians had adopted "German Austria" as the official designation of their state was that it pointed the way toward their desired incorporation in the new German Republic. On racial and economic grounds the union seemed a natural arrangement, and, in general, it was approved by the American delegation. The French, Czechoslovaks, and Italians were all, for various reasons, opposed to Germany's annexing the Austrian territory, however, and they were able to influence the peace conference on this point. It was stipulated in the treaty that the independence of

---

[9] The departure of Wilson and Lloyd George immediately after the signing of the treaty of Versailles brought about the dissolution of the "Big Four." Subsequent negotiations and treaty-drafting were under the direction of the Council of Five, which now became known as the Supreme Council and which continued to sit in Paris until January 21, 1920, when, upon Clemenceau's resignation, the Supreme Council as such formally ended. It was succeeded by the Council of Ambassadors composed of the American, British, Italian, and Japanese ambassadors at Paris and of a French representative.

Austria was inalienable except with the consent of the Council of the League of Nations. It was further specified that Austria must "abstain from any act which might directly or indirectly, or by any means whatever, compromise her independence."

In dealing with central Europe, the peace conference was "placed in the position of executor of the Habsburg estate." Czechoslovakia, Poland, Rumania, Yugoslavia, Austria, Hungary, and Italy were the heirs, and by the time the conference assembled in January, 1919, they had already divided the territories of the Habsburgs in a rough, provisional fashion. But the heirs were in general so jealous, grasping, and quarrelsome that the statesmen at Paris had a dual task. They had to adjust the conflicts which had begun between the different nationalities before they developed into actual war; and they had "to effect a definitive division of the Habsburg inheritance that would be just, practical, and conducive to the peace and security of Europe."

The drawing of international boundaries is not easy, at best. The principles that may be adopted for such work are many, and include ethnic, economic, geographic, historic, and strategic considerations. Perhaps most important of all is the factor of national safety. But few indeed are the instances where boundaries which afford adequate national safety at the same time conform to historic and ethnic rights. In central Europe the lines of nationality were rarely so clear-cut that boundaries could be drawn to the satisfaction of all involved. Few of the Habsburg races were separated from their neighbors by clearly marked natural frontiers. Lines of former administrative divisions were of little avail, for most of the provinces contained two or more races jumbled together. Questions of railway and canal communication as well as those of economic dependence had to be considered. It is little wonder, therefore, that the peace conference was obliged to work long and hard on this problem, only in the end to receive chiefly bitter criticism.

Again it must be emphasized that most of the provisions of the treaties were not drafted hastily by the statesmen of the great powers, but were rather the result of the careful investigation and study of a group of experts who were appointed for this purpose. Experts representing the United States, France, Great Britain, and Italy composed the commissions which drafted the new boundaries. When the report of a commission was unanimous, it was usually adopted without modification. Occasionally, however, when political considerations were involved or when a situation became especially acute, the "Big Four" took the whole problem into its own hands for settlement. Then "one might have seen President Wilson himself on all fours, kneeling on a gigantic map spread upon the floor and tracing with his finger a proposed boundary, other plenipotentiaries grouped around him, also on all fours."

The crisis which gained the greatest notoriety and which probably took up more time than any other one problem at the conference arose out of the need for allotting the former Habsburg territory. In the secret treaty of London Italy had been promised, in return for her entry into the war, the acquisition of certain territories around the head of the Adriatic and down the east shore, including the two ports of Trieste and Pola. Unfortunately, after the war the Italians were not content with the gains stipulated in the treaty of London. They demanded in addition the city of Fiume and territories of strategic and economic value which lay beyond the treaty of London line. A strong public sentiment was aroused in Italy to demand especially the annexation of Fiume, the population of which was declared to be for the most part of Italian blood. By many Italians it was believed that the acquisition of this city was necessary to complete, with Trieste and Avlona, the "triple bridgehead for expansion in the Danubian and Balkan system" which was contemplated by Italy.

Furthermore, Italy had long aspired to the complete control of the Adriatic. It was partly to obtain the ascendancy in this sea that she had entered the war against Austria. Although Italy's former rival in the Adriatic had now disappeared, to many Italians it seemed that a new competitor for the control of that sea was being raised by the creation of Yugoslavia. Italy had no desire for another strong commercial or naval rival. If she could secure the port of Fiume in addition to Trieste, Pola, and Avlona, she would obtain practically a monopoly of the maritime trade of the Dalmatian coast and would greatly handicap the commercial expansion of Yugoslavia, whose only practicable port was Fiume. Consequently, Orlando and Sonnino put forward the Italian claims to that city.

On the other hand, the Yugoslav statesmen were insistent that Fiume and the Dalmatian coast should be awarded to Yugoslavia. They based their claim on nationality and self-determination, quoting figures to show that the population of the region was over-whelmingly Yugoslav [10] and that before the war practically every popularly elected official had been Yugoslav. In respect to Fiume itself they based their claim particularly on the fact that it was their only practicable seaport. South of Fiume there was in Yugoslavia only one railway through to the coast, a winding rack-and-pinion road which came out at Ragusa but which would be very expensive to develop and operate as a first-class railway. Actually, nearly all the standard-gauge railways of Yugoslavia were in the latitude of Fiume and had their only direct outlet to the sea at that port. To hand over Fiume to Italy, it was maintained, would be an intolerable subjection of the Yugoslavs to foreign control.

President Wilson gave his support to the Yugoslavs. He not only opposed Italy's annexation of Fiume; he even opposed the complete execution of the Adriatic terms of the treaty of London, which he claimed was not in harmony with the "Fourteen Points." In fact, he himself drew a boundary, known as the "Wilson line," which cut down the London terms though it conceded to Italy for strategic reasons the three key positions of Pola, Lissa, and Avlona. A mem-orandum supporting this line was presented directly to the Italian delegation by Wilson, but, since it denied Fiume to Italy, Orlando and Sonnino refused to accept it, fearing to offend the aroused national spirit of the Italian people.

Finally Wilson gave to the press a statement of his reasons for opposing Italy's claim to Fiume. He concluded his statement with the assertion that the claim was contrary to the principles for which America had fought, contrary to the principles upon which she could consent to make peace, contrary to those upon which she hoped and believed "the people of Italy" would ask her to make peace. Orlando at once condemned Wilson's statement as an appeal "to the peoples outside of the governments which represent them, I should say, almost in opposition to their governments." Excite-ment reached a high pitch when, later in the same day, it was an-nounced that the Italian delegation had decided to leave Paris. Al-though the Italian delegates actually returned to Rome, they realized that their continued absence from the conference would exclude

---

[10] In Fiume itself the census of 1910 showed 24,000 Italians and 16,000 Yugoslavs. Serbia asserted that, if the population of Šušak, a suburb of Fiume, were counted, the Yugoslavs would have a majority in the municipal area.

Italy from the benefits of the treaty, and so, having found that the Italian people supported them in their opposition to Wilson, they returned to Paris. Orlando resumed his place in the Council of Four, but on June 19 his ministry fell, and he and Sonnino were succeeded in Paris by Nitti and Tittoni. The peace conference never succeeded in solving this problem but left it to be settled by direct negotiations between Italy and Yugoslavia.[11]

Aside from Fiume, however, the statesmen at Paris eventually succeeded in making some sort of provision for all the territory of the former Dual Monarchy. Austria lost not only her earlier subject peoples but even some of her own Germans as well. To Italy she ceded the Trentino, southern Tirol (although the latter included 250,000 Germans), Trieste, Istria, and two islands off the Dalmatian coast. To Czechoslovakia she lost part of Lower Austria, most of Austrian Silesia, Moravia, and Bohemia, with perhaps 3,000,000 Germans. To Poland she lost Galicia; to Rumania, Bukowina. The duchy of Teschen was divided between Poland and Czechoslovakia. To Yugoslavia she surrendered Bosnia and Herzegovina, together with the Dalmatian coast and islands. Austria shrank from an empire with a population of about 30,000,000 to a small landlocked state of only 6,500,000.

Most of the other provisions of the treaty were similar to those drawn up for Germany. Austria's army was reduced to 30,000 men and placed under various limitations. Her entire navy was surrendered, and in the future she was to have only three police boats on the Danube. She must make reparation, the amount to be determined by the Reparations Commission. States which contained territory of the former empire, however, were required to assume a proportional amount of the Austrian prewar national debt. In order that Austria might have free access to the Adriatic, she was given the right to transport goods over the territories and in the ports formerly in the empire and was to receive in those territories and ports national treatment in respect to charges, facilities, and all other matters. On the other hand, she was obliged to concede to Czecho-

[11] In September, 1919, perhaps in imitation of Garibaldi's exploits in the nineteenth century, Gabriele d'Annunzio, an ultrapatriotic poet and soldier-aviator, seized Fiume with the aid of a small band of volunteers. In November, 1920, however, Italy and Yugoslavia signed the treaty of Rapallo recognizing Fiume as a free city, and Italian troops compelled D'Annunzio's forces to withdraw. Still later (1924), by another Italo-Yugoslav treaty, Fiume was annexed by Italy and Šušak, its chief suburb, by Yugoslavia.

slovakia the right to send her own trains over certain Austrian lines toward the Adriatic. Although the Austrian assembly vigorously protested against the detachment of Germans in Bohemia and Tirol and against the prohibition of Austrian union with Germany, it eventually changed the name of the state from "German Austria" to "Austria," assented to the new boundaries as outlined in the treaty, and agreed to safeguard the rights of the racial, religious, and linguistic minorities of the republic. The completed treaty was finally signed on September 10, 1919.

Although it had been intended to open the peace negotiations with Hungary at the same time as with Austria, the signing of the Hungarian peace treaty did not occur until June, 1920. The chaotic domestic political situation in Hungary was the cause of this delay, for it was not until late in November, 1919, that a government was organized in Hungary which the Supreme Council at Paris would recognize. In January, 1920, the first draft of the proposed treaty was presented to the Hungarian delegation headed by Count Apponyi.

Former Hungarian territory was awarded to every surrounding state—Yugoslavia, Rumania, Czechoslovakia, even Austria. To Yugoslavia went Croatia-Slavonia and part of the Banat of Temesvar; [12] to Rumania, the rest of the Banat, Transylvania, and some of the Hungarian plain to the west; to the Czechoslovak republic, Slovakia and territory to the east and south of the Carpathians inhabited by some 500,000 Ukrainians; to Austria, German West Hungary, [13] the latter being the only case where one of the Central Powers was given additional territory. The fate of Fiume, Hungary's one direct outlet to the sea, was left to the negotiations of Italy and Yugoslavia, but at least it was lost to the Magyars. Hungary was reduced from a country with an area of over 125,000 square miles and a population of over 20,000,000 to a small landlocked state with only 35,000 square miles of territory and about 8,000,000 inhabitants; while outside these greatly contracted frontiers dwelt some 3,000,000 of their kinsmen. The territorial adjustments were difficult to reconcile with any one clear-cut principle.

[12] All of the Banat of Temesvar was claimed by Rumania on ethnic and geographic grounds, while Yugoslavia claimed the western and central part on historic grounds. The western third of the district was given to Yugoslavia, the rest to Rumania. For the ethnic characteristics of the Banat, see the map in I. Bowman, *The New World* (1921), page 272.

[13] As a result of a plebiscite held in December, 1921, the town of Sopron was later ceded to Hungary.

The rest of the terms of the treaty were substantially the same as those of the treaty of St. Germain. Count Apponyi resigned from the Hungarian delegation as a protest against the refusal of the Allies to make desired modifications, but the delegation was reorganized, and the Hungarian treaty was eventually signed on June 4, 1920, in the Long Gallery of the Grand Trianon Palace, adjoining the park of Versailles.

The peace treaty with Bulgaria was signed at Neuilly-sur-Seine on November 27, 1919. Although she suffered far less shrinkage in territory than any other of the defeated powers, she did not escape altogether. Her most serious loss was western Thrace, which she had gained from Turkey in 1913 and which provided her only direct access to the Aegean. This she was compelled to surrender to the Allies, who handed it over to Greece. In the west she was obliged for strategic reasons to cede three small areas to Yugoslavia. These were awarded to the latter in order that she might control certain mountain passes and thus obtain greater security in time of war for her Nish-Saloniki railway. Slight alterations were made also in the Greco-Bulgarian boundary line. In view of Bulgaria's loss of her coast line on the Aegean, the Allied powers undertook to insure her economic outlets to that sea. Bulgaria's military establishment was limited, like those of Germany, Austria, and Hungary, and her navy was surrendered. She was obliged to recognize her liability to make reparation, the amount in this case being fixed at $450,000,000, payable in thirty-seven years from January 1, 1921. As a result of the war and the peace treaties, Bulgaria became one of the least of the Balkan states in area, resources, population, and military power.

## THE MINORITIES TREATIES

In spite of the great advance toward nationalism which came as a result of the World War, Europe was still far from organized into purely national states. So many considerations entered into the drafting of the new boundary lines that, even with the best of intentions, it was impossible to prevent the inclusion of racial minorities in some states. Along almost every frontier there were these minorities, a fact which gave considerable concern to the statesmen at Paris. To provide for this situation the "Big Four" decided to incorporate minimum guarantees for racial, linguistic, or religious minorities in the fundamental law of several of the European states. To this end, appropriate provisions were inserted in the peace treaties with Austria, Hungary, Bulgaria, and Turkey, and special treaties for this purpose were signed by the principal Allies with Poland, Czechoslovakia, Rumania, Yugoslavia, and Greece.[14]

Although the minorities treaties differed slightly in details, they were very similar. In general, the various states agreed to assure full and complete protection of life and liberty to all their inhabitants without distinction of birth, nationality, language, race, or religion. All inhabitants were entitled to the free exercise, public and private, of any creed, religion, or belief the practice of which would not be inconsistent with public order or public morals. Such minorities were further granted the free use of any language in private business and in private schools, and the right to instruction in the public primary schools in their own language if they constituted a considerable proportion of the population. In some cases particular privileges, such as the right of Jews to observe their Sabbath as a holiday, were guaranteed. The protection of minority rights was placed in the hands of the League of Nations, and the guarantees might be modified only with the consent of a majority of the Council of the League.

The states which were thus called upon to grant guarantees to minorities vigorously opposed the demand, insisting that they were being compelled to do something which the great powers themselves would never be willing to do. They pointed out that such exactions were an infringement of their own sovereignty and would only help to perpetuate the separatist tendencies which already existed among the minorities. The "Big Four," however, insisted that the demands were in the interest of the peace of Europe, and forced the acceptance of the various guarantees.

## THE TREATIES WITH TURKEY

The last of the peace treaties to be concluded at Paris, and the only one never to be ratified, was that with the Ottoman Empire, signed at Sèvres on August 10, 1920. During the war several secret agreements had been made by the Allies looking to the eventual partition of the Turkish lands. Roughly, according to these, Russia was to obtain Constantinople and European Turkey from the Straits up to

[14] Lithuania, Latvia, Estonia, and Albania later entered into engagements with the League of Nations to observe toward their minorities obligations more or less identical with those laid down in the minorities treaties.

a line running from Enos on the Aegean to Midia on the Black Sea. In addition, she was to have the islands of Imbros and Tenedos in the Aegean, all the islands in the Sea of Marmora, territory on the Asiatic shore of the Bosporus, the provinces of Erzerum, Trebizond, Van, Bitlis, and part of Kurdistan. The other Entente powers were to share in the partition. Great Britain was to secure southern Mesopotamia with Bagdad, and the two Mediterranean ports of Haifa and Acre; France, the coastal strip of Syria, the vilayet of Adana, and an extensive hinterland; Italy, the Dodecanese in the Aegean, and an area in southwestern Asia Minor in the vicinity of Adalia which she hoped would include the coast from Adalia to Smyrna and the hinterland as far as Konia. Other agreements stipulated that the Arab population of the empire was to be freed and established as an independent Arab state, and that Palestine was to be internationalized. This disruptive program was never fully carried out, however, largely because of the Bolshevik revolution and the resultant uncertainty and differences of opinion which developed among the Allies as to the fate of those regions formerly assigned to Russia.

Eventually, under the provisions of the abortive treaty of Sèvres, Turkey surrendered sovereignty over practically all her non-Turkish populations. In Arabia the Kingdom of Hejaz was recognized as independent. Syria, Palestine, and Mesopotamia (with boundaries extended to include Mosul), were to be entrusted to, or "advised and assisted" by, mandatory powers.[15] Smyrna and its hinterland were to be administered by Greece for five years, at the end of which a plebiscite was to decide their future status. The Dodecanese and Rhodes were ceded to Italy, which by another treaty agreed to turn over the former to Greece. Other Greek islands in the Aegean, together with eastern Thrace up to the Chatalja line, were surrendered by Turkey to Greece. Turkey agreed to recognize the independence of an Armenian state to be constructed in the area of Erzerum, Trebizond, Van, and Bitlis, the frontiers of which were to be decided by the President of the United States. Kurdistan was to receive an autonomous government or, if a plebiscite so decided, independence. The Straits were to be internationalized and the adjoining territory demilitarized. Constantinople and a region in Europe up to the

---

[15] On May 5, 1920, the powers at San Remo named France as the mandatory for Syria and Great Britain for Mesopotamia and Palestine. In July, 1922, the Council of the League of Nations formally assigned the mandates.

Chatalja line remained under Turkish sovereignty. Turkey thus became little more than a shadow of her former self, a small Asiatic state in the Anatolian uplands around Angora.[16]

Although the sultan, in Constantinople within the range of Allied warships, might be content with the mere shadow of former things, there were those in Turkey who demanded more of the substance. Back in the hills of Anatolia, far beyond the reach of Allied guns, the spirit of Turkish nationalism and Moslem fanaticism had been aroused by an experienced army officer, Mustapha Kemal. The Turkish Nationalists demanded the retention by Turkey of all territory "inhabited by an Ottoman Moslem majority," a plebiscite in western Thrace, the security of Constantinople, and, by implication, the abolition of the capitulations. When the sultan, doubtless under Allied pressure, dissolved the parliament and denounced the Nationalists, the latter held a grand national assembly at Angora and organized a government with Mustapha Kemal at its head. By June, 1920, Nationalist armies were threatening the British on the Ismid peninsula, the French in Cilicia, and the Greeks in the Smyrna area.

In these circumstances Venizelos proposed, and the Allies approved, a Greek offensive against the Turks, and Great Britain advanced a loan to the Greek government. Greek armies at once began operations and before the end of the year succeeded in defeating the Nationalists and in occupying extensive regions of Anatolia including the city of Brusa. During 1921 further military successes brought the Greek armies within two hundred miles of Angora, but their supreme attempt to capture the Nationalist capital resulted in failure. A year later the Turkish Nationalists suddenly launched an attack and succeeded in administering a decisive defeat to the Greek forces; on September 9, 1922, the Nationalists entered Smyrna. Within a short time every Greek soldier in Anatolia was captured or driven off the mainland. Faced by this situation, the great powers invited Greece and Turkey to a conference to draft a new peace treaty with Turkey. Mustapha Kemal accepted their proposal, and an armistice was signed at Mudania on October 11.

The "revisionary" peace conference opened in Lausanne on No-

---

16 On the same day that the treaty of Sèvres was signed, a tripartite agreement was made between France, Italy, and Great Britain by which spheres of economic and political interest were mapped out in parts of the new Turkey. The French "sphere" was Cilicia, north of Syria; Italy's was the southwest part of Anatolia outside the Smyrna area.

vember 20, and was attended by delegates of Great Britain, France, Italy, Japan, the United States, Russia, Greece, Rumania, Yugoslavia, and Turkey. The inclusion of Turkish delegates made this the only one of the peace treaties which was negotiated and not dictated. A draft treaty was finally completed and presented to the conference on January 31, 1923; but at the last moment the Turkish delegates asked for further time to consider, and at length on February 4 definitely refused to sign because of certain economic and judicial clauses. It appeared that the conference had failed; the delegates returned home. But it turned out that the conference had only been interrupted. Although the Turkish National Assembly rejected the draft treaty, it authorized the continuance of negotiations. On April 24, therefore, the conference resumed its sessions. Three months later, after the Allies had yielded on enough points to satisfy the Turks, the treaty of Lausanne was signed on July 24, 1923.

The territorial extent of Turkey was slightly increased over what it was to have been according to the treaty of Sèvres. Although Mesopotamia, Arabia, Syria, and Palestine were still recognized as independent of Turkey, the latter advanced her frontier in Europe to the line of the Maritza River, plus a small district to the west of it in one place in order that she might control Karagach and its railway station. In the Aegean Turkey retained the Rabbit Islands, off the entrance to the Dardanelles, and the islands of Imbros and Tenedos. The Dodecanese,[17] Rhodes, and Castellorizo, Turkey ceded to Italy; and all her other Aegean islands to Greece. Turkey renounced all rights and titles over Libya, Egypt, and the Sudan, and recognized Great Britain's annexation of Cyprus. She also accepted articles for the protection of minorities similar to those signed by several of the European powers. On the other hand, she obtained the recognition by the signatory powers of the complete abolition of the capitulations in Turkey, suffered no restrictions of her military and naval forces, and was released from any claim on the part of the Allied powers to reparations on account of the World War.

In separate conventions a number of other agreements were entered into which had the same force as the treaty itself. The

---

[17] On October 8, 1922, Italy had announced that she considered her agreement to cede the Dodecanese to Greece had lapsed because of the nonratification of the treaty of Sèvres.

"principle of freedom of transit and of navigation by sea and by air in the strait of the Dardanelles, the sea of Marmora, and the Bosporus" was recognized, and an International Straits Commission was to operate under the auspices of the League of Nations. Both shores of the Dardanelles and of the Bosporus were demilitarized, as were the islands off the entrance to the Dardanelles and all the islands in the Sea of Marmora except Emir Ali Adasi.

A Greco-Turkish convention stipulated that there should "take place a compulsory exchange of Turkish nationals of the Greek Orthodox religion established in Turkish territory, and of Greek nationals of the Moslem religion established in Greek territory." Exceptions were made in the case of the Greeks on the islands of Imbros and Tenedos and of those who were established in Constantinople before October 30, 1918, and of the Moslem inhabitants in the district in western Thrace which Greece had obtained in 1913 by the treaty of Bucharest. Other conventions provided for the demilitarization of a region on both sides of the Greco-Turkish and Turco-Bulgarian frontier lines, and for the withdrawal of British, French, and Italian troops from Turkish territory immediately after the ratification of the treaty by the Turkish National Assembly. A comparison of the provisions of the treaty of Lausanne with the aims announced by the Nationalists reveals that the Turks obtained nearly everything for which they had fought—ethnographic frontiers, freedom from international servitudes, and national independence.

## THE CONFLICT OF IDEAS

The contents of these peace treaties drafted at the close of the World War clearly disclose the conflict which was waged within the peace conference between the diplomats and statesmen of the old, "practical," Machiavellian school, on the one hand, and those of the new, idealistic, "forward-looking" school, on the other. A comparison of the terms of the peace settlement with President Wilson's "Fourteen Points" [18] will reveal the extent to which the idealistic parts of his program were defeated. Certain of the provisions of the treaties seem to indicate that the preceding century had seen little progress in the principles of treaty-making. If a fear-inspired desire to protect Europe against France was one of the basic principles in the Vienna

[18] See page 454.

settlement of 1814, it was far more so in respect to Germany at Paris in 1919. If the principle of "compensations to the victors" prevailed in 1814, it dominated in a degree only slightly less in 1919-1920. Many of the terms imposed in these later years were worthy of Metternich, Castlereagh, or Wellington.

Nevertheless, the statesmen of the new school left their impress on the settlement. If the victors' desire for spoils deprived Germany of all her colonies and Turkey of much of her territory, the idealists dictated that those who gained control of these regions must hold them as mandates of a world society to which they must render account as stewards. If the desire for compensation or protection against Germany led to the demand for territory inhabited by an alien people, it encountered vigorous opposition, for nationalism was as much exalted in 1919-1920 as it had been suppressed in 1814. Although the statesmen at Paris failed to usher in the millennium in respect to nationalist aspirations, an examination of the map of post-war Europe discloses the marked advance which has been made toward the coincidence of national and political frontiers.

Despite the fact that there were some instances of arbitrary shifting of peoples from one state to another, which were reminiscent of the Congress of Vienna, such procedure was the exception rather than the rule. More frequently, when the will of the people was not fully known, it was determined through the use of a plebiscite. And in most cases where it was felt necessary, for strategic or economic or geographical reasons, to incorporate an alien people within the bounds of any state, the attempt was made to safeguard them in their political, religious, and linguistic rights by minorities treaties under the protection of the League of Nations.

Finally, the statesmen at Paris, in creating the League of Nations, succeeded in giving practical expression to something akin to that "Holy Alliance" which had been only vaguely conceived in the visionary mind of Alexander I, but which had been characterized by the statesmen of those days as a "sonorous nothing," a "piece of sublime mysticism and nonsense." Thus, in 1919-1920, though the statesmen failed to decide wisely and ideally in every instance, they took steps to provide a future means of correcting and remedying their own worst blunders. For the League of Nations was an integral part of the peace treaties, the keystone of the postwar settlement.

## THE UNITED STATES AND THE PEACE SETTLEMENT

The fact that the League of Nations was inextricably woven into the peace settlement largely accounts for the determined opposition which the treaty of Versailles encountered in the United States. Although many bitter "Hun-haters" in that country denounced it for its criminal leniency toward Germany, and many utopian idealists, on the other hand, condemned it for not being in full accord with Wilson's "Fourteen Points," the attack on the treaty was directed chiefly against Part I, which constituted the Covenant of the League of Nations. Within the Covenant the most bitter assault was made upon Article 10, in which members of the League guaranteed the territorial integrity and existing political independence of all the other members.

Many Americans denounced this article as an infringement on the right of Congress alone to declare war and to authorize the use of the military forces of the United States. Many feared that it might involve the country in war without any choice in the matter, that it transferred to the League "the right to send our boys into wars overseas." There was undoubtedly much misrepresentation and misunderstanding of the League and its powers, and Wilson upon his return to the United States decided [19] to undertake a speaking tour throughout the country in behalf of the treaty and the League. In clear and eloquent addresses the President explained that the League could only advise members regarding steps to be taken against a recalcitrant state. Again and again he pointed out that, with the necessity for unanimous vote in the Council, the United States could not be led into a war against her will. In ratifying the Covenant, he explained, the United States did not assume any legal but only a strong moral obligation to enforce the sanctions of the League. Whether popular opinion would have been won to the support of the treaty had the President carried through his extensive speaking campaign will never be known, for on September 26, 1919, his strength failed him and he suffered a slight paralytic stroke.

Meanwhile, on September 5, the Senate had begun its formal consideration of the treaty, and in the course of the ensuing debates four points of view toward the League Covenant became evident: (1) nonratification, (2) ratification with far-reaching reservations,

[19] Despite the advice of his physicians and friends.

(3) ratification with mild reservations, (4) ratification without reservations. Wilson declared that the reservations proposed by Senator Lodge, chairman of the foreign relations committee, would seriously impair the League. Although willing to accept "reservations of interpretation" so long as they were not incorporated in the ratification, he vigorously opposed reservations in the ratification itself, and urged Democratic senators to vote against the treaty with Lodge's reservations. Consequently, in November and again in March, 1920, when votes were taken in favor of ratifying with reservations, the opposing votes of those Democratic senators who followed Wilson's advice prevented the two-thirds vote necessary for ratification.

Wilson was confident, however, that the majority of Americans were with him and not with the Republican senators who had proposed the reservations. It was his hope that the presidential election of 1920 might be made a popular plebiscite on the League, and that the Democrats might win such a victory as to enable them to secure ratification of the treaty without reservations. By November, 1920, however, the American people had suffered a reaction from their war-time idealism, and were swayed chiefly by a feeling of disillusionment and discontent. Although the League played only a relatively minor part in the campaign, the Republicans interpreted their overwhelming victory in the election of President Harding as a popular mandate against the treaty and the League. The treaty of Versailles was therefore dropped, and the United States continued to be technically at war with Germany.

In July, 1921, Congress eventually passed a joint resolution which was designed to end hostilities immediately without waiting for a formal treaty. Early in the following month a new treaty was concluded with Germany (treaty of Berlin), in which the United States was guaranteed "all the rights and privileges stipulated" in the treaty of Versailles. Since the Covenant of the League of Nations was also an integral part of the treaties with Austria and Hungary, the latter were likewise never ratified by the United States. Instead, new treaties were concluded which, omitting the League Covenant, still guaranteed to the United States all the rights and privileges stipulated in the treaties of St. Germain and Trianon. Against Bulgaria and Turkey the United States had never declared war, and no action had to be taken on the treaties of Neuilly and Sèvres.

American repudiation of the treaty of Versailles and of the League of Nations had far-reaching and unfortunate results in the years immediately after the war. From the counsels of the Reparations Commission was removed the one power which had no direct and selfish interest in securing huge reparations payments from Germany. Had the United States been represented on this commission, as was originally intended, her weight might have been thrown into the scales on the side of moderation and reason. In still one other feature of the peace settlement, the action of the United States was a heavy handicap, for the state which was expected to be the most ardent and most powerful member of the new League of Nations held aloof during the critical formative years of that organization.

## CHAPTER XVI

# THE LEAGUE OF NATIONS AND THE PEACE SETTLEMENT

O NE of the notable features of the Paris peace conference was its recognition that many of the problems which confronted it could be solved only by some form of permanent international organization. In consequence, the League of Nations, which was at first advocated chiefly as an instrument for the maintenance of peace among the nations of the world, was eventually seized upon by the statesmen at Paris and pressed into service as an agency for carrying out certain features of the peace settlement. In fact, the League became so firmly woven into the very warp of the treaties that without it certain of their provisions become incomprehensible. An examination of the work of the League of Nations during the first decade of its existence reveals that its most spectacular activities had to do chiefly with the execution of various provisions of the peace treaties, the settling of international disputes arising out of postwar readjustments, the healing of national ills caused by the war and its aftermath—in other words, with liquidating the war and implementing the peace.

## The Structure of the League

The constitution of the League of Nations is the Covenant,[1] which comprises the first twenty-six articles of the various peace treaties drafted at the Paris conference. The Covenant may be amended by the unanimous vote of the members of the Council with a majority vote of the members of the Assembly, for the League was created to be not a fixed and static thing, but a living, growing organism. Its growth is not—may never be—complete, for new powers and new duties with new machinery for their execution may be added year by year. Already several articles of the Covenant have been amended to adapt it to altered conditions.

---

[1] It may be found in Carnegie Endowment for International Peace, *The Treaties of Peace, 1919–1923.*

The original or "charter" members of the League were the signatory states named in the Annex to the Covenant and such of those "invited" states there named as acceded without reservation to the Covenant within two months of its coming into force. Any fully self-governing state, dominion, or colony not named in the Annex may become a member of the League by a two-thirds vote of the Assembly. At the time of the first meeting of the Council there were twenty-four members; ultimately the number increased to nearly sixty. A member may withdraw from the League after two years' notice of its intention so to do. Several eventually withdrew, Japan, Germany, and Brazil being the most important.

The League functions through the instrumentality of an Assembly, a Council, and a permanent Secretariat. The Assembly is the representative body of the League and as such somewhat resembles the representative legislatures of national states, but with the essential difference that it has no real lawmaking power. It is the instrument by means of which the nations of the League confer, advise, and deliberate, and in it each member state has one vote and not more than three representatives. Meetings are held annually in Geneva beginning in September, the official languages being French and English. The Assembly is empowered to "deal at its meetings with any matter within the sphere of action of the League or affecting the peace of the world." More specifically, it controls the budget [2] of the League, selects the nonpermanent members of the Council, admits states into League membership, and participates in the election of the judges of the Permanent Court of International Justice.

The Council is composed of one delegate from each of the states entitled to representation. The Covenant of the League provided that the Council should have five permanent and four nonpermanent members, but the refusal of the United States to enter the League left only four permanent members. The total membership was thus only eight until in 1922 the Assembly increased the number of nonpermanent members to six. With the admission of Germany to the League in 1926, the number of permanent members was fixed at five and the number of nonpermanent members was increased to nine. In 1933 Japan and Germany gave notice of their withdrawal from the League and ceased to be represented in the Council. One of these two vacancies was filled in 1934, however, when the Soviet

[2] The annual budget of the League amounts to about thirty million Swiss francs.

Union was admitted to the League and assigned a permanent seat. Meanwhile, in 1933, the number of nonpermanent members had been increased to ten. In 1937, therefore, the Council consisted of four permanent members—France, Great Britain, Italy, and the Soviet Union—and ten regular nonpermanent members.[3] The latter hold seats for three-year terms, and a certain number of terms expire each year. Representatives of states not members of the Council may by invitation sit with the Council when questions concerning them are under consideration.

The scope of the Council's powers is the same as that of the Assembly's, but the Covenant delegates to it more specific tasks. It has the duty of formulating plans for the reduction of armaments, of advising on the means of protecting member states in time of foreign aggression, of mediating in case of international disputes, and of receiving reports from mandatory powers. In most cases the decision of the Council must be unanimous. From 1923 the Council followed the procedure of meeting four times yearly, with extraordinary sessions as required, but in September, 1929, it decided to reduce the number of its regular sessions from four to three annually. Special emergencies and current work throughout the year are handled by the Council, which has become to a certain extent the League's executive organ.

The permanent Secretariat comprises a secretary-general and a large staff. The first secretary-general, Sir Eric Drummond, was named in the Annex to the Covenant, but subsequent secretaries-general were to be appointed by the Council with the approval of a majority of the Assembly. Chosen in this way, Joseph Avenol, a Frenchman who had served the League in various capacities including deputy secretary-general, succeeded Sir Eric as secretary-general in 1933. The secretary-general is assisted by two deputy secretaries-general and three undersecretaries-general. These offices were distributed among the great powers, the first secretary-general being British, the deputy and undersecretaries being chosen from the other great powers. The body of the Secretariat is composed of eleven

[3] In 1936 the League Assembly voted that two additional nonpermanent seats should be added provisionally for three years. The League regulations provide, furthermore, that three of the nonpermanent seats shall be semipermanent. This means that the state concerned is eligible for re-election to the Council by a simple majority instead of a two-thirds vote.

sections,[4] which vary in size from six or seven persons to forty or fifty, the total personnel of the sections numbering about two hundred. In addition to the sections, there are numerous other units known as services, offices, or branches. The Secretariat as a whole requires a personnel of several hundred men and women who are gathered from more than forty different countries. In general it deals with what have been called the "civil-service duties of the League."

The preliminary organization of the League began even before the signing of the treaty of Versailles. At the time the peace conference approved the text of the Covenant, on April 28, 1919, it authorized the appointment of an organization committee consisting of representatives of the powers constituting the members of the Council. Provisional headquarters of the League were established in London, and the secretary-general with the committee's approval selected the staff of the Secretariat. Permanent headquarters were later established in Geneva, which thus became the administrative center of the League. In 1936 the Secretariat moved into a magnificent new League Palace, providing countless offices, numerous conference chambers, a large library and reading rooms, and auditoriums for meetings of the Assembly and Council.

The Permanent Court of International Justice, commonly called the "World Court," is also in a sense an agency of the League. It was stipulated in Article 14 of the Covenant:

The Council shall formulate and submit to the Members of the League for adoption plans for the establishment of a Permanent Court of International Justice. The Court shall be competent to hear and determine any dispute of an international character which the parties thereto submit to it. The Court may also give an advisory opinion upon any dispute or question referred to it by the Council or by the Assembly.

The Council, at its second meeting, began the execution of this article by naming a committee of eminent jurists to draft a plan for such a court. This committee, under the leadership of Elihu Root, former secretary of state of the United States, submitted its report to the League Council on August 5, 1920. With slight amendment,

[4] Political, information, legal, economic and financial, transit, administrative commissions and minorities questions, mandates, disarmament, health, social problems, international associations.

the Council in turn presented the report to the first Assembly, which, after adding a number of amendments, adopted the plan. A protocol of signature, to which the project for the court was annexed as a statute, was subsequently opened, and eventually it was ratified by about fifty states. The statute became effective in September, 1921. The court is composed of fifteen judges [5]—not necessarily nationals of members of the League—chosen for nine-year terms by an absolute majority in the Council and the Assembly, each voting separately. The seat of the court is at the Hague, where the first ordinary session began on June 15, 1922.

The court has both "compulsory" and "voluntary" jurisdiction. Attached to the protocol adopting the statute of the court was an "optional clause" which pledged the states acceding to it to "accept as compulsory, *ipso facto* and without special Convention" the jurisdiction of the court in all legal disputes concerning the interpretation of a treaty, a question of international law, or a breach of an international obligation. Only a few of the member states adopted this clause immediately, but by 1936 forty-one states had ratified it, some with reservations. In case of "compulsory" jurisdiction one state may summon another to appear before the court for trial, and, if the latter fails to respond, the court may give judgment by default. The jurisdiction of the court is "voluntary" when states having a dispute agree to refer it to the court. All questions are decided by a majority of the judges present at the hearing. The court has also the function of giving advisory opinions at the request of the Council or the Assembly, though this use of the court has been open to some criticism on the ground that such advisory opinions are somewhat in the nature of international politics.

The Permanent Court of International Justice should not be confused with the Hague Court of Arbitration, which was created by the Hague Convention of 1899 and is still in existence. The latter is not a permanent court to try cases, but exists only as a list of the names of 132 distinguished jurists from which disputing states may select arbitrators. The World Court, on the other hand, is a court of law and not of arbitration. Its decisions rest on legal principles and on the application of law and justice as found "in treaties, international practice and precedent, or accepted international teaching."

---

[5] The first judges elected were nationals of Brazil, Cuba, Denmark, France, Great Britain, Italy, Japan, the Netherlands, Spain, Switzerland, and the United States.

To a certain extent the International Labor Organization is part of the machinery of the League of Nations. The representatives of labor who were present among the delegations to the peace conference feared that the interests of labor might be completely overshadowed by political considerations and perhaps be mishandled if left to the general jurisdiction of the League. To free the League organs from this responsibility and to ensure proper attention and management for the affairs of labor, a separate organization was provided for by Part XIII of the treaty of Versailles and by similar sections in the other peace treaties of 1919–1920. The International Labor Organization is an integral but autonomous part of the League. Although it is supported by the funds contributed by member states for the maintenance of the League, and although membership in the League entails membership in the Labor Organization, the latter is completely self-directing. States may be members of the Labor Organization without being members of the League. The United States, for instance, became a member of the former in 1934, and various states which resigned from the League retained their membership in the Labor Organization. In 1937 there were about sixty member states.

The International Labor Organization consists of a General Conference, a Governing Body, and an International Labor Office. The General Conference meets annually and consists of four delegates from each member state, one representing labor, one representing the employers, and two representing the government of the state. In matters requiring a vote the delegates vote individually. The work of the conference generally takes one of two forms. It may draw up a recommendation in the form of general principles for the guidance of national governments in drafting legislation, or it may formulate a draft convention in more precise and detailed terms for ratification by the member states. The governments of these states are pledged at least to submit the conference proposals to their respective competent authorities for action.

The Governing Body of the Labor Organization consists of a group of thirty-two persons, eight of whom represent the workers, eight the employers, and sixteen the governments. Of the last group eight must (1937) represent the governments of Canada, France, Great Britain, India, Italy, Japan, the Soviet Union, and the United States, thus ensuring that half of the government representatives shall be from the states of greatest industrial importance. The other eight states represented are chosen by the government delegates in the conference, and the representatives of the workers and the employers are chosen by the delegates representing those groups respectively. The Governing Body elects its own chairman, and its members hold office for three years. It meets at least once in three months and has the task of preparing the agenda for the conference.

The director of the International Labor Office is appointed by and subject to the control of the Governing Body, but he chooses his own subordinates. The office is established at Geneva in a building erected for the purpose, the total personnel including about four hundred persons in Geneva and about fifty more located in branch offices in the principal cities of the world. The office collects information bearing upon the questions coming up for discussion, issues a journal dealing with labor matters, and keeps in touch with governments and various voluntary organizations throughout the world. Obviously the structure of the International Labor Organization is very similar to that of the League of Nations. Its General Conference is analogous to the League Assembly, its Governing Body to the Council, and its International Labor Office to the Secretariat.

During the period since the establishment of the International Labor Organization approximately one hundred recommendations and conventions have been drafted by the annual labor conferences. These have had to do with working hours, woman and child labor, night work, sanitary conditions, unemployment, public labor exchanges, rights of combination among agricultural workers, conditions of employment at sea, protection against occupational diseases, and the like. Many of the conventions have been ratified, many have not, at least by the industrial powers of the West. The greatest successes have been achieved in the East—in India, Japan, China, and Persia. Although the Labor Organization has no actual legislative or executive power, it makes a strong appeal to public opinion and gives to labor such a vigorous leadership as it has never before known.

### THE UNITED STATES AND THE LEAGUE

In the American political campaign of 1920, Warren G. Harding, the Republican candidate for the presidency, opposed the League of Nations, although pronouncing himself to be in favor of some sort of "free association of nations." His sweeping victory in the November elections of that year, however, appeared to drive from his mind all thoughts not only of a free association of nations but even of the existence of the League itself. For several months the new Republican administration completely ignored the League of Nations and refused to acknowledge notes and communications to the United States government from that organization. Only after this situation had been exposed in the American press did the state department bring itself to acknowledge in a formal way the receipt of the League's communications.

Toward the Permanent Court of International Justice, as distinct from the League, President Harding was more sympathetic. In fact, he recommended that the United States should become a member of the World Court, provided she were given an equal voice in the election of the judges with those states which were members of the League. President Harding died suddenly on August 2, 1923, before the Senate had acted on his recommendation. Calvin Coolidge, who succeeded to the presidency, also urged the Senate to ratify the World Court Protocol, and the Senate, after much delay, in 1926 finally voted to approve it with five reservations. The states that were members of the World Court practically accepted all of these reservations except that which stated the court should not "without the consent of the United States entertain any request for an advisory opinion touching any dispute or question in which the United States has or claims an interest." This reservation, it was maintained abroad, would give the United States a privileged position.

Apparently discouraged by his inability to bring the Senate and the members of the World Court together, President Coolidge after 1926 ceased to urge adherence. In 1929, however, a committee representing the states that were members of the court, in consultation with Elihu Root, formulated a series of amendments to the World Court Protocol to bring it into harmony with the American Senate's reservations. Herbert Hoover, who became President of the United States in 1929, thereupon authorized the signing of the Protocol and urged upon the Senate its ratification. Nevertheless, throughout President Hoover's term the Senate continued its dilatory policy and failed to take any action. Although in the presidential campaign of 1932 the political platforms of both the Republican and the Democratic Party advocated American adherence to the court, the Protocol was defeated by a close vote in the United States Senate in 1935. Meanwhile, the policy of the United States toward the League itself had gradually undergone a change. From an attitude of complete aloofness the government of that country advanced by 1922 to a willingness to send "unofficial observers" to conferences where matters of concern to the United States—such as customs formalities, traffic in women and children, opium traffic, and communications and transit—were to be discussed. As the years passed, the American policy of co-operation expanded. The various disarmament and economic conferences called by the League were attended by American delegates. The United States eventually began to contribute a small amount toward the expenses of the League, and from time to time Americans were chosen to serve on League commissions. Four distinguished Americans—John Bassett Moore, Charles Evans Hughes, Frank B. Kellogg, and Manley O. Hudson—have served as judges on the World Court. Beginning with the administration of President Coolidge, the United States government, as though a member of the League, voluntarily deposited with the League Secretariat copies of its treaties with other nations, and under Presidents Hoover and Roosevelt it made every effort to advance the cause of disarmament at the League's Geneva conference. Nevertheless, the lack of the official presence of the United States at the council tables of the League, and the ever-present uncertainty as to how far the United States might be relied upon to co-operate with the League, seriously militated against the latter's successful mediation in international disputes.

## THE LEAGUE AND THE PRESERVATION OF PEACE

Undoubtedly the chief purpose in the minds of those who formulated the League of Nations was the prevention of future international wars. To this end, the member states in accepting the Covenant agree "to respect and preserve as against external aggression the territorial integrity and existing political independence of all members of the League" (Article 10); to concede it "to be the friendly right of each member of the League to bring to the attention of the Assembly or of the Council any circumstance whatever affecting international relations which threatens to disturb international peace or the good understanding between nations upon which peace depends" (Article 11); to resort to arbitration or judicial settlement in case of failure to settle satisfactorily any dispute suitable for sub-mission to arbitration or judicial settlement, to carry out in full good faith any decision that may be rendered, and not to resort to war against a member which complies with such a decision (Article 13); to submit to the Council any dispute likely to lead to a rupture which is not submitted to arbitration or judicial settlement (Article 15).

In the case of mediation by the Council, the parties to the dispute submit to the secretary-general statements of their case, together with relevant facts and papers. If the Council makes a unanimous report (the votes of the interested parties not counting), it is considered conclusive, and members agree that they will not resort to war against any state which complies with the decision. If the Council fails to obtain unanimity, the members are free "to take such action as they shall consider necessary for the maintenance of right and justice." If the Council authorizes the Assembly to handle the dispute, a decision to be conclusive must be concurred in by the representatives of all those states which are represented in the Council and by a majority of the other members of the League. In case the Council finds that a dispute arises out of a matter which by international law is solely within the domestic jurisdiction of one of the states, it is forbidden to make any recommendation. In other words, the League has no right of intervention, no power within a state.

Penalties are stipulated for a member of the League which goes to war in disregard of its agreements to resort to arbitration, media-tion, or the World Court. All other members agree "immediately to subject it to the severance of all trade or financial relations" (Article 16). This is the so-called "economic weapon" and applies not only to the states involved but also to the nationals of those states. When the Covenant was adopted, it was expected that the League of Nations would be a universal organization. By 1935, however, when Article 16 was first invoked,[6] not only the United States but Japan and Germany as well were nonmembers, so that at that time it was found to be exceedingly difficult to make economic sanctions as effective as expected. In addition to the "economic weapon" the Council may also "recommend to the several governments concerned what effective military, naval, or air force the members of the League shall severally contribute to the armed forces to be used to protect the covenants of the League." The members of the League agree to

[6] See pages 647–649.

adopt similar measures to protect a member state against a non-member state which has resorted to war against it.

## THE LEAGUE'S ROLE IN POSTWAR ADJUSTMENTS

Even before the first Assembly convened, international disputes arising out of postwar adjustments had begun to force the League to take steps "to achieve international peace and security." The first occasion was that of the Åland Islands controversy between Finland and Sweden. The Åland Islands, an archipelago of about three hundred islands with a population of some 27,000, lie between Sweden and Finland and command the entrance to the Gulf of Bothnia. They belonged for many years to Sweden but were lost to Russia along with Finland during the Napoleonic wars. From 1809 to 1917 Finland and the Åland Islands were ruled by Russia as one administrative unit. Soon after Finland became independent, the inhabitants of the Åland Islands, chiefly of Swedish stock, began to talk of union with Sweden and even held two plebiscites in favor of this step. Finland naturally opposed such a movement, and, when at length open revolt seemed imminent, Finnish troops were landed in the islands and two of the separatist leaders were arrested. Public opinion in Sweden thereupon became aroused and began to demand some action on the part of the Swedish government. At this juncture Great Britain, acting under Article 11 of the Covenant, had the matter brought before the Council in July, 1920.[7]

The latter referred to a special committee of jurists the question whether or not the matter in hand was within domestic jurisdiction, together with the question of the present state of international obligations regarding the demilitarization of the islands, the treaty of Paris (1856) having declared that they should neither be fortified nor have any military or naval establishments upon them. The committee of jurists reported: (1) that, as Finland had not been recognized by Russia as a completely established state at the time the dispute in question arose, by international law the matter of determining the status of the islands did not fall within the exclusive competence of Finland, and therefore the Council had authority to recommend a solution; (2) that the terms of the treaty of 1856 were still in force, and whoever possessed the islands did so in conformity with the provisions of that treaty. The Council, having thus estab-

[7] This was some three months before Russia recognized Finland's independence.

lished the points of law, next sent a committee to visit Sweden, Finland, and the islands to obtain evidence upon which a decision could be based.

As a result of the committee's reports, the Council, on June 24, 1921, decided: (1) that Finland should have sovereignty over the islands; (2) that she should guarantee autonomy and the protection of the political rights of the islands; (3) that she should preserve the rights of private property and the use of the Swedish language in the schools; (4) that the islands should be neutralized and not fortified. A new international treaty neutralizing the islands became effective on April 6, 1922.

Most of the other political disputes which came before the League Council during these years arose from boundaries left unsettled by the failure of the peace conference to take definite action, the inability or reluctance of the Council of Ambassadors [8] to execute the decisions of the conference, or the failure of states to agree upon boundaries which had been left to them for settlement through the ordinary channels of diplomacy. One of the first of these was the long-drawn-out Polish-Lithuanian controversy regarding Vilna, which the League proved to be unable to settle with the same dispatch and success that had marked the Åland Islands dispute.

Prior to this controversy Vilna had had a varied history. Capital of the medieval kingdom of Lithuania, it had passed under Polish influence when the two countries became united by the marriage of the Grand Prince of Lithuania to the young Queen of Poland in the fourteenth century. This union, further cemented by the Act of Lublin in 1569, lasted until the close of the eighteenth century, and during this period the Polish language and people came to dominate in the region about Vilna; in fact, the latter became a center of Polish culture. By the partitions of Poland, Vilna next passed under Russian control.

Following the overthrow of the tsar and the defeat of the Central Powers, both Poles and Lithuanians declared their independence and set up their own governments—the former at Warsaw, the latter in the beginning at Vilna. In January, 1919, the Bolshevik army drove the Lithuanians out of Vilna, but the Bolsheviks in turn were driven out by the Poles, who then occupied the city themselves. No definite frontier between the two states was laid down by the peace confer-

8 See the footnote on page 498.

ence, but the treaty of Versailles provided (Article 87) that the boundaries of Poland not established by that treaty should be "subsequently determined by the Principal Allied and Associated Powers." Acting under this authority the Supreme Council on December 8, 1919, laid down a provisional boundary, the "Curzon line," which gave to Poland most of the territory in which the Poles predominated, but assigned the city and province of Vilna to Lithuania.

During the successful advance of the Bolsheviks in 1920, Vilna was again occupied by Russian forces. While the latter were still in possession of the city, the Russian and Lithuanian governments concluded the treaty of Moscow (July 12, 1920), by which Vilna and parts of the former provinces of Suwalki and Grodno were ceded to Lithuania. When the Poles again drove back the Russians, the former and the Lithuanians came into conflict over Vilna, and actual fighting began. Poland appealed to the League of Nations.

The League Council at once dispatched to the scene of conflict a military commission which not only put a stop to the fighting between the two countries but by its continued presence in the contested territory made a renewal of hostilities on a large scale impossible. In October the two governments were persuaded to sign an armistice agreement at Suwalki, accepting as a provisional boundary a revised "Curzon line" which still left Vilna to Lithuania. On the day before this agreement was to come into force, however, General Zeligowski, an independent Polish commander, with a large body of irregular Polish troops drove the Lithuanians out of Vilna and occupied the greater part of the province for the Poles.

The question once more came before the League Council, which eventually persuaded both countries to accept the principle of a plebiscite under the supervision of the League. A plebiscite commission was established, and preparations were made for the creation of an international force to ensure a proper vote. But numerous difficulties were encountered, and in March, 1921, the Council abandoned the idea of a plebiscite in favor of direct negotiations between the two governments. The latter were invited to undertake such negotiations at a conference under the presidency of a representative of the League, but the conference in turn failed to bring the two governments to an agreement. Finally, in January, 1922, the Council withdrew the League commission at Vilna, thus practically admitting its inability to settle the problem with its existing powers. An assembly elected in Vilna under Polish supervision voted in favor of union with Poland. On February 3, 1923, the Council again laid down a provisional boundary between the two states which assigned to Poland the district occupied by General Zeligowski's forces, and with this act washed its hands of the whole affair.[9] Lithuania's attempts to reopen the boundary question were unsuccessful.

The acquisition of Memel by Lithuania about this time may have mitigated to some extent the bitterness of defeat in the Vilna dispute. Memel, a city at the mouth of the Niemen, which is the natural outlet for Lithuania and part of Poland, in the treaty of Versailles was surrendered by Germany to the Allies. At first it was administered by an Allied high commissioner supported by French troops, for at the time of the treaty of Versailles the future extent of Lithuania had not been settled, nor had the latter received full recognition from the Allies. Years passed, but the city was not handed over to Lithuania. There were rumors that Poland desired the city as a Polish port in compensation for the loss of Danzig. Furthermore, there developed some feeling among the Allies that it might be better to give Memel a status like that of Danzig rather than to incorporate it in Lithuania. The Lithuanians became alarmed.

Early in January, 1923, Lithuanian troops entered the city, drove the French troops back, and set up a provisional government. Negotiations between the Council of Ambassadors and the Lithuanian government for a permanent settlement became deadlocked, and the whole problem was referred to the Council of the League. The latter appointed a special commission under Norman H. Davis, former undersecretary of state of the United States, whose report was approved by the Council and incorporated in a convention finally accepted by Lithuania and the Allies on March 15, 1924. Lithuania was given full sovereignty over the city, but the latter was accorded a large degree of autonomy in executive and legislative matters, and its port was to be administered by an international Harbor Board, composed of a Lithuanian, a Pole, and a citizen of Memel.

[9] On February 15, 1923, Poland appealed to the Council of Ambassadors for formal recognition of her frontiers. The latter, more or less in despair, finally established the permanent boundaries of Poland, adopting between the latter and Russia the line laid down by the treaty of Riga (1920) between those two countries, and between Poland and Lithuania the provisional lines drawn by the League Council on February 3, 1923. Lithuania protested, refused to accept the boundaries, and continued to regard herself as in a state of war with Poland.

In the meantime the League had also been called upon by the Council of Ambassadors to extricate it from the embarrassing position in which it found itself while attempting to execute the provisions of the treaty of Versailles regarding Upper Silesia. The treaty stated that the results of a plebiscite conducted by an Inter-Allied commission should be reported to the Council of Ambassadors, which in turn should undertake to settle the boundary between Germany and Poland in accordance with the wishes of the people, and "with consideration for the geographical and economic conditions of the locality." An Inter-Allied commission, composed of representatives of France, Great Britain, and Italy, supported by an Inter-Allied force of French and Italian troops, arranged and supervised the plebiscite which was held on March 20, 1921. The official figures showed 707,605 votes for Germany and 479,359 for Poland, with 754 of the communes in favor of Germany and 699 in favor of Poland. The Poles at once claimed that they should be given those districts having Polish majorities, while Germany contended that the province was economically indivisible and that its fate as a whole should be decided by the majority.

While the controversy continued to become more and more acute, Korfanty, a Pole, at the head of a force of irregular troops, overran a large part of the territory. The French portion of the occupying troops openly favored the Poles, and six British battalions had to be sent to the scene to restore order. The Inter-Allied commission, being unable to reach an agreement upon a boundary line, referred the problem to the Council of Ambassadors, which proved to be no more successful in solving it. The latter then availed itself of Article 11 of the Covenant and laid the whole question before the League Council, requesting it to recommend a solution.

The Council appointed a committee of four members—representing Belgium, Brazil, China, and Spain—to study the Upper Silesian problem with the aid of experts. In accordance with the report of this committee, the Council recommended that Upper Silesia be partitioned and unanimously approved a line which divided the territory so that the number of electors assigned to each state did not differ appreciably from the total number given in its favor in the plebiscite. This awarded the larger part of the population and territory to Germany, but gave Poland by far the greater proportion of the economic resources.[10] The Council further recommended that Poland and Germany should conclude a general convention which would place Upper Silesia under a special regime during a transitional period of fifteen years. The League's recommendations were adopted, and on July 9, 1922, the Inter-Allied troops left Upper Silesia, turning the region over to the Poles and Germans, who had already occupied those parts of the area to which they were entitled under the award.

No sooner had the League succeeded in solving the Upper Silesian problem than it was called upon to play a decisive role in preserving the territorial integrity of Albania. The peace conference had left unsettled the boundaries of this little Balkan state, it being understood that they would later be delimited by the Council of Ambassadors. For reasons of international politics the latter delayed taking action. Both Yugoslavia and Greece had occupied areas within the frontier delimited in 1913–1914, and efforts were made to stir up disaffection among the Albanian people. The question of the territorial integrity, even the existence, of Albania became acute. In 1920 Albania applied for admission to the League of Nations. The Assembly committee's recommendation that she should not be admitted pending the adjustment of her frontiers was overruled by the Assembly itself, which on December 18, 1920, admitted Albania to membership in the League. Her independence as a state was thus recognized.

While the Council of Ambassadors continued dilatory, in 1921 the Yugoslav-Albanian frontier became the scene of agitation. Disruptive revolutionary activities were instigated within Albania and assisted with money, arms, and munitions from the Yugoslav side of the line. They were successfully suppressed by Albanian forces. Then followed the actual invasion of Albania by a well-equipped Yugoslav army of 12,000 men, whose advance was applauded by the Yugoslav press. The danger of another Balkan war was imminent, and Italy's intense jealousy of Yugoslavia's position on the Adriatic made the situation doubly serious.

[10] To Poland went 53 of the 67 coal mines; 24,600,000 of the 31,700,000 tons of coal output of 1920; 91.5 per cent of the accumulated 60,000,000 tons of pit-head stocks; 11 of the 16 zinc and lead mines, with 70 per cent of the total German zinc output; 21 of the 37 blast furnaces; 9 of the 14 steel and rolling mills; and all of the zinc and lead foundries.

On November 7, 1921, Lloyd George, invoking Article 11 of the Covenant, asked the secretary-general of the League to call a special meeting of the League Council to consider the application to Yugoslavia of Article 16 relating to economic blockade. Within two days the Council of Ambassadors, after a two years' impasse, announced that it had fixed the boundary of Albania, with certain minor rectifications in favor of Yugoslavia. Along the northern frontier it laid out a temporary neutral zone and ordered that all Yugoslav and Albanian troops should be withdrawn from it until the work of the Delimitation Commission was finished. Pashich, Yugoslav premier, bowed to the inevitable and withdrew the Yugoslav forces. When the Council met in special session, there was no need to discuss the question of economic blockade—the mere threat to use it had proved sufficient.

The treaty of Lausanne stated that the frontier between Turkey and Iraq (Mesopotamia) should be "laid down in friendly arrangement to be concluded between Turkey and Great Britain within nine months," but that, failing such an agreement within the time mentioned, the dispute should be referred to the Council of the League of Nations. Representatives of the two states met at Constantinople in an attempt to settle the line but could reach no agreement, the chief difficulty arising over the vilayet of Mosul, which is rich in petroleum resources. On August 6, 1924, Great Britain referred the whole matter to the League of Nations. A commission of inquiry was at once created to study the situation and to lay before the Council information and suggestions. In the meantime the *status quo* in the disputed territory was to be maintained.

After clashes between Turkish troops and those of the mandated territory, the question came before the Council again at an extraordinary session at Brussels in October, 1924. At that time a committee of the Council laid down a line which was accepted by both parties and adopted by the Council as representing the *status quo*. The "Brussels line," which left in British control practically all of the vilayet of Mosul, was intended as only a provisional boundary to be observed until the permanent frontier should be fixed.

The commission on the Turco-Iraqi frontier next proceeded to the scene of the dispute and spent weeks on a tour of investigation. Its report was submitted to the Council in September, 1925. Because of the backward state of most of the population of the area, the commission rejected the Turkish argument for a plebiscite. It reported that the majority of the inhabitants south of the "Brussels line" had sentimental leanings toward Turkey but calculated that their economic interests would be better served by a union with Iraq as a British mandate. In case Iraq were to remain under the effective mandate of the League for a period "which may be put at twenty-five years," such union appeared to be the best solution, but if the League's control were to terminate on the expiration of the four-year treaty then in force, "it would be more advantageous for the territory to remain under the sovereignty of Turkey."

The Council next appointed General Laidoner, a distinguished Estonian soldier, to investigate the situation along the "Brussels line." In his report he stated that the Turks were driving Christians out of the provisional Turkish zone, and that atrocities were being committed similar to those which accompanied the Armenian deportations of 1915. Until the reading of this report certain members of the Council had favored a compromise division of the vilayet, on the ground that it would be unfortunate for the League to render a decision wholly favorable to a great power within the League against a small power outside. General Laidoner's report, however, produced unanimity. The Council decided on December 16, 1925, that the Turco-Iraqi frontier should be fixed at the "Brussels line," but that this decision was to be final only in case Great Britain undertook by treaty to ensure the continuance of the mandatory regime in Iraq for twenty-five years.

This decision was immediately accepted by both Great Britain and Iraq, which on January 13, 1926, concluded a treaty continuing the mandatory regime in the latter for the desired term of years. On March 11 the Council of the League of Nations pronounced definitive its previous decision. Although Mustapha Kemal had proclaimed, "Mosul is Turkish and nothing can ever change that fact, even bayonets," three months later Sir Austen Chamberlain informed the Council that a treaty between Great Britain and Turkey had put an end to the tension between them.

Undoubtedly the League of Nations proved to be invaluable during the period of postwar readjustment, even though its machinery and principles were not always nor uniformly successful. Differences in national viewpoint and character did not disappear with the institution of the League. International complications became no less complicated because they were presented to the League for settlement. Being a form of co-operation between states and not itself a superstate, it could do nothing except as the governments of its members willed.[11]

## THE SAAR

The peace treaties laid upon the League of Nations certain administrative and supervisory tasks having to do with the Saar basin, the Free City of Danzig, the mandatory system, and the protection of minorities. Early in 1920 the League Council appointed three members of the Saar Basin Delimitation Commission, naming nationals of Great Britain, Brazil, and Japan. France and Germany each appointed one additional member of the commission, which laid down the boundaries of the basin to fit the mines, their dependent industries, and the residences of the workmen locally employed. The result was an area of some 741 square miles with a population of approximately 770,000.

The Council next appointed the Governing Commission of the Saar basin. According to the terms of the treaty of Versailles, the commission was to consist of five members: one citizen of France, one inhabitant of the Saar territory, and three citizens of three countries other than France or Germany, all to be appointed by the Council for one-year terms subject to reappointment. The Council filled the three discretionary appointments with nationals of Belgium, Denmark, and Canada, and the commission entered upon its duties on February 25, 1920. The peace treaty also stipulated that an advisory council should be elected by the Saar inhabitants, and after considerable delay the commission finally ordered its election. This Advisory Council met every three months, and, although it could not enact laws, it served to make articulate native opinion.

The treaty of Versailles had envisaged an impartial commission which should administer the basin in the interests of the inhabitants themselves without interference from either France or Germany. Unfortunately, this proved not to be the case at first owing to the composition of the commission, in the appointment of which French

[11] A number of international disputes not directly connected with the peace settlement were referred to the League in later years. These are discussed in connection with the histories of the countries involved. Consult the index under "League of Nations" or under the names of the countries directly concerned.

influence had been paramount. The Belgian representative was sympathetic with France; the Dane had lived twenty years in Paris and had become French in his general outlook. The French representative, Rault, was made president of the commission, and, when the Saar representative perceived that the commission was adopting a pro-French policy, he resigned in protest. His successor co-operated with the French group. In consequence, the commission during the first few years was largely the instrument of French policy.

Rault remained head of the commission until 1926. It was he who attended Council meetings when Saar questions were under consideration, and, since the Council had ordered that all complaints should go first to the Saar Commission, which in turn should send them with comments to the Council, he was in a position to minimize all complaints. Although he was undoubtedly honest and upright in his administration of the Saar, he believed that the basin should go to France and that it was his duty to look after French interests there. Editors who protested against the pro-French policy were arrested, and many others who complained were sent out of the territory.

The commission, in spite of the vigorous protests of the inhabitants, retained a French armed force of 5,000 or more "for the protection of persons and property in the Saar basin." With the rapid depreciation of the German mark, French currency was adopted as the sole legal tender in the basin, and the basin was included in the French customs union. French schools were established for children of French people in the Saar in accordance with the peace treaty, but apparently various forms of persuasion or indirect coercion were used to get German children into them. The amount of taxes which France paid on her mines in the Saar was arbitrarily reduced following the French government's protest that it was too high.

For more than four months, early in 1923, the Saar miners were on a strike for higher wages. This coincided with the French occupation of the Ruhr, and the Saar miners showed their pro-German feeling by meetings and parades. The commission resorted to severe measures. It was made a penal offense to "utter sentiments likely to incite to a breach of the peace, and in this category was included speaking against the League of Nations." Picketing was forbidden, and France was called upon for military reinforcements. The press was muzzled, and various papers in the Saar were suspended temporarily. Protests were raised against the commission's actions, and the British government finally requested the League to investigate the situation.

The League Council, in consequence, invited the whole Governing Commission to attend its session in July, 1923. Although the Council was careful not to criticize the work of the commission adversely, it suggested that foreign troops should be withdrawn and their places be taken by a local gendarmerie. Rault's position was undoubtedly undermined and the policy of the pro-French group in the commission checked by being openly exposed. In the following year the commission was reorganized by the substitution of members more impartial in their viewpoints. In 1926 Rault resigned from the commission and was succeeded as president by a Canadian. With the ascendancy of Briand's more conciliatory ideas in French foreign policy, and with the expansion of the League Council to include a representative of Germany, the situation in the Saar became more in accord with that anticipated by the peace treaty. Had it not been for the prospective plebiscite to be held in 1935, the League would probably not have been so much handicapped by the play of international politics.

Active discussion of the Saar plebiscite began during the League Council meeting in January, 1934, when a committee of three, representing Argentina, Italy, and Spain, was appointed to study the preparations for the plebiscite. This committee's report was adopted at a special meeting of the Council in June, and January 13, 1935, was set as the date of the plebiscite. In further fulfillment of the recommendations of the committee, an international plebiscite commission —consisting of commissioners from Switzerland, the Netherlands, and Sweden, with a technical expert from the United States—was established to supervise preparations for the plebiscite. Action was taken, also, to set up a plebiscite tribunal to decide any disputes regarding the voting. Both Germany and France agreed to abstain from pressure of any kind which might affect the plebiscite, and not only to avoid reprisals and discriminations against persons because of their attitude toward the plebiscite but to take all necessary steps to prevent or punish any attitude of their nationals contrary to these undertakings.

Nevertheless, friction developed in the Saar, largely because of the aggressive tactics and terroristic activities of the German Front, an organization in sympathy with the Nazis of Germany. Because of the disturbed conditions, the chairman of the Governing Commission of the Saar requested the League Council to provide for a stronger police force. Eventually the League Council arranged for a League army of 3300 men—supplied by Great Britain, Italy, the Netherlands, and Sweden—to enter the Saar for the maintenance of law and order during the plebiscite. Germany, although stating her belief that no outside force was necessary, accepted the League's plan unconditionally.

One question which disturbed the minds of many was connected with the Saar mines. These were given to France by the treaty of Versailles, but with the proviso that, if the Saar voted to return to Germany, the latter was to repurchase the mines at a price fixed by a Frenchman, a German, and a representative of the League. It was widely feared that disagreement over the purchase price or Germany's inability to make payment might yet delay a final settlement of the Saar problem. Fortunately, an agreement was reached on this matter in December through negotiations carried on between Germany and France in consultation with the chairman of the League's committee of three. It was agreed that, should the plebiscite go in favor of Germany, the latter should pay France 900,000,000 francs as settlement for the mines and all other French credits in the Saar. Part of the payment was to be made in coal delivered to France during the next five years, and part was to be made in francs obtained by exchanging German marks for French francs circulating among the Saarlanders.

As the day for the plebiscite approached, preparations were made for the return of some 55,000 former Saarlanders now living abroad, for the treaty of Versailles provided that all those resident in the Saar on June 28, 1919, were entitled to vote, provided they were twenty years of age. Although the atmosphere in the Saar was somewhat tense in the days immediately preceding the plebiscite, the explicit rules laid down by the plebiscite commission and the presence of the League army discouraged any serious outbreaks of violence. On January 13 approximately 98 per cent of those registered participated in the plebiscite. Of the 528,005 votes cast, more than 90 per cent were in favor of returning the Saar to Germany. Only 46,513 voted in favor of continuing League rule, and only 2124 advocated annexation to France. Not a single voting district returned a majority against reunion with Germany. The Council of the League of Nations on January 17 awarded the entire Saar basin to Germany, and on March 1, 1935, the formal transfer of the district occurred. It was generally conceded that in handling this difficult task the League had done well.[12]

## MANDATES AND MINORITIES

The mandatory system created by the peace conference was placed under the supervision of the League of Nations. By the peace treaties Germany renounced in favor of the Allied powers all her overseas possessions, and Turkey renounced the possession of her Arab lands. All of the former and part of the latter were placed under the mandatory system, in accordance with which they were to be assigned to states which were members of the League, with the understanding that the mandates would be administered in the interests of their inhabitants.

As the territories were widely distributed over the globe, and as the peoples had reached varying degrees of civilization, the mandates were ranged into three classes, known as A, B, and C. Class A included the former Turkish possessions: Iraq, Syria and Lebanon, Palestine, and Transjordan. These territories were considered to "have reached a stage of development where their existence as independent nations can be provisionally recognized, subject to the rendering of administrative advice and assistance by a Mandatory until such time as they are able to stand alone." In Class B were the six mandates in central Africa, where a greater amount of supervision would be required, while Class C included Southwest Africa and the Pacific islands, which, "owing to the sparseness of their population or their small size, or their remoteness from the centers of civilization, or their geographical contiguity to the territory of the Mandatory, and other circumstances, can be best administered under the laws of the Mandatory as integral portions of its territory," subject to certain safeguards in the interests of the native population.

The distribution of the mandates was the work of the principal Allied powers. The allocation of the African and Pacific mandates was accomplished by the Council of Four at the peace conference in May, 1919. In general these areas were placed under the rule of the country nearest them. Thus, of the C group, Southwest Africa was

[12] For the League's relation to the Free City of Danzig, see pages 754–757.

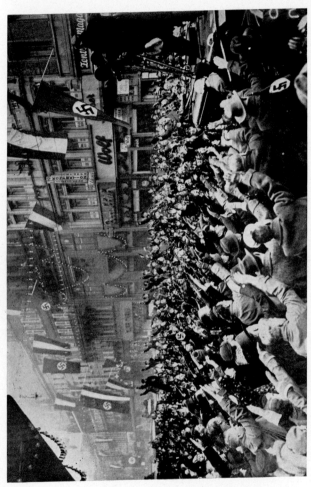

"THE SAAR IS GERMAN!"

Crowds in Saarbrücken giving the "Heil, Hitler!" after the announcement of the result of the Saar plebiscite.

assigned to the Union of South Africa; Samoa to New Zealand; Nauru to Great Britain, Australia, and New Zealand jointly; other former German islands south of the equator to Australia; and the former German islands north of the equator to Japan. Later in 1919 the Class B mandates were assigned. Kamerun (one sixth), East Africa (Tanganyika), and Togoland (one third) were allotted to Great Britain; Kamerun (five sixths) and Togoland (two thirds) to France; and Ruanda-Urundi to Belgium. The Class A mandates were not assigned until April, 1920. Palestine, Transjordan, and Iraq went to Great Britain, while France received Syria and Lebanon. The C mandates were approved by the League Council in December, 1920, the B mandates and Palestine and Syria in July, 1922, and Iraq in September, 1924.

Annually the mandatory powers present reports to the League regarding their mandates. These are examined by the Permanent Mandates Commission, which is composed not of governmental representatives but of ten independent experts, the majority of whom are citizens of nonmandatory states. This commission, which meets twice yearly, presents its observations to the Council of the League. Each year both the Council and the Assembly discuss the working of the mandates, and an opportunity is provided for the public opinion of the world to bring influence to bear upon the mandatory powers to protect the rights of the natives under their control. So far there has been no occasion for direct intervention of the League in case of maladministration of a mandate. The mandatories have sought to receive the approval of the League, and suggestions of the Mandates Commission have proved effective. After all, the mandatory system is a "great adventure in the difficult sphere of colonial government." It has at least provided an effective means of exchanging experience and establishing co-operation between powers burdened with the task of governing backward peoples.

The reconstruction of Europe following the war still left some thirty million of its inhabitants constituting racial minorities in various countries. Most of these people live under the protection of the minorities provisions of fourteen postwar treaties, in which the League of Nations was named as guardian. Violations of the rights of minorities may be brought to the attention of the Council, and petitions may be sent to the League. The usual procedure in these cases is for the head of the section of the League dealing with minorities to attempt to reach a settlement directly with the government involved, but more than once cases have been taken to the Council, and on two or three occasions they have been referred to the World Court.

The League's handling of the minorities problem has not met with the universal approval of its members. At the meeting of the League Council in December, 1928, the German representative, Stresemann, questioned the effectiveness of the League's action in respect to minorities, and at the next two meetings of the Council the minorities question occupied a prominent place on the agenda. The Council ultimately decided that all minorities petitions or communications should be submitted to minorities committees, consisting of the president of the Council and two (sometimes four) other members chosen by him. A new committee should be appointed for each petition, and this committee should decide whether any given petition should be placed on the Council's agenda. Individual members, however, still retained their right to call the Council's attention to any infractions of a minorities treaty. Nevertheless, dissatisfaction continued in some quarters, and in 1934 Poland announced that she would no longer feel obliged to co-operate with the League in respect to minorities until some new general system for their protection had been developed.[13] The whole system of protecting the rights of minorities is politically difficult, and the League, rather than try arbitrarily to impose its decisions upon the governments in question, has sought to develop the spirit of toleration and conciliation.

## HUMANITARIAN ACTIVITIES

Less spectacular and less widely acclaimed in the press than the activities discussed above have been the League's efforts to promote co-operation in matters of general humanitarian interest and concern. It supervised, for instance, the safe return to their homes of several hundred thousand prisoners of war; it helped to care for hundreds of thousands of Greek and Armenian refugees expelled from Turkey; it organized Europe's medical services to prevent the spread of typhus from Russia to the rest of the continent. It brought about the financial rehabilitation of Austria and Hungary,[14] and gave financial

---

[13] States bound by the minorities treaties felt aggrieved because certain other states with minorities—Germany and Italy, for example—were not bound to observe "as high a standard of justice" as they themselves were.

[14] See pages 766 and 779.

assistance to other countries—notably Greece, Bulgaria, Estonia—in time of economic stress. It brought about regular international co-operation in the drafting of sanitary, antiepidemic, and quarantine regulations; in the suppression of traffic in women and in the study of comparative legislation for the protection of the life and health of children; in the reduction and restriction of the sale of opium; in the abolition of slavery and forced labor; in economic, financial, transit, and trade matters; in the extension of intellectual relations. In these fields of endeavor international effort is no longer feeble and spasmodic as in prewar days, for under the League's direction these questions are systematically and continuously studied. Nor is the benefit of the League's activities limited to the problems involved. Repeated co-operation here means a wider extension of international contacts and closer understanding in many other spheres of action.[15]

[15] For the League's activities in respect to national disarmament and security, see pages 562–564 and 573–576.

## CHAPTER XVII

## REPARATIONS AND WAR DEBTS

ONE part of the peace settlement which immediately received severe criticism and denunciation was that dealing with the highly technical and deeply perplexing problem of reparations. No other feature of the peace treaties so intimately affected the lives of so many millions of people. Probably no other provisions were so much discussed on the platform, in the street, and in the press, and at first with so little understanding of the real problems involved. No other section of the treaty of Versailles came so near splitting the Entente front in the years immediately succeeding the war.

### GERMANY'S TOTAL OBLIGATION

It will be recalled that on the subject of reparations the final decision of the peace conference was that Germany must make compensation, in gold or in certain goods, for all damage done to the civilian population of the Allied powers and to their property during the war, but that the treaty did not stipulate the total amount which must be paid. This was left to be determined by a Reparations Commission,[1] but in the meantime Germany was to pay, in gold or otherwise as the Reparations Commission might determine, the equivalent of $5,000,000,000,[2] to be applied first on the expenses of the Allied armies of occupation, and then on the reparations account.

After the peace conference, therefore, the first problem was to determine the total amount which Germany must pay and the system of payments which she must adopt. Negotiations were carried

[1] The Reparations Commission was originally intended to have one representative each from the United States, France, Great Britain, and Italy, with a fifth representative from time to time as the interests of other powers were directly involved. But, because the United States did not ratify the treaty of Versailles, it was not represented on the commission.

[2] The reparations figures given in this chapter in dollars are only approximate, for the German mark and Reichsmark (normally worth 23.81 cents) are here counted as four to the dollar.

on between the Allies and Germany—in the course of which the former demanded $56,500,000,000—but no agreement was ever reached through the channels of diplomacy. When the negotiations broke down, the Allies proceeded to take both military and economic sanctions by occupying the industrial cities of Düsseldorf, Duisburg, and Ruhrort and by sequestrating German customs receipts on the western frontier.

When high politics failed to bring an agreement upon a definite total, the Reparations Commission took up the task and finally notified Germany, on April 28, 1921, that the amount of damage for which reparations were due was $33,000,000,000, in addition to Belgium's war debt. According to the "London schedule" drawn up later, $12,500,000,000 of this amount was to bear interest at 5 per cent, and payments were to be made in fixed annuities of $500,-000,000 plus variable annuities equal to a tax of 26 per cent on Germany's exports. Furthermore, despite Germany's claim to the contrary, the commission announced that Germany's total payments to date had not been more than sufficient to cover the expenses of the various Allied control commissions and armies of occupation, exclusive of the expenses of the United States army. According to the Reparations Commission, Germany had as yet paid nothing which could be credited toward reparations, and the total indebtedness therefore still remained intact.[3] An ultimatum was dispatched to Germany requiring her to accept without reserve the proposals of the commission under threat of Allied occupation of the Ruhr. On May 11, 1921, accordingly, Germany agreed to the total amount of reparations set by the commission and undertook to make payments according to the schedule the Allies had outlined.

### GERMANY'S DEFAULT

A number of circumstances made it almost impossible for the German government to fulfill the obligations which it had assumed. In the first place, postwar Germany had no international credit; and, even if she had had, no countries in the world, with the possible exception of the United States, were in a position to advance her any large amounts immediately. She could not, therefore, settle

[3] The Allies had agreed that of the reparations payments, France should receive 52 per cent, Great Britain 22 per cent, Italy 10 per cent, Belgium 8 per cent, all other participants 8 per cent. Belgium's right to preferential treatment was fixed at $500,-000,000.

the reparations demands at once by foreign loans. In the second place, owing to the Allied blockade which had so long cut her off from sources of raw materials and at the same time destroyed her prewar commercial system, Germany was faced with the necessity of buying extensively abroad, but was unable immediately to export an equivalent amount of goods. Her foreign trade, therefore, failed to bring into the country gold or foreign exchange which might have been used to make reparations payments. On the contrary, the adverse balance of trade was draining from Germany the little gold that she had. The necessity of buying gold and foreign currencies to meet reparations obligations led, in turn, to increased inflation of German currency.

In the third place, Germany was handicapped by a tremendous "flight" of capital from the country. Capitalists were fearful lest their wealth be attached for reparations payments, and hastened to put as much of it as possible safely out of the clutches of the tax-gatherer. Considerably more than a billion dollars was thus placed beyond the reach of the government. The "flight" of German capital led to a still further inflation of the currency. This, in turn, coupled with the then existing inefficient fiscal system, resulted in a continuous national deficit which again compelled a resort to still greater inflation. Thus a vicious circle was created in the matter of currency inflation and depreciation. Finally, there existed in Germany a very definite lack of "the will to pay." This was especially true of the great industrialists, who with the depreciation of the mark waxed in power and arrogance. They appeared to defy the Allies, and refused to co-operate with their own government in any serious attempt to fulfill the terms of the treaty.

The combination of circumstances just discussed resulted eventually in Germany's failure to meet the cash payments or even to make full deliveries in kind according to the London schedule. Although the first payment of $250,000,000 was made, it was accompanied by a very decided decline in the value of the paper mark. By the end of the year Germany concluded that she could not continue to make full payments without the assistance of foreign loans or a resort to much greater inflation of the currency. She therefore raised the question of a moratorium. A partial moratorium was granted for 1922, but, when Germany attempted to make her revised payments, the mark again sank rapidly in value. In

July, 1922, Germany requested a moratorium on all cash payments until January, 1925.

As a result of Germany's demand for a total moratorium, the reparations problem for a time ceased to be merely a question between the Allies and Germany, and resolved itself into a diplomatic conflict between the British and French governments. Fundamentally, the view of each in respect to the policy to be adopted toward Germany was based upon the economic situation in its own country, and the divergence which developed in the viewpoints of the two governments was caused chiefly by the changed economic situation in Great Britain.

For some time following the armistice, business had boomed in Great Britain, thanks to the immediate demand from European countries which had been cut off from the outside world by the war. But for various reasons which will be discussed later,[4] the boom collapsed in 1920. Exports fell off in that year approximately 50 per cent, and during the succeeding years Great Britain's foreign trade remained far below the prewar figure. With the decline in exports, the volume of shipping fell off, and factories curtailed production. Business stagnation ensued, accompanied by widespread unemployment. The latter, in turn, entailed the payment by the government of millions of dollars in unemployment "doles." British statesmen, therefore, were confronted with the task of rebuilding the nation's prosperity, and, since this was dependent chiefly upon the ability of foreign markets to consume British goods, they were particularly eager that Germany, normally Great Britain's best customer, should regain her prosperity and with it her ability to purchase British commodities. Therefore, while British statesmen willingly conceded the French right to receive and the German duty to pay reparations, in 1922 they began to put forward the view that the economic restoration of Germany must precede the adequate payment of reparations.

On the other hand, France had emerged from the war with a devastated region of nearly thirteen thousand square miles to be restored. This region, which in prewar days had contained about one eighth of the total population of the country, had been both an agricultural and an industrial area. Approximately three fourths of the land had been under cultivation or in pasturage, while at the

[4] See page 691.

same time it had yielded about 55 per cent of the coal production and more than 90 per cent of the ore production of France. Furthermore, it had been an important manufacturing region. The chief economic problem for France after the war, consequently, was to restore this devastated area to its former wealth-producing capacity. By the middle of 1922 France had spent $7,500,000,000 in reconstruction and pensions. It was expected that this would ultimately be recovered from Germany, for the latter by the treaty of Versailles had agreed to make compensation for such expenditures. But, up to May 1, 1921, France, because of the expenses of the Allied armies of occupation and because of priority payments to Belgium, had received nothing in reparations from Germany, and had been compelled to finance her reconstruction work mainly through short-term internal loans.

French statesmen, therefore, were not likely to look with favor upon Germany's demand for a moratorium. They believed that the German fiscal difficulties were chiefly caused not by the payment of reparations, but by Germany's bad administration of her finances and by the bad faith of her nationals, who were deliberately evading taxation and sending millions of dollars in gold and securities out of the country. Poincaré, speaking for France, asserted that no moratorium should be granted unless "productive guarantees" were secured. Furthermore, the French premier asserted that no greater amount of the reparations debt would be remitted to Germany than the amount of the French war debt which Great Britain might remit to France.

When, therefore, Germany on November 14, 1922, once more demanded a total moratorium for three or four years and a grant of bank credit from the Allies in order that she might stabilize the mark, it was practically inevitable that the Allies at their London conference in December would come to a deadlock. Poincaré was determined to have Germany declared in default in order that further sanctions might be exacted. On the other hand, Bonar Law, the British prime minister, believed that no step like the occupation of the Ruhr could possibly bring a satisfactory settlement of the reparations problem. Germany could not be declared in default in cash payments because she had been granted concessions in this respect by the Reparations Commission. She had, however, failed to meet all the requirements of deliveries in kind. The French government concentrated its attacks on deliveries of timber and coal, and by a vote of three to one, the British government dissenting, the Reparations Commission declared Germany in default in these respects. On January 10, 1923, the French government announced that a mission of control would be sent into the Ruhr.

## THE STRUGGLE IN THE RUHR

The French and Belgian governments, with the support of Italy, now sought a solution of the reparations problem through direct action. Within a few days the whole Ruhr and Lippe region was occupied as far east as Dortmund by French and Belgian troops. Although the occupied area was only about sixty by twenty-eight miles in extent, it constituted the industrial heart of Germany. It was estimated that, at the date of the occupation, 80 to 85 per cent of Germany's coal, 80 per cent of her steel and pig-iron production, and 70 per cent of the goods and mineral traffic on her railways came from this territory. Owing to the fact that almost all of her gun steel during the war had been produced here, the Ruhr had come to be called the "German arsenal." As might be expected, it was one of the most thickly populated regions in Europe, containing 10 per cent of the German people. These facts constituted the basis of Poincaré's policy. By holding this small area, France and Belgium would either secure reparations payments at first hand or so paralyze the industrial life of Germany as to force her to agree to their terms.

The German government now faced two alternatives: either to accept the French demand and make new proposals for the payment of reparations, or to refuse to co-operate with France and passively resist all French efforts. The German chancellor believed that without German assistance France would be unable to operate the Ruhr industries, that the cost of the profitless occupation would force the French treasury into bankruptcy, and that thus the French would be compelled to withdraw in defeat from the territory. His unhappy guess as to the outcome led him to choose a policy of passive resistance, and the German government now proceeded to do everything that it could, short of open resistance, to oppose French efforts. It stopped all deliveries of reparations in kind to France and Belgium. It ordered the inhabitants of the occupied area to pay no customs duties, coal taxes, or export duties which could come into French hands, and forbade them to render any assistance to the French under threat of severe penalties. Finally, it entered upon a program of financial aid to all those—officials, railwaymen, miners, and industrial workers—who by reason of passive resistance lost their means of support.

The French and Belgian authorities countered these measures by declaring a state of siege and by prohibiting the export of all manufactured goods from the occupied district. The economic isolation of the Ruhr became complete. Furthermore, they imposed heavy fines and prison sentences, placed a censorship on the press, seized private property and private funds, and expelled countless officials and leaders. Altogether, some 147,000 German citizens were expelled during the first eleven months of the occupation. Nor was this all. The French estimated that seventy-six Germans were killed and ninety-two wounded by the Allies, while twenty Allied soldiers were killed and sixty-six wounded by the Germans.

Large numbers of men in the Ruhr were thrown out of employment, and food became scarce, the French allowing only sufficient to come into the district to ration the population. The German government was ruining itself to sustain passive resistance by paying allowances to expelled officials, to miners "on strike," and in a multitude of other ways. The deterioration of the mark was catastrophic. Not only the workmen in the Ruhr but, because of the decline of the mark and the cutting off of goods from that district, millions outside the Ruhr suffered as well. Nevertheless, the German people rallied about their government largely because they believed that Poincaré was actuated not by a desire to secure reparations but by fear of the economic recovery of Germany, by the wish to tighten the French hold on the Rhineland and the Rhine frontier, and by the hope of building up a great industrial trust under French control, combining French iron ore with the Ruhr coal.

But the stranglehold which France held on German industry began to tell. France might not secure enough out of her occupation to pay for the cost of maintaining that occupation, but Germany could not go on indefinitely without free access to this great center of her national industrial life. Unemployment in other parts of Germany soon resulted from the loss of products from the Ruhr. The mark continued its precipitate decline. By the middle of June it stood at 100,000 to the dollar, a month later it had sunk to 200,-

000, and on August 8 it finally reached 5,000,000. Popular dissatisfaction with the complete failure of the policy of passive resistance brought the downfall of the Cuno ministry on August 12. A new cabinet was organized under Gustav Stresemann, who now had the unenviable task of extricating Germany from her embarrassing situation by the only possible course—the cessation of passive resistance. On September 26 the German government announced that resistance had been abandoned.

The effect of the occupation of the Ruhr was far-reaching. In Germany it brought a change in the attitude of the great industrialists. Formerly indifferent or hostile to the payment of reparations, they had been too often defiant in the face of the Allied demands for fulfillment. With the seizure of their industries in the Ruhr, however, their attitude gradually underwent a change, and with the utter collapse of the German currency they came to the place where they themselves were willing to make sacrifices to pay reparations in order that the French might be got out of the Ruhr and the way cleared for currency stabilization in Germany. The German people as a whole learned that France was really in earnest and had the upper hand. All this, in turn, made it easier for the German government to carry through the reparations program as later outlined.

In France the effect of the Ruhr occupation was equally important, for it revealed the fact that mere force could not wring from Germany the money so much desired. Although in the fall of 1923 the occupation actually did begin to prove profitable, the net returns for the first year were not great, and were accompanied by a decline in the value of the franc. The majority of the French were again ready to try the method of peaceable adjustment if there appeared to be any likelihood of its success. And in the negotiations which must precede a new program of fulfillment, France would no longer stand as a weak suppliant begging for her rights; she now held something with which to get them. The German need for relief from the situation caused by the Ruhr occupation now matched the French need for reparations payments.

## THE DAWES PLAN

On October 24, 1923, in a note to the Reparations Commission, Germany declared her willingness in principle to resume payments under the treaty of Versailles, and requested an examination of her capacity to pay. The Reparations Commission thereupon decided to appoint two committees of experts, one to consider the means of balancing the German budget and stabilizing the German currency, the other to estimate the amount of capital which had been exported from Germany and to recommend the means of bringing it back. In this nonpolitical investigation the United States government consented to the participation of American experts.

The first committee of experts, headed by Charles G. Dawes of the United States, came to be known as the Dawes Committee, and included two representatives each from the United States, Great Britain, France, Italy, and Belgium. The second committee was headed by Reginald McKenna of Great Britain, and had one representative each from the above-mentioned countries. On April 9, 1924, the two committees simultaneously submitted their reports to the Reparations Commission. The McKenna Committee's report estimated that the total amount of German capital abroad at the end of 1923 was about $1,687,500,000 and that the amount of foreign currency held in Germany was about $300,000,000. It stated that the return of the capital could be hastened by permanently stopping German inflation and in general by carrying into effect the recommendations of the Dawes Committee.

The task originally assigned to the latter was to recommend ways and means of balancing the German budget and stabilizing the German currency. But the committee stated that, unless the amount of reparations which was to be contributed from the ordinary budget resources was known, financial and currency stability could not be assured. It thus cleared the way for recommendations in regard to German reparations payments.

In brief, the Dawes report embodied the following recommendations: (1) the Ruhr should be evacuated; (2) Germany should pledge certain revenues as security for payment of reparations, the standard annuities to be paid from railway bonds and a transport tax, from industrial debentures, and from the ordinary budget; [5]

[5] The committee made very definite recommendations regarding the sources from which reparations payments were to come. In the first place, the 33,000 miles of state-owned German railways—valued conservatively at $6,500,000,000 and practically free from debt—were to be subject to a first-mortgage bond issue of $2,750,000,000. This at 6 per cent would yield annually $165,000,000 for reparations payments. A transport tax upon the railways was to yield an additional $72,000,000 annually. In the second place, the industries of Germany—which were valued at approximately

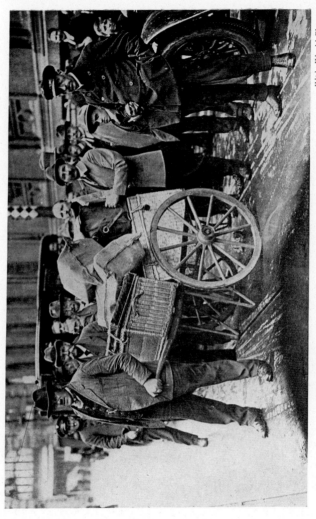

THE RESULT OF CURRENCY INFLATION

A Berlin firm's payroll in depreciated marks in August, 1923.

(3) the annual reparations payments should start at $250,000,000 and rise gradually over a four-year period to a normal figure of $625,-000,000; (4) future payments should be increased or decreased according to an index of prosperity; (5) a foreign loan of $200,000-000 should be made as a foundation for Germany's fiscal system; (6) a central bank should be established with a fifty-year monopoly for the issue of paper money, subject to the control of an international board of seven Germans and seven foreigners.

Two days after receiving the report, the Reparations Commission notified Germany that it considered it a practical basis for the solution of the reparations problem. Five days later Germany gave her full consent. In July a conference of the Allies, with American representatives participating unofficially, was opened in London for the purpose of drafting a protocol to put the Dawes plan into effect. On August 30, 1924, the protocol embodying the acceptance of the plan by the various governments and the Reparations Commission was signed in London. On September 1 the plan began to operate; on July 31, 1925, the last French and Belgian soldiers left the Ruhr.

## THE INTER-ALLIED WAR DEBTS

Meanwhile, not unrelated to the problem of reparations was that of the Inter-Allied war debts, which were also a legacy of the World War. During the early years of the conflict Great Britain, as the wealthiest of the Allies, advanced some billions of dollars in loans to Russia, France, Italy, and the lesser powers, and, after the United States became a belligerent, the latter loaned approximately $10,338,-000,000 to the Allies, including Great Britain, in return for their demand notes bearing interest at 5 per cent.

At the Paris peace conference the British proposed a general cancellation of all Inter-Allied debts; that is, Great Britain asserted her willingness to cancel the amounts owed her by the Allies if the United States would do the same. Such a step would of course have been to

---

$8,000,000,000 and were likewise practically debt-free, thanks to the inflation of the currency—were to assume a blanket mortgage of $1,250,000,000. This would provide another annual payment of $75,000,000. In the third place, certain specific revenues—customs, alcohol, tobacco, beer, and sugar—were to be assigned to Germany's creditors as a pledge for $312,500,000 annually. All revenues from these latter sources were to pass directly into the hands of an agent general for reparations payments, who, after deducting the above amount, would surrender the balance to the German government. It was estimated that these assigned revenues would yield between $425,000,000 and $535,000,000 annually when the plan came fully into effect.

the advantage of Great Britain, for her loss in canceling the Allied debts to herself would have been more than offset by the cancellation of her debt to the United States and by the general stimulation to world trade which would have followed such a reduction of international debts. On the other hand, such a step would, for all practical purposes, have placed a war indemnity of over ten billion dollars on American taxpayers.

Nevertheless, it was argued by many Europeans and even by some Americans that, since the war against Germany had been a common struggle, and since the United States had entered the conflict late and lost relatively very few men, she should consider the loans to the Allies as her contribution to the common cause. It was further pointed out that an amount even greater than that advanced in loans was spent in the United States by the Allies during the war and hence that the United States should be satisfied with the great wealth which had come to her from her war-time activities and should not try to collect the war debts. Finally, it was asserted that, since Europe could not pay her war debts without flooding the United States with foreign commodities, collection of the debts would greatly harm American manufacturers and merchants.

At the peace conference President Wilson declined the British proposal, however, and the American attitude during the succeeding decade was later succinctly summed up by President Coolidge when he explained that the Allies had "hired the money" and that they were therefore obliged to repay it with interest. In defense of the American position, it was argued that the war debts should be collected in order that European countries might learn that they themselves must pay for their wars even though they temporarily financed them by borrowing from abroad. Moreover, public opinion demanded that the war debts be collected in order to prevent the shifting of this heavy burden to the shoulders of American taxpayers, who otherwise would be obliged to retire the war bonds floated by the United States to obtain funds for the Allies. In 1922 the United States government, accordingly, officially requested all its debtors to take the necessary steps to fund their debts to the United States.

Once again the British attitude was shown in the Balfour note of August 1, 1922. In that note the British government declared that, although it still favored a general cancellation of both war debts and reparations claims, it was forced to adopt a different policy by the stand of the United States. The British government, according to the note, would seek to collect from its debtors only such sums as would in their aggregate equal the amount which Great Britain must pay to the United States. In other words, if the United States would reduce the amount of the British indebtedness, the British government would reduce the amount owed to it by the other Allies. The latter maintained, in general, that they could pay Great Britain and the United States only as they themselves received reparations from Germany.

This connection between reparations and war debts the American government consistently refused to admit, and in the end the debtor states entered into funding agreements with the United States. As a rule, no interest had been paid on the loans since their contraction, so that to each original loan was added, at the time of funding, the accrued interest. Consequently, the amount actually funded totaled approximately $11,500,000,000. The United States had earlier declared that, when final arrangements were made, each debtor nation's capacity to pay might be taken into consideration in determining the rate of interest. Such consideration was given, and, although the principal of each debt was maintained intact, the interest rate was in every case reduced from the original 5 per cent, that of Great Britain being reduced to an average of 3.3 per cent and that of Italy to as low as 0.4 per cent. In principal and interest the debtor nations agreed to pay the United States over a sixty-two-year period a total of approximately $22,000,000,000. Figured on the originally contracted rate of interest, approximately half of the total debt was thus remitted by the United States.

### The Linking of Reparations and War Debts in the Young Plan

With Germany regularly making her reparations payments to the Allies under the Dawes plan, the Allies were able in turn to make their war-debt payments to the United States. Between September, 1924, and September, 1928, about $1,350,000,000 was paid to the Allies by Germany without any noticeable strain on the Dawes machinery or upon the external value of the German mark.[6] With the opening of the fifth year the first standard annual payment of $625,000,000 fell due, the experts having assumed that by this time the financial and economic situation in Germany would have become normal.

The Dawes report had, of course, limited itself merely to pointing out the amount which Germany could pay annually over a period of years. It had said nothing about how long she should pay nor what the total should be. So far as Germany was concerned, she was still legally bound to pay $33,000,000,000 by the agreement which she had been forced to accept in May, 1921. But no one now considered it possible to exact any such amount, and the fact that there was still no real final determination of Germany's reparations liabilities left an element of uncertainty in the affairs of all the states concerned. The next step in the reparations problem, therefore, was to reach some new decision either as to a revised total which Germany must pay or as to the specific number of years over which the Dawes plan was to operate.

During the sessions of the League Assembly in September, 1928, conferences were held between representatives of France, Great Britain, Belgium, Italy, Japan, and Germany, which led to an agreement on the opening of official negotiations with a view to a complete and final settlement of the reparations problem. A new committee of experts was accordingly appointed which included in its personnel some of the best financial brains of the nations concerned and of the United States as well. Beginning in February, 1929, sessions of the committee were held in Paris under the chairmanship of Owen D. Young, one of the American delegates, who had played an important role in the drafting of the Dawes plan. As in the latter case, the committee soon became known from its chairman as the Young Committee.

The committee's task, however, was not simply economic. If it were to succeed, it had to draft a report that would be acceptable to the governments involved, to their parliaments, and in the last analysis to general public opinion. Naturally, the creditor states desired to obtain as large an amount as possible from Germany, while the latter sought to have her payments reduced below the

---

[6] During these years, although the fact was not generally recognized at the time, Germany was enabled to make her reparations payments largely because huge sums were being loaned to German interests by foreign bankers, chiefly American.

Dawes Committee's figures. More specifically, France desired such a settlement as would permit the early mobilization of some part of the reparations debt; Great Britain wished to have the existing system of deliveries in kind abolished or greatly limited; Germany sought the appointment of some sort of nonpolitical committee to function in case she should encounter difficult periods in the payment of reparations.

On June 7, after nearly four months of struggle and compromise, what has been characterized by one of its participants as "the grimmest conference on record" came to a close with the signing of the final report. The experts had, of course, been acting independently, and their decisions had to be approved by the governments concerned. To facilitate the ratification of the plan, diplomatic conferences met at the Hague in August and again in the following January. The final act was signed on January 20, 1930, and in the succeeding months it was ratified by the various governments.

The Young plan provided for thirty-seven payments by Germany averaging $512,500,000, to be followed by twenty-two further payments averaging $391,250,000.[7] Of each annuity, $165,000,000 was to be unconditional, that is, payable without any right of postponement of any kind; and of this amount $125,000,000 was assigned to France in order to allow her to mobilize a substantial part of her share in the total settlement. On the ground that the system of deliveries in kind had come to play an important role in the economic life of Germany and that its immediate cessation would not be in the interest of Germany or of the creditor powers, the plan provided for the continuance of the system for a period of ten years. Actually, however, the payments in kind were reduced to approximately half of what they had been.

The Dawes plan had begun the process of removing the reparations problem from the political to the financial sphere; the Young plan carried the process still further by the creation of the Bank for

---

[7] The experts recommended that the annuities during the first thirty-seven years should be derived from two sources: the German Railway Company and the budget of the republic. As its share in the annuity the railway company would pay a direct tax to the German government of $165,000,000. The railway bonds imposed by the Dawes plan would be abolished, together with the attendant circumstance of foreign participation in the management of the railway. The industrial debentures imposed by the Dawes plan would likewise be abolished, the contribution formerly made to the annuity from this source being transferred to the budget of the republic. After the thirty-seventh year the whole annuity would come from the German budget.

International Settlements. This institution was to perform the banking functions necessary in the sequence between the initial payment of the annuities and the final distribution of the funds. It was placed outside the field of political influences, and its powers and facilities were sufficiently broad to enable it to deal freely and promptly with the problems involved in the settlement of Germany's obligations. It was authorized, for example, to deal with the question of postponement of the conditional annuities if raised at any time by the German government. The control of the management of the bank was placed in the hands of the central banks of the countries involved in the reparations settlement, including Germany. Obviously, the reparations problem was lifted out of the political sphere, and the former political method of handling what was purely an economic problem now became obsolete.

In contrast with the Dawes plan, the Young plan definitely fixed the number and the amounts of the annuities necessary for a final settlement. It removed the uncertainty attendant upon the operation of the index of prosperity. It abolished the system of external controls, gave Germany full financial autonomy, and left to her the obligation of facing her engagements on her own responsibility. The system of deliveries in kind was greatly limited, and on the other hand the annuities were to be paid in a form lending themselves to mobilization. Finally, the whole scheme was placed in charge of a purely financial institution in the management of which Germany was to have an appropriate part.

Germany's payments, moreover, were fixed in relation to the sums owed by the Allied countries in war debts, and the *de facto* relationship between war debts and reparations was clearly recognized. If any of the creditor powers received any relief in its payments of war debts, during the first thirty-seven years Germany should benefit two thirds, and during the last twenty-two years the whole relief should be applied to the reduction of Germany's liabilities. Thus was destroyed the fiction that the problems of war debts and reparations were unconnected. Furthermore, it was agreed that the Inter-Allied occupation of the Rhineland should end. Evacuation began in September, 1929, and was completed by June 30, 1930. With the Allies and Germany at last in agreement regarding the number and amounts of the latter's future reparations payments, it was hoped that the settlement was "complete and final," and that at last the tortuous problem of reparations had been successfully solved.

## ECONOMIC DEPRESSION AND MORATORIUM

In 1929 the financial experts of the Young Committee had based their scheme for reparations payments on the assumption that world trade would expand both in volume and in value. Unfortunately, however, almost simultaneously with the inauguration of the Young Plan there came an economic depression on an unprecedented scale, bringing in its train a drastic shrinking in the volume of world trade and a rapid and steady fall in commodity prices.

The causes assigned for the depression were about as varied as the interests and outlooks of those who examined the situation. By many the inadequacy of the world's relatively small supply of gold as a basis for national and international exchange was held responsible for the catastrophic decline in the price of commodities. By others the blame was placed upon the oversupply and consequently decreasing value of silver. This development, it was asserted, greatly lessened the purchasing power of, and therefore the international trade with, those countries—particularly China and India—which were on a silver basis. A world-wide surplus of agricultural products, it was further pointed out, inevitably brought a decline in the price of these commodities and therefore diminished the farmers' ability to purchase manufactured goods; while, at the same time, the postwar revolution in industry by the introduction of labor-saving machines decreased the man power needed in certain types of manufacturing and so through unemployment brought a decline in the purchasing power of the proletariat. The new machinery, on the other hand, vastly increased the output of manufactured goods, so that inevitably there came an overproduction and the closing down of factories, with further loss of purchasing power on the part of those who were dismissed. Extreme nationalism, with its erection of high protective tariffs and its resultant interference with the flow of international trade, also came in for bitter criticism. But, whatever were the causes of the depression, the year 1930 witnessed a marked slowing down of industry and an alarming increase in unemployment.

In 1931 the continued economic depression at last brought the financial collapse of certain countries of Europe, which found themselves unable to dispose of their surplus products at prices that would enable them to meet their international obligations. The latter were of three types: (1) payments on reparations and war debts, (2) payments of interest and amortization charges on huge long-term loans which had been made for rehabilitation work, (3) repayments of short-term credits which had been lavishly advanced by American and British banks in order that Europe might be able to continue her importation of commodities from their countries.

From 1924 to 1929 Germany had been enabled to make her reparations payments largely because she had been advanced huge sums from abroad, chiefly by American bankers. The Allies, having received reparations payments from Germany, had in turn also been able to meet their war-debt payments to the United States. In 1929, however, the sources of these foreign loans had begun to dry up,[8] and Germany had been forced to resort to short-term loans and to her own budget in order to meet her international obligations. During 1930–1931, despite the strenuous efforts of the government to curtail expenditures and increase receipts, the German budget became more and more unbalanced, and another financial debacle seemed imminent.

The incident which precipitated the financial crisis in central Europe occurred in Austria, where in June, 1931, the Creditanstalt, by far the largest private bank in the republic, came to the verge of collapse and had to be rescued by the Austrian government. The difficulties of the Creditanstalt shook foreign confidence in the solvency of central Europe as a whole and reacted on Germany, where a banking crisis was already developing, largely because American bankers were recalling their short-term credits.[9] Once again Germany seemed to face national bankruptcy. To prevent such a catastrophe, with all its attendant evils to the world, President Hoover, on June 20, 1931, proposed a suspension of all payments on reparations and intergovernmental debts for one year beginning July 1.

The situation in Germany, nevertheless, grew worse in July with

---

[8] Partly because surplus capital in the United States was being devoted to speculation.
[9] In July, 1931, the short-term credits of Germany totaled approximately $3,000,-000,000.

the continued calling of short-term loans and the export of capital. Germans themselves, withdrawing money to hoard or to transfer abroad, precipitated a further crisis when on July 13 the Darmstädter und National-Bank, one of the largest financial institutions in the country, was forced to close its doors. This in turn evoked a governmental decree temporarily closing all banks and stock exchanges. In August a committee, headed by an American banker, Albert H. Wiggin, was convened by the Bank for International Settlements to study the German situation. This committee recommended that the existing short-term loans should be continued for a period of six months, and its recommendation was at once adopted by Germany's creditors, who negotiated a "standstill agreement" extending until February 29, 1932, all short-term credits.[10]

This "freezing" of short-term loans in turn reacted disastrously on Great Britain, whose bankers were fatally handicapped by their inability to recall the short-term credits they had advanced to Germany. During August and September gold was rapidly withdrawn from London, particularly by Dutch, Belgian, and Swiss bankers who feared that British banks would not be able to meet their obligations, and that the British government might even be forced to abandon the gold standard. On September 21 continued withdrawals finally forced Great Britain to go off the gold standard, a step in which she was soon followed by many other countries both in Europe and throughout the world.

World economic conditions in general and German conditions in particular soon convinced the German government that it would be impossible to resume reparations payments at the end of the Hoover moratorium. In November, 1931, therefore, availing itself of a provision of the Young plan, it requested the Bank for International Settlements to convene a special advisory committee of financial experts to investigate Germany's capacity to resume reparations payments in July, 1932. This committee on December 23 reported that Germany would be justified in declaring that she would not be able, in the year beginning in July, 1932, to transfer the conditional part of the reparations annuity. The committee also took occasion to

[10] In February, 1932, and yearly thereafter through 1937, the "standstill agreement" was extended. By 1937 short-term credits had been reduced, however, to about $440,000,000.

point out that a prompt adjustment of all intergovernmental debts to the existing situation of the world[11] was the only lasting step capable of re-establishing economic stability and real peace.

### The End of Reparations

On June 16, 1932, a reparations conference once more convened —this time at Lausanne—to decide upon "a lasting settlement" of the questions raised in the report of the most recent committee of financial experts, and to consider measures necessary to solve the other economic and financial difficulties which, it was felt, were responsible for and might prolong the existing world crisis. So far as the reparations problem was concerned, Germany, of course, sought to secure the complete cancellation of all reparations payments. France, on the other hand, desired to have the Young plan formally continued but with the payments specified therein greatly reduced. In the end an agreement was reached (July 9) that the reparations payments stipulated in the Young plan should be set aside and replaced by an obligation upon Germany to pay into a general fund for European reconstruction the sum of $750,000,000. To meet this obligation, the German government was to deliver to the Bank for International Settlements bonds to that amount. These bonds were to be held by the bank for three years, after which they might under certain restrictions be placed on the market. Such bonds as the bank had been unable to negotiate at the end of fifteen years, however, were to be canceled. Interest at the rate of 5 per cent was to be paid only on those bonds which were negotiated and only from the date of their negotiation.

The Lausanne agreement constituted one more recession in the series of ever-diminishing demands upon Germany for reparations. An Allied demand in 1921 that Germany assume an obligation to pay $56,500,000,000 was followed in the same year by the Reparations Commission's decision that the total figure should be $33,000,000,000. This stood legally as Germany's obligation until the Young plan reduced it to an amount which was equivalent to a cash payment of approximately $9,000,000,000. Two years later came the Hoover moratorium, and then in July, 1932, the Lausanne agreement drastically revised Germany's obligations to a total cash pay-

---

[11] The tremendous fall in commodity prices had obviously greatly increased the burden of all intergovernmental payments.

Underwood & Underwood

Another "Scrap of Paper"

The signing of the Briand-Kellogg pact, August 27, 1928.

ment of only $750,000,000, with the possibility that even this amount might never be paid.[12]

On the same day on which the Lausanne treaty was signed, Great Britain, France, Italy, and Belgium came to another agreement. By this so-called "gentlemen's agreement" these powers undertook not to ratify the Lausanne treaty until a satisfactory settlement had been reached between them and their own creditors. If such settlements were not obtained, the agreement with Germany was not to be ratified and Germany's position in regard to reparations would be legally that which existed before the Hoover moratorium. An effort was thus once more made to link the reparations question with the problem of Inter-Allied war debts, and to make the final solution of the reparations problem rest upon the willingness of the United States either to cancel or to reduce the debts due it from the Allies.[13]

## DEFAULT ON WAR-DEBT PAYMENTS

Although the Hoover moratorium in 1931 suspended all payments on war debts, the United States expected that with the expiration of the one-year period these payments would be resumed. Congress, in approving the moratorium in December, 1931, expressly declared that cancellation or reduction of any of the indebtedness of foreign countries to the United States was contrary to the policy of that body. On the other hand, the Allied governments maintained that the Lausanne agreement practically canceling Germany's reparations payments was made in the belief that the United States would consent to a revision of war-debts payments. In November, 1932, accordingly, Great Britain and France presented notes to the United States raising the question of debt revision. Both linked the questions of reparations and war debts, and both requested postponement of the payments due on December 15 as a preliminary to a general review of the debt agreements.

[12] Early in 1937 Chancellor Hitler announced in effect the German government's repudiation of these reparations bonds.
[13] In accordance with a suggestion of the Lausanne conference, a world monetary and economic conference convened in London in June, 1933. From the outset, unfortunately, the nations differed regarding the steps necessary to economic recovery. As the discussions proceeded it became clear that the settlement of the currency question was a prerequisite for agreement on other matters. When the United States declined to agree upon currency stabilization at that time, the conference came to an end without taking any notable step toward ending the world economic depression.

In reply, President Hoover pointed out that the American government still held that "reparations are a solely European question in which the United States is not concerned," and that it refused to recognize that the Lausanne settlement of German reparations "was made in reliance upon any commitments given by this government." He furthermore asserted that as President he had no jurisdiction to grant either a postponement of the payments due on December 15 or a review of the debt situation.

Although in both Great Britain and France strong minorities favored default, in neither country was the government willing to go so far. In the former the government was able to carry through its policy and on December 15 made its payment in full. Italy, Czechoslovakia, Finland, Latvia, and Lithuania followed Great Britain's example. Developments in France, however, were quite otherwise. The French had always strongly opposed the payment of war debts and had ratified the funding agreement with the United States with the reservation that the debt to that country was to be paid "exclusively by the sums that Germany shall pay France." Although Premier Herriot asserted that the honor of France required that she should make the debt payment as agreed, his request for authorization to pay the amount due on December 15 was voted down by the Chamber of Deputies, and he himself was obliged to resign. The payment was, in the words of the Chamber of Deputies, "deferred" until the United States should agree to enter a conference for the purpose of adjusting all international obligations and of putting an end to all international transfers for which there was no compensating transaction. Poland, Belgium, Estonia, and Hungary took the same stand as France.

On June 15, 1933, when payments again became due, Finland alone made her payment in full. Great Britain, Italy, Czechoslovakia, Rumania, and Latvia made "token" payments, the British payment being accompanied by a note indicating that the payment was to be considered "as an acknowledgment of the debt, pending a final settlement." France again defaulted completely and was joined in this step by Belgium, Poland, Yugoslavia, Estonia, Lithuania, and Hungary. Six months later only six of the countries scheduled to make payments to the United States actually did so, and five of them made merely "token" payments. Finland alone paid her full installment in December, 1933. Although, in an effort to bring pressure on the debtor governments, the United States Congress, in April, 1934, passed the Johnson Act forbidding nationals of the United States to make loans to foreign governments in default on their debt obligations to the United States, on June 15, 1934, the only payment received was from Finland. And in the succeeding years she was the only country to make any payments whatever to the United States.[14]

By 1934 it was becoming evident to most observers that the effort of the United States to collect some $22,000,000,000 of war debts and interest on the basis of settlements calling for payments over a period of sixty-two years had broken down. Just as the attempts of the former Allies to collect reparations payments from Germany in amounts ranging from $33,000,000,000 to $9,000,000,000 had collapsed in the face of the impossibility of transferring such tremendous sums, so, it appeared, had American efforts suffered a similar fate. As the year 1932 saw the practical ending of the payment of reparations, so the year 1934 saw apparently the ending of payments of war debts to the United States by the Allied countries.

For this eventuality the United States was not entirely blameless. In the first place, although most of the original ten billion dollars had been transferred to the Allies in the form of commodities, the United States had refused to accept payment in kind from the debtor nations. In the second place, she had raised high tariff barriers against foreign commodities and had thus greatly handicapped the debtor powers in their efforts to secure American currency with which to make payments. In the third place, she had vigorously sought to increase her own export trade and in so doing had inevitably lessened the sale of goods abroad by the debtor nations. Finally, by subsidizing the American merchant marine, she had indirectly reduced the income of foreign shipping. All of these things the United States had a right to do, but in doing them she went far toward preventing the European powers from being able to meet their war-debt obligations. To many it seemed that the United States had as yet an incomplete understanding of her new position as a creditor rather than a debtor nation.

[14] During these years Finland had a favorable balance of trade with the United States.

# CHAPTER XVIII

## DISARMAMENT AND SECURITY

THE outbreak of the World War in 1914 had clearly demonstrated that great armaments did not secure peace. It had, indeed, convinced many that great armaments, by engendering international fear and suspicion, actually constituted an underlying or fundamental cause of war. Reflecting this state of mind, the statesmen at the Paris peace conference admitted in the treaties there drafted "that the maintenance of peace requires the reduction of national armaments to the lowest point consistent with national safety and the enforcement by common action of international obligations." They went even further than this, and made a beginning of compulsory disarmament by forcing Germany, Austria, Hungary, and Bulgaria to accept definite limitations upon their military and naval establishments. These limitations, the Allies informed Germany, were only "the first steps towards that general reduction and limitation of armaments which they seek to bring about as one of the most fruitful preventives of war, and which it will be one of the first duties of the League of Nations to promote." Efforts to extend this program of disarmament to other countries in the postwar years, however, encountered almost insuperable obstacles, which eventually forced general recognition that national disarmament is inextricably intertwined with the problem of national security.

### THE LEAGUE'S EARLY EFFORTS TO PROVIDE SECURITY

Upon the Council of the League the statesmen at Paris imposed the duty of formulating plans for the reduction of armaments. Accordingly a commission was appointed in February, 1921, to make proposals, but the commission decided that no scheme for disarmament could be effective which did not provide some form of mutual security to be given in exchange. The third Assembly thereupon requested the commission to prepare a draft treaty embodying this idea of mutual security. The result was a draft treaty of mutual assistance, unanimously adopted by the fourth assembly in September, 1923.

The security provided in this proposed treaty consisted of the assurance given by the signatory powers that, if a state were attacked, the rest of the signatory powers would come to its assistance. The question of deciding which state was the aggressor in case of war was delegated to the Council of the League, which must render its decision within four days of its being summoned. In order to link together security and disarmament, the treaty further provided that no state should be entitled to claim the benefits of the mutual guarantee unless it had limited its armaments to a scale approved by the Council of the League.

This draft treaty was circulated to all states whether or not they were members of the League. The replies received indicated that sixteen states, including France, Italy, and Japan, accepted the treaty in principle, while twelve states, including Germany, Great Britain, the United States, and Russia, declared that they could not adhere to it. Nearly all the replies pointed out the absence of a definition of aggression and criticized the policy of giving full power to the League Council to determine the aggressor state. The various criticisms of the draft treaty convinced those interested in disarmament that such a treaty must include a definition of aggression and a clear-cut indication of the aggressor.

When, therefore, MacDonald and Herriot, premiers of Great Britain and France respectively, submitted to the fifth Assembly of the League a protocol for the pacific settlement of international disputes, they linked with disarmament and security a third feature, arbitration. This so-called Geneva Protocol provided that all legal disputes must go before the Permanent Court of International Justice and all nonlegal disputes must be submitted to arbitration. War was declared a criminal offense, and every state which resorted to war in violation of the undertakings contained in the Covenant or in the protocol became an aggressor. The definition of an aggressor state was thus made almost automatic, and one of the chief objections to the preceding treaty was overcome. The "sanctions" to be taken against an aggressor state remained those provided for in Article 16 of the Covenant; namely, economic boycott and possible military action. The definition of aggression, the system of arbitration, and the effective measures to be taken against an aggressor were supposed to create a threefold guarantee of security. The Geneva Protocol, however, had very much the same reception as the proposed treaty of mutual assistance and failed of adoption.

But the League of Nations did not cease in its efforts. The Council next appointed the Preparatory Commission for the Disarmament Conference. This commission, which consisted of representatives of all of the great powers, including Germany, the United States, and eventually even Soviet Russia, together with representatives of a number of the small powers in the League, began its work at Geneva in May, 1926.

## FRENCH SECURITY, 1920–1928

Meanwhile, some of the states of Europe were busy attempting to provide security for themselves by concluding treaties of alliance or nonaggression. France was especially disturbed after the war by the specter of a discontented and revengeful Germany.[1] To allay this fear President Wilson and Premier Lloyd George had signed at the peace conference a tripartite guarantee treaty pledging their countries to come to the aid of France in case of an unprovoked attack by Germany. When this alliance failed to become effective because of nonratification by the United States, France at once began to build a system of alliances centering about herself. First she concluded a defensive military convention with Belgium (1920). She then turned to Poland, whose statesmen naturally feared for the security of their country's western frontier, established as it had been at the expense of Germany. The result was a Franco-Polish defensive alliance against Germany, signed in 1921. In the following year France sought to obtain a defensive alliance with Great Britain. This time she failed, however, because Lloyd George and Poincaré, the prime ministers of the two countries, could not agree upon terms. Nevertheless, France persisted in her general scheme and turned next to Czechoslovakia, whose statesmen wished to guard against the union of Austria and Germany and against the restoration of either the Habsburgs or the Hohenzollerns. In 1924 a Franco-Czechoslovak treaty of alliance was formally signed in Paris.

The next step in strengthening French security came from across the Rhine. Early in 1925 Gustav Stresemann, German foreign minister, offered France a pact of mutual guarantee and nonaggression.

---

[1] For French efforts to obtain security at the peace conference, see pages 483 and 490.

During the extended exchange of notes which followed, France admitted that such an agreement might be possible provided (1) Germany became a member of the League, (2) Belgium became a party to the pact, and (3) nothing in the pact should be construed to prevent France from going to the aid of Poland, or the Allies from acting in accordance with the Covenant of the League. To draft such an agreement representatives of Germany, France, Great Britain, Italy, Belgium, Poland, and Czechoslovakia gathered in the little Swiss town of Locarno beside the blue waters of Lake Maggiore. After twelve days of negotiations the conference closed on October 16, 1925, with the initialing of a treaty of mutual guarantee, four arbitration treaties between Germany on the one side and France, Belgium, Poland, and Czechoslovakia on the other, and two treaties of guarantee between France on the one side and Poland and Czechoslovakia on the other.

By Article 1 of the treaty of mutual guarantee, Germany, Belgium, France, Great Britain, and Italy, as a group and individually, guaranteed the inviolability of the existing frontiers between Germany and Belgium, and between Germany and France, together with the demilitarization of German territory west of a line drawn fifty kilometers east of the Rhine. By Article 2 Germany and Belgium, and Germany and France, mutually agreed in no case to attack, invade, or resort to war against each other except (1) in case of legitimate defense against a violation of Article 2 of the treaty, (2) in case of a "flagrant breach" of the agreements regarding the demilitarized zone, (3) in case of being directed by the League against a state which had first attacked another member of the League.

In case of a "flagrant violation" of either Article 1 or Article 2, the signatory powers agreed to come immediately to the assistance of the injured party. In case of a doubtful violation, the question was to be considered by the Council of the League, and the signatory powers agreed to fulfill their obligations as above if the Council was satisfied that a violation or breach had been committed. The agreement was to come into force as soon as Germany became a member of the League of Nations, and was to remain in effect until the League Council should decide that "the League of Nations ensures sufficient protection to the high contracting parties."

By the network of arbitration agreements Germany on the one side and Belgium, France, Czechoslovakia, and Poland severally on the other engaged to settle by peaceful means all disputes, of every kind, which proved impossible of adjustment by the normal methods of diplomacy. By the guarantee treaties which France signed with Czechoslovakia and Poland it was agreed that in case Poland or Czechoslovakia or France should suffer from a failure to observe the undertakings arrived at between them and Germany, France and reciprocally Poland, or France and reciprocally Czechoslovakia, should "lend each other immediately aid and assistance, if such failure is accompanied by unprovoked recourse to arms."

In the succeeding years France sought to forge still more links for her chain of security treaties. In 1926 she signed with Rumania a treaty of friendship in which, among other things, the two states promised to consult each other in all matters which might threaten their external security or which might tend to subvert the situation created by the treaties of peace. If either state should be attacked without provocation, the two governments engaged immediately to consult each other as to the action to be taken by each "within the framework of the Covenant of the League of Nations" in order to safeguard their legitimate national interests and to maintain the order established by the peace treaties. The two states agreed to concert their policy in case of any attempted modification of the political status of the countries of Europe and to confer regarding the attitude to be taken in such an event. In the next year France signed an almost identical treaty with Yugoslavia.

In 1927 Aristide Briand, French foreign minister, proposed to the United States a declaration by the two powers condemning recourse to war, renouncing war as "an instrument of national policy," and agreeing that a settlement of all disputes arising between them should be brought about only by pacific means. The American secretary of state, Frank B. Kellogg, suggested that instead of a bilateral treaty a similar multilateral treaty should be drafted in order to extend "throughout the world the benefits of a covenant originally suggested as between France and the United States alone." In the course of negotiations which extended over the following months Kellogg's proposal was subjected to a number of reservations and interpretations, as a result of which it appeared that the nations were agreed that all war was to be renounced except (1) in self-defense, (2) against any treaty-breaking signatory state, (3) in the execution of any obligation consequent upon the signing of any treaty of neutrality, (4) in the case of Great Britain, in defense of certain strategic places which are considered vital to the safety of the empire, (5) in fulfillment of the obligations and responsibilities incurred by membership in the League of Nations and by the signing of the Locarno agreements.

Subject to these reservations, which were not, however, incorporated into the treaty, the plenipotentiaries of fifteen states gathered at the Quai d'Orsay on August 27, 1928, and there signed a general treaty for the renunciation of war, the so-called pact of Paris. In it the powers solemnly declared that they condemned recourse to war for the solution of international controversies, renounced it as an instrument of national policy in their relations with one another, and agreed that the settlement or solution of all disputes or conflicts which might arise among them should never be sought except by pacific means. Immediately following the signing of the treaty, it was opened to the adherence of all states, and ultimately it was accepted by practically every country in the world. The treaty was promulgated by President Hoover of the United States on July 24, 1929.

### Security in Central Europe and the Balkans

In central Europe fear of the return of the Habsburgs and of the destruction of the status established by the peace settlement was the motivating force in bringing about negotiations for security. Although Austria's desire to be united with Germany caused some concern, the most disturbing factor in the situation was the determination of the proud and aggressive Magyars to secure a modification of the treaty which separated from them not only their prewar minorities but even some 3,000,000 of their kinsmen. To check the outward thrust of Hungary's irredentism the surrounding states resorted to centripetal counteralliances. In this defensive movement the initiative was taken by Edward Beneš, Czechoslovak foreign minister, who made his first objective an understanding between Czechoslovakia, Yugoslavia, and Rumania.

In 1920 Czechoslovakia and Yugoslavia signed a convention in which each agreed to assist the other in case of an unprovoked attack by Hungary. A Czechoslovak-Rumanian convention with practically identical terms was signed in April of the following year, and the so-called Little Entente [2] was completed two months later by a Yugoslav-Rumanian alliance in which each agreed to aid the other if attacked by Hungary or Bulgaria. In 1933 a convention was signed with the purpose of transforming the Little Entente into a permanent "unified international organization." By the terms of this convention the earlier bilateral treaties between the members of the Little Entente were renewed for an indefinite period; a permanent council, consisting of the foreign ministers of the three states, was organized, and a permanent secretariat was established. Every political treaty and every economic agreement thereafter entered into by a member of the Little Entente was first to have the unanimous consent of the permanent council. This convention created in a sense—so far as international affairs were concerned—a new great power in Europe, with a population not far from 50,000,000 and with a combined military force of considerable size. By treaties which France had signed with Czechoslovakia, Rumania, and Yugoslavia the Little Entente was to some extent linked with that great power.

The security which the Little Entente agreements and the French treaties provided, in part, for the Balkans was considerably extended a few years later by still another treaty. In 1934 Greece, Rumania, Yugoslavia, and Turkey signed a mutual-assistance pact in which the signatory powers agreed to guarantee Balkan frontiers against aggression by any Balkan state, the pact to become effective against any Balkan state that might join an outside power that had committed an act of aggression against one of the signatories.[3] The Greek parliament, however, ratified the treaty with the reservations that the boundaries guaranteed were those internal to the Balkans and that under no circumstances were obligations arising from the pact to be so construed as to involve Greece in a war with any great power.[4] These reservations were accepted by the other signatories, though clearly they weakened the force of the pact. Provision was made for a permanent council like that of the Little Entente. Yugoslavia and Rumania, before they signed this Balkan treaty, were obliged to submit its terms to the approval of the Little Entente.

[2] Although not a member of the Little Entente, Poland from 1921 to 1926 had a diplomatic agreement with Czechoslovakia in which these two powers mutually guaranteed their frontiers with Germany.

[3] This would prevent an interpretation like that of King Constantine of Greece in 1915. See the footnote on page 407.

[4] In 1936 the Balkan Entente agreed that Albania should not be regarded as a Balkan state within the meaning of the Balkan pact.

## SECURITY IN EASTERN EUROPE

In eastern Europe the states which bordered upon Soviet Russia were likewise concerned with the problem of security. In view of the fact that they were created in whole or in part out of territory of the former Russian empire; that Riga, Libau, Windau, and Reval—ports now controlled by the Baltic republics—were before the war the outlets for the greater part of the seagoing trade of northern Russia; that the Russo-Polish boundary, forced from the Soviet government in a moment of military weakness, tore from Russia millions of her own kinsmen; that the annexation of Bessarabia by Rumania, though sanctioned by the principal Allied powers, was not recognized as legal by the Soviet government—in view of all these facts, it was not surprising that a number of attempts were made to arrive at some plan for mutual assistance.

Rumania, the power which had the most reason to fear an attack from Russia, took the first step, and in 1921 a Polish-Rumanian defensive alliance resulted. By the terms of this treaty an unprovoked attack on the eastern frontier [5] of either power would require the other to enter the war to assist the one attacked. Poland, from her geographical position, seemed naturally the power which should expand the Polish-Rumanian alliance into a system to include the Baltic states as well. This she failed to do, however, largely because she had alienated Lithuania by her arbitrary and unauthorized seizure of Vilna. Although these two states, carved in each case from former German and Russian territory, had need of a common policy toward the two greater powers, the Vilna dispute drove a wedge between them.

A treaty of defensive alliance was concluded, however, between two of the small Baltic republics. In 1923 Estonia and Latvia agreed to pursue a purely pacific policy toward all nations, to concert together and lend each other political and diplomatic support in their international relations, and to give armed assistance to each other in case of unprovoked attack. Eleven years later Lithuania was linked with these two in the so-called Baltic Entente when the three powers signed (September, 1934) a ten-year treaty agreeing to settle by peaceful means such questions as might arise among them and to hold conferences at least twice a year for the co-ordination of their foreign

---

[5] When the Polish-Rumanian alliance was renewed in 1926, it was extended to cover not only the eastern frontiers of the two states but all foreign aggressions.

policies. But Lithuania's unwillingness to unite in any common undertaking to which Poland was a party, and the general fear of the other Baltic states that in such a union Poland might come to dominate, effectively prevented anything like a common alliance for security among the Baltic republics.

During these years Soviet Russia had been endeavoring to obtain security for herself by proposing nonaggression pacts to her neighbors. Down to the close of the year 1925 her efforts were unavailing, but in December of that year she concluded with Turkey a treaty in which each agreed not to attack the other and to remain neutral in the event of the other's being attacked by any third power or group of powers. Each agreed further not to participate in any alliance or agreement—political, financial, or economic—directed against the other. This was typical of the treaties of nonaggression and neutrality which the Soviet government continued to conclude in the following years. In 1926 such a treaty was concluded with Germany. Early in 1929, by signing an anticipatory protocol, Russia, Estonia, Latvia, Poland, and Rumania put the Paris pact into immediate effect among themselves and thus "outlawed" war. During 1932 and 1933 further nonaggression pacts were signed by the Soviet government, and by the close of the latter year it had such agreements not only with all of Russia's immediate borderlands, but with Germany, France, Italy, and the states of the Little Entente as well.

## THE LIMITATION OF NAVAL ARMAMENTS

Meanwhile, although little had been achieved at Geneva in the matter of armament reductions, some progress had been made in the limitation of navies by direct negotiations between the principal naval powers themselves. At the close of the World War, with certain groups in the United States demanding that their country should have a navy second to none, it appeared for a time that Great Britain, Japan, and the United States were embarked upon a race for naval supremacy. With a view to preventing such a development, the United States invited Great Britain and Japan to a conference to consider the possibility of limiting naval armaments. Since this question was found to be bound up with questions and problems concerning the Far East, the United States extended the scope of the conference to include these matters also, and invited not only Great

Britain and Japan to send delegates, but France, Italy, China, Belgium, Portugal, and the Netherlands as well.

The Washington conference, in session from November 12, 1921, to February 6, 1922, resulted in the adoption of seven treaties which were designed to put an end to naval rivalry and to solve some of the difficulties in the Far East. Following the American proposal for a ten-year "naval holiday," two treaties were signed between the five most important naval powers: Great Britain, the United States, Japan, France, and Italy. The first treaty called for the scrapping of approximately 40 per cent of the capital ships already built or being constructed by the three great naval powers. For the future definite limits were placed upon the quota and tonnage of capital ships and aircraft carriers permitted to each state, the total tonnage being fixed at a ratio of approximately 5:5:3 for Great Britain, the United States, and Japan, and 1.67 for France and Italy. No new capital ships were to be constructed for ten years, and those built after 1931 were specifically limited in their tonnage and in the maximum size of their guns. The second treaty outlawed the use of poison gas in warfare and restricted the use of submarines.[6]

At the Washington conference Great Britain accepted the principle of "parity" with the United States, but, when the latter sought to extend the 5:5:3 ratio to all types of naval craft, an agreement was prevented largely by differences of opinion regarding the size of cruisers and the abolition of submarines. Another conference met in Geneva in 1927, upon the invitation of the United States, but again it was found impossible to reconcile the British program of a great number of small cruisers and the American program of a small number of large cruisers.

The failure of the Geneva conference engendered suspicion and ill will between Great Britain and the United States to such an extent that Anglo-American relations become more strained than they had been for a generation. In 1929, however, after Herbert Hoover had become President of the United States and Ramsay MacDonald had become prime minister of Great Britain for a second time, something of a *rapprochement* was effected between the two countries. Follow-

[6] The naval treaties also provided for restrictions on fortifications in the Pacific. Great Britain, the United States, and Japan agreed to maintain the *status quo* in the defenses on a number of their insular possessions and naval bases. In some regions there were to be no fortifications whatsoever.

ing MacDonald's visit to Washington, the British government invited the United States, France, Italy, and Japan to participate in a five-power naval conference in London in January, 1930. As the Washington conference had abolished the competitive building of capital ships, so it was hoped that the London conference might abolish or allay competition in all other categories.

Although Great Britain, the United States, and Japan ultimately succeeded in reaching an agreement regarding the size of the various categories of their naval establishments, it proved impossible to conclude a five-power agreement because of differences between Italy and France. The former demanded the right to have in all categories the parity with France which had been granted her in capital ships at the Washington conference. This France steadily refused to concede, asserting that to permit Italy parity with France would be to give Italy actual superiority in the Mediterranean, since France had two seacoasts to defend. France was determined to safeguard her national security even though her stand might spell failure for the London conference. Both France and Italy declined to be bound by the general treaty which was signed on April 27, 1930.

By the London naval treaty the existing naval holiday in capital ships was extended until 1936. The total tonnage of the three principal powers in cruisers, destroyers, and submarines was fixed, the United States being granted substantial parity with Great Britain in all categories. Japan gained parity in tonnage with these two in submarines, and in other categories was permitted a ratio slightly better than the 5:5:3 agreed upon for capital ships at Washington. The Anglo-American dispute over cruisers was solved by a compromise which permitted a greater number of large cruisers to the United States and a greater number of small cruisers to Great Britain. These terms, it was believed, gave each of the three powers sufficient naval strength to make a successful invasion of its home waters by either of the others practically impossible. The London conference resulted not so much in the reduction of armaments as in their limitation. The naval tonnage of the United States, for example, was fixed at a figure which was practically identical with her total naval strength before the conference. Parity with Great Britain was granted to the United States, but as a matter of fact actual parity would entail the expenditure of more than a billion dollars by 1936 if American tonnage was to equal that of Great Britain.

### The Failure of the Geneva Disarmament Conference

Meanwhile, the League's Preparatory Commission for the Disarmament Conference had been working to pave the way for the calling of a general disarmament conference, and eventually, on February 2, 1932, the conference convened in Geneva with sixty nations, including the United States and the Soviet Union, represented. In the debates which ensued a number of differences in viewpoint at once appeared.

One problem was how to estimate effectives. The countries that employed conscription in general objected to the counting of trained reserves as effectives, while those which had volunteer armies maintained that reserves should be included in this category. Another problem was that of international supervision. France and her allies desired to have an elaborate system of international control established, but the other states maintained that the execution of any disarmament program must in general depend upon the good faith of the nations involved. The United States would not consent to any limitation of expenditures for armaments; Germany refused to approve any limitation of effectives unless trained reserves were included, and rejected the articles stating that existing treaties providing for the limitation of armaments should remain in force; Italy maintained that an agreement must be reached by all the naval powers on the proportions and levels of maximum tonnage.

France, still insistent upon her postwar thesis that security must precede disarmament, proposed that an international force, principally aircraft, should be created and placed at the disposal of the League for use in case sanctions had to be applied under Article 16 of the Covenant. This proposal found little favor among the other great powers. Germany, in turn, demanded general recognition of her "equality of right" to possess the same armaments as other countries. Soviet Russia suggested a progressive and proportional reduction of armaments with a view ultimately to their complete and rapid abolition. As none of these proposals was generally acceptable, a deadlock ensued.

In June President Hoover of the United States sought to break the deadlock. "The time has come," he declared, "when we should cut through the brush and adopt some broad and definite method of reducing the overwhelming burden of arms which now lies upon the toilers of the world." He proposed that land forces should be differentiated into "police components" designed to maintain internal order and "defense components" designed to resist attack from abroad. The latter, he suggested, should be reduced by approximately one third. President Hoover's program received strong support from Germany, Italy, and Russia, but Great Britain, Japan, and France raised so many objections that the plan failed of adoption. When the conference adjourned in July, the German delegation let it be known that it would not return to the conference until Germany's demand for equality had been granted. In December, 1932, the German claim to equality was recognized by the powers.

In the following month Adolf Hitler, one of whose cardinal points was the repudiation of the treaty of Versailles, became chancellor of Germany. Nevertheless, when the delegates resumed their labors at Geneva in February, 1933, Germany was again represented. But by the end of the month, chiefly because of disagreements between the Germans and the French, another deadlock had resulted. To many it appeared that the disarmament conference was about to collapse. Such a disaster was prevented at the moment by the decisive action of Prime Minister Ramsay MacDonald, who came to Geneva with new proposals.

According to the British plan, which was to be effective for five years, all European armies should be recruited on a uniform basis of conscription with a short-term period of service. Soviet Russia would be allowed an army of 500,000 men; France, Italy, Germany, and Poland, each 200,000; Rumania, 150,000; Spain, 120,000; Czechoslovakia and Yugoslavia, each 100,000; and the other countries from 25,000 to 60,000 each. Under this scheme the total number of men under arms in Europe would be reduced by approximately 450,000, while the existing armies of Germany, Austria, Hungary, and Bulgaria would be increased by about 177,000 men. Powers having overseas possessions were to be permitted supplemental colonial troops ranging in number from 15,000 for Belgium to 200,000 for France. Limitations were to be placed on the use of heavy guns, military and naval aircraft, and bombing, and a permanent disarmament commission was to be established.

Although Germany was at first inclined to criticize the proposals and to increase her own demands, ultimately the German delegate declared that his government accepted the British plan as a basis for the proposed disarmament convention. Later he announced that

Germany was willing to accept equality in only those weapons which the conference should decide were defensive, provided those that were defined as offensive were completely abolished at the end of the five-year period. Disagreements persisted regarding the steps to be taken to achieve disarmament, however, and in June, 1933, the conference adjourned until the following October. In the meantime, it was hoped, informal discussions between the representatives of the great powers might eliminate some of the difficulties which prevented a general agreement.

Such discussions were actively carried on during September and October. Eventually a tentative agreement was reached by Great Britain, France, Italy, and the United States, providing that for a period of four years no powers—Germany included—should increase their armaments. At the end of that period, however, Germany should be permitted to have such tanks, military airplanes, and other weapons forbidden by the treaty of Versailles as the other powers then retained. Unfortunately, the chauvinistic utterances of the Nazis had so alarmed France and the various succession states that they were unwilling to permit Nazi Germany to increase her armaments at once. The latter, on the other hand, was determined to secure immediately the right to have a limited number of such "defensive" weapons—tanks and military airplanes—as the other great powers possessed. She asserted, furthermore, that the former Allies were by the treaty of Versailles bound to reduce their armaments as they had compelled the defeated powers to do.

On October 14, two days before the disarmament conference was to reconvene, the world was startled by Germany's announcement of her withdrawal from the conference and of her intended withdrawal from the League of Nations. It had become evident, the German foreign minister declared, that the conference would not bring about general disarmament in accordance with "the contractual obligations" of the powers, and that the "satisfactory fulfillment of Germany's recognized claim to equality" was therefore impossible. Since the latter constituted the condition upon which the German government had agreed to return to the conference in December, 1932, it was now compelled to withdraw.

In view of Germany's spectacular move the other powers decided to postpone the meeting of the conference temporarily and in the meantime to resort to diplomacy in an effort to overcome the impasse.

It was generally agreed to be futile to attempt to draft a general disarmament treaty before Germany and France had come to an agreement on the basic questions. The next four months, therefore, were devoted to an exchange of views between France and Germany, in the course of which each country submitted plans, only to have them rejected by the other.

Despite the failure to reconcile the differences between the two countries, however, the conference again convened on May 29, 1934. The views expressed by the leading speakers fell generally into two categories. On the one hand, British, American, Italian, and other delegates made clear their desire to place disarmament first and to consider defensive security as resulting from it. On the other hand, the French and Russian delegates argued for security first and disarmament second. On June 11 the conference, in despair of an agreement, again adjourned, and Arthur Henderson, chairman, openly charged France with responsibility for its failure to accomplish any practical results. After more than two years of effort the disarmament conference had not succeeded in scrapping a single gun, tank, or airplane.

## The Rearmament of Germany

Early in 1935 diplomatic conversations were inaugurated between Great Britain and France with a view to a joint proposal to Germany on the matter of armaments. Eventually, on February 3, Germany was invited by these two powers to join in a freely negotiated settlement for the purpose (1) of abolishing the provisions of Part V of the treaty of Versailles limiting Germany's armaments, and (2) of establishing in their place agreements regarding armaments generally. Apparently, however, equality of armaments for Germany must be accompanied or preceded by the latter's return to membership in the League and by her willingness to sign pacts of mutual assistance with countries in central and eastern Europe. Although Germany in a formal reply to the proposals cautiously promised to submit the whole matter to an exhaustive examination, the proposals were far from acceptable to the Nazi government.

That this was the fact became abundantly clear on March 16 when Chancellor Hitler proclaimed that, despite the treaty of Versailles, Germany would at once reintroduce compulsory military service and would increase the peace size of her army to more than 500,000 men.

In justification of Germany's unilateral action, Hitler claimed that the treaty of Versailles had already been nullified by the failure of the former Allies to carry out its promise of general disarmament. Furthermore, he asserted, Soviet Russia's huge peace-time army and France's restoration of two-year military service required Germany to take measures for her own national defense. Protests against Germany's action were at once filed in Berlin by the British, French, and Italian governments. One month later the Council of the League of Nations formally condemned Germany for her unilateral repudiation of the disarmament clauses of the treaty of Versailles.

The British government apparently decided to face in a realistic manner the situation created by Germany's rearmament. Anglo-German naval conversations were initiated in London, and on June 18, 1935, it was announced that a treaty had been concluded between the two powers giving Germany the right to a navy 35 per cent as large as that of Great Britain. Germany, which already had three powerful "pocket-battleships" limited to 10,000 tons each in accordance with the treaty of Versailles, would now be allowed to add a total of nearly 200,000 tons in capital ships. The treaty recognized, also, Germany's right to have submarines, although she expressed her willingness to abolish this type of fighting ship if the other powers would do the same.

Despite Hitler's solemn promises to observe the Locarno agreements, the natural corollary of Germany's rearmament was that she should seize upon some favorable occasion to remilitarize the Rhineland and thus remove the last restriction upon the Reich's territorial sovereignty. Such an occasion presented itself during the Italo-Ethiopian conflict when the Locarno front was broken so far as the great powers were concerned. Timing his act to fall when the international situation was particularly tense because of contemplated petroleum sanctions against Italy,[7] Hitler on March 7, 1936, announced Germany's repudiation of the treaty of Versailles and the Locarno mutual-guarantee treaty. Simultaneously with his announcement, 20,000 German troops marched into the Rhineland.

So far as the treaty of Versailles was concerned, Hitler asserted that the German people could not, should not, and would not bear the injustices of that dictated treaty. As to the Locarno treaty, voluntarily suggested and signed by Germany, he declared that it had been in

[7] See page 649.

effect nullified by the Franco-Soviet treaty of mutual assistance signed in 1935.[8] Germany, therefore, no longer considered herself bound by its provisions, and accordingly "restituted full, unmitigated sovereignty of the Reich in the demilitarized zone of the Rhineland." A memorandum to this effect was dispatched to the other signatories of the Locarno treaty—that is, to Belgium, France, Great Britain, and Italy. On March 12 the signatories of the Locarno treaty—minus Germany—met and unanimously agreed that Germany's action was "a clear violation of Articles 42 and 43 of the treaty of Versailles and the Locarno pact." One week later the Council of the League of Nations, after listening to Germany's case as presented by Joachim von Ribbentrop, Hitler's special ambassador, also voted that Germany was guilty of infringing the Locarno treaty.

Although demands for economic and financial sanctions against Germany were made by France, Poland, the Little Entente, and Soviet Russia, Great Britain opposed such a step. Under the Covenant sanctions were applicable only against a state which had illegally embarked upon a war. This Germany had not done. Furthermore, in view of the fact that France had opposed effective sanctions against Italy when the latter had deliberately embarked upon a war of conquest, she was at this time in no position to make a strong case for sanctions against Germany. It was generally recognized, moreover, that morally, if not legally, Germany had much to support her attempt to regain a status of national equality with the other great powers. Despite the fact that the Locarno treaty of mutual guarantee specifically stated that the signatory powers would come to the aid of the injured party in case of just such a "flagrant" violation of the demilitarized zone, no steps were taken to force the German troops out of the Rhineland, and Germany's sovereignty over her national territory was thus restored.

## Europe's Reaction to Hitler

Meanwhile, the establishment of the Nazi dictatorship in Germany and the subsequent repudiation of the Versailles and Locarno treaties had had very definite effects on Europe's international affairs. This became evident first in the case of Italy.

In the years prior to the triumph of the Nazis in Germany the European powers had gradually come to be divided into two general

[8] See page 581.

groups—those that insisted with ever-increasing vehemence upon a revision of the peace treaties, and those beneficiaries of the peace settlement which were ardent defenders of the status it had established. Italy, an unsatiated and ambitious power, had thrown her influence on the side of the revisionists, while France was the chief defender of the *status quo*. At the opening of the year 1933 France, Great Britain, the powers of the Little Entente, and Poland constituted one group of states, with Soviet Russia inclined to lean in their direction, while Italy, Germany, Austria, Hungary, Albania, and Bulgaria constituted a rival combination in opposition to the champions of the *status quo*. The international situation appeared to be moving toward a crisis, with Hitler seeking to bring about co-operation between the two fascist dictators.

But apparently the Nazi revolution in Germany had given Mussolini pause. The latter had no desire to see a union between Germany and Austria, especially under the nationalistic Nazis. Such a union would bring a powerful Germany into direct contact with Italy and might lead to an accentuation of the German irredentist activity in southern Tirol, which had been transferred from Austria to Italy by the treaty of St. Germain. Such a large Germanic bloc lying across central Europe might destroy Italy's influence in Hungary and menace her position in the Balkans. Furthermore, the Fascist leader was apparently loath to see Europe definitely split into two antagonistic groups with Italy lined up with Germany against France and Great Britain. In order to escape this embarrassing situation, Mussolini persuaded France, Germany, and Great Britain to sign with Italy (July, 1933) the so-called "four-power pact," which was designed to dissipate the "state of disquiet" prevailing throughout the world by reinforcing the solidarity of these four great powers. In view of subsequent developments, the pact appeared to have little significance other than to reveal a shift in Mussolini's foreign policy.

In the following year a number of diplomatic steps were taken by the powers to strengthen themselves against the threats of Nazi Germany. Since Hitler had openly announced a program of German expansion to the east, it is not surprising that Soviet Russia was among those states which were active. In June, 1934, Russia and Rumania completed a triangular understanding by which the Soviet Union, Poland, and Rumania mutually guaranteed their existing frontiers and thus ended the years-old friction caused by Russia's refusal to recognize Rumania's title to Bessarabia. Three months later the Soviet Union, apparently in order to be linked with fifty-seven other states in an organization for the defense of the *status quo,* accepted membership in the League of Nations.

France, too, was active. In 1934 she proposed for eastern Europe the adoption of a pact of mutual assistance similar to the Locarno pact of 1925. In this so-called eastern Locarno agreement, the Soviet Union, the Baltic states, Poland, Germany, and Czechoslovakia were to be included. Although Russia agreed to sign such a pact, Germany declined. She was willing to sign nonaggression treaties with most of the countries near her eastern frontier, but she was very definitely opposed to signing any treaty of mutual assistance in that region. Poland also refused to be drawn into an eastern Locarno. Her statesmen felt that such a step might arouse the resentment of Germany and that it might even require her to defend Russian territory. Furthermore, in time of crisis, Poland might become the battlefield of eastern Europe. The French plan for blocking German aggression in eastern Europe therefore met with failure.

One fear which particularly disturbed the French was the possibility that Hitler, by coming to terms with Mussolini, might place himself in a position to dominate the Continent. To prevent such a catastrophe negotiations were inaugurated in 1934 to remove the postwar causes of friction between France and Italy. These were successfully carried through by Pierre Laval and resulted in the signing of a number of pacts and conventions in January, 1935. Italian ill feeling arising from France's failure to grant Italy adequate colonial compensation in Africa following the World War was largely wiped out by two colonial conventions. France agreed to cede to Italy territory adjoining the latter's Libyan colony on the south and a strategic triangle of territory on the southern edge of Italy's Eritrea, so that the latter might have direct access to the Strait of Bab-El-Mandeb connecting the Red Sea and the Gulf of Aden. In addition, France also agreed that Italy should have a share in the railway from Jibuti in French Somaliland to Addis Ababa, the capital of Ethiopia. Another convention, dealing with the rights of Italians living in Tunis, was designed to remove Italy's dissatisfaction with the status of her citizens there. So far as Germany was concerned, the two powers agreed to consult in case Austrian independence should be seriously threatened. These various agreements went far toward removing the causes of ill feeling and friction between Italy and France, and resulted in Mussolini's moving from the revisionist group into the French camp. Later developments seemed to indicate that as his reward for this shift he obtained France's benevolent tolerance of his plans for the conquest of Ethiopia.

Hitler's spectacular moves in 1935 and 1936 had further repercussions in Europe. Within two months of his announcement of Germany's rearmament came the signing of a five-year pact of mutual assistance between France and the Soviet Union, and a little later a similar pact between the Soviet Union and Czechoslovakia. Germany's remilitarization of the Rhineland in 1936, in turn, had the effect of driving Great Britain into the arms of France. The former at once agreed to assist Belgium and France in case of a possible attack by Germany. In April, 1936, the general staffs of the three countries were instructed to consult regarding the best means to make their joint operations effective. In July, in the face of Germany's spectacular progress in rearmament, Great Britain apparently sought to reach an understanding with Mussolini in order to link Italy with the powers arrayed against Germany.

Italy, also, moved to strengthen her position against possible Nazi aggression in central Europe. A two-day conference at Rome between Mussolini and Chancellor Schuschnigg of Austria and Premier Gömbös of Hungary led to the decision to form a permanent council composed of the foreign ministers of the three countries to consult periodically on problems of mutual concern. Their immediate and fundamental aim was the maintenance of the *status quo* in central Europe by safeguarding the independence of Austria. Hitler's rise, furthermore, seems to have led Mussolini to advise the introduction of universal military conscription in Austria, for this step was taken by Chancellor Schuschnigg a few days later.

## DIPLOMATIC MANEUVERS, 1936–1937

After 1935 the international situation in Europe was rendered more complex and complicated by Italy's conquest of Ethiopia and by the Spanish civil war.[9] The former tended to drive a wedge between Italy on the one hand and Great Britain and France on the other, and Hitler was quick to seize upon this estrangement to advance his own plan for co-operation between the two fascist states. The Spanish civil war,

[9] For the former, see pages 642–646; for the latter, see pages 742–745.

which in some respects seemed to develop into a conflict between fascist and communist ideologies, further facilitated a *rapprochement* between Italy and Germany.

In 1936 Germany took steps to emerge from the state of isolation in which she had found herself in the preceding year. To placate Italy as well as to pave the way for her own economic *Drang nach Osten,* Germany on July 11, 1936, recognized the full sovereignty of Austria and agreed that the latter's political structure was an internal affair with which she would neither directly nor indirectly interfere. Three months later (October 25) Italy and Germany reached an accord which provided for (1) the collaboration of the two states in all matters affecting their "parallel interests," (2) the defense of European civilization against communism, (3) economic cooperation in the Danubian region, and (4) the maintenance of Spain's territorial and colonial integrity. Germany recognized Italy's Ethiopian empire and in return was promised economic concessions in that part of Africa. In December an Italo-German trade agreement implemented the October accord by extending to Italian colonies the economic privileges which Germany already enjoyed in Italy and by dividing the river and rail traffic of the Danubian states in such a way as to benefit Hamburg and Trieste.

Fortified by these understandings with Italy, Germany during 1936–1937 bent every effort to advance her economic penetration in central and eastern Europe. During the summer of 1936 Schacht, her minister of economics, visited the various Balkan capitals for the purpose of concluding new commercial treaties. Later in the year, in order to strengthen her position in relation to Soviet Russia, Germany concluded with Japan an agreement providing for common action against communist propaganda. According to reports, each pledged benevolent neutrality in case of war and agreed upon close technical collaboration between the military and industrial establishments of the two countries.

Meanwhile, Italy was taking steps to strengthen her position. In November, 1936, she signed a protocol with Austria and Hungary in which these powers formally recognized her annexation of Ethiopia. Four months later (March 26, 1937) she reached a number of agreements with Yugoslavia. The two powers (1) promised to respect each other's boundaries and to remain neutral in case one of them should be attacked by a third power; (2) agreed, in case of international complications, to confer on measures to protect their common interests; (3) recognized and guaranteed the independence of Albania, which had been something of an apple of discord between them; and (4) conceded cultural rights to each other's minorities within their own frontiers. It is possible that in concluding these agreements Italy desired to protect herself against an attack from the rear in case of a Mediterranean clash and to secure the friendly co-operation of Yugoslavia if Germany attempted to absorb Austria.

But the other states of Europe were not unmindful of their own security. In June, 1936, the powers of the Little Entente renewed their decision to oppose the union of Austria and Germany, and arranged to have their military staffs meet to discuss co-ordinated military action in central Europe. To make it easier for Soviet Russia to co-operate in blocking Germany if the latter should forcibly attempt to carry through her *Drang nach Osten,* Rumania in the following month agreed to construct—with the aid of a loan from Czechoslovakia—a military railway to facilitate the transport of Russian troops across Rumania to Czechoslovakia. In 1936, too, an exchange of visits by the Polish and French chiefs-of-staff bore witness to the fact that the Franco-Polish alliance was far from dead, even though Poland and Germany had in January, 1934, signed a ten-year nonaggression pact.

Belgium, disturbed by Germany's rearmament and by the failure of collective action to preserve peace, announced (October, 1936) her determination to resume a policy of neutrality in the near future and her decision meanwhile to increase her military establishment in order to discourage any attempt to violate Belgian territory. Although King Leopold's announcement may eventually bring the end of the Franco-Belgian alliance of 1920, the immediate effect of the decision to increase the Belgian armaments was to strengthen France and Great Britain against German aggression in the west.

Great Britain's contribution to the solution of the problem of security against the plots of aggressive powers was a program calling for a tremendous expansion of her naval and air forces. The British budget for 1936–1937 included the largest defense appropriation in peace-time history—nearly £200,000,000. And in February, 1937, the chancellor of the exchequer announced that Britain's rearmament program would necessitate the expenditure of £1,500,000,000 in the ensuing five years. It was hoped that a powerful Britain might give the fascist dictators pause. Not unconnected with these British preparations may have been the signing (January 2, 1937) of an Italo-British Mediterranean agreement in which the two powers recognized "that the freedom of entry into, exit from and transit through, the Mediterranean is a vital interest both to the different parts of the British Empire and to Italy, and that these interests are in no way inconsistent with each other," and disclaimed "any desire to modify, or to see modified, the *status quo* as regards national sovereignty of territory in the Mediterranean area."

## THE NEW ARMAMENTS RACE

Meanwhile, Germany had not been the only great power to object to permanent inferiority in the matter of national armaments. The Washington and London naval treaties, which were scheduled to expire at the end of 1936, provided for the holding of another conference for the limitation and reduction of naval armaments in 1935. In preliminary negotiations carried on in London between representatives of the United States, Great Britain, and Japan in preparation for a new conference, Japan proposed that she should have the right to naval equality with Great Britain and the United States. But the United States was unwilling to sign a new naval treaty granting parity to Japan, and in this stand was supported by Great Britain. These two powers argued that the 5:5:3 ratio gave Japan perfect equality for defense, that what should be sought was not equality in the size of navies but equality in security. They claimed that Japan's demand for parity was in reality a demand for effective superiority. This the Japanese denied, asserting that technical advances in the years since the Washington conference had increased the range of fleets and left Japan feeling no longer secure with her proportion of three to the five each for the other two great naval powers. Back of the Japanese proposal many saw, however, the desire to be prepared for a more aggressive policy on the Asiatic mainland as well as the desire to be able to enforce her new "Monroe Doctrine for the Far East." With a deadlock very soon reached on the matter of naval parity, the preliminary negotiations were finally adjourned, and on December 29, 1934, Japan notified the United States that the Washington treaty of 1922 would terminate on December 31, 1936. Although there seemed to be little likelihood of success, a new naval conference convened at London on December 9, 1935, with representatives of the five powers in attendance. The early discussions concerned themselves with Japan's proposal that the new treaty should be based upon the fundamental idea of setting up a common limit of naval armaments which the signatory powers should not be allowed to exceed. This, of course, was merely another way of saying parity among the great powers. On January 8, 1936, the Japanese declined to engage in further discussion until Japan's demand for parity had been granted. One week later, after the other four powers had rejected their demand, the Japanese announced that they could no longer "usefully continue" in attendance, and withdrew from the conference. Despite Japan's withdrawal, the other four powers continued the conference and gradually reached agreements on a number of points. Late in February, however, the Italian delegation announced that Italy would not be bound by the treaty. Consequently, the naval treaty which was drafted was in the end signed on March 25, 1936, by only three powers—France, Great Britain, and the United States. In July, 1937, however, Germany and the Soviet Union also signed treaties with Great Britain adhering to the new naval treaty.

This three-power naval treaty provided for a quantitative limitation for naval armaments only in respect to heavy cruisers of between 8000 and 17,500 tons. In this category a five-year building holiday was accepted. A qualitative limitation in regard to size of ships and caliber of guns was agreed upon, however, in the categories other than that just mentioned. In general the effect of the treaty was to limit the tonnage and gun caliber of most types of ships but to permit unrestricted construction of naval armaments within these specifications. But with the Washington and London naval treaties expiring on December 31, 1936, and the capital-ship holiday ending on that date, the way for a new era of naval construction was obviously opened.

Everywhere in the world the year 1937 saw tremendously increased military and naval budgets.[10] Everywhere were being created more powerful navies and larger peace-time armies. Everywhere were being made efforts to secure equality if not superiority in air forces. Armies numbering millions were being supported by the powers.[11] Military airplanes by the thousands were being prepared to shower destruction upon possible enemy countries. As in the hectic prewar

---

[10] In 1934 the world expenditure for military purposes was $5,000,000,000; in 1936 it was nearly $11,000,000,000.

[11] In 1937 a total of 6,000,000 men were in Europe's peace-time armed forces.

days,[12] the vicious circle of national fear and resultant increased armaments was once more present to undermine the peace of the world. Despite the lesson of the World War, the powers apparently still clung to the idea that great armaments can secure peace. Apparently they were determined to ignore the fact that great armaments engender international fear and suspicion, that they may actually constitute one of the fundamental causes of war.

[12] For the situation in 1913–1914, see pages 363–365.

# PART FIVE

# NATIONAL PROBLEMS AND EXPERIMENTS OF THE POSTWAR PERIOD

Preceding chapters have shown how the World War released or engendered certain revolutionary forces which in 1917 and 1918 overturned the existing political regimes in one European country after another and brought into existence a number of new states. But the World War also brought in its train tremendously heavy burdens and seemingly insuperable difficulties which in the postwar period caused the collapse of several national governments. The creation of new states and the establishment of new regimes in some of the older states in turn opened the way for the inauguration of political and economic experiments of a sweeping nature. The chapters in Part Five discuss somewhat fully the Communist, Fascist, and Nazi regimes in Russia, Italy, and Germany as well as in a number of the lesser states. But attention is also given to the serious problems which confronted those countries which continued to maintain liberal traditions and to the ways in which they met their difficulties without abandoning their long-cherished ideals. In other words, Part Five describes how the different countries of Europe reacted to the serious problems arising from the World War.

## CHAPTER XIX

## SOVIET RUSSIA

THE national reconstruction which occurred in so many countries as a result of the World War saw the inauguration of a number of new experiments in the political and economic life of Europe. The first of the great powers to embark upon a new course was Russia, where, with the establishment of the Soviet regime, there developed a "dictatorship of the proletariat." In the succeeding years private enterprise largely disappeared from the economic life of Russia, to be succeeded by a system which may be described as state capitalism or state socialism. It was in order that they might be free to inaugurate undisturbed their sweeping political, economic, and social reforms that the Bolsheviks had signed the humiliating treaty of Brest-Litovsk in March, 1918.

### FAILURE TO DISLODGE THE BOLSHEVIKS

The Bolshevik hope of being left in peace to introduce their new regime in Russia was soon blasted, for both within and without the country numerous movements were at once begun for the purpose of driving the Bolsheviks from power. Many Russians believed that Bolshevism was but a passing phase in the Russian upheaval and hoped, by counterrevolutionary measures supported by the Allies, to be able to overthrow the Bolshevik regime. The Allies were at first not averse to intervention. Great stores of military supplies had been landed at Murmansk, Archangel, and Vladivostok for use against the Central Powers. Unless preventive measures were at once taken, it seemed likely in 1918 that these might be seized by the Germans and turned against the Allies themselves. Furthermore, France particularly was eager for the downfall of the political regime which had repudiated both the highly valued Franco-Russian alliance and the gilt-edged government bonds in which billions of francs had been invested by the French people.

After Russia's signing of the treaty of Brest-Litovsk, therefore, Allied expeditionary forces were dispatched to Murmansk, Archangel, and Vladivostok. In November, 1918, after the collapse of Turkey, French forces seized Odessa, and British forces occupied the various Transcaucasian republics. Each of the regions seized by the Allied armies served as a rallying ground for anti-Bolshevik Russians who were plotting to overthrow the Soviet government. With "White" armies planning to advance from the east, from the south, and from the west, it was hoped in anti-Bolshevik circles that the year 1919 would see the final downfall of the Soviet government.

Menaced by innumerable revolutionary plots from within and threatened by Allied armies of intervention from abroad, the Bolshevik leaders depended for defense chiefly upon two agencies—the "Cheka" and the "Red Army." The Cheka was organized immediately after the November revolution to maintain order in the capital, but it was soon transformed into an agency of terror which was used to force the population into passivity or active support. In order to purge Russia of all elements dangerous to the revolution, the Cheka was empowered to arrest, try, and shoot all who were considered dangerous. In August, 1918, an organized Red Terror was begun which in the following years surpassed the bloody Reign of Terror in France. Thousands of tsarist sympathizers and bourgeois were ruthlessly put to death. But while Red Terror might suppress internal opposition, it could not unaided defeat the advancing White armies, subsidized and equipped by foreign powers. For a short time the Soviet government had almost no organized forces at its command. A volunteer Red Army was soon organized, however, by Trotsky, commissar for war, and it was developed during 1918 into a well-equipped, well-trained force of more than 100,000 men, commanded for the most part by former tsarist officers whose loyalty to Russia led them to fight against what they looked upon as foreign invasion.

In 1919 the simultaneous advance of the White armies began. Some of the forces actually got within sight of Leningrad (the name given to Petrograd by the Soviet government on April 22, 1920), only to be defeated and driven back. Perhaps the greatest single cause of the miserable failure of the White armies was the fact that the Russian people, especially the peasants, came to view them as the agents of reaction who were seeking to restore lands to the landlords and the old system of privileges to the aristocracy. The Russian peasants were not anxious to be "liberated" by armies of the landlords. The advance of the White armies had been accompanied, too, by looting, disorder,

A PRODUCT OF THE FIRST FIVE-YEAR PLAN

The dedication of the dam at Dnepropetrovsk in 1932.

and a White Terror almost as ruthless as that of the Reds; and, as between Bolshevism and extreme military reaction, the Russian masses preferred the former temporarily as the less of two evils. The conduct of the counterrevolutionary armies and the bloody repressive measures of the White leaders also alienated popular sympathy in the Allied countries. By the close of 1919 all Allied forces had been withdrawn from European Russia, though the Japanese remained for a time in Vladivostok.

But the Soviet government was not yet freed from the need for military campaigns. The White forces of the south were actively supported by the French government, and during the early months of 1920 they once more moved northward in the Ukraine. At the same time the Poles, recalling the medieval grandeur of their state and desiring to push their Russian frontier as far east as possible, began an invasion of Russia. In May they succeeded in occupying the city of Kiev. Again the Russians rallied to support the Soviet government, and the Poles were hurled back almost to Warsaw. Only the timely aid of French men and munitions prevented a debacle. In October a preliminary treaty brought peace between the two countries and a settlement of the boundary question. By this time the Soviet government had concluded similar treaties with Estonia, Lithuania, Latvia, and Finland, and was finally free to give its attention once more to the White armies in the south. By the close of the year 1920 European Russia was cleared of active counterrevolutionary armies.

## The Establishment of the Union of Soviet Socialist Republics

Meanwhile, the Bolsheviks had profoundly altered the political life of Russia. In the summer of 1918 a new constitution, adopted by the fifth All-Russian Congress of Soviets, established the Russian Soviet Federated Socialist Republic (R.S.F.S.R.). Russia became a federal state in which all power belonged to the workers "united in urban and rural Soviets." The new republic was declared to be "a free socialist society of the working people of Russia."

For a time, after the November revolution of 1917, it appeared that Russia might be reduced in size to a territory little larger than that ruled by Ivan the Terrible in the sixteenth century. By the treaty of Brest-Litovsk she had been compelled to renounce her sovereignty over a great strip of territory in the west—Finland, Estonia, Latvia,

Lithuania, Poland—and over the whole of the Ukraine in the south. In the Transcaucasus her rule had been repudiated by Azerbaijan, Georgia, and Armenia, which had established themselves as independent states. In September, 1918, all Siberia had been organized under an anti-Bolshevik directorate at Omsk.

Nevertheless, with the exception of Poland and the new Baltic republics which the Soviet government definitely recognized as independent in 1920, all of these apparently lost territories were regained. The reintegration of the Ukraine and the Transcaucasus was achieved by bringing into existence in those states governments organized on the soviet model, which, while nominally independent, entered into close relations with the R.S.F.S.R. In Siberia the Red armies succeeded in capturing Omsk, Tomsk, and Irkutsk, and all the territory west of Lake Baikal was incorporated into the R.S.F.S.R. The region to the east, however, remained independent and in 1920 was established as the Far Eastern Republic. When two years later a constituent assembly of the Far Eastern Republic declared its absorption into the R.S.F.S.R., Russia's control once more extended to the Pacific.

During the years of civil war and reintegration the constitution of the R.S.F.S.R. had been modified to meet the expanding territory and new needs. In December, 1922, conditions were deemed propitious for taking a further step. The tenth All-Russian Congress of Soviets in the R.S.F.S.R. accordingly declared in favor of a Union of Soviet Socialist Republics and appointed a delegation to collaborate with delegations from the other members of the proposed federation in the drafting of the terms of union. Shortly thereafter a declaration of the Union of Soviet Socialist Republics (U.S.S.R.) and a treaty of union were signed in Moscow, the latter being in reality the federal constitution of the union which it established. During the following months the treaty was ratified by the constituent states and became effective on July 6, 1923.

The U.S.S.R. became a federation of republics which varied in size and population from the R.S.F.S.R. with its more than 100,000,000 inhabitants to the smallest with less than one million. Its political machinery consisted principally of a Union Congress of Soviets, a Union Central Executive Committee, and a Union Council of Commissars. The Union Congress consisted of some 1500 members elected indirectly as shown in the accompanying diagram, and met for about a week once in two years to decide on general policies. It also appointed the members of the Union Central Executive Committee.

The latter was a bicameral body composed of a Soviet of the Union representing the republics in proportion to population and a Soviet of Nationalities representing the ethnic units of the union on the basis of approximate equality. The Soviet of Nationalities was created to reflect the needs and consciousness of the innumerable ethnic units within the union, and it was so constructed that it might easily be expanded to include other and different ethnic groups which might later be sovietized. The two chambers co-operated in the drafting of legislation and administrative ordinances and in the exercise of political control in the union; and they had a joint presidium of some twenty members, which, between sessions of the Union Congress or Central Executive Committee, acted as the supreme authority.

The Union Council of Commissars, appointed by and responsible to the Union Central Executive Committee, consisted of a president, a vice-president, the chairman of the Supreme Economic Council, and the commissars for foreign affairs, war and marine, foreign trade, ways and communications, posts and telegraphs, workers' and peasants' inspection, labor, food, and finance. The first five commissars had sole jurisdiction throughout the union; the others had to do with matters in which the union and the constituent republics had concurrent jurisdiction. Since, however, the administrative ordinances of the union usually prevailed, the union had practically a monopoly of political power except as to local government. The union government had the right to abrogate any decisions of the congresses of soviets, central executive committees, and councils of people's commissars in the constituent republics which infringed the treaty of union. The federal character of the union, therefore, was extremely limited, one Russian scholar asserting that the constituent republics retained merely the right to legislate on social insurance, public health, education, minor courts, and agriculture except for land distribution.

The political machinery of the R.S.F.S.R. was typical of that of the various constituent republics. The right to participate in the government was given to citizens of both sexes who were eighteen years of age, provided they were productive workers, the housekeepers of productive workers, or soldiers or sailors.[1] Local government was en-

---

[1] Numerous classes were deprived of the right to vote or be voted for: (1) persons who employed hired labor for their own profit; (2) persons who had an income from

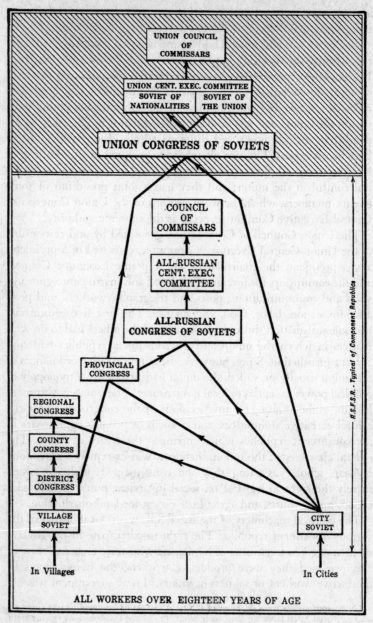

POLITICAL STRUCTURE OF THE U.S.S.R. UNTIL 1936

trusted to rural and urban soviets. In villages the peasants, together with the home workers and local teachers and doctors, met and elected the deputies of the local soviet. In cities deputies were elected to the urban soviet from the factories and shops according to the different types of industry. Representation was in general by vocation, people of different employments voting separately, the ironworkers in one group, the miners in another, the soldiers in another, and so on. Housewives and independent handicraftsmen met ordinarily by districts. Until 1936 voting in these local elections was by show of hands rather than by secret written ballot. All representation above the village and city soviets was indirect, as shown in the accompanying diagram.

Supreme power in the R.S.F.S.R. resided theoretically in the All-Russian Congress of Soviets, composed of representatives chosen directly by the urban soviets in the ratio of one for every 25,000 voters, and by the provincial congresses in the ratio of one for every 125,000 inhabitants. A discrepancy in regard to representation was made in favor of the urban centers, where Communism had its greatest strength. The All-Russian Congress was originally supposed to meet twice yearly, but after 1921 it held only annual sessions. Its principal function was to elect the All-Russian Central Executive Committee, which was in theory responsible to it. This Central Executive Committee was "the supreme legislative, executive and controlling organ of the R.S.F.S.R." It convoked the All-Russian Congress and appointed the Council of People's Commissars, which was "entrusted with the general management of the affairs of the R.S.F.S.R." The Council of Commissars was a small group of about seventeen members which resembled the ministry in a parliamentary state. It had authority to issue decrees and to take the necessary measures to secure prompt and orderly administration, but its action was subject to annulment or approval by the Central Executive Committee.

The Soviet system of government as found in the separate republics and in the union had three distinguishing characteristics. In the first place, the Soviet state was controlled by only one class—the proletariat. During what was expected to be merely a transitional stage from capitalism to pure communism the government of the Soviet Union

some other source than their own labor; (3) private merchants, trade and commercial brokers; (4) monks and clergy of all denominations; (5) employees and agents of the former tsarist police, gendarmerie, or secret service; (6) members of the former reigning family; (7) criminals, lunatics, and those under guardianship

was a dictatorship of the proletariat. That is to say, only the industrial workers and poor peasants had political power. The ultimate goal, of course, was the abolition of all classes and the destruction of the causes of class struggle. A second characteristic of the soviet system was the extensive use of indirect representation and the great distance which separated the voters from the supreme seat of authority. The peasants, who constituted perhaps 80 per cent of the people, were six steps removed from the Union Council of Commissars, and the urban proletariat were four. The third characteristic of the soviet system was the complete lack of separation of powers. The same set of agencies was used to perform all the functions of government—legislative, executive, administrative, and even, at times, judicial. The judiciary in the Soviet Union was "not an independent organ of the government, but an administrative department charged with the defense of the social order established by the proletarian revolution."

## The Constitution of 1936

In February, 1935, the Union Congress of Soviets voted that the constitution of the union should be amended to give more direct popular control of the political machinery. The Union Central Executive Committee, accordingly, appointed a constitutional commission, which, instead of merely preparing amendments to the existing constitution, drafted a complete new document, which was ultimately adopted with amendments by the Union Congress on December 5, 1936.

The new constitution changed the political machinery slightly. The Union Congress of Soviets was abolished, and supreme power was lodged in the Supreme Council of the U.S.S.R., a bicameral legislature which is practically the former Union Central Executive Committee under a new name. A similar change was proposed for each of the constituent republics also. Much more significant were the modifications made in regard to franchise, method of voting, and system of representation.

In the new constitution every citizen at least eighteen years of age was given "the right to elect and be elected irrespective of his race or nationality, his religion, educational qualifications, residential qualifications, his social origins, property status and past activity." Voting at elections was no longer to be by show of hands but by secret ballot. Moreover, the old system of indirect representation was completely

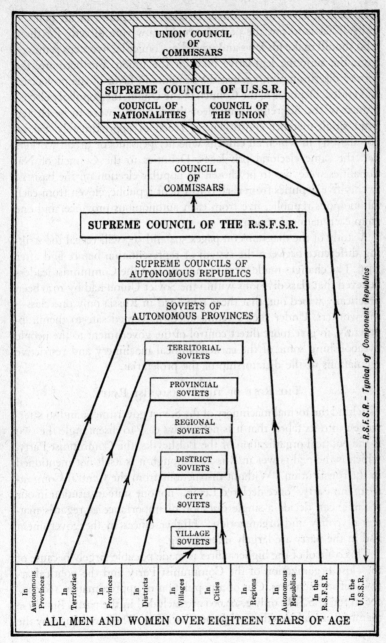

UNION COUNCIL
OF
COMMISSARS

SUPREME COUNCIL OF U.S.S.R.

COUNCIL OF
NATIONALITIES

COUNCIL OF
THE UNION

COUNCIL
OF
COMMISSARS

SUPREME COUNCIL OF THE R.S.F.S.R.

SUPREME COUNCILS OF
AUTONOMOUS REPUBLICS

SOVIETS OF
AUTONOMOUS PROVINCES

TERRITORIAL
SOVIETS

PROVINCIAL
SOVIETS

REGIONAL
SOVIETS

DISTRICT
SOVIETS

CITY
SOVIETS

VILLAGE
SOVIETS

R.S.F.S.R. – *Typical of Component Republics*

In
Autonomous
Provinces

In
Territories

In
Provinces

In
Districts

In
Villages

In
Cities

In
Regions

In
Autonomous
Republics

In the
R.S.F.S.R.

In the
U.S.S.R.

ALL MEN AND WOMEN OVER EIGHTEEN YEARS OF AGE

POLITICAL STRUCTURE OF THE U.S.S.R. AFTER 1936

abolished in favor of the direct election of deputies in all political units. That is to say, the peasant would now vote directly for those who should make his laws and would no longer be five steps removed from the supreme legislative body of the union. Furthermore, the former discrimination against the peasants in favor of the proletariat was ended. Deputies to the Council of the Union, the popularly elected branch of the Supreme Council of the U.S.S.R., were to be elected from single-member constituencies (each of approximately 300,000 population) in which all citizens whether peasants or urban workers had the same electoral privileges. Deputies to the Council of Nationalities were also to be chosen by popular election on the basis of twenty-five deputies from each constituent republic, eleven from each autonomous republic, five from each autonomous province, and one from each national region.

A study of the diagrams on pages 594 and 597 will reveal the striking difference between the system of representation before and after 1936. The changes made seem to indicate that the Communist leaders believed that class divisions within the Soviet Union had by 1936 been practically wiped out, that there remained in Russia only one class— the workers. Under such circumstances it seemed safe to them, apparently, to give more direct control of the government to the people by abolishing some of the earlier political machinery and restrictive regulations of the dictatorship of the proletariat.

## The Role of the Communist Party

Behind the formal machinery of the Soviet government and so interwoven into its fabric that it is not always easy to disentangle the two is the political organization of the Bolsheviks, the Communist Party, which is the real power in Russia, although it is itself not mentioned in the constitution. "Without instructions from the Central Committee of our party," once declared Lenin, "not one state institution in our republic can decide a single question of importance as regards matters of policy and organization." Higher offices in the government and in the party are largely interlocking.

This control of the higher offices is made possible largely because of the close organization of the Communist Party and the political activity of its members. Out of a population of approximately 160,000,-000 in the U.S.S.R., only 2,500,000 are included in the party. But these members are subjected to a rigorous discipline. They are bound by the decisions of the party and may be expelled from the organization for failure to accept them. They are expected to be active in the trade unions and other organizations. In every soviet their aim must be to organize the Communist members into efficient, disciplined groups for the purpose of winning control by the election of Communist members to the higher positions. Candidates for membership are required to pass through a probationary period before admission. The Communist Party, therefore, is "a carefully selected body of active workers with a definite goal, who are willing to make great sacrifices for its success and who are bound together by a centralized discipline." The party, too, has various youth organizations. For the purpose of perpetuating the enthusiasm and sacrificial quality of the older Communists who suffered exile or imprisonment for their principles, three junior Communist societies were created. The Octobrists (eight to ten years of age), the Pioneers (ten to sixteen), and the Communist Youth (sixteen to twenty-three) had in 1937 an enrollment of over 11,000,000 members, drawn from both sexes.

Aside from the Communist Party no other parties are permitted. All opposition is suppressed. Freedom of speech and of the press has been abolished. Even "movies" are subject to government censorship. Although the Cheka was formally abolished in 1922, a state political department was created to take its place. The new organization of espionage was usually referred to by its initials as the "Ogpu," and according to some the only difference between it and the Cheka was the change of letters. In 1934 the Ogpu, in turn, was abolished, and its functions were entrusted to a commissariat of internal affairs which was supposed to be organized along civil instead of semimilitary lines. Opposition continued to be crushed from time to time, however, by arbitrary imprisonment, exile to Siberia, or death.

## EARLY ECONOMIC EXPERIMENTS

Far more revolutionary than the changes introduced into the political system were those made in the economic life of Russia by the Bolsheviks during the first three years of their regime. The fundamental concept of their economic thought—prevention of the exploitation of the workers by the capitalists and landlords—demanded the nationalization of all land, forests, and minerals, together with all means of production, transportation, trade, banking, and insurance. These would then belong to the state, and under the soviet system the workers constituted the state. All profits which formerly went to landlords and capitalists would accrue to the state—in other words, to the workers. The surplus products of both peasants and proletariat would be turned over to state agencies from which each would in return secure those commodities which he needed; that is to say, money and wages would be abolished, and the state would take all output and in turn reward each according to his needs. In greatly simplified form, this was the economic system envisaged by the Bolshevik leaders.

It had been the original intention of the Bolsheviks to nationalize only large industrial establishments at first, and then only after they had been concentrated in trusts. But this plan for gradual and systematic nationalization broke down almost immediately. Instead, there began a haphazard and punitive nationalization of all sorts of industries. The effect of this procedure upon Russia's economic life was disastrous. The workers were prepared neither by education nor by training to take over the responsibilities of management. The efficient conduct of the factories, the procuring of regular supplies of raw materials, and the distribution of the finished products were beyond their ability. There was little effort at co-ordination; each factory was run by its own committee independently of all others. Industrial chaos naturally ensued.

Because of the collapse of industry, an attempt was made in June, 1918, to escape further haphazard nationalization and to develop a system of industrial administration under centralized control. Practically all industry was nationalized. Furthermore, all agencies of domestic and foreign trade, the merchant marine, and the banks were nationalized and their total assets confiscated. To control and co-ordinate the industrial life of the country the Supreme Economic Council was established. It was to see that all factories were supplied with necessary raw materials, fuel, and machinery, as well as the money and food needed for their workers. As might have been expected under the circumstances, the Supreme Economic Council proved altogether unable to accomplish so gigantic a task. Industrial production fell off alarmingly. Moreover, costs of production everywhere rose because of increased demands of the workers, scarcity of raw materials, and uneconomical management.

Meanwhile, the government had become involved in a struggle with the peasants. In accordance with the Bolshevik economic plan, as briefly outlined above, the Soviet government in May, 1918, established a food dictatorship and ordered every peasant to turn over to the state all grain above a certain minimum needed for seed and for the consumption of his family. This at once encountered the opposition of the peasants, who either failed to understand or refused to adopt the role which had been assigned to them in the Bolshevik economic scheme. If in return for the grain which they surrendered to the state they could have received an equivalent value in the manufactured goods which they needed for their farms and their homes, they might have acquiesced. But this was impossible, both because of the cutting off of the importation of manufactured goods from abroad and because of the demoralization of Russian industries at home. The peasants, therefore, refused to surrender their grain. When the government seized grain by force, the peasants were further antagonized and thereupon resorted to passive resistance. They raised only enough grain for themselves. The harvest in 1921 amounted to only 42 per cent of the average harvest in the four years preceding the war, and a severe famine resulted. Naturally, in the circumstances, the government's system of rationing the urban workers broke down.

The first large-scale communist experiment in history was headed for disaster. The industrial workers had failed to produce the manufactured goods needed by the peasants. The peasants, failing to obtain tangible goods in exchange for their grain, had curtailed their planting. This had contributed to produce a shortage of grain, and the government was now unable to provide adequate food supplies for the industrial proletariat. And unless the urban workers were supplied with food, they would certainly turn against the government, for hunger is ever a powerful provocative of revolution. Pure communism was doomed.

## THE NEW ECONOMIC POLICY

In the spring of 1921 the Bolsheviks thus faced the possibility of losing their political power as a consequence of having antagonized the great body of peasants. They had made practically no headway in their efforts to win this class to their economic scheme, and so were forced to conclude that it was "easier to change their policy than to change the peasants." They decided that, while retaining complete control of the administration of the government, the means of transport, large-scale industry, and foreign trade, they would make a number of minor concessions in other phases of economic life. They began their economic retreat by inaugurating a "New Economic Policy" (Nep).

Perhaps the most important feature of this Nep was the abandonment of the system of requisitioning grain from the peasants and the substitution of a fixed tax. Whatever a peasant produced over and above the amount of his tax was his to retain or to dispose of freely in the open market. The incentive which had been destroyed by the communistic scheme was thus restored, and there at once followed a gradual increase in the area under cultivation. Existing conditions of land ownership were stabilized. Although the Soviet government continued to insist that the state was the sole owner of the land and that the peasants were merely tenants, the right of usage and the right to dispose of products became so unrestricted that for all practical purposes the land belonged to the peasants. In 1925 the Nep was extended to permit the renting of land for limited periods of time and the employment of a certain number of wage laborers. Some of the richer, more enterprising peasants (the *kulaks*) at once benefited by renting land to increase their holdings and by farming intensively with hired labor. As the years passed, therefore, just as before the revolution some peasants added to their wealth, while others became impoverished and sought employment once more as hired agricultural laborers.

In industry the Nep brought the denationalization of establishments employing fewer than twenty workers. With the exception of small factories and shops, however, the state still reserved to itself the monopoly of industrial production, though it introduced the principle of sweeping decentralization. Industries were organized into large independent units or "trusts," each with its board of managers acting as trustee of the state. These trusts were given freedom to dispose of their products and to obtain their raw materials and fuel in the open market, subject only to prices fixed by the state and to the obligation of preferred service to the state. In order to overcome the lack of liquid capital, the Soviet government even granted foreign capitalists concessions for mining, manufacturing, transportation, trade, and agricultural activity.

In the realm of commerce, foreign trade remained fundamentally a state monopoly, carried on through a number of organizations to which the government gave the right to conduct export and import operations within prescribed limits under its own control. Domestic trade was opened to private capital but was subject to taxation and, as it revived, to more and more state regulation. Private trade developed so rapidly that the government, beginning in 1924, began to exert great pressure against it in favor of state and co-operative agencies, with the result that the Nep-men were to a large extent forced out of business.

The re-establishment of banking and credit operations began with the opening of a state bank in November, 1921. This was followed after 1924 by the opening of other banks—municipal, agricultural, co-operative, savings—throughout the union. In 1921 insurance of private property was instituted as a state monopoly, and three years later life insurance was restored. A new currency was introduced (the *chervonets*), a gold reserve was accumulated, and in 1924 the new currency was stabilized on a gold basis. Money wages were once more paid, and the system of governmental rationing of the cities was abandoned. A capitalistic system of taxation was inaugurated and eventually a balanced national budget obtained.

To summarize, then, under the Nep the state retained control of production in the large and middle-sized industrial plants and completely monopolized foreign trade, but restored agriculture, small industrial establishments, and domestic trade to private enterprise, subject to some degree of state control. Russia's economic life, as a consequence, came to present a strange picture of intermingled state socialism, state capitalism, and private capitalism. Nevertheless, under it that economic life came to be almost fully restored; some branches indeed even rose above prewar levels of production.

## THE RISE OF JOSEPH STALIN

Meanwhile, a bitter conflict had been going on within the ranks of the Communist Party. So long as Lenin was able to take an active part in the direction of Russian affairs, this conflict had been held in abeyance, for his prestige and influence were of such magnitude that his policies found ready acceptance among his followers. But after illness had removed him from active participation in Russian affairs early in 1922, and especially after his death in January, 1924, differences between the Communist leaders became pronounced and constituted the basis of a struggle to determine who should assume Lenin's position as head of the Communist Party.

Prominent among those who became involved in the struggle over policies and power were: Trotsky, the first commissar for foreign affairs and later organizer of the "Red" army, a brilliant revolutionary leader, orator, and writer, the one looked upon by most foreigners as the logical successor of Lenin; Zinoviev, the organizer and head of the Communist or Third International, enthusiastic in his plans to carry out the international propaganda of Bolshevik ideas in order to achieve the world proletarian revolution; Dzerzhinsky, a descendant of Polish-Lithuanian nobility, the organizer and head of the Cheka, skilled agitator and organizer of strikes who had twice suffered exile to Siberia under the tsarist regime; Stalin, the son of a Georgian shoemaker, a stalwart of the Bolshevik "Old Guard" who had frequently suffered imprisonment and exile for his beliefs, former editor of the Bolshevik newspaper *Pravda,* characterized by Lenin as "too cruel" and "too brutal" and as having concentrated too much power in his hands as general secretary of the Communist Party; Rykov, who as a young man had early come under Lenin's influence and had repeatedly suffered imprisonment and exile in his service, Lenin's private secretary, at one time head of the Supreme Economic Council, the successor of Lenin as president of the Council of People's Commissars; Kamenev, a former law student under President Millerand in France, vice-president of the Union Council of People's Commissars and chairman of the Council for Labor and Defense, suspected by Lenin of not being 100-per-cent Bolshevik; Bukharin, an ardent supporter of Lenin, characterized as "the evangelist of Bolshevism," who from the words of his master had created "the gospel of Communism," yet considered by Lenin as having "stuffed his head too full of books." Within this small group there developed a powerful triumvirate composed of Stalin, Zinoviev, and Kamenev, the political genius of the group being Stalin. From this inner circle Trotsky was excluded, for he had joined the party only in 1917 and was looked upon as a newcomer by the "Old Guard," who consistently sought to discredit him.

Lenin's death at once precipitated a conflict within the party between a group led by the triumvirate and another led by Trotsky. The Stalin group believed that the capitalist regime outside Russia had become stabilized and that it was not likely to be overturned in the immediate future; the Trotsky opposition still clung to the hope of a world revolution "in our time." The former desired to cater to the interests of the peasants on the ground that their support was necessary for the success of the great Bolshevik economic experiment; the latter wished to emphasize the interests of the urban workers as being paramount in a proletarian state. The group led by Stalin maintained that Russia's welfare demanded the assistance of foreign capital; the opposition denounced such a policy as treason to the Communist ideal. Briefly, the policies of the Stalin group were in the direction of stabilization; those of the opposition, in the direction of revolution. Trotsky was defeated. Early in 1925 he was dismissed as commissar for war and removed from the Council of Labor and Defense, and his active adherents were expelled from the army and navy.

Next the members of the triumvirate began to quarrel among themselves. Stalin was alarmed by the continued unrest among the peasants and advocated further concessions to win their support. He also advocated additional measures to attract foreign capital. Such concessions and measures were vigorously opposed by a Left group led by Zinoviev and Kamenev. In the Communist Party congress in 1925 Stalin, supported by Rykov, Dzerzhinsky, and Bukharin, succeeded in winning the support of the majority, and Zinoviev and Kamenev were ordered to discontinue their opposition. As they had humiliated Trotsky in the preceding year, so they themselves were now humiliated.

Trotsky then joined forces with Zinoviev and Kamenev in an attempt to oust Stalin and his group from control of the Communist Party. But again the Stalin group won out. In 1926 the Trotsky-Zinoviev opposition was ordered to submit to the party discipline or withdraw from the organization. When in the following year the opposition once more began its attacks, Trotsky, Zinoviev, Kamenev, and some fourscore of their associates were expelled from the Communist Party and sent into exile. But Trotsky from his place of exile in Turkestan continued his opposition, and during the winter of 1928–1929 his influence with the urban workers resulted in spasmodic agitation in the factories in his behalf. Eventually, on the ground that Trotsky was still carrying on illegal propaganda against the government, the latter decided to expel him from the union. Had it not been for the danger of creating a martyr to Trotskyism, it is possible he might have been executed. In February, 1929, he took up his residence in Turkey. In April the Communist Party once more approved Stalin's leadership.

In 1929–1930, a Right group, led by Rykov, Bukharin, and Tomsky, attacked Stalin on the ground that his ruthless "liquidation" of the kulaks and his rapid and compulsory collectivization of peasant estates—in connection with the first Five-Year Plan—were altogether too radical. This so-called Right deviation was in turn crushed, however, much as had been the earlier Left opposition led by Trotsky. As the first decade after Lenin's death drew to a close, it became more and more evident that that great Communist leader's mantle had fallen to Joseph Stalin.

This heir to Lenin's power in Russia was born in 1879 in Gori, a town in the Caucasus. The son of a Georgian shoemaker, he had been christened Joseph Visserionovich Dzhugashvili. Destined by his parents for the priesthood, he had been sent to a theological seminary, but from this clerical institution he had been ultimately expelled because of his Marxian ideas. Soon thereafter he became a member of the Social Democratic Party, and in 1902 he was arrested and exiled to Siberia for his part in a demonstration at Batum. Although an exile in 1903, when the Social Democratic Party split, Dzhugashvili sided with Lenin and thus at once entered the ranks of the Bolsheviks.

In 1904 Dzhugashvili escaped from Siberia and returned to his home district under an assumed name, and during the ensuing decade his career was filled with repeated arrests, exiles, escapes, and new aliases. Of the latter, the one by which he became best known was Stalin (Steel), conferred upon him by his fellow Bolsheviks because of his strength, coolness, ruthlessness, and taciturnity. Always plotting, agitating, writing, or editing, he persistently worked against the tsarist regime from within Russia. Six times arrested and exiled, he five times escaped, thanks to his cleverness and to his physical powers of endurance. During the years after 1913, however, he was successfully kept in exile in northern Siberia within the Arctic Circle. Isolation, prison tortures, forced labor, and severe deprivation were the lot of this "man of steel."

Freed by the March revolution of 1917 with its political amnesty, and permitted to return to Petrograd, Stalin at once became active in organizing soviets. Not an impassioned and eloquent orator, he interested himself primarily in the practical affairs of organization and thus helped to rebuild the Communist Party. When the November revolution occurred, he became one of the first commissars in the new Communist government. During the period of White invasions, he played a prominent part in defense of the Bolshevik regime, and to commemorate his success at Tzaritzin on the lower Volga, that city was rechristened Stalingrad. From 1920 to 1923 he was commissar of nationalities and left his impress upon the constitution of the U.S.S.R. with its Soviet of Nationalities. As secretary-general of the Russian Communist Party, Stalin directed and maintained discipline within that organization and ruthlessly eliminated all disruptive personalities. Quietly but solidly he built up a political machine which enabled him to dominate the party—and through it the Soviet Union.

The fate of those who might dare to challenge Stalin's supremacy in subsequent years was startlingly revealed in 1934 when Sergius Kirov, a prominent member of the Communist Party and one of Stalin's close associates, was assassinated on December 1 in Leningrad. The Soviet authorities struck with terrifying speed. Within a few weeks the assassin and nearly a hundred others who were charged with complicity were executed. After the first wave of alarm had subsided, it was charged that the plot was the work of an anti-Stalin faction within the Communist Party. The conspirators were represented as consisting of remnants of the old Trotsky-Kamenev group who were seeking to prepare the way for Trotsky's return. Accordingly, a thoroughgoing purge of the party was at once inaugurated. A considerable number of Communists were arrested and, on the ground of their heretical beliefs, were ordered imprisoned for terms varying from five to ten years. As the result of new trials inaugurated in 1936 prominent Communist leaders, including Zinoviev and Kamenev, were condemned to death; while Tomsky, who was among the accused, committed suicide before the trial ended. Apparently earlier friendships counted for nothing when Russians were found to be opposing Stalin's regime.

In 1937 hundreds more, including several prominent generals in the Soviet army and some high officials in the state governments, were summarily tried and executed on the ground that they were either Japanese or German spies. The former were charged with plotting to sabotage the Soviet railways in the Far East; the latter, with plotting to co-operate with Nazi Germany to facilitate Hitler's projected push eastward into the Ukraine. Foreign observers were somewhat at a loss to reconcile these executions with the reputed strength of Stalin's government.

## THE FIVE-YEAR PLANS

During the struggle between Trotsky and Stalin the former had frequently denounced the latter on the ground that his policies were threatening Russia with a reversion to capitalism, permitting as they did the growth of Nep-men and kulaks. Although Trotsky and his followers were expelled from the party and in some cases even arrested or exiled, their attitude toward kulaks and Nep-men was actually adopted by the victorious Stalin, and a program of swift industrialization and ruthless elimination of these classes ensued in the years after 1928. Stalin's new policies became effective through the so-called Five-Year Plan (*Piatiletka*), which sounded the death knell of both Nep-men and kulaks.

As early as 1925 the Soviet government had contemplated the introduction of a more organized and planned system of national economy. Eventually, on October 1, 1928, an official Five-Year Plan, prepared by the State Planning Commission (*Gosplan*), was inaugurated for the years 1928-1933. This plan laid down a schedule for practically every phase of the country's activities—production, distribution, and finance. It called for an enormous amount of new industrial construction—huge tractor factories, gigantic agricultural machinery factories, immense steel plants, extensive hydroelectric works, and new railways. Capital investments during the five-year period were to amount to billions of dollars. Control figures for each of the five years included quantity and quality of products, cost of production, efficiency of labor, wages, cost of living, and so forth.

Agriculture was to be reorganized on a large-scale mechanized basis through the institution of huge state and collective farms. Through the organization of such farms it was planned to mechanize and socialize the agrarian system and thus at last bring agriculture, which had long been a stumbling block in the way of socialism, into the sphere of planned economic life. The state farms were to be experiments in the application of the most modern mechanized methods of agriculture to huge expanses of fresh land. Managers were to be appointed by the grain trust, a state organization, and labor was to be hired on a wage basis. The state farms were to be financed by the government, and their total agricultural product would belong to the state.

The collective farm, on the other hand, was to result from the combination of a number of peasants' small holdings into one large farm. Although there might be different types of such collective farms, in general the peasants were to retain their homes, gardens, cows, pigs, and chickens, but were to surrender their lands, machinery, and horses to common ownership. The peasants would then work together under the direction of an elected managerial board. After certain amounts were set aside for seeds and fodder, taxes and insurance, purchase of new machinery and construction of new buildings, debt payments, contributions for education and charity, and administrative expenses, the balance of income from the collective farm would be divided among the peasants in proportion to the amount of property which each contributed and the amount and quality of the work each had performed. This type of collective was called an "artel." By eliminating the ditches which separated the small individual plots, thousands of acres could be combined into huge fields in which tractors and modern agricultural machinery could be used to advantage.

The adoption of the Five-Year Plan marked a shift from the relatively loose and easygoing system of the Nep to a much more strictly regulated and definitely socialist phase of the revolution. Various earlier concessions to private initiative were to be annulled or rigorously restricted. The two principal capitalist classes which had grown up under the Nep—the private traders in the towns and the kulaks in the villages—were to be "liquidated." Ultimately, it was hoped, the Five-Year Plan, with its emphasis on all phases of industrial development and with its anticipated expansion of agricultural production, would bring Soviet Russia close to the goal of self-sufficiency in basic and essential commodities. In this sense, the Five-Year Plan was "a declaration of economic independence against the outside world."

The inauguration of the plan inevitably raised a number of serious problems. Obviously, one was the matter of finance. The government planned to finance its undertakings chiefly by means of taxes, internal loans, profits from state trusts, and capital savings resulting from the reduced costs of production. To pay for the necessary importation of machinery and other needed articles from abroad, the government proposed to rely largely upon the export of the country's increased surplus of grain. In this connection a second problem was raised by the drastic decline in the world price of grain. Although in 1929–1930, for example, Russia's exports rose almost 50 per cent—thanks to increased production of grain—the world decline in prices prevented this increase from being reflected in the country's monetary income. To meet this unexpected crisis, the Soviet government ruthlessly stripped the country of articles which had export value, and the world beheld the curious anomaly of a people forced to live on short rations while millions of tons of grain were being exported from the land.

Another problem in connection with the successful execution of the plan was that of securing an adequate number of well-trained engineers, technicians, and skilled workers. The plan called for the introduction of new specialized courses in schools and universities and for the establishment of many new technical and vocational schools. To solve the immediate problem, the services of foreign engineering firms and individual specialists were engaged. Foreign engineers and technicians became important, almost indispensable, cogs in Russia's industrialization machine. Still another problem was that of securing industrial efficiency from untrained or ill-trained workers. Machines were often injured and products ruined. The factory management itself was seriously handicapped by the necessity of discussing first with the workers any new plans they wished to inaugurate or orders which they wished to give. In the early period all incentive to speed and efficiency was largely lacking because of the policy of treating all workers alike.

The inevitable result of all these factors was that the scheduled decreased cost of production, increased efficiency of labor, and improved quality of goods were not attained. Although the quantity of goods produced in the ensuing years was frequently in excess of the control figures, the quality was usually below the required standards. Beginning with the year 1930, efforts were made by the government to remedy this situation. The Supreme Economic Council threatened severe punishment for individuals responsible for producing goods of low quality. Differential wage scales and piece work were introduced as an incentive to greater effort, and the work day was lengthened. To improve the efficiency of factory managements, their control over the workers was increased, and the authority of workers' committees was lessened.

Nevertheless, despite all handicaps and obstacles, the Five-Year Plan for industry moved steadily forward, in many cases more rapidly than had been dreamed possible in 1928. In the production of oil, automobiles, tractors, agricultural machinery, sugar, coal, and electrical equipment the five-year goal was attained within three years. In April, 1930, the 1100-mile Turkestan-Siberian Railway was completed more than a year ahead of schedule. The year 1932 saw a 900,000-horsepower hydroelectric plant, built at a cost of more than $100,000,-000, dedicated at Dnepropetrovsk, and the first blast furnace fired in the Magnitogorsk steel works, which when completed would be the largest steel plant in the world.

In agriculture astonishing changes were being introduced. Principally in southeastern Russia, Siberia, and Kazakstan huge state farms were established on previously unused lands. These great farms averaged between 100,000 and 200,000 acres, and the largest, the "Giant," located in the northern Caucasus, put under the plow nearly 300,000 acres in 1930. Tens of thousands of tractors and hundreds of combines—great machines which reaped and threshed the grain at the same time—were put into service.

Great advances were made, also, in the collectivization of peasant holdings. Special inducements—such as lower taxes, easier credit facilities, precedence in the acquisition of machinery and manufactured goods—were offered to those who joined the collectives. On the other hand, heavier taxes and a ruthless requisitioning of grain at fixed prices were the lot of the more prosperous peasants, who were loath to merge their holdings in a collective. The houses, livestock, and tools of thousands of these kulaks were confiscated, and they themselves were torn from their homes and banished to remote regions where they were compelled to work at hard labor. Thousands more were arrested and thrown into prison. The government was determined to liquidate the kulaks. The effectiveness of the new large-scale farming was shown in 1930 when, after a lapse of four years, Russia was once more able to export grain in substantial quantities.

In 1930 the government decided that the Soviet economic year should coincide with the calendar year, and so it was decreed that the Five-Year Plan should include only four and one quarter years in order that it might close on December 31, 1932. With the official ending of the plan it became possible to form some judgment regarding its success. Great strides had certainly been made toward transforming Soviet Russia into a powerful industrial country. The union was dotted with enormous new factories and magnificent new power plants. No other important country could show a rate of quantitative industrial progress to compare with that of the Soviet Union during these years. In the production of machinery, tractors, and petroleum the original plan had been exceeded. On the other hand, in certain industries like iron, steel, and coal, and in some of the consumption industries like textiles, the production had failed to meet the schedule of the original plan. Furthermore, it had been discovered that huge industrial plants were far easier to construct than to operate efficiently.

In agriculture the plan, so far as acreage in state and collective farms was concerned, had been far exceeded. Nearly 30,000,000 acres had been organized into state farms, and more than 15,000,000 peasant households had been brought into the collective farms. Mechanization and collectivization of agriculture had made great advances. Nevertheless, here, too, not all the goals set up by the plan had been attained, for it had been found easier to bring the peasants into collective farms than to make them efficiently productive. As a stimulus to hard work and careful handling of tools and animals no adequate substitute had been found for private ownership.

For the great mass of the Russians, perhaps the worst failure of the plan was in the matter of wages and living standards. Although money wages went up faster than had been contemplated, a number of factors prevented a reduction of the cost of living and a corresponding rise in living standards. In the first place, when expected economies in production did not materialize and when the export income of the government did not reach the desired figure because of the decline in world prices, the currency was inflated by a resort to the printing press. Prices, therefore, became high in terms of the rubles which the Russians received for their products or labor. In the second place, there was a very real shortage of foodstuffs and of manufactured articles for daily consumption. The great majority of Russians were worse off in 1932 so far as food supply was concerned than they had been in 1927. In fact, the year 1932–1933 saw something of a famine in parts of Russia. Furthermore, consumption goods were sacrificed to the production of factories, power plants, and basic articles like steel, petroleum, and coal, with the result that many manufactured necessities of daily life became so scarce that they could not be generally obtained at any price. The Five-Year Plan, nevertheless, undoubtedly constituted a landmark in Russian industrial history.

Early in 1934 the Communist Party congress approved an outline of a second Five-Year Plan covering the years 1933–1937. Under the second plan more attention was to be given to consumers' goods.

Greater emphasis was to be laid, also, upon the efficiency of labor, the reduction in production costs, and the improvement in the quality of goods. The material welfare of the masses was one of the major concerns of the second period. Thousands of houses and apartments were to be erected in the industrial centers, together with theaters, clubs, stadiums, and parks. The crying need for such construction was caused by the great shift in population from the farms to the cities, the number of industrial wage-earners having increased from 11,500,000 in 1928 to 23,500,000 in 1934. These figures likewise explain the Soviet problem of increasing efficiency in industrial production with workers many of whom were inexperienced. To help solve this last problem provision was made in the second Five-Year Plan for still greater expansion of facilities for vocational and technical training. In the interests of greater efficiency a decree in 1934 abolished fixed minimum wages and ordered reductions for inefficient workers.

The results obtained under the second Five-Year Plan were distinctly encouraging. In the basic heavy industries—mining, iron and steel, petroleum, machinery, railway equipment, and the like—the specifications of the plan were generally exceeded. In fact, in 1934 the Soviet Union occupied second place in the world production of pig iron and third place in steel production, in each case ranking ahead of Great Britain. More encouraging still, perhaps, was the increase in workers' efficiency and the reduction in production costs; it appeared that the Russians had begun to master industrial technique. In agricultural production the gains were also notable. The grain harvest for 1933 was the largest in Russian history, that for 1934 was still larger, and that for 1935 again set a record. The last year saw record harvests in other products than cereals, too. Sugar beets, tobacco, fruit, cotton, and flax also established new records. The increased production of cotton was particularly significant in view of Russia's enlarged facilities for textile manufacturing. In 1937 cotton and coal were exported to the United States.

In contrast with the first Five-Year Plan, which imposed many privations upon the masses in order that the foundations might be laid for an industrialized country, the second Five-Year Plan began to bring to the Russian people some of the fruits of their long and arduous toil. This was evident, for instance, in the matter of foodstuffs. In 1935 the whole food-rationing system was abandoned, and all foodstuffs—meat, potatoes, butter, eggs, sugar, and the like—were made available to purchasers without restrictions. Moreover, prices were reduced by government decree. Nor were improvements in living standards limited to the matter of food. Since the industries producing textiles and footwear had exceeded their quotas under the plan, articles of wearing apparel were both more plentiful and lower-priced. In general, the retail stores were better supplied with goods than in previous years.

The peasants, too, participated in the rising standard of living. Higher official prices for farm products and freedom to sell surplus produce in the open market naturally increased their purchasing power. They thus found themselves in a position to buy in the village stores many consumers' goods which they had been unable to obtain in preceding years. And—what was equally important—more consumers' goods were available for purchase. It may therefore be stated with a fair degree of certainty that the real incomes of the Russian people and consequently their general standard of living rose during the years after 1933, although the rate of improvement was somewhat checked in 1936 because of increased emphasis upon military and naval armaments.

In 1936 the Communist leaders announced that the Soviet state had largely achieved the first of its objectives in its march toward communism. The productive means of the country, it was asserted, had at length been almost entirely socialized. Furthermore, it was pointed out, with the socialization of industry and the collectivization of agriculture, there remained in Russia only one class—the workers. Among the peasants—the most difficult of the Russians to be absorbed into the communist state—there were, it was reported, no longer rich, middle-class, and poor. All had become "members of a collectivized and socialized agricultural society." Although the Communist leaders were doubtless slightly overenthusiastic about the extent of their achievements, it seemed fairly clear in 1936 that the struggle to establish in Russia a collectivized and mechanized system of agriculture had been largely won.

The new constitution of that year stated that the "economic foundation of the U.S.S.R. consists in the socialist ownership of the implements and means of production" (Article 4), and that socialist ownership has either the form of state ownership or the form of co-operative and collective-farm ownership (Article 5). Alongside the socialist system of economy, however, "the law allows small private economy of individual peasants and handicraftsmen based on individual labor and excluding the exploitation of the labor of others" (Article 9). That the Soviet Union had by 1936 departed from the ideals of pure communism is apparent in the statement that the "personal owner-ship by citizens of their income from work and savings, of home and auxiliaries pertaining thereto, of objects of domestic and household use, of objects of personal use and comfort, as well as the right to in-herit private property are protected by law" (Article 10). This de-parture is further revealed by the declaration that in the U.S.S.R. "the principle of socialism is being realized: 'From each according to his ability, to each according to his work'" (Article 12). Apparently the earlier communist ideal of taking from each according to his ability and giving to each according to his needs has been abandoned.

## EDUCATION AND RELIGION

Not unrelated to the economic life of Russia was the attitude of the Soviet government toward public education. Upon the schools the Bolsheviks relied for two important achievements. By them must be prepared the well-trained, skilled technicians who were expected to assume in the economic and administrative life of the union the places left vacant by the overthrow of the bourgeoisie. In this sense there was in Russia a "race between education and catastrophe." Then, as Lenin pointed out, the Bolshevik economic scheme was not possible without "an intellectual revolution." From this point of view the Bol-sheviks looked to the schools to produce a generation which should be thoroughly versed in and loyal to the communist ideal.

Just how these aims should be accomplished the Bolsheviks were not altogether sure, so that the Soviet Union came to constitute a great laboratory for educational experiments. On one thing they were deter-mined, however: that the illiteracy of the tsarist period should be wiped out, that no more generations of Russian children should grow up in ignorance. Under the old regime the higher schools and in many places the secondary schools were closed to the workers and peasants. This the Soviet government would change. In the old days education was for the privileged classes only; henceforth it must be for the masses.

In general the Soviet educational program called for free, obligatory, and universal education between the ages of three and sixteen, and for the right of every Russian citizen to a higher education, though financial bankruptcy, civil wars, famine, and economic disorganization all contributed to prevent much progress until after 1921. The school system was secularized and "communized" to the extent that nothing contrary to Communist principles might be taught. Much progress was made, too, in educational work among the minority populations of Russia. Under the tsarist regime most of the minor nationalities in the country had no schools, and many of them no written language. With the aid of anthropologists and linguistic scholars the Soviet government had the different languages reduced to written forms. It then provided textbooks in these local languages and laid the foundations of a school system in these scattered districts.

As already pointed out, the Five-Year Plans outlined programs of educational as well as industrial expansion. During the years 1928–1932 great strides were made in developing the public-school system, the aim being to have compulsory elementary education a fact and not merely a theory by 1933. By the latter year nearly 22,000,000 children—three times the number in tsarist days—were enrolled in elementary schools; four fifths of all children between the ages of eight and fourteen were receiving education at the hands of the government; and illiteracy in the adult population had been to a considerable extent eliminated. By 1933, too, an extensive system of vocational and technical training had been developed, with factory schools to give instruction in the operation of machines and technical colleges for the training of engineers.

With the Communist Party officially atheistic and believing that religion is an "opiate of the people," it is not surprising that the position of the Orthodox Church in Russia was profoundly altered by the Soviet government. All lands belonging to the church or to monastic institutions were at once nationalized, and it was decreed that no ecclesiastical or religious association had the right to possess property. All church buildings became the property of the state. Many were transformed into schools or clubrooms, and some of the most famous cathedrals were turned into national museums. In general, however, buildings needed specifically for purposes of worship were turned over to associations of twenty or more persons for use free of charge.

The church was separated from the state, and government subsidies were abolished. The church was forced to depend henceforth, as in the United States, upon the voluntary contributions of its adherents.

Public religious processions were forbidden, and the old church calendar—thirteen days behind that in use in the Western world—was abolished in favor of the latter. The church was deprived of its control of marriage and divorce, registration of births and deaths, and cemeteries. The control of all these was confided to the civil government. The schools were separated from the church, and it was originally decreed that Christian churches might not give organized religious instruction to minors under eighteen years of age. No religious instruction was permitted in any public or private school, but children in groups of three or less might receive religious instruction, provided it was given outside the schools and churches. Although the influence of the government was thus thrown against religion, attendance at religious services was unrestricted, except to members of the Communist Party.

In the beginning the Soviet government proclaimed that "the liberty of religious as well as antireligious propaganda is guaranteed to all citizens." Protestant churches—particularly the Baptists, Methodists, and Lutherans—took advantage of the new situation to extend their activities and entered upon programs of social and educational work among young people. The Orthodox Church, stimulated by this vigorous competition, likewise embarked upon a program of social-welfare work. By 1929 Communist leaders, who desired to have a monopoly of the training of Russian youth, became alarmed, and the Soviet government promulgated a new code for the regulation of religious institutions. Atheism was practically made a state dogma, for to the atheists was granted a monopoly of the right to teach their beliefs. Believers in religion might still hold any creed, but they were deprived of the right to propagate their views, and the commissariat for education was instructed to organize a special inspectorate to superintend the enforcement of these new laws. Communist leaders constantly urged the necessity of intensifying the work of the "godless societies," on the ground that the fight against religion was also a fight against counterrevolution.

## SOVIET FOREIGN POLICY

For the sake of convenience and clarity the history of the Soviet Union's foreign policy will be discussed in relation to the different aims which seem to have predominated in successive periods since

1917. In the first three years after the November revolution the dominant aim of the Soviet government was to bring about the overthrow of all capitalist governments. During this period the Bolshevik leaders were far from confident of their ability to retain control in Russia. To them a world proletarian revolution which should everywhere supplant capitalism by a Communist regime seemed absolutely essential to their own continuance in power. The Soviet government's foreign policy during these early years, therefore, may be characterized as primarily that of revolutionary propaganda.

To facilitate the carrying on of this propaganda the Bolshevik leaders in March, 1919, founded the Third or Communist International (*Comintern*).[2] This new organization was designed (1) to carry on an international propaganda of Bolshevik ideas, (2) to unite and strengthen the Communist parties in all countries, (3) to win the leadership of all labor and socialist movements, and (4) "to accelerate the development of events toward world revolution." Once the revolution had been accomplished, the Third International was to direct the future efforts of the working classes. In the meantime it was to constitute the "headquarters for the world army of the proletariat." Its headquarters were set up in Moscow, and it was liberally subsidized by the Soviet government.

Sometimes through its own officials, but more often through the instrumentality of the Third International, the Soviet government during its first years attempted to launch anticapitalist offensives in various countries of Europe. It played a part in the Communist uprisings in Germany in 1918 and 1919, in the establishment of the Bela Kun regime in Hungary (1919), in the communistic experiments in Italy (1920), and in spasmodic outbreaks in some of the Baltic republics. Its efforts to establish strong connections with the workers of Great Britain, France, Austria, and Czechoslovakia, however, proved futile. Equally futile, too, were the government's efforts to win the good will and co-operation of the Asiatic peoples in the hope that they might be converted to Communism and a gigantic coalition be created against Western capitalism. Despite all efforts of the Soviet

[2] The "First International," officially the "International Workingman's Association," was organized in 1864 under the influence of Karl Marx to advance the rights of labor in all countries. As a result of the reaction against socialism in Europe a decade later, it fell to pieces about 1874. With the gradual revival of socialism came in 1889 the founding of the "Second International," with which the various Socialist and Labor parties of the world soon became affiliated. The World War temporarily put a stop to its activities.

government and of the Third International, the world proletarian revolution failed to materialize.

At home, after three years of almost constant fighting against the forces of counterrevolution, the Bolsheviks found themselves at last in complete control, but in control of a Russia which, because of their communist experiments, was fast sinking into economic chaos. The New Economic Policy which Lenin thereupon decided to inaugurate has already been discussed. This change in economic policy at home was accompanied by a change in the Soviet government's policy abroad. In order to rescue Russia from its complete industrial and commercial collapse, there was need for the influx of capital, machinery, and experts from abroad. But these could hardly be obtained so long as Russia remained isolated among the nations. Early in 1918 the diplomatic representatives of all the powers had been withdrawn because of Bolshevik policies, and until the opening of the year 1921 the only states which had recognized the Soviet government were the Baltic republics—Finland, Latvia, Estonia, and Lithuania. While not abandoning completely its purpose of undermining the capitalist governments by Communist propaganda, the predominant aim of the Soviet government next came to be the opening of trade relations with foreign countries as a means of hastening Russia's economic revival. A provisional trade agreement between Russia and Great Britain was signed on March 16, 1921, and by the end of the year the Soviet government had suceeded in obtaining similar agreements with Germany, Norway, Austria, and Italy.

But one serious obstacle in the way of Russia's complete reestablishment of diplomatic and commercial relations with other countries was the Soviet government's repudiation of all Russia's foreign debts. Late in 1921, accordingly, the Soviet government notified the powers that, though it was neither legally nor morally bound by the debts of the former regime, it was willing to consider what could be done toward meeting foreign claims. It proposed that an international congress should be held for the purpose of recognizing the Soviet government, devising some means of bringing about Russia's economic revival, and considering the problem of repudiated debts. In April, 1922, such a conference opened at Genoa with representatives of thirty-four states in attendance, all of Russia's creditors being present except the United States. After a number of weeks of negotiation, however, the conference finally broke down because the demands and counterdemands were so far apart as to prevent an agreement. The only immediate gain for the Soviet government was the fact that it had at least won the *de facto* recognition of Europe. During the negotiations at Genoa, moreover, Russia, by the treaty of Rapallo,[3] did secure *de jure* recognition by Germany.

Nevertheless, Russia had made little real progress toward regaining her former place in the states system of Europe. Six years after the November revolution she was still largely an outlaw nation. Her government was recognized *de jure* in Europe by only Poland, Germany, and the Baltic republics, and elsewhere in the world by only Turkey, Persia, and Afghanistan. The Soviet government became increasingly anxious to remedy this situation.

By 1924 the dominant and openly declared aim of its foreign policy became, therefore, *de jure* recognition. It let it be known that it was prepared to conclude a commercial treaty on especially favorable terms with the first great power to grant it such recognition. On February 1 Ramsay MacDonald, head of the new Labor government in Great Britain, telegraphed unconditional *de jure* recognition of the Soviet government. Italian recognition came officially six days later, and in the following months the U.S.S.R. received the *de jure* recognition of Norway, Austria, Greece, Hejaz, China, Denmark, Mexico, Hungary, and even France. At the close of the year 1924 the Soviet government had been recognized by fifteen European states as compared with only six at its beginning, and every European great power had re-established diplomatic relations with it. In the succeeding years *de jure* recognition was eventually obtained from most of the important states of the world, including the United States.

Meanwhile, the year 1925 had seen the successful conclusion of the Locarno negotiations among the other great powers of Europe. The Locarno treaties were looked upon in Moscow as a serious menace to Russia's position, and from the close of the year 1925 the Soviet government's primary aim in foreign affairs was the creation of a protective barrier of states which could not be drawn into any concerted attack upon Russia. So successful were the Bolsheviks in this phase of their foreign policy that by the summer of 1933 they had concluded pacts of neutrality and nonaggression not only with all their neighbors to the west and south but with a number of the leading

[3] See page 659.

powers of Europe as well.[4] After 1933, because of alarm over the policies of Nazi Germany in the west and imperialistic Japan in the east, the Soviet government sought even more definitely to obtain national security. In 1934, despite the fact that the Communists had professed to believe the League of Nations an organization of capitalist states conspiring against them, the Soviet Union joined the League. In the following year it concluded defensive military alliances against Germany with both France and Czechoslovakia.

Nevertheless, from time to time after 1921 there still appeared evidence of the continued desire to bring about a world proletarian revolution and the downfall of the capitalist regime. Communist revolts were encouraged in Germany, Estonia, Latvia, Finland, and Bulgaria. During the strike in Great Britain in 1926 large subsidies were offered the miners in the hope of converting that strike into a Communist movement. During these years, too, extensive assistance was given to the rising Nationalist movement in China in the hope that it might be won to communism and turned against Western capitalism. Continued anti-British propaganda both in Asia and within the British Empire led in May, 1927, to the Arcos raid and Great Britain's subsequent severing of diplomatic relations with the Soviet government for more than two years.[5] In the Spanish civil war which began in 1936 aid was given to the loyalists in order that the Communist forces in that country might be strengthened.[6]

It would thus appear that during these years there were conflicts between those policies of the Soviet government which were dictated by the desire to advance Russia's national welfare and Bolshevik propaganda dedicated to the object of world revolution. Frequently the latter embarrassed the former, as in Great Britain in 1927. This apparent inconsistency in Russia's foreign policy was caused by a division within the ranks of the Bolsheviks—some desiring to consider Russia's interests first, others seeking to use Russia primarily as an agent for bringing about world revolution. The former, at the head of the Soviet government, attempted to disclaim all responsibility for foreign propaganda and placed the blame upon the Third International, which they asserted was in no way connected with the

[4] For this phase of Russia's foreign policy, see page 570.
[5] For the Arcos raid, see page 701.
[6] See page 743.

Russian government. But since behind both the Soviet government and the Third International there stood the Russian Communist Party as the supreme authority, foreign governments were reluctant to believe that the two were as distinctly separated as the Bolsheviks maintained.

## CHAPTER XX

# FASCIST ITALY

THE second of the great powers to inaugurate a sweeping program of political and economic reform during the postwar years was Italy, where Fascism launched a counteroffensive against Communism and established what many have called a "dictatorship of the middle class." Fascism has often been represented as "the last stand of capitalism," and it is true that in Italy the means of production, though extensively regulated and regimented, do remain for the most part in private hands with the profit system continuing. Nevertheless, it will become obvious that the regime which Fascism introduced in Italy has many characteristics in common with that which Communism established in Soviet Russia.

## POPULAR DISSATISFACTION WITH THE GOVERNMENT

Probably the chief reason for Italy's embarking upon a new course in 1922 was that in the years immediately following the armistice a great portion of the Italian people came to feel that their existing political regime was able neither to preserve and defend Italy's just national interests abroad nor to provide law, order, and efficient government at home. More than the people of any other power, perhaps, the Italians entered the World War for the purpose of securing certain definite additions of territory, and during the conflict their territorial ambitions further increased. They emerged from the war with the high hope and confident expectation of territorial acquisitions which should meet their nationalistic and imperialistic aspirations. Their first disappointment came in the case of Fiume. The failure of the statesmen at Paris to award that city to Italy bitterly disappointed the Italian people, and, when the Italian government later signed with Yugoslavia the treaty of Rapallo (November, 1920), recognizing "in perpetuity" the independence of the Free State of Fiume, the nationalists of Italy denounced the government for its weakness and pusillanimity.

Their second disappointment had to do with Albania, where the

plan to make of the Adriatic an Italian lake called for the establishment of Italian control. But the Italian forces which had entered
Albania during the war were gradually forced back into Avlona by
the Albanians, and the Italian government was obliged to withdraw
its troops and recognize Albanian independence. This withdrawal
constituted for Italian nationalists an "inglorious page of our political and military history." A third disappointment came in the
colonial sphere. After the war Italians aspired to territorial acquisitions in the eastern Mediterranean and in Africa. But by the Treaty
of Sèvres and complementary treaties, Smyrna with its hinterland
was allotted to Greece, and Italy was forced to agree that the Greek-
inhabited Dodecanese Islands, which she had occupied since 1912,
should likewise be surrendered to Greece. In Africa Italy fared little
better, for the German African colonies were granted as mandates
to Great Britain, France, and Belgium, while Italy, with her lack of
raw materials and her scanty colonies, failed to obtain one square
inch of German territory.

These disappointments and humiliations in foreign affairs led many
Italian nationalists to believe that "the sacrifies made in the war were
in vain," that the Allies "were robbing Italy of the fruits of the victory." The bitter hostility which was thus aroused against Italy's
"faithless allies" was turned eventually even against their own government itself because of its inability to protect Italian national interests. Discontent and exasperation brought at length a strong nationalist reaction.

Nor were conditions within the country such as to win popular
support for the government. Like so many other European countries, Italy faced a serious economic situation immediately after the
war. Her national fiscal system was in a hopeless state. Staggering
national deficits succeeded one another yearly, and the national
currency fell steadily to less than a third of its face value. Living costs,
in terms of paper currency, rose to six or seven times their prewar
level. Furthermore, many soldiers, returning to civil life at a time
of industrial crisis, failed to regain their old jobs or to obtain new
ones.

Socialism profited by these circumstances. The Socialists from the
beginning had denounced the war and had repeatedly prophesied
ultimate disaster. Demobilized soldiers, contrasting their actual conditions with the extravagant promises made to them by politicians

in the last months of the struggle, were profoundly disillusioned and went over to socialism almost *en masse*. In the parliamentary elections of November, 1919, the Socialists practically doubled their numbers in the Chamber of Deputies, where they constituted a controlling force and helped to paralyze the government. Meanwhile, the emissaries of Bolshevism had been preaching strikes, the seizure of factories and the land, and the dictatorship of the proletariat. Influenced by the Russian Revolution, the extreme Socialists abandoned their prewar law-abiding character and evolutionary methods and planned by revolution to transplant into Italy the soviet system. During the winter of 1919–1920, it is asserted, a good third of Italy was "Red." Thousands of the most flourishing communes were seized by extreme Socialists. Soon in the parliament itself Socialists were "singing the 'Red Flag,' giving cheers for Lenin, and hissing the King."

The extremists sought to accomplish their ends by direct action, and as early as August, 1919, disorders broke out in the rural districts. During the war many had advocated land for the peasants, and it was in an attempt to bring this about by direct action that land-raiding was begun. In some instances former service men sought to obtain plots of idle land for cultivation; in others tenants refused to pay rent to the owners; while in still others rural laborers sought to introduce the eight-hour day. Outrages were perpetrated—people were killed, houses were burned, cattle were slaughtered, harvests were destroyed. Although the total amount of land seized was relatively small, the psychological effect on the property-owning classes was great.

In industry, too, strikes became frequent and occurred in such essential services as the railways, tramways, and postal and telegraph systems, and even in the light and food-supply systems of the large towns. Enterprises dependent upon such services became demoralized. The strike movement reached its peak in August and September, 1920, when more than 600 factories involving some 500,000 employees were suddenly seized by the workers. Throughout the country the "dictatorship of the proletariat" was hourly expected. The government, paralyzed by divisions in the parliament and embarrassed by difficulties abroad, was powerless to intervene. Anarchists and Communists sought to extend the scope of the movement and to give it definitely revolutionary aims, but their proposal was vigorously opposed by the more moderate element. Ultimately the factories were returned to their owners, the trade unions accepting the government's proposal to bring in a bill for the establishment of factory councils.

Although the crisis passed, sporadic strikes continued, and the fear which the short communist experiment had engendered remained. The proletariat had failed to carry through its program, in fact had abandoned its attempt; but it had succeeded in further demoralizing the already unstable commercial and industrial life of the country. Without permanently injuring the other classes, it had aroused their fear, hostility, and exasperation. Landlords and industrialists, who had looked in vain to the state for protection, denounced the supineness and inability of the government. All Italians who felt they had anything to lose by a communist revolution urgently desired a firm government, and were ready to support any movement which might promise to provide it.

### Mussolini and the Rise of Fascism

The group which benefited most from this situation was the new organization which had been founded by Benito Mussolini. This vigorous Italian was born in 1883, the son of a village blacksmith in northern Italy. His mother was a school teacher, and at the age of eighteen he himself became a teacher. Deciding that he needed further education, he later went to Switzerland, where he attended the Universities of Lausanne and Geneva, working to pay his expenses. While in Switzerland his innate organizing ability and his interest in socialism led him to participate in the founding of trade unions and the fomenting of strikes, activities for which he was ultimately expelled from the republic by the Swiss government.

Back in Italy he once more took up teaching. His continued interest in socialism, however, led him to become involved in agrarian disorders, and in 1908 he was arrested and temporarily imprisoned as a dangerous revolutionary. Later, after having been expelled from Trent by the Austrian government because of his irredentist propaganda, he drifted into journalism and in 1912 became editor of *Avanti,* the official organ of the Italian Socialist Party.

Upon the outbreak of the World War Mussolini advocated Italian neutrality, urged the workers to resist being drawn into a "bourgeois" war, and preached preparation for a social revolution. Suddenly, in October, 1914, he changed his views and began to urge Italian intervention in the war. The Socialists thereupon repudiated him and forced him to resign from *Avanti*. In the following month he established in Milan the daily paper, *Il Popolo d'Italia,* which under his editorship became an interventionist organ. In September, 1915, when his class was called to the colors, Mussolini entered active service and served as a private on the Isonzo front. Early in 1917 he was wounded by the explosion of a trench mortar, and upon his recovery he procured exemption from further military service on the ground of being indispensable to the management of *Il Popolo d'Italia.* In the days following the Caporetto disaster its columns were used to combat the spirit of national depression.

At the conclusion of the war Mussolini, in March, 1919, issued a call for a meeting of former service men who "desire to express their attitude toward the country's postwar problems." A small group gathered about him—chiefly young men, mostly ex-Socialists—and under his leadership was founded the *Fascio di Combattimento* (Union of Combat). Its program of proposed political, economic, and religious changes was extremely democratic,·even revolutionary, but at the same time strongly nationalistic. At first Fascism made little headway. In the parliamentary elections of 1919 it put forward two candidates—Mussolini was one—but neither was successful. Nevertheless, through pamphlets, speeches, and patriotic demonstrations the Fascisti denounced the government for its weakness both at home and abroad.

During the occupation of the factories Mussolini took no sides, though in the previous year he had approved a similar step. Following the collapse of the occupation, however, he threw the weight of his organization into a drive against the Communists. In northern and central Italy Fascist branches were established by ex-officers of the army and agents of the industrial and landowning classes. While Mussolini aroused enthusiasm by articles in his newspaper, *squadristi* of young men—wearing black shirts—were sent out to combat Communism. Guns, clubs, and castor oil were their weapons. In the beginning the Giolitti government, wishing to destroy Communism, apparently connived with the Fascist forces. They were quietly supplied with arms, given free transportation on the railways, and rarely punished for their misdeeds. Early in 1921 many of D'Annunzio's legionaries joined the Fascist movement. They added a more pronounced military and nationalistic element to Fascism and contributed certain Roman terms, symbols, and war cries. The fighting groups of "Black Shirts" rapidly increased during the first half of this year. Punitive expeditions, with their beatings, attacks on Communist and trade-union headquarters, and destruction of printing establishments continued. The Communists countered with ambuscades and mass attacks. Much blood was shed on each side during the conflict.

Great numbers now welcomed the new organization. To the employers it meant the restoration of discipline among workmen and the reduction of wages; to landowners, possible protection against further peasant outbreaks; to helpless and terrified professional men, middle classes, and intelligentsia, the restoration of law and order; to patriots, the purification of the civil life and the strengthening of the state. From all these classes young men hastened to enroll in the *squadristi*. Tired of violence and factional fights, the majority of Italians began to look to Mussolini to bring in an era of social peace. The failure of the communist experiment, the weakness of the government, the subsidies of the rich, the revival of the middle class, the spread of patriotism, and the longing for a strong government, all these—together with Fascist willingness to resort to violence to attain its ends—contributed to bring success.

In November, 1921, the Fascist movement was transformed into the Fascist Party. A new and more elaborate as well as less radical program was drawn up. The succeeding months were spent in strengthening the party and in winning public opinion. The idea was spread abroad that Fascism had been responsible for the defeat of Bolshevism, and that it alone stood between Italy and the return of that dread evil. The classes which had rallied to Fascism in order to rid the country of the threat of Communism now continued to support it for fear that the danger had not been permanently removed. The government remained unstable, weak, and inefficient. Its services were overstaffed, its budget unbalanced. Tremendous fiscal deficits piled up, and further currency inflation followed. Disorders continued at home, and the path of empire in Asia Minor and northern Africa was beset with difficulties. Ministerial instability discredited parliamentary government. During the summer of 1922 Fascism began its conquest of political power by the ejection of executive officials in the outlying provinces.

### The "Fascistization" of the Government

During the fall of 1922 Mussolini repeatedly demanded that Facta, the premier who had succeeded Giolitti, either dissolve the parliament or resign in favor of a new cabinet which should include five Fascist ministers, but Facta refused to do either. In October, at a great congress of Fascisti in Naples, Mussolini delivered his ultimatum: "Either the government will be given to us or we shall seize it by marching on Rome." A ministerial crisis ensued. A tardy attempt was made to bring the Fascisti into the ministry by offering them certain positions. They declined. Instead they began their "march on Rome." The Facta government proclaimed a state of siege, but the king, in order to avoid civil war, refused to sign the decree. Instead he called upon Mussolini to form a new ministry. The government which the latter established on October 30 was a coalition in which the Fascisti were predominant.

Immediately upon assuming the premiership Mussolini demanded and received from the parliament what practically amounted to dictatorial powers until the end of 1923. Then followed the "fascistization" of the administrative offices of the government. Eventually a law was enacted giving the government authority to dismiss any civil servant who held political views contrary to those of Mussolini. Next came the "fascistization" of the parliament. An electoral reform bill was forced through the parliament, under the provisions of which the party obtaining the largest vote in a parliamentary election would receive two thirds of all the seats. In April, 1924, the plan was tested in a general election. The Fascist Party won over 60 per cent of the seats regardless of the provisions of the new electoral law, though the opposition declared that this was not accomplished without violence and intimidation. However that may be, the parliament was at any rate "fascistized." During 1925–1926 popular control of local government was also gradually abolished. Local machinery of government was suppressed in all municipalities of less than 5000 population, and these districts were placed under the control of *podestas* appointed by the government at Rome. Later all provincial, communal, and municipal elections were indefinitely suspended, and *podestas* took the place of popular government in all towns and cities.

Meanwhile, Mussolini's position as premier had been transformed into that of a dictator. He was freed from dependence upon the parliament and made responsible to the king alone. He was given permanent control of the national military, naval, and air forces. No item might be placed on the order of the day in either house of the parliament without his consent. The authority to issue governmental decrees with the force of law was placed in his hands. His title was changed to "Head of the Government," and the members of the ministry were made definitely subordinate to him, his relation to the ministry coming to resemble that of the President of the United States to his cabinet.

All these changes were not accomplished without opposition, but wherever it appeared drastic steps were immediately taken to suppress it. Newspapers were so rigorously censored that eventually nothing but a Fascist press remained. University presidents and deans and public-school principals were required (1930) to be chosen from the Fascisti, and professors were dismissed for holding views contrary to Mussolini's. A secret police, the O.V.R.A. (*Organizzazione Volontaria per la Repressione dell' Antifascismo*), was established to ferret out those who plotted against the existing regime, and military tribunals were set up to try such offenders. Many were exiled to the Lipari Islands off the north coast of Sicily for holding political views contrary to Mussolini's. Many who desired to leave the country were prevented from going. In general, freedom of speech, of the press, and of association—the pillars of liberal government—were destroyed. Mussolini's *Il Popolo d'Italia* declared: "There is no longer any room for many things which were excellent in other times."

In addition there was, especially in the early years, frequent resort to violence to suppress the opposition. Doubtless much of this was carried on by irresponsible elements in the party, for all sorts of men had been drawn into the movement from a variety of motives. On the other hand, on at least one occasion members of the party in high standing became involved. In June, 1924, Giacomo Matteotti, a Socialist member of the Chamber of Deputies, was abducted and murdered, apparently because he had announced that he was going to expose the corruption of the Fascist minister of the interior. Although Mussolini, in an attempt to "purify" Fascism, at once removed from office all those known to be involved in the crime, they were later defended by high officers of the Fascist Party and escaped with almost no punishment.

## FASCISM CONSTITUTIONALIZED

The Fascist Party is a centralized, hierarchical organization with nearly two million members. At its apex is the Fascist Grand Council presided over by Mussolini, *Il Duce* (The Leader). This council is the supreme Fascist organ, and, since Mussolini has the right to add to it at will any who have been of special service to Fascism or the nation, he is always able to control a majority. The party consists of some ten thousand branches (*fasci*), which are grouped into provincial federations with councils similar to the Grand Council. The secretary-general of the party is appointed by the king upon the nomination of Mussolini; the provincial secretaries are appointed by Mussolini on the nomination of the secretary-general; the local secretaries are appointed by the provincial secretaries.

In order that Italy and Fascism might have a well-trained and disciplined youth, Fascism established three auxiliary organizations, the *Balilla,* the *Avanguardia,* and the *Giovani Fascisti,* for boys from eight to fourteen, fourteen to eighteen, and eighteen to twenty-one respectively; and two, the *Piccole Italiane* and the *Giovane Italiane,* for girls under and over twelve years respectively. In 1928 the government ordered the suppression of all non-Fascist institutions for the physical, moral, or spiritual training of Italian youth, and the ranks of Fascism were eventually closed (1933) except to "graduates" of the *Balilla* and *Avanguardia.*

The militant character of Fascism during the early years expressed itself through *squadristi* of "Black Shirts." These were the armed forces of the movement in the years when it was fighting for existence and crushing opposition. It was the "Black Shirts" who conducted the "march on Rome." In 1923 the *squadristi* were disbanded, and from them was recruited the Voluntary Militia for National Security. This militia is now part of the armed forces of the state and subject to the army discipline code. It is open to all citizens from seventeen to fifty years of age who possess certain "physical, moral, and political" qualifications. It has charge of the preliminary training of the *Avanguardisti,* and some of its number are assigned to duty in connection with railways, ports, and postal and telegraph offices. Most of its members, however, now remain in civil life subject to call.

Although, from 1923 on, the policies which were enacted into law

by the Italian parliament were in general formulated and enforced
by the leaders of the Fascist Party, the latter as such had no constitutional place in the Italian government. In 1928, however, the Fascist
Party was written into the Italian constitution. By the provisions of the
Electoral Reform Act of that year, discussed below, the Fascist Grand
Council was given the legal right to draw up the list of candidates
for the Chamber of Deputies. Later it was also given the right to nominate candidates for the office of prime minister and for the other
high government positions. At the same time it was made the chief
advisory body of the government on all questions of a constitutional
character, such as proposed legislation affecting succession to the
throne, the royal powers and prerogatives, the composition of the
two houses of the parliament, the powers of the prime minister, and
the relations between church and state. International treaties which
involve changes in the national territory became subject to its delibera-
tion. The Fascist Grand Council was changed, therefore, from a mere
organ of the Fascist Party unofficially consulted by the prime minister
into an openly recognized *de jure* part of the political machinery of
the state.

### FASCIST SYNDICALISM AND THE CORPORATIVE STATE

At the very beginning of the Fascist movement Fascist trade
unions were organized in opposition to the existing Socialist unions.
In 1923 a Federation of Fascist Syndical Corporations was created,
and two years later the Fascist syndicates were recognized by the
Italian Industrial Employers' Federation as the sole representatives
of their employees. Late in 1925 legislation was formulated which
became the Legal Discipline of Collective Labor Relations Law on
April 3, 1926. Under the provisions of this law as later modified there
are in Italy nine national confederations, four for employers and four
for employees in the fields of agriculture, industry, credit and insurance, and commerce, and one for professional men and artists.
Each confederation has subdivisions or syndicates for regions, provinces, and municipalities.

These syndicates are given authority to enter into collective contracts regulating hours of labor, wages, apprenticeship, and the like.
They have power over all workers and employers in a given industry
and district regardless of whether the latter are members of the syndicates. The contracts which the syndicates make are binding upon

all, and each syndicate has the right to exact an annual contribution to the common fund from all, whether members or not. Strikes and lockouts are illegal. When trouble arises between employer and employees, the syndicates to which they belong seek an amicable settlement. In case of failure, the dispute is referred to the minister of corporations, an appointee of Mussolini. Failure here is followed by an appeal to one of the sixteen Italian courts of appeal, each of which has a labor section. From its decision there is no appeal.

In 1928 the syndicalist system was linked with the political system of Italy when an electoral reform law was passed. By this law the right to nominate deputies was given to the syndicates and to certain legally recognized "cultural, educational, charitable, or propagandist" associations. The national confederations were authorized to propose 800 candidates and the other associations 200 more. These names were then to be sent to the Fascist Grand Council, which, with full power to accept or reject any name or even to choose one outside those submitted, should draw up a list of 400 candidates. This list was finally to be submitted to a plebiscite of the voters who, as a single national constituency, must vote "yes" or "no" on the list as a whole. Men twenty-one (or eighteen if they were married and had children) might vote if they paid syndicate dues or 100 lire in taxes, if they received pensions from the government, or if they belonged to the clergy.

The electoral scheme was given its first test early in 1929 when an election or plebiscite, as it was called, was held on March 24. During the preceding two weeks a campaign in favor of the Fascist nominees was conducted by means of speeches, proclamations, and posters. No opposition speeches were permitted. The question which was put to the electorate was: "Do you approve of the list of deputies chosen by the Fascist Grand Council?" Of the 9,460,727 male voters who composed the electorate, 8,663,412 voted in favor of the Fascist list. Only 135,761 had the temerity to cast their votes against it. Five years later a second election (March 25, 1934) had similar results. Of the 10,041,998 votes cast, only 15,265 votes were in the negative.

A still further step in the development of the corporative state was taken in 1934 when Mussolini announced the formation of twenty-two corporations or guilds designed to represent every phase of Italy's economic life. The corporations, each of which has Mussolini as president and members of the Fascist Party among its officers, consist of representatives of employers, and employees, and technicians in the twenty-two branches of Italy's economic life.[1] They are based on "cycles of production," and each corporation is to concern itself with the whole process by which a raw product is transformed into a finished article. Each is charged with the task of analyzing costs of production, reducing them whenever possible by rationalization, and establishing a price which must: (1) assure a profit for the employer, (2) give proper remuneration to the worker, (3) safeguard against overcharging the consumer, and (4) permit Italian exports to compete successfully abroad. It would appear perfectly clear that the establishment of the corporative system marks the end of *laissez faire* in Italy's economic life.

A final step was taken in March, 1939, when the Chamber of Deputies was supplanted by the Chamber of Fasces and Corporations. This new legislative body consists of the Duce, the members of the Fascist Grand Council and the Fascist National Council, and the members of the National Council of Corporations. It thus represents politically the Fascist Party and economically the Italian corporative system. Members of the new national legislature have no fixed terms and surrender their seats when they are no longer members of the constituent bodies. The corporative system, according to Mussolini, is an honest attempt to advance in constitutional legislation along lines best calculated to promote smooth collaboration of all classes of society for the good of the state. Each art, craft, trade, and profession is represented in this legislative body.

That the corporative system is thoroughly subordinated to Mussolini and the Fascist Party is obvious. At the top of the pyramid is the minister of corporations under Mussolini. Then come the twenty-two corporations, each of which has the Duce as its president. Below them come the nine national confederations of syndicates, the president and council of each of which are appointed by the government. The local syndicates, in turn, are subject to the control of the provincial prefect if their activities are limited to a single province, or to that of the minister of corporations if they include two or more provinces. Although in theory the syndicates and federations are elective bodies, actually all syndical officials are appointed by the Fascist Party, sub-

[1] The twenty-two corporations are: Cereals; Horticulture, Flowers, and Fruit; Vines and Wine; Oils; Beets and Sugar; Zootechnics and Fisheries; Wood; Textile Products; Metallurgy and Engineering; Chemicals; Clothing; Paper and Printing; Building and Public Works; Water, Gas, and Electricity; Mining Industries; Glass and Ceramics; Insurance and Credit; Professions and Arts; Sea and Air; Internal Communications; Theater; Tourist Industry.

ject to ratification by the minister of corporations, and may be removed whenever their work is unsatisfactory to party leaders.

### THE SETTLEMENT OF THE ROMAN QUESTION

Fascism inherited from its predecessors the long-standing problem
of Italy's relations with the Vatican, a problem which Mussolini was
especially eager to solve. In 1926 the Duce through an intermediary
expressed to Pope Pius XI his strong desire to enter into negotiations
for the purpose of eliminating the existing state of hostility between
the church and the state. The delicate negotiations which ensued
eventually resulted in an agreement between the papacy and the
Italian government, and on February 11, 1929, a treaty, a concordat,
and a financial convention were signed in the Lateran Palace by Cardinal Gasparri, papal secretary of state, and by Mussolini.

By the terms of the treaty Italy recognized the state of Vatican City
under the sovereignty of the pope. The Vatican City—the smallest of
sovereign states, with an area of only slightly more than a hundred
acres and with less than five hundred citizens—thus took its place
among the states of the world. It was to have its own coinage system,
postage stamps, wireless, and railway station, and the right to send
and receive ambassadors. Its territory was always to be considered
neutral and inviolable; freedom of access to the Holy See was guaranteed for bishops from all parts of the world; and freedom of correspondence with all states, even with states which might be at war
with Italy, was assured. Furthermore, the privilege of extraterritoriality was granted outside the Vatican City to certain churches and
buildings used by the Holy See for its administration. Finally, the
person of the pope was declared to be as sacred and inviolable as that
of the king.

In the concordat Italy recognized the Holy Catholic Apostolic and
Roman religion as the only state religion in the country. The Italian
government bound itself to enforce within its territory the canon law
—that is to say, the laws relating to faith, morals, conduct, and discipline prescribed for Catholics by church authority. Matrimony was
recognized by the state as a sacrament regulated by canon law, and
thereafter, if certain regulations were observed, the state would recognize the legality of marriages performed by priests. Religious instruction, formerly excluded from the secondary schools, now became
compulsory in both elementary and secondary schools, and was to be

given by instructors selected by the bishops and maintained by the
state. The election of bishops was also further regulated. Formerly
they were appointed by the church subject to the approval of the state,
which paid their salaries; thereafter the state's role would be restricted
to the right of objecting to an appointee for political reasons. Ordained
priests, moreover, were exempted from military obligations.

In the financial convention the pope accepted 750,000,000 lire ($39,-
375,000) in cash and 1,000,000,000 lire ($52,500,000) in 5-per-cent gov-
ernment bonds "as a definite settlement of all its financial relations
with Italy in consequence of the fall of temporal power." Finally, the
"Holy See . . . declares the Roman question definitely and irrevoca-
bly settled and therefore eliminated, and recognizes the Kingdom of
Italy under the Dynasty of the House of Savoy, with Rome as the
capital of the Italian State."

On June 7 ratifications of the treaties comprising the settlement
were exchanged in the Vatican by Cardinal Gasparri and Mussolini.
Immediately after the ceremony Pope Pius XI sent a telegram to King
Victor Emmanuel III imparting his apostolic benediction to the king,
the queen, the royal family, Italy and the world. A papal nuncio was
at once appointed to the Quirinal and an Italian ambassador to the
Holy See. A few weeks later a pope left the Vatican for the first time
in almost two generations, thus recognizing the settlement of the
Roman question. Then followed a number of efforts to emphasize the
new spirit which existed between the Italian government and the
Vatican. In December, 1929, the king and queen paid their first visit
to the pope. On the twelfth of the same month the Chamber of Deputies voted that September 20, the anniversary of the taking of Rome in
1870, should be supplanted as a national holiday by February 11, the
anniversary of the signing of the Lateran treaties.

### ECONOMIC AND FISCAL PROBLEMS

Perhaps the most pressing problem which confronted Fascism immediately upon assuming control of the government was the threatening state of the national finances. The budget was tremendously out
of balance, the national debt was rapidly increasing, and the inflated
national currency stood at twenty-four (normally five) to the dollar.
Bankruptcy faced the state unless remedial measures were taken. Fascism at once began an extensive reorganization and modernization of
the fiscal system in the interest of efficiency. Expenditures were rig-

orously scrutinized, and superfluous bureaucratic offices were abolished. The national railways, which had a deficit of over one billion lire in 1922, were made self-supporting and were even able to turn over a surplus to the national treasury. Taxes were increased until, in proportion to national income, they became heavier than those of any other country. The effects of these reforms soon became evident in the national balance sheet. Finally, after heroic efforts in 1926–1927, the national currency, which had declined to 31.6 to the dollar, was raised to 19 to the dollar, where it was legally stabilized on a gold basis in 1928.

Nevertheless, the most difficult and at the same time the most fundamental problem with which Fascism had to wrestle continued to be Italy's general economic situation. The seriousness of the problem rested chiefly on two basic facts: (1) the denseness of Italy's population, and (2) her lack of those natural resources which are essential to the upbuilding of a great industrial country. The pressure of Italian population against Italian resources was great, and it seemed likely to increase, for the nationalist philosophy of Fascism demanded a powerful Italy, and this, it was believed, was dependent upon a populous Italy. Numerous measures were taken to encourage large families. Mussolini's aim was a nation of 60,000,000 inhabitants by 1950.

With so dense a population and such inadequate natural resources, it is not surprising that Italy was far from self-sufficient economically. She had long had a deficit in her foreign trade. To overcome this situation, Mussolini mapped out a program which called, in the first place, for a decrease in Italy's dependence upon foreign raw products. To this end, efforts were directed toward increasing the home production of foodstuffs and toward developing extensively Italian hydroelectric projects. At the end of the first decade of the "battle of the wheat," which was waged in the succeeding years, the production of wheat in Italy had increased by 70 per cent over that in 1922. At the same time, increases in the production of rice, corn, and oats ranged from 40 to 60 per cent, and further lessened Italy's need to import foodstuffs. The possibility of freeing the country from dependence upon foreign fuel, however, was not so favorable. Although hydroelectric projects were advanced until Italy stood first in Europe in this type of development, she was still forced to import large quantities of coal.

As the second part of his economic program, Mussolini sought to increase the production and export of Italy's manufactured goods, to expand her merchant marine, and to attract tourist trade. Under his new syndical system the number of days lost by strikes was greatly lessened, and the material forces of the nation were largely fused into "a single dynamo of production." As a result, Italy's industries expanded and her exports increased. To assist in the expansion of the Italian merchant marine, the government advanced subsidies to new lines. Fascism's restoration of economic and political stability, together with its fiscal reforms, restored foreign investors' confidence in Italy, and much-needed foreign capital began to flow into the country. In order to hold out further attractions, legislation was enacted abolishing inheritance taxes and exempting foreign capital for a time from various other kinds of taxes. By the opening of the second decade of Fascist rule Italy had advanced to the place where she had, at least temporarily, a favorable balance of trade.

Inevitably, however, despite Mussolini's efforts, the world depression took its toll. In 1933 Italy once more had an adverse balance of trade. This disturbing situation, which grew steadily worse in 1934, was further aggravated by decreased income from tourists and from remittances from Italians living abroad. To make the matter still worse, the country was confronted with serious budgetary problems caused by increasing national deficits. These circumstances, taken together, threatened to impair Italy's international credit, for during the year the country suffered increasingly heavy losses of gold. The situation became so menacing that the government in 1935 ordered that all foreign credits, foreign securities, and foreign currencies held by Italian nationals should be deposited with the National Exchange Institute, the holders to receive thereafter their interest and other payments in lire. By this measure, it was estimated, a sum of between 3,000,000,000 and 6,000,000,000 lire in foreign currencies would be mobilized for the government's use, if necessary, to make good the country's deficit in the balance of international payments, and thus stop the drain on Italy's gold reserves. Finally, in the summer of 1935, when Mussolini was preparing to conquer Ethiopia, the struggle to maintain the gold coverage was abandoned, and the law requiring 40 per cent was suspended. Thereafter the Bank of Italy's gold reserves steadily diminished until in October, when the publication of the monthly financial statement of the Bank of Italy was discontinued, the gold coverage stood at 28 per cent.

## Recovery of International Prestige

Whether or not Mussolini improved the economic condition of Italy, there is little doubt that he raised her international prestige. In the early years of the Fascist regime he was fortunate enough to recover for Italy some of the territories and concessions which had been lost through the "weakness" of preceding Italian governments. The first gain came with the Dodecanese Islands which Italy had agreed to surrender to Greece by the Italo-Greek treaty of 1920. Mussolini maintained that this agreement was no longer valid because the treaty of Sèvres, with which it was linked, had lapsed. In the treaty of Lausanne (1923) Italy obtained legal recognition of her possession of the Dodecanese. A fortified naval base was at once constructed, and the foundation was laid for Italy's hoped-for predominance in the eastern Mediterranean.

Later in the year 1923 Mussolini delighted Italian nationalists by his spectacular action in the crisis arising out of the murder of an Italian who was head of the Delimitation Commission engaged in locating the boundary between Greece and Albania. On August 27 the head of the commission and four companions, of whom three were Italians, were killed on Greek soil near Janina. The Italian government at once presented an ultimatum to Greece, demanding among other things a strict inquiry with the assistance of the Italian military attaché and the payment of an indemnity of 50,000,000 lire. The other demands Greece offered to accept, but these two she regarded as "outraging the honor and violating the sovereignty of the state." The answer of the Italian government was the bombardment and occupation of the Greek island of Corfu on August 31. Mussolini announced that the occupation of Corfu was only temporary, but many saw in the affair a strange similarity to the events of July, 1914.

Greece, acting under Articles 12 and 15 of the Covenant, immediately appealed to the League of Nations, but Salandra, the Italian representative on the Council, denied the competence of the League to deal with the affair. He asserted that the Delimitation Commission had represented the Council of Ambassadors, which should therefore handle the matter. Mussolini at first contended that the affair would be settled without outside interference, but popular indignation throughout the world led him to retreat to the position already taken by Salandra.

The League Council thereupon urged the Council of Ambassadors to find a solution of the crisis. The latter stipulated that an Inter-Allied commission should supervise the preliminary investigation undertaken by Greece and complete its work by the date which Mussolini had set for the evacuation of Corfu, and that, if the Council of Ambassadors considered the commission's report sufficient, it should at once assess damages. The commission reported that the persons guilty of the crime had not been discovered, and the ambassadors ordered Greece to pay to the Italian government 50,000,000 lire. The money was paid, and Corfu was evacuated on September 27. The government's seeming defiance of the League of Nations convinced Italian nationalists that the whole affair had been a distinct triumph for Mussolini.

The Duce's settlement of the Fiume question, while no less satisfactory to Italian nationalism, was much more skillfully and quietly accomplished. By the treaty of Rapallo (1920) Fiume had been made an independent free city. The arrangement was satisfactory neither to the Italians nor to the Yugoslavs, and it proved unworkable. Mussolini made suggestions regarding a new solution of the Fiume question, and eventually his suggestions were incorporated in the treaty of Rome, signed on January 27, 1924. By the provisions of this treaty the Free State of Fiume was divided between Italy and Yugoslavia. Fiume proper went to Italy. Port Baros, which had been originally constructed especially to handle the trade of Croatia and which is separated from Fiume by only a small stream, went to Yugoslavia. On March 16, 1924, final Italian annexation of the much-discussed city was officially celebrated at Fiume in the presence of King Victor Emmanuel. Another "catastrophic abandonment" of Italian interests was rectified.

The settlement of the Fiume question brought about an improvement in Italo-Yugoslav relations, and a five-year pact of friendship and co-operation was entered into between the two countries. This was followed in 1925 by the Nettuno convention, in which Yugoslavia in return for certain commercial advantages in Italy recognized the right of Italians to buy land within thirty miles of the Yugoslav frontier and the right of Italian firms in Yugoslavia to import Italian labor. In accordance with this general policy of eastward orientation, Italy in 1926 signed the treaty of Tirana with Albania, gaining economic concessions in return for guaranteeing "the *status quo,* political, juridical, and territorial, of Albania." The latter, furthermore, agreed not to conclude with other powers political and military agreements prejudicial to Italian interests. During 1927 internal improvements were carried out in Albania under Italian supervision and with Italian loans, and the Albanian army was reorganized by Italian officers. Later in the year Italy signed with Albania a twenty-year defensive alliance in which each agreed that, "when all the means of conciliation have been exhausted," she would come to the aid of the other in case of unprovoked attack. At last, it appeared, Italy had obtained the protectorate over Albania which Italian nationalists had been seeking ever since the outbreak of the World War.

In 1927, too, Fascism sought to assert Italy's position as a great power in the western Mediterranean by securing the right to participate in the international regime at Tangier, a port in Morocco near the Strait of Gibraltar. In October of that year, on the eve of the opening of negotiations between France and Spain regarding the modification of the international regime in Tangier, three Italian warships made an ostentatious visit to that port. From Rome came the unofficial announcement that Italy as a Mediterranean power considered herself to be vitally concerned in the status of Tangier. There were not lacking those who perceived in Mussolini's gesture a striking similarity to the action of the German Kaiser William II when he precipitated the first Moroccan crisis in 1905. Briand's policy of conciliation was in the ascendancy in Paris at this time, however, and Italy was invited to participate in the ensuing conference. A new agreement concerning Tangier was reached in 1928, and by it Italy was given a larger share in the administrative machinery of that city. Italy's position as a great power had been protected, and in Rome the outcome was looked upon as a great diplomatic triumph for Mussolini. His attempts to advance Italy's position in the Mediterranean still further by demanding naval parity with France at the London naval conference in 1930 and in negotiations during the succeeding years were not, however, so successful. Nevertheless, Mussolini in the years after 1922 undoubtedly did succeed in strengthening Italy's hold on the Adriatic, in increasing her prestige in the Mediterranean, and in extending her diplomatic and commercial influence in southeastern Europe.

## ITALY'S CONQUEST OF ETHIOPIA

On December 5, 1934, Italian and Ethopian border patrols clashed at Ualual, an oasis in a disputed area between Ethiopia and Italian Somaliland. Ethiopia immediately filed a protest with Italy and requested that the affair be arbitrated in accordance with an Italo-Ethiopian treaty of 1928. Italy, however, refused to arbitrate and demanded instead a formal apology, an indemnity for Italian soldiers slain, and the arrest and punishment of the Ethiopian officers involved.

Many believed that Mussolini was about to seize upon this incident to right another Italian "wrong" by "avenging" the humiliating disaster which had befallen Italy at Adowa in 1896 at the hands of Ethiopia. By "avenging" Adowa he might arouse still greater enthusiasm for the Fascist regime; by conquering a considerable portion of Ethiopia he might acquire for Italians more room for expansion and much-needed raw materials and natural resources. Furthermore, since the League of Nations had failed to take any effective step to prevent Japan from seizing Manchuria, he probably believed that a weaker League—minus both Japan and Germany—would not dare to interfere with his venture. Possibly he felt doubly sure that the powers would not interfere because of their need for his support in Europe against an increasingly powerful Nazi Germany. Whatever the factors influencing his decision, however, it seems fairly clear that Mussolini began definitely planning to embark upon a military campaign against Ethiopia. By midsummer of 1935 more than 240,000 troops and laborers had been sent to Italy's East African colonies.

Efforts were made to settle the dispute by peaceful means, however. On January 3, 1935, Ethiopia formally appealed to the League under Article 11 of the Covenant, but the League Council in its January meeting postponed its consideration of the incident until its next session, hoping that it might in the meantime be settled by direct negotiations between the two governments. In May the League Council was informed that the two governments, acting under the treaty of 1928, had agreed to arbitrate. But when the arbitration commission failed to agree upon the fifth arbitrator, the Council again met, instructed the commission to proceed to the choice of a fifth member, and set September 4 as the date upon which the Council would begin a general examination of Italo-Ethiopian relations. The arbitration commission's unanimous decision, announced on September 3, was that neither side was to blame for the Ualual clash, since each believed that it was fighting on its own soil. Obviously this report eliminated the incident as a pretext for Italian reprisals.

Meanwhile, on the suggestion of the League Council, Great Britain, France, and Italy had entered into negotiations for the purpose of facilitating a solution of the differences between Italy and Ethiopia. The negotiations were brought to a sudden end, however, when Mussolini rejected the Anglo-French proposal to entrust to Italy an economic mandate under the League for the financial and administrative organization of Ethiopia. Mussolini announced that Italy's need for colonial expansion and security of Italian colonists could not be satisfied by anything less than annexation of the large portion of Ethiopia bordering upon Eritrea and Somaliland and military occupation of the rest.

Following Mussolini's rejection of the Anglo-French proposal, the British government decided to leave the dispute to the League and to invoke collective action and the use of sanctions against Italy if the latter attacked Ethiopia in violation of the League Covenant. Although France desired if possible to retain the newly won friendship of Italy even at the cost of permitting her to take part of Ethiopia, she wanted the support of Great Britain even more than that of Italy in case of another German war. Consequently, after the British government definitely determined to support collective action at Geneva, France was practically forced to take the same stand. When the League Council met in September, therefore, sanctions against Italy appeared to be almost inevitable unless Mussolini was willing to withdraw from his Ethiopian venture. One more effort was made, however, to settle the dispute without war and yet at the same time to meet Italy's economic needs in Ethiopia. After hearing statements by the Italian and Ethiopian delegates, the Council appointed a committee of five—representing Great Britain, France, Spain, Poland, and Turkey—to find a way to a peaceful settlement.

While the committee was deliberating, Great Britain took active measures to strengthen her position in the Mediterranean. The British Mediterranean fleet was suddenly transferred from Malta to the Suez Canal, and most of the mighty British home fleet was concentrated at Gibraltar. Italy countered these moves by strengthening the fortifications of Pantellara, an island between Sicily and North Africa, so that she might be in a position to cut British communications in the

Mediterranean if necessary, and by concentrating her warships near the Dodecanese Islands in the eastern Mediterranean.

The international situation was exceedingly tense, therefore, when the Council's committee of five submitted its plan for conciliation on September 18. The committee recommended that far-reaching international assistance be extended to Ethiopia through the League, with five foreign advisers nominated by the League Council with the consent of Emperor Haile Selassie. To facilitate the acceptance of the plan by both governments, Great Britain and France announced that (1) they were ready to aid in territorial adjustments between Italy and Ethiopia by themselves consenting to certain sacrifices in the region of the Somali coast in order to give Ethiopia an outlet to the sea, and (2) they would look with favor on the conclusion of economic agreements between Italy and Ethiopia, provided the two powers recognized and safeguarded the existing rights of Great Britain and France. Ethiopia at once accepted the proposals in principle, but Mussolini again rejected the plan on the ground that the concessions to Italy were inadequate. The Council next voted to proceed under Article 15 of the Covenant and entrusted to a committee composed of all Council members except the two disputants (the so-called Committee of Thirteen) the drafting of a report.

Before the report could be drafted, however, the Italian forces began their advance into Ethiopia. On October 3 Adowa and Adigrat were bombed by Italian airplanes, and within three days both were taken without resistance, thus "avenging" the defeat of 1896. The Italian forces continued their advance and on November 8 captured Makale—about sixty miles southeast of Adowa—without resistance. Meanwhile, in the south other Italian forces under General Rudolfo Graziani had captured Gerlogubi, near Ualual, on October 6 and later had occupied Gorahai and Gabredarre.

Thereafter the Italian advance slowed down. Time was required apparently to construct roads through the wild and mountainous country. Roads were necessary to make possible the bringing up of powerful heavy artillery and to prepare the way for the future advance of mechanized and motorized forces. Eventually, after nearly three months of inaction, however, the Italian forces were again ready to advance. In the middle of January, 1936, Graziani's forces suddenly launched an attack northwest from Dolo on the border of Italian Somaliland. With mechanized and motorized forces and with little resistance they pushed rapidly forward until they reached Noghelli, some 250 miles distant. From here they were in a position to strike at the chief caravan routes between Addis Ababa and Kenya. Later in the same month the Italian armies near Makale resumed operations.

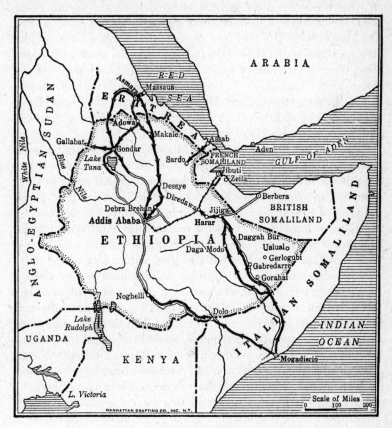

How Italy Conducted Her Invasion of Ethiopia

Within a few weeks they had routed the last well-organized Ethiopian army in the north. Developments seemed to indicate that the period of seeming inaction had been advantageously used by the Italians to create disaffection among the enemy chieftains through the judicious bestowal of large cash bribes.

In April the primitive Ethiopian resistance completely collapsed in the face of Italian heavy artillery, tanks, airplanes, bombs, and poison gas. Haile Selassie, his armies demoralized and his retreat to the west cut off by disaffected tribal chiefs, on May 2 fled to French Somaliland, where he boarded a British warship. Meanwhile, 30,000 Italian troops in what was perhaps the greatest motorized column yet organized rolled slowly and steadily on by two main routes toward Addis Ababa. On May 5, with fifty airplanes roaring overhead, they entered the Ethiopian capital and hoisted the Italian flag. In the south, at the same time, General Graziani's forces had also advanced. Here, too, Ethiopian resistance quickly collapsed, and on May 8, again with numerous airplanes flying overhead, Graziani's forces marched into Harar, the second city of Ethiopia. A vanguard at once pushed on and cut the Addis Ababa-Jibuti railroad at Diredawa.

Meanwhile, in Rome, on May 5 Mussolini, in addressing a great victory celebration, had announced "Ethiopia is Italian." Four days later the Duce decreed that all of Ethiopia was "placed under full and complete sovereignty of the Kingdom of Italy," and that the "title of Emperor of Ethiopia is assumed for himself and for his successors by the King of Italy." By a further decree on June 1 Ethiopia, Eritrea, and Italian Somaliland were organized into a single unit to be known as Italian East Africa. Marshal Badoglio, commander of the army which had captured the Ethiopian capital, was made the first viceroy.

Within an incredibly short time and at the cost of a billion dollars Mussolini thus secured for Italy an empire of 350,000 square miles with a population of approximately ten million. Whether the gains made warranted the expenditures required, only a careful geological survey of Ethiopia's resources could tell. Some coal, iron, and other metals are to be found in the territory, and there have been repeated rumors of gold and petroleum, though the presence of the latter remains to be ascertained. There seems little doubt that the region can be developed to produce cereals, cotton, coffee, and livestock, all of which Italy is at present compelled to import. That the conquest will appreciably relieve Italy's overpopulation seems doubtful, however. Fascist leaders spoke confidently of locating half a million colonists in the fertile lands of Ethiopia within a very few years. Even granted that such colonization is possible, it is perfectly obvious that in itself this will not relieve Italy's pressure of population, which is still increasing at the rate of 400,000 each year. Italy's economic difficulties, it appears, still remain to be solved.

## ITALY VERSUS THE LEAGUE

When her troops advanced into Ethiopia on October 3, Italy embarked upon a struggle not only against the Ethiopians but against the League of Nations as well. In world history the latter was probably much more important than the former in so far as the issues at stake were concerned. In the ensuing months was tested whether the nations through collective action but without resort to military measures could successfully protect a weak country against a strong and aggressive power.

On October 7 the League Council decided that "the Italian government has resorted to war [2] in disregard of its covenants under Article 12 of the Covenant of the League of Nations." The Council's decision was then referred to the Assembly, which at once concurred in the verdict. The latter thereupon appointed a committee to consider what measures should be taken under Article 16 dealing with sanctions. By October 19 five proposals had been drafted. The first provided for immediately placing an arms embargo against Italy and lifting any existing embargo against Ethiopia. The second provided for financial sanctions which were to become completely effective by October 31. The third forbade the importation—directly or indirectly—of all Italian goods. The fourth forbade the exportation to Italy—directly or indirectly—of a list of key war materials,[3] and the fifth provided that League members would try to replace imports from Italy by imports from states which normally had profitable markets in Italy. These proposals were accepted by most of the member states, and the Assembly committee eventually declared that all sanctions against Italy should be in effect by November 18.

[2] As in the case of Japan in Manchuria, Italy did not actually declare war upon Ethiopia.

[3] Included were transport animals of various kinds, rubber, tin and tin ore, and other metals and minerals. The Canadian delegate to the League proposed that an embargo be placed upon petroleum, coal, iron, and steel, also, and the suggestion was adopted "in principle," provided the plan would not come into force "until conditions for rendering it effective appear to be realized." It was generally felt that such an embargo could not be effective if the United States and Germany did not co-operate with the League. Early in October President Roosevelt, acting under the terms of a neutrality resolution passed by Congress in the summer of 1935, had announced that Italy and Ethiopia were at war and had placed an embargo on arms shipments to both belligerents. Furthermore, he had warned United States citizens not to travel on ships of either belligerent and had declared that Americans trading with either country did so at their own risk. It was vigorously maintained by many, however, that the President possessed no authority to embargo such commodities as petroleum.

To counteract these proposed sanctions, numerous steps were being taken by the Italian government to conserve resources. Scores of decrees were issued to control the supplies of foodstuffs and raw materials. Drastic economies were introduced to save food, coal, and other commodities. Certain days, for instance, became meatless days. Mussolini had said that economic sanctions would be met by discipline, sobriety, and a spirit of sacrifice. Probably the most spectacular instance of this last was the nation-wide donation of gold wedding rings on "Faith Day" in December, 1935, in order to swell the nation's gold reserve. Foreign trade was placed entirely in the hands of the government, and all private banking was abolished. At the same time desperate efforts were made to nullify the program of sanctions by increasing Italy's trade with the nonsanctionist countries—the United States, Germany, Austria, Hungary, Switzerland, and Albania.

Nevertheless, by the beginning of 1936 the effect of sanctions began to be seriously felt in Italy. The latter's exports to sanctionist countries for the first three months of 1936 fell terrifically. But unfortunately for the success of the sanctionist policy, Italy's trade with nonsanctionist countries either increased or remained relatively the same as in the preceding year. Despite the cutting off of trade in war munitions, for instance, the exports of the United States to Italy for the first three months of 1936 were practically the same in dollars as in the corresponding period of the preceding year. Nevertheless, the drain on Italy's meager gold reserves continued, the known net loss of gold from the beginning of sanctions until May 1, 1936, being computed at $156,602,500. By September, 1936, it was estimated, Italy's gold reserves might be exhausted. What the effect upon Italy would have been had the League in November at once adopted the Canadian proposal to put oil, coal, steel, and iron on the embargo list may well be imagined.

Meanwhile, the League's committee on sanctions had met in January, 1936, to consider the possible application of a petroleum embargo and had decided that the question needed further study. But the demand for an oil embargo continued to grow, and on March 2 British Foreign Secretary Eden announced that Great Britain favored such an embargo and was prepared to join in its early application. French Foreign Minister Flandin, on the other hand, desired that one more attempt at conciliation be made before resort to the embargo. Consequently, action on the oil sanction was deferred for forty-eight hours in order that the Committee of Thirteen might make a fresh appeal to Italy and Ethiopia to end the war on terms "within the League Covenant's framework." This appeal was sent on March 3 and stated that the Committee of Thirteen would meet one week later to consider the replies. Before that date, however, Hitler's announcement (March 7) of the remilitarization of the Rhineland introduced a new element into an already complicated situation and definitely ended the possibility of France's supporting an oil embargo.

Italy's annexation of Ethiopia on May 5 presented a new problem— should the League recognize Italy's conquest as a *fait accompli* which it had failed to prevent, and now remove sanctions, or should it maintain that Italy had gone to war in disregard of her League obligations and continue economic sanctions against her, regardless of her victory? The British government appeared to favor the "common-sense" policy of abandoning sanctions. On the other hand, the Little Entente, the Balkan Entente, and the so-called neutrals all pronounced in favor of continuing sanctions. When the Council convened on May 11, it decided that further time was necessary "to permit its members to consider the situation created by the serious new steps taken by the Italian government," and voted to resume its discussion of the Italo-Ethiopian conflict on June 15. In the meantime sanctions would continue. It appeared to be the general opinion, however, that, if on June 15 the Council failed to abandon its sanctionist policy, Italy would quit the League.

On June 2 Argentina formally requested the League to convoke the Assembly to examine the situation brought about by the annexation of Ethiopia, and four weeks later a special meeting of the Assembly opened in Geneva. On July 4 the Assembly adopted a resolution in which, while "remaining firmly attached to the principles of the Covenant . . . excluding the settlement of territorial questions by force," it recommended that its committee on sanctions should make the necessary proposals to bring the sanctions to an end. Two days later this committee fixed July 15 as the date on which economic and financial sanctions against Italy should be suspended. Italy, it appeared, had won.

# LIBERAL AND NAZI GERMANY

GERMANY emerged from the World War defeated but with a new political regime which was distinguished for its liberalism and democracy. Although compelled to wrestle with almost insuperable problems, the liberal republic survived until it was fatally hit by the world-wide economic collapse of 1929. During the depression years which followed, conditions in Germany came to be not unlike those existing in Italy from 1920 to 1922, and the popular reaction in the former was very similar to that which had occurred in the latter. In 1933 Germany finally came into the control of the Nazis, who in their so-called Third Reich inaugurated a regime in many ways like that of the Fascists in Italy, one which was vastly different from that set up by the German constitution of 1919.

## THE WEIMAR CONSTITUTION

For a time, after the downfall of the empire,[1] it looked as though Germany might adopt a soviet form of government, for tens of thousands of Communists—called Spartacists in 1918—were determined to establish in Germany the rule of the proletariat on the Russian Bolshevik model. Karl Liebknecht was the "voice," Rosa Luxemburg the "brain," of this group during the early weeks of the republic. In December, 1918, they stirred up a revolt among the sailors stationed in Berlin, but the Majority Socialist Friedrich Ebert, who had succeeded Prince Max as chancellor, successfully suppressed the uprising by calling upon the veteran troops of the old regime. A month later the Communists and Independent Socialists together attempted to overthrow the republican government, but after ten days of bitter fighting their movement collapsed. Liebknecht, "while attempting to escape," was shot; and Rosa Luxemburg, attacked on the way to prison, was likewise killed. The political future of Germany, it appeared, was to be decided not by street fighting but by the legally chosen representatives of the German people.

[1] For the collapse of the German Empire, see pages 464–471.

As the time for the election of the National Assembly approached, political parties became active. The German Nationalist Party, composed of the conservatives, the Pan-Germans, the militarists, and the majority of the Junker class, succeeded to the old Conservative Party. During the election campaign its leaders openly avowed their monarchical sentiments. The Right wing of the old National Liberal Party organized itself into the German People's Party, which posed as the champion of liberalism in the new state. Although it preferred monarchy, it announced its acceptance of republican government. It specifically denounced all class rule, strikes, socialization, communism, and anarchy. It was the party of "big business" and was ably led by Gustav Stresemann. The Center Party supported the democratic republic but was strongly opposed to all attempts to establish a socialistic regime. It favored the maintenance of the federal character of Germany, universal suffrage, proportional representation, opening of all offices to all classes, and the adoption of a bill of rights. Its outstanding leader was Matthias Erzberger.

The Left wing of the old National Liberals united with the former Progressive Party to form the German Democratic Party, the first bourgeois party to organize after the revolution. In addition to supporting the republic it advocated the partial socialization of industry, the prosecution of war profiteers, and the adoption of a single progressive capital tax. It denounced the "divine right" of kings, the "squirearchy," and the military bureaucracy. The Majority Socialists proposed a scientific and gradual policy of socialization to be accomplished through the ordinary channels of parliamentary government. Of all the parties in opposition to the existing provisional government, the Independent Socialists conducted the most bitter campaign, accusing the Majority Socialists of treason to the cause of socialism. The Communists, because of their aversion to parliamentary tactics in any form, refused to take part in the election.

On January 19, 1919, national elections were held, with over 30,500,-000 men and women voting in this first German election under universal suffrage. Because of the system of proportional representation the strength of each party was fairly represented in the number of seats it obtained. The Majority Socialists stood first, followed by the Centrists, the Democrats, the Nationalists, the Independent Socialists, and the People's Party. Although the Majority Socialists elected by far the largest number of delegates to the assembly, they did not control a majority, so that a coalition now became necessary. When the National Assembly met at Weimar in February, the Majority Socialist government therefore gave way to the "Weimar Coalition," composed of Majority Socialists, Centrists, and Democrats, under the leadership of the Majority Socialist Scheidemann. Friedrich Ebert, who since the preceding November had served as chancellor, was then elected the first president of the German Republic.

Following the establishment of a temporary government, the National Assembly at once turned its attention to constitution-making. It could not, however, devote its whole attention to this task, for it was called upon to maintain internal order, to provide food for the starving population, to re-establish the national economic life, and to conclude peace with the Allies. Nor was it left to fulfill these arduous duties in peace and quiet. A Communist revolt in Berlin early in March was put down only after twelve hundred persons had been killed and property to the value of millions had been destroyed. In Munich another Communist uprising, provoked by a Nationalist's murder of Kurt Eisner, the Bavarian premier, led to the proclamation of a soviet republic which was not suppressed for two months.

Eventually, however, a constitution was drafted and accepted on July 31 by a vote of 262 (Majority Socialists, Centrists, Democrats) to 75 (Independent Socialists, People's Party, Nationalists). On August 11 it received the signature of President Ebert, and three days later it came into force by presidential proclamation. On August 21 President Ebert took the oath of office required by the new constitution before the last session of the National Assembly at Weimar. The assembly, however, did not dissolve with the conclusion of its constituent work but constituted itself a legislative body, which from September 30, 1919, sat in the Reichstag building in Berlin.

It has been said that "the constitution of a nation is its apparel, its mantle." The German people replaced their former royal robe with the latest mode of the plainer garb of democracy, choosing a republic in which political authority was derived from the people.[2] Every member state had to have a republican constitution, and representatives had to "be elected by the universal, equal, direct and secret suffrage of all German citizens, both men and women, according to the

---

[2] The government as here discussed is that which existed prior to the drastic changes which were introduced in consequence of the National Socialist revolution of 1933. For subsequent modifications, see pages 676–678.

principles of proportional representation." The chancellor and the ministers required for the administration of their offices the confidence of the Reichstag and had to resign if the latter by formal resolution withdrew its confidence. The republic was therefore a truly representative democracy.

The executive of the republic consisted of the president and the cabinet, composed of the chancellor and other ministers. The president was elected by the direct vote of the people, held office for seven years, and might be re-elected. Like the French president and the British king, the German president had little real power, every executive order requiring the countersignature of the chancellor or some other minister. The chancellor, responsible to the Reichstag, was the one who determined the general course of policy and assumed responsibility therefor.

The national legislature consisted of two houses, the Reichstag and the Reichsrat. The former was composed of members elected for a term of four years by the direct vote of all men and women over twenty years of age. It might be dissolved by the president, but only once for the same cause. The Reichsrat, like the former Bundesrat, represented the states. In it each state had at least one vote, the larger states having one vote for each 700,000 inhabitants; but no state might have more than two fifths of all the votes. The Reichsrat functioned merely as a sort of "brake on legislation," and contrary to the condition under the empire, the Reichstag was by far the more powerful branch of the legislature.

The constitution contained many compromises, but in general it reflected the more moderate desires of the Democratic and Social Democratic parties, with numerous concessions to the Centrists in matters relating to education and religion. The finished document was, as might have been expected, far too conservative to please the Independent Socialists and much too liberal to suit the parties of the Right; yet, in view of the manifold difficulties which confronted the republic in the years following its adoption, the new framework of government proved reasonably strong.

## THE DEFENSE OF THE REPUBLIC

To draft and set up a republican form of government for Germany was one thing; to defend it against the onslaughts of domestic foes of the Left and Right was quite another. From the day of its proclamation the republic encountered the bitter opposition of the Communists, who believed, not in democracy, but in the rule of the proletariat organized in soviets on the Russian model. The first open attempts to overthrow the republic came from this group, but their numerous riots, strikes, military uprisings, and political *coups d'état* during 1919 were eventually quelled by the government. Although the Communists continued to exist and fluctuated in political strength according to the exigencies of the republic, it was not until after 1930, when economic conditions became critical, that their numbers became so great as to be an important political factor.

Somewhat in proportion as the threat from the Communists declined in the early years of the republic, that from the reactionaries of the extreme Right increased. So long as Germany was actually threatened by communism, the reactionaries delayed their attack on the republic, for they feared communism more than bourgeois republicanism. But by 1920 the immediate danger from communism seemed to have passed, and the Junkers, Pan-Germanists, irreconcilable militarists, and remnants of the prewar Conservative Party took heart. If the Germans rejected communism, perhaps they would accept monarchism.

In March, 1920, the reactionaries struck their first blow against the republic in what is known as the Kapp-Lüttwitz *Putsch*. General Baron von Lüttwitz, commander-in-chief of Berlin, suddenly seized the capital, and his confederate, Dr. Wolfgang von Kapp, was proclaimed chancellor. But, though President Ebert's government fled precipitately to Dresden and then on to Stuttgart, the *Putsch* proved a miserable failure. Some of the monarchist leaders refused their active support, and the bulk of the army and of the propertied classes failed to rally to it. At the same time it encountered the determined opposition of the working classes, to whom President Ebert issued a passionate appeal to inaugurate a general strike. Necessities like water, gas, and electricity were suddenly shut off; railway and tramway services ceased. The revolutionary government was paralyzed and collapsed within a week, Kapp fleeing to Sweden.

During the next three years events in connection with the fulfillment of the peace treaty provided numerous opportunities for the reactionary monarchists to criticize the republican regime and to seek to weaken and discredit it. The losses of territory by plebiscites, the Allied demand for the punishment of German "war criminals"—

many of whom were looked upon as national heroes in the fatherland, the reparations and disarmament demands, the forced disbandment of the Bavarian *Einwohnerwehr* (citizen guard), all presented points of attack for the monarchists. A "stab in the back" legend was developed to the effect that all the postwar ills arose from the military defeat, which in turn had been caused by the prearmistice revolutionary intrigues of the present republicans. The past glories of the Hohenzollern monarchy were constantly placed over against the existing ills of the democratic republic. A campaign of agitation, centering in Bavaria, was directed against all who had played a part in the events leading to the signing of the Versailles treaty, and a series of political murders began which eventually claimed such distinguished figures as Matthias Erzberger, the Centrist leader, and Walther Rathenau, a Democrat who at the time of his assassination was minister for foreign affairs.

In 1923, when Germany was in chaos as a result of French occupation of the Ruhr and German passive resistance, various plots were hatched in Bavaria looking toward the overthrow of the Berlin government. One reactionary group under the leadership of Gustav von Kahr plotted the establishment of a directory which, backed by the military, would assume control of the Reich. Another group led by Ludendorff and Adolf Hitler, the latter destined to become the Nazi dictator of Germany, planned to march on Berlin, where Hitler would be proclaimed president under the military dictatorship of Ludendorff. Hitler's plans conflicted with those of Kahr, with the result that the two factions consumed their ardor in quarreling between themselves, and the "beer-cellar rebellion" of November 8 collapsed without having seriously threatened the republic. The chief conspirators were arrested and tried, but friendly courts let them off with lenient treatment.

In the midst of the republic's struggles against domestic foes of the Left and the Right its territorial integrity was seriously threatened. Almost simultaneously with the Hitler-Ludendorff *Putsch* in Bavaria came a separatist movement in the Rhineland which aimed, not to overthrow the German Republic, but to bring about its disintegration. The first blow was struck in September, 1923, when the separatists seized Düsseldorf in the Ruhr. During the following month Aachen, Coblenz, Bonn, Wiesbaden, Trier, and Mainz were occupied by separatist forces. The "Autonomous Government of the Palatinate" was proclaimed at Speyer in November and was at once officially recognized by the French high commissioner. Approximately 19,000 officials who refused to make declarations of loyalty to the Palatinate government were deported. But the unnatural Rhineland movement failed. Its leaders soon fell to quarreling with one another; the great majority of the lawful officials and population of the region refused to support it; the Belgian and British governments opposed it. In January, 1924, the president of the "Autonomous Government of the Palatinate" was assassinated. In February the French officials withdrew their support, and by the end of the month the separatist regime in the Rhineland had ended.

### THE CURRENCY DEBACLE

While German statesmen of the new regime were engaged in a life-and-death struggle to prevent the destruction or disintegration of the republic, they were forced to deal also with the reparations problem, which has already been discussed. At the same time they were compelled to wrestle with the perplexing and baffling problem of a currency rapidly depreciating toward the vanishing point. The republic had inherited a currency which was already greatly inflated, but the exigencies of the period of demobilization and readjustment had brought further inflation, as had the necessity of making reparations payments. By May, 1921, the mark had declined to 60 (normally 4.2) to the dollar. On June 1, 1921, the Reichsbank for the first time began to pay a premium for gold coin, thus officially recognizing the inflation. This depreciation of the mark in turn operated to keep the national budget unbalanced, for taxes assessed with the mark at one figure were paid later with a mark depreciated below that figure. The continued deficits which resulted led to still more inflation. By November, 1922, the mark had sunk to 7000 to the dollar.

The occupation of the Ruhr by the French and the Belgians and the adoption by Germany of the policy of passive resistance, with the accompanying need for subsidizing the idle workers, started the mark upon its toboggan slide. By the close of January, 1923, it stood at 50,000 to the dollar. By July it stood at 160,000, and during the month it declined to 1,100,000 to the dollar. From this date began the so-called repudiation of the mark. By the middle of November it had become practically worthless, being quoted in Berlin at 2,520,000,000,000 and in Cologne at about 4,000,000,000,000 to the dollar. Even to print the currency needed was a tremendous task.

The economic and social results of this practical repudiation of the mark were terrific. The obvious effect of the devaluation was the destruction of savings, pensions, and insurance. Those who had laid by or inherited a sum sufficient to maintain them in comfort according to the standards of their class suddenly discovered their capital dwindling. Of what value were 100,000 marks invested in banks, bonds, or fixed annuities when the mark declined until it took 1,000,000,000 to buy a dollar's worth of food? The inevitable consequence of such a declining currency was the forced transfer of wealth from the creditor to the debtor class. Mortgages were lifted, bonds retired, and notes paid off with currency worth only an infinitesimal fraction of its face value.

Undoubtedly the most lasting of the disastrous results of the currency inflation was the destruction or disintegration of a great part of the previously prosperous middle class. This vital class was, in the words of one German, "economically guillotined," and many of its members were forced into the ranks of the working people. On the other hand, the wealth and power of some of the great industrialists increased enormously. Availing themselves of artificially cheap labor, extensive Reichsbank loans, and a rapidly falling currency, they piled up tremendous paper profits. With these they purchased substantial assets abroad, enlarged and modernized their plants at home, or paid off loans and bonded indebtedness. Thus the mighty capitalists and industrialists profited enormously by the inflation and showed no great concern to check it until the mark had become worthless.

When, however, farmers and merchants began to refuse to sell food for worthless currency, when "the catastrophe of currency developed into a catastrophe of the food and other supplies, which was worse than in the worst periods of the war," when plunderings and riots began to be of daily occurrence, the German government in desperation decided to create a new bank of issue and a new currency. On October 15, 1923, a decree for the establishment of the bank was issued. In November Hjalmar Schacht, general manager of one of Germany's largest banks, was appointed special currency commissioner with the task of stabilizing the mark and introducing the new currency. His first step was to stop the printing presses in order to prevent further inflation. Simultaneously he issued a new currency, supposedly based upon a blanket mortgage on all productive lands and industries of Germany to the amount of 3,200,000,000 gold marks. The new currency was stabilized at the old rate of 4.2 to the dollar and circulated along with the old mark at the ratio of one to one trillion. At the same time Finance Minister Luther by heroic measures balanced the budget and ended the need for inflation. Eventually, in October, 1924, the Dawes plan loan [3] added to the working capital of the country and provided the economic backing which the situation required. With the organization of the new Reichsbank, the new currency became known as the Reichsmark. Provision was made that the old depreciated marks might, until July 5, 1925, be converted into the new Reichsmark at the ratio of one trillion to one.

## STRESEMANN'S POLICY OF CONCILIATION

Meanwhile, German statesmen had been compelled to formulate a national foreign policy. The latter was inevitably based upon certain definite features of Germany's postwar situation. To begin with, an important part of her national territory was occupied by alien troops. Her military and naval forces had been drastically curtailed and were under the supervision of Inter-Allied commissions of control. Her Rhineland had been demilitarized. Her overseas colonies had been taken from her, and in Europe her territory had been dismembered and reduced by cessions to other countries. She had been denied the right to have her Austrian kinsmen unite with her even when they so desired. Furthermore, she was weighted down with the burden of an indefinitely large reparations obligation and with the odium of "war guilt." She found herself isolated, almost an outcast among the powers of Europe. Her former Habsburg ally had been utterly destroyed; her lesser allies had been defeated and rendered insignificant in European affairs. She had been refused an invitation to become a member of the League of Nations.

These fundamental facts practically dictated Germany's foreign policy, the fundamental aim of which was to throw off the various limitations on her sovereignty in order that she might regain her prewar position of power and influence in world affairs. More specifically, she sought (1) to reduce and ultimately to escape from the reparations indemnity which she was obligated to pay, (2) to liberate her territory

[3] For the Dawes plan, see pages 547–549.

from foreign occupation, (3) to secure the removal of the Inter-Allied commissions of control, (4) to regain her freedom in military and naval matters, (5) to restore her right to fortify and protect the Rhineland, and (6) to emerge from isolation and once more hold a place as an equal among the great powers. Ultimately, she sought to redeem the Saar, to secure a union with Austria, to bridge the gap between Germany and East Prussia, and to regain at least some of her colonies.

Immediately after the war many German statesmen were inclined to look to the east for their country's salvation. They cordially hated the victorious Allies, spurned any move toward reconciliation with them, repudiated their dictated peace treaty, declined to adopt a policy of fulfillment, and hoped eventually, by forming an alliance with Russia, to be able to defy them and overthrow the treaty. The economic recovery of Germany they would hasten by re-establishing trade relations with Russia and by extending German economic control over the boundless resources of the Soviet Union. The most spectacular step taken in this policy of eastern orientation was the signing of the treaty of Rapallo with Russia in April, 1922. Germany accorded *de jure* recognition to the Soviet government, and each renounced all war claims and prewar indebtedness. Probably the most important articles of the treaty, so far as Germany was concerned, were those providing for the extension of mutual facilities of trade. The results of the attitude of defiance were unfortunate, however. Not only were none of the immediate ends of her foreign policy attained, but in 1923 Germany found herself further limited and weakened by the Franco-Belgian occupation of the Ruhr.

Those in Germany who favored a policy of western orientation believed that the republic's salvation was to be found only with the aid and co-operation of the Allies. They demanded a "policy of fulfillment and reconciliation." The one who more than all others developed a constructive foreign policy for Germany based on the idea of western orientation was Gustav Stresemann, who assumed the office of foreign minister in the critical days of August, 1923, and held it through ten shifting ministries down to his regrettable death on October 3, 1929. A member of the bourgeoisie, associated with big business, he belonged before the war to the National Liberal Party. During the revolutionary days he formed the German People's Party and became its leader. Content during the early years of the republic to assume a more or less negative policy of opportunism, his assumption of a share of the governmental burden of responsibility in 1923 led him to become increasingly constructive in his policies. Under his guidance the republic chose the path leading toward fulfillment and reconciliation.

Real gains came to Germany from Stresemann's policy. The Dawes Committee's investigation brought the settling of the method and amounts of reparations payments in accordance with the views of impartial experts, and the introduction of the Dawes plan brought financial assistance which made the economic rehabilitation of Germany possible. It led within a year to the military evacuation of the Ruhr area and the cities of Ruhrort, Duisburg, and Düsseldorf. It secured for Germany admission to the League of Nations (1926) with a permanent seat on the Council. Early in the following year it brought the abolition of the Inter-Allied commissions of control, their duties being transferred to the League, of which Germany was now an influential member.

In 1928 Stresemann secured the initiation of negotiations looking toward a final settlement of the reparations problem and the early evacuation of the Rhineland. As a result, the definite total which was fixed for German reparations liabilities was placed far below that originally fixed by the Reparations Commission in 1921; and it was agreed that all Allied forces of occupation should be withdrawn from the Rhineland by June 30, 1930. But the influence of Stresemann's policy of fulfillment and reconciliation did not end with his death. It continued for a number of years to affect the Allied attitude toward Germany and undoubtedly played a part in the practical cancellation of reparations payments at Lausanne in 1932.

### Economic Recovery and Decline

Not unrelated to Stresemann's successful foreign policy was the rapid economic recovery which the republic experienced during the five years after 1924. Prewar Germany had been the third most powerful wealth-producing organism in the world, possessing an abundance of coal and iron, a closely unified and efficient railway system, a profitable merchant marine, extensive colonies, and large foreign investments. It has been pointed out how the treaty of Versailles drastically changed all this.[4]

[4] See page 496.

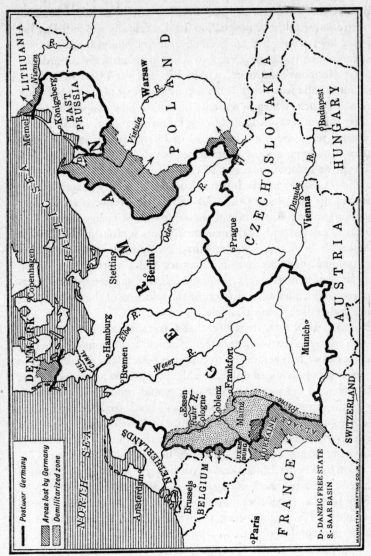

GERMANY BEFORE AND AFTER THE WORLD WAR

Postwar Germany
Areas lost by Germany
Demilitarized zone

D - DANZIG FREE STATE
S - SAAR BASIN

But Germany set resolutely to work to rebuild or adapt her economic machine to the new situation. In this task she was aided by the fact that her territory had not been devastated by the war and that she had, consequently, no great reconstruction problem such as burdened France. Germany's factories, within her postwar frontiers at least, were intact. She was aided in the second place, strange to say, by her currency debacle, which in no sense diminished the real wealth of the country but rather contributed to the industrial recovery of Germany in several ways. By the sale abroad of German currency, drafts in marks, banknotes, and other securities which became worthless as a result of the inflation, real wealth estimated as high as $2,000,000,000 came into German hands. Inflation enabled Germany to compete for a time in the markets of the world with goods produced at home by labor unusually cheap, while at the same time it enabled her industrialists to expand and modernize their plants with loans which were repaid with an almost worthless currency. By 1924, as the Dawes experts pointed out, Germany's industries and transportation system were in admirable physical condition. All that she needed was international credit, and, as a result of the introduction of the Dawes plan, abundant credit became available.

It is not surprising, therefore, that Germany's economic recovery was rapid in the years that followed. She had lost a considerable proportion of her coal resources; to compensate for this, she resorted to the more extensive use of electricity. She possessed water power whose total potential output, it is calculated, would produce in power annually the equivalent of 32,000,000 tons of black coal; this she began to develop. She had vast beds of lignite or "brown coal"; these she began to transform into electricity, constructing in their vicinity great generating plants. In her steel industry new methods of furnace construction and better utilization of coal brought lower costs. She soon reached the place where she again had a surplus of coal for export, and by 1927 her production of steel ingots was back nearly to the prewar figure. The rolling stock in her railways became superior in quality and condition to that of prewar days. The gross tonnage of her merchant vessels rose from 400,000 to 3,738,067 by 1928, and possessed the great advantage of being nearly all new.

German industrialists felt confident of their ability to achieve success. They planned to resume their prewar commercial and industrial relations and hoped to regain the place in the world's markets which they had held in 1914. To hasten the republic's economic recovery they introduced into German industrial life the "rationalization movement," to which they ascribed the rapid rise of American industry. Mass production and industrial efficiency became their watchwords. Standardization of products and materials, scientific planning and management, elimination of duplication and useless competition by the formation of trusts and combines—these became their goals. Undoubtedly greater efficiency was achieved. The average output per man was considerably increased in various types of industry and even in agriculture. Furthermore, greater protection was given to home industry by modifying the German customs tariff act, and German interests abroad were advanced by the conclusion of commercial treaties with all of the important powers. By 1929 the total volume of industrial output in Germany exceeded that of 1913.

In 1929, however, it began to be apparent that the republic's rapid economic recovery could not continue. That recovery had been facilitated in part by extensive loans which had been obtained from foreign bankers. In 1929 the sources of these loans began to dry up. Continued economic recovery required a further extension of German markets abroad. But the high tariff walls raised by other countries, the successful competition of the United States, Great Britain, and France, and the inability to regain to any great extent the prewar markets in Russia, operated to prevent that necessary extension. Moreover, the loss of wages by those who were rendered superfluous in industry by the introduction of "rationalization," and the decrease in prices of agricultural products resulting from world overproduction, both brought a noticeable decline in the purchasing power of the home market. In 1929 German industrial activity began to decline, and unemployment began to rise. The resultant situation raised serious problems for the German government and inevitably reacted upon the political situation.

## THE FIRST DECADE OF POLITICS

During the first decade of the republic Germany had one presidential campaign and four parliamentary elections. On February 28, 1925, President Ebert died. As chancellor or president he had been at the head of the government ever since the proclamation of the republic on November 9, 1918. Although originally favoring a democratic parliamentary monarchy like Great Britain's, he had accepted the republic after its proclamation by the proletariat and had used the influence of his unselfish patriotism to strengthen and stabilize it. An artisan and the son of an artisan, lacking the academic training so highly esteemed in Germany, a plain man of the people, his presence at the head of the state had gone far toward winning the radical proletariat from Bolshevism to the support of the republic. President Ebert's term of office had been provisional. The unsettled conditions during the early months of the republic had convinced the members of the Weimar assembly that it would be unwise to hold a popular election at that time. They had therefore elected Ebert president without referring the question to the people. His death precipitated the first popular presidential election, for the German constitution made no provision for a vice-president.

German electoral procedure called for one or two elections to determine the popular choice. In the first balloting a candidate to be successful had to receive a clear majority of all votes cast. If no candidate received such a majority, a second election had to be held in which the candidate receiving the largest number of votes, whether a majority or not, was elected. Seven candidates were presented in the election of March 29, 1925, and none received the requisite majority. A second vote therefore became necessary, and party coalitions were the result. The Centrists, Democrats, and Social Democrats, who together had polled over 13,000,000 votes in the first election, finally agreed to support Wilhelm Marx, leader of the Centrists. The Communists refused to join this coalition and persisted in running their own candidate. The combined vote of the parties of the Right in the first election had been less than 12,000,000, so that they were now confronted with a serious problem. They solved it unexpectedly by dropping all their earlier nominees and naming as their common candidate the aged Field Marshal Paul von Hindenburg, the idolized hero of the German people.

In the first poll some 12,000,000 qualified voters had failed to participate. In the final election on April 26, between three and four million of these lethargic citizens were galvanized into action by the dynamic magic of Hindenburg's name, and nearly three million of them cast their ballots for the war hero—enough to turn the scale in his favor. By many it was feared that the election of Field Marshal von Hindenburg to the presidency by "militarists" and "monarchists" would lead to the overthrow of the republic. But the new president took the oath of loyalty to the republic without qualification and apparently sought sincerely to fulfill it—at least until 1932.

In the early parliamentary elections the voting usually resolved itself into a contest between the so-called Weimar parties, which had been responsible for Germany's liberal constitution, and the parties on the Right and Left, which were theoretically opposed to the acceptance of the democratic republic. The outcome of the elections varied with the exigencies of the economic situation. In June, 1920, and again in May, 1924, the parties of the extreme Right and the extreme Left gained at the expense of the middle groups, although the latter, with the aid of the People's Party, were able to retain a bare working majority. In a special election of December, 1924, the Nationalists on the Right increased their Reichstag representation so much that they stood second only to the Social Democrats. The cabinet which assumed control of the government after this election was a Right-Center group consisting of members of the Nationalist, People's, and Center parties.

The number of ministries which the German Republic had during the first decade of its existence was in marked contrast with the few which served during the period of the empire. Germany had a multiparty system. The multiplicity of parties was a direct advantage to the chancellor under the old imperial regime, since he was responsible only to the Kaiser and could play off one party against another. But now that the chancellor had to have a majority of the Reichstag behind him, the multiparty system resulted in frequent changes of the ministry. In the shifting of the ministries the Center Party well exemplified its name. Its strong sense of moderation and responsibility made it the nucleus of practically all of the coalition governments of the postwar period. Its chief task was to determine whether it would ally itself with the Left or the Right. The trend, however, during the first nine years was steadily toward the Right. Although the first four ministries, beginning in November, 1918, were headed by Socialist chancellors, during the eight years after June, 1920, there was not a single Socialist chancellor, and only twice during that period were Socialists even included in the ministry. On the other hand, the People's Party four times had the chancellorship, and Nationalists were twice included in the government. In other words, the drift in German politics during these years was distinctly toward bourgeois control.

The fourth general elections for the Reichstag, in May, 1928, brought a swing back from the Right. The Nationalists lost heavily, while the Social Democrats and the Communists both increased, the latter outnumbering the People's Party and becoming the fourth largest group in the Reichstag. A Socialist, Hermann Müller, became chancellor and a "grand coalition," consisting of the People's Party, Centrists, Bavarian People's Party (an offshoot of the Centrists), Democrats, and Social Democrats, was organized under his leadership. Social Democratic dissatisfaction with financial reforms which were pushed through the Reichstag in an effort to solve the republic's pressing economic problems after 1929 brought the downfall of the Müller government in March, 1930. In the new government, headed by Heinrich Brüning, leader of the Centrists, the Social Democrats refused to participate. It consisted, therefore, of only the middle parties, and marked a renewed swing back toward the Right.

The chief task of Brüning's government was to secure the adoption of a budget which would wipe out the steadily increasing national deficit, but conflicts between party, class, and local interests in the Reichstag constituted a serious handicap. Finally, in July, 1930, after the Reichstag had rejected the government's budget, President Hindenburg dissolved that body and called for new elections to be held in September. In the meantime, availing himself of the "emergency clause" (Article 48) of the constitution, the president inaugurated a financial program which differed little from the one the Reichstag had rejected.

## HITLER AND THE NATIONAL SOCIALISTS

The political group which benefited most from the economic depression and the growing spirit of unrest in Germany was the National Socialist Party,[5] whose chief was Adolf Hitler. This extremely nationalistic German leader was born (1889) not in Germany but in Austria, and was the son of a humble customs inspector of the Dual Monarchy. His formal education was somewhat limited, for he had been obliged to leave school at an early age because of financial difficulties. While yet a mere youth he went to Vienna for the purpose of studying architecture, but finding himself unable to enter the Painting Academy, he had had to be content with a position as

[5] The members of the party were often called Hitlerites, Nazis, or fascists.

draftsman and decorator. The Austrian capital Hitler had abhorred as a "racial Babylon," and it was during his years in Vienna, apparently, that he developed his bitter anti-Marxist and anti-Semitic hatreds.

Shortly before the World War began, Hitler moved to Munich, where he worked as a house painter. During the war he fought in the Bavarian army as a private and later as a sergeant, and acquitted himself so well that he was awarded the Iron Cross. Soon after the war he helped to organize in Munich the National Socialist German Workers' Party, and in February, 1920, a program of twenty-five points, formulated by Gottfried Feder, was adopted by the party.[6] This early program, somewhat analogous to the early platform of the Italian Fascists, was modified by later pronouncements of Hitler and was ultimately much expanded in a volume of memoirs entitled *Mein Kampf* (My Struggle). In 1921 Hitler began to harangue the crowds in the Munich beer gardens, especially denouncing the Jews, the capitalists, the French, the treaty of Versailles, and the German Republic. In 1923, as already pointed out, he co-operated with Ludendorff and others in an unsuccessful attempt to overthrow the German government, and was consequently sentenced to five years' imprisonment. After a prison term of only a few months, he was released but was forbidden for a time to make public speeches.

Hitler then devoted himself primarily to the task of organizing his followers, and in this work he closely followed the plans of Mussolini, whom he greatly admired. The swastika or hooked cross (卐) was adopted as the emblem of the National Socialist Party, which was further provided with an elaborate ritual and a military organization. Party members were required to pay small monthly dues and were permitted in turn to wear the party uniform—a brown shirt with a black swastika on an armband. Like Mussolini's *squadristi*, Hitler had his "storm troops" (*Sturmabteilungen*), whose duties in the beginning were to protect Nazi meetings and to interfere with Communist gatherings. In addition, the organization had its smaller group of "defense squads" (*Schutzstaffeln*), which constituted a sort of party police for protecting Nazi leaders and for executing unusually difficult tasks. In order to reach the whole German people with the Nazi program the country was organized into

[6] The text of this document may be found in *Current History*, Volume XXXVI, pages 170–172.

twenty-six districts, each in turn subdivided into "cells" to which a number of trained Nazi speakers were assigned.

So far as organization was concerned, therefore, the National Socialists were in a position to make great gains in the election of 1930. Their program, too, was of such a nature as to attract large numbers of adherents in a time of national humiliation and economic depression. They were extremely nationalistic in their aims, seeking to stimulate German patriotism, to unite all Germans (those in Austria, Czechoslovakia, Poland, Holland, and Alsace included) in a common state, to regain for Germany her lost colonies and her parity with the other great powers in national armaments, to secure the cancellation of the peace treaties and thereby the refutation of war guilt and the repudiation of reparations obligations. They advocated, too, certain social and economic reforms such as the abolition of all unearned income, the confiscation of war profits, the nationalization of the great trusts and large department stores, the guarantee by the government of employment and decent living conditions for German citizens (Jews could not be citizens), the abolition of speculation in land, the inauguration of agrarian reform, and the shifting of tax burdens from the workers and lower middle classes to the rich. All these reforms and achievements were to be the fruits of the "Third Reich" [7] which the National Socialists aimed to establish.

At a time when the number of unemployed in Germany was close to 4,000,000, when the burden of taxation was becoming constantly heavier, when no ray of hope for a way out of the economic depression was visible, it is not surprising, perhaps, that great numbers were won to the National Socialist standard by the magnetic oratory of Adolf Hitler. Although labor, in general, remained deaf to the Nazi leader's siren song, millions of others who were alarmed at the prospect of pauperization responded. From the German youth great numbers of university students and university graduates, moved by their discontent with a situation which failed to provide employment for the educated classes, joined the Nazi ranks. From the professional classes many who suffered from the keen competition of the Jews in medicine, law, banking, and trade were cheered

[7] The first Reich was the Holy Roman Empire; the second was created by Bismarck in 1871.

by the promise of the National Socialist anti-Semitic program. Unorganized retail shopkeepers and lesser capitalists, fearful of the encroachments of the great trusts, department stores, and chain stores,
found hope in the Nazi plan to nationalize such enterprises. Even
the peasants, burdened with debt and prevented by their concept
of private property from supporting the Communists and Socialists,
in many cases as a protest threw their support to the Nazis. Finally,
the great ranks of the white-collar classes, unemployed or poorly
paid, joined the Hitler movement almost *en masse*. When the votes
were finally counted at the close of the election of September 14,
1930, therefore, it was found that the National Socialists had made
tremendous gains. The 12 seats which they had held in the Reichstag at the time of its dissolution were now increased to 107, thus
giving to the Nazis a strength in the national legislature second
only to that of the Social Democrats.

### GOVERNMENT BY EMERGENCY DECREES

Despite the losses of the middle parties, Brüning's government
was enabled to continue in office through the support of the Social
Democrats, who threw their strength to it on a vote of confidence.
Again in December, 1930, however, President Hindenburg was
compelled to resort to emergency decrees in order to put into effect
the financial program of the government. But Brüning was confronted by a national financial crisis which grew steadily worse,
and in 1931 emergency decrees were once more issued in an attempt to increase income and reduce expenditures. The financial
crisis which was precipitated in that year and the efforts of the
powers through a moratorium and "standstill agreements" to prevent
a complete debacle have already been discussed.[8] Nevertheless, the
situation in Germany—both economic and political—continued to
be so critical that late in 1931 President Hindenburg felt compelled
to issue a new set of emergency decrees.

In order to spare the country the cost and excitement of a presidential election in a time of such political and economic distress,
Brüning suggested to the various party leaders early in 1932 that
Hindenburg's term be extended beyond the legal seven years. Hitler
opposed the suggestion, however, and, since the president declined

[8] See pages 556–557.

to use his emergency powers to prolong his own term, an election was called for March 13. Hindenburg and Hitler [9] were the principal candidates for the presidency in an election which witnessed a notable shift in party loyalties when contrasted with the campaign of 1925. The Social Democrats and the Centrists, who on the former occasion had opposed Hindenburg's election as a menace to the republic, were now his most stanch and active supporters; while the Nationalists and the monarchists, who had put forward the marshal as their candidate in 1925, now became his most determined opponents.

The voting on March 13 failed to bring the election of any candidate, for President Hindenburg lacked by approximately one half of one per cent the necessary majority of the votes. In the second election, held on April 10, Hitler increased his vote—this time to more than 13,400,000—but Hindenburg received a majority of approximately 2,200,000 over the combined votes for Hitler and Thälmann, the Communist candidate, and thus in his eighty-fifth year began his second term as president of the German Republic.

Although the outcome of the presidential election was by many interpreted as a popular mandate in favor of Brüning's policies, gains by the Nazis in state elections during the succeeding weeks indicated that there was a widespread and growing dissatisfaction with his government. Naturally, his attempts to enforce rigid economies in the government, coupled with his increases in taxation, reacted against his popularity. Furthermore, the feeling was becoming somewhat general that Brüning's system of governing by executive decree was a failure. In 1932 the unemployment figures rose to nearly 6,000,000, and the budgetary deficit mounted to $400,000,000. On May 30 Brüning finally resigned. [10]

The new chancellor chosen by Hindenburg was Colonel Franz von Papen, who as military attaché in Washington in 1915 had been recalled at President Wilson's request because of alleged violations of American neutrality. [11] The ministry which he selected was composed for the most part of nationalists and conservatives, and con-

[9] In February, 1932, Hitler became a German citizen by accepting appointment as an attaché of the Brunswick legation in Berlin.

[10] The immediate cause of Brüning's resignation was the president's refusal to sanction the chancellor's plan to provide relief by carving up into small farms some of the large estates of East Prussia.

[11] See page 425.

stituted a decided swing to the Right. Realizing that he could not hope to control a majority in the existing Reichstag, Chancellor von Papen had it dissolved immediately. Nothing, however, seemed to be able to stem the rising tide of Hitlerism. In the ensuing elections the Nazis more than doubled the number of seats in the Reichstag which they had obtained in 1930. Their new total of 230 seats gave them the largest number that any party had ever had in the history of the republic. Nevertheless, President Hindenburg rejected Hitler's demand that he be made chancellor. To escape a vote of no confidence Papen at once dissolved the recently elected Reichstag and again called for elections. On this occasion the Nazis lost some 2,000,000 votes, but still retained first place in the number of seats in the national legislature. On the other hand, the Communists increased their total number of seats to 100 and came within striking distance of the strength of the Social Democrats. It appeared that the workers were deserting the moderate Social Democratic Party to join the ranks of the more radical Communists.

President Hindenburg now invited Adolf Hitler to undertake to construct a government of national concentration, but the Nazi leader found himself unable to obtain the promise of majority support. The president in turn declined to entertain Hitler's proposal that he be appointed with dictatorial powers, and instead called to the chancellorship General Kurt von Schleicher, minister of defense in the Papen government. Schleicher's ministry, which was recruited largely from that of Papen, proved to be no more able to handle the situation than its predecessors. After less than two months in office General von Schleicher resigned on January 28, 1933.

### The National Socialist Revolution

Two days later Adolf Hitler was appointed chancellor at the head of a ministry in which two of the appointments were highly significant. The important post of minister of the interior was given to Wilhelm Frick, one of Hitler's Nazi colleagues in the Munich *Putsch* of 1923. An appointment as minister without portfolio went to Hermann Göring, next to Hitler the most powerful personality in the Nazi movement. Göring had also participated in the "beer-cellar rebellion," and to escape punishment at that time he had fled to Italy, where he spent two years in studying Fascism.

Regardless of the fact that they constituted a decided minority in the government, the Nazis at once set out to secure complete control. In the hope of gaining ascendancy in the Reichstag Hitler dissolved that body and called for new elections. During the ensuing five weeks Hitler's government resorted to strong-arm methods against the opposition, particularly the Communists, the Social Democrats, and the Centrists. Opposition newspapers were suspended or suppressed; opposition meetings were forbidden or broken up; opposition speakers were denied access to the radio, which became a Nazi monopoly. Five days before the elections a fire of incendiary origin nearly destroyed the Reichstag building.[12] The Communists were at once accused by the Nazis of being the perpetrators of this act of vandalism, and hundreds of Communist leaders were arrested. By dwelling upon the dangers of a Communist-Socialist plot to overthrow the government, the Nazis sought to cause a wave of anti-Communist hysteria to sweep the country. An emergency decree of the president suspended all constitutional provisions guaranteeing personal liberty, freedom of the press, liberty to hold meetings, and even secrecy of the mails.

On March 5, stirred by the propaganda and excitement of the preceding week, more than 39,000,000 German citizens went to the polls. Although the German workers still showed their militancy and strength by polling 7,000,000 votes for the Social Democrats and 4,800,000 for the Communists, although the Catholic Center parties showed their opposition to the Nazi program of suppression and intimidation by casting 5,500,000 votes and even increasing their Reichstag representation, the millions of ordinary "stay-at-homes" who participated in this election turned the tide in favor of the National Socialists. In the country as a whole the latter secured more than 17,000,000 votes, which, with the 3,000,000 votes of the Nationalists, gave the Hitler-Papen government about 52 per cent of the popular vote. With 288 Nazi representatives and 53 Nationalists, Hitler controlled a majority of the 648 seats in the new Reichstag.

Wearing his Nazi uniform, Chancellor Hitler appeared before the newly elected Reichstag at its first session and, much as Mussolini had done in 1922, demanded dictatorial powers for four years. In a single session the Reichstag rushed the enabling act granting these powers through the required three readings, and then adjourned

---

[12] The Hitlerites have been accused of deliberately burning the building in order to arouse fear of the Communists.

indefinitely.[13] Adolf Hitler thus after more than a decade of fighting achieved by constitutional methods the great triumph toward which he had looked forward. He was now chancellor of Germany and possessed of power greater by far than even the "iron chancellor," Bismarck, had ever wielded.

Any attempt to appraise the forces which brought about the National Socialist revolution must take into account four or five major factors. Perhaps first in importance was the world economic depression. In the years from 1924 to 1929, when Germany was experiencing an economic recovery, the Nazi movement made relatively little headway. But the misery and suffering resulting from four years of economic depression inevitably caused in Germany as in every other country a reaction against those in power. A second factor was the resurgence of a militant German nationalism, carefully cultivated by Hitler's exaltation of German racial superiority. With the rise of nationalism came a strong reaction (1) against the sense of humiliation resulting from defeat in the World War and from the harsh terms of the treaty of Versailles, (2) against the doctrines of men like Stresemann and Brüning, who had preached that the only pathway open to Germany was acknowledgment of defeat and fulfillment of the demands of the victors, (3) against the Weimar middle parties, which had pursued a policy of conciliation and fulfillment, and (4) in favor of the Nazis, who promised to repair for Germany the losses resulting from defeat and to regain for her that proud place among the powers of the world which she had held before 1914.

A third factor in the situation was the temporary collapse of parliamentary government caused by the German multiparty system and the adoption of proportional representation under the Weimar constitution. As already pointed out, for more than two years before the elections of March, 1933, there was a deadlock in the Reichstag resulting from the fact that no party or group of parties controlled a majority. When a resort to the "presidential" type of government failed to end the crisis, many became convinced that only a "strong man" could bring back to Germany the domestic peace and prosperity of prewar days. This desire for a "strong man" was further increased by fear of the rising tide of Communism, which was winning millions of discontented and despairing workmen into its ranks.

[13] On January 30, 1937, the Reichstag extended this enabling act for four more years.

After the burning of the Reichstag building by alleged Communists, the anti-Communist feeling mounted almost to hysteria among the upper and middle classes, who saw in the Nazis a bulwark against the "Reds."

Finally, Hitler's own contribution to the forces which brought the revolution must not be overlooked. The Nazi leader was apparently not particularly original in his methods or ideas, but he was certainly a skillful imitator. He undoubtedly understood the temper of the German people, particularly of the younger generation. He was an adept psychologist, a clever demagogue, and a master showman. At the same time, he was a resourceful agitator, a tireless worker, and an able organizer. Above all, he was a captivating and inspiring orator and knew how to sway people in the mass. With the conditions which existed in Germany and with Hitler's ability to exploit them to the full through popular propaganda, the outcome was almost inevitable, especially when the Nazis resorted to repression and intimidation in the weeks before the election.

## ANTI-SEMITISM

For years Hitler and his colleagues, in order to popularize their program and win members to the National Socialist Party, had carried on a bitter anti-Semitic campaign. Again and again in their efforts to whip up an anti-Semitic frenzy they had threatened the German Jews with physical violence, civil and political degradation, and economic repression once the Nazis should come into power. It was not surprising, therefore, that the Nazi political victory in March was at once followed by numerous attacks upon Jews by Nazi storm troopers. Apparently the government and the police made little effort to afford protection. "The police," said Göring, "are not a defense squad for Jewish stores or there to protect rogues, vagabonds, swindlers, profiteers, and traitors."

These early outbursts of physical violence were soon followed by many measures which, while not so violent, nevertheless made the Jews objects of persecution and deliberate discrimination. It was decreed that no person of non-Aryan descent [14] or married to one of non-Aryan descent could be eligible for appointment as an official

---

[14] "Non-Aryan descent means descent from non-Ayran, and especially Jewish, parents or grandparents, even though only one of the parents or grandparents was of the Jewish religion."

of the national government, the states, the municipalities, or any kind of public or legal corporation, institution, or endowment. Non-Aryan civil servants were required to resign unless they had been already employed at the outbreak of the World War or unless they had fought at the front or lost a father or son in the war. Likewise—subject to the same conditions—it was decreed that admission to the bar might be refused to Jewish lawyers, that Jews might be struck off the roll of patent-lawyers, that Jewish notaries should be "urgently advised" to refrain from exercising their calling. All Jewish judges were "invited" to apply for leaves without delay, and all Jewish court clerks and court attachés were ordered dismissed. Similar steps were taken in the medical profession, where Jewish doctors were deprived of the right to serve as panel doctors in the national health-insurance service [15] and were excluded from practice on clients of private companies insuring against illness. Various state and municipal authorities went so far as to issue orders expelling Jewish physicians from hospitals and forbidding Jewish nurses to practice.

In the realm of education it was decreed that Jewish students must not comprise more than 1.5 per cent of those entering schools, colleges, and universities, and that all Jewish students already attending such institutions should be dismissed in so far as their numbers exceeded 5 per cent of the total attendance. Jewish university professors and teachers in secondary schools were progressively dismissed from their positions and deprived of their licenses to teach or lecture.[16] Even such a world-renowned scholar as Professor Albert Einstein, the physicist, incurred the wrath of the German Nazis.

In an attempt to "extirpate the un-German spirit" from the public libraries a public burning of un-German books was announced for May 10, at which time the books of some 160 writers were burned at inquisitional stakes in various university towns. During the ensuing months measures were taken—too many to be enumerated here in detail—to bar Jews from an increasing number of activities —economic, social, and cultural. Tens of thousands of Jewish professional men, business men, teachers, writers, musicians, artists,

[15] Great numbers of the younger physicians and many of the older ones received a large part of their professional income from their panel practice.
[16] So also were many liberals who were not Jews.

and artisans felt the heavy hand of the Nazi regime as it ruthlessly deprived them of their accustomed means of livelihood. The
seeds of anti-Semitism, so lavishly sown by Nazi agitators before
1933, thus bore abundant fruit.

Additional steps were taken in 1935 to define the status of Jews
in Germany and to restrict them further in their political and social
life. Only three classes of persons were thenceforth to be recognized
under German law: (1) Germans, (2) Jews, who were defined as
those having more than two Jewish grandparents, (3) Jewish "mix-
tures" or "hybrids," those having less than three Jewish grandparents. Jews were specifically deprived of German citizenship.
They were, however, to be subjects of the state; that is to say, although barred from voting and holding office, they would still have
obligations to the state. Among the Jewish "hybrids" those might be
citizens who were (1) only 25-per-cent Jewish, or (2) half-Jews who
did not belong to a Jewish religious community, or (3) half-Jews
who were not married to Jews. A decree "for the protection of German blood and honor" forbade marriages between Germans and
Jews and between Germans and Jewish "hybrids" who were half-
Jews.

## THE TOTALITARIAN STATE

Meanwhile, vigorous measures had been taken to create in Germany a totalitarian state in which there should be but one political
party, the National Socialist. Some of the parties—notably the Communist, Social Democratic, and Democratic—were forcibly outlawed by the government; the others voluntarily dissolved. On
July 14, 1933, Hitler's government decreed that the National Socialist
Party was the only legal party in Germany, and that the formation
of any new parties would constitute high treason. Furthermore, in
order that the administrative offices of the republic might be filled
with Nazis, a new civil-service law, applying to the federal, state,
and municipal services, was promulgated, making it possible to dismiss all civil servants who were not acceptable to the central authorities.

The Nazi government also inaugurated a program designed to
centralize all political authority in Berlin. Within a year it had
progressed so far that on January 30, 1934—the first anniversary of
Hitler's appointment as chancellor—the Reichstag passed unani-

mously Hitler's measure transferring the sovereign powers of the various German states to the Reich government. The legislative functions of the states were definitely abolished, and the governors appointed over the states by the Reich government were placed under the jurisdiction of the Reich minister of the interior. The situation of the states and governors in Germany thus came to be not unlike that of the French provinces and prefects. The act also empowered the Reich to promulgate a new constitution and to dispose of the Reichsrat, which had originally been instituted to give the states parliamentary representation. The formal abolition of the Reichsrat occurred in February, 1934.

Even the municipal governments were "co-ordinated." The burgomasters of the cities and the presidents of the villages in Prussia, which constitutes two thirds of all Germany, were made appointees of the Reich minister of the interior. Full power to make all decisions was to rest with these appointed executives. Members of the city and village councils—thereafter to be merely advisory bodies—were also to be appointed by the minister of the interior in agreement with local Nazi leaders. A year later cities and towns in the other German states were made subordinate to the Nazi central regime in a somewhat similar manner. These various measures resembled in effect those taken in Italy by Mussolini in 1925–1926.

Steps were also taken to secure undisputed control of the German youth. In 1926 Hitler had organized the Hitler Youth, an organization which came to include boys from ten to twenty years of age. After coming into power Hitler created the position of "Leader of the Youth of the German Reich" and appointed to this office the director of the Hitler Youth organization. This new official was made head of all German youth organizations and was authorized to take over the administrative functions of all the governing bodies which had hitherto existed. Furthermore, no new youth organization or junior auxiliary of an adult organization might be formed without his consent. Membership in the Hitler Youth was eventually made a prerequisite for admission to the Nazi Party and for appointment to government offices. Late in 1936, in fact, it was decreed that all youth—boys and girls—within the Reich were to be included in the Hitler Youth organization.

Thus Hitler attained his goal of a completely centralized, totalitarian, or one-party, state. The federal, state, and local governments had been brought wholly under his control; the parliamentary system had been entirely destroyed; the various military organizations had been either absorbed into the Nazi ranks or suppressed; the German youth movements had been restricted and centralized under Nazi leadership. As in Italy all political life was centralized in and controlled by Mussolini's Fascist Party, so at last in Germany the political life of the republic was monopolized by the Nazis. "The National Socialist Party," Hitler announced, "is the state." The Nazi party flag—the black hooked cross in a white circle on a red field—in 1935 became the official flag of the Third Reich.

To expedite the creation of the totalitarian state, Hitler had utilized two different agencies: propaganda to popularize the Nazi regime, and force to suppress all opposition to it. The former was placed in the hands of Paul Joseph Goebbels as minister of propaganda and enlightenment; the exercise of the latter was confided to Göring, Prussian premier and minister of police. Freedom of speech and of the press was abolished, and even the secrecy of telephone conversations and of the mails was disregarded. The whole educational system was placed in the hands of the Nazis, and all teachers and officials known to be in opposition to the Hitlerite regime were removed. Many famous German scholars and scientists were deprived of their positions and forced to take refuge abroad. By a national decree of July 14, 1933, all critics of the government living abroad were made subject to loss of citizenship and seizure of property unless they returned to Germany, and their relatives in Germany might be held as hostages for their good behavior. A secret state police (*Gestapo*), independent of the regular police, was created and placed under the command of Göring. To trace and fight all political activities dangerous to the state was declared to be its peculiar task. Thousands were arrested and placed in "concentration camps."

## THE "CO-ORDINATION" OF THE CHURCH

In Germany there were, before the National Socialist revolution, some twenty-nine major Protestant churches, a situation which, according to the Nazis, tended to make for disunity and inefficiency. Hitler desired instead that Germany should have one national church (*Reichskirche*) with a national bishop (*Reichsbischof*) at its head, and that it should be subordinate to the state. Threats of "co-ordinating" the Protestant churches with the Nazi regime were made early in 1933. A preliminary step toward this end was taken by Nazi Protestants when they organized into a group known as "German Christians."

In order to forestall any possible interference by Hitler, the various Protestant churches took steps in 1933 to create a new organization which should bring them all into one German Evangelical Church. The new constitution provided that at the head of the new church there should be a Lutheran bishop and that he should have co-operating with him a spiritual cabinet representing the non-Lutheran evangelical bodies. There was to be also a national synod to co-operate in promulgating church legislation and in appointing church heads. Representatives of the twenty-nine Protestant churches chose as the first bishop of the new church Friedrich von Bodelschwingh, a clergyman widely known for his social-welfare work. The new bishop had never been actively identified with any political party, and it was hoped by those who elected him that his choice would satisfy Hitler and lead the government to keep its hands out of church affairs.

Unfortunately, Ludwig Müller, a Nazi army chaplain and one of Hitler's chief advisers on religious matters, desired to be bishop of the new church, and, when he failed to secure the position, he at once issued a statement announcing that the "German Christians" could not accept the election. His opposition to Bodelschwingh's election was seconded by the head of the "German Christians," and their attitude boded ill for the freedom and independence of the German Evangelical Church. Hitler appointed Wilhelm Frick, minister of the interior, to mediate between the two groups, and under his direction Müller, Bodelschwingh, and other representatives of the two Protestant factions sought a solution of the problem. On July 11 a new constitution for the German Evangelical Church was approved by the representatives of the Protestant churches of Germany. A referendum on the new constitution was ordered, at which time delegates to the national synod and members of local church boards were also to be elected.

In the days before the church elections the Nazis turned the full force of their political machine to the advantage of the "German Christians," who called themselves the "storm troops of Jesus Christ." Press and radio publicity was limited to the pronouncements of the latter, and the government ruled that all persons over twenty-four years of age, who had baptismal certificates showing them to be Protestants, were entitled to vote. On the eve of the elections Hitler, in a radio address, once more raised the specter of Communism and appealed to the Protestants to elect representatives who would support the new political regime. The result was a foregone conclusion; the "German Christians" won by a landslide. It was therefore not surprising that the national synod, when constituted, chose as Reich bishop Ludwig Müller, the candidate of the Nazi "German Christians."

Extremists in this latter group now sought to make a number of radical changes. They advocated the rejection of the Old Testament, the removal of crucifixes from the churches, and even a revision of the New Testament in such a way as to repudiate the divinity of Jesus Christ. They further demanded the insertion in the church constitution of a so-called "Aryan paragraph" which was designed to force out of the pulpit all Christian clergy having Jewish blood in their veins and to segregate in a separate church all Christians with Jewish blood. To prevent such innovations in the church several thousand clergy, led by Martin Niemöller, organized the Pastors' Emergency League. Their opposition resulted in the elimination of the "Aryan paragraph" from the church constitution, but further efforts on the part of Reich Bishop Müller to co-ordinate the church led to continued conflict.

Although the Pastors' Emergency League was disbanded, its work was carried on by a Confessional Synod, to which, rather than to Müller, the opposition looked for direction in matters of doctrine and discipline. Hundreds of pastors were thereupon arrested, suspended, transferred, or deprived of their incomes because of their refusal to obey the Reich bishop. Eventually, in September, 1935, Hitler definitely placed the Evangelical Church under state control. Reich Bishop Müller was deprived of his authority, and Hanns Kerrl was made minister for church affairs with full control of all nondoctrinal church matters. Three months later Kerrl decreed that all groups which in the future attempted to interfere with state control of the church would be suppressed.

Throughout 1936 the government sought to obtain unity within the Evangelical Church, but failed. Thereupon, early in 1937, Hitler ordered the election of another national synod, which should frame a new church constitution. Differences of opinion at once arose between the "German Christians" and the "Confessional Christians" regarding a number of details of the election, especially in regard to those who should compose the electorate, and in April Hitler postponed the church elections indefinitely. In the following months the Nazi government renewed its campaign against the Confessional Synod. All five members of the executive committee of the Confessional Synod's provisional church government, together with Niemöller, were suddenly arrested by the secret state police, and it was made a crime to collect or to contribute money for the work of the synod. In the summer of 1937 one result of four years of Nazi effort to "co-ordinate" the Evangelical Church was the conviction among a growing number of the clergy that church and state should be completely separated.

Relations between the Nazi government and the Catholic Church have also been far from peaceful. Soon after coming into power Hitler sought to secure a single concordat with the Holy See to replace the existing three concordats between the church and the governments of Prussia, Bavaria, and Baden. Ultimately, on July 20, 1933, a concordat was signed, by the terms of which Catholic clergy were forbidden to take any part in German politics, and the Vatican withdrew any support it had previously given to the German Center parties. The Catholic religion in Germany was placed on an even footing with the Protestant faith and was guaranteed the same rights and privileges as the latter. Catholic chaplains were to serve with the German armed forces and were to be placed under a military archbishop appointed by the pope. All bishops and archbishops in Germany were to be German citizens and were to be appointed by the Holy See after consultation with the German government. The latter, for its part, recognized the Catholic Action as a nonpolitical organization under the leadership of which the Vatican might concentrate its efforts on the development of nonpolitical Catholic groups. Catholic schools, youth organizations, workers' associations, and cultural societies were to be unmolested so long as they did not concern themselves with politics.

As might perhaps have been expected, friction soon developed between the Nazi state and the Catholic Church over the interpretation of certain articles of the concordat dealing with schools and youth organizations. In the last analysis, the Nazis were determined to limit the activities of the Catholic Action, to absorb the Catholic Youth Movement, to suppress the confessional schools, to destroy the Catholic workingmen's societies, and to abolish freedom of the Catholic press. On the other hand, prominent Catholic clergy publicly denounced the Nazi sterilization law and the Nazi attacks on the crucifix and on the Old Testament. Friction was further increased in 1935 when the Nazis charged that money and foreign exchange were being smuggled out of Germany by members of the Catholic secular and regular clergy contrary to German decrees. Millions of marks in fines were levied by the government.

During 1936, despite the provisions of the concordat, the government continued its efforts to enlist all Catholic children in the Hitler Youth and to put an end to education by Catholic schools. By pressure upon parents the Nazis succeeded in reducing registrations for Catholic schools in some parts of southern Germany almost to the vanishing point. Ultimately the pope was led to protest, and in an encyclical on March 21, 1937, he declared that the concordat had been both misinterpreted and openly violated by the Nazi government. At the same time he called upon German Catholics to rally to defend the freedom of the church. The government, on the other hand, sought to discredit the Catholic Church by bringing numerous priests and members of religious orders to trial on charges of immorality. Furthermore, in June it went so far as to dissolve the hundreds of Catholic schools in Bavaria, converting them into secular institutions. That the relations between the Reich and the Vatican might be strained to the breaking point appeared possible in the summer of 1937.

## THE "CO-ORDINATION" OF GERMANY'S ECONOMIC LIFE

But the Nazi program of co-ordination was not limited to the political and religious realms alone. Steps were taken to bring Germany's economic life likewise into harmony with Nazi principles. In 1933 all the previously existing trade unions in Germany were suppressed, and in the following year the employers' associations were likewise dissolved. To replace these former organizations of workers and employers a new organization, the German Labor Front, was established to represent capital and labor in the realm of commerce, industry, and the professions. Under a new labor law, effective from May 1, 1934, the principle of the solidarity of capital and labor was accepted, and the idea of an inevitable conflict between the two was rejected. Collective bargaining, strikes, and lockouts were forbidden. The workers thus lost their ultimate safeguard against exploitation—the right to strike—and became dependent for their well-being upon labor trustees, political appointees of the Nazi government, who have full authority to issue regulations, binding upon both workers and employers, "establishing the conditions for the concluding of wage agreements."

Under the law of 1934 the Nazi principle of "leadership" was introduced into the economic life of the Reich. In each enterprise with more than twenty employees the employer became the "leader"; the employees became the "followers." A "confidential council," chosen yearly, was authorized to advise on the running of the business, on working conditions, and on the maintenance of efficiency and a spirit of co-operation. The members of this council are nominated by the leader in consultation with the head of the Nazi cell organization among the workers. The list of nominees is then submitted to the workers. In case no satisfactory election can be made, the workers may then appeal to the labor trustee for their district to appoint the members of the council. To these trustees is confided the task of maintaining industrial peace. They have authority to interfere in cases where large dismissals of workers are contemplated. They have authority also to draft general regulations for the fixing of wages and to enforce existing contracts on both the employer and the workers. They even have power to oust the employer from his business if he is too inefficient or too inconsiderate of the welfare of his employees.

Private property and private initiative were thus still retained as in the orthodox capitalistic system. The owner or manager of an enterprise, as the leader, however, was made not only responsible for carrying on his business as efficiently as possible, but equally responsible for the welfare of his workers or followers. The latter in turn were to have confidence in their employer and assist him in every way possible. Reciprocal confidence, common responsibility, and Nazi leadership were expected to create an economic system in which the welfare of society should prevail over that of the individual.

Despite their earlier promises of agrarian reform, the Nazis made no attempt to confiscate or to divide the great landed estates of the

Junkers of East Prussia and Pomerania. They did, however, introduce some changes in the German system of landholding. A law—called the Hereditary Farms Law—was promulgated with the purpose of elevating the independent farmers into a new "nobility." By this law estates of less than 278 acres, capable of supporting a family and owned by a German citizen of Aryan descent, became hereditary farms. A hereditary farm cannot be sold, mortgaged, or attached for debt and must pass undivided upon the owner's death to the eldest son or nearest male heir. The new owner, however, is held responsible for the support and educational training of his younger brothers and sisters. The law was in a sense designed to create a peasant aristocracy, only the owners of hereditary farms being entitled to be termed peasants.

In its attitude toward agriculture the Nazi government was influenced to a considerable extent by its desire to realize national self-sufficiency (*Autarkie*). In view of Germany's experience during the World War, the Nazis were particularly determined that the Third Reich should become completely independent of the outside world for its food supplies. In addition to measures designed to "ennoble" the independent farmer, the government established for agriculture an organization called the Food Estate (*Nährstand*) under the direction of the Reich minister of agriculture. This organization has introduced a sort of planned economy for agriculture and has regulated the price and distribution of most foodstuffs.

In the realm of foreign trade the Nazis encountered difficulties. The large export surplus which Germany had enjoyed at the time the Nazis came into power decreased—partly as a result of boycotts in foreign countries because of the Nazi anti-Semitic measures—until in 1934 it finally became an import surplus instead. The resultant drain on the gold reserves of the Reichsbank was so severe that they became depleted, and the gold coverage fell to the dangerously low figure of 2.1 per cent. Once more the fear of currency depreciation haunted the German people. Immediate and drastic steps were needed, and Hjalmar Schacht, president of the Reichsbank, was appointed minister of economics with dictatorial power.

Three types of measures were taken by Schacht to meet the threatening situation: (1) default in whole or in part on foreign interest payments in order to stop one of the drains on Germany's gold, (2) rigid curtailment of imports into Germany from abroad in order to reduce another drain on the country's gold reserves, and (3) extensive subsidies to industries manufacturing for export in order that they might reduce their prices, increase their foreign sales, and thus bring gold or goods into Germany. As a result of these measures, the year 1935 closed with a favorable trade balance of 111,000,000 marks, which rose to 550,000,000 marks in 1936.

The years after 1934 saw a rapid recovery in German industry, production rising until by the opening of the year 1937 it was running 12 per cent ahead of the boom year 1928. This improvement was largely the result of credit-financed programs of rearmament and public works. To secure the funds for these extensive programs the government resorted not to increased taxes or direct currency inflation but to what amounted to a system of forced loans from banks, industries, and various organizations which had funds that might be used for investment. In other words, the German government went more and more into debt. The amount borrowed was not revealed, for after 1934 the Reich budget was not published. There was certainly, however, a growing credit inflation in Germany with a rise in the price of many commodities. Within the country the mark was arbitrarily kept at a gold parity, but the fear of currency depreciation seemed to be indicated by a government order in December, 1935, which forbade the importation of marks or their domestic acceptance for the settlement of foreigners' debts. The German mark thus took its place alongside the Soviet ruble and the Italian lira as a purely domestic currency.

In September, 1936, Hitler announced the inauguration of a Four-Year Plan designed to increase Germany's self-sufficiency and at the same time to provide productive employment for those released by the gradual completion of the Reich's rearmament program. During the ensuing four years all of Germany's resources— land, labor, capital—were to be mobilized to serve the campaign for greater self-sufficiency. Since Germany was at that time largely dependent upon foreign countries for all important industrial raw materials except coal, the plan placed upon German scientists what Hitler called a "stupendous task." Göring, the Nazi strong man, was placed in charge with plenary powers to issue all decrees necessary for the execution of the plan. That Hitler's Four-Year Plan would exact burdensome sacrifices from the German people seemed practically inevitable.

## Nazi Foreign Policy

When the Nazis came into power Germany had not yet attained some of the primary objects of her postwar foreign policy. Although she had escaped from reparations payments, liberated her territory from foreign occupation, secured the removal of the Inter-Allied commissions of control, and gained a permanent seat in the Council of the League of Nations along with the other great powers, she was still restricted in military and naval matters and still prevented from fortifying the Rhineland. Furthermore, she had not yet redeemed the Saar, and had made no apparent progress toward union with Austria [17] or toward the reacquisition of the territory lost to Poland. But all of these aims and more were included in the Nazi program as proclaimed in the years before 1933.

Whereas Stresemann's foreign policy had been based on conciliation and fulfillment, Hitler's appeared to be founded on recalcitrance and opportunism. That Nazi Germany would not meekly submit to national inferiority was soon indicated when, in October, 1933, she withdrew from the Disarmament Conference, the League of Nations, and the Labor Organization because of the delay in granting the Reich equality in armaments. This step was followed in 1935 by her repudiation of the military and naval restrictions of the treaty of Versailles and in 1936 by her remilitarization of the Rhineland in defiance of the same treaty and of the Locarno pact as well.[18] In the latter year, too, Germany denounced the clauses of the peace treaty which internationalized the Rhine, Elbe, Danube, and Oder Rivers and the Kiel Canal. On January 30, 1937, Hitler announced that those parts of the treaty of Versailles which deprived Germany of equality had finally been liquidated and that the Reich had been emancipated from its status of an inferior nation.

Meanwhile, the Nazis had attempted to advance toward their goal of bringing all Germans into the Third Reich. Apparently in order that Germany might be undisturbed in her efforts to consummate the *Anschluss* with Austria and to redeem the Saar, the Reich government in January, 1934, signed with Poland a ten-year nonaggression pact recognizing temporarily the inviolability of Germany's

[17] For the abortive attempt to establish an Austro-German customs union, see page 768.

[18] See pages 576–578.

*Wide World Photos*

The "Rome-Berlin Axis"

The close co-operation between Fascist Italy and Nazi Germany was emphasized by Mussolini's visit to Hitler in September, 1937.

eastern frontiers. The Nazis then concentrated their attention on Austria and sought to "co-ordinate" that little German republic by a Nazi terror which culminated in the murder of the Austrian Chancellor Dollfuss and the abortive Nazi *Putsch* of July, 1934.[19] But the failure of the Austrians to support the *Putsch* and more especially Mussolini's prompt action in rushing Italian troops to the Austro-Italian frontier prevented the Nazis from seizing the Austrian government. The Reich government hastened to deny any connection with these events in Austria. In the Saar plebiscite in the following January, however, the Nazis were more successful, and in March, 1935, that German territory was incorporated in the Third Reich.[20] In other territory lost to Germany by the treaty of Versailles Hitler's policy was one of "Nazification." In 1935 the governments of Danzig and of Memel both came under the control of local Nazi parties which were linked with the Hitler organization in Germany.[21]

In addition to the union of all Germans in one powerful Reich, Hitler in *Mein Kampf* emphasized Germany's need to acquire new territory in Europe on which Germans might settle. The Reich, according to Hitler, must turn its eyes toward the east, for only in Russia and along the Baltic could Germany obtain the new territory so necessary to provide for her rapidly increasing population. The Ukraine appeared to be the region toward which the Nazis cast their covetous eyes. But this territory, obviously, could not be secured except by military measures; hence the determination to create for the Reich a powerful military machine. Hence, also, the suspicion that the German-Japanese agreement (November 25, 1936) to combat the activities of the Third International includes secret protocols providing for military co-operation.

Although the Nazi foreign policy emancipated and strengthened Germany as a military power, it had for a time an unfortunate effect upon her international position. Before 1933 both Italy and Russia had been inclined to support Germany, and even Great Britain had been sympathetic with German policies. By 1936, on the other hand, the Nazi drive against Communists and the Nazi program for eastern expansion had driven Russia into a Franco-Soviet military alliance; the Nazi attempt to absorb Austria had alienated Italy and facilitated a Franco-Italian *rapprochement;* and the Nazi rearmament program had alarmed Great Britain and forced her into

[19] See page 771.        [20] See page 535.        [21] See pages 757 and 759.

what was practically an Anglo-Franco-Belgian alliance against Germany. In 1936 Germany stood practically isolated among the great powers of Europe.

But Hitler soon removed the chief cause of friction between Mussolini and himself. In July, 1936, Germany signed an agreement with Austria recognizing the independence of the latter and pledging herself not to interfere in Austria's domestic political life. Thereafter the two fascist states co-operated to a large extent in their foreign policies. Germany joined Italy in aiding the Spanish insurgents,[22] and Italy in turn supported Germany by signing the German-Japanese anti-Communist treaty. A "Rome-Berlin axis" was thus created.

## POLITICAL DEVELOPMENTS UNDER THE NAZIS

It might reasonably have been expected that, after Hitler received dictatorial powers, he would not feel called upon to consult the German electorate. This proved not to be true, however. Twice, when the nationalism of the German people had been roused to a high pitch as a result of some step taken by the Führer, elections or plebiscites were held to prove the popular support of the Nazi regime. On one other occasion, after stirring events within the Reich, a plebiscite was held to show that Hitler's deeds were sanctioned by the German people. The latter, therefore, though ruled by a dictator, continued to have the privilege—the duty, according to the Nazis—of expressing themselves in favor of the dictatorship through popular elections.

In October, 1933, at the time that Hitler announced Germany's withdrawal from the Disarmament Conference and from the League of Nations, the Reichstag was dissolved and new elections were set for November 12. In the weeks preceding the plebiscite Hitler pleaded with the Germans to cast their votes in such a way as to show the world that they were "solidly behind the stand formulated by me against our country's accepting a position of inferiority to other countries." Undoubtedly swayed by Hitler's masterful oratory, some 43,000,000 Germans participated in the first national plebiscite and election under the Nazi regime. Of this number, more than 40,-500,000 gave their approval of the policy of the Reich government, and more than 39,500,000 voted in favor of the Nazi list of Reichstag candidates.

[22] See pages 742–745.

Although on the surface the elections of November, 1933, appeared to indicate that Hitler's party was functioning efficiently and harmoniously, a dangerous cleavage was developing within the ranks of the Nazis, who had been drawn from widely differing economic and social groups. Anyone who seriously studied the Nazi program realized that it contained goals that were distinctly in conflict one with another, and that, when the time should come to put the program into effect, some of the groups that had rallied to Hitler's standard would inevitably be disappointed. In 1934 the Left elements of the party became restless because of Hitler's failure to carry into effect his earlier socialistic, anticapitalistic, and anti-Junker promises. Apparently Ernst Röhm, chief of staff of the Nazi storm troops, assumed leadership among the discontented elements of the party, who desired a "second revolution" which should carry into fuller effect the socialistic features of the original Nazi program.

According to Hitler's official statement, issued later, Röhm and a small group of ambitious storm-troop leaders spent some months in preparing for action. They feared that Hitler planned to lessen the importance of the storm troops and therefore plotted to forestall Hitler's action by seizing power for themselves. The discontented Left elements, they hoped, would rally to their side against the existing regime. During the day of June 29 alarming messages reached Hitler informing him that the "plot" was about to be carried out. Instructing Göring to take vigorous steps in Berlin and elsewhere in Prussia, Hitler at once flew by airplane to Munich and proceeded against the alleged plotters. Apparently lists of those to be killed had been carefully prepared in advance, for Hitler's agents seemed to know exactly who were to be found. Within a few hours, in a reign of terror, seventy-four persons, according to the official statement, were summarily killed with little or no hearing. Prominent among those murdered, shot, or "permitted to commit suicide" were Röhm, former Chancellor Kurt von Schleicher and his wife, Erich Klausener, leader of the Catholic Action group, and three of Papen's secretaries.[23] The complete list was never published. Hitler's defense of his summary action was that "I was responsible for the fate of the German nation and therefore I myself was the German people's Supreme Tribunal for those twenty-four hours."

---

[23] For some days Papen's fate was in doubt. President Hindenburg came to his aid by ordering the *Reichswehr* to be responsible for his safety.

Germany had hardly had time to calm down when on August 2, 1934, President Hindenburg died. Hitler at once assumed the functions of the president in addition to those of chancellor and thus became probably the world's most powerful ruler. He declined to assume the title of president, however, and requested that he be addressed as in the past as "Leader" or "Reich Chancellor." Desiring that the cabinet's action in combining the presidency and the chancellorship should have the approval of the German people, Hitler ordered another plebiscite to be held. Once again all the oratorical artillery of the Nazis was brought into action. A document described as the "political testament" of the late president, indicating Hindenburg's approval of Hitler's policies, was published on August 15. Two days later the chancellor made an appeal to the people in a national broadcast. Of the 43,529,710 ballots cast in the plebiscite, 38,362,760, or approximately 88 per cent, were in the affirmative; 5,166,950 ballots, or approximately 12 per cent, were either in the negative or invalid. The number voting against Hitler in this plebiscite was approximately twice as great as in that of November, 1933.

This registered opposition was practically eliminated in the next plebiscite, which was held in March, 1936, after Hitler had remilitarized the Rhineland and extended the sovereignty of the Reich over all its territory. On this occasion 98.5 per cent of the eligible voters—nearly 45,000,000—went to the polls. As a matter of fact, Nazi storm troops saw to it that the electorate was mobilized. After the votes were counted, it was announced that 99 per cent had been cast in favor of the Führer's foreign policy.

During the first three years of his dictatorship it thus appears that Hitler, with his showman's instinct, unerringly seized upon various occasions to galvanize the German people into an enthusiastic blanket approval of his regime. The issue on each occasion was made to be directly or indirectly the Führer's defiance of the former Allies and not his domestic economic, religious, or racial policies. In each case it was inevitable that the Germans would support their government in its attempt to regain for the fatherland its prewar place as a sovereign power. The fact that no opposition parties existed and that no opposition could be voiced in public speeches or newspapers made the outcome in each plebiscite hardly a matter of doubt.

## CHAPTER XXII

# GREAT BRITAIN AND IRELAND

THE European great power which has wavered least in its loyalty to the liberal tradition during the postwar years is Great Britain. Although a monarchy, Great Britain probably more than any other country in Europe has displayed a deep attachment to political democracy and a continued concern for social justice. The quest of the latter was made particularly difficult after the war because Great Britain found it impossible to increase her foreign trade to its prewar level. The chronic unemployment which resulted from this failure became such a serious problem that it repeatedly affected the policies of the British government both at home and abroad. Like a scarlet thread it can be traced through the history of the postwar period.

### TRADE DECLINE AND UNEMPLOYMENT

For a time after the armistice, thanks to the great demand for commodities in European countries long isolated from the rest of the world by the war, British trade prospered. But toward the close of 1920 the business boom collapsed, and in the next year exports fell off by about one half. During the succeeding years, though some improvement occurred, Great Britain's foreign trade never reached its prewar figure.

Various circumstances account for this decline. Great Britain's foreign trade is obviously dependent upon world and especially European conditions. But the war had impoverished the world's purchasing power so that, after the first spurt in buying, purchases were greatly curtailed. The situation was further aggravated by the depreciation of so many Continental currencies. At the very time when Great Britain was trying to deflate her own currency, most European countries were resorting to inflation. This situation worked to the great disadvantage of British manufacturers, who were forced to compete in foreign markets with goods produced where labor was relatively cheaper because of the depreciated currency in which it was paid. Furthermore, the war had ended in the creation of numerous new states, and each, led by an excessive national zeal, began to erect "political dams across the economic streams of Europe." National tariffs inevitably interfered with the flow of British goods to their accustomed markets.

The British coal industry was particularly hard hit. In prewar years Great Britain had been accustomed to export some 62,500,000 tons of coal annually, but the rapid development of new sources of power—hydroelectric plants, petroleum oil, and low-temperature carbonization of coal and lignite—decreased the demand for raw coal. Between 1920 and 1923 the output of Europe's water-power plants increased by over 3,000,000 horse power. Germany's delivery of coal to France and Italy as part of her reparations payments further lessened the demand for British coal. But the staple industries were also seriously affected, in this case chiefly because the spread of the Industrial Revolution was depriving British industries of long-monopolized markets. The expansion of cotton manufacturing in India, China, and Japan, for example, was seriously felt in Lancashire. Outside Europe, Britain's exports of cotton cloth in the postwar years were only about half as great as before 1914. Old plants and antiquated methods, furthermore, handicapped many British industries in meeting competition.

Because of the decline in export trade, factories were forced to curtail production. The volume of British shipping naturally decreased, and the demand for new ships for a time largely disappeared. The important shipbuilding industry was therefore also adversely affected. But the welfare of most of the British was bound up with industry and commerce, for only 6 per cent of the people of England were directly dependent upon agriculture for a living. Nearly 80 per cent (1921) of the population was urban in England and Wales. Anything affecting the industrial or commercial life of the country, therefore, was bound to affect to a greater or less degree the majority of the British people.

The reduction in British foreign trade was even more serious at this time because in the decade after 1913 the total population of Great Britain had increased by about two million. The natural increase in the number of workers which this brought was further augmented by contingents of women who during the war had entered the industrial field, and by part of the former "leisure class" who had been driven, by the increased cost of living and the relative decline in their incomes, to join the ranks of the workers. With the collapse of Britain's commerce in 1921, therefore, came a rapid increase in unemployment. At the beginning of the year over one million were out of work; by the middle of the year the number had considerably more than doubled; and in subsequent years it rose as high as three million. The various British governments as they succeeded one another were inevitably compelled to wrestle with this unemployment problem.

## THE LLOYD GEORGE COALITION

Great Britain emerged from the World War with a coalition government. The exigencies of the war had brought a reorganization of the government in 1915, when Asquith had become the head of a coalition ministry composed of representatives of the Liberal, Conservative, and Labor parties. In 1916 a further change had occurred when Lloyd George forced Asquith out of the premiership and himself assumed the office. Politics had been "adjourned" in Great Britain for the duration of the war, so that the dissolution of Parliament which should regularly have occurred in 1915 had been postponed. When the armistice was signed, therefore, eight years had elapsed since the last election. It was high time for the electorate to be consulted. Parliament was at once dissolved, and new elections were set for December 14, 1918.

On a platform which called for the punishment of German "war criminals," the full payment of the Allied war costs by the defeated powers, the protection of "essential" British industries, the prevention of dumping in Great Britain of goods produced by cheap foreign labor, the improvement of housing and labor conditions, and the settlement of the Irish question, Lloyd George appealed for the continuation of the war coalition. Asquith, however, denounced the coalition and entered the lists at the head of a party known as the Independent Liberals, and the Labor Party, declining longer to participate in the coalition, waged a campaign to increase its own parliamentary strength. The elections of 1918 were particularly notable, since they provided the first opportunity for nearly 8,000,000 new voters to register their views.

Earlier in the year Great Britain had taken another great stride toward political democracy by passing the Representation of the

People Act. Aside from certain temporary provisions this act conferred a parliamentary vote on all men twenty-one years of age who could qualify by six months' residence or by the occupation of business premises, and on all women thirty years of age who were local government electors or wives of such electors. The act also provided for the redistribution of representatives in accordance with the principle of single-member constituencies of approximately equal size, and the limiting of an elector's vote to not more than two constituencies. The number of electors participating in this election, therefore, was far greater than in any other in the previous history of Great Britain.

The result of the voting was an overwhelming victory for the Lloyd George coalition. Asquith's Independent Liberals managed to capture only 28 seats, but Labor increased its representation to 63. Lloyd George therefore had a large majority over all opposition groups. But the character of the majority must have given the Liberal leader pause, for it was made up five to two of Conservatives. In the reconstitution of the ministry in January, 1919, this fact was reflected. The proportion of Conservatives became so great that the coalition ceased to be predominantly Liberal in tone, and Great Britain was presented with the anomalous spectacle of an extreme Liberal at the head of a government consisting largely of Conservatives.

A number of steps were taken by Lloyd George's government in an effort to meet the unemployment situation. The Unemployment Insurance Act was modified to give greater relief, and the government itself contributed millions in "doles" to the unemployed. Such measures, however, could at best be only temporary palliatives. They did not strike at the root of the evil. Lloyd George therefore advocated the resumption of trade relations with Soviet Russia in order to rehabilitate British trade and industry. On March 16, 1921, a trade agreement was signed with Russia providing for the resumption of trade and commerce between the two countries pending the conclusion of a formal general peace treaty which should regulate their economic and political relations in the future. Later in the year the Safeguarding of Industries Act was passed. This measure was designed to protect key industries which would be vital in the event of future war, and to protect British workmen against the competition of cheap foreign commodities. For these purposes the act provided for a 33⅓ per cent duty to safeguard certain special industries, and for a tax on imports from countries with depreciated currencies. This partial abandonment of Great Britain's traditional policy of free trade aroused much opposition throughout the country.

Meanwhile, as the years passed, Lloyd George discovered that the Conservative portion of his coalition was becoming restless. The effect of the partial adoption of the old Conservative policy of protection in 1921 was nullified by his conclusion late in that same year of the Anglo-Irish treaty recognizing the Irish Free State.[1] The protests of the Conservatives against this treaty were vigorous and undisguised, and their threat to secede from the coalition early in 1922 nearly overthrew the government. Conservative leaders like Bonar Law and Stanley Baldwin, eager to secure freedom of action for their party, quietly fostered a movement looking toward secession. Finally, in October, 1922, the Conservative Party declared its independence and decided to enter the approaching electoral campaign as a separate party with its own leader and its own program.

With the defection of the Conservatives the coalition government was doomed. Lloyd George immediately resigned, and Bonar Law was called upon to head a new ministry. The government which the latter organized was drawn entirely from the ranks of the Conservatives and was the first homogeneous ministry since 1915. Parliament was dissolved, and new elections were called for November. In the ensuing campaign Lloyd George led what was known as the National Liberal Party, but Asquith and his Independent Liberals continued their active opposition and held aloof. The real struggle was between the Conservatives and the Laborites, with the outcome complicated by the possibility of the return of many minority candidates. Fear of the supposed radical tendencies of the Labor Party and hope of obtaining once more a one-party parliamentary government both helped to place the Conservatives in power with a majority over all opposition parties. Although the Conservatives won a great electoral victory, the achievement of the Labor Party was of even greater note. With the 142 seats which the Labor Party now controlled it became the second largest group in Parliament and therefore stepped into the position of "His Majesty's Opposition."

1 See page 714.

### Free Trade or Protection?

The chief task of the Conservative leaders when they assumed control of the government was to formulate some program which would solve the unemployment problem. In May, 1923, Bonar Law resigned the premiership because of ill health, and was succeeded by Stanley Baldwin. The latter, haunted by the specter of unemployment, resolved that some drastic step must be taken to meet the situation. While he was in this state of mind, the extremists of his party apparently suggested protection as a solution. Without consulting his party as a whole, Baldwin suddenly announced his determination to introduce a protective tariff. But the Conservatives had taken office with the general understanding that they would embark upon no aggressive or radical program without further consulting the electorate. Such a radical departure from the long-accepted British policy of free trade, therefore, called for an appeal to the people, and Baldwin, recognizing this, dissolved Parliament and went to the country on the issue of protection. In order to relieve British unemployment and maintain a reasonable level of wages for British workers, he demanded the defense of the home market by means of a tariff on manufactured goods.

The Conservatives argued that the whole world was erecting tariff barriers against British goods and that British duties might be utilized as a means of forcing reductions in these foreign tariffs. They asserted that the British Empire was economically sufficient unto itself and advocated Chamberlain's old scheme of imperial preference. They promised to keep raw materials on the free list, to place no tax on such foodstuffs as wheat and meat, and to reduce duties on tea and sugar. The opposition parties argued, on the other hand, that in an exporting country like Great Britain protection could not cure chronic unemployment. Among the Liberals personalities were subordinated in the face of Baldwin's attack upon their cherished free-trade principle, and a reconciliation, at least superficial, was brought about between the followers of Asquith and the Welsh leader. Although as a result of the election the Conservatives still retained the largest number of seats, their former safe majority over all opposing parties was transformed into a decided minority. Labor maintained its position as the chief opposition party by raising its total representation in the Commons to 192. The reunited Liberals stood third with 158. A majority of the electorate appeared to favor the traditional policy of free trade.

## BRITAIN'S FIRST LABOR GOVERNMENT

The outcome of the election entailed a change in the government. Clearly Baldwin had been rejected on the platform of protection, but on the other hand no single party now controlled a majority. Either a coalition or a minority government therefore became necessary. But none of the parties appeared anxious to merge its identity in a coalition again. The final outcome was the resignation of the Baldwin ministry and the elevation of Ramsay MacDonald to the premiership as the head of Great Britain's first Labor government, the highest point yet reached by Labor in its rapid rise from a minor parliamentary group with only twenty-nine seats in 1906.

But the change in government entailed no radical departure from well-established British policies by the introduction of anything suggestive of Bolshevism, for, in the words of MacDonald, "Our Labor movement has never had the least inclination to try short cuts to the millennium." In fact, one of the reasons why the Labor Party had increased so rapidly was the growing recognition by the British people of the essentially constitutional character of the movement. A second reason why nothing radical was to be expected in the way of legislation was the fact that Labor was dependent upon one of the other parties for the support necessary to enact any measure. Consequently Labor was compelled to defer its more far-reaching proposals such as the capital levy, for lack of an adequate majority. No bill could be pushed through Parliament by party discipline alone; it would have to win the support of more than one political group. MacDonald's government was therefore bound to cut a rather sorry figure in domestic affairs, especially since the economic situation was largely out of the power of any British government to control.

The Laborites were almost immediately confronted with an epidemic of serious strikes, but by their firmness in handling the strikers, who came from their own ranks, they gained the confidence and respect of the country at large. This confidence was retained by their handling of the fiscal problem, in which nothing especially radical was undertaken. The tax on cheap amusements was repealed, and, in spite of the vigorous protests of the protected interests, the protective duties inaugurated by Lloyd George were abolished. No attempt was made to introduce a capital levy. In accordance with their platform a bill was passed providing a scheme for building inexpensive houses with the aid of government subsidies. They proved to be unable to lessen noticeably the number of unemployed, however.

It was in the realm of foreign affairs that MacDonald achieved his outstanding successes. His most spectacular move was his unconditional *de jure* recognition of the Soviet government of Russia on February 1, 1924. This was in full accord with his earlier pronouncement that the first step in the process of settling affairs with Russia should be recognition, which was the key for reopening the markets of that country to British goods. The immediate sequel of this move was the Anglo-Russian conference, which opened in London in April, 1924, in an attempt to negotiate a general treaty of amity and commerce to replace the trade agreement of 1921, and to effect a settlement of the claims arising out of the Soviet government's repudiation of Russia's debts and the confiscation of private property. Two treaties were finally drafted and signed,[2] the immediate effect of which would be merely the favorable treatment of British goods in Russian markets.

The Russian treaties were immediately attacked not only by the Conservatives but even by Lloyd George, who had been responsible for the first trade agreement of 1921. In fact, the desertion of MacDonald by the Liberals at this time was the beginning of the end. A little later he was again attacked by them because his government had abandoned the prosecution of a Communist accused of inciting British soldiers to mutiny. Without a majority to support him, MacDonald dissolved Parliament and appealed to the electorate. For the third time in two years the British voters were called upon for a decision. In this campaign both the Conservatives and the Liberals directed their attacks against Labor. The latter's prospects were injured by the publication, shortly before the election, of a letter purporting to be from Zinoviev, the head of the Third International, urging British Communists to prepare the way for a revolution in Great Britain. Moderates were frightened by the specter of what

[2] In a treaty of commerce and navigation Russia gave unconditional most-favored-nation treatment to British goods. In a general treaty she admitted liability for the claims of British bondholders and promised to negotiate with them, and agreed that such other claims as were established by a joint commission should be embodied in a subsequent treaty. The British government for its part, agreed that, as soon as the British claims had been settled by a subsequent treaty, it would submit to Parliament a proposal to guarantee a loan to the Soviet government.

might follow if the detested Socialists were returned to power. At the same time many workers were disappointed by the continuance of unemployment even under a Labor government.

In the election, although Labor piled up a total of 5,500,000 popular votes, its parliamentary representation was reduced to 155. Since the Liberals elected only 36 members, the Conservatives were swept back into power with a top-heavy parliamentary majority of over two hundred, though they obtained less than a majority of the popular vote. With such a Conservative majority in the House, Baldwin of course returned to Downing Street, and MacDonald stepped down to his earlier position of leader of the opposition.

## FIVE YEARS OF CONSERVATIVE GOVERNMENT

But the change in government brought no immediate improvement in Britain's economic situation. During the ensuing year the production of coal, iron ore, and pig iron, the basic industries of the kingdom, remained considerably below the prewar figure. In the hope of "safeguarding employment" and, incidentally, of satisfying certain British industrial interests, Baldwin returned to the tariff policy inaugurated by Lloyd George and afterward repealed by the Labor government. Over the protests of the opposition, who declared that he was violating his campaign pledges, a plan for partial protection was enacted.

The coal industry, in which the industrial depression was most pronounced, profited little from this scheme, however. The price of coal continued to fall, and the operators, in order to cut the cost of production, asked the miners to lengthen the working day from seven to eight hours and to accept a cut in wages. The miners refused to agree to these proposals, whereupon the operators availed themselves of a provision of the existing wage agreement to terminate it on July 31, 1925. In order to prevent a coal strike the government then subsidized the industry until May 1, 1926, pending a permanent settlement. Before that date a royal commission under Sir Herbert Samuel made an investigation of the coal industry. In its report it stated that three fourths of the coal raised was being produced at a loss. It recommended national ownership of the mines [3] and an extensive reorganization of the industry, including

[3] Eventually, in April, 1937, Prime Minister Baldwin announced that the government had agreed to pay the 4300 mine owners of the country £66,450,000 in return

the closing of the pits which were permanently impossible of operation at a profit. It declared that the coal industry was facing disaster and that, to restore the industry to solvency, wage reductions were necessary.

When the mine operators notified the miners that the existing wage agreement would end on May 1, the latter decided to strike. The Trades Union Congress, in order to assist the miners, thereupon called a sympathetic strike in certain vital industries, including the transport services and the printing trade. In popular belief Great Britain faced a "general strike," but this was hardly the case. Less than half of the six million trade-union members were called out, and it was specifically ordered that work should not cease in electric and gas, sanitary, and health and food services. The government at once declared a state of emergency and issued an appeal for volunteers to maintain the essential services. The generous response to this appeal more than any other factor contributed to the failure of the sympathetic strike.

The "general strike" lasted only nine days. On May 12 the Trades Union Congress announced the decision to end it with the understanding that negotiations would be resumed regarding the wages of miners. These, however, resulted in no agreement. The operators demanded lower wages; the miners refused to return to work. In July Parliament passed a law providing for an eight-hour day in the coal industry, but the act produced no coal, and it became necessary to import large quantities from Germany and the United States. Finally, after more than seven months, the strike came officially to an end on November 19 with the complete surrender of the miners' unions. Their submission was forced by the exhaustion of their resources and by their inability to prevent numbers of miners from returning to work. With winter coming on, longer hours and lower wages seemed preferable to no work at all.

The Conservative Party, never particularly sympathetic with trade unions or the labor movement, availed itself of the state of public opinion and the exhaustion of labor after the great strike of 1926 to pass the Trades Disputes and Trades Union Act in the following year. By the terms of this law, a general strike became illegal, picket-

for the extinction of their claims to all future royalties. This nationalization of coal royalties was expected to clear the way for a systematic reorganization of the coal industry by a central government authority, for after 1950 the British government will own all the coal deposits.

ing was forbidden, and no member might be disciplined by a trade union for refusing to participate in an illegal strike. The Trades Dispute Act of 1906 was repealed in so far as it exempted trade unions from legal suit, and trade-union funds might be enjoined by the attorney-general. A blow was struck at the Labor Party by including a provision that trade unions might make political levies on their members only if the latter gave specific permission in writing. Formerly the law had stated that such levies might be made unless a member formally protested.

In 1928 Baldwin carried out his campaign pledge to extend the ballot to all women on the same age basis as to men. Another five million voters, it was estimated, were thus added to the registers. An attempt to reorganize the House of Lords so as to increase its strength and importance had to be abandoned in the face of the strong opposition which was aroused. A number of measures of social legislation were enacted, undoubtedly the most important being the act for widows', orphans', and old-age pensions. Based on the principle that the state, the employer, and the worker should each contribute to the fund, it provided that every insured worker should receive a pension at the age of sixty-five, and that, if he died before that age, his widow and children should receive pensions.

In foreign affairs the Conservative government largely continued the spirit of co-operation and conciliation so happily inaugurated by the Labor premier. Only in respect to Russia was the latter's foreign policy completely reversed. Baldwin refused to submit to Parliament the treaties which the Labor government had negotiated, so that both lapsed, and the trade agreement of 1921 remained the basis of relations between Russia and Great Britain. On May 12, 1927, in the belief that certain secret documents which had disappeared from the British War Office had come into Russian possession, the government raided the offices of Arcos, Ltd., the headquarters of Russia's trading agency in Great Britain. Although the lost documents were not discovered, the government declared that considerable evidence was found of Russian military espionage in Great Britain and of other revolutionary activities in the British Empire. As a result, Parliament voted to sever all relations with the Soviet government.

Meanwhile, despite the establishment of many new industries in southern England and the noticeable shift of industrial population into that region, and despite the fact that London in general was prosperous, the unemployment problem continued unsolved. The year 1928 saw a considerable increase in the number out of work, and ended with close to 2,000,000 unemployed—the highest number since the worst days of 1921–1922. The unparalleled distress and suffering, especially in the coal fields, aroused public generosity to supplement government grants in the work of alleviation.

So far as the government was concerned, the chief measures taken to meet the unsatisfactory economic condition of the country were designed to safeguard certain British industries from foreign competition and to relieve them from the burden of local taxation. By 1929 industries producing motorcars, silk and artificial yarns, clocks and watches, cinematograph films, gloves, cutlery, china, and rubber tires and tubes were being safeguarded or, as critics asserted, "protected by the back door." By the reform in local taxation the great basic industries were freed from the oppressive burden which they declared was strangling them. As a consequence of the new legislation they were relieved to the extent of 75 per cent of the local taxes. In general, however, Baldwin advocated a policy of *laissez faire* toward business as a cure for unemployment.

Inevitably the problem of unemployment and rehabilitation of British trade was again the outstanding issue in the general election of May, 1929. "The great need of the day," declared one influential journal, "is a positive policy for dealing with unemployment by promoting industrial recovery as well as by providing immediate work. The party that has the best unemployment policy deserves to be the next Government." This fact the leaders of all three parties well realized, and in the campaign to win public favor each stated its position in respect to this problem. The solution put forward by the Liberal Party was national works on a colossal scale, including roads and bridges, telephone and electrical development, land drainage, London passenger traffic, and housing. This program, Lloyd George asserted, would reduce the terrible figures of unemployment to normal proportions in a single year.

Labor, which was hopeful of obtaining a clear majority over both of the other parties, offered a much more extensive and detailed program. The Labor Party advocated nationalization of the coal, transport, and power industries and of life insurance; the fostering of the migration of miners into other districts and other occupations, and the prohibition of the recruitment of adults from other industries into mining; the immediate raising of the school-leaving age; and a great national scheme for development of electrical power. To the workingmen it specifically promised the repeal of the Mines Act (1926) and the Trades Disputes Act (1927), the creation of a superannuation scheme for aged miners, a forty-eight-hour week, and steeply graded inheritance taxes and high supertaxes on the rich. The Conservative Party was disposed to stand on its record and to appeal to the conservative electorate. "Safety first!" was its slogan, and it asked the voters to support it as the defender of the constitution against the threat of the general strike and against the perils of socialism, and as the only party which could secure stable conditions and ordered progress along sound, practical lines.

The elections brought an increase in Labor's representation in the Commons from 160 to 289, while the Conservatives declined from 396 to 259. Owing to the fact that the Liberal Party elected 58 candidates, however, no party controlled a majority. But it was apparent that the Conservatives had been rejected, and Stanley Baldwin at once resigned the premiership. On June 5, 1929, Ramsay MacDonald for the second time accepted the king's invitation to form a government.

## The Second Labor Government

The second Labor government, like the first, was handicapped in carrying out its domestic policies by dependence upon either the Liberals or the Conservatives for support. But of the various pledges which the Labor leader had made regarding domestic legislation, he was able to carry out a few. A widows' pension bill was enacted to extend a weekly pension to approximately 500,000 widows unprovided for by the original measure passed by Baldwin's government. A new unemployment insurance act was passed with provisions designed to care for 1,000,000 unemployed at any time. A bill for the rehabilitation of the coal-mining industry became law, thus providing for price-fixing agreements, compulsory marketing schemes, and the possibility of compulsory amalgamation of mining enterprises in the same area. A bill for raising the compulsory school age was introduced, but in the face of the determined opposition of the Catholics, whose schools could not accommodate the increased numbers, the measure was dropped. Similarly, an amendment to the Trades Disputes Act was introduced to restore to Labor its privileges under the act of 1906, but again MacDonald was unable to carry his measure through Parliament.

In foreign affairs MacDonald returned to his earlier policy toward Soviet Russia. In December, 1929, full diplomatic relations were resumed with the Soviet government, on the latter's promise to abstain from subversive propaganda within the British Empire. This step led in April, 1930, to an Anglo-Russian trade treaty which provided for most-favored-nation treatment in commerce between the two countries. The treaty further stipulated that the general offices of the Russian trading corporation in Great Britain should be inviolate, thus obviating the possibility of another raid like that on the offices of Arcos, Ltd., in 1927. Finally, the treaty provided that the British government would guarantee a credit of $150,000,000 to be employed in financing Russian purchases in Great Britain during the ensuing two years.

Meanwhile, general business conditions in Great Britain improved not at all. Exports of manufactured goods declined in 1929. In 1930 the iron and steel trade fell to the lowest point in four years, and the depression in cotton manufacturing was considered the worst since the American Civil War. In 1930 the country's foreign trade declined by over $1,650,000,000. Naturally, these figures were reflected in the growth of unemployment. When Labor took office the unemployed numbered approximately 1,000,000; within a year the number had increased to over 1,700,000; and early in 1931 it reached the highest point since the war with more than 2,600,000 out of work. The government was, in general, helpless to remedy the economic situation. It did, however, take care of those without work. It not only contributed tens of millions of dollars, as its share, to the unemployment insurance fund, but advanced hundreds of millions more in the form of loans to the fund, which went steadily further into debt.

The severe drain upon the British budget, resulting from increasing expenditures and decreasing tax receipts, became evident when the fiscal year 1929–1930 closed with a deficit instead of the contemplated surplus. The deficit in the following year was still greater, and that for the year 1931–1932 appeared likely to reach $600,000,000. The prospect of such a seriously unbalanced budget caused alarm both within and without the kingdom. Gold began to flow in large amounts from Great Britain to the Continent. London, which served as a bank of deposit for foreign funds, had over a long period of years built up the tradition of meeting every obligation promptly and in full. But on this occasion it was fatally handicapped by the Hoover moratorium, which temporarily "froze" large sums that had been loaned by British bankers to Germany and other countries. With the British supply of liquid credit thus seriously impaired by inability to call in many short-term loans, it was imperative that steps be taken to increase confidence in British financial integrity.

At this point came the report of a committee of financial experts (May Committee) which had been appointed to make recommendations to the chancellor of the exchequer regarding the budget. To meet the prospective deficit the experts recommended severe reductions in expenditures for pensions, salaries, defense, public works, and social services. In order definitely to balance the budget, they suggested that some slight additional taxation would be necessary. Laborites immediately denounced the report on the ground that approximately 90 per cent of the reductions suggested would be at the expense of the classes from which the Labor Party drew its chief support. Economies such as these, they claimed, did not constitute "a general sacrifice." They demanded, instead, that the deficit be met chiefly by increased taxation. When Ramsay MacDonald and Philip Snowden, chancellor of the exchequer, decided to accept the experts' recommendations, the Labor Party split, and the Labor government was forced to resign.

MacDonald, apparently placing loyalty to Britain's welfare above loyalty to party pledges, undertook to organize a new ministry. For the third time he became premier, this time in a coalition of Laborites, Conservatives, and Liberals which became known as the National government. Philip Snowden, J. H. Thomas, and Lord Sankey followed their leader into the new government, and for this step they and MacDonald were read out of the Labor Party, which chose Arthur Henderson as its official leader.

## THE NATIONAL GOVERNMENT

In September, 1931, Snowden submitted a supplementary budget by means of which the prospective deficit was to be converted into a slight surplus. In general, the recommendations of the May Committee were followed. Drastic economies were effected in national expenditures by decreasing the amount spent on social services, on

army, navy, and air forces, and on government salaries. More than
half of the retrenchment was to be made by reductions in unemployment insurance payments and by increases in unemployment
insurance premiums. Meanwhile, the flow of gold from London
had continued. Fear that Great Britain might not be able to balance her budget, that she might be adversely affected by the critical
financial situation in central Europe, that she might have to abandon the gold standard, that a new election might bring further instability, led many foreigners and even Britishers themselves to
sell sterling. Speedy action was needed, and on September 21 Parliament suspended the gold standard. The British pound (normally
$4.86) at once depreciated, and in the succeeding months fluctuated
between $3 and $4.

In October the National government went to the country in a general election. This occasioned a split in the Liberal Party, for Lloyd
George and a number of his free-trade followers refused to give the
National government their support. On the other hand, Sir Herbert Samuel, acting leader of the Liberals, and Sir John Simon, who
had long been restless under Lloyd George's leadership, both threw
their lot in with the Nationalists and led what were called the
National Liberals. A few of the Laborites, generally referred to as
National Laborites, gave their support to MacDonald. The election, consequently, was a three-cornered struggle between the Nationalists (Conservatives, National Liberals, and National Laborites), the Laborites, and the free-trade Liberals.

The outcome of the election was an amazing triumph for Mac-
Donald's National government, which received 554 seats in a House
of Commons of 615. This huge total was composed of 471 Conservatives, 68 National Liberals, 13 National Laborites, and 2 independents. The 267 seats which the Labor Party had held before dissolution were cut to 52. Lloyd George's free-trade Liberals captured
only four seats. With the Conservatives so overwhelmingly returned
it was thought that Stanley Baldwin might head a new government, but instead he gave MacDonald free rein to choose his ministers. The latter's fourth cabinet, as finally organized in November, 1931, consisted of eleven Conservatives, five National Liberals,
and four National Laborites.

Three major domestic problems confronted the National government in the years that followed. The first was that of maintaining

a balanced national budget. The year 1931–1932 closed with a balance in the treasury, and the following year would have done likewise except for the war-debt payment to the United States for which no provision had been made in the budget.[4] The next four years, however, closed with surpluses. At the same time taxes were slightly reduced, and the reductions in unemployment insurance and in government salaries were gradually restored. When the budget for 1936–1937 was introduced, however, a reversal in the trend toward lower taxation was revealed. Because of German rearmament, Italy's aggressive policy in Africa and in the Mediterranean, and the apparent break-down of collective security, the government felt compelled to inaugurate an extensive defense program. In the so-called defense or rearmament budget, therefore, increases were made in income taxes, and a new tax was placed on tea. Despite considerable increases in taxes again in the following year, huge expenditures for armaments resulted in a budget for 1937–1938 which was slightly unbalanced.

The second problem with which the government wrestled was that of reducing the country's adverse balance of trade. A committee of the cabinet, appointed to consider ways and means, concluded that imports into the country must be restricted, and recommended a 10-per-cent tariff on a very wide range of manufactured and semi-manufactured articles. The new tariff was finally approved, and on March 1, 1932, after some eighty years of free trade, Great Britain again became a protectionist country. As a result of this step there followed a considerable decrease in British imports.

In the matter of increasing British exports, one step had already been taken which it was hoped would help, namely, the abandonment of the gold standard with the subsequent depreciation of the British pound. This move was expected to lower the cost of production in Great Britain and thus enable British goods to compete on more favorable terms in world markets. In the hope of increasing still further the demand for British goods, the government sent a delegation to the Imperial Economic Conference which met at Ottawa during the summer of 1932. At this conference Great Britain made a number of treaties with various parts of her empire, as a result of which she gained slight advantages for some of her manufactured goods at the expense of non-empire countries. But the ad-

[4] The government had expected the Hoover moratorium to be extended.

vantages which Great Britain extended to the dominions—particularly the duty on foreign wheat—aroused opposition in the cabinet and led in September, 1932, to the resignation of Lord Snowden,[5] Sir Herbert Samuel, and a number of others.

In subsequent years, by using the British protective tariff as a basis for bargaining, new reciprocal commercial agreements were negotiated with a number of countries for the purpose of increasing British exports, and these agreements were further supplemented by a system of import quotas designed to assure exports to some home industries and to control imports in favor of others. Partly in consequence of these steps the value of British exports rose after 1933. Although the visible balance of trade continued to be adverse, increases in returns from British shipping and from British investments abroad—coupled with the policy of making no war-debt payments to the United States—gave Great Britain a net favorable balance in international payments.

Meanwhile, the condition of industries manufacturing for home consumption and of agriculture had considerably improved, thanks in part to government policies, some of which strongly resembled those of the NRA and the AAA in the United States. Obligatory agreements to fix prices and wages, to control marketing, to abandon inefficient plants and out-of-date equipment, and to set up machinery for the self-regulation of industry were instigated or encouraged by the government. Financial assistance was granted to aid in the rationalization of some of the backward industries. Agricultural subsidies, processing taxes, protective tariffs, and import quotas were used to preserve the home markets against foreign competition. In addition, the whole recovery movement was accelerated by an extensive slum-clearance and housing program. In the summer of 1935 the index of general business activity reached the 1929 level.

The third major problem which faced the government during these years was the perennial one of unemployment. Despite all the efforts of the government to improve the situation, at the end of 1932 the number of unemployed had risen to the highest point reached at any time since the war, over 3,000,000 being out of work. Improvement came in the succeeding years, however. By 1937 the number of unemployed had fallen below 1,500,000. One has but to

[5] In 1931 Philip Snowden was created Viscount Snowden of Ickornshaw, and took a seat in the House of Lords.

recall that the unemployed numbered only about one million when the second Labor government took office in 1929 to realize that Britain's unemployment problem still persists.[6] In certain "depressed areas" in South Wales, in the north of England, and in Scotland the situation remains particularly bad.

Politically, the position of the National government appeared to be weakening in 1934. In by-elections the Labor Party was usually able to reduce the immense majorities received by the National government in 1931. Probably most spectacular was the triumph of the Labor Party in the London County Council election in March, when Labor won a majority for the first time in its history, and displaced the Conservatives who had controlled the Council for a generation. In November Labor repeated its victory by extending its control from four to fifteen of London's twenty-eight boroughs. In other parts of the kingdom somewhat similar shifts in electoral strength were evident, so that it appeared that the Labor Party would be a much stronger contender for power in the next parliamentary election than it had been in 1931.

On June 7, 1935, Ramsay MacDonald submitted his resignation and that of his cabinet. Although the prime minister's ill health was given as the reason for this step, it is possible that beneath that lay MacDonald's declining popularity and loss of effectiveness as a political leader. Stanley Baldwin, head of the Conservative Party, which had dominated the National government, at once accepted the premiership and organized a ministry which for the most part consisted of those who had already been serving. MacDonald remained in the cabinet as lord president of the council. Four months later, the new premier cleverly seized upon a critical international situation to retain control of the government for another term of years. A huge unofficial peace ballot taken earlier in the year had showed that at least 10,000,000 voters favored the League of Nations and the use of economic sanctions against a warring nation. These millions might be expected to look with favor upon a government which had apparently dared to take the lead at Geneva against Italy's Ethiopian venture.[7] Moreover, the Labor Party had just approved the use of sanctions, but at the cost of a split in the party

---

[6] Of course, even before the war Great Britain had hundreds of thousands of unemployed.

[7] See pages 643 and 648.

and the loss of three of its outstanding leaders. Thus the most serious rival of the Conservatives was in no good position to wage an effective campaign. On October 25 Parliament was dissolved, and an election was called for November 14, 1935.

As was expected, the election resulted in an easy victory for the National government, although its previous majority was reduced to approximately 250. The Conservatives themselves had a majority of more than 150 over all the other parties combined. As was also expected, the Labor Party increased its representation considerably, adding nearly 100 seats to the number it had had before the election. The Liberal Party secured only 20 seats. The situation in the House of Commons again came to resemble the two-party system which most Englishmen prefer. Although both Ramsay MacDonald and his son, Malcolm, were defeated, they were included in the new cabinet, which remained very much as it had been before the election.

## EDWARD VIII AND GEORGE VI

During the summer of 1935 various celebrations were held in Great Britain to commemorate the twenty-fifth anniversary of George V's accession to the throne. The king held a high place in the affections of his people both because of his recognition of the limitations of his position as a constitutional ruler and because of his modesty, patriotism, and readiness to perform the duties which fell to him. During his Silver Jubilee the kingdom and empire united to show their high esteem for the monarch. Not many months after the completion of the festivities connected with his jubilee, however, the king was taken ill, and a few days later, on January 20, 1936, he died at the age of seventy. His eldest son, the former Prince of Wales, at once succeeded him as Edward VIII. But before the date set for the new monarch's coronation a constitutional crisis had forced him from the throne.

The crisis was precipitated in December, 1936, when the Baldwin government resisted the king's desire to marry a twice-divorced American woman. Edward argued that his marriage was a private matter on which he was not limited by the advice of his ministers, but the cabinet maintained that it was a public act which was bound to affect seriously the monarch's standing not only in Great Britain but in the dominions overseas. Baldwin insisted that the elevation to the British throne of a twice-divorced woman would undermine the prestige of the crown to such an extent that he was doubtful "if anything could restore it."

The king's proposal that Parliament should legalize a morganatic marriage which would not raise his wife to the rank of queen and would exclude their children from the succession was also refused by the government. The House of Commons, realizing that the issue was fundamentally a question of whether the will of the king should prevail over the advice of the cabinet representing Parliament, supported Prime Minister Baldwin.

Faced by this impasse, Edward VIII on December 10 informed Parliament of his decision to renounce the throne. On the next day Parliament passed the Abdication Act giving effect to the king's abdication and regulating the succession to the throne. Edward VIII then gave his official assent to the measure, and that night left England. On December 12 the accession of King George VI and Queen Elizabeth was proclaimed in London. The new king's first act was to confer upon Edward a dukedom and the title of Duke of Windsor. Five months later (May 12, 1937) King George and Queen Elizabeth were crowned at Westminster Abbey in the presence of thousands of representatives of the kingdom, commonwealth, and empire.

Shortly after the coronation Prime Minister Baldwin, who had been so much responsible for the change in monarchs, tendered his resignation and that of his cabinet, and retired from public life.[8] A new ministry was organized on May 28 by Neville Chamberlain, son of the Joseph Chamberlain who had led the Unionist secession from the Liberal Party in 1886. Although the Conservatives retained fifteen of the twenty-one major posts, the government was still "National" in the sense that it included National Laborites and National Liberals.

## THE BRITISH COMMONWEALTH OF NATIONS

According to Prime Minister Baldwin, the British government was guided to a great degree during the constitutional crisis of 1936 by the advice of the various dominion governments. The fact that it asked the assent of the dominion parliaments to the Abdication

---

[8] Stanley Baldwin was made an earl and took his place in the House of Lords. Ramsay MacDonald was also offered an earldom but declined.

Act is in itself indicative of a change which has occurred since 1914 in the constitutional organization of the empire ,over which Great Britain has so long presided. During the war an imperial conference recommended that the self-governing dominions be recognized as autonomous nations of an imperial commonwealth. Another conference in 1926 actually declared (Balfour Report) that Great Britain and the dominions were "autonomous communities within the British Empire, equal in status, in no way subordinate one to another . . . though united by a common allegiance to the Crown." A committee representing the "autonomous communities" was appointed (1929) to recommend the steps that should be taken to carry into effect this declaration, and its report was adopted by an imperial conference in 1930. This report was then transformed into law by the action of the parliaments of Great Britain and the dominions. In accordance with this procedure the Statute of Westminster was passed in December, 1931, by the British Parliament.

By the terms of this statute it was agreed that (1) no law passed by a dominion parliament could in the future be declared void because it was contrary to a law of Great Britain; (2) no law of the British Parliament could apply to any dominion unless the latter specifically requested it; (3) no longer might the king on the advice of his British ministers set aside an act of a dominion parliament; (4) no change in the laws concerning succession to the British throne might be made without the consent of the dominion parliaments. As early as 1930 the dominions had successfully contended that their choice of governor-generalship should be accepted.

As the Statute of Westminster legalized the dominions' independence in their domestic affairs, custom and practice has brought a notable change in their status so far as international relations are concerned. Whereas before the war the foreign policy of the empire as a whole was directed by a British ministry responsible to the Parliament in Westminster alone, in succeeding years it came to be directed to a large extent by the advice of the dominion ministers. At the same time, the dominions gained practical independence in their own foreign relations, being represented individually in the League of Nations, being allowed to administer mandates of the League in their own names, and having their own diplomatic representatives in many foreign capitals. Furthermore, they obtained the right to negotiate treaties for themselves and to refuse to ratify treaties entered into by Great Britain.

In other words, the British Empire in the years since 1914 has been transformed into something like a league of independent states bound together by a symbol, the crown, and co-operating through periodic imperial conferences of the prime ministers of the several states. Great Britain has thus ceased to be the ruling head of an empire and has become merely an equal member of the "British Commonwealth of Nations."

## THE IRISH FREE STATE

The postwar years saw a new dominion added to the British Commonwealth of Nations in an effort to solve the perplexing Irish question. The crisis which was provoked in Ireland at the time of the enactment of the Home Rule Bill in 1914 has already been discussed.[9] During the war the situation in Ireland improved not at all. Irish demands became more radical, and, under the direction of Sinn Fein leaders, home rule came to mean for many not a parliament for an Ireland which would still constitute a part of the British Empire, but the establishment of a republic under which Ireland should be as independent of Great Britain as is the United States. This desire for independence resulted in an Irish revolt in 1916, planned in conjunction with the military leaders of Germany.

Although the rebellion was quickly suppressed, a very decided drift into the ranks of Sinn Fein continued. This was clearly revealed in the parliamentary elections of 1918 when the Sinn Feiners won an overwhelming victory outside Ulster. The newly elected Sinn Fein representatives thereupon asserted that the elections constituted a mandate in favor of an independent republic, and proceeded to organize themselves into an Irish parliament, the Dail Eireann. In January, 1919, the latter elected Eamon De Valera "President of the Irish Republic." During the following months what practically amounted to a state of war existed between the "Irish Republic" and Great Britain.

In December, 1920, a new Home Rule Bill was passed by the British Parliament. This measure provided for two parliaments in Ireland, one for the six counties in northeast Ulster and one for the

<hr>

[9] See pages 209–211.

rest of the island. It conferred greater powers upon the Irish legislatures than those given by the act of 1914, but reserved certain imperial services such as the army, navy, foreign relations, customs, and excise to the parliament at Westminster. In this latter body the two divisions of Ireland were still to be represented by duly elected though somewhat less numerous members. Northern Ireland at once accepted this plan as preferable to subordination to a parliament at Dublin, and proceeded to carry it out. On June 22, 1921, the parliament of Northern Ireland was formally opened by King George V. In Ireland, outside Ulster, however, the act was generally repudiated, for the Sinn Feiners refused to have anything to do with a scheme which seemed to make permanent the partition of the island.

Two days after the opening of the Ulster parliament Lloyd George invited De Valera to confer with him regarding the possibility of a settlement. But the proposals which the British prime minister made in the ensuing conference were characterized as unacceptable by De Valera and were rejected by the Irish Dail Eireann. Nevertheless, Lloyd George extended a second invitation, and in October, 1921, another conference met in the prime minister's official residence in London. Representing the Sinn Feiners were such Irish leaders as Arthur Griffith, Michael Collins, Eamon J. Duggan, and Gavan Duffy. De Valera did not attend. After eight weeks of intermittent negotiations the signatures of the plenipotentiaries were eventually affixed to a treaty providing for the establishment of the Irish Free State.

Under this agreement the Irish Free State was to have "the same constitutional status in the community of nations known as the British Empire as the Dominion of Canada" and the other self-governing dominions. The crown was to be represented in Ireland by an officer "to be appointed in like manner as the Governor-General of Canada." The Free State assumed responsibility for a share of the British national debt, the amount to be determined later. It was to have its own military forces, and its own armed vessels for the protection of revenue and fisheries. Certain harbor facilities were conceded by the Free State to the imperial government, and the coast of Ireland was to be defended by the British fleet, pending an arrangement to be negotiated later. Northern Ireland was not to be included in the Free State if it declared its desire to continue under the act of 1920.

The treaty at once created a schism in the ranks of Sinn Fein. De Valera denounced it as in violent conflict with the wishes of the majority of the Irish and urged its rejection. Arthur Griffith, on the other hand, asserted that the treaty would lay the foundation of peace and friendship between Ireland and England, that the end of the conflict of centuries was at hand. In the Dail the treaty, after much debate, was accepted. De Valera thereupon resigned from the presidency, and Arthur Griffith was chosen to succeed him. A few days later De Valera and his followers withdrew from the Dail. The bare majority which remained set up a provisional government under the chairmanship of Michael Collins.

De Valera next plunged Ireland into civil war. The "Irregulars," as the men in his Irish republican army came to be called, subjected southern Ireland to an orgy of destruction, in the course of which the country was desolated. Bridges and viaducts were blown up, railways and roads were destroyed, houses were burned, supplies were requisitioned, "traitors to the republic" were "executed." On August 12, 1922, came the unexpected death of Arthur Griffith, founder of Sinn Fein but since 1921 a loyal supporter of the Irish Free State treaty. Four days later Michael Collins, a Sinn Feiner who had turned his unbounded courage and energy to the defense of the Free State, was ambushed and killed. Ireland presented, in the words of Kevin O'Higgins, "the spectacle of a country bleeding to death, of a country steering straight for anarchy, futility, and chaos." But under the guidance of William Cosgrave and Kevin O'Higgins the provisional government resorted to vigorous measures to restore order. In the spring of 1923 De Valera finally admitted the impossibility of continuing the struggle, and ordered his followers to put aside their arms.

Some months before this the Irish Free State had been legally established. In September, 1922, a provisional parliament had met and elected Cosgrave president of the provisional government. The parliament at once gave its attention to its constituent duties and on October 25 adopted a constitution. As in the other dominions, the executive authority was vested nominally in the king, represented in the Free State by a governor-general. Actual executive power was placed in the hands of an executive council, directly responsible to the lower house of the legislature. The legislature (*Oireachtas*) was to consist of two houses, the Chamber of Deputies (*Dail Eireann*) and the Senate (*Seanad Eireann*). The latter was to be elected indirectly for twelve years, one fourth of the mem-

IRELAND TODAY

bers being chosen every three years. The Chamber of Deputies was to be chosen by a system of proportional representation with universal suffrage.

Early in December the constitution received the assent of King George, and on December 6, 1922, the Irish Free State was established by royal proclamation. In September, 1923, representatives of the Free State were received into the Assembly of the League of Nations; in October Cosgrave for the first time attended a dominion conference in London. Diplomatic representatives of the Free

State were established in Washington, Geneva, Paris, Berlin, and Brussels, and a high commissioner took up his residence in London. In a reaction against the use of English, Gaelic was made compulsory for civil servants and for lawyers, and the Irish representative in the League of Nations Assembly was even instructed to make his speeches in Gaelic. Family and place names were Gaelicized, the best-known example being the change from Queenstown to Cobh. The difficulty of using Gaelic, however, prevented the universal adoption of the language. Irish nationalism did obtain some satisfaction, however, in the adoption of Irish coins and postage stamps.

In the summer of 1927, when it began to seem that Ireland was at last settling down to a somewhat ordered life, the world was shocked by the recurrence of assassination. On July 10 Kevin O'Higgins, vice-president of the executive council of the Free State and the "strong man" of the government, was deliberately shot and killed by three assailants. O'Higgins had been Cosgrave's chief lieutenant since the assassination of Collins and the death of Griffith. As minister of justice he had been largely responsible for the vigorous measures which had suppressed the republican opposition. The "Irregulars" had long hated him. Although De Valera and his followers disclaimed any connection with the assassination of O'Higgins, popular opinion throughout the world was inclined to place part of the responsibility for the deed upon the obstructionist tactics of the republican leader.

Soon after this event De Valera changed his tactics. Until then he and his republican followers had refused to take the oath of allegiance to the British king and in consequence had been excluded from the Chamber of Deputies. In August, 1927, De Valera announced that he would take the oath and would undertake to become the head of a constitutional opposition. In parliamentary elections held in the following month his Fianna Fail Party increased its representation, but Cosgrave's Free State Party won the largest number of seats, and with the support of some of the lesser groups President Cosgrave was enabled to remain in office.

Nevertheless, despite the very real material and nationalistic gains which came to the Irish as a result of Cosgrave's administration, the world depression inevitably affected the popularity of his government. As sentiment in practically all countries where democratic government prevailed turned against the parties in power during the years of the depression, so it was in Ireland. Furthermore, De Valera constantly appealed to the Irish with a very definitely anti-British—and therefore popular—program. The extreme republicans were attracted by his demand for the abolition of the oath of allegiance to the British king. Small landholders were won by his promise to withhold the land annuities which they were compelled to pay under the land-purchase agreements of earlier years.

De Valera entered the political campaign of 1932 with a platform which called for the abolition of the oath to the British king, the retention by the Irish treasury of the land annuities which were due under agreements of 1921, 1923, and 1926, and the enactment of a protective tariff. In general, he advocated a policy of political and economic self-sufficiency for Ireland. The subsequent voting resulted in the election of 72 members of Fianna Fail and 65 followers of Cosgrave, but representatives of lesser parties held the balance of power. When the Laborites threw their support to De Valera, the latter was elected president of the executive council in March, 1932.

De Valera at once undertook to carry out his promises. In April a bill was introduced in the Chamber to remove the oath from the Irish constitution, but opposition in the Senate, which Cosgrave's followers controlled, prevented the bill from becoming a law.[10] On July 1 De Valera withheld the payment of £1,500,000 due on the land annuities. This action the British government declared was a violation of a binding engagement of the Irish Free State, and the British parliament passed a law empowering the government to levy a duty up to 100 per cent on Irish goods coming into Great Britain, in order to secure funds equivalent to the defaulted land annuities. De Valera retaliated with Irish duties which were almost prohibitive on certain British goods, and a tariff war therefore ensued. That De Valera's policy had the support of a majority of the Irish seemed apparent when new elections in January, 1933, returned the Fianna Fail Party with a clear majority over all opposition.

In an effort to make the Irish Free State less dependent upon Great Britain economically, De Valera encouraged the expansion of local industry and sought to persuade farmers to strike a more reasonable balance between grazing and tillage. Undoubtedly a

[10] In 1936 the Senate was abolished.

DESTRUCTION IN MADRID

Loyalists made homeless by insurgents' bombs.

considerable development of industry occurred, and many commodities which formerly had to be imported came to be manufactured in the Free State. But the attempt to make Ireland economically more self-sufficient, although perhaps beneficial in the long run, had unfortunately the effect of raising the cost of living in the Free State. De Valera, nevertheless, stoutly asserted that Ireland was "prepared to take the full consequences of being an independent nation."

What these consequences might be economically was revealed when the annual trade reports were published. In 1933–1934 the country's adverse balance of trade was the highest in the history of the Free State; in 1934–1935 it was still higher. Indeed, the Free State's total foreign trade for 1934–1935 was only 60 per cent of that for 1930–1931, the year before De Valera became president. Obviously, no adequate substitute market for Free State produce had been found to take the place of Great Britain. By 1936 it was becoming apparent that De Valera's hope of making the Free State economically independent of Great Britain was destined to be blasted, and early in that year the Free State president practically admitted the failure of his plan. In a trade agreement signed in 1936 the Free State government removed the duty on British coal and gave the British practically a monopoly of the market for that commodity within its territory. It also reduced the duties on a great number of other commodities usually imported from Great Britain and agreed to purchase one third of its cement from British firms. In return Great Britain, although still retaining high duties on many Irish products, reduced them somewhat on livestock and meats.

Meanwhile De Valera had been taking steps to emphasize the political independence of the Irish Free State. In May, 1933, the Chamber of Deputies again passed the bill abolishing the oath of allegiance, and this time it became law. Next the governor-general's approval was made unnecessary for the legalization of acts passed by the Irish parliament. Later in the year the right of appeal from Irish courts to the British Privy Council was abolished. In March, 1934, De Valera arranged that the new United States minister to the Irish Free State should present his credentials, not to the governor-general as the representative of the British crown, but to the president of the executive council. Later in the same year he introduced a bill in the Chamber to create a separate Free State citizenship and to abolish British citizenship in the Irish Free State. In 1935 no Free State delegate attended the celebration of the twenty-fifth anniversary of King George's accession to the throne. The absence of such a delegate was doubtless one more gesture designed to emphasize De Valera's determination to cut the Free State off from Great Britain. A similar gesture was made again in January, 1936, when King George died. The Irish Free State government took no step to proclaim King Edward VIII in Dublin and sent no official representative to the funeral of the deceased ruler. In December, 1936, during the constitutional crisis in Great Britain, the Chamber of Deputies abolished the office of governor-general and the British king's prerogatives in Ireland's domestic affairs. Although the Chamber gave its necessary official assent to the Abdication Act, the Free State government refused to proclaim the new king in Dublin or to send an official representative to his coronation in the following May.

In April, 1937, De Valera published a new Irish Free State constitution which proclaimed the Irish nation's "indefeasible and sovereign right to choose its own form of government, to determine its relations with other nations and to develop its life, political, economic and cultural, in accordance with its own genius and traditions." Nowhere in the constitution was there any mention of Great Britain or the British king. The new constitution provided for a president who should be elected by direct vote of the people for a seven-year term and who in a sense was to occupy the titular position formerly held by the governor-general. Executive power was to be exercised chiefly by a prime minister and cabinet responsible to the Chamber of Deputies. The parliament was to consist of a popularly elected Chamber of Deputies and an indirectly elected or nominated Senate.

After consideration of the draft of the new constitution by the Chamber, the latter was dissolved and an election was called with De Valera's policies as the issue. At the same time the proposed constitution was submitted to the voters for their approval or rejection. Although the constitution was approved by slightly more than 56 per cent of those who voted, De Valera's Fianna Fail Party did not fare so well. Its representation in the Chamber was reduced from 77 to 69, and De Valera found himself dependent upon the Labor Party for a working majority in the Chamber of Deputies.

## CHAPTER XXIII

## FRANCE AND SPAIN

FRANCE was the only great power on the Continent which in the postwar period continued to hold to the liberal tradition despite the many serious problems which confronted her. Though the uncertainties, anxieties, and hardships inevitably accompanying the attempts to solve these problems led many to advocate and support communism or fascism, the bulk of the French people stood loyally by their liberal republic. In France's neighbor, Spain, the postwar years saw a valiant attempt to introduce a liberal regime which resulted in the downfall of monarchy and the establishment of a republic. The Spanish liberals, however, were handicapped from the start by strong opposition from both the reactionary Rightists and the radical Leftists, and ultimately the republic succumbed to a civil war which threatened at times to engulf all Europe.

### ALSACE-LORRAINE'S RETURN TO FRANCE

One of the first problems which confronted the French Republic after the war was that of assimilating into a unitary state the provinces of Alsace-Lorraine, whose institutions in the years after 1871 had come to differ from those of France. Friction soon developed between the inhabitants of the "redeemed" provinces and the French government because of political changes. Under Germany the provinces had constituted a single political unit which, though ruled arbitrarily by the imperial government until 1911, had in that year been granted a local legislature with considerable power. But in a unitary state like France there is no place for provincial legislatures. In accordance with the French system of government Alsace-Lorraine in 1919 was divided into three departments, and the legislature was ignored. Strasbourg ceased to be a capital with governmental powers and organs and became simply a prefecture. The inhabitants of the provinces were naturally reluctant to lose their local rights. Furthermore, they complained that officials sent out from

Paris knew no German, the language most nearly akin to that spoken by the majority of the people.

The matter of language also caused ill feeling in the provinces. The great majority of Alsatians and Lorrainers speak patois or dialects closely related to high German, which is used in printing and writing. Only German was taught in the elementary schools during the years in which the provinces were included in the German Empire, but with the return to France the official language of the schools of Alsace-Lorraine became French. It was required that during the first two years of the elementary schools French should be studied exclusively; after that three hours a week of instruction in German was also provided. The French government insisted that French should have a primary place in the school system and discouraged the use of German, despite the desire of many Alsatians for language equality.

The greatest dissatisfaction arose from the government's efforts to change the religious and educational situation in Alsace-Lorraine. At the time when the provinces were taken from France in 1871, these matters were regulated by the concordat which Napoleon had concluded with the pope in 1801. Under this agreement the salaries of the clergy were paid by the government, which had a voice in their appointment, and education was almost entirely under the control of the church. The German government had respected these arrangements in Alsace-Lorraine when it annexed the provinces and had permitted them to continue. In France, on the other hand, subsequent anticlerical legislation had completely altered the situation.[1]

France, a highly centralized unitary state, has no provision for local differences in such matters as education. Nevertheless, President Poincaré at the time of the recovery of Alsace and Lorraine had pledged the retention of their religious system, and the government had winked at the anomalous situation created in France when it permitted the religious and educational situation in Alsace-Lorraine to continue undisturbed. But the government which came into power in France in 1924 was definitely anticlerical, and determined to introduce in Alsace-Lorraine the same regime as existed elsewhere in France. When it attempted to disestablish the churches

[1] See pages 120–124.

and to introduce secular schools, however, it encountered the active obstruction of the people. The Catholic school children of Alsace-Lorraine united in a great strike, and Catholics in many other parts of France vigorously protested. In the end a compromise solution was adopted. An "interconfessional" school system was introduced in accordance with which the children were to be sent for their academic instruction to a common school without regard to their religious beliefs but were to be separated for their religious instruction.

Many of those in Alsace-Lorraine who had welcomed French troops so enthusiastically as "liberators" who would bring in "a new era of liberty, prosperity, and happiness" later had serious doubts as to whether their return to France was altogether an unmixed blessing. In fact, stimulated by grievances and fears as well as by a highly financed propaganda, disgruntled elements of the Alsatian population were gradually won over to an autonomist movement which sought home rule or even separation from France. So serious did the situation become that early in 1929 the Chamber of Deputies devoted itself for more than two weeks to a consideration of the problems connected with the administration of Alsace-Lorraine. In the succeeding years, however, and especially after the Nazis came into power in Germany, autonomist agitation largely ceased.

While the political, religious, and educational problems raised by the return of Alsace-Lorraine were largely temporary and might be expected to disappear with the passing of the years, the economic benefits brought to France by the "redeemed" provinces were likely to be permanent. Although the provinces were rich agriculturally, their chief contributions to French economic well-being were their mineral and industrial resources. The iron mines of Lorraine more than doubled the production of iron ore in France, and the coal mines of the provinces contributed several millions of tons of coal yearly. The provinces also brought France rich potash deposits and some petroleum. Moreover, Lorraine had great iron and steel industries, and the textile mills of Alsace increased the number of spindles in France by more than 20 per cent. In natural resources and industrial equipment, therefore, France was stronger after 1918 than she had been before the World War.

### THE PROBLEM OF RECONSTRUCTION IN FRANCE

Nevertheless, at the close of the World War, throughout some 12,884 square miles of northern France chaos reigned. Here in prewar days had dwelt one eighth of France's population. Here had been concentrated the greater part of her industries and mines. But as a result of the war hundreds of towns and villages had become deserted wastes of shapeless ruins. Hundreds of thousands of homes had been wrecked or totally destroyed. Thousands of factories had been looted or blown up; mines had been allowed to fill with water or been deliberately destroyed; railways had become dilapidated and worn out. Millions of acres of once smiling farmland had been cut and torn and scarred with trenches and shell holes. Orchards and forests had been shot to pieces or razed by the retreating Germans; thousands of wells had been damaged, contaminated, or destroyed; hundreds of thousands of cattle and other stock had been carried off; and everywhere mile upon mile of barbed-wire entanglements and heaps of debris had been left to encumber the ground.

The restoration of this territory to its prewar state constituted a gigantic problem for France. During the war the French government had promised to reimburse its citizens for all direct and material losses occasioned by the war; in other words, it took the stand that losses occasioned by war were to be reimbursed by the state as a matter of right. With the cost of replacement of damaged and destroyed property averaging five times its estimated value in 1914, partly in consequence of the decline of the franc, the French government was thus called upon to expend billions in the work of restoration. But it was hoped and expected that whatever was spent for this purpose would ultimately be recovered from Germany under the treaty of Versailles.

The procedure of the French government, therefore, was to create for the reconstruction of the devastated area a special budget known as the "budget of recoverable expenditures." To this budget were charged all expenditures for restoration, and for this purpose money was spent freely and, some said, not without fraud. Since reparations payments were not immediately forthcoming, however, income for the special budget was provided from loans floated by the French government with the understanding that they would ultimately be retired when German reparations payments began to come in. By

May, 1921, great strides had been made in the work of restoration, in the course of which the French government had spent over 20,-000,000,000 francs, but up to that date France had actually received nothing from Germany to apply on her reparations account.

## The Problem of National Finance in France

It was inevitable that the reparations problem should become involved in French politics. Briand, the premier in 1921, stood for a policy of reasonable moderation and conciliation. But with France's failure to receive reparations payments of any size, Frenchmen became restless. When at the close of 1921 Germany asked and was later granted a partial moratorium, the Nationalists, led by such men as Raymond Poincaré and André Tardieu, took up cudgels against Briand, and in January, 1922, he was forced out of office and was succeeded by Poincaré. The latter's policy, culminating in the French occupation of the Ruhr and the subsequent appointment of the Dawes Committee, has already been traced.

By 1924, however, a number of circumstances conspired to weaken Poincaré's position. The continued fall of the franc reacted against him, as did the accompanying rise in the cost of living. The failure to secure reparations from Germany, the increase in the national debt, the heavier taxes being laid upon Frenchmen, and the inability of the government to balance the national budget gave his opponents numerous opportunities to attack him. Through the efforts of Briand a Left bloc was finally organized with the purpose of defeating Poincaré, and in the general parliamentary elections in May, 1924, the parties of the Left were returned in a majority, the Radical Socialists constituting the largest single group in the new Chamber.

The immediate result of this reversal in French politics was the downfall of both Premier Poincaré and President Millerand. That Poincaré should be forced to resign was, of course, quite to be expected under the French parliamentary system. But the French president was constitutionally considered to be in somewhat the same position as the king of England relative to party politics, that is, not affected by the fluctuations in party strength or by the rise and fall of ministries. The leaders of the Left bloc, however, now resolved that Millerand must resign because he had overstepped his presidential prerogatives by pursuing a personal policy and by openly supporting the National bloc during the preceding electoral campaign.

When, therefore, following Poincaré's resignation, President Millerand called upon Édouard Herriot, leader of the Radical Socialists, to form a government, the latter declined. The president then invited another member of the Chamber to assume the premiership, but the latter's cabinet when presented failed to secure the support of the Chamber. An impasse was thus created which was surmounted only when President Millerand resigned his office on June 11. Gaston Doumergue, president of the Senate and a member of the Left group, was elected president, and Herriot then accepted the new president's invitation to form a cabinet.

Herriot's most difficult problem was that of national finance. Four factors united to produce a serious crisis in the French fiscal system: the tremendous increase in the service charges on the debt of France, which had risen from 35 billion francs to 180 billion francs during the war; the enormous current expenditures required for the reconstruction of the devastated area in the early years of the postwar period; the relatively insignificant amounts actually received in reparations payments prior to 1926; and the failure of the government's system of taxation to bring in revenue sufficient to balance the budget. During the five years before Herriot came into power annual deficits had added a total of 150 billion francs to the already gigantic national debt. The national currency had become greatly inflated, and the franc, normally worth 19.3 cents, had depreciated until by March, 1924, it was worth less than 5 cents.

In 1924 the French people began to show a reluctance to make further loans to the government, and holders of short-term bills displayed an unwillingness to renew their loans as they came due. The government was unable to increase the national revenue materially because of the bitter conflict in the parliament over the method of taxation. The extreme Socialists asserted that French capital had not been subjected to as heavy income and excess-profit taxes as had British and American capital and now demanded that it be forced to help solve the fiscal problem of France by a capital levy. The government, unwilling to adopt such a measure, resorted to increases in the paper currency until in April, 1925, Herriot fell when the Chamber of Deputies refused to support his plan for further inflation. In the ensuing fifteen months no less than six ministries followed one another in rapid succession while the fiscal impasse remained.

By July, 1926, French bonds were selling far below par, the treasury was practically empty, the budget was still unbalanced, an enormous floating debt was maturing at the rate of 7,500,000,000 francs a month, the franc had fallen to 48 to the dollar, and the confidence of the French people in the integrity of the financial measures of their government had become seriously impaired. The crisis brought a radical change in the government. Party lines were at last obliterated, and a ministry of National Union was organized to include six former premiers under the leadership of France's "strong man," Poincaré, who was given practically dictatorial powers in the realm of finance.

Drastic measures were at once taken. The budget of recoverable expenditures was absorbed into the national budget, which in turn was greatly simplified. New tax measures were enacted, increasing the state's revenue by 9,300,000,000 francs. Extensive reforms in the administrative system reduced expenditures. The budget—the largest in the nation's history—was balanced, and the year 1926 closed with a surplus of over 1,500,000,000 francs in the treasury. The franc was gradually raised in value until by December 20, 1926, it stood at 25.19 to the dollar, where it was given *de facto* stabilization. These measures brought a return of investors' confidence in the government, which enabled the latter to adjust its floating debt advantageously. Renewed confidence in the government made it possible to reduce interest rates so that by 1928 the service charges on the floating debt had been decreased by over 300,000,000 francs yearly. Furthermore, the reconstruction of the devastated area was practically completed so that extraordinary expenditures for this purpose became negligible, while income from reparations payments under the Dawes plan increased.

In 1928 France had an opportunity to pass upon Poincaré's achievements in the parliamentary elections which were held in April. As in the elections four years earlier, the chief issue was Poincaré and his policies, but on this occasion the elections constituted a victory for his government. Poincaré continued to hold the premiership until ill health forced his resignation in July, 1929, when the removal of his strong hand from the helm of state brought a return of the republic's traditional ministerial instability. Party politics again became active, and the succeeding years saw numerous ministries come and go, the most prominent premiers between 1929 and 1932 being

André Tardieu and Pierre Laval. As a result of parliamentary elections in May, 1932, the Radical Socialists again became the largest single group in the Chamber of Deputies, and in June of that year Herriot once more assumed the premiership.

### DEFLATION AND UNREST IN FRANCE

In the succeeding years the rise and fall of ministries was generally connected with some phase of the republic's perplexing budgetary, fiscal, or economic problems. France, because of her adhering to the gold standard, found herself obliged to compete with devalued British pounds and American dollars. In consequence, her foreign trade greatly decreased, as did tourist expenditures which formerly brought into the country hundreds of millions of dollars. Industrial output declined in most categories, the railways incurred deficits, and unemployment from the autumn of 1934 on progressively reached new high peaks for the postwar period. By bankers, exporters, and those catering to tourist trade the government was urged to devalue the franc once more in order to enable France to compete more successfully with foreign currencies. On the other hand, the *rentier* class, having learned by experience the effect of currency depreciation upon it, was unalterably opposed to any further experiments of that nature.

In general, the policy of French statesmen during the ensuing four years was that of deflation. That is, they sought by reductions in the wages of government employees, in the pensions of war veterans, and in the interest rate on government bonds to lessen the national expenditures, while at the same time they attempted by higher taxes to balance the budget and thus remove the necessity for increasing the national debt or inflating the currency. Such a policy inevitably incurred the opposition of many taxpayers, government employees, and war veterans. Furthermore, many in France argued that the government's fiscal system should be balanced not by deflation of the budget but by inflation of the currency. There was, accordingly, much dissatisfaction with the various attempts at deflation. Moreover, the governments' revenues regularly fell below budgetary estimates, so that deficits continued and the national debt mounted. Alarm at this latter development in turn occasionally created fear of monetary inflation and a consequent run on gold. Altogether, the position of the premiers who succeeded one another during these years was far from enviable. Édouard Herriot, Joseph Paul-Boncour, Édouard Daladier, Albert Sarraut, and Camille Chautemps, all Radical Socialists, held the premiership between June, 1932, and January, 1934.

During the winter of 1933–1934 the government became linked in the public mind with a pawnshop scandal which caused a loss of 200,000,000 francs to French investors. The failure of the police to find the absconder, Alexander Stavisky, led to charges of corruption against the administration of justice, and, when Stavisky killed himself, it was rumored that he had been shot by the police to prevent his revealing embarrassing information. Public demand for a complete reorganization of the government, accompanied by riots in the streets of Paris, eventually forced Chautemps out of office late in January, 1934.

But the disorders did not cease when he was succeeded by Daladier. Newspapers representing various elements in France, apparently seeking to embarrass the government, called upon their readers to gather for demonstrations on the day that the new cabinet was to appear before the Chamber of Deputies. On the one hand, royalists, war veterans, and members of the Patriotic Youth were urged to gather for a demonstration "to oppose the thieves and this abject regime"; on the other, Socialists and Communists were incited to defend their interests against "the forces of fascism" which were said to be seeking to destroy democracy.

Daladier, feeling that the police might not be able to cope with the situation unaided, had ordered some 3000 troops to Paris. Soldiers with machine guns were stationed on the steps of the Palais Bourbon where the Chamber of Deputies meets. On the night of February 6, while the crowds were milling about the Place de la Concorde and fighting the police, the floodlights suddenly went out. In the confusion that ensued police and troops, apparently without orders from their officers and actuated by "spontaneous personal reaction" under the impression that they were fighting in self-defense, began to use their pistols. Seventeen civilians were killed and more than six hundred were wounded. Of the police and military, one was killed and more than 1600 were wounded.

In view of these developments in Paris, the Daladier ministry was forced at once to resign. The situation was highly critical and demanded immediate and extraordinary steps if calm were to be restored. Prominent political leaders united in urging that former President Gaston Doumergue be made premier. In answer to their appeal this veteran statesman agreed to form a ministry on condition that he be given complete freedom in regard to his program and choice of ministers. Hailed as a "national savior," Doumergue arrived in Paris on February 8 and immediately organized a cabinet which included among its members six former premiers and Marshal Pétain. Nearly every shade of political opinion except the extremes was represented, only the royalists, Socialists, and Communists being omitted. The new ministry inspired confidence, political harmony was attained, and government economies were introduced.

But, when Doumergue sought to have the French constitution amended in order that the frequently repeated overthrow of cabinets might be checked, fear of a movement toward dictatorial rule caused opposition and brought the fall of his ministry in November, 1934. Again came a rapid succession of governments, headed by Pierre-Étienne Flandin, Fernand Bouisson, Pierre Laval, and Albert Sarraut.

The reluctance of the Chamber of Deputies to vote new powers to the premiers during these years was caused, in part, by the fear that a movement toward a fascist dictatorship was under way in France. The one most suspected was Colonel François de la Rocque, leader of the *Croix de Feu,* an organization of war veterans. Although Colonel de la Rocque for his program had been content with such vague statements as "Take France away from the politicians and give it back to the French people," he had been able by his oratory and personal magnetism to weld together an organization of several hundred thousand men. More or less allied with him were two other organizations of the Right, the royalist *Action Française* and the blue-shirted *Solidarité Française.* Not unmindful of the way in which fascist dictatorships had arisen in other countries during the postwar period, the Socialists and Communists, in turn, began more effectively to organize their ranks. Clashes inevitably occurred between the Right and Left groups, and each side accused the other of preparing to overthrow the government. So strained did the situation become that a law was passed forbidding the carrying of arms to public meetings and authorizing the dissolution of semimilitary organizations with uniforms, insignia, and arms. Following an unprovoked assault on Léon Blum, leader of the Socialist Party, by

members of the *Action Française,* President Lebrun [2] on February
13, 1936, decreed the dissolution of the *Action Française* and its two
subsidiary groups, the *Camelots du Roi* and the National Federation
of Students of the *Action Française.*

## THE POPULAR FRONT IN FRANCE

In preparation for the parliamentary elections to be held in the
spring of 1936 the Radical Socialists, the Socialists, and the Communists organized the Popular Front. Although the parties differed
among themselves on many points, on one fundamental they were
agreed—that a united and militant front must be organized against
the threat of fascism. Apparently the French electorate felt similarly,
for the elections resulted in a decisive victory for the Popular Front.
For the first time in French history the Socialists secured the largest
number of seats in the Chamber of Deputies. Léon Blum, the Socialist leader who was destined to be the next premier, sought to construct a ministry which would include representatives of all of the
Popular Front parties, but the Communists declined to enter such a
coalition. Blum's cabinet, therefore, when it finally took over the
reins of government on June 5, consisted of only Socialists and Radical Socialists and was partly dependent for its continued life upon
the support of the Communists.

At the time that the Blum government took office, France was
seriously disturbed by "sit-down" strikes involving hundreds of
thousands of workers who demanded wage increases, shorter hours,
and a two-week annual holiday with pay. Immediately upon assuming office the new premier arranged a settlement between the
workers and employers which granted wage increases. He also secured the enactment of legislation providing for a forty-hour week,
holidays with pay, and collective labor contracts. The strike situation
thereupon improved, although it was some months before all of
the major labor disputes were settled. Eventually the parliament empowered the government to provide by decree for the compulsory
mediation and arbitration of industrial conflicts. Meanwhile, on the
ground that its members were precipitating clashes by interfering

---

[2] In 1931 Doumergue was succeeded as president by Paul Doumer. On May 6, 1932,
the latter was assassinated by a Russian émigré, and Albert Lebrun was then elected
to be president of France.

with strikers, Blum in June, 1936, had ordered the dissolution of the *Croix de Feu*.[3]

During the summer two notable acts of reform legislation were passed. One provided for the nationalization of the country's armament industries; the other altered the composition and selection of the governing body of the powerful Bank of France so that all classes of French economic life would have representation and a majority of its members would be appointed by the government. In September, in an attempt to solve the republic's economic and fiscal problems, the government took the important step of reducing the gold content of the franc by about 30 per cent in order to align it with British and American currencies.

By depreciating the franc Blum hoped to stimulate business through the expansion of the French export trade. Unfortunately for his hopes, however, the economic situation did not respond to devaluation as favorably as had been expected. He had also hoped that devaluation would bring the return of French capital in sufficient amounts to enable the government to meet its needs by floating loans. But here, too, he met disappointment. In June, 1937, France still had an unbalanced budget, her bonds were selling below par, and the republic's credit was at the lowest point since the fiscal crisis of 1926.

To meet the new crisis the government asked the parliament for authority until July 31, 1937, to take by decree all measures needed to assure the recovery of public finances and to meet attacks against the public credit. Apparently Blum sought temporary dictatorial powers in the realm of finance like those conferred upon Poincaré in 1926. Although such powers were voted by the Chamber of Deputies, the more conservative Senate refused to pass the bill. In consequence, the Blum government resigned on June 20, after having been in office slightly more than a year. He was succeeded by Camille Chautemps, a leader of the Radical Socialists and a member of Blum's cabinet. The Socialists agreed to maintain the Popular Front government, and Blum and eight other Socialists accepted places in Chautemps' ministry. As in the case of Blum, the Communists gave the government their support.

On June 30 the parliament voted the Chautemps government, until August 31, 1937, the full powers which it had denied Blum.

[3] The *Croix de Feu* soon reappeared as the French Social Party.

Thereupon the new government gave up its attempt to maintain the French currency on a gold basis, and the franc very soon fell in value to less than 3.40 cents. Other emergency measures included authorization for the government to increase its borrowings from the Bank of France, higher taxes to increase the government's revenue, and higher fares on the government's railways. But whether the Popular Front government could solve the republic's fiscal problems, whether indeed the Popular Front could long be maintained in power, were questions which only the future could reveal.

## UNREST AND DISCONTENT IN SPAIN

During the war and early postwar years Spanish labor, plied with socialist and syndicalist propaganda, became more and more aggressive. Costly and sometimes bloody strikes ensued, especially in the industrial region of Barcelona. The years 1919–1921 were especially disturbed by general strikes and street fighting; in March, 1921, the Spanish premier was even assassinated; and in the next two years hundreds were killed or wounded in the recurring industrial disputes.

In addition to widespread labor unrest, Spain was disturbed during these years by a growing autonomist movement in Catalonia, the northeastern section of the country including the populous city of Barcelona. Even before the World War Catalan nationalism had begun to rally to a states' rights program, and during the war, when so much was said about nationalism and the rights of self-determination, the autonomist movement waxed stronger. One group, the autonomists, demanded that Catalonia should have its own parliament, its own executive, its own judiciary, and its own official language. It should be united with the other provinces of Spain only in a federal union. Another group, even more extreme than the autonomists, went so far as to demand complete independence. Regionalism and separatism, therefore, were seriously disturbing factors in the history of Spain during these years. Ministerial instability, caused by industrial strikes and autonomist agitation, was further increased by the repeated interference in political affairs of the military juntas, that is, councils of army officers.

The lot of the government was made still more difficult by the course of events in Spanish Morocco. Native resistance had begun as soon as Spain had attempted to extend her sway over the region, and, despite the vigorous military campaigns finally undertaken by the Spaniards in 1918, Abd-el-Krim, the Riffian chieftain, continued to defeat the Spanish forces. King Alfonso took it upon himself to meddle personally in the Moroccan situation, and thus became involved in one of the most disgraceful military disasters in Spanish history. This debacle precipitated a crisis in Spanish affairs. Demands were made that those responsible should be summarily punished, and a parliamentary committee was appointed to investigate the tragedy. The committee's report was at once suppressed, but rumor said that a considerable number of high officials—even Alfonso himself—were implicated.

When the parliament, the press, and the populace began to protest against the action of the government in withholding the report, when they began to demand that punishment be meted out where punishment was due, King Alfonso seemingly decided to forestall the attempts to find scapegoats for the Moroccan disaster. At the same time, apparently, he hoped to strengthen the government to deal with the continuing industrial and regional unrest. Having given his consent to the establishment of a military dictatorship in the country, he tactfully arranged to be visiting in France when the blow was struck.

On September 13, 1923, General Miguel Primo de Rivera overthrew the ministry, suspended the constitution, organized a military directorate, proclaimed martial law, and established himself as military dictator of Spain. Rivera was an army man of long standing. He had served with the Spanish troops in Cuba and the Philippines during the Spanish-American War; he had fought in Morocco in later years; and after 1915 he had been military governor of various districts of Spain. At the time of his *coup d'état* he held this position in Barcelona. As dictator, he at once dissolved the parliament, suppressed freedom of speech and of the press, and abolished trial by jury. To prevent incriminating evidence regarding the Moroccan catastrophe from leaking out, he seized the documents resulting from the parliamentary investigation.

For the next two years Rivera ruled by strong-arm methods. Provincial legislatures were arbitrarily dismissed, leaders of the republican group were exiled, severe fines were exacted for minor offenses, and the censorship was tightened. In spite of these developments—or perhaps because of them—popular hostility toward the dictatorship increased instead of diminishing, and, unfortunately for King Alfonso, it tended to rise against the monarchy as well. After 1928 popular dissatisfaction grew rapidly. In 1929 a mutiny occurred in the army, and riots of university students and the working classes became frequent. Gradually Rivera was deserted by nearly all classes. Plans were made in some circles for a revolution which should usher in a republic early in 1930. The dictator became discouraged. Suffering from ill health, discovering that he had lost the confidence and support not only of his king but of the army as well, Rivera suddenly resigned his office on January 28, 1930, and left the country. On March 16 he died

Upon Rivera's resignation, King Alfonso at once announced that the constitution of 1876 would be restored, the demands of university students and professors would be granted, all officers who had suffered at the dictator's hands would be given their former status, all political prisoners would be pardoned, and free and honest elections would be held late in 1930 for a new national parliament. The Socialists insisted, however, that the new government differed not essentially from that of Rivera, and before long shouts of "Down with the king and the monarchy!" began to be heard. The shouts were soon followed by the definite demand that a national assembly be called to draft a new constitution and to determine whether Spain should remain a monarchy or become a republic. In December a serious military uprising and a republican revolt were suppressed only after thousands had been arrested and martial law had again been proclaimed throughout the country.

In February, 1931, Alfonso restored the constitution and called for parliamentary elections to be held in March. So great was the popular demand for a constituent assembly rather than a parliament, however, that the government later suspended the call for the March elections. It announced instead plans for municipal and provincial elections in April, to be followed by the election of a constituent assembly. Apparently Premier Aznar and King Alfonso desired to learn popular sentiment by local elections before proceeding with plans for a constituent assembly. If so, they were not left in doubt. The municipal elections of April 12 constituted a veritable republican landslide. On the next day the Aznar government resigned, and a republican junta headed by Niceto Alcalá Zamora, leader of the unsuccessful republican revolt of December, 1930, issued an ulti-

matum stating that a revolution would be called if Alfonso refused
to abdicate. That night the king without formal abdication left for
France, merely suspending "the exercise of the royal power" until he
should "learn the real expression of the collective opinion of his
people."

## THE ESTABLISHMENT OF THE SPANISH REPUBLIC

Following the flight of the king, Zamora at once proclaimed a
republic with himself as provisional president. A carefully selected
cabinet of the best moderate republican and Socialist talent available
took charge of the government, which was soon recognized by most
of the leading powers. The provisional government hastened to outline its program, for it faced the necessity of meeting the demands of
the various groups which had been responsible for the development
of the strong antimonarchical sentiment: the intellectuals, who denounced the church and deplored its medieval influence in Spanish
affairs; the republicans, who sought a constitutional democracy in
which the military should be subordinated to the civil authorities;
the Socialists, who had as their goal a new economic and social
order; and the autonomists, who wished to throw off the old detested
centralized regime.

The republican government immediately guaranteed religious and
civil liberty and recognized the rights of private property. It proclaimed an amnesty for all political prisoners and invited all exiles
to return to Spain. It abolished all titles of nobility and arrested a
number of former royal officials. It announced that it would inaugurate comprehensive agrarian reforms with a view to modernizing the system of land tenure and improving the methods of
farming, which were hopelessly antiquated. It promised to hold
elections for a national constituent assembly in the near future and
modified the electoral system to make it conform with modern conditions. It extended the franchise to the clergy, but at the same time
it abolished compulsory religious education in the public schools.

Elections for the constituent assembly were held in June, 1931, and
resulted in an overwhelming victory for the Left Republicans and
the Socialists. The assembly at once took up its task and, after nearly
five months of consideration and debate, finally completed the republican constitution which on December 9, 1931, was adopted.
Spain was declared "a republic of the workers of all classes," in

which the franchise was extended to all men and women over twenty-three years of age. A single-chamber parliament (*Cortes*) was provided for, its members being elected directly for four years by popular vote. The president of the republic was to be chosen for a six-year term by an electoral college, consisting of the members of parliament and an equal number of electors chosen by the voters. No active or reserve army officer and no member of the clergy might be a candidate for the presidency. Executive power was placed in the hands of a ministry directly responsible to the parliament. In other words, Spain became politically a democratic, parliamentary republic. So far as decentralization was concerned, the constitution provided that any area which desired autonomy must submit for the approval of the parliament a regional charter, and that the parliament in turn might delegate to the local authorities power to administer certain national laws.

Wide as was the break between Spain's former political system and that established in 1931, the departure from the former regime in social, cultural, and economic matters was perhaps even more pronounced. Spain was to have complete religious freedom and no state church. Education was to be secularized. Divorce was to be made easy, and illegitimate and legitimate children were to have equal rights. The state was to have authority (1) to expropriate, with compensation, all kinds of private property, (2) to socialize large estates, (3) to nationalize public utilities, and (4) to "participate in the development and co-ordination of industries." In general, therefore, all the wealth of the country was to be subordinated to the interests of the national economy. Spain, it appeared, was to be transformed from a semifeudal nation into a modern state with somewhat socialistic tendencies.

A special clause of the constitution provided that the first president of the Spanish Republic should be chosen by the national convention which had drafted the constitution. Accordingly, on December 10, 1931, Niceto Alcalá Zamora was elected to this office; on the next day he received the oath of office and took up his official residence in Alfonso's former palace. The provisional government at once resigned, and a new cabinet headed by Manuel Azaña took office. As has frequently been the case in the history of other countries, the constituent assembly did not resign upon the completion of its constituent duties, but continued to sit thereafter as the national parliament. The members of the assembly desired themselves to launch the program of reform which by laws should carry into effect the general principles laid down in the constitution. "We have finished the first step," said Premier Azaña. "We must now complete the revolution by drafting supplementary laws."

In January, 1932, the Jesuit order was dissolved; its property, valued at $30,000,000, was confiscated by the state and later ordered to be distributed for purposes of social-welfare. In May, 1933, the drastic Associations Law was passed, stipulating that the heads of the various religious orders in Spain must be Spanish citizens and must submit to Spanish laws, and that the state reserved the right to pass upon their appointment. Members of religious orders were forbidden to teach anything except religion. Church schools were suppressed, and all teaching by members of religious orders was to cease. All church property was nationalized; although placed under the custody of the clergy, it was subject to the disposition of the government. All government support of priests—of whom there were 40,000 in Spain—was to cease after November 11, 1933.

The pope, in the early days of the revolution, had directed the clergy to accept the republic but to offer determined resistance through constitutional means to the enactment of laws hostile to the church. The Spanish clergy, in turn, urged loyal Catholics to participate actively in the civil and political life of the republic in order to defend the rights of the church. As soon as the Associations Act was passed, however, the pope issued a vigorous protest in an encyclical in which he condemned the separation of church and state and denounced the prohibition of teaching by religious orders.

The government also made a beginning of agrarian and labor reform. The great estates of Spain's grandees [4] were confiscated, for the most part without compensation, and the parliament enacted a measure for distributing over fifty million acres of land held before the revolution by the king or under his royal grant. It was expected that a million Spaniards would be settled on these lands, and that they would be assisted with government subsidies. Furthermore, in the interests of the peasants and industrial workers alike, a new charter of economic independence and freedom was adopted,

---

[4] A grandee was a person who had the right to appear in the presence of the king of Spain without removing his hat.

providing for a national schedule of working hours and wages and for mixed courts to settle labor disputes.

Finally, the problem of Catalan autonomy was settled to the apparent satisfaction of most of the Catalans when in 1932 Premier Azaña presented an autonomy statute to the president of the Catalan *generalidad* in Barcelona. By the terms of this statute Catalonia secured the right to have its own state government, which was given power to tax and to enact social legislation within certain restrictions. The enforcement of law and order in Catalonia was left to the local government, and the execution of national laws was in general confided to Catalan authorities. Without destroying the integrity of the republic, a considerable measure of self-government was thus extended to Catalonia. As further concessions to the national sentiment of the Catalans, they were granted the right to have a national anthem and their own flag. The Catalan language was made official in the province and was given equality with Castilian in official communications with the rest of Spain. On December 6, 1932, the Catalan parliament met for the first time since 1705.

## THE STRUGGLE TO CONTROL THE SPANISH REPUBLIC

But not all Spaniards were content with the course of events in the new republic. On the Right were the clericals and the royalists, who looked back with longing upon their positions and privileges in the old regime and who fervently prayed for the collapse of the republic and the return of the monarchy. On the extreme Left were the Syndicalists and Communists, who felt that the Spanish revolution had stopped altogether too soon, that the republican government should be displaced by a regime more like that in Soviet Russia. Abortive attempts to overthrow the government were made by both the royalists and the Communists in the years 1932 and 1933.

In November of the latter year the republic had its first parliamentary elections. The result was a disastrous defeat for the moderate Left parties which had been in control of Spain since the overthrow of the monarchy. The combined opposition of the Catholic Popular Action Party, led by the brilliant young editor José María Gil Robles, of the commercial, industrial, and financial leaders, and of the landlord classes had carried the day. The ensuing year was marked by a succession of minority governments which leaned more and more to the Right. The relations between the government and the Vatican were improved, legislation designed to ameliorate the lot of the clergy was passed, the educational measures and land reforms enacted in 1932–1933 were modified and weakened, and many grandees were permitted to return to their landed estates. The leaders of the Left became convinced that the parliament was undermining the republic and threatening to turn Spain back again to men who were monarchists at heart.

In October, 1934, a new ministry included three members of the Popular Action Party. This was particularly alarming to the Left groups, for in the national assembly those who later organized this party had been frankly antirepublican and hostile to nearly every article in the constitution which was adopted. They had refused to vote for the constitution and had from the day of its adoption been revisionists. In the elections of 1933 the Popular Action Party had been allied with the royalists, and, although Gil Robles had later announced his acceptance of the republic, the party was still suspected by those on the Left of remaining monarchist at heart. The Left parties at once called a general strike against what they claimed was a shift toward fascism in Spain. At the same time, President Companys of Catalonia proclaimed that state a free and independent republic. Open revolt spread rapidly through central and northern Spain, causing the death of thousands and the destruction of millions of dollars in property.

Unfortunately for the revolutionists, there was lack of solidarity among the Left elements and in many parts of the country relatively little support from the rural districts. The uprising in Catalonia was almost immediately crushed by the use of the army, the navy, and the civil guard. President Companys, former Premier Azaña, and hundreds of others were arrested and held for courtmartial. In the reaction which followed, Socialist provincial governors and municipal councilors were throughout the country largely replaced by men loyal to the government at Madrid. The Catalan statute, moreover, was set aside and made subject to a thorough revision, while outstanding Catalonian leaders were held for trial by court-martial.

The Center and Right groups next sought to alter Spanish institutions to conform with their ideas, claiming that those who drafted the constitution had gone beyond the wishes of a majority of the Spanish people in matters relating to the church, education, and agrarian reform. In 1935 the government began to draft a number of constitutional amendments to carry out the policies of the Right. But ministerial instability continued, and when in December of that year the government was again overturned, President Zamora, who had apparently begun to fear for the safety of the liberal republic, passed over Gil Robles, who could have formed a government commanding a majority in the parliament, and instead appointed as premier Manuel Portela Valladares, a loyal moderate republican. In January, 1936, President Zamora dissolved the parliament and called for new elections.

In the ensuing elections the score or more of political parties in Spain combined into two major groups. On the Left the Syndicalists, Communists, Socialists, Left Republicans, and Republican Unionists fought together as the Popular Front. They were determined to prevent the Rightists from securing control of the parliament lest they should liquidate completely the achievements of the republic. On the Right the Conservative Republicans, the clericals, and the royalists combined in an effort to prevent the triumph of those who were suspected of desiring to introduce a proletarian regime. The election resulted in a decisive majority in favor of the Left; within this coalition the Socialists won the most seats. Of all the parties, however, Gil Robles' Popular Action still had the greatest number of deputies.

Manuel Portela, who was himself defeated in the election, at once resigned the premiership and was succeeded as head of the government by Manuel Azaña. The latter's ministry consisted of eleven Left Republicans and two Republican Unionists, the Socialists declining to participate in the government. Amnesty was at once proclaimed for 30,000 political prisoners and exiles, among whom was Louis Companys, former president of Catalonia. The Catalonian parliament, suspended since the revolt of October, 1934, reassembled, and steps were taken by the central government to restore Catalonian autonomy. Agrarian reform was again pushed, and thousands of tracts of land were distributed among the peasants. Anticlericalism once more surged to the front as scores of churches, schools, and convents were attacked and burned, and street clashes resulted in the death of some forty or fifty persons. In April the parliament voted to remove President Zamora from office on the ground that he had exceeded his powers in dissolving the parliament, and Manuel Azaña was elected to succeed him as president.

## THE SPANISH CIVIL WAR

Meanwhile, the Popular Front government had been taking steps to rid the army of officers whose loyalty to the existing regime was suspected. In April a decree stipulated that all officers known to have been politically active should be retired at once upon pensions. Some with monarchist or conservative sympathies were transferred to Spain's overseas possessions; General Francisco Franco, who had been chief of staff when Gil Robles was minister of war, was sent to the Canary Islands. In July the government further ordered the removal from their posts of many of the officers of the Foreign Legion in Morocco. These various measures threatened the control of Spain's military forces by the ruling clique of officers, and apparently led the latter to decide to overthrow the government. They knew that in a rebellion they could count on the support of most of the royalists, clericals, Conservative Republicans, and great landowners; and, in view of later developments, it is possible that they had the encouragement of Fascist and Nazi leaders in Italy and Germany.

On July 17 a number of regiments in Morocco raised the standard of revolt, and General Franco, the leader of the insurrection, flew to Morocco to take charge. In Spain garrisons in various parts of the country at once mutinied under the leadership of their generals. The insurgents, it appeared, had the support of approximately 90 per cent of the officers and two thirds of Spain's organized military forces. In August, furthermore, they began to receive aid from Italy and Germany; ultimately thousands of well-trained officers and men from these countries joined the insurgents as "volunteers."

The government, with only a small part of the organized military forces loyal to it, was obliged to turn to the left-wing labor groups for assistance. A Popular Militia of workers was hastily created, and thanks to its efforts Madrid and Catalonia were saved. But the loyalist forces were unable to stop the advance of General Franco's disciplined units. In November the insurgents were at the gates of Madrid, and the seat of the loyalist government was transferred to

Valencia. Germany and Italy thereupon extended *de jure* recognition to the insurgent government which had been set up by General Franco at Burgos. But by this time the Popular Militia had been strengthened by antifascist volunteers from many foreign countries, and by supplies—particularly airplanes and tanks—presumably from Soviet Russia. In the succeeding months the attempts of the insurgents to capture Madrid were successfully defeated.

In March, 1937, the insurgents launched a determined offensive on the Guadalajara front, about sixty miles northeast of Madrid. Although Italian troops took the lead in this attack, the loyalists not only stopped the advance but routed both the insurgents and their Italian "volunteers." Three months later, however, the insurgents, after a long and desperate siege, in which they were greatly aided by German and Italian airplanes, men, and munitions, succeeded in capturing the Basque city of Bilbao on the Bay of Biscay. In October, 1937, they captured Gijón, the last loyalist stronghold in northwestern Spain, and it appeared that the insurgents might thereafter be free to concentrate all their forces on the capture of Madrid.

Throughout the first year of the Spanish civil war it was constantly feared that the struggle might precipitate a general European conflict. Apparently all of the powers were reluctant to be drawn into such a conflict, however, and in August, 1936, France initiated negotiations looking toward a general European agreement against intervention in the civil war. Eventually twenty-seven countries, including all the great powers of Europe, agreed to set up a committee in London to apply a policy of nonintervention in Spain. Early in 1937, on the suggestion of Great Britain and France, all of these countries further agreed to prohibit the flow of foreign volunteers to Spain and to this end decided to establish a system of international control.

Finally, in March, a naval cordon, consisting of ships provided by Great Britain, France, Italy, and Germany, was thrown around Spain, and inspectors were stationed along the French and Portuguese land frontiers. All went well with the international blockade until the latter part of May, when the German warship *Deutschland* and the Italian warship *Barletta* were bombed by loyalist airplanes. Five German warships thereupon at once bombarded the loyalist city of Almeria in retaliation, and Germany and Italy withdrew from the nonintervention patrol. These events tended to make the fascist states more aggressive and recalcitrant. Although in June, following a new agreement between the four great powers, Germany and Italy rejoined the naval patrol, an alleged attempt of the loyalists to torpedo the German cruiser *Leipzig* led the two fascist powers again to withdraw their warships from the international patrol and to intimate that they considered themselves freed of nonintervention obligations.

During the summer a number of neutral merchant ships suspected of carrying cargoes to Valencia were attacked by submarines in the Mediterranean. Although the submarines were unidentified, they were widely suspected of being Italian, and in September the Soviet government openly charged Italy with responsibility for the torpedoing of two Soviet freighters. In order to consider measures for dealing with these acts of "piracy," a conference of all the Mediterranean and Black Sea powers and Germany was called to meet on September 10 at Nyon in Switzerland. Italy and Germany, however, declined to attend because the Soviet Union was to be represented. Nevertheless, the powers at Nyon agreed to establish an antisubmarine patrol of warships and airplanes to protect neutral merchant ships in the Mediterranean and the Black Sea, the greater part of the Mediterranean to be patrolled by ships of Great Britain and France. After the Nyon agreement the submarine attacks soon ceased.

On October 2 a Franco-British note to Italy pointed out that no improvement in the general European situation could be expected until the policy of nonintervention in Spain had been made fully effective by the withdrawal of foreign nationals from the Spanish armies. It emphasized the failure of the London nonintervention committee to solve this problem and proposed a three-power conference between France, Great Britain, and Italy. Italy, however, declined the invitation to such a conference and proposed instead that the question of foreign volunteers be dealt with by the London committee. Italy further stated that she would not participate in any conversations or conferences to which Germany had not been invited.

The question of the withdrawal of volunteers was therefore considered by the nonintervention committee, but the discussions were deadlocked by the fascist powers' demand that at the same time belligerent rights should be extended to the insurgents. Eventually, however, after the fall of Gijon and the loyalists' decision to transfer their government from Valencia to Barcelona, Italy and Germany, on October 20, agreed to defer the grant of belligerent rights until after "token" withdrawals of foreign fighters had been made from both sides. It was expected, however, that the drafting of the plans for the actual withdrawals would require long negotiations, and some saw in the fascist powers' concession merely a move to postpone action until General Franco's forces had gained a decisive victory. An account of the triumph of General Franco and the institution of a fascist corporate state in Spain is found on pages 882–886.

## CHAPTER XXIV

## POLAND AND THE BALTIC REPUBLICS

STRETCHING across Europe from Czechoslovakia and Rumania on the south to the Arctic Ocean on the north, effectively cutting off the great Soviet Union from direct contact with most of western Europe, lie Poland and the Baltic republics. These states resemble one another not only in their proximity to the Soviet Union but in the fact that the present territory of each was carved wholly or in part from prewar Russia. All of these states were newly created at the beginning of the postwar period, and each consequently faced the problem of establishing its government and building up its national economic structure. Each of them contained within its new frontiers the racial minorities of other nations to complicate its already difficult situation; each as an agricultural country was confronted with the problem of agrarian reform.

### POLAND

History, which is frequently said to repeat itself, occasionally has a way of reversing itself. In the closing years of the eighteenth century Poland, partitioned by powerful Romanov, Hohenzollern, and Habsburg monarchs, disappeared as a state from the map of Europe. When at the close of the World War those same proud dynasties were hurled from their thrones, the three separated portions of the Polish people once more became united, and their state again assumed an important position in the political system of Europe.

Probably no other postwar territorial settlement in Europe led to so much actual fighting or to such bitter and prolonged controversy as did the definition of Poland's boundaries. The difficulties in connection with the problem of Danzig and the Polish Corridor, the partition of Upper Silesia, and the seizure of Vilna have been discussed.[1] The acquisition of eastern Galicia, like that of Vilna, resulted largely from the use of force. Although the inhabitants of western Galicia readily united in the establishment of the Polish

---

[1] See pages 486–488 and 525–529.

Republic at the close of the World War, the Ukrainians who constitute the bulk of the population in eastern Galicia were opposed to such a step. Many desired to unite with their kinsmen in the Ukrainian People's Republic, while others organized a national council in Lemberg and sought to establish an independent state.

The Poles refused to recognize Ukrainian self-determination, immediately invaded the region, occupied Lemberg on November 5, 1918, and during 1919 completed their conquest of the province. The peace conference at first planned to give eastern Galicia the right of self-determination, but finally decided in December, 1919, that it should be granted autonomy for twenty-five years under a Polish protectorate, its status after that period to be determined by the League of Nations. Regardless of the peace conference, however, the Poles treated eastern Galicia as part of Poland and eventually in March, 1923, succeeded in having the Conference of Ambassadors settle the questions of Vilna and eastern Galicia by recognizing the *de facto* frontiers of the republic.

Between Russia and Poland the peace conference originally laid down a provisional frontier known as the "Curzon line," which was in general accord with the ethnographic situation. This, however, was not satisfactory to the Poles, who undertook a military campaign to regain their frontier of 1772. The treaty which was finally signed with Russia at Riga in March, 1921, gave Poland an eastern boundary which, except for the territory that had become the new Republic of Lithuania, corresponded roughly with the one she had had just before the partition of 1795. The peace of Riga and the decision of the Conference of Ambassadors to sanction the northern, eastern, and southeastern boundaries (1923) closed the period of acute controversy over Poland's frontiers. As finally stabilized, they include a territory four fifths as large as Germany.

Meanwhile, Poland had begun the organization of her political life in the hope of establishing a stable and efficient regime. In her efforts she was handicapped, however, by the lack of political experience on the part of most of her leaders, by the diversity of administration in the three formerly separated parts of the country, by the tendency of German and Austrian Poles to consider themselves the superiors of the Russian Poles, and by the great multiplicity of petty political parties which immediately sprang into existence. But eventually, in March, 1921, the Polish constitution was adopted. As in France, the president was to be elected for a seven-year term by a majority vote of the two legislative houses meeting together as a national assembly. The president was given no power over legislation, and in general his authority was greatly limited. All his official acts required the countersignature of some member of the ministry, which in turn was made responsible to the legislature. Both houses of the parliament were to be elected directly by universal suffrage with an age requirement of thirty years for electors of the Senate. Real power in legislation was placed in the lower house, the *Sejm,* which was empowered to pass any measure over the veto of the Senate by a bare eleven-twentieths majority of those voting.

Twenty months elapsed between the adoption of the constitution and the first parliamentary elections held under it in November, 1922. A score or more of political parties then presented candidates, and at least fifteen of them succeeded in obtaining representation in the first Sejm. To Polish nationalists perhaps the most disturbing feature of the election was the fact that parties of various national minorities succeeded in winning 20 per cent of the seats in the lower house. In December of that year the two houses of parliament, meeting as the National Assembly, chose Stanislas Wojciechowski as President of Poland.

Poland was now urgently in need of a strong, efficient government to deal with her serious economic and political situation. But the first Sejm hindered rather than provided the efficiency needed. The multiplicity of parties produced ministerial instability, for no majority could be found that would consistently support a ministry. Governments changed in personnel and policies at frequent intervals, six ministries following one another within three and a half years. The policy of restricted expenditures, increased taxation, and cessation of inflation for the sake of fiscal reform was for two years prevented because the parliament would not support it. Agrarian reform was sacrificed to the interests of the great landed proprietors, capitalists, and rich peasants.

National politics became a series of crises and personal and party struggles. Many became convinced of the incapacity of the parliament; many began to assert that it did not really represent the desires of the electorate. Demands for new elections were heard on many sides. But Poland's constitution made it impossible for the government to dissolve the legislature and hold new elections without the consent of the Senate, and the latter, reluctant to face a new election, withheld its consent. An obstructive legislature and an obstructive constitution seemed to stand in the way of a strong government, and there were not lacking those to point out that Poland's downfall in the eighteenth century had been due to causes of a similar type.

The political situation in Poland greatly disturbed Pilsudski, who became alarmed by the weakness of the government of the state which he had done so much to create. Eventually, in May, 1926, he decided that the situation called for drastic action, and he and his followers began a march on the capital somewhat in the manner of the Fascist march on Rome. They aimed by an armed demonstration to force the prime minister from office, but the latter was not at once persuaded. A three days' siege of Warsaw was necessary to convince him of the necessity of resigning, but his resignation finally came and with it that of President Wojciechowski. On May 15 a new government was established with Charles Bartel as prime minister, Pilsudski as minister of war, and the other members chiefly professors and technical experts. Two weeks later the National Assembly elected Pilsudski President of Poland, but he declined to accept the office, suggesting instead that Professor Ignace Moszicki, a chemist of undoubted integrity, be elected.

In August the constitution was amended in order to strengthen the executive control of the budget, provide the president with authority to dissolve the parliament with the consent of his cabinet, and give him power within limits to issue ordinances with the force of law. By the use of such presidential decrees steps were at once taken to balance the budget, stabilize the currency, reorganize the Polish Bank, and improve the national credit. When in October, 1926, Bartel proved to be unable to command a parliamentary majority, Pilsudski himself assumed the office of premier, organized a strong ministry, and threatened the Sejm with dissolution if it did not comply with his wishes. Finally, on November 3, 1927, he ordered its dissolution to prevent discussion of the budget. In June of the following year Pilsudski resigned the premiership but retained the positions of minister of war and inspector-general of the army. He still dictated the policies of the republic, however, and constantly urged that the constitution be revised in order to increase the powers of the president. Ministries came and went, but the premiers were regularly lieutenants of Pilsudski.

Finally, in August, 1930, doubtless in the hope of attaining political stability for the republic, the marshal himself once more assumed the premiership. He immediately dissolved the parliament and called for new elections. With grim determination the government bloc set out to win control of the new Sejm, a feat which no party or bloc had yet been able to achieve in the history of the republic. A systematic attempt was made to handicap and suppress the opposition. The rather natural outcome of elections held under such conditions was the victory of Pilsudski's national bloc, which won a safe majority in both houses. Having largely succeeded in the task which he had set for himself, Pilsudski, after the elections, again resigned the premiership, handing it over to one of his military colleagues.

Pilsudski's followers had long desired to reform the constitution in order to establish in effect a presidential dictatorship with a docile legislature. As early as 1929 they had submitted such a project, but it had been rejected by the parliament. They had hoped that the elections of 1930 would give them the necessary control to accomplish their ends, but in this they were disappointed. In the spring of 1931 the national bloc's project for constitutional reform was again presented and was again rejected. Once more in 1934 the government submitted its proposals, and this time, by methods which the opposition denounced as illegal, it secured the adoption of a new constitution, which was promulgated on April 23, 1935.

Under the new frame of government the president is elected by universal suffrage from two candidates, one nominated by the retiring president, the other by an assembly of eighty electors of whom fifty are chosen by the Sejm and twenty-five by the Senate. Should the retiring president fail to make a nomination, however, the candidate of the Assembly of Electors shall be recognized as president without a popular election. The president appoints the ministers, who practically are responsible only to him; he convenes, adjourns, and dissolves the parliament; he is head of the army, and appoints and dismisses the commander-in-chief and the inspector-general; he appoints one third of the members of the Senate, the others being chosen by a very limited electorate. The new basis of government obviously provides for a powerful executive.

On May 12, 1935, less than three weeks after the promulgation of the new constitution, Marshal Pilsudski, the outstanding exponent of strong government for Poland, died on the ninth anniversary of the bold coup by which he had seized control of the government. In the years after 1926 Pilsudski had lived in semiseclusion, constantly watching over the welfare of Poland but content that others should have the titular authority. Firmly convinced that his country's woes in the eighteenth century had resulted from its military weakness and its inefficient government, he had patriotically sought to build up Poland's armed forces and to strengthen the republic's international position by favorable treaties and alliances. The new constitution provided more nearly the type of government which he thought Poland required than had the one which it supplanted. General Edward Rydz-Smigly, inspector-general of the army, was elevated to the place formerly held by Marshal Pilsudski as the virtual dictator of Poland.

But political problems were not the only ones to complicate Poland's domestic affairs, for the republic contains within its borders the largest minorities population of all the countries of Europe. The most numerous minority group consists of the Ukrainians. The Ukrainians insist that the local autonomy which was extended in 1922 to eastern Galicia is greatly restricted and not at all consonant with that stipulated by the Council of Ambassadors. Furthermore, the Ukrainians assert that Poland is not observing her obligations under the minorities treaty but is rather steadily carrying on a campaign to "Polonize" the eastern provinces. Although in 1924 some concessions were made in matters of language and schools, the Ukrainians have continued to complain of the way they are being treated, and at times have even resorted to passive resistance by refusing to pay their taxes.

The second largest minority group consists of the Jews. Unlike the other minorities, they are not segregated in one area, but constitute a large percentage of the population in all towns and cities. In the early years of the republic they were subjected to harsh treatment at the hands of the Poles, who denounced them as not being good patriots on the ground that they put personal profit above national welfare. In 1925, however, the government negotiated with representatives of the Jews an agreement which became known as the "Declaration of Warsaw." In consequence of the Jews'

recognition of their duties to the republic, measures were introduced giving them the same linguistic privileges as had been granted
to the border peoples, legalizing their observance of Jewish religious
holidays, and recognizing their schools. The agreement went far
toward removing the causes of friction between the government and
one of the republic's most numerous minorities. Nevertheless, in the
succeeding years, and especially after the rise of anti-Semitism in
Germany in 1933, there were occasional anti-Jewish outbreaks in
Poland. In fact, in 1936–1937 Jews in foreign countries were active
in calling attention to the woes of their kinsmen not only in Germany but in Poland as well.

The third major minority group in Poland consists of Germans,
and between Poland and Germany friction has been occasioned by
the former's treatment of these Germans within her territory. Poland
was eager to regain as much as possible of the land which had passed
from Polish into German hands while Posen was in the German
Empire, and in 1920 decided to cancel all contracts of tenants who
held land from the former German government unless they could
show clear legal titles. Germany appealed to the League, and the
question went finally to the World Court, which decided that
Poland must respect private rights. Poland eventually agreed to
compensate the German colonists who had been evicted.

A second cause of friction between Poland and Germany arose
from the complaints of the German minority in that part of Upper
Silesia which was awarded to Poland in 1922. Germans here asserted
that they were being subjected to mistreatment and unfair discrimination. The Polish government, it was alleged, failed to provide adequate protection to the Germans, who were exposed to terrorism at
the hands of the Poles, particularly during political campaigns. Germans in Poland sought the sympathy of the German Republic,
which on several occasions brought the Silesian troubles before the
League.

Poland claimed that she was attempting to live up to her obligations under the minorities treaty which she had signed, and submitted much evidence to prove her contention. She asserted, on the
other hand, that the more than one million Poles in Germany were
being consistently mistreated. What particularly irked Poland was
the fact that, while the German minority in Poland had a statutory
right to appeal to the League of Nations whenever they felt that

they had been wronged by the Polish government, the Poles in Germany had no similar right. Finally, at the meeting of the League of Nations Assembly in September, 1934, Poland announced that she found herself "compelled to refuse as from today all co-operation with the international organizations in the matter of supervision of the application by Poland of the system of minority protection" until "a general and uniform system for the protection of minorities" had been created. In 1937 the German-Polish treaty of 1922 governing each country's treatment of the other's nationals in Upper Silesia expired, and Poland announced her determination not to renew it. The way was thus opened for further possible friction with Germany over the question of Poland's treatment of her German minority.

Meanwhile, progress had been made in the economic life of the country. Poland is primarily agricultural, 65 per cent of her inhabitants earning their living from the soil. Before the war a very large part of the land was in the hands of a few owners, most of whom belonged to the nobility. Only one third of the peasant farms were self-supporting, the peasants in most cases being obliged to work outside their own farms in order to earn a livelihood. This situation the peasants hoped to change under the republic. Some progress was made in land redistribution at the close of the war, but it was far from satisfactory to the peasant parties. But eventually, in December, 1925, a land act was passed providing for the distribution among peasants of some 500,000 acres yearly for a period of ten years. Compensation was to be based upon the existing value of the land, and payment was to be made partly in cash and partly in government bonds. Although not entirely satisfactory to any of those directly concerned, the agrarian legislation facilitated the recovery of the country. Practically all tillable land was again brought under cultivation, thousands of farm buildings were constructed, and farms were eventually restocked to the prewar level.

Industry was somewhat slower to recover from the war destruction and revolutionary disruption. By 1927, however, new postwar records were established in coal, pig iron, crude steel, and zinc production. The railways, completely demoralized after the war, were rebuilt and greatly extended. To free the republic from complete dependence upon Danzig, the construction of a new port was begun in 1925 at Gdynia on Polish territory in the extreme western corner of the Bay of Danzig. By 1929 what was formerly an obscure fishing hamlet had become a city of 15,000 inhabitants with a port capable of handling 2,000,000 tons of freight yearly.

Although Poland, like other countries, suffered from the effects of the world depression, she continued to develop her new Baltic port. In 1930 the government inaugurated regular steamship service between Gdynia and New York. In the fall of that year a new railway was opened between Gdynia and Bromberg on the southern edge of the Polish Corridor. In 1931 Poland turned to the bankers of her ally, France, and entered into an agreement with them to finance the building and operation of a railway to connect Upper Silesia with Gdynia. Such a direct line between the rich coal fields of Upper Silesia and Gdynia would greatly facilitate the exportation of Polish coal. By 1933 Gdynia had surpassed Danzig in total trading volume and had come to monopolize practically all of Poland's overseas passenger traffic.

## DANZIG, POLAND, AND THE LEAGUE

By the treaty of Versailles Danzig was constituted a free city under the protection of the League of Nations. According to the provisions of the subsequently drafted constitution and the Danzig-Polish convention which supplemented it, the free city was given a popular Assembly of 120 members and a Senate of 22 members. The latter, which contained eight administrative heads, constituted the government. The city's foreign relations as well as the protection of its nationals abroad were committed to Poland. The control of the port of Danzig was entrusted to a commission composed of an equal number of Poles and Danzigers with a neutral chairman, and Poland was given "free use and service of the port."

A League high commissioner serves as a court of first instance for disputes between Poland and Danzig, which have the right of appeal to the Council. A great number of disputes have arisen, owing to the complex intermingling of economic and political prerogatives in the free city. Many of the disputes have been settled by direct negotiations between the two parties through the good offices of the high commissioner, but many others have been referred to the high commissioner himself. Occasionally appeals have been carried to the Council, and in one case the World Court was invoked to decide Poland's right to maintain a postal service in Danzig.

Economically, during the first decade of its new regime, the

THE BALTIC REPUBLICS AND CENTRAL EUROPE, 1919-1937

free city prospered. Its importance as a port increased. In 1925 the total tonnage of seagoing vessels entering and leaving Danzig was about twice as much as in 1912, and the total import and export trade of the port for 1927 was more than four times as great as for any prewar year. Poland's determination to create a great port of her own, however, caused considerable alarm in Danzig, which felt that its own economic position as the chief outlet for Polish commerce was threatened. In 1930 Danzig appealed to the League of Nations, seeking to have Poland compelled to use the port of Danzig either exclusively or preferentially for her sea-borne trade. But Poland refused to consider any arrangements involving the compulsory dependence of her trade upon Danzig, and steadily proceeded with the development of Gdynia. In 1933, however, a convention was signed between Poland and Danzig which stated definitely that Poland would direct 45 per cent of her foreign trade through Danzig and 55 per cent through Gdynia.

In the succeeding years the organization of a Nazi party in Danzig greatly disturbed the situation in the free city. The election of members of the Danzig Assembly on April 7, 1935, was preceded by an exciting electoral campaign in which the issue was the degree of success which the Nazis might attain. Their aim was to secure two thirds of the seats in order that the constitution of the free city might be amended to bring that territory into conformity with the totalitarian regime in Germany. Electioneering speeches were made by some of the outstanding Nazi leaders of the Third Reich, including Göring, premier of Prussia, Goebbels, minister of propaganda, and Hess, deputy chancellor. A Nazi campaign of terrorism, moreover, sought to intimidate the Socialists and Poles. Although the Nazis increased their representation in the Assembly, they fell slightly short of the two thirds which they needed to enable them to change the constitution.

In 1936 considerable friction developed between the League of Nations and the Nazi government of Danzig. In January of that year, Anthony Eden, British representative on the League Council, informed that body of the Danzig government's disregard of freedom of the press, election safeguards, and other opposition rights, and of its failure to execute certain Council recommendations. The Nazi president of the Danzig Senate, who represented the free city before the Council, was inclined to be recalcitrant. Under the threat of a League investigation and a possible resort to sanctions, however, the Nazi government gave in and promised to respect the Council's orders to obey the free city's constitution. But six months later the head of the Danzig government again appeared before the Council of the League and in the course of his address demanded that the Council should send a new high commissioner to Danzig with instructions to abstain from interfering in internal affairs and to deal only with external policy.

In Danzig it was officially announced that the government of the free city would thereafter ignore Sean Lester, the League high commissioner, and would have no more official dealings with him. Apparently the League felt that Lester's usefulness was seriously impaired by the Danzig government's attitude toward him, for in February, 1937, a new high commissioner—a citizen of Switzerland —was appointed, and it was generally believed that he had been instructed not to intervene in the free city's domestic affairs unless its government interfered with Poland's interests.

During 1936 and 1937 the Nazis by administrative measures transformed the government of the free city from a democratic to a totalitarian regime. The Communist, Social Democratic, German Nationalist, and Center parties were all dissolved or suppressed. After October, 1937, the National Socialist Party was the only German party permitted in the free city. Thus the Nazis eventually accomplished in Danzig that co-ordination with the Third Reich which they had sought but failed to achieve in Austria in 1934.

## LITHUANIA, VILNA, AND MEMEL

To the north of Poland lies Lithuania, a diminutive reminder and remnant of the once large and powerful grand duchy of the same name. The Lithuanians were so long merged with the Poles that the idea of their constituting a separate political entity was for a time forgotten. Gradually during the nineteenth century, however, the Lithuanians awoke to a consciousness of their separate nationality, and by 1905 they were demanding autonomy within a Russian federation. During the World War their national sentiment increased. A movement for independence was begun, and Lithuanians living in other lands gave their efforts to a campaign of propaganda to advance the cause. National independence was finally and formally proclaimed on February 16, 1918. Powerful German influences succeeded in directing the political current into monarchical channels, and in July a German prince accepted the Lithuanian crown. The monarchy was but an ephemeral thing, however, and with the defeat of Germany it was speedily replaced by a republic.

The new Lithuanian state faced a difficult situation. It had to contend not only with the Russian "Reds" to the east but with the aggressive Poles to the south. Bolshevik armies were soon advancing into Lithuania, and the government was forced to retire from Vilna to Kaunas (Kovno). A few months of fighting eventually drove the Bolsheviks out of the country, but not until July 12, 1920, was peace actually obtained. In the treaty of Moscow the Soviet government recognized the independence of Lithuania and defined its boundary with the latter, ceding to it the district of Vilna. The struggle which immediately ensued with Poland over the possession of this capital of medieval Lithuania has already been discussed.[2] Although the Conference of Ambassadors, in March, 1923, confirmed Poland's possession of Vilna, the Lithuanian government continued to claim it on the basis of the treaty of Moscow. "The act of a sovereign state cannot be set aside by any Council of Ambassadors," declared the Lithuanian premier. The Vilna question remained a disturbing irritant constantly inflaming the Lithuanian body politic and preventing normal diplomatic relations between Lithuania and Poland.

While the neighboring Poles were busy "Polonizing" Vilna, the Lithuanians were apparently engaged in an effort quietly to "Lithuanianize" the city and district of Memel, which the League of Nations had awarded to them in 1924 with a stipulation for local autonomy. Their efforts in this respect were seriously checked after 1932, however, by the vigilance and activity of the Nazis of Germany, who extended their political organization into Memel. In February, 1934, the Lithuanian government outlawed two Nazi political parties in Memel on the ground that they were treasonable. Later it arrested more than a hundred German Nazis in the Memel district on charges of plotting to restore that city to Germany by force. In December the Nazis were brought to trial, and, since Lithuania was at that time under emergency law, the cases were brought before a court-martial.

During the ensuing weeks, while the trials were being conducted,

[2] See pages 525–527.

national sentiment in Germany was aroused, and demands that the "Saar of the East" be redeemed by the fatherland were frequently voiced. The international situation became strained; German and Lithuanian troops were mobilized along the border. When in March, 1935, the Lithuanian court condemned four of the accused to death [3] and eighty-seven to prison terms, indignation in Germany rose to great heights with many popular demonstrations protesting the verdict. In May, fortunately, the tension between Germany and Lithuania was lessened when the death sentences were commuted to life imprisonment and most of the prison terms were reduced in length.

In 1935 demands were made in Germany that the powers which had signed the Memel convention [4] should see that the rights of Germans under Lithuanian rule were observed in accordance with that agreement. A directorate of five members responsible to a chamber of deputies was supposed to exist in Memel, but no chamber had functioned for practically a year, and no directorate existed. In April, 1935, the British, French, and Italian governments in a joint note to Lithuania declared that the latter should take steps at once to reintroduce representative government in Memel.

It so happened that in May the terms of the Memel deputies expired, and an election was called for September. In the election, which assumed somewhat the character of a plebiscite, the Germans won control of the Memel chamber of deputies. Consequently, a directorate controlled by German Memelanders was set up under the presidency of the Lithuanian-born head of the German group. The government at Kaunas thus failed in its efforts to "Lithuanianize" Memel and to secure Lithuanian ascendancy in that territory.

## ESTONIA AND LATVIA

To the north of Lithuania and Poland, along the east shore of the Baltic, lies a territory inhabited chiefly by Estonians and Letts, who, after having been dominated by Danes, Germans, Swedes, and Poles, came in the course of the eighteenth century under the rule of the Romanov dynasty. Until 1819 they were serfs, tilling the soil on the great estates of the German barons, or Balts, the successors of

---

[3] On the charge of murdering a so-called Nazi traitor.
[4] See page 528.

the medieval Teutonic Knights who had originally conquered the territory and established there an "upper crust of Germanic civilization." Although both Estonians and Letts eventually rose from serfdom to the status of a free peasantry, the greater part of the land remained, until the World War, in the hands of the Balts, who constituted an insignificant fraction of the population. Both peoples were filled with a bitter hostility toward these foreign masters of their soil, as well as toward their political rulers, the Slavs, who sought to "Russify" them.

As might have been expected, after the Bolshevik revolution in Russia the Estonians declared their independence on November 28, 1917. This action led to an immediate "Red" invasion from Russia, but in 1918 advancing German armies put the Bolsheviks to flight and subjected the country to German occupation. This was highly satisfactory to the Baltic barons, who were as eager as were the Germans to bring this territory under Teutonic control. But all attempts to force an Estonian representative assembly to elect a Hohenzollern duke were in vain. Finally the Balts, acting in the name of Estonia, invited the Kaiser to be their ruler, and in April, 1918, William II, through his chancellor, accepted the invitation. The defeat of the Central Powers, however, brought the collapse of monarchical and pro-German plans.

The withdrawal of German troops was in turn followed by a second Bolshevik invasion, which swept over most of the little country. Two months of severe fighting eventually freed Estonia of "Red" armies, but the war dragged on until an armistice was signed with the Soviet government in December, 1919. This was transformed into the definitive peace of Dorpat (Tartu) on February 2, 1920. By it Russia recognized the independence of Estonia, while the latter in turn granted Russia free transit to Estonian ports. On June 15, 1920, a permanent constitution was adopted establishing Estonia as an independent "republic in which the power of the state is in the hands of the people."

Meanwhile the Letts had fared in a somewhat similar way. From 1915 on, most of their territory was occupied by the Germans, who planned to bring it permanently under Teutonic rule. In this they incurred the determined opposition of the Letts, and, as elsewhere in the Baltic regions, German influence and control were destroyed by the outcome of the war. On November 18, 1918, Latvian independence was proclaimed and a provisional government established. The new government, however, was soon confronted with a formidable task, for the Bolshevik armies began an invasion of Latvia and occupied most of the country. At the same time the Baltic barons seized the opportunity to intrigue with the remaining German forces to overturn the government in order to establish one favorable to their interests. But the Balts' attempts failed, and after a year's struggle the Bolsheviks were finally driven from the country in February, 1920. Six months later Russia by the treaty of Riga (August 11) recognized the independence of Latvia. In February, 1922, a permanent form of government was adopted which followed rather closely the Estonian constitution.

On January 26, 1921, Estonia and Latvia received the *de jure* recognition of the principal Allied powers, and in September of the same year both were admitted to the League of Nations. Both countries during their early years had to contend with Communist intrigues and uprisings fostered beyond their frontiers, and both in the end outlawed Communism. Because of the devastation wrought by German and Bolshevik forces and because of the cutting-off of the great Russian hinterland, the economic recovery of both countries was greatly handicapped. In order to hasten it and at the same time remove all need for Russia's plotting against them, both countries sought to foster the transit trade between their ports and Russian territory and provided every facility for Russian commerce. The close relations between these two republics and the fears which were common to them resulted in their concluding (November 1, 1923) a treaty of defensive alliance. Under its terms the two states agreed to pursue a purely pacific policy toward all nations, to concert together and lend each other political and diplomatic support in their international relations, and to give armed assistance to each other in case of unprovoked attack.

Both Estonia and Latvia carried through a program of agrarian reform during the early years of their independence. In these two states the reform assumed the guise of a peasant revolt against the German Balt landlords, so that the movement was racial and national as well as economic and social. In the former, according to official statistics, 33,438 farms comprising some 2,560,000 acres were parceled out. In the latter approximately 125,000 new holdings—ranging from 25 to 55 acres each—were created.[5]

## FINLAND

The northernmost, the largest, and the strongest of the Baltic republics is Finland, a country nearly two thirds as large as France, lying just east of the Scandinavian peninsula and extending from the Baltic to the Arctic Ocean. Before the war the territory was under the control of the Russian tsars, and the attempts of the latter to "Russify" the inhabitants have been discussed. The latter, however, succeeded in preserving their own individuality, and reached a high level of literacy with a superior type of culture. They were thrifty and capable, and their educational and economic standards were far above those of the Russians. The Finns were therefore quick to seize upon the deposition of the tsar in 1917 as an opportunity for severing their union with Russia. In December, 1917, Finland formally declared her independence, and within a few weeks received the recognition of Soviet Russia, Sweden, France, Germany, Norway, and Denmark.

For a time it appeared that Finland, like Russia, might become a soviet republic. A radical wing of the Finnish Social Democrats attempted to introduce the soviet regime and was actively assisted with Russian soldiers, arms, and munitions. Early in 1918 "Red Guards" gained control of Helsinki, the capital, and all southern Finland. A class war ensued. The bourgeois and landowning classes took up arms to resist and organized "White" armies under Baron Mannerheim, a Swedish Finn who had been a cavalry commander in the Russian army. Foreign aid was sought by these "Whites," and in April German troops landed, to be joyously acclaimed by the bourgeoisie as the "liberators" of their country. By the early part of May, 1918, the "Red Guards" had been defeated and expelled

---

[5] Agrarian reform was also inaugurated in Lithuania. Before the war 36 per cent of the agricultural area of Lithuania had belonged to large landowners, chiefly Poles, most of whom held estates of more than 5000 acres. Of the agricultural population, on the other hand, between 15 and 20 per cent was landless. By a law of February, 1922, lands in private estates in excess of 200 acres were expropriated, together with the church lands and those belonging to the former Russian nobles' and peasants' agricultural banks. These were added to the existing state lands to form a land reserve from which small holdings were formed for some 300,000 new proprietors.

from the country. Then followed a German attempt to bring Finland within the sphere of Teutonic influence. With the end of the World War, however, a reaction against things German began. In June, 1919, the Finnish diet finally decided in favor of a republic, and in the following month a republican constitution was adopted. In December, 1920, Finland was admitted to the League of Nations.

The peace treaty which was signed with Soviet Russia at Dorpat on October 14, 1920, ceded to Finland a narrow strip of territory between Murmansk and the eastern frontier of Norway so that the new republic might have an ice-free port at Pechenga. In the treaty negotiations Finland likewise sought the annexation of Eastern Karelia, a district lying outside the frontiers of the old grand duchy but inhabited by people ethnically affiliated with the Finns. The Soviet government refused to permit this enlargement of Finland's territory, however, because the possession of Eastern Karelia was essential to Russia's control of the recently constructed Petrograd-Murmansk railway. Finland was forced to content herself with the Soviet government's promise to give political, economic, and cultural autonomy to the district.

In the summer of 1921 Finland complained to the Soviet government that it was not carrying out the stipulations of the treaty of Dorpat regarding Eastern Karelia. A few months later a rebellion against Russia broke out in the district, but was suppressed. After having appealed in vain to the League of Nations, Finland finally asked to have the case referred to the Permanent Court of International Justice. Russia, however, refused to recognize the court's competence, and the case gave the court an opportunity to hand down an important ruling, namely, that it could not express an opinion in a dispute between a member of the League and a state not a member, without the consent of the latter. Finland therefore was unsuccessful in her efforts to reopen the Karelian question. In the Åland Islands dispute she fared decidedly better.[6]

Despite the political and social struggle which accompanied the acquisition of her independence, despite the early need to suppress both the Left group with its sovietism and social revolution and the Right group with its monarchical tendencies, Finland soon became economically and politically stabilized. A sturdy race of yeo-

[6] See pages 524–525.

man farmers, an influential middle class, and an educated citizenry all helped to maintain a liberal bourgeois republic. Agrarian legislation paved the way to still further economic progress, for about two thirds of the population is engaged in agriculture and dairying.

## CHAPTER XXV

# THE SUCCESSION STATES OF CENTRAL EUROPE

POSTWAR central Europe differs radically from what it was before the war. Although the former Habsburg empire had long been a political anachronism, yet, stretching from the plains of the Vistula to the shores of the Adriatic and from the heart of the Alps to the bounds of Rumania, it had constituted a strong economic unit. Within its confines had been found grain fields, pasturelands, and forests; oil wells and coal mines; iron, copper, lead, silver, and gold ores; breweries, distilleries, and sugar refineries; steel mills and textile factories; glass works and potteries. All had been included within a common tariff union. This relatively balanced and unified economic organism was utterly disrupted by the nationalistic upheaval which followed the war. Most of the periphery of what had been Europe's second largest country was absorbed into surrounding states—Italy, Yugoslavia, Rumania, and re-created Poland; the center fell to Austria, Hungary, and Czechoslovakia. This chapter discusses the postwar history of the last three of these states.

## AUSTRIA

In the early months of 1919 vigorous attempts were made to bring Austria into the ranks of the soviet republics. In the midst of acute food shortage and widespread unemployment, emissaries from Soviet Hungary and Soviet Russia preached communism in the streets of Vienna. Disciples of Lenin invaded workmen's councils and waged a mighty struggle for control. But, thanks to the efforts of moderate Socialists like Otto Bauer and Victor Adler, there was in Austria no bitter communist conflict between the proletariat and the bourgeoisie. The issue was settled within the ranks of the workers. The forces of moderation won out; Bolshevism was rejected. Elections in February, 1919, gave the Social Democrats the largest representation in the National Constituent Assembly, whose first act was to announce that Austria was a democratic republic. The Habs-

burgs were banished from the country, and all possessions of the
dynasty were confiscated.

On October 1, 1920, a constitution was adopted. Under it Austria
became a federal republic with nine provinces, each with its own
local diet. The national government had a bicameral legislature consisting of the Federal Council, elected by the diets, and the National
Council, elected by popular vote. In 1929 provision was made for the
popular election of the president also. Real executive power, however, resided in a ministry responsible to the National Council,
which, furthermore, had authority to enact legislation over the veto
of the upper house. The whole political structure rested on proportional representation and universal suffrage. On December 9 Michael Hainisch, a liberal bourgeois, was elected first president of the
republic, which, in the same month, was admitted to membership
in the League of Nations.

The disruption of the Habsburg empire had particularly unfortunate economic results for Austria. The latter, which inherited the
populous capital of the former empire, was left with inadequate
food supplies for her population and with insufficient coal and raw
materials for her industries. She therefore faced the necessity of importing these commodities. But the free exchange of goods, which
might have enabled her to pay for her imports by the exportation of
her manufactured products, was prevented when each of the succession states of central Europe at once erected tariff barriers against
its neighbors.

By 1922 Austria's plight was so serious that Chancellor Ignaz
Seipel proposed a currency and customs union with Italy as a cure
for the republic's economic woes. But this proposal was so distasteful to Czechoslovakia that Beneš, the Czechoslovak foreign minister,
did his utmost to persuade the League of Nations to save Austria
from bankruptcy. In September, 1922, Seipel made a personal appeal to the League, stating Austria's willingness to accept a system
of control if assistance were forthcoming, but warning that Austria
unaided would constitute a grave danger to the peace of the world,
a danger which it was the duty of the League of Nations to avert.

The League decided to undertake the financial rehabilitation of
the little republic, and on October 4, 1922, three protocols embodying
the Council's scheme were signed by representatives of Great Britain, France, Italy, Czechoslovakia, and Austria. The first protocol con-

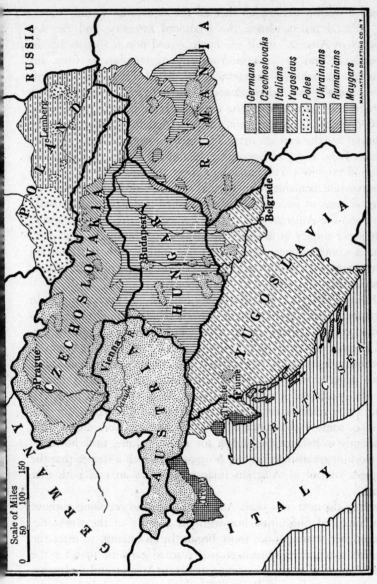

ETHNOGRAPHIC MAP OF THE FORMER DUAL MONARCHY, SHOWING THE SUCCESSION STATES, 1919–1937

tained a solemn declaration that all the signatories would "respect the political independence, the territorial integrity, and the sovereignty of Austria," while the latter agreed not to alienate her independence and to "abstain from any negotiations or from any economic or financial engagement calculated directly or indirectly to compromise this independence." Austria agreed to carry through a program of reform, involving increased revenue from taxation and rigid economy in expenditure, in order that her budget might be balanced by the end of 1924. The governments of Great Britain, France, Italy, and Czechoslovakia guaranteed a loan up to 650,000,-000 gold crowns ($135,000,000) to cover the excess of expenditure over revenue available from normal resources during the next two years. A bank of issue was to be established under prescribed conditions, and the Austrian government agreed to surrender all right to issue paper money or to negotiate loans except by special authorization. A commissioner-general, in collaboration with the Austrian government, was to supervise the execution of the plan. In a sense Austria went into the hands of a receiver.

During November the inflationary issue of notes was stopped. In December Alfred Zimmerman, a Netherlander who had been appointed commissioner-general, arrived in Vienna to take up his duties. From January 2, 1923, a new national bank of issue began to function independently of the state; the currency was stabilized at 14,400 paper crowns to one gold crown, and the monetary reform of 1924 established a new unit, the schilling, on a gold basis. Although the reforms occasioned considerable suffering by the dismissal of some 80,000 public officials, expenditures were not reduced sufficiently to balance the budget for 1924. By June, 1926, however, the work of reconstruction had progressed to such a degree that the League's control of Austrian finances came to an end with that month.

During the next four years Austria managed to get along without great financial difficulties, but with the coming of the world depression her troubles once more began. In an attempt to meet the situation a tentative agreement was reached early in 1931 for the establishment of a customs union between Austria and Germany. But the nationalists of France, Czechoslovakia, and Poland—envisioning the consummation of the political union of the two countries which they so much feared—were immediately aroused, for to them the plan seemed to resemble the customs union which had helped Prussia to create the German political union in the nineteenth century. They therefore denounced the Austro-German proposal as contrary to the treaty of Versailles, the treaty of St. Germain, and the Geneva protocol of 1922. France and Great Britain brought the matter before the League of Nations, which in turn referred the question—one of interpreting treaty obligations—to the World Court for an advisory opinion. On September 5, 1931, the latter by an eight-to-seven vote decided that the proposed customs union was incompatible with the Geneva protocol.

In order to strengthen Austria's economic position, France in 1932 proposed that the five Danubian states should arrange among themselves a close economic collaboration based on preferential prices and quotas. The French plan was approved by the Little Entente, but Austria opposed it because it did not provide for the inclusion of Germany and Italy, Austria's best customers. France insisted that such a commercial union should exclude these great powers, and many believed that the French had in mind the creation of a Danubian economic unit under the domination of French financial and commercial influences. Antagonism between the Little Entente and France, on the one hand, and Austria, Germany, and Italy, on the other, prevented any tangible results.

Again Austria had to turn to the League of Nations for help, and in the summer of 1932 a twenty-year loan of $42,000,000 was made to the republic through the Bank for International Settlements. One third was guaranteed by France, one third by Great Britain, and one third by several other states. Certain conditions were attached to the loan. The national budget must be balanced, and the republic must once more submit to the financial supervision of a League representative. It must not, furthermore, enter into any economic union with Germany during the duration of the loan. This loan again rescued Austria from the economic abyss, but left her future still in doubt. Although to many the situation of the little republic appeared hopeless, some agreed with Chancellor Engelbert Dollfuss, who in 1933 asserted that, if Austria could obtain markets and reasonable facilities for the discharge of her debts, she could stand by herself "as Switzerland does."

To many, however, the only solution for Austria's economic difficulties appeared to be union with Germany. Therefore, although

Austria in the treaty of St. Germain had been compelled to agree not to alienate her sovereignty without the consent of the League Council, the desire for union with Germany persisted. Not all Austrians, to be sure, were thoroughly in sympathy with the movement. Some disliked the idea of being linked with a Germany so strongly Lutheran; others feared the dominance of aggressive and militaristic Prussia; while still others were disturbed by the prospect that their glorious Vienna might be relegated to the position of a second-rate provincial city like Munich. Those who favored the *Anschluss* argued, on the other hand, that all Germans should be in one state, that Austria's domestic markets would be greatly extended if she were part of Germany, and that, when it came to negotiating commercial treaties with foreign states, Austria as part of Germany could secure far better terms.

In 1921 an attempt was made to circumvent the provisions of the treaty of St. Germain when two Austrian provinces held plebiscites and voted for union with Germany. Although the peace treaty forbade Austria to unite with Germany, it was argued, no restraint had been placed upon the individual provinces. Vigorous protests from the Allies, however, soon put an end to this movement. Nevertheless, the desire for union was not destroyed, and during the succeeding decade a number of steps, official and unofficial, were taken to bind the two peoples closer together both in spirit and in fact. Government officials and university professors exchanged visits. Austro-German cartels were established in various branches of production. Tariff concessions were granted to each other in respect to certain commodities. In many fields legislation and codes were made uniform. Thus a sort of "progressive assimilation" took place. But when an Austro-German customs union was proposed in 1931, it was, as pointed out above, prevented by the opposition of the powers.

After 1931 the *Anschluss* question developed a new phase, largely because of the spectacular rise of Adolf Hitler in Germany. Even before the Nazi leader came into power at Berlin, a subdivision of his National Socialist Party was established in Austria, and the situation in the little republic became complicated by the organization of Nazi "Brown Shirts." Hitler's success in Germany in 1933 at once had its repercussion in Austria, where Austrian Nazis immediately began to work for the *Anschluss*. German Nazis, doubtless realizing that the outright annexation of Austria—which they had always advocated—would cause international complications, apparently determined to achieve the same end indirectly. Since the Austrian Nazis belonged to Hitler's party and took their orders from him, a Nazi political victory in Austria would bring the *de facto* union of the two republics. That this might be accomplished, the German Nazis spent millions of dollars on propaganda in Austria. Skilled agitators were sent into the little republic, while German Nazis dropped from airplanes over Austria and broadcast from Bavarian radio stations attacks upon the Dollfuss government.

But in Chancellor Dollfuss they encountered a serious obstacle to their success. Although he was originally in sympathy with the *Anschluss,* the activities of the Hitlerites drove him into open opposition. Boldly and resolutely he struck back at the Nazis. He at once dissolved the parliament, abolished freedom of the press and of assembly, forbade Nazi propaganda over the radio, forced German Nazi agitators to leave the country, prohibited the wearing of the Nazi uniform and the display of any flag or political symbol except the Austrian flag, and finally, in June, 1933, outlawed the Nazi party in Austria altogether. During that summer Dollfuss sought to build up a spirit of Austrian patriotism by creating the so-called Fatherland Front, an organization designed to replace all political parties for the purpose of unifying the Austrian people.

The Nazis continued their activities, however, and on July 25, 1934, a small group of them seized the government radio station and forced the announcer to broadcast a statement that the Dollfuss cabinet had fallen. Another group seized the chancellory, mortally wounded Dollfuss, and held other members of the cabinet captive. Apparently their plan was to force a reorganization of the government in order to give the Nazis prominent places in the new cabinet. Their plot was not well organized, however, and quickly collapsed. By July 28 the Austrian government had the situation well in hand, and on the next day a new cabinet was formed, headed by Kurt Schuschnigg, a Christian Socialist colleague of the former premier and a member of Dolfuss's last cabinet. Between ten and fifteen of the Nazi leaders were eventually put to death, while hundreds were sentenced to prison terms of various lengths.

Events in Austria had their repercussions abroad, where it was widely believed that the German Nazis were back of the attempted revolt. Mussolini promptly mobilized troops along the Austrian frontier, as did also Yugoslavia. Fortunately for the peace of Europe, Hitler's government carefully maintained a "correct" attitude. It officially denied any connection with the Austrian revolt, closed the roads across the frontier into Austria, recalled the German minister in Vienna on the ground that he had overstepped his authority during the uprising, and dismissed the Nazi head of the radio station at Munich. Nevertheless, Austria's dependence upon outside support for the maintenance of her independence was made emphatically clear. Had it not been for Mussolini's swift dispatch of Italian troops to the Brenner Pass, the Nazi *Putsch* might have succeeded. Mussolini's announcement in 1937 that Italy could not give military assistance to protect Austria against a German attempt to consummate the *Anschluss* was particularly alarming, therefore, to those who desired to maintain the independence of the little state.

But Austria was not disturbed merely by the German Nazis. In the second decade of its existence the republic was shaken by bitter conflicts between the urban proletariat and the rural classes. The republic comprises roughly two districts which are nearly equal in population though not in area. The eastern end, including Vienna, the plain between the capital and Wiener-Neustadt, and the ore-bearing districts of Styria, constitutes a great industrial region. The rest of the republic is agricultural and is largely in the hands of peasant proprietors. As a consequence of these differences there at once developed in postwar Austria a fairly clear-cut antagonism between the socialism of the factory and the individualism of the farm, between the skepticism of the city and the clericalism of the province, more specifically, between the "Reds" of Vienna and the "Blacks" of the countryside. The federalization of the republic had been caused chiefly by these differences, for decentralization had been demanded by the conservative Christian Socialists as a means of protection against the radical Social Democrats of the capital.

Although the Social Democrats originally favored the unity of the state, federalism eventually worked to their great advantage in at least one respect. Vienna, a city of nearly 2,000,000 inhabitants, was detached from Lower Austria and established as a separate province. As such the municipality became wealthy, for one half of the taxes raised in each province went to the local government. Under Social Democratic control the capital raised and spent money freely on social welfare, public health, education, and city improvements. Large sums were devoted by the municipality to the construction of model tenements and public baths for the proletariat, the money being raised largely by confiscatory taxes levied upon property holders. Public utilities were taken over by the municipality, former palaces were transformed into office buildings or museums, and pre-war royal gardens were opened as public parks.

The enmity between the proletariat of Vienna and the peasants of the provinces led to the creation of two hostile militant organizations, the *Schutzbund* and the *Heimwehr*. The former, with its strength in the industrial districts, came to have a well-disciplined membership of nearly 100,000 men, and managed to store in secret hiding places large quantities of arms and munitions for use in time of crisis. The rural Heimwehr, on the other hand, was a type of fascist organization which was not only strongly anti-Socialist but inclined to be monarchical as well. Financed to some extent by the wealthy Prince Ernst von Starhemberg, the Heimwehr ultimately enrolled some 60,000 well-armed men. Frequent clashes occurred between the rival bodies, and at times the government with its very small army had difficulty in maintaining order.

Ultimately the government's attitude toward this domestic conflict was influenced by its desire to prevent Austria from coming under the control of the Third Reich. At the close of the year 1933 Chancellor Dollfuss was looking for some way to strengthen his hand against the Nazis. The Social Democrats, the largest political group in Austria, would have been glad to unite with him in a common front against their common foe. But Mussolini, who had been supporting Dollfuss in his struggle to prevent the consummation of the *Anschluss,* apparently opposed an alliance with the Socialists and favored instead a government in Austria which should include the Heimwehr. The latter, in turn, made the destruction of the Socialists the price of their support. On February 12, 1934, police and Heimwehr men began raiding Social Democratic headquarters.

When a general strike was called by Social Democratic leaders, Dollfuss at once outlawed the Social Democratic Party, declared martial law, ordered civilians with firearms to be executed, and began military measures against the Socialists. Although the Heimwehr succeeded almost at once in getting possession of the city hall in Vienna, the Socialists held out until the government gave a promise of amnesty to all except certain of their leaders. In the end the Social Democratic Party was completely suppressed. Some of its leaders fled to Czechoslovakia; hundreds, including Mayor Seitz of Vienna, were arrested and thrown into prison; a few were hanged. On April 1 a new municipal constitution was decreed for Vienna, removing the last vestiges of self-government for that city, which had been governed since 1918 by the Socialists.

Four weeks later the Austrian parliament without opportunity for debate—and with more than half of its members, including the Social Democrats, absent—approved a new constitution submitted to it by the Dollfuss government. An authoritarian corporative state was outlined. The word "republic" nowhere appeared in the new constitution, which abolished universal suffrage and political representation of the people. In April, 1935, the anti-Habsburg laws of 1919 were repealed, and the government was authorized to restore to the Habsburgs some of the property which had been earlier confiscated. This action was thought by many to presage the early restoration of the monarchy. The well-known opposition of the Little Entente to a Habsburg restoration remained, however, and in 1937 even Mussolini announced himself as opposed to such a move.

Beginning in 1935 there occurred in Austria a struggle for power between the extreme fascist and pro-Italian Starhemberg and the clerical and slightly less extreme Schuschnigg. The two leaders had not always seen eye to eye. Some years earlier Schuschnigg had organized the Catholic Storm Troops to counterbalance Starhemberg's Heimwehr, and, although their two private armies had co-operated in 1934 to crush the Socialists and Nazis, the leaders differed on a number of policies. Schuschnigg was apparently willing to make some conciliatory moves toward the former Socialists and was even ready for a *rapprochement* with Germany if the latter would unreservedly recognize Austria's independence. Both of these policies were anathema to Prince Starhemberg.

On April 1, 1936, evidently after consultation with Mussolini, who desired to strengthen Austria against the increasingly more militant Germany, Chancellor Schuschnigg proclaimed the introduction of universal conscription in defiance of the limitations of the treaty of St. Germain. This step had been opposed by Starhemberg, for it was apparent that it would sound the death-knell of private armies like his Heimwehr. The conflict between the two leaders finally reached a climax in May when a bloodless coup ousted Starhemberg from the vice-chancellorship and from the headship of the Fatherland Front. Chancellor Schuschnigg himself assumed the portfolios of foreign affairs and the interior, in addition to those of war and public instruction which he had formerly held. He also assumed command of the Fatherland Front and of the Fatherland Front Militia, the only military force thereafter to be permitted in the republic.

With the support of Mussolini Schuschnigg next sought that *rapprochement* with Germany which had been opposed by Starhemberg. In July, 1936, an agreement was ultimately reached with Hitler by the terms of which Germany reaffirmed her recognition of Austria's independence, Austria declared herself to be "a German state," and each agreed not to try to influence the other's internal affairs but to co-operate in the stabilization of the situation in central Europe. On the surface it appeared that at last Austria might for a time be permitted to live in peace without interference from the German Nazis.

## HUNGARY

When, on November 16, 1918, the Hungarian People's Republic was proclaimed in Budapest, it seemed that Hungary was to join Czechoslovakia and Austria in the ranks of the new democratic republics of postwar Europe. The government in power was headed by the liberal Count Michael Karolyi, who believed that concessions to the subject nationalities and a friendly attitude toward the Allied powers might preserve the Hungarian state from disruption. With feverish haste long-overdue reforms were initiated. Democratic federation, universal suffrage, secret ballot, proportional representation, freedom of speech and of the press, trial by jury, separation of church and state, genuine liberal education, expropriation of the large estates—all these were included in the aims of the new government.

But Karolyi's program, liberal though it was, failed to win the support of the people. The concessions came too late. No longer would the subject races be content with federation within a Hungarian republic. They now demanded complete independence or union with their kinsmen in neighboring states. Moreover, the prospect of agrarian reform frightened many of Karolyi's followers, who thereupon withdrew their support. Finally, the Allies had no sympathy with Karolyi's plan to retain the subject peoples in a federalized Hungary and in March, 1919, ordered Hungarian troops to withdraw from Transylvania. Karolyi at once resigned his position as provisional president.

Meanwhile, radicalism had rapidly increased, fostered by the hardships resulting from the continued Allied blockade and by Bolshevik ideas brought back by soldiers returning from the Russian front. The Socialists and Communists decided to seize upon Karolyi's resignation as an occasion to set up a soviet state. Actual power came into the hands of the new commissar for foreign affairs, Bela Kun. This young middle-class Jew had been an active Socialist ever since his graduation from the Transylvanian University of Kolozsvár. During the war he had been an officer in the Austro-Hungarian army on the Galician front, where he had been taken captive in 1915. He was in Russia during the revolution of 1917 and became an ardent admirer of Bolshevism. Supplied with money from Russia, Bela Kun had returned to Hungary with the avowed object of overthrowing the People's Republic and of establishing soviet rule in its place.

All branches of the government now came into the hands of soviet officials, who assumed practically dictatorial powers. The immediate nationalization of large industrial establishments, railways, banks, and mines was ordered. A drastic land-reform scheme was adopted which nationalized the large estates without compensation. An elective soviet system was introduced, with the franchise limited to productive workers. Education was separated from church control and reorganized on a strictly proletarian basis. The Communists, comprising only a very small minority of the population, resorted to terror in order to maintain themselves in power. Revolutionary tribunals replaced the existing judicial system, and a "Red" army was created. The press was muzzled, the right of public meeting was denied to all except Communists, hundreds were imprisoned, and political murders became frequent.

But even "Red Terror" could not maintain the Communists in power against the rising tide of opposition. The peasants refused to sell their produce for Bolshevik currency. The situation of the capital, blockaded by the Allies and boycotted by the peasants, became daily more and more desperate. The majority of the trade unionists, not extreme Communists at heart, turned against the new regime. The Allied powers demanded the resignation of the soviet government to make way for one elected by the people. A counter-revolutionary movement was inaugurated, and in the French zone an opposition government was set up. A Rumanian army defeated the Hungarian "Red" army and in August, 1919, captured Budapest. Bela Kun fled to Russia.

In November, 1919, counterrevolutionary forces, led by Nicholas Horthy, a rear admiral in the former Habsburg navy, entered the Hungarian capital. Early in 1920 elections were held for a national assembly to decide upon the future constitution of the country. Sentiment for a monarchy was once more strong, and the first law enacted by the assembly restored the former monarchical constitution. Although Charles IV had never legally abdicated the throne, his return was temporarily prevented by the attitude of the Allies. Consequently, on March 1 the National Assembly elected Admiral Horthy to act as regent during the enforced absence of the king. Three weeks later an executive order formally declared Hungary a monarchy. Reactionary legislation followed, and a "White Terror" continued for many months to punish those in any way connected with the soviet regime.

Influenced by the hope that the strong monarchical reaction in Hungary presaged an enthusiastic welcome to his return and by the belief that a *fait accompli* would receive no more than a formal protest from the Allied powers, King Charles suddenly returned to Hungary in 1921 and on March 21 demanded back his throne. The result was most disappointing and disillusioning to Charles. There was no outburst of popular acclaim; Horthy declined to surrender his power until ordered to do so by the National Assembly; the Little Entente powers and the principal Allies vigorously protested. The Hungarian National Assembly joined Horthy in urging Charles to leave the country immediately. Confronted by great opposition and accorded little support, the ex-monarch reluctantly withdrew.

But Charles was neither convinced nor contented. On October 20, 1921, he escaped from Switzerland by airplane and made his second return to Hungary. There he placed himself at the head of a band of armed royalists and marched on the capital. Two days later Beneš, foreign minister of Czechoslovakia, announced that the return of Charles constituted a *casus belli*, that preparations for mobilization were going forward, that energetic measures would be taken in concert with the other Little Entente powers, and that military force would be used, if necessary, "to obtain the final settlement of the Habsburg question in Hungary."

Hungarian troops were dispatched against Charles, who was defeated and taken prisoner. Horthy's government then demanded that Charles abdicate, but he resolutely refused to comply. Upon representations from the Allies, the ex-monarch and his wife were eventually delivered on board a British monitor in the Danube for removal to a definitive place of residence. The Allies demanded the deposition of Charles, but the Little Entente powers went further and demanded the permanent exclusion from the throne of the whole Habsburg dynasty. The Hungarian National Assembly was obliged to pass a law carrying these demands into effect, and the government agreed to permit no election to the throne without previously coming to an understanding with the principal Allies. Hungary thus remained a monarchy, but with the election to the throne indefinitely adjourned.

Although Charles IV died in exile in April, 1922, there continued to be in Hungary a Legitimist Party which advocated the immediate coronation of his son, Otto. As the day approached when the latter would reach his majority (November 20, 1930) and, in the eyes of the Legitimists, become entitled to rule at Budapest, some nervousness was felt among those opposed to a Habsburg restoration. The Hungarian government prepared to defend itself against a *coup d'état*, but when the day arrived no untoward events occurred. By the members of the Habsburg family Otto's headship was acknowledged; but the youthful archduke, following a picturesque ceremony at his mother's home in Belgium, returned to the University of Louvain to continue his education. Hungarian governments since 1930 have shown little active interest in a Habsburg restoration.

Although Regent Horthy was more often in the limelight and was usually considered the "strong man" of Hungary, the statesman who really directed the policies of the monarchy during the decade after 1921 was Count Bethlen. The latter was the descendant of a wealthy noble family of prewar Transylvania, but the World War and the treaty of Trianon had forced him to choose between Ru-

manian and Hungarian citizenship. As one of the Hungarian op-
tants, he had lost his estates in Transylvania and had become relatively an impoverished man. Though of the conservative aristocracy,
Bethlen recognized that the prewar order in Hungary could not be
fully restored, and his Union Party—representing the interests of
the landowners, the well-to-do peasants, and some of the clergy—
constituted a middle group between the Socialists on the Left and
the reactionaries on the Right.

Nevertheless, Hungary has remained generally conservative in
her institutions. Soon after proclamation of the monarchy an executive decree restricted the suffrage and restored open voting in most
districts. In 1926 an upper legislative chamber was created, with
forty life members and with the rest not popularly elected but drawn
from the nobility, county and municipal councils, church organizations, universities, and commercial and industrial bodies. Although
an agricultural country, Hungary has experienced little in the way
of agrarian reform in the postwar period, remaining a land of large
estates. While nearly 40 per cent of the land is held in estates of
more than 1400 acres each, the great majority of the peasants consist of landless agricultural laborers or of owners whose tiny holdings place them in practically the same category.

In the early years Hungary, like Austria, had a difficult time with
her finances, and in 1923 Bethlen's government appealed to the
League of Nations for assistance. In the following year the League
inaugurated in Hungary a financial regime similar to that instituted in 1922 in Austria. Hungary's recovery was rapid, and by
June, 1926, she was again possessed of a sound fiscal system, though
the situation became difficult during the world depression.

Like so many other statesmen throughout the world who were
retired from office during the depression largely because of popular
economic discontent, Count Bethlen was forced to resign the premiership in August, 1931. Although the national treasury had had
a budget surplus of $15,000,000 when the League of Nations with-
drew its commissioner in 1926, five years later the surplus had been
converted into a budget deficit of twice as much. France then came
to Hungary's assistance with a loan, but insisted in return that the
government should cease its revisionist agitation. Ever since the
peace conference the spirited Magyars had been ardent revisionists,
for they deplored their loss of territory and the inclusion of some

three million of their kinsmen within the frontiers of other states. Denunciation of the treaty of Trianon had been vigorous, and the determination to overthrow the settlement established by that treaty had been openly proclaimed by such nationalist organizations as the "Awakening Magyars."

The next outstanding personality in postwar Hungary was General Julius Gömbös, a personal friend of Regent Horthy and former minister of war. Gömbös had the distinction of being one of the very few commoners to become prominent in Hungarian political life. He had played an active part in elevating Horthy to the regency and had organized an officers' national defense society to support the Horthy regime. It was Gömbös with his defense society who was chiefly responsible for preventing Charles's enthronement at Budapest in 1921. He had been a violent anti-Semitic in former years and had been closely connected with the propaganda of the "Awakening Magyars." In the autumn of 1932 Gömbös became premier and head of the Union party.

The Legitimists were disappointed by Gömbös's elevation to the premiership, and subsequent events only confirmed their belief that the new premier was not of their number. When the Legitimists became active in Otto's behalf in 1933, Gömbös openly declared that the revival of the kingship could in no way help to alleviate the country's ills. Unlike the Legitimists, however, Hungarian nationalists had no cause for disappointment. Although, upon becoming premier, Gömbös renounced his earlier anti-Semitic views, he did not hesitate to summon all Magyars to prepare for that day of Hungary's resurrection which should be ushered in by the peaceful revision of the treaty of Trianon. The economic rehabilitation of the Danubian area, he asserted, could not be accomplished without a revision of the postwar treaties. In the succeeding years he sought to link Hungary closely with Fascist Italy, but his career was cut short by death in October, 1936, before he had been able to alter the situation in central Europe. His place as premier was taken by Koloman Daranyi.

## CZECHOSLOVAKIA

The third of the succession states of central Europe, the one which has enjoyed the most ordered and prosperous national development, is Czechoslovakia. The relative stability of this republic came chiefly

from its advantageous economic situation as an industrial and agricultural country, from the Western outlook of its dominant races,
and from the great ability, wisdom, and moderation of its leading
statesmen. No other of the new states of postwar Europe enjoyed
during its first decade of existence the continuous guidance of two
such capable national leaders as Thomas Garrigue Masaryk and
Edward Beneš. The former, rising above political and racial groups,
steadily pointed the way toward co-operation and unity within the
republic; the latter won and held for Czechoslovakia a prominent
place in the councils of Europe.

On February 29, 1920, the Czechoslovak National Assembly approved a constitution, providing for a democratic parliamentary regime. Under this constitution the National Assembly consists of a
Chamber of Deputies and a Senate, both elected by universal, equal,
secret, and compulsory suffrage, the former for six years and the latter for eight. Real power in the government rests in the Chamber of
Deputies, which has both the right to enact legislation over the veto
of the Senate and the right to compel the resignation of the ministry
by a vote of no confidence. The president of the republic is elected
for a seven-year term by the National Assembly. On May 27, 1920,
Masaryk was elected president.

Next to the revolution itself the greatest accomplishment of the
republic, according to President Masaryk, was the land reform,
which, in his words, constituted the "crowning work and the genuine realization" of the revolution. Before the reform, 2 per cent
of the landowners of Bohemia owned more than 25 per cent of the
land; less than one per cent of the landowners of Moravia owned
nearly a third of the land; and in Slovakia about a thousand persons
owned nearly half of the land. Most of these great estates owned by
Germans had belonged to Czechs before the Bohemian Protestants
were dispossessed by Emperor Ferdinand back in 1620. Land reform, therefore, had the double object of improving the lot of the
peasants and righting a great historic wrong.

In April, 1919, a law providing for expropriation was passed. The
maximum above which land might be expropriated was fixed at
375 acres for arable land and at 625 acres for other types. Peasant
holdings were fixed usually at from 15 to 25 acres. Peasants might
either lease or buy the land, but in the latter case they might not
resell it within ten years without the consent of the state. The

thinly settled sections of Slovakia presented a suitable field for colonization, and a number of colonies were planted in that province. Three months later a law providing for compensation was passed. All expropriated estates, except those belonging to the former royal family, were to be paid for at a rate based upon the average market price during the years 1913–1915, with a reduction from this price for estates of more than 2500 acres. The depreciated Czech crown was to be considered as the equivalent of the prewar Austro-Hungarian crown in compensating the landowners. Peasants were required to pay in cash only one tenth of the purchase price, the state extending credit for the rest. By 1935 some 4,395,000 acres had been transferred to new peasant proprietors. A total of 1913 estates, including some 27 per cent of the tillable land of the country, had been involved. In place of a few hundred large agrarians, more than half a million peasants had become owners of land.

Undoubtedly the most difficult domestic problem of the republic arose from the great number of its racial minorities, about a third of the total population being Germans, Magyars, Ukrainians, Jews, or Poles. The political and racial heterogeneity of parts of the country was well illustrated by elections for the Chamber of Deputies in March, 1924. In one province thirteen different parties contested the eight seats, five of them succeeded in electing candidates, and the oath of office was taken in Ukrainian by four, in Magyar by two, and in Slovak and in Czech by one each. The rights of these minorities are protected by a minorities treaty signed by Czechoslovakia and by specific provisions of the Czechoslovak constitution which guarantee the rights of all citizens without regard to language, race, or religion. Special schools for the minorities are provided, and official business may be transacted in a minority language in districts where 20 per cent of the population belongs to that minority.

One phase of the minorities problem arose in Ruthenia (Pod-karpatska Rus), a province lying at the eastern tip of the republic. This province, providing Czechoslovakia and Rumania with the direct connections which were considered essential to complete the territorial ring about Hungary, was assigned to Czechoslovakia by the peace conference with the provision that it should be granted extensive local autonomy. The population is composed largely of Ukrainians, who in 1919 were for the most part illiterate as a consequence of prewar Magyar oppression. The Czechoslovak government feared that a

Ukrainian diet, if established at once, would be dominated by the well-organized Magyars and Jews rather than by the Ukrainians, and therefore delayed establishing it. In the meantime the government began the rapid introduction of an educational system and instituted throughout the province special courses of instruction in the Ukrainian language for government officials. The first governor appointed was an American of Ukrainian extraction, but in 1923 a native Ukrainian succeeded to the office. Although in the beginning most of the state officials of the district were not Ukrainians, by 1922 more than half were natives of the district. Nevertheless, the government's delay in granting full autonomy to Ruthenia caused bitter complaints.

The Czechs and Slovaks are officially regarded as forming one Czechoslovak nationality and as such constitute the racial majority in the republic. Nevertheless, the differences between them are marked. The Czechs have a very high degree of literacy and are inclined to be both socialistic in politics and agnostic in religion. The Slovaks, on the other hand, had in 1918 a high degree of illiteracy and as a conservative peasantry are for the most part loyal and pious Roman Catholics. It is perhaps not surprising, therefore, that friction developed between them. In the early years of the republic the Slovaks complained that the Czechs were monopolizing the administrative offices. The Slovak Popular Party (Catholic) began to demand semiautonomy for the province, and in 1924 went even so far as to hold meetings calling for a boycott of everything of Czech origin until the demand should be granted. Eventually, in 1929, a new local autonomy law went into effect under which the country —except for Ruthenia, which now has an elective diet—is divided for administrative purposes into three districts. Bohemia, Moravia and Silesia, and Slovakia were given three local councils which are partly elected and partly nominated.

Meanwhile, the aim of the government, under the direction of Masaryk and Beneš, was not only fair treatment of the minorities but such a union of all groups of the population that distinctions of majority and minority would not be felt. In general that policy seems to have succeeded. In October, 1926, two Germans became members of the government, and three months later they were joined by two representatives of the Slovak Popular Party. Nevertheless, continued unrest in Slovakia led in September, 1929, to the dissolution of the parliament and to the Slovak Popular Party's decision to co-operate with the German and Magyar minorities in an effort to throw off Czech domination. That the party did not reflect the viewpoint of all the Slovaks, however, became apparent when it emerged from the election of October, 1929, with a loss of six seats.

In 1932–1933 the German Nazi movement penetrated Czechoslovakia as it did Austria, and tended to interfere with the co-operation of the German parties in the parliament. The Czechoslovak government realized the menace of Hitlerism, with its Pan-German program, and sought, by restricting the use of the radio and prohibiting the circulation of many foreign newspapers from Germany and Austria, to handicap Hitlerite propaganda in the republic. In October, 1933, the Czech Nazi Party announced its own dissolution, just before a government order was issued proscribing it and the German National Party, with which it was apparently about to amalgamate. The *Sudetendeutsch* Party was organized to succeed the proscribed parties, and under the leadership of Konrad Henlein it polled the largest number of votes in the republic in the parliamentary elections of May, 1935. The Nazi movement, therefore, continued to be a force in Czechoslovakia.

Early in 1937 the government in an effort further to conciliate the three million Germans, whose presence within Czechoslovakia constitutes the republic's chief minority problem, reached an agreement with them providing for cultural autonomy, a fair share of government contracts, a greater proportion of German officials, larger appropriations for social services, and an extension of the official use of German. Although Henlein refused to approve these concessions on the ground that they fell short of the political autonomy which the *Sudetendeutsch* Party demanded, they appeared to satisfy the million or more members of the German Social Democratic Party and the German Agrarian League.

Meanwhile, on December 13, 1935, after having held the office for seventeen years, Thomas Garrigue Masaryk, founder of the Czechoslovak Republic, had resigned the presidential office. Eighty-five years of age, he felt that he was no longer strong enough for the task which he had handled so well in the difficult formative period of the republic.[1] "Four times I have been elected president of

[1] Masaryk died on September 14, 1937.

the republic," he said. "This fact may give me the right to ask you . . . always to remember that states can be maintained only by respecting those ideals which brought them into being." Justice, he emphasized, must "be equal for all citizens regardless of race and religion." Five days later in Vladislav Hall of Prague Castle, where formerly the kings of Bohemia had been crowned, Edward Beneš was chosen by the National Assembly to be Czechoslovakia's new president.

## CHAPTER XXVI

# THE TURBULENT BALKANS

THAT the Balkans constituted before the war the storm center of Europe, and that the crisis which precipitated the world conflict had its beginning in that quarter of the Continent, are notorious. Local nationalist aspirations and conflicting imperialist intrigues of the great powers for years kept the Balkans in an unsettled and chaotic state. When the World War ended with the elimination of the long-standing Austro-Russian rivalry, when the victory of the Allies brought the final attainment of Yugoslav union, it was optimistically hoped that the Balkans might at last settle down to an orderly and peaceful existence. But repeated *coups d'état,* revolutions, dictatorships, border clashes, assassinations, and executions during the postwar period have given constant evidence of continued unrest in the turbulent Balkans.

## GREECE

For repeated and spectacular reversals of political life, no Balkan state better exemplifies these unsettled conditions than Greece. The conflict between King Constantine and Venizelos during the war sharply divided the Greeks into two hostile groups, and after the king's forced abdication in 1917 [1] Greek politics became subject to sudden and unexpected shifts. For the most part the issues were in some way related to the outstanding Greek statesman of the period, Eleutherios Venizelos, and eventually all Greeks became either Venizelists or anti-Venizelists.

In 1919–1920 Venizelos's prestige was great as a result of the Allied victory and the territorial gains which were apparently to come to Greece. But during his prolonged absence in Paris in the interests of Greece, his numerous opponents at home were busily undermining his position. The royalists declared that his place at the head of the government was the result of Allied intervention, not popular choice, and accused him of resorting to dictatorial methods in order to maintain

[1] See page 432.

himself in power. Popular discontent was given an opportunity to express itself in the parliamentary elections of November 14, 1920—the first in more than five years. The unexpected death of King Alexander in the preceding month injected into the campaign the question of Constantine's return and made the elections a test of the immediate relative popularity of the premier and the ex-monarch. The premier's Liberal Party was decisively defeated, and Venizelos withdrew from Greece. In December a plebiscite was held on the return of Constantine, and, despite the announced opposition of the Allies, it proved to be almost unanimously in favor of the deposed monarch, who entered Athens amid great popular enthusiasm on December 19, 1920. The Allies refused to recognize the restored ruler and immediately ceased their subsidies to the Greek government.

Unfortunately for Constantine, he inherited a difficult military campaign in Asia Minor, a campaign undertaken on the assumption of Allied assistance which was now no longer forthcoming. His presence on the throne came to be connected in the public mind with the appalling Greek military disaster of 1922.[2] Disappointment at the loss of Smyrna, alarm over the threatened loss of Thrace, belief that the army had been betrayed by the government and that Constantine was the obstacle in the way of close relations with the Allies, all reacted against the king, whose abdication was at once demanded by the military chiefs. On September 27, 1922, Constantine surrendered his throne for the second time in a little over five years. In despair, the Greeks turned to Venizelos; the earlier repudiated statesman was recalled to the service of his country and sent to salvage all that was possible for Greece at the Conference of Lausanne.[3]

Although Constantine's eldest son succeeded to the throne as George II, sentiment in favor of transforming Greece into a republic grew rapidly. Following parliamentary elections in December, 1923, in which the Venizelists won a decisive victory, the king was requested to withdraw from the country. Venizelos opposed the parliament's desire to depose the king and advocated instead a popular plebiscite on the question. When the parliament persisted in its desire, Venizelos also withdrew from Greece, and in his absence the parliament voted to overthrow the Glücksburg dynasty. A popular plebiscite on April 13, 1924, then approved the establishment of a republic.

[2] See page 507.          [3] See pages 507–509.

During the next four years conditions in Greece were far from stable. A succession of republican governments held office until, in June, 1925, General Pangalos seized power. Later he dissolved the parliament, proclaimed himself a temporary dictator, and made a feeble attempt to emulate Mussolini. But his career was in turn cut short by a *coup d'état* in August, 1926, and Greece once more had a series of republican governments. In 1927 Venizelos returned to his native land, and, disturbed by rumors of an intended royalist revolt, in May, 1928, he announced that he would again enter politics. In July he became prime minister, and in new parliamentary elections his Liberal Party secured about 90 per cent of the seats. The electorate, apparently weary of the endless succession of weak governments, had turned again to the country's only dominant personality. During the next four years Greece enjoyed a period of political stability and progress.

Along with the problem of securing political stability, Greece after 1922 was compelled to wrestle with the necessity of assimilating some 1,200,000 refugees who came to her chiefly from Asia Minor and eastern Thrace as a consequence of the Greek military disaster of 1922 and the resultant treaties with Turkey in the following year. The exigency which arose when the population of the country was thus suddenly increased by one quarter forced the republic to appeal to the League of Nations for assistance, but in the course of succeeding years the refugees were accommodated.

Despite the misery and suffering which this forced migration brought to those involved, the ultimate result for Greece was undoubtedly beneficial. Most of the naturally industrious Greeks from Asia Minor were settled in Greek Macedonia and western Thrace, to whose long-neglected regions they brought benefits somewhat analogous to those brought to the sandy wastes of Brandenburg by French Huguenots in the days of the Great Elector. New territories were put under cultivation, new crops were introduced, new industries were established, and the economic center of gravity in the republic was shifted in the direction of Saloniki.

But the effect of the influx of Greek refugees was not alone economic. It conferred a predominantly Greek character upon the republic's territory in Macedonia and western Thrace and thus removed from the agenda of international disputes the question of the racial composition of the districts. In this way it probably increased

The Balkans, 1923–1937

the stability of the political frontiers in that region of Greece, where for economic reasons both Bulgaria and Yugoslavia have long desired to establish themselves. Furthermore, the exchange of Greek and Turkish populations ended, for the immediate future at least, the century-long Greco-Turkish territorial conflict. With the ancient feud between the Greeks and the Turks laid to rest, the two republics in 1930 signed a treaty of friendship and arbitration, reaffirmed their acceptance of the territorial *status quo,* and pledged neutrality in case of a war to overthrow the treaty settlement. Attached to the treaty was a protocol providing for the maintenance also of the *status quo* in naval armaments. Three years later the two powers signed a ten-year pact of nonaggression, mutually guaranteeing the inviolability of their common frontiers.

Meanwhile, in 1932 political conditions had once more become unstable. In parliamentary elections held in the autumn of that year the Liberals lost heavily and the royalist People's Party gained accordingly. In November Panayoti Tsaldaris, leader of the latter party, became premier, but two months later he was forced out of office by an adverse vote of the National Assembly, and Venizelos for the seventh time became the head of the government. New elections in March, 1933, however, gave the People's Party a clear majority. Thereupon General Plastiras, who had been the organizer of the military coup in 1922, immediately proclaimed a military dictatorship in defense of the republic. When his movement collapsed within twenty-four hours, Plastiras fled from the country, and Tsaldaris again came into power at the head of a royalist ministry.

Two years later fear that the Tsaldaris government was planning to restore the monarchy again led to a republican revolt. Civil war broke out in Macedonia and Thrace, and the islands of Crete, Samos, Mytilene, and Chios went over to the revolutionists. Five warships in the harbor of the Piraeus were seized by the rebels and forced to head for Crete, where the republican leader, Venizelos, was living. Vigorous measures were taken by the government, however, and in less than two weeks the revolt had been crushed. Venizelos fled from Crete. A few of the leaders were put to death, and a considerable number of the rebels were imprisoned.

That there was some basis for the fear of the republicans soon became evident. Although the royalists were overwhelmingly defeated in the parliamentary elections held in June, 1935, Premier Tsaldaris later endorsed the proposal to hold a plebiscite on the question of restoring the monarchy. In July the parliament voted to have a plebiscite in which the electorate should decide whether to continue the republican regime. The republicans confidently declared that they would win if a fair vote was permitted.

Possibly that was what General George Kondylis feared, for he desired that the plebiscite should be held only after the republic had been abolished. However that may be, on October 10 when the parliament reassembled, a military *coup d'état* led by Kondylis forced Tsaldaris to resign the premiership. Martial law was proclaimed. By bills which were rushed through the National Assembly the republic was abolished and the monarchical constitution of 1911 was restored. General Kondylis himself became premier and also regent until King George should return. On November 3, 1935, the plebiscite was held. Since the republicans felt that they could have little real influence on the outcome of the vote, in view of the fact that avowed monarchists were in control, they boycotted the plebiscite. The vote, therefore, proved to be almost unanimously monarchist. On November 25, 1935, George II, after an absence of some twelve years, returned to Athens as king.

The restored monarch's difficulties began almost at once. The king, who desired a general and inclusive amnesty, disagreed with Premier Kondylis, and, before a week had passed, the latter had resigned the premiership. Constantine Demerdjis, a professor at the University of Athens, thereupon organized a nonpartisan stop-gap government and immediately signed an amnesty pardoning several hundred prisoners and exiles, including even Venizelos. In the election of January 26, 1936, the Venizelist Liberals won a striking victory, but failed to secure a majority over all the other parties in the National Assembly. While attempts were being made to construct a new cabinet, General Kondylis suddenly died on January 31. The death of the one who was perhaps Venizelos's most bitter foe in Greece was followed within a few weeks by that of Venizelos himself. The veteran Greek statesman died on March 18, 1936, while still in exile in Paris. On April 13 the situation was complicated still further when Premier Demerdjis suddenly died.

King George thereupon appointed as head of the government General John Metaxas, vice-premier and war minister in the preceding cabinet. On August 5, 1936, the latter, after announcing that

Greece was threatened by a Communist uprising, declared martial law, dissolved the National Assembly, and postponed elections indefinitely. In the succeeding months he established a dictatorship in Greece in accordance with fascist ideals.

## YUGOSLAVIA

The kingdom of the Serbs, Croats, and Slovenes—after 1929 officially called Yugoslavia—comprises principally the descendants of three Slavic tribes which pushed their way into the Danube valley and into the northwestern part of the Balkan peninsula in the seventh century. Despite their proximity and their kinship in race and language, the three peoples never before 1918 constituted parts of the same state. Furthermore, with the Serbs looking eastward to Constantinople, and the Croats and Slovenes looking westward and northward to Rome, Vienna, and Budapest, the three groups in the course of centuries developed many differences in customs, culture, and religion.

Nevertheless, a common racial heritage as Yugoslavs, a common hatred of the ruling Habsburgs, and a vigorous nationalist propaganda emanating from Serbia gradually brought the three groups to believe in a common nationality and to envisage their future in a common Yugoslav state. Existing differences were recognized, and the Corfu Manifesto of 1917, the so-called "birth certificate of Yugoslavia," seemed to take them all into consideration when it proclaimed to the world that the three peoples constituted a single nation; that their future state would be called "The Kingdom of the Serbs, Croats, and Slovenes"; that it would be "a constitutional, democratic, and parliamentary monarchy" under the ruling house of Serbia; that the new state would have a flag of its own and the three constituent members would in addition have their own flags, which would "rank equally" and might "be freely hoisted on all occasions"; that the two alphabets and the three religions prevalent among the Yugoslavs would likewise be of equal rank; that suffrage in the new state would be universal, equal, direct, and secret; and that the future constitution would be framed by a special constituent assembly elected by universal suffrage.

But the spirit of conciliation and co-operation, which the Corfu Manifesto so happily seemed to promise, failed to materialize. One question that famous document left to be decided, and the inability to settle it to the satisfaction of all caused continuous political unrest and occasional crises in the kingdom. Should Yugoslavia be a unitary or a federal state? Immediately after the collapse of the Central Powers and the disappearance of the Habsburg menace, the Yugoslavs split into two groups: those advocating a centralized state which should be in a general way an expansion of the former Serbian kingdom, and those demanding a federal state with a considerable degree of local autonomy. The leader of the former was Nikolas Pashich, the "grand old man of Serbia"; of the latter, Stefan Radich, the "uncrowned king of Croatia."

The advocates of a unitary state argued that the former Hungarian territories were hopelessly backward politically, and that to create autonomous states of such districts would be most unwise. They pointed out that as a matter of fact Yugoslavia could not well be a federation of equals and that even in a federal system Serbian hegemony would inevitably result. They declared that the difficult and pressing task of national reconstruction and unification required the utmost use of all the forces at the disposal of the state, and asserted that these could be best marshaled under a strong central regime. But to all of these arguments the Croats, who had had self-government within the Habsburg empire, replied that the marked differences between the various territories composing the new state made a federal system the only possible solution.

For a time the question remained largely in the realm of the academic, since Alexander, Prince Regent of Yugoslavia, refused to convoke a constituent assembly or to set a date for elections until the frontiers of the kingdom were definitely decided. After the signing of the treaty of Rapallo with Italy had apparently settled the question of Yugoslavia's Adriatic territory, however, elections for a constituent assembly were held on November 28, 1920. Radich's Croatian Peasant Party succeeded in electing fifty deputies, but they refused to take their seats, so that Pashich was able to create a working majority. The Serbian statesman was determined to secure the adoption of a centralist constitution, and he succeeded in carrying through his program. The Yugoslav constitution of June 28, 1921, therefore, provided for a centralized government which should apply equally to all parts of the country in order eventually to do away with localism and obliterate regional differences. Historic frontiers were erased, and provincial diets were supplanted by one national parliament

(*Skupshtina*) in Belgrade. Local officials were to be chosen directly by the people, but in the conduct of their offices they were to be subject to national supervision exercised by the minister of finance and by prefects appointed by him.

The first elections to the parliament were held in March, 1923, and resulted in large gains for the parties of the two opponents, Pashich and Radich. The former attempted to come to some agreement with the Croatian peasant leader, but his efforts were unavailing. Radich again refused to allow the Croatian Peasant deputies to take their seats, and Pashich was thus once more enabled to form a ministry. After another year of boycott, Radich apparently came to the conclusion that the only result of his party's abstention was to perpetuate Pashich in power. Accordingly, the deputies of the Croatian Party returned to the parliament and caused Pashich's resignation in March, 1924. The continued intransigence of the Croatian Peasant leader made parliamentary government difficult during the next four years, especially after the country was deprived of its most experienced statesman by the death of Pashich in December, 1926.

Affairs came to a crisis on June 20, 1928, when Radich attacked the government for its proposal to ratify the Nettuno convention with Italy, which Croatians declared was inimical to their interests. Angered by the speech, a supporter of the government fired upon leaders and members of the Croatian Peasant Party, killing two and wounding several others. Among the latter was Radich himself, who died from the effects of his wound on August 8, 1928. The Croatian deputies thereupon withdrew from the parliament and set up a rival body at Zagreb, where they passed resolutions refusing to recognize laws enacted by the "rump" parliament at Belgrade. On October 1 delegates representing Croatia and Dalmatia met at Zagreb and decided to establish a close union to work independently of the Belgrade government and to boycott Serbia. Two months later the Croatians refused to participate in the national celebration of the tenth anniversary of the founding of the Yugoslav state.

King Alexander decided to resort to drastic measures. Declaring that the nation's confidence in the parliament had been undermined by recent events, that parliamentarism, instead of developing and strengthening the feeling of national union, had begun to provoke moral disorganization and national disunion, the king on January 5, 1929, dissolved the parliament, abrogated the constitution of 1921, and called upon General Zhivkovich, commander of the guard division stationed in Belgrade, to head the government. The new ministry, which was to govern the country by decree pending the complete reform of the constitution, was composed of representatives from Serbia, Croatia, Bosnia, Slovenia, and Dalmatia.

Yugoslavia was temporarily transformed into an absolute monarchy, the king assuming complete and sole authority over every officer of state. Very definite efforts were made to wipe out particularism in the kingdom and to replace it by a genuine national sentiment. The use of the names of the separate races was frowned upon, the display of the flags of the separate peoples was prohibited, and the old historic boundaries were obliterated by the creation of nine new administrative districts—in six of which the Serbs constituted a majority—with entirely new boundaries and names. Finally, in October, 1929, even the name of the state was changed by royal proclamation to the "Kingdom of Yugoslavia." King Alexander hoped that the Serbs, Croats, and Slovenes would organize themselves nonracially into Yugoslav groups based on social, economic, and other class interests.

After nearly three years of arbitrary rule, during which some economic and cultural gains were undoubtedly made, Alexander announced on September 3, 1931, that the dictatorship was ended, and that the country would return to constitutional government. A new constitution—not the work of a popularly elected constituent assembly but the product of the king and his advisers—was proclaimed. According to this document the Kingdom of Yugoslavia was to have a bicameral parliament instead of its former one-house legislature. The Chamber of Deputies was to be elected for four years by the direct vote of all men and women at least twenty-one years of age. Half of the members of the Senate were to be elected for six-year terms in a similar manner, and the other half were to be appointed by the king. The administrative districts and municipalities of the kingdom were given a considerable degree of autonomy, but the governors of the nine districts were to be appointed by the king on the nomination of the premier.

But the electoral law, promulgated on September 12, caused great dismay. To participate in an election a party must have at least sixty supporters in each election district in the country, a condition which none of the former Yugoslav parties could fulfill. The voting was to be for national rather than district lists, and the party which received the largest vote in the kingdom was to receive two thirds of the seats in the Chamber of Deputies. Furthermore, voting was to be by open ballot; that is, each voter must declare his choice orally and in public.

The first parliamentary elections under the new constitution were held on November 8, 1931. Most of the former political parties, notably the Croatian Peasant Party and Serbian Peasant Party, were urged by their leaders to boycott the election. The only party which had fulfilled the requirements of the electoral law was the National Party headed by Premier Zhivkovich. The election, of course, resulted in a "victory" for the government party. When the new parliament convened in January, 1932, it expressed its full approval of the government's work "from January 6, 1928, to the present day." The Croats, however, continued to resist the royal attempts to bring about the "Serbianization" of the government and the people.

The centralizing tendencies of King Alexander's government were apparently responsible for the assassination of the forty-five-year-old monarch on October 9, 1934. On that day, the king disembarked at Marseilles from the Yugoslav destroyer *Dubrovnik,* bound on an official visit to France. As he and Foreign Minister Barthou of France were riding together through the city, an assassin leaped upon the running-board and shot the king dead. The French foreign minister also received injuries from which he died shortly afterward. The assassin was killed on the spot even before he could shoot himself. Investigations disclosed that he had entered France under a forged Hungarian passport, and that the plot was the work of a Croatian terrorist organization which worked in conjunction with Mihailov's Macedonian revolutionists.[4]

Since the headquarters of the Croatian extremists were in Hungary near the Yugoslav border, and since prior to the assassination Yugoslavia's efforts to have the Hungarian government take steps to put an end to the organization had been unavailing, the Yugoslavs were naturally incensed by the assassination. The government began to expel from the country Hungarians who had not acquired Yugoslav citizenship. This in turn aroused resentment in Hungary, and for a time the danger of an armed clash between frontier guards of the two countries was imminent. Fortunately for the peace of Europe, however, the League Council was able to solve the crisis to the satis-

[4] For the Macedonian revolutionary movement, see pages 802–804.

faction of both Yugoslavia and Hungary, and ultimately the former stated her willingness to rely on Hungary's promise to take all necessary measures against terrorist activities.

Meanwhile, in Yugoslavia, Alexander's oldest son, a boy of eleven years, had been proclaimed King Peter II, and a regency council had been established. In May, 1935, elections were held for a new parliament. Although opposition parties were permitted to present candidates, vigorous steps were taken by the government to prevent their having much success. Opposition leaders were arrested, and antigovernment meetings were broken up. On the other hand, considerable pressure was exerted in favor of the government party, which, as might be expected, won a decisive victory. When the parliament met, it was boycotted by all of the opposition members. Thanks, perhaps, to the conciliatory temper of Prince Paul Karageorgevich, the chief regent, Vladko Matchek, the Croatian leader, was called to the capital to aid in settling the crisis.

A new ministry on a national basis—broad enough to include not only Croats but Serbian Radicals, Bosnian Moslems, and Slovene Clericals—was formed with the former finance minister, Milan Stoyandinovich, as premier. Stoyandinovich's statement of policy, however, was disappointing to the Croats, for, although he advocated a gradual transition from the dictatorship to a free parliamentary regime, he announced his adherence to the unitary rather than the federal form of government. When the premier organized a new political party—the Yugoslav Radical Union—pledged to maintain Yugoslav unity, the three Croatian members of the cabinet resigned, and Matchek announced that the Croats would never be satisfied until Croatia was granted an autonomous position in Yugoslavia analogous to that of Hungary in the Dual Monarchy before the war. In the summer of 1937 the conflict between federalism and centralization seemed little nearer to a settlement than it had been in 1920.

## ALBANIA

To the west of Yugoslavia and Greece lies Albania, the smallest and weakest of the Balkan states, with an area equal to that of Denmark but with only a quarter of the latter's population. The country, which gained its independence in 1913, was at that time a most backward and primitive region, having no railways and very few roads. Schools and newspapers were exceedingly scarce, and illiteracy was general. The population was for the most part agricultural or pastoral, organized on an almost feudal basis, and largely lacking in national sentiment. In fact, the question was raised then, and was subsequently repeatedly raised, whether there should be an independent Albania. In 1913 Serbia and Russia, on the one hand, and Austria and Italy, on the other, had nearly come to blows on this point. Albania's independent existence, therefore, resulted principally from the jealousies of her neighbors. Had it not been for the opposition of Italy and Austria, her territory might have been divided between Greece, Serbia, and Montenegro at the time of the Balkan wars.

During the World War the dismemberment of Albania was contemplated, but at the peace conference President Wilson steadily opposed its partition. Italy sought a mandate for the region, most of which she had occupied in the course of the war, but the military opposition of the Albanians led the Italians to recognize their independence and to withdraw from the country in the fall of 1920. Despite the desire of Greece and Yugoslavia to partition the country, Albania's independence was recognized by her admission to membership in the League of Nations in December, 1920. During the following year, while the question of boundaries was still unsettled, repeated incursions into Albania were made by bands from Yugoslavia, and disruptive revolutionary movements were encouraged and assisted with money, arms, and ammunition sent in from that country. This menacing situation was eventually ended by action of the League of Nations.

Meanwhile, within Albania the question of future government was being settled. A monarchical regime had been originally set up with a German prince as ruler, but he had been forced to leave the country soon after the outbreak of the World War. Early in 1920 a temporary regency council of notables was elected in place of the monarch, and a struggle for control ensued. After frequent changes in the government during a period of three years, Ahmed Zogu, a young tribal chieftain who from the age of sixteen had been fighting in the cause of the Albanian mountaineers, at length won out. In 1925 a national assembly was convoked, a republic proclaimed, and Zogu elected president for a seven-year term. The constitution subsequently adopted provided for a bicameral legislature but placed the chief power in the hands of the president, who had an absolute veto on legislation, the sole right to initiate changes in the constitution, authority to dissolve the parliament at will, and the right to apply the previous year's budget in case of the parliament's failure to vote a new one. The president differed little from a dictator; in fact, in 1928 the National Assembly proclaimed him King Zog I.

The Albanian ruler's chief task was to create a modern state. To secure the capital which he so much needed, he entered into close relations with Italy. To secure an entering wedge for the economic domination of this weak state on the opposite shore of the Strait of Otranto, Italy gladly advanced the necessary funds. The treaty of Tirana (1926) granted Italy extensive economic concessions in Albania, and the Italo-Albanian defensive alliance (1927) drew the two states still closer together.[5] Albanian finances and the Albanian army were placed under the supervision of Italian experts. For all practical purposes Albania became an Italian protectorate and an outpost for Mussolini's desired economic penetration of the Balkans.

## BULGARIA

The political history of Bulgaria since the war, although not so kaleidoscopic as that of Greece, has been far from calm and uneventful. The military defeat of Bulgaria brought the immediate abdication and flight of King Ferdinand, who had been largely responsible for the country's joining the Central Powers, and the elevation to the throne of his young son, Boris III, who in succeeding years proved to be as democratic as his father before him had been autocratic. Military defeat likewise brought the downfall of the existing government and eventually (October, 1919) the elevation to the premiership of the leader of the Agrarian Party, Alexander Stambolisky, who had dared to oppose the royal proposal to join the Central Powers in 1915 and had been imprisoned for his temerity. The collapse of the Bulgarian front in the fall of 1918 had been followed by Stambolisky's release from prison and his return to active leadership of the peasants. Under his guidance the Agrarian Party won a decisive victory in the parliamentary elections of March, 1920, in consequence of which a homogeneous Agrarian ministry was established.

Then followed a three-year period of Agrarian rule in which the role of Stambolisky differed not materially from that of dictator. The

[5] For the terms of these agreements, see page 641.

great weakness of his regime was its devotion to the interests of practically one class, to the exclusion of the so-called upper classes. In 1923 the premier declared that the Agrarian Party would "keep at the head of national affairs until the country is rid of the old and pernicious parties, until the peasantry and the working classes get rid of their parasites, the lawyers, bankers, profiteers, idle politicians, and mischievous doctrinaires, and the people in general of its frenzied partisans." The Agrarian leaders became ever more overbearing and intolerant. Freedom of the press was abolished, leaders of bourgeois parties were imprisoned, universities were closed, the church was defied.

Inevitably the neglected and oppressed classes drew together. The bourgeoisie, the intelligentsia, and the military discovered a common bond in their hatred of the Agrarian regime. A conspiracy was entered into and plans were laid for the overthrow of Stambolisky's government. On June 9, 1923, all the ministers were suddenly arrested except Stambolisky, who was absent from the capital. A new government representing all opposition parties but the Communists was formed with Alexander Tsankov, a professor in the University of Sofia, as premier. Stambolisky was later captured and shot, and his parliament, on the ground that it had been elected by fraud and violence, was at once dissolved.

A serious threat to the political stability of Bulgaria in the ensuing years came from the Communists. In September, 1923, they instigated a revolt in an attempt to replace the monarchy with a soviet republic, and thousands of peasants, bereft of their former leader, gave it their support. Although the uprising became so serious that at one time Sofia was practically surrounded, it was in the end successfully suppressed. In April, 1925, came a second Communist attempt when a bomb was exploded in the cathedral in Sofia at a time when it was crowded for the funeral of a recently assassinated general. Most of the members of the government were in attendance. More than a hundred persons were killed, and several hundred were injured, including Prime Minister Tsankov and some of his associates. A counterterrorism was at once inaugurated by the government; martial law was proclaimed; thousands were arrested; many were put to death. Communist plots continued, however, and in February, 1929, over one hundred Communists were arrested as a result of the discovery of a plan to overthrow the government.

In 1932 the Communists again surged to the fore. Naturally, the severe hardships of the peasants, resulting from the deflated prices of agricultural products, caused widespread and deep discontent. This reflected itself in successes of the Communists in municipal elections in February, 1932, and again in September of the same year when they won 19 of the 35 seats in the municipal council of Sofia. Fear of Communism led the bourgeoisie to take defensive measures. The League of Reserve Officers, which had played a leading role in overthrowing Stambolisky, called for a rallying of all forces opposed to Communism, and in 1934 Bulgaria finally succumbed to a dictatorship when on May 19 the government was overturned by a *coup d'état* executed by a group of army officers and politicians.

Two major policies, it was announced, would receive the particular attention of the government, namely, the abolition of all political parties, and the complete suppression of the Macedonian revolutionary movement. All political parties were formally outlawed, and all forms of party activity were forbidden. Sweeping measures were taken in the interests of national recovery. Decrees were issued reducing debts of peasants 40 per cent, those of artisans 30 per cent, and those of merchants 20 per cent. Furthermore, moratoriums on all payments for periods ranging up to two years were proclaimed for these various classes. Most of the losses entailed by these decrees were to be assumed by the state and ultimately made good from supplementary income and occupational taxes. Eventually the government decided to cancel payment of all foreign debts, a step which led the League of Nations financial commissioner to leave Sofia immediately in protest.

Gradually relations between King Boris and the government became more and more strained. According to reports, the premier insisted that the king should be deprived of his influence over government policies and converted into a figurehead. Boris naturally resented such plans, and in January, 1935, forced the resignation of the cabinet. Another military man then became head of the government, but, when he had two former premiers arrested for attempting to keep their political parties alive, a schism in the cabinet developed and brought its downfall. King Boris then called to the premiership a civilian who had not been active in politics, and he organized a distinctly civilian government. Apparently the military were dissastified with this move, for in October, 1935, the discovery of an alleged plot to overthrow the monarchy led to the proclamation of martial law and to the arrest of Colonel Veltchev, a former premier, and a number of army officers. In February, 1936, Veltchev and a colleague were found guilty of treason and condemned to death, and nine other army officers were sentenced to prison terms. Five months later a new ministry was organized ostensibly to prepare the way for a return to constitutional government. Nevertheless, little progress appeared to have been made in that direction by the summer of 1937.

Meanwhile, throughout the postwar period, Bulgaria's domestic history and international relations had been repeatedly disturbed by the "Macedonian question." Bulgaria's long-standing interest in Macedonia has already been discussed, as has her failure to obtain the territory as the result of wars in 1877–1878, 1912–1913, and 1916–1918.[6] After the World War over 200,000 refugees and exiles from Greek and Serbian Macedonia flocked into Bulgaria, where they formed a well-organized and well-armed group. These homeless masses constituted a grave domestic problem for Bulgaria, embarrassing the government's foreign policy by their constant demands for the redemption of their "Bulgaria irredenta," complicating the political situation by providing a fertile field for Communist propaganda, and frequently disturbing the ordered existence of the country by their brigandage. In that district of Bulgaria which is located near the convergence of the frontiers of Greece, Yugoslavia, and Bulgaria, the Macedonian *comitadjis* established a base of operations for guerrilla warfare, and their revolutionary activities repeatedly excited alarms and protests on the part of neighboring states.

Numerous clashes occurred along the Greco-Bulgarian and Yugoslav-Bulgarian frontiers, but the most serious occurred in 1925. On October 19 shots were exchanged between Greek and Bulgarian sentinels. A Greek soldier was killed, his body remaining on Bulgarian territory. Companions from each side came to the scene, and further firing occurred. Reports reached Athens of a serious premeditated attack by the Bulgarians, and, without confirming these reports, the Greek minister of war ordered the Third Army Corps to march on the Bulgarian town of Petrich. Greek troops under orders crossed the frontier early on the morning of the twenty-second

[6] See pages 252, 351–352, and 406.

and occupied during the following days some seventy square miles of Bulgarian territory.

The Bulgarian government, after the Greek invasion began, requested the secretary-general of the League of Nations to convene the Council to consider what steps should be taken in view of the Greek violation of Bulgarian territory. On October 23 Briand, acting president of the Council, informed the governments at Athens and Sofia of the coming meeting and demanded immediate withdrawal of the troops of each government within their respective frontiers and the cessation of hostilities pending the decision of the Council. When the latter convened on the twenty-sixth, it gave the two powers sixty hours within which to inform it that all troops had been withdrawn within the national frontiers, that all hostilities had ceased, and that the troops had been warned that the resumption of firing would be visited with severe punishment. On the twenty-eighth the Council declared itself satisfied that orders had been given within the time limit set, and on the next day Briand announced that the withdrawal of the Greek troops had been completed. The danger of war was averted.

A commission of inquiry was appointed, and on November 28 its report was submitted to the Council and to the Greek and Bulgarian governments. It decided that there had been no premeditation on either side but that the invasion of Bulgarian territory had been unjustified, and recommended that the Greek government should pay to the Bulgarian government about $220,000 as indemnity. On December 14 the commission's report was adopted with slight modifications by the Council, and on March 1, 1926, the last installment of the indemnity was paid by the Greek government.

In the summer of 1926 an attack on a Yugoslav village by a band of *comitadjis* provoked a joint note of protest from Yugoslavia, Greece, and Rumania. The Bulgarian government did what it could to restore order on the frontiers, affirmed its sincere desire to keep the peace, pointed out the difficulties under which it labored, and invited the co-operation of its neighbors. The great numbers of unsettled refugees in Bulgaria who looked forward either to returning to their former homes across the border or to avenging themselves on those who had driven them out made the situation extremely difficult for Bulgaria to control. A year later renewed *comitadji*

804 POSTWAR PROBLEMS AND EXPERIMENTS

activities culminated in the assassination of a famous Serbian general.
Yugoslavia thereupon closed her frontier against Bulgarians. Raids
and assassinations continued throughout 1928, but suggestions of a
conference of representatives of the Yugoslav, Greek, and Bulgarian
governments were futile.

Finally, in February, 1929, after the establishment of the dictatorship in Yugoslavia, the Belgrade government took a conciliatory step
by reopening the Bulgarian frontier. The new government's desire
for better relations with its neighbor and for some joint means of
combating the *comitadji* evil was reciprocated by Bulgaria, and negotiations between the two governments led in 1930 to a protocol for
the regulation of the frontier. Relations were further improved by the
vigorous steps taken by Bulgaria to suppress the intrigues and activities of the Macedonian revolutionary organization within her territory. In 1930 Ivan Mihailov, the "uncrowned king of Bulgarian
Macedonia," was arrested, and during the winter of 1930–1931 some
of the Macedonian assassins who had been guilty of political murders were brought to trial.

In the succeeding years the Macedonian revolutionists seriously
weakened themselves by splitting into two warring and bitterly
hostile factions, the Mihailovists and Protogerovists—the revival of
a feud which dates back to 1907. Scores of members of each faction
were assassinated, and in December, 1932, a miniature battle between
the two groups occurred on the principal street in Sofia in front of
the royal palace. In the early summer of 1933 Macedonian murders
and abductions became so frequent in the Bulgarian capital that
drastic steps had to be taken by the government to protect its citizens.
A new law was enacted, providing that the penalty for committing,
instigating, or being accessory to, a political murder should be death.
Large numbers of suspected Macedonian terrorists were arrested and
interned in concentration camps. All Macedonians having arms were
ordered to surrender them, and leaders of the Macedonian revolutionary organization were imprisoned or ordered out of the Macedonian areas. In 1934 the Protogerovist organization announced its
dissolution, and Ivan Mihailov with a number of colleagues fled
across the border into Turkey. In proportion to the weakening of the
Macedonians the good relations between Bulgaria and Yugoslavia
were strengthened, and eventually, January, 1937, the two powers
concluded a pact of nonaggression.

## RUMANIA

Rumania's acquisition of territory as a result of the World War surpassed the fondest expectations of her extreme nationalists. That she might gain territory from either the Habsburgs or the Romanovs if she were fortunate in her choice of sides in the war was readily conceivable; but that she might in the end gain from both these mighty empires the territory which each had offered her at the expense of the other was, it seemed, utterly foolish to expect. And yet this is precisely what happened. Rumania emerged from the war with her territory practically doubled in extent, her frontiers very nearly attaining those of the province of Dacia to which Trajan sent the Roman colonists from whom the Rumanians love to trace their lineage.

In view of Rumania's joining the Entente powers in the war, the least-expected territorial acquisition was Bessarabia, the district between the river Pruth, the river Dniester, and the Black Sea, which Russia had taken from Turkey in 1812. The population was chiefly Rumanian (Moldavian) in 1812, and in spite of a policy of "Russification" the largest element in it—the peasantry—remained Rumanian in 1914. In December, 1917, after the Bolshevik revolution, a Supreme Council in Bessarabia proclaimed an independent Moldavian republic and requested the Rumanian government to send troops to preserve order and to provide protection against the Bolsheviks. In April, 1918, the Supreme Council voted for political union with Rumania with the understanding that the district should retain a large degree of local autonomy. The Soviet government, claiming that this council was not a truly representative body and that it was intimidated by the presence of Rumanian military forces, refused to recognize the legality of this action. In November, after the defeat of the Central Powers, the Supreme Council, with only about a third of its members present, passed a new motion which canceled the conditions regarding local autonomy laid down in April and merged Bessarabia with Rumania. On the next day the council was permanently dissolved.

At the Paris peace conference Rumania included Bessarabia among her claims for territory, but the "Big Four" long delayed to take action. Not until October 28, 1920, did the principal Allied powers—France, Great Britain, Italy, Japan—sign a treaty recognizing Rumania's sovereignty over the district, and then they did so only in the face of Russia's protest and warning that she would not recognize the action. Rumania's acquisition of Transylvania, Bukowina, and part of the Banat of Temesvar by the treaties of St. Germain and Trianon has already been mentioned. In these regions there lived perhaps twice as many Rumanians as in Bessarabia, and they brought to the kingdom a higher culture and a greater political self-consciousness than the latter. The assimilation of all these territories taxed the Rumanian administrative system to the limit, and the succeeding years heard many complaints of inefficiency, corruption, and poor government, aggravated by dissatisfaction with economic conditions.

In 1917 universal suffrage had been introduced for parliamentary elections, and Jews had been admitted to citizenship rights. The political situation in Rumania was radically altered by this extension of the franchise to some millions who had previously not voted as well as by the addition of so much new territory. The Liberal Party, the organ of the industrial, commercial, and banking interests, centralistic, and nationalistic in its opposition to the influx of foreign capital, continued under the domination of the wealthy and clever John Bratianu. Another party, the People's Party, was organized by General Averescu after the enactment of the new franchise law, but its policies seemed to differ little from those of the Liberal Party, with which it became accustomed to co-operate. The political power of the peasants and minor nationalities was at once reflected in the organization of many new parties.

In the first elections held in Rumania after the war the peasant groups won a large majority, and a coalition government was organized under a Transylvanian leader. The conservative elements of the country at once became alarmed because of proposed expropriation of land and the fear of Bolshevik propaganda. King Ferdinand, who maintained that he had the right to appoint and dismiss his ministers regardless of the parliamentary situation, now dismissed the peasant government and called General Averescu, leader of the People's Party, to be prime minister. During the next eight years, despite the undoubted numerical superiority of the peasant electorate, the government was kept almost constantly in the hands of Averescu or Bratianu, leaders of the parties whose chief strength was in the territory of prewar Rumania.

During these years a program of agrarian reform was inaugurated in Rumania. To bring about a wider distribution of land, legislation enacted between 1917 and 1921 provided for the expropriation of all landed property of absentee and foreign owners, all the arable lands of the crown, and all large estates in excess of 1250 acres. The original proprietors were to be compensated in state bonds on the basis of prewar values when the Rumanian leu was worth a gold franc. The greatly depreciated value of the leu after the war, however, made the compensation quite illusory, so that almost the entire burden fell upon the dispossessed landlords. By 1932 approximately 90 per cent of the land was in the hands of small peasant proprietors.

Meanwhile, despite agrarian reform, the peasants were becoming more and more restless because of their inability to obtain control of the government. In May, 1928, a peasant convention in Transylvania was attended by some 200,000 members of the National Peasant Party. Some had come equipped with arms, expecting that force would be employed, and the more spirited proposed a march on Bucharest. Their leader, Julius Maniu, wisely counseled moderation and, after resolutions demanding Premier Bratianu's resignation were passed, directed his followers to return to their homes. During the succeeding weeks the situation grew more tense. Plans for a rival National Peasant parliament and for a republican movement in Transylvania seemed to endanger not only the existing government but the monarchy itself. On November 4 the premier grudgingly laid down the reins of office, and the long rule of the Bratianus was broken. Two days later Maniu became premier. Parliamentary elections confirmed the peasants' victory by returning an overwhelming majority for the National Peasant Party. It appeared that the half century of almost continuous rule by aristocratic landed and capitalistic classes had come to an end, that Rumania's 14,000,000 peasants had at last come into their own.

The years 1929 and 1930 saw an increasing sentiment in behalf of Prince Carol, who in 1925 had renounced his right of succession to the throne, choosing instead to keep his mistress, Magda Lupescu. At that time the Rumanian parliament had recognized as crown prince five-year-old Michael, Carol's son by his wife, the former Princess Helen of Greece. Upon the death of King Ferdinand in July, 1927, Michael had succeeded to the throne, with a regency to govern during his minority. But the exiled Carol was popular with the army, and his return and accession to the throne were favored not only by his brother, Prince Nicholas, but by the veteran politician, General Averescu, and by the National Peasant Party as well. In fact, only his mother, Queen Marie, and Bratianu's Liberal Party very vigorously opposed his restoration. In June, 1930, following an announcement that he had broken with Magda Lupescu,[7] Carol arrived in Bucharest by airplane. The parliament at once annulled all acts which had been passed relating to his abdication, recognized him as having been the *de jure* king of Rumania since the death of his father in 1927, and proclaimed him as Carol II. Plans for the king's coronation were held in abeyance, pending a possible reconciliation with his wife, Helen. Such a reconciliation failed to materialize, however, and in 1931 Helen was obliged to renounce her queenly title and to agree to be known henceforth merely as Princess Helen of Rumania. Later she was exiled from the country.

For some months after Carol's return the government remained in the control of the National Peasant Party, but in April, 1931, the king forced the resignation of the ministry and replaced it with one headed by Professor Nicholas Jorga. The latter, a prominent historian, had been Carol's personal tutor. The parliament, in which the National Peasant Party held an overwhelming majority, was at once dissolved. In the ensuing election the National Union, organized by the premier to support his announced program of economy and efficiency in government, secured only 48 per cent of the votes, but under the existing electoral law the National Union was given 75 per cent of the seats in the new Chamber. Carol and his premier then inaugurated a thinly veiled dictatorship, and it was feared by many that the peasants had again been definitely pushed aside.

Despite its party platform, however, the Jorga ministry proved to be far from efficient and economical. The government offices were overstaffed, expensive public works were lavishly initiated, expenditures regularly exceeded income, and the national deficit steadily mounted. Obviously, too, the world economic depression with its low price of grain constituted a serious handicap to the economic and financial recovery of the country. Ultimately the government's inability to secure a foreign loan did what the peasants' votes had failed to do a year earlier. In May, 1932, the Jorga ministry was forced to resign. Alexander Vaida-Voevod, who had succeeded Maniu as leader of the National Peasant Party, became premier at the head of

[7] Subsequent events proved that this was not true.

a cabinet consisting of members of his party. New elections in July gave the premier's followers control of the parliament. Rumania continued to be embarrassed by her financial difficulties, however, and in 1933 the government was obliged to accept the assistance of the League of Nations.

The Vaida-Voevod government's chief contribution to Rumanian history was the conclusion of a nonaggression pact with Soviet Russia. The active agitation for revision of the peace treaties; especially in Italy and in Germany, alarmed Rumania, which had made such large territorial gains by the peace settlement; and the rise of Hitlerism, with its subsequent vigorous suppression of the Communists in Germany, disturbed Russia. In self-defense the two countries moved closer together, and in June, 1934, they signed a pact mutually guaranteeing their existing frontiers. By this amicable settlement of the Bessarabian question in favor of Rumania, the position of the latter in relation to Hungary was much strengthened. Should a revisionist quarrel with Hungary occur, forces which might otherwise have been required to protect Bessarabia against Russia would be available for use in central Europe. To the extent that Rumania was thus strengthened, so also was the Little Entente.

Not all Rumanians favored cordial relations with the Soviet government, however. Opposition to the government's foreign policy was particularly strong from the "Iron Guard," a violently anti-Semitic organization which had developed in the postwar period and which had come to be fascist and pro-German in its outlook. Vaida-Voevod's failure to curb the Iron Guard and other fascist organizations was largely responsible for Carol's dismissal of the National Peasant government in November, 1933, and for his appointment of a Liberal cabinet headed by Ian G. Duca. Elections for a new parliament were set for the following month, and in order to check the activities of the Iron Guard the new premier suppressed its meetings and publications and canceled its parliamentary nominations. Hundreds of those suspected of membership were arrested. The Liberals won the elections, but in retaliation for the repressive measures which had been used by the government a former university student assassinated Premier Duca in December, 1933. Three months later a plot was discovered to kill the king, the crown prince, and the members of the cabinet in order to set up a military dictatorship, but it was nipped in the bud, and those implicated were sentenced to prison.

In the ensuing years the Liberal government, headed by George Tatarescu, was compelled to wrestle with difficulties arising from the spread of fascism within the country. Despite the opposition of the premier and King Carol, the fascist Iron Guard, subsidized by the German Nazis, continued to grow. This was startlingly revealed by the parliamentary elections of December, 1937, in which the government—contrary to all precedent—was defeated. Tatarescu was succeeded as premier by Octavian Goga, who was known to be anti-Semitic, antiparliamentarian, anti-Russian, and anti-French. But Goga's government was short-lived, for he in turn was forced to resign on February 10, 1938.

King Carol thereupon apparently decided to inaugurate something in the nature of a totalitarian state with greater authority in the hands of the king. A new constitution was proclaimed which provided for "a juster representation" of the farmers, workers, and other productive elements. At the same time the king was given the right to declare war and make peace, to conclude treaties, and to issue decrees when the parliament was not in session. Early in 1938 all political parties were ordered dissolved. Codreanu, leader of the Iron Guard, and hundreds of his followers were arrested on charges of plotting to overthrow the government. The Iron Guard leader was sentenced to ten years' imprisonment, but on November 30 he and thirteen subordinates were killed "while attempting to escape from their prison guards." Carol, it appeared, was determined to crush the Iron Guard movement in Rumania.

# PART SIX

# THE EAST IN REVOLT

During the postwar years a widespread revolt against the domination of the West swept through northern Africa, western and central Asia, India, China, and Japan—in other words, through those regions of the world which, because of their type of civilization, are usually referred to as the East. In consequence, several European powers emerged from the World War only to find themselves almost immediately confronted or threatened in distant parts of the world with uprisings of native populations. Where these powers were forced to resort to military operations, the efficiency of their modern weapons in the end brought victory. In some cases European countries, in preference to actual war, made sweeping concessions to discontented peoples, and occasionally even military success was followed by measures designed to placate the conquered. Full political independence, extensive national autonomy, or a measure of local self-government was obtained by various non-European groups, accompanied in some instances by the abolition of capitulations, the cancellation of foreign privileges, and the grant of economic freedom.

## CHAPTER XXVII

# THE NEAR AND MIDDLE EAST

THE Turkish nationalist movement, with its repudiation of the treaty of Sèvres, its opposition to the loss of Turkish territory, and its determination to throw off the servitude of the capitulations, was the first clear indication of the revolt of the East at the close of the war. It was also probably the most successful. In the succeeding years, however, Turkey sought voluntarily to adopt many features of the civilization of the West against which she had revolted.

## THE TURKISH REPUBLIC

As already pointed out, the Turkish Grand National Assembly on November 1, 1922, deposed Sultan Mohammed VI. Some three months after the signing of the treaty of Lausanne that same body, on October 29, 1923, proclaimed Turkey a republic and unanimously elected Mustapha Kemal the first president.[1] Despite the name "republic," however, Turkey was in reality a dictatorship. Kemal's Nationalist People's Party was for years the only organized political group permitted in the country; and after 1927 Kemal, as president-general, had the right to name all of the party's candidates for the National Assembly. But though the general government remained a dictatorship, laws were enacted to bring its judicial system into step with the Western world. A Supreme Court was established, and in 1926 all the old law codes were supplanted by new civil, penal, and commercial codes which were based on European models. In 1932 Turkey became a member of the League of Nations.

The strong national spirit of Kemal and his associates led to efforts to free the Turks from non-Turkish influences. Cities were given new Turkish names, for example, Constantinople becoming Istanbul; Angora, Ankara; Smyrna, Izmir, and so on. The national capital was removed from the Bosporus, where it had been for centuries, and located at Ankara, which consequently grew from a small

---

[1] In 1927 and again in 1931 he was unanimously re-elected to the presidency.

town into a modern city. To assist in the nationalizing movement, the language of the people was purified of Arabic influences. A national law in 1928 provided that in the course of the following fifteen years the Latin alphabet should supplant the old Arabic. Newspapers and books were ordered to cease publication in Arabic characters after January, 1929.

Meanwhile, the religious institutions of the country had been fundamentally changed. In March, 1924, the National Assembly abolished the Turkish caliphate and exiled from the country all members of the former Osman dynasty. Four years later that same body decided that Islam should no longer be the state religion of Turkey, that in fact the republic thereafter should tolerate all religions on an equal footing. Although Islam continued to be the religion of the bulk of the Turks, republican officials were no longer required, upon taking office, to swear by Allah. Severe restrictions were placed on the teaching of religion—Mohammedan or Christian—in public or private elementary schools. Early in 1933, in order to force the Moslem clergy to have a more liberal training, the theological faculty and curriculum of the University of Istanbul were modified by the government. The next year the government again struck at the influence of the Moslem clergy by a decree forbidding the wearing of clerical garb except at religious rites.

Sweeping social changes were introduced by Kemal, especially in the position of women. In 1925 legal polygamy was abolished and divorce was made permissible. In the next year civil marriage was made compulsory, and the legal age for marriage was raised to seventeen for women and eighteen for men. Western clothing was introduced, the wearing of the veil was made optional, and many occupations were opened to women. In 1929 women gained the right to vote in local elections and to hold office in municipalities; in December, 1934, an amendment to the constitution gave them the right to vote for and become deputies. In February of the next year seventeen women were elected to the Grand National Assembly. By another law passed in 1934 all persons were required to assume family names, which were to be registered with the authorities by January 1, 1935. The National Assembly suggested that Mustapha Kemal assume the surname "Atatürk" ("Father of the Turks"). This the president did.

In the realm of education considerable progress was made. Al-

THE "WESTERNIZATION" OF THE EAST

Six of the seventeen Turkish women elected to the Grand National
Assembly in 1935.

though handicapped by a shortage of money, teachers, and educational facilities, the government increased the number of schools to 7000 by 1936. Its goal was compulsory school attendance for all children between seven and sixteen years of age. Attempts were made to compel all Turks under forty years of age to take lessons in reading and writing, and beginning in June, 1931, literacy was in general necessary to obtain the full rights of citizenship. Nevertheless, although illiteracy, according to reports, had been reduced by half, in 1937 a considerable percentage of the population was still illiterate.

Some advance was made by Turkey in her economic life also. In this realm, too, Kemal's aim was modernization and Westernization. The government itself in many ways sought to assist directly in the economic upbuilding of the country. Special departments were established to study commerce, shipping, industry, and agriculture. Large appropriations for public works were made, railways and highways were constructed, and a strong central bank was established. To encourage infant industries, a protective tariff was adopted in 1929; and in succeeding years, in order to overcome the republic's adverse trade balance, a quota system of imports was inaugurated. State control or state ownership of various enterprises was secured. The results of the government's efforts seemed justified. Gradually between 1928 and 1931 the value of Turkish manufactured goods rose from $20,000,000 to $50,000,000.

To Westernize and industrialize the country further a five-year industrial plan was adopted in January, 1934, providing for the building of fifteen factories, twelve of which were to be owned and operated by the government. The new enterprises were designed, in part, to free Turkey from the need of importing certain types of manufactured goods. The government announced that it had decided upon the adoption of a form of state capitalism and that, as rapidly as the resources of the government permitted, private enterprises would be taken over. To make the raw materials of the country more available, 1681 miles of railway were constructed by 1937, and plans called for building of some thousands of miles of additional railways by 1940.

In 1934 the desire to free Turkey from foreign control again manifested itself in several ways. In March the government announced its decision to purchase the 450-mile Smyrna-Kassaba Railway, which was owned by French interests. Later in the year the government made arrangements to take over from the French companies their concessions for operating the port facilities at Istanbul, and in 1935 it acquired the Istanbul Telephone Company from British interests. Meanwhile, in 1934, the minister of public works had announced that, in the future, enterprises undertaken by foreign capital in Turkey must register as Turkish companies, that no new concessions would be granted to foreign companies having their headquarters abroad. Furthermore, in that same year a law had gone into effect ousting all aliens from the professions, the trades, and jobs involving manual labor. Only by becoming naturalized citizens of Turkey could the thousands of persons affected escape the provisions of the law, regardless of the fact that they might have lived in Turkey for years.

In 1934 it was rumored that Turkey was becoming desirous of refortifying the Straits, a move which had been for some time strongly advocated by the Turkish press. After having sounded out the other powers, the Turkish government on April 11, 1936, laid before the states signatory to the treaty of Lausanne, and before the League of Nations also, a formal request for the revision of those clauses of the treaty relating to nonfortification of the Dardanelles and the demilitarized zones.[2] The strong feeling against Italy because of the latter's high-handed conquest of Ethiopia in disregard of treaty obligations doubtless reacted in favor of Turkey when the latter sought thus to secure treaty revision in accordance with legal procedure. In July an international conference, meeting at Montreux, Switzerland, approved a new convention authorizing Turkey to proceed with the fortification of the Straits immediately.

A year later, on the initiative of the Turkish government, a Middle Eastern Entente was established when a nonaggression treaty was signed by Turkey, Iraq, Iran (Persia), and Afghanistan. The four Moslem powers pledged themselves to guarantee security in the Middle East by fulfilling their obligations under the League Covenant and the Briand-Kellogg pact. They specifically promised to abstain from interfering in one another's affairs and undertook to prevent the formation within their territories of bands or associations seeking to disturb the peace of any of them. Thereafter Turkey was in a position to foster co-operation between the Balkan countries

[2] For the treaty of Lausanne, see page 508.

and those of the Middle East, for she was included in ententes with both groups of powers.[3]

## EGYPT

British control in Egypt, inaugurated in 1882, had been in no way legalized when the World War began, but on December 18, 1914, a proclamation was issued by the British government declaring a protectorate over Egypt. On the succeeding day the ruling khedive was deposed by a proclamation which stated that the succession had been accepted by Prince Hussein Kamel, whose title was to be Sultan of Egypt. The title indicated independence of Turkey, but actual control still rested in the hands of Great Britain.

British rule during the war caused much discontent. Egyptians were forced to serve in the army labor corps under a form of conscription; grain and animals were commandeered; the supply of cotton was controlled. The natural discontent because of arbitrary foreign rule was further stimulated by the Arab movement for independence, the Wilsonian theory of self-determination, and Moslem dislike for Christians. General unrest gradually crystallized into an Egyptian nationalist movement against British rule. Led by Saad Zaghlul Pasha, the Nationalists in 1918 began demanding complete autonomy. Sporadic rioting, strikes, and continuous agitation throughout 1919 finally led the British government to send to Egypt a mission to investigate the situation and to suggest a form of constitution. The mission recommended that Great Britain recognize Egypt as a sovereign state, provided the latter would recognize Great Britain's special interests in the Suez Canal as a link in the system of British imperial communications. Such a proposal, however, was unacceptable to the Egyptian Nationalists.

At length, on February 28, 1922, the British government by proclamation terminated the protectorate, abolished martial law, and recognized Egypt as "an independent sovereign state," but reserved for future discussion (1) the security of British communications, (2) the defense of Egypt, (3) the protection of foreigners and minorities in Egypt, and (4) the Sudan.[4] This arrangement was characterized

[3] For the Balkan Entente, see page 568.
[4] The chief interest of both Great Britain and Egypt in the Sudan was economic, arising from the development of irrigation projects which make possible the extensive growth of cotton. Because the Assuan dam marked the limit of easy exploitation of the Egyptian Nile, and because of deterioration in the quality of Egyptian cotton in recent

by Lord Allenby, British high commissioner, as equivalent "to the declaration of a British Monroe Doctrine over Egypt." The sultan, in order to give formal expression to Egypt's new international status, on March 15 assumed the title of king, and in April, 1923, a constitution was enacted by a royal rescript. In the first general elections for the Egyptian parliament Zaghlul's party won an overwhelming majority, and in January, 1924, he became premier. Zaghlul still demanded Egypt's complete freedom from Britain's control.

In November, 1924, Anglo-Egyptian relations were suddenly subjected to a severe strain when Sir Lee Stack, commander-in-chief of the Egyptian army and governor-general of the Sudan, was killed by assassins in Cairo. The act came as the culmination of a long campaign against British officers and British sympathizers. Both the king and Premier Zaghlul immediately expressed their profound sorrow and their horror at the crime, and in the name of the Egyptian government Zaghlul pledged himself to put forth every effort to bring the criminals to justice and to inflict exemplary punishment.

Nevertheless, on November 22 the British government presented an ultimatum, demanding an apology, punishment of the criminals, prohibition of political demonstrations, and the payment of an indemnity of $2,500,000. It further required the withdrawal of all Egyptian troops from the Sudan within twenty-four hours, the removal of limitations which in Egyptian interests had been placed on the area to be irrigated in the Gezira, and the withdrawal of all opposition to Great Britain's wishes in regard to the protection of foreign interests within Egypt. Zaghlul's government at once accepted all the demands except those referring to the Sudan and to the protection of foreign interests, and paid the indemnity within twenty-four hours. Failure to accept all the demands, however, brought the British announcement that the Alexandria customs office would be occupied. Zaghlul thereupon resigned, and a new premier accepted the British requirements in full.

But the Nationalists continued to win whenever parliamentary elections were held and likewise continued to reject Anglo-Egyptian treaties when they were submitted to them. In 1930, apparently in an attempt to weaken the Nationalists, the government issued a new

years, the Nationalists were eager to incorporate the Sudan in Egypt. This would entail the withdrawal of the British, for an Anglo-Egyptian condominium had governed the Sudan since 1899.

constitution, but the promulgation of this document had the effect of bringing about a union of the forces of the Nationalists and the Liberal Constitutionalists, both of whom wished to retain the constitution of 1923. Preceded by the threat of a Nationalist boycott and by a resort to repressive measures against Nationalist meetings, and accompanied by riots in which hundreds were reported killed or wounded, the first elections under the new constitution were held in May, 1931. In the following month King Fuad pointed out in his speech from the throne that much had been done to improve the economic condition of the country and that, in spite of the depression, the national budget had been balanced. During the next three years, however, the government continued to wield dictatorial powers, resorting to severe measures to suppress the opposition, and calling and proroguing the parliament about as it pleased. Nevertheless, after a protracted political crisis late in 1934, King Fuad's semiautocratic regime came to an end with the abrogation of the constitution of 1930 and the dissolution of the parliament.

Tension between Great Britain and Italy arising from the Italo-Ethiopian conflict in 1935 gave the Egyptian Nationalists an excellent opportunity to bring pressure to bear upon Great Britain. Their nationalism was further aroused, moreover, by the apparent disregard with which Great Britain treated the Egyptian government in the military and naval steps which the former took in Egypt to prepare for a possible Italo-British clash, and by the fear that Egypt might be drawn into the Italo-Ethiopian conflict through Britain's actions. Anti-British demonstrations were staged in Cairo and other cities. Anti-British sentiment rose to new heights when Sir Samuel Hoare, British foreign secretary, admitted in a speech in London on November 9, 1935, that the British government had advised against the restoration of the constitution of 1923 on the ground that it was unworkable.

Three days later the Nationalist Party decided to withdraw its support from the government. In the succeeding days anti-British demonstrations of Egyptian students led to frequent riots and clashes with the police, in the course of which the British consulate in Cairo was stoned. Eventually all parties in opposition to the government organized a "united front" under the leadership of the former Nationalist premier, Mustapha Nahas Pasha, to force the restoration of the constitution. Faced by the possibility of political chaos in Egypt, so important a strategic spot for Britain's activities in the Mediterranean, the British government surrendered to the Nationalist demands. On December 12 King Fuad issued a royal rescript restoring the constitution of 1923.[5]

In the ensuing elections the Nationalists again won a decisive victory at the polls, and on May 10, 1936, Mustapha Nahas Pasha became premier in a ministry consisting entirely of Nationalists. Meanwhile, scenting the possibility of a still greater victory, the Nationalists had demanded a treaty of alliance with Great Britain which would recognize Egypt's complete independence. On August 26 such a treaty was signed in London, the terms differing little from those of the treaty of 1930 which the Nationalists had rejected. Apparently the attitude of the latter was influenced by the Italian conquest of Ethiopia, which emphasized Egypt's need of military protection against possible threats from Italian Libya and Italian East Africa.

By the terms of the treaty (1) the administration of the Sudan reverted to the prewar status, (2) Great Britain agreed to withdraw her troops from Egypt except from the vicinity of the Suez Canal, (3) Egypt gave the British the right to use Alexandria and Port Said as naval bases and the right to move their troops through Egyptian territory in case of war or the threat of war, (4) Egypt agreed to have her army instructed by the British and equipped with British arms, (5) both agreed that should either be at war the other would come to its assistance, (6) in recognition of Egypt's complete independence Great Britain agreed to replace her high commissioner by an ambassador and to support Egypt in her request for the abolition of capitulations and for membership in the League of Nations. The treaty was ratified by the Egyptian and British parliaments in November, 1936.

In May, 1937, a convention was signed at Montreux, Switzerland, by the capitulatory powers, providing (1) that after October 15, 1937, foreigners in Egypt would be subject to Egyptian-made law and taxation, and consular courts would surrender most of their powers to mixed tribunals, and (2) that after a transitional period the mixed tribunals would be abolished and in 1949 foreigners in Egypt would be subject to the Egyptian courts and laws in all mat-

---

[5] On April 28, 1936, King Fuad died and was succeeded by his sixteen-year-old son, who was proclaimed King Farouk.

ters. In the same month Egypt was admitted to membership in the League of Nations.

## SYRIA, PALESTINE, AND IRAQ

In western Asia at the close of the World War most of the non-Turkish regions of the former Ottoman Empire were entrusted to France and Great Britain as Class A mandates of the League of Nations. As such they were considered to have reached a stage of development where their existence as independent nations could be provisionally recognized, subject to the rendering of administrative advice and assistance by the mandatory power until they should be able to stand alone. The eagerness of the native peoples to secure complete independence and the reluctance of the advisory powers to recognize such a status at times precipitated serious armed clashes.

The iron-handed methods of the French administration of Syria and Lebanon ultimately led in 1925 to open revolt by the Druse tribesmen. The French retaliated by bombarding some of the native villages, and the uprising in consequence spread rapidly. When natives in the vicinity of Damascus attempted to cut the French line of communication, French forces countered by burning several villages. In fact, they ultimately subjected the city of Damascus to a bombardment and to bombing by airplanes, causing the loss of a thousand lives. The revolt continued, however, and in 1926 a second bombardment of Damascus, with the loss of another thousand lives, led the Mandates Commission of the League to remonstrate. In the guerrilla war which ensued, the French maintained control of the cities but for a time made little headway in the rural districts. The high commissioner continued to refuse to recognize the tribesmen as belligerents, and the latter continued to demand independence, with admission to the League of Nations.

Eventually, in 1928, the French permitted elections to be held for a constituent assembly which should draft a Syrian constitution, the understanding being that the adoption of the constitution would be followed by a Franco-Syrian treaty defining the relations between the two countries and giving Syria her place among the nations of the world. In the constituent assembly which opened on June 9 of that year a substantial majority was held by the Syrian Nationalists, who wanted a completely independent republic. But the French were unwilling to permit the adoption of such a constitution, and so the high commissioner at first suspended and then adjourned the constituent assembly *sine die*.

In May, 1930, a constitution promulgated by the high commissioner himself established a republic, subject only to the mandatory powers of the French government and to the latter's control of its foreign policy. Syria was to have her own president and her own parliament. The president was to be elected for a five-year term by the parliament and was to be a Moslem. Not until January, 1932, were popular elections held under this constitution, and then they were accompanied by considerable disorder. Thanks, many claimed, to French pressure, a majority of moderate Nationalists was returned. In June the parliament elected as president of Syria a wealthy Arab who had been practically nominated by the French.

Late in 1933 France negotiated and signed a Franco-Syrian treaty of friendship and alliance, apparently as a step preliminary toward ending her mandate over Syria. The treaty was strongly denounced by Syrian patriots, however, because it did not include all the territory which they desired to see incorporated in Syria, and because for twenty-five years Syria's foreign policy as well as her financial and military affairs were to be under French supervision. When it became clear that the treaty would not be ratified, the French high commissioner withdrew it and prorogued the parliament.

But the success of anti-British agitation in Egypt had its effect in Syria, where early in 1936 the Syrian campaign for independence was revived. When the French authorities sought to prevent trouble by ordering the dissolution of the Syrian Nationalist Party, violent street fighting broke out which brought the death of a number of persons and the arrest of hundreds more. A general strike by the Syrians finally compelled the French authorities to permit the establishment of a Nationalist cabinet. Léon Blum's government, which came into power in France in the summer of 1936, at once sought to bring about better relations with the natives and in the fall of that year signed with the Nationalist governments of Syria and Lebanon treaties of alliance and friendship which closely resembled the Anglo-Egyptian treaty of August, 1936. By the terms of these treaties both were to become independent nations at the end of a three-year transition period, and France was to sponsor their admission to the League of Nations. The French, however, were to maintain troops in the republics for a time and to train and equip their armies.

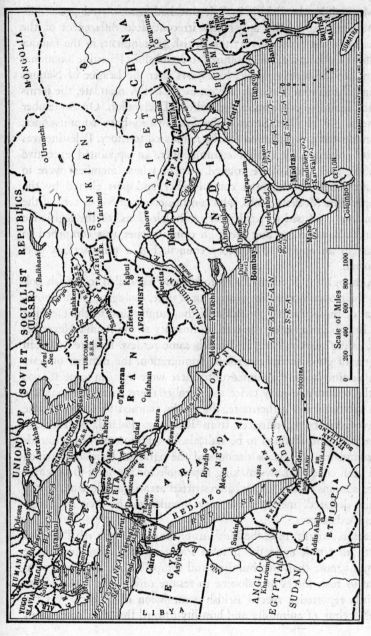

THE NEAR AND MIDDLE EAST

Meanwhile, the British in Palestine had encountered great difficulties because of the apparently irreconcilable differences of the Arabs and the Jews. In 1917 the British government, in the famous Balfour Declaration, had promised to establish in Palestine a national home for the Jewish people. Five years later the League of Nations assigned Palestine to Great Britain as a Class A mandate, the terms of the mandate confirming the Balfour Declaration. On September 1, 1922, Sir Herbert Samuel, the first British high commissioner, promulgated a constitution for the mandated territory. Palestine was to be governed by a high commissioner, an appointed executive council, and a legislative council, part of whose members were to be appointed by the high commissioner and part elected by the people. The Moslem Arabs, who constituted about 80 per cent of the population, refused to participate in the elections for the legislative council, however, so that the high commissioner was compelled to resort to an appointed advisory council. For a time serious riots occurred.

Although the Moslems failed to become reconciled to British policy, their open opposition abated for a time, owing to the improvement of the economic condition of the country and to the fact that the British government showed no hostility to the Arabs. Nevertheless, as the years passed, the latter became restless. Despite a certain degree of government control of immigration, the number of Jews in Palestine steadily mounted until there were by 1929 some 160,000 in the territory—nearly twice the number there when the mandate was established. Furthermore, the Arabs claimed that most of the newcomers—being refugees from Rumania, Poland, or Russia—were poor and inclined to be radicals. In addition to these grounds of complaint, the Arabs denounced the agrarian legislation which had been enacted. Laws making it possible for the Jews to purchase large sections of the somewhat restricted area of arable land, so the Arabs declared, menaced the very foundations of their own economic existence.

Late in August, 1929, the Moslems broke out in open rebellion and began an attack upon the Jews in Palestine which resulted in the death of more than two hundred and compelled the British government to rush forces to Palestine to restore order. The cause of the rioting, reported a special British commission of inquiry, was the Arab feeling of animosity and hostility toward the Jews, consequent upon the disappointment of their political and national aspirations, and fear for their economic future. Investigation brought to light the fact that while, by the natural increase in population, the number of Arabs was mounting, the land available for their sustenance, because of the area which had passed into Jewish hands, had decreased by about 250,000 acres. In the light of Arab methods of cultivation, there was, it was reported, no margin of land available for agricultural development by new immigrants. It was further pointed out that the Jewish Foundation Fund, which rented land to the Jews, forbade the employment of Arab labor on its soil, and that the policy of the General Federation of Jewish Labor was to import Jewish workers rather than to hire landless Arabs.

Despite the protests of the Jews, the British authorities for a time suspended immigration. In 1931, therefore, the Arabs became more conciliatory and displayed a willingness to co-operate in the election of a legislative council. When the project of such a council was accordingly revived, it next encountered the opposition of the Jews, who declared they would have nothing to do with it unless they were guaranteed at least an equality in membership with the Arabs. Once more the project had to be dropped.

Although some attempts were made by the British authorities to control the type of Jewish immigrant, by 1933 there were in Palestine, according to Jewish authorities, more than 200,000 Jews, and the amount of land held by the latter had increased twelvefold since the close of the war. One new Jewish city, Tel Aviv, was reported to have a population of 60,000 in 1933 and to be increasing at the rate of 12,000 a year. Meanwhile, in 1925, a Hebrew University had been opened in Jerusalem. Thanks to the influx of capital from abroad, to the increased application of scientific methods to agriculture, industry, and business, and to the initiative and energy of the Jewish Agency, Palestine was relatively unaffected by the world depression. Millions of dollars of Jewish capital flowed into the country, projects for electrification were started, Haifa was improved into a deep-water port, a pipe line was begun to connect this port with the rich Mosul oil fields, and a survey was completed for a future Haifa-Bagdad railway. Many believed that, when these various projects were completed, Palestine would come to play an important role in the trade of the Near and Middle East.

Nevertheless, the opposition of the Moslems continued. When in

February, 1933, the high commissioner declined to place further restrictions on Jewish immigration or to forbid the sale of Arab lands to Jews, Arab leaders once more announced a policy of non-co-operation with the British authorities. Three years later anti-Jewish outbreaks on the part of the Arabs again became serious. Clashes occurred which caused over three hundred fatalities, and increased British forces were sent to Palestine in an effort to restore order. To enforce their demand that further Jewish immigration be halted, the Arabs resorted to widespread strikes and to a campaign of civil disobedience.

In May, 1936, the British government again decided to send a royal commission to Palestine to investigate Arab and Jewish grievances. The commission's report, published in July, 1937, declared that the aspirations of the 400,000 Jews and the 1,000,000 Arabs in Palestine were irreconcilable and the existing British mandate unworkable. It therefore recommended that Palestine be divided into three parts. Nazareth, Jerusalem, and a corridor from the latter to the Mediterranean at Jaffa should continue to be a British mandate; a section including about one third of Palestine should be converted into a Jewish state; and the rest of the territory should become an Arab state linked with Trans-Jordan. The Jewish state would have ports at Haifa and Tel Aviv, the latter having by 1937 a population of 125,000. The Arab state would have an outlet to the Mediterranean at Gaza. Both states would have to enter into military alliances with Great Britain, and the important naval base and pipe-line terminus at Haifa would be left temporarily under British control. The commission's proposals were at once vigorously denounced by both Arabs and Jews, though the Zionist Congress eventually empowered its executive to negotiate for partition.

Although the British government at once approved the commission's report, opposition was so strong in the House of Commons that it was voted to have the plan for partition studied further before final parliamentary action. In August, however, the mandates commission of the League of Nations approved in principle the attempt to solve the problem in Palestine by partition but insisted that the new Jewish and Arab states should continue under mandate. The League Council thereupon adopted a resolution which provided authority for the British to carry on negotiations. The way therefore appeared to be open for the British government to seek the support of Parliament for a scheme to implement the report of the royal commission.

Although the British met little opposition in assuming their mandate over Trans-Jordan, where they confided the local government to Abdullah—son of Hussein, the first king of Hejaz—in Iraq, where they installed Faisal, another son of Hussein, as king, they encountered open revolt. Hostility to British rule was so great that, despite the suppression of open resistance, the mandate had to be transformed into an Anglo-Iraqi treaty of alliance (1922). Not until 1924 was the treaty ratified by the constituent assembly of Iraq, and then only after Great Britain had threatened to bring the matter before the League Council. Late in 1925, in accordance with the League's decision in the Turco-Iraqi boundary dispute, Great Britain and Iraq negotiated another treaty, which was to run for twenty-five years or until Iraq should become a member of the League of Nations. This treaty was signed on January 13, 1926.

Iraq, however, was eager to throw off the mandatory status as soon as possible. In 1927 the Iraqi government attempted to persuade Great Britain that Iraq should be admitted to the League at once. Although the British were unwilling to support this step so soon, they did sign a new treaty (December, 1927) agreeing to recognize the independence of Iraq within five years and—if Iraq's existing rate of progress continued—to support her candidacy for admission to the League in 1932. Iraq, on her part, agreed to lease three new air bases to Great Britain and to turn over to a British military commission the training of the Iraqi army, which would use British equipment. It was further agreed that Great Britain should be represented in Iraq by an ambassador who should have precedence over all other diplomats.

Five years later the British mandate was ended, and Iraq became independent. The Mandates Commission in 1932 drew up a list of guarantees which Iraq had to accept before she could become a member of the League. These included protection of minorities, freedom of conscience and religion, recognition of rights acquired and debts contracted during the mandatory regime, and the guarantee of the rights of foreigners before the courts. Iraq promised, furthermore, in case of actual or imminent war, to aid Great Britain to the extent of her ability. On October 3, 1932, Iraq was admitted to the League as an independent power, and the European states surrendered their privileges under the capitulations.

## PERSIA

Meanwhile, to the east of Iraq, the Persians had become imbued with the same nationalistic spirit which had led the Turks to rebel against the West. They had every reason to fear the extinction of their independence as a sovereign state, for the Anglo-Russian treaties of 1907 and 1915 had practically divided Persia between these two great powers. The withdrawal of Russian forces after the Bolshevik revolution gave little encouragement to Persian nationalists, since their place was taken by the British, and in 1919 an Anglo-Persian treaty made Persia dependent upon Great Britain in political and military matters.

The weak Persian government which consented to this treaty came to be regarded by Persian nationalists as an instrument of foreign rule. In February, 1921, this government was overthrown by a military revolution led by Riza Khan, who, like Mustapha Kemal, was a soldier who had risen from the ranks to be head of a small and efficient military force. Riza Khan at once became commander-in-chief of the Persian army and the real power in the government, which promptly denounced the Anglo-Persian treaty. Soon after the *coup d'état* of February, 1921, Riza Khan became minister of war, and, after making and unmaking several ministries, he finally assumed the premiership in October, 1923. The shah was induced to leave Persia for Europe, and on December 12, 1925, a Persian constituent assembly made Riza Khan hereditary shah.

By this time the reconstruction of Persia had been largely accomplished. The Russian-officered Cossacks, British-officered South Persian Rifles, and Swedish-officered gendarmerie had given way to a well-organized and well-equipped national Persian army of some 40,000 men. With this force Riza Khan had succeeded in restoring order and in asserting the authority of the Teheran government over many tribes which had been enjoying *de facto* independence. In 1921 the Persian government had sought foreign assistance in its task of remodeling its public finances and promoting the economic development of the country, and in the succeeding years Riza Khan sought further to modernize Persia. The legal age for marriage for girls was made sixteen years, and women were given an equal right with men to secure a divorce. Railway construction was begun, highways were extended, an air force was created, and in 1932 a small Persian navy was placed in the Persian Gulf.

The attempt to throw off outside control continued. All foreign capitulations in Persia were abolished, and national tariff autonomy was secured. Foreign mission schools in the country were forbidden to teach Persian children in the primary grades. In 1931 the Persian government took over control of all the country's telegraph lines, which were formerly in the hands of the Indo-European Telegraph Department of the British India Office. In the next year the Junkers Aircraft Company, a German concern, was forced to discontinue its air services in Persia, largely because the Persian government placed difficulties in the way of a renewed concession; at the same time the government refused to allow the Imperial Airways Company of Great Britain to have landing fields in Persia on the route to India.

Finally, in November, 1932, the Persian council of ministers, presided over by Riza Khan, decided to cancel the concession of the Anglo-Persian Oil Company, a majority of whose stock was held by the British government. Great Britain at once denied Persia's right to cancel the concession, but proposed that the whole question be referred to the World Court. Persia refused to admit the competence of the court in a dispute between herself and a commercial company. Thereupon Great Britain requested that the matter be submitted to the League Council. At the meeting of the Council in February, 1933, however, the two countries agreed that the League proceedings should be suspended for three months while direct negotiations regarding a new concession were carried on between Persia and the Anglo-Persian Oil Company. This step marked a distinct victory for Persia, for throughout the dispute she had steadily maintained that the company should negotiate directly with Persia.

The Persian government ultimately won a victory in its dispute with the powerful British company. On April 30, 1933, a new sixty-year lease was signed with drastically altered terms. In place of the former 16 per cent of the net profits of the company, Persia was to receive one dollar per ton of oil extracted regardless of the price and, in addition, was to receive 20 per cent of the company's total net profits above a stated minimum. Furthermore, the company was to pay Persia in taxation about $1,125,000 annually for the first fifteen years and about $1,500,000 for the second fifteen years. Persia gained much better financial terms than she formerly enjoyed. Moreover, she made other nationalistic gains. The company's area of exploitation was drastically curtailed; it was to replace progressively its foreign employees by Persians; it was to spend some $50,000 annually educating Persians in Great Britain; and it was to sell oil to Persians and to the Persian government at a discount from the world prices. By many it was considered that Persia's victory in this dispute constituted an important precedent in the relations between "backward" nations and powerful concessionaries.

## INDIA

The World War directly affected India, for nearly a million and a half men were sent overseas, more than a third of them actually becoming combatants. As a consequence of the war, India incurred or assumed a financial burden of about $700,000,000. Out of this contact with the war came a sense of added prestige and an increased desire for freedom from European control, for a place as an equal among the states of the world. A great impetus was thus given to the nationalist movement which had already begun in India before 1914.

In December, 1916, a meeting of representatives of both Hindus and Moslems in India drafted a scheme of reform for which the National Party in India should stand, and the British government soon took steps to recognize the national awakening. Two Indians were included among the four delegates from India at the imperial conference of 1917. In August of that year E. S. Montagu, secretary of state for India, announced that the British government was planning to increase the association of Indians in the administrative branches of the government and to develop gradually self-governing institutions. In July, 1918, came a report on the reforms which had been drafted as a result of consultations between Montagu and Lord Chelmsford, the viceroy of India. The moderate parties in India accepted the scheme outlined, but in December the National Congress, now the organ of the extreme National Party, wholly condemned the proposals and demanded immediate and full autonomy.

For the time being, however, the constitutional question was eclipsed by the course of events in India, where Mohandas K. Gandhi, a Hindu social and religious reformer, became the spokesman and leader of the agitation and initiated a movement of passive resistance. The Indian government, alarmed by the unrest and revolutionary agitation, hurriedly passed certain emergency measures. These the Nationalist press and Nationalist politicians at once denounced as attacks upon popular liberties and as instruments of tyranny and oppression. A wave of excitement spread over the Punjab and reached its height when on April 13, 1919, the "Amritsar massacre" occurred. Military forces employed to disperse an unlawful gathering in Amritsar caused the death of about 400 Indians and the wounding of three times that number.

In Great Britain it was hoped that the admission of Indian claims to self-government would alleviate Indian unrest and Indian hostility. The Montagu-Chelmsford scheme of constitutional reform was accordingly pushed through Parliament and became the Government of India Act in December, 1919. This act applied not to the three hundred or more Indian principalities which have relations with the British government, but only to the 230,000,000 people living in British India.

The Government of India Act fundamentally altered the political situation in India. In the first place, it provided for decentralization through the establishment of provincial governments which should have charge of such matters as education, public health, agriculture, irrigation, criminal law, prisons, and labor legislation. For most administrative purposes, the provinces were treated as separate states within a kind of federation. Each of these provinces had a legislative council in which at least 70 per cent of the members were elected and not more than 20 per cent were officials. All men over twenty-one years of age had the vote, provided they met certain property or occupational requirements, but these were of such a character that only about 5,350,000 persons had the franchise.

Within each province the functions of government were divided, under a system known as dyarchy, into reserved and transferred subjects. The reserved departments, including irrigation, land revenue, factory inspection, and police, were administered by the provincial governor and his executive council; the transferred departments, including public health, education, public works, and agriculture, were administered by ministers chosen from the provincial assembly and responsible to it. In this way it was planned to provide a field in which Indian leaders could be trained in the actual practice of government; and the dyarchical scheme was intended to be only transitory and experimental.

No dyarchy was provided for the central government, however, which consisted of the governor-general in council and two advisory bodies—the Legislative Assembly and the Council of State. The governor-general and his executive council remained directly responsible to the British Parliament for the government of India, but the two advisory bodies were chosen by very restricted Indian electorates. Those entitled to vote for the Legislative Assembly numbered less than a million men, while the electorate for the Council of State included less than eighteen thousand. The Legislative Assembly developed into the chief agency for crystallizing and voicing Indian opinion, and came to be something of a parliament without power.

The Government of India Act stipulated that ten years after its passage a parliamentary commission should go to India to inquire into the working of the plan and to report on the desirability of extending or modifying the degree of responsible government already existing. Two years before the expiration of the designated decade, the British government appointed an interparty parliamentary commission under Sir John Simon to consider possible amendments to the act of 1919. The exclusion of Indians from the commission led to dissatisfaction among the Nationalists, who demanded that responsible Indians should themselves devise the future system of government in India or at least be treated as equal co-operators. The commission attempted to give Indian statesmen an opportunity to help construct the future constitution of India by proposing that Indians should work with them "on equal terms in joint conference."

During the early months of 1929 the Simon Commission continued its investigations, while Indian radicals did their utmost to awaken a widespread distrust of it and its objects. Gandhi again conducted a vigorous campaign against the use or sale of British cloth in India, resulting in the seizure and burning of such cloth, and in subsequent riots and arrests. In 1930 he inaugurated a new campaign of civil disobedience. Setting an example by himself violating the laws establishing a government salt monopoly, he brought about a general defiance of laws in India. The collection of taxes was resisted, railway and street traffic was obstructed, and many Hindu officials resigned. Although Gandhi counseled his followers to avoid violence, disorders broke out, and in May, 1930, the government finally took the step of arresting and imprisoning Gandhi and a number of his more important followers.

In 1930 the report of the Simon Commission was published. The document carefully avoided any mention of dominion status or independence and appeared to seek an increase in the executive powers of the secretary of state for India, the governor-general, and the various provincial governors. It was thoroughly unsatisfactory to the Indian Nationalists. In an attempt to work out some compromise solution of the Indian problem the British government next called a number of round-table conferences to meet in London. The first, which assembled in November, 1930, was attended by representatives of the three British political parties, the native Indian states, and various groups in British India. In September, 1931, a second conference convened, and this time Gandhi himself attended. This conference was notable chiefly for its disagreements. Hindus and Moslems disagreed on means of protecting the latter; British Indians and the native princes disagreed on the type of federation to be adopted; high-caste Hindus and the "untouchables" disagreed on the future status of the latter; and, finally, Britishers and Indians disagreed on the extent of self-government which India was to have. The conference ultimately adjourned in December, after Premier MacDonald had pointed out that disagreements among the Indians themselves constituted a serious handicap to the drafting of a constitution.

Meanwhile, during 1931, India had been greatly disturbed by violence on the part of the Nationalists. So serious did the situation become that the governor-general issued a number of ordinances of a severely repressive nature. Upon his refusal to recall them, Gandhi once more launched a campaign of civil disobedience. The Nationalist leader, in consequence, was again imprisoned, and during the first half of 1932 nearly 50,000 Indians were arrested for violation of special ordinances. Ultimately the British government announced that it would itself work out a plan to solve the minorities problem, and that when it had done this it would summon a third round table to draw up a new constitution for India.

In November, 1932, this conference convened in London for a final consideration of the projected Indian constitution. When it

adjourned late in December, a complete and definite form of government had at last been drafted. In March, 1933, the British government issued a white paper containing the new Indian federal constitution. This was in turn submitted for consideration and revision
to an India Joint Select Committee, chosen from both houses of the
British Parliament. Although many Labor members of the British
Parliament and some extreme Conservatives were opposed to the
projected scheme of government—though, obviously, for far different reasons—the Government of India Bill was passed by the House
of Commons, and on August 2, 1935, it became law. The Marquess
of Linlithgow, chairman of the India Joint Select Committee, was
thereupon appointed to be the new viceroy of India and entrusted
with the task of putting the act into effect.

Under her new constitution India still failed to attain dominion
status, for the governor-general was to control defense and foreign relations and was to possess a number of emergency powers in case of
domestic crises arising from conflicts over religion, minorities, currency, or justice to foreigners. British India was to have a central
government and eleven provincial governments, and the general
purpose of the constitution seemed to be to place the chief responsibility for domestic administration on the latter. In each of the self-
governing provinces a ministry, selected from its legislature, was
normally to conduct all provincial affairs, including even the maintenance of law and order. Over the ministry, however, was to be
placed a British governor, as formerly, with special responsibilities.
If circumstances demanded, the governor might take charge of any
branch of the provincial government, might issue ordinances with
the force of law, might even override the provincial legislature on appropriation bills. The electorate for the provincial legislatures, according to figures which were published, was to include some 38,000,000
men and women, and therefore marked a considerable extension of
the franchise over that existing under the act of 1919. The Council
of State, the upper house of the national legislature, was to have
150 members elected by the provincial legislatures, 100 members appointed by the princes, and 10 appointed by the government. The
Legislative Assembly, the lower house, was to have 250 members
elected directly by the voters, and 125 members appointed by the
princes. The national electorate was to consist of some 6,000,000
voters, which likewise constituted an advance over the provisions of

the act of 1919. Nowhere, of course, was universal suffrage provided. The new constitution, being a compromise, naturally pleased nobody. In general, the Indian view was that it in no sense substantiated agreements reached at the first two round tables. The Congress Nationalists at once decided to boycott the new regime.

When elections were held in the eleven provinces in January and February, 1937, however, the Congress party participated and won a decisive victory, securing an absolute majority in six and a plurality in three of them. In March the All-India Congress committee resolved that Congress ministers should accept office only if each governor would agree not to "use his special powers of interference or set aside the advice of ministers in regard to their constitutional activities." The provincial governors, however, declared it constitutionally impossible for them to accept this formula. On April 1, when the new constitution was formally introduced, a general strike and a protest demonstration were organized against it. Nevertheless, many saw reasons for great encouragement in the fact that, in the six provinces in which the Nationalist Party had won majorities, Nationalist leaders organized governments and in the succeeding months showed a desire to make their administrations function successfully.

## CHAPTER XXVIII

## THE FAR EAST

ALTHOUGH native unrest and nascent rebellion in French Indo-China, the Dutch East Indies, and the American Philippines were phases of the East's revolt against the West, the chief exponents of this movement in the Far East were the Chinese and Japanese. The former persistently sought to rid themselves of Western domination and exploitation, but unfortunately were seriously handicapped by their own inability to unite and present a common front. The latter, nationally united and militarily modernized, ultimately revolted against Western interference in their imperialistic plans, and successfully defied both the League of Nations and the United States.

### CHINA, JAPAN, AND THE WORLD WAR

Shortly before the World War began, the Emperor of China—a boy six years of age—was deposed, and a republic was proclaimed (1912). Sun Yat-sen, who for years had worked to bring about the republic, was elected provisional president, but in the interest of Chinese harmony and unity he resigned in favor of Yuan Shih-k'ai, the last premier under the empire. The Chinese liberals, organized as the Nationalist Party (*Kuomintang*), were from the beginning suspicious of the new president and soon came into open conflict with him. While the Nationalists sought to establish in China a democratic regime, based upon a broad franchise, a strong parliament, and a relatively weak executive, Yuan aimed to set up a powerful executive and a weak parliament. Friction developed between the two groups, and, after an attempt had been made to overthrow Yuan, the latter ordered the unseating of the Nationalist members of the parliament (1913), and took steps looking toward the re-establishment of the monarchy. In 1916, before he had succeeded in doing this, he died, and after his death a succession of presidents held office in Peking. Although the Nationalists, denouncing the Peking government as illegal, in 1917 proclaimed a new provisional government in Canton and asserted that the latter was the only constitutional government in China, foreign powers continued to recognize and deal with the authorities in Peking. The real power in China fell more and more into the hands of various military chiefs (*tuchuns*), who devoted themselves primarily to the advancement of personal rather than national interests.

Meanwhile, in August, 1914, as has already been pointed out,[1] Japan demanded that Germany surrender her leased territory of Kiaochow "with a view to the eventual restoration of the same to China," and, when Germany refused to comply with this demand, Japan declared war upon her. In November the German base was surrendered to the Japanese. Not content with the acquisition of this former German stronghold on Chinese soil, the Japanese in January, 1915, presented to President Yuan a list of twenty-one demands designed to transform China into a Japanese protectorate. Menaced by a Japanese threat of war and well aware that the European powers were too preoccupied with their own affairs to intervene effectively in her behalf, China on May 25, 1915, finally signed two treaties which in a modified form embodied most of the points of Japan's original demands. The latter obtained special concessions in South Manchuria and Inner Mongolia. The Chinese Nationalists denounced the treaties and declared that they would never recognize their validity; the agreements, in fact, were never ratified by the Chinese parliament. Japan, nevertheless, claimed that her rights were valid because the treaties contained clauses providing that they should become effective the day they were signed.

In the early years of the war China three times contemplated entering the conflict on the side of the Allies, but on each occasion the Japanese government—reluctant to have China build up an efficient army or participate in the eventual peace conference—managed to prevent the step. After Japan's position in China had been strengthened by various agreements with the Allies in 1917, however, she began to urge the latter to enter the struggle, and in this she was seconded by the United States. Eventually, in 1917, the authorities at both Peking and Canton declared war on Germany and Austria-Hungary.

At the peace conference China presented demands which included tariff autonomy, the abolition of extraterritoriality, the cancellation

[1] See pages 389 and 400.

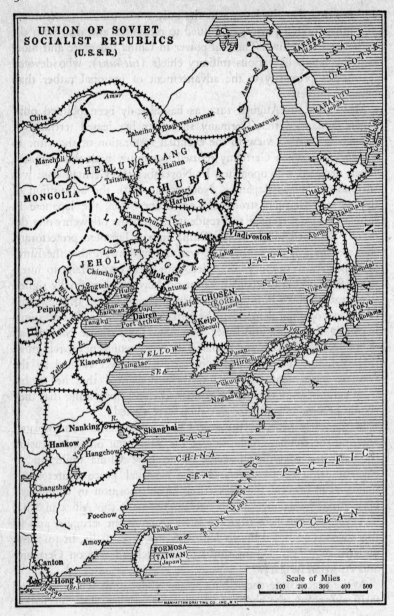

UNION OF SOVIET
SOCIALIST REPUBLICS
(U.S.S.R.)

THE FAR EAST, 1920–1931

of foreign spheres of influence, the withdrawal of foreign troops, and the surrender of leased territories. The statesmen at Paris, however, held that they had no power to deal with these questions. On the other hand, the peace conference, shackled by secret treaty agreements, decided to award the former German rights in Shantung to Japan. In China a violent popular movement against foreigners resulted, and numerous student demonstrations were organized in protest. A widespread and vigorous boycott of Japanese goods was instituted, and Japanese trade in China suffered severely. China scorned the direct negotiations with Japan concerning Shantung which the peace conference recommended, and on June 28 she refused to sign the treaty of Versailles.

Nevertheless, some nationalist gains came to China as a result of the war. She obtained membership in the League of Nations by signing the treaty of St. Germain, and by a separate treaty with Germany she secured the cancellation of the latter's extraterritorial rights. Furthermore, China saw to it that treaties with the new states of Europe made no extraterritorial concessions.

## THE WASHINGTON CONFERENCE

The next real gains for China in her struggle for the recognition of her integrity and independence and for the abolition of all special privileges of foreigners in her territory came at the Washington conference on the limitation of armaments. In 1921 the United States government, besides wishing to check a possible naval race with Great Britain, desired to secure the satisfactory settlement of certain questions in the Pacific and the Far East. It therefore invited Japan, China, Great Britain, France, Italy, the Netherlands, Belgium, and Portugal to a conference at Washington. The conference sat from November 12, 1921, to February 6, 1922, and as a result of its deliberations a number of treaties were concluded. The two which had to do with naval disarmament have already been discussed.[2] The others dealt with questions which concerned the Pacific and the Far East.

Although China failed to obtain all that she demanded in the way of national rights, she appeared to make a number of gains. A nine-power treaty guaranteed her territorial integrity and independence and again proclaimed the policy of the "open door." The signatory

[2] See pages 570–571.

powers agreed to respect China's rights as a neutral in time of war and promised not to support any agreements between their respective nationals which were "designed to create spheres of influence or to provide for the enjoyment of mutually exclusive opportunities in designated parts of Chinese territories." China, for her part, promised not to exercise or permit unfair discrimination of any kind on her railways. A second nine-power treaty permitted China to make an increase in her tariff rates and gave her greater control of the expenditure of the proceeds. Provision was also made for the appointment of two commissions to study the problems of Chinese tariff autonomy and extraterritoriality. A separate agreement between China and Japan, signed outside the conference, provided that Japan should return Shantung and all former German property rights in that province, and that China should reimburse Japan for the amounts which the latter had spent for railway and other improvements since 1914. In December, 1923, Shantung was restored to Chinese control.

The commission on customs, decided upon at Washington, eventually met in Peking in October, 1925. It passed a resolution agreeing that Chinese tariff autonomy ought to be restored, but, in view of the chaotic conditions within China, it adjourned without taking positive action. The commission on extraterritoriality met in Peking early in 1926. Although China during the four years after the Washington conference had been laboriously attempting to introduce judicial reform, the commission reported that the republic was not yet in a condition to administer justice in accord with Western ideas. It therefore recommended the postponement of the abolition of extraterritoriality until a later date. The Peking government, nevertheless, began denouncing all treaties granting extraterritoriality as they expired.

## NATIONALIST EFFORTS TO UNITE AND EMANCIPATE CHINA

In the years after 1921 it appeared for a time that the Nationalists, who had established a constitutional government at Canton, might be the salvation of China. Their aim was not only to unite the whole country under one administration, but to emancipate it from all foreign restrictions as well. For assistance against both Western imperialism and the opposing Chinese forces in the north they turned to the Soviet government, which in those days was eager to assist in the fight against Western capitalism. Early in 1924 a Nationalist congress offered party membership to all Chinese communists who were willing to accept the Kuomintang program.

By 1926, however, a serious schism had developed among the Nationalists, for the Right wing of the party was opposed to communism and desired to break with the Soviet government. Chiang Kai-shek, a successful general who became leader of the Nationalists after the death of Sun Yat-sen in March, 1925, threw his lot in with the Right wing of the party, repudiated communism, and began to persecute the communist members of the Nationalist Party. Nevertheless, despite division within their ranks, the Nationalists successfully carried on their northward advance against the opposing military chiefs. In September, 1926, they captured Hankow and early in the following year Shanghai and Nanking. In April, 1928, Chiang moved his Nationalist government to the latter city, and, after Nationalist troops captured Peking in June of that year, the northern government was abolished, and Nanking was made the new national capital of China. The name of Peking (Northern Capital) was thereupon changed to Peiping (Northern Peace). In August the Nanking government was recognized *de jure* by the League of Nations, which accepted its representative at the meeting of the League Council in that month.

In October, 1928, the central executive committee of the Nationalist Party issued an organic law for the national government of China. This document provided that the supreme administrative body in China should be a Council of State; and on October 10 the central executive committee, under whose supervision the organic law was to be executed, chose Chiang to be chairman of this council. Chiang thus came to hold in China a position analogous to that of president. By the close of the year 1928 the Nanking government had secured recognition from Japan and most of the Western states.

By this time the Nationalist government had begun its campaign to emancipate China from her international servitudes and had announced that it would abrogate all the "unequal treaties" as they expired. In 1928 the United States concluded a treaty restoring to China complete national tariff autonomy. Other Western powers took the same step, and the year closed with practically all countries recognizing Chinese tariff autonomy. Early in 1929 a new national tariff was put into effect by China, raising the basic rate from the former 5 per cent to 12½ per cent. A new criminal code and a new code of criminal procedure in accordance with Western ideas were introduced in September, 1928, and in October the Chinese government sent identical notes to all powers which still held extraterritorial privileges, asking them to take steps to abolish such privileges as soon as possible. Germany and Russia had already surrendered their extraterritorial rights, and late in 1928 Belgium, Italy, Denmark, and Portugal did the same. Again in April, 1929, the Chinese foreign minister, in a note to the foreign powers, requested action toward the relinquishment of the rights then held under treaties, so that steps might "be taken to enable China, now unified and with a strong central government, to rightfully assume jurisdiction over all nationals within her domain."

Unfortunately for China, she was neither so unified nor possessed of so strong a central government as the Nationalist foreign minister asserted. Although Chiang earnestly sought to create a united and powerful Chinese state, his handicaps were great. South of the Yangtse, in Kiangsi, Hunan, and North Fukien provinces, Chinese communists, taking advantage of the hardships resulting from floods and famines, won great numbers into their ranks and endeavored to establish a soviet regime. In other parts of China rival military leaders still sought to benefit from the central government's weakness by securing control of one or more valuable provinces for their own advantage. Worst of all, perhaps, was the fact that the Nationalist Party itself definitely split in the spring of 1931. Because of dissatisfaction with what they termed Chiang Kai-shek's "dictatorship," Kwantung and Kwangsi provinces joined in a rebellion against the Nanking government and set up a separate regime at Canton. With China again in chaos and with the world as a whole in the throes of a disastrous economic depression, it was small wonder, perhaps, that Japan should decide that the situation was favorable for further advancing her own position in Manchuria.

## JAPANESE PENETRATION OF MANCHURIA

In 1931 what was described on maps as Manchuria consisted of the three eastern provinces of China—Liaoning, Kirin, and Heilungkiang—with a total area about equivalent to that of France and Germany combined, and with a population of approximately 30,-000,000. The control of the district rested in the military power of the local war lord and not in the central government of China. The war lord and governor of Manchuria, Chang Tso-lin, had repeatedly declined to take orders from those who seized authority in Peiping and had actually declared Manchuria's independence of China at various times. Chang apparently looked upon Manchuria as possessing extensive autonomy under his personal rule, though his son and successor, Chang Hsiao-liang, after 1928 recognized the sovereignty of the Chinese national government.

Manchuria is rich in mineral resources—such as iron, coal, gold, silver, copper, lead, and asbestos—and numerous agricultural products are raised in abundance. It had therefore long been looked upon as a rich prize by the imperialistic powers of the world.[3] The Japanese had steadily increased their economic interests in the region until by 1931 their investments in Manchuria amounted to approximately a billion dollars. The foreign banking business of the district was practically a monopoly of the Japanese, who also controlled the South Manchuria Railway. Much of the foreign trade of Manchuria was diverted from the Russian port of Vladivostok to the Japanese-controlled port of Dairen.

By 1931, therefore, Japan had acquired or claimed in Manchuria rights the effect of which was to restrict the exercise of Chinese sovereignty in a manner and to a degree quite exceptional. She governed the leased territory of Kwantung, exercising therein what amounted to practically full sovereignty. Through the medium of the South Manchuria Railway she administered the railway zones, including several towns and important parts of populous cities such as Mukden and Changchun. In these areas she controlled the police, taxes, education, and public utilities. She maintained armed forces in certain parts of the country—the army of Kwantung in the leased territory, railway guards in the railway zones, and consular police in the various districts.

The Japanese were eager and determined to strengthen their hold on Manchuria in order that they might continue and increase their exploitation of that region. Japan's own natural resources were not overabundant, and her population was relatively dense. Less in area than California, Japan proper had a population of approximately 65,000,000, more than 40 per cent of which gained its livelihood directly from the soil. Unfortunately, however, less than one fifth of

[3] See pages 262–269.

the country's area was tillable, so that the number of inhabitants in proportion to cultivated area was nearly four times as great as that in England. Even including Korea, the Japanese Empire had an area less in extent than Texas; yet it had to support a population of over 90,000,000, a population which was increasing by about one million annually. Obviously there was in Japan, therefore, a heavy pressure of population upon resources. The introduction of modern industrialism had afforded some relief from this pressure; but machines—if they were to be kept running—required plentiful supplies of raw products and profitable markets. Hence the Japanese were vitally interested in the future development of Manchuria.

It was almost inevitable, therefore, that friction should develop between the imperialistic Japanese and the nationalistic Chinese. The interconnection of respective rights, the uncertainty at times of the legal situation, the increasing opposition between the conception held by the Japanese of their "special position" in Manchuria and the claims of the Chinese nationalists were a source of numerous disturbing incidents and disputes. Japan consistently sought to advance her interests in Manchuria by taking advantage of rights open to question. The Chinese authorities, on the other hand, repeatedly put obstacles in the way of the exercise of rights which unquestionably belonged to Japan.

Japan complained that the Chinese were placing obstacles in the way of the former's leasing of land and exercising of other treaty rights. Undoubtedly the Chinese, refusing to admit the validity of the agreements of 1915, were seeking to prevent the South Manchuria Railway from steadily increasing the amount of land being brought under its administration by leases. Moreover, the Chinese after 1925 were more than ever determined to develop in Manchuria their own railway system with the port at Hulutao as an outlet. The rapid development of this system and port caused alarm among the officials of the South Manchuria Railway, who became equally determined to prevent the Chinese from "strangling" their line.

## THE ESTABLISHMENT OF MANCHUKUO

In the late summer and early fall of 1931 the situation in Manchuria reached a crisis. On the night of September 18 a section of the South Manchuria Railway near Mukden was destroyed by explosives, placed there—the Japanese army leaders asserted—by

Chinese soldiers from neighboring barracks. The Japanese army had already carefully prepared a plan of action in case of possible hostilities between the Japanese and the Chinese in Manchuria, and this plan was at once put into operation with swiftness and precision and without any prior consultation with the government in Tokyo.[4] The next morning the population of Mukden awoke to find their city in the control of Japanese troops.

The Nanking government at once made strong protests at Tokyo, and on September 19 the Chinese representative at Geneva placed the Manchurian situation before the Council of the League of Nations. While the latter and the United States sought a satisfactory solution of the crisis,[5] Japanese military authorities in Manchuria, apparently with political motives and often without authorization from Tokyo, steadily extended the area of occupation. Following each occupation the civil administration was reorganized, loyal Chinese officials being replaced by friends of Japan. A separatist movement was encouraged by the Japanese military authorities, who capitalized grievances held against the former administration by certain minorities among the inhabitants.

With this encouragement from the Japanese, an "administrative committee" in Manchuria in February, 1932, issued a formal declaration of the independence of Manchuria and Inner Mongolia. On March 9, 1932, Henry Pu-yi—who as emperor had been deposed by the Chinese in 1912—was inaugurated as regent of the new state of Manchukuo.[6] A few days later the Manchukuo authorities notified the Chinese government that all political connection with China was ended, and proceeded themselves to take over the administration of the customs duties and salt tax. Changchun, with its name changed

[4] In Japan the army and navy departments were practically independent of civil authorities and had the right to go directly to the emperor without regard for the cabinet. The army leaders had little sympathy for parliamentary rule and little respect for civil government, and looked upon many of the politicians as scheming individuals who were primarily concerned in advancing the interests of certain business groups. During the years 1931–1933 the military succeeded in dominating the civil government, even to the extent of forcing it to defy the world. In 1932 the Japanese premier was deliberately killed in his home by a group of cadets and army officers as a "patriotic protest" against the government's policies.

[5] The next section of this chapter discusses the various attempts at mediation and settlement.

[6] On March 1, 1934—the second anniversary of the creation of Manchukuo—Henry Pu-yi was enthroned as Emperor of Manchukuo, with the title of Emperor Kang Teh. Regardless of his title, however, real authority in Manchukuo continued to rest in the hands of Japanese military authorities.

to Hsinching (New Capital), became the official capital of the new state.

Meanwhile, the Chinese, in addition to appealing to the League of Nations and to the United States for aid against the Japanese, had once more resorted to their powerful economic weapon, the boycott. Since Japan's interest in Chinese trade was much greater than China's interest in trade with Japan, this weapon could be extremely effective. In the four months from September, 1931, to January, 1932, Japan's exports to China fell to one third of what they had been in the corresponding period of the preceding year. Many Japanese textile mills in China were obliged to suspend operations; Japanese shipping engaged in China's coastwise and river traffic was seriously crippled; and Japanese bankers and shopkeepers in China faced ruin.

In response to the plea of Japanese residents of Shanghai, the most important foreign-trade center of China, Japanese consular and naval authorities in that city demanded a cessation of the boycott and of other anti-Japanese activities and the dissolution of the Chinese organizations responsible therefor. To support this demand a score or more of Japanese warships were at once dispatched to Shanghai. Faced by this demonstration, the Chinese accepted the ultimatum and acquiesced in the Japanese demands. Nevertheless, the Japanese admiral, apparently eager to gain glory for the navy, decided to occupy certain sections of Shanghai in order "to protect" the Japanese residents there. When marines were landed, a clash with the local Chinese garrison resulted, and fighting began. The local Chinese troops showed unexpected ability and courage. Five weeks of stiff fighting, accompanied by artillery duels and air bombings and the dispatch of nearly 100,000 Japanese soldiers, were necessary to force the Chinese to retreat. In May an armistice was signed providing for the evacuation of the Japanese forces and the abandonment of the boycott. Property damages resulting from the fighting were estimated at over half a billion dollars.

Many of the Japanese troops withdrawn from Shanghai were sent to reinforce those in Manchukuo, where an attempt was being made to pacify the country and to extend the area of effective occupation. Japanese operations in Manchukuo were greatly facilitated by an agreement made with the government of that new state on September 15, 1932. In a protocol signed on that date Japan recognized Manchukuo as an independent state, and in return secured not only the right to station in Manchukuo "such Japanese forces as may be necessary" for the maintenance of the national security of either country, but Manchukuo's promise "to confirm and respect . . . all rights and interests possessed by Japan or her subjects within the territory of Manchukuo by virtue of the Sino-Japanese treaties, agreements, or other arrangements, or through Sino-Japanese contracts, private as well as public." Manchukuo, it appeared, was to be a profitable Japanese protectorate. In March, 1933, Japan's troops added still a fourth province—Jehol in Inner Mongolia—to her puppet state.

Early in April the Japanese next launched a drive against the Chinese and advanced south of the Great Wall to within a few miles of Peiping and Tientsin. In May the Nanking government ordered the Chinese troops to evacuate Peiping, and shortly thereafter the "Peiping Political Council," composed of men holding moderate or pro-Japanese views, was constituted with administrative authority over an undefined area in North China. Negotiations were opened between this council and the Japanese, and on May 31 a truce was signed at Tangku, near Tientsin. By the terms of this truce it was agreed that Chinese troops should withdraw south and west of a line running roughly from Tientsin to Peiping and that Japanese troops should withdraw north of the Great Wall. These measures resulted in the creation between Manchukuo and China of a demilitarized zone administered by Chinese friendly to Japan—the possible future nucleus of another state with pro-Japanese sympathies. A few weeks later an agreement regarding the administration of this demilitarized area was signed at Dairen between representatives of China, Manchukuo, and Japan. Apparently the Chinese had been driven to realize the futility of struggling against Japanese military forces and had come to the conclusion that, to prevent the possible spoliation of China proper, they would have to recognize that Manchukuo had gone the way of Burma, Annam, Tonkin, Formosa, and Korea.

## THE INTERNATIONAL CRISIS OF 1931–1933

When the Chinese representative brought the Manchurian affair before the Council of the League of Nations by invoking Article 11 of the Covenant, he transformed what might have been merely a local conflict in the Far East into what became probably the most important international crisis since July, 1914. On September 22, 1931, the League Council adopted a resolution calling upon both China and Japan to withdraw their troops from the zone of conflict and to abstain from acts liable to aggravate the situation, and on the next day the United States sent identical notes of the same tenor to the two governments. Japanese military operations, however, still continued. On October 13 the United States government urged the League not to fail to exert all pressure and authority within its competence toward regulating the action of China and Japan, stated that, acting independently through its diplomatic representatives, it would endeavor to re-inforce what the League did, and offered to appoint an observer to sit with the League Council if invited to do so. Two days later the Council, with only the Japanese representative opposing, invited the United States to participate in its deliberations.

From the very outset Japan maintained that her military operations in Manchuria had no relation to anything but self-defense, and that she could not allow either their necessity or their appropriateness to be the subject of discussion.[7] When it came to a discussion of how the situation should be met, however, both Japan and China submitted what they considered should constitute the bases of a settlement. According to the former these were: (1) mutual repudiation of aggressive policy and conduct, (2) respect for China's territorial integrity, (3) complete suppression of all organized movements interfering with freedom of trade and stirring up international hatred, (4) effective protection throughout Manchuria of all peaceful pursuits undertaken by Japanese subjects, (5) respect for treaty rights of Japan in Manchuria. China, on the other hand, insisted that there must be: (1) no negotiations until the Japanese troops were withdrawn, (2) a neutral investigation during and after the withdrawal, (3) reparations for the damage committed, (4) establishment of a permanent board of arbitration and conciliation between China and Japan.

On the withdrawal of Japanese troops China and Japan were

[7] During the negotiations leading to the pact of Paris the American secretary of state, Frank B. Kellogg, had stated not only that the right of self-defense was inherent in every sovereign state and implicit in every treaty but that "every nation is free at all times and regardless of treaty provisions to defend its territories from attack and invasion, and it alone is competent to decide whether circumstances require recourse to war in self-defense." The United States Senate went even further by declaring that measures of self-defense might also involve military operations outside the territorial boundaries of the state.

diametrically opposed. China insisted that evacuation must precede any negotiations; Japan maintained that negotiation must precede and provide the bases for evacuation. The Council seemed to be more in sympathy with the Chinese viewpoint and on October 24 passed (Japan dissenting) a resolution calling upon Japan to evacuate the occupied territory in Manchuria by November 16, 1931, "on the basis of Chinese guarantees for the safety of Japanese nationals." On the ground that this resolution had not been adopted by a unanimous vote, however, Japan declined to recognize its validity, and continued her military operations in Manchuria.

On November 16 the Council once more convened, but, apparently as a concession to Senate isolationists in the United States, the American government declined to have an official observer sit with it. This change in policy appeared to indicate that the United States was faltering in its support of the League. During the ensuing three weeks futile efforts were made to draft a resolution which would reconcile the conflicting demands of the Chinese and Japanese governments. Finally, on December 10, the Council, acting on a proposal made by Japan, resolved to appoint a commission which should investigate the Sino-Japanese conflict in the Far East. This commission, which was composed of representatives of Great Britain, Italy, France, Germany, and the United States, with the British Earl of Lytton as chairman, soon became known as the Lytton Commission.

The Lytton Commission, with a group of expert advisers, spent several months visiting Japan, China, and Manchuria, and received extensive memoranda prepared by both the Japanese and the Chinese governments. In Manchuria, however, its investigations were gravely embarrassed by the fact that no one was allowed to come near it without a permit from the police. Thus, under the guise of protecting the members of the commission, Japan evidently sought to prevent it from obtaining first-hand information from those opposed to the new regime. The commission's report, completed and signed at Peiping on September 4, 1932, was rushed by airplane to the League Secretariat.

On October 2, 1932, the Lytton Report—a two-volume document of some 100,000 words—was published at Geneva. It consisted of an introduction and ten chapters, most of which were devoted to tracing the background and the course of the crisis. A number of conclusions were the result of its investigations: (1) no wish to separate from China had ever been expressed by the population of Manchuria; (2) to cut off Manchuria permanently from China would create a serious irredentist problem; (3) the maintenance and recognition of the existing regime in Manchuria would be in the interests of neither China nor Japan; (4) a Sino-Japanese conference, with the League standing behind to help, but keeping hands off as much as possible, should work out a new status; (5) Sino-Japanese relations as a whole were much more important to Japan than Manchuria alone; (6) the disruption of China—of which a separate Manchuria would be the beginning—would lead to bitter rivalries between many powers; (7) Japan required the good will of China and would find better, less costly security against Chinese nationalism in friendly co-operation and enforcement of treaties; (8) China needed the help of the whole world, especially Japan, and should curb its intolerant nationalism and co-operate with the latter; (9) the considerations producing the Washington treaties still held good. In view of these conclusions the commission recommended, among other things, that, although Japan's special interests must be recognized, Manchuria should be autonomous under Chinese sovereignty and should be policed only by gendarmerie. Japan did not question the conscientious nature of the report, but she argued that it was essentially superficial.

On December 6, 1932, a Special Assembly of the League of Nations met to consider the Sino-Japanese dispute, and before that body the Chinese and Japanese representatives presented the views of their respective governments. After considerable general discussion, the Assembly referred the dispute to a committee of nineteen with the request that it draw up a plan of settlement for submission to the Assembly at the earliest possible moment. This committee approved a resolution to serve as a basis of conciliation and communicated it—without publishing it—to the Chinese and Japanese governments. According to reports, the plan laid down as one of its basic points the nonrecognition of Manchukuo. Japan at once declared herself opposed to any plan of conciliation which condemned the setting up of the Manchukuo government.

The committee of nineteen therefore came to the conclusion that it could not formulate any plan which would be acceptable to both China and Japan, and proceeded to draw up a report on the dispute in accordance with Paragraph 4 of Article 16 of the League Covenant.[8] On February 14, 1933, the draft report was approved by the committee of nineteen; three days later it was broadcast to the world in a spectacular manner by radio. The first two sections once more discussed the general problem and dealt with events from September 18, 1931; the third listed twelve conclusions which were held to be justified by the preceding explanations; the last section contained four recommendations for settling the dispute. These provided in essence that the principles laid down by the Lytton Report should be executed through a committee which should supervise the subsequent Sino-Japanese negotiations. All League members were urged to continue nonrecognition of Manchukuo [9] and to refrain from any action liable to prejudice the situation.

On February 24 the League Assembly met to approve or reject the report of the committee of nineteen. Before the vote was taken, the Chinese and Japanese delegates addressed the Assembly, the former expressing gratification at the courageous verdict which the report contained, the latter announcing that the Japanese government disagreed with it and could not possibly accept it. When the rollcall on approving the report was finally taken, forty-two member states, including all the great powers, voted "Yes"; Japan alone voted "No." By this action the Assembly exonerated China of blame for the development of events, denied that Japan's military measures as a whole could be regarded as measures of self-defense, asserted that the sovereignty of Manchuria belonged to China and that the "Government of Manchukuo" was made possible only by the presence of Japanese troops, declared that the presence of Japanese troops outside the zone of the South Manchuria Railway was incompatible with the legal principles which should govern the settlement of the dispute, and recommended the evacuation of all Japanese troops outside the treaty zones. Never before had such a universal vote of censure been passed upon any sovereign state. Yosuke Matsuoka, the Japanese

[8] This article reads: "If the dispute is not thus settled, the Council either unanimously or by a majority vote shall make and publish a report containing a statement of the facts of the dispute and the recommendations which are deemed just and proper in regard thereto."

[9] On January 7, 1932, the United State secretary of state, Stimson, in identic notes to Japan and China had stated that the United States "does not intend to recognize any situation, treaty or agreement which may be brought about by means contrary to the covenants and obligations of the pact of Paris of August 27, 1928," and in March, 1932, the League Assembly had resolved that its members should not recognize any situation, treaty, or agreement which might be brought about by means contrary to the Covenant.

representative, thereupon read a brief statement in which he expressed profound regret at the vote which had just been taken and emphasized that Japan had "reached the limit of endeavors to co-operate with the League regarding the Sino-Japanese dispute." With firm step he then walked down the center aisle and withdrew from the Assembly, followed by the other members of the Japanese delegation. On March 27 the Japanese government gave notice of Japan's intention to withdraw from the League.

Doubtless a punitive war, conducted jointly by all of the great powers of the West, might eventually have crushed Japan, compelled her to observe her treaty obligations, and forced her to withdraw from Manchuria. But such a conflict would have been a costly struggle and would have entailed sacrifices far greater than the peoples of the West were willing to make. Possibly, had the great powers been able to suppress their economic rivalries long enough to subject Japan to the rigors of a general worldwide financial and commercial boycott, they might have compelled her to surrender her ill-gotten gains. Such a boycott, to be effective, however, would probably have necessitated in the end a resort to military and naval measures, and these would have led to war. But in the years 1931–1933 no Western people sufficiently resented Japan's conquest of Manchuria to be willing to wage war to prevent it, and no responsible statesman of the great powers went so far as to urge measures which might conceivably have precipitated such a war.

### Japan and Soviet Russia

Japan's occupation of Manchuria very definitely weakened Russia's position in the Far East by threatening her hold on Vladivostok and eastern Siberia. Early in 1933 the entire state railway system of Manchukuo was consolidated under the South Manchuria Railway administration, and construction was rushed on a new railway to connect Hailun, on a branch of the Chinese Eastern Railway, with Taheiho, which is just across the Amur River from Blagoveshchensk, the southern terminus of a branch line of the trans-Siberian railway. The completion of this Hailun-Taheiho Railway fundamentally altered the strategic situation in eastern Siberia and northern Manchuria, for it left the Russian maritime province and Vladivostok at the mercy of the Japanese. In case of a conflict with Russia the Japanese army, by utilizing this new line, could sever the trans-Siberian railway and block practically all traffic from Russia to Vladivostok.

In 1933 Russia offered to sell her half interest in the Chinese Eastern Railway to Manchukuo. Negotiations carried on in Tokyo
eventually led to an agreement in January, 1935, and in March the
Soviet interests in the railway were transferred. The railway, with its
name changed to North Manchuria Railway, became part of the

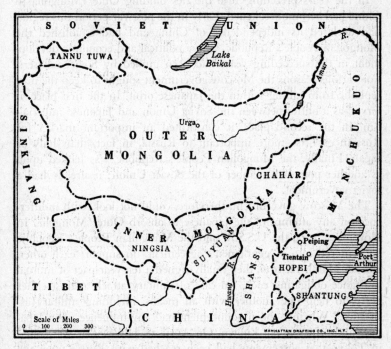

THE SCENE OF JAPAN'S AGGRESSION AFTER 1934

Manchurian railway system, which, in turn, is operated by the Japanese South Manchuria Railway Company. The Chinese government
refused to acknowledge the validity of the sale and filed a formal
protest with the powers.

Although the sale of the Chinese Eastern Railway removed one
possible cause for friction between Japan and Soviet Russia, the
winter of 1935–1936 saw renewed tension between the two countries
caused by clashes along the Manchukuan-Soviet border and along
the border between Manchukuo and Outer Mongolia. The Soviet

government seemed to be more concerned over the latter, for Soviet authorities were apparently convinced that, with Japanese hegemony being gradually extended over Inner Mongolia, Japanese imperialists envisaged eventual penetration into Outer Mongolia also. Uncertainty regarding the border between Outer Mongolia and Manchukuo served to complicate the situation.

In the years preceding 1936 the ties binding Outer Mongolia to China had become weakened. Early in the postwar period this region had declared its independence of China and had established the Mongolian People's Republic, whose political and economic development in the succeeding years had been guided by Soviet advisers. For various reasons the Moscow government sought to keep the new republic from falling within the Japanese orbit. In the first place, it served as a buffer between the Soviet Union and Japanese imperialism. In the second place, it constituted an important market for Russian exports—more important to Russia, in fact, than Italy or Japan. Finally, the Mongolian People's Republic was looked upon as another potential member of the Soviet Union; it already had a soviet government.

The Moscow government, therefore, could not look with indifference on any attempt of the Japanese to absorb Outer Mongolia. In November, 1934, the U.S.S.R. and the Mongolian People's Republic had entered into a "gentlemen's agreement" to support each other, and on March 12, 1936, they finally signed a ten-year pact of mutual assistance obligating each, "in case of military attack against either party, to help one another with all means, including military assistance." Whether the announcement had any influence upon Japanese authorities is not known. On April 28, however, it was stated in Tokyo that agreements had been reached with Russia upon the appointment of two commissions to investigate and settle border disputes and to resurvey and demarcate the international boundary between Manchukuo and the Soviet Union. The Soviet government desired also the appointment of a commission to adjudicate similarly boundary disputes and clashes on the line between Outer Mongolia and Manchukuo, but the Japanese secured a postponement of consideration of these matters.

After 1932, by double-tracking the trans-Siberian railway from Chita east to the Pacific, by rushing construction on a new railway paralleling the trans-Siberian line on the north, by pushing motor-road construction in the maritime province of Siberia, by building local factories for supplying its troops with war materials, and by increasing its air and submarine forces at Vladivostok, the Soviet government sought to strengthen itself for the defense of its own territorial integrity in the Far East. In the summer of 1937 serious border clashes again occurred on the Amur River, the boundary between Siberia and Manchukuo.

## JAPAN'S ADVANCE INTO NORTH CHINA

Meanwhile, Japan continued to strengthen her dominant position in the Far East and to announce with ever-increasing clearness and decision her thesis "that Japan, serving as only a cornerstone for the edifice of peace in eastern Asia, bears the entire burden of responsibilities." In April, 1934, the Japanese foreign office emphasized this viewpoint once more when it announced that the activities of the League of Nations for the rehabilitation of China, American loans to China, and the presence of foreigners as instructors in the Chinese army were considered by the Japanese government as tending to support in China a resistance to Japan which threatened the peace of Asia. All of these measures, it was declared, were objectionable to Japan, and, if they were continued and supported by force, then "Japan herself may be compelled to resort to force." It seemed clear that Japan was determined to assert her exclusive right to control China in the interests of Japanese security and Japanese economic penetration. Her interest in and control of China seemed to be indicated in the latter's new tariff schedules, which became effective in July, 1934, for rates on goods imported for the most part from the West were raised, while those on goods imported from Japan were lowered.

During 1935 Japan began to encroach upon several of the northern provinces of China. In consequence of demands made upon the Nanking government, the governors of Hopei and Chahar provinces were removed, all branch offices of the Nationalist Party in North China were closed, all anti-Japanese organizations in Chahar were abolished, troops of the Nanking government were withdrawn from Hopei province and from the Chahar-Jehol frontier, and a new mayor, police commissioner, and garrison commander—all acceptable to the Japanese—were installed in Tientsin. On November 25 eighteen counties in and near the demilitarized zone along the Great Wall declared their independence and set up an autonomous state under Yin Ju-keng, the pro-Japanese administrative commissioner of the demilitarized zone. In the following month the Nanking government agreed to the establishment of a semi-independent regime in Hopei and Chahar provinces, which include Peiping, the old Chinese capital, and Tientsin, North China's commercial city. The newly organized government, called the Hopei-Chahar Political Council, had as its head General Sung Cheh-yuan, a North China military leader, and consisted chiefly of pro-Japanese members. During 1936 this council permitted the smuggling of Japanese goods into North China upon payment of only one eighth of the national tariff dues, and agreed to the principle of joint Sino-Japanese economic development of that region. Late in 1936 troops from Manchukuo and Chahar attempted to extend the area of Japanese domination by an invasion of Suiyan province.

Despite the measures taken by the Nanking government to guard against the possibility of popular opposition to its policy of capitulation, a strong nationalist and anti-Japanese sentiment developed in 1936 in China, thanks largely to the activities of Chinese students. So strong did this nationalist movement become that even the semi-independent Canton government in South China demanded that the government in Nanking should resist Japanese aggression with armed force. Of China's important military leaders, Chiang Kai-shek alone appeared to remain opposed to the adoption of a strong anti-Japanese program. Possibly he believed that no effective resistance could be offered to Japan until China was thoroughly united and militarily prepared. Whatever his motives, however, an emergency law was issued in 1936 by the Nanking government authorizing Chinese troops and police to use force or any other effective means to dissolve meetings and parades, to suppress anti-Japanese propaganda, and to punish those who aided violators of these provisions.

During 1936 some progress was made in unifying China when the rebellious provinces of Kwantung and Kwangsi were brought to recognize again the Nationalist government at Nanking. Nevertheless, in December it was revealed that the latter had again accepted further Japanese demands: to suppress anti-Japanese movements, to engage Japanese advisers, and to reduce Chinese tariffs. In that month Nanking ordered twelve of the provincial governments to inaugurate an anti-Communist campaign in accordance with the Japanese desire to check the growing strength of the Communist forces in the northwest provinces of China. General Chiang himself proceeded to Shensi province because he was dissatisfied with General Chang Hsueh-liang's conduct of the campaign against the Communists. But on December 12 by a sudden *coup d'état* Chang Hsueh-liang captured General Chiang and held him a prisoner at Sian, the capital of Shensi. As conditions for release he demanded a declaration of war against Japan, the Nanking government's promise to recover all lost territories, and the readmission of Chinese Communists to the Nationalist Party.

Although much about the coup still remains a mystery, after a detention of two weeks Chiang Kai-shek was released, and he returned to Nanking bringing General Chang as a prisoner. In January, 1937, however, the latter received a full pardon for his part in the rebellion, and later in the month an agreement between the rebellious Shensi forces and the Nanking government permitted occupation of northern Shensi by Communist troops. During the succeeding months negotiations were carried on between the Nanking government and the Communist leaders. The latter declared their willingness to modify their social program and to place their armies under Chiang Kai-shek's command, if the Nationalist government would adopt an anti-Japanese policy and introduce a more democratic regime in China.

During the first half of 1937 the Nanking government, with the whole of China united at least temporarily by a wave of nationalism, sought increasingly to assert its influence over North China officials. It also interfered with the Japanese-protected smuggling into North China, and it even ordered the suspension of a new Tientsin-Tokyo air line which had been established without Chinese consent. Undoubtedly the strong anti-Japanese sentiment in China and the apparently growing military strength of the latter were disturbing to Japanese military leaders, who planned to establish a pro-Japanese regime in China's five northern provinces.

On July 7, 1937, a clash occurred a short distance west of Peiping between Japanese troops and units of the Chinese army. After some diplomatic temporizing by both the Chinese and the Japanese, the latter on July 19 demanded (1) the withdrawal of the Chinese army from its position west of Peiping, (2) the punishment of the Chinese responsible for the clash, (3) the suppression of all anti-Japanese activities in North China, and (4) the enforcement of measures against communism. Chinese acceptance of these demands would obviously go far toward giving the Japanese that ascendancy which they sought in North China. The Nanking government refused to accept the Japanese demands.

Late in July, following an ultimatum, Japanese troops began an advance in the coveted northern provinces. Within a few days the eastern part of Hopei province, including Tientsin, Peiping, and the area between the latter and the sea, had been effectively occupied, and provisional governments favorable to Japan had been established. In August Japanese troops moved southward in Hopei province and northwestward toward Chahar. In Japan there was every indication that preparations were being made for war on a large scale. In China the Nanking government called for resistance to Japanese aggression, and Chiang Kai-shek announced that China would surrender no more territory "even though this means fighting inadequately and to the death." Chinese troops were rushed northward toward the area of hostilities.

But the fighting was not confined to North China. The killing of two Japanese naval men by Chinese in Shanghai on August 10 was the signal for the dispatch of a fleet of Japanese warships and the landing of Japanese marines. The latter took up positions within the International Settlement. The Chinese in turn moved some of their finest German-trained soldiers into the vicinity of the International Settlement, and hostilities soon began. The Japanese utilized their airplanes, warships, and troops in an effort to drive the Chinese back from the city, and the Chinese with their airplanes attempted to bombard Japanese positions. Thousands of civilians in the crowded city of Shanghai were killed or wounded, including a number of foreigners. Neutral powers protested and began the evacuation of their nationals from the area of fighting.

When Great Britain, France, and the United States requested the suspension of hostilities in the Shanghai area, Japan declared that fighting there could not be brought to an end except by the withdrawal of the Chinese troops. Since the Chinese refused to withdraw, hostilities continued, and the undeclared Sino-Japanese war was thereafter waged on two fronts. To handicap the Chinese, Japan ordered a blockade of all Chinese shipping on the Chinese coast, exempting from the blockade only British Hong Kong, Portuguese Macao, and French Kwangchowan. Such a blockade not only cut off supplies from China but deprived the Nanking government of a large part of the revenue which it normally derived from customs payments.

While the Japanese forces around Shanghai slowly battled their way forward to victory during the next two months, significant gains were also made in North China by Japan's armies, which were engaged in operations to extend their zone of occupation. A drive to the northwest was temporarily halted by the Chinese in an eleven-day battle at Nankow Pass, but eventually the pass was taken, and the Japanese moved on to Kalgan, the capital of Chahar. From this province the invading forces then pushed westward, and in October they captured Kweisui, the capital of Suiyuan province. Other Japanese armies, driving south from Peiping and Tientsin, forced the Chinese to retreat in a battle near Chowchow and later routed them in another battle near Shihkiachwang. By the middle of October the Japanese had captured most of Hopei province and had made important gains in Shantung, Shansi, Suiyuan, and Chahar provinces. They were, in fact, well on their way to control of the five provinces north of the Yellow River. The Japanese-dominated administration of Peiping thereupon decided to change the name of that city back to Peking.

As in 1931, the Chinese government in 1937 appealed to the League of Nations against Japan. When the Assembly convened in September, China's appeal was referred to the League's Far Eastern advisory committee, which unanimously condemned Japan as an invader and a treaty-breaker. It recommended that the Assembly should invite those members of the League which were signatories of the Washington nine-power treaty to meet as soon as possible to initiate consultation regarding the agreement to respect China's sovereignty, independence, and territorial integrity. On October 6 the League Assembly adopted the advisory committee's resolution, expressed its moral support for China, and recommended that League members should refrain from taking any action which might weaken China's power of resistance and should consider how they could individually extend aid to her. On the same day the United States government announced that its conclusions were "in general accord with those of the Assembly of the League of Nations."

Upon the League's invitation the representatives of nineteen nations convened at Brussels on November 3, 1937, to consider what might be done under the nine-power treaties to safeguard peace in the Far East. Japan declined to be represented at the meeting, however, and insisted that China was responsible for the existing conflict, that China, not Japan, was "violating the spirit of the pact against war." Japan further maintained that "the most just and equitable solution" could be reached through direct negotiations between herself and China. The delegates thereupon adopted a declaration expressing regret over Japan's refusal to participate in the conference, and characterizing Japan's military action in China as illegal. China's appeal for the withholding of war materials and credits to Japan went unheeded. Late in November, just before adjourning indefinitely, the conference admitted that for the time being it could do nothing to re-establish peace. No group of states was willing to pay the price in life or wealth which would be necessary to save China from the invading armies of the Japanese.

In September, 1938, China appealed to the League of Nations for assistance under the terms of Article 17 of the Covenant. The Council thereupon decided that Japan's invasion of China was a violation of the Briand-Kellogg treaty and of the nine-power treaty of 1922. It further decided that Article 16 regarding sanctions became applicable, but held that the time was not suitable for collective action. The net result of China's appeal was the Council's invitation to members of the League individually to support China. Once again collective security had been proved to be a broken reed.

# PART SEVEN

# THE SECOND WORLD WAR

Although the great mass of the people of Europe had emerged from the First World War fervently hoping that the new international order which the League of Nations was to establish would forever banish war from the face of the earth, by 1938 it seemed clear that forces were once more operating in Europe which would plunge that continent, and part of the outside world with it, into another great war. International crises followed one another with monotonous regularity as the tension between the powers constantly increased. In August, 1939, international relations were finally strained to the breaking point, and the nations plunged into the Second World War.

## CHAPTER XXIX

# THE IMMEDIATE BACKGROUND OF THE WAR

IT is well known now that the First World War was not caused primarily by the assassination of the Austrian archduke at Sarajevo. Similarly, the war into which Europe plunged in September, 1939, did not arise merely from Poland's refusal to accede to Hitler's demand for Danzig and a corridor to East Prussia. The causes of the Second World War were deeper-lying and more profound; they were not greatly different from those which have been pointed out[1] as the fundamental causes of the First World War.

## THE CONTINUING CAUSES OF WAR

Perhaps foremost among the causes which precipitated the war which finally plunged Europe into another blood bath in September, 1939, was German nationalism—the desire to incorporate in the Reich the German-speaking peoples of Europe, particularly those in Austria, the Sudetenland of Czechoslovakia, Polish Upper Silesia, Danzig, the Polish Corridor, and Memel. But nationalism was a force to a less extent in some of the other countries of Europe, also. Italian Fascisti occasionally murmured of a new *Italia Irredenta*—Corsica, Nice, and even Savoy, and Communist leaders in Soviet Russia recalled that millions of White Russians and Little Russians (Ukrainians) had been conquered by Poland in 1920. It was likewise a factor in Hungary and Bulgaria, which wished to regain territories and peoples lost in the years from 1913 to 1920. The nationalism of these lesser states might lead them to take advantage of a crisis or war among the great powers if by so doing they could gain their nationalistic aims, but it seemed extremely doubtful that either would move alone.

A second dynamic cause of the new war was imperialism. In Germany the Nazis never ceased demanding the return of the colonies lost at the close of the World War. But more important than this was

[1] See pages 361–367.

the fact that under the inspiration of Hitler they came to advocate a program for the Reich which was similar to that of the Pan-Germans before 1914.[2] They were eager to create a *Mittel-Europa* and to execute a *Drang nach Osten*. In fact, Hitler even urged Germany's need to acquire the fertile Russian Ukraine as part of the Reich's *Lebensraum* (living space). Soviet leaders, on the other hand, cast covetous eyes on the small Baltic republics and southern Finland, whose territories dominated the Gulf of Finland and threatened the security of Leningrad; nor had they forgotten Russia's historic mission to push through the Balkans to the Mediterranean. Italian imperialists, bitterly disappointed with the colonial realm which their country had received by the peace treaties of 1919–1920, hoped to strengthen their hold upon Albania across the Adriatic, and to obtain French Tunisia, where many Italians dwelt, the French port of Jibuti, which was the terminus of the only railway connecting Ethiopia with the outside world, and a place on the board of directors of the Suez Canal. Ultimately, they hoped some day to destroy completely Great Britain's control of the Mediterranean so that Italy should cease to be a "prisoner in her own sea."

Out of such territorial ambitions there arose, as before the World War, a number of entangling alliances. The various attempts to obtain security, made chiefly by the countries possessing the territories coveted by the unsatiated powers, have already been discussed.[3] It was more or less natural, too, that some of the "have not" powers should likewise come together in mutual agreements. At the close of 1935, it will be recalled, as the result of various acts and policies of the Nazi government, Germany stood practically isolated among the great powers of Europe. Russia, prior to 1933 inclined to be friendly with Germany, had been alarmed by Hitler's undisguised desire for eastern expansion and had united with France in a defensive military alliance against the Third Reich. Italy, as one of the unsatiated powers, had tended before 1933 to support Germany in the latter's demands for treaty revision, but the Nazi attempt to absorb Austria in 1934 had alienated Mussolini and facilitated a Franco-Italian *rapprochement*. Even Great Britain, disturbed by Germany's rearmament program, had been forced into what was practically a defensive Anglo-Franco-Belgian alliance against the Reich.

[2] See pages 82–83.
[3] See pages 564–570, 578–584.

During 1936, however, Hitler took steps to remove Germany from her state of isolation. In his endeavors he was aided by the complicated international situation in Europe resulting from Italy's invasion of Ethiopia and the outbreak in July of civil war in Spain. The imposition of sanctions in connection with the former drove a wedge between Italy on the one hand and Great Britain and France on the other, while Mussolini could hardly help being grateful for the indirect aid which came to him in a critical situation from Hitler's remilitarizing the Rhineland. The Spanish civil war further facilitated a *rapprochement* between Italy and Germany, both of which actively supported General Franco.

Hitler was not slow to take advantage of the international situation to advance his own plan for co-operation between the two fascist states. In that year what was popularly referred to as the Rome-Berlin Axis was created when Italy and Germany reached a number of agreements in matters of foreign policy.[4] And when, in 1937, Italy adhered to the anti-Communist pact which Germany and Japan had signed on November 25, 1936,[5] three of the important totalitarian and unsatiated states were brought together in the so-called Rome-Berlin-Tokyo Axis.

Evidence of the spirit of co-operation which developed among these authoritarian states was forthcoming on several occasions. Italy's adhesion to the Rome-Berlin Axis was confirmed in 1937 by the Duce's statement that Italy could not give military assistance to protect Austria against a German attempt to consummate the *Anschluss*, by Mussolini's visit to Germany as Hitler's guest in September of that year, and by Italy's announcement of her withdrawal from the League of Nations in the following December. The cordial relations between the two Western powers and Japan were confirmed by Italy's recognition of Manchukuo as an independent state in November, 1937, and by Germany's similar action on May 12, 1938. Further evidence of the operation of the Rome-Berlin-Tokyo Axis seemed indicated in 1938 by Hitler's order that all German military advisers to the Nationalist government in China should leave that country. Thus it is evident that by 1938 the great powers, as in 1914, were once more coming to be divided into two increasingly antagonistic groups.

It has frequently been pointed out that the existence of huge

[4] See page 582.
[5] See page 582.

national armaments was one of the fundamental causes of the World War.[6] But in the years from 1936 to 1939 military and naval budgets rose far above those of the prewar days. The unsatiated powers strained themselves to the utmost to create more powerful navies and larger armies in order that they might strike effectively if occasion should arise. In the Reich Germans were told that there must be "cannon before butter." In Italy Mussolini impregnated his people with a militaristic spirit by his speeches, and kept the national budget unbalanced by his heavy expenditures on the country's military, naval, and air forces. In the Soviet Union the rate of improvement in the general standard of living, as outlined in the Five-Year Plans, was checked after 1936 because of the increased emphasis upon military and naval armaments. And although France and Great Britain, unfortunately for them, did not direct their energies and resources to the increase of armaments with the same fanatical zeal as did the Reich, nevertheless these years saw tremendous increases in military expenditures even in these states. By 1938 millions of men were being kept under arms by the European powers. Thousands of tanks were being built to facilitate the invasion of enemy territory, and other thousands of military airplanes were being rushed to completion that they might be ready to shower destruction from the skies. As in the days before 1914, the vicious circle of increased armaments and increased national fear again operated to undermine the peace of Europe.

Finally, if the nations of the world were living in a state of "international anarchy" in 1914, it was little less true in 1938. Although in the years after 1920 practically all states had pledged themselves not to resort to war as an instrument of national policy but to settle international disputes by recourse to some pacific means, these pledges had not been kept. Japan ignored them when she conquered Manchuria in 1931 and invaded China in 1937,[7] and received censure but no punishment from the League of Nations. Germany by unilateral action broke not only the "dictated" treaty of Versailles but the voluntarily negotiated Locarno treaties when she remilitarized the Rhineland in 1936,[8] and she, too, received nothing but censure. Italy de-

[6] See pages 364–365.
[7] See pages 844–852, 857–860.
[8] See page 686.

liberately launched an imperialistic war against Ethiopia in 1935 [9] and, thanks in part to Hitler's remilitarization of the Rhineland, carried it through to a successful conquest despite the League's half-hearted imposition of sanctions. One by one the unsatiated powers, as they broke their pledges, withdrew from the League of Nations, until by 1938 only three great states—France, Britain, and Russia— still remained in the League. As in 1914, so in 1938 there were "sovereign" states which refused to recognize any authority higher than their own will and their own interests. One of these was Hitler's Third Reich.

### Hitler's "Drang nach Osten"

In Germany, although the merciless purge of June, 1934, had eliminated one Left group which had threatened to embarrass the Führer, in the succeeding years another Left group—with which apparently Hitler was this time largely in sympathy—had developed. Led by Heinrich Himmler, chief of the *Schutzstaffeln* and of the *Gestapo,* Joseph Goebbels, minister of propaganda, and Joachim von Ribbentrop, German ambassador to Great Britain, this Left group advocated a more revolutionary policy both at home and abroad. They favored the pursuit of more active policies in behalf of the Germans in Austria and Czechoslovakia, urged that more help be given General Franco in Spain, and wished to see the Rome-Berlin Axis and the anti-Communist pact more forcefully implemented. In internal affairs the Leftists wanted an intensification of the anti-Jewish campaign and the extension of the control of the Nazi Party over the army.

Most of these policies the Right group—supported by the conservatives of the general staff and of the foreign office and by the great industrial and financial leaders—strongly opposed. Furthermore, the military looked upon Field Marshal von Blomberg, the war minister, as a political soldier, too closely associated with the Nazi Party to be good for the army. A clash between Hitler and the conservative army leaders was precipitated when General von Fritsch, the commander-in-chief, demanded that the war minister be retired because, contrary to the army traditions of "caste and class," he had married the daughter of a humble carpenter. At the same time Fritsch made other demands—that the army should have a status above politics, that it

[9] See pages 642–649.

should not be subjected to the Nazi anti-Christian doctrines, and that the government should restrict its "activist" foreign policy. Thus the question was raised: was the army to be under the control of the Nazi Party or was it to stand above domestic politics?

Although the military were strong enough to force the removal of Field Marshal von Blomberg, Hitler struck back. On February 4, 1938, he suddenly dismissed General von Fritsch and thirteen senior generals in the army and air force, and announced that he himself had assumed "personal and direct command over all the armed forces." At the same time he removed from the foreign ministry Baron von Neurath, who had held that position since before the Nazis came into power, and appointed in his place the 100 per cent Nazi, Joachim von Ribbentrop. The "conservative" ambassadors to Italy, Japan, and Austria were also recalled. By this purge it appeared that Hitler had definitely strengthened the Nazi control of the Reich's army and foreign policy.

### GERMANY'S ABSORPTION OF AUSTRIA

Evidence that the Left group was in control was soon forthcoming. Although in July, 1936, an Austro-German agreement had been reached in which Germany had reaffirmed her recognition of Austria's independence and had promised not to interfere in the little republic's internal affairs, Hitler now apparently believed that the time had come when he could safely disregard this treaty. Italy, involved in Ethiopia and in Spain, was in no position to break with her partner in the Rome-Berlin Axis. France appeared to be in a weakened condition internationally because of her domestic difficulties, and Great Britain under Chamberlain's guidance [10] was thought to look with some tolerance upon Germany's desire to absorb Austria.

[10] The conduct of British foreign policy occasioned a cabinet crisis in Great Britain in February, 1938. Prime Minister Chamberlain and a majority of the cabinet wished to attempt to negotiate with Italy and Germany in order to discover "whether there was any common ground on which we might build up a general scheme of appeasement in Europe." Foreign Secretary Eden, on the other hand, believed that it was time for Great Britain to stand firm rather than to undertake negotiations under an implied threat of pressure from abroad. He considered that there had lately been too keen a desire on the part of the British government to make terms with others rather than that others should make terms with Britain. He did not believe that progress could be made in European appeasement "if we allow the impression to gain currency abroad that we yield to constant pressure." Consequently he resigned on February 20, and was succeeded as foreign secretary by Viscount Halifax.

The first step in Hitler's program came on February 12, 1938, when an interview between the Austrian Chancellor Schuschnigg and Hitler occurred at the latter's Bavarian mountain chalet at Berchtesgaden. As the result of the Führer's threats, Schuschnigg was forced to agree to admit members of the Austrian Nazi Party into his government. Four days later a new cabinet was organized in Vienna with Arthur Seyss-Inquart, the Austrian Nazi leader, as minister of the interior, and with other Nazis as ministers of justice and of foreign affairs.

While the Austrian Nazis speedily took advantage of their new position and freedom to urge and work for the early consummation of the *Anschluss,* many Austrians hastened to proclaim their loyalty to an independent Austria. Schuschnigg still hoped to maintain the republic's independence and on March 9 suddenly announced that a plebiscite on the question would be held in Austria four days later. Evidently he believed that the interval before election would be too short for the Nazis to mobilize their high-pressure speakers and terroristic methods effectively, and that the subsequent vote would prove to the world that the majority of Austrians had no desire to be absorbed by Germany.

But Hitler and the Austrian Nazis were determined that no plebiscite should be held under such conditions. Nazi riots against the vote at once began to occur. Then, on March 11, Seyss-Inquart presented Schuschnigg with an ultimatum demanding his resignation and the postponement of the plebiscite, threatening that otherwise German troops, already mobilized on the border, would invade Austria. Confronted by this situation, Schuschnigg, "in order to save bloodshed," canceled the plebiscite and resigned. Seyss-Inquart was thereupon appointed head of the new cabinet, which at once invited the German government to send troops into Austria "to preserve order."

On March 12 Hitler returned to Linz, his former home in Austria. On the next day the German government issued a law declaring Austria to be a state of the German Reich. President Miklas resigned, and Chancellor Schuschnigg was placed under arrest. On March 14 Hitler arrived in Vienna, preceded by German mechanized and air forces, and was given an enthusiastic reception. "All Germany is living through this hour of victory—seventy-four millions in one united Reich," he shouted. "No threats, no hardships, no force can make us break our oath to be united forever." Although France and Great

Britain lodged formal protests with Berlin, no state raised a hand in defense of Austria's sovereignty. A particularly marked contrast with the swift mobilization of Italian troops on the Brenner Pass in 1934 [11] was Italy's immobility in March, 1938.

To many it appeared that Hitler's swift consummation of the *Anschluss* had taken Mussolini by surprise. On this assumption, what seemed like a British attempt to further weaken the Rome-Berlin Axis came on April 16, 1938, when Italy and Great Britain signed a number of agreements regarding the *status quo* of the Mediterranean and Red Seas and the Suez Canal. In addition Italy agreed to Great Britain's formula [12] for the proportional evacuation of the foreign volunteers from Spain, promised that all Italian volunteers would be removed from Spanish territory at the close of the civil war, and disclaimed any territorial or political aims or desire for a privileged economic position anywhere in Spanish territory. Great Britain, on the other hand, promised to take steps in the League Council to free states that were members of the League from their obligation not to recognize Italian sovereignty over Ethiopia. Nevertheless, despite this apparent Anglo-Italian *rapprochement,* Hitler's visit to Italy as Mussolini's guest in May, 1938, indicated the continuance of the Rome-Berlin Axis.

During 1938, in view of Germany's absorption of Austria and her subsequent press and diplomatic campaign against Czechoslovakia, the lesser powers of central and southeastern Europe sought to put their relations with their neighbors on a friendly basis in order to check the *Drang nach Osten*. On July 31 the Balkan Entente permitted Bulgaria to rearm and to remilitarize her frontiers with Greece and Turkey in return for Bulgaria's pledge of nonaggression against the countries of the Balkan Entente. A few weeks later the Little Entente permitted Hungary to rearm in return for a similar pledge. While these lesser states were thus promising to live in good neighborliness together, Hitler in August, 1938, openly courted the favor of Hungary by having Admiral Horthy make a state visit to Berlin. During this period, too, Great Britain was drawn more and more into alignment with France. On April 28 and 29 the premiers and foreign ministers of the two states conferred in London, and decided to continue the contacts between their general staffs as arranged for in 1936.

[11] See page 772.
[12] See page 744.

They also agreed upon further co-ordination between the defense forces of the two countries, the details to be worked out by experts. In July the cordial and close relations existing between the two countries were emphasized by the state visit which the British king and queen made to the President of France.

The absorption of Austria greatly strengthened Germany's position in central Europe and at the same time advanced her *Drang nach Osten*. She was now in direct contact with Italy at the Brenner Pass and also in direct touch with Yugoslavia and Hungary. Furthermore, domination in Austria gave the Third Reich military and economic control of practically all the communications of southeastern Europe. Czechoslovakia was almost isolated. Her trade outlets through Germany were at the mercy of the latter, and her communications by rail and river to the south and southeast could be severed almost at will. It is not surprising, with Czechoslovakia's position thus weakened, that the Nazis of Germany next turned their attention to "alleviating the wrongs" suffered by their 3,500,000 kinsmen in Czechoslovakia.

### GERMANY'S ANNEXATION OF THE SUDETENLAND

It has already been pointed out [13] that the Nazi movement had entered Czechoslovakia, where it was organized politically as the Sudeten German (*Sudetendeutsch*) Party under the leadership of Konrad Henlein. From 1935 on the latter had denounced the government at Prague for its treatment of minorities and had accused it of denying to the Germans their rightful economic and cultural opportunities. After Hitler's success in Austria the Sudeten German leader called on all Germans in Czechoslovakia "to join the great political front of our people's party." The party, it was announced, would admit new members until May 31, 1938, and there was the thinly veiled threat that after that it would be too late to "get in" on the winning side. The intensive propaganda campaign soon bore fruit. On March 22 the German Agrarian Party withdrew its representative from the cabinet and joined the Sudeten German Party; two days later the German Clericals did the same; on March 26 the German Social Democrats withdrew their representative but did not join the Sudeten German Party. Henlein thereupon announced that

[13] See page 784.

the Social Democrats could no longer be included in the German race group.

On April 23 at the Sudeten German Party congress at Karlsbad Henlein announced an eight-point program: (1) equality of status for Germans and Czechs; (2) recognition of the Sudeten Germans as a legal body incorporate; (3) legal recognition of the German areas within the state; (4) full self-government for the German areas; (5) legal protection for citizens living outside the area of their own nationality; (6) removal of injustices inflicted since 1918 and reparation therefor; (7) recognition of the principle that within the German area there must be German officials; (8) full liberty to profess German nationality and political philosophy. The fulfillment of the third, fourth, and eighth points seemed to make possible the establishment within a democratic republic of a totalitarian state taking its orders from a foreign ruler. This the Czechoslovak government was unwilling to consider.

In May the tension both in Czechoslovakia and in Europe reached a high point when elections were held in some 11,000 communities of the republic. Preceding the elections a vigorous campaign against Czechoslovakia was waged in the German press, and it was feared by many that the Nazi government might avail itself of some of the clashes between rival nationals in connection with the elections to go to the aid of the Germans in Czechoslovakia. On May 19 there were rumors of German troop movements near the border, and the Czechoslovak general staff countered these by making military dispositions along the German frontier.

Although the French government urged Czechoslovakia to go to the limit of concession to the Sudeten Germans, it left no doubt that France would fulfill her military obligations if Czechoslovakia were attacked. Russia also stated her readiness to go to the aid of the Czechs, should the need arise. The British government kept in constant touch with Paris and sought to bring pressure at both Berlin and Prague in favor of peace. The Nazi government informed Great Britain that the stories of German troop movements were unfounded, and subsequently the German press accused Great Britain of seeking to pose as saving the peace of Europe, which had not in fact been threatened by Germany. However that may be, the elections passed off without the feared German intervention.

Meanwhile, the Czechoslovak government had approved a nationalities statute, had communicated its provisions in confidence to Henlein, and had formally invited the latter to negotiate regarding it. The government proposed a substantial increase of local autonomy for communes, districts, and even regions in matters such as education, social work, and communications, with local elected diets in which the minority elements would have their own representatives. The statute did not, however, provide for autonomy for the Sudeten areas as such. On June 7 the Sudeten German Party, in turn, submitted its demands, which were somewhat more detailed than the previously announced eight-point program. A rather wide gap separated the two sets of proposals.

In July the British government asked Premier Hodža whether the Czechoslovak government would accept a British adviser in the dispute with the Sudeten German Party, and was informed that it would do so. Lord Runciman was then appointed as such an adviser, and both President Beneš and Premier Hodža stated that Czechoslovakia was prepared to go to the full limit of Lord Runciman's advice, provided the sovereignty of the state was protected. On August 3 Lord Runciman arrived in Prague to assist in the negotiations between the Czechoslovak government and the leaders of the Sudeten German Party.

During August the international tension greatly increased. The German government arranged for fall maneuvers of its armed forces, with the result that fighting men variously estimated at between 1,350,000 and 1,500,000 would be ready for action when the annual congress of the Nazi Party was held in Nuremberg in September. Shortly before the congress opened, Hitler made an ostentatious inspection of the fortifications of the West Wall or Siegfried Line, which had been constructed along the Rhine from Switzerland to the Netherlands by the labor of hundreds of thousands of men working under pressure since the German-Czech crisis of the preceding May. By many it was believed that these gigantic fortifications were designed to halt France in the west while Germany pursued her *Drang nach Osten* at Czechoslovakia's expense.

France and Great Britain also took steps to strengthen their positions in case of a war. French reserves were moved up to man the powerful Maginot Line, which had been built along the German frontier between 1929 and 1936, and Great Britain concentrated forty warships—her biggest Home Fleet since the World War—at the

North Sea base of Invergordon for autumn maneuvers at the time when the Nazi congress would be in session. It was evidently feared in many quarters that the prolonged international crisis might be brought to the breaking point at the time of the Nuremberg congress.

In this strained atmosphere negotiations were meanwhile being carried on between the Czechoslovak government and the Sudeten German leaders. One by one the proposals made by the government were rejected by Henlein and his associates after conferences with Hitler. It became perfectly obvious that fundamentally the negotiations were between the Führer and the Czechoslovak government. On September 7 the latter offered a fourth plan, which was said to constitute the limit of possible concessions, and which, according to Lord Runciman, granted practically everything in the Karlsbad program of the Sudeten Germans.

The world awaited with considerable concern what Hitler would say in reply to these proposals when, on September 12, he made his final address to the hundreds of thousands gathered at the Nazi congress. In an impassioned speech the Führer then demanded the "right of self-determination" for the Sudeten Germans of Czechoslovakia, and announced that if the latter could not defend themselves, "they will receive help from us." The German Nazis, he declared, "will not remain indifferent for long if these tortured and oppressed creatures cannot defend themselves."

Immediately after Hitler's address the Sudeten Germans, as though operated by a push-button from Nuremberg, began demonstrating in favor of union with Germany. Riots and clashes with the Czechoslovak gendarmerie ensued, and a number of casualties occurred. These incidents were at once seized upon and exaggerated by the German press, which denounced the Czechoslovak government for its brutal oppression of the Sudeten Germans. A campaign of bitter vilification was also launched against President Beneš. On September 13 the Sudeten leaders broke off negotiations with the Czechoslovak government on the basis of the latter's fourth proposal, and on the next day Henlein announced that even the Karlsbad points were no longer satisfactory to the Germans. Declaring Sudetens and Czechs could no longer live in the same state, he hastily fled to Germany, where he at once began to organize a "Sudeten Free Corps." Events seemed to indicate that a situation was being created to provide an opportunity for German troops to invade Czechoslovakia in order to protect the "tortured and oppressed" Germans living in that republic. Such an invasion would place upon France and Russia the obligation to go to the aid of Czechoslovakia and so might precipitate a general European war.

In this highly critical situation Prime Minister Chamberlain of Great Britain decided upon an unprecedented step. Desiring to ascertain whether Hitler was correctly informed of the British attitude and whether there was any possibility of saving the peace, he asked the German Führer for a personal interview. Hitler was willing to hold such a conference, and so on September 15 Chamberlain, with the approval of France, flew to Munich and proceeded to the mountain chalet at Berchtesgaden where the fateful interview between Hitler and Schuschnigg had occurred seven months earlier. Here Chamberlain learned that Hitler had decided that the Sudeten Germans should have the right to unite with the Reich, if they wished, and that he would aid them if necessary even at the risk of a general European war.

Upon the prime minister's return to London he met with the British cabinet and also with Premier Daladier [14] and Foreign Minister Bonnet of France, who came from Paris to London for the conference. It was decided, in accordance with Lord Runciman's conclusions, that the only way to avoid a general European war was to accept the principle of self-determination. On September 19 Great Britain and France therefore asked Czechoslovakia to agree to the immediate transfer to the Reich of areas inhabited by a population more than 50 per cent German. The proposals envisaged the adjustment of frontiers by an international body including a Czech representative. It was further proposed that Czechoslovakia's future independence should be safeguarded by a general guarantee against unprovoked aggression, and Great Britain stated her willingness to join in such a guarantee.

When Czechoslovakia suggested that the matter be submitted to arbitration, Great Britain declared that she must accept or reject the Anglo-French proposals at once. Faced by this necessity, the Czechoslovak government on September 21 accepted the proposals. So great was the dissatisfaction with this step in Czechoslovakia, however,

[14] Early in 1938 the Popular Front government, which had taken office in France in 1936, disintegrated, and on April 10 Edouard Daladier had become premier in a government consisting of Radical Socialists and representatives of certain moderate center groups.

that the Hodža ministry felt compelled to resign. It was succeeded by a government of national concentration, headed by General Jan Syrovy, the chief of the Czechoslovak general staff.

On September 22 Chamberlain returned to Germany for another interview with Hitler, this time at Godesberg in the Rhineland. The British prime minister informed the Führer that Czechoslovakia had agreed to cede the German areas to the Reich, and explained the plans which the British and French governments had worked out for effecting the transfer and for delimiting the new frontier. These plans Hitler at once rejected on the ground that they were too dilatory and offered too many opportunities for Czechoslovak evasion.

On September 23 he, in turn, presented other proposals which were ultimately drafted in the form of a memorandum to be transmitted to Czechoslovakia. These called for the withdrawal by October 1 of all Czech armed forces, police, gendarmerie, customs officials, and frontier guards from the Sudeten German area as shown on an accompanying map, the evacuated territory to be handed over to Germany as it stood without any military, economic, or traffic establishments being damaged or removed. In certain areas, to be more definitely defined, plebiscites were to be held before November 25 under the control of an international commission, all persons residing in the areas on October 28, 1918, or who were born in those areas prior to that date, being permitted to vote.

Hitler's proposals, which according to the Führer constituted his "final" stand on the Sudeten question, confronted Chamberlain with what the latter called a "totally unexpected situation." Apparently what shocked the British prime minister most was Hitler's threat to occupy the entire Sudeten area by force on October 1 without waiting for its delimitation by an international commission. Hitler's memorandum was described as an ultimatum by Chamberlain, and, even while the latter was at Godesberg, France and Great Britain informed the Czechoslovak government that they could not continue to take the responsibility of advising it not to mobilize.

On September 24 the government at Prague informed Chamberlain that Hitler's demands "in their present form" were "absolutely and unconditionally unacceptable," since they would deprive the republic of every safeguard for its national existence by admitting German armies deep into Czechoslovakia before the latter had been able to organize its defenses on a new basis, and because the whole process of moving the population would be reduced to panic and flight on the part of those who would not accept the German Nazi regime. Great Britain and France likewise held the demands to be unacceptable and agreed that no pressure would be exerted on Czechoslovakia to secure their acceptance. It appeared that Hitler might be compelled to carry out his threat to use force.

But Premier Daladier had stated that if Czechoslovakia were the victim of an unprovoked aggression France would immediately take the necessary measures to assist her, and on September 26 Great Britain, while declaring that she would guarantee the surrender of the Sudeten area to Germany if the latter did not go to war, announced that she and Russia would certainly stand by France if the latter went to the defense of Czechoslovakia. Meanwhile, Mussolini had declared that should a general war break out over Czechoslovakia, Italy's place was already chosen at the side of her partner in the Rome-Berlin Axis. Another general European war seemed imminent.

Already, on the night of September 23, President Beneš had ordered general mobilization of the Czechoslovak army, bringing its total strength to an estimated 1,500,000 men. On the next day France ordered partial mobilization by calling to the colors two full classes, which brought the French armed strength to more than 2,000,000 men. The British Home Fleet left Invergordon, its destination unknown. In Belgium 270,000 men were called to the colors for "reasons of security and a desire for peace." War fears mounted as German merchant ships canceled their sailings and others turned about in midocean and steamed for home ports. On September 27 it became known that Germany had decided to order mobilization against Czechoslovakia if the latter had not accepted the Hitler memorandum by 2 P. M. on the following day. In London Prime Minister Chamberlain in a radio address to the empire and the world declared that he would continue to work for peace, but asserted that he would fight if it became clear that "any nation had made up its mind to dominate the world by fear of its force."

On the twenty-seventh President Roosevelt of the United States made a direct appeal to Hitler urging an international conference to settle the controversy. At the same time Chamberlain, Daladier, and Roosevelt all appealed to Mussolini to use his influence with Hitler in the cause of peace. Apparently Mussolini, despite his warlike speeches, was at heart not eager to be drawn into a general war at a time when Italy was already involved in Ethiopia and Spain—especially when his partner in the Axis could secure what he desired without resort to arms. On the morning of September 28 Mussolini had a personal telephone conversation with Hitler, as the result of which the Führer agreed to an international conference to settle the Sudeten controversy. Chamberlain, Daladier, and Mussolini were invited to meet with the Führer at Munich on September 29.

The meeting of the four statesmen in the Führerhaus at Munich must have been dramatic; Mussolini and Chamberlain had never seen each other, and Daladier had never met either Mussolini or Hitler. In less than nine hours, however, they had worked out an agreement regarding the Sudetenland. By the terms of this pact the Czechs were to begin to evacuate the Sudetenland on October 1, and on the same day the Germans were to begin their progressive occupation of four zones which were known to be predominantly German. The evacuation would be supervised by an international commission representing Germany, Great Britain, France, Italy, and Czechoslovakia, which commission should decide by October 7 the remaining territory of preponderantly German character. This fifth zone should then come into German occupation by October 10. The Czechoslovak government was to be held responsible for carrying out the evacuation without damage to any "existing installations." The final determination of the frontiers between Germany and Czechoslovakia was to be made by the international commission, which should decide in which territories plebiscites should be held. Great Britain and France promised to guarantee the new frontiers of Czechoslovakia against unprovoked aggression, and Germany and Italy promised to do the same "when the question of the Polish and Hungarian minorities in Czechoslovakia has been settled."

There was nothing for Czechoslovakia to do but submit to the Munich agreement. Early on the morning of October 1 German troops marched across the frontier into zone number one. Two days later Adolf Hitler made a triumphal entry into Eger, which had served as the unofficial capital of the Sudeten Germans. "Never again," he declared, "shall the Sudetenland be torn from the Reich. . . . For you the nation was prepared to draw swords. You will also be as ready in the same spirit to assist if ever our German land and German people are threatened."

On October 5 the international commission awarded Germany the

THE PRINCIPALS AT GODESBERG

Neville Chamberlain and Adolf Hitler.

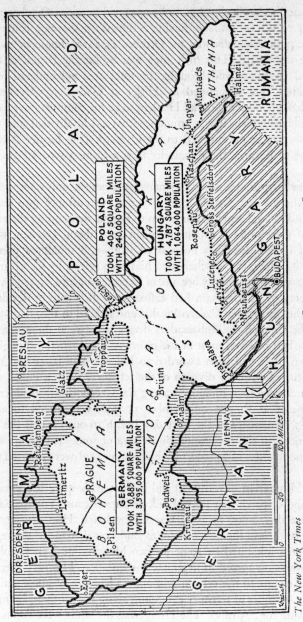

POLAND
TOOK 405 SQUARE MILES
WITH 240,000 POPULATION

HUNGARY
TOOK 4,787 SQUARE MILES
WITH 1,064,000 POPULATION

GERMANY
TOOK 10,885 SQUARE MILES
WITH 3,595,000 POPULATION

THE PARTITION OF CZECHOSLOVAKIA, 1938

The New York Times

fifth zone in Czechoslovakia, to be occupied between October 7 and October 10, the commission having accepted the German contention that the population statistics for October 28, 1918, should be used in making the award. This fifth zone was by far the largest of those awarded Germany and brought the total area surrendered to approximately that demanded by Hitler at Godesberg. Meanwhile, Hitler had appointed Konrad Henlein to be his commissioner for the Sudetenland, which, it was announced, would be divided into three sections—part being annexed to the Ostmark (the former Austria) and part to Bavaria, the remainder to constitute a separate Sudeten district.

But the territorial losses to Germany were not the only ones suffered by Czechoslovakia. On the eve of Germany's entrance into the Sudetenland Poland sent an ultimatum to Prague demanding the evacuation of Czechoslovak troops from an area about Teschen, where most of Czechoslovakia's Poles lived. Although inhabited predominantly by Poles, the Teschen area had been seized by Czech troops in January, 1919, primarily because of its economic and strategic value. The treaty of St. Germain had called for a plebiscite to decide the fate of the district, but Czechoslovakia and Poland in 1920 had agreed to let the Council of Ambassadors divide it between them. Czechoslovakia had received most of the mines of the district, although the old town itself had been awarded to Poland. The latter had never been satisfied with the division of the territory. With a Polish army of some 200,000 men mobilized along the Czechoslovak frontier, the government at Prague on October 1, 1938, was forced to accept Poland's demands. On the next day Polish troops crossed the Olsa River to begin the occupation of an area of some 400 square miles with a population of 240,000, of which 65 per cent were asserted to be Poles.

The Hungarian government did not act with quite the same decision and dispatch that Poland did, perhaps because Yugoslavia and Rumania threatened to assist Czechoslovakia if Hungary attacked her. Nevertheless, the government at Budapest demanded the cession of the area inhabited by some 800,000 Magyars, and on October 2 Czechoslovakia agreed to negotiate the question. Hungary then put forward claims to the cession without a plebiscite of approximately 6000 square miles of territory extending along the southern boundary of Slovakia for 275 miles. The Hungarian demands were denounced as excessive by Czechoslovakia, and the negotiations became dead-locked. Late in October, however, the two countries agreed that their territorial dispute should be arbitrated by Germany and Italy, and on November 2 the arbitrators awarded to Hungary approximately 4800 square miles of Czechoslovak territory with a population of about one million. Some important cities were included, but Bratislava, the republic's only outlet on the Danube, was left to Czechoslovakia. Hungarian troops began their occupation of the ceded territory on November 5.

The crisis of September, 1938, had far-reaching effects on the international situation in Europe, for it largely wrecked the system of security which France had constructed on the continent. Czechoslovakia, deserted by her powerful ally in the west, passed at once into the German orbit. Poland, Rumania, and Yugoslavia, with which France had long been linked in agreements to defend the *status quo* set up by the peace settlement, had every reason to question the value of collective security in general and of French commitments in particular. From Moscow came unofficial statements that the Soviet government considered its alliance with France as having come to an end. To many it seemed inevitable that France must thereafter follow ever more closely in the wake of Great Britain.

The French government at once attempted to bring about a *rapprochement* with Italy, which, it seemed, could not help being disturbed by Germany's ever-increasing strength in central Europe. In October France recognized Italy's conquest of Ethiopia. But apparently Mussolini was eager to take advantage of any French weakness to advance his own imperialistic plans. On November 30 there were frenzied—and probably inspired—shouts for Tunisia, Corsica, Savoy, and Nice in the Italian Chamber of Deputies. Almost simultaneously Fascist demonstrations occurred among the Italians in Tunis. In December the Italian government denounced the Franco-Italian colonial agreements of January, 1935.[15] Mussolini was apparently determined to force France to make territorial concessions as the price of Italian friendship. There were rumors, indeed, that his demands included the cession to Italy of Jibuti, the terminus of the only railway connecting Addis Ababa with the sea.

At the same time, despite Hitler's assertion that with the acquisition of the Sudetenland his territorial ambitions in Europe would be satis-

[15] See page 580.

fied, it appeared that the Third Reich under his leadership was just as determined to push the *Drang nach Osten* as had been the German Empire under the Kaiser. Hitler announced on October 9 that he had "decided to continue construction of our fortifications in the west with increased energy," and many, recalling how Germany's *Drang nach Osten* had been related to the World War, feared that the Munich settlement had not brought peace to Europe, but merely the postponement of war.

### Franco's Triumph in Spain

In Spain, on the other hand, the threat to the peace of Europe seemed to be in the process of liquidation, thanks to the military victories of the Insurgents, or the Nationalists, as they called themselves. With the capture of Gijón [16] in October, 1937, the Nationalists had completed their conquest of the northwestern part of the country. During 1938 they therefore concentrated their forces against the Loyalist lines in the east. Directing their drives from Saragossa, with the aim of cutting the coast road connecting Barcelona with Madrid and the rest of Spain, the Nationalist troops advanced until on April 15 they reached the coast south of Tortosa. In July, however, when General Franco, with the strongest army yet assembled in the war, was planning to launch a drive southward against Sagunto and Valencia, the Loyalist forces suddenly crossed the Ebro and struck the Nationalists in the rear and flank. So successful was the Loyalist attack that Franco was compelled to halt his campaign in the south in order to protect his lines on the Ebro front.

For a number of months the military situation appeared deadlocked, but in December, 1938, the Nationalists with a well-equipped army of some 300,000 men again struck—this time toward Barcelona. The Loyalist forces, greatly weakened by their Ebro campaign and greatly inferior in guns, tanks, and airplanes, were unable to check the Nationalist advance. On January 13, 1939, Franco's forces crossed the Ebro, and twelve days later they reached the outskirts of Barcelona. Here they met no such determined fighting as they had encountered when they reached Madrid in November, 1936. The Loyalist government withdrew to Figueras, President Azaña fled to the Spanish embassy in Paris, and Barcelona surrendered without offering resistance on January 26. As the Nationalists pushed forward in

[16] See page 743.

pursuit of the retreating and demoralized Loyalists, the territory held by the latter in Catalonia rapidly contracted. Hundreds of thousands of refugees and Loyalist troops fled across the frontier into France after the downfall of Figueras early in February.

With the extensive industries, munitions plants, and harbor facilities of Catalonia in the hands of the Nationalists, President Azaña and most of the cabinet ministers realized the futility of further resistance and urged the opening of negotiations with General Franco. Premier Negrín, however, was determined to continue the struggle and in this determination was supported by the Cortes. But only central Spain with the two important cities of Madrid and Valencia longer remained in Loyalist hands. To Madrid, therefore, Premier Negrín now returned by airplane, only to discover that the military leaders there believed that further resistance was useless. The latter not only differed with the premier; they ignored his government and set up a Council of National Defense to supersede it. Threatened by arrest, on March 6 Negrín and his ministers fled by airplane to France.

On the same day General Miaja, commander-in-chief of all remaining Loyalist forces, arrived in Madrid and broadcast an appeal for peace. This broadcast precipitated a series of Communist uprisings within Madrid with the aim of overthrowing the Council of National Defense, but after more than a week of bloody fighting the Communists were eventually suppressed. Then, following futile attempts to obtain a negotiated peace, General Miaja withdrew from Madrid, and on March 28, 1939, General Franco's victorious troops entered the capital unresisted. Four days later a Nationalist communiqué announced: "Today the Red army is captive and disarmed, and the Nationalist troops have achieved their military objectives. The war is over." Already, on February 27, Great Britain and France had extended recognition to the Nationalist government in Burgos. The specter of a general European war rising out of foreign intervention in the Spanish struggle seemed at last to be definitely laid.

Within Spain, however, the situation was summed up by the Nationalist minister of the interior in his victory speech: "Now our real job begins. The military war is over; the political battle starts." A Law of Political Responsibilities, designed "to liquidate the political crimes of those who, through their acts or through their serious failure to act, have contributed to . . . the present plight of Spain," outlawed twenty-six specified organizations, including supporters of the Popular Front, autonomist organizations, and Masonic lodges. Even before the war ended, General Franco had stated that he had "more than 2,000,000 persons card-indexed, with proofs of their crimes and names of witnesses," and tens of thousands of new arrests were made immediately following the fall of Madrid. A year after the close of the civil war it was reported that there were still some 500,000 political prisoners in Spain.

As might be expected, a number of decrees of a reactionary nature were issued. It was ordered, for example, that the grandees should be given back all land seized under the Agrarian Reform Law of 1932.[17] The Catholic Church also regained many of the privileges which it had held in Spain before the downfall of the monarchy. Catholicism was made the official state religion, government subsidies were restored to the clergy, all confiscated property was returned to the Jesuits, civil marriage and divorce were prohibited, and religious instruction was required in all public schools, colleges, and universities. One cause of friction developed between the Nationalist government and the papacy, however. Franco desired the continuation of the concordat of 1851, under which all religious controversies in Spain were settled by a Spanish court and the Spanish ruler appointed the bishops in Spain. The pope, on the other hand, desired a new concordat which, in accordance with the code of canon law issued in 1918, would deny the Spanish government the right to hold its own ecclesiastical tribunals or to name bishops.

In March, 1938, the Falange (*Falange Española Tradicionalista*) had issued a labor charter, and at the conclusion of the war the Nationalist government announced that this charter was thereafter to be applied throughout Spain. Labor unions were abolished, and strikes and lockouts were forbidden. All workers, including executives, were incorporated in vertical syndicates, restrictions were imposed on workers and employers alike, and each industry was organized under supervision of the syndicalist state, somewhat as in Italy under Mussolini.[18] As in Italy, too, the government, in January, 1940, authorized plans for draining marshy tracts and irrigating arid areas in order to improve the country's agriculture and increase peasant holdings. Regions in which private enterprise could not pro-

17 See page 738.
18 See pages 632–633.

vide the needed drainage and irrigation projects—including lands held by the grandees—were to be taken over by the government for the colonization of peasants.

During the civil war Franco had received his greatest support from the fascist Falangists, the landed nobility, the monarchists, the army leaders, and the clergy. Following the defeat of the Loyalists the chief problem of the Nationalists was to reconcile the conflicting aims of these varied groups. As early as April, 1937, General Franco had adopted most of the program of the Falangists as his official platform. Thereafter he omitted any public mention of plans for the restoration of the monarchy, though by a decree of December, 1938, he restored to Alfonso XIII all his rights of Spanish citizenship as well as his private properties in Spain. The monarchists were seriously weakened, as they were in France after 1870,[19] by divisions among themselves. The Alphonsists were split into two groups, those supporting Alfonso XIII and those in favor of his son Prince Juan, and the situation was further complicated by the Carlists,[20] who had a strong candidate in Prince Xavier of Bourbon-Parma. All efforts to bring agreement among the monarchists seemed to fail.

Politically, Nationalist Spain was organized about the Falangist Party, in which by a decree of July, 1939, officers and men of the army were incorporated as "affiliated members." At the head of the state stands the *Caudillo* (Leader)—General Franco—who on August 4, 1939, assumed "absolute authority . . . . responsible only to God and to history." Assisting him is the Falange National Council, part of whose members are named by the Caudillo, and the Falange Political Junta, the permanent governing body of the Falange, which has the right to present to the Caudillo any proposals it may think fit. Wide powers were also conferred on the secretary-general of the Falangist Party, a permanent official appointed by the Caudillo. In January, 1940, by the Law of Syndical Unity, all organizations representing economic or class interests—whether composed of employers or of workers—were incorporated in the Falange. The similarities between the Falangist system of Spain and the Fascist system of Italy are readily apparent.[21]

Nationalist Spain's leaning toward the Axis powers was evident

---

[19] See pages 103–106.
[20] See page 227, note.
[21] For the Fascist system, see pages 631–632.

not only in its political and economic organization but in its foreign policy also. At the close of the civil war Franco's government signed the anti-Communist pact, and in May, 1939, Spain withdrew from the League of Nations. The occasional demands of Spanish imperialists for the return of Gibraltar indicated that Spain under favorable circumstances might join the totalitarian states against the "possessing" powers, though financial weakness and need for physical rehabilitation militated against the country's hasty entrance into war in the immediate future.

### The Renewal of the "Drang nach Osten"

If the course of events in Spain during 1939 augured well for the peace of Europe, the same could not be said for developments in Czechoslovakia. Following the Sudeten crisis drastic changes had occurred in the political organization and life of that country. On October 4, 1938, Foreign Minister Krofta, who had been pro-French and pro-Russian, was dropped from the cabinet. His place was taken by Frantisek Chvalkovsky, who had served as Czech minister to Germany and Italy, and who was believed to be more satisfactory to their authoritarian governments. On October 5 came a resignation of still greater significance—that of President Beneš. A believer in the idea of collective security, he had founded the Little Entente and had loyally supported the League of Nations. Under his guidance Czechoslovakia's foreign policy had been based upon the promise and the expectation of French support in maintaining the *status quo*. But the Munich four-power accord revealed how little Czechoslovakia could expect from the western democracies in time of crisis, and foreshadowed the passing of his state into the orbit of the Third Reich. Recognizing that Hitler considered him an obstacle to friendly relations with Czechoslovakia, Beneš therefore surrendered his office. On November 30 the National Assembly elected Emil Hacha, former president of the supreme court administration, to be the third President of the republic, and on the same day Rudolf Beran, former leader of the Agrarians, succeeded Syrovy as premier.

Meanwhile, the Slovak Popular Party, which had long agitated for Slovak autonomy, had seized upon the crisis of 1938 to push its demands, and, in what was virtually an ultimatum to the Prague government, it insisted upon an immediate solution of the autonomy question. With Hungary and Poland both clamoring for the annexation or division of Slovakia, the government hastened to satisfy the Slovaks. On October 6 it announced that the Slovaks' autonomy demands had been conceded in their entirety; that is, Slovakia was granted full autonomy within the framework of the republic. Joseph Tiso was at once appointed prime minister for Slovakia, and to his government was surrendered full control of all matters affecting Slovakia with the exception of foreign affairs, national defense, and national finance. As a result of the crisis, too, Ruthenia (Carpatho-Ukraine) was made autonomous with its own premier and ministry. Czechoslovakia became, therefore, practically a loose federation of three states—Czechia, Slovakia, and Carpatho-Ukraine. Slovakian and Ukrainian were declared the official languages respectively in the last two.

Premier Beran's program resembled that of the totalitarian states in its emphasis on the need for co-ordinating and unifying all political, economic, and cultural organizations, for state control of all means of influencing public opinion, and for a "solution" of the Jewish problem. Following the example of the national legislatures of Italy and Germany, the parliament in Prague on December 14, 1938, passed an act authorizing Beran's government to legislate by decree for a period of two years, and thereupon adjourned *sine die*. In Slovakia the government and diet were composed exclusively of members of the Popular Party led by Tiso. All opposition groups were dissolved, a single-party system was established, and a vigorous anti-Semitic policy was pursued. In Carpatho-Ukraine, also, a single-party system was established, and only the Ukrainian National Union was permitted to nominate candidates in the elections to the local diet in February, 1939.

Despite this transformation of Czechoslovakia into a rather loose federation, relations between the autonomous governments and the authorities in Prague continued to be strained. An aggressive Ukrainian nationalist propaganda, conducted from Carpatho-Ukraine apparently with the approval of Germany, antagonized Poland, and eventually President Hacha intervened to dismiss a prominent Carpatho-Ukraine minister whom he held to be responsible for the propaganda. The Slovaks, meanwhile, were demanding further rights, and it was rumored that Slovak separatists were plotting to overthrow the Czechoslovak republic. In view of this situation, Premier Beran, on March 10, 1939, took the drastic step of dismissing the Slovak premier, Tiso, and of proclaiming martial law in Bratislava. Tiso at once appealed to Hitler for aid, while the leader of the Germans in Slovakia proclaimed that the interests of the Germans were endangered and "must be protected." From Vienna, meanwhile, a stream of anti-Czech propaganda was being broadcast in the Ukrainian and Slovak languages. As in September, 1938, reports were circulated in Berlin of violent attacks on the German minority by Czech mobs or police.

On March 13 Tiso was summoned to Berlin by Hitler, and on the following day, after the former had given the Slovak diet an account of his conversations with the Führer, the governments of both Slovakia and Carpatho-Ukraine declared their independence. On March 14 President Hacha and the Czechoslovak foreign minister were also summoned to Berlin, and during discussions with Hitler which lasted till 4 A. M. on the fifteenth President Hacha was persuaded—by what threats one can imagine—to place "the fate of the Czech people and the land trustingly in the hands of the Führer of the German Reich," to quote the language of the German communiqué. Early on the morning of the fifteenth Nazi troops occupied western Czechoslovakia, the President of that country first having issued orders that their advance must nowhere be resisted.

On March 16 Hitler announced that Czechia thereafter belonged to the territory of the German Reich and would be known as the "Protectorate of Bohemia and Moravia." Although the protectorate was permitted to retain its own government under the nominal presidency of Hacha, for all practical purposes it became an integral part of Germany under a "Reich protector," a position at first assigned to the former German foreign minister von Neurath. In the protectorate a one-party authoritarian system, based on the German pattern, was at once inaugurated. President Hacha appealed for popular support for this new system and warned that opposition might mean the death of the Czech people.

Meanwhile Tiso, who had once more become premier of Slovakia, had invited Hitler to become the protector of that state. On March 23 a treaty was accordingly signed between Germany and Slovakia providing that the former would protect the political independence and territorial integrity of the latter. The German army was authorized to construct and use military works along the state's frontiers, and the Slovak government agreed (1) to organize its own military forces in close co-operation with those of the Reich, and (2) to conduct its foreign policy at all times in close agreement with the German government. Obviously Slovakia had become a vassal state of the Reich and possessed a degree of independence little greater than that of Bohemia-Moravia.[22] One result of Germany's military occupation of both Czechia and Slovakia was crystal-clear—she was now in a stronger position than ever to continue her *Drang nach Osten,* for she now had new bases from which she could strike either northward against Poland or southward against Hungary.

While these events were following one another in· swift succession, on March 14 troops of the latter country had crossed the Carpatho-Ukraine frontier, and two days later the Budapest government had announced the incorporation of Carpatho-Ukraine in Hungary. Border clashes ensued between Hungarian and Slovak forces which eventually resulted in Hungary's further acquisition of some 400 square miles of Slovak territory, giving her full control of the Ung valley and of the railway connecting Hungary and Poland. The common frontier which these two states had sought and failed to gain in October, 1938, was thus obtained, and the Magyars were once more in control of a people whom they had consistently oppressed in the years prior to 1914.

While Czechoslovakia was thus in the process of destruction, Hitler seized upon the confusion in Europe to redeem still another German area. On March 21 he presented an ultimatum to Lithuania demanding the immediate return to the Reich of the Memel territory. Lithuania was of course in no position to defy the Führer, and an agreement to this effect was at once signed in Berlin.[23] Lithuanian troops and police were immediately withdrawn, and on March 23 Hitler arrived in Memel on board the battleship *Deutschland.*

Hitler's partner in the Rome-Berlin Axis now decided that, regardless of pledges made in the Anglo-Italian treaty of 1938, he should strengthen Italy's position in the Balkans. For some time there had been serious differences of opinion between King Zog of Albania and Mussolini, and, persuasion having failed, the Duce decided to resort to force. Italian troops were landed in Albania, and on April 8, 1939, they captured Scutari and Tirana, from which King Zog and his

---

[22] The Slovaks were permitted separate foreign representation and some form of local defense force, rights which were denied to the Czechs. In October, 1939, Tiso was elected President of the Slovak Republic.

[23] The agreement stipulated that Lithuania should have a free zone in the port.

family had already fled across the frontier into Greece. Count Ciano, Italian foreign minister, announced that the Italian forces had come merely to restore order, prosperity, and progress, and disclaimed any desire to interfere with the existence of Albania as a nation. An Albanian constituent assembly then met and voted to abrogate the existing constitution and regime and to offer the Albanian crown to the King of Italy. On April 15 the Italian parliament decided that Victor Emmanuel's title thereafter should be "King of Italy and Albania, Emperor of Ethiopia," and on the following day the Italian king accepted the Albanian crown at the hands of the Albanian premier. In theory, at least, Albania and Italy became united merely in a personal union,[24] Victor Emmanuel being represented in Albania by a lieutenant-general resident at Tirana. But Albania was soon included in an Italian customs union, and by a constitutional statute her diplomatic services were taken over by Italy and her soldiers were absorbed into the Italian army. Obviously Mussolini had improved his position in the Balkans should he thereafter decide to push his own *Drang nach Osten*.

## THE END OF "APPEASEMENT"

In his proclamation of March 16, 1939, stating the terms of his protectorate over Bohemia-Moravia, Hitler had justified his action not on the ground of self-determination, as he had done in the case of Austria and the Sudetenland, but on the basis of history and the principle of self-preservation. "Bohemia and Moravia," he proclaimed, "have for thousands of years belonged to the *Lebensraum* of the German people." Further, he explained, "It is in accordance . . . with the principle of self-preservation that the Reich is resolved to intervene decisively, to re-establish the bases of a reasonable Central European order, and to take all measures which in consequence arise." To many observers it began to appear that Hitler was determined not merely to bring all Germans in adjacent areas into the Reich but to construct something analogous to the Holy Roman Empire of the German People (the First Reich), which had been destroyed by Napoleon at the opening of the nineteenth century. And some were not slow to point out that Hitler's practical incorporation of Slovakia within his realm indicated that the Führer's ambitions were not even limited to the former Holy Roman Empire, for Slovakia had never

[24] The natives were permitted to retain Albanian as their official language.

been a part of that realm. In either case, however, there appeared to be plenty of cause for alarm to the statesmen of the other countries of Europe.

Certainly Hitler's repudiation of his own principles and of the formal pledges he had given Chamberlain in September, 1938, seems at last to have convinced the British prime minister that no reliance could be placed upon any assurances that might come from the Führer. At the time of the Sudeten crisis Chamberlain had asserted that he would fight if it became clear that any nation had made up its mind "to dominate the world by fear of its force." It now seemed apparent that Hitler had undertaken to dominate, if not the world, at least Europe by his might or the fear of it, and many believed that the next victim of his aggression would be Poland or Rumania. Consultations were accordingly at once begun by Great Britain, France, Russia, and some of the states of eastern Europe regarding measures to be taken in case of such an eventuality. Chamberlain hastened to make clear that ideological differences would not influence the British government's view as to what states should be consulted for mutual defense.

The first step in the new movement to "stop Hitler" came on March 31 when Great Britain and France announced that, "in the event of any action which clearly threatened Polish independence and which the Polish government accordingly considered it vital to resist with their national forces," they would at once lend Poland all support in their power. On April 5 Great Britain's unilateral commitment to Poland was transformed by a joint Anglo-Polish declaration into a reciprocal guarantee and took its place with the already existing Franco-Polish treaty of mutual guarantee. Consultations had meanwhile continued with other states, and, after Mussolini's seizure of Albania, Great Britain and France announced on April 13 that they had extended to Greece and Rumania guarantees identical with that given Poland two weeks earlier. British and French conversations were continued with Russia and with Poland and Rumania in an attempt to overcome the latter's reluctance to be associated with Russia in any arrangement which permitted the presence of Soviet troops on their soil.

In May the number of states becoming linked together in the attempt to preserve their national security was further increased when Great Britain and Turkey declared that "in the event of an act of aggression leading to war in the Mediterranean area, they would be prepared to co-operate effectively, and to lend each other all the aid and assistance in their power." France sought to conclude a similar pact, but in her case Turkey seized upon the occasion to exact territorial concessions. In 1937 the Syrian Sanjak of Alexandretta [25] had been detached from Syria and established as an independent state because Turkey insisted that its population was chiefly Turks. The first assembly of this new state in September, 1938, had adopted the name Republic of Hatay. Having succeeded in detaching the district from Syria, Turkey next sought to absorb it into her own territory, and this was the price exacted of France. On June 23, 1939, a Franco-Turkish convention ceded Hatay to Turkey except for a small section inhabited by Armenians, which was returned to Syria. The latter protested against the cession, but the parliament of Hatay approved the transfer and voted itself out of existence.[26] On the same day the French and Turkish governments signed a declaration of mutual assistance analogous to that made by Great Britain and Turkey.

Meanwhile, the indications pointing to Poland's becoming the next storm center of Europe increased. In a manner which experience had taught was the usual prelude to Hitler's execution of some new stroke, the German press in March had begun reporting attacks upon Germans in the Polish Corridor and denouncing the intolerable terror to which the German minority in Poland was subjected. Next, using the British-Polish declaration of mutual guarantee as a justification, Hitler on April 28 abrogated the German-Polish treaty of nonaggression of 1934 and the Anglo-German naval agreement of 1935. On the same day in a speech to the Reichstag he reiterated an earlier demand that Danzig be returned to Germany and that the latter be given a motor road and a railway line through the Polish Corridor possessing the same extraterritorial status for Germany as the Corridor itself had for Poland. In return he stated his willingness, among other things, to give Poland a free harbor in Danzig, to regard the existing boundaries between Germany and Poland as final, and to conclude a new nonaggression treaty with Warsaw. On May 5

[25] The Sanjak included the important city of Antioch.

[26] On July 7 the President of Syria declared that the new policy of France was "in clear contradiction with existing agreements" and thereupon resigned. On the next day the French high commissioner in Syria dissolved the parliament, suspended the constitution, and ordered the establishment of a council of officials to exercise executive authority under his supervision.

Poland denied the German demands for Danzig and for extraterritorial rights in the Corridor, but suggested a common guarantee of the existence and rights of the Free City and pointed out that Poland already allowed German citizens to travel across the Corridor without customs or passport formalities.

The Axis powers next made a countermove. In an apparent effort to strengthen themselves in the face of Great Britain's guarantee to Poland and the latter's resistance to German demands, or possibly in the hope of intimidating Chamberlain into returning to his policy of appeasement, Italy and Germany on May 22 signed a military alliance. This ten-year agreement provided for consultation whenever the interests of one of the signatory powers were threatened, coordination of their economies for wartime purposes, and military aid in case either became involved in war.[27] It also stipulated that neither power would conclude a separate armistice or peace in the event of their being at war. The alliance was at once implemented by conferences between German and Italian military leaders. Further, to remove one possible cause of dissension between the Axis partners, negotiations were carried on during the early summer of 1939 with a view to transferring the Germans from the South Tirol. On July 4 it was announced in Berlin that such an agreement had been reached.[28]

Meanwhile, it was obvious to most observers that the Anglo-French guarantees to Poland, Rumania, and Greece were greatly weakened by the practical difficulty of sending military aid to eastern Europe. To solve this strategic problem the British government, under pressure from France, in April, 1939, had initiated negotiations for a mu-

[27] According to the statement made by Italian Foreign Minister Ciano on December 16, 1939, Germany and Italy agreed on the necessity of maintaining peace for a considerable time in order to allow the two powers to perfect their internal reconstruction and to complete their military preparations. The period was estimated by Italy at three and by Germany at four or five years, and the German government agreed on the advisability of not raising any seriously controversial questions for this period.

[28] The agreement was not actually signed until October 21, 1939. It then provided that German citizens should be transferred without option within three months, and that Germans who had earlier accepted Italian citizenship should until December 31, 1939, have the choice of becoming German citizens again and emigrating or reaffirming their loyalty to Italy. Those who chose German citizenship must leave before January 1, 1943. Early in 1940 it was reported that more than 70 per cent of the German inhabitants of the South Tirol had opted for Germany, and that a convention had been signed settling the amount which Italy should pay in compensation for the property of the people emigrating. It was estimated that the transfer of the Tirolese to Germany would provide the latter with credits in Italy equal to more than 7,000,-000,000 lire, for those who returned to Germany would receive their compensation either in paper currency of the Reich or in property of deported aliens.

tual assistance pact with Russia similar to the Franco-Soviet pact of
May, 1935. By early summer it had become clear that the Soviet government was determined that any such pact not only must provide
for mutual assistance between Britain, France, and the U.S.S.R.,
but must also give to all the European states bordering on the Soviet
Union a three-power guarantee against attack by aggressors. Furthermore, the pact must be accompanied by a military alliance, fully implemented by consultations of the general staffs of the three countries.[29]

The point upon which the negotiations tended to break down was
Russia's demand that the three-power guarantee should be extended
to Finland, Estonia, and Latvia, and the difficulty arose from the unwillingness of these states to accept such a guarantee and Great Britain's unwillingness to force one upon them.[30] The governments and
ruling classes in the Baltic republics genuinely feared Russia and the
infiltration of communism. They feared that if they accepted a guarantee from the Soviet Union the latter might seize upon some pretext
for a military intervention which might result in permanent occupation and the overthrow of the existing regimes. The Baltic states
wished to preserve their neutrality, but apparently, if it became necessary for them to have the protection of any great power, they preferred
that of Germany.

On the other hand, Soviet military leaders feared that in case of a
Russo-German war Germany might quickly seize the small Baltic
republics and use them as an advantageous base for an advance upon
Leningrad or Moscow. Furthermore, they realized that, if Germany
should secure control of the ports of these republics and of the Dagoe
Islands or the Åland Islands, she would be in an excellent position to
bottle up the Soviet fleet in the Gulf of Finland. Finally, there is no
doubt that the Soviet government, since the surrender at Munich,
had been deeply suspicious of the motives of British and French
statesmen. In March, 1939, Stalin himself had voiced the belief
that the Western powers hoped that Germany might become deeply
involved in a war with Russia so that when both belligerents were

[29] The Franco-Soviet pact of 1935 had never been so implemented.
[30] On December 2, 1939, it was stated semiofficially in London that during the
negotiations with the Soviet government the Russians had stipulated that, as the
price of their alliance, Britain and France should persuade Finland and the Baltic
countries to put naval bases on the coast and on the islands of Oesel and Dagoe at the
disposal of Russia. Britain and France refused to agree.

sufficiently exhausted France and Britain might enter the stage with fresh forces and dictate their own terms. Russia therefore was determined not to enter into any mutual defense pact unless it provided for her own protection in the Baltic. Nevertheless, regardless of the delay in agreeing upon the terms of such a pact, France and Great Britain, acting upon Russia's suggestion, in July decided to send military missions to Moscow for staff consultations.

Unknown to the British and French governments, Russia had meanwhile been carrying on negotiations for a pact of nonaggression with Nazi Germany, negotiations initiated apparently by the Reich early in the spring of 1939. Some indication that a change in the course of Russia's foreign policy was possibly in the offing came on May 3 when Maxim Litvinov was superseded as Soviet foreign commissar by Premier Molotov. The former had been associated with the idea of collective security, and had been responsible for the conclusion of the Franco-Soviet pact of 1935 and for Russia's entrance into the League of Nations. France and Britain ignored this change of commissars, however, and proceeded in a leisurely way with their negotiations. In the course of the latter the Soviet government apparently came to the conclusion that it could expect no tangible assistance from France or Great Britain if Russia were attacked by Germany. Possibly it decided, also, that it might be much more to Russia's advantage to have Germany become involved in a long and costly war with the Western powers, in the course of which the Soviet Union might be able with more or less impunity to secure territorial gains and at the close of which, in case Germany, France, and Britain became exhausted, communism itself might make great gains in western Europe.

On his side, Hitler, as a result of Britain's pledge to Poland, had apparently concluded that his hope of an Anglo-German friendship was futile. His next hope was, apparently, that an announcement of the signing of a Soviet-German nonaggression pact would cause Great Britain and France to repudiate their pledges to Poland as they had repudiated those to Czechoslovakia in 1938. Then he would be in a position either to gain a bloodless victory once more or to wage a short victorious war against the Poles.

The first tangible result of the German-Soviet *rapprochement* came on August 20, just ten days after the Anglo-French military missions arrived in Moscow, when a trade agreement was signed between the Soviet Union and the Reich. The former agreed to supply Germany during the ensuing two years with raw materials valued at 180,000,000 marks. The Reich, on its part, promised to send Russia on credit machines and manufactured goods to the value of 200,-000,000 marks. Three days later came the signing in Moscow of a nonaggression pact, by the terms of which Russia and Germany agreed to refrain from any act of force against each other and to remain neutral should the other become "the object of warlike action on the part of a third power." Subsequent events indicate that there may have been an understanding—tacit or otherwise—that Russia should share in the spoils in case of a Polish war and should be given a free hand in the Baltic republics.

### THE CRISIS OF AUGUST, 1939

On August 22, as soon as it had become known that the German-Soviet nonaggression treaty was to be signed, Chamberlain warned Hitler that that pact would in no way alter Great Britain's obligation to Poland, and stated that the British government was determined that there should be no misunderstanding on this point. He argued, however, that there was nothing in the German-Polish question which could not be settled without resort to force, and urged direct negotiations between Germany and Poland, possibly with the aid of a neutral intermediary. But he declared that any settlement which was reached should be guaranteed by other powers.

Hitler, in his reply on the following day, pointed out that Germany had never interfered in Britain's interests but had for years sought to win her friendship. Danzig and the Corridor, however, were among the interests which it was impossible for the Reich to renounce. Germany was prepared to settle this problem with Poland "on a basis of a proposal of truly unparalleled magnanimity," but Britain's guarantee had made the Poles unwilling to negotiate and had encouraged them to unloose "a wave of appalling terrorism against the one and a half million Germans living in Poland." The British decision to assist Poland in case of war, Hitler maintained, could not change the Reich's determination to safeguard the interests of Germany. "The questions of Danzig and the Corridor must and shall be solved."

Two days later, in a conference with Sir Nevile Henderson, British ambassador to Germany, the Führer declared that after the solution of the German-Polish problem he would "approach England once more with a large comprehensive offer." He accepted the British Empire, he said, and, if his colonial demands were fulfilled and his obligations toward Italy were not touched, he was ready to pledge himself personally for its continued existence. He was, furthermore, willing to accept a limitation of armaments which corresponded to the new political situation, and was not interested in western problems, the Reich's new fortifications constituting its final western frontier. If Great Britain would consider these ideas, he declared, a blessing for Germany and also for the British Empire might result. If she rejected them, there would be war. This was his last offer.

On the same day that this conversation occurred (August 25) the Anglo-Polish declaration of April 5 was transformed into a definite five-year treaty for mutual assistance and was formally signed in London. On the next day Premier Daladier informed Hitler of France's determination to stand by Poland, but offered to co-operate in seeking a direct settlement between Poland and the Reich. Hitler replied that he saw no way of inducing Poland to accept a peaceful settlement, and once more restated his claims to Danzig and the Corridor. After several consultations between the British and French governments, the British answer to Hitler's proposals of the twenty-fifth was delivered on August 28. It reiterated Britain's contention that a reasonable solution of the German-Polish problem could be reached which would also safeguard Poland's essential interests, and declared that Poland had already agreed to enter into direct negotiations with the Reich on this basis, the settlement to be guaranteed by other powers. Great Britain hoped that Germany, too, would consent to such negotiations. When once the differences between the Reich and Poland were peacefully settled, Great Britain was prepared to accept Hitler's recent proposals for a general understanding as subjects for discussion. But the British government, the note stated, "could not, for any advantage offered to Great Britain, acquiesce in a settlement which put in jeopardy the independence of a state to which it had given its guarantee."

On August 29 Hitler declared that Germany was prepared to accept the British proposal for direct discussion, and stated that Germany never had any intention of touching Poland's vital interests or questioning the existence of an independent state. He explained, however, that in the event of a territorial rearrangement in Poland, the Reich would no longer be able to give guarantees or to participate in guarantees unless the Soviet Union were associated therewith, and thus seemed to indicate that Germany had already made some commitment to Russia regarding the division of Polish territory. The German government, Hitler declared, accepted Great Britain's good offices in securing the dispatch to Berlin of a Polish emissary "with full powers," and it counted on the arrival of this emissary on the next day (August 30).

At 2:30 A.M. on August 30 the British government telegraphed its ambassador in Berlin to inform the Reich government that careful consideration would be given to Hitler's reply but that the latter must not expect that the British government could produce a Polish representative in Berlin that same day. At 6:50 P.M. another telegram suggested that Germany adopt the normal procedure of handing the Polish ambassador the proposals for transmission to Warsaw, and stated that if the British government thought, after seeing the proposals, that they offered a reasonable basis, it would do its best in Warsaw to facilitate negotiations. When Sir Nevile Henderson called on Foreign Minister von Ribbentrop to deliver this message, the latter "produced a lengthy document which he read out in German aloud at top speed." This document was a sixteen-point program [31] for the settlement of all German-Polish problems. When the British ambassador asked for the text of the proposals, he was informed that "it was now too late, as the Polish representative had not arrived in Berlin by midnight."

The formal British reply to Hitler's proposal of August 29 finally reached Berlin in time to be presented to the German foreign minister about midnight of the thirtieth. It stated that the British govern-

[31] The following are the main points in the proposals: the Free City of Danzig to return to the Reich; the Corridor to decide by plebiscite whether it should belong to Poland or to Germany, all domiciled there on January 1, 1918, or born there up to that date having the right to vote; the territory to be evacuated by the Polish authorities and armed forces and to be placed under the supervision of an international commission on which France, England, Italy, and the U.S.S.R. would be represented; Gdynia to be excluded from the plebiscite area; the plebiscite not to take place before the lapse of twelve months, and the question of ownership to be decided by a simple majority; if the plebiscite area went to Poland, Germany to have an extraterritorial traffic zone, one kilometer wide, in which to lay down a motor road and a four-track railway; if the area went to Germany, Poland to have an analogous communication with Gdynia; in this case, Germany to have the right to proceed to an exchange of populations; Danzig and Gdynia both to have the character of exclusively mercantile towns; an international commission of inquiry to examine complaints of both sides as to treatment of their minorities; Germany and Poland to guarantee the rights of the minorities by the most comprehensive and binding agreement; in the event of agreement on these proposals, both countries to demobilize immediately.

ment understood that Germany was preparing proposals, and it could determine, after examination, how far these agreed with the essential conditions stated by Great Britain and accepted in principle by Germany. The British government would at once transmit Germany's reply to Warsaw. While it was urgent that negotiations should be undertaken, Great Britain believed that they would probably not be practicable on the thirtieth. The British government shared Hitler's fear of border incidents which might arise from the proximity of two mobilized armies standing face to face and therefore strongly urged that both Germany and Poland should agree that during the negotiations no aggressive military movements would take place. This last suggestion, which was repeated to Poland, brought a reply from the latter on August 31 stating that Poland would not violate the frontiers of the Reich during the negotiations, provided Germany made a reciprocal pledge, but Germany never replied to this proposal.

Apparently the German note of August 29 and the British reply of the thirtieth were not communicated to Poland until August 31. In the afternoon of that day the Polish government informed the British that it would authorize its ambassador in Berlin to inform the German foreign office that Poland had accepted Great Britain's proposals for direct negotiations. The Polish foreign minister stated, however, that the Polish ambassador would not be authorized to accept the proposals, which the earlier experience of the Austrian Chancellor Schuschnigg and the Czechoslovak President Hacha indicated might be accompanied by "some sort of ultimatum." Foreign Minister von Ribbentrop refused to see the Polish ambassador until the evening of the thirty-first. When at that time Ribbentrop learned that the Polish ambassador was authorized to receive Germany's proposals but had no plenary powers to negotiate, the interview was abruptly closed, and the German government at once broadcast its sixteen-point program, which had not yet been communicated officially to Poland. When the Polish ambassador tried to get in touch with Warsaw, he was unable to do so because all means of communication had been closed by the German government.

On that same evening Germany informed Britain that Hitler for two days had waited in vain for the arrival of a fully empowered Polish negotiator, and that therefore the German government regarded its proposals as having been "to all intents and purposes rejected." Apparently, as the British foreign secretary later pointed out, Hitler conceived of a negotiation between Germany and Poland as nothing more than the summoning of a Polish plenipotentiary to Berlin, at twenty-four hours' notice, to discuss terms not previously communicated to him. At this time, too, Germany at last provided Britain with the sixteen points in full, but before these could be considered Hitler had ordered the German army to advance across the Polish frontier. At about 5 A. M. on September 1, 1939, German airplanes began raining bombs upon numerous Polish cities. Later in the day Danzig by Hitler's order was incorporated in the Reich, and the Nazi leader in that city was appointed head of the civil administration. Great Britain and France thereupon immediately presented ultimatums to Germany stating that unless the latter suspended all aggressive action against the Poles and withdrew her forces from Polish territory, they would at once fulfill their obligations to Poland.

Although a general war now seemed inevitable, one avenue to peace still remained open. On August 31 Mussolini had notified Great Britain and France that he could call an international conference on September 5 for the purpose of revising the clauses of the treaty of Versailles "which are the cause of the actual disturbance of European life," but he could do so only on condition that he had a previous assurance of Anglo-French adherence and that the participation of Poland was guaranteed by Great Britain and France. On September 1 Italy received replies from the latter which the Italians characterized as "favorable in principle." On September 2 Italy informed Hitler that the convocation of a conference preceded by an armistice was still a possibility. The Führer then inquired whether the earlier Anglo-French note demanding German evacuation of Polish territory was in the nature of an ultimatum. Italy was informed that it was and that German withdrawal from the occupied territory was a fundamental condition of Anglo-French participation in such a conference. "In this state of affairs the Italian government," according to its own communiqué, "contented itself with informing the Führer of the above mentioned conditions, adding that unless it heard to the contrary from the German government it would assume that the latter was unable to proceed with the withdrawal of its forces."

At 9 A. M. on September 3, after having received no reply to the ultimatum of September 1, the British ambassador in Berlin notified Germany that unless satisfactory assurances had been received by

Great Britain by 11 A. M., a state of war would exist between the two countries. Such assurances were not given, and at 11:15 A. M. Chamberlain announced that Great Britain was at war with Germany. France made a similar announcement at 5 P. M. the same day. Already on September 1 the Italian government had stated that Italy would take no initiative in military operations.

## CHAPTER XXX

## WARFARE—NEW STYLE

**M**OST people—at least outside Germany—rather confidently expected the Second World War to be conducted like that of 1914–1918. Few realized how the mechanization and motorization of military forces had altered the strategy and tactics of land warfare. Nor did they comprehend how vastly different war would be as a result of the perfection of the airplane and its utilization for military purposes. They failed to understand how bombers in the air and tanks and motorized units on land had outmoded the old style of conflict. This was quickly revealed, however, by the German invasion of Poland.

### THE NAZI-SOVIET PARTITION OF POLAND

In the postwar period military experts had come to regard the Polish army rather highly, and it was believed that the conquest of Poland by Germany might not be an easy task. The Poles had an army of thirty regular divisions and thirty reserve divisions with a total fighting strength of some 1,500,000 men. But, unfortunately for the Poles, in the war of 1939 man power was not the important factor. The Germans were vastly superior to the Poles in aircraft, tanks, motorized equipment, artillery, and antitank and antiaircraft guns. And in the *Blitzkrieg* (lightning war) which the German General von Brauchitsch had planned, it was the latter which actually counted.

On September 1 Germany's motorized armies advanced into Poland from East Prussia, Pomerania, Silesia, and Slovakia while German airplanes at once subjected Polish airdromes to severe bombardments which largely crippled the inferior Polish air force at the very outset of the conflict. Within a week the "eyes" of the Polish army had been blinded by the destruction of its airplanes and its bases. By the use of its own air force, the German high command could then learn what the Polish armies were doing, while the Poles, on the contrary, could not learn what the Germans were doing until some new blow was struck. Meanwhile, German bombers ranged constantly far and wide, behind the Polish lines, disrupting Polish communications and interfering with Polish concentrations, while German *Panzer* (armored) and motorized divisions pushed steadily forward. The resisting Polish units gradually became "mere islands in an ocean of confusion."

Great Britain and France, meanwhile, did practically nothing to aid Poland in her death struggle with Germany. At the outbreak of the war it was thought that there were two ways, perhaps, in which they could give assistance. In the first place, they might give direct aid by sending a great air force to Poland to combat the German advance. Actually, however, Germany had an air superiority over Great Britain and France combined. Furthermore, the Polish landing fields, airdromes, and fuel supplies were almost immediately so damaged or destroyed by German bombings that there would not have been adequate facilities for servicing a large Anglo-French air force even had it been sent. In the second place, it was believed that France might give indirect aid to Poland by launching such a terrific blow against Germany from the west that Nazi troops would have to be diverted from the east to meet the French attack. But the French high command was apparently so confident of the impregnability of the Maginot Line that it convinced itself that it would likewise be futile to attempt to break through the German West Wall or Siegfried Line. Only feeble attacks were made by the French during the whole Polish campaign.

At the end of the second week of hostilities the Poles had lost almost all of their western provinces, and Warsaw was practically surrounded. During the third week, while the Germans were attacking such advanced points as Brest-Litovsk and Lwow (Lemberg), the Polish armies in desperation hastily withdrew to the east and south in the hope that they might establish a front along the Dniester River where they could possibly be supported through Rumania by aid from France and Great Britain. But suddenly, on September 17, Soviet armies began advancing into Poland from the east to protect "the Ukrainians and White Russians, who . . . now have been abandoned entirely to their fate." This move brought the collapse of all effective Polish resistance except at Warsaw, which under its mayor, Stefan Starzynski, heroically endured terrific artillery and air bombardments until September 27, when an armistice was concluded. A week earlier than this the Polish government had fled to Rumania, where President Moscicki and Marshal Smigly-Rydz were interned.[1] Thus in the unbelievedly short period of twenty-seven days was completed the military destruction of a nation of 34,000,000 people, inhabiting a country 150,000 square miles in extent, defended by an army of 1,500,000 men.

Two days after the signing of the armistice the German and Soviet governments concluded a treaty of friendship which fixed the frontier of their interests in the former territory of Poland. Generally speaking, the line ran from the Hungarian frontier on the south along the San, the Bug, and the Narew Rivers to East Prussia, and roughly approximated the "Curzon Line" of 1919.[2] The fate of all former Polish territory west of the demarcation line was left to Hitler. The provinces of Poznan (Posen), Pomorze (Pomerania), and Upper Silesia, which prior to 1918 were German, together with parts of the provinces of Warsaw and Lodz, including the industrial city of Lodz, were at once incorporated in the Reich. The rest of the territory under German control was constituted a separate unit known as the "Government General," with its capital at Cracow. By reason of the new situation in the East, Ribbentrop declared on October 24, Germany had gained *Siedlungsraum* (colonizing space) for generations, and in this area she would attempt to relocate some 1,500,000 Germans scattered in other parts of Europe. To Heinrich Himmler, head of the *Gestapo,* was confided the task of organizing the transfer of populations.

To prepare the way for this German colonization in the areas immediately annexed to the Reich, the Nazis sought by mass deportations to transfer every non-German into the Polish Government General. Polish inhabitants were driven from their farms and from their homes, and Polish businesses were expropriated without compensation. By November, 1939, it was reported, the Polish inhabitants (128,000) of Gdynia had already been deported "to make room for newcomers from Germany, South Tirol, and the Baltic states,

---

[1] A new Polish government was soon constituted in France under President Raczkiewicz and Prime Minister Sikorski. It established the capital of the Polish state at Angers, but after Germany conquered France in June, 1940, the capital was moved to England. Meanwhile, a Polish army of volunteers was created to fight on the side of the Allies.

[2] See page 747.

leaving the houses furnished ready for the new occupants." In the
closing months of 1939 tens of thousands of Germans were brought
from the Baltic republics, each being promised that he would re-

THE PARTITION OF POLAND, 1939

ceive in former Polish territory as far as possible the equivalent of
what he left behind—for instance, a farm or a store. Others were
brought from the Polish Government General, from Russian-occupied
Poland, and from the Italian South Tirol, all of which, in the words
of Hitler, were "partly filled up with splinters of German nationality

that cannot be maintained." Systematic efforts were made to Germanize as rapidly as possible the newly annexed provinces. The public use of the Polish language was suppressed, and place names were changed. Gdynia became Gotenhafen, a German naval base.

The uprooting of Germans from regions in which they and their ancestors had lived for generations or even centuries could not but be accompanied by hardships and heartaches. But the sufferings of the repatriated Germans were as nothing in comparison with those of the Poles and Jews who were being driven from their homes in the territory annexed to the Reich. The sorrow and privations inevitably linked with such a transfer of population were immeasurably increased by the reign of terror which was instituted by the *Gestapo* and by former German residents in Poland. According to a report to the pope by Cardinal Hlond, who had escaped from the area annexed by Germany, mass shootings and plunderings were conducted with cold-blooded brutality. The intellectual leaders of the Poles—professors, teachers, clergy, bourgeoisie—were especially singled out for execution or deportation. Hundreds of thousands of able-bodied men were torn from their families and sent to work in Germany, while thousands of old people, women, and children were jammed into freight cars or motor trucks and transported to the Government General, where they were dumped in the dead of winter with little or no provision for their welfare. But in a speech at Lodz in January, 1940, the Germans were admonished by Dr. Ley, leader of the German Labor Front: "You must remain hard. Then the wish of the Führer will be fulfilled . . . that in fifty years this will be a flourishing German farmland in which there will be not a single Pole or Jew."

Meanwhile, the Government General, constituting an area of some 42,500 square miles with a population of about 13,000,000, was being organized. Over this province Hitler appointed Dr. Hans Frank, formerly deputy Reich protector of Bohemia-Moravia, to rule as governor general, with authority to administer justice and issue decrees in his own name. The Government General was divided into four major districts—Cracow, Warsaw, Radom, and Lublin—each governed by a German civil official responsible to the governor general. Each district in turn was divided into ten "circles" ruled by German officials, and each of the larger towns was assigned a German civil chief responsible to the district governor. The rest of the civil administration was left in the hands of the Poles, who constituted a large percentage of the civil servants.

It was generally assumed that the Government General would probably be a protectorate of the Reich similar to Bohemia-Moravia. That this was a mistaken assumption, however, became apparent when on August 16, 1940, Governor General Frank declared that the Germans would never leave Poland, that "the swastika will fly over this land forever." On the first anniversary of the beginning of the war, he further announced, the main square in each of the four district capitals would be renamed Adolf-Hitler-Platz. Nine days later it was reported from Berlin that the Polish Government General had been incorporated into the Reich by Hitler's decree. That the conditions of the Poles in this region had been deplorable seemed indicated, meanwhile, by protests from the Vatican and by Germany's refusal to permit foreign journalists to enter the area.

To the east of the German-controlled Government General the territory given to Soviet Russia constituted an area of approximately 75,000 square miles. It included the former Polish provinces of Vilna, Nowogrodek, Polesia, Volhynia, Tarnopol, and Stanislawow, and most of the provinces of Bialystok and Lwow, regions whose chief resources were forests and agricultural lands except for the oil fields in the province of Lwow. Save in the province of Bialystok, a large part of the population (about 14,000,000) of these new territories was closely akin racially to the neighboring peoples in the Soviet Union, and was predominantly of the agricultural and laboring class.[3] In October the newly acquired territory was organized as Western White Russia and the Western Ukraine. In each a national assembly petitioned for admission into the U.S.S.R. In November Western White Russia became part of the White Russian Soviet Socialist Republic and the Western Ukraine was absorbed by the Ukrainian Soviet Socialist Republic. Thus at last Russia regained the territory which Poland had taken from her when the Communists were fighting against "White" armies and foreign intervention in 1920.[4] But whether Russia's acquisition of this territory would be recognized at the close of the war remained open to question, especially after Hitler's attack upon the Soviet Union in 1941.

[3] Many of the Polish and Jewish minorities acquired, however, belonged to the professional, landowning, and commercial classes.

[4] See page 747.

## Russia's Return to the Baltic

By this time, too, Soviet Russia had extended her influence into the Baltic republics and had established her armed forces on strategic islands and coastal points of the eastern Baltic. Hitler's order for the withdrawal of the German Balts from these republics seemed to indicate that he knew of Stalin's intentions and had possibly given his consent at the time of the conclusion of the Soviet-German nonaggression treaty. However that may be, during September and October the foreign ministers of Estonia, Latvia, and Lithuania successively were summoned to Moscow for conferences from which came in each case a pact of mutual assistance against an attack by a third power. By each of the treaties Russia undertook to supply arms and war materials on advantageous conditions. To Lithuania it made a special gesture by agreeing to transfer to it the city and district of Vilna, which had just been obtained by Russia in the partition of Poland.

The most significant features of these treaties were the military and naval concessions which Russia obtained. Each of the republics granted the Soviet Union the right to maintain land and air armed forces "of strictly limited strength" within its territory. Estonia further gave permission for Russia to maintain naval bases and airdromes on the Estonian islands of Oesel and Dagoe and on the mainland at Baltiski. Similarly, Latvia granted the right to establish naval bases in the ports of Libau (Liepaja) and Windau (Ventspils), to set up artillery bases along the coast, and to build airdromes for the Soviet air force.

Although each of the three pacts solemnly declared that nothing in it should be allowed to impair the sovereign rights of the parties nor affect their internal regime, to most observers it was obvious that the Baltic republics—once they had carried out the terms of these agreements—would be powerless to prevent their permanent occupation by Russia. If these moves by the Soviet Union were made with the consent of Germany, it seems clear that Hitler was willing to go much further than Chamberlain and Daladier in his efforts to gain the good will of Stalin's government. During October and November Soviet armed forces began occupying their new bases along the Baltic, and during the summer of 1940 the three states were finally absorbed altogether by the Soviet Union.[5]

[5] In August, 1940, they were "admitted" as constituent republics of the U.S.S.R.

Undoubtedly by the acquisition of these air and naval bases Russia greatly strengthened her defensive position in the west. But Soviet leaders felt that the security of Leningrad was still menaced so long as Russia did not fully control the sea and land approaches to that city. The Soviet government therefore in October initiated negotiations with Finland, apparently expecting the latter to make concessions similar to those which had been made by the Baltic states. The Russian demands were presented on October 14 and included: (1) a thirty-year lease of the port of Hangoe and adjoining territory for the purpose of establishing a naval base; (2) Hogland and other islands at the eastern end of the Gulf of Finland; (3) Björkö island, commanding the entrance to the bay of Viborg (Viipuri); (4) a new frontier from Björko eastward to join the existing Finnish-Soviet frontier crossing Lake Ladoga; (5) the Finnish part of the Rybachi peninsula, which would enable Russia to dominate Petsamo, Finland's outlet on the Arctic Ocean. In exchange the Soviet government offered to surrender some 2134 square miles of territory in Soviet Karelia along the eastern frontier of Finland. The latter was willing to cede the various islands demanded except Hogland, but was determined not to lease nor sell to Russia the port of Hangoe, which, the Finns contended, would give Russia complete domination of their country.

Negotiations eventually reached a deadlock on November 14, when the Finnish delegation withdrew from Moscow, whereupon the Soviet press became more violent in its attack on Finland and frontier incidents were alleged. On November 26 Russia demanded that Finnish troops be withdrawn some twelve to fifteen miles from the frontier near Leningrad, and two days later denounced the Finnish-Soviet nonaggression treaty of 1932 on the ground that Finnish troop concentrations in the "neighborhood of Leningrad" were an act of hostility to the Soviet Union. On November 29 the Soviet government broke off diplomatic relations, and on the next day Russian troops and airplanes crossed the border. On December 1 a "People's Government" headed by Otto Kuusinen, a Finnish Communist who had lived as an exile in Russia since the collapse of the "Red" movement in Finland in 1918,[6] was organized in a small Finnish village near the Soviet frontier. This new puppet government at once concluded with Moscow a treaty of mutual assistance

[6] See page 762.

in which it agreed to make the territorial concessions earlier demanded of the *de jure* Finnish government by Russia.

On December 2 Finland appealed to the League of Nations, which on the fourteenth condemned the Soviet invasion, expelled the Soviet Union from the League, and authorized the League secretariat to co-ordinate all offers of assistance received from League members. Foodstuffs and medical supplies were sent by many neutral countries, and Sweden, Great Britain, France, and even Italy contributed airplanes and military materials to aid the Finns. Moreover, the brave stand of the latter inspired many foreigners to enlist as "volunteers," as had been done in the case of the Spanish civil war, though such volunteers were not enough to enable Finland to put into the field more than a fraction of the troops which Russia threw against her. Furthermore, the neighboring Scandinavian countries, although unofficially they sent assistance to the Finns, officially adopted an attitude of strict neutrality. Norway and Sweden steadfastly refused to consent to the passage of any Allied force across their territory. Despite the Finnish parliament's declaration that Finland was fighting as "an outpost of Western civilization" and despite its appeal for "active help from other civilized nations," Finland with less than 4,000,000 inhabitants was left to fight largely unaided against the vast Soviet Union with its 170,000,000.

The Russian attack was made at four points. The right wing of a force based on Murmansk sought to capture Petsamo and the narrow strip of territory giving Finland access to the Arctic, while the left wing struck southwest toward Kemijaervi in the hope of capturing the Tornea-Kemijaervi railway, thus cutting Finnish railway connection with Sweden. About midway on the eastern frontier of Finland a second Russian force launched a heavy attack on Suomussalmi, apparently designed to reach Uleaborg on the Gulf of Bothnia and thus to cut Finland in two at the narrowest point. A third Russian army operated north of Lake Ladoga in an attempt to flank the strong Mannerheim Line, which defended Viborg and the Karelian Isthmus. The largest Russian force was eventually concentrated for an attack on this famous line, which was a "fortification in depth," consisting of a system of blockhouses, pillboxes, and other kinds of ingenious fortifications like those in the German West Wall and in the French Maginot Line.

WINSTON CHURCHILL IN THE BOMBED HOUSE OF COMMONS

"We would rather see London in ruins and ashes than that it
should be tamely and abjectly enslaved."

Although the Russians for weeks made little progress against the Mannerheim Line, in the north Soviet troops captured Petsamo and penetrated a considerable distance into Finnish territory. The Finns fought heroically, and as they retreated they deliberately devastated the region and left the Russians to face subzero blizzards without shelter or adequate supplies. During the latter part of December the Finns in turn launched counterattacks which not only stopped the Russian advance but in some cases drove the Soviet troops back onto Russian soil. Thus the Russian attempts at a war of movement were checked in the north with heavy losses. Apparently the Soviet high command was unable to solve the problem of transport security over bleak forest lanes and roads far from the Murmansk railway.

In January the Russians turned their special attention to the Karelian front. Heavy guns, which could outrange the Finnish artillery, there began to take their toll, and late in January Soviet troops made the first breach in the Mannerheim Line. A relentless pressure was maintained against the bravely fighting Finns by replacing tired or decimated Soviet divisions by fresh troops. But for the Finns there could be no such replacements. The weight of man power and munitions gradually turned the scale. For some days on the Summa sector in February the Russians fired 300,000 shells daily, while from overhead hundreds of airplanes dropped their deadly bombs. On February 26 the Russians finally captured the fortress island Koivisto, which served as the western anchor of the Mannerheim Line, and a few days later they were approaching Viborg. Meanwhile, whenever the weather permitted, Soviet airplanes operating from the new Russian bases in Estonia constantly bombed Helsinki and the southern Finnish cities. With their most powerful line broken, their second largest city about to fall into the hands of the enemy, and little prospect of securing from abroad sufficient assistance [7] to stop the Russian "steam roller," the Finnish government sued for peace. At Mos-

---

[7] According to statements made by Chamberlain and Daladier, the Finnish Field Marshal Mannerheim in January had said that he had men enough to last until the spring thaw came, but that he would be glad to have 30,000 trained soldiers in May. Before that time, however, the Allied supreme war council decided to offer Finland a fully equipped expeditionary force, and the Finnish government was told in February that if Finland appealed for help before March 5 the Allied force would be dispatched. At the beginning of March an Allied army of 100,000 men was ready to be sent. But Norway and Sweden would not grant passage to the Allied troops because of threats of German intervention, and Finland therefore never requested Allied aid.

cow on March 12 Finnish plenipotentiaries accepted the Russian-dictated terms. Said the Finnish foreign minister: "Our only fault was that we are too small a nation." [8]

By the treaty of Moscow Finland ceded to Russia the whole Karelian Isthmus, including the Mannerheim Line, Viborg and its bay and islands, and a number of islands in the Gulf of Finland. She also surrendered territory west, north, and northeast of Lake Ladoga, so that that lake became entirely Russian. By these cessions Finland lost one of her most densely populated regions, formerly containing more than 10 per cent of the republic's population and the country's second most important port.[9] Finland also lost territory north of Markajaervi and Kuolajaervi, which had the effect of moving the frontier farther west from Russia's Murmansk railway where formerly Finnish territory came nearest to it. This cession therefore helped Russia to protect her communications with Murmansk. In the extreme north, Finland's part of the peninsula of Rybachi was also surrendered. On the other hand, the Soviet government agreed to evacuate the Petsamo area, thus leaving Finland in possession of her nickel mines and a port on the Arctic.

But Russia acquired a number of concessions other than territorial. She secured the right of transit traffic to and from Sweden, and for this purpose the Finnish and Soviet governments agreed to build at once, each in its own territory, a railway connecting Kandalaksha, a Russian port on the White Sea and on the Murmansk railway, with Kemijaervi. Such a railway might conceivably facilitate a Russian advance to the Gulf of Bothnia, where Soviet troops could cut rail communication between Finland and Sweden or even move upon the valuable Swedish iron mines beyond Lulea. Similarly, in the far north Russia obtained the right of free transit for her citizens through the Petsamo region into Norway and the right to send goods to and from Norway free from control and free from transit duties. Russian commercial aircraft were also given the right to fly over the Petsamo territory. On the other hand, as a safeguard against any possible Finnish threat to Murmansk, Finland was compelled to agree

[8] According to official Finnish and Russian statements respectively 15,700 Finns and 48,745 Russians were killed during the Soviet invasion.

[9] On March 31, 1940, the Soviet government incorporated the Karelian Isthmus in the Karelian Soviet Republic to form the "Karelian-Finnish Soviet Socialist Republic." It was estimated in Helsinki that some 400,000 people from the ceded territory would have to be resettled in Finland and provided with work.

SCANDINAVIA AND THE BALTIC, 1939

not to keep any submarines or military aircraft in the Arctic waters and to refrain from establishing there naval ports, bases, or shipyards in excess of those required for the few ships of not more than 400 tons each permitted to her.

Finally, Finland agreed to give Russia a thirty-year lease of the peninsula of Hangoe, with territory within a radius of from three to five miles, together with a number of islands. Here Russia was to be permitted to establish a naval base and maintain land and air forces for the protection of the entrance to the Gulf of Finland. Coastal artillery at Hangoe, in conjunction with that at the Soviet naval base at Baltiski in Estonia, could easily command the entrance to the gulf.[10] It is obvious that the terms forced upon Finland in March, 1940, were much more severe than the demands made in the previous October. It seems clear, too, that once the terms of the treaty had been executed Finland would be as little able to resist future Russian aggression as was Czechoslovakia in the case of Germany after the Munich settlement. Certainly the Soviet Union by its steps in Lithuania, Latvia, Estonia, and Finland had immensely improved its defensive position in the west. It had advanced its air and naval outposts down the Baltic, had gained complete control of the Gulf of Finland, had extended Soviet territory to surround Lake Ladoga, and had destroyed the threat of the Mannerheim Line to the important Leningrad district. By other concessions wrenched from Finland, it had prepared the way for a possible drive across northern Scandinavia to the open Atlantic at some future time.

### THE "PHONY" WAR IN THE WEST

Meanwhile, on October 6, after his armies had victoriously completed their conquest of Poland, Hitler in a speech before the Reichstag had launched a peace offensive. Possibly hoping that the Western democracies, confronted by his *fait accompli* in the East, might be willing to consider a cessation of hostilities, he asked, "Why should there be any war in the West?" It could not change the new situation in the East. The Poland of the Versailles treaty would never rise again, for, he declared, "two of the greatest states of the world

[10] In July, 1940, Russia demanded and received military transit facilities through Finland to the naval base at Hangoe by way of Finnish railways. The original peace treaty provided that Russia could contact Hangoe only by sea.

guarantee that." So far as the West was concerned, he continued, the treaty of Versailles was now "extinct," and Germany saw "no cause for any further revision except for the demand for such colonial possessions as are due to the Reich and correspond to it." Hitler proposed removing "step by step the obstacles to free trade" and creating "an absolutely guaranteed peace and a feeling of security among all the peoples" by "a final sanctioning of the status of Europe" and by "the reduction of armaments to a reasonable and economically tolerable extent." But, he threatened, if the war continued in the West, it would not be limited to the continent. There were, he asserted, "no longer any islands."

Neither Great Britain nor France, however, was in a mood to accept Hitler's peace terms, which, in the view of Prime Minister Chamberlain, were "based on recognition of his conquests and his right to do what he pleases with the conquered." "Peace conditions," he vehemently declared, "cannot be acceptable which begin by condoning aggression." The British knew all too well that in modern war between great powers victor and vanquished must alike suffer cruel loss. "But surrender to wrongdoing would spell the extinction of all hope and the annihilation of all those values of life which have, through centuries, been at once the mark and the inspiration of human progress." Furthermore, the British prime minister continued, the peace for which the Western democracies were fighting "must be a real and settled peace, not an uneasy truce interrupted by constant alarms and repeated threats." As to Hitler's fresh assurances, Chamberlain asserted, the "plain truth is that . . . it is no longer possible to rely upon the unsupported word of the present German government." "The issue is therefore plain," he concluded. "Either the German government must give convincing proof of the sincerity of its desire for peace by definite acts and by the provision of effective guarantees of its intention to fulfill its undertakings, or we must persevere in our duty to the end." Obviously the day of appeasement had passed. The war therefore continued.

But in the ensuing six months there was relatively little activity on the western front, although by the beginning of October 158,000 men of the British Expeditionary Force had arrived in France and had taken up their assigned positions. At the outset of the war the Western democracies adopted the principle of a unified command, and the French General Maurice Gamelin was given supreme control of the forces in France. Allied operations at sea were placed under the direction of the British Admirals Chatfield and Pound, and the Allied air force was put in charge of Sir Cyril Newall of the Royal Air Force. But, as already pointed out, even during the Nazi invasion of Poland the French made little effort to smash the German West Wall. General Gamelin was reported as saying that he had no intention of starting "a new Battle of Verdun." If this was undesirable while seventy or eighty divisions of Germans were involved in the Polish campaign, it appeared doubly so after the German forces along the West Wall, reinforced by troops freed in the East, had gained superiority in numbers over the Anglo-French.

Nor did the much-dreaded war in the air develop as had been predicted. The German air force made little attempt to destroy French communications back of the Maginot Line, and on the other hand the Allied bombers left untouched the great German munition industries in the Ruhr not far behind the West Wall. At the opening of the war the children of London were hastily evacuated to escape the expected air bombardments, and civilians in London, Paris, and elsewhere were instructed to carry gas masks and to take refuge in air-raid shelters when the sirens warned of the approach of enemy airplanes. Nightly the larger cities were subjected to precautionary "blackouts." But the great mass attacks on cities so frequently predicted did not occur. Allied warplanes bombed the German civilian population, but the bombs were propaganda leaflets informing the Germans that the Allies had no war with them, that if they would rid themselves of Hitler peace could be easily achieved.

On the sea the war proceeded more nearly in accord with expectations. As in 1914, the overwhelming British sea power drove German shipping into home or neutral ports. Except in the Baltic the German flag disappeared from the seas. And, as in 1914, the Germans struck back with submarines, of which they had an estimated sixty or seventy at the outbreak of hostilities. Nor did they delay in starting their "unrestricted" campaign. As early as September 4 the British passenger ship *Athenia* was sunk with 1400 persons on board, of whom more than 300 were Americans. Thereafter neutral as well as Allied shipping was sunk without discrimination by submarines, mines, and airplanes, but the total losses of the Allies and neutrals in the first nine months of the war were only a third as great as in the same period after February 1, 1917.[11]

Also, to prey upon Allied and neutral shipping, German pocket battleships slipped through the British blockade and roamed the high seas. One of these, the *Deutschland,* accompanied by the light cruiser *Emden,* encountered the British converted merchant cruiser *Rawalpindi,* manned by reservists and carrying only six-inch guns. Under the devastating fire from the German eleven-inch and six-inch guns the *Rawalpindi* went down with the loss of 250 lives. On December 13 the British navy more than evened the score, however, when the British cruisers *Exeter, Achilles,* and *Ajax,* despite inferior armaments, outmaneuvered and outgunned the Reich's newest pocket battleship, the *Graf Spee,* and so damaged her that she fled for refuge into Montevideo harbor. Faced by the necessity of leaving the neutral port and renewing the battle at the end of four days, the Nazi ship on orders from Hitler was sailed out of the harbor on December 17 and deliberately scuttled.

By this time it seemed to be abundantly clear that the Allies had decided to wage a war of attrition, relying upon the increasing pressure of economic strangulation to force Germany to her knees. That it was recognized that this would be a slow process was indicated by the British government's announcement that it was basing its policy on the assumption that the war would continue three years or more. To strengthen themselves for the long struggle the Western democracies resorted to diplomacy and on October 19, 1939, signed a tripartite treaty of alliance with Turkey.

By the terms of this treaty France and Britain agreed to help Turkey if the latter were attacked by a European power or if she were involved in war through an act of aggression leading to war in the Mediterranean area. Turkey on her part promised to aid France and Britain if an act of aggression by a European power involved them in a Mediterranean war or if they were engaged in hostilities in pursuance of their guarantees to Rumania and Greece. Turkey's obligations were not to become effective, however, if as a consequence they would involve her in a war with Soviet Russia. It appeared, therefore, that the alliance was designed primarily to immobilize Italy in the

[11] But the British suffered the loss of two first-line warships during the first two months of the war.

Mediterranean and to provide the Allies with aid in case Germany should attack Rumania or Greece. Further to guard against possible contingencies a French force under General Weygand was concentrated in Syria, and troops from Australia, New Zealand, and India began to arrive in Egypt and Palestine early in 1940.

In order to strengthen the Allied economic position, an Anglo-French Co-ordinating Committee was established in November, 1939, to supervise all purchases required by the Allies and to provide for the best use in the common interest of the resources of both countries. At the same time, to weaken the Reich's economic position, a British order in council, issued in retaliation for illegal acts [12] ascribed to Germany, on November 27 provided for the blockade of German exports whether coming directly from German-controlled ports or indirectly through neutral ports. Thereafter both imports to and exports from the Reich were, so far as possible, to be intercepted by the Allies.

Meanwhile, legislative action of the United States Congress had the effect of increasing the military resources available to the Allies. On November 4 the American neutrality act of 1937 was repealed and a new "cash and carry" neutrality act became effective. By the provisions of the former act the export of arms to belligerent powers had been forbidden, and airplane deliveries to the extent of more than $70,000,000 had been embargoed even though the orders had been placed by Great Britain and France before the outbreak of the war. By the new act the United States returned to its "traditional neutrality," which permitted the sale of American goods to all belligerents who were in a position to obtain them, though certain restrictions were placed upon such purchases. The export of all goods must be preceded by transfer of title to a foreign government or national; no goods might be carried to a belligerent country [13] in American ships or airplanes; and all loans and credits to belligerent governments were forbidden. Other provisions of the act forbade American ships and American citizens to enter combat areas in the war zones, and closed the ports and territorial waters of the United States to the sub-

---

[12] Among these acts were the sinking of Allied and neutral vessels in violation of the submarine protocol of 1936, signed by Germany, and the sinking by mines laid indiscriminately and without notification of Allied and neutral vessels in contravention of the Hague convention of 1907.

[13] In effect this prohibition applied only to European belligerents, the bill expressly exempting ports in the western hemisphere, in the Pacific and Indian Oceans, the Bay of Bengal, the China, Tasman, and Arabian Seas, and the South Atlantic.

marines of foreign belligerent powers. Although the withdrawal of all American ships from trade with the Allies inevitably decreased the tonnage available for conveying goods from the United States to Great Britain and France, the opening of the United States to purchases by the Allies provided the latter with industrial plants for the manufacture of war materials which were safely outside the range of German bombing airplanes. In the succeeding months orders to the extent of more than $1,000,000,000 were placed in the United States by the Anglo-French Co-ordinating Committee.

In December Great Britain, Australia, Canada, and New Zealand launched a scheme for training pilots and air crews safely beyond the reach of German bombers also. Their plans called for the establishment of sixty-seven training schools with staffs of 40,000 men in Canada. The twenty existing air fields in that country were to be enlarged, and sixty new ones were to be constructed. Canada was to become the greatest air training center in the world, and it was planned that when in operation the schools in Canada, Australia, and New Zealand [14] would produce 20,000 pilots and 30,000 air crews yearly. But the scheme was expected to take some years to carry to completion.

To many observers there seemed to be a leisureliness about Allied long-range plans for the war that was at times extremely disturbing. Although the British were gradually being called to the colors under the system of conscription, there were, according to the French,[15] only ten divisions of British troops on the western front by May, 1940. Although the Germans had for years been working at a full wartime pace in the production of military supplies, and in the six years prior to the war had spent 90,000,000,000 marks ($36,000,-000,000) in war preparation, Great Britain, as Winston Churchill pointed out in January, 1940, had much slack to take up, and had not yet done this or there would not be 1,300,000 unemployed. The complacent assumption prevailed in high quarters that France was protected by the impregnability of the mighty Maginot Line and that Britain was safe behind her mastery of the sea. In the words of British War Secretary Hore-Belisha, this was "a fortress war," a war of endurance in which the Germans, to win, must break through the

[14] The schools in Australia and New Zealand would give a certain amount of training to candidates before they were sent to Canada.

[15] According to the British prime minister there were 400,000 British soldiers in France in May, 1940.

Allied defenses, "an assault upon which was awaited with confidence by the French high command." The eyes of most of those in authority appeared to be turned toward the past, and to believe that the system of trench warfare and the slow war of attrition which had won in 1918 must inevitably win again.[16] They seemed blinded to the significance of the *Blitzkrieg* which the German armored divisions and bombers had waged in Poland.

That there was some uneasiness in the Allied countries over this complacency seemed to be indicated when, on March 19, 1940, Daladier was forced to resign as premier in France. A strong feeling prevailed that his government had not been sufficiently aggressive and bold in its prosecution of the war, that, specifically, it had failed to give adequate support to Finland. The new premier, Paul Reynaud, had long been an uncompromising opponent of Nazi Germany. He was not associated with the futile policy of "appeasement" which Daladier had pursued in conjunction with Chamberlain. Nor was he one of those who looked upon the Allied situation with complete satisfaction. "It must not be thought," he had earlier declared, "that all to be done is to wait patiently for victory. It is not patience but ardor that is required. . . . What the democracies have lacked during twenty years to win peace has not been material means, but lucidity and daring." Reynaud retained Daladier and many former ministers in his cabinet, but transformed it into more of a national government by persuading the Socialists to accept three places. Significantly, he appointed as undersecretary of war General Charles de Gaulle, who for years had preached almost unheeded the doctrine of motorizing and mechanizing the French armed forces. Within a month the tremendous importance of such mechanized divisions was again revealed by Germany's invasion of Norway.

## Hitler's Seizure of Norway and Denmark

For some time the situation in Norway had been a cause of concern to the Allies, especially to the British. The latter, determined to make their blockade of Germany as tight as possible, realized that the 800-mile corridor of territorial waters along Norway's much-indented

---

[16] The distinguished British historian, Arnold J. Toynbee, pointed out before the war that history teaches that once a nation wins wars or makes conquests by a particular ephemeral technique which may have been revolutionary in its formation, it ends by idolizing that technique and stubbornly adheres to it long after it has outworn its usefulness.

coast constituted a serious threat to their success. German warships and submarines moved up and down it as they desired. Stray German liners [17] and merchant ships, seeking to return to Germany from the outer seas, followed this route. German importation of much-needed Swedish iron ore was made possible by use of the Norwegian port of Narvik and Norwegian territorial waters. Often the ships were escorted and supposedly protected by Norwegian torpedo boats.

The first indication that the British might interfere with the free use of this corridor by German ships came in February, 1940, when it was discovered that the *Altmark* was moving down the Norwegian coast. This ship had acted as an auxiliary to the *Graf Spee* and was known to have some 300 British seamen imprisoned aboard. On February 16 two British destroyers tried to stop the German ship, but the commander of the escorting Norwegian torpedo boat protested, and the British ships withdrew. That night, however, a British destroyer entered the fjord where the *Altmark* had taken refuge. The latter was boarded and the British prisoners were rescued. Although Great Britain at first maintained that the Norwegian government had failed in its duty as a neutral by not searching the German ship and releasing the British prisoners, Chamberlain admitted later that Great Britain had committed "a mere technical breach of neutrality" which took no neutral lives and touched no neutral property. "Merchant vessels may be sunk, cargoes may be destroyed, the crew may be turned adrift to drown or perish of exposure, and the neutral country must not complain." Why then, asked Chamberlain, should the Nazis now "exhaust themselves in exclamations of hysterical indignation"?

Eventually the British government decided that Germany's use of Norwegian territorial waters should be interrupted and that German shipping should be made to come out into the open sea. More than 150 neutral vessels had already been destroyed by German action, the Allied governments asserted, and "a heavy proportion of the losses inflicted had fallen on Norwegian shipping; yet Germany continued to demand from the Norwegian government the fullest use of Norwegian territorial waters, and the Norwegian government had even

[17] The most famous instance was the German liner *Bremen*, which had sailed from New York just before the Nazis invaded Poland. She at first took refuge in Murmansk and then eventually reached home on December 12 by using the Norwegian territorial waters.

been obliged to provide armed escort in their own waters for German ships." The Allied governments felt unable to acquiesce in that state of affairs and on April 8 notified Norway that mine fields had been laid off three specified points along her coast and that British patrol craft would be stationed near them to warn ships over the dangerous areas.

It so happened that Hitler had concluded that Germany could not win a long war of attrition and that she must and could smash the Allies in the west. He had already decided, as a preliminary step, to seize Norway and Denmark, and on the very next night after Britain announced her new mine fields German troops suddenly landed at the Norwegian ports of Narvik, Trondheim, Bergen, Stavanger, Egersund, and Arendal, and on the Oslo estuary, and early the next morning Denmark was similarly invaded by land and sea. Some of the "Trojan horse" troop transports, disguised as innocent merchant or ore ships operating through the territorial waters of Norway, must have left Germany at least a week before this blow was struck.[18] Warships must have been so dispatched as to reach all the Norwegian ports simultaneously,[19] and the requisite air force must have been carefully assembled to protect the troop transports against possible attack.

But German military efficiency was not the sole explanation of the astounding success of the attack. Apparently the way had also been carefully prepared within Norway by the creation of a "fifth column" [20] of Nazi sympathizers led by Major Vidkun Quisling and Colonel Konrad Sundlo. The easy conquest of the almost impregnable Oslo fjord was made possible because fake orders were sent to garrison commanders and naval units not to resist the Germans. At Narvik, in fact, the port was turned over to the Germans by Colonel Sundlo without resistance. Once more the world was given an example of Nazi success in boring from within.

Early on the morning of the ninth identical German notes were

[18] Reports from Narvik on the eighth had stated that there were seven German ships in the harbor there and eight others inside territorial waters south of the port.

[19] The British had learned on April 7 that a large German naval force was moving along the Norwegian coast, and that night the British battle fleet and the second cruiser squadron had sailed in the hope of engaging the enemy.

[20] This term seems to have originated during the Spanish civil war, when a Nationalist general stated that besides the four columns converging upon Madrid the Nationalists had a fifth column of sympathizers within that city who would co-operate with the forces outside when the right time came.

handed to the Danish and Norwegian governments, that to the latter being presented at 5 A. M., after the Nazi landings had already been effected. Both notes alleged that the German government had learned of the Allied decision to seize ports in Norway, and explained that Germany believed that the Norwegians would not or could not successfully resist. Germany therefore felt it necessary to take action for the protection of Scandinavia, and any attempt to block German efforts would be crushed. The notes were accompanied by demands that the government (in the case of Norway) should, among other things, instruct the people not to resist German troops; order the Norwegian army to co-operate with the Germans; surrender all military establishments and fortifications; disclose the exact location of all Norwegian mines; turn over all means of communication, including radio; prohibit all ships and airplanes from leaving the country; forbid all external mail; and submit immediately to German censorship.

King Christian and the Danish government at once submitted to German control, and Denmark became, at least temporarily, a German protectorate. But King Haakon and the Norwegian government decided that no independent country could accept such demands, and fled from Oslo to avoid capture by the Germans. On the next day the German government increased its demands upon Norway, insisting that a new government must be created headed by Major Quisling and other Nazi sympathizers. King Haakon declined to accede to this demand, and was thereafter forced to flee from place to place to escape pursuing German airplanes.

The British and French governments immediately announced that they would "extend their full aid to Norway." In a British naval action in the Skagerrak, carried out chiefly by submarines, several German transports were sunk, but Nazi supremacy in the air deterred the British surface fleet from attempting to cut off German reinforcements by that route. In the far north, however, the British battleship *Warspite* led a destroyer flotilla into Narvik fjord and sank the seven German destroyers there. On April 15 British military forces arrived in the Narvik area.[21]

The initial stroke of the Germans gave them a tremendous advantage over the Allies in the subsequent struggle for the control

21 The British eventually captured Narvik but abandoned it on June 9 when the Germans were advancing into France.

of Norway. In Oslo they possessed an excellent port to which they could ferry reinforcements protected by submarines and by airplanes operated from captured Danish and Norwegian air fields. Although they lost some transports as the result of Allied mines placed in the Skagerrak and Kattegat, they were able to land sufficient men and adequate military equipment for a swift campaign. Their chief objective was to open a route between their Oslo forces and the German units at Trondheim.

The Allied expeditionary forces were handicapped from the very outset. All the better ports were in the hands of the Germans, and the Allied troops were compelled to land in small ports without proper harbor facilities for handling heavy military equipment and without neighboring air bases. The chief Allied objective was to isolate Trondheim from rail communication with the German base at Oslo. Despite German superiority in the air, an Allied force landed at Namsos between April 14 and 18 and moved southward, only to be thrown back by better-equipped German troops supported by German aircraft and by German warships in the adjoining fjord. The Allied force lacked both antiaircraft guns and fighter aircraft of their own, and before long Namsos itself was nearly destroyed by German bombing airplanes. Meanwhile, a second Allied force landed at Andalsnes between April 17 and 19 and attempted to cut the railways linking Oslo and Trondheim. But German mechanized units moved swiftly up from Oslo through both the Osterdaal and the Gudbrandsdaal, encountering relatively little resistance,[22] and on April 30 these units met the German forces pushing southward from Trondheim. From that moment the fate of the 12,000 Allied troops in central Norway was sealed. By May 3 they had evacuated both Namsos and Andalsnes, and the German control of southern Norway was assured. The operations of German tanks and armored cars had clearly shown that a *Blitzkrieg* could be carried through even in mountainous country if air superiority was assured.[23]

By their seizure of Norway and Denmark the Germans had gained valuable submarine and air bases for use in their campaign

[22] The Norwegian failure to blow up bridges and tunnels greatly facilitated the German advance.

[23] On June 9 the war in Norway ended with the capitulation of the Norwegian army and the flight of King Haakon and his government to London. On April 16 British troops had landed in the Faroe Islands, and on May 10 they landed in Iceland.

against the British navy, and excellent ports from which they might operate in any future attempt to invade Great Britain. Furthermore, they had taken steps to safeguard themselves against an attack from the rear, should they decide to launch a *Blitzkrieg* on the western front. Incidentally, they had increased their resources temporarily by commandeering foodstuffs and other supplies which Norway and Denmark had at the time of the invasion.

That the German seizure of Norway might have far-reaching results politically for the latter was indicated a few months later. On September 25 the German commissioner for Norway announced that effective from that date King Haakon had been removed as the head of the state, the royal succession had been broken, all political parties had been abolished, and Major Quisling would thereafter be the sole political leader. Temporarily a council of fifteen, selected by the German commissioner, was placed in charge of the Norwegian government, and legal provision was made for the indefinite occupation of the country by troops of the Reich. Moreover, Norway was deprived of all control of her foreign policy and foreign relations. What the ultimate fate of this unhappy land would be—whether it would be treated like Bohemia-Moravia or like the Polish Government-General —remained for the future to unfold.

But one political result of Hitler's victory in Norway came swiftly and at once, namely, the downfall of Neville Chamberlain's government in Great Britain. On May 11 Winston Churchill, who during the preceding years had repeatedly pointed out the disaster that awaited Britain unless she awoke and prepared for the coming conflict with Hitler, became prime minister. Included in his new government were outstanding representatives of all three British political parties, the Labor Party receiving a number of important positions. Clement Atlee and Arthur Greenwood—Labor leader and deputy-leader respectively—were among the five members of the new war cabinet in which Chamberlain was retained in a position of minor responsibility. Two of Chamberlain's former critics were also included in the ministry, Anthony Eden becoming secretary for war and Duff Cooper minister of information. It was generally believed that Churchill would inject new life into Britain's military, economic, and diplomatic efforts. That there was need for every effort, if defeat was to be avoided, was already apparent.

## "Blitzkrieg" in the West

The day before Churchill became prime minister the Nazis unleashed another terrific attack which Hitler in a proclamation to his troops asserted would "decide the fate of the German people for a thousand years." At approximately 3 a. m. on May 10 German troops began to cross the frontiers of the Netherlands, Belgium, and Luxembourg. An hour later German parachute troops landed and seized the airport of Rotterdam, and before 5 a. m. seaplanes had alighted on the Maas (Meuse) River in the heart of that city and Nazi forces had occupied the bridges and two railway stations. Other parachute troops were landed at Dordrecht, at Delft, and near The Hague, and the airdrome at Amsterdam was heavily bombed. At the very outset of the invasion, therefore, the small Dutch air force was rendered practically useless by the capture or destruction of its landing fields. Thereafter Nazi reconnaissance planes informed the German high command where Dutch reinforcements were proceeding and might be bombed, and where Nazi troops could advance with the least opposition.

While Dutch troops heroically fought near the frontiers to stem the tide of the invasion, bombing and parachute attacks destroyed large parts of Rotterdam, damaged Amsterdam and The Hague, and caused general confusion in the rear of the defending armies. Apparently there was again in this case, too, a certain amount of "fifth column" activity to assist the Germans. The important Moerdiik bridge across the estuary of the Maas and Waal Rivers, for instance, fell undamaged into German hands. German mechanized forces drove swiftly through the Dutch defense lines and on May 14 reached Rotterdam, while to the north the important city of Amsterdam was being bombed and attacked by parachutists. Overwhelmed by the sheer number of German bombers, tanks, parachutists, and troops, General Winckelman, commander-in-chief of the Dutch forces, realized the futility of further resistance and on May 15 suspended hostilities. Queen Wilhelmina and the royal family had already fled to England. As the result of only five days of *Blitzkrieg* the Netherlands lay powerless before the Nazi invaders. The country was at once placed under the control of Reich Commissioner Seyss-Inquart, who had played such a prominent role in bringing about the *Anschluss* with Austria.

Simultaneously with their attack on the Netherlands the Germans struck at Belgium and Luxembourg. The latter was completely overrun on the first day of the attack. But the Belgians hoped that their strong defense line along the Meuse River and the Albert Canal from Givet on the French frontier to Antwerp on the Scheldt would enable them to hold off the invaders until Allied forces could come to their aid. By 6 A. M. on May 10 British and French mechanized units were moving toward Belgium, and before the day was over the Allied forces were advancing on the front extending from the North Sea to the Moselle River. On the next day, however, the powerful Belgian fort commanding the passage of the Meuse River and the Albert Canal fell to the Nazis, and their capture of bridges over the Albert Canal permitted the Belgian defense line to be outflanked. One week after the opening attack German troops marched into Brussels, and Antwerp was thereupon at once abandoned by the Belgian forces. On May 18 Hitler incorporated the former German districts of Eupen, Malmédy, and Moresnet in the Reich.[24]

But it was farther south that the Allies suffered a gigantic military disaster. As soon as the French forces had moved hastily forward to assist the Belgians, the Germans concentrated the full force of their terrific attack against the relatively weak but vital Sedan-Montmédy sector defended by the French Ninth Army under General Corap. For some incredible reason the bridges over the Meuse were not destroyed, and on May 15 the Nazis crossed the river north of Mézières at three points. By the next day the battle from Namur to Sedan had become open warfare with motorized units and aircraft participating. By May 19 the German forces had opened a sixty-mile gap through the weaker extension of the Maginot Line and had reached St. Quentin and Rethel. These German successes came, it appeared, as the result of "an effective combination of shock infantry, repair engineers, followed by tank squadrons and armored troop carriers, behind which came petrol carriers and supply trains, working in perfect co-ordination with air squadrons and artillery support."

In the face of this disaster Premier Reynaud took prompt measures. General Gamelin was at once replaced by General Weygand, who had been hastily summoned from his army in the Near East, and General Corap was supplanted as commander of the Ninth Army by

---

[24] For the circumstances under which these districts had become Belgian, see page 486.

General Giraud, who, however, was almost immediately captured while reconnoitering in a tank. But the German mechanized forces could not be stopped. Protected by swarms of bombers, they broke through the French lines near Péronne, captured Amiens on May 21, and then sped on to Abbeville near the mouth of the Somme. By completing this advance the Germans had succeeded in isolating the Allied forces in Belgium and northern France from the main body of the French armies. German troops and supplies were rushed through the Somme gap in the Allied lines so that pressure might be brought from both south and north against the Anglo-French armies in Flanders. The Nazis envisaged the complete annihilation or capture of these forces.

From the south the Germans swiftly began to close in. The important port of Boulogne was occupied by their mechanized forces on the night of May 23, and Calais was attacked on the twenty-seventh. Meanwhile, other German armies were constantly pounding the Allied forces in Belgium, where the northern flank was held by the Belgian army led by King Leopold. This army was subjected to terrific punishment by the Germans, who appeared to have singled it out for their most severe attack in the north. General Weygand flew to King Leopold's headquarters to discuss the situation and was informed that the Belgians could not hold out without "substantial new assistance." But such new assistance could not, of course, be given. On May 27 the Belgian king, against the advice of his ministers, finally asked the Germans for armistice terms, and was told that his army must surrender unconditionally. Leopold agreed, and early on the morning of May 28 the Belgian troops were ordered to cease fighting.

The collapse of Belgian resistance exposed the left flank of the Anglo-French forces in Belgium and made desperate the efforts to withdraw them through Dunkirk before their annihilation. Their escape was aided by the valiant stand of a small British force at Calais, which held back for four precious days the German mechanized columns pushing up from the south. It was made possible by the mobilization of 220 war vessels and 650 other craft of all descriptions, by the British air force, which in the limited area around Dunkirk gained a superiority in the air, and by foggy weather, which helped to reduce the casualties suffered in the evacuation. Although the British and French admitted the loss of twelve destroyers and twenty other craft, War Secretary Eden announced that 350,000 of the 400,000 men in the British Expeditionary Force had been rescued before the Germans eventually captured Dunkirk on June 3. But the British admitted that their army in Flanders had lost 30,000 men, 1000 guns, and all its mechanized equipment in what Prime Minister Churchill characterized as a "colossal military disaster."

With the German capture of Calais and Dunkirk the Battle of the Ports ended and the first phase of the German drive on the western front was over. In twenty-four days Hitler's armies had overrun and conquered the Netherlands, Belgium, Luxembourg, and an important section of France extending from Montmédy to Abbeville north of the Somme and the Aisne. The victory was the most crushing German military triumph since Hindenburg's battle of Tannenberg.[25] Not only had the channel coast opposite England fallen to the Nazis; all the ports in western Europe from Abbeville to Narvik beyond the Arctic Circle were now within their hands. The diplomatic as well as military effect of these conquests was far-reaching.

During the last two weeks of the Battle of the Ports the French had hastily prepared defensive positions extending roughly along the Somme, the Oise-Aisne canal, and the Aisne to Montmédy at the western end of the Maginot Line. This new position was hopefully called by the populace the Weygand Line. Preceded by a large-scale air attack on Paris two days before, the Germans launched their new offensive against this Weygand Line at 4 A. M. on June 5. The Battle of France, destined to decide the fate of the Third Republic, had begun. To meet the invader the French army stood practically alone, for most of the shattered British forces which had escaped from the Flanders trap were in England, recuperating and seeking new equipment to take the place of that abandoned in the hasty evacuation from Dunkirk. One British division held the extreme left of the French line south of Abbeville.

As in Poland and in the Netherlands and Belgium, the German strategy was to cut through the enemy position with armored divisions, assisted by deadly dive bombers. Although the French troops fought valiantly and tirelessly to stem the Nazi tide, they not only were decisively outnumbered by the attacking troops but were overwhelmed by German superiority in airplanes and tanks. Courage alone could not check the terrific onslaught. By June 10 the Nazis

[25] See page 399.

had driven a wedge to the Seine near Rouen and had thus isolated Paris from the important port of Havre. On that day Mussolini, who had been becoming more and more bellicose with each advance of the Germans, took Italy into the war against France and Great Britain. This step removed all possibility of sending any of the million men on the Italian front to relieve the weary French soldiers before Paris, many of whom had not slept for five days and nights.

Northeast of Paris on June 11 a German armored column forced the French to withdraw to positions south of the Marne in the vicinity of Château-Thierry. The Nazis were beginning to encircle the capital, and the French government fled to Tours and then on to Bordeaux. In order that Paris might be spared the fate of Warsaw and Rotterdam, the government withdrew all troops and declared the capital an open city. German troops made a peaceful entry into the city on June 14. The fall of the capital undoubtedly had a disastrous effect upon the morale of the French, especially upon some of the political leaders.

Already on June 12 General Weygand had informed the French cabinet that the military situation was practically hopeless, and most of the ministers believed that the total occupation of France was therefore inevitable. Some urged an immediate armistice, but Premier Reynaud was determined that France should continue to fight as the ally of Great Britain, should never make a separate peace even if the government had to be transferred to northern Africa. On June 10 he had sent an impassioned plea for help to President Roosevelt, and two days later he personally explained the seriousness of the French situation to Prime Minister Churchill and War Secretary Eden. Churchill promised to rush all available men and equipment to France, and even proposed that France and Great Britain should thereafter constitute "one Franco-British Union" with a common citizenship and "joint organs of defense, foreign, financial, and economic policies." But such promises and offers, it appeared, could do little immediately to stem the onrushing Germans. What France needed, at once, as Reynaud had informed President Roosevelt, was "clouds of airplanes." But neither Great Britain nor the United States could send such aid.

On June 16, after the German armies had captured Verdun, had begun to cut off the Maginot Line from the rear, and had penetrated it in frontal attacks from the north and east, Reynaud was forced to resign. His place as premier was taken by the 84-year-old Marshal Pétain, the hero of the first Battle of Verdun. By this time the industrial life of France was demoralized. In German hands were

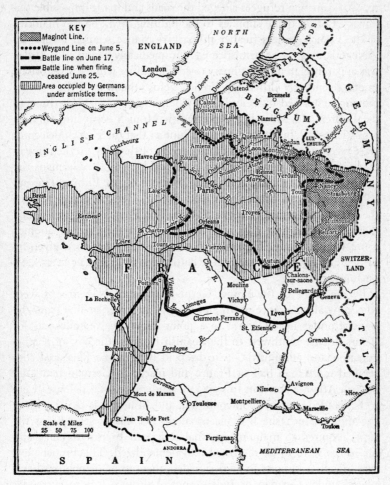

THE COLLAPSE OF FRANCE, 1940

80 per cent of her coal production, most of the Briey iron-ore field, ports that formerly handled 50 per cent of her foreign trade, the textile center of Lille, the oil centers of Rouen and Havre, one of the

main plants of the Schneider-Creusot arms works at Havre, and the Paris area, which included most of her automobile, tank, and airplane-engine factories. And in the rear of the French armies more than 10,000,000 civilian refugees clogged the roads and made impossible the transport of adequate supplies to the fighting men. To the majority of the French leaders further military resistance seemed futile.

Negotiations for an armistice were immediately begun. But Hitler was apparently in no great hurry to end hostilities while his victorious troops relentlessly drove the French before them with their swift-moving motorized units and deadly bombing airplanes. On June 18 the Führer and Mussolini conferred in Munich regarding suitable armistice terms, but it was not until June 21 that the French delegates were received by Hitler. On the afternoon of that day, in the railway coach [26] at Compiègne in which Foch had handed the Germans the armistice terms in 1918, and in the presence of the Führer, Göring, Ribbentrop, Hess, Brauchitsch, and Raeder, General Keitel read to the French the armistice terms of 1940. The French delegates signed these terms the next day, and two days later they signed another armistice with Italy. The order to stop hostilities was then given by Hitler, and fighting ceased on the battlefields of France at 12:35 A. M. on June 25.

By the terms of the Franco-German armistice Nazi troops were to occupy all of France north and west of an irregular line from the Swiss frontier near Geneva to a point about twelve miles east of Tours, thence southwest to the Spanish frontier, the cost of the occupation and administration to be paid by France. This area constituted more than half of France and placed in German hands all French Atlantic ports. In this area all land and coastal defenses were to be handed over in good condition, and France was to clear away the mines which she had placed along her coasts. Except for the units required to maintain internal order, all French military and air forces were to be disarmed and demobilized. The French fleet was to collect in ports to be designated, there to be demobilized and placed under German or Italian control. France was to surrender

[26] After the armistice terms had been presented, Hitler ordered that the historic car and the near-by monument to France's World War triumph should be taken to Berlin, that the stones which marked the places where both the car and the train of the German plenipotentiaries of 1918 had stood should be destroyed, but that the monument to Marshal Foch should be preserved unharmed.

undamaged as much of the artillery, tanks, warplanes, antitank and antiaircraft guns, and mechanized equipment of her army at the front as Germany might demand, and all military equipment in the unoccupied area was to be placed under German or Italian control. Further manufacture of war materials was to be stopped, and no Frenchman might serve against Germany in the army of another power. All German prisoners held by France were to be surrendered, but French prisoners were to be held by Germany until the end of the war. France, furthermore, was to surrender any Germans on French territory whom the Reich government might designate, in order, apparently, that the Reich might arrest those anti-Nazi Germans who had sought refuge in France. French radio stations were to be silenced, flight by airplanes over French territory was to be prohibited, and all French landing fields were to be under German or Italian control. Finally, France was to facilitate freight traffic between Germany and Italy.

By the Franco-Italian armistice Italian troops were permitted to occupy a very narrow Alpine strip of French territory extending from Switzerland to the Mediterranean,[27] and a thirty-mile strip beyond the occupied area was to be demilitarized. Demilitarized zones were also to be established on the French side of the Franco-Libyan frontier and along the coast of French Somaliland. Italy was granted full right to use the port of Jibuti and the French section of the Jibuti–Addis Ababa railway. For the duration of the war France was also to demilitarize her fortified areas and naval bases at Toulon, Bizerte, Ajaccio, and Oran. As in the case of the armistice with Germany, France was to surrender upon Italian demand all the equipment of the army which had faced Italy, and was to hand over all Italians who had been taken prisoners.

The terms of these two armistices clearly indicated that France had become a conquered land. On June 20 Marshal Pétain, in a broadcast to the French people, had explained the reasons by contrasting the situation in 1917–1918 with that in 1940. "On May 1, 1917," he declared, "we still had 3,280,000 men under arms, in spite of three years of murderous fighting. On the eve of the present bat-

---

[27] On the day after France asked Italy for an armistice the Italians finally launched what they called a "general attack" from Mt. Blanc to the sea and succeeded in occupying a strip of French territory to a depth ranging from one to five miles. This "conquered" territory constituted the area of occupation.

tle we had 500,000 fewer. In May, 1918, we had 85 British divisions; in May, 1940, we only had 10.[28] In 1918 we had with us 58 Italian divisions and 42 American divisions. The inferiority of our material was even greater than that of our effectives. French aviation has fought at odds of one to six. Not so strong as 22 years ago, we had also fewer friends, too few children, too few arms, too few allies. There is the cause of our defeat."

But Pétain might have said more. He might have pointed out that those at the head of the French military forces had had little conception of the revolutionary changes introduced into warfare by airplanes and motorized equipment; that they had failed to keep pace with Germany's production of these essential instruments of modern warfare, mistakenly putting their reliance in the defensive strength of heavily fortified lines; that, despite the German blow through Belgium in 1914, they had incredibly failed to extend the Maginot Line in its full strength along the Belgian frontier. He might have pointed out that the political leaders of France had failed to grasp the significance of the Nazi revolution or the determination of the Nazi leaders to remake the map of Europe; that in the years when they should have been devoting their united efforts to preparing their country for defense, they had kept France weak by their continual maneuvering for personal political preferment. He might have pointed out that during the period when capital and labor were sternly regimented in Germany in order that the nation's industry might pour out military equipment for use in a future war, French industrial and economic life was repeatedly demoralized by strife between workers and employers, with disastrous results for the production of war supplies. He might have pointed out, finally, that if France and Britain were determined to prevent German hegemony over western Europe they should have moved against Hitler in 1936—when he remilitarized the Rhineland in disregard of the Versailles and Locarno treaties—before he had had time to gain for the Reich such a superiority in mechanized and armored equipment and in bombing and fighting airplanes, before he had absorbed Austria and destroyed Czechoslovakia, and while Russia and Italy were still suspicious of him. Then, perhaps, Nazi aggression might have been checked.

[28] The British government maintained that there were 400,000 British troops in France in May, 1940.

### The Battle of Britain

Spectacular though Hitler's military successes had been against Poland, Norway, the Netherlands, Belgium, and France, they had not by the midsummer of 1940 attained for him his principal objective—the end of the war on his own terms. Though Great Britain had seen five states, including her chief ally, crushed in a few weeks by the mighty power of Hitler's war machine, she was determined to fight on. "Bearing ourselves humbly before God," Prime Minister Churchill declared on July 14, "but conscious that we serve an unfolding purpose, we are ready to defend our native land against the invasion by which it is threatened. We are fighting by ourselves alone. But we are not fighting for ourselves alone." "Should the invader come to Britain," he warned, "there will be no placid lying down of the people in submission before him. . . . We shall defend every village, every town, and every city . . . we would rather see London in ruins and ashes than that it should be tamely and abjectly enslaved. . . . Thus only, in times like these, can nations preserve their freedom."

But once again, on July 19, Hitler launched a peace offensive, as he had done in the preceding October after the German conquest of Poland. At the close of a long address in which he outlined to the Reichstag the astounding successes of the Nazis during the preceding months, he declared:

I . . . realize that this struggle if it continues can end only with the complete annihilation of one or the other of the two adversaries. . . . In this hour I feel it to be my duty before my own conscience to appeal once more to reason and common sense in Great Britain as much as elsewhere. I consider myself in a position to make this appeal since I am not the vanquished seeking favors but the victor speaking in the name of reason. I can see no reason why this war must go on. I am grieved to think of the sacrifices which it will claim. I should like to avert them also for my own people. I know that millions of German men, young and old alike, are burning with a desire at last to settle accounts with the enemy, who for the second time has declared war upon us for no reason whatever. But I also know that at home there are many women and mothers who, ready as they are to sacrifice all they have in life, are yet bound to it by their very hearts. Possibly Mr. Churchill will again brush aside this statement of mine by saying that it is merely born of fear and of doubt in our final victory. In that case I shall have relieved my conscience with regard to the things to come.

There was a close similarity between Hitler's peace plea of 1940 and that of the Kaiser's government in 1916.[29] Both were issued just after the Germans had won a decisive military triumph, at a time when German military successes had reached their highest point, when on the map of Europe German power seemed most widely extended. Both pointed out the invincibility of German arms and declared that there could be no doubt of the final outcome if the war continued. But both failed to offer any specific peace proposals, any definite terms upon which Germany would be willing to end the war. There was in the Führer's speech no suggestion that peace must be based on justice, no word of recognition that the other nations of Europe had the same right to self-determination that Hitler had so often invoked for the Germans.[30] The picture of Europe was one of Germany lording it over the peoples who had been deprived of their freedom.

As the Allies in 1916 considered the German peace offer an attempt to undermine the morale of the Allied peoples, so in 1940 the British characterized Hitler's speech as an effort to divide opinion in Britain, purposely designed to weaken the will power of the British people. At the same time, as in 1916, it seemed aimed to remove from the shoulders of the Berlin government, in the eyes of the Germans, the blame for the continuation of the war. If severe hardships and suffering came to Germany in the following months, Hitler would be in a position to assert that his was not the responsibility. But if he hoped that Britain, faced by his threats, would immediately sue for peace, he was disappointed. "We realize that the struggle may cost us everything," Foreign Secretary Halifax declared. "But we shall not stop fighting till freedom, for ourselves and others, is secure."

[29] See page 419.

[30] On July 26 it was reported from "reliable sources" in Berlin that Hitler's peace terms included the following points: (1) the British Empire to stay out of Europe proper; (2) the Kamerun and former German East Africa to be returned to Germany but former German Southwest Africa to remain with the Union of South Africa; (3) the Belgian Congo to go to Germany; (4) Germany to guarantee the British Empire protection of its colonies from the "Yellow Peril"; (5) Norway to remain a German province; (6) Belgium to become a protectorate under King Leopold; (7) Germany to keep that part of France already occupied, except Paris; (8) the Netherlands to be a protectorate, with no molestation of the Netherland colonial possessions; (9) Italy to have a free hand in the affairs of Spain and Greece under German supervision; (10) Italy to have all the Adriatic coast.

In the ensuing Battle of Britain which, according to many, might decide the fate of the world, each side had certain advantages. In man power Germany with a population of more than 80,000,000 held a distinct advantage over Great Britain, which without her overseas empire had only some 48,000,000. The British regular army at home, despite the adoption of conscription in March, 1939, consisted in July, 1940, of only 1,500,000 men. These were supported by another million "Home Guard" volunteers who had been hastily organized to destroy parachutists and other air-borne invaders. But the great bulk of the British troops were men who had never campaigned under actual war conditions, and many of them were incompletely armed and equipped. Moreover, the British suffered from a serious shortage of tanks, artillery, antitank guns, and even small arms. The German army, on the other hand, consisted of approximately 3,500,000 men, all well trained and fully armed and equipped. It was a veteran force, by most observers considered in July the best and most powerful in the world. Of course, a large part of Germany's troops had to be kept in the various conquered territories—Bohemia-Moravia, Poland, Norway, Denmark, the Netherlands, Belgium, and France. Nevertheless, it seemed rather certain that, if Great Britain in July had been merely another country on the Continent, adjacent to France, she would have been overrun and conquered by the Germans.

But, regardless of Hitler's declaration that there were "no more islands," Great Britain remained separated from the Continent by a moat of water twenty miles or more in width. And she had, moreover, the most powerful navy in the world, greater by far than the navies of Germany and Italy combined. With more than a thousand armed ships this royal navy was determined to risk complete destruction, if necessary, to prevent the landing of an invading army in Britain. The warships did more than defend the British Isles against a foreign foe, however. Day and night they blockaded the coast of Europe from the Arctic Circle to the Dardanelles, completely isolating the Axis powers from extra-European trade except for the small amount that might come by the overland route through Russia. The inclusion of Spain and Portugal within the scope of this blockade, following the collapse of France, closed the last sea door against the Axis powers.

While part of the navy was thus used to sever Europe's commercial contacts with the rest of the world, another part kept the lanes of commerce open for British trade. Obviously, if Great Britain were cut off from her overseas trade, she would inevitably collapse for want of food and the necessary materials for her industries. Many ships of the royal navy, especially destroyers, were used to convoy British and neutral ships carrying cargoes to or from the island kingdom.[31] The difficulty of the task of obtaining goods from abroad was greatly increased by Germany's conquest of some of the European countries which were formerly sources of British supply. The longer hauls required to secure commodities from the New World or other overseas regions placed an added burden upon the British merchant marine. Nevertheless, it was upon the effective work of her navy and her merchant ships that Great Britain counted for ultimate victory in what she expected to be a long war of endurance.

But the war of 1939 had proved to be entirely different on land from that of 1914, largely because of airplanes, and Hitler counted upon superiority in the air to make the outcome at sea likewise different. Although in some categories British airplanes were superior to the German in quality, there seemed little doubt that at the opening of the Battle of Britain Germany possessed an air superiority of three or four to one in the number of warplanes. Here again, of course, not all German airplanes could be used in operations against Britain, for many of them had to be distributed throughout the conquered territories, and many others had to be maintained at the hundreds of air bases at home.

But the Germans possessed not only the advantage of a superior number of airplanes. Thanks to the conquests they had made from April to July, they held a great advantage geographically. Scores of new air fields in southern Norway, Denmark, the Netherlands, Belgium, and France gave German airplanes admirable bases for attacking the southern and eastern coasts of Britain. As a result, the latter was geographically and industrially much more vulnerable to air attack than Germany. The distance which German bombers had to fly to reach their commercial and industrial objectives in Britain was far less than that necessary for the British to strike at German industrial

---

[31] Great Britain's need for added destroyers for convoy duty led to a deal between the British and the United States governments which President Roosevelt announced to Congress on September 3. In return for fifty over-age American destroyers, Great Britain gave the United States ninety-nine-year leases on a number of shore and island bases stretching from Newfoundland to British Guiana, and at the same time pledged herself not to scuttle or surrender her fleet under any conditions.

areas. Furthermore, industry in Britain was more concentrated than in Germany. Although the British had a highly organized air-defense system, consisting chiefly of fighter airplanes, antiaircraft guns, and balloon barrages, the effectiveness of these defenses against mass attacks by thousands of airplanes had yet to be proved.

Another advantage Hitler possessed in having Mussolini as an active ally, at least if the war against Britain were to be relatively short. Although many considered that Italy might prove to be the Achilles' heel of the Axis in case of a long war, it was undoubtedly true that in the early months of the Battle of Britain Italian activities in the Mediterranean and in Africa kept in those regions many British fighting ships and airplanes which might otherwise have been used for defensive purposes at home.

Since Hitler could not capitalize on his victories on the Continent until Great Britain had been forced to make peace, and since it seemed that the latter could better stand a long war of relative inaction and economic attrition, it devolved upon the Axis powers to take the offensive. And the most important objective in that offensive must be the conquest of Great Britain herself, for Italy's seizure of British territory here and there in Africa could not of itself put Britain out of the conflict so long as she retained control of the sea and continued to have access to her dominions and to the United States. The chief role, therefore, in the war against Britain fell to the Germans, and particularly to their air forces.

Experts believed that there were three ways in which the Germans might attack and ultimately conquer Britain. In view of the great air superiority of the Nazis, it was thought that the German airplanes by terrific offensives in which thousands of bombers would be used might overwhelm the British air forces as they had overwhelmed those of Poland and the Netherlands. Then, once British air fields had been destroyed and British airplanes had been grounded or wrecked, the Germans would do to the industrial cities of Great Britain what they had done to Warsaw and Rotterdam. Factories, power plants, warehouses, business centers, means of communication, if necessary the homes of the people, would be destroyed, and Britain would merely collapse internally.

A second plan envisaged by the experts was the concentration of Nazi air attacks upon the various British ports and upon the convoys of ships bringing supplies from overseas. Through the Thames estuary, for example, nearly 30,000 ships normally passed each year carrying goods to and from London's 1700 wharves. According to the proponents of this plan, most of these wharves would be destroyed and most of these ships would be sunk, and what was done there would be done also at Southampton, Plymouth, Bristol, Liverpool, Glasgow, and the other British ports. Furthermore, it was thought that from Norwegian ports and airdromes German submarines and warplanes would operate against shipping entering the Irish Sea from the north, while others from French coastal bases would destroy those ships which tried to enter that sea from the south. If these "siege" actions were carried through successfully, Great Britain would be forced to surrender or starve.

The third plan which experts considered likely was the actual invasion of the island by the German army. In this case, it was believed, the Germans would attempt to "pulverize" a comparatively small area near the English Channel. At the same time they would seek to gain control of the air over the Channel so that airplanes, assisted by submarines, would drive all defending British ships out of the narrow waters where a crossing would be possible. A "bridgehead" would then be established in Britain by troops landed at first, perhaps, by parachutes, transport airplanes, and small, speedy boats, and to it subsequently large motorized forces would be transferred. The military conquest would then proceed as it had previously done on the Continent. In preparation for such an invasion the British converted a twenty-mile stretch along the east and south coasts of Britain into a defense zone, from which, in some places, civilians were evacuated. In that zone defense works were erected—antiaircraft guns, coastal artillery, concrete "pillboxes," trenches, barbed-wire entanglements —and day and night the British troops kept guard against the invader. Behind this defense zone, throughout the island, innumerable measures were also taken to prevent or hinder the landing of enemy airplanes.

Even before the signing of the Franco-German armistice, Hitler launched his attack upon Britain. During the night of June 18–19 German warplanes bombed the Thames estuary and southern England. On the following night British airplanes struck back, bombing Hamburg, Bremen, Cologne, Düsseldorf, Frankfort, and other places. Thus was inaugurated the long-expected and much dreaded air war between the Reich and Great Britain. Daily and nightly, during the ensuing weeks, the raids regularly continued, each country using relatively few airplanes, and each apparently seeking to bomb merely military objectives.

During the latter part of July, after Hitler's second peace offensive had failed, the Germans increased somewhat the intensity of their air attack. In place of the previous regular but relatively small raids they launched continuous and unremitting assaults on a considerably larger scale, designed, the Germans asserted, to "soften up" the British by reducing munitions and aircraft production, by forcing increased rationing of food, by terrorizing the people and lowering their morale. Special efforts, too, were made to destroy the shipping being convoyed along the British east coast. The number of airplanes shot down or otherwise destroyed rapidly increased on both sides, though the British claimed they were inflicting losses upon the Germans at a ratio of three or four to one. Meanwhile, deep into Germany British bombing squadrons continued nightly to attack munitions factories, oil refineries, and hydrogenation plants. Nightly the air-raid sirens screamed, and not only British civilians, who had never experienced the horrors of war on their own soil, but Germans, whose country had not known foreign invasion for more than a century, came to feel the terrors of war in the homeland.

With the opening of the second week in August the Germans further increased the number of airplanes being sent over Britain. On August 8 the biggest air combat yet fought occurred over a British naval convoy in the Channel when several hundred German airplanes attacked in successive waves. Three days later a mass attack on a still larger scale was made along a 200-mile stretch of British coast from Portland to the Thames estuary. All the next day, too, hundreds of German airplanes bombed Britain's southern coast, and at night ranged inland to every corner of the kingdom. On the thirteenth, again, wave after wave of German airplanes attacked, bombing particularly Southampton and the British air bases in southeastern England. On August 15—the day when it was rumored that the Germans might land a force in England—from early morning until late into the night the most powerful Nazi bombers and fighters swarmed by the hundreds over the island from all directions, hurling destruction upon England, Wales, and Scotland. For the first time the suburbs of London were attacked when scores of dive bombers struck at Tilbury docks on the Thames and at the great

Croydon airport. For three more days the mass raids continued with great waves of airplanes roaring across the Channel. But the German military invasion failed to materialize.

Late in August the Germans declared that the "preliminaries" to the Battle of Britain were over and announced that "systematic destruction" would soon start. Beginning on September 6 the Nazi bombing attacks were greatly increased, and, though other parts of Britain were not wholly neglected, special efforts were made to destroy or "erase" London. German bombers, directed personally from an airdrome in France by Marshal Göring, unleashed furious attacks upon the British capital. In the beginning the docks and factories along the Thames and the adjoining slums of the East End of London suffered especially. But gradually the Germans extended their attacks, dropping incendiary as well as explosive bombs. Fires in various parts of the city illumined the skies almost nightly, and much destruction resulted not only in the industrial and commercial sections of the city but in the residential areas as well. The German bombers, it appeared, were dropping their loads of explosives upon the city with little discrimination as to targets, and delayed-action bombs were used from time to time to increase the nervous tension of the Londoners. Berlin announced that waves of bombers would continue to strike at London until the British people set up a government which would be willing to accept German terms. After London, the nerve center of Great Britain, had been destroyed, the Nazis asserted, the less important cities would suffer a similar fate. During the ensuing months German bombers did their utmost to make good this threat.

Meanwhile, the British air force had been striking back, not only in the air over Britain but far over Germany and even down into northern Italy. Nightly the British bombed various objectives as far east as Berlin. After mid-September, when the fear of a heavy full-scale German invasion increased, the R.A.F. heavily bombed Nazi barges and supply ships in Calais, Boulogne, Dunkirk, Havre, Ostend, Antwerp, and other ports as well as supply depots and railway junctions in the Ruhr and the Rhineland. When the Germans unloosed their long-range guns against the coast of Kent, British airplanes and British warships answered by bombing their emplacements. Whether or not the strong British air offensive against the points of German embarkation was responsible, certain it is that a year after the capitulation of France no German army had yet landed in Britain. Although London, Coventry, Birmingham, Bristol, Liverpool, and other cities had suffered heavy property damage, they had not been "erased." Nor had the British air force been put out of the conflict. On the other hand, there seemed little hope of being able to stop the endless hammering at Britain by the German airplanes.

By June, 1941, however, it appeared that more serious than the threat of a Nazi invasion of Britain was the German campaign against British and neutral shipping. In May the British admiralty revealed that German mines and air and sea raiders on British ships and ships in British service had, since the beginning of the war, sunk more than 1400 merchantmen, totaling more than 6,000,000 tons.[32] Of this number 885 were British ships. What was particularly disturbing was the fact that the acknowledged losses for the months of March and April, 1941, each exceeded those for any month except June, 1940, which included the costly evacuation from Dunkirk. Although the rate of destruction was not so great as in the first six months of unrestricted submarine warfare in 1917, it was great enough to constitute a very real threat to Britain's ability to transport to her shores the foodstuffs and supplies without which she could not hope to continue the war.

To wage the Battle of the Atlantic Germany was more favorably situated than in the World War. She had many more submarines and airplane bases, and they were more widely scattered—from Norway to the Pyrenees. It was much more difficult than in the previous conflict, therefore, for Great Britain to block German submarines by mine fields, nets, and the like. Her airplanes did, however, almost nightly bomb the most menacing submarine bases on the Continent. The Germans had another advantage over 1917 in the ability of their reconnaissance airplanes to inform submarine commanders of the location of British merchant ships which might otherwise have escaped detection. Great Britain, on the other hand, actually needed more merchant ships than in 1917 because of the longer hauls necessary to secure her supplies. At the same time she was woefully short of ships for use in convoy duty, so that many convoys became relatively easy prey through lack of adequate protection.

In June, 1941, it appeared that Britain's greatest difficulties in the Battle of the Atlantic could be solved only if she obtained more mer-

[32] The Germans put the figure much higher.

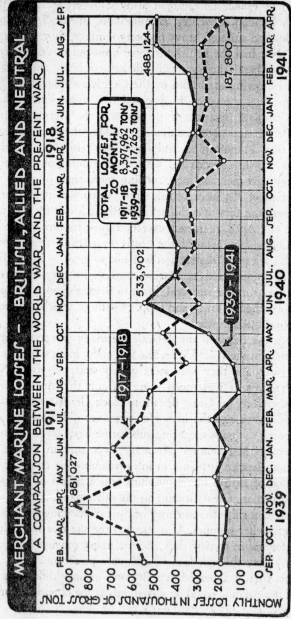

MERCHANT MARINE LOSSES – BRITISH, ALLIED AND NEUTRAL

A COMPARISON BETWEEN THE WORLD WAR AND THE PRESENT WAR

| TOTAL LOSSES FOR 20 MONTHS | |
| --- | --- |
| 1917-18 | 8,397,962 TONS |
| 1939-41 | 6,117,263 TONS |

488,124

187,800

533,902

1939-1941

1917-1918

881,027

1917    1918

1939    1940    1941

MONTHLY LOSSES IN THOUSANDS OF GROSS TONS

900 800 700 600 500 400 300 200 100 0

SEP. OCT. NOV. DEC. JAN. FEB. MAR. APR. MAY JUN. JUL. AUG. SEP. OCT. NOV. DEC. JAN. FEB. MAR. APR.

FEB. MAR. APR. MAY JUN. JUL. AUG. SEP. OCT. NOV. DEC. JAN. FEB. MAR. APR. MAY JUN. JUL. AUG. SEP.

*The New York Times*

chant ships and more aerial and naval protection. How far the various measures taken by the United States [33] might help the British in their struggle to keep the sea lanes open still remained to be seen. That Britain still remained supreme on the *high* seas when it came to naval combat, however, was spectacularly emphasized when the *Bismarck,* Germany's newest and most powerful battleship—by some reputed the most powerful battleship afloat—was sunk on May 27.[34]

## CONQUERED FRANCE

The Nazi *Blitzkrieg* which demoralized and destroyed the French military forces at the same time delivered a mortal blow to French democracy. The Third Republic, born of a humiliating defeat by the Germans in 1870-1871, died as the result of a similar military disaster suffered at their hands in 1940. On July 9 the two houses of the French parliament, meeting at Vichy outside the German-occupied zone, by overwhelming votes approved a draft resolution conferring upon Marshal Pétain full power to draw up a new constitution establishing an authoritarian regime. On the next day the same two houses, sitting as the French National Assembly, officially adopted the resolution, merely adding a proviso that the new constitution should be submitted to a national plebiscite.

On July 11 Pétain issued three constitutional decrees. By the first he assumed the functions of Chief of the French State and abolished the position of President of France. By the second he conferred upon the Chief of State plenary governmental powers both executive and legislative. By the third he adjourned the Senate and Chamber of Deputies *sine die,* and decreed that they should thereafter be convened only on call of the Chief of State. On the next day he appointed what was considered a strongly fascist cabinet, and named former Premier Laval—a friend of Mussolini's—as vice-premier and his even-

[33] See pages 985-988.
[34] A British reconnaissance airplane had reported the *Bismarck's* departure from a Norwegian port. The *Prince of Wales,* one of Britain's newest battleships, and the battle cruiser *Hood,* the largest capital ship afloat, were sent out to engage her. In Denmark Strait between Iceland and Greenland an engagement took place on May 24 in which the *Prince of Wales* was damaged and the *Hood* was sunk with all hands when an enemy shot hit the ship's magazine. A heavy fog enabled the *Bismarck* to escape. The British air force and navy were at once ordered out to scour the seas in search of her, and on May 26 an airplane finally located her some 550 miles off the southwestern coast of England. On the following day she was attacked by British airplanes, destroyers, and battleships and was sunk with almost her entire crew.

tual successor. Later by still another decree (January 27, 1941) all high officials in France were required to swear fidelity to Pétain's person, and the Chief of State was given authority to punish any official who betrayed his duties. Thus by legal steps the Third Republic was converted into the Pétain dictatorship.

Statements by those in authority at Vichy indicated that France's future parliament would probably consist of an upper house appointed by the government and a lower house, similar to Italy's Chamber of Fasces and Corporations,[35] representing trade groups, industry, agriculture, and other divisions of the national life. This parliament would meet only when summoned by the Chief of State, and its duties would apparently be largely advisory. Apparently, too, the French multiparty system, which caused so much ministerial instability between 1875 and 1940, was to be abolished in favor of a single-party system as found in the authoritarian states. Especially significant was Laval's declaration that all "international doctrines" would be banished and all persons who had had any role in the Popular Front government would be eliminated from power.

French economic life, it was stated, would be organized around corporate groups of workers and employers, and strikes and lockouts would be forbidden. In the future, according to the minister of labor, France would abandon her "exaggerated industrialism" and become a peasant country once more. Agricultural renovation would be the basis of national reconstruction. These statements, it seemed, might possibly be interpreted to mean that authoritarian France expected to accept an economic position subordinate to and linked with industrial Germany. Anti-Semitism raised its head, too, when a new paper, *France at Work,* began to advocate the isolation of all Jews, and a number of decrees issued later by the Vichy government showed a distinct anti-Jewish bias.

On July 23 the Pétain government, as the first step in a "moral purge" of the nation, ordered a judicial investigation of the roles played by a number of French statesmen in the Republic's military catastrophe. A few days later a supreme court of justice was created by decree, and before it, according to reports, former Premiers Daladier, Reynaud, and Blum, General Gamelin, and several former ministers in the government were to be tried for taking France into war when

[35] See page 634.

they knew the French were not prepared to fight.[36] A number of prominent men were also arrested and deprived of their citizenship for having fled from Bordeaux to Casablanca, just before the signing of the armistice, in the hope of continuing the war.

Whether these revolutionary measures were taken because the members of the Pétain government believed that France could surmount her crisis only by temporarily submitting to a dictatorship or whether they arose from the conviction that the day of democracy had definitely passed, there was no way of knowing. They might have resulted from the hope that an authoritarian France would receive more lenient treatment than a democratic France at the hands of her authoritarian conquerors. Or they might have been merely forced by irresistible Nazi pressure exerted behind the scenes. On the surface, however, it appeared that France was only the latest victim to succumb to the new revolution which was sweeping over Europe, that under the impact of Nazi ideology and Nazi military victories the French had abandoned their own earlier revolutionary ideals—liberty, equality, fraternity—for the totalitarian ideas of the Nazis.[37]

Not all Frenchmen approved of the actions and policies of the Pétain government. General Charles de Gaulle, Reynaud's undersecretary of war, was one who did not. He believed that France, though conquered on the Continent, should still fight as the ally of Great Britain, continuing to use her navy, her air force, and her vast colonial realm. Upon the collapse of the French army he had fled to London, where on June 22 he had issued a radio appeal urging all Frenchmen outside France to continue the war against Hitler. The interest of France demanded, he declared, "that all free Frenchmen should fight wherever they are." After the signing of the armistice General de Gaulle appointed himself leader of the French outside France and established a Provisional French National Committee. On July 1 he announced the appointment of Vice-Admiral Muselier as

---

[36] Minister of Interior Adrien Marquet declared: "When a country has 1000 airplanes and knows its possible adversary has 15,000, when a country has 4000 tanks and knows its possible adversary has 15,000, the responsible heads of that country should never lead it into war."

[37] The constitutional law of July 10 stated that the new constitution "shall guarantee the rights of work, family, and native land." On July 17 Foreign Minister Baudouin declared: "The world existing before May 10 is definitely buried. Soon new relations will be instituted between capital and labor, and there will be new conceptions of life based on authority, order and obedience."

commander of both the "Free French" naval force and the "Free French" air force.

Meanwhile, relations between Great Britain and the Pétain government had become severely strained. As soon as the armistice went into effect, Great Britain had extended her economic blockade to the occupied areas in France, and on June 28 the British government had recognized General de Gaulle as "leader of all free Frenchmen . . . who rally to him in support of the Allied cause." Eventually a definite break between Great Britain and her former ally resulted when on July 3 the British took drastic steps to safeguard their position on the sea.

As allies Great Britain and France had each agreed not to negotiate for an armistice or peace without the consent of the other, but on June 16 Premier Reynaud had asked the British government to release France from this obligation. Great Britain had reluctantly given her consent, but on condition that the French fleet should be dispatched to British ports and remain there while negotiations were taking place. Following the downfall of Reynaud the British reminded the Pétain government, also, of this condition and were promised that the French fleet would never be allowed to fall into German hands. But the armistice terms which France signed stipulated, as already pointed out, that French warships should be collected in ports to be specified and be demobilized and disarmed under German or Italian control.

Although the German government solemnly declared that it had no intention of using the French fleet during the war, the British felt that Hitler's word was of little value and therefore feared that the situation on the seas might be seriously altered to Great Britain's detriment by the union of the French, Italian, and German fleets. Churchill's government accordingly decided to take drastic measures to prevent this eventuality. Early on the morning of July 3 two French battleships, two light cruisers, eight destroyers, a number of submarines, and about 200 smaller craft which lay in British harbors were seized by superior British forces. This operation encountered little opposition, the combined casualties on both sides being only six. At the same time, at the Egyptian port of Alexandria, a French fleet, consisting of a battleship, four cruisers, and a number of smaller vessels, was informed that it would not be permitted to leave the harbor and fall into German hands. After some days of negotiation, the commander of these French units eventually agreed to a program which would immobilize them for the duration of the war.

But at Oran, the French naval base in Algeria, the situation was not so easily handled. Lying in the harbor there were the two powerful battle cruisers, *Dunkerque* and *Strasbourg,* two smaller battleships, several light cruisers, and a number of destroyers, submarines, and other vessels. To Admiral Gensoul, who was in command of this fleet, the British presented an ultimatum, also on the morning of July 3. Four alternatives were offered. The French fleet might (1) sail with the British and continue the war, (2) sail with reduced crews to a British port, (3) sail with reduced crews to some French port in the West Indies, there to be demilitarized, or (4) be scuttled within six hours. If none of these alternatives were accepted the British battle squadron off the harbor would "use whatever force may be necessary to prevent your ships falling into German or Italian hands." After conversations lasting all day, Admiral Gensoul refused to comply and declared his intention to fight. The British thereupon opened fire and all but destroyed the French fleet as an effective fighting force, though as darkness came on the damaged *Strasbourg* escaped and with some other ships fled across the Mediterranean to the French base at Toulon. A few days later France's mightiest battleship, the 35,000 ton *Richelieu,* after her commander had refused to comply with any of the same alternatives, was disabled by depth charges and aerial bombs as she lay in the harbor of Dakar, French West Africa. By these various actions against the French fleet [38] Great Britain safeguarded her supremacy at sea, a supremacy which obviously might prove decisive in the impending Battle of Britain. Following the British action at Oran the French government broke off diplomatic relations with Britain, and at the same time Germany and Italy mitigated the armistice terms by permitting the temporary nonapplication of those terms regarding the French naval and air forces. Until further notice the French naval bases in the Mediterranean need not be demilitarized.

The spread of General de Gaulle's "Free French" movement to the French overseas empire ultimately strained Anglo-French relations still further. During August and September revolts against the Vichy government in favor of continuing the war in conjunction with Great

[38] In the French West Indies were the French cruiser *Emile Bertin,* the training cruiser *Jeanne d'Arc,* and the aircraft carrier *Béarn* with some 140 airplanes. These ships were blockaded by the British, and eventually in August an agreement was reached that the French ships should be disarmed.

Britain occurred in Chad, French Kamerun, French West Africa, French Equatorial Africa, and some of the scattered French islands. Unrest was also apparent in Morocco and Indo-China. In the latter part of September General de Gaulle decided to assume personal leadership of this movement in Africa, and set out with a small force of "Free Frenchmen" for Dakar, the most important port on the west coast of that continent. He was accompanied by a number of "Free French" and British warships.

But the French high commissioner at Dakar on September 23 refused to permit the landing of the "Free Frenchmen" and shelled not only the landing forces but the British warships as well. The latter returned the fire, and a bombardment of the French colonial seaport ensued. When it became obvious, however, that only a major operation could effect the capitulation of Dakar, hostilities were discontinued, and the expedition withdrew two days later. General de Gaulle declared that he had no wish to be the cause of bloodshed between Frenchmen, and the British disclaimed any desire to enter into serious warlike operations against Frenchmen who were loyal to the Vichy government. Whether General de Gaulle had been misled regarding the strength of the "Free French" movement in Senegal or whether German Nazis, active in strategic Dakar, had been able to force the French authorities to resist seemed uncertain. Indeed, much connected with the expedition was at the time obscured in a mist of uncertainty. It was clear, however, that General de Gaulle's prestige had suffered considerably, although his successful landing in the French Kamerun a fortnight later and the French governor's pledge to aid his "Free French" movement softened the blow somewhat.

But within conquered France not everything was harmonious. In June, 1940, Pétain, Laval, and their associates undoubtedly believed that the war was lost and that when France withdrew from the conflict Great Britain would inevitably be forced to do the same. Britain's determination to fight on altered the situation and caused friction among the French leaders. Laval apparently wished to have France join Germany against Britain, whereas Marshal Pétain maintained that "honor forbids us to take any action against our former allies." But Laval was convinced that the Nazis would win the war, and was determined that France should "collaborate" with Hitler's "new order." Eventually he succeeded in arranging an interview between Hitler and Pétain (October 25, 1940), as a result of which the latter did agree in principle to collaborate with Germany in the reconstruction of Europe.

During the ensuing weeks negotiations regarding the details of collaboration were carried on between Laval and Nazi authorities in Paris. It was rumored that the Nazis demanded that France's collaboration should take the form of handing over the French navy and Mediterranean ports for German use against Britain. These steps Pétain apparently refused to take, although they were urged by his vice-premier. Suddenly, without announcement of any reasons for such a step, Pétain on December 13 dismissed Laval from the government and placed him under arrest.[39] Although he was subsequently released and permitted to take up his residence in Paris, following a hasty visit to Vichy by Otto Abetz, German Commissioner to France, the constitutional decree of July 12 designating him as Pétain's successor was rescinded.

Negotiations for French collaboration were broken off for a time following Laval's dismissal. Hitler had no immediate military plans that were pressing and could afford to let the French wait and suffer "while the cruel wounds inflicted by the conqueror—the partition of the country, the separation of families, the economic bleeding— had time to fester and reduce resistance." At the same time two million French soldiers were held as prisoners by the Reich, while within France stocks of food and materials declined, the budget situation became almost hopeless, and the lack of free communication between the occupied and unoccupied zones tended to split the country in two morally and politically.

Small wonder that early in 1941 the Pétain government sought again to resume negotiations. This time they were intrusted to Laval's successor, Admiral Jean François Darlan, an Anglophobe who bitterly resented the British attack on the French fleet at Oran. Darlan's views regarding collaboration were not greatly different from those of Laval, and eventually he apparently gained the confidence of the Nazi conquerors. After three months of negotiations between the French vice-premier and some of the lesser Nazi officials in Paris, on May 12, 1941, an interview finally occurred at Berchtesgaden between Hitler and Darlan. Pétain had earlier stated that conquered France was not free, that a German noose was hung

[39] According to rumors, Laval had planned to execute some kind of *coup d'état* against Pétain in favor of the Nazis.

around her neck, and that the Nazis gave it a twist whenever they wished to exert pressure. Apparently in May, 1941, Hitler tightened the noose.

After Darlan's return to Vichy Pétain in a broadcast to the French people stated that he approved in principle of what had been agreed upon at Berchtesgaden, and declared that it "is no longer a question today of public opinion . . . being able to estimate the chances we are taking . . . or judge our acts. For you, the French people, it is simply a question of following me without mental reservations along the path of honor and national interest. If through our close discipline and our public spirit we can conduct the negotiations in progress, France will surmount her defeat and preserve in the world her rank as a European and colonial power." The spirit of Pétain's utterance was not greatly different from what might have been expected from the Führer or the Duce.

What French collaboration might entail seemed revealed in part when on May 15 it was reported that German and Italian warplanes had begun using Syrian airdromes as bases from which to attack the British in Iraq. When in turn the British attempted to bomb Axis airplanes in Syria, they were met by antiaircraft fire from French guns in that country. That the French collaboration policy might assist Hitler in his effort to gain control of the Mediterranean seemed probable; that it might actually lead to a Franco-British war did not seem beyond the realm of possibility.

## THE NAZI ADVANCE INTO THE MEDITERRANEAN

From the moment that France had begun to reel before the Nazi attack in June, 1940, the Balkans had become more and more the center of diplomatic intrigue and aggression. Soviet Russia had been the first to disturb the *status quo* in that part of Europe. On June 26, 1940, Foreign Commissar Molotov had presented Rumania with a twenty-four-hour ultimatum demanding the immediate cession to Russia of Bessarabia and northern Bukowina. After frantically seeking the advice of Hitler and Mussolini, who had urged acceptance in order to prevent a new war, the Rumanian government had acceded to the demands, and Russian forces at once occupied these additional territories.

This experience, coupled with the startling successes of the Nazis in the West, had its effect upon the political situation in Rumania, which for a year had wavered back and forth between the Axis powers and the Western democracies, appearing to favor first one side and then the other. In June, after the collapse of France, she threw in her lot with the totalitarian powers. King Carol by decree converted Rumania into a totalitarian state with only one legal political party, the "National Union Party," headed by the king. Jews were forbidden to join this party, and subsequent developments indicated that the government would pursue an anti-Semitic policy. An amnesty for political criminals was declared, and imprisoned members of the fascist Iron Guard [40] were freed. On July 1 the government renounced the Anglo-French guarantee of April 13, 1939, and ten days later it announced Rumania's decision to withdraw from the League of Nations.

On July 4 a new cabinet was organized which included several members of the Iron Guard and several others who had been in the pro-Axis, anti-Semitic government set up by Octavian Goga in December, 1937.[41] The new foreign minister, an Iron Guard member, had recently returned from Germany. A government statement at once declared that in foreign affairs Rumania would follow a policy of integration with the Axis. "By this policy," Prime Minister Jon Gigurti asserted, "we return to the old traditions of the Rumanian state.[42] It means the total transformation of the internal political structure, dominated by an effective and creative nationalist conception." This pro-German attitude was soon further revealed by the dismissal from the oil fields and the expulsion from the country of forty British subjects, by the government's expropriation of the country's largest oil company, in which the British had large holdings, and by the seizure of British barges on the Danube.

Probably Rumania's quick decision to align herself with the Axis powers was motivated in part by her hope that they would protect her from further loss of territory. At the time that Russia took Bessarabia and northern Bukowina, Hungary and Bulgaria both showed signs of a determination to regain the territories which Rumania had taken from them. Troops were rushed to both frontiers, and the possibility of another Balkan war seemed imminent. This Hitler and

[40] For a discussion of the Iron Guard, see pages 809–810.
[41] See page 810.
[42] For Rumania's pro-German attitude before the World War, see pages 70, 316.

Mussolini at the moment wished to avoid at almost all costs. In July Hungary's premier and foreign minister were therefore summoned to Munich to confer with Ribbentrop and Ciano and apparently were told that Hungary must not resort to military measures to regain Transylvania. Later in the month the leaders of the Rumanian and Bulgarian governments were likewise summoned to Germany and

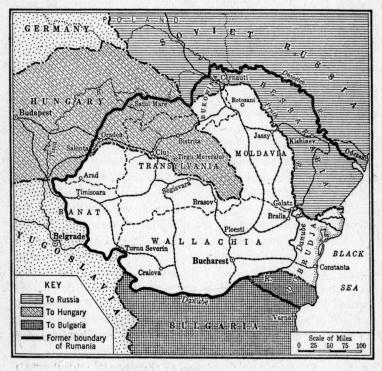

THE PARTITION OF RUMANIA, 1940

Italy for conferences, shortly after which it was announced that Rumania was prepared to cede some of the disputed territory to Hungary and Bulgaria.

Negotiations in regard to the exact extent of the cessions were initiated in August. Apparently without great difficulty an agreement was reached by which Rumania ceded to Bulgaria that part of the Dobrudja which the former had taken from the latter in 1913 at the close of the Second Balkan War.[43] The official entry of the Bulgarian civil administration into the southern Dobrudja began on September 15.

But not so quickly nor so easily did the Rumanians and the Hungarians reach an accord. Instead, their discussions became deadlocked, and on August 25 Hungary referred the whole question to the Axis powers for "arbitration." The latter hastened to impose a settlement. On August 29 the German and Italian foreign ministers met in Vienna with representatives of Rumania and Hungary. On the next day Hungary was awarded the northern half of the province of Transylvania—about 19,300 square miles—which enabled her to push her frontier to the Carpathian Mountains. Rumanian troops, it was agreed, should withdraw from this territory within two weeks. Germany and Italy assumed the responsibility of guaranteeing the new frontiers of both Hungary and Rumania, and the latter powers, in turn, agreed to permit German minorities to accept Nazi ideology without hindrance. Obviously the way was thus opened for Hitler to avail himself of "fifth columnists" within these two states if he should later have occasion to use them.

Within Rumania strong opposition to the settlement at once developed among the peasants of Transylvania, who threatened to resist the Hungarian occupation. In Bucharest, too, much dissatisfaction was manifest, and the Iron Guard sought to take advantage of the situation to stage a coup against King Carol. In an effort to strengthen his position, the latter thereupon dismissed the Gigurti government and invited General Jon Antonescu, a strong nationalist who was held in high esteem by the Iron Guard, to form a ministry. But Antonescu, only recently released from prison, where he had been placed because of prohibited political activity, forced King Carol to surrender practically all his powers, and on September 6 compelled him to abdicate in favor of his son, who for the second time became King Michael V. While the latter immediately called back to Rumania his exiled mother, former Queen Helen, the newly exiled Carol and Magda Lupescu fled precipitously from the country in a special train. General Antonescu assumed the title of "Chief of State," set up a government in which power was largely concentrated in his own hands, and on September 14 decreed the establishment of an Iron Guard totalitarian state whose foreign policy would be in com-

[43] See page 352.

plete accord with that of the Rome-Berlin Axis. Early in October German troops entered Rumania and began the occupation of that country with the permission of Antonescu's government. Another state, it appeared, had succumbed to Nazi forces, and Rumania's lot appeared to be little better than that of Denmark. In the case of Rumania, however, no protest against the Nazi action was lodged.

Germany's military occupation of this Balkan country, it was explained, resulted from the need to police the Ploesti oil fields in order that they might be protected against British sabotage, and from the need to train Rumanian soldiers in German methods and efficiency. The occupation was designed further, it was stated, to implement the guarantee of Rumania's borders which had been given by the Axis powers at the time of the Vienna award of Rumanian territory to Hungary. Whatever the explanation, the fact was self-evident that at last Hitler had reached the Black Sea, one of the principal objectives which he had outlined in *Mein Kampf*. Airplanes, tanks, and submarines were reported being sent to the Russian-Rumanian frontier and to Rumanian Black Sea ports during the rest of October.

The next move in the Balkans was made by Hitler's partner in the Axis. Following an ultimatum which accused Greece of aiding Great Britain and which demanded permission for Italian troops to occupy strategic Greek bases in order to guarantee Greece's "neutrality," Mussolini on October 28 ordered his troops to advance across the Greco-Albanian frontier. The invasion was no great surprise. Ever since Italy's entrance into the war, the Duce's government had been building up a case for an attack upon the Greeks, and for weeks prior to October 28 Italian troops had been massing on the Greco-Albanian frontier. What occasioned surprise was the successful resistance of the outnumbered and poorly equipped Greeks.

Mussolini's forces launched their invasion on two fronts—eastward from Koritza in Albania toward Florina, Edessa, and Saloniki, and southward from Albania paralleling the coastline of the Ionian Sea. The former campaign, if successful, would put them in possession of probably the most important commercial city in the Balkans and would enable them to cut the important railway connecting Yugoslavia with the Aegean. A successful southward thrust might isolate Corfu, Cephalonia, and other strategically important Greek islands in the Ionian Sea.

But the Italians did not reach these objectives. Instead they themselves were at first forced to stand on the defensive, and then later they were compelled to retreat into Albania. Whether this sudden reversal of the situation arose from the Duce's expectation of little Greek resistance and from Italy's consequent lack of preparation for a difficult campaign was not clear. The Italians apparently were able to make little headway with their mechanized equipment over the mountain roads rendered more impassable by the winter weather. Furthermore, British ships and bombing planes helped the Greeks to interfere with the shipment of Italian men and supplies across the Adriatic. On November 12, 1940, for instance, British bombers and torpedo planes made a spectacular raid from aircraft carriers against the Duce's fleet in the Italian naval base at Taranto, badly damaging a number of enemy fighting ships. Moreover, from the Greek island of Crete, where the British secured naval and air bases, the British air force launched bombing attacks upon Naples and southern Italy. For their part, during the first three months of 1941 the Greeks fought stubbornly on over difficult terrain toward Avlona, the chief port of Albania.

During the winter of 1940–1941 there was much speculation as to whether and how Hitler might go to the assistance of his ally. German airplanes and aviators were sent to Italy and Sicily, and a considerable number of German troops of various categories apparently entered the country, also. It was even rumored that there was increasing dissatisfaction among Italians at the presence of these German forces, and some observers reported that Italy had become subordinated to the Reich to a degree little less than conquered France.

Meanwhile, it appeared, Hitler had been attempting to persuade the small states of central Europe and the Balkans to support the "new order" which the Nazis had announced for postwar Europe. In November he had made some headway, for within a week (November 20, 23, 24) Hungary, Rumania, and Slovakia had signed the tripartite agreement of September 27, 1940, which Germany, Italy, and Japan had made to facilitate the establishment of "a new order in Europe" and "in Greater East Asia." [44] Additional Nazi troops were soon sent to Rumania, and during the opening weeks of 1941 they were gradually concentrated on the frontiers of Bulgaria

[44] See page 980.

and Yugoslavia, apparently in the hope that pressure might force these states, also, to join the Axis powers and thus open the way to an attack upon Greece down the Struma and Vardar valleys.

Despite Churchill's warning to Bulgaria not to forget the misfortunes which came to her from choosing the wrong side in the World War, those elements in the country gained the ascendancy which believed that the Nazis would win the present war, that it would be futile for Bulgaria to try to resist the German military machine, and that Bulgaria might, in fact, regain some of the territory lost in 1913 and 1919 if she allied herself with the Reich. During February there occurred a considerable infiltration of German forces into Bulgaria, and on March 1 the Bulgarian government finally joined the Axis powers by signing the tripartite agreement in Vienna. Within a few hours Nazi forces were reported in occupation of Sofia. Great Britain, which had broken off diplomatic relations with Rumania on February 10, did the same with Bulgaria on March 5.

Everything now pointed to the further spread of the war in the Balkans, for the Nazis were now able to concentrate on the Bulgarian-Greek frontier, from which they could menace Saloniki. Great Britain, in turn, began to transfer men and equipment from the army in Egypt to Greece, largely, no doubt, to encourage the Yugoslavs to hold out against the Axis. Both sides exerted pressure upon the government at Belgrade. As early as February 13 the Yugoslav prime minister, Dragisha Cvetkovich, had conferred with Hitler at Berchtesgaden, where he had undoubtedly been both threatened and cajoled. After Bulgaria had succumbed to Hitler's pressure and Nazi forces in consequence were able to concentrate on nearly all sides of Yugoslavia, the regent, Prince Paul, and Cvetkovich and his ministers apparently came to the conclusion that discretion would be the better part of valor.

They knew that if they defied Hitler and war resulted, the only route by which Yugoslavia could receive assistance and supplies was up the Vardar valley from Saloniki—and this route might be speedily cut by German mechanized forces. Furthermore, they feared that if they went to war against the Axis it might mean the end of Yugoslavia, for Bulgaria would be quick to demand the territory which she had lost in 1913 and 1919, Mussolini would undoubtedly seek to extend Albania at Yugoslavia's expense, and dissident Croats might throw their lot in with the Nazis in the hope that a dismembered Yugoslavia might result in an independent Croat state. The long-standing quarrel between the Croats and Serbs has already been discussed.[45] Although the moderate Croats were fairly well satisfied by the autonomy which had been granted Croatia in 1939,[46] Vice-Premier Matchek, the leader of the Croatian Peasant Party, feared that the Germans might incite the radical elements among the Croats to desert the Serbs in case of war. He therefore favored "collaboration" with the Third Reich as a means of preserving the territorial integrity of Yugoslavia.

On March 25 the Yugoslav government formally signed the tripartite pact in Vienna. Apparently the Axis powers gave assurances that Yugoslavia's sovereignty and territorial integrity would be respected, and received in return the promise of economic advantages and transit facilities for Nazi war materials through Yugoslavia. It was rumored, also, that Cvetkovich had agreed to demobilize the Yugoslav army. The news of this capitulation to the Axis was received in Yugoslavia—at least in the districts which had constituted Serbia and Montenegro—with anger and resentment, which finally culminated in a bloodless *coup d'état* in the early morning hours of March 27. The regency of Prince Paul and the government of Premier Cvetkovich were both overturned. On the next day the seventeen-year-old son of former King Alexander was elevated to the throne as King Peter II, and General Dusan Simovich, commander of Yugoslavia's air force and leader of the coup against Cvetkovich, became premier. Although the new government announced that it would maintain a policy of strict neutrality as regarded the European war, it began to mobilize Yugoslav troops along the country's frontiers.

But Hitler struck before the Yugoslavs had time to complete their

---

[45] See pages 792–797.

[46] On August 24, 1939, an agreement had been reached settling the long-standing Croatian problem. The Yugoslav government was immediately reorganized. Matchek became vice-premier, and five members of his Croatian Peasant Party were included in the new cabinet. Under the terms of the new agreement about 26 per cent of the Yugoslav territory, with 4,423,000 inhabitants, was organized into the *banovina* of Croatia under a governor to be appointed and dismissed by the Crown. Croatia was to have its own legislative body at Zagreb, and was to have full autonomy in all matters except foreign affairs, the army, foreign trade, state communications, public security, and religion. On September 23, 1939, the governor and the departmental heads of government of Croatia were appointed—nine Croats and two Serbs, none of them politicians—and Matchek announced that he was completely satisfied with the new arrangement.

mobilization. On April 6 the Nazis with a million troops launched invasions into both Yugoslavia and Greece, using their usual *Blitzkrieg* pattern. With their overwhelming superiority in mechanized equipment and air force, they were able to carry out a campaign against Yugoslavia very much like the one they had waged against France in 1940. At various points the Yugoslav lines were pierced by "mechanized infiltration"; the Yugoslav armies were separated from one another and then encircled. At the same time a powerful German thrust down the Struma and into the Vardar valley effectively cut off the Yugoslavs from outside aid, even had such aid been available. Eventually the Germans, driving westward, made contact with the Italians fighting in Albania, and on April 17—after a twelve-day campaign—the defeated and disorganized Yugoslav army laid down its arms without conditions.[47]

Meanwhile, the Germans had been pushing their invasion into Greece, which—aided by 60,000 British, Australian, and New Zealand troops and some heavy equipment from the Army of the Nile—was now compelled to meet blows from two major European powers. As in all their other campaigns, the Nazis possessed an overwhelming superiority in air and mechanized forces which inevitably weighed in the balance despite the more difficult terrain and the valiant stands of the Greek and Anzac troops. Almost at once the Nazis drove through Thrace from the Bulgarian frontier to the Aegean and thus cut off the Greeks from contact by land with Turkey. At the end of the third day of the campaign the defeat of the Yugoslavs in the lower Vardar valley opened the way for a German advance upon the important Greek port of Saloniki, whose capture in turn entrapped the Greek army east of the Vardar.

[47] The Yugoslav defeat brought the disintegration of Yugoslavia. Even before the fighting had ceased, Regent Horthy ordered Hungarian troops to reoccupy territories in Yugoslavia which had been taken from Hungary in 1918. At Zagreb a separate, independent state was proclaimed by the pro-Axis Croatian terrorist, Ante Pavelich, who assumed the title of Poglavnik (leader). The new state was at once recognized by both Hitler and Mussolini, and on May 18, 1941, the Duke of Spoleto, nephew of the Italian King Victor Emmanuel, was chosen to be king. By various political, military, and economic agreements signed on that day the Kingdom of Croatia in turn became an Italian protectorate. Italy gained in other ways by the defeat of Yugoslavia. She annexed Ljubiana, capital of Slovenia, and a district surrounding it; Šušak, adjoining Fiume; Spalato and the Dalmatian coast north to Zara; Cattaro and the Adriatic coast south to Albania; and all but three of the former Yugoslav islands in the Adriatic. She thus obtained what she had sought but failed to secure at Paris in 1919. What territories Bulgaria and Germany might take from the prostrate Yugoslavia had not been announced at the time this was written.

The Germans next began blasting the Anglo-Greek defense line extending through the mountains from Mount Olympus on the Gulf of Saloniki northwestward to Lake Ochrida on the Albanian frontier. While Australian troops held tenaciously to the Mount Olympus anchor of this line, the Allies were forced by Nazi pressure in the ensuing week twice to retire to new positions in the west. The Greeks in Albania, who had so valiantly driven the Italians back in the preceding months, now found themselves in a precarious position. Although they sought by hastily abandoning their hard-won gains to join their retreating compatriots to the southeast, the German capture of Janina cut them off. Meanwhile, on April 19, the Nazi armored divisions, at the cost of heavy casualties, had eventually forced the passes to the west of Mount Olympus. Thereupon the Allies again fell back, this time to a short line extending from the heights of Thermopylae to the Gulf of Corinth. The German conquest of Greece now seemed inevitable, but the fierce resistance of New Zealand troops at historic Thermopylae Pass enabled the British Expeditionary Force to evacuate 45,000 of its men. Most of its heavy equipment, however, as at Dunkirk, had to be abandoned. On April 27, after a three weeks' campaign, the Nazis occupied Athens, from which King George II and the Greek government had already fled to Crete. In the ensuing days they completed their conquest of the Peloponnesus.

Although Hitler's invasion of the Balkans brought rather heavy casualties for the German armies, the expenditure of petroleum and other war materials, and the necessity of providing German garrisons for two more conquered countries, it perpetuated the legend of the invincibility of his *Panzer* divisions and air force. Furthermore, his success destroyed the immediate possibility of a new military front in Europe, for except for Gibraltar the British and their allies now had no foothold anywhere on the Continent. The conquest of Yugoslavia assured that country's mineral and agricultural resources for the Reich, and the occupation of Greece and some of the Greek islands in the northern Aegean placed the Nazis in a position not only to dominate that sea and the Dardanelles but to challenge Great Britain's domination of the whole eastern Mediterranean. The Nazi victory, too, seemed bound to have an effect upon the policies of Turkey, Russia, and France. The net result of the campaign appeared to be distinctly favorable to Hitler.

But the Führer was not content to stop with the conquest of the Balkans. On May 20 he launched the first completely air-borne invasion in history against the strategic British-occupied Greek island of Crete, some sixty miles from the European mainland. Following a terrific attack by hundreds of bombing planes which prepared the way for them, thousands of Nazi troops were landed in Crete by parachutes, gliders, and transport planes. After a day of fighting with the British and Greek forces the Nazis, though having suffered heavy casualties, had gained a foothold on the island. Then followed a contest between air power and sea power, for the British undoubtedly had a naval superiority while the Nazis soon gained complete mastery of the air.

The British navy, though repeatedly attacked by Nazi dive bombers, shattered all German attempts to land troops and heavy equipment by sea, but hundreds of airplanes, shuttling back and forth between Greece and Crete, carried men, supplies, and light equipment to the Nazi "bridgeheads" on the island. Within two days the Germans had succeeded in capturing the Maleme airdrome between strategically important Suda Bay and Canea, the Cretan capital. Strengthened by ever-increasing reinforcements, the Nazis captured Canea on May 28, and Suda Bay and Candia on the next day. King George II and his government had already fled for the second time, this time to Egypt. By early June the Nazis had occupied most of the island, the British without aerial protection being almost helpless. For the third time, however, they were able to carry out an overseas evacuation with some degree of success. Some 15,000 of the British and Greek troops on the island were reported to have been removed to Egypt, although the British admitted the loss of 15,000 men.

The outcome of the battle for Crete seemed to be a clear-cut victory for air power. Although the British had an army there with defended positions, artillery, and some tanks and other heavy equipment, the Germans by air power alone succeeded in landing on the island men, equipment, and supplies enough to overpower the defenders. The great British weakness at Crete was the woeful lack of airplanes to defend the island against an aerial invasion. Furthermore, they lacked the hundreds of aviation transports which would have been required to land reinforcements fast enough to match the Germans. Finally, even had adequate transportation been avail-

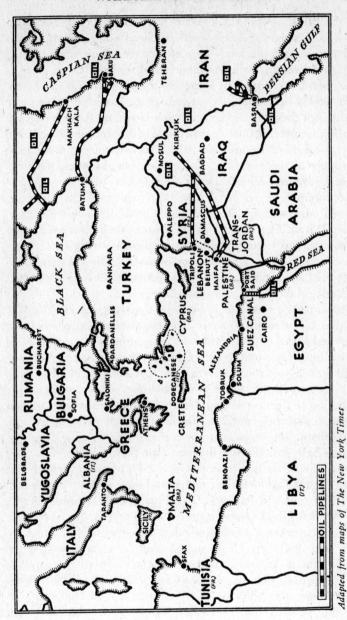

The Eastern Mediterranean and the Near East

Adapted from maps of The New York Times

able, the British probably felt themselves to be in too precarious a position to weaken the Army of the Nile by sending reinforcements to Crete when another Axis force in western Egypt stood already poised to deliver a blow at Alexandria and the Suez Canal.

The German conquest of Crete deprived the British of the excellent naval base at Suda Bay as well as the few airdromes on the island which they had used since Italy's attack upon Greece in the preceding October. It thus destroyed one of Britain's important outposts for offensive action against the Axis lines of communication and supply in the eastern Mediterranean. On the other hand, its conquest advanced Hitler's *Drang nach Osten* one more step, and provided him with an aerial base from which attacks might be launched against Egypt and the Suez Canal, or against Palestine, Syria, and Iraq. The loss of fighting ships in the operations around both Greece and Crete undoubtedly weakened Britain's sea power in the eastern Mediterranean at a time when the Axis was strengthening its hold by acquiring new bases for its air forces both on the mainland and on the Aegean islands.

In June, 1941, it was thought by many observers that Hitler might next turn his attention to Syria and Iraq, both in order to obtain the coveted Mosul oil fields and to secure a military base in the Near East for an advance on the Suez Canal. In Syria, when negotiations for the Franco-German armistice were first initiated in June, 1940, the French residents, General Mittelhauser, commander of the French forces there, and the French high commissioner all had announced that they would continue the struggle in company with Great Britain. Ten days later, however, the French authorities had reversed their position and declared that they would enforce the orders of the Pétain government. General Mittelhauser was relieved of his command and left the country, and some of his troops joined the British forces in Palestine. The French high commissioner in 1941, General Henri Dentz, appeared to be wholly in accord with the Vichy government's policy of collaboration with Hitler. In Iraq, which since its independence in 1932 had been allied with Great Britain,[48] the government in June, 1940, had showed its sympathy with the British by closing the pipeline from the Mosul oil fields to Syria and diverting all oil to the Palestinian port of Haifa.

During the early months of 1941, however, German and Italian

48 See page 827.

agents had apparently been busy in Iraq. On April 4 the regent for six-year-old King Faisal II and his prime minister were ousted by a *coup d'état* when the pro-Axis Rashid Ali Beg Gailani seized control. The coup seemed to presage ill for Great Britain, and to counter possible Axis penetration in this important oil-producing country the British on April 19 began to land troops at Basra, the Iraqi port on the Persian Gulf. Although by the Anglo-Iraqi treaty of alliance the British had the right to use the Iraqi "railways, rivers, ports, airdromes, and means of communication" in case of war, Rashid Ali objected. Hostilities broke out on May 2 when Iraqi troops attacked the British air base at Habbania, some sixty-five miles west of Bagdad, and Rashid Ali appealed to Hitler for aid.

British reinforcements were rushed by air and land from Palestine and from Basra, and transport airplanes, recently received from the United States, brought troops over from India. Although Hitler dispatched some bombing and fighting planes to Iraq, utilizing Syrian airdromes as bases, he was apparently preparing for his conquest of Crete and failed to send sufficient aid to enable Rashid Ali to gain superiority in the air. British and "Free French" airplanes not only attacked the Iraqi forces but also repeatedly bombed the airdromes in Syria which were being used by the Germans.

During the period when the Nazis were assailing Crete, British motorized units pushed steadily on toward Bagdad. Rashid Ali's government collapsed, the pro-Axis premier himself fled to Iran, and on June 1 all fighting between the British and the Axis-inspired Iraqi came to an end under the terms of an armistice signed on the previous day. The pro-British government, which had been overthrown in April, returned to power and agreed, according to reports, to permit the transit of British troops through the country. Basra, Bagdad, and Mosul—the only Iraqi towns of any size—came into the hands of the British, who, it appeared, had secured possession of the "backdoor to the Near East." The pro-Axis outbreak, it seemed, had been ill-timed and premature from the Nazi viewpoint.

Nevertheless, in June, 1941, there were continued reports of Nazi infiltration into Syria and even rumors of the landing of German troops. Accusing the Vichy government of having surrendered to Axis domination in Syria, on June 8 British imperial and "Free French" forces launched an invasion into that French-mandated territory, moving in from Palestine, Trans-Jordan, and Iraq. At the same time General Georges Catroux, the "Free French" leader in the Middle East, proclaimed the independence of Syria and Lebanon and promised to negotiate a treaty to that effect. The immediate objectives of the Allied advance were Damascus and Beirut, but although the Allies had superiority in air force and motorized equipment and had the assistance of warships along the coast, it was not until June 21 that they captured Damascus. The slowness of the advance was attributed in part to the opposition of General Dentz's French troops and in part to the British and "Free French" desire to win over the opposition by propaganda if possible. What effect Hitler's decision to attack Russia might have on the situation in Syria was problematical.

## THE NAZI INVASION OF RUSSIA

After the Nazi victory in Crete there was considerable speculation as to where Hitler would strike next, for it was felt that he could not be content to let his gigantic military machine lie idle. As already pointed out, it was thought that he might strike through Syria into Iraq in order to secure the Mosul oil or that he might drive across North Africa in order to oust the British from Egypt and the control of the Suez Canal. To those who expected these developments, the failure of the Nazis to come to the assistance of the Vichy forces in Syria seemed especially baffling. Events, however, soon revealed that Hitler had plans for operations on a much vaster scale.

Soon after the British invasion of Syria there were increasing reports of the massing of Nazi troops along the Russian frontier from Finland to the Black Sea. Although denied in both Berlin and Moscow, it was repeatedly rumored that Hitler by military pressure was seeking to exact from Stalin economic, and perhaps political, territorial, and military, concessions. If so, Stalin apparently remained obdurate. On June 18 Hitler next resorted to diplomacy in his "war of nerves" when the Reich and Turkey concluded a treaty of friendship and nonaggression. On the next day the Rumanian army was reported completely mobilized, and Finland was said to be rushing military preparations. But from Berlin no word came to reveal the seriousness of the situation.

Suddenly, on June 22, without a declaration of war, the Nazi air and land forces struck at Russia. Although attacks were made along the whole western frontier of the Soviet Union, the hardest blows appeared to be aimed at Bessarabia and the Ukraine. Here the Nazis had also the co-operation of the Rumanian army. The Soviet government at once announced that the might of its Red army would be hurled against Hitler's forces. What the ultimate outcome of this great military struggle would be, none could foretell.

It seemed clear, however, that one immediate result would be the temporary lessening of Nazi pressure upon Britain, whose prime minister immediately promised that the British would give whatever help they could to Russia and the Russian people, on the ground that "any man or state who fights against Naziism will have our aid." The R.A.F. redoubled the force of its attacks upon Germany and German-held points. Whether the British would be able to use this opportunity to clear up the military situation in North Africa, also, only time could tell.

### THE WAR IN AFRICA

There had already been considerable fighting in Africa. In view of Great Britain's determination to fight on to the end regardless of the French collapse, Mussolini in the summer of 1940 seemed to be presented with a golden opportunity to wrest from the British the rich territories of Egypt, the Anglo-Egyptian Sudan, Somaliland, and Kenya Colony. These regions, if obtained, would give Italy an immense semicircular empire stretching from Tripoli and perhaps Tunis on the Mediterranean to the middle of Africa's east coast, together with a stranglehold on the Suez Canal and an open road to India. Thanks to France's withdrawal from the war, Italy was free to throw all her African forces against Britain's colonies and protectorates in the northern part of that continent. Libyan troops, no longer required to defend the frontier facing Tunis, could devote their whole attention to preparations for an attack upon Egypt. The opening of Jibuti and French Somaliland to Italian troops, moreover, exposed the western flank of British Somaliland to an Italian invasion.

In the first two months of the Duce's war against Britain his forces operated chiefly from Italian East Africa. Slight advances were made at three places into the Anglo-Egyptian Sudan, and that part of Kenya Colony which projected northeastward as a salient into Italian East Africa was cleared of British troops. But the first important objective of the Italians was to conquer British Somaliland and thus not only to round out Italy's empire in East Africa but to gain a valuable strategic coastline on the Gulf of Aden. On August 6, 1940, Mussolini's forces launched an attack upon British Somaliland from the east, the west, and the south.

Heavily outweighed in man power, tanks, and airplanes, the British fought merely rear-guard actions in an attempt to make the Italians pay as dearly as possible for their gains. Within a few days the Duce's troops were closing in on Berbera, the chief port and capital of the colony, and ultimately on August 20 they occupied that city after the British defenders had been evacuated. But the British comforted themselves with the thought that the ultimate fate of Somaliland would depend upon the outcome of the war in Europe, that Britain still controlled the Suez Canal, through which not an Italian ship had been permitted to pass since Italy entered the war. Except by air the Italian forces in East Africa were completely cut off from the rest of the world, and though they might win early victories their future fate was still in doubt.

This became evident early in 1941 when the British in turn launched offensives into Italian East Africa from both Kenya and the Sudan. Troops advancing from Kenya conquered Italian Somaliland, recaptured British Somaliland, cut the Jibuti–Addis Ababa railway, and finally entered the Ethiopian capital on April 5. One month later Emperor Haile Selassie returned to his throne in Addis Ababa. In the north, meanwhile, other British forces, advancing from the Sudan, had met stubborn resistance in Eritrea, but on April 1 they captured Asmara, the capital, and one week later Massawa, the chief Italian port on the Red Sea. The Italians continued to fight delaying actions in order to keep British forces involved as long as possible, but on May 19 their last large military unit in East Africa was surrounded and captured at Alagi. The Duke of Aosta, Italian viceroy of Ethiopia, and a number of Italian generals and staff officers were among those who surrendered.

By June, 1941, practically all of East Africa had been cleared of Italian troops, and the British were free to transfer some of their land and air forces to the Egyptian or Near Eastern fronts. Whether Great Britain could marshal and supply sufficient forces—and more especially air forces and heavy land equipment—to meet an Axis advance upon Egypt and the Suez, was the great question. The fact that on April 11 President Roosevelt had declared that the Red Sea was no longer a combat zone, and had thus opened it to American ships carrying supplies to the British, seemed important in this regard.

Meanwhile, another Italian army had attempted to advance from Libya into Egypt in an attempt to break Great Britain's hold on the Suez Canal and the eastern Mediterranean. On September 12, 1940, Marshal Rodolfo Graziani, a veteran in conducting desert campaigns, launched a drive into Egypt with a force reputed to number 300,000 men. In five days the Italians reached Sidi Barrani, approximately sixty miles beyond the Libyan frontier. The British, distinctly inferior in numbers, were apparently content to fall back, exacting as heavy a toll as possible as they retreated.

At Sidi Barrani the Italian forces stopped to try to consolidate their gains, a task in which they were handicapped by bombing from the British air force in Egypt and shelling from the British navy in the eastern Mediterranean. Not only Sidi Barrani but Bardia and Tobruk, important bases in Libya, were pounded by the British fleet, which was definitely superior to the Italian naval forces in the eastern Mediterranean. This British naval superiority was plainly revealed early in September when a convoy of troop transports from Britain safely landed some thousands of reinforcements in Egypt. It was further revealed by the fact that the Italian navy avoided major engagements with the British fleet and fled precipitately to the protection of shore batteries whenever a British squadron was sighted.

But on this campaign the Italians never got beyond Sidi Barrani, for on December 9 the British Army of the Nile, under the command of General Sir Archibald P. Wavell, struck back in a well-planned and well-executed counterattack. Five days later the Italians were back in Libya and still in retreat. Step by step during the ensuing weeks the British advanced, capturing Bardia, Tobruk, and Derna as they went. On February 6, 1941, they finally took Bengazi, the last important stronghold in eastern Libya. In the course of their advance, also, the British captured more than 100,000 prisoners and considerable quantities of war supplies.

Several factors seem to have caused this sudden reversal of the situation in North Africa. Probably British superiority on the sea was the most important, for it not only enabled General Wavell to receive heavy reinforcements of men and supplies but prevented the Italians from readily increasing their own supplies. In this campaign, for the first time, the British showed their ability to wage a *Blitzkrieg* under favorable circumstances. Land, sea, and air units were carefully co-ordinated in a well-planned advance. On the other hand, the Italian fighting spirit appeared to be poor, perhaps because the army suffered from a shortage of water, gasoline, and other supplies. Furthermore, as the Italians retreated over an almost roadless and waterless desert, they were demoralized by British aerial and naval bombardments in their rear. Finally, the fact that the Italians had become involved in an unsuccessful war against the Greeks prevented them from giving their undivided attention to the campaign in North Africa.

General Wavell now had to consider whether his forces should push on hundreds of miles over the desert to Tripoli, the last important port in Libya, or whether he should weaken the Army of the Nile by sending troops and equipment to aid the Greeks in their stand against the Axis. In favor of the latter course was the possibility of influencing the governments of Yugoslavia and Turkey to stand firm against Hitler. The British therefore halted their advance at El Agheila, to the west of Bengazi, and began to ship some of their African forces to Greece. Some British troops were also transferred to the Sudan to strengthen the forces operating against Eritrea. On the other hand, in the succeeding weeks many Nazi troops were flown across to Tripoli from Sicily in airplanes. Apparently, too, some Axis ships succeeded in slipping through the British naval blockade—perhaps by using French territorial waters off Tunisia—and landed tanks, trucks, and other equipment. By April the Italians in Libya had been reinforced by three German armored divisions.

Suddenly, just as the Germans launched their offensives against Yugoslavia and Greece, the Axis forces in North Africa struck. In nine days the German *Panzer* divisions roared 350 miles eastward, capturing El Agheila, Bengazi, Derna, Bardia, and Solum. Only the British infantry division at Tobruk, behind strong fortified lines, held out against them. On April 14 the Germans were inside Egypt and had nullified all the British gains in North Africa during the preceding winter. But by this time the German advance appeared to have spent itself, at least temporarily.

The Nazis had to contend with the same sort of difficulties that had plagued the Italians some months earlier. They were dependent upon a 1000-mile land supply line stretching back over the desert to Tripoli, which in turn was dependent upon supplies received for the most part in ships from Sicily and southern Italy. The vulnerability of this supply line was revealed on the night of April 15 when British ships sank an entire Axis convoy between Sicily and Tripoli. Furthermore, Tripoli, Bengazi, and the coastal road to the Egyptian frontier were repeatedly bombed from the air or from the sea. Early in June, 1941, the British were still holding in the vicinity of Solum, and the important port of Tobruk was still in their hands. Whether the Nazi conquest of Crete would have an important effect on the situation in North Africa remained to be seen.

## THE WAR IN THE FAR EAST

The war in Europe had very obvious repercussions in the Far East, where Japan, at the time Germany invaded Poland, had already been engaged for more than two years in an undeclared war against China. In July, 1937, after an "incident," the Japanese began what their military leaders apparently expected to be a relatively short decisive campaign in North China. Within a few days they had occupied both Tientsin and Peiping. In August a campaign was also launched against the important commercial city of Shanghai, which, after three months of hard fighting, was captured on November 8, 1937. Following this success the Japanese next advanced up the Yangtze, and in December captured Nanking, the political capital of China. General Chiang Kai-shek and the Chinese Nationalist government thereupon established their headquarters in Hankow.

In 1938, while one Japanese army fought its way southward from Hopei and Shansi provinces along the Peiping-Hankow railway and another moved westward from Shantung and Kiangsu provinces along the Lung-hai railway, the Japanese forces in the Yangtze valley, assisted by Japanese gunboats on the river, undertook an advance upon Hankow. In June a general exodus from that city began, and the Nationalist government was again moved, this time to Chungking. But the Chinese fighting to protect Hankow continued to offer stiff resistance, and in October, 1938, the Japanese, in an effort to prevent military supplies from reaching these Chinese forces, launched an offensive in South China. On October 11 Japanese troops landed at Bias Bay, some twenty-five miles north of Hong Kong; ten days later Japanese tanks rumbled through the streets of Canton.

By the capture of this city the Japanese severed the last remaining railway link between the Chinese Nationalist forces and the outside world. But the occupation of Canton seemed to be significant for more than military reasons. It appeared to indicate the ascendancy in Japan of those who desired to convert all China into a Japanese protectorate. It seemed, also, to indicate that Japan was even willing to challenge Great Britain's position in China, for the hinterland about Canton had long been considered a British sphere of influence. It is possible that the Tokyo government concluded from Great Britain's passive role in the Sudeten crisis a few days earlier that the British would not go to war even to protect their own interests in China.

Meanwhile, in the Yangtze valley the Japanese had continued to advance, and on October 25 Hankow, too, at last fell into their hands. Many believed that with the Japanese holding the great commercial cities of Tientsin, Peiping, Shanghai, Nanking, Hankow, and Canton, and controlling the main railways of China, Chiang Kai-shek might be forced to make peace. Outside the great cities, however, in practically every "occupied" province, Chinese guerrilla forces were operating only a few miles from the railway lines. If the Chinese continued to carry on their guerrilla activities, it appeared possible that years might elapse before the Japanese had fully pacified the country.

During the first half of 1939 the Japanese continued their military activities in China, but while they extended their area of occupation in some regions they were unable to gain any decisive advantages. Off the mainland, however, they did make one or two moves of special significance. On February 10, in defiance of a stern warning issued by France and Great Britain in the preceding summer, Japanese forces seized the large and valuable Chinese island of Hainan, which dominates the coast of French Indo-China and lies in a position to menace the sea line from Singapore to Hong Kong. "Military necessity" was given as the reason for the step. On March 31, after Germany's absorption of Bohemia-Moravia, the Japanese further announced the annexation of the Spratley Islands [49] lying

49 Japan claimed that they had long been ownerless and that in 1917 the Japanese were the first to begin their economic development.

to the west of the Philippines midway between Indo-China and Borneo. France protested, but to no avail. By these annexations Japan moved nearer the Netherlands East Indies, rich in petroleum, rubber, tin, and other resources, and many speculated as to what might happen in the Far East if the great European powers should again go to war.

With France and Great Britain becoming involved more and more deeply in developments in Europe in 1939, it appeared that the United States constituted the chief obstacle to Japan's southward expansion. As though indicating the American attitude toward Tokyo's recent moves, the United States on April 15 suddenly transferred its fleet from the Atlantic to the Pacific. Then, on July 26, apparently as a step to place the United States in a position to use economic pressure, if necessary, to retard Japan's plan for the "new order in East Asia," the American State Department abruptly gave the six months' notice necessary to abrogate the existing Japanese-American commercial treaty. It was well known that for some time the United States had been the economic "life line" for Japan in her effort to conquer China.

By the late summer of 1939 it seemed that the only country other than the United States that might put an obstacle in the way of Japan's execution of her program for the Far East was the Soviet Union. For more than a year there had been Russo-Japanese clashes along the Outer Mongolia–Manchukuo border. Particularly disturbing therefore was the German-Soviet nonaggression treaty of August 23, which freed Russia of the threat of a German attack in the west and at the same time deprived Japan of possible German military assistance against the Soviet Union. A swift Japanese cabinet crisis ensued. On August 29 a new government, headed by General Nobuyuki Abe, took office with a program designed to carry out Japan's "immutable policy" in China. But almost immediately thereafter the Japanese forces operating on the Mongolian border of Manchukuo suffered a serious reverse in what the Japanese admitted was "a disastrous, bitter battle."

Obviously, if Japan were to settle the "China incident" with speed, she must not become involved in a large-scale war with Russia. The latter, at the same time, desired to be free from embarrassments in the Far East so that she might seize every opportunity to push her way westward and southward in Europe as opportunities might offer. On September 16, the day before Soviet troops began advancing into Poland, a Russo-Japanese truce temporarily fixed the Outer Mongolia–Manchukuo border at a line which represented the Soviet conception of the frontier.[50]

Meanwhile, the Tokyo government had issued a significant statement of policy. Japan, it declared, did not intend to be involved in the European war that had just broken out; she would "concentrate her efforts upon the settlement of the China affair." The war in Europe, it seemed, would certainly offer the Japanese an opportunity for increased freedom of action in the Far East if they could only force the Chinese Nationalist government to make peace. With a force of some 200,000 men Japan in September launched a new offensive southward from Yochow with the purpose of gaining control of the Canton-Hankow railway, most of whose 400-mile stretch was in the hands of the Chinese. Although by October 1 the vanguard of the Japanese army was reported at the gates of Changsha, a Chinese counterattack five days later turned the Japanese advance into a retreat. By October 15 the Chinese were themselves attacking Yochow. In December the Japanese attempted an attack from the southern end of the railway and advanced northward from Canton nearly a hundred miles. But again the Chinese counterattacked, and again they beat back the Japanese until by the middle of January, 1940, they were within twenty-five miles of Canton.

The Chinese, it seemed, could fight if they could continue to secure munitions and war supplies in sufficient quantities. There still remained to them three major avenues of importation—from Indo-China, from Burma, and from Soviet Russia through Outer Mongolia. Against one of these routes the Japanese had already moved. On November 15, 1939, troops had been landed on the southernmost coast of the province of Kwangtung, east of the border of French Indo-China, and nine days later they entered Nanning, in Kwangsi province, about one hundred miles inland. By this action the Japanese cut the Hanoi-Nanning-Kweilin motor road over which much of China's foreign trade was being carried. Furthermore, from Nanning as a base Japanese airplanes could the more easily bomb the Hanoi-Kunming railway still farther west. In the north the Japanese made an effort also to cut the route from Soviet Russia

---

[50] On June 9, 1940, a Soviet-Japanese agreement regarding the disputed Mongolian frontier was signed in Moscow.

to China by a thrust west from Paotou in Suiyuan province, but after an initial success against the Chinese forces the latter early in 1940 checked the advance and gradually drove the Japanese back toward Paotou.

For some time the Japanese had planned to establish in the occupied area of China a puppet government like that set up in 1932 in Manchuria under Henry Pu-Yi.[51] In accordance with this plan, on March 30, 1940, a new "Chinese National Government" was inaugurated in Nanking under Wang Ching-wei.[52] As might be expected, one of the points in Wang Ching-wei's immediately announced program was the "establishment of a new order in East Asia." As might be expected, too, the Tokyo government in a formal declaration pledged "whole-hearted co-operation and support" to the new regime. Thereafter Japan could, if she wished, avoid dealing with embarrassing protests from Western powers regarding the administration of the lower Yangtze valley by politely referring them to Wang Ching-wei's government in Nanking. The United States, however, immediately announced that it would continue to recognize the government at Chungking as the government of China.

Germany's successful *Blitzkrieg* in western Europe in May and June had pronounced repercussions in the Far East, where Japan at once moved toward establishing her hegemony not only over the East Asiatic mainland but over the South Seas, too. "The present international situation is developing in a manner advantageous to Japan's national policy," declared the Japanese war minister on June 25. "We should not miss the present opportunity or we shall be blamed by posterity." The destiny of the Far East and the South Seas, any development in them, and any disposal of them, Foreign Minister Arita broadcast four days later, was a matter of grave concern to Japan. "It is most natural," he asserted, "that peoples most closely related geographically, racially, culturally, and economically should form a single sphere of their own and establish peace and order within it. It is in this spirit that Japan is now engaged in the task of establishing a new order in East Asia."

[51] See page 845.
[52] The whole of the occupied area in China was not centralized under the new government in Nanking, however. The northern provinces of Hopei, Shansi, and Shantung were given a semi-independent position under a "Political Affairs Commission," and Inner Mongolia was given an independent status under the domination of the Japanese army of Kwantung.

On July 18 Prince Konoye, who had been premier of Japan's first war cabinet in 1937–1938 and who more recently had been attempting to organize a totalitarian party, became head of a new government in which the foreign minister was Yosuke Matsuoka, a firm expansionist and head of a Japanese fascist party. This Konoye government, it was believed, would try to capitalize upon every opportunity for further Japanese expansion which the European war might present, and might convert Japan into a totalitarian corporative state in order to strengthen the country for its new tasks. On August 15 the last of Japan's political parties formally dissolved itself to clear the way for a new political structure. Said one of the party's representatives: "Japan now stands at the crossroads of her destiny to rise or fall with the double burden of building Greater East Asia and completing the China affair. There is a nation-wide desire for a new national structure in which the minds of the people and the nation's total power can be regimented for the attainment of those great aims." On August 27 Premier Konoye appointed a preparatory committee for the new structure, and three weeks later this committee presented plans for establishing a corporative state.

Meanwhile, the Japanese had been taking definite steps to weaken or eliminate Great Britain, the Netherlands, and France as potent factors in the Far East. Britain's extensive commercial and imperial interests in occupied China and at Hong Kong made her particularly vulnerable to pressure. A year earlier, on June 14, 1939, the Japanese had begun a blockade of the British and French concessions in Tientsin, ostensibly because the British had given asylum to four alleged anti-Japanese terrorists. The first result of this pressure had been Great Britain's assent on July 26, 1939, to the Craigie-Arita formula by which the British granted virtual belligerent rights to the Japanese forces in the "regions under their control" in China. Two weeks later Great Britain had agreed to surrender the four alleged terrorists. But Japan's demand that Britain surrender the silver deposited by Chiang Kai-shek's government in the Tientsin concession and prevent Chinese national currency from circulating within the concession limits the British government had refused.

But after Germany's advance to the Channel ports in June, 1940, the British felt obliged to meet Tokyo's demands. It was agreed (June 19) that Japanese gendarmes should collaborate with the concession police in the suppression of "activities prejudicial to the security of the Japanese forces," that Japanese-sponsored North China currency—valueless as foreign exchange—should circulate in the concession on the same basis as China's national currency, and that Chinese-Nationalist silver to the value of 5,000,000 yen should be surrendered to the Japanese army for famine relief. Japan did not relax her pressure, however. On June 22 Japanese forces began to concentrate upon the border of British Kowloon on the mainland opposite Hong Kong, and two days later the Tokyo government demanded that Britain stop all movement of supplies to Chiang Kai-shek by way of Hong Kong and Burma. The British hastily dynamited the bridges connecting Hong Kong and Kowloon and began to evacuate their women and children to Manila.

Great Britain was forced to accede to Japan's newest demands. In the words of Prime Minister Churchill, at a time when the British Empire was "engaged in a life and death struggle" it was necessary to remove Anglo-Japanese tension. It was accordingly agreed that for a period of three months beginning on July 18, 1940, the Burma government would suspend the transit to China of gasoline, trucks, railway material, arms, and ammunitions. Within the three months it was hoped that a Sino-Japanese settlement might be achieved. Shipment of the same goods was to be prohibited from Hong Kong, but, according to the British, this had been done long before the Japanese demand was presented. Further to conciliate the Japanese, it appeared, Great Britain in August withdrew her troops from Shanghai and other places in North China "for service elsewhere."

In regard to the Netherlands East Indies, Japan had taken a preliminary step as early as February 12, 1940, when she had denounced her arbitration treaty with the Netherlands. Two months later, on April 15, Foreign Minister Arita let it be known that "the Japanese government cannot but be deeply concerned over any development accompanying the aggravation of the war in Europe that may effect the *status quo* of the Netherlands East Indies." Secretary Hull of the United States at once called attention to the four-power pact of 1921, under which Japan had agreed to respect the integrity of the Netherlands East Indies, and declared that "any alteration of their *status quo* by other than peaceful processes would be prejudicial to the cause of stability, peace and security not only in the region of the Netherlands Indies but in the entire Pacific area." The government at The Hague notified Tokyo that in case the Netherlands became involved in the European war, it would neither request nor accept aid from any power in protecting the East Indies, and this statement, the Japanese stated, was satisfactory to them.

Nevertheless, on May 11, after Germany had invaded the Netherlands, Japan notified the belligerent powers and the United States and Italy that she was deeply concerned over the *status quo* of the Netherlands Indies. Again Secretary Hull called attention to the four-power pact and stated that the United States assumed that each of the governments which had made commitments would continue to abide by them. On May 22, however, Germany informed Japan that she was not interested in the question of the Netherlands Indies, and this statement was apparently regarded in Tokyo as offering Japan a free hand in the Far East. Subsequently there developed in Japan an increasing sentiment in favor of a Japanese "protective occupation" of the Netherlands Indies, and on June 3 the Japanese foreign minister stated in an address that Japan's national mission to stabilize East Asia involved not only China but also the South Seas.

Pressure was also being exerted against France. In June, 1940, at the moment when Marshal Pétain was seeking to obtain an armistice with Germany, Japan forced France to agree that Japanese inspectors might be stationed at key points in Indo-China with power to supervise and control all traffic through that French colony. At the same time the French were obliged to recognize Japan's "special needs" in China by signing an agreement similar to the Craigie-Arita formula of July, 1939. Moreover, Japanese troops moved up to the frontier of Cochin-China, Japanese warships began patrolling its coast, and the Tokyo government called to the attention of Hitler and Mussolini Japan's claims for consideration in the disposal of French possessions in the Far East. In August Japan made demands on French Indo-China which included not only closer economic relations but the right to move Japanese troops across the country, to use the French Hanoi-Kunming railway into South China, and to establish naval and air bases.

Despite Secretary Hull's statement to the Japanese government that any change in the status of French Indo-China would have an "unfortunate effect" on American public opinion, and despite the British foreign secretary's announcement of Britain's interest in the

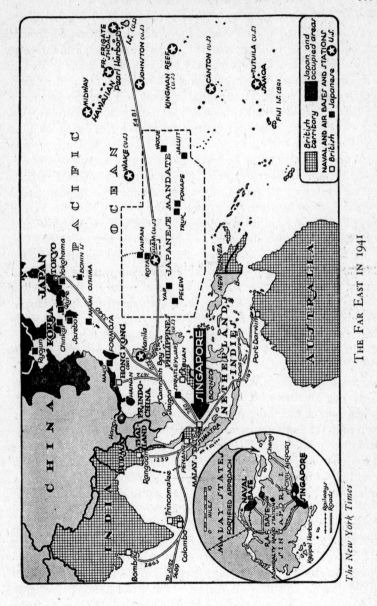

The New York Times

The Far East in 1941

preservation of the *status quo* in the Pacific, the Tokyo government continued to exert pressure upon France. Eventually, on September 22, the latter agreed to permit the Japanese to establish three air bases in northern Indo-China and to maintain a limited number of troops at Haiphong, the chief port in that region. In return Japan guaranteed to respect the territorial integrity and French sovereignty of Indo-China. To most observers it seemed obvious, however, that once the Japanese had established their air forces in Indo-China the French army in that colony would have great difficulty in preventing further Japanese encroachments.

As though to counter Japan's aggressive moves in the Far East, on September 25 one agency of the United States government agreed to buy $30,000,000 worth of tungsten from China and another agreed to loan Chiang Kai-shek's government $25,000,000, and on the next day President Roosevelt placed an embargo, effective on October 16, on the export of all scrap steel and iron except to the Western Hemisphere and Great Britain. Although Japan was not mentioned in the announcement, it was well known that during the preceding two years she had obtained nearly all such metal from the United States. According to the Japanese press the American embargo made inevitable a clash between Japan and the United States.

The next move in the diplomatic chess game came at once. On September 27 in Berlin representatives of Germany, Italy, and Japan signed a ten-year military alliance in which they undertook "to assist one another with all political, economic, and military means when one of the three is attacked by a power at present not involved in the European war or in the Chinese-Japanese conflict." The basis upon which the alliance rested was, on the one hand, Japan's agreement to recognize and respect "the leadership of Germany and Italy in the establishment of a new order in Europe" and, on the other, the agreement of the last two powers to recognize and respect "the leadership of Japan in the establishment of a new order in Greater East Asia." It was pointed out that the pact was aimed at the United States and was designed to keep the latter from entering the European war on the side of Britain or resorting to force to stop Japan's creation of her "Greater East Asia." But obviously the pact could operate equally well against Soviet Russia, should the latter enter the European war to check Hitler's *Drang nach Osten* or strike at Japan through Manchukuo or China while Tokyo's forces were involved in pushing their way into Indo-China or the Netherlands East Indies.

If the announcement of the military alliance of the totalitarian states was designed primarily to immobilize the United States in the Far East, it seemed destined to failure. It appeared, on the contrary, to have the effect of bringing that country and Great Britain into closer collaboration and of convincing the latter that further efforts to appease Japan would be futile. Thereafter there were repeated indications of a growing Anglo-American determination to extend aid to China and to exert pressure upon Japan. On October 8 the State Department at Washington advised Americans to leave China, Japan, Manchukuo, Hong Kong, and French Indo-China, and on the same day Prime Minister Churchill informed the British House of Commons that the Burma road would be reopened on October 18. On that date hundreds of trucks began rolling over that highway with war supplies for Chiang Kai-shek's armies.

During the closing months of 1940 Japan made no further aggressive move in Indo-China, but there was some suspicion that she had a hand in inciting Thailand (Siam) to seize upon France's weakness as an opportunity to regain some of the lands taken from Siam by an imperialistic France in the nineteenth century. Sporadic and local fighting along the frontier was followed in January, 1941, by Thai infantry attacks, which were supported by extensive bombing operations. It was rumored that Thailand was being assisted by military advisers, airplanes, and pilots from Japan. Eventually, on January 21, the latter offered to mediate the dispute between Thailand and France, and ten days later an armistice was concluded. By the subsequent peace treaty, which was signed in Tokyo on March 11, Thailand was reported to have received some 21,750 square miles in the Indo-Chinese provinces of Laos and Cambodia, the ceded territory to constitute a demilitarized zone. To what extent Japan had benefited by the whole incident remained to be disclosed.

Soon after the conclusion of this peace Japanese Foreign Minister Matsuoka left for conferences with his Axis partners in Berlin and Rome, and for a conference with Soviet officials in Moscow. Just what his purpose was in personally visiting Hitler and Mussolini and just what agreements or understandings were reached was not divulged. What did become known, however, was the fact that in Moscow on April 13 the Japanese and Soviet governments signed a five-year pact of nonaggression and neutrality. In addition, the Soviet Union agreed to respect the territorial integrity and inviolability of Manchukuo, while Japan promised to do the same toward the Mongolian People's Republic.

What effect the signing of this agreement might have upon Japan's future moves in the Far East was problematical. On the surface it appeared that she was now free to move against the British and the Americans without fear of an attack by Soviet Russia from the rear. It seemed quite possible that Soviet leaders might welcome a war between Japan and Great Britain and the United States in the Far East as they had probably welcomed the outbreak of war between Germany and Great Britain and France in the West. Whether the Soviet-Japanese treaty relieved Japan of her obligations toward the Axis in case of a Soviet-German war, was also not clear. But that it did not improve her position in China seemed apparent, for the U.S.S.R. assured the Chungking government that it would continue to send it war supplies.

The signing of the Soviet-Japanese pact may have hastened the conclusion of further agreements between Japan and France regarding Indo-China, concerning which negotiations had been carried on for months. On May 5, 1941, two agreements were signed providing for economic "collaboration" between Japan and Indo-China. Certain provisions seemed especially significant, namely, that Japanese capital should be permitted to participate in the development of Indo-Chinese agriculture, mining, and hydraulic concessions, that Japanese commercial firms should be admitted into the Indo-Chinese Federation of Importers and Exporters, and that Japanese schools should be established in Indo-China. The conclusion of the pact with Russia may have been responsible, too, for the much more aggressive attitude of the Japanese government in its negotiations with the government of the Netherlands East Indies. In June, 1941, relations between the two were becoming particularly strained.

## The War and the United States

In September, 1939, the great majority of Americans had certain definite ideas regarding the war which had broken out in Europe. One was that there was little doubt as to where "war guilt" lay. They had watched Hitler's increasing disregard of Germany's treaty obligations and had seen him become ever more and more aggressive.

At the same time they had seen the leaders of Great Britain and France make numerous efforts to appease the Führer in order to prevent the outbreak of another war, even when such appeasement had entailed the destruction or dismemberment of certain weaker states. Most Americans were convinced, therefore, that the war was the direct outcome of Nazi principles and technique, and, since they abhorred these, most Americans were openly sympathetic with the Allies and hoped they would win what was feared would be a long war.

But the great majority of Americans fervently hoped that the United States would not be drawn into this war as it had been in 1917. During the postwar years much had been said and written about the way the American people had been dragged into the World War by propagandists, financiers, and war profiteers. The fact that the United States had entered the war only after German submarines had deliberately sunk American vessels was almost forgotten. Furthermore, postwar agitators had emphasized that the peace settlement had been bad, that "the war to end war had ended in a peace to end peace," and that therefore the sacrifices resulting from the World War had been entirely futile. Many Americans maintained that the United States' entrance into the World War had been a mistake; most of them were determined that the country should not again be drawn into a European conflict. President Roosevelt, in a radio address on September 3, 1939, to some extent expressed these two ideas when he stated that he could not "ask that every American remain neutral in thought," but at the same time stated his hope and belief that "the United States will keep out of this war."

These two fundamental ideas of the American people were further expressed in a new Neutrality Act which was passed on November 4, 1939. Under the Neutrality Act of 1937 the United States government was compelled to place an embargo on the shipment of implements of war to belligerent powers. Obviously, because of Britain's control of the sea, this act operated not to the detriment of Germany but to that of the Allies. Most Americans were willing to supply the Allies with the sinews of war if it could be done without involving the United States in war. The new act was designed to accomplish these two ends.[53] The Allies were free to purchase war

[53] For the provisions of this act, see page 918.

materials in the United States but such materials might not be carried to a belligerent country in American ships. Furthermore, the act empowered the President to forbid American citizens and ships to enter combat areas in war zones. Thus, it was hoped, there would be no occasion for the United States to be dragged into this war as in 1917 because of the sinking of American ships by German submarines. Most Americans, it appeared, were willing to sit on the sidelines and watch the Allies defeat the Nazi dictator.

From this somewhat placid state the United States was rudely shaken by the startling developments in Europe in the spring and early summer of 1940. After the fall of France the feeling grew among Americans that Great Britain was their first line of defense against the Nazi and Fascist dictators, and that the British must be assisted with all aid "short of war." Following Dunkirk the United States government turned back to manufacturers—who rushed them to England—rifles, machine guns, field guns, and airplanes, which were needed to re-equip the evacuated British troops. In September, in a similar manner, some 229 tanks were sent to Canada. In that same month, also, fifty over-age American destroyers were transferred to Great Britain in return for ninety-nine-year leases of naval and air bases in the islands of Newfoundland, Bermuda, the Bahamas, Jamaica, St. Lucia, Trinidad, and Antigua, and in British Guiana. By this transaction Great Britain was strengthened to defend her overseas lifeline and the United States secured advance bases for the defense of North America and the Caribbean.

While there was some difference of opinion among Americans regarding the policy of all aid to Great Britain "short of war," there were few who doubted that the United States should itself embark upon a sweeping program of national preparedness. In September, 1940, Congress passed and President Roosevelt approved the first American law to prescribe compulsory military service in time of peace. By the terms of the Selective Training and Service Act every male citizen who was between the ages of twenty-one and thirty-six on the date to be set for registration was "liable for training and service in the land or naval forces of the United States." Normally the period of service would be one year, after which each man was to enter a reserve component which might be called into active service under prescribed conditions. Provision was also made for calling the National Guard into federal service, and in the ensuing months this step was taken. Meanwhile, on October 16, 1940, some 16,000,000 men registered for the draft. The act had set an upper limit of 900,000 to be the number of men who might be called each year, and the order of selection was determined by lot. On November 18, 1940, the first groups of drafted men were inducted into the army.

But men without weapons would, of course, be of little use in defending the country. During the year 1940 the government authorized the expenditure of more than $17,000,000,000 for a "two-ocean navy" and for all the latest and most efficient weapons for land and air warfare, and in the first six months of 1941 more billions of dollars were voted for similar purposes. In May, 1940, the task of organizing and co-ordinating the country's industrial resources had been given to the National Defense Advisory Commission, but despite the ability and sincere efforts of its members defense production lagged. Ultimately, in December, 1940, the President created a new body, the Office of Production Management for Defense, popularly referred to as the OPM. The head of this body was William S. Knudsen, former president of the General Motors Corporation, and the other members were Sidney Hillman, a prominent labor leader, Henry L. Stimson, secretary of war, and Frank Knox, secretary of the navy. To the OPM was given the authority to take over industrial plants for the government under certain conditions.

On December 29, 1940, President Roosevelt in a radio address pointed out that the American people faced the possibility of an Axis victory which would mean "a new and terrible era in which the whole world, our hemisphere included, would be run by threats of brute force." In that address the President defined what many considered a doctrine worthy to rank alongside the Monroe Doctrine, namely, that the American people were determined not to permit control of the seaways leading to their coasts to pass into the hands of a power hostile to their own democratic way of life and bent on its destruction. British sea power in the Atlantic was recognized as a bulwark friendly to democracy, and in order that it should not be destroyed an administration bill "to promote the defense of the United States" was introduced in Congress in January, 1941.

This bill, which was popularly called the Lease-Lend Bill, after long debate in both houses of Congress finally became law on March 11. The act authorized the President, "notwithstanding the provisions of any other law," to manufacture for, exchange with, sell,

lease, lend, or in other ways make available any defense article to
"the government of any country whose defense the President deems
vital to the defense of the United States." Payment might be made by
any means which the President deemed satisfactory. The act was
to be financed through appropriations made from time to time, and
carried with it an initial appropriation of $1,300,000,000. Immedi-
ately, however, the President asked for an additional appropriation
of $7,000,000,000 for aid to Britain under the provisions of the act,
and this amount was authorized by Congress late in March. The
United States was to become the great "arsenal of democracy."

But it soon began to be clear to Americans that to produce the
weapons of war was not enough. They must be put in Britain's hands
if they were to be used in the fight in defense of democracy. For, as
already pointed out, the German campaign against shipping in 1941
was taking a heavy toll in the Battle of the Atlantic, and it appeared
that it might defeat the whole purpose of the Lease-Lend Act. The
United States navy had already inaugurated a "neutrality patrol system" to warn peaceful shipping of the presence of raiding submarines
and airplanes. On April 9 Secretary of State Hull took a step which
was designed to facilitate this patrol system and further to safeguard
the Western Hemisphere against Nazi invasion. On that day he
and the Danish minister to the United States signed an agreement
giving the United States the right to establish air bases and other
military and naval facilities in Greenland. For all practical purposes
the island was placed under the protective custody of the United
States for the duration of the war. American bases in Greenland
would flank the "Great Circle" shipping route between North America and Britain and would greatly strengthen the American naval
and air patrol eastward to within three miles of the Nazi-proclaimed
blockade zone. The increased efficiency of the American patrol might
make possible the shifting to other zones of some British naval vessels which had been operating in the western Atlantic.

Other steps to strengthen Britain in the Battle of the Atlantic were
taken by President Roosevelt. On April 10 he asked Congress for
legislation to permit him to requisition for American service any
foreign ships in American waters deemed necessary for national
defense, due compensation to be paid, and early in June he was given
the necessary authorization. On April 30 he asked the United States
Maritime Commission to create a pool of at least 2,000,000 tons of

merchant shipping whose operation should be so planned as to make this cargo space "immediately effective in accomplishing our objective of all-out aid to the democracies." He further asked that American shipping be reallocated so as to make every cargo count in the battle against the dictatorships. By the early part of June the Maritime Commission had secured some 1,275,000 toward the 2,000,000 tons.

In another address to the American people on May 27 President Roosevelt re-emphasized and expanded the doctrine which he had enunciated five months earlier. "It is," he asserted, "unmistakably apparent . . . that unless the advance of Hitlerism is forcibly checked now, the Western Hemisphere will be within range of the Nazi weapons of destruction." The Nazis, he declared, had the armed power at any moment to occupy Spain and Portugal, and that threat extended "to the island outposts of the New World—the Azores and Cape Verde Islands." The President climaxed his speech by the announcement that he had issued a proclamation of an unlimited national emergency, the reason for which was contained in the proclamation itself, namely, that "common prudence requires that for the security of this nation and of this hemisphere we should pass from peacetime authorizations of military strength to such a basis as will enable us to cope instantly and decisively with any attempt at hostile encirclement of this hemisphere, or the establishment of any base for aggression against it, as well as to repel the threat of predatory incursion by foreign agents into our territory and society."

In carefully chosen words President Roosevelt pointed out the essential requirements of the defense of the United States. In the first place, the American industrial defense program would have to be further speeded up, and to this end powers authorized under the proclamation of unlimited emergency would be invoked if necessary. In the second place, the sea lanes to Britain should be, must be, and would be, kept open. "From the point of view of strict military and naval necessity," he declared, "we shall give every possible assistance to Britain and to all who, with Britain, are resisting Hitlerism." In the third place, the United States would resist Nazi attempts to occupy points from which the Western Hemisphere could be threatened. "We in the Americas will decide for ourselves whether and when and where our American interests are attacked and our security threatened," the President announced. "We are placing our armed forces in strategic military position. . . . We will not accept a Hitler-dominated world."

Whether this challenge to Hitler would ultimately lead the United States into the war as an active participant, was not clear at the time the challenge was issued. Various polls of popular opinion revealed, however, that in May, 1941, although most Americans opposed entering the war, the overwhelming majority of them favored fighting, if necessary, to defend the whole Western Hemisphere, and most of them regarded the ultimate defeat of Hitler as essentially more important than staying at peace.

Events in June further strained relations between the United States and the Axis. On June 9 it was learned that a German submarine had deliberately sunk the *Robin Moor,* an American freighter, in the mid-Atlantic outside the combat zone on May 21. Passengers and crew had been left in open boats far from land. The United States government at once prepared to make a stern protest. But it did more than that. On June 14 President Roosevelt ordered the immediate "freezing" of the assets in the United States of Germany and Italy and eight other states occupied or controlled by them. Two days later the American government ordered the closing of all German consulates and bureaus of information in the United States because their "improper and unwarranted" activities were inimical to the welfare of the United States. Customs and immigration officials were also instructed to detain temporarily any German nationals seeking to leave the country. On June 19 both Germany and Italy ordered American consulates in their countries closed, whereupon the United States ordered the closing of Italian consulates also. That these steps were but the preliminaries to a complete break in the diplomatic relations between the United States and the Axis powers was the belief of many.

# SELECT BIBLIOGRAPHY
## AND
## INDEX

# SELECT BIBLIOGRAPHY

No attempt has been made to include in this bibliography all of the thousands of books which deal in one way or another with the history of Europe since 1870. For more complete bibliographies, including works published in foreign languages, the reader is referred to: W. H. Allison and others, *A Guide to Historical Literature* (1931); G. P. Gooch, *Recent Revelations of European Diplomacy* (1930); R. J. Kerner, *Slavic Europe, A Selected Bibliography in the Western European Languages* (1918); W. L. Langer and H. F. Armstrong, *Foreign Affairs Bibliography* (1933); I. G. Mudge, *New Guide to Reference Books* (1929); J. Nield, *Guide to the Best Historical Novels and Tales* (1929); K. S. Pinson, *Bibliographical Introduction to Nationalism* (1935); H. W. V. Temperley and L. M. Penson, *A Short Bibliography of Modern European History, 1789–1935* (1936).

The following texts also have helpful bibliographies for the period since 1870: V. L. and M. H. Albjerg, *From Sedan to Stresa* (1937); F. L. Benns, *Europe Since 1914* (1936); G. P. Gooch, *History of Modern Europe, 1878–1919* (1923); C. D. Hazen, *Fifty Years of Europe, 1870–1919* (1919); L. H. Holt and A. W. Chilton, *The History of Europe from 1862 to 1914* (1917); W. C. Langsam, *The World Since 1914* (1936); J. A. R. Marriott, *Europe and Beyond, 1870–1920* (1921); R. B. Mowat, *European History, 1878–1923* (1924); J. H. Rose, *The Development of the European Nations, 1870–1921* (1922); P. W. Slosson, *Twentieth Century Europe* (1927) and *Europe Since 1870* (1935); J. W. Swain, *Beginning the Twentieth Century* (1933); E. R. Turner, *Europe Since 1870* (1927); A. W. Ward and others (eds.), *Cambridge Modern History*, Vol. XII (1912).

General discussions of international relations since 1870 may be found in: F. M. Anderson and A. S. Hershey, *Handbook for Diplomatic History* (1918); R. Beazley, *The Road to Ruin in Europe, 1890–1914* (1932); E. Brandenburg, *From Bismarck to the World War* (1933); G. L. Dickinson, *The International Anarchy, 1904–14* (1926); S. B. Fay, *The Origins of the World War*, Vol. I (1928); G. P. Gooch, *History of Modern Europe, 1878–1919* (1923) and *Before the War, Studies in Diplomacy* (1936); W. L. Langer, *European Alliances and Alignments, 1871–1890* (1931) and *The Diplomacy of Imperialism*, 2 vols. (1935); R. J. Mowat, *History of European Diplomacy, 1815–1914* (1922) and *History of European Diplomacy, 1914–1925* (1927) and *The Concert of Europe* (1931);

B. E. Schmitt, *Triple Alliance and Triple Entente* (1934); C. Seymour, *The Diplomatic Background of the War, 1870–1914* (1916); R. J. Sontag, *European Diplomatic History, 1871–1932* (1933). The following collections of source materials are available for the period: A. N. Cook, *Readings in Modern and Contemporary History* (1937); W. H. Cooke and E. P. Stickney, *Readings in European International Relations Since 1879* (1931); W. P. Hall and E. A. Beller, *Historical Readings in Nineteenth Century Thought* (1928); E. Hertslet, *The Map of Africa by Treaty*, 3 vols. (1909); J. MacMurray, *Treaties Concerning China, 1894–1919*, 2 vols. (1921); G. B. Manhart, *Alliance and Entente, 1871–1914* (1932); D. P. Myers, *Manual of Collections of Treaties* (1922); J. H. Robinson and C. A. Beard, *Readings in Modern European History*, Vol. II (1909); F. J. Scott and A. Baltzly, *Readings in European History since 1814* (1930).

For the very recent period much material may be found in such annuals as *The Statesman's Year Book, The New International Year Book, The Annual Register, Political Handbook of the World* (ed. by W. H. Mallory), and *Survey of International Affairs* (ed. by A. J. Toynbee), and in such periodicals as *Foreign Affairs, Current History, Political Science Quarterly, The Journal of Modern History, The Round Table, Fortnightly Review, Nineteenth Century,* and *Contemporary Review.*

CHAPTER I

INDUSTRIALISM, IMPERIALISM, AND WORLD POLITICS

SCIENCE, INVENTION, AND INDUSTRY: E. W. Byrn, *The Progress of Invention in the Nineteenth Century* (1900); S. Chase, *Men and Machines* (1929); E. Cressy, *Discoveries and Inventions of the Twentieth Century* (1915); R. C. Epstein, *The Automobile Industry, Its Economic and Commercial Development* (1928); H. de B. Gibbins, *Economic and Industrial Progress of the Century* (1903); J. A. Hobson, *The Evolution of Modern Capitalism* (1913); E. E. Howe (ed.), *Chemistry in Industry* (1924); W. B. Kaempffert, *Popular History of Invention*, 2 vols. (1924) and *Invention and Society* (1930); S. C. A. Knowles, *Industrial and Commercial Revolutions during the Nineteenth Century* (1926); M. Luckiesh, *Artificial Light* (1920); D. H. MacGregor, *Evolution of Industry* (1912); W. Meakin, *The New Industrial Revolution* (1928); L. Mumford, *Technics and Civilization* (1934); V. Ross, *The Evolution of the Oil Industry* (1920); H. O. Rugg, *The Great Technocracy* (1933); H. Sée, *Modern Capitalism* (1926); E. E. Slosson, *Creative Chemistry* (1921); A. P. Usher, *History of Mechanical Invention* (1929); A. R. Wallace, *Wonderful Century* (1898); F. W. Wile (ed.), *Century of Industrial Progress*

(1928); H. S. Williams, *Story of Nineteenth Century Science* (1900).

TRANSPORTATION AND COMMUNICATION: A. Berglund, *Ocean Transportation* (1931); F. C. Bowen, *A Century of Atlantic Travel* (1930); C. L. M. Brown, *The Conquest of the Air* (1927); C. R. Gibson and W. B. Cole, *Wireless of To-Day* (1923); R. S. Holland, *Historic Airships* (1928); T. F. Manus and W. Beasley, *Men, Money, and Motors, The Drama of the Automobile* (1929); L. G. MacPherson, *Transportation in Europe* (1910); A. J. Maginnis, *The Atlantic Ferry* (1892); F. A. Talbot, *Railway Conquest of the World* (1911) and *Steamship Conquest of the World* (1912).

IMPERIALISM: H. Feis, *Europe: the World's Banker, 1870–1914* (1930); C. W. Halberg, *The Suez Canal* (1931); C. K. Hobson, *The Export of Capital* (1914); J. A. Hobson, *Imperialism* (1905); W. L. Langer, *The Diplomacy of Imperialism*, 2 vols. (1935); P. T. Moon, *Imperialism and World Politics* (1926); P. Reinsch, *World Politics at the End of the Nineteenth Century* (1900); F. H. Simonds and B. Emeny, *The Great Powers in World Politics* (1935); I. Tucker, *History of Imperialism* (1920); L. Woolf, *Economic Imperialism* (1921) and *Imperialism and Civilization* (1928).

EUROPE IN AFRICA: R. Brown, *The Story of Africa and Its Explorers,* 4 vols. (1911); R. L. Buell, *The Native Problem in Africa*, 2 vols. (1928); N. D. Harris, *Europe and Africa* (1927); H. L. Hoskins, *European Imperialism in Africa* (1930); H. H. Johnston, *Livingstone* (1891) and *The Opening Up of Africa* (1911) and *A History of the Colonization of Africa by Alien Races* (1913); A. B. Keith, *The Belgian Congo and the Berlin Act* (1919); J. S. Keltie, *The Partition of Africa* (1895); H. W. Little, *H. M. Stanley* (1890); D. Livingstone, *Missionary Travels and Research in South Africa* (1858) and *The Last Journals of David Livingstone in Central Africa* (1875); C. Lucas, *The Partition and Colonization of Africa* (1922); L. Middleton, *The Rape of Africa* (1936); E. D. Morel, *Red Rubber* (1907) and *The Black Man's Burden* (1920); H. M. Stanley, *Through the Dark Continent* (1878) and *The Congo and the Founding of Its Free State*, 2 vols. (1885) and *How I Found Livingstone* (1913); L. S. Woolf, *Empire and Commerce in Africa* (1919).

EUROPE IN THE FAR EAST: H. F. Bain, *Ores and Industry in the Far East* (1927); G. Bienstock, *The Struggle for the Pacific* (1937); G. H. Blakeslee, *The Pacific Area* (1929); R. K. Douglas, *Europe and the Far East* (1928); C. B. Fletcher, *The Problem of the Pacific* (1919); N. D. Harris, *Europe and the East* (1926); T. F. Millard, *The New Far East* (1907); H. B. Morse and H. F. MacNair, *Far Eastern International Relations* (1931); D. E. Owen, *Imperialism and Nationalism in the Far East* (1929); G. H. Scholefield, *The Pacific, Its Past and Future* (1919);

P. J. Treat, *The Far East, A Political and Diplomatic History* (1928); H. M. Vinacke, *History of the Far East in Modern Times* (3d ed., 1936); H. Webster, *History of the Far East* (1923).

JAPAN: E. Baelz, *Awakening Japan* (1932); H. Dyer, *Japan in World Politics* (1909); H. H. Gowen, *Outline History of Japan* (1927); J. H. Gubbins, *The Making of Modern Japan* (1922); A. S. and W. S. Hershey, *Modern Japan* (1919); K. S. Latourette, *The Development of Japan* (1918); N. Matsunami, *The Constitution of Japan* (1930); W. W. McLaren, *Political History of Japan, 1867–1912* (1916); J. Murdoch, *A History of Japan* (1926); S. Okuma, *Fifty Years of New Japan* (1909); J. E. Orchard, *Japan's Economic Position* (1930); R. P. Porter, *Japan, The Rise of a Modern Power* (1918); S. Uyehara, *Industry and Trade of Japan since 1868* (1926).

CHINA: M. J. Bau, *The Foreign Relations of China* (1921) and *The Open Door Doctrine in Relation to China* (1923); J. O. P. Bland and E. Backhouse, *China under the Empress Dowager* (1910); P. H. Clements, *The Boxer Rebellion* (1915); E. J. Dingle, *China's Revolution, 1911–12* (1912); A. N. Holcombe, *The Chinese Revolution* (1930); G. W. Keeton, *Development of Extraterritoriality in China*, 2 vols. (1928); P. H. Kent, *Passing of the Manchus* (1912); V. K. W. Koo, *The Status of Aliens in China* (1912); K. S. Latourette, *The Development of China* (1929); T. W. Overlach, *Foreign Financial Control in China* (1919); A. H. Smith, *China in Convulsion*, 2 vols. (1910); E. S. Tai, *Treaty Ports in China* (1918); T. Williams, *A Short History of China* (1928); W. W. Willoughby, *Foreign Rights and Interests in China*, 2 vols. (1927).

CHAPTER II

SOCIAL CHANGES, PROBLEMS, AND PROGRAMS

DISEASE, FOOD, AND POPULATION: J. S. Chamberlain, *Chemistry in Agriculture* (1926); J. H. Collins, *The Story of Canned Food* (1924); J. B. Davidson, *Agricultural Machinery* (1931); P. de Kruif, *Microbe Hunters* (1926); E. Duclaux, *Pasteur* (1920); F. N. G. Kranich, *Farm Equipment for Mechanical Power* (1923); E. S. Mead and B. Ostrolenk, *A Study of the Agricultural Revolution* (1928); S. Paget, *Pasteur and After* (1914); L. Rogin, *Introduction of Farm Machinery* (1931); E. A. Ross, *Standing Room Only?* (1927); J. F. Steward, *The Reaper* (1931); R. Vallery-Radot, *Pasteur* (1923); A. F. Weber, *Growth of Cities in the Nineteenth Century* (1899); H. Wright, *Population* (1923).

SOCIALISM, SYNDICALISM, AND ANARCHISM: A. Bebel, *My Life* (1925); M. Beer, *Life of Karl Marx* (1924); E. Bernstein, *Ferdinand Lassalle as a Social Reformer* (1893) and *Evolutionary Socialism* (1912); M. M.

Bober, *Karl Marx's Interpretation of History* (1927); V. Cathrein, *Socialism, Its Theoretical Basis and Practical Application* (1904); B. Croce, *Historical Materialism and the Economics of Karl Marx* (1914); P. Elzbacher, *Anarchism* (1900); R. C. K. Ensor, *Modern Socialism as Set Forth by Socialists in Their Speeches, Writings and Programs* (1910); J. H. Harley, *Syndicalism* (1912); S. Hook, *Towards the Understanding of Karl Marx* (1933); K. Kautsky, *Economic Doctrines of Karl Marx* (1925); H. W. Laidler, *Socialism in Thought and Action* (1930); L. L. Lorwin, *Syndicalism* (1914) and *Labor and Internationalism* (1929); J. R. MacDonald, *The Socialist Movement* (1911); S. Markham, *A History of Socialism* (1930); K. Marx, *Capital*, 3 vols. (1906-09); F. Mehring, *Karl Marx, The Story of His Life* (1936); S. P. Orth, *Socialism and Democracy in Europe* (1913); C. W. Pipkin, *Social Politics and Modern Democracies*, 2 vols. (1927); P. J. Proudhon, *What is Property?* (1840); D. Riazanov (ed.), *Karl Marx and Friedrich Engels* (1927); O. Rühle, *Karl Marx* (1929); B. Russell, *Roads to Freedom* (1918), an examination of socialist, syndicalist, and anarchist ideals; W. Sombart, *Socialism and the Social Movement* (1909); J. Spargo, *Syndicalism, Industrial Unionism and Socialism* (1913); I. M. Steklov, *History of the First International* (1928); D. O. Wagner, *Social Reformers* (1934); S. and B. Webb, *Socialism and Individualism* (1911); E. V. Zenker, *Anarchism* (1897).

FEMINISM: K. Anthony, *Feminism in Germany and Scandinavia* (1915); M. Booth, *Women and Society* (1929); R. F. Bres, *Maids, Wives and Widows* (1918); E. R. Hecker, *Short History of Women's Rights* (1914); H. L. Mencken, *In Defense of Women* (1922); H. G. Mozans, *Woman in Science* (1913); O. Schreiner, *Woman and Labor* (1911).

CHAPTER III

THE GERMAN EMPIRE

GENERAL: J. E. Barker, *Modern Germany* (1907) and *The Foundations of Germany* (1919); Prince von Bülow, *Imperial Germany* (1917); B. Cerf, *Alsace-Lorraine since 1870* (1919); W. H. Dawson, *Municipal Life and Government in Germany* (1916) and *The Evolution of Modern Germany* (1919) and *The German Empire, 1867-1914*, 2 vols. (1919); R. H. Fife, *The German Empire between Two Wars* (1916); G. P. Gooch, *Germany* (1925); C. D. Hazen, *Alsace-Lorraine under German Rule* (1917); E. F. Henderson, *A Short History of Germany*, 2 vols. (1916); B. E. Howard, *The German Empire* (1906); F. K. Krüger, *Government and Politics of the German Empire* (1915); H. Lichtenberger, *Germany and Its Evolution in Modern Times* (1913); H. Oncken, *Germany under*

*Wilhelm II* (1913); G. H. Perris, *Germany and the German Emperor* (1912); C. Phillipson, *Alsace-Lorraine* (1918); F. Schevill, *The Making of Modern Germany* (1916); L. L. Snyder, *From Bismarck to Hitler, Background of Modern German Nationalism* (1935); A. W. Ward and S. Wilkinson, *Germany, 1815-90,* 3 vols. (1916-18).

ECONOMIC PROGRESS: P. W. L. Ashley, *Modern Tariff History: Germany, United States, France* (1904); J. H. Clapham, *Economic Development of France and Germany, 1815-1914* (1921); W. H. Dawson, *Protection in Germany* (1904) and *Industrial Germany* (1912); H. H. Farrell, *The Franco-German War Indemnity and Its Economic Results* (1913); H. Hauser, *Germany's Commercial Grip on the World* (1918); K. Helfferich, *Germany's Economic Progress and National Wealth, 1888-1915* (1915); R. Hoffman, *Great Britain and the German Trade Rivalry, 1875-1914* (1933); E. D. Howard, *The Cause and Extent of the Recent Industrial Progress of Germany* (1907); C. D. Snow, *German Foreign Trade Organization* (1917); T. Veblen, *Imperial Germany and the Industrial Revolution* (1915).

SOCIALISM AND SOCIAL LEGISLATION: W. J. Ashley, *The Progress of German Working Classes* (1904); A. Bebel, *Reminiscences,* 2 vols. (1910-14); E. Bernstein, *Ferdinand Lassalle as a Social Reformer* (1893); G. Brandes, *Ferdinand Lassalle* (1877); W. H. Dawson, *Bismarck and State Socialism* (1891) and *German Socialism and Ferdinand Lassalle* (1899) and *The German Workman* (1906) and *Social Insurance in Germany* (1911); F. C. Howe, *Socialized Germany* (1915); A. Schirokauer, *Lassalle* (1932).

FOREIGN POLICY: E. F. Benson, *The Kaiser and English Relations* (1937); E. Brandenburg, *From Bismarck to the World War* (1933); A. C. Coolidge, *The Origins of the Triple Alliance* (1926); J. V. Fuller, *Bismarck's Diplomacy at Its Zenith* (1922); G. P. Gooch, *Franco-German Relations* (1923); O. J. Hale, *Germany and the Diplomatic Revolution, 1904-1906* (1931); O. Hammann, *World Policy of Germany, 1890-1912* (1925); W. L. Langer, *European Alliances and Alignments, 1871-1890* (1931) and *The Diplomacy of Imperialism,* 2 vols. (1935); P. B. Mitchell, *The Bismarckian Policy of Conciliation with France, 1875-1885* (1936); F. Neumann, *Central Europe* (trans. 1916); K. Nowak, *Germany's Road to Ruin* (1932); A. F. Pribram, *The Secret Treaties of Austria-Hungary, 1879-1914,* 2 vols. (1920-22); P. Rohrback, *German World Politics* (trans. 1915); C. Sarolea, *The Anglo-German Problem* (1912); B. E. Schmitt, *England and Germany, 1740-1914* (1916); J. Simpson (ed.), *The Saburov Memoirs or Bismarck versus Russia* (1929); O. H. Wedel, *Austro-German Diplomatic Relations, 1908-1914* (1932); E. L. Woodward, *The Congress of Berlin* (1920).

IMPERIALISM AND NAVALISM: A. F. Calvert, *The German African Empire* (1916); E. M. Earle, *Turkey, the Great Powers and the Bagdad Railway* (1923); A. S. Hurd and H. Castle, *German Sea Power* (1913); P. E. Lewin, *The Germans and Africa* (1915); R. A. Norem, *Kiaochow Leased Territory* (1936); H. Schnee, *German Colonization Past and Present* (1926); M. E. Townsend, *The Origins of Modern German Colonialism* (1921) and *The Rise and Fall of Germany's Colonial Empire* (1930); Mildred Wertheimer, *The Pan-German League, 1890–1914* (1924); A. T. Wilson, *The Persian Gulf* (1928); J. B. Wolf, *The Diplomatic History of the Bagdad Railroad* (1936); E. L. Woodward, *Great Britain and the German Navy* (1935).

BIOGRAPHIES AND MEMOIRS: O. von Bismarck, *Reflections and Reminiscences,* 3 vols. (1898–1922); Prince von Bülow, *Letters* (1930) and *Memoirs,* 4 vols. (1931–32); M. Busch, *Bismarck, Some Secret Papers of His History,* 2 vols. (1898); G. Egelhaaf, *Bismarck* (1922); A. U. Davis, *The Kaiser as I Knew Him* (1918); E. Dombrowski, *German Leaders* (1919); C. Gauss (ed.), *The German Emperor as Shown in His Public Utterances* (1915); S. C. Hammer, *William the Second* (1915); Prince Hohenlohe, *Memoirs,* 2 vols. (1906); B. Hulderman, *Albert Ballin* (1922); E. Ludwig, *Kaiser Wilhelm II* (1925); K. F. Nowak, *Kaiser and Chancellor* (1930); F. Ponsonby, *Letters of the Empress Frederick* (1929), mother of William II; C. G. Robertson, *Bismarck* (1918); S. Shaw, *William of Germany* (1913); A. von Tirpitz, *My Memoirs,* 2 vols. (1919); F. W. Wile, *Men Around the Kaiser* (1913); Wilhelm II, *The Kaiser's Speeches* (1903) and *Letters from the Kaiser to the Czar* (1920) and *The Kaiser's Memoirs* (1922); R. Zedlitz-Trutzschler, *Twelve Years at the Imperial German Court* (1923).

CHAPTER IV

## THE THIRD FRENCH REPUBLIC

GENERAL: E. Bourgeois, *History of Modern France, 1815–1913,* 2 vols. (1919); J. C. Bracq, *France under the Republic* (1916); P. de Coubertin, *The Evolution of France under the Third Republic* (1897); A. L. Guérard, *French Civilization in the Nineteenth Century* (1914); G. Hanotaux, *Contemporary France,* 4 vols. (1903–09); F. Lawton, *The Third French Republic* (1909); R. Recouly, *The Third Republic* (1927); C. Seignobos, *The Evolution of the French People* (1932); A. Tilley, *Modern France* (1922); E. A. Vizetelly, *Republican France, 1870–1912* (1913); B. Wendell, *The France of Today* (1912); C. H. C. Wright, *History of the Third French Republic* (1916).

SPECIAL: J. P. T. Bury, *Gambetta and the National Defense, a Re-*

*publican Dictatorship in France* (1936); A. and P. Dreyfus, *The Dreyfus Case* (1937); C. J. H. Hayes, *France, a Nation of Patriots* (1930); P. O. Lissagaray, *History of the Commune* (1886); E. S. Mason, *The Paris Commune* (1930); C. T. Muret, *French Royalist Doctrines since the Revolution* (1933); C. S. Phillips, *The Church in France, 1848–1907* (1936); P. Sabatier, *Disestablishment in France* (1906); A. Siegfried, *France, A Study in Nationality* (1930); J. Simon, *The Government of M. Thiers,* 2 vols. (1879).

Politics: J. Barthélemy, *Government of France* (1924); J. Bodley, *France,* 2 vols. (1907); R. Poincaré, *How France Is Governed* (1914); E. M. Sait, *Government and Politics of France* (1920); R. H. Soltau, *French Parties and Politics, 1871–1930* (1930).

Economic and Social: S. Bernstein, *Beginnings of Marxian Socialism in France* (1933); J. H. Clapham, *The Economic Development of France and Germany, 1815–1914* (1921); A Girault, *The Colonial Tariff Policy of France* (1916); L. Levine, *The Labor Movement in France* (1912); L. Lorwin, *Syndicalism in France* (1914); H. O. Meredith, *Protection in France* (1904); P. T. Moon, *The Labor Problem and the Social Catholic Movement in France* (1925); D. J. Saposs, *The Labor Movement in France* (1931).

Imperialism and Foreign Affairs: E. N. Anderson, *The First Morocco Crisis, 1904–1906* (1930); E. M. Carroll, *French Public Opinion and Foreign Affairs, 1870–1914* (1931); M. B. Giffen, *Fashoda, the Incident and Its Diplomatic Setting* (1930); G. P. Gooch, *Franco-German Relations, 1871–1914* (1923); O. J. Hale, *Germany and the Diplomatic Revolution, 1904–1906* (1931); W. L. Langer, *The Franco-Russian Alliance, 1890–1894* (1929) and *The Diplomacy of Imperialism, 1890–1905* (1935); G. Michon, *The Franco-Russian Alliance, 1891–1917* (1929); E. D. Morel, *Morocco in Diplomacy* (1912); S. H. Roberts, *History of French Colonial Policy, 1870–1925,* 2 vols. (1929); F. L. Schuman, *War and Diplomacy in the French Republic* (1931); W. M. Sloane, *Greater France in Africa* (1923); C. Southworth, *The French Colonial Adventure* (1931); G. H. Stuart, *French Foreign Policy, 1898–1914* (1921); A. Tardieu, *France and the Alliances* (1908); R. H. Wienefeld, *Franco-German Relations, 1878–1885* (1929).

Biographies and Memoirs: G. Adam, *The Tiger: Georges Clemenceau, 1841–1929* (1930); G. Clemenceau, *In the Evening of My Thoughts,* 2 vols. (1929); P. Deschanel, *Gambetta* (1920); L. Gambetta, *Gambetta: Life and Letters* (1909); S. Huddleston, *Poincaré* (1924); H. M. Hyndman, *Clemenceau* (1919); G. C. Lecomte, *Georges Clemenceau: the Tiger of France* (1919); J. Martet, *Georges Clemenceau* (1930); F. T. Marzials, *Life of Léon Gambetta* (1890) and *Memoirs of M. Thiers, 1870–1873*

(1915); G. Michon, *Clemenceau* (1931); M. Pease, *Jean Jaurès* (1917); Poincaré, *Memoirs,* 4 vols. (1926–30); C. W. Porter, *The Career of Théophile Delcassé* (1935); A. N. Rambaud, *Jules Ferry* (1903); P. de Rémusat, *Thiers* (1889); H. Stannard, *Gambetta* (1921); V. Thomson, *Briand, Man of Peace* (1930); H. R. Weinstein, *Jean Jaurès, A Study of Patriotism in the French Socialist Movement* (1936).

CHAPTER V

## The Kingdom of Italy

T. Barclay, *Turco-Italian War* (1912); F. Crispi, *Memoirs,* 3 vols. (1912–14); B. Croce, *History of Italy, 1871–1915* (1929); W. Deecke, *Italy, A Popular Account of the Country* (1899); G. Giolitti, *Memoirs* (1923); B. King and T. Okey, *Italy To-Day* (1909); C. Lapworth, *Tripoli and Young Italy* (1912); A. L. Lowell, *The Governments of France, Italy, and Germany* (1914); G. B. McClellan, *Modern Italy* (1933); W. K. McClure, *Italy in North Africa* (1913); J. A. R. Marriott, *Makers of Modern Italy* (1931); E. A. Mowrer, *Immortal Italy* (1922); A. Robertson, *Victor Emmanuel III* (1925); W. J. Stillman, *Francesco Crispi* (1899); T. Tittoni, *Modern Italy* (1922); F. M. Underwood, *United Italy* (1915); L. Villari, *Italian Life* (1902); W. K. Wallace, *Greater Italy* (1920); H. Zimmern and A. Agresti, *New Italy* (1920).

CHAPTER VI

## The United Kingdom and the British Empire

GENERAL: A. L. Cross, *Shorter History of England and Great Britain* (1929); R. C. K. Ensor, *England, 1870–1914* (1936); J. A. Farrer, *England under Edward VII* (1922); J. M. Gaus, *Great Britain, A Study of Civic Loyalty* (1929); R. H. Gretton, *A Modern History of the English People, 1880–1910,* 2 vols. (1913); E. Halévy, *History of the English, 1895–1905* (1924); S. Low and L. C. Sanders, *Political History of England, 1837–1901* (1907); J. A. R. Marriott, *England since Waterloo* (1913); H. Maxwell, *A Century of Empire, 1801–1900,* 3 vols. (1909–11); J. McCarthy, *Short History of Our Own Times,* 4 vols. (1879–1905); T. C. Meech, *This Generation,* 2 vols. (1928); H. W. Paul, *History of Modern England,* 5 vols. (1904–06); G. M. Trevelyan, *British History in the Nineteenth Century, 1782–1901* (1922); S. Walpole, *History of Twenty-Five Years, 1856–1880,* 4 vols. (1904–08).

GOVERNMENT AND PARTIES: G. B. Adams and R. L. Schuyler, *Constitutional History of England* (1934); P. Alden, *Democratic England*

(1912); C. Allyn, *Lords versus Commons* (1931); W. R. Anson, *The Law and Custom of the Constitution,* 3 vols. (1909); H. Belloc and C. Chesterton, *The Party System* (1911); W. L. Blease, *Short History of English Liberalism* (1913); H. Cecil, *Conservatism* (1912); L. Courtney, *The Working Constitution of the United Kingdom* (1910); H. Fyfe, *The British Liberal Party* (1928); L. T. Hobhouse, *Liberalism* (1911); A. W. Humphrey, *History of Labour Representation* (1912); S. J. M. Low, *Governance of England* (1915); A. L. Lowell, *The Government of England* (1912); J. Marriott, *How England is Governed* (1928) and *The English Constitution in Transition, 1910–1924* (1925); F. A. Ogg, *English Government* (1929); J. H. Park, *English Reform Bill of 1867* (1920); A. F. Pollard, *The Evolution of Parliament* (1920); C. Seymour, *Electoral Reform in England and Wales, 1832–1885* (1915); T. P. Taswell-Langmead, *English Constitutional History* (1919); C. Trevelyan, *From Liberalism to Labour* (1921); E. M. Violette (ed.), *English Constitutional Documents since 1832* (1936).

ECONOMIC AND SOCIAL: Lord Aberconway, *The Basic Industries of Great Britain* (1927); W. J. Ashley, *British Industries* (1903); M. Beer, *History of British Socialism,* 2 vols. (1919–20); P. Blanshard, *Outline of the British Labor Movement* (1923); E. P. Cheyney, *Introduction to the Industrial and Social History of England* (1920); J. Clayton, *The Rise and Decline of Socialism in Great Britain, 1894–1924* (1926); G. D. H. Cole, *A Short History of the British Working Class Movement,* 3 vols. (1927); Lord Ernle, *English Farming, Past and Present* (1927); C. J. Fuchs, *The Trade Policy of Great Britain* (1893); F. E. Green, *History of the English Agricultural Labourer, 1870–1920* (1920); H. R. Haggard, *Rural England,* 2 vols. (1902); C. J. H. Hayes, *British Social Politics* (1913); F. G. Heath, *British Rural Life* (1911); G. J. Holyoake, *History of Coöperation in England,* 2 vols. (1906); R. Hoffman, *Great Britain and the German Trade Rivalry* (1934); E. R. Pease, *History of the Fabian Society* (1916); G. H. Perris, *Industrial History of Modern England* (1914); C. W. Pipkin, *Social Politics and Modern Democracies,* 2 vols. (1931); M. E. Seebohm, *The Evolution of the English Farm* (1927); G. Slater, *The Making of Modern England* (1915); A. P. Usher, *The Industrial History of England* (1920); D. O. Wagner, *Church of England and Social Reforms since 1854* (1930); S. and B. Webb, *History of Trade Unionism* (1920); W. J. Wilkinson, *Tory Democracy* (1924).

THE IRISH QUESTION: A. Balfour, *Aspects of Home Rule* (1912); E. Barker, *Ireland in the Last Fifty Years, 1866–1916* (1919); F. L. Benns, *The Irish Question, 1912–1914* (1928); J. D. Clarkson, *Labor and Nationalism in Ireland* (1925); I. D. Colvin, *Carson the Statesman* (1935); A. V. Dicey, *England's Case against Home Rule* (1887); S. Ervine,

*Parnell* (1925); Lord Eversley, *Gladstone and Ireland* (1912); F. Hackett, *Ireland, A Study in Nationalism* (1918); J. Haslip, *Parnell, A Biography* (1936); E. Hull, *A History of Ireland and Her People* (1931); Margaret Leamy, *Parnell's Faithful Few* (1936); M. MacDonagh, *Home Rule Movement* (1920); R. McNeill, *Ulster's Stand for Union* (1922); J. E. Morris, *Great Britain and Ireland, 1845–1910* (1914); R. B. O'Brien, *Life of Charles Stewart Parnell,* 3 vols. (1899); J. O'Connor, *History of Ireland, 1798–1924,* 2 vols. (1925); K. O'Shea, *Charles Stewart Parnell* (1914); G. de C. Parmiter, *Roger Casement* (1936); L. Paul-Dubois, *Contemporary Ireland* (1908); W. A. Phillips, *The Revolution in Ireland, 1906–1923* (1926); J. E. Pomfret, *The Struggle for Land in Ireland, 1800–1923* (1930); L. G. Redmond-Howard, *John Redmond, The Man and the Demand* (1911); D. D. Sheehan, *Ireland since Parnell* (1921); E. R. Turner, *Ireland and England in the Past and at Present* (1920).

FOREIGN POLICY: A. L. P. Dennis, *The Anglo-Japanese Alliance* (1923); C. F. Chang, *The Anglo-Japanese Alliance* (1931); H. E. Egerton, *British Foreign Policy* (1917); G. P. Gooch and J. H. B. Masterman, *A Century of British Foreign Policy* (1917); P. Knaplund, *Foreign Policy* (1935); H. Lutz, *Lord Grey and the World War* (1928); M. Montgelas, *British Foreign Policy under Sir Edward Grey* (1928); A. F. Pribram, *England and the Great Powers, 1871–1914* (1931); A. W. Ward and G. P. Gooch, *Cambridge History of British Foreign Policy, 1783–1919,* 3 vols. (1922–23); E. L. Woodward, *Great Britain and the German Navy* (1935).

BIOGRAPHIES AND MEMOIRS: H. H. Asquith, Earl of Oxford, *Fifty Years of British Parliament,* 2 vols. (1926); Harold Beeley, *Disraeli* (1936); A. C. Benson and Viscount Esher (ed.), *Letters of Queen Victoria, 1837–1861,* 3 vols. (1907); J. Bryce, *William E. Gladstone* (1898); G. E. Buckle (ed.), *Letters of Queen Victoria* (Second Series, 1926); O. Burdett, *Gladstone* (1927); G. Cecil, *Life of Robert, Marquis of Salisbury,* 2 vols. (1921); A. Chamberlain, *Politics from Inside, An Epistolary Chronicle, 1906–1914* (1936); E. Clarke, *Benjamin Disraeli* (1926); B. Disraeli *Letters,* 2 vols. (1929); B. E. C. Dugdale, *Arthur James Balfour,* 2 vols. (1937); W. H. Edwards, *The Tragedy of Edward VII* (1928); G. T. Garratt, *The Two Mr. Gladstone* (1936); J. L. Garvin, *Life of Joseph Chamberlain,* 3 vols. (1932–34); H. Gladstone, *Gladstone After Thirty Years* (1928); Viscount Grey, *Twenty-Five Years,* 2 vols. (1925); Viscount Haldane, *Before the War* (1920) and *The Autobiography of Richard Burdon Haldane* (1929); W. P. Hall, *Mr. Gladstone* (1931); Arthur Hodges, *Lord Kitchener* (1936); S. H. Jeyes, *Mr. Chamberlain* (1903); T. E. Kebbel, *Lord Beaconsfield and Other Tory Memoirs* (1907); S. Lee, *Queen Victoria, A Biography* (1903) and *King Edward VII,* 2 vols. (1927); A. Maurois, *Disraeli* (1927); W. F. Monypenny and G. E.

Buckle, *Life of Benjamin Disraeli, Earl of Beaconsfield,* 6 vols. (1910–20); J. Morley, *The Life of W. E. Gladstone,* 3 vols. (1903) and *Recollections,* 2 vols. (1917); T. P. O'Connor, *Lord Beaconsfield* (1884); E. T. Raymond, *Life of Arthur James Balfour* (1920) and *Mr. Lloyd George* (1922) and *Disraeli* (1925); D. C. Somervell, *Disraeli and Gladstone* (1926); H. Spender, *The Prime Minister, Lloyd George* (1920) and *Life of Sir Henry Campbell-Bannerman,* 2 vols. (1923); J. A. Spender and C. Asquith, *Life of Lord Oxford and Asquith,* 2 vols. (1932); L. Strachey, *Eminent Victorians* (1918) and *Queen Victoria* (1921); H. D. Traill, *The Marquis of Salisbury* (1891); G. M. Trevelyan, *Grey of Fallodon, The Life and Letters of Sir Edward Grey, afterwards Viscount Grey of Fallodon* (1937).

BRITISH IMPERIALISM: C. A. Bodelsen, *Studies in Mid-Victorian Imperialism* (1925); D. C. Boulger, *England and Russia in Central Asia,* 2 vols. (1879); C. H. Currey, *British Colonial Policy, 1783–1915* (1916); H. E. Egerton, *Short History of British Colonial Policy* (1918); R. H. Gretton, *Imperialism and Mr. Gladstone, 1876–1887* (1923); C. W. Hallberg, *Suez Canal* (1931); G. H. Holdich, *The Indian Borderland, 1880–90* (1909); P. Knaplund, *Gladstone and Britain's Imperial Policy* (1927); C. P. Lucas (ed.), *Cambridge History of the British Empire* (1930 ff.); A. F. Pollard, *The British Empire* (1909); H. Robinson, *The Development of the British Empire* (1922); W. M. Shuster, *Strangling of Persia* (1912); L. Weinthal (ed.), *The Story of the Cape to Cairo Railway,* 4 vols. (1923); J. A. Williamson, *Builders of the Empire* (1925) and *Short History of British Expansion,* 2 vols. (1930).

EGYPT: W. S. Blunt, *Secret History of the English Occupation of Egypt* (1907); D. C. Boulger, *Life of Gordon,* 2 vols. (1896); Lord Cromer, *Modern Egypt,* 2 vols. (1908); S. Low, *Egypt in Transition* (1914); P. F. Martin, *The Sudan in Evolution* (1921); Lord Milner, *England in Egypt* (1920); H. D. Traill, *England, Egypt, and the Sudan* (1900).

THE BOER WAR AND SOUTH AFRICA: R. H. Brand, *The Union of South Africa* (1909); E. H. Brookes, *The History of Native Policy in South Africa* (1927); W. H. Dawson, *South Africa* (1925); C. R. De Wet, *Three Years' War* (1902); A. C. Doyle, *Great Boer War* (1903); J. A. Hobson, *The War in South Africa* (1900); H. M. Hole, *The Making of Rhodesia* (1916); Paul Kruger, *Memoirs* (1902); W. J. Leyds, *The Transvaal Surrounded* (1919); R. I. Lovell, *The Struggle for South Africa, 1875–99* (1934); J. F. Maurice and M. H. Grant, *History of the War in South Africa, 1899–1902,* 4 vols. (1906–10); S. G. Millan, *Rhodes* (1933); A. P. Newton, *Select Documents Relating to the Unification of South Africa,* 2 vols. (1924); W. Plomer, *Cecil Rhodes* (1933); H. Spender, *General Botha* (1916); G. M. Theal, *South Africa* (1916); E. A. Walker,

*A History of South Africa* (1928); B. Williams, *Cecil Rhodes* (1921); W. B. Worsfold, *Lord Milner's Work in South Africa* (1906) and *Union of South Africa* (1912).

The Other Dominions: Earl of Birkenhead, *Story of Newfoundland* (1920); J. B. Condliffe, *Short History of New Zealand* (1925); H. D. Hall, *British Commonwealth of Nations* (1920); W. P. Hall, *Empire to Commonwealth, Thirty Years of a British Imperial History* (1927); R. Jebb, *Imperial Conference, A History and a Study*, 2 vols. (1911); E. Jenks, *History of the Australasian Colonies* (1912) and *The Government of the British Empire* (1918); A. B. Keith, *Imperial Unity and the Dominions* (1916) and *Responsible Government in the Dominions* (1928); C. Martin, *Empire and Commonwealth* (1929); R. Muir, *Short History of the British Commonwealth*, 2 vols. (1922–23); W. P. Reeves, *State Experiments in Australia and New Zealand* (1925); G. W. Rusden, *History of New Zealand*, 3 vols. (1895) and *History of Australia*, 3 vols. (1908); G. H. Scholefield, *New Zealand in Evolution* (1909); R. G. Trotter, *The British Empire-Commonwealth* (1932); H. G. Turner, *First Decade of the Australian Commonwealth* (1911); B. R. Wise, *Making of the Australian Commonwealth, 1889–1900* (1913); C. A. Wittke, *A History of Canada* (1928); G. M. Wrong, *Canada* (1924).

India: C. Burdett (ed.), *The Cambridge History of India* (1922–29); V. Chirol, *India* (1921); C. Cross, *The Development of Self-Government in India, 1858–1914* (1922); Lord Curzon, *British Government in India*, 2 vols. (1925); H. H. Dodwell, *A Sketch of the History of India from 1858–1918* (1925); R. C. Dutt, *Economic History of British India*, 2 vols. (1916); V. A. Smith, *Oxford History of India* (1921); L. J. Trotter, *History of British India under Queen Victoria*, 2 vols. (1886).

CHAPTER VII

The Lesser States of Western Europe

The Scandinavian Monarchies: R. N. Bain, *Scandinavia, A Political History of Norway, Denmark and Sweden, 1513–1900* (1905); M. Childs, *Sweden: The Middle Way* (1936); P. Drachmann and H. Westergaard, *Industrial Development and Policies of the Three Scandinavian Countries* (1915); G. Gathorne-Hardy, *Norway* (1925); K. Gjerset, *History of the Norwegian People*, 2 vols. (1915) and *History of Iceland* (1924); C. Hallendorf and A. Schück, *History of Sweden* (1929); F. C. Howe, *Denmark, A Co-operative Commonwealth* (1921); H. G. Leach, *Scandinavia of the Scandinavians* (1915); F. Nansen, *Norway and the Union with Sweden* (1905); A. Rothery, *Denmark: Kingdom of Reason* (1937);

J. Stefansson, *Denmark and Sweden, with Iceland and Finland* (1917); A. Stromberg, *History of Sweden* (1931).

HOLLAND AND BELGIUM: A. J. Barnouw, *Holland under Queen Wilhelmina* (1923); P. J. Blok, *History of the People of the Netherlands,* Vol. V (1912); E. Cammaerts, *Belgium* (1921) and *Albert I* (1935); S. B. Clough, *History of the Flemish Movement in Belgium* (1930); Count Corti, *Leopold I of Belgium* (1923); C. Day, *The Policy and Administration of the Dutch in Java* (1904); G. Edmundson, *History of Holland, 1361–1913* (1922); R. C. K. Ensor, *Belgium* (1915); A. Holden, *Uncle Leopold, A Life of the First King of the Belgians* (1936); A. C. J. Jitta, *Holland's Modern Renascence* (1930); L. de Lichtervelde, *Leopold of the Belgians* (1929); R. Putnam, *Luxemburg and Her Neighbors* (1919); T. H. Reed, *The Government and Politics of Belgium* (1924); A. Vandenbosch, *The Dutch East Indies* (1934); L. van der Essen, *Short History of Belgium* (1920); H. van der Linden, *Belgium, The Making of a Nation* (1920).

SWITZERLAND: R. C. Brooks, *Government and Politics of Switzerland* (1918) and *Civic Training in Switzerland* (1930); W. D. McCrackan, *Rise of the Swiss Republic* (1901); W. Martin, *History of Switzerland* (1931); W. Oechsli, *History of Switzerland, 1499–1914* (1922); W. E. Rappard, *The Government of Switzerland* (1937).

SPAIN AND PORTUGAL: J. A. Brandt, *Toward the New Spain* (1933); C. Chapman, *History of Spain* (1918); H. B. Clarke, *Modern Spain, 1815–1898* (1906); C. S. Cooper, *Understanding Spain* (1928); P. Crabitès, *Unhappy Spain* (1937); M. Hume, *Modern Spain* (1923); J. McCabe, *Spain in Revolt, 1814–1931* (1931); S. de Madariaga, *Spain* (1930); H. D. Sedgwick, *Spain, A Short History of Its Politics, Literature and Art* (1923); R. Sencourt, *The Spanish Crown, 1808–1931* (1932); H. M. Stephens, *Portugal* (1908); E. Stewart, *Twenty-Nine Years* (1931), a biography of Alfonso XIII; E. H. Strobel, *Spanish Revolution, 1868–1875* (1898); G. M. Theal, *The Portuguese in South Africa* (1896); J. B. Trend, *The Origins of Modern Spain* (1934); George Young, *Portugal, Old and Young* (1917).

CHAPTER VIII

THE RUSSIAN EMPIRE

GENERAL: G. Alexinsky, *Modern Russia* (1913); R. Beazley and others, *Russia from the Varangians to the Bolsheviks* (1918); V. Berard, *The Russian Empire and Czarism* (1905); B. Chaninov, *A History of Russia* (1930); G. Drage, *Russian Affairs* (1904); A. Fortescue, *The Orthodox Eastern Church* (1911) and *The Uniate Eastern Churches* (1923); M.

Karpovich, *Imperial Russia, 1801–1917* (1932); A. Kornilov, *Modern Russian History*, 2 vols. (1924); M. M. Kovalevsky, *Russian Political Institutions* (1902); A. Leroy-Beaulieu, *The Empire of the Tsars,* 3 vols. (1893–96); N. Makeef and V. O'Hara, *Russia* (1925); T. G. Masaryk, *Spirit of Russia,* 2 vols. (1919); B. Pares, *History of Russia* (1930); S. F. Platonov, *History of Russia* (1925); G. Vernadsky, *A History of Russia* (1929); H. W. Williams, *Russia of the Russians* (1914).

THE ROMANOVS: G. Botkin, *The Real Romanovs* (1931); P. Gilliard, *Thirteen Years at the Russian Court* (n.d.); C. Lowe, *Alexander III* (1895); J. H. Williams, *The Emperor Nicholas as I Knew Him* (1920).

ECONOMIC AND SOCIAL: M. Baring, *The Russian People* (1914); M. G. Hindus, *The Russian Peasant and the Revolution* (1920); J. Mavor, *Economic History of Russia,* 2 vols. (1926); M. S. Miller, *The Economic Development of Russia, 1905–1914* (1926); D. S. Mirsky, *Russia: A Social History* (1932); G. Pavlovsky, *Agricultural Russia on the Eve of the Revolution* (1930); A. Raffalovich (ed.), *Russia, Its Trade and Commerce* (1918); G. T. Robinson, *Rural Russia under the Old Régime* (1932); D. M. Wallace, *Russia* (1912); L. Wiener, *Interpretation of the Russian People* (1915).

FOREIGN POLICY: G. Alexinsky, *Russia and Europe* (1917); A. P. Izvolsky, *Recollections of a Foreign Minister* (1921); S. A. Korff, *Russia's Foreign Relations during the Last Half Century* (1922); W. L. Langer, *The Franco-Russian Alliance, 1890–1894* (1929) and *The Diplomacy of Imperialism,* 2 vols. (1935); S. D. Sazonov, *Fateful Years* (1928); F. Stieve, *Izvolsky and the World War* (1926).

EXPANSION OF RUSSIA: J. F. Baddeley, *The Russian Conquest of the Caucasus* (1908); G. N. Curzon, *Russia in Central Asia* (1889); A. Lobanov-Rostovsky, *Russia and Asia* (1933); M. P. Price, *Siberia* (1912); E. G. Ravenstein, *The Russians on the Amur* (1861); A. Rambaud, *The Expansion of Russia* (1904); F. H. Skrine, *Expansion of Russia, 1815–1900* (1915); A. Vamberry, *Central Asia and the Anglo-Russia Frontier Question* (1874); G. F. Wright, *Asiatic Russia,* 2 vols. (1902).

SUBJECT PEOPLES: G. Brandes, *Poland, A Study of the Land, People, and Literature* (1903); S. M. Dubnow, *History of the Jews in Russia and Poland,* 3 vols. (1916–20); J. R. Fisher, *Finland and the Tsars* (1901); I. Friedlaender, *The Jews of Russia and Poland* (1905); J. S. Orvis, *Brief History of Poland* (1916); A. Reade, *Finland* (1917); N. D. Sergeevsky, *Finland* (1911); J. H. Wuorinen, *Nationalism in Modern Finland* (1931).

RUSSO-TURKISH WAR: D. Harris, *A Diplomatic History of the Balkan Crisis of 1875–78* (1936); T. E. Holland, *The European Concert in the Eastern Question, A Collection of Treaties and Other Public Acts* (1885); J. F. Maurice, *The Russo-Turkish War of 1877* (1905); H. W. V. Temperley, *The Bulgarian Atrocities, 1875–1878* (1931); E. L. Woodward, *The Congress of Berlin* (1920).

RUSSO-JAPANESE WAR: K. Asakawa, *The Russo-Japanese Conflict* (1904); T. Dennett, *Roosevelt and the Russo-Japanese War* (1925); A. S. Hershey, *International Law and Diplomacy of the Russo-Japanese War* (1906); A. Kuropatkin, *The Russian Army and the Japanese War*, 2 vols. (1909); D. Murray, *The Official History of the Russo-Japanese War*, 5 vols. (1908–10); E. B. Price, *Russo-Japanese Treaties of 1907–1916 concerning Manchuria and Mongolia* (1933); Z. Volpicelli, *The China-Japan War* (1896) and *British Official History of the Russo-Japanese War*, 6 vols. (1910–16); S. I. Witte, *The Memoirs of Count Witte* (1921). See also the books listed on pp. 865–866.

REPRESSION AND REVOLUTION: H. Barbusse, *Stalin* (1935); S. Graham, *Stalin* (1931); A. Herzen, *Memoirs*, 4 vols. (1924–25); G. Kennan, *Siberia and the Exile System*, 2 vols. (1891); S. A. Korff, *Autocracy and Revolution in Russia* (1923); P. A. Kropotkin, *Memoirs of a Revolutionist* (1899); I. D. Levine, *The Man Lenin* (1924) and *Stalin* (1931); R. Lévy, *Trotsky* (1920); V. Marcu, *Lenin: Thirty Years of Russia* (1928); P. N. Miliukov, *Russia and Its Crisis* (1905); D. S. Mirsky, *Lenin* (1931); H. W. Nevinson, *The Dawn in Russia* (1906); M. J. Olgin, *The Soul of the Russian Revolution* (1917); B. Pares, *Russia and Reform* (1907); G. H. Perris, *Russia in Revolution* (1905); K. P. Pobiedonostev, *Reflections of a Russian Statesman* (1898); A. S. Rappoport, *Pioneers of the Russian Revolution* (1918); S. Stepniak, *Underground Russia* (1883) and *Career of a Nihilist* (1901); L. Trotsky, *My Life* (1930); W. C. White, *Lenin* (1936).

CHAPTER IX

THE AUSTRO-HUNGARIAN DUAL MONARCHY

GENERAL: G. Drage, *Austria-Hungary* (1909); V. Gayda, *Modern Austria* (1915); O. Jaszi, *Dissolution of the Hapsburg Monarchy* (1929); L. P. M. Léger, *History of Austria-Hungary* (1907); J. Redlich, *Austrian War Government* (1927); W. von Schierbrand, *Austria-Hungary* (1917); H. W. Steed, *The Hapsburg Monarchy* (1919).

HUNGARY: T. Capek, *The Slovaks of Hungary* (1906); F. Eckart, *A Short History of the Hungarian People* (1931); F. A. Forster, *Francis Deák* (1880); A. de Hevesy, *Nationalities in Hungary* (1919); C. M. Knatchbull-Hugesson, *Political Evolution of the Hungarian Nation*, 2 vols. (1908); R. W. Seton-Watson, *Racial Problems in Hungary* (1908) and *Corruption and Reform in Hungary* (1911); P. Teleki, *Evolution of Hungary* (1923); A. B. Yolland, *Hungary* (1917).

FOREIGN POLICY: J. Goričar and L. B. Stowe, *The Inside Story of the Austro-German Intrigue* (1920); A. F. Pribram, *Austrian Foreign Policy, 1908–1918* (1923) and *Secret Treaties of Austria-Hungary, 1879–1914,* 2 vols. (1920–22); B. E. Schmitt, *The Annexation of Bosnia, 1908–1909* (1937); R. W. Seton-Watson, *The Southern Slav Question and the Hapsburg Monarchy* (1911) and *German, Slav, and Magyar* (1916); A. H. E. Taylor, *The Future of the Southern Slavs* (1917); O. H. Wedel, *Austro-German Diplomatic Relations, 1908–1914* (1932).

FRANCIS JOSEPH: E. Bagger, *Francis Joseph, Emperor of Austria* (1927); O. Ernst, *Franz Joseph as Revealed by His Letters* (1927); E. Ketterl, *The Emperor Francis Joseph* (1929); R. P. Mahaffy, *Francis Joseph I* (1915); A. Margutti, *The Emperor Francis Joseph and His Times* (1921); J. Redlich, *Emperor Francis Joseph of Austria* (1929); H. Rumbold, *Francis Joseph and His Times* (1909); K. Tschuppki, *Francis Joseph* (1930).

CHAPTER X

TURKEY AND THE BALKANS

GENERAL: H. N. Brailsford, *Macedonia, Its Races and Their Future* (1906); C. A. Chekrezi, *Albania, Past and Present* (1919); A. C. Coolidge, *Claimants to Constantinople* (1917); S. P. Duggan, *The Eastern Question: A Study in Diplomacy* (1902); M. E. Durham, *Twenty Years of the Balkan Tangle* (1920); N. Forbes and others, *The Balkans, A History of Bulgaria, Serbia, Greece, Rumania, and Turkey* (1915); W. M. Gewehr, *The Rise of Nationalism in the Balkans* (1931); P. P. Graves, *The Question of the Straits* (1931); H. Kohn, *History of Nationalism in the Near East* (1929); J. A. R. Marriott, *The Eastern Question* (1930); W. Miller, *The Balkans* (1908); W. S. Murray, *The Making of the Balkan States* (1910); M. I. Newbigin, *Geographical Aspects of Balkan Problems* (1915); S. Panaretoff, *Near Eastern Affairs and Conditions* (1922); C. Phillipson and N. Buxton, *The Question of the Bosphorous and Dardanelles* (1917); F. Schevill, *A History of the Balkan Peninsula from the Earliest Times to the Present Day* (1922); B. E. Schmitt, *The Annexation of Bosnia, 1908–1909* (1937); R. W. Seton-Watson, *The Rise of Nationality in the Balkans* (1917); W. M. Sloane, *The Balkans, a Laboratory of History* (1920); M. W. Tyler, *The European Powers and the Near East, 1875–1908* (1925); George Young, *Nationalism and War in the Near East* (1915).

THE BALKAN WARS: E. Ashmead-Bartlett, *With the Turks in Thrace* (1913); M. E. Durham, *The Struggle for Scutari* (1914); I. Gueshoff, *The Balkan League* (1915); H. Howard, *The Partition of Turkey, 1913–*

*1923* (1931); R. Rankin, *The Inner History of the Balkan War* (1914);
J. G. Schurman, *The Balkan Wars, 1912–1913* (1916); E. P. Stickney,
*Southern Albania or Northern Epirus, 1912–1923* (1926).

BULGARIA: A. H. Beaman, *Stambuloff* (1895); E. Dicey, *The Peasant
State* (1894); E. Gleichen, *Bulgaria and Roumania* (1924); A. E. von
Huhn, *The Kidnapping of Prince Alexander of Battenberg* (1887); A.
Koch, *Prince Alexander of Battenberg* (1887); J. MacDonald, *Czar
Ferdinand and His People* (1913); W. S. Monroe, *Bulgaria and Her People*
(1914); S. Panaretoff, *Bulgaria and Her Neighbors* (1917); S. Protich,
*Aspirations of Bulgaria* (1915).

GREECE: S. B. Chester, *Life of Venizelos* (1921); H. A. Gibbons,
*Venizelos* (1923); P. Hibben, *Constantine I and the Greek People* (1920);
P. F. Martin, *Greece of the Twentieth Century* (1913); W. Miller, *A
History of the Greek People, 1821–1921* (1922) and *Greece* (1928); L.
Sergeant, *Greece in the Nineteenth Century* (1897).

RUMANIA: O. Brilliant, *Roumania* (1915): C. U. Clark, *Greater Roumania* (1922) and *Bessarabia, Russia and Roumania on the Black Sea*
(1927); N. Jorga, *History of Roumania* (1926); D. Mitrany, *Rumania,
Her History and Politics* (1917); T. W. Riker, *The Making of Roumania*
(1931); R. W. Seton-Watson, *A History of the Roumanians* (1934).

SERBIA AND MONTENEGRO: W. M. Petrovitch, *Serbia* (1915); A. Stead,
*Servia by the Servians* (1909); F. S. Stevenson, *A History of Montenegro*
(1912); H. W. V. Temperley, *History of Serbia* (1917).

TURKEY: W. E. D. Allen, *The Turks in Europe* (1920); D. C. Blais-
dell, *European Financial Control in the Ottoman Empire* (1929); E. S.
Creasy, *History of the Ottoman Turks*, 2 vols. (1906); C. N. E. Eliot,
*Turkey in Europe* (1908); G. Eversley, *The Turkish Empire, Its Growth
and Decay* (1923); E. G. Mears, *Modern Turkey, A Politico-Economic
Interpretation, 1908–1923* (1924); W. Miller, *The Ottoman Empire and
Its Successors, 1801–1927* (1934); E. Pears, *Turkey and Its People* (1912)
and *Life of Abdul Hamid* (1917); S. L. Poole, *Story of Turkey* (1922);
L. von Sanders, *Five Years in Turkey* (1927).

CHAPTER XI

## THE OUTBREAK OF THE WAR

HOPES OF PEACE: D. Allen, *The Fight For Peace* (1930); N. Angell,
*The Great Illusion* (1913); A. C. F. Beales, *History of Peace* (1931);
J. S. Bloch, *The Future of War . . . Is War Now Possible?* (1899); H.
N. Brailsford, *War of Steel and Gold* (1914); J. B. Bury, *The Idea of
Progress* (1920); G. G. Coulton, *Main Illusions of Pacifism* (1916); A.
P. Higgins, *The Hague Peace Conferences and Other International Con-*

*ferences Concerning the Laws and Usages of War* (1909); W. I. Hull, *The Two Hague Conferences* (1908); Ellen Key, *War, Peace, and the Future* (1914); F. S. Marvin, *Century of Hope* (1919); J. B. Scott, *The Hague Peace Conferences*, 2 vols. (1909); T. Veblen, *An Inquiry into the Nature of Peace* (1919).

CAUSES OF WAR: J. Bakeless, *Economic Causes of Modern War* (1921); C. J. H. Hayes, *Essays on Nationalism* (1926); E. Krehbiel, *Nationalism, War and Society* (1916); K. Liebknecht, *Militarism* (1917); A. T. Mahan, *Armaments and Arbitration or the Place of Force in the International Relations of States* (1912); W. Millis, *Martial Spirit* (1931); R. Muir, *Nationalism and Internationalism* (1916); G. F. Nicolai, *The Biology of War* (1917); H. H. Powers, *The Things Men Fight For* (1916); E. H. Reisner, *Nationalism and Education since 1789* (1922); M. Smith, *Militarism and Statecraft* (1918).

THE CRISIS OF 1914: H. E. Barnes, *The Genesis of the World War* (1928), by an American; E. F. Benson, *The Outbreak of War, 1914* (1934); C. Bloch, *The Causes of the World War* (1935), by a Frenchman; M. E. Durham, *The Serajevo Crime* (1925); J. S. Ewart, *The Roots and Causes of the Wars, 1914–1918*, 2 vols. (1925), by a Canadian; M. Bogichevich, *Causes of the War* (1919); A. Fabre-Luce, *The Limitations of Victory* (1926), by a Frenchman; S. B. Fay, *The Origins of the World War*, 2 vols. (1928), by an American; K. Kautsky, *The Guilt of William Hohenzollern* (1920), by a German; H. Lutz, *Lord Grey and the World War* (1928), by a German; Count M. Montgelas, *The Case for the Central Powers* (1925); A. J. Nock, *The Myth of a Guilty Nation* (1922); P. Renouvin, *The Immediate Origins of the War* (1928), by a Frenchman; B. E. Schmitt, *The Coming of the War: 1914* (1930), by an American; J. F. Scott, *Five Weeks* (1927), public opinion during the crisis; R. W. Seton-Watson, *Sarajevo, A Study in the Origins of the Great War* (1926); F. Stieve, *Isvolsky and the World War* (1926); A. von Wegerer, *A Refutation of the Versailles War Guilt Thesis* (1930); H. W. Wilson, *The War Guilt* (1928), by an Englishman; T. Wolff, *The Eve of 1914* (1936), by a German.

MEMOIRS AND RECOLLECTIONS: H. H. Asquith, *Genesis of the War* (1924), by the British prime minister in 1914; F. L. B. Bertie, *A Diary of Lord Bertie*, 2 vols. (1924), by the British ambassador at Paris in 1914; T. von Bethmann-Hollweg, *Reflections on the World War* (1920), by the German chancellor in 1914; G. Buchanan, *My Mission to Russia*, 2 vols. (1923), by the British ambassador to Russia in 1914; W. S. Churchill, *The World Crisis, 1911–1918*, 4 vols. (1923–27), by the British first lord of the admiralty in 1914; Viscount Grey of Fallodon, *Twenty-Five Years, 1892–1916*, 2 vols. (1925), by the British foreign minister in 1914; K. M.

Lichnowsky, *Heading for the Abyss* (1928), by the German ambassador to Great Britain in 1914; G. M. Paléologue, *An Ambassador's Memoirs,* 3 vols. (1924–26), by the French ambassador to Russia in 1914; R. Poincaré, *The Origins of the War* (1922), by the President of the French Republic in 1914; S. D. Sazonov, *Fateful Years, 1909–1916* (1928), by the Russian foreign minister in 1914; W. E. Freiherr von Schoen, *The Memoirs of an Ambassador* (1922), by the German ambassador to France in 1914; R. Viviani, *As We See It* (1923), by the French premier in 1914; Wilhelm II, *The Kaiser's Memoirs, 1887–1918* (1922).

DOCUMENTS: W. C. Bridge (ed.), *How the War Began in 1914, Being the Diary of the Russian Foreign Office* (1925); W. H. Cooke and E. P. Stickney, *Readings in European International Relations since 1879* (1931); E. T. S. Dugdale (ed.), *German Diplomatic Documents, 1871–1914,* 4 vols. (1928–31); J. W. Headlam-Morley (ed.), *Foreign Office Documents, June 28th–August 4th, 1914* (1926); M. Montgelas and W. Schücking (eds.), *Outbreak of the World War, German Documents Collected by Karl Kautsky* (1924); *Official Files Pertaining to Pre-War History,* 3 vols. (1920–21), a fuller edition of the Austrian "red book" of 1914; *Official German Documents Relating to the World War,* 2 vols. (1923); G. von Romberg, *Falsifications of the Russian Orange Book* (1923); J. B. Scott (ed.), *Diplomatic Documents Relating to the Outbreak of the European War,* 2 vols. (1916) and *The German White Book Concerning the Responsibility of the Authors of the War* (1924).

CHAPTER XII

THE PERIOD OF TEUTONIC ASCENDANCY

GENERAL: J. Buchan, *A History of the Great War,* 4 vols. (1922); C. R. M. Cruttwell, *A History of the Great War, 1914–1918* (1934); C. J. H. Hayes, *A Brief History of the Great War* (1926); B. H. Liddell Hart, *A History of the World War, 1914–1918* (1935); E. Ludendorff, *The Nation at War* (1936); A. F. Pollard, *A Short History of the Great War* (1928); F. H. Simonds, *A History of the World War,* 5 vols. (1917–20); L. Stallings (ed.), *The First World War: A Photographic History* (1933); W. S. Woods, *Colossal Blunders of the War* (1930).

SPECIAL AREAS OR BATTLES: G. F. Abbott, *Greece and the Allies 1914–1922* (1922); E. Ashmead-Bartlett, *The Uncensored Dardanelles* (1928); P. Coblentz, *The Silence of Sarrail* (1930); C. T. E. Edmonds, *Lawrence of Arabia* (1935); A. Emin, *Turkey in the World War* (1930); L. van der Essen, *The Invasion and the War in Belgium* (1917); R. Evans, *A*

*Brief Outline of the Campaign in Mesopotamia* (1926); N. N. Golovine, *The Russian Army in the World War* (1931) and *The Russian Campaign of 1914: The Beginning of War and Operations in East Prussia* (1933); E. Ironside, *Tannenberg, The First Thirty Days in East Prussia* (1925); H. Kannengiesser, *The Campaign in Gallipoli* (1928); A. von Kluck, *The March on Paris, 1914* (1920); T. E. Lawrence, *Revolt in the Desert* (1927); O. Liman von Sanders, *Five Years in Turkey* (1927); G. L. Mc-Entee, *Italy's Part in Winning the World War* (1934); H. P. Pétain, *Verdun* (1930); L. J. Thomas, *With Lawrence in Arabia* (1924); C. Townshend, *My Campaign in Mesopotamia* (1920); G. M. Trevelyan, *Scenes from Italy's War* (1919); S. Tyng, *The Campaign of the Marne, 1914* (1935); L. Villari, *The War on the Italian Front* (1932); A. P. Wavell, *The Palestine Campaigns* (1928).

THE WAR ON THE SEA AND IN THE AIR: W. G. Carr, *By Guess and by God* (1930); E. K. Chatterton, *Sea-Raiders* (n.d.); J. S. Corbett and H. Newbolt, *Naval Operations*, 5 vols. (1920–31); C. Domville, *Submarines and Sea-Power* (1919); H. W. Fawcett and G. W. W. Hooper (eds.), *The Fighting at Jutland* (1929); J. A. Fisher, *Memories and Records*, 2 vols. (1920); G. G. von Forstner, *The Journal of Submarine Commander von Forstner* (1917); L. Gibson and J. E. T. Harper, *The Riddle of Jutland* (1934); R. H. Gibson and M. Prendergast, *The German Submarine War, 1914–1918* (1931); L. Guichard, *The Naval Blockade* (1930); J. E. T. Harper, *The Truth about Jutland* (1927); G. von Hase, *Kiel and Jutland* (n.d.); E. Hashagen, *The Log of a U-Boat Commander* (1931); J. R. Jellicoe, *The Grand Fleet, 1914–1916* (1919) and *The Submarine Peril* (1934); E. A. Lehmann and H. Mingos, *The Zeppelins* (1928); H. Newbolt, *A Naval History of the War, 1914–1918* (1920); H. Poch-hammer, *Before Jutland: Admiral von Spee's Last Voyage* (1931); W. Raleigh, *The War in the Air*, 2 vols. (1922–28); R. Scheer, *Germany's High Sea Fleet in the World War* (1920); L. Thomas, *Raiders of the Deep* (1928); A. von Tirpitz, *My Memoirs*, 2 vols. (1919); C. C. Turner, *The Struggle in the Air, 1914–1918* (1919); R. E. W. Wester-Wemyss, *The Navy in the Dardanelles Campaign* (n.d.).

ESPIONAGE AND PROPAGANDA: G. G. Aston, *Secret Service* (1930); H. R. Berndorff, *Espionage!* (1930); J. Crozier, *In the Enemy's Country* (1931); H. Landau, *All's Fair* (1934); H. D. Lasswell, *Propaganda Technique in the World War* (1927); W. Nicolai, *The German Secret Service* (1924); C. E. Playne, *Society at War, 1914–1916* (1931); A. Ponsonby, *Falsehood in Wartime* (1928); J. D. Squires, *British Propaganda at Home and in the United States from 1914 to 1917* (1935); C. Stuart, *Secrets of Crewe House* (1920); G. S. Viereck, *Spreading Germs of Hate* (1930).

MISCELLANEOUS: G. H. Clark (ed.), *Treasury of War Poetry* (1917); H. Cobb, *Paths of Glory* (1935); F. C. Cocks, *The Secret Treaties and Understandings* (1918); G. A. B. Dewar, *The Great Munition Feat, 1914–1918* (1921); C. H. Foulkes, *Gas! The Story of the Special Brigade* (1934); E. Fradkin, *Chemical Warfare* (1929); J. F. C. Fuller, *Tanks in the Great War* (1920); H. L. Gray, *War Time Control of Industry* (1918); M. Hardie and A. K. Sabin (eds.), *War Posters Issued by Belligerent and Neutral Nations, 1914–1919* (1920); B. H. Liddell Hart, *Reputations Ten Years After* (1928); W. Martin, *Statesmen of the War in Retrospect, 1918–1928* (1928); H. W. Miller, *The Paris Gun* (1930); W. Molony, *Prisoners and Captives* (1933); E. M. Remarque, *All Quiet on the Western Front* (1929); R. C. Sherriff, *Journey's End* (1929); A. Zweig, *The Case of Sergeant Grischa* (1928).

BIOGRAPHIES, MEMOIRS, AND RECOLLECTIONS: G. C. A. Arthur, *The Life of Lord Kitchener*, 3 vols. (1920); H. H. Asquith, *Memories and Reflections, 1852–1927*, 2 vols. (1928); G. G. Aston, *The Biography of the Late Marshal Foch* (1929); A. A. Brusilov, *A Soldier's Notebook* (1930); C. E. Callwell, *Field Marshal Sir Henry Wilson*, 2 vols. (1927) and *The Life of Sir Stanley Maude* (1920); J. Charteris, *Field Marshal Earl Haig* (1929); S. B. Chester, *Life of Venizelos* (1921); W. S. Churchill, *The World Crisis, 1911–1918*, 4 vols. (1923–27); G. A. B. Dewar and J. H. Boraston, *Sir Douglas Haig's Command*, 2 vols. (1922); A. Djemal, *Memories of a Turkish Statesman, 1913–1919* (1922); E. von Falkenhayn, *General Headquarters and Its Critical Decisions* (1919); F. Foch, *Memoirs* (1931); G. French, *The Life of Field Marshal Sir John French* (1931); J. French, *1914* (1919); E. J. Galet, *Albert, King of the Belgians, in the Great War* (1931); H. A. Gibbons, *Venizelos* (1923); G. Giolitti, *Memoirs of My Life* (1923); I. Hamilton, *Gallipoli Diary*, 2 vols. (1920); P. von Hindenburg, *Out of My Life*, 2 vols. (1921); J. J. C. Joffre, *Personal Memoirs*, 2 vols. (1932); B. H. Liddell Hart, *Foch, the Man of Orleans* (1932) and *Colonel Lawrence: The Man Behind the Legend* (1934); D. Lloyd George, *War Memoirs of David Lloyd George*, 6 vols. (1933–37); E. Ludendorff, *Ludendorff's Own Story, August 1914–November 1918*, 2 vols. (1920); L. Madelin, *Foch* (1929); H. Morgenthau, *Ambassador Morgenthau's Story* (1919), war-time Turkey as seen by the American ambassador; R. Recouly, *Joffre* (1931); W. Robertson, *Soldiers and Statesmen, 1914–1918*, 2 vols. (1926); A. Salandra, *Italy and the Great War: From Neutrality to Intervention* (1932); E. Sherson, *Townshend of Chitral and Kut* (1928); J. W. Wheeler-Bennett, *Wooden Titan, Hindenburg in Twenty Years of German History, 1914–1934* (1936); B. Whitlock, *Belgium: A Personal Narrative*, 2 vols. (1919).

CHAPTER XIII

AMERICA'S INTERVENTION AND RUSSIA'S WITHDRAWAL

AMERICA'S ENTRANCE INTO THE WAR: N. D. Baker, *Why We Went to War* (1937); R. S. Baker, *Neutrality: 1914–1915* (1935); R. S. Baker and W. Dodd (eds.), *The Public Papers of Woodrow Wilson*, 6 vols. (1925–27); J. S. Bassett, *Our War With Germany* (1919); J. von Bernstorff, *My Three Years in America* (1920) and *Memoirs of Count Bernstorff* (1937); T. Dennett and J. V. Fuller (eds.), *Papers Relating to the Foreign Relations of the United States: Supplements: The World War* (1928 ff.); K. Dumba, *Memories of a Diplomat* (1932); J. W. Gerard, *My Four Years in Germany* (1917); C. H. Grattan, *Why We Fought* (1929); S. Gwynn (ed.), *The Letters and Friendships of Sir Cecil Spring-Rice*, 2 vols. (1929); B. J. Hendrick, *Life and Letters of Walter H. Page*, 2 vols. (1922); R. Lansing, *War Memoirs* (1935); W. Millis, *Road to War: America, 1914–1917* (1935); J. B. Scott, *A Survey of International Relations Between the United States and Germany, 1914–1917* (1917); C. Seymour, *Woodrow Wilson and the World War* (1922) and *American Neutrality: 1914–1917* (1936) and *American Diplomacy During the World War* (1934); C. Seymour (ed.), *The Intimate Papers of Colonel House*, 2 vols. (1926–28); W. G. Sharp, *The War Memoirs of William Graves Sharp, American Ambassador to France, 1914–1919* (1931); P. W. Slosson, *The Great Crusade and After, 1914–1928* (1930).

THE UNITED STATES IN THE WAR: L. P. Ayers, *The War with Germany, A Statistical Summary* (1920); Col. de Chambrun and Capt. de Marenches, *The American Army in the European Conflict* (1919); G. B. Clarkson, *Industrial America in the World War* (1923); G. Creel, *How We Advertised America* (1920); J. Daniels, *Our Navy at War* (1922); H. P. Davison, *The American Red Cross in the Great War* (1919); T. G. Frothingham, *The American Reinforcement in the World War* (1927) and *The Naval History of the World War*, III (1926); A. Gleaves, *A History of the Transport Service* (1921); J. G. Harbord, *The American Army in France* (1936); E. N. Hurley, *The Bridge to France* (1927); H. Liggett, *Commanding an American Army* (1925) and *A.E.F.* (1928); P. C. March, *The Nation at War* (1932); W. G. McAdoo, *Crowded Years* (1931); J. B. McMaster, *The United States in the World War*, 2 vols. (1918–20); S. T. Moore, *America and the World War* (1937); A. W. Page, *Our 110 Days Fighting* (1920); F. Palmer, *Newton D. Baker*, 2 vols. (1931) and *Our Greatest Battle* (1919); M. M. Patrick, *The United States in the Air* (1928); J. J. Pershing, *My Experiences in the World War*, 2 vols. (1931); W. S. Sims, *The American Navy in the*

*War* (1920); W. S. Sims and B. J. Hendrick, *The Victory at Sea* (1920); S. Thomas, *History of the A.E.F.* (1920); D. Van Every, *The A.E.F. in Battle* (1928).

THE RUSSIAN REVOLUTION: E. K. Breshko-Breshkovskaia, *Hidden Springs of the Russian Revolution* (1931); J. Bunyan and H. H. Fisher (eds.), *The Bolshevik Revolution, 1917–1918* (1934); W. H. Chamberlin, *History of the Russian Revolution*, 2 vols. (1935); V. Chernov, *The Great Russian Revolution* (1936); A. J. Denikin, *The Russian Turmoil* (1922); M. T. Florinsky, *The End of the Russian Empire* (1931); R. Fülöp-Miller, *Rasputin: The Holy Devil* (1928); F. A. Golder (ed.), *Documents of Russian History, 1914–1917* (1927); P. P. Gronsky and N. J. Astrov, *The War and the Russian Government* (1929); M. G. Hindus, *The Russian Peasant and the Revolution* (1920); F. F. Iusupov, *Rasputin* (1927); A. F. Kerensky, *The Prelude to Bolshevism* (1919) and *The Catastrophe* (1927); N. Lenin, *Preparing for Revolt* (1929); *Letters of the Tsaritsa to the Tsar, 1914–1916* (1923); *The Letters of the Tsar to the Tsaritsa, 1914–1917* (1929); V. Marcu, *Lenin: Thirty Years of Russia* (1928); G. T. Marye, *Nearing the End in Imperial Russia* (1929); J. Mavor, *The Russian Revolution* (1928); A. F. Meyendorff, *The Background of the Russian Revolution* (1929); P. Miliukov, *History of the Second Russian Revolution* (1920); A. S. Rappoport, *Pioneers of the Russian Revolution* (1918); M. V. Rodzianko, *The Reign of Rasputin: An Empire's Collapse* (1927); E. A. Ross, *The Russian Bolshevik Revolution* (1921); A. Trachtenberg (ed.), *Lenin: Toward the Seizure of Power*, 2 vols. (1932); L. Trotsky, *From October to Brest-Litovsk* (1919) and *Lenin* (1925) and *The History of the Russian Revolution* (1934); C. E. Vulliamy (ed.), *The Red Archives* (1929); E. A. Walsh, *The Fall of the Russian Empire, The Story of the Last Romanovs and the Coming of the Bolsheviki* (1928).

CHAPTER XIV

THE COLLAPSE OF THE CENTRAL POWERS

In addition to the references for Chapter XII the following are suggested:

GENERAL: E. Dahlin, *French and German Public Opinion on Declared War Aims, 1914–1918* (1933); G. A. B. Dewar, *Sir Douglas Haig's Command*, 2 vols. (1923); G. L. Dickinson (ed.), *Documents and Statements Relating to Peace Proposals and War Aims, 1916–1918* (1919); H. Gough, *The Fifth Army* (1931); E. de Manteyer (ed.), *Austria's Peace Offer, 1916–1917* (1921); F. Maurice, *The Last Four Months* (1919); J.

B. Scott (ed.), *Preliminary History of the Armistice* (1924); J. C. Wise, *Turn of the Tide* (1920).

THE DISINTEGRATION OF AUSTRIA-HUNGARY: H. Baerlein, *The Birth of Yugoslavia*, 2 vols. (1922); I. Balassa, *Death of an Empire: Life of Karl IV* (1936); O. Bauer, *The Austrian Revolution* (1925); E. Beneš, *My War Memories* (1928); S. Burian, *Austria in Dissolution* (1925); K. Capek (ed.), *Masaryk Tells His Story* (1935); T. Capek, Jr., *Origins of the Czechoslovak State* (1926); O. Czernin, *In the World War* (1920); E. Glaise von Horstenau, *The Collapse of the Austro-Hungarian Empire* (1930); M. W. Graham, *The New Governments of Central Europe* (1924); O. Jaszi, *Revolution and Counter-Revolution in Hungary* (1924) and *The Dissolution of the Hapsburg Monarchy* (1929); M. Karolyi, *Fighting the World: The Struggle for Peace* (1924); R. J. Kerner, *The Jugo-Slav Movement* (1918); T. G. Masaryk, *The Making of a State* (1927); K. F. Nowak, *The Collapse of Central Europe* (1924); J. Opočenský, *The Collapse of the Austro-Hungarian Monarchy and the Rise of the Czechoslovak State* (1928); J. Papoušek, *The Czechoslovak Nation's Struggle for Independence* (1928); C. Pergler, *America in the Struggle for Czechoslovak Independence* (1926); J. Pilsudski, *The Memories of a Polish Revolutionary and Soldier* (1931); A. Polzer-Hoditz, *The Emperor Karl* (1931); J. Redlich, *Austrian War Government* (1929); C. von Werkmann, *The Tragedy of Charles of Hapsburg* (1924); L. Windisch-Graetz, *My Memoirs* (1921).

DOWNFALL OF THE GERMAN EMPIRE: M. Baumont, *The Fall of the Kaiser* (1931); E. Bevan, *German Social Democracy during the War* (1919); S. M. Bouton, *And the Kaiser Abdicates: The German Revolution, November 1918–August 1919* (1921); G. P. Gooch, *Germany* (1925); R. H. Lutz (ed.), *The Causes of the German Collapse in 1918* (1934) and *Fall of the German Empire, 1914–1918: Documents of the German Revolution,* 2 vols. (1930); R. H. Lutz, *The German Revolution of 1918–19* (1922); Maximilian, Prinz von Baden, *The Memoirs of Prince Max of Baden,* 2 vols. (1928); A. Rosenberg, *The Birth of the German Republic* (1931); P. Scheidemann, *The Making of New Germany: The Memoirs of Philipp Scheidemann* (1929); H. Stroebel, *The German Revolution and After* (1923).

COSTS AND CONSEQUENCES OF THE WAR: E. L. Bogart, *Direct and Indirect Costs of the Great World War* (1919); A. L. Bowley, *Some Economic Consequences of the War* (1930); J. M. Clark, *The Costs of the World War to the American People* (1931); H. Folks, *The Human Costs of the War* (1920); F. W. Hirst, *The Consequences of the War to Great Britain* (1934); S. Kohn and A. F. Meyendorff, *The Cost of the War to*

*Russia* (1932); D. Mitrany, *The Effect of the War in Southeastern Europe* (1937).

CHAPTER XV

THE PARIS PEACE SETTLEMENT

GENERAL: G. Adam, *The Tiger: Georges Clemenceau, 1841–1929* (1930); R. S. Baker, *Woodrow Wilson and the World Settlement*, 3 vols. (1922–23); B. M. Baruch, *The Making of the Reparation and Economic Sections of the Treaty* (1920); G. Clemenceau, *Grandeur and Misery of Victory* (1930); E. J. Dillon, *The Inside Story of the Peace Conference* (1920); W. E. Dodd, *Woodrow Wilson and His Work* (1932); C. H. Haskins and R. H. Lord, *Some Problems of the Peace Conference* (1920); E. M. House and C. Seymour (eds.), *What Really Happened at Paris: The Story of the Peace Conference, 1918–1919, by American Delegates* (1921); H. Howard, *The Partition of Turkey, 1913–1923* (1931); R. Lansing, *The Big Four and Others of the Peace Conference* (1921) and *The Peace Negotiations: A Personal Narrative* (1921); D. H. Miller, *The Drafting of the Covenant* (1928); H. Nicolson, *Peace-Making, 1919* (1933); G. B. Noble, *Policies and Opinions at Paris, 1919* (1935); K. F. Nowak, *Versailles* (1929); V. Schiff, *The Germans at Versailles* (1930); C. Seymour (ed.), *The Intimate Papers of Colonel House*, 4 vols. (1926–28); A. Tardieu, *The Truth about the Treaty* (1921); H. W. V. Temperley (ed.), *A History of the Peace Conference of Paris*, 6 vols. (1920–24); C. T. Thompson, *The Peace Conference Day by Day* (1920); F. Wilson, *The Origins of the League Covenant* (1928); Wood Ge Zay, *The Shantung Question* (1922); E. J. and C. G. Woodhouse, *Italy and the Jugoslavs* (1920).

THE TREATIES: N. Almond and R. H. Lutz (eds.), *The Treaty of St. Germain* (1934); J. F. Bass, *The Peace Tangle* (1920); S. Bethlen, *The Treaty of Trianon and European Peace* (1934); Carnegie Endowment for International Peace, *The Treaties of Peace, 1919–1923*, 2 vols. (1924), the texts with maps; R. Donald, *The Tragedy of Trianon* (1928); A. Ebray, *A Frenchman Looks at the Peace* (1927); J. M. Keynes, *The Economic Consequences of the Peace* (1920); F. S. Nitti, *The Wreck of Europe* (1922); A. P. Scott, *An Introduction to the Peace Treaties* (1920); R. W. Seton-Watson, *Treaty Revision and the Hungarian Frontiers* (1934); H. Stegeman, *The Mirage of Versailles* (1928); A. J. Toynbee, *The World After the Peace Conference* (1925).

THE UNITED STATES AND THE PEACE SETTLEMENT: T. H. Dickinson, *The United States and the League* (1923), an indictment of the men held responsible for defeating ratification; D. F. Fleming, *The United*

*States and the League of Nations* (1932), an account of the conflict between President Wilson and the Senate; H. Foley (comp.), *Woodrow Wilson's Case for the League of Nations* (1923), the President's speeches and explanations; H. C. Lodge, *The Senate and the League of Nations* (1925); P. W. Slosson, *The Great Crusade and After, 1914–1918* (1930).

CHAPTER XVI

THE LEAGUE OF NATIONS AND THE PEACE SETTLEMENT

GENERAL: J. S. Bassett, *The League of Nations, A Chapter in World Politics* (1928); M. Beer, *The League on Trial* (1933); T. P. Conwell-Evans, *The League Council in Action* (1929); J. Eppstein (comp.), *Ten Years' Life of the League of Nations* (1930); C. Howard-Ellis, *The Origin, Structure and Working of the League of Nations* (1928); W. H. Kelchner, *Latin American Relations with the League of Nations* (1930); League of Nations, *Ten Years of World Co-operation* (1930); T. Marburg, *Development of the League of Nations Idea*, 2 vols. (1932); M. Matsushita, *Japan in the League of Nations* (1929); F. Morley, *The Society of Nations* (1932); W. E. Rappard, *The Geneva Experiment* (1932); C. K. Webster, *The League of Nations in Theory and Practice* (1933); A. Zimmern, *The League of Nations and the Rule of Law, 1918–1935* (1936).

WORLD COURT: A. S. de Bustamente, *The World Court* (1925); M. O. Hudson, *The Permanent Court of International Justice* (1934); E. Lindsey, *The International Court* (1931); J. W. Wheeler-Bennett, *Information on the World Court, 1918–1928* (1929).

INTERNATIONAL LABOR ORGANIZATION: National Industrial Conference Board, *The Work of the International Labor Organization* (1928); E. M. Oliver, *The World's Industrial Parliament* (1925); J. T. Shotwell (ed.), *The Origins of the International Labor Organization*, 2 vols. (1934); F. G. Wilson, *Labor in the League System* (1935); World Peace Foundation, *The International Labor Organization* (1931).

THE UNITED STATES AND THE LEAGUE: C. A. Berdahl, *The Policy of the United States with Respect to the League of Nations* (1932); M. O. Hudson, *The Permanent Court of International Justice and the Question of American Participation* (1925); P. C. Jessup, *The United States and the World Court* (1929); F. A. Kellor and A. Hatvany, *The United States Senate and the International Court* (1925).

THE SAAR: T. Balk, *The Saar at First Hand* (1934); W. R. Bisschop, *The Saar Controversy* (1924); R. Donald, *A Danger Spot in Europe and Its Government by the League of Nations* (1925); M. T. Florinsky, *The Saar Struggle* (1934); M. Lambert, *The Saar* (1934); B. T. Reynolds, *The*

*Saar and the Franco-German Problem* (1934); F. M. Russell, *International Government of the Saar* (1926).

MANDATES AND MINORITIES: N. de M. Bentwich, *The Mandates System* (1930); B. Gerig, *The Open Door and the Mandates System* (1930); O. Junghann, *National Minorities in Europe* (1932); E. van Maanen-Helmer, *The Mandates System in Relation to Africa and the Pacific Islands* (1929); L. D. Mair, *The Protection of Minorities* (1928); A. M. Margalith, *The International Mandates* (1930); W. O. Molony, *Nationality and the Peace Treaties* (1934); E. Noel-Buxton and T. P. Conwell-Evans, *Oppressed Peoples and the League of Nations* (1922); J. S. Rouček, *The Working of the Minorities System under the League of Nations* (1929); Q. Wright, *Mandates under the League of Nations* (1930).

OFFICIAL PUBLICATIONS: M. J. Carroll, *Key to League of Nations Documents Placed on Public Sale, 1920–1929* (1930); International Labor Office, *Monthly Summary of the International Labor Organization;* League of Nations, *Monthly Summary of the League of Nations* and *Official Journal* and *Records of the Assembly* and *Treaty Series.*

CHAPTER XVII

REPARATIONS AND WAR DEBTS

REPARATIONS: C. Bergmann, *The History of Reparations* (1927); R. C. Dawes, *The Dawes Plan in the Making* (1925); G. Greer, *The Ruhr-Lorraine Industrial Problem* (1925); J. M. Keynes, *The Economic Consequences of the Peace* (1920) and *A Revision of the Treaty* (1922); H. Lichtenberger, *The Ruhr Conflict* (1923); D. Lloyd George, *The Truth about Reparations and War Debts* (1932); R. E. C. Long, *The Mythology of Reparations* (1928); H. G. Moulton and C. E. McGuire, *Germany's Capacity to Pay* (1923); H. G. Moulton, *The Reparation Plan* (1924), the Dawes plan; D. P. Myers, *The Reparation Settlement* (1929), the Young plan; H. Schacht, *The End of Reparations* (1931); M. Sering, *Germany under the Dawes Plan* (1929); C. J. C. Street, *Rhineland and Ruhr* (1923); J. W. Wheeler-Bennett and H. Latimer, *Information on the Reparation Settlement* (1930); J. W. Wheeler-Bennett, *The Wreck of Reparations* (1933).

INTER-ALLIED WAR DEBTS: P. Dexter and J. H. Sedgwick, *The War Debts: An American View* (1928); H. E. Fisk, *The Inter-Ally Debts* (1924); H. G. Moulton and L. Pasvolsky, *War Debts and World Prosperity* (1932) and *World War Debt Settlements* (1926).

WORLD ECONOMIC DEPRESSION: P. Einzig, *The World Economic Crisis, 1929–1932* (1932) and *The Sterling-Dollar-Franc Tangle* (1933);

R. R. Kuczynski, *American Loans to Germany* (1927); League of Nations, *World Production and Prices, 1925–1933* (1934); E. M. Patterson, *The World's Economic Dilemma* (1930); L. Robbins, *The Great Depression* (1934); J. C. Stamp, *The Financial Aftermath of War* (1932); E. Varga, *The Great Crisis and Its Political Consequences* (1935); Q. Wright (ed.), *Unemployment as a World Problem* (1931).

CHAPTER XVIII

DISARMAMENT AND SECURITY

DISARMAMENT: *Armaments Year-Book* (1924 ff.); R. L. Buell, *The Washington Conference* (1922); P. Einzig, *The Economics of Rearmament* (1934); H. C. Engelbrecht and F. C. Hanighen, *Merchants of Death: A Study of the International Armament Industry* (1934); G. Engely, *The Politics of Naval Disarmament* (1932); Y. Ichihashi, *The Washington Conference and After* (1928); V. Lefebure, *Common Sense about Disarmament* (1932); D. P. Myers, *World Disarmament* (1932); R. Neumann, *Zaharoff: The Armaments King* (1935); J. W. Wheeler-Bennett, *Information on the Reduction of Armaments* (1925) and *Disarmament and Security since Locarno* (1932); B. H. Williams, *The United States and Disarmament* (1931).

SECURITY: R. P. Arnot, *Soviet Russia and Her Neighbors* (1927); P. J. N. Baker, *The Geneva Protocol for the Pacific Settlement of International Disputes* (1925); V. de Balla, *The New Balance of Power in Europe* (1932); J. Cambon and others, *The Foreign Policy of the Powers* (1935); E. H. Carr, *International Relations since the Peace Treaties* (1937); A Cippico, *Italy, the Central Problem of the Mediterranean* (1926); J. O. Crane, *The Little Entente* (1931); G. M. Gathorne-Hardy, *A Short History of International Affairs, 1920–1934* (1935); G. Glasgow, *From Dawes to Locarno, 1924–1925* (1925); M. W. Graham, *The Soviet Security System* (1929); M. Habicht, *Post-War Treaties for the Pacific Settlement of International Disputes* (1930); J. W. Headlam-Morley, *Studies in Diplomatic History* (1930); H. Lichtenberger, *Relations between France and Germany* (1923); N. L. Hill, *Post-War Treaties of Security and Mutual Guarantee* (1928); League of Nations, *Ten Years of World Co-operation* (1930); C. A. Macartney and others, *Survey of International Affairs, 1925*, 2 vols. (1928); R. Machray, *The Little Entente* (1929); D. H. Miller, *The Peace Pact of Paris* (1928) and *The Geneva Protocol* (1925); R. B. Mowat and others, *Problems of Peace: Anarchy or World Order* (1936); D. P. Myers, *Origin and Conclusion of the Paris Pact* (1929); J. P. Selsam, *The Attempts to Form an Anglo-French Alliance, 1919–1924* (1936); J. T. Shotwell, *War as an Instru-*

*ment of National Policy* (1929); F. H. Simonds and B. Emeny, *The Great Powers in World Politics* (1935); A. J. Toynbee, *Survey of International Affairs* (1925 ff.); J. W. Wheeler-Bennett and F. E. Langermann, *Information on the Problem of Security, 1917–1926* (1927); J. W. Wheeler-Bennett (ed.), *Documents on International Affairs* (1934 ff.); J. W. Wheeler-Bennett, *Information on the Renunciation of War, 1927–1928* (1928), an analysis of the pact of Paris.

CHAPTER XIX

SOVIET RUSSIA

GENERAL: American-Russian Chamber of Commerce, *Handbook of the Soviet Union* (1936); K. Borders, *Village Life under the Soviets* (1927); W. H. Chamberlin, *Soviet Russia* (1931); R. W. Dunn, *Soviet Trade Unions* (1928); W. Duranty, *Duranty Reports Russia* (1934); H. von Eckardt, *Russia* (1932); A. W. Field, *Protection of Women and Children in Soviet Russia* (1932); F. W. Halle, *Woman in Soviet Russia* (1933); M. G. Hindus, *Broken Earth* (1926); A. Karlgren, *Bolshevist Russia* (1927); P. Malevsky-Malevitch (ed.), *Russia-U.S.S.R.* (1933); A. Newsholme and J. A. Kingsbury, *Red Medicine: Socialized Health in Soviet Russia* (1933); G. M. Price, *Labor Protection in Soviet Russia* (1928); T. Siebert, *Red Russia* (1932); J. Smith, *Woman in Soviet Russia* (1928); L. Trotsky, *The Real Situation in Russia* (1928); S. and B. Webb, *Soviet Communism: A New Civilization?*, 2 vols. (1936); A. Wicksteed, *My Russian Neighbors* (1934); A. Yarmolinsky, *The Jews and Other Minor Nationalists under the Soviets* (1929).

BOLSHEVIK THEORY AND PRACTICE: W. R. Batsell, *Soviet Rule in Russia* (1929); H. N. Brailsford, *How the Soviets Work* (1927); W. Gurian, *Bolshevism: Theory and Practice* (1932); B. W. Maxwell, *The Soviet State* (1934); M. Parmelee, *Bolshevism, Fascism and the Liberal-Democratic State* (1934); N. Popov, *Outline History of the Communist Party of the Soviet Union,* 2 vols. (1935); A. Rosenberg, *A History of Bolshevism* (1934); A. L. Strong, *The New Soviet Constitution: A Study in Socialist Democracy* (1937).

INTERVENTION AND COUNTERREVOLUTION: P. Bulygin, *The Murder of the Romanovs* (1935); W. P. and Z. K. Coates, *Armed Intervention in Russia, 1918–1922* (1935); J. Cudahy, *Archangel: The American War with Russia* (1924); A. I. Denikin, *The White Army* (1930); W. S. Graves, *America's Siberian Adventure* (1931); C. C. M. Maynard, *The Murmansk Venture* (1928); G. Stewart, *The White Armies of Russia, A Chronicle of Counter-Revolution and Allied Intervention* (1933); G. G.

Telberg and R. Wilton, *The Last Days of the Romanovs* (1920); P. N. Wrangel, *Memoirs* (1929).

SECRET POLICE AND TERROR: G. Agabekov, *Ogpu* (1931); R. N. Baldwin, *Liberty under the Soviets* (1928); V. K. Brunovskii, *The Methods of the Ogpu* (1931); B. Cedarholm, *In the Clutches of the Tcheka* (1929); G. K. Popov, *The Tcheka: The Red Inquisition* (1925); T. Tchernavin, *Escape from the Soviets* (1934); L. Trotsky, *The Defense of Terrorism* (1920).

ECONOMIC LIFE: J. Beauchamp, *Agriculture in Soviet Russia* (1931); W. H. Chamberlin, *Russia's Iron Age* (1934) and *The Soviet Planned Economic Order* (1931); G. S. Counts, *The Soviet Challenge to America* (1931); M. Dobb and H. C. Stevens, *Russian Economic Development since the Revolution* (1928); L. Fischer, *Machines and Men in Russia* (1932); M. S. Farbman, *Bolshevism in Retreat* (1923); F. Golder and L. Hutchinson, *On the Trail of the Russian Famine* (1927); P. P. Haensel, *The Economic Policy of Soviet Russia* (1930); A. Hirsch, *Industrialized Russia* (1934); C. B. Hoover, *The Economic Life of Soviet Russia* (1931); E. W. Hullinger, *The Reforging of Russia* (1925); International Labor Office, *Industrial Life in Russia, 1917–1924* (1924); L. Lawton, *An Economic History of Soviet Russia*, 2 vols. (1932); V. M. Molotov, *The Success of the Five Year Plan* (1931); A. L. Strong, *The Soviets Conquer Wheat* (1931).

EDUCATION AND RELIGION: E. J. Dillon, *Russia Today and Yesterday* (1930); W. C. Emhardt, *Religion in Soviet Russia* (1929); G. P. Fedotov, *The Russian Church since the Revolution* (1928); R. Fülöp-Miller, *The Mind and Face of Bolshevism* (1928); S. N. Harper, *Civic Training in Soviet Russia* (1929) and *Making Bolsheviks* (1931); J. F. Hecker, *Religion and Communism* (1935); S. Nearing, *Education in Soviet Russia* (1926); A. P. Pinkevich, *The New Education in the Soviet Republic* (1929); M. Spinka, *The Church and the Russian Revolution* (1927); T. Woody, *New Minds: New Men?* (1932).

FOREIGN POLICY: R. P. Arnot, *Soviet Russia and Her Neighbors* (1927); K. W. Davis, *The Soviets at Geneva* (1934); A. L. P. Dennis, *The Foreign Policies of Soviet Russia* (1924); L. Fischer, *The Soviets in World Affairs*, 2 vols. (1930); S. N. Harper, *The Soviet Union and World Problems* (1935); C. L. R. James, *World Revolution, 1917–1936* (1937), the Third International; J. S. Mills, *The Genoa Conference* (1922); L. Trotsky, *The Third International after Lenin* (1936); V. A. Yakhontoff, *Russia and the Soviet Union in the Far East* (1931).

BIOGRAPHIES: H. Barbusse, *Stalin: A New World Seen through One Man* (1935); R. W. Fox, *Lenin* (1934); S. Graham, *Stalin* (1931); N. K.

1022

BIBLIOGRAPHY AND INDEX

Krupskaia, *Memories of Lenin* (1930); I. D. Levine, *Stalin* (1931); R.
Lévy, *Trotsky* (1920); V. Marcu, *Lenin* (1928); D. S. Mirsky, *Lenin*
(1931); L. Trotsky, *My Life* (1930); F. J. P. Veale, *The Man from the
Volga* (1932); G. V. Vernadsky, *Lenin, Red Dictator* (1931).

CHAPTER XX

## Fascist Italy

GENERAL: I. Bonomi, *From Socialism to Fascism* (1924); H. L. Childs
(ed.), *Propaganda and Dictatorship* (1936); C. M. Cresswell, *The Keystone of Fascism* (1929); R. P. Dutt, *Fascism and Social Revolution*
(1935); W. Elwin, *Fascism at Work* (1934); G. Ferrero, *Four Years of
Fascism* (1924); H. Finer, *Mussolini's Italy* (1935); H. N. Gay, *Strenuous Italy* (1927); P. Gorgolini, *The Fascist Movement in Italian Life*
(1923); E. W. Hullinger, *The New Fascist State* (1928); B. King, *Fascism in Italy* (1931); R. Muriello, *Mussolini: His Work and the New
Syndical Law* (1928); P. Nenni, *Ten Years of Tyranny in Italy* (1932);
F. F. Nitti, *Escape* (1930); F. Nitti, *Bolshevism, Fascism and Democracy*
(1927); M. Parmelee, *Bolshevism, Fascism and the Liberal-Democratic
State* (1934); W. Parsons, *The Pope and Italy* (1929); G. Prezzolini,
*Fascism* (1926); E. Reut-Nicolussi, *Tyrol under the Axe of Italian Fas-
cism* (1930); A. Robertson, *Mussolini and the New Italy* (1928); G.
Salvemini, *The Fascist Dictatorship in Italy* (1927) and *Under the Axe
of Fascism* (1936); H. W. Schneider and S. B. Clough, *Making Fascists*
(1929); H. W. Schneider, *Making the Fascist State* (1928) and *The Fas-
cist Government of Italy* (1936); T. Sillani (ed.), *What is Fascism and
Why?* (1931); H. R. Spencer, *Government and Politics of Italy* (1932);
B. Williamson, *The Treaty of the Lateran* (1929).

ECONOMIC: H. E. Goad, *The Making of the Corporate State* (1932);
C. Haider, *Capital and Labor under Fascism* (1930); C. E. McGuire,
*Italy's International Economic Position* (1926); F. Pitigliani, *The Italian
Corporative State* (1934).

IMPERIALISM: C. D. G. Booth and I. Bridge, *Italy's Aegean Possessions*
(1928); M. Currey, *Italian Foreign Policy, 1918–1932* (1932); A. H. M.
Jones and E. Monroe, *History of Abyssinia* (1935); E. P. McCallum,
*Rivalries in Ethiopia* (1935); D. Mitrany, *The Problem of International
Sanctions* (1925); Royal Institute of International Affairs, *Abyssinia and
Italy* (1935); G. L. Steer, *Caesar in Abyssinia* (1937); A. J. Toynbee,
*Survey of International Affairs, 1935*, II (1936); L. Villari, *The Expan-
sion of Italy* (1930); E. Work, *Ethiopia: A Pawn in European Diplomacy*
(1935).

MUSSOLINI: V. E. de Fiori, *Mussolini: The Man of Destiny* (1928); B.

Mussolini, *My Autobiography* (1928); C. A. Petrie, *Mussolini* (1931); M. C. Sarfatti, *The Life of Benito Mussolini* (1925); G. Seldes, *Sawdust Caesar* (1935).

CHAPTER XXI

LIBERAL AND NAZI GERMANY

EARLY YEARS: R. Brunet, *The New German Constitution* (1922); J. F. Coar, *The Old and New Germany* (1924); O. H. Fisk, *Germany's Constitutions of 1871 and 1919* (1928); G. P. Gooch, *Germany* (1925); H. Kraus, *Germany in Transition* (1924); W. B. Munro, *The Governments of Europe* (1926); M. P. Price, *Germany in Transition* (1924); P. Scheidemann, *The Making of New Germany: The Memoirs of Philipp Scheidemann* (1929); H. Stroebel, *The German Revolution and After* (1923).

GENERAL WORKS ON THE REPUBLICAN REGIME: J. W. Angell, *The Recovery of Germany* (1932); H. G. Daniels, *The Rise of the German Republic* (1928); W. H. Dawson, *Germany under the Treaty* (1933); O. Hoetzsch, *Germany's Domestic and Foreign Policies* (1929); J. B. Holt, *German Agricultural Policy, 1918–1934* (1936); H. R. Knickerbocker, *The German Crisis* (1932); E. Koch-Weser, *Germany in the Post-War World* (1930); H. Lowenstein, *The Tragedy of a Nation: Germany, 1918–1934* (1934); E. Ludwig, *Hindenburg and the Saga of the German Republic* (1935); E. Luehr, *The New German Republic* (1929); R. Olden, *Stresemann* (1930); H. Quigley and R. J. Clark, *Republican Germany* (1928); R. von Rheinbaben, *Stresemann, the Man and the Statesman* (1929); H. Schacht, *The Stabilization of the Mark* (1927); G. Schultze-Pfaelzer, *Hindenburg* (1931); E. Sutton (ed.), *Gustav Stresemann: His Diaries, Letters, and Papers* (1935); A. Vallentin, *Stresemann* (1931); R. Weterstetten and A. M. K. Watson, *The Biography of President von Hindenburg* (1930); J. W. Wheeler-Bennett, *Wooden Titan, Hindenburg in Twenty Years of German History, 1914–1934* (1936); T. R. Ybarra, *Hindenburg, the Man with Three Lives* (1932).

THE THIRD REICH: H. F. Armstrong, *Hitler's Reich: The First Phase* (1933); R. A. Brady, *The Spirit and Structure of German Fascism* (1937); R. T. Clark, *The Fall of the German Republic* (1935); P. Einzig, *Germany's Default: The Economics of Hitlerism* (1934); F. Ermarth, *The New Germany* (1936); G. Feder, *Hitler's Official Programme and Its Fundamental Ideas* (1934); M. T. Florinsky, *Fascism and National Socialism* (1936); H. P. Greenwood, *The German Revolution* (1934); W. Gurian, *Hitler and the Christians* (1936); K. Heiden, *Hitler* (1936) and *A History of National Socialism* (1935); A. Hitler, *My Battle* (1933);

J. B. Holt, *Under the Swastika* (1936); C. B. Hoover, *Germany Enters the Third Reich* (1933); J. Kastein, *Jews in Germany* (1934); E. Lengyel, *Hitler* (1932); H. Lichtenberger, *The Third Reich* (1937); S. Lorant, *I Was Hitler's Prisoner* (1935); F. M. Marx, *Government in the Third Reich* (1936); J. B. Mason, *Hitler's First Foes* (1936); J. Murphy, *Adolf Hitler: The Drama of His Career* (1934); R. Olden, *Hitler* (1936); R. Pascal, *The Nazi Dictatorship* (1934); D. Reed, *The Burning of the Reichstag* (1934); F. L. Schuman, *The Nazi Dictatorship* (1935); G. Segar, *A Nation Terrorized* (1935); F. Seidler, *The Bloodless Pogrom* (1934); W. Steed, *The Meaning of Hitlerism* (1934).

CHAPTER XXII

GREAT BRITAIN AND IRELAND

GENERAL: H. Begbie, *The Mirrors of Downing Street* (1932); R. Berkeley, *England's Opportunity* (1931); J. Clayton, *The Rise and Decline of Socialism in Great Britain, 1894–1924* (1926); G. D. H. Cole, *A Short History of the British Working Class Movement* (1927); H. Dalton, *Practical Socialism for Britain* (1935); W. Dibelius, *England* (1933); J. P. Dickie, *The Coal Problem: 1910–1936* (1936); H. Fyfe, *The British Liberal Party* (1928); G. Glasgow, *The Foreign Policy of the First Labour Government in Great Britain* (1925); G. A. Greenwood, *England Today* (1922); H. Heaton, *The British Way to Recovery* (1934); A. C. C. Hill, Jr., and I. Lubin, *The British Attack on Unemployment* (1934); W. R. Inge, *England* (1926); G. Lansbury, *Labour's Way with the Commonwealth* (1935); F. W. P. Lawrence, *The Gold Crisis* (1931); A. Loveday, *Britain and the World Trade* (1931); I. Lubin and H. Everett, *The British Coal Dilemma* (1927); C. F. G. Masterman, *England after War* (1922); G. Peel, *The Economic War* (1930); J. B. Priestley, *An English Journey* (1934); A. Siegfried, *England's Crisis* (1931); C. E. Sipple, *British Foreign Policy since the World War* (1932); A. Willert, *Aspects of British Foreign Policy* (1928); J. L. White, *The Abdication of Edward VIII* (1936).

BIOGRAPHIES: A. M. Andreadés, *Philip Snowden* (1930); H. Bolitho, *King Edward VIII: An Intimate Biography* (1937); J. Buchan, *The People's King* (1935), George V; J. H. Edwards, *David Lloyd George,* 2 vols. (1929); Ephesian, *Philip Snowden* (1929); G. Glasgow, *MacDonald as a Diplomatist* (1924); P. Guedalla, *A Gallery* (1924); Iconoclast, *England's Labour Rulers* (1924); Iconoclast, *James Ramsay MacDonald* (1931); C. E. Mallet, *Mr. Lloyd George: A Study* (1930); B. Roberts, *Stanley Baldwin, Man or Miracle* (1937); E. H. Short, *King George the Well-Beloved* (1936); P. Snowden, *An Autobiography,* 2 vols. (1934);

H. W. Steed, *The Real Stanley Baldwin* (1930); H. H. Tiltman, *Ramsay MacDonald: Labor's Man of Destiny* (1929).

EMPIRE-COMMONWEALTH: P. J. N. Baker, *The Present Judicial Status of the British Dominions in International Law* (1929); W. Y. Elliott, *The New British Empire* (1932); H. D. Hall, *The British Commonwealth of Nations* (1920); W. P. Hall, *Empire to Commonwealth* (1928); W. K. Hancock, *Survey of British Commonwealth Affairs*, I (1937); A. B. Keith, *Dominion Autonomy in Practice* (1930); J. A. Spender, *Great Britain, Empire and Commonwealth, 1886–1935* (1936); R. G. Trotter, *The British Empire-Commonwealth, A Study in Political Evolution* (1933); A. E. Zimmern, *The Third British Empire* (1926).

IRELAND: P. Beasley, *Michael Collins and the Making of New Ireland* (1926); H. D. Butler, *Irish Free State: Economic Survey* (1928); M. Collins, *The Path of Freedom* (1923); D. Figgis, *Recollections of the Irish War* (1927); J. W. Good, *Ulster and Ireland* (1919); D. Gwynn, *De Valera* (1933); D. R. Gwynn, *The Irish Free State, 1922–1927* (1928); R. M. Henry, *The Evolution of Sinn Fein* (1920); E. Hull, *A History of Ireland and Her People* (1931); F. P. Jones, *History of the Sinn Fein Movement and the Irish Rebellion of 1916* (1917); W. Moss, *Political Parties in the Irish Free State* (1933); W. O'Brien, *The Irish Revolution* (1923); B. O'Connor, *With Michael Collins in the Fight for Irish Independence* (1930); L. Paul-Dubois and T. P. Gill, *The Irish Struggle and Its Results* (1934); W. A. Phillips, *The Revolution in Ireland, 1906–1923* (1926); A. S. Quekett, *The Constitution of Northern Ireland* (1928); H. Talbot, *Michael Collins' Own Story* (1923); W. B. Wells and N. Marlowe, *A History of the Irish Rebellion of 1916* (1916).

CHAPTER XXIII

FRANCE AND SPAIN

FRANCE: R. Cahill, *Economic Conditions in France* (1934); G. Clemenceau, *In the Evening of My Thought*, 2 vols. (1929); E. L. Dulles, *The French Franc, 1914–1928* (1929); R. K. Gooch, *Regionalism in France* (1931); D. R. Gwynn, *The Catholic Reaction in France* (1924); R. M. Haig, *The Public Finances of Post-War France* (1929); C. J. H. Hayes, *France: A Nation of Patriots* (1930); H. Hill, *The Spirit of Modern France* (1934); S. Huddleston, *France* (1927) and *Poincaré: A Biographical Portrait* (1924); W. MacDonald, *Reconstruction in France* (1922); W. L. Middleton, *The French Political System* (1933); H. G. Moulton and C. Lewis, *The French Debt Problem* (1925); W. F. Ogburn and W. Jaffé, *The Economic Development of Post-War France* (1929); D. J. Saposs, *The Labor Movement in Post-War France* (1931);

F. Sieburg, *Who Are These French?* (1932); A. Siegfried, *France: A Study in Nationality* (1930); R. H. Soltau, *French Parties and Politics* (1930); R. L. Stokes, *Léon Blum: Poet to Premier* (1937); A. Tardieu, *France in Danger!* (1935); V. Thomson, *Briand, Man of Peace* (1930); P. Vaucher, *Post-War France* (1934); A. Werth, *Which Way France?* (1937).

SPAIN: V. Blasco Ibáñez, *Alfonso XIII Unmasked: The Military Terror in Spain* (1924); J. A. Brandt, *Toward the New Spain* (1933); C. S. Cooper, *Understanding Spain* (1928); P. Crabitès, *Unhappy Spain* (1937); F. B. Deakin, *Spain Today* (1924); H. Gannes and T. Repard, *Spain in Revolt* (1937); W. B. Harris, *France, Spain and the Riff* (1927); J. McCabe, *Spain in Revolt, 1814–1931* (1931); E. A. Peers, *The Spanish Tragedy, 1930–1936* (1937); Princess Pilar and D. Chapman-Huston, *Every Inch a King* (1931); F. T. Rogers, *Spain: A Tragic Journey* (1937); D. A. de Santillan, *After the Revolution* (1937); W. B. Wells, *The Last King* (1934); G. Young, *The New Spain* (1933).

CHAPTER XXIV

POLAND AND THE BALTIC REPUBLICS

POLAND: S. J. Boncza, *The Founder of Polish Independence, Joseph Pilsudski* (1921); A. B. Boswell, *Poland and the Poles* (1919); F. Bujak, *Poland's Economic Development* (1926) and *The Jewish Question in Poland* (1919); R. Devereux, *Poland Reborn* (1922); R. Donald, *The Polish Corridor and the Consequences* (1929); R. Dyboski, *Outlines of Polish History* (1931); M. Felinski, *The Ukrainians in Poland* (1931); D. R. Gillie, *Joseph Pilsudski* (1931); A. L. Goodhart, *Poland and the Minority Races* (1922); G. Humphrey, *Pilsudski: Builder of Poland* (1936); S. Karski, *Poland, Past and Present* (1927); R. Landau, *Pilsudski and Poland* (1929) and *Ignace Paderewski, Musician and Statesman* (1934); R. Machray, *Poland, 1914–1931* (1932); R. Martel, *The Eastern Frontiers of Germany* (1930); E. J. Patterson, *Poland* (1934) and *Pilsudski, Marshal of Poland* (1935); J. Pilsudski, *Joseph Pilsudski: The Memories of a Polish Revolutionary and Soldier* (1931); A. Skrzynski, *Poland and Peace* (1923); N. O. Winter, *The New Poland* (1923).

THE BALTIC REPUBLICS: T. W. Atchley, *Finland* (1931); A. Bihlmans, *Latvia in the Making, 1918–1928* (1928); M. W. Graham, *New Governments of Eastern Europe* (1927); E. J. Harrison (ed.), *Lithuania* (1928); H. Leoke, *Facts about Esthonia* (1924); H. L. McBain and L. Rogers, *The New Constitutions of Europe* (1922); R. M. McBride, *Finland and Its People* (1925); P. Meyer, *Latvia's Economic Life* (1925); J. A. Osolin, *Latvia in the Making* (1922); A. Rothery, *Finland, the New Nation*

(1936); A. Ruhl, *The New Masters of the Baltic* (1921); O. Rutter, *The New Baltic States and Their Future* (1925); E. van Cleef, *Finland: The Republic Farthest North* (1929); J. H. Wuorinen, *Nationalism in Modern Finland* (1931); A. Zalts, *Latvian Political Economy* (1928).

CHAPTER XXV

THE SUCCESSION STATES OF CENTRAL EUROPE

GENERAL: J. O. Crane, *The Little Entente* (1931); J. D. E. Evans, *That Blue Danube* (1935); G. E. R. Gedye, *Heirs to the Hapsburgs* (1932); M. W. Graham, *The New Governments of Central Europe* (1927); R. Machray, *The Little Entente* (1929); L. Pasvolsky, *Economic Nationalism of the Danubian States* (1929); G. Schacher, *Central Europe and the Western World* (1936).

AUSTRIA: A. Basch and J. Dvořáček, *Austria and Its Economic Existence* (1925); O. Bauer, *The Austrian Revolution* (1925); M. Bitterman, *Austria and the Customs Union* (1931); V. W. Germains, *Austria Today* (1932); J. D. Gregory, *Dollfuss and His Times* (1935); C. Hamilton, *Modern Austria* (1935); C. O. Hardy and R. R. Kuczynski, *The Housing Program of the City of Vienna* (1934); K. Hudeczek, *The Economic Resources of Austria* (1922); F. F. G. Kleinwächter, *Self-Determination for Austria* (1929); League of Nations, *The Financial Reconstruction of Austria* (1926); C. A. Macartney, *The Social Revolution in Austria* (1926); P. W. Slosson, *The Problem of Austro-German Union* (1929).

HUNGARY: S. Apponyi and others, *Justice for Hungary* (1928); E. Ashmead-Bartlett, *The Tragedy of Central Europe* (1923); K. Buday, *The International Position of Hungary and the Succession States* (1931); R. Donald, *The Tragedy of Trianon* (1928); F. A. Eckhart, *Short History of the Hungarian People* (1931); O. Jaszi, *Revolution and Counter-Revolution in Hungary* (1924); League of Nations, *The Financial Reconstruction of Hungary* (1926); R. W. Seton-Watson, *Treaty Revision and the Hungarian Frontiers* (1934); C. J. C. Street, *Hungary and Democracy* (1923); C. Tisseyre, *An Error in Diplomacy, Dismembered Hungary* (1924).

CZECHOSLOVAKIA: J. Borovicka, *Ten Years of Czechoslovak Politics* (1929); P. Crabitès, *Beneš* (1934); C. Holland, *Czechoslovakia: The Land and Its People* (1931); K. Krofta, *A Short History of Czechoslovakia* (1934); D. A. Lowrie, *Masaryk of Czechoslovakia* (1930); T. G. Masaryk, *The Making of a State* (1927); J. Mothersole, *Czechoslovakia, the Land of an Unconquerable Ideal* (1926); R. W. Seton-Watson (ed.), *Slovakia, Then and Now* (1931); C. J. C. Street, *President Masaryk*

(1930); L. E. Textor, *Land Reform in Czecho-Slovakia* (1923); F. J. Vondracek, *The Foreign Policy of Czechoslovakia* (1937).

CHAPTER XXVI

THE TURBULENT BALKANS

GENERAL: H. F. Armstrong, *The New Balkans* (1926) and *Where the East Begins* (1929); R. J. Kerner and H. N. Howard, *The Balkan Conferences and the Balkan Entente, 1930–1935* (1936); H. T. Montague-Bell (ed.), *The Near East Year Book and Who's Who* (1931–32); N. J. Padelford, *Peace in the Balkans* (1935); S. Panaretoff, *Near Eastern Affairs and Conditions* (1922).

GREECE: C. B. Chester, *Life of Venizelos* (1921); S. Cosmin, *The Tragedy of Greece* (1928); B. Cunliffe-Owen, *Silhouettes of Republican Greece* (1928); C. B. Eddy, *Greece and the Greek Refugees* (1931); H. A. Gibbons, *Venizelos* (1923); S. P. Ladas, *The Exchange of Minorities* (1932); League of Nations, *The Greek Refugee Settlement* (1926); C. A. Macartney, *Refugees* (1931); J. Mavrogordato, *Modern Greece* (1931); E. G. Mears, *Greece Today* (1929); W. Miller, *Greece* (1928); H. Morgenthau, *I Was Sent to Athens* (1929).

YUGOSLAVIA: C. A. Beard and G. Radin, *The Balkan Pivot: Yugoslavia* (1929); J. Buchan (ed.), *Yugoslavia* (1923); G. Ellison, *Yugoslavia: A New Country and Its People* (1935); M. W. Graham, *The New Governments of Central Europe* (1924); R. G. D. Laffan, *Yugoslavia since 1918* (1929); K. S. Patton, *Kingdom of the Serbs, Croats, and Slovenes: Commercial and Industrial Handbook* (1928).

ALBANIA: B. Bareilles and others, *Albania and the Albanians* (1920); C. A. Chekrezi, *Albania, Past and Present* (1919); E. P. Stickney, *Southern Albania or Northern Epirus in European Affairs, 1912–1923* (1926); J. Swire, *Albania: The Rise of a Kingdom* (1929).

BULGARIA: J. Buchan (ed.), *Bulgaria and Roumania* (1924); S. Christowe, *Heroes and Assassins* (1935); H. Leslie, *Where East is West: Life in Bulgaria* (1933); A. Londres, *Terror in the Balkans* (1935); G. C. Logio, *Bulgaria, Problems and Politics* (1919); L. Pasvolsky, *Bulgaria's Economic Position* (1930).

RUMANIA: J. M. Cabot, *The Racial Conflict in Transylvania* (1926); C. U. Clark, *Bessarabia* (1927) and *United Roumania* (1932); F. Deák, *The Hungarian-Rumanian Land Dispute* (1928); S. Dragomir, *The Ethnical Minorities in Transylvania* (1927); I. L. Evans, *The Agrarian Revolution in Roumania* (1924); N. A. Jorga, *History of Rumania* (1925); D. Mitrany, *The Land and the Peasant in Rumania* (1930); A. Popovici, *The Political Status of Bessarabia* (1925); C. G. Rakovsky,

*Roumania and Bessarabia* (1925); J. S. Rouček, *Contemporary Roumania and Her Problems* (1932); Z. Szasz, *The Minorities in Roumanian Transylvania* (1927).

CHAPTER XXVII

THE NEAR AND MIDDLE EAST

GENERAL: V. Chirol, *The Occident and the Orient* (1924); G. M. Dutcher, *The Political Awakening of the East* (1925); W. E. Hocking, *The Spirit of World Politics* (1932); J. A. Spender, *The Changing East* (1926); A. J. Toynbee, *The Western Question in Greece and Turkey: A Study in the Contact of Civilisations* (1922) and *Survey of International Affairs, 1925: Part I, The Islamic World Since the Peace Settlement* (1927).

TURKEY: Ali Shah Ikbal, *Kamal: Maker of Modern Turkey* (1934); H. E. Allen, *The Turkish Transformation* (1935); H. Armstrong, *Turkey and Syria Reborn* (1930); H. C. Armstrong, *Gray Wolf: Mustapha Kemal* (1933); G. Ellison, *Turkey Today* (1928); Hālidah Adīb, *Turkey Faces West* (1930); T. L. Jarman, *Turkey* (1935); K. Krüger, *Kemalist Turkey and the Middle East* (1932); L. Linke, *Allah Dethroned* (1937); E. G. Mears, *Modern Turkey* (1924); D. von Mikusch, *Mustapha Kemal* (1931); W. Miller, *The Ottoman Empire and Its Successors* (1934); F. Nansen, *Armenia and the Near East* (1928); L. Ostroróg, *The Angora Reform* (1928); C. Price, *The Rebirth of Turkey* (1923); A. J. Toynbee and K. Kirkwood, *Turkey* (1927); H. E. Wortham, *Mustapha Kemal of Turkey* (1931).

EGYPT: P. E. Elgood, *Egypt and the Army* (1924); M. Harris, *Egypt under the Egyptians* (1925); E. W. P. Newman, *Great Britain in Egypt* (1928); M. T. Symons, *Britain and Egypt: The Rise of Egyptian Nationalism* (1925); G. Young, *Egypt* (1927).

SYRIA AND PALESTINE: F. F. Andrews, *The Holy Land under Mandate*, 2 vols. (1931); N. de M. Bentwich, *England in Palestine* (1932); A. Granovsky, *Land Problems in Palestine* (1926) and *Land Settlement in Palestine* (1930); H. M. Kallen, *Zionism and World Politics* (1921); E. P. McCallum, *The Nationalist Crusade in Syria* (1928); L. Preiss and P. Rohrbach, *Palestine and Transjordania* (1926); Royal Institute of International Affairs, *Great Britain and Palestine, 1915–1936* (1937); L. Stein, *Syria* (1926); J. Stoyanovsky, *The Mandate for Palestine* (1928).

IRAQ AND PERSIA: H. A. Foster, *The Making of Modern Iraq* (1935); E. Main, *Iraq* (1935); O. A. Merritt-Hawkes, *Persia: Romance and Reality* (1935); A. C. Millspaugh, *The American Task in Persia* (1925); E. D. Ross, *The Persians* (1931).

INDIA: P. S. S. Aiyer, *Indian Constitutional Problems* (1929); C. F. Andrews, *Mahatma Gandhi's Ideas* (1930); C. F. Andrews (ed.), *Mahatma Gandhi, His Own Story* (1930); V. Anstey, *The Economic Development of India* (1931); D. N. Banerjee, *The Indian Constitution and Its Actual Working* (1926); J. Beauchamp, *British Imperialism in India* (1934); P. L. Chudgar, *Indian Princes under British Protection* (1929); A. Duncan, *India in Crisis* (1931); J. F. C. Fuller, *India in Revolt* (1931); M. K. Gandhi, *The Story of My Experiments with Truth,* 2 vols. (1927–29); Kerala Putra, *The Working of Dyarchy in India* (1928); K. Mayo, *Mother India* (1927); C. S. Ranga Iyer, *India in the Crucible* (1928); R. Rolland, *Mahatma Gandhi* (1924); J. Simon, *India and the Simon Report* (1930); E. Thompson, *Reconstructing India* (1930); C. H. Van Tyne, *India in Ferment* (1923); H. Whitehead, *Indian Problems in Religion, Education and Politics* (1924); F. E. Younghusband, *Dawn in India* (1931); G. M. Williams, *Understanding India* (1928).

CHAPTER XXVIII

THE FAR EAST

GENERAL: G. Bienstock, *The Struggle for the Pacific* (1937); G. H. Blakeslee, *The Pacific Area* (1929); U. Close, *The Revolt of Asia* (1927); F. V. Field (ed.), *Economic Handbook of the Pacific Area* (1934); H. B. Morse and H. F. MacNair, *Far Eastern International Relations* (1931); P. J. Treat, *The Far East* (1928); H. M. Vinacke, *A History of the Far East in Modern Times* (3d ed., 1936).

CHINA: M. J. Bau, *Modern Democracy in China* (1924) and *China and World Peace* (1928); Chen Tsung Hsi and others, *General Chiang Kai-shek: The Builder of the New China* (1929); G. Clark, *The Great Wall Crumbles* (1935); J. H. Dolsen, *The Awakening of China* (1927); A. N. Holcombe, *The Chinese Revolution* (1930); H. F. MacNair, *China in Revolution* (1931); P. Monroe, *China: A Nation in Evolution* ('1928); H. K. Norton, *China and the Powers* (1927); C. H. Peake, *Nationalism and Education in Modern China* (1932); R. T. Pollard, *China's Foreign Relations, 1917–1931* (1933); H. B. Restarick, *Sun Yat-sen* (1931); C. F. Remer, *Foreign Investments in China* (1933); L. Sharman, *Sun Yat-sen* (1934); H. A. Van Dorn, *Twenty Years of the Chinese Republic* (1932); W. W. Willoughby, *China at the Conference* (1922) and *Foreign Rights and Interests in China,* 2 vols. (1927); T. T. C. Woo, *The Kuomintang and the Future of the Chinese Revolution* (1928).

JAPAN: W. R. Crocker, *The Japanese Population Problem* (1931); P. T. Etherton and H. H. Tiltman, *Japan: Mistress of the Pacific* (1933); A. E. Hindmarsh, *The Basis of Japanese Foreign Policy* (1936); M. D.

Kennedy, *The Changing Fabric of Japan* (1930); N. T. Kitazawa, *The Government of Japan* (1929); N. Matsunami, *The Constitution of Japan* (1930); H. G. Moulton and J. Ko, *Japan* (1931); H. Saito, *Japan's Policies and Purposes* (1935); G. Stein, *Made in Japan* (1935); T. Takeuchi, *War and Diplomacy in the Japanese Empire* (1935); O. Tanin and E. Yohan, *Militarism and Fascism in Japan* (1934); H. E. Wildes, *Japan in Crisis* (1934).

MANCHURIA: P. T. Etherton and H. H. Tiltman, *Manchuria, the Cockpit of Asia* (1932); K. K. Kawakami, *Manchukuo: Child of Conflict* (1933); O. Lattimore, *Manchuria: Cradle of Conflict* (1935) and *The Puppet State of Manchukuo* (1935); G. B. Rea, *The Case of Manchoukuo* (1935) and *The Verdict of the League* (1933), official documents; W. W. Willoughby, *The Sino-Japanese Controversy and the League of Nations* (1935); C. W. Young, *The International Relations of Manchuria* (1929) and *The International Legal Status of the Kwangtung Leased Territory* (1931).

CHAPTER XXIX

THE IMMEDIATE BACKGROUND OF THE WAR

INTERNATIONAL RELATIONS, 1919–1939: P. Birdsall, *Versailles Twenty Years After* (1941); E. H. Carr, *Britain: A Study of Foreign Policy from the Treaty of Versailles to the Outbreak of the War* (1939); W. S. Churchill, *While England Slept: A Survey of World Affairs, 1932–1938* (1938); and *Step by Step: 1936–1939* (1939); V. M. Dean, *Europe in Retreat* (1939); M. Foot, *Armistice, 1919–1939* (1940); C. Golding, *From Versailles to Danzig* (1941); S. Graham, *From War to War, 1917–1940: A Datebook of the Years Between* (1940); R. S. Kain, *Europe: Versailles to Warsaw* (1939); W. N. Medlicott, *British Foreign Policy Since Versailles* (1940); C. Scarfoglio, *England and the Continent* (1939); F. L. Schuman, *Europe on the Eve: The Crises of Diplomacy, 1933–1939* (1939); R. W. Seton-Watson, *Britain and the Dictators* (1938), and *From Munich to Danzig* (1939); A. Wolfers, *Britain and France Between Two Wars: Conflicting Strategies of Peace Since Versailles* (1940).

AUSTRIA AND CZECHOSLOVAKIA: H. F. Armstrong, *When There Is No Peace* (1939); V. Beneš and R. Ginsburg, *Ten Million Prisoners* (1940); M. Bullock, *Austria, 1918–1938* (1939); W. Frischauer, *Twilight in Vienna* (1938); M. Fuchs, *Showdown in Vienna: The Death of Austria* (1939); G. E. R. Gedye, *Betrayal in Central Europe* (1939); M. Hindus, *We Shall Live Again* (1939); E. B. Hitchcock, *"I Built a Temple for Peace": The Life of Edward Beneš* (1940); S. Hodgson,

*The Man Who Made the Peace: Neville Chamberlain* (1938); G. Hutton, *Survey After Munich* (1939); E. Lennhoff, *The Last Five Hours of Austria* (1938); B. E. Schmitt, *From Versailles to Munich* (1938); K. Schuschnigg, *My Austria* (1938); F. G. Vondracek, *The Foreign Policy of Czechoslovakia, 1918–1935* (1937); A. Werth, *France and Munich: Before and After the Surrender* (1939); E. Wiskemann, *Czechs and Germans: A Study of the Struggle in the Historic Provinces of Bohemia and Moravia* (1938).

SPAIN: J. Arraras, *Francisco Franco, the Times and the Man* (1938); F. Davis, *My Shadow in the Sun* (1940); A. Mendizabal, *The Martyrdom of Spain* (1938); N. J. Padelford, *International Law and Diplomacy in the Spanish Civil Strife* (1939); G. Regler, *The Great Crusade* (1940); A. M. Smith, *The Day of the Liberals in Spain* (1938); A. L. Strong, *Spain in Arms* (1937); E. White, *War in Spain* (1937).

NAZI LEADERS AND AIMS: W. D. Bayles, *Caesars in Goose Step* (1940); W. E. and M. Dodd (eds.), *Ambassador Dodd's Diary, 1933–1938* (1941); O. Dutch, *The Errant Diplomat: The Life of Franz von Papen* (1940); K. Loewenstein, *Hitler's Germany: The Nazi Background to War* (1939); H. Rauschning, *The Revolution of Nihilism: Warning to the West* (1939); and *The Voice of Destruction (Hitler Speaks)* (1940); K. Singer, *Göring: Germany's Most Dangerous Man* (1940); O. Strasser, *Hitler and I* (1940); O. D. Tolischus, *They Wanted War* (1940); H. C. Wolfe, *The German Octopus* (1938).

THE CRISIS OF 1939: Finland, *The Finnish Blue Book* (1940); France, *Papers Relative to the Events and Negotiations Which Preceded the Opening of Hostilities Between Germany on the One Hand, and Poland, Great Britain, and France on the Other* (1940); Germany, *Documents on Events Preceding the Outbreak of the War* (1940); Great Britain, *Documents Concerning German-Polish Relations and the Outbreak of Hostilities between Great Britain and Germany on September 3, 1939* (1939); C. H. Grattan (ed.), *The German White Paper. Full Text of the Polish Documents Issued by the Berlin Foreign Office* (1940); N. Henderson, *Failure of a Mission: Berlin, 1937–1939* (1940); Poland, *Official Documents Concerning Polish-German and Polish-Soviet Relations, 1938–1939* (1940).

CAUSES AND ISSUES OF THE WAR: N. Angell, *For What Do We Fight?* (1940); P. Benson, *Through the Diplomatic Looking-Glass: Immediate Origins of the War in Europe* (1939); F. T. Birchall, *The Storm Breaks: A Panorama of Europe and the Forces That Have Wrecked Its Peace* (1940); H. A. L. Fisher et al., *The Background and Issues of the War* (1940); S. E. Hooper (ed.), *The Deeper Causes of the War and Its*

*Issues* (1940); J. Mackintosh, *The Paths That Led to War* (1940); W. Millis, *Why Europe Fights* (1940).

MISCELLANEOUS: R. L. Buell, *Poland: Key to Europe* (1939); N. Chamberlain, *In Search of Peace* (1939); E. Daladier, *In Defense of France* (1939); R. E. Dupuy, *World in Arms* (1939); A. C. Johnson, *Anthony Eden* (1939); J. F. Kennedy, *Why England Slept* (1940); S. B. Leeds, *These Rule France. The Story of Edouard Daladier and the Men Around Him* (1940); J. T. Shotwell, *What Germany Forgot* (1940); C. K. Streit, *Union Now: A Proposal for a Federal Union of Democracies of the North Atlantic* (1939); D. Walker-Smith, *Neville Chamberlain* (1940).

CHAPTER XXX

WARFARE—NEW STYLE

GENERAL: M. Boveri, *Minaret and Pipe-Line; Yesterday and To-day in the Near East* (1939); G. T. Garratt, *Europe's Dance of Death* (1940); J. Marlow, *De Gaulle and the Coming Invasion of Germany* (1940); E. McInnis, *The War: First Year* (1940); W. O'D. Pierce, *Air War: Its Psychological, Technical and Social Implications* (1939); H. Rosinski, *The German Army* (1940); F. L. Schuman, *Night over Europe: The Diplomacy of Nemesis, 1939–1940* (1940); J. T. Shotwell and F. Deák, *Turkey at the Straits* (1940); B. Souvarine, *Stalin: A Critical Survey of Bolshevism* (1939); T. A. Taracouzio, *War and Peace in Soviet Diplomacy* (1940); W. Waller (ed.), *War in the Twentieth Century* (1940); R. M. Werner (ed.), *Stalin's Kampf: Joseph Stalin's Credo Written by Himself* (1940); A. Williams, *Airpower* (1940).

POLAND AND SCANDINAVIA: J. Bryan, *Siege* (1940); H. B. Elliston, *Finland Fights* (1940); C. J. Hambro, *I Saw It Happen in Norway* (1940); J. O. Hannula, *Finland's War of Independence* (1939); J. H. Jackson, *Finland* (1940); S. de Ullman, *The Epic of the Finnish Nation* (1940).

BLITZKRIEG IN THE WEST. H. F. Armstrong, *Chronology of Failure: The Last Days of the French Republic* (1940); Belgian American Educational Foundation, *The Belgian Campaign and the Surrender of the Belgian Army, May 10–28, 1940* (1940); R. de Chambrun, *I Saw France Fall: Will She Rise Again?* (1940); D. van der Heide, *My Sister and I. Diary of a Dutch Boy Refugee* (1941); E. N. van Kleffens, *Juggernaut over Holland. The Dutch Foreign Minister's Personal Story of the Invasion of the Netherlands* (1941); A. Maurois, *Tragedy in*

*France* (1940); L. Moën, *Under the Iron Heel* (1941); H. Pol, *Suicide of a Democracy* (1940); A. Simone, *J'Accuse! The Men Who Betrayed France* (1940); E. Taylor, *The Strategy of Terror* (1940); E. Wiskemann, *Prologue to War* (1940).

THE BATTLE OF BRITAIN: V. Brittain, *England's Hour* (1941); W. S. Churchill, *Blood, Sweat, and Tears* (1941); D. Forbes-Robertson and R. W. Straus (eds.), *War Letters from Britain* (1941); G. T. Garratt, *Gibraltar and the Mediterranean* (1939); R. Ingersoll, *Report on England, November, 1940* (1940); R. Kraus, *Winston Churchill* (1940); F. Pratt, *Sea Power and Today's War* (1939).

THE FAR EAST: R. Berkov, *Strong Man of China* (1938); T. A. Bisson, *American Policy in the Far East: 1931–1940* (1940); K. Block, *German Interests and Policies in the Far East* (1939); E. F. Carlson, *The Chinese Army* (1940); W. H. Chamberlin, *Japan over Asia* (1937); A. W. Griswold, *The Far Eastern Policy of the United States* (1939); H. Hanson, *"Humane Endeavor": The Story of the China War* (1939); A. R. M. Lower, *Canada and the Far East—1940* (1941); A. Smedley, *China Fights Back* (1938); E. Snow, *The Battle for Asia* (1941); G. E. Taylor, *The Struggle for North China* (1941).

THE UNITED STATES: D. Aikman, *The All-American Front* (1940); J. Alsop and R. Kintner, *American White Paper: The Story of American Diplomacy and the Second World War* (1940); C. A. Beard, *Foreign Policy for America* (1940); R. L. Buell, *Isolated America* (1940); M. Dies, *The Trojan Horse in America* (1940); A. W. Dulles and H. F. Armstrong, *Can America Stay Neutral?* (1939); L. Hartley, *Our Maginot Line. The Defense of the Americas* (1939); W. T. Stone, *America Rearms* (1941); H. J. Tobin and P. W. Bidwell, *Mobilizing Civilian America* (1940).

# INDEX

Abbeville, 928, 929
Abd-el-Krim, 734
Abdication Act, 711
Abdul Hamid II, 247-248, 334, 336-338, 344-345
Abdullah, 827
Abe, 973
Abetz, 951
Abyssinia: see Ethiopia
*Achilles,* 917
Acre, 506
*Action Française,* 730, 731
Adalia, 402, 506
Adana, 506
Addis Ababa, 580, 645, 646, 881, 968
Aden, 114, 968
Adigrat, 644
Adler, 765
Adolphus of Nassau, 222
Adowa, 155-156, 644
Adrianople, 248, 348, 350, 351, 352, 463
Adriatic, 957, 960 n.
Aegean, 960, 961, 964
Aehrenthal, 339-341, 344
Afghan War, 179
Afghanistan, 183, 212, 235, 816
Africa, 967-971
Afrikander Bond, 191, 204
Agadir, 135
Agram, 307, 311; see also Zagreb
Agrarian reform: Baltic republics, 761-762; Czechoslovakia, 781-782; Poland, 753; Rumania, 806-807; Spain, 736, 738, 741
Agriculture: new methods, 30; Austria-Hungary, 288-290, 302; Bulgaria, 323; Denmark, 217; France, 126-127; Germany, 684; Great Britain, 185-186, 205-206; Holland, 221; Ireland, 173, 176, 181; Italy, 140, 637; Palestine, 825; Rumania, 318; Russia, 236, 280, 608-609, 611-613; Switzerland, 226; Turkey, 335
Air power decisive in Crete, 962
Airplanes, 11-13; in war on shipping, 943
Aisne, 397, 428, 929
Ajaccio, 933
*Ajax,* 917
*Alabama* case, 177-178
Alagi, 968

Åland Islands, 450, 524-525, 894
Alaska, 233
Albania, 161, 315, 347-348, 349, 351, 352-354, 374, 406, 505, 529-530, 583, 623-624, 639, 797-799, 864, 889, 890, 956, 957, 958, 960, 961
Albert Canal, 927
Albrecht, 72
Alcock, 11
Aleppo, 83, 463
Alessio, 349
Alexander of Bulgaria, 319-322
Alexander of Greece, 787
Alexander II of Russia, 66, 233, 238-243, 247, 253-254, 292, 320
Alexander III of Russia, 70, 254-256, 259-260, 443
Alexander I of Serbia, 328
Alexander of Yugoslavia, 793-796
Alexandretta, 892
Alexandria, 820, 948, 964
Alexis, 439-440
Alfonso XII of Spain, 227
Alfonso XIII of Spain, 228, 734-736, 885
Algeciras conference, 132, 368
Algeria, 113, 949
Allenby, 430
Allenstein, 488-489
Alliance of the three emperors, 68, 70, 294
Allies in World War I: advantages, 395-396; retreat in the west, 397; Dardanelles-Gallipoli failure, 401-402; failures in the Balkans, 407; drives in 1916, 414-416; defeatism, 433-434; war aims, 454-455; victories in the Near East, 429-432; final triumph, 461, 472-474
Almeria, 743
Alsace-Lorraine: before 1914, 61, 66, 96-97; in the peace negotiations, 419, 483, 496; after 1918, 721-723
*Altmark,* 921
Amadeo, 227
Amiens, 928
Amsterdam, 221, 926
Anarchism, 40-41
Anatolia, 86, 507
Anatolian Railway, 83, 85
Andalsnes, 924
Andrássy, 293, 303
Angell, 359

Angers, 904
Anglican Church, 170
Anglo-Egyptian Sudan, 967
Anglo-French Co-ordinating Committee, 918, 919
Anglo-French entente: see Entente Cordiale
Anglo-French military and naval agreements (before 1914), 211, 214-215
Anglo-German commercial rivalry (before 1914), 193-195, 213
Anglo-German naval rivalry, 213-214
Anglo-Iraqi alliance, 965
Anglo-Japanese alliance, 200, 265
Anglo-Persian Oil Company, dispute with Persia, 829-830
Anglophobia, in Germany, 90
Anglo-Russian entente (see Triple Entente)
Anglo-Russian naval conversations (before 1914), 215
Angola, 80
Angora, 84, 507, 813-814
Ankara: see Angora
Annam, 24, 26, 113
Annunzio, 160, 502, 627
Anschluss movement, 686-687, 770-772, 865, 869
Anticlericalism: in France, 112, 120-124; in Germany, 58-59; in Spain, 229, 736, 737, 738, 741; in Turkey, 814
Anti-Communist pact, 865, 867, 886
Antigua, 984
Antioch, 892
Anti-Semitism: in France, 118-120, 946; in Germany, 669, 674-676, 867; in Poland, 751-752; in Rumania, 318-319, 953; in Russia, 258-259
Antivari, 161, 293
Antonescu, 955, 956
Antwerp, 927, 942
Anzac troops in World War II, 960
Aosta, Duke of, 968
Appeasement, 868 n., 890, 983
Apponyi, 503-504
Arabs, 83, 430, 506; in Palestine, 824-826
Archangel, 599
Arcos raid, 621, 701
Ardahan, 252, 451
Arendal, 922
Arita, 975, 976, 977
Armaments, 363-365, 490-492, 502, 508, 562, 583-584; Washington naval treaty (1922), 570-571; Geneva naval conference (1927), 571; London naval treaty (1930), 572; Geneva disarmament conference (1932-1934), 573-

576; London naval treaty (1936), 584-585; rearmament after 1936, 584-586, 866
Armenians, 336-337, 346, 506, 592
Armentières, 458
Armistice: World War I (1918), 472-473; Franco-German (1940), 932-933, 948; Franco-Italian (1940), 933
Army of the Nile, 960, 964, 969, 970
Arras, 411, 427, 458
Artel: see Collective farms
Asmara, 968
Asquith, 90, 202, 207, 208, 210, 694-696
Assab, 155
Associations Law: in France, 121-122; in Spain, 738
Assuan dam, 817 n.
Atatürk: see Kemal
Atheism in Soviet Russia, 616-617
Athenia, 916
Athens, 961
Atlee, 925
Ausgleich, 287-288
Australia, 165, 192, 401, 478 n., 489-490, 537, 647 n., 918, 919
Australian troops in World War II, 960, 961
Austria: before 1914, 287-289, 295-301; and the peace settlement, 494, 498-503, 505; political history after 1918, 765-766, 771-775; economic difficulties, 766-769; Anschluss question, 769-772, 863, 865, 867, 868-871
Austria, treaties with: Germany, 582, 688, 775; Italy, 582; Russia, 619
Austria-Hungary, 284-312, 371, 374; and the Balkans, 292-294, 339-344; and Russia, 246-252; and World War I, 399, 402, 403-404, 413-415, 417-418, 432-433, 459-460; disintegration of, 463-464
Austria-Hungary, treaties with: Germany, 67-69; Italy, 69, 153, 154, 161; Rumania, 70, 294; Russia, 68, 337; Serbia, 293-294; Turkey, 342
Austro-German alliance, 67
Austro-German customs union, 768-769
Austro-Prussian War, 53, 99, 139
Austro-Sardinian War, 139
Automobiles, 9-10
Avanguardia, 631
Avanti!, 151, 163, 626, 627
Avenol, 516
Averescu, 806
Avlona, 402, 500, 501, 957
Awakening Magyars, 780
Azaña, 737, 738, 740, 741, 882
Azerbaijan, 592

Aznar, 735
Azores, 987

Badeni, 298-299
Badoglio, 646
Bagdad, 83, 85, 430, 506, 965
Bagdad Railway, 83-85
Bagdadbahn, Die, 84
Bahamas, 984
Baku, 260
Bakunin, 41, 150, 243, 245
Baldwin, 695-697, 699-703, 706, 709, 710-711
Balfour, 184, 196, 201, 478
Balfour Declaration, 824
Balfour note, 550
Balfour Report, 712
Balilla, 631
Balkan Alliance (1934), 568, 649
Balkan Entente, 870
Balkan League (1912), 346-347, 369, 373
Balkan Wars, 348-352
Baltic Entente, 569-570
Baltiski, 908, 914
Balts, 756-760, 761, 908
Baluchistan, 26, 179
Banat, 287, 416, 503, 806
Bank for International Settlements, 553-554, 557
Bank of France, 732
Bapaume, 461
Barcelona, 733, 739, 745, 882
Bardia, 969, 970
Barker, 213
Barletta, 743
Bartel, 749
Barthou, 796
Bases, naval and air, leased to U.S., 984
Basra, 86, 965
Battle of Britain, 937-943
Battle of France, 929-932
Battle of the Atlantic, 943, 986
Battle of the Ports, 926-929
Battle of the wheat, 637
Batum, 252, 451
Baudoin, 947 n.
Bauer, G., 496
Bauer, O., 765
Bavaria, 55, 655, 880
Beaconsfield: see Disraeli
Béarn, 949 n.
Beatty, 412
Bebel, 59
Beersheba, 430
Beirut, 463, 966
Belfort, 396
Belgian Congo, 936 n.
Belgium: before World War I, 26, 211, 220, 222-225; and World War I, 383-385, 396-398; after World War I, 486, 490, 494, 537, 545-547; treaties, 564, 565, 583; in World War II, 926-928, 936 n.
Belgrade, 339, 380, 381, 406, 464
Bell, 496
Beneš, 462, 463, 478, 567, 777, 781, 783, 785, 873, 874, 877, 886
Bengazi, 969, 970, 971
Beran, 886, 887
Berbera, 968
Berchtesgaden, 869, 875, 951, 952, 958
Berchtold, 373, 376, 377, 379, 381, 386-388
Bergen, 922
Berlin: Congress of (1878), 67, 179-180, 252; Congress of (1884-1885), 20, 74; treaty of (1878), 251-253, 293, 316, 319, 335; treaty of (1921), 512
Berlin-Bagdad railway, 8, 84-85, 319, 371
Bermuda, 984
Bernhardi, 90
Bernstorff, 409, 420
Berry-au-Bac, 428
Bessarabia, 234, 247, 249, 252, 331, 388, 569, 805-806, 952, 967
Bessemer process, 4
Bethlen, 778-779
Bethmann-Hollweg, 89-90, 95, 96, 135, 381, 384, 409, 433
Beust, 292
Bey: see Enver Bey
Bhutan, 26
Bialystok, 907
Bias Bay, 972
Bicycle, 46
Big Four at the Paris peace conference, 480-481, 486, 493, 495, 498, 500, 502, 504, 505, 536
Bilbao, 743
Birmingham, 943
Bismarck, 56-76, 82-83, 99, 102, 113, 261
Bismarck, 945
Bismarck Archipelago, 74
Bissolati, 151
Bitlis, 506
Bizerte, 933
Björkö, 92, 909
Black Hundreds, 276
Black Sea, 966
Black Shirts, 628, 631
Blackouts, 916
Blanc, 37-38
Blank check (July, 1914), 376
Blériot, 11
Blitzkrieg, 902, 924, 926-932, 960, 970
Bloch, 359

Blockade, British (World War II), 948
Blomberg, 867, 868
Blood purge, Nazi, 689
Bloody Sunday, 272-273
Blum, 730-732, 946
Bodelschwingh, 679
Boer War, 192-193
Boers, 79, 91, 165, 189-192, 204
Bohemia, 287, 290, 295-301, 461, 464, 502, 503, 781
Bohemia-Moravia, 888, 889, 890
Bokhara, 234
Bolsheviks (Bolsheviki), 270-271, 275-276, 442-444, 445, 446-447, 448
Bonapartists, 103, 118
Bonar Law, 478, 544, 695, 696
Bonnet, 875
Bordeaux, 100, 104, 930, 947
Boris III, 799, 801
Borneo, 187, 973
Bosnia-Herzegovina, 247, 249, 253, 293, 294, 307, 308, 310, 332, 339-344, 368-369, 400, 502
Bosnian crisis, 338-344, 368-369
Botha, 204, 478
Bothnia, Gulf of, 912
Bouisson, 730
Boulanger, 116-118
Boulé in Greece, 324
Boulogne, 397, 928, 942
Bourse Gazette, 375
Boxer War, 23
Brailsford, 364
Bratianu, 478, 806
Bratislava, 881, 888
Brauchitsch, 902, 932
Bremen, 470, 940
Bremen, 921 n.
Brenner Pass, 772, 870
Brest-Litovsk, 404, 449-451, 497, 903
Briand, 120, 121, 123, 125, 534, 566, 725, 803
Briand-Kellogg pact: see Paris, pact of
Bright, 183
Bristol, 940, 943
British Commonwealth of Nations, 711-713
British Empire, 164-167, 187-193
British Expeditionary Force: World War I, 397; World War II, 915, 929
British Guiana, 938 n., 984
British peace ballot (1935), 709
British Somaliland, 187, 967, 968
Bromberg, 754
Brown, 11
Bruges, 397
Brüning, 666, 670
Brunswick, 470

Brusa, 507
Brussels, 927
Brussels conference: (1876), 20; (1937), 860
Brussels line, 530, 531
Bryce, 202
Bucharest, treaty of, 352
Buchlau, 341
Budapest, 777
Bug River, 904
Bukharin, 444, 604, 605
Bukowina, 286, 291, 331, 414, 416, 417, 502, 806, 952
Bulgaria: before World War I, 247-252, 314, 315, 319-323, 331-332, 333, 344, 347-354, 370; and World War I, 406, 417-418, 463; and the peace settlement, 504, 505, 509; after World War I, 799-804, 863, 870; in World War II, 953, 954, 957, 958
Bülow, 89, 92-95, 130-131, 199, 341
Bundesrat, 54
Burgos, 743, 883
Burma, 24, 26, 974, 977, 981
Burns, 203
Byrd, 12

Cadets, 275
Cadorna, 413-414, 434-435
Caillaux, 135, 136, 370, 434
Cairo, 818, 819
Calais, 397, 928, 942
Caliphate, 814
Cambodia, 22, 113, 981
Cambon, 371, 372, 384, 478
Cambrai, 427, 429
Camelots du Roi, 731
Camorra, 140, 146
Campbell-Bannerman, 201, 202
Canada, 164-165, 174, 192, 196, 919, 984
Candia, 962
Canea, 962
Canovas, 227-228
Cantigny, 459
Canton, 836, 837, 842, 856, 972, 974
Cape Colony, 165, 189, 190, 204
Cape to Cairo railway, 187, 188
Cape Verde Islands, 987
Capital, 39, 150
Capitalist class, 32-33, 34
Capitulations: see Extraterritoriality
Caporetto, 434-436
Caprivi, 76
Caribbean, 984
Carinthia, 287, 290
Carlists, 227, 885
Carlos I of Portugal, 230

Carnegie, 360, 361
Carniola, 287, 332
Carnot, 116
Carol I of Rumania, 307, 316, 318, 331, 388, 416
Carol II of Rumania, 807, 810, 953, 955
Caroline Islands, 80
Carpatho-Ukraine, 887, 888, 889
Carson, 209-210
Cartel, 7
Casablanca, 134, 947
Cassel, 90
Castellorizo, 508
Castelnau, 397
Catalonia, 230, 733, 739, 740, 741, 742, 883
Catholic Association in Ireland, 174
Catholic Church: in France, 722-723; in Germany, 58-59, 681-682, 689; in Italy, 143-144, 635-636; in Portugal, 231; in Spain, 738, 740
Catholic Party in Belgium, 223-224
Catroux, 966
Cattaro, 960 n.
Caucasus, 273, 276
Caudillo, the, 885; see Franco
Cavour, 139, 143
Cecil, 482
Central Powers in World War I: advantages, 395; military plans, 396; advance halted in France, 397; position at the close of 1914, 398-399; successes of 1915, 403-407; failure to end the war in 1916, 410-418; peace proposals, 418-421; submarine campaigns, 407-409, 423, 425, 452-453; final drives, 456-460; collapse, 461, 472-474
Cephalonia, 956
Chad, 950
Chad, Lake, 136, 188
Chahar, 855, 856, 859
Chamber of Deputies, French, 945
Chamber of Deputies, Italian, 634
Chamber of Fasces and Corporations, Italian, 634, 946
Chamberlain, A., 531
Chamberlain, J., 80, 183, 184-185, 191-192, 196, 198-199
Chamberlain, N., 711, 868, 875, 876, 877, 878, 891, 896, 911 n., 915, 921, 925
Chambord, Count of, 103, 105, 118
Chang Hsiao-liang, 843
Chang Hsueh-liang, 857
Chang Tso-lin, 843
Changchun, 269, 843, 845
Changsha, 974
Charleroi, 397

Charles: Archduke of Austria, 413; Emperor of Austria, 433, 463, 464, 777-778
Charles of Hesse, 450
Château-Thierry, 460-461, 930
Chatfield, 916
Chautemps, 729, 732-733
Cheka, 590, 599
Chervonets, 603
Chiang Kai-shek, 841, 842, 856, 857, 858, 971, 981
Chicherin, 444
Chief of the French State, 945
China: under the empire, 22-24, 198-200, 263-265; establishment of the republic, 24, 836-837; and World War I, 389, 400, 837; and the peace settlement, 490, 496, 837-839; at the Washington Conference, 839-840; under the Nationalists, 840-842; loss of Manchuria, 844-852; war with Japan, 855-860, 866, 971-975, 980, 981, 982
Chinese Eastern Railway, 264, 267, 852-853
Ching-wei: see Wang Ching-wei
Chita, 854
Chosen: see Korea
Chowchow, 859
Christian IX of Denmark, 217
Christian X of Denmark, 217 n., 923
Chungking, 971, 982
Church of Ireland, 174, 176
Churchill, 203, 211, 919, 925, 929, 930, 935, 958, 967, 977, 981
Chvalkovsky, 886
Ciano, 890, 893 n., 954
Cilicia, 507
Clemenceau, 110, 116, 136, 434, 477, 480, 483, 484, 487, 490, 493, 496
Clyde, 169
Coal strike in Great Britain, 699-700
Cobh, 717
Coblenz, 495
Cochin-China, 22, 113, 978
Codreanu, 810
Collaboration, French-German, 950-952
Collective farms in Russia, 608-609, 611, 612
Collective Labor Relations Law in Italy, 632
Collins, 714, 715
Cologne, 470, 495, 657, 940
Colonial Society in Germany, 73, 78, 87, 93
Colonies and colonial policies: see Imperialism
Comintern: see Third International
Comitadjis, 802, 803, 804

Commons, British House of, characterization, 171

Communards, 100-102

Commune of Paris, 100-102, 120

Communism: in Austria, 765; in Baltic republics, 758, 760, 761, 762; in Bulgaria, 800-801; in China, 857; in France, 729, 730, 731, 732; in Germany, 650, 652, 654, 672; in Great Britain, 698; in Hungary, 776-777; in Italy, 625, 628; in Russia, 270-271, 275-276, 442-451, 598-599, 603-606, 607; in Spain, 739, 741

Communist International: see Third International

*Communist Manifesto*, 38, 39, 150

Communist Youth in Russia, 599

Companys, 740, 741

Compiègne, 474, 932

Compulsory military service (1940) in U.S., 984

Concordat of 1801, 121

Conference of Ambassadors: see Council of Ambassadors

Confessional Synod in Germany, 680

Congo, French, 81, 135-136

Congo Act, 74

Congo Free State, 20, 188, 222-223

Congress of the United States, 425, 426, 559, 561

Conscription: in World War I, 415, 426, 458; in World War II (U.S), 984

Constantine, 407, 432, 786, 787

Constantinople, 248, 419, 505

Constanza, 418

Constitutional decrees in France (1940), 945

Constitutional law of July 10, 1940, in France, 947 n.

Consulates: American, closed in Germany and Italy, 988; German and Italian, closed in U.S., 988

Convoys, 943

Coolidge, 521

Cooper, 925

Corap, 927

Corfu, 406, 956

Corfu affair, 639-640

Corfu Manifesto, 462, 792

Corinth, 432; Gulf of, 961

Corn Laws in Great Britain, 175

Coronel, 400

Corporations, National Council of, in Italy, 634

Corporative state in Italy, 632-635

Corrupt Practices Act in Great Britain, 181

Corsica, 863, 881

Cortes, 883

Cosgrave, 715, 716, 717

Council of Ambassadors, 498, 527, 528, 529, 530, 639-640, 747, 751, 758

Council of National Defense, in Spain, 883

Council of Ten, 479-480

County Councils Act in Great Britain, 185

Courland, 404, 450

Covenant of the League of Nations, 514-517, 522-523

Coventry, 943

Cracow, 904, 906

Craigie-Arita formula, 976

Creditanstalt, 556

Crete, 314, 324-326, 344, 352, 790, 957, 961, 962, 964

Crimean War, 115, 197, 233-234, 239

Crispi, 146, 151, 152, 155-156

Croatia, 959, 960 n.

Croatian Peasant Party, 959

Croats: in the Dual Monarchy, 286, 287, 303, 307-311, 332, 503; in Yugoslavia, 793, 794, 797, 958, 959

Croce, 156

*Croix de Feu*, 730, 732

Crown colonies (British), 166, 167

Croydon, 942

Cuba, 228

Cuno, 547

Currency inflation: Austria, 768; France, 726-727; Germany, 656-657; Great Britain, 706; Italy, 624, 637

Curzon line, 526, 747, 904

Cvetkovich, 958, 959

Cyprus, 180, 253, 508

Cyrenaica: see Tripoli

Czechia, 887, 888

Czechoslovakia: establishment of, 462-463; and the peace settlement (1918), 489, 494, 502, 503, 505; political history, 780-781, 783-785; agrarian reform, 781-782; minorities problem, 782-783, 784, 863, 867, 870, 871-881; partition of, 878-881

Czechoslovakia, treaties with: France, 564, 566; Germany, 565; Poland, 568; Rumania, 567; Russia, 581; Yugoslavia, 567

Czechs in the Dual Monarchy, 286, 287, 291, 295, 296, 297, 298, 462, 463

Czernin, 433, 455

Czernowitz, 414

Dagoe Islands, 894 n., 908

Dahomey, 114

Dail Eireann, 713, 714

Daimler, 9

Dairen, 843, 847

Dakar, 949, 950
Daladier, 729, 875, 877, 878, 897, 911 n., 920, 946
Dalmatia, 287, 307, 309, 310, 332, 402, 960 n.
Dalny, 264
Damascus, 463, 821, 966
D'Annunzio, 160, 502, 627
Danube, internationalized, 494
Danzig, 487-489, 754-757, 863, 892, 893, 896, 900
Daranyi, 780
Dardanelles: attack on the, 401-402; demilitarized, 509; refortified, 816; in World War II, 961
Darlan, 951, 952
Darmstädter und National-Bank, 557
Davis, 527
Dawes plan, 547-549
Deák, 302, 303
Debts, Inter-Allied: see War debts
Dedeagach, 352
Defeatism, 433-434
Defense Squads, Nazi, 667
Delagoa Bay, 79, 189, 190
Delcassé, 128-132
Delegations, Austro-Hungarian, 288
Delft, 926
Demerdjis, 791
Demilitarized zone: Rhineland, 484, 491; the Straits, 509, 816; Greco-Turkish frontier, 509; Turco-Bulgarian frontier, 509
Denmark, 216-218, 486, 922, 923
Denmark Strait, 945 n.
Dentz, 964, 966
Depression, economic (of 1929), 555-558
Depretis, 146, 150, 155
*Der Führer:* see Hitler
Derna, 969, 970
Destroyers transferred to Britain by U.S. (1940), 984
*Deutschland,* 743, 889, 917
De Valera, 713-720
Dewey, 80
Diaz, 435, 460
*Die Flotte,* 88
Diederichs, 80
Dimitriyevich, 376
Diredawa, 646
Disarmament: see Armaments
Disraeli, 178-180, 252
Dixmude, 465
Dmowski, 478
Dnepropetrovsk dam, 611
Dniester River, 903
Dobrudja, 249, 352, 388, 406, 416, 418, 954, 955

Dodecanese Islands, 162, 352, 402, 506, 508, 624, 639, 644
Dogali, 155
Dollfuss, 687, 769, 771
Dolo, 644
Donets basin, 260
Dordrecht, 926
Dormans, 460
Dorpat, peace of: Estonia, 760; Finland, 763
Dortmund, 545
Doumer, 731
Doumergue, 726, 730, 731
Draft, military, in U.S., 984-985
Draga, Queen of Serbia, 328
*Drang nach Osten,* 86, 341, 344, 362, 409, 430, 582, 583, 864, 870, 871, 873, 882, 889, 890, 964
Dreadnoughts, 88-89
Dresden, 654
Dreyfus affair, 118-120
Drummond, 516
Drumont, 118
Dual Monarchy: see Austria-Hungary
Dubno, 414
*Dubrovnik,* 796
Duca, 809
*Duce, il,* 631; see also Mussolini
Duffy, 714
Duggan, 714
Duisburg, 541
Dumas: municipal, 241, 256, 272; national, 274-278, 437, 439
*Dunkerque,* 949
Dunkirk, 397, 928, 942, 943, 984
Durazzo, 161, 349, 406, 464
Düsseldorf, 470, 541, 655, 940
Dzerzhinsky, 444, 604, 605
Dzhugashvili: see Stalin

East Africa, 968; German, 74, 401 n., 537, 936 n.; Italian, 968
East Prussia, 94, 487, 902
Eastern Karelia, 763
Eastern Locarno, proposed agreement, 580
Eastern Question, 313
Eastern Rumelia, 252, 314, 315, 320-321; see also Rumelia
Ebert, 471, 472, 650, 652, 654, 663
Ebro River, 882
Eckener, 12
Eden, 648, 756, 868 n., 925, 929, 930
Edessa, 956
Edison, 6
Education: Austria, 297; Bulgaria, 323; France, 111-112; Great Britain, 176-177, 181, 185; Hungary, 303; Italy,

Education (*continued*)
146, 158; Russia, 255-256, 615; Spain, 229, 737-738
Edward VII, 210
Edward VIII, 710-711
Eger, 878
Egersund, 922
Egypt, 83, 129-130, 180, 182-183, 508, 817-821, 918, 958, 962, 964, 966, 967, 968, 969, 970
Einstein, 675
*Einwohnerwehr,* 655
Eisner, 652
El Agheila, 970
Elbe, 494
Electoral Reform Act in Italy, 632
Elementary Education Act in Great Britain, 185
Embargo, 983
*Emden,* 917
Emigration: from Austria-Hungary, 304; from Italy, 149-150
*Emile Bertin,* 949 n.
Engels, 38
England: see Great Britain
English Channel, 940, 941, 942
Entente Cordiale, 91, 129, 200, 371
Enver Bey, 345, 350
Epirus, 315, 352
Eritrea, 155, 580, 968, 970
Erzberger, 433, 472, 651, 655
Erzerum, 506
Esterhazy, 119
Estonia, 257, 450, 505, 569, 759-762, 894, 908, 911
Ethiopia, 21, 114, 127, 155-156, 580, 581, 642-649, 864, 865, 867, 870, 881, 968
Eupen, 486, 927
Evangelical Church, German, 679
*Exeter,* 917
Extraterritoriality: China, 24, 839-840, 841; Egypt, 820-821; Persia, 829; Turkey, 508

Facta, 629
Faisal I, 827
Faisal II, 965
Faith Day in Italy, 648
Falange, 884-885
*Falange Española Tradicionalista,* 884
Falange National Council, 885
Falange Political Junta, 885
Falangist Party, 885
Falk Laws in Germany, 58, 60
Falkenhayn, 412, 416, 417, 430
Falkland Islands, 400
Far East, 22-26, 79-80, 113, 221, 262-269, 281, 389, 490, 570-571, 584-585, 836-860; see also Japan, China, Russia, Germany
Faroe Islands, 218, 924
Faruk, 820 n.
Fasces and Corporations, Italian Chamber of, 634, 946
*Fascio di Combattimento,* 627
Fascism: early program, 627, 628; seizure of the government, 629; suppression of opposition, 630; constitutionalized, 631-632; syndicalist program, 632-633; the corporative state, 633-634
Fascist Grand Council, 631, 632, 634
Fascist National Council, 634
Fascist Party, 628, 629, 631-632, 634
Fashoda affair, 128, 188
Fatherland Front in Austria, 771, 775
Feder, 667
Federation of Importers and Exporters, in Indo-China, 982
Federation of the Left in France, 107, 110
Feminism, 49
Fenian Brotherhood in Ireland, 174
Ferdinand of Bulgaria, 322-323, 352, 799
Ferdinand of Rumania, 806
Fergana, 234
Ferry, 110, 111, 112, 113, 115
Fez, 134
Fianna Fail in Ireland, 718
Fifth Column, 922, 926, 955
Figueras, 882
Finland: under the tsars, 256-257, 272, 274, 279; after 1917, 450, 524-525, 561, 762-764, 894; in war with Russia, 909-914, 966
Finland, Gulf of, 912
First International: see International Workingman's Association
First World War (1914-1918): underlying causes, 361-367; July crisis, 375-387; mobilization of belligerents, 390-392; propaganda, 392-394; question of guilt, 385-387; naval engagements, 400, 401, 412-413; aims of the Allies, 422-423, 456; aims of the Central Powers, 420, 456-457; aims of President Wilson, 419, 454-455; casualties, 474; costs, 474; see also Allies, Central Powers, and United States
Fismes, 461
Fiume, 286, 287, 307, 309, 500-502, 623, 640, 960 n.
Five-Year Plan: in Soviet Russia, 608-614; in Turkey, 815
Flanders, 928, 929
Flandin, 648, 730
Flemings in Belgium, 223
*Flotte, Die,* 88

Foch, 397, 428, 429, 458, 460, 461, 472
Food Estate in Germany, 684
Ford, 9
Formosa, 24, 263
Forster Education Act in Great Britain, 176
Fourier, 37
Four-power pact, Mussolini's, 579
Fourteen Points, President Wilson's, 454-456, 465, 481, 501, 509, 511
Four-Year Plan in Germany, 685
France before 1914: war with Germany (1870–1871), 99-100; the Commune of Paris, 100-102; recovery under Thiers, 102-103; establishment of the republic, 103-107; constitutional laws, 108-110; anticlericalism, 111-112, 120-124; imperialism, 112-114, 127, 129-136; pre-war international relations, 114-115, 129-136, 160, 261, 263; Boulanger affair, 116-117; Dreyfus affair, 118-120; economic conditions, 124-127; militarism, 136-138
France after 1914: World War I, 396-397, 401, 428-429, 434, 459, 460-461; the peace settlement, 483-486, 490-491, 493; reparations, 543-547; disarmament, 570-572, 573-576, 584-585; the Italo-Ethiopian affair, 643, 648; problem of Alsace-Lorraine, 721-723; material reconstruction, 724-725; fiscal and economic problems, 725-727, 728, 731; elections, 725, 727, 728, 731; search for security, 483 n., 490-491, 564-567, 881
France in World War II: on eve of war, 865, 866, 867, 868, 869, 873, 875, 877, 881, 883, 891, 892, 893, 894, 895, 900, 901, 983; collapse of, 929-932; reasons for collapse, 933-934; armistice terms, 932-933; Vichy government, 945-947, 961, 978, 981, 982
France, treaties with: Belgium, 564, 583; Czechoslovakia, 564, 566; Germany, 565, 579; Great Britain, 129-130, 565, 579; Italy, 129, 565, 579, 580-581; Poland, 564, 566; Rumania, 566; Soviet Russia, 570, 581; Spain, 130; Syria, 822; Yugoslavia, 566
Franchise laws: Austria, 296, 298; Denmark, 217; Great Britain, 171, 181, 694, 701; Greece, 324; Italy, 142, 146-147, 158-159, 633; Netherlands, 222; Norway, 219; Russia, 274, 278; Soviet Union, 593, 596; Spain, 737; Sweden, 220
Francis Ferdinand, 311-312, 375-376
Francis Joseph, 66, 247, 284-286, 290, 292, 294, 295, 296, 297, 299, 305, 306, 307, 312, 343, 367, 379, 381, 416, 433
Franco, 742, 743, 745, 865, 867, 882-886
Franco-British Union, 930
Franco-German War, 53, 139
Franco-Italian tariff war, 148
Franco-Russian alliance, 115, 261, 263
Frank, 906
Frankfort: treaty of, 102; bombed by British, 940
Frederick VIII of Denmark, 217
Frederick III of Germany, 75
Free French movement, 947-948, 949-950, 965, 966
Freedom of the seas, 454-455
Freezing of assets of Axis countries, in U.S., 988
French Congo, 81, 135-136
French Equatorial Africa, 950
French Somaliland, 114, 580, 933, 967
French West Africa, 950
Frick, 671, 679
*Friedensturm*, 460
Friedjung, 309-310
Fritsch, 867, 868
F's, the three, 173, 181
Fuad, 819, 820
*Führer, der*: see Hitler
*Future of War, The,* 359

Gabredarre, 644
Galicia, 286, 290, 291, 295, 399, 404, 414, 445, 502, 746-747
Galitzin, 438
Gallieni, 397
Gallipoli, 401-402
Gambetta, 100, 104, 106, 107, 110, 115
Gamelin, 916, 927, 946
Gandhi, 830, 832, 833
Gapon, 272
Garibaldi, 139
Gasparri, 635-636
Gaulle, 920, 947, 948, 949-950
Gaza, 430
Gdynia, 753-754, 904, 906
General Confederation of Labor: in France, 125; in Italy, 157
General Motors Corporation, 985
Geneva, seat of the League of Nations, 517
Geneva disarmament conference, 573-576
Geneva Protocol, 563-564
Genoa conference, 619-620
Gensoul, 949
George V of Great Britain, 210, 710, 716
George VI of Great Britain, 711
George I of Greece, 324

George II of Greece, 787, 791-792, 961, 962

*George Washington,* 481

Georgia, 592

Gerlogubi, 644

German Christians, 679, 680, 681

German Confederation, 53

German East Africa, 74, 401 n., 537

German Labor Front, 682

German Southwest Africa, 74, 188 n., 401 n., 536

Germans: Austria-Hungary, 286, 287, 291, 296, 299; Czechoslovakia, 502, 784; Danzig, 487, 756-757; Italy, 502; Memel, 758-759; Poland, 752-753; Russia, 257

Germany before 1914: constitution of the empire, 53-56; political history (to 1890), 56-61; economic progress and social legislation, 61-65, 77; diplomacy under Bismarck, 65-71; imperialism, 71-75, 78-86; political history (1890-1914), 75, 76, 93-98; Alsace-Lorraine, 96-97; diplomacy under William II, 76-77, 91-92, 198-199; navalism, 78, 86-91; militarism, 98

Germany after 1914: World War I, 396-399, 400-401, 403-406, 407-409, 410-413, 415-416, 417-421, 423-425, 433, 455-459, 460-461; the peace settlement, 483-497; reparations, 540-549, 551-559; rearmament, 573-578, 585; postwar political parties, 650-651; Weimar constitution, 652-653; elections, 651, 664-666, 669, 670, 671, 672, 688, 690; antirepublican plots, 653-656; currency debacle, 656-658; foreign policy, 658-660, 686-688, 863-865; economic conditions, 660-663, 682-685; rise of the National Socialists, 666-671; National Socialist revolution, 671-674; political changes, 676-678; conflict with the church, 678-682; and Spanish civil war, 742-745; *Drang nach Osten,* 867-882, 886-890; absorption of Austria, 868-871; destruction of Czechoslovakia, 871-881, 886-889

Germany in World War II: on eve of war, 894, 895, 896-901; conquers Poland, 902-907; launches peace offensive, 914-915; attacks shipping, 916-917, 943; seizes Norway and Denmark, 920-925; conquers Netherlands, Belgium, and Luxembourg, 926-928; conquers France, 927-933; second peace offensive, 935-936; attacks Britain by air, 940-943; occupies Rumania, 956; occupies Bulgaria, 958; conquers Yugoslavia, 959-960; conquers Greece, 960-961; takes Crete, 962; attacks Russia, 966-967; helps Italy in North Africa, 970-971; sinks American freighter, 988; assets in U.S. frozen, 988; consulates in U.S. closed, 988; closes American consulates, 988

Germany, treaties with: Austria, 582, 688, 775; Austria-Hungary, 67-69; Belgium, 224, 565; Czechoslovakia, 565; France, 565, 579; Great Britain, 565, 579; Italy, 69, 153-154, 565, 579, 582; Japan, 582, 687; the papacy, 681; Poland, 565, 583, 684; Rumania, 70; Russia, 68, 570, 619-620, 659, 895-896

*Germany and the Next War,* 90

*Gestapo,* 678, 867, 904, 906

Gevgeli, 352

Gezira, 818

Ghent, 397

"Giant" state farm, 611

Gibraltar, 886, 961

Gigurti, 953, 955

Gijón, 743, 882

Gil Robles, 739, 740, 741, 742

Giolitti, 156-163, 627, 629

*Giovane Italiane,* 631

*Giovani Fascisti,* 631

Giraud, 928

Givet, 927

Gladstone, 75, 175-178, 180-184, 247

Glasgow, 940

Gliders, military use of, 962

Godesberg, 876

Goebbels, 678, 756, 867

Goering: see Göring

Goga, 810

Gold standard, abandonment of, 557, 638, 707, 732, 733

Gömbös, 780

Gorahai, 644

Gorchakov, 234

Gordon, 183

Goremykin, 277, 279

Göring, 671, 674, 678, 689, 756, 932, 942

Gorizia, 287, 402, 415, 434

Gorlice, 404

*Gosplan,* 608

Gotenhafen, 906; see also Gdynia

Government General, Polish, 904, 905, 906, 907

Government of National Defense in France, 99

Gradisca, 287, 402

*Graf Spee,* 917, 921

Graziani, 644, 646, 969

Great Britain before 1914: economic development, 168-169, 193-194, 205-206; government, 169-171, 207-208; political parties, 171-173; Liberal governments, 175-178, 180-184, 201-215; Conservative governments, 178-180, 184-201; imperialism, 164-167, 179-180, 182-183, 187-193; foreign relations, 197-200, 211-215; Irish problem, 172-174, 176, 180-181, 183-184, 186, 209-211; social legislation, 186, 204-205

Great Britain after 1914: World War I, 415-416, 427-428, 429-430, 457-459; the peace settlement, 490, 506, 508, 537; reparations and war debts, 543, 549-551, 559-560; disarmament, 570-572, 574-576, 577, 584-585; rearmament, 583-584; the Italo-Ethiopian affair, 643, 648, 649; postwar elections, 693-694, 696-697, 699, 703, 710; postwar economic conditions, 691-692, 699, 701-702, 704, 706-708; unemployment, 692-693, 702, 708-709; Lloyd George government, 693-696; Labor governments, 697-699, 703-705; Conservative governments, 696-703; National governments, 705-713; adoption of protective tariff, 707; constitutional crisis (1936), 710-711; and France, 864, 865, 875, 877; and Italy, 870; and Czechoslovakia, 872-873, 875-878; and Spain, 883; and Poland, 891, 895, 896, 897, 898, 899; and Turkey, 891, 892; and Russia, 893-895; and Germany, 896-901; and Finland, 910-911

Great Britain in World War II: on eve of war, 890-901; answers first German peace offer, 915; alliance with Turkey, 917; and Norway, 920-925; and France, 929-930, 948-949; Battle of Britain, 937-943; and Greece, 958, 960-961, 962, 970; and Syria, 964-966; and Iraq, 965; and Russia, 967; and Italy, 967-969; and Japan, 976-977, 981; and United States, 984-987

Great Britain, treaties with: Egypt, 820; France, 129-130, 565, 579; Germany, 565, 579; Iraq, 827; Italy, 565, 579, 584; Japan, 200, 265; Persia, 828; Russia, 212-213, 281-282, 619, 694, 704

Great Circle shipping route, 986

Great Illusion, The, 359

Great Wall of China, 847, 855

Greater East Asia program, 976

Greco-Italian clash (1923), 639-640

Greco-Serbian alliance (1913), 351

Greece: before 1914, 252, 314, 321, 323-326, 327, 332, 347-354, 370; World War I, 407, 430-432; the peace settlement, 504, 505, 506-509; downfall of the monarchy, 786-787; the republic, 788-791; restoration of the monarchy, 791-792; refugee problem, 788-789; treaties, 351, 568, 639, 790; alliance with Britain and France, 891; attacked by Italy, 956-957; conquered by Axis powers, 960-961

Greek Orthodox Church in Russia, 237-238, 616-617

Greenland, 218, 945 n., 986

Greenwood, 925

Grévy, 107, 116

Grey, 89, 90, 135, 203, 211-212, 343, 350, 368, 371, 372, 378, 379, 384

Griffith, 714, 715

Grodno, 404

Guadalajara, 743

Guchkov, 275, 440, 442

Gudbrandsdaal, 924

Guesde, 120, 121

Guinea, 114

Gustavus V of Sweden, 220

Haakon VII of Norway, 219, 923, 924 n., 925

Haase, 465

Habbania, 965

Habsburg empire: see Austria-Hungary

Hacha, 886, 887, 888

Hague, The, 926

Hague Court, 134, 360-361, 378, 518

Hague Peace Conference: first, 360, 364; second, 364

Haifa, 506, 826, 964

Haig, 459

Haile Selassie, 644, 646, 968

Hailun-Taheiho Railway, 852

Hainan, 972

Hainisch, 766

Haiphong, 980

Haldane, 90, 203, 370

Halicz, 399

Halifax, 868 n., 936

Hall of Mirrors, 496

Hamburg, 470, 494, 582, 940

Hangoe, 909, 914

Hankow, 841, 971, 972

Hanoi, 974, 978

Hanover, 470

Harar, 646

Harbin, 264

Harding, 512, 520

Hatay, 892

Havre, 930, 931, 942

Hegel, 243
*Heimwehr,* 773, 775
Hejaz, 430, 506, 827
Helen of Rumania, 807-808, 955
Helgoland, 188, 413, 470
Helsinki, 762, 911
Hemisphere defense, 985, 986, 987, 988
Henderson, A., 576, 705
Henderson, N., 896, 898
Henlein, 784, 871, 872, 874, 880
Hereditary Farms Law in Germany, 684
Herriot, 560, 563, 726, 728, 729
Hertling, 455-456, 462, 465
Hertz, 113
Herzegovina: see Bosnia-Herzegovina
Herzen, 243
Hess, 756, 932
Hillman, 985
Himmler, 867, 904
Hindenburg, 399, 412, 423, 453, 456, 457, 465, 664, 669, 670, 671, 689, 690
*Hindenburg,* 12
Hindenburg Line, 427, 464, 472
Hindus, 833
Hipper, 412
Hitler, 559, 576, 577, 581, 649, 655, 666-674, 676-678, 680, 686, 689, 864, 865, 867-868, 869-870, 873-880, 888, 889, 890, 891, 892, 895, 896, 897, 898, 900, 901, 914-915, 922, 925, 926, 932, 935-936, 950, 951, 952, 953, 956, 957, 958, 959, 960 n., 961, 962, 964, 965, 966, 967, 981, 982, 988
Hitler-Ludendorff *Putsch,* 655
Hitler Youth, 677, 682
Hlond, 906
Hoare, 819
Hodža, 873, 876
Hogland, 909
Hohenlohe, 78
Holland: see Netherlands
Holstein, 92, 131
Home rule: see Irish home rule
Hongkong, 22, 859, 972, 977, 981
*Hood,* 945 n.
Hoover, 426, 521, 560, 567, 571, 573-574; moratorium, 556, 559, 705
Hopei, 855, 856, 858, 859, 971, 975 n.
Hore-Belisha, 919
Horthy, 777-778, 870, 960 n.
Hötzendorf, 311-312, 339, 386
House, 98, 375, 418-419, 478, 489
Hsiao-liang: see Chang Hsiao-liang
Hsinching, 846; see also Changchun
Hsueh-liang: see Chang Hsueh-liang
Hudson, 522
Hughes, 522
Hull, 977, 978, 986

Hulutao, 844
Humbert I of Italy, 156
Hungary: in the Dual Monarchy, 287, 288, 289, 291, 301-312; the peace settlement, 503-505; People's Republic, 775-776; soviet regime, 776-777; attempted Habsburg restoration, 777-778; political history after 1922, 778-780; economic problems, 779; nationalism in, 863; takes parts of Czechoslovakia, 880-881, 889; takes part of Rumania, 954-955; joins Axis, 957; takes part of Yugoslavia, 960 n.
Hussein, 817
Hymans, 478

Iceland, 218, 924, 945 n.
*Il Duce,* 631; see also Mussolini
*Il Popolo d'Italia,* 627, 630
Imbros, 506, 508, 509
Imperialism: revival of interest in, 14-27; Austro-Hungarian, 292-294, 338-344, 362; Belgian, 222-223; British, 164-167, 179-180, 182-183, 187-193, 817-820, 824-828, 829-830, 830-835; Dutch, 221; French, 112-114, 127, 129-136, 821-822; German, 71-75, 78-86, 362; Italian, 152-156, 162-163, 362, 639-649; Japanese, 262-264, 265-269, 842-860; Portuguese, 231; Russian, 232-235, 245-253, 262-269, 281-283, 340-343, 362, 853-855; Spanish, 228, 733-734; as cause of World War II, 863-864
Independence Party in Hungary before 1914, 304-306
India, 84, 166, 179, 401, 429, 831-835, 918, 965, 967
India Act, Government of: (1919), 831-832; (1935), 834-835
Indo-China, 22, 950, 972, 973, 974, 978-980, 981, 982
Industrialism, 3-13; Austria-Hungary, 290; Belgium, 222; Denmark, 217-218; France, 124-125; Germany, 61-62, 77, 662-663; Great Britain, 167-168, 196, 691-692, 699, 708; Italy, 139-140, 147-148, 638; Japan, 22, 844; Russia, 259-262, 608, 610-611, 612, 613; Spain, 228-229; Sweden, 220; Switzerland, 226
Inner Mongolia: see Mongolia
Insurgents, in Spain: see Nationalists
International anarchy, 361-362, 866
International Labor Organization, 519-520
International Settlement in Shanghai, 858
International Workingman's Association, 39-40, 618

Invergordon, 874, 877
Ionian Islands, 324
Ionian Sea, 956
Iran: see Persia
Iraq, 530-531, 536, 537, 816, 827-828, 952, 964, 966
Ireland: in the United Kingdom, 172-174; Church of, 174, 176
Irish Free State: treaty, 714-715; constitution (1922), 715-716; constitution (1936), 720; Cosgrave government, 715-718; De Valera government, 718-720
Irish home-rule bills, 183-184, 209-211, 713
Irish land acts, 176, 181, 186-187
Irish Nationalists, 172, 174, 180, 183-184, 207, 209-211
Irish Republic, 713
Irkutsk, 592
Iron Guard in Rumania, 809, 810, 953, 955
Isabella II of Spain, 227
Ishtip, 347
Isonzo, 403, 413, 414, 415, 434
Istanbul: see Constantinople
Istria, 287, 309, 402, 502
*Italia Irredenta,* 151-152, 159-160, 388, 402, 419, 863
Italian East Africa, 646, 967-968
Italian Somaliland, 155, 646, 968
Italy before 1914: conditions in 1870, 139-142; the Roman question, 143-144; government of Depretis and Crispi, 145-156; era of Giolitti, 156-163; economic progress, 139-140, 144-145, 147-149; emigration, 150; imperialism, 152-156, 162-163, 362; irredentism, 151-152, 159-160
Italy after 1914: World War I, 387-388, 402-403, 413-415, 434-436, 459-460, 464; the peace settlement, 500-502, 506; disarmament, 570-572, 573-576, 584-585; background of Fascism, 623-628; fascistization of the government, 629-630, 632, 633; Fascist Party organization, 631; the corporative system, 632-635; settlement of the Roman question, 635-636; postwar economic problems, 624-626, 636-639; postwar international relations, 639-641; conquest of Ethiopia, 642-649, 866-867; the Spanish civil war, 742-745; rapprochement with Germany, 865; militarism in, 866; agreements with Britain (1938), 870; takes part in Munich conference, 877-878; wants French territory, 881; conquers Albania, 889-890

Italy in World War II: on eve of war, 893, 900; enters war, 930; armistice with France, 932, 933; attacks Greece, 956-957; takes parts of Yugoslavia, 960 n.; fights British in North Africa, 967-970; assets in U.S. frozen, 988; closes American consulates, 988; consulates in U.S. closed, 988
Italy, treaties with: Albania, 641, 799; Austria, 582; Austria-Hungary, 68-69, 152-153, 161; France, 129, 565, 579, 580-581; Germany, 68-69, 152-154, 565, 579, 582, 688; Great Britain, 154, 155, 565, 579, 584; Greece, 639; Hungary, 582; Japan, 688; the papacy, 635-636; Rumania, 70; Russia, 161, 619; Yugoslavia, 582-583, 640
Ivangorod, 404
Ivanov, 439
Ivory Coast, 114
Izmir: see Smyrna
Izvolsky, 281-283, 340-343, 372

Jaffa, 430, 826
Jagow, 382
Jamaica, 984
Jameson raid, 190, 191
Janina, 348, 350, 352, 639, 961
Japan: modernization of, 22; war with China (1894–1895), 263-264; alliance with Great Britain, 199-200, 265; war with Russia, 267-269; World War I, 389, 400, 837; the peace settlement, 490, 537; the Washington Conference, 839-840; and London naval treaties, 570-572, 584; in Manchuria, 842-844; and Manchukuo, 844-847; and the League of Nations, 847-852; and Soviet Russia, 852-855; and North China, 855-860; anticommunism treaty, 582, 687, 688, 865; extends war on China, 971-981; opposed by U.S., 973, 975, 978, 981; opposed by U.S.S.R., 973; gets bases in Indo-China, 980; signs alliance with Germany and Italy, 980; signs nonaggression pact with U.S.S.R., 981-982
Jassy, 418
Jaurès, 120, 121, 126, 137-138
*Jeanne d'Arc,* 949 n.
Jehol, 847
Jerusalem, 430, 825, 826
Jesuits, 58, 112, 738
Jewish Agency in Palestine, 825
Jews: Germany, 669, 674-676; Palestine, 824-826; Poland, 751-752; Rumania, 318-319, 806; Russia, 258-259, 279

Jibuti, 114, 127, 128, 155, 580, 864, 881, 933, 967, 968
Jibuti–Addis Ababa railway, 968
Joffre, 372, 397, 411, 428
Johannesburg, 190
Johnson Act, 561
Jorga, 808
Juan, Prince, 885
Junkers, 56, 654
Jutland, 412-413

Kabul, 234
Kahr, 655
Kaiser: see William II
Kaiser Wilhelmsland, 74
Kai-shek: see Chiang Kai-shek
Kalgan, 859
Kamenev, 444, 604, 605, 607
Kamerun, 74, 81, 114, 136, 188, 401, 537, 936 n., 950
Kandalaksha, 912
Kang Teh, 845 n.; see also Pu-yi
Kapp-Lüttwitz Putsch, 654
Kara George, 327
Karageorgevich dynasty, 327, 328
Karelian-Finnish Soviet Socialist Republic, 912 n.
Karelian Isthmus, 910, 912
Karelian Soviet Republic, 912 n.
Karlsbad program, 872
Karolyi, 775, 776
Kars, 248, 252, 451
Kattegat, 924
Kauffmann, 234
Kaunas: see Kovno
Kavalla, 352
Kazakstan, 611
Keitel, 932
Kellogg, 522, 566, 848 n.
Kellogg-Briand pact: see Paris, pact of
Kemal, 507, 813-815
Kemijaervi, 910, 912
Kent, 942
Kenya Colony, 187, 967, 968
Kerensky, 281, 439, 442, 444-448
Kerrl, 680
Khan: see Riza Khan
Khiva, 234
Kiangsu, 971
Kiaochow, 79, 389, 400, 490, 837
Kiderlen, 134
Kiel, 470
Kiel Canal, 494, 686
Kiev, 591
Kirk Kilissé, 348, 352
Kirov, 607
Kishinev, 259
Kitchener, 128, 188, 192, 390

Klausener, 689
Knox, 985
Knudsen, 985
Koivisto, 911
Kokand, 234
Kolokol, 243
Kolonialzeitung, 73
Kondylis, 791
Konia, 83, 84, 504
Königsberg, 399
Konoye, 976
Korea, 24, 200, 262, 263, 265, 267, 269
Korfanty, 528
Koritza, 956
Kornilov, 446
Kossova, 348
Kossuth, 304
Kovno, 404, 758, 759
Koweit, 85
Kowloon, 977
Kramář, 478
Krofta, 886
Kruger, 190, 191, 192
Kruger telegram, 79, 190-191
Kulaks, 280, 602, 608, 609, 611
Kulturkampf, 58-59, 60-61
Kumanova, 347
Kun, Bela, 776, 777
Kunming, 974, 978
Kuolajaervi, 912
Kuomintang, 836, 841
Kurdistan, 506
Kuropatkin, 268
Kut-el-Amara, 409, 429
Kuusinen, 909
Kwangchowan, 264, 859
Kwangsi, 974
Kwangtung, 974
Kwantung, 975 n.
Kweilin, 974
Kweisui, 859

La Bassée, 458
Labor legislation, 63-65, 125, 126, 158, 186, 204, 205, 297, 520, 632-633, 682-683, 694, 701, 703
Labrador, 165
Labriola, 150
Laconia, 425
Ladoga, Lake, 909, 912, 914
La Fère, 458
Laidoner, 531
Lancashire, 168, 174
Landtag in Prussia, 94
Lansdowne, 132
Lansing, 478
Laon, 428
Laos, 26, 113, 981

Lassalle, 59
Lateran treaties, 635-636
Latvia, 257, 505, 759, 760-762, 894, 908
Lausanne: treaty (1912), 162; treaty
(1923), 507-509, 530, 639; reparations
treaty (1932), 558; "gentlemen's agreement" (1932), 559
Laval, 580, 728, 730, 945, 946, 950, 951
Law, Bonar, 478, 544, 695, 696
Law of Syndical Unity, in Spain, 885
Lawrence, 430
League of Nations: Covenant, 481-483,
490, 514-517, 522-524; structure, 515-
517; and the peace treaties (1918), 486,
487-488, 489-490, 494, 499, 505, 506,
509, 510; the mandatory system, 536-
537; the minorities treaties, 537-538;
humanitarian work, 538-539; national
security, 562-564; Austria, 766-768,
769; Danzig, 754-757; Greece, 788;
Hungary, 779; Palestine, 826-827; Rumania, 809; the Saar, 532-536; Åland
Islands dispute, 524-525; Vilna dispute, 525-527; Memel dispute, 527;
Upper Silesian dispute, 528-529; Albanian dispute, 529-530; Mosul dispute, 530-531; Greco-Italian dispute,
639-640; Greco-Bulgarian clash, 802-
803; Yugoslav-Hungarian crisis, 796-
797; Italo-Ethiopian war, 642-644, 647-
649, 866; Sino-Japanese clashes, 845,
847-852, 859-860, 866; Germany's re-
armament, 577-578; unsatiated powers
withdraw, 866; Spain withdraws, 886;
expels Soviet Union, 910; Rumania
withdraws, 953
League of Patriots in France, 116-117
League of the Three Emperors, 66-67, 246
Lease-Lend Bill (Act), 985-986
Lebanon, 536, 537, 821-822, 966
Lebrun, 731
Leghorn, 145
Legion of Honor, 116, 120
Legitimists: in France, 103, 104, 105, 118;
in Hungary, 778, 780
Leicester, 199
Leipzig, 470, 494
Leipzig, 744
Lemberg, 301, 399, 747; see also Lwow
Lenin, 270, 275-276, 443-444, 445, 447,
448, 450, 598, 615, 619
Leningrad, 590, 864, 894, 909, 914; see
also St. Petersburg and Petrograd
Leninsk, 443
Lens, 465
Leo XIII, 60, 118
Leopold II of Belgium, 20, 188, 222-223
Leopold III of Belgium, 583, 928, 936 n.

Leopold of Hohenzollern-Sigmaringen,
227
Leroy-Beaulieu, 113
Lesseps, 179
Lester, 757
Ley, 906
L'Humanité, 121
Liao-tung peninsula, 263, 264, 269
Liaoyang, 268
Libau, 569, 908
Liberia, 21
Liberty Loans, 426
Libya, 508, 580, 933, 969, 970
Liebknecht, K., 466, 656
Liebknecht, W., 59
Liége, 225, 396
Liepaja: see Libau
Lille, 931
Lindbergh, 12
Linlithgow, 836
Linotype, 46
Linz, 869
Lissa, 501
Lister, 29
Lithuania (Lithuanians), 258, 273, 450,
489, 505, 525-527, 757-759, 889, 908
Little Entente, 568, 583, 649, 769, 777-
778, 870, 886
Litvinov, 895
Livenza, 435
Liverpool, 940, 943
Livingstone, 16, 17, 20
Livonia, 450
Ljubiana, 960 n.
Lloyd George, 135, 203, 455, 477, 478,
480, 484, 485, 487, 490, 493, 498, 530,
564, 693-695, 696, 698, 706, 714;
budget (1909), 205-207
Locarno treaties, 565, 577-578, 620, 866
Lodge, 512
Lodz, 904, 906
London: declaration of (1909), 408;
treaty of (1913), 350-351; pact of
(1914), 385, 403; treaty of (1915),
402, 500; economic conference (1932),
559 n.; treaty of (1936), 820; as a
commercial and banking center, 169;
Anglo-French military conference
(1938), 870-871; Anglo-French conference on Sudeten crisis, 875; air-raid
precautions (1939), 916; as shipping
center, 940; bombed, 941-943
London Daily Telegraph incident, 95
Lords, House of, in Great Britain, 170,
207-208
Loubet, 119, 160
Louis I of Portugal, 230
Lower Austria, 287, 290, 502, 772

Loyalists, in Spain, 742-744, 882-883
Lübeck, 470
Lublin, 906
Ludendorff, 399, 412, 423, 453, 456, 459, 460, 461, 655, 667
Lüderitz, 74
Lule Burgas, 348
Lulea, 912
Lung-hai railway, 971
Lupescu, 808, 955
*Lusitania,* 408-409
Lutsk, 414
Lüttwitz, 654
Luxemburg, 222, 383, 396, 486, 494, 496, 926, 927
Luxemburg, R., 466, 656
Lvov, Prince, 440, 446
Lwow, 903, 907
Lyons, 125
Lytton Commission, 849
Lytton Report, 849-850

Maas: see Meuse
Macao, 859
MacDonald, M., 710
MacDonald, R., 563, 571-572, 620, 697-699, 703-710
Macedonia, 248, 315, 332-333, 337, 347, 348, 352, 406, 788-789; revolutionary movement in, 801, 802-804
McKenna Committee, 548
Mackensen, 404, 406, 417
MacMahon, 105, 107, 109
Madagascar, 114
*Made in Germany,* 195
Madrid: conference (1880), 131; in civil war, 742, 743, 882, 883
Mafia, 140, 146
Magdeburg, 470
Maginot Line, 873, 903, 919, 929, 930
Magnitogorsk, 611
Magyarization, 303-305
Magyars, 286, 287, 301-307, 464
Mainz, 495
Majuba Hill, 182
Makale, 645
Malay states, 26
Maleme, 962
Malmédy, 486, 927
Malta, 643
Manchukuo, 844-847, 853, 854, 855, 856, 865, 973, 974, 980, 982
Manchuria, 91, 198, 262, 264, 265, 267, 268, 269, 281, 842-844, 866
Mandates Commission, 821, 826, 827
Mandatory system, 489-490, 506, 536-537
Manila, 80, 977
Maniu, 807, 808

Mannerheim, 762, 911 n.
Mannerheim Line, 910, 911, 912, 914
Manuel II of Portugal, 230
March on Rome, 629
Marchand, 128
Marconi, 13
Marianne Islands, 80
Marie of Rumania, 808
Marienwerder, 487, 488, 489
Maritime Commission, U.S., 986-987
Maritza, 348
Markajaervi, 912
Marne, 388, 397, 459, 460-461, 930
Marquet, 947 n.
Marseillaise, 110
Marseilles, 194
Marx, K., 38-40, 59, 120, 150
Marx, W., 664
Masaryk, 298, 310, 462, 463, 781, 784
Massaua, 155, 968
Matchek, 797, 959
Matsuoka, 851, 976, 981
Matteotti, 630
Maude, 429-430
Max of Baden, 465, 468, 471, 472
May Committee, 705
May Laws, 58, 60
Mazzini, 139
Mecca, 430
Medicine, 29
Mediterranean, 952, 961, 964, 967, 969
*Mein Kampf,* 667, 687, 956
Melikov, 253
Memel, 489, 527, 758-759, 863, 889
Menelik, 155
Mensheviks (*Mensheviki*), 270-271, 275, 441, 442
Mesopotamia, 83, 429, 506
Metaxas, 791
Meuse River, 926, 927
Meuse-Argonne offensive, 472
Mexico, 423
Mézières, 927
Miaja, 883
Michael, Grand Duke of Russia, 439-440
Michael: Prince of Rumania, 807; King (V), 955
Michael Obrenovich, 327
Middle Eastern Entente, 816
Mihailov, 796, 804
Miklas, 869
Milan Obrenovich, 327-328
Militarism, 363-365, 866; see also Preparedness
Miliukov, 275, 440, 441-442
Millerand, 120, 121, 725-726
Milner, 191
Milosh Obrenovich, 327

Minorities treaties, 504-505, 508, 510, 537-538
*Mir,* 236, 239, 240, 280
Mirsky, 272, 273
*Mittel-Europa,* 82, 83, 409, 418, 464, 864
Mittelhauser, 964
Mobilization in World War I, 380, 381-382, 384, 390-392
Moerdiik, 926
Mohammed V of Turkey, 345
Mohammed Ahmed of the Sudan, 183
Moldavia, 234, 316, 418; see also Bessarabia
Molotov, 895, 952
Moltke, H. J. L. von, 381, 382
Moltke, H. K. B. von, 53
Monastir, 347, 348, 352, 406
Mongolia: Inner, 845, 847, 854, 975 n.; Outer, 24, 853, 854, 973, 974
Mongolian People's Republic, 854, 982
Monroe Doctrine, 483, 985
Mons, 397
Montagu-Chelmsford Report, 830-831
Montdidier, 459, 461
Montenegro, 161, 242, 252, 314, 330, 332, 347, 349-354, 374, 406, 959
Montevideo, 917
Montgolfier, 11
Montmédy, 927, 929
Montreux conference: (1936), 816; (1937), 820-821
Moore, 522
Moravia, 287, 290, 298, 402, 781
Moresnet, 486, 927
Morley, 202
Morocco, 81, 129-136, 211, 367-368, 369-370, 950; Spanish, 136, 733-734, 742
Moscow, 618, 894, 895, 896, 908, 909, 981
Moselle River, 927
Mosul, 463, 506, 530-531, 964, 965, 966
Moszicki, 749, 904
"Movies," 46
Mozambique, 81, 189
Mudania, 507
Mukden, 268, 843, 844, 845
Müller, H., 496, 666
Müller, L., 679, 680
Munich, 470, 652, 875, 878, 932, 954
Munich agreement, 878
Municipal Corporations Act in Great Britain, 182
Murmansk, 589, 763, 910, 912, 921 n.
Murray, 430
Mürsteg program, 337
Muselier, 947
Mussolini, 163, 579, 581, 626-630, 633, 634, 635, 636, 637, 638, 639, 640, 641,

646, 687, 772, 773, 774, 864, 865, 866, 870, 877, 878, 881, 889, 890, 900, 930, 932, 945, 956, 958, 960 n., 967, 981
Mustapha Kemal: see Kemal
Mutsuhito, 22
Mutual assistance, proposed treaty of, 563

Nahas, 819, 820
Namsos, 924
Namur, 225, 396, 927
Nancy, 460
Nanking, 841, 845, 847, 855, 856, 857, 858, 971, 975
Nankow Pass, 859
Nanning, 974
Naples, 957
Napoleon III, 99, 118
Narew River, 904
*Narodniki,* 244-245
Narvik, 921, 922, 923
Natal, 165, 204
National aspirations in 1914: Bulgaria, 366; France, 366; Greece, 366; Italy, 366; Rumania, 366; Serbia, 366
National Assembly in France, 99-102, 104-106, 945
National Council of Corporations in Italy, 634
National Defense Advisory Commission, in U.S., 985
National Defense society in Serbia, 375
National Exchange Institute in Italy, 638
National Guard, in U.S., 984
National Socialists: Germany, 666-669, 671-690; Austria, 770-772; Danzig, 756-757; Memel, 758-759; Rumania, 810; the Saar, 535
National Union Party, in Rumania, 953
Nationalism: a cause of World War I, 366-367; a cause of World War II, 863
Nationalists, in Spain, 882-886
Nauru, 537
Naval engagements: in World War I, 400, 401, 412-413; in World War II, 917, 923, 945, 949, 957
Navalism: in Germany, 78, 86-91; in Great Britain, 89, 187, 213-214
Navy League in Germany, 78, 93
Nazareth, 826
Nazis: see National Socialists
Near East, 83-86, 179-180, 182, 245-253, 292-294, 313-354, 368-369, 370-371, 813-828
Negrín, 883
Nep, 601, 603
Nepal, 26
Nep-men, 603, 608, 609

Netherlands, 220-222, 926, 927, 936 n.
Netherlands East Indies, 973, 977-978, 982
Nettuno convention, 640, 794
Neuilly, treaty of, 504
Neurath, 868, 888
Neutrality Act (U.S.): (1937), 918, 983; (1939), 918-919, 983
Neutrality patrol, 986
New Guinea, 74
"New order": in Europe, 950, 957, 980; in "Greater East Asia," 957, 980
New Zealand, 165, 192, 401, 489-490, 537, 918, 919, 960, 961
Newall, 916
Newfoundland, 165, 938 n., 984
Newspapers, 46
Nice, 863, 881
Nicholas, Grand Duke of Russia, 404
Nicholas, Prince of Rumania, 808, 810
Nicholas of Montenegro, 330
Nicholas II of Russia, 92, 254, 272, 273, 276, 322, 364, 374, 437, 439-440
Niemen, internationalized, 494
Niemöller, 680, 681
Niger River, 114
Nigeria, 187
Nihilists, 244, 254
Nine-power treaty, 839-840, 859-860
Nish, 339, 406, 464
Nitti, 502
Nivelle, 428, 429
Nobel, 360
Noghelli, 645
Non Expedit, 143
Non Licet, 144, 158
Nonintervention committee for Spain, 743-745
Norddeutsche Allgemeine Zeitung, 93
North Africa, 966, 967, 969, 970
North German Confederation, 53
North Manchuria Railway, 853
Northern Ireland: see Ulster
Norway, 50, 218-220, 910, 911 n., 912, 920-925, 943
Novibazar, 253, 293, 308, 314, 339, 341, 352, 369, 406, 464
Nowogrodek, 907
Noyon, 459, 461
Nuremberg, 873
Nyasaland, 187
Nyon conference, 744

Obrenovich dynasty, 327-328
Ochrida, Lake, 961
O'Connell, 174
October manifesto, 274

Octobrists: in tsarist Russia, 274, 277, 278, 279, 440; in Soviet Russia, 599
Oder, internationalized, 494
Odessa, 194, 390, 590
Oesel, 894 n., 908
Office of Production Management for Defense, in U.S., 985
Ogpu, 599
O'Higgins, 715, 717
Okhrida, 347
Old Catholics, 58
Old Czechs, 298
Olsa River, 880
Olympus, Mount, 961
Omsk, 592
OPM, 985
Opolu, 81
Optional clause of World Court protocol, 518
Oran, 933, 949, 951
Orange Free State, 165, 191, 192, 204
Oriental Railway, 83
Orlando, 478, 480, 481, 500, 501, 502
Orleanists, 103, 104, 105, 106, 118
Osborne judgment, 208
Oscar II of Sweden, 219
Oslo, 922, 923, 924
Ostend, 397, 942
Osterdaal, 924
Ostmark, 880; see also Austria
Ottawa conference, 707-708
Otto I of Greece, 323
Otto of Habsburg, 778, 780
Ottoman Empire: see Turkey
O.V.R.A. in Italy, 630
Owen, 36-37

Pacifism, 357-361
Paderewski, 462, 478
Painlevé, 428
Palatinate, Autonomous Government of the, 655-656
Pale, Jewish, in Russia, 258
Palestine, 430, 506, 536, 537; under mandate, 824-827; plan for the partition of, 826; in World War II, 918, 964, 966
Palmerston, 175
Panama Canal, 11; scandal, 118
Pangalos, 788
Pan-German League, 78-79, 82, 87, 93
Pan-Germanists, 433, 651, 654, 864
Pan-Hellenism, 326, 332, 370
Pan-Serbianism, 308-309, 332-333
Pan-Slavism, 98, 282, 300, 342
Pantellara, 643
Panther, 135
Panzer divisions, 903, 961, 970
Paotou, 975

Papacy, relations of: France, 122-123; Germany, 58-59, 60; Italy, 143-144, 635-636; Portugal, 231; Spain, 738
Papal Guarantees, Law of, 143
Papen, 424-425, 670, 671, 689
Parachute troops, 926, 962
Paris, 99, 397, 459, 460-461; pact of, 566-567; treaty of, 246, 316; in World War II, 916, 930, 932, 936 n.
Paris, Count of, 103, 105, 118
Paris peace conference, 477-513
Parliament Act (1911) in Great Britain, 207-208
Parnell, 180, 183
Pashich, 328, 330, 374, 462, 478, 530, 793, 794
Passchendaele Ridge, 429
Pasteur, 29
Pastors' Emergency League, 680
Patrimony of St. Peter, 139
Patriotic Youth in France, 729
Paul, Prince of Yugoslavia, 797, 958, 959
Paul-Boncour, 729
Pavelich, 960 n.
Peace movement: see Pacifism
Peace proposals: of the Central Powers (1916), 419-420; of Hitler (1939), 914-915; of Hitler (1940), 935-936
Peel, 175
Peiping, 22, 23, 841, 847, 856, 857, 858, 859, 971; see also Peking
Peiping Political Council, 847
Peking, 836, 837, 840, 841; see also Peiping
Pelew Islands, 80
Peloponnesus, 961
Pemba, 188
Permanent Court of Arbitration: see Hague Court
Permanent Court of International Justice: see World Court
Péronne, 465, 928
Persia, 26, 86, 212, 261-262, 816, 828-830
Persian Gulf, 83, 84, 86, 429, 965
Pétain, 411, 428, 429, 458, 730, 931, 933, 934, 945, 948, 950, 951, 952
Peter I of Serbia, 308, 328, 329
Peter II of Yugoslavia, 797, 959
Petrich, 802
Petrograd, 437, 438, 439, 441, 446, 448; see also St. Petersburg and Leningrad
Petsamo, 910, 911, 912
Philippine Islands, 26, 228, 973
"Phony" war, 914-920
Physiocrats, 33
Piatiletka, 608
Piave, 435, 460, 464

Piccole Italiane, 631
Pichon, 478
Picquart, 119
Pig war, 308-309, 330
Pilsudski, 749, 750, 751
Pinsk, 404
Pioneers (Communist), 599
Pius IX, 58, 143-144
Pius X, 122
Pius XI, 635-636
Plastiras, 790
Plebiscites: Allenstein, 488-489; Eupen, 486; German West Hungary, 503 n.; Malmédy, 486; Marienwerder, 488-489; Moresnet, 486; the Saar, 534-536; Schleswig, 486
Pledge plan in the 1914 crisis, 380
Plehve, 255, 272
Plekhanov, 270
Plevna, 248
Ploesti oil fields, 956
Plymouth, 940
Pobiedonostsev, 254-255, 274
Podestas, 629
Poglavnik (leader), 960 n.
Pogroms, 259, 276
Poincaré, 136-137, 349, 370, 372, 544, 545, 546, 564, 722, 725, 727
Pola, 500, 501
Poland: before 1914, 242, 243, 257-258; during World War I, 404, 419, 450; and the peace settlement, 486-489, 502, 505, 525-527, 528, 529; problem of boundaries, 486-488, 525-529, 746-747; political history, 747-751; minorities problem, 538, 751-753, 863; economic progress, 753-754; treaties, 564-566, 568-569, 579, 583, 684, 747, 754, 756; takes part of Czechoslovakia, 880; guaranteed by Britain and France, 891; German pressure on, 892-893, 896-900; conquered by Germany, 900-903; partition of, 903-907
Poles: in Austria-Hungary, 295, 300-301; in Germany, 96; in Russia, 272, 273, 276, 279
Polesia, 907
Polish Corridor, 487-489, 863, 892, 893, 896
Polish National Committee during World War I, 462
Pomerania, 94, 902, 904
Pomorze: see Pomerania
Popolo d'Italia, Il, 627, 630
Popular Front: in France, 731-733, 875 n., 946; in Spain, 741-742, 884
Population: growth of, 28-30, 260; urbanization of, 30-31

Port Arthur, 263, 264, 265, 267, 268, 269
Port Baros, 640
Port Said, 820
Portela, 741
Portland, 941
Portsmouth, treaty of, 269
Portugal, 26, 80-81, 230-231, 937, 987
Posen, 488, 904
*Potemkin,* 273
Potsdam, 85
Pound, 916
Poznan: see Posen
Prague, 291, 295, 296, 299, 461, 873
Preparedness for World War I: Austro-Hungarian, 312, 373; Belgian, 225; British, 368, 371-372; French, 136-138, 372; German, 98, 373; Italian, 373; Russian, 283, 372; see also Armaments and Navalism
Preparedness for World War II: in Europe, 866; in U.S., 984
Pribram, 284
*Prince of Wales,* 945 n.
Pripet marshes, 404
Prisrend, 406
Proletariat, 32, 34, 35
Propaganda in World War I, 392-393, 424, 463, 467
Protectorate of Bohemia and Moravia, 888
Protogerov, 804
Proudhon, 40-41, 243
Provisional French National Committee, 947
Prussia, 55-56, 58
Przemysl, 399
Punjab, 831
Pu-yi, 845, 975; see also Kang Teh
Pyrenees, 943

Quisling, 922, 923, 925

Rabbit Islands, 508
Racconigi, 161, 369
Raczkiewicz, 904 n.
Radich, 793, 794
Radio, 13, 46
Radom, 906
Raeder, 932
Ragusa, 501
Rainbow books, 392
Rapallo, 436; treaty (1920), 502, 623; treaty (1922), 619-620, 659
Rashid Ali Beg Gailani, 965
Rasputin, 437
Rathenau, 655
Rault, 533
*Rawalpindi,* 917
*Rayahs,* 246

Rearmament: see Armaments
Red Army, 590, 967
Red Cross, 436
Red Sea, 968, 969
Red Terror, 590
Redistribution Act in Great Britain, 181
Redmond, 210
Reform Act in Great Britain: second, 171; third, 181
Refrigeration, 15, 45
Reichsbank, 57, 656, 658
Reichsmark, 658
Reichsrat: Austrian, 288, 299, 301, 461, 463; German, 653, 677
Reichstadt, 247, 293
Reichstag: in German Empire, 54; in German Republic, 653
Reichstag building fire, 672
Reims, 459, 460
Reinsurance treaty (German-Russian), 71
*Rentier* class in France, 127
Reparations, 492-494, 502, 504, 540-549, 551-559; British attitude toward, 543; French attitude toward, 543-547
Reparations Commission, 493, 513, 540, 541, 544, 545, 547, 548, 549, 558
Representation of the People Act in Great Britain, 693-694
Rethel, 927
Reval, 569
*Revanche,* 103, 112-113, 116
Revisionism, 579, 779
Reynaud, 920, 927, 930, 946, 948
Rhine, internationalized, 494
Rhineland, 483-486, 495, 554, 577-578, 655-656, 660, 865, 866, 867, 942
Rhiza Khan, 828
Rhodes, 352, 506, 508
Rhodes, C., 190
Rhodesia, 187
Ribbentrop, 578, 867, 868, 898, 899, 904, 932, 954
*Richelieu,* 949
Riga, 569, 747
Rivera, 734-735
Rivet law in France, 102, 104
*Robin Moor,* 988
Robles: see Gil Robles
Rocque, de la, 730
Rodzianko, 437, 438
Röhm, 689
Rohrbach, 85
Romagna, 163
Roman question, 143-144; settlement of, 635-636
Rome, treaty of (1924), 640
Rome-Berlin Axis, 688, 865, 867, 870, 877
Rome-Berlin-Tokyo Axis, 865

Roon, 53
Roosevelt, F. D., 877, 930, 938 n., 983, 985, 986, 987
Roosevelt, T., 269
Root, 517, 521
Rotterdam, 221, 926
Rouen, 930, 931
Rouvier, 132
Royal Air Force, 940, 941, 942, 943
Royalists in France, 103-104, 115-120
Rozhestvensky, 268
R.S.F.S.R., 592, 593-595; see also Russia, Soviet
Ruandi-Urundi, 537
Ruhr, 541, 545-547, 656, 916, 942
Ruhrort, 541
Rumania: before 1914, 249, 252, 313, 316-319, 331, 352; and World War I, 388-389, 416-418, 453; and the peace settlement, 502, 505, 805-806; political history after 1918, 806, 807-810; agrarian reform, 806-807; on eve of World War II, 891, 918; partition of, 952, 953-955; becomes totalitarian, 953; occupied by Germany, 956; joins Axis, 957; mobilizes, 966; joins Germany in war on Russia, 967
Rumania, treaties with: the Allies, 416-417; Austria-Hungary, 70, 294; Czechoslovakia, 567, 880; France, 566, 881; Germany, 70; Greece, 568; Italy, 70; Poland, 569, 579; Russia, 579, 809; Turkey, 568; Yugoslavia, 568
Rumanians in Austria-Hungary, 303, 304, 307, 331, 464
Rumelia, 247; see also Eastern Rumelia
Runciman, 873, 874, 875
Rupprecht, 433
Russia, Soviet: the Bolshevik revolution, 442-449; peace of Brest-Litovsk, 449-451; White plots and intervention, 589-591; political structure, 591-598; constitution of 1936, 596-598, 614-615; Communist Party, 598-599; economic communism, 599-601; Nep, 601-603; five-year plans, 608-614; the peasants, 600-601, 611, 612, 614; intraparty conflicts, 603-606, 607; education, 615-616; religion, 616-617; foreign policy, 617-622, 840-841, 864; and the Geneva disarmament conference, 573-576, 585; rearmament, 866; end of alliance with France, 881; consults with Britain and France, 891, 894-895; nonaggression pact with Germany, 895-896; takes part of Poland, 903, 904, 907; returns to Baltic, 908-914; takes Bessarabia and northern Bukowina, 952; attacked by

Germany, 966-967; clashes with Japan, 973-974; signs nonaggression pact with Japan, 981-982
Russia, Soviet, treaties with: Austria, 619; the borderlands, 570; Czechoslovakia, 581; Estonia, 760; Finland, 763, 912-918; France, 570, 581, 881; Germany, 570, 619, 620, 659, 895-896; Great Britain, 619, 694, 704; Italy, 570, 619; Japan, 981-982; Latvia, 761; Little Entente, 570; Mongolian People's Republic, 854; Norway, 619; Poland, 579, 747; Rumania, 579, 809; Turkey, 570
Russia, tsarist: vastness of, 232-235; backwardness of (in 1855), 235-238; reign of Alexander II, 238-254; reigns of Alexander III and Nicholas II, 254-283; emancipation of the serfs, 239-240; economic conditions in, 236, 259-262, 279-280, 437; repression and Russification, 242-243, 254-259, 279; radicalism, 243-245, 253-254, 270-272, 280-281; revolution of 1905, 270-278; and the Balkans, 233-234, 245-253, 282, 340-344, 368-369; and the Far East, 198-199, 235, 262-270, 281; and World War I, 399, 403-404, 414, 436-438, 444-445, 449-451; the revolution of 1917, 436-451
Russification, 256-259, 279
Russo-Chinese Bank, 264
Russo-Japanese War, 88, 92, 267-269
Russo-Turkish War (1877-1878), 247-248
Ruthenia, 782; see also Carpatho-Ukraine
Rybachi peninsula, 909, 912
Rydz-Smigly, 751, 904
Rykov, 444, 604, 605

Saar basin, 484-485, 496, 532-536; plebiscite in, 534-536
Saar Basin Delimitation Commission, 532-534
Sabotage, 42
Safeguarding of Industries Act in Great Britain, 694-695
Sagasta, 228
Sagunto, 882
St. Germain, treaty of, 498-503
St. Lucia, 984
St. Mihiel, 464
St. Petersburg, 272, 275, 437; see also Petrograd and Leningrad
St. Quentin, 427, 927
Saint-Simon, 37
Sakhalin, 235, 269
Salandra, 163, 388, 639

Salisbury, 184, 199

Saloniki, 293, 314, 330, 339, 348, 351, 352, 406, 407, 417, 430-431, 463, 788, 956, 958, 960; Gulf of, 961

Salzburg, 287, 290

Samarkand, 234

Samoa, 81, 537

Samuel, 699, 706, 708, 824

San Remo, 506

San River, 904

San Stefano, treaty of, 67, 248-250

Sanctions, 523, 563; against Italy, 647-649

Sanders, 373

Sanjak of Alexandretta, 892

Sankey, 705

Saragossa, 882

Sarajevo, 374-375

Sarrail, 407, 417

Sarraut, 729, 730

Savoy, 863, 881

Sawai, 81

Saxony, 55

Sazonov, 283, 372, 374, 378, 379, 380

Schacht, 582, 657, 684

Scheer, 412

Scheidemann, 652

Scheldt River, 927

Schleicher, 671, 689

Schleswig, 218, 486

Schlieffen plan, 396

Schneider-Creusot works, 932

Schuschnigg, 581, 771, 774, 869

Schutzbund, 773

Schutzstaffeln, 667, 867

Schwartzenberg, 290

Scotland, 941

Scrap of paper, 385

Scutari, 161, 348, 349, 350, 889

Scutari, Lake, 161

Sea power, 962, 964, 969, 985

Second International, 40, 358, 618

Second World War: causes, 863-867; U.S. attitude toward, 982-984

Security League in Germany, 58

Sedan, 99, 472, 927

Seine River, 930

Seipel, 766

Seitz, 774

Sejm in Poland, 748

Selective Service Act in the United States (1917), 426

Selective Training and Service Act, in U.S. (1940), 984

Senate, French, 945

Separation Law in France, 123

Serbia: before 1914, 246, 252, 293, 294, 309, 314, 321, 327-330, 332, 333, 339, 342-343, 347-354, 368, 370, 374, 376, 377; and World War I, 399-400, 405-407, 463, 464, 959; see also Yugo-slavia

Serbo-Bulgarian War (1885), 321

Serfs, emancipation of, in Russia, 238-240

Sergius, 273

Seven Weeks' War: see Austro-Prussian War

Sèvres, treaty of, 505-507

Seyss-Inquart, 869, 926

Shanghai, 841, 846, 858, 859, 971, 977

Shansi, 859, 971, 975 n.

Shantung, 79, 264, 490, 840, 859, 971, 975 n.

Shensi, 857

Sherif of Mecca, 430

Shih-k'ai: see Yuan Shih-k'ai

Shihkiachwang, 859

Shimonoseki, treaty of, 263

Shipping, in World War II: British, German campaign against, 943, 986; Axis, requisitioned by U.S., 986; American, reallocated, 987

Shogun, 22

Siam, 113, 981

Sian, 857

Siberia, 279, 280, 592, 855

Sicily, 957, 970, 971

Sidi Barrani, 969

Siegfried Line, 427; see also West Wall

Siemens process, 4

Sienkiewicz, 462

Sikorski, 904 n.

Silesia, 287, 290, 502, 902

Simbirsk, 443

Simon Commission, 832-833

Simovich, 959

Singapore, 972

Sinn Fein, 713, 714

Sino-Japanese War: (1894–1895), 263; (1931–1933), 844-847; (1937), 857-860

Sixteen-point program, German, 898

Skagerrak, 923, 924

Skoropadski, 450 n.

Skupshtina in Yugoslavia, 794

Slavophiles, 256, 260

Slovak Popular Party, 886, 887

Slovakia (Slovaks), 286, 287, 303, 503, 781, 782, 783-784, 886, 887, 888, 889, 902, 957; see also Czechoslovakia

Slovenes, 286, 310

Slovenia, 960 n.

Small Holdings Act in Great Britain, 185

Smigly-Rydz, 751, 904

Smith, Adam, 33

Smuts, 478, 482, 489, 493
Smyrna, 506, 507, 624
Smyrna-Kassaba Railway, 815-816
Snowden, 705, 708
Social insurance: Austria, 297; France, 126; Germany, 63-65; Great Britain, 186, 204-205, 694, 701, 703; Italy, 158
Socialism: rise of, 35-40; Austria, 300, 765, 772-774; Belgium, 223-224; France, 120-121, 126, 731-732; Germany, 59-61, 64, 88, 93-96, 465, 470, 650, 676, 682; Great Britain, 201-202, 695, 697-699, 703-705; Italy, 150-151, 157-158, 163, 624-625; the Netherlands, 222; Russia, 270-271, 273, 275, 279, 438-439, 441-449, 589-622; Spain, 229, 736, 741; Sweden, 220
Sofia, 800, 801, 958
Soissons, 428, 459, 461
Solidarité Française, 730
Solomon Islands, 74
Solum, 970, 971
Somaliland: British, 187, 967, 968; French, 114, 580, 933, 967; Italian, 155, 646, 968
Somme, 411, 415-416, 458, 461, 928, 929
Sonnino, 478, 500, 502
Sopron, 503 n.
South Africa, Union of, 204, 489-490, 537, 936 n.
South Africa Act, 204
South African Republic: see Transvaal Republic
South Manchuria Railway, 843, 844, 852, 853
South Tirol, 893, 904
Southampton, 940, 941
Southwest Africa, German, 74, 188 n., 401 n., 536, 936 n.
Soviet of Nationalities in Russia, 593, 598
Soviet Russia: see Russia, Soviet
Soviet Union, established, 592; see also Russia, Soviet
Soviets in Russia: (1905-1906), 275-276; (1917), 438, 439, 440, 441-442, 447
Spa, 461, 465, 469, 471
Spain: before 1914, 130, 136 n., 227-230; dictatorship (1923), 733-736; republic, 736-745; elections, 736, 739, 740, 741; civil war, 581-582, 743-745; 865, 870, 882-886; Italy and, 936 n.; blockaded, 937; Germany and, 987
Spalato, 960 n.
Spanish-American War, 80, 228
Spartacists, 466, 467
Spartacus letters, 466
Speyer, 656
Spezia, 145

Splendid isolation, British, 197; abandonment of, 200
Spoleto, Duke of, 960 n.
Spratley Islands, 972
Squadristi, 627, 628, 631
Stack, 818
Stalin, 444, 603-607, 894, 966
Stambolisky, 799-800
Stambulov, 322-323
Standstill agreement, 557
Stanislawow, 907
Stanley, 20
Starhemberg, 774-775
Starzynski, 903
State farms in Russia, 608, 611, 612
Stavanger, 922
Stavisky scandal in France, 729
Steamship Subsidy Bill in Germany, 74
Štefanik, 462, 463
Stettin, 494
Stimson, 985
Stimson doctrine of the United States, 851 n.
Stolypin, 279-280, 342
Storm Troops, Nazi, 667
Straits at Constantinople, 161, 212, 233, 248, 249, 281, 340, 346, 374, 379, 390, 505, 506, 509, 816
Strasbourg, 721
Strasbourg, 949
Stresemann, 538, 547, 564, 651, 659-660
Struga, 347
Struma valley, 958, 960
Strumitsa, 352
Sturmabteilungen, 667
Stürmer, 436
Stuttgart, 470, 654
Styria, 287, 290, 772
Submarine warfare, 407-409, 423-425, 452-453, 943
Suda Bay, 962, 964
Sudan, 128, 183, 188, 508, 817, 818, 967, 968, 970
Sudeten Free Corps, 874
Sudeten German Party, 784, 871, 872, 873
Sudeten Germans, 871, 872, 873, 874, 875, 876, 878
Sudetendeutsch Party in Czechoslovakia, 784
Sudetenland, 863, 878, 880, 881
Suez Canal, 11, 179, 194, 430, 643, 817, 820, 864, 870, 964, 966, 967, 968, 969
Suffrage: see Franchise
Suiyuan, 859, 975
Sultan: of Turkey, 247-248, 334, 336-338, 344-345, 813; of Egypt, 817
Summa, 911

Sun Yat-sen, 836, 841
Sundlo, 922
Suomussalmi, 910
Supilo, 310
Supreme Council in Versailles peace settlement, 498, 526
Supreme Economic Council in Russia, 600, 610
Supreme War Council, 436
Šušak, 501 n., 960 n.
Suwalki, 526
Swastika, 667, 678
Sweden, 218-220, 524-525, 910, 911, 912
Switzerland, 225-226
Syllabus of Errors, 58
Syndicalism, 41-42; in Italy, 163; in Spain, 739, 741
Syndicates in Italy, 632-633
Syria, 83, 86, 506, 536, 537, 821-822, 892, 918, 952, 964, 965, 966
Syrian Sanjak, 892
Syrovy, 876, 886

Taafe, 297, 298
Taff Vale decision, 201
Tagliamento, 434-435
Taheiho, 852
Tanganyika, 188
Tangier, 131, 136, 367, 641
Tangku, 847
Tanks: in World War I, 429; in World War II, 902, 924, 926, 929, 933, 962, 968
Tannenberg, 399
Taranto, 145, 957
Tardieu, 478, 725, 728
Tariff Reform League in Great Britain, 196
Tarnopol, 399, 445, 907
Tartu: see Dorpat
Tashkend, 234
Tasmania, 165
Tatarescu, 810
Teh: see Kang Teh
Tel Aviv, 825
Telephone, 13
Temesvar: see Banat
Tenedos, 506, 508, 509
Terrorists in Russia, 245
Teschen, 502, 880
Thailand (Siam), 981
Thames River, 939, 940, 941
Thermopylae, 961
Thessaly, 252, 314, 324
Thiers, 100-105
Third International, 618, 621-622
Third Reich, 668; see Germany
Third Section in Russia, 255

Thomas, 705
Thomas-Gilchrist process, 5, 61, 124
Thrace, 315, 351, 352, 406, 504, 506, 788-789, 960
Tibet, 26, 212
Tientsin, 847, 855, 856, 858, 859, 971, 976
Tirana, 641, 889, 890
Tirol, 287, 290, 402, 502, 503, 893, 904
Tirpitz, 87, 90
Tiso, 887, 888
Tisza, 303, 305, 306, 307, 377, 416
Tittoni, 502
Tobruk, 969, 970, 971
Togo, 268-269
Togoland, 74, 93, 188, 400, 537
Tokyo, 845, 853, 854, 981
Tolstoi, 360
Tomsk, 592
Tomsky, 605, 607
Tonkin, 24, 26, 113
Tornea, 910
Tortosa, 882
Totalitarian state in Germany, 676-678
Toul, 383
Toulon, 933, 949
Tours, 930, 932
Townshend, 409
Toynbee, 324, 920 n.
Trade Union Act (1913) in Great Britain, 208
Trade unions, rise of, 34-35
Trades Dispute Act (1906) in Great Britain, 204, 701
Trades Disputes and Trades Union Act (1926) in Great Britain, 700-701, 703
Transcaucasus, 592
Transjordan, 536, 537, 826, 827, 966
Trans-Siberian railway, 8, 262, 264, 267, 852-853, 854
Transvaal Republic, 79, 165, 180, 182, 190-192, 204
Transylvania, 287, 291, 304, 307, 331, 388, 416, 417, 418, 503, 806, 954, 955
Trebizond, 506
Trentino, 151, 160, 287, 388, 402, 403, 413, 415, 464, 502
Trepov, 273
Trialism in Austria-Hungary, 311-312
Trianon, treaty of, 503-504
Trieste, 151, 160, 163, 194, 286, 287, 301, 402, 464, 500, 502, 582
Trinidad, 984
Tripartite agreement, Sept. 27, 1940 (Germany, Italy, Japan), 957, 958, 959
Triple Alliance, 68-70, 91, 152-154, 372-373, 388
Triple Entente, 132, 213, 282, 377

Tripoli (in Africa), 161, 162, 967, 970, 971; see also Libya
Tripoli (in Asia), 463
Tripolitan War, 162, 346
"Trojan horse," 922
Trondheim, 922, 924
Trotsky, 275, 444, 445, 448, 449, 450, 590, 604, 605
Trumbich, 462, 478
Tsaldaris, 790-791
Tsankov, 800
Tsingtao, 490
Tso-lin: see Chang Tso-lin
Tsushima, 263, 269
*Tuchuns* in China, 837
Tuileries, 101
Tunis, 69, 114, 152, 580, 967
Tunisia, 864, 881, 970
Turati, 150, 157, 163
Turgenev, 244
Turin, 434
Turkestan, 234
Turkestan-Siberian Railway, 611
Turkey: the Kaiser's interest in, 83-86; war with Italy, 162, 346; war with Russia, 245-253; Abdul Hamid's regime, 334-338; the Young Turk movement, 338, 345; the loss of Bosnia-Herzegovina, 252-253, 338-344; the Balkan Wars (1912–1913), 347-354; World War I, 389-390, 401-402, 429-430, 451, 463; the peace settlement, 505-509, 530-531; the establishment of the republic, 813; postwar nationalism, 813-814, 815-816; anticlericalism, 814; Westernization, 813, 814-815; economic progress, 815; absorbs Hatay, 892; mutual-assistance declarations with Britain and France (1939), 892; non-aggression treaty with Germany (1941), 966; treaties, 342, 568, 570, 790, 816, 966
Turkification, 345-346
Tutuila, 81
Twenty-one demands, 837
"Two-ocean navy," for U.S., 985
Tzaritzin, 607

Ualual, 642
Ucciali, treaty of, 155
Uganda, 187, 188
Uitlanders, 189
Ukraine, 243, 450-451, 591-592, 687, 864, 967
Ukrainian National Union, 887
Ukrainian People's Republic, 451
Ukrainian Soviet Socialist Republic, 90⌐

Ukrainians: in Austria-Hungary, 287, 295, 301, 303; in Czechoslovakia, 503, 782-783; in Poland, 747, 751, 863
Uleaborg, 910
Ulianov: see Lenin
Ulster, 209-211, 713-714
Ung River, 889
Uniate Catholics in Russia, 258
Union and Progress, Committee of, in Turkey, 338
Union of Liberation society in Russia, 271
Union or Death society in Serbia, 375
Unionists in Great Britain, 183, 209-210
United Irishmen society, 174
United Kingdom: see Great Britain
United States, 26, 132; and World War I, 408-409, 418-419, 422-427, 453, 458, 459, 464, 472; the peace settlement, 511-513; the League of Nations, 511-512, 520-522; disarmament, 570-572, 573-576, 584-585; the Italo-Ethiopian affair, 647-648; the Far East, 848, 849, 858, 859, 860, 973, 975, 977, 978, 980, 981, 982; the Sudeten crisis, 877; and World War II, 982-988
United States Shipping Board Emergency Fleet Corporation, 426
Unlimited national emergency, proclamation of, in U.S., 987
Untouchables, 833
Upper Austria, 287, 290
Upper Silesia, 489, 497, 528-529, 863, 904
Uskub, 347, 348
U.S.S.R., 592-593; see also Russia, Soviet

Vaida-Voevod, 808
Valencia, 743, 744, 745, 882, 883
Valera: see De Valera
Van, 506
Vardar, 339, 348, 382, 463, 958, 960
Vatican, 907
Vatican City, 635
Vatican Council, 58
Veltchev, 802
Venetia, 139
Venice, 194
Venizelos, 326, 344, 407, 432, 478, 507, 786, 787, 788, 790, 791
Ventspils: see Windau
Verdun, 383, 410-412, 930
Vereeniging, treaty of, 192
Versailles, 100, 110, 496, 504; treaty of, 481-497, 866
Viborg, 277-278, 909, 910, 912
Vicenza, 413
Vichy government, 945, 946, 951, 952, 964, 965

Victor Emmanuel II of Italy, 139, 142
Victor Emmanuel III of Italy, 156, 160, 629, 636, 640, 890, 960 n.
Victoria, Queen of the United Kingdom, Empress of India, 169, 179, 187, 196
Vienna, 772-774, 869, 888, 955, 958
Viipuri: see Viborg
Vilna, 404, 525-527, 758, 907, 908
Vimy Ridge, 427
Virgin Islands, 218
Viviani, 120
Vlachs, 333
Vladivostok, 235, 262, 263, 264, 269, 589, 591, 843, 852, 855
Volhynia, 907
Vorarlberg, 287
*Vorwärts,* 151

Waal River, 926
Waldeck-Rousseau, 111, 121
Wales, 206, 208-209, 941
Wallachia, 316, 418; see also Rumania
Walloons in Belgium, 223
Wang Ching-wei, 975
War debts, Inter-Allied, 549-551, 554, 559-561; British view, 549, 550, 551; French view, 550, 551; American view, 550-551; default, 559
War Finance Act in the United States, 426
*War of Steel and Gold, The,* 364
Warsaw, 404, 463, 487, 591, 749; Declaration of, 751; in World War II, 903, 904, 906
*Warspite,* 923
War-weariness, 432
Washington naval conference, 570-571; treaties, 839-840
Wavell, 969, 970
Weihaiwei, 264
Weimar Assembly, 652
Weimar Coalition, 652
Weimar Constitution, 652-653
Wekerle, 305
*Weltpolitik,* 80, 88, 93, 94
West Prussia, 487, 488
West Wall, 873, 903, 916
Western Ukraine, 907
Western White Russia, 907
Westminster, Statute of, 712
Weygand, 918, 927, 928, 930
Weygand Line, 929
White armies in Russia, 590, 591
White Russian Soviet Socialist Republic, 907
White Russians, 863
Wiener-Neustadt, 772
Wiggin Committee, 557

Wilhelmina, Queen of the Netherlands, 222, 926
Wilhelmshafen, 470
William of Albania, 354
William I of Germany, 57, 66, 75
William II of Germany, 75, 91, 92, 93, 95, 131-132, 135, 190, 263, 269, 341, 367, 375, 381, 421, 433, 450, 465, 469, 471, 494, 760
William of Urach, 450
Wilson, President, 98; and World War I, 418, 420, 423, 425, 454-455, 461, 465, 469, 472; and the peace settlement, 477, 480, 482, 483, 484, 485, 487, 489, 490, 492, 496, 497, 498, 500, 501, 511, 564, 798
Winckelman, 926
Windau, 569, 908
Windsor, Duke of, 711; see also Edward VIII
Witte, 260-262, 269, 274, 276, 277, 279
Wojciechowski, 748, 749
Women, progress of, 47-50
World Court, 517-518, 521-522, 563, 752, 754, 763, 769
World War: see First World War and Second World War
Wright brothers, 11
Württemberg, 55

Xavier, Prince of Bourbon-Parma, 885

Yangtze River, 971, 972
Yat-sen: see Sun Yat-sen
Yin Ju-keng, 856
Yochow, 974
Yorkshire, 168
Young Czechs, 298
Young Ireland, 174
Young plan, 551-555, 558
Young Turks, 338, 341, 344, 345, 346
Ypres, 397
Yuan Shih-k'ai, 836, 837
Yugoslav question in Austria-Hungary, 307-312, 462-464
Yugoslavia: and the peace settlement (1918), 500-502, 503, 504, 505; the question of federalism, 792-794, 797; dictatorship, 794-795; the constitution of 1931, 795-796; the assassination of King Alexander, 796-797; and Albania, 529-530; in Czechoslovak crisis, 880, 881; pressure on, by belligerents (1941), 958-959; joins Axis, 959; *coup d'état* in, 959; conquered by Germany, 959-960, 961; partitioned, 960 n.; treaties,

566-568, 582-583, 640, 959; see also Serbia

Zaghlul, 817, 818
Zagreb, 463, 794, 959, 960 n.; see also Agram
Zambesi, 188
Zamora, 735, 737, 741
Zanzibar, 72, 188
Zara, 960 n.
Zeebrugge, 397
Zeligowski, 526-527

Zemstvos, 240, 242, 256, 272
Zeppelins, 12
Zhivkovich, 795, 796
Zimmerman, 768
Zimmermann note, 423, 425
Zinoviev, 444, 445, 604, 605, 607
Zinoviev letter, 698
Zionist Congress (1937), 826
Zog, 798, 799, 889
Zogu: see Zog
Zola, 119
Zulus, 180

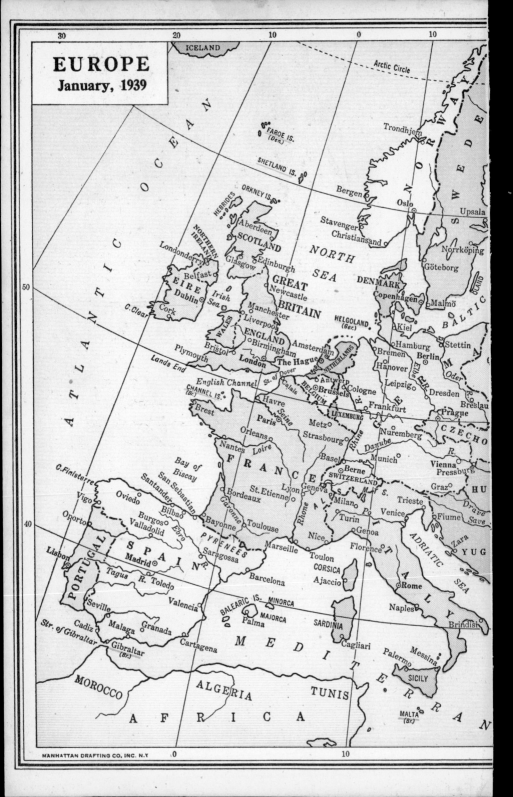